# 1 MONTH OF
# FREE
# READING

## at

## www.ForgottenBooks.com

By purchasing this book you are eligible for one month membership to ForgottenBooks.com, giving you unlimited access to our entire collection of over 1,000,000 titles via our web site and mobile apps.

To claim your free month visit:
www.forgottenbooks.com/free1121830

ISBN 978-0-331-42305-1
PIBN 11121830

Forgotten Books is a registered trademark of FB &c Ltd.
Copyright © 2018 FB &c Ltd.
FB &c Ltd, Dalton House, 60 Windsor Avenue, London, SW19 2RR.
Company number 08720141. Registered in England and Wales.

For support please visit www.forgottenbooks.com

# COMMERCIAL RELATIONS

OF THE

*117565*

# UNITED STATES

WITH

# FOREIGN COUNTRIES

DURING

# THE YEAR 1902.

IN TWO VOLUMES.
## VOLUME II.

ISSUED FROM THE BUREAU OF FOREIGN COMMERCE,
DEPARTMENT OF STATE.

WASHINGTON:
GOVERNMENT PRINTING OFFICE.
1903.

# CONTENTS.

3

# EUROPE.

## AUSTRIA-HUNGARY.

### REPORT FROM CONSULATE GENERAL AT VIENNA.[a]

#### EXPORT AND IMPORT FLUCTUATIONS.

Statistics of the foreign commerce of Austria-Hungary for the first six months of 1902 show that the imports amount to $175,240,000, being $1,220,000 more than for the same period in 1901, while the exports represent a value of $180,620,000, exceeding by $3,780,000 the value of the exports of the preceding year. There is, therefore, a resulting balance of exports over imports of $5,380,000, while the first six months of 1901 showed a balance of $13,800,000 of exports over imports.

Of the imports from all countries, the value of bale cotton is $19,180,000, an increase of $380,000 over the same period of the preceding year; machinery, $4,200,000, an increase of $120,000; grain, $4,440,000, an increase of $980,000; neat cattle, $2,260,000, an increase of $70,000; coffee and tea, $4,860,000, an increase of $400,000; cotton yarns, $2,780,000, an increase of $860,000; raw silk, $4,860,000, an increase of $640,000; wine, $2,120,000, an increase of $160,000; wool, $3,680,000, an increase of $620,000; manufactured woolen goods, $2,460,000, an increase of $220,000; coal, coke, and peat, $9,380,000, a decrease of $860,000; copper, $2,480,000, a decrease of $660,000; leather, $4,060,000, a decrease of $400,000; pig iron, $560,000, a decrease of $62,000; manufactured silk goods, $3,040,000, a decrease of $180,000; tobacco, $5,400,000, a decrease of $360,000.

Among the exports, the noteworthy fluctuations are the following: The value of neat cattle exported during the first half of 1902 amounts to $8,460,000, being an increase of $2,020,000 over the same period of 1901; clocks and fancy goods, $6,200,000, an increase of $400,000; clothing, $4,460,000, an increase of $480,000; cotton yarns and goods thereof, $2,620,000 an increase of $460,000; grain, $4,460,000, an increase of $60,000; horses, $6,240,000, an increase of $320,000; paper, $2,480,000, an increase of $160,000; pig iron, $1,120,000, an increase of $400,000; silk and silk textiles, $3,520,000, an increase of $200,000; hides, $4,600,000, an increase of $480,000; wool and woolen textiles, $5,700,000, an increase of $480,000.

The following articles were exported in values less than during the first semester of 1901; Coal, coke, and peat, $9,300,000, a decrease of $1,380,000; flax, hemp, jute, and goods thereof, $4,720,000, a decrease of $180,000; glassware, $4,740,000, a decrease of $120,000; seed, $2,360,000, a decrease of $280,000; sugar, $14,380,000, a decrease of $1,860,000; lumber, $19,740,000, a decrease of $2,540,000.

[a] For a fuller report from Vienna (received too late for insertion in its proper place) see appendix.

Of the various means employed in Austria-Hungary to further the commercial welfare of the Empire, some of the more important are the following: There is a vast system of canals in course of construction that will open up several provinces hitherto difficult of access; certain railroad lines are passing under State control; a ship-subsidy act is in full operation; the Austro-Hungarian consular service has been reorganized, honorary officials being replaced by trained consuls; there is an export academy for the education, by a rigorous curriculum, of commercial workers for foreign fields; very recently a war ship has gone abroad, carrying an Austro-Hungarian consul-general, who will study commercial conditions in various countries, with a view to benefiting Austro-Hungarian exports; official export associations are organized in Vienna and in Budapest; a commercial expedition under private auspices, taking orders for Austro-Hungarian manufactures, has just returned from a tour around the world; there are excellent colleges of agriculture, of mining, and of forestry; and 128 trade schools, with some 24,000 attendants, one half of which are subsidized by the Government. In addition to these schools, which are devoted to certain branches of industry in which the country excels, such as porcelain, glass, lace making, metal work, weaving, and stone and wood work, there are some 750 other trade schools of a general character, attended by about 150,000 pupils; and the latest Austrian budget contains the item of $1,609,000 for industrial education.

It will thus be seen that nothing is left undone to advance the internal development of the Empire; and every means that can be employed with a reasonable prospect of success the Government is readily inclined to foster, by beneficent legislation. But in spite of these various measures, trade conditions are not altogether satisfactory; business has extended somewhat, but is capable of much further expansion. The quality of the production is good, but the quantity disposed of in the world's markets is relatively small.

Perhaps the most striking feature of the present commercial history of Austria-Hungary is the organization of various trusts, which, with their ramifications, control the manufacture and output of sugar, petroleum, iron, and other important products. It is claimed that the first trust known to the modern business world was formed in Austria; and the great local producers have not given up this tendency to business combination. To illustrate the characteristics of Austrian trusts, the sugar trust, which is, perhaps, as interesting as any other trade combination just now may be cited.

The sugar interests of Austria-Hungary are controlled by a committee of the associated raw and refined sugar manufacturers which consists of six members and has its seat at Vienna. It calculates, collects, and distributes compensations and back payments. Resolutions are carried by a two-thirds majority. A board of umpires has been nominated to adjust any differences, but its rights are closely circumscribed.

The associated raw-sugar manufactories agree that all the raw sugar produced by them which is to be refined or used in the Austro-Hungarian Monarchy is to be delivered to the plants of the associated refineries exclusively; furthermore, that they will produce no refined sugar except granulated sugar, which is to be exported; deliver no sugar of any kind for inland consumption; take no sugar except that produced by the trust refineries; make no sale or purchase on time, sooner than two months before this agreement shall expire, and not create or assist in creating any new factories or sugar refineries in Austria-Hungary.

On the other hand, the manufacturers may acquire plants from other members of the trust, on certain conditions prescribed by the original agreement entered into by them. Fines are assessed for violation of the provisions of the trust. "Compensations" are to be paid by the refineries to the raw-sugar factories, if the average price for raw sugar does not reach $6 for 220 pounds at the Aussig, Bohemia, docks. The difference is turned over by the refineries to the general committee; the amount, which is calculated according to the monthly average price, being paid every thirty days. On the other side, a compensation is to be paid to each refinery if the official price for refined loaf sugar be less than $16.90 for 220 pounds, either by reason of new laws or imported sugar being sold below that price. The amount to be paid is to be equal to the margin between the official price of $16.90 for 220 pounds and the market value below the price of $16.90. If the official price be higher than $16.90 for 220 pounds for refined loaf sugar or $17.30 for refined lump sugar, the refineries are to pay 40 cents per 220 pounds, which amount may be raised by resolution of the committee. The raw-sugar factories are to receive 60 per cent of this sum, and such payments shall take place each month after the common committee has fixed the rate. Rates of interest and fines are fixed for delay in making such payments. The refineries are allowed every month to dispose of 1,207 tons of refined sugar, free of any payment of compensation, which is to be employed for industrial purposes; and plants which produce no more than 3,503 tons may dispose of the whole of that quantity.

This agreement will be valid from November 1, 1902, until November 1, 1903; it will become invalid if the tariff union between Austria and Hungary should not be renewed, or if any monopolizing measure in regard to sugar production should be adopted by the Government. When a refinery exceeds its monthly quota by more than 10,020 tons, or when the price for raw sugar sinks below $3.20 for 220 pounds, or if the agreement should be rendered void by the authorities, the refineries will be entitled to give warning of their intention to withdraw from the trust. On the other hand, the the raw-sugar factories will have the same right of withdrawing if the refineries reduce unjustly the price for refined sugar below $16.90 per 220 pounds for loaf or $17.30 for lump sugar.

## SUBSIDIZED MERCHANT MARINE.

Important subsidies are granted by the Government, that have a beneficial influence on the merchant marine of Austria-Hungary. By a recent act, steamers and sailing vessels under the national flag, and owned, two-thirds or more, by subjects of the country, are entitled to aid from the State. This grant from the Government is of two kinds, namely, a working subsidy and a subsidy for the voyage. The first consists in a sum to be paid every year during the first fifteen years after the launching of the vessel, according to the tonnage registered, in the following gradations: $2.40 for steamers of iron and steel; $1.80 for sailing ships of iron and steel; $1.20 for sailing ships of wood or mixed construction.

Beginning with the second year of this agreement, the amount to be paid is lessened by 5 per cent each year. Vessels constructed in Austria-Hungary receive an additional 10 per cent as a working subsidy; and if at least one-half of the material used in their building is of domestic production, they are entitled to 25 per cent more. Vessels also receive a traveling subsidy for voyages beyond the small coasting trips to and from Austro-Hungarian ports. Such voyages must be undertaken in the interests of home commerce, and not to any port to which a regular line is established and already in receipt of aid from the Government. The rate of this assistance is fixed at 2 cents for every registered ton of freight per 100 sea miles traveled. By a late decree, the words "in the interest of home commerce" are construed to mean that a traveling subsidy can be granted only when at least one-quarter of the cargo of the vessel is taken in or discharged in an Austro-Hungarian port. By virtue of this law, vessels of a regular line which are already in receipt of grants from the State are not entitled to any further subsidy.

Figures covering the merchant marine for the period from 1881 to 1894 show a decrease in the registered tonnage of sailing vessels from 50,229 to 39,641 tons, and in that of the large coasters from 6,062 to 4,852 tons. This decrease continued during the subsidy period of 1894 to 1900. In the year 1900, the registered tonnage for sailing vessels for long voyages was only 13,427 tons and that of large coasting vessels 946 tons. In 1881, the number of steamers for long voyages was 70, with 62,387 tons. In 1894, the same number of steamers comprised a tonnage of 87,073 tons. But during the subsidy period 1895–1900, there is an improvement, and the decrease to 12,778 tons in sailing vessels is met by an increase of steamer tonnage aggregating 80,465 tons, of which 12,671 tons belong to the Austrian Lloyd line. During a period of thirty years, the tonnage of the Austro-Hungarian vessels entering Trieste has increased by 484,238 tons, or about 92.5 per cent, while the tonnage of the vessels under foreign flags entering the same port has increased 148 per cent. Perhaps, the prosperity of the merchant marine should not be ascribed entirely to the beneficial results of the ship-subsidy law. In a great measure, it is also due to the opening afforded for shipping by the increase of German commerce, the large freights incident to foreign wars, and the development of trade with America.

CARL BAILEY HURST, Consul-General.

VIENNA, *October 15, 1902.*

--------

### PRAGUE.

Since the latest report on the commerce and industries of this district, in March, 1900 [a]—when labor and trade were greatly disturbed by serious "strikes" among the coal miners and riotous disputes between the two racial and political factions, the Czechs and the Germans—the country has enjoyed a period of rest and quiet.

During that time, business has, on the whole, been reasonably pros-

--------

[a] Consular Reports No. 237 (Advance Sheets No. 721).

perous; but in certain branches of trade, there has been, and still is, great stagnation, more particularly among the iron and steel works, some of which are working short hours, while others are completely idle.

Serious depression also prevails in the sugar industry, owing to the heavy decline in the price of this commodity throughout Europe.

## IMPORTS.

As no statistics of imports from the United States into this district are kept separately, it is impossible to give accurate information on the subject. There is good reason to believe, however, that this trade is increasing, although there is still much need for the exercise of a little more energy on the part of our exporters, particularly those interested in the following wares: Agricultural and other machines, petroleum, lubricating oils, raw cotton, typewriters, boots and shoes, electrical supplies, walnut wood for cabinetmakers, canned vegetables, and leather.

Many staple articles, such as beef, bacon, canned meat, hams, and California fruit, are almost wholly excluded from this market by the imposition of prohibitive import duties.

## EXPORTS.

Export business with the United States is increasing steadily. The declared value of merchandise consigned from this consular district to our country during the fiscal year ended June 30, 1902, was $3,414,596.58, which is the record.

The export of raw beet sugar has entirely ceased, but this decline is to a great extent covered by the increased shipments of refined sugar.

The export of beans has fallen off greatly, owing to partial failure of the crop. Wool, gloves, and chemicals likewise show decreases. On the other hand, the shipments of machinery, hops, paper, beer, porcelain, glassware, and glue have increased largely. The exportation of steel wire rods has also become quite extensive. A comparative statement of the principal exports from this district to the United States during the years 1901 and 1902 is appended.

ETHELBERT WATTS, *Consul.*

PRAGUE, *October 18, 1902.*

---

*Comparative statement of exports of principal articles from the consular district of Prague, Bohemia, to the United States during the last two fiscal years, ended June 30, 1901 and 1902.*

| Articles. | 1901. | 1902. | Articles. | 1901. | 1902. |
|---|---|---|---|---|---|
| Beans | $234,462.37 | $116,787.55 | Chemicals | $107,678.89 | $82,257.92 |
| Bed feathers | 17,238.85 | 43,360.60 | Carlsbad Sprudelsalt. | 32,853.32 | 37,148.59 |
| Beer | 241,367.53 | 300,108.09 | Cotton goods | 7,118.09 | 9,804.83 |
| Beet sugar: | | | Glue | 9,103.08 | 20,787.48 |
| Raw | 784,829.69 | | Glycerin | 41,734.40 | 27,215.00 |
| Refined | 495,004.01 | 1,189,879.36 | Linen goods | 24,840.82 | 36,659.37 |
| Books | 52,265.61 | 58,922.80 | Machinery | 8,769.09 | 23,869.34 |
| Earthenware | 47,031.60 | 52,888.31 | Musical instruments. | 68,705.64 | 60,964.63 |
| Gloves | 59,380.00 | 31,586.73 | Paper | 13,891.20 | 20,065.03 |
| Buttons | 7,372.68 | 17,753.07 | Plate glass | | 10,971.63 |
| Glassware | 117,805.96 | 123,222.87 | Steel wire rods | | 128,686.50 |
| Hops | 91,517.79 | 137,322.71 | Syphon bottles | 51,502.34 | 41,082.85 |
| Porcelain | 494,688.89 | 565,080.16 | Wool | 137,665.83 | 112,974.96 |

Declared value of all exports from this district during fiscal year ended June 30, 1902, $3,414,596.58.

### REICHENBERG.

A slight improvement is noticeable in the commerce and industry of the Reichenberg consular district this year in comparison with 1901, but on the whole, the situation is unsatisfactory.

#### COAL.

Austria has two great coal districts—northwestern Bohemia, which produces soft coal, and Moravian-Silesia, which produces "stove" coal. In the demand for stove coal, there is a decrease of 25 per cent this year, due, it is alleged, to reduced consumption by machinery, vehicle, and locomotive factories, which have been insufficiently employed, and by railroads, because of decreased business. The hesitating course of the sugar factories, which, influenced by the present uncertain situation, provide for only pressing necessities, has also tended to minimize the demand for this kind of coal.

In the Bohemian soft-coal district, the condition is not so bad. The principal mines suspend work two days in the week, and this has caused a reduction of about 15 per cent in the product. Neither the export of coal to Germany nor the demand from local factories, however, has decreased. Prices in both coal-producing districts are depressed.

#### LABOR.

The labor situation continues deplorable. Many thousands of hands, especially in the machine-making industries, are out of work. Uncertainty as to the renewal of the agreement between Austria and Hungary, it is explained, deters many factories from ordering new machinery. Orders are also wanting from the great sugar works, which, in times of good business, frequently renew and improve their appliances.

#### TEXTILES.

Cheerful reports come from the textile industries. The woolen spinning and weaving mills are doing an excellent business, production and demand having decidedly increased in the first six months of this year. Cotton-goods printers are busily employed. Weavers, however, complain of great overproduction and that the selling price of their product often fails to cover its cost. The import of cotton into this district is very heavy, that from the United States maintaining its full standard of about 250,000 bales per annum.

#### BROADCLOTHS.

In broadcloths and the like, business is excellent, better than last year, though profits are small. The high prices of wool and yarn, coupled with the possibility of still higher rates, stimulate orders but decrease profits. Exports have materially increased, notably to Roumania, where good crops caused general prosperity. Female fashions, besides, are at present favorable for these cloths. Good crop prospects make the near future bright for the home trade.

## LINEN TRADE.

The linen business is fairly good this year, decidedly better than in 1901. The mills are fully engaged, though at reduced prices, and in spite of unstable prices of raw materials. The outlook is cheerful, with good crops, hope of renewal of the ausgleich with Hungary, and good times in the United States; but stability in prices is an important factor in taking account of the future.

## CARPETS AND RUGS.

Of carpets and rugs, there is a decided increase of exports from this district to the United States, while the business generally is very satisfactory.

On the whole, there is no reduction of working force in the textile industries, although most ironworks, mines, machine and vehicle factories have discharged some of their hands.

Notwithstanding the general complaint last year in textile circles, evidence appears that the business was, after all, uncommonly good. The usual day's work in Austrian textile industries is eleven hours. As appears from recently published statistics, the extra hours of work in 1901 in those industries aggregated 1,111,367, or 418,602 more than in 1900. But in Austria's manufacturing industries, as a whole, the number of extra hours was 25 per cent less in 1901 than in 1900. Every branch of textiles showed an increase in this respect last year, as compared with 1900.

## GLASS PRODUCTS.

Altogether, business this year is unsatisfactory—worse than in 1901—though exports to the United States are unusually large. As to details: Trade in buttons is improving, while the demand for glass pearls far exceeds production. The former large trade in bangles with India is very much reduced and apparently will gradually die out altogether. The imitation precious stones sold this year to America are mainly of cheap grades. Fashion is unfavorable to some kinds and French competition is injurious in many cases. The demand for cut glassware is less than last year, while that for hat ornaments is greater.

Producers differ in opinion as to the future. Some consider it promising, but others are gloomy, especially regarding trade with the United States, which they say is steadily decreasing because we are manufacturing more and more for our own use. Those are not wanting who assert the belief that, two or three decades hence, the United States will be sending glass goods to Austria and taking practically none therefrom.

The depression in Germany—Austria's chief market—has seriously affected trade in that direction.

Spain has always been a great market for Bohemian glass products and still is, but complaint is heard that loss is caused by the placing of orders in Paris and Berlin. It is noticed that the goods do not go direct from the manufacturing section, but in larger part through foreign commission men. It is alleged that this seriously reduces the manufacturer's profit, and means of stopping the practice are discussed.

The union of glassware and porcelain dealers in Hungary asks all its members to boycott the Austrian producers of these articles, because the latter persist in selling goods to speculators, whereby prices are generally increased. The sale of such pr ucts to Hungary being very large, a boycott of that sort would be calamitous to Bohemia. But the manufacturers profess to be undisturbed, relying upon the fact that Hungary is virtually compelled to buy Bohemian glassware, itself making practically none, and to import from foreign countries would be unsatisfactory as well as very expensive.

### GENERAL TRADE WITH HUNGARY.

Notwithstanding that Hungary is distinctively an agricultural country and its exports are almost entirely farm products, its trade with Austria gives yearly a balance in its favor—small, but hardly to be expected, since Hungary draws from Austria most of the manufactures that it uses. Austria's trade with Hungary, sales and purchases, is in value about half the amount of its aggregate business with all foreign countries. Hungary is, however, making approaches toward supplying its own needs in textile products, having now 112,000 cotton spindles and 4,500 looms in operation. But the estimate that it requires 1,600,000 spindles and 36,000 looms to supply its demand for cotton goods indicates that it is still a long way from being self-sustaining in that respect. These observations also apply generally to other textiles.

### BEER PRODUCT.

In extent, beer making ranks among the very first of Bohemia's industries. It is a business, too, which varies little unless by way of increase, and from which hard times keep aloof. The product of the 67 breweries in Bohemia in 1901 was 4,620,000 hectoliters (122,046,540 gallons). One-fourth of this aggregate was produced by three breweries at Pilsen, one of which is claimed to exceed in annual output any other brewery in Europe. Pilsener beer is consumed in every European country, ranking in favor with the black beer of Munich, and gives a name to the pale, transparent beers made in the United States. The brewery in this city made over 3,000,000 gallons last year. Every Bohemian city feels that it must have a brewery—if not through private enterprise, then through municipal appropriation.

### PAPER GOODS.

Doleful reports come from the paper-goods factories in this district, of which there are 28, besides as many pulp mills. Business is reported exceedingly bad—worse even than last year. The future is uncertain. No betterment is deemed possible until the world's markets improve. Bad crops in India and the trouble in China have narrowed the foreign market, while imports of paper goods and enlargement of several factories have caused accumulations of unsalable stocks.

## EXPORTS.

The exports from the Reichenberg consular district (exclusive of the Haida agency) to the United States during the last two fiscal years were:

| Articles. | 1901. | 1902. |
|---|---|---|
| Artificial flowers.......................................... | $2,103.52 | ............ |
| Beads, and articles of..................................... | 28,232.80 | $66,287.19 |
| Buttons.................................................... | 49,155.97 | 86,597.80 |
| Cane and umbrella handles................................. | 238.63 | 655.41 |
| Chinaware................................................. | 2,727.61 | 3,511.38 |
| Colors.................................................... | | 1,871.56 |
| Cutlery................................................... | 560.61 | 211.45 |
| Glassware, cut and decorated.............................. | 77,314.44 | 81,321.67 |
| Hair (human).............................................. | 3,346.86 | 1,112.12 |
| Hops...................................................... | 1,512.98 | ............ |
| Jewelry, and imitation of................................. | 196,882.86 | 282,804.69 |
| Metal ware................................................ | 898.01 | 4,989.02 |
| Miscellaneous............................................. | 321.23 | 336.79 |
| Musical instruments....................................... | 1,456.43 | 277.50 |
| Oil paintings............................................. | 710.69 | ............ |
| Paper, and articles of.................................... | 209.50 | 170.16 |
| Paste figures and ornaments............................... | 459.63 | 201.38 |
| Picture frames............................................ | 1,159.92 | 746.24 |
| Pictures, framed.......................................... | 412.80 | 21.92 |
| Potash, carbonate of...................................... | 3,707.81 | ............ |
| Precious stones, and imitation of......................... | 177,800.43 | 165,321.25 |
| Textiles— | | |
|   Bed and table covers .................................. | ............ | 407.54 |
|   Blankets............................................... | ............ | 2,588.24 |
|   Carpets................................................ | 8,563.76 | 28,864.55 |
|   Cotton cloth........................................... | 10,506.58 | 5,947.08 |
|   Handkerchiefs.......................................... | ............ | 260.59 |
|   Head shawls............................................ | ............ | 1,831.62 |
|   Linens................................................. | 575,083.09 | 543,078.94 |
|   Linen yarn............................................. | 389.23 | ............ |
|   Velveteen.............................................. | ............ | 1,121.43 |
|   Woolen dress cloth..................................... | 12,990.13 | 49,483.22 |
| Thermometers.............................................. | 362.07 | 620.92 |
| Toilet cases.............................................. | ............ | 346.12 |
| Toothpick knives.......................................... | 257.20 | 429.95 |
| Wine and brandy........................................... | 217.23 | ............ |
|     Total..................................... | 1,151,459.52 | 1,306,417.68 |

During the last fiscal year, compared with its predecessor, exports of linens and several other articles declined; but this was more than offset by notable increases in exports of beads, buttons, imitation jewelry, carpets, and woolen dress goods.

There has been no marked change in exports to other countries. No local statistics are obtainable, but the report for the entire monarchy indicates the drift locally. According to these figures, the exports for the half year ending June 30, 1902, were slightly more than for the first six months of 1901. Germany continues, as heretofore, to be Austria's chief market, taking nearly half its total exports. The imports from Germany are but 70 per cent of this country's exports thereto. The chief export from this section to Germany is soft coal.

Special efforts are being made to enlarge trade with Japan, in furtherance of which arrangements are suggested whereby the steamers of the Yokohama-London line shall call at Trieste.

Excepting linen, the yarn used in the Austrian textile manufactories is mainly imported. But in finished goods, except silks, Austria's exports of textiles far exceed her imports, especially of linens, whereof her imports are practically nil. Austria's sale of textiles to Hungary is, however, nearly three times greater than her entire exports thereof to foreign countries.

During the past eight months, considerable quantities of raw sugar have been shipped into Bohemia from Germany, and after paying the import duty of 6 florins gold ($2.89) per 100 kilograms (220.46 pounds), has been sold at a lower price than the domestic article. It is used by makers of candy and sweetmeats. Such an import would be impossible were it not for the agreement between Bohemian raw-sugar producers, whereby they can sell only to refiners or foreign buyers.

### AMERICAN PRODUCTS.

Some progress has been made this year in introducing American goods into this district. A local shoe store has found a ready sale for American footwear, the first ever brought to this market. American thread is also sold at the local stores. An agency has just been established for American machine tools, and it is the intention to vigorously push their sale. As heretofore, large quantities of American petroleum, lard, bacon, dried fruits, etc., are imported, but any great extension of our trade in this district is, as I have before remarked, hindered by the comparatively illiberal terms offered by our exporters, and by their seeming indifference in many cases. The greatest opportunity still remains in the line of factory and agricultural machinery.

### MISCELLANEOUS.

#### NEW RAILWAYS.

During the present year, two short railway lines have been constructed in the northern part of this district, connecting certain towns with others just over the border in Germany. Next year, a branch line will be laid to fill a 15-mile gap in the eastern part of the district.

Several railways in Austria are State property, and, for reasons of policy and profit, there is much talk this year of taking over others (and possibly in time all the railways in the dual monarchy) by the State.

The soft-coal product of this section for the first half of the current year was 6,260,000 tons, against 6,750,000 for the first six months of 1901.

#### PUBLIC BATH.

An important new institution in this city, completed this year, is the Kaiser Franz Josef Bad, claimed to be the finest and most perfect bath in Europe. It cost 1,000,000 crowns ($200,000) and is the gift of a local savings bank to the city. The building contains a swimming pool and baths of all kinds. The number of patrons exceeds 2,000 a week.

#### WATERWORKS.

A waterworks system is just being installed in this city, the water coming from mountain springs 5 miles distant. Wells and brooks have heretofore furnished the supply.

#### CROPS.

The crops at this writing promise exceedingly well, notwithstanding the summer has been unusually cold and rainy, even for this always cool and damp climate. But the principal farm product of this district is small grain, which can flourish in such weather.   Since 1896, crops have not been generally good throughout the monarchy, and if present indications are realized, business of all kinds will be greatly stimulated.

The iron trade continues much depressed, and most works are unable to dispose of all the product for which they have capacity.   But it is expected that the increase of prices by the recently formed combine of all the iron industries of Austria-Hungary will better conditions, for the producers, at least.

FRANK W. MAHIN, *Consul.*

REICHENBERG, *August 26, 1902.*

---

## REPORT FROM CONSULAR AGENCY AT HAIDA.

The comparative statement, hereto appended, of declared exports for the fiscal years ended June 30, 1901, and June 30, 1902, respectively, requires some explanation.

The $95,000 decrease in porcelain and pottery shipments is due largely to the fact that a good deal of the porcelain of the Karlsbad region, which, previous to January 1, 1901, was declared at Haida, has since been declared invariably at Prague.

The $90,000 decrease in glassware shipments is actual, and is caused by the improvement of the glass-refining industry in the United States. During the past four years, a number of good glass painters and engravers from this district have been induced to emigrate to the United States.   This fact, together with a nearly 30 per cent increase in the exports of glass paints, shows that some of the glass refining, formerly done in this district, is now done in the United States.

### ARTIFICIAL FLOWERS.

The almost doubling of the exports of artificial flowers shows that a large demand exists for this article.   Artificial flowers are manufactured by the farmers and their children in the agricultural districts, during the long winter evenings.   The work is done by hand and extremely low wages are paid; for this reason, the industry is hardly likely ever to become popular in the United States.

### GLASSWARE.

The fragility of the glassware shipped from the Haida consular district makes it imperative that the very carefully packed goods should not be opened until they reach their final destination.   For this reason, the Haida agency is called upon to authenticate probably a larger number of invoices for shipments to interior points in America than any other United States consular office.   The writer has counted 50 different ports of entry in the United States for which glassware shipments were declared during the last year.   Hence, Haida has become widely known in the United States; and now that American glassware is being largely exported to Europe, many of our manufacturers are writing letters of inquiry to this office.   The replies to such letters, however, must be almost invariably disappointing, since

Haida, with its sister town of Arnsdorf, has only about 6,000 inhabitants, no wholesale trade of any kind, but one railroad and that not a trunk line, no water communication, and no regular custom-house.

But Northwestern Bohemia, forming the Haida consular district, one of the most thickly populated regions in all Europe, has, opposite each other on the Elbe River, and in direct water and railroad communication with the port of Hamburg, the towns of Bodenbach and Tetschen. There, all goods imported into Bohemia by the river and its adjacent railway lines have to be examined for customs duty, unless shipped "in bond."

Then, also, about 18 miles farther up the river is the city of Aussig, containing over 40,000 inhabitants, the chief shipping point of coal and iron in Bohemia. These are the points through which American manufacturers should work their wares into Northwestern Bohemia and districts to the south.

FRANK SILLER, *Consular Agent.*

HAIDA, *July 10, 1902.*

---

*Declared exports from the consular agency district of Haida, Austria, to the United States during the four quarters of the fiscal year ended June 30, 1902, as compared with the preceding year.*

[Value in American gold.]

| Articles. | Quarter ended— | | | | Total for fiscal year. | | Increase (+) or decrease (−). |
|---|---|---|---|---|---|---|---|
| | Sept. 30, 1901. | Dec. 31, 1901. | March 31, 1902. | June 30, 1902. | 1901–2. | 1900–1901. | |
| Artificial flowers ............ | $7,812.96 | $25,371.15 | $16,561.01 | $5,383.07 | $55,128.18 | $30,762.92 | +$24,365.26 |
| Buttons (mostly ivory)...... | 3,784.21 | 3,618.72 | 7,012.21 | 5,589.75 | 20,004.89 | 20,244.84 | − 239.95 |
| Chemicals (glass paints) .... | 615.06 | 2,386.41 | 3,188.42 | 5,415.26 | 11,605.14 | 8,987.94 | + 2,617.20 |
| Cotton goods (velveteen and corduroy) ................ | 4,244.06 | 147.47 | 1,500.50 | 9,270.36 | 15,162.39 | 16,059.79 | − 897.40 |
| Cutlery (pocket knives) .... | 9,333.78 | 13,706.30 | 6,397.87 | 14,514.62 | 43,957.57 | 43,813.75 | + 143.82 |
| Glassware ................... | 156,834.98 | 53,528.06 | 30,538.52 | 87,836.30 | 328,737.81 | 419,384.46 | − 90,646.65 |
| Metal ware................. | 8,078.72 | 5,753.60 | 4,448.70 | 8,936.87 | 27,217.89 | 14,343.38 | + 12,874.51 |
| Porcelain and pottery....... | 33,191.73 | 8,492.58 | 9,535.06 | 21,512.10 | 72,731.47 | 167,737.06 | − 95,005.59 |
| Skins (an unusual shipment). | .......... | .......... | .......... | .......... | .......... | 6,786.80 | − 6,786.80 |
| Smokers' articles (cigarette holders)................. | .......... | .......... | .......... | 431.44 | 431.44 | 1,678.89 | − 1,247.45 |
| Sparterie ................... | 5,926.60 | 604.73 | 4,615.14 | 4,317.52 | 15,463.99 | 9,883.76 | + 5,580.23 |
| Sundries .................. | 538.25 | 56.43 | 8.00 | 59.39 | 662.07 | 909.45 | − 247.38 |
| Total ............... | 230,635.28 | 113,665.45 | 83,805.43 | 168,266.68 | 591,102.84 | 740,593.04 | −149,490.20 |

## TRIESTE.

### MERCHANT MARINE.

The merchant fleet of Austria, inclusive of all registered fishing vessels, lighters, etc., consisted, in 1901, of 12,928 vessels which had an aggregate net tonnage of 280,285 and were manned by 34,548 men. The increase over the year 1900 was 28 vessels, 35,984 tons, and 1,045 men. The number of deep-sea and large coasting steamers in 1901 was 134, with an aggregate net tonnage of 219,446, which is a gain of 7 steamers and 35,497 tons over 1900. Ten years ago, nearly all the deep-sea and large coasting steamers of Austrian register were owned by the Austrian Lloyd Navigation Company, but since the adoption by the Empire of the ship-subsidy policy, in 1893, the increase in the number of sea steamers owned by smaller companies, syndicates, and private individuals has been quite remarkable, as the following table will show:

| Year | Deep-sea and large coasting steamers. | | Belonging to— | | | |
|---|---|---|---|---|---|---|
| | | | Austrian Lloyd. | | Other owners. | |
| | Number. | Net tonnage. | Number. | Net tonnage. | Number. | Net tonnage. |
| 1891 | 88 | 85,387 | 76 | 80,012 | 12 | 5,375 |
| 1892 | 91 | 87,187 | 71 | 75,222 | 20 | 11,965 |
| 1893 | 96 | 95,522 | 74 | 83,318 | 22 | 12,204 |
| 1894 | 93 | 94,160 | 72 | 82,006 | 21 | 12,154 |
| 1895 | 99 | 105,793 | 72 | 85,243 | 27 | 20,550 |
| 1896 | 110 | 119,969 | 71 | 86,282 | 39 | 33,687 |
| 1897 | 114 | 136,662 | 65 | 88,257 | 49 | 48,405 |
| 1898 | 113 | 142,086 | 61 | 84,115 | 52 | 57,971 |
| 1899 | 112 | 154,460 | 55 | 88,525 | 57 | 65,935 |
| 1900 | 123 | 183,949 | 58 | 95,721 | 65 | 88,228 |
| 1901 | 134 | 219,446 | 54 | 97,012 | 80 | 122,434 |

In 1890, the 76 steamers of the Lloyd Company, with a tonnage of 80,012, represented 94 per cent of the entire tonnage of the deep-sea and large coasting steamers of Austria. In 1901, the Lloyd's tonnage of 97,012 was only 44 per cent of the total. During the same period, the average Lloyd steamer increased from 844 to 1,796 tons, and the average non-Lloyd steamer of the foreign-service class from 448 to 1,530 tons. The merchant fleet contained, besides the larger steamers, 77 small coasting steamers, with an aggregate tonnage of 7,245. The average displacement of these local coasters was 94.1 tons.

The sailing fleet proper consisted of of 33 deep-sea vessels, with an aggregate tonnage of 21,461, and of 1,544 coasters, with an aggregate tonnage of 20,182. The number of vessels employed in the fisheries was 3,818, with an aggregate tonnage of 8,859 and an aggregate crew of 13,924 men. The number of lighters, pilot, and other boats was about 7,500.

### TRAINING SHIPS.

The constant decline of the deep-sea sailing fleet has made it almost impossible for nautical apprentices to get a thorough training on Austrian ships, and it is not at all unusual for young men desirous of fitting themselves for a nautical career to serve their apprenticeship on foreign sailing vessels. The Adria Steamship Company, of Fiume, recognizing this want of training facilities for its own and the country's future navigators, has decided to purchase a training ship for the exclusive use of nautical pupils. It is the company's intention to use the ship in carrying coal from Great Britain to Austro-Hungarian ports. It is stated that the Austrian Lloyd Steamship Company has been requested by the Government to make similar provision for the training of nautical pupils, and has decided to build two training ships in its own shipyard. As there are already good nautical schools at Trieste and Fiume, the training of the future navigators for Austrian vessels promises soon to be well provided for.

### MOVEMENT OF SHIPS AT THE PORT OF TRIESTE.

Port statistics for 1901 show a considerable increase in the movement of vessels over the year 1900. There arrived here last year 9,970

H. Doc. 305, pt 2——2

vessels, with an aggregate tonnage of 2,278,801, and departed 10,042 vessels, with an aggregate tonnage of 2,291,964.   The total number of vessels that arrived from the United States was 67, viz, 57 steamer and 10 sailing vessels.

Bills of health were issued at this consulate to 38 steamers and 4 sailing vessels bound for United States ports.   No American merchant vessel called at Trieste during the year.   In fact, not a single merchant ship flying the Stars and Stripes has been seen in this port since the summer of 1897.

The following table shows the entries and departures of vessels during the year under review:

*Statement showing the movement of vessels at the port of Trieste for the year ended December 31, 1901.*

| Flag. | Sailing vessels. | | Steamships. | | Total. | |
|---|---|---|---|---|---|---|
| | Number. | Tons. | Number. | Tons. | Number. | Tons. |
| ENTERED. | | | | | | |
| Austria-Hungary | 822 | 29,498 | 6,581 | 1,554,493 | 7,408 | 1,583,991 |
| Belgium | | | 3 | 3,894 | 3 | 3,894 |
| Denmark | | | 4 | 4,768 | 4 | 4,768 |
| France | | | 1 | 1,896 | 1 | 1,896 |
| Germany | | | 25 | 26,821 | 25 | 26,821 |
| Great Britain | | | 140 | 195,410 | 140 | 195,410 |
| Greece | 84 | 10,811 | 67 | 58,148 | 151 | 68,959 |
| Italy | 1,673 | 65,528 | 475 | 280,317 | 2,148 | 345,845 |
| Montenegro | 18 | 546 | | | 18 | 546 |
| Russia | | | 11 | 14,040 | 11 | 14,040 |
| Spain | | | 3 | 6,514 | 3 | 6,514 |
| Sweden and Norway | | | 3 | 3,562 | 3 | 3,562 |
| Tunis | 1 | 30 | | | 1 | 30 |
| Turkey | 33 | 2,124 | 26 | 20,401 | 59 | 22,525 |
| Total | 2,631 | 108,537 | 7,339 | 2,170,264 | 9,970 | 2,278,801 |
| CLEARED. | | | | | | |
| Austria-Hungary | 838 | 29,276 | 6,585 | 1,558,368 | 7,423 | 1,587,644 |
| Belgium | | | 3 | 3,894 | 3 | 3,894 |
| Denmark | | | 4 | 4,768 | 4 | 4,768 |
| France | | | 1 | 1,896 | 1 | 1,896 |
| Germany | | | 26 | 27,650 | 26 | 27,650 |
| Great Britain | | | 142 | 197,416 | 142 | 197,416 |
| Greece | 86 | 11,127 | 67 | 57,922 | 153 | 69,049 |
| Italy | 1,711 | 68,191 | 477 | 280,156 | 2,188 | 348,347 |
| Montenegro | 17 | 513 | 1 | 25 | 18 | 538 |
| Russia | | | 14 | 19,225 | 14 | 19,225 |
| Spain | | | 2 | 3,916 | 2 | 3,916 |
| Sweden and Norway | | | 3 | 3,562 | 3 | 3,562 |
| Tunis | 1 | 30 | | | 1 | 30 |
| Turkey | 37 | 2,787 | 27 | 21,242 | 64 | 24,029 |
| Total | 2,690 | 111,924 | 7,352 | 2,180,040 | 10,042 | 2,291,964 |

## COMMUNICATION WITH THE UNITED STATES.

The two lines of steamers mentioned in my last annual report, viz, the Austro-Americana and the New York and Mediterranean Steamship Company, continue the freight service between Trieste and United States ports.   The Austro-Americana, with 12 steamers, has from one to two sailings a month to New York.   From New York, the steamers of this line sail alternately to Savannah and to Tampa and New Orleans, to load cotton, phosphates, and cotton-seed oil for Mediterranean and Adriatic ports.   The New York and Mediterranean Steamship Company, with 7 steamers, has fairly regular semimonthly sailings from Trieste and intermediate ports to New York, and vice versa. Their west-bound cargo consists chiefly of fruit, while for the return voyage, the steamers load general merchandise at New York. Both companies issue through bills of lading to any city in the United States or southern Europe. Their present rates from Trieste to New York vary from 6 to 50 shillings ($1.46 to $12.15) per ton; magnesite paying from 6 to 8, iron from 8 to 12, rice 15, and skins 50 shillings per ton, all with 5 per cent primage.

The Austro-Americana line has contracted for the construction of 2 new steamers, each of 5,500 tons burden. These vessels, which are to be completed next March, will each have accommodations for several hundred steerage passengers, it being the company's intention to engage in the emigrant business, if the Government can be prevailed upon to open this port to emigration. It is believed that a considerable portion of the emigration business, which now goes to Hamburg, Bremen, and Genoa, could be drawn to Trieste, and that this step would greatly improve the communication between this port and the United States by insuring more frequent and regular sailings and lower freights.

### THE AUSTRIAN LLOYD STEAMSHIP COMPANY.

In these days of our commercial expansion, the American exports to the Levant have also greatly increased. But our trade in the East would probably be several times larger than it is at present if we had regular and direct communication with that part of the world. I have no doubt that many an order has to be refused because of the impossibility of prompt delivery.

As direct communication with the various ports of the Levant is as yet out of the question, our exporters and importers will do well to bear in mind that Trieste, as the headquarters of the Austrian Lloyd, is the principal port of transshipment in southern Europe for goods destined for Egypt, Greece, Turkey, and southern Russia, as well as for India and southeastern Africa. With a fairly regular steamship service existing between New York and Trieste, which promises to be greatly improved in the near future, shippers of wares intended for oriental markets could probably often save freight and time by selecting the Trieste route.

The Lloyd company has direct lines to Alexandria, the Adriatic ports of Turkey, Patras, Piraeus, and Constantinople, and connecting lines to Odessa, Candia, Port Said, Cyprus, and the principal ports of Roumania and Asia Minor.

A fast steamer runs to Alexandria weekly, making the journey in less than four days. From Alexandria, the Lloyd has a connecting line to Port Said and Cyprus, and another to Port Said, and thence along the coast of Asia Minor to Constantinople. The company has, furthermore, several weekly steamers between this port and Constantinople. The fastest of these vessels makes the trip in less than six days, calling only at Brindisi, Corfu, Patras, Piraeus, and Dardanelles. From Constantinople, the Lloyd runs weekly steamers to Batum and the principal intermediate ports on the north coast of Asia Minor, as well as to Odessa and the Turkish and Roumanian ports on the western coast of the Black Sea. The Thessalian and Graeco-Oriental lines give to this city connection with nearly all the ports of Turkey and Greece, with Candia, the principal isles of the Grecian Archipelago, and Smyrna.

The Lloyd also has regular semimonthly sailings to India and monthly sailings to Japan and China, and issues direct bills of lading to Suez, Aden, Karachi, Bombay, Colombo, Penang, Rangoon, Singapore, Hongkong, Shanghai, Yokohama, and Kobe.

During the South African war, the Lloyd's line to East Africa was discontinued. The regular monthly sailings will, however, be resumed at the end of the present month. With Durban (Natal) as the southern terminus of this line, the steamers call at Aden, Mombasa, Zanzibar, Beira, and Delagoa Bay. Passenger and freight rates for all these lines may be had by applying to the commercial department of the Austrian-Lloyd Navigation Company at Trieste.

### RAILROAD FREIGHT TARIFF.

I have given in former reports tables of railroad freight rates from Trieste to the various inland cities of Austria-Hungary, on the principal commodities imported from the United States. As numerous changes in the rates have been made during the past year, I have prepared the following revised statement for the benefit of American exporters and forwarding agents:

| Articles. | Rate per 100 kilograms (220 lbs.) from Trieste to— | | | | | |
|---|---|---|---|---|---|---|
| | Vienna. | | Budapest. | | Prague. | |
| Iron and steel ware: | *Crowns.* | | *Crowns.* | | *Crowns.* | |
| Less than 5,000 kilograms (11,023 lbs.) .......... | 2.90 | $0.58 | 3.34 | $0.68 | 4.30 | $0.87 |
| 5,000 kilograms and over...................... | 2.38 | .48 | 2.87 | .58 | 2.82 | .57 |
| 10,000 kilograms (22,046 lbs.) and over.......... | 2.22 | .45 | 2.87 | .58 | 2.82 | .57 |
| Agricultural machinery: | | | | | | |
| Less than 5,000 kilograms...................... | 4.49 | .91 | 3.34 | .68 | 5.98 | 1.21 |
| 5,000 kilograms and over...................... | 3.43 | .69 | 2.87 | .58 | 4.30 | .87 |
| 10,000 kilograms and over...................... | 2.36 | .48 | 1.97 | .40 | 2.82 | .57 |
| Bicycles: | | | | | | |
| Less than 5,000 kilograms...................... | 7.50 | 1.52 | 7.41 | 1.50 | 9.97 | 1.82 |
| 5,000 kilograms and over...................... | 7.50 | 1.52 | 7.41 | 1.50 | 8.97 | 1.82 |
| 10,000 kilograms and over...................... | 7.50 | 1.52 | 7.41 | 1.50 | 8.97 | 1.82 |
| Paper: | | | | | | |
| Less than 5,000 kilograms...................... | 3.16 | .64 | 3.34 | .68 | 5.98 | 1.21 |
| 5,000 kilograms and over...................... | 3.16 | .64 | 2.87 | .58 | 4.30 | .87 |
| 10,000 kilograms and over...................... | 2.60 | .52 | 2.87 | .58 | 3.28 | .67 |
| Cotton: | | | | | | |
| Less than 5,000 kilograms...................... | 3.92 | .80 | 3.34 | .68 | 4.84 | .98 |
| 5,000 kilograms and over...................... | 3.43 | .70 | 2.87 | .58 | 4.30 | .87 |
| 10,000 kilograms and over...................... | 2.56 | .52 | 2.87 | .58 | 2.73 | .55 |
| Oil, linseed, etc.: | | | | | | |
| Less than 5,000 kilograms...................... | 3.93 | .80 | 3.34 | .68 | 5.98 | 1.21 |
| 5,000 kilograms and over...................... | 3.43 | .70 | 2.87 | .58 | 4.30 | .87 |
| 10,000 kilograms and over...................... | 2.36 | .48 | 2.87 | .58 | 2.82 | .57 |
| Cotton-seed oil: | | | | | | |
| Less than 5,000 kilograms...................... | 3.93 | .80 | 3.34 | .68 | 5.98 | 1.21 |
| 5,000 kilograms and over...................... | 3.43 | .70 | 2.87 | .58 | 4.30 | .87 |
| 10,000 kilograms and over...................... | 2.88 | .58 | 2.42 | .49 | 3.28 | .67 |
| Raw iron: | | | | | | |
| Less than 5,000 kilograms...................... | 2.90 | .59 | 3.34 | .68 | 4.30 | .87 |
| 5,000 kilograms and over ...................... | 2.38 | .48 | 2.87 | .58 | 2.82 | .57 |
| 10,000 kilograms and over ...................... | 1.57 | .32 | 1.57 | .32 | 2.18 | .44 |
| Blue vitriol: | | | | | | |
| Less than 5,000 kilograms...................... | 4.08 | .83 | 3.34 | .68 | 5.98 | 1.21 |
| 5,000 kilograms and over ...................... | 3.43 | .70 | 2.87 | .58 | 4.30 | .87 |
| 10,000 kilograms and over...................... | 2.88 | .58 | 2.87 | .58 | 3.28 | .67 |
| Smoked and salted meats: | | | | | | |
| Less than 5,000 kilograms...................... | 4.08 | .83 | 3.34 | .68 | 5.98 | 1.21 |
| 5,000 kilograms and over ...................... | 3.90 | .80 | 2.98 | .60 | 4.80 | .97 |
| 10,000 kilograms and over ...................... | 3.42 | .69 | 2.98 | .60 | 3.76 | .76 |
| Bacon: | | | | | | |
| Less than 5,000 kilograms...................... | 4.08 | .83 | 3.34 | .68 | 5.98 | 1.21 |
| 5,000 kilograms and over ...................... | 3.90 | .80 | 2.98 | .60 | 4.80 | .97 |
| 10,000 kilograms and over ...................... | 3.42 | .69 | 2.98 | .60 | 3.76 | .76 |
| Lard: | | | | | | |
| Less than 5,000 kilograms...................... | 3.92 | .80 | 3.34 | .68 | 5.98 | 1.21 |
| 5,000 kilograms and over ...................... | 3.43 | .70 | 2.87 | .58 | 4.30 | .87 |
| 10,000 kilograms and over ...................... | 2.88 | .58 | 2.87 | .58 | 3.28 | .67 |

| Articles. | Rate per 100 kilograms from Trieste to— | | | | | |
|---|---|---|---|---|---|---|
| | Graz. | | Linz. | | Salzburg. | |
| | *Crowns.* | | *Crowns.* | | *Crowns.* | |
| Iron and steel ware: | | | | | | |
| Less than 5,000 kilograms | 1.97 | $0.40 | 3.26 | $0.66 | 3.22 | $0.65 |
| 5,000 kilograms and over | 1.74 | .35 | 2.20 | .45 | 2.18 | .44 |
| 10,000 kilograms and over | 1.56 | .31 | 2.16 | .44 | 2.18 | .44 |
| Agricultural machinery: | | | | | | |
| Less than 5,000 kilograms | 3.28 | .66 | 5.08 | 1.03 | 4.96 | 1.00 |
| 5,000 kilograms and over | 2.60 | .52 | 2.64 | .53 | 3.22 | .65 |
| 10,000 kilograms and over | 1.56 | .31 | 2.64 | .53 | 2.18 | .44 |
| Bicycles: | | | | | | |
| Less than 5,000 kilograms | 6.64 | 1.35 | 8.86 | 1.80 | 9.72 | 1.97 |
| 5,000 kilograms and over | 6.64 | 1.35 | 8.86 | 1.80 | 9.72 | 1.97 |
| 10,000 kilograms and over | 6.64 | 1.35 | 8.86 | 1.80 | 9.72 | 1.97 |
| Paper: | | | | | | |
| Less than 5,000 kilograms | 3.28 | .66 | 5.08 | 1.03 | 4.96 | 1.00 |
| 5,000 kilograms and over | 2.60 | .52 | 4.38 | .89 | 3.22 | .65 |
| 10,000 kilograms and over | 2.60 | .52 | 3.56 | .72 | 2.46 | .50 |
| Cotton: | | | | | | |
| Less than 5,000 kilograms | 2.40 | .49 | 4.40 | .89 | 4.96 | 1.00 |
| 5,000 kilograms and over | 2.40 | .49 | 3.26 | .66 | 3.22 | .65 |
| 10,000 kilograms and over | 2.14 | .43 | 2.60 | .52 | 2.46 | .50 |
| Oil, linseed, etc.: | | | | | | |
| Less than 5,000 kilograms | 2.40 | .49 | 4.76 | .96 | 4.96 | 1.00 |
| 5,000 kilograms and over | 2.40 | .49 | 3.26 | .66 | 3.22 | .65 |
| 10,000 kilograms and over | 2.12 | .43 | 2.60 | .52 | 2.18 | .44 |
| Cotton-seed oil: | | | | | | |
| Less than 5,000 kilograms | 2.40 | .49 | 4.76 | .96 | 4.96 | 1.00 |
| 5,000 kilograms and over | 2.40 | .49 | 3.26 | .66 | 3.22 | .65 |
| 10,000 kilograms and over | 2.12 | .43 | 2.60 | .52 | 2.46 | .50 |
| Raw iron: | | | | | | |
| Less than 5,000 kilograms | 1.97 | .40 | 3.26 | .66 | 3.22 | .65 |
| 5,000 kilograms and over | 1.74 | .35 | 2.20 | .45 | 2.18 | .44 |
| 10,000 kilograms and over | 1.21 | .24 | 1.68 | .34 | 1.64 | .33 |
| Blue vitriol: | | | | | | |
| Less than 5,000 kilograms | 3.28 | .66 | 5.08 | 1.03 | 4.96 | 1.00 |
| 5,000 kilograms and over | 2.60 | .52 | 3.30 | .67 | 3.22 | .65 |
| 10,000 kilograms and over | 2.14 | .43 | 2.64 | .53 | 2.46 | .50 |
| Smoked and salted meats: | | | | | | |
| Less than 5,000 kilograms | 3.28 | .66 | 5.08 | 1.03 | 4.96 | 1.00 |
| 5,000 kilograms and over | 2.81 | .57 | 4.38 | .89 | 4.28 | .87 |
| 10,000 kilograms and over | 2.47 | .50 | 3.56 | .72 | 3.76 | .76 |
| Bacon: | | | | | | |
| Less than 5,000 kilograms | 3.28 | .66 | 5.08 | 1.03 | 4.96 | 1.00 |
| 5,000 kilograms and over | 2.81 | .57 | 4.38 | .89 | 4.28 | .87 |
| 10,000 kilograms and over | 2.47 | .50 | 3.56 | .72 | 3.76 | .76 |
| Lard: | | | | | | |
| Less than 5,000 kilograms | 3.28 | .66 | 5.08 | 1.03 | 4.96 | 1.00 |
| 5,000 kilograms and over | 2.60 | .52 | 3.30 | .67 | 3.22 | .65 |
| 10,000 kilograms and over | 2.14 | .43 | 2.64 | .53 | 2.46 | .40 |

## COMMERCE.

The aggregate value of the commerce of Trieste was 4.6 per cent greater in 1901 than in 1900, having increased from 1,396,819,719 crowns ($283,554,403) to 1,461,068,899 crowns ($296,596,986). The value of the total imports by land and sea was 769,050,241 crowns ($156,117,199), and that of the total exports by land and sea 692,018,658 crowns ($140,479,787), as against 731,370,100 crowns ($148,468,130), and 665,449,619 crowns ($135,086,273), respectively, in 1900. The trade in textiles, cotton, sugar, tobacco, and several other commodities showed a considerable increase, while only a few important articles, among them rice and iron, suffered a noticeable loss. The price of sugar declined sharply during the year, but the trade was brisk and exceeded in volume that of the previous year by 30 per cent.

The following table shows the values of the various imports and exports:

| Articles. | Imports. | | Exports. | |
|---|---|---|---|---|
| | Quantity. | Value. | Quantity. | Value. |
| | *Quintals.a* | | *Quintals.a* | |
| Alcohol and distilled liquors | 123,712 | $1,660,414 | 133,890 | $1,959,062 |
| Animals (cattle) | b 22,490 | 1,369,641 | | |
| Beer | 144,514 | 528,054 | 138,162 | 304,844 |
| Bones and bone dust | | | 25,261 | 46,152 |
| Books and other printed matter | 8,574 | 399,047 | 2,487 | 277,674 |
| Bran | 225,194 | 599,243 | 211,320 | 428,980 |
| Bricks and tiles | 394,419 | 160,134 | | |
| Brushes, brooms, and similar manufactures | 1,913 | 148,495 | 4,241 | 148,829 |
| Butter, bacon, and lard | 12,103 | 264,938 | 7,459 | 158,360 |
| Candles | 3,839 | 72,927 | 2,422 | 55,096 |
| Caoutchouc | 8,724 | 544,300 | 8,994 | 584,867 |
| Cement and cement ware | 157,560 | 11,221 | 70,332 | 44,791 |
| Charcoal | 272,287 | 331,646 | 66,480 | 80,912 |
| Chemical products | 8,997 | 219,178 | 2,302 | 56,077 |
| Cheese | 12,712 | 387,080 | 5,080 | 54,686 |
| Chocolate, and surrogates of | 1,766 | 78,870 | 1,642 | 73,332 |
| Clothing and millinery | 6,851 | 1,668,904 | 12,340 | 3,006,024 |
| Coal and coke | 3,114,616 | 1,569,789 | 515,472 | 275,639 |
| Cocoa | 9,562 | 271,752 | 9,154 | 260,157 |
| Cocoons, silk | | | 776 | 110,270 |
| Coffee | 555,548 | 9,478,204 | 503,407 | 8,583,896 |
| Colors, prepared | 11,216 | 318,759 | 9,464 | 268,967 |
| Cork and cork ware | 13,458 | 114,486 | 14,057 | 120,715 |
| Corn | 327,046 | 912,650 | 206,263 | 564,805 |
| Cotton, raw | 578,984 | 11,753,375 | 578,521 | 11,743,976 |
| Dough | 6,325 | 64,199 | 21,494 | 218,174 |
| Drugs | 33,928 | 916,744 | 43,976 | 1,154,337 |
| Dyewood | 26,660 | 86,586 | 23,612 | 76,692 |
| Earths, diverse | 114,574 | 51,169 | | |
| Earthenware | 17,985 | 179,576 | 9,708 | 111,046 |
| Eggs | 9,577 | 126,868 | | |
| Engravings and chromos | 370 | 63,844 | | |
| Explosive materials and powder | 1,585 | 61,259 | 1,756 | 101,294 |
| Extracts for tanning and dyeing | 16,403 | 99,794 | 16,757 | 102,050 |
| Fish, fresh and canned | 22,197 | 396,160 | 21,212 | 377,557 |
| Flour | 536,347 | 2,395,825 | 257,305 | 1,149,124 |
| Fowl, domestic | 4,711 | 105,197 | | |
| Fruit | 1,311,861 | 7,104,268 | 1,269,604 | 6,847,425 |
| Furs, diverse | 649 | 111,985 | 478 | 96,191 |
| Glassware, etc | 97,752 | 997,238 | 71,144 | 734,941 |
| Glues, diverse | 4,653 | 75,565 | 2,937 | 47,697 |
| Gold coin | | | 2 | 105,501 |
| Gum and rosin | 23,527 | 659,606 | 23,186 | 576,435 |
| Hardware | 23,828 | 2,262,577 | 23,400 | 2,924,093 |
| Hats, diverse | 1,034 | 293,863 | 1,109 | 357,178 |
| Hemp | 22,519 | 365,709 | 18,466 | 299,888 |
| Indigo | 6,008 | 1,036,680 | 6,087 | 1,050,312 |
| Insect flowers and powder | 9,631 | 414,480 | 7,669 | 330,043 |
| Instruments, scientific | 887 | 258,098 | 746 | 242,301 |
| Instruments, musical | 3,558 | 264,938 | 3,871 | 216,252 |
| Intestines and bladders | 3,540 | 129,452 | 3,498 | 127,634 |
| Iron and ironware | 646,707 | 4,841,121 | 803,821 | 3,748,501 |
| Jet goods | 3,562 | 115,694 | 7,373 | 239,475 |
| Jute | 242,344 | 884,745 | 234,911 | 1,603,086 |
| Leather goods | 3,357 | 288,518 | 3,232 | 557,131 |
| Oilcloth, asphalt cloth, linoleum, etc | | | 6,290 | 247,718 |
| Machines and parts of machines | 43,348 | 884,745 | 17,983 | 377,112 |
| Magnesite | 284,254 | 288,518 | 292,730 | 297,121 |
| Malt | 17,153 | 90,584 | | |
| Manganese | 31,934 | 45,378 | | |
| Manure | | | 72,845 | 79,161 |
| Matches, etc | 49,967 | 517,205 | 47,349 | 490,204 |
| Meat, fresh, canned, and dried | 11,974 | 319,603 | 1,903 | 54,217 |
| Medicines, prepared | 953 | 96,730 | 8,082 | 312,823 |
| Meerschaum | 1,979 | 281,216 | 1,899 | 269,848 |
| Metal and metal ware | 180,204 | 5,167,971 | 160,146 | 4,578,794 |
| Metal coin | 989 | 60,230 | 999 | 60,839 |
| Minerals, diverse | 707,810 | 360,905 | | |
| Mineral water | 28,479 | 185,000 | 19,725 | 128,134 |
| Mother-of-pearl | 5,908 | 239,865 | 6,897 | 280,018 |
| Nutgall, etc | 135,143 | 689,738 | 159,699 | 808,575 |
| Oils: | | | | |
| Cotton, sesame, etc | 200,944 | 2,492,796 | 124,400 | 1,745,556 |
| Ethereal, essences (aromatic), and perfumery | 2,538 | 223,786 | 2,164 | 348,338 |
| Fish | 6,903 | 63,069 | 5,361 | 48,973 |
| Mineral and lubricating | 337,098 | 828,010 | 329,561 | 1,338,001 |
| Palm, cocoa, etc | 19,780 | 208,798 | 27,016 | 285,181 |

a Of 220 pounds.                 b Number.

| Articles. | Imports. | | Exports. | |
|---|---|---|---|---|
| | Quantity. | Value. | Quantity. | Value. |
| Oils—Continued. | *Quintals.a* | | *Quintals.a* | |
| Olive | 61,966 | $1,157,277 | 154,586 | $2,887,048 |
| Turpentine, etc | 4,187 | 55,247 | | |
| Opium | 131 | 58,505 | 117 | 52,252 |
| Paper, pasteboard, etc | 483,602 | 3,706,052 | 401,107 | 3,578,428 |
| Paraffin, ceresin, etc | 34,332 | 522,333 | 36,419 | 746,820 |
| Pease, dried | 110,822 | 411,059 | 88,787 | 331,008 |
| Phosphates | 43,111 | 43,758 | 50,777 | 51,539 |
| Plants and parts of | 10,518 | 170,812 | 19,520 | 317,005 |
| Porcelain | 13,616 | 304,045 | 9,305 | 207,781 |
| Pulse, potatoes, etc | 350,815 | 646,515 | 282,241 | 495,291 |
| Quicksilver | 1,873 | 199,615 | 1,964 | 209,313 |
| Quinine, etc | 99 | 60,291 | 102 | 62,118 |
| Rags | | | 12,069 | 72,463 |
| Rice | 581,972 | 2,608,081 | 541,879 | 3,491,038 |
| Ropes, manufactured (cordage) | 4,844 | 127,833 | 5,717 | 150,872 |
| Rosin, etc | 81,391 | 198,268 | 76,065 | 185,294 |
| Saltpeter | 16,353 | 82,991 | 16,484 | 3,346 |
| Seeds, diverse | 278,177 | 1,609,741 | 93,820 | 19,045 |
| Silk, scraps of | 4,335 | 352,002 | 6,127 | 497,512 |
| Silver and silver coin | 139 | 220,493 | 313 | 497,673 |
| Skins, raw | 128,843 | 4,314,784 | 145,828 | 5,176,208 |
| Skins, tanned | 11,847 | 807,487 | 11,009 | 783,947 |
| Soap | 6,700 | 88,005 | 33,024 | 335,194 |
| Sponges | 2,834 | 575,302 | 1,639 | 332,718 |
| Stone and stoneware | 168,234 | 97,670 | 48,136 | 61,680 |
| Sugar | 1,850,690 | 9,571,424 | 1,758,816 | 9,096,142 |
| Sulphur | 129,772 | 237,093 | 128,120 | 234,075 |
| Sumac | 23,135 | 75,142 | 22,119 | 718,425 |
| Surrogates of coffee | 8,035 | 71,769 | | |
| Tallow | 6,768 | 82,434 | 11,260 | 187,147 |
| Tar coloring, extracts of | 3,126 | 158,645 | 816 | 41,412 |
| Tartar | 18,994 | 462,694 | 26,385 | 642,789 |
| Tea | 12,973 | 1,448,435 | 11,488 | 1,282,629 |
| Textile fabrics and yarn | 279,063 | 29,541,388 | 209,172 | 22,630,520 |
| Tobacco, etc | 116,090 | 10,208,440 | 102,883 | 7,384,921 |
| Turners' work, etc. | 3,772 | 153,143 | 1,521 | 61,753 |
| Upholstery, etc | 521 | 105,763 | 447 | 90,741 |
| Ultramarine | 2,826 | 103,262 | 2,188 | 79,949 |
| Varnish | 2,329 | 47,279 | 2,544 | 51,643 |
| Vegetable hair | 26,981 | 60,249 | 28,787 | 64,281 |
| Viands | 14,212 | 403,905 | 25,091 | 713,086 |
| Vitriol | 25,574 | 208,492 | 23,418 | 183,659 |
| Watches, and parts of | 8,082 | 375,388 | 2,402 | 292,564 |
| Wax, animal and vegetable | 2,437 | 143,466 | 2,762 | 162,599 |
| Wine | 531,492 | 3,187,094 | 419,130 | 2,529,177 |
| Wood | 2,207,508 | 3,654,758 | 2,508,277 | 4,072,696 |
| Wooden ware | 173,171 | 1,447,619 | 124,096 | 1,425,458 |
| Wool, raw | 22,833 | 1,158,775 | 21,965 | 1,114,724 |
| Yeast | 2,511 | 61,168 | | |

*a* Of 220 pounds.

## COMMERCIAL RELATIONS WITH THE UNITED STATES.

The statistics of the Trieste Chamber of Commerce show a decline in the value of the imports from the United States at Trieste. In 1899, these imports amounted to $7,876,999, decreasing in 1900 to $7,285,485, and in 1901 to $6,701,772.

As all Austrian customs duties are specific, no declaration of value is required when merchandise is entered. At Trieste, the values of imports are estimated by the secretary of the chamber of commerce, according to a fixed schedule, on the basis of the records of the custom-house. The above figures are therefore only approximately correct.

There was a decrease in the imports of copper, blue vitriol, paraffin, lumber, coffee, and cotton oil; and an increase in those of coal, iron, lead, rosin, and cotton.

The decrease in the importation of blue vitriol is due to the fact that with the gradual disappearance of phylloxera from Austrian vineyards, the consumption of Bordeaux mixture, and its principal ingredient, blue vitriol, has greatly diminished. In the case of coffee, a large quantity of which had in 1899 and 1900 been shipped here from New York, freight rates and prices had in 1901 so adjusted themselves as to render the direct shipment from Brazil more profitable. The comparatively unimportant loss in the imports of American cotton oil is to be accounted for by the increased home production of olive oil and the great rise in the price of the American product. As regards the several other commodities in which decreases are noted, the loss seems to have been due solely to the great rise of prices in the United States, which, in many instances, compelled the American exporter to withdraw from the foreign market.

The following table gives the imports from the United States at Trieste for the year 1901 and the first six months of 1902:

*Imports from the United States at Trieste for the year 1901 and the first six months of 1902.*

| Articles. | Year 1901. | First six months of 1902. | Articles. | Year 1901. | First six months of 1902. |
|---|---|---|---|---|---|
| | *Pounds.* | *Pounds.* | | *Pounds.* | *Pounds.* |
| Allspice | 58,186 | 47,386 | Machines, and parts of. | 241,118 | 163,537 |
| Arms and parts of arms. | 441 | | Maize | | 2,399,274 |
| Automobiles | 2,645 | | Margarine | 89,482 | |
| Bacon and lard | 162,435 | 28,432 | Meat, canned | 53,778 | 43,689 |
| Blacking | 8,596 | | Metals and alloys | 11,240 | |
| Books, etc | 1,322 | | Metal ware, common | 661 | |
| Boots and shoes | 1,543 | | Molasses and sirups | 10,359 | |
| Bicycles | 2,645 | | Mother-of-pearl | 8,155 | |
| Caoutchouc | 1,102 | | Nails | 133,562 | 39,011 |
| Carriages | a 4 | | Oils: | | |
| Caviar | 221 | | Cotton-seed | 33,654,419 | 8,289,685 |
| Clothing and millinery. | 661 | | Fish | 242,220 | 98,298 |
| Coal | 122,467,244 | 18,568,920 | Lubricating | 641,584 | 513,506 |
| Cocoa | 5,510 | | Mineral | 221 | |
| Codfish | 1,984 | | Palm, cocoa, etc | 1,223,661 | 109,759 |
| Coffee | 641,584 | 646,654 | Turpentine, etc | 311,646 | 85,295 |
| Copper | 8,004,487 | 5,468,565 | Other | 210,041 | 87,499 |
| Cotton | 19,072,975 | 13,553,278 | Paper, pasteboard, etc | 136,868 | 804,813 |
| Dyewood | 169,928 | | Paraffin | 3,745,037 | 2,706,292 |
| Earths and minerals not otherwise mentioned | 111,963 | 111,963 | Phosphate | 4,505,417 | |
| | | | Plants, dried, etc | 6,832 | |
| Felt | 9,257 | | Roots for tanning and dyeing | 8,375 | |
| Flour | 59,949 | | Rosin | 17,298,755 | 8,893,581 |
| Fruit, dried and canned. | 11,902 | | Rum, etc | 661 | |
| Glassware | 13,004 | 20,056 | Skins, raw | 1,763 | |
| Glue | 2,424 | | Sponges | 47,606 | |
| Greases, diverse | 466,366 | 59,508 | Staves | 1,178,258 | b 90,473 |
| Hair, diverse | 6,892 | | Stearin | 132,240 | 201,225 |
| Hardware | 8,155 | | Talc | 2,050,381 | 503,614 |
| Instruments. | | | Tallow | 260,733 | |
| Musical | 1,984 | | Varnish | 18,973 | |
| Scientific | 441 | | Viands | 17,852 | 35,925 |
| Intestines and bladders. | 1,763 | | Vitrol, copper and zinc. | 3,475,047 | 8,256,190 |
| Iron, raw, pig, ferro-manganese, etc | 9,619,358 | 94,772 | Watches, and parts of. | 882 | |
| | | | Wood | 2,868,286 | 881,600 |
| Iron and steel strips, tempered and filed | 233,401 | | Wooden ware | 42,978 | 18,073 |
| Iron and steel ware | 48,708 | | Woolen ware | 221 | |
| Lead | 11,350,380 | 4,879,876 | Zinc | 13,845 | 22,922 |
| Leather goods | 2,204 | | Total | 245,193,460 | 72,163,148 |

a Number.          b Pieces.

The exports from this consular district to the United States increased in value from $714,026 in 1900 to $821,452 in 1901. Beans and fruit showed a slight decrease, and skins, wool, and tobacco leaves a not inconsiderable increase. The exports of skins, in particular, grew in value about $85,000 over those of the year 1900. A new and very important article of export was milled rice, of which commodity the local mills shipped to the United States nearly $80,000 worth during the year.

The following table shows the declared value of exports from Trieste to the United States during the year 1901 and the first six months of 1902:

*Exports from Trieste to the United States for the year 1901 and the first six months of 1902.*

| Articles. | Year 1901. | First six months of 1902. | Articles. | Year 1901. | First six months of 1902. |
|---|---|---|---|---|---|
| Antimony .................... | ............ | $2,881.82 | Lemon peel ............. | 11.19 | ............ |
| Barberry juice.......... | $676.40 | ............ | Macaroni.............. | 2,194.60 | ............ |
| Beans .................. | 15,388.63 | 8,347.30 | Mineral wax ............ | 510.86 | ............ |
| Books ................. | ............ | 244.64 | Mustard seed........... | 3,454.43 | 985.70 |
| Cedars, myrtles, and | | | Nuts..................... | 2,552.08 | 41.67 |
|   palms ................. | 2,769.95 | ............ | Oils...................... | 2,811.75 | 1,157.41 |
| Cheese ................. | 427.08 | 1,930.34 | Olives .................. | ............ | 158.69 |
| Citrons in brine ........ | 381.43 | 1,056.96 | Orange peel ............. | 476.77 | 505.71 |
| Cloth................... | 310.30 | ............ | Paint ...... | 563.08 | ............ |
| Cuttlefish bones........ | 26,478.02 | 10,616.66 | Pepper, red........... | 818.03 | ............ |
| Drugs (herbs, roots, | | | Polishing earth........ | 1,554.42 | 3,368.80 |
|   leaves, etc.) .......... | 49,516.88 | 9,622.91 | Red lead ............... | 174.70 | ............ |
| Filberts ............... | 10,059.59 | 2,566.94 | Rice and rice flour ..... | 79,969.98 | 60,996.22 |
| Fish: | | | Rosin...................... | ............ | 37.53 |
|   In oil ................ | 3,100.00 | 1,516.20 | Seeds..................... | 629.34 | ............ |
|   Salted ............... | ............ | 257.96 | Skins..................... | 416,830.33 | 231,479.45 |
| Fruit, dried ........... | 11,770.54 | 11,382.39 | Sponges ................. | 5,968.88 | 2,299.95 |
| Fustic wood and roots.. | 6,602.26 | 3,115.36 | Sticks ................ | 541.71 | ............ |
| Galls.................. | 2,130.36 | 215.19 | St. John's bread ....... | 1,390.92 | 852.96 |
| Glycerin .............. | 2,518.76 | 3,751.49 | Tobacco leaves........ | 36,322.74 | 15,466.42 |
| Gum.............../... | 58,417.93 | 36,658.22 | Turpentine.............. | 6,290.78 | 3,271.23 |
| Insect flowers and pow- | | | White lead ............ | 3,134.68 | 3,266.22 |
|   der .............. | 55,624.47 | 41,902.49 | Wine and other liquors. | 2,883.29 | 3,043.29 |
| Intestines, salted...... | ............ | 1,410.85 | Wool ............... | ............ | 20,254.33 |
| Iron .................. | 6,299.50 | ............ | Returned goods ...... | ............ | 101.50 |
| Iron oxide............. | ............ | 291.77 | | | |
| Household goods and | | | Total ............. | 821,452.46 | 484,579.06 |
|   personal effects ...... | 395.85 | 572.46 | | | |

## SUGAR.

Sugar continues to be Trieste's principal article of export. While in the year under review the exports were unusually large, there was an unprecedented fall in prices, and the campaign proved to both manufacturer and dealer one of the most unsatisfactory on record.

Quotations at the beginning of the present year were fully 20 per cent lower than they had been twelve months before. Week after week, lower prices were offered. This condition invited speculation, and contracts for future delivery took to a large extent the place of cash sales.

Long-term deliveries and sharp declines led to differences and repudiations, and the year closed with a well-developed demoralization of the market.

### SUGAR FREIGHTS.

About a year ago, Trieste's sugar export to the Balkan States and the Levant seemed for a time to be seriously imperiled. Trieste had always been able to control this eastern trade, being greatly aided in the maintenance of her supremacy by the fact that the Austrian Lloyd Steamship Company has for many years had regular sailings and fixed freight rates to the principal Levantine ports. The Lloyd rates were comparatively high but, in the absence of competition in the eastern sugar market, not prohibitive. In the spring of 1901, however, a new factor appeared in the equation. Hungarian and Roumanian sugar producers, who had long had their eyes on the eastern market, pre-

vailed upon, the Danube steamship companies to arrange with the
various Hungarian and Roumanian railways a joint tariff, whose low
rates enabled them to undersell Trieste exporters in all the ports on
eastern and southern shores of the Black Sea.   The situation soon
became critical for Trieste, and the Lloyd finally found itself compelled to rearrange its tariff to meet the changed conditions.   The
company, however, at the same time advanced its sugar rates to India
1s. (24 cts.) per ton, probably to reimburse itself for the decrease in
the earnings of its Levantine lines.

### RECEIPTS.

No sugar is produced in this consular district; in fact, none is produced south of Vienna; and Trieste's stocks come from the provinces
north of the capital and from Hungary.
The following table shows the arrival of sugar from the various
provinces during the past three years:

| From. | Tons.ᵃ | | |
|---|---|---|---|
| | 1901. | 1900. | 1899. |
| Moravia | 103,500 | 77,600 | 100,930 |
| Bohemia | 35,500 | 24,000 | 26,500 |
| Hungary | 26,000 | 23,530 | 18,000 |
| Lower Austria (including the shipments from Vienna warehouses) | 12,000 | 9,000 | 9,840 |
| Silesia | 6,000 | 6,900 | 5,600 |
| Galicia | 1,600 | 400 | |
| Total | 184,600 | 141,430 | 160,870 |

ᵃ Of 2,205 pounds.

It will be noticed that last year's receipts were more than 30 per cent
larger than those of 1900.
Classified as to quality, the receipts of the last three years were:

| Quality: | Tons. | | |
|---|---|---|---|
| | 1901. | 1900. | 1899. |
| Pulverized and granulated | 77,700 | 50,050 | 582,400 |
| Melispilé and lump | 48,500 | 37,600 | 576,000 |
| Crushed | 48,200 | 46,000 | 480,000 |
| Cut loaf | 4,200 | 5,000 | 51,000 |
| Loaf | 6,000 | 2,780 | 19,000 |
| Total | 184,600 | 141,430 | 160,840 |

### EXPORTS.

The exports to the East Indies were almost twice as large as in the
year 1900.   Those to Japan and China also increased materially; that
is to say, nearly 15 per cent.   It is feared, however, that the recent
increase in the sugar duty of India and the growing home production
of Japan will in the future seriously curtail Austria-Hungary's exports
of sugar to the Far East.
Strenuous efforts have been made in recent years to increase the
exports to northern Africa, and especially to Morocco, but in spite of
these steps, last year's shipments showed an increase of only about
1,000 tons over those of 1900.   Nearly a year ago, the Hungarian
steamship company "Adria" opened a line of steamers to the principal ports of Morocco, to enable Austro-Hungarian sugar to com-

pete successfully in the Moroccan markets with French and Belgian products, which enjoy exceedingly favorable freights. The statement is, however, freely made in local sugar circles that the Adria's present rates will not enable the Austrian product to make any material gains in the north African markets.

## COFFEE.

The coffee trade of 1901 showed a slight increase over that of the previous year, due partly to the growing home consumption and partly to an extension of Trieste's market in the East. The imports of 1901 were the largest on record, being 550,090 quintals (1,212,728 pounds), against 527,297 quintals (1,162,685 pounds) in 1900. Over 70 per cent of the total imports was of Brazilian origin. The remainder was chiefly the product of Central America, Porto Rico, and the East Indies.

Wholesale dealers assert that Porto Rican coffee is growing more popular in Austria every year, and that the demand for it is constantly increasing. It is not possible, however, to obtain exact figures showing the total imports of Porto Rican coffee at Trieste, as the greater part of it is shipped via German ports and classed in the Austrian customs statistics as a German import. The article, of course, never loses its identity for the dealers.

Of the total imports, only 20 per cent was reexported. The principal markets for the coffee export of Trieste are the Balkan States and the Levant.

### INSECT FLOWERS AND POWDER.

Trieste continues to be the principal and almost only market for Dalmatian insect flowers. Between June 1, 1901, and May 31, 1902, Dalmatia shipped here 4,650 quintals (1,023,000 pounds) of this article, and arrivals of over 4,500 quintals may be said to be indicative of a good harvest. Prices varied from 96 to 250 crowns per quintal ($19 to $50 per 220 pounds), first cost; some lots of so-called "bogus" flowers and stems were sold as low as 50 crowns ($10) per quintal. The latter article is, however, absolutely worthless.

The present export quotations for genuine flowers are:

|  |  | Crowns. |
|---|---|---|
| Open flowers | per quintal [a].. | 150 to 200 |
| Half-closed flowers | do.... | 200 to 230 |
| Closed flowers | do.... | 230 to 280 |

Even at the present comparatively low price of flowers, the genuineness of insect powder offered at less than 200 crowns ($40) per quintal must be questioned, as a really good quality of powder can not be sold for less than from 250 to 275 crowns per quintal ($50 to $56 per 220 pounds). The total quantity of insect flowers and powder exported to the United States was about 450,000 pounds, valued at $55,624.

### OAK STAVES.

Austria-Hungary still produces large quantities of oak staves. These staves are shipped from the interior to Trieste and Fiume, whence they are exported, chiefly to France. The average price of staves at Trieste is about $100 per 1,000 pieces, the so-called normal stave (36 by 1 by 4

[a] 220.46 pounds.

inches) being taken as the standard, and the cubic contents of staves
of all other dimensions being reduced to this unit of measure.

The following table gives the exports of Austria-Hungary during
1901, according to destination and ports of shipment:

| Destination. | From Trieste. | From Fiume. | Total. |
|---|---|---|---|
| | *Pieces.* | *Pieces.* | *Pieces.* |
| France | 2,295,783 | 40,953,614 | 43,249,397 |
| Portugal | 405,609 | 105,293 | 510,902 |
| Italy | 84,511 | 248,247 | 332,758 |
| England | 17,080 | 246,300 | 263,380 |
| Algiers | | 185,057 | 185,057 |
| Holland | | 77,627 | 77,627 |
| Turkey | | 57,034 | 57,034 |
| Tunis | | 9,969 | 9,969 |
| Greece | | 2,017 | 2,017 |
| Spain | | 1,406 | 1,406 |
| Total | 2,802,983 | 41,886,564 | 44,689,547 |

## COAL.

The total imports of foreign coal at Trieste amounted to about
284,000 tons, of which the United States furnished 555,659 quintals
(61,122 tons) against 458,246 quintals (50,452 tons) in 1900. The Austrian Lloyd Steamship Company imported from the United States about
57,000 tons for its own use. The coal proved so satisfactory that,
nearly a year ago, the Lloyd commenced negotiations for the purchase
of 100,000 tons of the American product, to be delivered during the
present year. However, owing partly to the sharp advance in the
price of coal in the United States, and partly to the lowering of
British freights, these negotiations finally came to naught, and the
Lloyd placed its coal order with English colliers. During the first six
months of the present year, only one cargo of American coal reached
Trieste, and the present condition of our home market leaves further
shipments of coal to the Adriatic out of the question for the remainder of the year.

## COTTON.

The total importation of raw cotton into Austria-Hungary in 1901
increased 130 tons over 1900, exceeding the imports of all previous
years, with the exception of 1898, which year holds the record. Of
the three cotton-producing countries, British India exported to Austria 130 tons more than in 1900, the United States about held its
own, and Egypt lost some ground. The indirect importation from
such nonproducing countries as Germany, England, and France was
not insignificant, the cotton thus imported being almost all of American origin. The United States furnished in all 69½ per cent of the
total cotton imports of Austria-Hungary, East India 22 per cent,
and Egypt 8½ per cent, against 74½, 13½, and 12 per cent, respectively,
in 1900.

The increase in the importation of Indian cotton must be accounted
for by its low price and the fact that there is a demand in this country
for the inferior grades of goods manufactured therefrom. It is expected, however, that, owing to the continual establishment of new
mills in India, as well as in China and Japan, nearly the entire East
Indian product will within a few years be consumed in Asia.

The import of cotton via Trieste amounted to 376 tons, which was an increase of 120 tons over the previous year. Of the American cotton, 86 tons came through Trieste, against 86 tons in 1900.

Our poor bagging and loose baling continue to be the subject of general complaint. The former constantly exposes the cotton to damage, and the latter causes needless extra expense in transportation. The Indian bale of cotton, which is not as well pressed as the Egyptian, weighs about 410 pounds, and measures 49 by 21 by 18 inches. Fifty-five such bales, with a total weight of 22,500 pounds, can be loaded in an Austrian so-called 10-ton freight car, while but 25 American bales, weighing only about 12,100 pounds, can be loaded in a car of the same capacity. Our cotton is of course at the same disadvantage as concerns sea freight.

### COTTON-SEED OIL.

The quantity of cotton-seed oil imported from the United States in 1901 amounted to 157,697 quintals (34,765,880 pounds) which was a decrease of about 2,270,000 pounds from the imports of the previous year. The total imports of that kind of merchandise at Trieste during the year under review were 161,105 quintals (35,517,000 pounds), as against 171,001 quintals (37,698,000 pounds) in 1900. Shipments from Great Britain showed a gain of 1,757 quintals (388,300 pounds), but this was due solely to the high prices of the American oil, which averaged during the year from 3 to 5 francs ($0.58 to $0.96) above the prices of the British product.

The refined American cotton-seed oil is in every respect superior to all others, and is from year to year growing in popularity in Southern Europe. Retail oil dealers declare that it is getting to be difficult to sell the pure olive oil, the majority of consumers preferring the blended article.

The prospects for the coming season are unusually good, and it is expected that the imports will come up to those of 1899, which was the banner year.

The present prices for prime refined American oil are rather high, but I do not believe that they need be lowered. Such oil has no really serious competitor in this market, and as long as its price is below the quotations for medium olive oil, it is sure to find a ready market in southern Europe.

### AMERICAN LEATHER.

Hemlock sole leather, which only a few years ago ranked among the principal imports at Trieste, is fast losing ground in Austria. In 1899, the value of the imports of that commodity was still above $100,000; in 1900 it decreased to $60,000, and in 1901 to $18,000. This decrease is due to the fact that the prices of hemlock leather have advanced in the United States so much that the article can no longer compete in Austria with the home-made leather. Calfskin, I am sorry to state, has fared even worse here than hemlock sole leather, for its importation has entirely ceased. Austrian tanneries have in recent years adopted American methods of tanning and introduced American machinery. As a result, calf leather equal in quality to the American product is now produced here and can be sold at a much lower price than the imported article, the duty on which is 4 cents per pound.

In the better markets, there is a growing demand for American glazed skins.   In former years, all the glazed leather was furnished by France, but the beauty of American ladies' shoes caused European consumers to desire American kid.

### SULPHATE OF COPPER.

As has been already stated, there was a large decrease in the imports of sulphate of copper.   The total amount imported at Trieste in 1901 was only 22 tons, as against 36 tons in 1900.   This decrease is chiefly due to the extermination of the phylloxera and the general introduction of immune American grape vines.   Imports from the United States fell from 26 tons in 1900 to 16 tons in 1901.   Dealers complain that the American product passes through too many hands before it reaches the consumer, and that its price is thus needlessly increased. It is claimed that if our exporters would sell directly to Trieste firms, instead of through British or German middlemen, the entire market of Southern Austria could readily be controlled by the American article.

### SHIPBUILDING IN TRIESTE.

The shipyards of Trieste were kept well employed during the year. The Stabilimento Tecnico Triestino completed a battleship of 8,340 tons displacement for the Austrian navy, and commenced work on two other similar vessels of equal tonnage.   It also built two mail and passenger steamers of 4,000 tons each for the Chinese and Eastern Railway, of Russia.   One cargo and passenger steamer of 3,000 tons and three smaller vessels were still under construction at the end of the year.

In the yard of the Austrian Lloyd, six steamers were building, three of which were completed in 1901 and the remaining three during the current year.   At present, there are four ships building in this yard, two of 5,000 tons and two of 3,000 tons each.

A good deal of repair work has also been done by both companies.

### FLOATING DOCK.

A section of the floating dock of Fiume was purchased last year by a Trieste syndicate.

The dock has been towed here and, with the permission of the Imperial port authorities, has been anchored at the end of the large break-water.   To secure the dock for Trieste, and thus draw here for docking purposes the small craft of the Adriatic, the Government granted to the docks yndicate exemption from taxation.

The dock is 60 meters (196.8 feet) long and 17 meters (55.7 feet) wide, and can float a steamer of 2,000 tons.

There is as yet no repair shop connected with this dock, but it is intended to erect one very soon on the breakwater adjoining it.

The floating dock is a great convenience to small vessels which can ill afford the cost of frequent dry docking; it also offers the advantage of being always dry, while the graving docks are more or less wet and muddy.

It is the intention of the syndicate to buy also the remaining smaller section of this dock.   The two sections together will be capable of lifting steamers of 3,500 tons.

So far, from two to three steamers a week have been docked, and the demand for the use of the floating dock is more likely to increase than to diminish in the future.

Unfortunately, the dock has been anchored in one of the most exposed positions in the bay, and it is the general opinion of seamen that in winter, when the Bora often blows for days at the rate of from 40 to 60 miles an hour, docking will at times be seriously interfered with.

### HARBOR IMPROVEMENTS.

I stated in my last year's report that an appropriation of 12,000,000 crowns ($2,436,000) had been made by the Government for the improvement of the Trieste Harbor. This work, which is to extend over a period of eight years, was commenced last January, and is progressing in accordance with the Government's plans. The mole which is being constructed before the quarantine office for the accommodation of coasting vessels is expected to be completed next year.

### NEW RAILROADS.

Several short lines of railroad have been opened in this consular district during the past year, chief among which are an independent line of the State railway system along the Istrian coast from Trieste to Pirano, and a so-called "secondary" or branch road from Gorizia to Aidussina. The latter place possesses excellent water power, and is the center of an incipient cotton industry. Heretofore, all the cotton consumed in the mills, as well as the entire finished product, had to be hauled on wagons to and from Gorizia, a distance of 20 miles. The mills consume principally American cotton. The improved transportation facilities will greatly increase the efficiency and output of the mills, and no doubt an increased demand for raw material will follow.

### LABOR.

The relations between capital and labor at Trieste have, for the last few years, left much to be desired. The laborers claim that they are underpaid, inasmuch as their wages are far below those given for similar labor elsewhere. Capital replies that, on the basis of efficiency, labor receives here a higher reward than even in Germany or Great Britain, since greater skill, intelligence, and endurance enable the British and German workmen to do on an average twice as much work, while they do not receive twice as much pay as Triestine laborers. Capital further points to the fact that the Austrian Lloyd Steamship Company, although it owns a large shipyard and could easily build all its own ships, has had a considerable number of its vessels constructed in Great Britain.

How labor and material figure in the expenses of shipbuilding in Austria has been well illustrated in a recent statement of the Lloyd concerning the cost of its steamer *Erzherzog Franz Ferdinand*, which was built in its own yard. Work was commenced June 7, 1898, and the vessel was launched on April 1, 1899, and was turned over to the traffic department on August 4 of the same year.

The steamer has a length of 426 and a width of 51 feet. Its gross tonnage is 6,043; net tonnage, 3,680; displacement, 9,640 tons; indicated horsepower, 3,859; average speed, 12 knots.

The total cost of the ship's hull was 1,333,929.40 crowns ($270,787.67), in which labor and material participated as shown:

| | Wages paid. | Cost of material used. | | Wages paid. | Cost of material used. |
|---|---|---|---|---|---|
| Machinists for rough work | $270 | $547 | Locksmiths | $1,611 | $1,787 |
| Machinists for fine work | 1,392 | 186 | Upholsterers | 289 | 2,588 |
| Fitters (on board) | 577 | 1,048 | Tinsmiths | 871 | 2,071 |
| Pattern makers | 263 | 30 | Masons | 1,496 | 915 |
| Coppersmiths | 331 | 2,427 | Sailors | 634 | 2,599 |
| Blacksmiths and galvanizers | 6,544 | 5,449 | Carpenters | 11,864 | 12,802 |
| Cabinetmakers | 9,079 | 6,682 | Sailmakers | 273 | 1,554 |
| Mast makers | 148 | 638 | Riveters | 83,558 | 100,483 |
| Boiler makers | 340 | 35 | Common laborers | 8,984 | 2,597 |
| Painters | 1,565 | 757 | Sundry labor | 863 | 136 |
| | | | Total | 125,454 | 145,333 |

The total cost of the engines was 464,532.28 crowns ($94,300), divided between labor and material as follows:

| | Wages paid. | Cost of material used. | | Wages paid. | Cost of material used. |
|---|---|---|---|---|---|
| Machinists for rough work | $12,785 | $20,687 | Masons | $349 | $696 |
| Machinists for fine work | 6,221 | 5,660 | Sailors | 22 | 3 |
| Fitters (on board) | 3,998 | 1,481 | Tinsmiths | 483 | 545 |
| Pattern makers | 1,094 | 162 | Riveters | 14,389 | 2,954 |
| Coppersmiths | 1,886 | 4,389 | Common laborers | 1,059 | 102 |
| Locksmiths | 1,866 | 1,821 | Sundry labor | 28 | 252 |
| Cabinetmakers | 121 | 195 | Total | 49,536 | 44,764 |
| Boiler makers | 5,243 | 5,807 | | | |

It will thus be seen that in the construction of the ship's hull and engines the cost of labor (which included, however, the cost of supervision, etc.) was nearly equal to the cost of material used.

The following table shows the daily wages paid at the Lloyd's arsenal:

| Trade. | Amount. | Trade. | Amount. |
|---|---|---|---|
| *Daily wages.* | | *Daily wages*—Cont'd. | |
| Machinists for rough work | $0.446-$0.974 | Laundrymen | $0.527-$0.747 |
| Machinists for fine work | .406- .933 | Coopers and wheelwrights | .649- .690 |
| Fitters (on board) | .527- 1.096 | Masons | .487- .812 |
| Assistants (for lifting gear) | .487- .730 | Sailmakers | .665- .730 |
| Crane men | .503- .706 | Calkers | .503- .609 |
| Pattern makers | .487- .852 | Common laborers | .406- .730 |
| Foundry men | .503- .974 | Teamsters and extra laborers | .507- .609 |
| Boiler makers | .406- 1.218 | Servants for officers and storehouses | .503- .690 |
| Boiler makers (for repair work) | .446- .828 | Watchmen | .527- .690 |
| Riveters | .406- 1.015 | Stokers | .300- .609 |
| Galvanizers | .503- .690 | Sawmill men | .527- .787 |
| Coppersmiths | .503- .893 | Engineers | .503- .933 |
| Blacksmiths | .446- 1.218 | Nurses (in the sanitary service) | .609- ...... |
| Locksmiths | .406- .893 | Clerks (timekeepers and draftsmen) | .487- .690 |
| Tinsmiths | .446- .852 | | |
| Painters | .406- .812 | *Monthly wages.* | |
| Bellows makers | .527- .544 | | |
| Upholsterers | .544- .665 | Sailors | 16.24 -17.05 |
| Cabinetmakers | .406- .852 | Night watchmen | -16.64 |
| Carpenters | .406- 1.218 | Porters | 11.77 -19.48 |
| Ship carpenters | .446- .812 | | |
| Mast makers | .649- .812 | | |

The wages paid by the Lloyd compare favorably with those paid by other employers of labor. Low wages and long hours are the rule throughout southern Austria.

### GENERAL STRIKE AT TRIESTE.

For years, labor has made strenuous efforts to improve its condition. Strikes have been frequent, but their results have, in the majority of cases, not been favorable to the strikers, want compelling them to return to their work without obtaining the ends for which they struck. Recently, however, there has been one notable exception to this rule. Last February, the firemen of the Austrian Lloyd demanded that, while in port, their daily watch be reduced from eleven and one-half to eight hours, and they be released from duty at night. The company declining to accede to these demands, all the men struck. The Lloyd, being under contract to carry the Imperial mails, then applied to the naval authorities for a detail of firemen to do duty on the outgoing mail steamers; and when this request was complied with, all the Lloyd's laborers and artisans, to the number of about 2,000, joined the strikers. Meetings were called by the various labor organizations and resolutions were adopted assuring the strikers of the sympathy of their fellow-laborers in the city, demanding that the differences between the Lloyd and its firemen be settled by arbitration, and threatening a general labor strike in case the company should refuse to submit to arbitration. The Lloyd, however, remained obstinate, and on the morning of February 13, 1902, all labor, and with it all business in the city and harbor of Trieste, came to a standstill. All the factories, restaurants, cafés, and stores were compelled to close their doors, and thousands of riotous people paraded the streets, demolishing windows, tearing up lamp-posts, and in a few instances, even plundering stores. The police tried in vain to restore order, and were frequently attacked by the mob. The Government finally found itself compelled to order out the troops; but still the rioting continued. The mob repeatedly charged the soldiery, who finally were compelled to fire in self-defense. In the various encounters between the military and the mob, 16 persons were killed and from 50 to 60 more or less seriously wounded. The gravity of the situation finally compelled the Government to proclaim martial law; but the Lloyd Company, at about the same time, notified the strikers that it was ready to submit the questions at issue to such a court of arbitration as the latter had demanded. The judges, who were promptly selected, assembled and practically granted every demand that the strikers had made. The strike was thereupon declared off, and peace was restored after three days of rioting.

One of the more remote results of the strike has been a greater solidarity in Trieste's labor circles. A general union of labor has recently been formed, whose object is stated to be to guard the moral and material interests of the working classes of this city "in all contingencies of life." The union is divided into sections which represent the various trades or categories of labor. An executive committee of three is practically given arbitrary power to order a general strike whenever it may see fit.

### COMMERCIAL TRAVELERS.

The Austrian Government has recently issued a decree placing greater restrictions upon the business of soliciting orders, either on one's own account or for others. Commercial agents will not be permitted hereafter to call, for the purpose of exhibiting samples or soliciting orders, on persons who have not expressly invited them or their firms to do so, unless such persons be manufacturers or retailers using in their business the goods offered for sale.  These restrictions do not apply, however, to the sale of the following articles:  Machinery, building material, crude cork, material for street pavements, technical appliances for heating and lighting, wooden window shades, curtains and rollers, sewing and typewriting machines.

A commercial agent is not permitted to do any business until he has first obtained a special license (Legitimationskarte) from the industrial board of his province.  To obtain this card, for which only a nominal fee is to be paid, he must furnish the following:

*a.* Full information as to the line of goods for which he intends to solicit orders.

*b.* A certificate of good conduct from the police or municipal authorities.

*c.* A physician's certificate that the applicant is not affected with any loathsome or contagious disease.

*d.* Proof that he is not deformed or disfigured.

*e.* A- photographic picture of the applicant, to be attached to his license.

Foreign traveling agents are required to be in possession of only such documents as the commercial treaties with their respective countries may stipulate.

As this decree has encountered general opposition in commercial circles, no effort has so far been made to enforce it, and it is believed that none will be made until some of its most obnoxious features have been modified.

### EXCHANGE.

The balance of trade having for several years been in favor of the monarchy, gold has become quite abundant, and Austrian currency may now be said to be at par.  American drafts are at present purchased at 4.95 and sold at 4.85 crowns per dollar.

### PROSPECTS FOR AMERICAN TRADE.

Little can be said as yet as to the present prospects for the extension of American trade in Austria.  The Austro-Hungarian customs union expires in 1903, and negotiations for a new treaty are now pending between the Governments of the dual monarchy.  Austria is preeminently a manufacturing and Hungary an agricultural State.  It is therefore but natural that the former should demand the greatest possible protection for its manufactures and the latter for its agricultural products.  The monarchy as a whole adopted the principle of high protection more than twenty years ago, and it is not likely that it will at this juncture lower its tariff in any important particular.  Some increases may, however, be looked for, and these increases, I fear, will fall more heavily upon the imports from the United States than upon those from any other country.

FRED'K W. HOSSFELD, *Consul.*

TRIESTE, *October 30, 1902.*

## HUNGARY.

The total value, according to final estimates, of Hungary's imports in the calendar year 1901 was $232,962,800, and of exports in the same period, $256,835,600. Although the excess in value of the exports was less than the excess in 1900, the result is officially pointed out to be the best for twenty years, i. e., since 1882. But the State statist notes that the imports in 1901 increased by $7,511,000, and that the exports decreased by $12,586,000. In other words, Hungary has paid better prices for her imported goods than she has received for her exports, provided the averaging system in determining the values is correct throughout. While textiles formed the chief cause of the increased value of imports, Americans will be interested to know that the import of grain products, leather goods, and ironware also reached higher figures. Yet Hungary was of old a storehouse of grain and hides, and has rich iron resources not properly worked.

Sugar, wine, and agricultural machines were imported in less quantities in 1901, for which no other reasons can be given than that in the case of the first two products, Hungary has been producing for some decades better qualities, while in the case of agricultural machines, both the overstocking of the stores and the continued efforts to improve home manufactures have to be taken into account.

Hungary's diminished export was chiefly in agricultural, textile, and iron products. A good corn crop and a good flour output failed to compensate for the decrease in export of animals, especially oxen and horses, and in animal products, particularly eggs.

### TRADE WITH AUSTRIA.

Hungary's trade with Austria, of which, internally, it is commercially independent, has been the subject of long and laborious investigations on the part of the two "merchandise-valuing committees," as they are called. These committees, it seems, have honestly differed in their estimation of the interstate trade of the two countries, as follows:

The Austrians figure the imports from Austria into Hungary at $6,353,900 less than the Hungarians; on the other hand, they figure the exports from Hungary to Austria at $933,800 higher. And in comparing the trade for the years 1900 and 1901, Austria claims an excess of exports from Hungary into her territory of $5,643,400, while Hungary finds an excess of imports from Austria into her dominions of $1,644,300.

The Hungarian committee openly declares that it differs from the Austrian in the valuation it places on some fifty different articles of trade.

FRANK DYER CHESTER, *Consul.*

BUDAPEST, *July 30, 1902.*

----

### TRADE OF HUNGARY WITH THE UNITED STATES IN 1901.

Neither the imports of Hungary from the United States nor its exports to that country amounted in 1901 to 1 per cent of the whole trade of Hungary. Nevertheless, the United States, like Austria, Servia, Brazil, and British East India, exported more, in value, to

Hungary than it imported therefrom.  In this respect, it compares favorably with Germany, whose imports from Hungary are more valuable than its exports to the Kingdom.

The average value of the total imports from the United States in 1901 was $1,808,924.07—somewhat less than the average value of the imports in 1900, but still twice that of 1899.

### PHOSPHATES.

The import of phosphates heads the list with 15,021,166.8 pounds, being almost the figure reached in 1898, nearly twice that of 1900, and three times as great as that of 1897 and 1899.  The average price paid for these phosphates was, however, less than that in 1898.  From statistics, it is clear that Austria received nearly a third more, while the import from Algeria—which, with Russia, competes most closely with the United States—was obtained at a price one-third lower.

### ROSIN.

The United States supplied Hungary with one-half of its imports of rosin in 1901.  In 1899 and 1900, these imports were attributed to Trieste, but last year they were correctly given as 7,343,963.5 pounds. The average price fell from $3.45 to $2.23 per 220.46 pounds.  The other half of the imports was supplied by Austria, at an average price of $4.06 per 220.46 pounds.  It is evident that the American exporters must be realizing less, even if they now export more of this product.

### COTTON, COPPER, AND OIL.

The imports of raw cotton and raw copper were well maintained. The average price paid for the former has increased; that paid for the latter slightly lowered.  Mineral oil was imported in about the same quantity as in 1901, and at the average price of previous years. Owing to the withdrawal of the American representative in this line, the imports next year will doubtless be decreased.

### TOBACCO.

The imports of raw tobacco fell off 60 per cent in value, yet the amount in weight (1,214,955 pounds) was nearly the same.  The only explanation is that Hungary bought better tobacco in 1900 than it did in 1899 and 1901, paying an average value of $53.19 per 220.46 pounds, instead of $17.30 and $20.30 respectively.  In this connection, it is noticeable that the import of raw tobacco from the Philippine Islands, which is still shown separately in the Hungarian statistics, did not fall off in value, while that from Cuba and Porto Rico did.

### LEAD.

The year 1901 is remarkable for the imports of American crude lead into Hungary—993,172.3 pounds, at an average value of $7.21 per 220.46 pounds.  The United States had to compete with Austria and Germany, the first-mentioned country receiving the highest average price—$8.06 per 220.46 pounds.

## PARAFFIN.

Hungary still imports half of her paraffin from the United States, and the average price has risen from $14.21 to $15.02 per 220.46. Germany, however, sold her small supply at the old rates, so that the figures may be reversed in 1902.

### TYPEWRITERS AND CALCULATING MACHINES.

For writing and calculating machines, the Hungarian statistician opened a new column in 1900. The imports of these machines from the United States, Germany, and Great Britain have been steadily increasing, while the shipments from Austria have fallen off, perhaps because independent branches of manufacture in these lines have been opened in Budapest. The principal imports, however, are still put down as coming from Austria.

### MUSICAL INSTRUMENTS.

In musical instruments, it is worthy of notice that Hungary imported eleven of her own national instrument, the "czimbalom," from Austria. There is no reason why an American firm should not undertake to supply this trade. The present average import price is $40.60. Hungary exported many of these instruments to Germany, France, Bosnia, and Switzerland.

### SEWING MACHINES.

The principal imports from the United States, in the mechanical line, were sewing machines and parts. The number of whole machines purchased increased 100 per cent, but the average price fell off—a fact not true of other lines of useful instruments, the prices paid for which have slowly risen.

### CHEMICALS: ACETATE OF LIME.

The United States, while ceasing to export saltpeter, sent Hungary, in 1901, a fair amount of a new chemical, acetate of lime (330,690 pounds, at an average value of $5,937.75), competing successfully with Bosnia (330,244.9 pounds), and with Austria, Italy, and Belgium. This was in addition to the regular export of blue vitriol.

In the chemical products, glues and ultramarine have to be added to the list, which includes shoe blacking, lampblack, drugs, perfumes, and cosmetics.

### IRONWARE.

In iron and ironwares, Hungary credits the United States with raw iron, 1,359,797.3 pounds; steel in bars, 8,377.5 pounds; plate and other iron, 440.9 pounds; stoves and the like, 1,543.2 pounds; sheet-iron products, 1,763.7 pounds; wire netting, muzzles, and bird cages, 1,763.7 pounds; cast-iron goods, 23,589.2 pounds; wrought-iron goods, including locksmiths' and blacksmiths' supplies 3,527.4 pounds; iron hoops, 220.46 pounds; iron piping, 661.38 pounds; hoes, spades, and shovels, 2,866 pounds; pitchforks, 220.46 pounds; handsaws, 220.46 pounds; files, 7,936.6 pounds; planes, 661.38 pounds; other fine hardware, 8,377.5 pounds; ordinary hardware, 1,763.7 pounds; fine steel ware, 881.8 pounds; revolvers, 661.38 pounds; cutlery, 1,322.8 pounds, and iron furniture, 1,102.3 pounds; which shows that in all these lines America is beginning to compete with Austria and Germany, and can always benefit by retaining the most-favored-nation clause, as the dutv is fairly high.

## LUMBER.

The export of wood from the United States to Hungary continues to be officially unnoticed here. Timber, 567,905 pounds; cork, 440.92 pounds, and staves, 167,108.7 pounds, sold at former rates; the last named at a better price than the imports from Bosnia, Roumania, Servia, and Austria, viz, $3.65 instead of $2.74 or $2.13 per 220.46 pounds.

### TRADE WITH CUBA AND PORTO RICO.

Hungary exported nothing, so far as is known, to Cuba and Porto Rico in the year 1901.
The imports from those islands were:

| Article. | Weight. | Value. |
|---|---|---|
| | *Pounds.* | |
| Coffee and tea | 171,077 | $25, 235. 95 |
| Pepper | 40 | 43. 65 |
| Raisins | 882 | 82. 62 |
| Tobacco and cigars | 1, 320, 335 | 359, 747. 06 |
| Rum | 1, 102 | 243. 60 |
| Rope | 6, 393 | 647. 57 |
| Total | 1, 500, 230 | 386, 000. 45 |

### TRADE WITH THE PHILIPPINE ISLANDS.

Hungary exported, in 1901, 54,453 pounds of minerals (dolomite) to the Philippine Islands, at an average value of $175.39. The invoice was not presented at this consulate.
The imports from that group were:

| Article. | Weight. | Value. |
|---|---|---|
| | *Pounds.* | |
| Tobacco | 3, 378, 550 | $601, 104. 32 |
| Manila hemp | 62, 611 | 5, 534. 59 |
| Total | 3, 441 161 | 606, 638. 91 |

### INDUSTRIES.

The industrial conditions in Hungary in 1901 were considered by local economic writers to have been as bad as during preceding years. A crisis existed in the building line and industries connected therewith, such as iron and machine manufactures. To afford relief, the National Government promised large appropriations for public works, to be begun as soon as possible.

Of 30 new industrial undertakings, 21 were factories established, with a total force of 3,149 workmen. The other 9 were rather enlargements of old plants. The increase in capital of the latter was $1,000,000. The Government gra te subsidies to 23 of the 30 new factories, 4 of which are engaged inmwœbdworking, 8 in the manufacture of textiles, 6 in metal working (including a scythe and sickle factory), 4 in producing chemicals (including 2 vegetable-oil factories, a degras, and a turpentine plant), two in making collars and cuffs, and 2 in the manufacture of food products (meat preserving and chocolate).

For the domestic industries, only about $19,000 could be appropriated, which went for school courses, plants, committees of arrangement, machines, and tools. More, however, was done than in previous years to improve the direction of this branch.

The export of domestic Hungarian embroideries and clay ware to America is still limited, but continues to increase from year to year, in proportion to the greater number of tourists who visit Hungary.

### SUBSIDIES.

The total amount of industrial subsidy given by the minister of commerce in 1901 was only $200,000. In the face of this small amount, it can not be wondered that as much as 12½ per cent of the industrial enterprise of Hungary in 1901 was of foreign capitalization. In 1892, however, the foreigners maintained 19$\frac{7}{15}$ per cent of the total industrial activity.

FRANK DYER CHESTER, *Consul.*

BUDAPEST, *November 12, 1902.*

### TRADE OF HUNGARY IN 1902.

Figures just published by the Hungarian state statistical bureau exhibit the trade of Hungary for the first half of the current year as follows:

There were 343,917,600 pounds less and 276,000 pieces more of merchandise imported, and 326,280,800 pounds less and 657,000 pieces more of merchandise exported, than in the corresponding period of 1901.

The total export exceeded the total import in value by $6,656,370 (the figures being $120,762,670 and $114,106,300, respectively). In spite of this favorable balance, the statistician sees with regret that in the trade of Hungary with Austria, there was a balance in favor of the latter of $1,597,610.

Among the items of the balance, $35,516,730 is found to have been paid by Hungary to foreign countries for textile goods, of which Austria alone received $34,302,940. Likewise, of $6,485,850 paid for clothing and underwear, Austria received $6,390,440. In leather and iron and wares thereof, the statistician notes the same fact.

Americans would do well to compete for the Hungarian trade in artistic and musical instruments, a branch of import for which $4,374,650 was paid last year.

Hungary's export of grain, flour, and animals amounted for the first half of 1902 to $23,142,000.

FRANK DYER CHESTER, *Consul.*

BUDAPEST, *July 26, 1902.*

### GOLD CIRCULATION IN HUNGARY.

Hungary's new gold coins of crown denomination (principally 20's and 10's) were first brought into common use on August 22, 1901. In the sixteen months since that date, coins to a total value of 245,740,000 crowns ($65,858,320) have been put into circulation, but of this 116,170,000 crowns ($31,133,560) worth have found their way back into the Hungarian treasury, so that tne present circulation is only 129,570,000 gold crowns ($32.952,476). But the Hungarian Government of its own initiative put into circulation 20,000,000 crowns ($5,360,000) worth of gold, so that the present amount of gold in common use is nearly 150,000,000 crowns ($40,200,000). The Hungarian Government feels certain that the continuous circulation of this amount is a proof that the public has become accustomed to the use of gold coins, and there will be no financial embarrassments when coin payments are assumed by the Government.

FRANK DYER CHESTER, *Consul.*

BUDAPEST, *December 29, 1902.*

## BELGIUM.

### REPORT FROM CONSULATE-GENERAL AT ANTWERP.

The result of the commercial movement of Belgium with all other countries during 1901 shows an increase of importation over 1900, but a decrease in exportation, as indicated below:

| Period. | Imports. | | Exports. | |
|---|---|---|---|---|
| | General commerce. | Special commerce. | General commerce. | Special commerce. |
| 1885–89 | $553,562,600 | $278,093,700 | $519,556,000 | $244,145,000 |
| 1890–94 | 565,123,800 | 314,898,800 | 519,343,700 | 269,621,000 |
| 1895–99 | 618,429,900 | 371,911,000 | 563,251,200 | 317,137,600 |
| 1900 | 693,719,200 | 427,649,400 | 636,417,500 | 371,119,700 |
| 1901 | 701,644,548 | 428,651,383 | 625.212,497 | 352,842,600 |

Importations from the United States into Belgium during 1901 amounted in value to $64,785,275, as compared with $51,473,100 in the preceding year, or an increase of $13,312,175. The articles principally affected were: Timber other than oak or walnut, $665,271; grains, $11,539,277; grease, $1,282,099; raw mineral matter, $610,845; chemical products not specially classified, $630,338; oleaginous grains, $583,053; vegetables and vegetable substances, $584,404.

The following classes of merchandise were received in lesser quantities: Starch, $159,418; living animals, horses, and foals, $222,529; drugs, $949,946; cottons, $456,638.

Exportations to the United States from Belgium during 1901 were $15,141,043, as contrasted with $14,841,700 in 1900, an increase of $299,343.

The most important items showing an increase were: Raw rubber, $639,602; raw textile matter, $280,043; unworked lead, $54,812; works of art and collections not otherwise specified, $109,238; raw hides, $612,582; vegetables, $131,819; other articles, $478,640.

The principal diminutions were: Tanned hides, $134,521; raw sugar, $2,206,762.

Tables showing the imports of Belgium from the United States during the year 1901, compared with those of 1900 and 1899, and the exports to the United States in the same years, follow:

*Imports from the United States into Belgium.*

| Articles. | 1901. | 1900. | 1899. |
|---|---|---|---|
| Barley .............................................pounds.. | 52,372,804 | 129,029,110 | 134,396,260 |
| Bran .................................................do.... | 120,230 | 4,164,710 | 11,816,491 |
| Buckwheat ........................................do.... | 9,618,620 | 2,174,110 | 5,684,878 |
| Indian corn........................................do.... | 315,686,839 | 648,730,820 | 480,966,649 |
| Rye ..................................................do.... | 14,859,116 | 21,101,740 | 28,677,358 |
| Oats.................................................do.... | 45,702,982 | 62,919,963 | 52,612,545 |
| Forage ..............................................do.... | 23,547,568 | 346,575,565 | 158,747,144 |
| Flour: | | | |
|   Wheat ............................................do.... | 7,942,536 | 7,555,715 | 5,489,573 |
|   Barley, oats, corn............................do.... | 469,128 | 611,406 | 810,495 |
|   Unclassified....................................do.... | 57,037 | 40,388 | 109,822 |
| Nonalimentary fecula...........................do.... | 7,942,536 | 7,096,460 | 11,297,389 |
| Coffee................................................do.... | 11,002,378 | 1,133,250 | 568,555 |
| Cotton ..............................................do.... | 79,399,390 | 74,707,700 | 65,340,063 |
| Hops.................................................do.... | | 46,935 | 200,654 |
| Malt .................................................do.... | 1,471,056 | 1,796,140 | 1,587,061 |
| Raw animal substances, such as lard...do.... | 27,208,559 | 20,696,830 | 20,376,604 |
| Animal fat, not specified......................do.... | 12,469,120 | 14,728,580 | 9,409,131 |
| Raw animal substances, horse hair, shells, etc ....dollars.. | 211,072 | 230,720 | 144,908 |
| Fruits: | | | |
|   Prunes............................................pounds.. | 750,239 | 1,144,550 | 743,140 |
|   Dried, unclassified ........................dollars.. | 108,050 | 103,720 | 106,367 |
| Honey...............................................pounds.. | 1,102,430 | 1,064,930 | 1,206,240 |
| Meats: | | | |
|   Salted or smoked, ham, tongue, etc .............do.... | 25,339,089 | 26,141,270 | 33,204,624 |
|   Preserved.......................................do.... | 1,145,687 | 1,129,040 | 1,273,306 |
| Raw animal matter, unclassified, grease.......do.... | 211,074 | 941,720 | 701,528 |
| Petroleum, refined ...............................do.... | 346,575,555 | 269,229,720 | 302,678,410 |
| Rushes, bamboo, etc.............................dollars.. | 59,528 | 78,358 | 170,397 |
| Stones, unclassified ............................pounds.. | 46,435,609 | 35,802,700 | 40,404,042 |
| Tar, asphalt.......................................do.... | 88,861,523 | 79,989,700 | 97,634,149 |
| Copper and nickel: | | | |
|   Unworked.......................................do.... | 9,123,756 | 10,650,380 | 4,735,478 |
|   Worked..........................................do.... | 141,090 | 138,560 | 106,874 |
| Iron: | | | |
|   Cast.............................................do.... | 4,220,750 | 27,028,400 | 36,468,056 |
|   Wrought.........................................do.... | 166,850 | 819,120 | 1,138,742 |
|   Old ..............................................do.... | 2,927,456 | 3,644,045 | 748,233 |
|   Not specified...................................do.... | 100,166 | 147,520 | 202,331 |
| Lead..................................................do.... | 171,969,556 | 6,057,965 | 6,520,265 |
| Steel in bars, sheets, and wire, unspecified.............do.... | 11,442 | 233,190 | 360,609 |
| Tools, machines of iron and steel, unclassified........do.... | 103,160 | 2,905,175 | 583,176 |
| Machines and machinery, unclassified .............do.... | 722,950 | 5,277,615 | 4,107,278 |
| Machines and machinery in cast iron, unclassified..do.... | 3,637,254 | 5,923,630 | 4,501,678 |
| Bicycles and parts ...............................dollars.. | 12,136 | 22,422 | 92,932 |
| Firearms............................................do.... | 25,499 | 43,250 | 9,820 |
| Hemp................................................pounds.. | 528,659 | 597,325 | 2,592,255 |
| Cordage.............................................do.... | 172,271 | 155,360 | 180,356 |
| India rubber, manufactured .................dollars.. | 15,040 | 8,273 | 4,717 |
| Hides, raw ........................................pounds.. | 334,580 | 204,137 | 755,891 |
| Leather, tanned .................................do.... | 137,159 | 144,490 | 94,103 |
| Furniture ..........................................dollars.. | 13,423 | 30,160 | 20,915 |
| Haberdashery and hardware: | | | |
|   10 per cent.....................................do.... | | 1,988 | 1,698 |
|   15 per cent.....................................do.... | 34,235 | 18,422 | 23,388 |
| Paper, not specified.............................pounds.. | 421,863 | 244,855 | 1,006,210 |
| Chemical products, unspecified................do.... | 1,646,868 | 1,036,930 | 973,805 |
| Dyes and colors, unspecified...................do.... | 1,643,980 | 4,475,830 | 1,661,896 |
| Drugs, unclassified, plants, roots, etc.................do.... | 30,078,450 | 38,392,910 | 28,605,031 |
| Drugs, glue........................................do.... | 252,590 | 98,965 | 16,728 |
| Tobacco: | | | |
|   Unmanufactured ..............................do.... | 9,745,507 | 10,362,320 | 11,341,662 |
|   Smoking and snuff............................do.... | 28,170 | 34,506 | 25,968 |
| Cigars and cigarettes ..........................do.... | 17,842 | 9,960 | 13,805 |
| Vegetable oils, nonalimentry..................do.... | 39,845,498 | 40,151,050 | 36,246,906 |
| Vegetable substances: | | | |
|   Unspecified.....................................do.... | 1,835,890 | 977,740 | 1,521,474 |
|   Seeds ...........................................do.... | 33,094,369 | 9,532,350 | 18,443,381 |
| Oil cakes...........................................do.... | 178,552,719 | 152,806,140 | 154,712,071 |
| Wood: | | | |
|   Oak and walnut— | | | |
|     Split...........................................feet.. | 16,132 | 1,055,081 | 848,647 |
|     Sawn..........................................do.... | 834,280 | 86,570 | 81,013 |
|   For building purposes other than oak and walnut, | | | |
|     unsawn, feet..................................... | 2,274,891 | 1,609,620 | 1,469,502 |
|   For building purposes other than oak and walnut, | | | |
|     beams, etc., sawn, dollars ..................... | 33,196 | 109,624 | 40,337 |
|   Manufactured ..................................pounds.. | 8,900 | 11,899 | 10,736 |
|   Pulp .............................................do.... | 7,250,502 | 4,501,570 | 4,983,361 |
| Horses..............................................number.. | 600 | 2,330 | 3,932 |
| Wool .................................................pounds.. | 362,397 | 125,630 | 1,454,141 |
| Raw mineral matter, unclassified...............dollars.. | 1,085,561 | 469,456 | 476,871 |
| Works of art........................................do.... | 791 | 1,939 | 6,111 |

*Exports from Belgium to the United States.*

| | 1901. | 1900. | 1899. |
|---|---|---|---|
| Alcoholic liquors, brandy of every description in bottles.............................................gallons.. | 660 | 3,646 | 1,828 |
| Brandy of every description in casks.................do.... | 4,431 | 4,150 | 5,864 |
| Beer, bottled.............................................do.... | 42,622 | 29,561 | 54,128 |
| Chicory.............................................pounds.. | 58,940 | 8,090 | 328,529 |
| Cocoa butter.............................................do.... | 1,718 | 12,550 | 822 |
| Coke.............................................do.... | 26,037,000 | 14,065,000 | 12,397,000 |
| Coal: | | | |
| In bricks.............................................do.... | 180,213,000 | 74,250,000 | 125,943,000 |
| Undenominated.............................................do.... | 80,506,800 | 138,974,000 | 112,303,400 |
| Chemical products not specified, as carbonic acid and sulphuric acid.............................................dollars.. | 810,174 | 766,825 | 791,118 |
| Sal soda.............................................pounds.. | 572,660 | 905,850 | 261,981 |
| Sulphur.............................................do.... | 987,080 | 889,760 | 522,708 |
| Raw mineral matter, unclassified, as tin, copper, lead, zinc, etc.............................................dollars.. | 164,040 | 172,130 | 128,024 |
| Salt: | | | |
| Raw.............................................pounds.. | 132,948 | ............ | 110,230 |
| Refined.............................................do.... | 1,077,670 | ............ | 108,834 |
| Lead, raw.............................................do.... | 2,109,679 | 1,374,582 | 823,248 |
| Steel rails.............................................do.... | 5,166,689 | 3,968,215 | 1,249,012 |
| Steel in bars, sheets, and wire.............................................do.... | 50,835 | 35,975 | ............ |
| Iron: | | | |
| Small beams.............................................do.... | 407,440 | 2,271,720 | 1,594,477 |
| Beaten in wire or rolled.............................................do.... | 617,155 | 1,391,510 | 824,970 |
| Wrought.............................................do.... | 681,296 | 727,275 | ............ |
| Coppered, galvanized, and nickeled.............................................do.... | 71,863 | 62,081 | ............ |
| Machines and tools: | | | |
| In cast iron and steel, not specified.............................................do.... | 217,712 | 486,368 | 399,482 |
| In iron and steel, unspecified.............................................do.... | 97,704 | 263,845 | 1,026,607 |
| In other metals.............................................do.... | 11,404 | 47,245 | 46,867 |
| Firearms.............................................dollars.. | 617,082 | 537,673 | 484,084 |
| Haberdashery and hardware.............................................do.... | 19,902 | 32,710 | 16,766 |
| Furniture.............................................do.... | 7,633 | 8,505 | 6,781 |
| Cement.............................................pounds.. | 148,792,470 | 234,202,110 | 242,288,986 |
| Sulphur.............................................do.... | 987,080 | 889,760 | 522,708 |
| Stones for building purposes.............................................do.... | 1,114,852 | 1,078,335 | 621,377 |
| Paper, not specified.............................................do.... | 9,900,919 | 1,506,425 | 972,029 |
| Books: | | | |
| Paper or bound.............................................do.... | 141,365 | 112,962 | 120,894 |
| Unbound.............................................do.... | 2,426 | 4,140 | 1,475 |
| Clothing of all kinds, ready made.............................................dollars.. | 70,998 | 6,959 | 139,618 |
| Underclothing of every description.............................................do.... | 398 | 100 | 23 |
| Cotton tulles, laces, etc.............................................pounds.. | 21,688 | 20,254 | 14,658 |
| Cotton textures, total value.............................................dollars.. | 3,446 | 88,420 | 70,657 |
| Woolen textures.............................................do.... | 131,819 | 194,505 | 216,607 |
| Woolen thread, carded, twisted, etc.............................................pounds.. | 35,741 | 8,573 | 25,004 |
| Wool, raw.............................................do.... | 1,183,094 | 2,595,465 | 1,974,852 |
| Silk textures.............................................dollars.. | ............ | 40 | 58 |
| Flax.............................................pounds.. | 3,442,533 | 1,976,065 | 1,582,885 |
| Hemp.............................................do.... | 43,747 | 122,192 | 584,716 |
| Oakum.............................................do.... | 664,732 | 244,490 | 398,217 |
| Cordage.............................................do.... | 236,981 | 176,368 | 147,834 |
| Oilcloths of all kinds.............................................dollars.. | ............ | 1,720 | 956 |
| Textures.............................................do.... | 772 | 2,943 | 3,435 |
| Horsehair, bristles, shells, etc.............................................do.... | 59,760 | 87,150 | 80,890 |
| Live plants and flowers.............................................do.... | 71,641 | 71,443 | 86,543 |
| Hides, raw.............................................pounds.. | 16,517,509 | 9,258,600 | 11,742,991 |
| Skins, dyed and tanned.............................................do.... | 43,861 | 221,650 | 203,275 |
| Gloves.............................................dollars.. | 38,566 | 109,705 | 118,315 |
| Rags.............................................pounds.. | 28,001,708 | 26,141,695 | 19,928,594 |
| Medicinal plants, essences, etc.............................................do.... | 337,110 | 118,450 | 104,954 |
| Meats, preserved.............................................do.... | 219,764 | 274,510 | 294,627 |
| Mineral water of all kinds.............................................dollars.. | 49,720 | 66,037 | 370,985 |
| India rubber: | | | |
| Raw.............................................pounds.. | 5,649,463 | 3,953,100 | 2,335,516 |
| Manufactured.............................................dollars.. | 4,063 | 568 | 946 |
| Rice, hulled.............................................pounds.. | 62,312 | 2,780 | 300,807 |
| Resin and bitumen, unclassified.............................................do.... | 1,502,204 | 1,771,045 | 2,677,506 |
| Glass: | | | |
| Window.............................................dollars.. | 1,118,383 | 809,976 | 1,043,644 |
| Ordinary.............................................do.... | 171,106 | 112,915 | 123,973 |
| Mirrors.............................................do.... | 747,084 | 498,970 | 205,292 |
| Ivory.............................................pounds.. | 125,481 | 127,900 | 120,761 |
| Works of art.............................................dollars.. | 64,154 | 13,818 | 10,915 |
| Sugar, raw, beet-root.............................................pounds.. | 10,392,665 | 113,544,595 | 24,531,470 |
| Vegetables: | | | |
| Preserved.............................................do.... | 1,444,823 | 880,840 | 385,926 |
| Not specified.............................................do.... | 742,907 | ............ | 283,540 |
| Vegetables and vegetable substances, not specified...do.... | 44,739 | 101,510 | 217,380 |

*Exports from Belgium to the United States*—Continued.

| | 1901. | 1900. | 1899. |
|---|---|---|---|
| Vegetable oils: | | | |
| Alimentary ...............................pounds.. | 373,665 | 79,450 | 37,478 |
| Nonalimentary ...............................do.... | 2,654,806 | 895,555 | 650,946 |
| Animal fat...............................do.... | 4,314,327 | 8,650,465 | 6,546,989 |
| Wood pulp...............................do.... | 807,571 | 1,087,710 | 1,042,500 |
| Wood, worked...............................dollars.. | 221,548 | 334,430 | 246,191 |
| Dye woods...............................pounds.. | ............ | 220,500 | 1,388,098 |
| Various products for commercial use ...............dollars.. | 3,440 | 1,177 | 93 |
| Dyes and colors...............................do.... | 5,851,157 | 5,639,180 | 8,524,227 |

## ECONOMIC CONDITIONS.

Following a period of great industrial prosperity, Belgium, like her neighbors, encountered in 1900 a serious depression; but she overcame her difficulties more easily than most of the other European countries. The national bank maintained a rate of discount considerably inferior to that of the Bank of England and the Bank of the German Empire, thus greatly alleviating the situation.

The general commercial movement in 1901 was only a little less as regards importations than that of 1900, but much inferior as far as exportations were concerned. Quantities, however, were larger than the preceding year, the difference being due especially to the fall in price of coal, iron, steel, and chemical products.

The total tonnage of vessels entering Belgian ports increased in 1901 by 734,544, of which 711,976 belonged to the port of Antwerp. The importations into Belgium for home consumption reached 13,333,110 tons, of which 4,700,000 tons were shipped to Antwerp.

The proportion of special commerce per inhabitant, which was only 80 francs ($15.44) in 1835, reached 857 francs ($165.40) in 1899.

In the development of Belgium's relations with transoceanic countries, very important progress was made. China, notwithstanding the disturbances, held, in 1900, the twelfth place among the markets for Belgian goods, with a total importation from Belgium of 17,250,000 tons for her own consumption. Twenty years ago, Belgium's commercial movement with China was nil. In 1880, Belgium's direct exportations to the Australian States, Canada, the Cape of Good Hope, the Indies, Japan, or the French colonies did not reach $200,000. In 1900, the values of exportations to these countries were:

| Countries. | Value. | Countries. | Value. |
|---|---|---|---|
| British India........................... | $3,395,642 | Morocco............................... | $497,361 |
| Canada ................................. | 3,045,926 | Victoria .............................. | 461,551 |
| Japan................................... | 2,161,021 | French West Africa Colonies......... | 437,724 |
| South Australia......................... | 1,113,031 | French Indo-China.................... | 324,433 |
| New South Wales........................ | 845,919 | Transvaal ............................ | 222,915 |
| Dutch East Indies ...................... | 625,127 | Natal ................................ | 210,370 |
| The Cape .............................. | 610,652 | New Zealand.......................... | 176,402 |

The exports to South and Central America remain much inferior to imports therefrom into Belgium.

However great may be the development of Belgium's commerce

with distant markets, its industrial condition is governed by its relations with its immediate neighbors and the United States.

Of a total importation of $427,640,329 in special commerce, i. e., for home consumption, the shipments from France, Germany, England, Holland, and the United States amounted to two-thirds, and to these same countries Belgium sends more than three-fourths of her total exports.

In the last ten years, trade with Germany has doubled. This is a result not only of the development of German industry, but also of the commercial treaty of December 6, 1891, instituting a special tariff in favor of Belgium. The same may be said of Austria-Hungary. These treaties cease to have effect on the 31st of December, 1903.

The production of coal in Belgium diminished by 1,389,077 tons in 1901 and that of cast iron by 254,291 tons. The exportation of combustible minerals reached 6,365,321 tons (coal 4,890,755 tons, coke 830,625 tons, briquettes 714,941 tons) against 6,939,162 tons in 1900 and 6,103,323 tons in 1899. The importation reached 3,096,630 tons (coal 2,927,452 tons, coke 152,223 tons, briquettes 17,155 tons), against 3,509,996 in 1900, and 3,151,504 in 1899.

The exportation of window glass reached 38,236 tons, as against 37,825 tons in 1900 and 46,135 tons in 1899; that of plate glass reached $4,891,064, as against $4,258,484 in 1900 and $4,769,317 in 1899. There now exist in Belgium in all 32 glassworks, employing about 7,200 hands. This industry, which prior to 1900 was one of the most important of the country, has not yet recovered from the prolonged and disastrous strikes which broke out in August, 1900.

The exportation of steel and iron in 1901 increased, respectively, by 36,000 and 23,500 tons.

In the autumn of 1901, there was a remarkable development in the potato trade, this being extended for the first time to our country, the value of Belgian potatoes exported to the United States from the 1st of October to the 31st of December being $145,552.81. It appears that the Belgian crop in 1901 was not only unusually abundant, but also of exceptionally good quality, the result being that a new trade sprang into existence, and it is hoped by the merchants here that although the crop of 1902 will not be quite so large, this trade may be, in a measure, maintained.

An extraordinary increase in the diamond trade with the United States is shown by the figures for export from Antwerp to the United States in 1900 and 1901. In 1900, the total value exported was $513,889.83, whereas in 1901 the total value was $1,376,377.92, an ncrease of $862,488.09.

### TRADE IN THE KONGO FREE STATE.

The Kongo Free State, notwithstanding the frequent attacks upon its administration, continues to progress. The last statistics of plantations show 2,631,183 coffee plants and 490,695 cocoa plants, besides 1,175,000 coffee plants and 132,000 cocoa plants in nurseries.

A brewery was built at Leopoldville, and began manufacture on the 1st of January, 1902.

Simultaneously with the development of the waterways, routes for automobiles have been constructed to complete the communications by railway.

The Matadi-Leopoldville railway reduced its tariff by 25 per cent on the 1st of July, 1902, and has agreed to transport at cost price all the material necessary for the construction of the Central African line, which has already been commenced.

The new railway will be 1,800 kilometers (1,117.8 miles) in length, and is destined to connect the Kongo with the Nile and Lake Tanganyika.

The special commerce of the Free State amounted in value to $9,744,260 for exportations, and $4,458,698.35 for importations. In these totals, Belgium figured for $9,083,536.50 and $3,226,226.79, respectively.

### DETAILS OF COMMERCE.

#### LUMBER AND HARD WOODS.

[Duty on oak and walnut, 19.3 cents per cubic meter; others, unsawn, 19.3; wood, sawn, all dimensions, $1.15; planed wood, $1.73.]

The year 1901 began with an enormous stock at Antwerp and a fall in price. Sales were very difficult during the greater part of the year, and the consumption small. The importations were much less than those of the preceding year, the respective figures being 539,264 cubic meters[a] and 590,264 cubic meters. The decrease was especially marked in the importations from Norway, Finland, and the Riga, while from America and India there was an increase.

The total importations during 1901 were—

| Pine: | Cubic meters. |
|---|---|
| Unsawn | 21,894 |
| Sawn | 391,392 |
| Planks | 37,223 |
| Oak and teak | 81,600 |
| Cottonwood, yellow pine, hickory, ash, elm, beech | 7,155 |
| Total | 539,264 |

#### COFFEE.

[Duty, $1.93 per 220.46 pounds.,

*Résumé of importations at Antwerp since 1850.*

| | Bales. | | Bales. |
|---|---|---|---|
| 1850 | 247,303 | 1898 | 728,497 |
| 1860 | 197,581 | 1899 | 655,670 |
| 1870 | 320,229 | 1900 | 540,015 |
| 1880 | 743,667 | 1901 | 752,059 |
| 1890 | 669,631 | | |

Thanks to the abundant crops at Rio and Santos, the above table shows a very considerable increase over the preceding years. The year closed in an unsettled condition with good average Santos quoted at $8.88. Haitian coffees began at $4.82 for Aux Cayes, $5.11 for Jacmel, and $5.40 for Petit-Goaves, falling to $4.15, $4.44, and $4.92 in the month of August, reaching their highest point at $5.21, $5.45, and $5.60 in November, and falling again to $5.07, $5.11, and $5.30 at the end of December.

---

a 1 cubic meter = 35.3 cubic feet.

### INDIA RUBBER.

[Free of duty.]

Importations of crude india rubber during 1901 from the Kongo Free State amounted to 11,918,403 pounds, as compared with 10,806,949 pounds in 1900; from other sources, 949,841 pounds, as compared with 1,751,270 pounds.

Following are the statistics of the Antwerp rubber market since 1893:

| Year. | Imports. | Sales. | Stock at end of year. | Year. | Imports. | Sales. | Stock at end of year. |
|---|---|---|---|---|---|---|---|
| | Tons. | Tons. | Tons. | | Tons. | Tons. | Tons. |
| 1893 | 164.563 | 160.319 | 8.060 | 1898 | 1,982.865 | 1,816.648 | 259.198 |
| 1894 | 270.256 | 231.441 | 38.840 | 1899 | 3,349.212 | 3,321.091 | 287.392 |
| 1895 | 522.711 | 435.256 | 87.455 | 1900 | 5,608.302 | 5,291.326 | 604.369 |
| 1896 | 1,098.802 | 1,048.328 | 137.429 | 1901 | 5,762.760 | 5,959.056 | 408.580 |
| 1897 | 1,652.710 | 1,697.164 | 92.975 | | | | |

The market has continued to develop, thanks to the activity of Belgian cultivators in Africa. Prices, rather weak during the first month of the year, rose in April as the result of large purchases for American account. Owing to heavy arrivals in the summer, they fell again until the December sale, when once more the intervention of American buyers caused them to rise. The year closed with a fall in price of about 6 per cent, as compared with that in December, 1900.

### COPAL GUM.

The importation of this article at Antwerp is becoming extensive. The total arrivals amounted to 180 tons, compared with 19 tons in 1900.

### CEREALS.

[Duty. Oats, 57 cents per 220.46 pounds, flour of oats, 77 cents; other, 38 cents; malt, 28 cents; other cereals, free.]

*Imports at Antwerp during 1901.*

| Whence imported. | Wheat. | Rye. | Barley. | Maize. | Oats. | Flour. |
|---|---|---|---|---|---|---|
| | Bushels. | Bushels. | Bushels. | Bushels. | Bushels. | Bags. |
| Australia | 1,473,590 | | | | | 2,020 |
| California and Oregon | 7,407,897 | 297,308 | 898,570 | | | |
| Canada | 2,237,715 | 36,617 | 105,621 | 85,512 | 729,962 | 300 |
| United States | 17,581,131 | 70,588 | 549,984 | 5,477,519 | 2,521,041 | 125,768 |
| East Indies | 1,763,748 | | | | | |
| Plata | 8,490,756 | 5,804 | 41,053 | 5,117,590 | | |
| Turkey | 221,902 | 24,500 | 1,896,333 | 106,039 | 158,804 | |
| Danube | 24,461,434 | 1,454,202 | 1,309,846 | 2,967,250 | 920,010 | |
| Black Sea and Azov | 461,630 | 358,878 | 2,094,943 | 316,316 | 73,880 | |
| Russia (northern) | 21,391 | 104,526 | 343,574 | | 1,822,941 | 325 |
| Germany | 160,717 | 43,761 | 170,346 | 20,930 | 50,131 | 13,309 |
| England | 20,213 | | 1,400 | | 840 | 1,190 |
| France | | | 14,042 | 19,781 | | 805 |
| Hungary | | | 82,536 | | | 4,252 |
| Denmark | | | 56,353 | | 1,663 | |

*Wheat.*—The year 1901 commenced with about the same prices as those of 1900, American wheat beginning at $3.14 and $3.18 and ending in December at $3.23.

*Maize.*—In the months of February and March, the activity of important American houses made prices very firm, and in May they reached $2.36 for American maize. Prices then fell until August, when they rose again to $2.70 in September for American maize, closing the year from $2.89 to $2.99.

## COAL.

### [Free of duty.]

At the beginning of the new century, the fall in prices was so great that it may be estimated at 50 per cent. Briquettes, which cost at the end of 1900 $6.18 per ton, were quoted at the end of 1901 at $3.09.

Attempts have been made to introduce American coal, but inasmuch as prices have fallen to such an extent on the European markets, it would not seem to be in the interest of American mines to export their coal here.

The following table shows the coal production of Belgium since 1850, compared with that of Germany, France, England, and the United States:

| Year. | Belgium. | Germany. | France. | Great Britain. | United States. |
|---|---|---|---|---|---|
| | *Tons.* | *Tons.* | *Tons.* | *Tons.* | *Tons.* |
| 1850 | 5,820,588 | 18,194,132 | 4,500,000 | 65,000,000 | 7,359,899 |
| 1870 | 13,697,118 | 26,397,800 | 13,179,000 | 112,200,000 | 25,000,000 |
| 1880 | 16,866,698 | 46,973,566 | 18,804,767 | 146,969,189 | 66,831,213 |
| 1890 | 20,465,960 | 64,373,545 | 26,083,118 | 181,614,288 | 141,657,596 |
| 1898 | 22,088,335 | 96,279,992 | 32,356,104 | 205,274,000 | 197,852,394 |
| 1899 | 22,072,068 | 101,622,000 | 32,862,712 | 223,616,208 | 221,882,677 |
| 1900 | 23,462,817 | 109,290,237 | 32,721,502 | 228,784,200 | 240,965,917 |
| 1901 | 22,073,740 | 107,825,009 | 31,613,036 | 225,181,000 | 267,850,000 |

## COTTON.

### [Free of duty.]

After a steady rise in price during nearly two years, the market has become stagnant. The price of $12.55 for American middling at the beginning of the year was not maintained, and fell gradually to $10.42 in the month of May. There was a temporary rise of $0.58 in June and July, but prices fell again to $10.42 in August. The year closed at $10.57.

*Imports for the last six years.*

| Whence imported. | 1896. | 1897. | 1898. | 1899. | 1900. | 1901. |
|---|---|---|---|---|---|---|
| | *Bales.* | *Bales.* | *Bales.* | *Bales.* | *Bales.* | *Bales.* |
| New York | 40,555 | 21,312 | 34,396 | 20,685 | 38,956 | 30,913 |
| New Orleans | 17,829 | 27,003 | 21,000 | 13,853 | 16,857 | 21,331 |
| Newport News | | | 2,483 | 610 | 1,014 | 750 |
| Boston | 40 | | | | | |
| Galveston | 2,194 | 20,093 | 39,723 | 51,380 | 56,907 | 57,397 |
| Philadelphia | 1,099 | 1,251 | 804 | | | |
| Baltimore | 3,508 | 4,111 | 7,553 | 336 | 4,161 | 150 |
| Norfolk | 4,000 | 300 | 1,898 | 100 | | |
| Savannah | | 6,674 | | | 15,712 | 7,978 |
| Pensacola | | | 5,014 | 4,424 | 2,413 | 7,450 |
| Bombay | 150,261 | 107,514 | 72,936 | 85,570 | 46,173 | 119,525 |
| Kurrachee | 15,043 | 15,087 | 38,378 | 16,838 | | |
| Madras | 410 | 435 | 440 | 1,593 | 1,550 | 1,639 |
| Calcutta | 2,093 | 2,972 | 991 | 2,406 | 2,125 | 3,100 |
| Colombo | | | 1,670 | 100 | | 1,631 |
| Alexandria | 2,560 | 3,219 | 5,436 | 8,655 | 11,034 | 4,743 |
| Hamburg | 459 | 730 | 241 | 458 | 9,186 | 1,713 |
| Smyrna | 125 | 100 | | | 1,363 | |
| England | 15,079 | 20,761 | 11,359 | 23,108 | 15,614 | 9,076 |
| France | 11,133 | 5,768 | 4,691 | 7,022 | 17,651 | 2,577 |
| Various | | 225 | 310 | 1,670 | 3,920 | 3,154 |
| Total | 266,388 | 237,455 | 249,822 | 237,808 | 244,576 | 276,136 |

### HIDES.

[Free of duty.]

The year was not marked by the fluctuations that characterized the prices of 1900. The demands of England, however, were so large that prices generally increased 5 per cent. They rose steadily until spring, when the dead season set in and business practically stopped. From July to September, the demand so advanced that the prices for saladeros rose 10 per cent above those at the end of December. The year closed with a stock at Antwerp and Havre of 188,000 hides, as against 377,000 in 1900. At Antwerp, 168,000 hides were sold, as against 33,000 in 1900. Plata dry hides were imported to the number of 110,000, as against 151,000 in 1900.

The importations of the year 1901 were in greater part pessados and dry calfskins. The last article was not subject to any notable fluctuation. The following were the prices at the end of December:

| Description. | 1901. | 1900. | Increase. |
|---|---|---|---|
| Bullocks, mataderos | $20.26 to $21.23 | $19.68 to $20.65 | $0.57 |
| Cows, mataderos | 20.26      21.23 | 19.68      20.65 | .57 |
| Bullock, campos | 17.37      18.91 | 17.75      18.33 | .57 |
| Cows, campos | 17.37      18.91 | 15.63      18.33 | .57 |

Australian salted hides were imported to the number of 19,300, as against 19,600 in 1900. Of parings and clippings, 1,392 bales were imported, as compared with 2,007 in 1900.

### ESSENCE OF TURPENTINE.

[Free of duty.]

*Importations at Antwerp since 1860.*

FROM UNITED STATES.

| | 1860. | 1870. | 1880. | 1890. | 1900. | 1901. |
|---|---|---|---|---|---|---|
| | *Barrels.* | *Barrels.* | *Barrels.* | *Barrels.* | *Barrels.* | *Barrels.* |
| Wilmington | | 1,585 | 14,595 | 2,941 | | |
| Charleston | 200 | | 2,751 | | | |
| New York | 12,314 | 3,914 | 2,857 | | | 100 |
| Savannah | | | 900 | 16,438 | 44,666 | 48,452 |
| Brunswick | | | | 1,500 | | |
| New Orleans | | | | | 500 | |
| Via England | | | 1,421 | 1,280 | 150 | 850 |
| Via Hamburg | | | 150 | | | |
| Via Rotterdam | | | | | 75 | |
| Total | 12,514 | 5,499 | 22,674 | 22,150 | 45,391 | 49,402 |

FROM FRANCE AND SPAIN.

| | *Packages.* | *Packages.* | *Packages.* | *Packages.* | *Packages.* | *Packages.* |
|---|---|---|---|---|---|---|
| Bordeaux | 21 | 382 | 5,399 | 3,893 | 2,850 | 1,350 |
| Bayonne | | 5,951 | 3,336 | 8,093 | 1,075 | 1,545 |
| Bilbao and Santander | | | | 1,000 | 3,287 | 4,855 |
| Total | 21 | 6,333 | 8,735 | 12,986 | 7,212 | 7,750 |

## PRUNES.

[Duty $4.82 p r 220.46 pounds packed in barrels of 400 pounds minimum, or sacks of 180 pounds, $2.89.]

While the French crop of prunes was limited, that of California, although not so abundant as usual, supplied an excellent fruit. In Bosnia and Servia, the crops were good, but the quality mediocre. The average prices throughout the year were from $10.42 to $12.54.

## APRICOTS.

[Duty, evaporated California, 10 per cent ad valorem.]

The California crop was practically nil, in consequence of which prices remained very high, and American exporters took advantage of the situation to sell the accumulated stock of 1900 at very remunerative prices, which ranged from $21.23 to $27.02.

## APPLES, EVAPORATED.

[Duty, 10 per cent ad valorem.]

The American crop of prime apples being very limited, second qualities were exported in abundance. The prices varied from $22.97 to $24.12.

## IVORY.

[Free of duty.]

The movement of the ivory market for 1901 shows a slight decrease as compared with that of 1900. The quantities of ivory imported and sold since 1888 are shown in the following table:

| Year. | Imports. | Sales. | Year. | Imports. | Sales |
|---|---|---|---|---|---|
| | Tons. | Tons. | | Tons. | Tons. |
| 1888 | 6¼ | 6¼ | 1897 | 261 | 277 |
| 1890 | 76¼ | 76¼ | 1898 | 227¼ | 202 |
| 1894 | 260¼ | 183¼ | 1899 | 328 | 287¼ |
| 1895 | 356¼ | 270 | 1900 | 328 | 331 |
| 1896 | 197 | 261 | 1901 | 322¼ | 307¼ |

## LARD.

[Free of duty.]

A rise in prices was expected at the end of 1900, but not what was realized during 1901. The reasons for this were the high price of maize, which is the natural food for hogs in America, and the constantly increasing requirements of the American population, which leave a smaller quantity free for exportation; also the falling off in the number of hog breeders in Europe. The year was therefore very satisfactory for those who had a stock of lard in hand, especially for speculators.

H. Doc. 305, pt 2——4

*Importations during 1900 and 1901.*

| Whence imported. | 1901. | | 1901. | |
|---|---|---|---|---|
| | *Tierces.* | *Packages.* | *Tierces.* | *Packages.* |
| New York | 8,670 | 99,507 | 13,788 | 123,528 |
| Philadelphia | 2,227 | 25,377 | 535 | 25,765 |
| Baltimore | 3,855 | 21,525 | 6,951 | 42,206 |
| Boston | 50 | | 1,415 | 4,798 |
| Newport News | 1,390 | 28,458 | 4,518 | 44,701 |
| Montreal | 2,490 | 12,493 | 1,034 | 18,362 |
| Portland | 850 | 9,409 | 140 | 4,425 |
| Chicago | | 850 | | |
| Total | 19,032 | 197,814 | 28,729 | 263,885 |

## WOOL.

[Free of duty.]

The year 1901 contrasted strangely with 1900. By reason of its calmness and the slight fluctuations of the market, it may be considered as a period of convalescence after the disasters of 1900.

The auction in January showed an increase of from 2 to 3 cents over the prices of the preceding November. At the end of March, prices reached $0.80 to $0.81. In April merinos rose 1 to 2 cents, and crossbreds fell 1 cent. At the end of June, combed wool was quoted at $0.78 to $0.80; at the end of August, $0.82 to $0.825; at the end of October, $0.77 to $0.79; at the end of November, $0.79 to $0.80; at the end of December, $0.80 to $0.82.

*Imports at Antwerp since 1850.*

| | Bales. | | | Bales. |
|---|---|---|---|---|
| 1850 | 21,294 | | 1890 | 294,931 |
| 1860 | 16,245 | | 1899 | 238,776 |
| 1870 | 135,586 | | 1900 | 215,531 |
| 1880 | 159,015 | | 1901 | 178,823 |

*Movement of the Antwerp market in 1900 and 1901.*

| From— | Imports. | | Sales. | | Transit. | | Stock, Dec. 31. | |
|---|---|---|---|---|---|---|---|---|
| | 1900. | 1901. | 1900. | 1901. | 1900. | 1901. | 1900. | 1901. |
| | *Bales.* | *Bales.* | *Bales.* | *Bales.* | *Bales.* | *Bales.* | *Bales.* | *Bales.* |
| La Plata | 86,130 | 88,795 | 25,999 | 36,752 | 58,310 | 55,233 | 7,844 | 4,654 |
| Chile and Peru | 173 | 14 | 24 | 98 | 40 | 25 | 109 | |
| Cape | 15,767 | 15,969 | 4,083 | 1,023 | 11,742 | 15,432 | 698 | 212 |
| Africa | 134 | 76 | 33 | 77 | 73 | 17 | 28 | 10 |
| Spain | 358 | 57 | 4 | 17 | 349 | | 5 | 45 |
| Australia | 112,969 | 73,912 | 1,284 | 2,139 | 111,470 | 71,777 | 236 | 232 |
| Total | 215,531 | 178,823 | 31,428 | 40,106 | 181,990 | 142,484 | 8,920 | 5,153 |
| Sheepskins: | | | | | | | | |
| La Plata | 1,948 | 2,139 | 334 | 582 | 1,513 | 1,599 | 102 | 60 |
| Various | 7,132 | 7,590 | 357 | 55 | 6,775 | 7,535 | | |
| Total | 9,080 | 9,729 | 691 | 637 | 8,288 | 9,134 | 102 | 60 |

## PETROLEUM.

[Free of duty.]

The use of petroleum for heating purposes has advanced very largely of late, because of the extraordinary rise in coal prices during the past two or three years. Petroleum is now considered a serious rival to coal, its use being already extended to the industries. Russian refined petroleum fluctuated to the extent of $0.48 only, the low prices being in April, May, and June.

*Importations of refined petroleum at Antwerp since 1862.*

| From— | 1862. | 1870. | 1880. | 1890. | 1899. | 1900. | 1901. |
|---|---|---|---|---|---|---|---|
| United States ......packages.. | 36,000 | 400,000 | 752,803 | 718,497 | 854,351 | 767,165 | 884,560 |
| Russia.................barrels.. | .......... | .......... | .......... | 167,400 | 191,500 | 201,805 | 194,000 |

The prices of the American product during 1901 (per 220.46 pounds) were—

| Month | Price. | Month. | Price. |
|---|---|---|---|
| January.................................. | $3.47.4 | July ...................................... | $3.42.5. |
| February ................................ | 3.61.8 | August ................................... | 3.42.5 |
| March .................................... | 3.61.8 | September............................... | 3.42.5 |
| April...................................... | 3.32.9 | October................................... | 3.47.4 |
| May....................................... | 3.06.8 | November................................ | 3.47.4 |
| June ...................................... | 3.06.8 | December ................................ | 3.37.7 |

### RESIN AND BITUMEN.

[Free of duty.]

The quantities imported during last year showed an increase over those of 1900. Although the demand was weaker, prices rose steadily, especially for the finer qualities, which have rarely reached such heights. The importations were:

### FROM FRANCE.

| | 1850. | 1860. | 1870. | 1880. | 1890. | 1899. | 1900. | 1901. |
|---|---|---|---|---|---|---|---|---|
| | *Barrels.* | *Barrels.* | *Barrels.* | *Barrels.* | *Barrels.* | *Barrels.* | *Barrels.* | *Barrels.* |
| Bordeaux ........... | .......... | .......... | 10,597 | 10,769 | 6,243 | .......... | 9,340 | 12,225 |
| Bayonne ........... | .......... | .......... | 15,356 | 11,542 | 10,018 | .......... | 2,716 | 2,570 |
| Total........... | .......... | .......... | 25,953 | 22,311 | 16,261 | .......... | 12,056 | 14,795 |

### FROM UNITED STATES.

| | | | | | | | | |
|---|---|---|---|---|---|---|---|---|
| New York........... | 13,500 | 63,270 | 19,582 | .......... | 24,626 | 5,520 | 8,400 | 2,000 |
| Wilmington........... | .......... | .......... | .......... | 31,248 | 11,065 | .......... | .......... | .......... |
| Charleston ........... | .......... | .......... | .......... | 908 | .......... | .......... | .......... | .......... |
| Savannah ........... | .......... | .......... | .......... | 5,669 | 12,109 | 48,012 | 47,040 | 58,070 |
| New Orleans........ | .......... | .......... | 216 | .......... | .......... | .......... | 3,000 | .......... |
| Brunswick........... | .......... | .......... | .......... | .......... | 1,297 | .......... | .......... | 4,000 |
| Baltimore........... | .......... | .......... | .......... | .......... | 500 | 2,200 | 3,700 | 3,300 |
| Via Hamburg....... | .......... | .......... | .......... | .......... | .......... | 200 | 450 | .......... |
| Via England and Holland ........... | .......... | .......... | 3,876 | .......... | .......... | .......... | .......... | .......... |
| Total........... | 13,500 | 63,270 | 23,624 | 37,258 | 49,597 | 55,932 | 62,590 | 67,370 |

### SALTED PROVISIONS.

[Free of duty.]

Salted provisions began the year at prices from $17.37 to $18.33, rising steadily until they reached $22.19 to $22.96 during the last month of the year. In November only, was there a slight fall, December making up for the loss.

*Importations at Antwerp since 1880.*

| From— | 1880. | | 1890. | | 1900. | | 1901. | |
|---|---|---|---|---|---|---|---|---|
| | *Cases.* | *Barrels.* | *Cases.* | *Barrels.* | *Cases.* | *Barrels.* | *Cases.* | *Barrels.* |
| New York............ | 122,583 | 8,807 | 65,767 | 829 | 41,932 | 997 | 23,628 | 416 |
| Philadelphia........ | 12,371 | 664 | 1,775 | .......... | 650 | .......... | 500 | .......... |
| Boston ............. | 2,995 | .......... | 25,415 | .......... | 13,036 | 50 | 5,756 | .......... |
| Baltimore........... | .......... | .......... | 6,561 | .......... | 771 | 150 | 465 | .......... |
| New Orleans........ | .......... | .......... | .......... | .......... | .......... | .......... | .......... | .......... |
| Newport News...... | .......... | .......... | .......... | .......... | 50 | .......... | 874 | 20 |
| Portland ........... | .......... | .......... | .......... | .......... | 50 | .......... | 150 | .......... |
| Montreal............ | .......... | .......... | .......... | .......... | 50 | .......... | .......... | 150 |
| Hamburg and Bremen............ | 65 | 352 | 29 | 515 | 1,904 | .......... | .......... | 2,174 |
| France.............. | 3,126 | 8 | 22 | .......... | .......... | .......... | .......... | .......... |
| England ............ | 12,609 | 164 | 5,466 | 54 | 1,056 | .......... | 3,975 | .......... |
| Others .............. | 499 | .......... | .......... | .......... | .......... | .......... | .......... | .......... |
| Total.......... | 154,248 | 9,995 | 105,035 | 1,398 | 58,599 | 1,197 | 36,348 | 2,760 |
| Packages ..... | 164,243 | | 106,433 | | 59,696 | | 38,108 | |

### TOBACCO.

[Duty $10.61, excise $2.89, per 220.46 pounds.]

*Movement of the Antwerp market for the year 1901.*

| | Kentucky. | Virginia. | Maryland and Ohio. | Total. |
|---|---|---|---|---|
| | *Hogsheads.* | *Hogsheads.* | *Hogsheads.* | *Hogsheads.* |
| Stock, Jan. 1............................................. | 1,040 | 402 | 79 | 1,611 |
| Importations............................................. | 5,860 | 1,021 | 130 | 7,011 |
| Total................................................ | 6,900 | 1,513 | 209 | 8,622 |
| Sales.................................................. | 5,723 | 1,329 | 209 | 7,261 |
| Stock at end of December ............................. | 1,177 | 184 | ............ | 1,361 |

The stock on hand in the warehouses on the 31st of December, 1901, was 2,568 hogsheads.

*Tobacco in hogsheads.*—The firmness in prices continued throughout the year, but the American trusts controlled the market to such an extent that importation was rendered most difficult.

*Seed leaf.*—Transactions greatly diminished in 1901, and the bad crops scarcely permitted the importation of the necessary quantity, while the complete lack of Manila tobacco and the destruction of the stock of Mexican tobacco in the great fire of the bonded warehouses in June precluded the transactions hoped for.

### INDUSTRIES.

#### SHIPYARDS.

The John Cockerill yards at Hoboken turned out, in 1901, 1 screw steamer of 4,000 tons, 6 stern wheelers, 2 screw tugs, 1 screw ferry-boat, and 7 whaling vessels; and at the beginning of the year they were constructing a 4,000-ton steamer, 5 screw steamers, and 3 side wheelers. The number of workmen employed at the present moment is about 800.

The Antwerp shipbuilding yards were constituted in February, 1900. The filling in of the land was begun in June of the same year. In December the workshops were constructed, and the machinery placed in March, 1901. The keel of the first steamer, of 2,200 tons, ordered by a Belgian firm, was laid in August, 1901; that of the second in

October, and that of the third in December. The number of workmen employed is about 480.

The Antwerp Boiler Works undertake the manufacture of boilers of all systems and sorts; also of reservoirs, gasometers, beams, joists, etc. The shipbuilding is limited to the construction of tugs, lighters, and stern wheelers. This establishment has a thoroughly modern plant, using steam, electricity, hydraulic, and pneumatic force. The company employs about 500 workmen.

### BREWERIES.

The number of breweries is increasing rapidly. In 1898, there were 3,141 breweries in activity; in 1899, 3,181; in 1900, 3,223, and in 1901, the number was 3,253.

The quantities of flour used are approximately the following:

|  | Pounds. |
|---|---|
| 1898 | 180,492,958 |
| 1899 | 187,937,792 |
| 1900 | 189,647,370 |
| 1901 | 188,259,414 |

### DISTILLERIES.

The question of distilleries has become more complex than ever. Some wish this branch of industry to flourish, while others urge its total suppression. The Government, however, requires the revenue and the population demands distillery products without prohibitive taxation. The following was the situation of Belgian distilleries during 1901:

| Provinces. | Number of working distilleries. | Production at 50 degrees. |
|---|---|---|
|  |  | *Gallons.* |
| Antwerp | 23 | 4,633,116 |
| Brabant | 44 | 3,596,271 |
| West Flanders | 38 | 2,145,647 |
| East Flanders | 79 | 2,101,261 |
| Hainaut | 15 | 3,746,778 |
| Liege | 18 | 799,601 |
| Limburg | 29 | 1,972,966 |
| Luxemburg | 1 | 471,385 |
| Namur | 16 | |
| Total | 263 | 19,469,025 |

### MANUFACTURE OF SUGAR.

Prices began on the 2d of January at $4.27, reaching the highest point—$4.77—on June 26, and falling gradually to $3.14 on December 13. The following table shows the exportation of raw sugar from Belgium during 1901, 1900, and 1899:

| Destination. | 1901. | 1900. | 1899. |
|---|---|---|---|
|  | *Tons.* | *Tons.* | *Tons.* |
| England | 93,405 | 109,944 | 100,886 |
| Canada | 26,586 | 43,177 | 27,797 |
| United States | 4,724 | 51,554 | 11,127 |
| Japan | 3,795 | 411 | |
| Netherlands | 47,584 | 37,812 | 40,090 |
| Other countries | 844 | 205 | 3,332 |
| Total | 176,888 | 243,103 | 183,132 |

The following figures show the quantity of exports during the October-December quarter of the last three years:

|      | Tons. |
|------|------:|
| 1901 | 96,330 |
| 1900 | 129,444 |
| 1899 | 77,268 |

## CEMENT.

The exportations of Belgian Portland cement amounted to 491,673 tons in 1901, as compared with 408,284 tons in 1900.

The first artificial cement factory was started in Belgium in 1874, and there are at the present time 12 working plants in the country.

## PORT OF ANTWERP; MERCHANT MARINE.

Of the 2,000 running meters (6,570 feet) of quays in course of construction by the Government at the south river front, 835 (3,277 feet) have been formally handed over to the city, the latter immediately constructing the necessary sheds, hydraulic cranes, etc.

During the year 1901, the works in connection with the new petroleum installation at the south were well advanced. The gates of the dry docks are being renewed, and new sheds, covering an area of 6,120 square meters (67,584 square feet), have been erected at the Kattindyck dock. At the Asia dock, a new warehouse for ores has been constructed.

Thirty new 2-ton cranes have been purchased for the river and dock quays. The bonded warehouses destroyed by fire in June, 1901, are now in course of reconstruction and are expected to be completed by the end of 1902. They will be of noncombustible material, and the different buildings will be isolated.

The Belgian merchant marine is composed as follows:

| Year. | Number of vessels. | | | Tonnage of vessels. | | | Average tonnage per vessel. | |
|-------|-------|------|--------|--------|---------|---------|--------|--------|
|       | Steam. | Sail. | Total. | Steam. | Sail. | Total. | Steam. | Sail. |
| 1870 | 55 | 12 | 67 | 20,648 | 9,501 | 30,149 | 375 | 791 |
| 1880 | 24 | 42 | 66 | 10,442 | 65,224 | 75,666 | 435 | 1,553 |
| 1890 | 10 | 46 | 56 | 4,393 | 71,553 | 75,946 | 439 | 1,555 |
| 1900 | 4 | 69 | 73 | 741 | 112,518 | 113,259 | 185 | 1,631 |
| 1901 | 6 | 66 | 72 | 1,121 | 109,336 | 110,457 | 187 | 1,657 |

The number of steamers arriving at Antwerp since 1860 has been:

|         | 1860. | 1870. | 1880. | 1890. | 1896. | 1899. | 1900. | 1901. |
|---------|-------|-------|-------|-------|-------|-------|-------|-------|
| Voyages | 410 | 1,745 | 3,158 | 3,879 | 4,721 | 4,943 | 4,843 | 4,740 |
| Tons | 139,610 | 722,865 | 2,500,562 | 4,257,027 | 6,144,810 | 6,556,770 | 6,442,347 | 7,197,839 |

| Arrivals by sea, for— | 1900. | | 1901. | |
|-----------------------|---------|--------|---------|--------|
|                       | Vessels. | Tons. | Vessels. | Tons. |
| Brussels | 164 | 31,056 | 136 | 23,804 |
| Louvain | | | 3 | 315 |
| Termonde | 1 | 112 | 2 | 214 |
| Total | 165 | 31,168 | 141 | 24,333 |

The totals of sailing vessels and steamers entered at Antwerp were:

|  | 1900. | 1901. |
|---|---|---|
| Vessels. | 5,414 | 5,267 |
| Tons. | 6,720,150 | 7,432,126 |

The totals of vessels entered at all Belgian ports were:

|  | 1900. | 1901. |
|---|---|---|
| Vessels. | 8,709 | 8,571 |
| Tons. | 8,558,162 | 9,287,706 |

## NATIONAL BANK.

The mercantile paper in Belgium discounted in 1901 amounted to $492,425,305.56. The branch bank discounted 243,118 bills of exchange, amounting to $77,087,330.85. If to the sum total of Belgian bills of exchange discounted be added 22,848 bills of exchange on foreign countries (amounting to $158,146,603), it is seen that the National Bank received, in 1901, 3,892,835 bills of exchange, amounting to $650,571,908.63.

In 1901, the bank refused 3,728 bills of exchange, which did not fulfill the required statutory conditions. These bills amounted to $862,216.50. Acceptances on December 31, 1901, amounted to $92,310,678.53; foreign mercantile paper included in this sum was valued at $31,370,700.43.

The movement of the bank and branches was:

| At— | Receipts. | Payments. |
|---|---|---|
| Brussels. | $841,177,856.20 | $835,642,987.97 |
| Agencies. | 1,276,809,640.69 | 1,214,804,726.98 |
| Branch bank. | 340,764,354.79 | 339,588,445.66 |
|  | 2,458,751,851.70 | 2,390,036,196.61 |

Receipts on account of the treasury.............................. $376,126,944.83
Payments............................................................. 374,468,417.83

    General movement....................................... 750,595,362.66

The balance in the bank on December 31, 1901, was $4,245,295.61. The credit of the savings bank figures to the extent of $1,613,728.52 in the general balance of accounts current.

The bills of exchange credited on account at Brussels during 1901 reached the number of 158,512, for a sum of $136,829,221.75; the bills of exchange credited on account in the provinces was 276,696, for the sum of $125,473,950.18; total, $261,303,171.88.

On December 31, 1901, the declared value of voluntary deposits was $91,548,175.71. In this sum was included $14,329,532.30, the deposits in the branch bank. The tax on deposit was $51,148.89.

The public funds belonging to the bank amounted to $9,633,291.50 on December 31, 1901. They included the following:

Belgian debt:

| | |
|---|---:|
| 2½ nominal value capital | $1,283,700.90 |
| 3 (first series) | 1,698,438.60 |
| 3 (second series) | 6,581,415.80 |
| 3 (third series) | 1,218,119.50 |
| Amount of notes payable to bearer | 152,022,240.00 |
| Notes in treasury | 26,701,486.31 |
| Bills in circulation on December 31, 1900 | 125,320,753.69 |
| | |
| Earnings on the stock for both half years. | 28.17 |
| Earnings of the stock of reserve fund | 3.42 |
| | |
| Together | 31.59 |

GEO. F. LINCOLN,
*Consul-General.*

ANTWERP, *October 17, 1902.*

## BELGIAN COMMERCE IN 1902.

### IMPORTS.

The quantity of barley imported from the United States into this country during the first six months of 1902 was 15,937,688 pounds, a decrease of 6,804,568 pounds from the figures of the preceding year.

Shipments of Indian corn fell off about 213,000,000 pounds, the figures being over 5,000,000 in 1902, 219,600,000 in 1901, and 281,000,000 in 1900, thus showing a decline for the past three years.

Wheat, which rose from 261,389,016 pounds in 1900 to 691,555,064 in 1901, fell to 460,144,887 pounds for the same period of 1902. Wheat flour also fell from 4,412,473 pounds in 1901 to 1,972,209 pounds for the same period in 1902.

Coffee, which fell about 273,000 pounds in 1901, reached 348,088 pounds, an increase of 4,000 pounds for the same period in 1902.

Importations of cotton, which increased by about 3,000,000 pounds in 1901, fell to 30,067,415 pounds in 1902, a decrease of 14,803,095 pounds.

Importations of lard decreased by 1,000,000 pounds in 1902. Animal fat, including fish oil, fell 4,000,000 pounds in 1902, while in 1901 it showed an increase of 1,000,000. The importations of raw animal substances, such as horsehair, shells, etc., fell from $112,816 in 1901 to $76,035 in 1902.

The fruit trade from the United States, which decreased by about 760,000 pounds last year, increased this year by 654,549 pounds. Unclassified dried fruits have increased in value by $15,813.

The notable gain in preserved meats in 1901 has been maintained and enlarged by about 89,000 pounds. Animal grease, which advanced by about 1,100,000 pounds in 1901, decreased about 4,000,000 pounds in 1902.

The importations of petroleum rose from 109,874,159 pounds to 127,937,103 pounds, an increase of 18,062,944 pounds

In copper and nickel, unworked, there was an increase of about 4,000,000 pounds, while in the same metals, worked, there was a decrease of about 33,000 pounds in 1902. The heavy fall in cast iron seems to continue, the total this year being 303,600 pounds, against 4,201,968 in 1901, a decrease of about 3,800,000 pounds. Wrought iron, on the contrary, advanced by 84,107 pounds. Old iron shows a very heavy falling off, the total of this year being 618,970 pounds, against 1,025,140 in 1901.

Lead, which reached last year 12,857,359 pounds, fell again to 6,724,383, a decrease of about 6,000,000 pounds. Tools and machinery of iron and steel increased by 72,003 pounds. The bicycle trade shows an advance, the increase being $5,865. The gain in firearms was not maintained, the totals being $19,660 in 1901 and $6,748 in 1902, a decrease of $12,912. Hemp, though amounting to 318,668 pounds in 1901, reached this year 721,501 pounds. Raw hides fell slightly— 17,000 pounds. Paper, unclassified, which fell from 228,218 pounds in 1900 to 42,844 in 1901, rose to 352,169 pounds for the same period in 1902. There is an increase over the figures of both 1900 and 1901 in the importations of chemical products, such as carbonic acid gas, of some $74,000. Dyes and colors increased from 975,094 pounds in 1901 to 1,095,934 in 1902. Drugs, such as plants, roots, flowers, etc., show a very heavy falling off, the totals being 20,220,216 pounds in 1901 and 10,278,097 in 1902, a decrease of 9,942,119 pounds. Unmanufactured tobacco shows a slight decrease, the figures being 4,791,728 pounds in 1901 and 4,370,557 pounds in 1902. Vegetable oils, nonalimentary, fell from 19,000,000 pounds to 11,000,000 pounds. Vegetable substances, such as oleaginous seeds, increased by 1,000,000 pounds, while vegetable substances unclassified, as well as seeds, fell from 1,030,297 pounds to 174,946 pounds. Importations of oil cakes have risen from 89,000,000 to 125,000,000 pounds. Oak and walnut, sawn, have shown a decline of about 153,000 feet as compared with the figures of the previous year. Wood pulp has increased by 176,530 pounds. The number of horses imported during the past three years has been: 1900, 1,867; 1901, 433; 1902, 169. Wool imports have risen from 187,000 pounds in 1901 to 381,000 pounds in 1902.

*Imports from the United States into Belgium for the first six months of the years 1902, 1901, 1900.*

[Amounts given in pounds unless otherwise stated.]

| Articles. | 1902. | 1901. | 1900. |
|---|---|---|---|
| Barley................................................. | 15,987,688 | 22,742,256 | 112,051,550 |
| Bran .................................................. | ............ | 120,481 | 4,047,072 |
| Buckwheat............................................ | 1,221,840 | 1,638,057 | 2,174,110 |
| Indian corn........................................... | 5,331,590 | 219,119,448 | 281,121,905 |
| Rye................................................... | 12,469,600 | 5,131,962 | 15,516,955 |
| Oats.................................................. | 332,375 | 39,800,194 | 23,747,257 |
| Wheat, spelt, and meslin............................. | 460,144,887 | 691,565,064 | 261,389,016 |
| Forage ............................................... | 12,721,913 | 5,184,752 | 5,623,488 |
| Flour, wheat.......................................... | 1,972,209 | 4,412,473 | 5,831,304 |
| Flour of barley, oats, corn, and buckwheat........... | 21,355 | 310,255 | 236,387 |
| Flour, unclassified................................... | 63,776 | 22,632 | 26,587 |
| Nonalimentary fecula................................. | 201,113 | 2,411,727 | 4,963,612 |
| Coffee ............................................... | 848,088 | 344,016 | 617,288 |
| Cotton ............................................... | 30,067,415 | 44,870,510 | 41,708,911 |
| Hops ................................................. | 1,280 | ............ | 18,611 |
| Malt.................................................. | 226,622 | 1,220,840 | 963,912 |
| Raw animal matter, such as lard...................... | 10,603,423 | 11,950,044 | 9,178,190 |
| Animal fat, not specified, fish oil.................. | 3,344,324 | 7,529,977 | 6,433,948 |
| Raw animal substances, horsehair, shells, etc........ | $76,035 | $112,816 | $66,492 |
| Fruits: | | | |
|   Prunes .......................................... | 827,114 | 172,565 | 939,050 |
|   Dried, unclassified ............................. | $65,623 | $49,810 | $69,178 |
| Honey................................................ | 511,544 | 619,278 | 608,182 |

*Imports from the United States into Belgium for the first six months of the years 1902, 1901, 1900—Continued.*

| Articles. | 1902. | 1901. | 1900. |
|---|---|---|---|
| **Meats:** | | | |
| Salted or smoked, ham, tongue, etc | 10,648,765 | 11,089,578 | 11,870,448 |
| Preserved | 690,784 | 601,348 | 485,452 |
| Raw animal matter, grease | 3,344,334 | 7,529,877 | 6,433,948 |
| Petroleum, refined | 127,987,103 | 109,874,159 | 107,035,975 |
| Rushes, bamboo, etc | $27,684 | $24,867 | $57,045 |
| Stones, unclassified | 21,789,264 | 23,932,917 | 28,373,200 |
| Tar, asphalt, etc | 51,059,708 | 42,158,142 | 33,872,671 |
| **Copper and nickel:** | | | |
| Unworked | 9,115,408 | 4,935,614 | 6,462,361 |
| Worked | 26,109 | 59,250 | 98,638 |
| **Iron:** | | | |
| Cast | 308,600 | 4,201,968 | 13,903,155 |
| Wrought | 85,129 | 1,022 | 133,250 |
| Old | 618,970 | 1,025,140 | 1,937,678 |
| Not specified | 157,678 | 37,290 | 106,669 |
| Lead | 6,724,383 | 12,857,359 | 3,244,891 |
| Steel in bars, sheets, and wire, unspecified | 63,113 | 49,630 | 155,127 |
| Tools, machines of iron and steel, unclassified | 435,894 | 863,891 | 704,336 |
| **Machines and machinery:** | | | |
| Unclassified | 83,241 | 79,564 | 26,402 |
| In cast iron, unclassified | 1,454,356 | 1,981,240 | 4,187,086 |
| Bicycles and parts | $12,023 | $6,158 | $15,987 |
| Firearms | $6,748 | $19,660 | $11,614 |
| Hemp | 721,501 | 318,668 | 89,021 |
| Cordage | 76,744 | 78,914 | 10,692 |
| India rubber, manufactured | $1,812 | $1,404 | $2,300 |
| Hides, raw | 251,852 | 268,325 | 78,089 |
| Leather, tanned | 70,877 | 80,067 | 37,588 |
| Furniture | $10,782 | $10,753 | $11,777 |
| Haberdashery and hardware | $27,875 | $14,582 | $10,683 |
| Paper, not specified | 352,169 | 42,844 | 228,218 |
| Chemical products, unspecified, as carbonic-acid gas, etc | $700,016 | $626,245 | $564,652 |
| Dyes and colors, unspecified | 1,095,934 | 975,094 | 2,932,547 |
| Drugs, unclassified, plants, roots, flowers, etc | 10,278,097 | 20,220,216 | 22,275,520 |
| Drugs, glue | 27,062 | 31,591 | 41,610 |
| **Tobacco:** | | | |
| Unmanufactured | 4,370,557 | 4,791,728 | 5,248,220 |
| Smoking and snuff | 9,974 | 11,640 | 23,950 |
| Cigars and cigarettes | 10,799 | 9,909 | 6,460 |
| Vegetable oils, nonalimentary | 11,419,892 | 19,328,782 | 21,241,761 |
| **Vegetable oils and substances:** | | | |
| Oleaginous grains | 1,628,628 | 357,575 | 853,246 |
| Unspecified grains | 174,946 | 1,080,297 | 245,266 |
| Oil cakes | 125,010,648 | 89,421,000 | 85,692,800 |
| **Wood, oak and walnut:** | | | |
| Split ............................feet | 7,836 | 13,237 | 12,390 |
| Sawed ..............................do | 259,396 | 412,384 | 500,024 |
| **Wood for building purposes other than oak and walnut:** | | | |
| Unsawed ...........................feet | 25,168 | 36,207 | 19,697 |
| Sawed, beams, etc ..................do | 89,167 | 344,062 | 111,795 |
| Wood, worked | 3,292 | 3,108 | 7,267 |
| Wood pulp | 4,014,484 | 3,837,954 | 906,707 |
| Horses .........................number | 169 | 433 | 1,867 |
| Wool | 381,132 | 187,800 | 125,662 |
| Raw mineral matter, unclassified, as mineral, copper, lead, zinc, etc | $512,944 | $707,937 | $220,318 |
| Works of art | $3,142 | $376 | $497 |

## EXPORTS.

The exportations of chicory for the first six months of this year were nil. Chemical products, not specified, such as carbonic acid and sulphuric acid, increased slightl , the totals being $347,731 in 1901 and $362,546 for the same periodÿin 1902. The exportation of soda and carbonate shows a decrease of about 93,000 pounds as compared with 1901. Steel rails, which decreased by 1,000,000 pounds in 1901, reached this year 6,623,931 pounds, an increase of 5,481,949 pounds. Small iron beams rose from 200,000 to 202,811 pounds. Wrought iron, such as wire or rolled iron, which fell 870,000 pounds in 1901, reached this year 1,228,581 pounds. Machines and machinery in cast iron, unspecified, which attained 74,603 pounds in 1901, fell to 39,061 pounds in

1902. In iron and steel, the figures were 82,365 pounds in 1902, 54,674 in 1901, and 158,246 in 1900. The increase in firearms exported to the United States was maintained, the figures being $214,503 in 1900, $245,915 in 1901, and $329,881 in 1902. Cement, which fell last year, advanced again in 1902, the figures being 65,917,540 pounds and 94,454,824 pounds, respectively. Stones for building purposes amount to 597,764 pounds, instead of 811,544 pounds in 1901. Paper, not specified, rose from 530,603 pounds to 593,012 pounds. Cotton textiles exported show an increase of about $14,000, the figures being $26,332 in 1901 and $40,882 in 1902. Raw wool shows 515,700 pounds in 1901 as compared with 999,604 in 1902. Flax held its own much better, the figures being 2,630,860 pounds in 1901 and 2,648,760 pounds in 1902. Exportations of jute and hemp textiles decreased by $14,000, though far exceeding the figures of 1900. Raw hemp has increased from 5,346 pounds in 1901 to 650,274 pounds in 1902. Rawhides, which increased in 1901, fell again, the figures being 6,621,832 pounds in 1901 and 4,703,067 pounds in 1902. Skins, dyed and varnished, rose from 26,534 pounds in 1901 to 325,579 pounds in 1902. Rags, which diminished last year, increased from 12,144,898 pounds in 1901 to 14,052,636 pounds in 1902. India rubber shows 2,391,241 pounds in 1901 and 1,185,540 in 1902. Exportations of window glass rose from $242,131 in 1901 to $628,704 in 1902. Raw beet sugar shows, for 1900, 38,757,222 pounds; for 1901, 10,060,856 pounds; and for 1902, 9,071,299 pounds.

*Exports from Belgium to the United States for the first six months of the years 1902, 1901, and 1900.*

[Amounts given in pounds, unless otherwise stated.]

| | 1902. | 1901. | 1900. |
|---|---|---|---|
| Alcoholic liquors, brandy of every description in casks, gallons | 3,854 | 2,084 | 2,192 |
| Beers | 9,771 | 14,457 | 19,411 |
| Chicory | | 47,046 | 8,101 |
| Cocoa butter | 109,782 | | 5,136 |
| Coke tons | 6,205 | 2,390 | 1,400 |
| Coal, ordinary pit do | 23,022 | 18,426 | 22,070 |
| Coal in bricks | 28,800 | 25,610 | 24,500 |
| Chemical products, not specified, as carbonic acid and sulphuric acid | $362,546 | $347,781 | $430,978 |
| Sal soda, carbonate | 146,150 | 239,207 | 567,788 |
| Sulphur | 497,090 | 119,290 | 357,398 |
| Raw mineral matter, unclassified, as tin, copper, lead, zinc, etc | $67,717 | $32,914 | $65,928 |
| Lead, unclassified | 1,878,800 | 1,062,495 | 22,411 |
| Steel rails | 6,628,931 | 1,141,982 | 2,590,497 |
| Iron: | | | |
| Small beams, cast | 202,811 | 200,618 | 1,719,590 |
| Beaten in wire or rolled | 1,228,581 | 344,821 | 1,214,403 |
| Wrought | 588,062 | 622,188 | 177,371 |
| Coppered, galvanized, and nickeled | | | 11,375 |
| Machines and machinery: | | | |
| In cast iron, unspecified | 39,061 | 74,603 | 54,169 |
| In iron and steel, not specified | 82,365 | 54,674 | 158,246 |
| In other metal | 9,405 | 3,820 | 42,277 |
| Firearms | $329,881 | $245,915 | $214,503 |
| Haberdashery and hardware | $6,603 | $9,155 | $17,090 |
| Furniture | $428 | $3,571 | $1,617 |
| Cement | 94,454,824 | 65,917,540 | 143,855,217 |
| Stones for building purposes | 597,764 | 811,544 | 597,446 |
| Paper, not specified | 593,012 | 530,603 | 922,845 |
| Books, paper back and bound | 68,923 | 60,306 | 35,604 |
| Books, unbound | 3,603 | 1,027 | 1,516 |
| Clothing of all kinds, ready-made | $40,801 | $44,544 | $76,700 |
| Cotton textiles | $40,882 | $26,332 | $36,332 |
| Woolen textiles | $48,170 | $61,455 | $88,780 |
| Woolen thread. carded, twisted, etc | 14,724 | 26,964 | 8,377 |
| Wool, raw | 999,604 | 515,700 | 1,055,734 |
| Flax | 2,648,760 | 2,630,866 | 1,220,037 |

*Exports from Belgium to the United States for the first six months of the years 1902, 1901, and 1900—Continued.*

|  | 1902. | 1901. | 1900. |
|---|---|---|---|
| Jute, hemp, etc., textiles | $130,956 | $144,238 | $107,192 |
| Rope | 83,927 | 34,336 | 30,302 |
| Hemp, raw | 650,274 | 5,346 | 24,700 |
| Oilcloth textiles | | | $1,698 |
| Horse hair, bristles, shells, etc | $26,500 | $31,373 | $29,196 |
| Live plants and flowers | $40,481 | $33,205 | $29,196 |
| Hides, raw | 4,703,067 | 6,621,832 | 4,731,986 |
| Skins, dyed and varnished | 32,579 | 26,684 | 181,680 |
| Gloves | $28,412 | $13,821 | $63,062 |
| Rags | 11,052,636 | 12,141,898 | 13,369,744 |
| Medicinal plants, essences, etc | 488,037 | 122,740 | 86,927 |
| Meats, preserved | 106,815 | 73,016 | 78,082 |
| Mineral waters of every description | $22,822 | $27,193 | $57,562 |
| India rubber, raw | 1,184,540 | 2,391,241 | 1,488,590 |
| Resins and bitumen, unclassified | 948,521 | 1,745,090 | 1,088,146 |
| Glass: | | | |
| Window | $628,704 | $242,131 | $369,000 |
| Ordinary | $39,686 | $103,193 | $49,446 |
| Mirrors | $248,917 | $102,618 | $66,202 |
| Ivory | 80,159 | 74,665 | 61,287 |
| Works of art | $636 | $111,509 | $2,528 |
| Sugar, raw beet-root | 9,071,299 | 10,060,856 | 38,757,222 |
| Vegetables, preserved | 225,935 | 156,520 | 145,746 |
| Vegetables and substances not specified | 674,746 | 86,640 | 54,563 |
| Vegetable oils, nonalimentary | 1,065,290 | 1,535,062 | 518,345 |
| Animal fat | 1,654,198 | 1,692,162 | 1,799,085 |
| Wood pulp | 3,925,396 | 165,091 | 570,991 |
| Wood, wrought feet | 35,326,969 | 11,575,046 | 33,371,631 |
| Dyewoods | | | 220,460 |
| Various products for industrial purposes | $289 | $1,486 | $96 |
| Dyes and colors | 3,290,672 | 2,301,326 | 2,526,295 |

## EXTENSION OF THE PORT OF ANTWERP.

After years of futile debate, something has been done with a view to relieving the port of pressure. A step in advance has been taken; but in order that it may be understood, it is necessary to trace the history of the knotty extension question that has troubled shipping circles here for some years.

Ever since the abolition of light dues and the reduction of dock dues at Antwerp, the tonnage entered at this port has increased so much that for some time past the area has been quite inadequate, with the result that annoying delays have been of daily occurrence. Projects have been advanced for extending the port, but owing to misunderstandings between the municipality of Antwerp and the central Government and the interference of politics, no definite plan has ever been approved. The river Scheldt is under the jurisdiction of the Government, whereas the docks and basins belong to the city; consequently any plan of the Government which interfered with the property of the city and did not meet with approval was vetoed in the city council. On the other hand, all plans submitted by the city to the Government affecting any part of the river met with a decided check from the central Government at Brussels. The city, confident in its knowledge of the river Scheldt, at first conceived the idea of extending the port to the left bank of the river at the Tête de Flandre, where, in fact, Napoleon I began the construction of quays. In this, however, the city received no support from the Government, which adhered to a plan of extension known as the "great cutting." Of all the schemes submitted by the Chambers of Deputies, by army officers, engineers, and private citizens, none received general approval; and it was not until 1897 that the Belgian Government, after exhaustive investigation and after consultation with some of the most eminent engineers of the

world—among them those responsible for the dredging of the Missis-
sippi—decided in favor of the scheme of the deputy from Antwerp.
This plan, which has become among engineers one of the interesting
problems of the day, comprises the increase of the superficial area of
the docks at the north, and the alteration of the course of the river.
The river is turned from its natural bed at a point known as the Kruys-
chaus, just below Lillo, where now exists the first sharp turning, the
new course continuing with a gradual curve to the America and Lefebvre docks.   Here it joins the present bed of the river.   The America
dock will be absorbed in the new river bed, while the Lefebvre dock
will remain intact.   The fortifications on the north will have to be
thrown out and rebuilt, considerably enlarging the boundary of Antwerp.   The cutting of the new bed would form a vast island between the
new channel and the old, where a free port, so earnestly desired by the
chamber of commerce, could easily be constructed.   The island thus
formed and the extension of the city limits to the north as well as to
the south will more than double the area of the port of Antwerp, making it one of the largest of the world.

So gigantic a project, however, can not be realized for some time,
and the Government well understood that something must be done at
once to relieve the pressure.   Accordingly, its first step was to undertake the construction of 6,500 feet of running river quays at the south
end of the river front, of which about half have already been handed
over and are ready to receive tonnage.   The Government also decided
to construct new docks at the north of the Lefebvre dock and the
America dock, to be known as the "intercalary works."   On the
construction of these docks the city and the Government now agreed
in principle, and this agreement is due to the efforts of the Antwerp
Shipping Federation, which, after vain attempts on the part of the
Antwerp deputies, the Antwerp Chamber of Commerce, etc., was able
to present the matter in such an impartial light that the municipal
and Government authorities were compelled to act.

The construction of the large docks referred to, at the north of the
Lefebvre dock and directly connected with the latter, would be, however, like that of a huge house without an entrance, for the single
sluice gate connecting the river with the Kattendyck dock is not even
sufficient for the present dock system.   Then arose the knotty problem of a third sluice.   This has now been decided, and it may be concluded that the work will soon begin, to the great relief of the community, for the continuation of the present state of things means
eventual ruin.

The minister of public works has decided that the new sluice should
be almost alongside of the present "Sas dock," cutting through and
doing away with two of the dry docks.   This, however, gave a sluice
with only 21 feet of water, whereas 28 feet are necessary; for under
present conditions, vessels drawing over 21 feet have to complete loading in the river.   Finally, the entire plans were again submitted to
the city engineer of Antwerp, Mr. Royers, one of the most competent
authorities in Belgium, who conceived the idea of cutting the new
sluice directly into the Lefebvre dock, giving the required 28 feet,
and saving incoming vessels the loss of time in getting round the
Kattendyck.   Knowing the susceptibilities of the Government regarding its project for cutting a new bed for the river, Mr. Royers has so
disposed the new sluice that, in the event of the new cutting being carried out, his work need in no way be interfered with.

The minister has seen no objection to Mr. Royers's plan, and at a meeting in Brussels between the authorities and Mr. De Smet de Nayer, the minister of public works, the matter was settled. Besides this, the minister agreed to a new dock for lighters and small coasting vessels, to be built at the south end.

The Antwerp Shipping Federation was formed in December, 1900, composed of all the shipbroking and shipowning houses of Antwerp, which united for the purpose of putting an end to labor troubles which at that time threatened the annihilation of the port. This federation practically put an end to the dockers' unions, by creating its own union (in which the men are much better off) by virtue of which a dockers' strike is now almost an impossibility. The federation then took up other matters of importance, and in its first annual meeting, on December 16, 1901, turned its attention seriously to the port extension. The following paragraph occurs in the annual report read at the meeting:

We might say that the year ends with the brightest prospects for the port of Antwerp, were the vital question of its extension solved, or even in the way of being solved by an understanding between the authorities. Unfortunately, we have learned of nothing encouraging so far. The intercalary works are soon to be adjudicated, so it is said. Although these new docks will not be sufficient, yet their construction will give some satisfaction, provided it is not forgotten that they will be of no service (unless at the same time direct communications between them and the river is established) if vessels of deep draft can not enter them. We must have the new docks, but at the same time we must have a new deep-water sluice.

This categorical report caught the attention of the authorities, where the chamber of commerce and even the deputies from Antwerp had failed. On April 29, the question was brought up in the Chamber of Deputies by an interpellation on the part of the Antwerp bench. The debate was adjourned, and in the interval a meeting of the Antwerp Shipping Federation was held, and the declaration was made that the present situation was disastrous, and that the 6,500 running feet of quays at the south end of the river front were absolutely inadequate to meet the requirements of the port. It further urged the authorities to come to an agreement.

This declaration of the Antwerp Shipping Federation placed the matter before the Chamber of Deputies in a clearer light than ever before, and was instrumental in bringing about the decision of the minister of public works to consent to a third sluice. At the last meeting of the Antwerp municipal council, the alderman of commerce announced that the agreement had been arrived at between the minister of finance and public works, Count De Smet de Nayer, and the city government with regard to the port extension at the north, while the question of the great cutting remains in abeyance. This official communication of news has been received with the greatest satisfaction by the entire shipping community. The new sluices, planned by Mr. Royers, will be 552 feet in width. The sluice and the new docks will be constructed at the same time, so that the latter may be accessible as soon as completed. In answer to a question, the alderman stated that the work would in all probability be completed in four years. It was further announced that the new bonded warehouses on the site of the enormous conflagration of June, 1901, would be finished before the end of the year.

GEO. F. LINCOLN, *Consul-General.*

ANTWERP, *October 17, 1902.*

## BRUSSELS.

The general results of the commercial movement of Belgium with foreign countries during 1901 were inferior to those of the preceding year. The general importations and exportations together amounted to 6,880,000,000 francs ($1,327,840,000).

### GENERAL COMMERCE.

The total weight of merchandise imported amounted to 16,421,139 tons, valued at 3,640,600,000 francs ($702,000,000). The total weight of merchandise exported amounted to 17,232,357 tons, valued at 3,239,400,000 francs ($625,200,000).

### SPECIAL COMMERCE.

The total weight of merchandise imported amounted to 13,549,961 tons, valued at 2,221,000,000 francs ($428,651,000). The total weight of merchandise exported was 14,352,905 tons, valued at 1,828,200,000 francs ($352,842,600).

The importations from the United States into Belgium during the year 1901 amounted to 335,700,000 francs ($64,790,100), and the exportations to 78,500,000 francs ($15,140,000). The declared value of exports from the consular district of Brussels to the United States for the year ending December 31, 1900, was $4,217,247.96, and for the same period of 1901, $4,486,989.34, an increase of $269,741.38.

The declared value of exports for the first six months of 1902 was $2,727,877.15, showing an increase of $948,976.40, as compared with the corresponding period of 1901.

### INDUSTRIES IN THE CONSULAR DISTRICT OF BRUSSELS FOR 1902.

In the various branches of trade, the situation in this consular district during the first eight months of 1902 has been, approximately, good.

*Bricks.*—There was great demand, but unfavorable weather prevented a normal production. Sales were active at high figures. The average price for ordinary bricks is $3 per thousand. Special bricks manufactured by mechanical process are in demand.

*Bronze and gas fixtures.*—The situation is normal. Bronze, copper, and white-metal foundries are in good condition, with full orders and prices steady.

*Cement.*—In the district of Mons, the production is very active, amounting to about 60 tons per day. The product is recognized as being of excellent quality and finds quick sale. At La Louvière, great activity prevails. At Tournai, which is an important cement center, the situation is bad. The exportation from Brussels to the United States during the year 1901, shows a decrease of $284,673.32 as compared with the year 1900; but for the six months ended June 30, 1902, this exportation amounted to $138,798.57, an increase of $8,624.06 as compared with the corresponding period of 1901.

*Cotton spinning.*—The situation is bad and sales are slow.

*Engraving.*—Work is abundant.

*Felt manufactures.*—The situation is unsatisfactory. At St. Nicolas, several factories are idle. At Ruysbrock, near Brussels, where a new factory has been built, orders are few and work insufficient. The decrease in the exportation for the year ended December 31, 1901, amounted to $19,927.07 as compared with the year 1900.

*Foundries.*—At Charleroi, Soignies, and Mons, cast-iron foundries are working short hours. The situation as regards steel foundries is more satisfactory, although there are some unemployed workmen. At La Louviére, orders are sufficient to keep the foundries running, but profits are small.

*Furniture.*—The trade poor at Brussels; at Mons, activity is normal.

*Glass trade.*—The situation is bad. Prices are upset, and, though quotations were lowered, orders are not sufficient to keep the works in a normal state of activity. Exportation is poor, though shipments from this consular district to the United States show an increase for 1901 of $694,141.51 as compared with 1900. At Mons, selling prices leave little profit. At an international meeting of glass manufacturers, held at Dusseldorf in the month of June, 1902, it was decided to maintain the increase of 15 per cent on prices for all export markets excepting England and its colonies. As concerns this market, the most absolute liberty was accorded as regards prices. In spite of the unfavorable situation, wages remain at old rates. At La Louviére, orders are scarce and stocks are increasing; buyers dispute prices, and sales are frequently made at great sacrifices. All workmen are employed, and goblet manufacturing is increasing. At Mons, a slight decrease in the price of window glass is reported, due to insufficient orders. The price of production is always very high and will increase further. Glass manufacturers are looking forward to a more flourishing state of affairs now that the war in South Africa is ended. England and China have been poor customers, and, at present, only a few orders are booked for America, owing to the shutting down of glassworks in the United States during the summer months. At Charleroi, the market is very dull. At La Louviére, overproduction renders sales difficult, and profits are below the normal.

*Electricity.*—Workshops are running with short force; orders are few and unimportant. The total length of streets laid with wires now amounts to 59,381 meters, 3,215 meters more than at this period last year. In a certain number of streets, the wires are laid under both sidewalks. The present total length of lines is 66,394 meters. There are 36 feeders, with a total length of 29,124 meters, sufficient to supply 64,752 lamps of 16 candlepower. The total length of cables is 330 kilometers, 24 kilometers more than last year. The number of branch lines serving subscribers is 2,120.

*Automobiles and bicycles.*—This industry is prosperous in Brussels, and the construction of motocycles is increasing. The communal administration, believing that the circulation of automobiles and motocycles presents grave dangers on the Avenue Victoria, especially on days when there is an unusual number of promenaders, has prohibited access to these vehicles from the Avenue du Champs des Courses to the Chaussée de La Hulpe.

*Breweries.*—The situation is normal and wages are satisfactory.

*Marble.*—The situation is very good in Brussels and wages are increasing.

*Matches.*—The situation is normal, but the workmen complain of their low wages, on account of the danger of their work.

*Metallurgy.*—Prices are rather low, while rates for fuel and raw material remain high. At Mons, the rolling mills have no orders. At Charleroi, prices remain steady for the home market, but are much too low for exportation, and manufacturers hesitate to book orders. The trade in steel rails and beams shows a slight improvement. Blooms and billets, however, maintain their prices with difficulty, and suffer from German competition. At Mons, the situation for boiler makers is bad, and a few workshops will probably shut down next winter. At Charleroi, orders for bridges and framework are numerous. At Mons, Charleroi, and Soignies, important contracts have been signed for railway material and engines.

*Painting.*—Work is abundant.

*Printing.*—Work is regular; printers are in demand.

*Rubber.*—Work is steady. The exportation of rubber toys from Brussels, as compared with that of 1900, shows an increase of $4,307.65.

*Soap.*—Trade is calm, with slight increase in prices of raw material.

*Shoemaking.*—The situation is satisfactory. In the factories, work is steady. Skilled workmen are scarce. The sale of American shoes, especially for ladies, is increasing.

*Sugar.*—In the Mons district, sugar plants will not work this year. Many farmers have abandoned beet growing and transformed their fields into meadows for cattle grazing. Sugar manufacturers consider that this crisis will probably last two years. At Soignies, manufacturers have repaired their plants, but have bought only small quantities of fuel. The outlook for the next season is discouraging, with a poor yeild and reduced prices for beets and sugar.

*Tobacco.*—Work is dull in cigar and cigarette making in Brussels. At St. Nicolas, the situation is satisfactory, with all hands employed and orders numerous. A great deal of the tobacco used in the factories at Brussels comes indirectly from the United States.

*Textile industry.*—There is great activity in the spinning mills of combed wool. An important increase of work is noted at Tournai, with insufficiency of spinners. At St. Nicolas, work in the weaving mills is regular, but sales are difficult. Workmen complain that they have to do double the amount of work to earn the same wages as formerly. Hosiery manufacturers report a slight falling off in sales.

*Tack and nail industry.*—Work is regular at Brussels, Mons, and Charleroi. Orders are abundant, but prices are still too low, although there has been a slight increase. Prices for raw material are high. At Charleroi, nail manufacturers contemplate the creation of a syndicate.

*Phosphate.*—Exportation is insignificant, and the manufacture of chemical manures is unimportant. There is an increase in the consumption of nitrate of soda for sugar beets.

*Vegetables, preserved.*—The exportation of preserved vegetables, especially "green peas," is constantly increasing. The year 1901 shows a gain of $10,343.42, as compared with 1900.

*Quarries.*—The situation is satisfactory for blue stone (small granite), but prices are low. White stone is much in demand, and sandstone quarries show great activity. Skillful stonecutters are rare.

*Linen trade.*—There is great activity in the spinning mills, but sales are difficult.   The exportation of linen goods from this consular district to the United States for 1901 shows an increase of $13,755.60, as compared with 1900, and for the first six months of 1902 the shipments amounted to $222,730.49, as against $196,064.78 for the corresponding period of 1901, being an increase of $26,665.71.

*Gloves.*—Conditions are unsatisfactory.   The exportation to the United States in 1901 shows a decrease of $335,336.85, as compared with 1900, and for the first six months of 1902 an increase of $44,107.96, as compared with the corresponding period of 1901.   Notwithstanding the fact of this increase, glove manufacturers regard the future of their industry as menaced by privileges granted by this Government to foreign glove manufacturers.   In order to supply work to a large part of the population, the privilege of introducing into Belgium unsewed gloves was accorded foreign manufacturers.   The unfinished goods are sent to a bonded warehouse, addressed to agents of foreign houses in Brussels, who deposit with the customs authorities bonds covering the value of the gloves.   These are then removed and distributed among the working women.   As glove sewing is more skillfully and economically done in Belgium than in Germany, German manufacturers not only secure a better finish for their gloves, but effect a decided saving in wages.   The gloves are packed and returned to the customs-house, stamped with the customs seal, and sent to Germany.   Belgian glove manufacturers contend that this stamp is used as a certificate of Belgian origin, to the detriment of Belgian gloves, and ask the abolition of these privileges, and also that a high duty be levied on foreign gloves sewed in Belgium, so as to equalize the cost price of German and Belgian gloves.

*Paper.*—Work is abundant, but skilled workmen are rare.

*Book binding* and manufacture of registers, cashbooks, etc., show satisfactory conditions.

*Hats.*—The situation is fair.

*Hatter's fur.*—Work is slack and some few workmen are unemployed.

*Rope making.*—The situation is excellent; full work and no idle hands.

*Locksmiths, ironwork, and stoves.*—Orders are abundant.

*Barrel making.*—Conditions are normal.

*Sawmills.*—Work is steady and orders are abundant.

*Joinery and carpentry.*—The situation is excellent.

*Chocolate.*—The situation is satisfactory.

*Oil.*—Conditions are very good.

*Tanneries.*—At Brussels, the situation is normal, but in other sections of this district, slack work and few orders are reported.

*Flour.*—The milling industry in this consular district appears to be passing through an acute crisis.   At La Louviere, there was a considerable rise in price, which, however, lasted only a short time, and just now the quotations are unusually low, as production exceeds demand.   Bran, though offered at reduced prices, sells slowly.   At Brussels, the situation is bad, owing to overproduction.

*Carriages.*—In certain localities of this district, work and orders are abundant, but at Brussels very little is being done.

*Coal.*—In Mons, extraction and expedition continue normal.   Sugar refiners buy from day to day in preference to giving orders for large quantities.   Owing to a decrease in wages, labor is scarce, miners having sought work in districts where the pay is more remunerative. Work on new installations is being actively pushed, and the surface works at the Nord du Rien-du-Coeur are nearly finished.

At Charleroi, one pit has discontinued extraction, but the 300 miners who were employed there readily found work in neighboring mines. The keeping up of prices, as the result of an understanding among coal producers, excites recrimination on the part of consumers, especially among iron and steel manufacturers. Foreign competition has fallen off. Stocks are reported to be some 200,000 tons less than at this time last year.

The average prices contracted for by the Government railways at the last bid were:

| Class. | Contract price per ton. | | Class. | Contract price per ton. | |
|---|---|---|---|---|---|
| | Francs. | U. S. equivalent. | | Francs. | U. S. equivalent. |
| Close-burning coal ........... | 8. 90 | $1,717 | Nut coal ...................... | 16. 00 | $3,088 |
| Rubby half-soft coal ......... | 10. 90 | 2,103 | Small nut coal ............... | 27. 75 | 5,355 |
| Rubby soft coal .............. | 12. 48 | 2,408 | Coal for ovens ............... | 15. 72 | 3,038 |
| Soft coal...................... | 13. 33 | 2,572 | | | |

*Coke.*—The manufacture is very active, with orders sufficiently abundant to warrant putting all the ovens into operation. Prices are relatively high, but steady.

*Coal agglomerates.*—The situation remains good as to prices, activity, and production.

*Agriculture.*—Throughout this consular district, early vegetables and fruits suffered from bad weather and night frosts.

Rye, barley, and flax pr m se abundant yields.

Hay is abundant, and haymaking was rapidly finished, owing to favorable weather. Although clover and lucern produced a remarkable yield, prices will not exceed 5 francs ($0.965) per 100 kilos (220 pounds). The potato crop is satisfactory. Wheat and oats are excellent. Beets in certain localities are comparatively good. As in prece years, farmers experienced difficulty in securing labor and werdinforced to supply themselves with agricultural implements.

Cattle are in excellent demand, owing to the abundance of forage. Prices for horses, cattle, and hogs remain high.

Cooperative dairy farms are in a prosperous condition.

Horse breeding is annually assuming more importance in Belgium. On one small farm not exceeding in extent 2½ acres there were foaled last year nearly 39,000 colts and fillies, while five years ago the number barely reached 30,000.

## LACE.

In 1860, Belgium counted 50,000 women who earned their living by lace making. This fine art is principally confined to Flanders. Owing to the intermediary agent system prevailing here, by which the agent rapidly grows rich and the maker receives barely sufficient wages to keep soul and body together, the profession is yearly less and less sought, and lace makers are ready to accept ruder and more difficult labor, with more remunerative wages. The lace maker never comes in contact with the manufacturer for whom she works. She receives her designs and pay from the intermediary agent. The latest census shows that there are 49,000 lace makers in Belgium and 900 intermediary agents operating in the interest of 126 manufacturers. It may be interesting to mention that in a recent interview with one of the lace makers at Bruges, it was shown that, out of 15,000 lace workers in that city, there was only one skillful enough to make the rare Bruges point, which is so difficult to find at present. A sort of imitation is made, showing the three clover leaves—the distinctive sign of Bruges—but it has nothing in common with the old point of large mesh of the fourteenth century, a marvelous sample of which was recently exhibited at Bruges, as was also a wonderful piece in the form of an apron, said to have belonged to Jeanne la Folle, mother of Charles V.

Large quantities of Flemish (or more properly speaking, Valenciennes) Duchesse, with applications of Brussels needle-point, and torchon laces are made in and around Bruges. The majority of the lace makers earn from 50 to 85 centimes ($0.0965 to $0.1640) per day. Exceptionally good workers earn 1 franc ($0.193), and expert workers (of whom there are only 10 or 12 out of the 15,000) 2 francs ($0.386) per day for no matter what kind of lace. The one lace maker above referred to stated with pride that she made lace flounces for which she received as high as 600 to 750 francs ($115.80 to $144.75) per meter, but added that it required a year of faithful labor to make one meter.

The year 1901 was remarkable for an extraordinary demand for "real laces" of all kinds, and there being no corresponding increase in the production, a considerable rise in prices resulted. Another reason for the higher prices may be ascribed to the fact that many fancy goods, both in real and partly real lace (Luxenil, Renaissance, and similar kinds), have come to the front in the last few years. They have to be quickly made in order to meet a transitory fashion, and in consequence higher wages were demanded and received by the lace makers. As above mentioned, all descriptions of lace have been in favor.

*Point Gaze laces.*—The making of this class of goods is greatly restricted, owing to the constant demand from various countries for Luxenil and Renaissance, which are made just now in the Point Gaze districts.

*Duchesse laces.*—Both by the piece and by the ar , these enjoyed great popularity, and United States buyers, as well as others, did not hesitate to pa the advanced prices. Narrow laces, up to 3 inches, were exceedingly scarce.

*Bruges goods in the corded make.*—These were in very good demand and were readily bought for the United States and European continental markets.

*Flat Bruges goods.*—These were not so much asked for, except fancy galloons, medallions, etc., as well as collars and godets (berthas), the latter articles being bought in very important quantities by England for home and colonial trade.

*Valenciennes.*—Prices in this make were firmer, and the demand from all countries kept brisk.

*Torchons.*—The same is true of this article.

*Luxenil and Renaissance.*—For these goods, made with French or German braid, there still exists a good demand in several countries, although they are no longer in favor in the United States. Such staple goods as bands, lace by the yard, flounces, godets, scarfs, collars, handkerchiefs, etc., continue in favor with buyers of collars and berthas (godets). There was frequently an insufficient supply.

*Lace dresses.*—The moderate demand for lace dresses remains unchanged. The Belgian lace manufacturers have been most successful in putting upon the market tasteful novelties in duchesse, appliqué, Bruges (corded and flat), point, valenciennes, etc., to meet the exigencies of fashion, which call for such articles as galloons (wavy and straight patterns), detachable medallions (round or square), garlands, festoons, etc. Although it is difficult to speak with certainty regarding the future, the prospects for the lace trade appear bright, especially as fashion favors the article in a marked degree. I am indebted to the firms of Jeanne Luig & Co. and Muser Brothers, late manufacturers at Brussels, for part of the above information. The exportation of laces to the United States from this district for the year 1901 shows an increase of $5,870.30 as compared with 1900. The exportation for the six months ended June 30, 1902, amounted to $58,658.25, showing an increase of $13,723.84 as compared with same period of 1901.

### TARIFF CHANGES.

The following is a summary of the changes made in the tariff during the year:

Wooden skipping-rope handles, which are at present included under the heading "small wares (mercerie) and hardware," shall be classed in the category of various products for industries, dutiable at 5 per cent ad valorem. This decree entered into force February 15, 1901.

The undermentioned articles, which are at present classed under the heading "small wares (mercerie) and hardware," shall be placed under the category of various products for industries, dutiable at 5 per cent ad valorem, namely:

1. Beads of steel or mother of pearl for embroidery, trimmings, knittings, rosaries, necklaces, etc.

2. Small chains, hearts, and crosses of steel, copper, or maillechort, and wooden and copper crosses, for manufacturing rosaries and necklaces. This decree entered into force October 20, 1901.

Felt rolls for affixing to brick-molding machines are classed in the category of various products for industries, dutiable at 5 per cent ad valorem. This decree entered into force November 15, 1901.

An import duty at the rate of 5 francs ($0.965) per 100 kilograms (220 pounds) is assessed upon sulphuric ether and of 8 francs ($1.544) per 100 kilograms (220 pounds) on acetic ether.

Gunstocks, furnished or not with parts of metal and flint stones, are free of duty.

Sheepskins, called straw skins ("peaux pailles"), are dutiable at 15 francs ($2.895) per 100 kilograms (220 pounds).

The Government may, in the interests of industry, exempt from import duty the following products:

Vegetable essences or natural essential oils of bitter almonds, bergamot, cananga (vetiver or ylang-ylang), lemons and their varieties, geranium, orris, jasmine, lavender, lemon-grass (Indian vervain), linaloe, oranges and their varieties, origanum, sandalwood, sassafras, tuberose, geraniol and safrol, scented greases imported in receptacles of 10 kilograms (22 pounds) at least.

Grease consisting of a mixture of vegetable butter (cocoa), oil, and a neutral lard or other neutral fats, with a certain proportion of water, is dutiable as "margarin and other artificial butter" at 20 francs ($3.86) per 100 kilograms (220 pounds).

Blinds formed of slender bamboo, cane, rush, or rattan stalks, entirely plaited with textile threads, both extremities being furnished with wooden rods and fitted at the top with faience-headed nails, also with rings likewise of faience and hooks wherein a cord slides to operate the blind, are classed under "wood, other manufactures," 10 per cent ad valorem.

Falliére's phosphatine is comprised in "cocoa prepared," and dutiable at 50 francs ($9.65) per 100 kilograms (220 pounds).

Packets of chicory, inside which, for every two packets, is found a small tablet of chocolate (3 grammes), these tablets being distributed as an advertisement. Same régime as above as to the quantities of chocolate so brought in, such tablets, for the purposes of the tariff, not being considered as samples entitled to free entry.

Kepler's cod-liver oil is comprised in "Preserves, other," and is dutiable at 12 francs ($2.316) per 100 kilograms (220 pounds).

Cigarettes, called "cigarillos balsamicos contro el asma," consisting of waste of various nightshade leaves more or less impregnated with niter, prepared by Dr. Andrea, of Barcelona, are classed under "drugs," free.

Canned preserves, called "champignons aux truffles," consisting of a mixture of mushrooms and truffles preserved in water, are dutiable as "groceries: truffles;" 300 francs ($57.90) per 100 kilogrames (220 pounds).

Cocoanuts entirely covered with their fibrous peels are included in "fruits not specially classed, fresh," at 30 francs ($5.79), or 12 francs ($2.316) per 100 kilograms (220 pounds), according as they are imported in cases, boxes, bocals, baskets, or other packages weighing 3 kilograms (6.6 pounds) or less, or otherwise.

Cocoanuts in the shell, or partly stripped of their fibrous peels, are dutiable as "fruits not specially classed, dried," at 10 per cent ad valorem.

Bands cut from a piece woven in great width, a kind of woolen plush, undulated when hot so as to have the appearance of fur, said bands being afterwards folded upon the borders and lined with another band of tissue, and, generally, all bands of plushed tissue (imitation fur), hemmed, lined, padded, sewn in form of rolls, or otherwise manufactured, are classed under "wearing apparel, * * * articles made up wholly or in part," etc., 15 per cent ad valorem.

Calorimeters of Junkers & Co.'s system, principally used for ascertaining the caloric power and lighting power of illuminating gas, and solely employed in laboratories, are included in "scientific instruments and apparatus," free. This also applies to the boxes in which the apparatus is imported.

Glasses of special shape, serving to manufacture water-level indicators of the Klinger system, and also water-level indicators generally, are included in "scientific instruments and apparatus," free.

Mechanical thrashers and straw presses imported together are dutiable as "machines, implements, and tools," taxed according to the component material predominating in weight in each of such machines.

Gerber's acido-butyrometers for testing the fatty matter of milk, when the different pieces and accessories constituting a complete acido-butyrometer are imported at the same time, pay as "machines, implements, and tools," taxed according to component material of which manufactured or chiefly composed. When certain parts are imported separately, they must be classified according to kind or composition as per tariff, namely:

Thermometer: Dutiable as "scientific instruments and apparatus," free.

Centrifugal: Classed under "machines, implements, and tools," according to the kind.

Brushes: Classed under "small wares (mercerie), etc., articles, other," 15 per cent ad valorem.

Copper cans: Classed under "copper, wrought," 10 per cent ad valorem.

Enameled pan: Classed under "iron, wrought," 4 francs ($0.772) per 100 kilograms (220 pounds).

Water bath, classed under "tin plate, wrought," 10 per cent ad valorem.

Lamps, classed under "furniture," 10 per cent ad valorem.

Butyrometers and small pipes, classed under "glassware, other," 10 per cent ad valorem.

Porous jars for mounting electric piles are comprised in "machines, implements, and tools of copper or any other material," at 12 francs ($2.316) per 100 kilograms (220 pounds); or, if the importer desires, in "earthenware, faïence and porcelain not specially mentioned," 10 per cent ad valorem.

Lifts comprising a mechanical motor, cabin, pulleys, etc., are included in "machines, implements, and tools" taxed according to the component material predominating in weight.

Bags of cow hair, open worked, for pressing stearin in candle factories, are dutiable as "machines, implements, and tools of copper or any other material," 12 francs ($2.316) per 100 kilograms (220 pounds).

Paper filters, consisting of small conical tubes, are classed under "small wares (mercerie) and hardware; articles, other," 15 per cent ad valorem.

Articles in the form of hollow seals, serving to affix a trade-mark upon wax plates for the use of dentists in taking the stamp of teeth; same régime as foregoing.

Portable copying presses, called traveling presses; same régime as above.

Glass cutters composed of a handle of cast iron and a small metal wheel; same régime as above.

Spangles for making ladies' dress trimmings, consisting of two small superposed rings, one of velvet, the other of canvas; same régime as above.

Brooms with handles, whatever be the composition of the broom; same régime as above.

Crank-working bottle washers; same régime as above.

Sheets of gelatin, colored or not in the paste, for manufacturing spangles, labels, etc., and bearing impressions or designs; also address cards, printed bands, religious pictures, boxes, lanterns, etc., of gelatine; same régime as above.

Electric cigar lighters are dutiable as small wares (mercerie) and hardware. Articles, other, at 15 per cent ad valorem, whether intended or not to be placed on counters.

Trimmings of metal, formed of a fancy hook and a back plate, placed upon a card, for ornamenting ladies' belts; same régime as above. If the hooks referred to are imported separately they shall be dutiable as "small wares and hardware, articles specially mentioned," at 10 per cent ad valorem.

Apparatus called "collar showers," consisting of a water reservoir connected by a rubber tube with a lance provided with a hollow ring having holes, to rest on the shoulders around the neck, same régime as above.

Puzzles, consisting of various cards bearing images and numbers, same régime as above.

Kettles on stand holding a spirit lamp, same régime as above.

Flanged conical tubes, for boilers of the Galloway system, are comprised in "Metals: iron, hammered, drawn, or rolled," at 1 franc ($0.193) per 100 kilograms (220 pounds).

Post-card and letter-card automatic distributers are dutiable as "furniture," 10 per cent ad valorem.

Gas-heating apparatus called "radiators," same régime as above.

Towel horses with 10 branches, called "drying racks of wood or metal, to be fixed to the wall," same régime as above.

Envelopes in the form of bags of transparent paper, not bearing impressions and more specially intended to contain photographs, are included in "paper, other," at 4 francs ($0.772) per 100 kilograms (220 pounds).

Disinfectants composed of colored or noncolored sawdust, and of antiseptics with addition of perfumery essence, are comprised in "perfumery, other," 15 per cent ad valorem.

Pieces of varnished leather suitable to be employed in leather wares and proceeding from skins included in the category of "skins, dyed, varnished, etc.," are classed under "skins, dyed, varnished, lacquered, or morocco leather and prepared furs," at 30 francs ($5.79) per 100 kilograms (220 pounds).

List or felt shoes, with leather soles, are dutiable as "hides and skins, manufactured," at 10 per cent ad valorem.

Single colored cubes of ceramic, imported in bulk or assembled in designs glued on paper for mosaic work, are included in "Earthenware: paving and building tiles and slabs, etc., of one color," at 1 franc ($0.193) per 100 kilograms (220 pounds).

Panels, slabs, or tiles of xylolithe for wall lining and paving are included in "Earthenware: ceramic tiles and slabs, etc., of one or several colors," at 1 franc ($0.193) or 2 francs ($0.386) per 100 kilograms, as the case may be.

Product called "tropon" is comprised in "chemical products, not specially classed," free.

Paste in small sticks for temporarily stopping teeth, composed of gutta percha, a fat body and chiefly of oxide of zinc, known under the name of ".Dr. Gilbert's provisional plugging," same régime as above.

Casein, intended for industrial purposes, and adulterated by means of mirban essence, same régime as above.

Sheets of gelatin, colored or not, in the paste, and intended for the manufacture of spangles, labels, are included in "various products for industries," at 5 per cent ad valorem.

Cards with the words printed on the face: "Union Postale Universelle," "Post-card," and on the back a picture obtained by a special photographic process, are dutiable as "typographical products, typographical impressions," 18 francs per 100 kilograms ($3.474 per 220 pounds).

Cardboard sheets covered with drawings to cut out and unite, same being colored with the brush or on the plate, same régime as above.

Lithographed invoice forms on which the mechanical ruler has made blue and red columns and lines are comprised in "typographical products, lithographs, etc., of one or two colors, on paper," at 35 francs ($6.755) per 100 kilograms (220 pounds).

Books called "cinematographs," "himematographs," whose leaves, each bearing a picture, successively reflect a series of motions, are classed in "typographical products, albums and picture or drawing books, typographic, colored or not with the brush or on the plate," at 30 francs ($5.79) per 100 kilograms (220 pounds).

Small trays, newspaper holders, etc., formed of chromolithographs glued on cardboard, stamped and cut out, are included in "typographical products, lithographs, chromolithographs, etc., on cardboard or on paper," at 18 francs ($3.474) and 40 francs ($7.72) per 100 kilograms, according as they are printed in one, two, or more colors.

Pastilles called "pasta pectoral balsamica," Dr. Andreos, of Barcelona, are comprised in "sugar, refined, in powder, etc.," at 50 francs 50 centimes ($9.74) per 100 kilograms, with a surtax of 10 per cent.

Traveling rugs made with cow hair are taxed as "tissues not specially classed," at 10 per cent ad valorem.

Tissues composed of cotton, silk, and copper threads are taxed as "tissues of cotton, all other," at 15 per cent ad valorem.

Bed covers stuffed with eiderdown, declared as "foot covers," are taxed as "tissues," according to kind."

Glass apparatus called "Fraenkel's nose douches" are included in "glassware, other," at 10 per cent ad valorem.

## The law of January 6, 1902, amending the sugar legislation, reads:

ARTICLE 1, SECTION 1.—Raw native sugars declared for export or deposit in bonded warehouses shall be classed in three categories and be entitled to discharge of excise duty, as follows: First category, Nos. 11 and above, Dutch standard, 45 francs ($8.685); second category, Nos. 8 to 11, Dutch standard, 40 francs 95 centimes ($7.903); third category, below No. 8, Dutch standard, 38 francs 43 centimes ($7.416).

SEC. 2. No sugars shall be admitted to exportation or deposit in bonded warehouse, under the discharge fixed in paragraph 1, except such as, on refining, are capable of yielding per 100 kilograms (220 pounds) of raw sugar the following rates, viz:

Sugars of the first category, 88 kilograms (193.60 pounds) at least; sugars of the second category, 80 kilograms (176 pounds) at least; sugars of the third category, 76 kilograms (167.20 pounds) at least.

ART. 2. Sugars exported or deposited in bonded warehouse and ascertained to show, on refining, a yield inferior by more than 2 kilograms (4.40 pounds) to the rate relating to the category declared, shall be classed officially in pursuance of article 1, without prejudice to the penalties incurred on account of wrong declaration.

ART. 3. The minister of finance will determine the method of testing the sugars as regards their yield on refining.

ART. 4. The words "not moist," ending littera d of article 176, section 1, of law dated April 16, 1887, are suppressed.

ART. 5. Articles 7 to 9, sections 1, littera b, and 5 of article 10 and article 12, of law dated August 9, 1897, are rendered applicable to sugar employed in biscuit making.

### TRANSITORY PROVISIONS.

ART. 6, SEC. 1. Notwithstanding the terms of section 2 of article 8 of the law dated September 11, 1895, any excess of receipts for the year 1902 shall be passed to account only for such part over 3,000,000 francs ($579,000).

SEC. 2. Manufacturers of raw beet sugar shall be allowed a bounty of 2 francs ($0.386) per 100 kilograms (220 pounds) of sugar entered to their debit during the year 1902-3, save that the total bounty shall not exceed 5,000,000 francs ($965,000).

In case the debited quantity exceeds 250,000,000 kilograms, the bounty per 100 kilograms shall be reduced proportionally to the excess ascertained.

## AGRICULTURE IN THE PROVINCE OF HAINAUT.

The yields of winter and spring cereals, potatoes, tobacco, chicory, sugar beets, and of beets for forage are reported good. Forage and flax are bad.

*Winter wheat.*—The yield was good. The cultivation of winter wheat is yearly decreasing, and is replaced by oats and winter barley. Varieties of English wheat were planted in 1901, but owing to the scarcity, as well as shortness, of stalks, farmers have this year employed native wheat, which yields long straw.

*Summer wheat.*—The cultivation of summer wheat has been completely abandoned.

*Rye.*—The grain is well developed and somewhat heavier than that of the preceding year. If the price of straw is considered, this cereal gave the best return per acre.

*Winter barley.*—There is a good yield both as to quality and quantity. Oats and winter barley are the principal cereals in use in Hainaut, and find ready sale.

*Oats.*—The yield of oats is good; the grain is fine and heavy, but straw is short. Growing oats is increasing on large farms. Russian, Swedish, Dutch, and Flemish oats are much in favor. Black oats are less cultivated than yellow oats.

*Potatoes.*—The crop is very satisfactory, both as to weight and quality. Potato disease occasioned very little damage on account of the drought.

*Beets.*—There was an average yield as to quantity and saccharine richness from 13.75 to 14 per cent. Prices are from 18 to 19 francs ($3.476 to $3.667) for 100 kilos (220 pounds).

*Hay.*—On account of an unusually dry spring, the yield may be considered bad. In view of the more remunerative occupation of cattle breeding and the constantly increasing scarcity of farm hands, farmers have to a considerable extent abandoned the cultivation of cereals and turned their attention to meadow crops. During the past few years, the area of meadow land under cultivation has greatly increased.

*Sainfoin* (French grass).—There was an average yield. The cultivation of this crop, like Lucern, is limited to argilous or calcareous soils.

*Flax.*—The yield of flax was only average, stalks being unusually short. The prices for the average quality were very low, 12 to 15 francs ($2.316 to $2.895) per 100 kilos (220 pounds). The growing of flax was again taken up last year, but owing to risks and the high wages demanded by laborers, the cultivation is again on the decrease.

*Tobacco.*—The yield of tobacco is very good, but prices are going down. Numerous species are cultivated, but the two principal kinds are the large leaf or "Flemish tobacco," and the narrow leaf called "Dog's tongue," giving a smaller yield but of superior flavor. The yield per hectare (2.474 acres) amounted to 1,900 kilos (4,180 pounds) against 1,875 kilos (4,125 p u s) in the previous year. The color is fine and the crop sells well.o nd

*Lumber.*—Wood for building, wheelwright work, carriage making, and boat building sells at very high prices, ranging from 20 to 40 francs ($3.86 to $7.72) per cubic meter (35.816 cubic feet) for soft wood, and from 40 to 120 francs ($7.72 to $23.16) per cubic meter for hard woods. Northern pine, for which there is very little demand, has fallen off in price.

*Butter.*—On account of the scarcity of feed, especially pasturage, the price of butter increased somewhat. Good butter is always profitable. Butter making is increasing among small farmers, and improved machinery is found on nearly every farm. Cooperative dairies suffer from the competition of margarine and other alimentary fats, and it is stated that a considerable number of members have withdrawn from dairy associations so as to make more profit by adding margarine to the butter they produce on their farms.

*Honey.*—The yield may be considered good, although the cold, wet spring was very injurious to the bees. Notwithstanding a succession of bad years, those engaged in apiculture are not discouraged. The average retail price of honey per kilo (2.20 pounds) 1.80 to 2 is francs ($0.347 to $0.386); average retail price of wax per kilo (2.20 pounds), 3.50 to 4 francs ($0.675 to $0.772); average wholesale price of wax per kilo (2.20 pounds), 3 to 3.50 francs ($0.579 to $0.675).

*Horse breeding.*—Little care is used in selecting brood mares, but the breeding of draft horses is still prosperous, although prices have decreased and the sale of colts is almost nil.

Horses of good race and pedigree still sell at high figures. Buyers from the United States have again appeared on the market, but have not bought the best horses.

*Hogs.*—Hogs sell well and at remunerative prices. Sucking pigs, from six weeks to two months old, sell from 15 to 25 francs ($2.895 to $4.825). Pigs from four to six months old, weighing from 80 to 120 kilos (176 to 264 pounds), sell from 0.95 to 1.10 francs (18 to 21 cents) per kilo (2.20 pounds).

*Sheep.*—Sheep breeding is not very important. Large numbers are imported from Germany, fattened, and sold on the Belgian market. The average price of mutton on foot is 0.85 franc (16 cents) per kilo, and for wool (raw) 1.20 francs (23 cents) per kilo (2.20 pounds).

### COAL MINES IN THE PROVINCE OF HAINAUT.

In the province of Hainaut, there are 66 coal mines in operation, comprising 183 extraction pits in activity, 16 in reserve, and 8 in preparation. Seventy thousand two hundred and sixty-five miners were employed in the pits and 25,872 in surface work. The gross production was 15,683,500 tons, amounting to 237,933,500 francs ($45,921,165.50). The total amount of profits was 36,574,700 francs ($7,058,917.10), and of deficit 2,269,900 francs ($438,090.70). It will thus be seen that the profits exceeded the losses by 36,404,800 francs ($6,620,826.40) against 65,583,300 francs ($12,657,576.90) in 1900. The average depth of veins worked was 0.65 centimeter (25.59 inches) against 0.66 centimeter (25.98 inches) in 1900 and 1899.

*Coke.*—There are in the province of Hainaut 34 plants for the production of coke, having 3,261 coke ovens and employing 2,058 workmen. One million six hundred and ninety-four thousand seven hundred and fifty tons of coal were consumed to produce 1,268,900 tons of coke, amounting to a total value of 27,956,600 francs ($5,385,623.80). The price of coke fell to 22.03 francs ($4.25), a decrease of 4.17 francs ($0.80) as compared with the preceding year.

The 27 agglomerate works (briquettes), including 60 presses, employed 1,237 workmen and consumed 1,130,460 tons of coal. The total value of agglomerates produced was 23,876,000 francs ($4,608,068), or 19.31 francs ($3.73) per ton.

*Quarries.*—There are 398 open quarries and 107 underground quarries, employing 16,312 workmen. The production amounted to bluestone, 8,000,000 francs ($1,544,000); porphyry paving blocks, 3,000,000 francs ($579,000); lime, 4,500,000 francs ($868,500). The general production was valued at 24,565,900 francs ($4,741,218.70), or 1,699,300 francs ($327,964.90) less than in 1900.

Ten smelting furnaces were in active operation and 9 shut down. These works employed 804 workmen. The output in cost, refined

iron and steel, amounted to 11,488,300 francs ($2,217,241.90). The
output of the 25 iron and steel works and rolling mills was valued at
22,083,000 francs ($4,262,019); wrought iron at 671,600 francs
($129,618.80); forged iron at 29,279,700 francs ($5,650,982.10); finished iron to 11,000,000 francs ($2,123,000). ·

### COAL MINES IN THE PROVINCE OF NAMUR.

There were 35 coal-mine concessions, of which only 11 were in active
operation. The total production of the mines was 745,780 tons, representing a round sum of 10,227,100 francs ($1,973,830.30). The
increase of net production over 1900 was 6,485 tons, but the value
shows a decrease of 1,247,650 francs ($240,796.45). The average price
per rough ton was 13.71 francs ($2.65) against 15.52 francs ($2.99) in
1900, a decrease of 1.81 francs ($0.34) per ton, or 11.7 per cent. The
quantity of coal sold, including coal for manufacture of agglomerates,
was 644,530 tons, representing a sum of 9,953,800 francs ($1,921,083.40)
or 15.44 francs ($2.97) per ton. The general result of working the
mines in the province of Namur during the year 1901 shows a bonus
of 1,027,950 francs ($198,394.35) against 2,122,600 francs ($409,661.80)
in 1900, giving a profit of 1.38 francs ($0.266) against 2.87 francs
($0.553) per ton; decrease, 1.49 francs ($0.287).

*Number of workmen.*—Three thousand seven hundred and fifty-one
workmen were employed in the coal mines of the Namur district. Of
this number, 2,682 were employed in the pits and 1,069 in surface
extraction.

The number of miners engaged in vein extraction was 690 against
671 in 1900. The average production per miner was 1,081 tons
against 1,102 tons in 1900, a decrease of 21 tons. The average production per miner working in the pits increased slightly, averaging
from 275 to 278 tons.

*Average wages.*—A net sum of 5,101,500 francs ($984,589.50), rep-
resenting 1,115,600 days of work, was paid for wages, showing an
average daily wage of 4.75 francs ($0.916) against 5.12 francs ($0.988)
in 1900. The average daily wage of miners working in the pits, which
had been 5.88 francs ($1.13), fell to 5.18 francs ($0.999). The wages
of surface miners remained unchanged at 3.09 francs ($0.596). The
average daily wage of vein extractors, which in 1900 had reached 6.84
francs ($1.32) fell to 5.82 francs ($1.12), a decrease of 1.02 francs
($0.196), or 14.9 per cent.

The following tables give further data:

*Results of the coal industry in the provinces of Hainaut and Namur in 1901.*

| Province. | Production. | | | Profitable mines. | |
|---|---|---|---|---|---|
| | Tons. | Value. | | Number. | Profits. |
| | | *Francs.* | | | *Francs.* |
| Hainaut ............... | 15,683,500 | 237,983,500 | $45,921,165.50 | 55 | 86,574,700 | $7,058,917.10 |
| Namur................. | 745,780 | 10,227,100 | 1,973,830.30 | 4 | 1,202,100 | 232,005.30 |

| Province. | Losing mines. | | | Labor-ers, num-ber. | Total annual wages paid. | | Other expenses. | |
|---|---|---|---|---|---|---|---|---|
| | Num-ber. | Loss. | | | | | | |
| | | *Francs.* | | | *Francs.* | | *Francs.* | |
| Hainaut .. | 11 | 2,299,900 | $438,090.70 | 96,137 | 121,919,740 | $23,530,509.82 | 81,708,960 | $15,769,829.28 |
| Namur.... | 7 | 174,150 | 33,610.95 | 3,751 | 5,131,350 | 990,850.55 | 4,067,800 | 785,085.40 |

*Results of the coal industry in the provinces of Hainaut and Naimur in 1901*—Continued.

| Province. | Total expenses. | | Total profits. | | Selling price of coal at mine, per ton. | | Profits per ton. | |
|---|---|---|---|---|---|---|---|---|
| | *Francs.* | | *Francs.* | | *Francs.* | | *Francs.* | |
| Hainaut ..... | 208,628,700 | $39,300,339.10 | 34,304,800 | $6,620,826.40 | 15.17 | $2.93 | 2.19 | $0.422 |
| Namur....... | 9,199,150 | 1,775,435.95 | 1,027,950 | 198,394.35 | 13.71 | 2.65 | 1.38 | .266 |

*Production of coal in the provinces of Hainaut and Namur in 1900 and 1901.*

| Year. | Production. | Value. | |
|---|---|---|---|
| Hainaut: | *Tons.* | *Francs.* | |
| 1900.................................... | 16,582,630 | 289,516,500 | $55,876,684.50 |
| 1901.................................... | 15,683,500 | 237,933,500 | 45,921,165.50 |
| Decrease............................... | 849,130 | 51,583,000 | 9,955,519.00 |
| Namur: | | | |
| 1900.................................... | 739,295 | 11,474,750 | 2,214,626.75 |
| 1901.................................... | 745,780 | 10,227,100 | 1,973,830.30 |
| Decrease............................... | ............. | 1,247,650 | 240,796.45 |
| Increase............................... | 6,485 | ............. | ............. |

| Year. | Profit. | | Value per ton. | | Profit per ton. | |
|---|---|---|---|---|---|---|
| Hainaut: | *Francs.* | | *Francs.* | | *Francs.* | |
| 1900 ......................... | 65,583,300 | $12,657,576.90 | 17.51 | $3.38 | 3.97 | $0.766 |
| 1901 ......................... | 34,304,800 | 6,620,826.40 | 15.17 | 2.93 | 2.19 | .422 |
| Decrease................... | 31,278,500 | 6,036,750.50 | 2.34 | .45 | 1.78 | .344 |
| Namur: | | | | | | |
| 1900 ......................... | 2,122,600 | 409,661.80 | 15.52 | 2.99 | 2.87 | .553 |
| 1901 ......................... | 1,027,950 | 198,394.35 | 13.71 | 2.65 | 1.38 | .266 |
| Decrease................... | 1,094,650 | 211,267.45 | 1.81 | .34 | 1.49 | .287 |

*Average wages per day in the province of Hainaut from 1894 to 1901.*

| For— | 1894. | | 1895. | | 1896. | | 1897. | |
|---|---|---|---|---|---|---|---|---|
| Laborers on the surface and in the mines...................... | *Francs.* 3.12 | $0.602 | *Francs.* 3.13 | $0.604 | *Francs.* 3.21 | $0.619 | *Francs.* 3.41 | $0.658 |
| Laborers working by the vein... | 3.85 | .743 | 3.85 | .743 | 3.97 | .766 | 4.30 | .829 |

| For— | 1898. | | 1899. | | 1900. | | 1901. | |
|---|---|---|---|---|---|---|---|---|
| Laborers on the surface and in the mines...................... | *Francs.* 3 61 | $0.696 | *Francs.* 4.01 | $0.773 | *Francs.* 4.72 | $0.910 | *Francs.* 4.31 | $0.831 |
| Laborers working by the vein ... | 4.62 | .891 | 5.28 | 1.019 | 6.41 | 1.237 | 5.53 | 1.067 |

*Laborers employed in the coal mines of the provinces of Hainaut and Namur during the year 1901.*

| Laborers | In the mines. | | On the surface. | | Total. | |
|---|---|---|---|---|---|---|
| | Hainaut. | Namur. | Hainaut. | Namur. | Hainaut. | Namur. |
| Men ........................... | 65,119 | 2,519 | 18,141 | 782 | 83,260 | 3,301 |
| Women........................... | 99 | ......... | 681 | 18 | 780 | 18 |
| Boys from 14 to 16 years ................. | 3,282 | 122 | 1,129 | 76 | 4,411 | 198 |
| Boys from 12 to 14 years ................. | 1,765 | 41 | 961 | 77 | 2,726 | 118 |
| Girls from 16 to 21 years............ .... | ............. | ............. | 2,915 | 77 | 2,915 | 77 |
| Girls from 12 to 16 years ............... | ............. | ............. | 2,045 | 39 | 2,045 | 39 |
| Total ..................... | 70,265 | 2,682 | 25,872 | 1,069 | 96,137 | 3,751 |

*Production of all the coal mines of Hainaut.*

| Year. | Production. | Profit. | | Profit per ton. | |
|---|---|---|---|---|---|
| | *Tons.* | *Francs.* | | *Francs.* | |
| 1898 | 15,861,160 | 15,431,400 | $2,978,260.20 | 0.97 | $0.187 |
| 1899 | 15,581,380 | 24,720,600 | 4,771,075.80 | 1.59 | .306 |
| 1900 | 16,532,630 | 65,583,300 | 12,657,576.90 | 3.97 | .766 |
| 1901 | 15,683,500 | 34,304,800 | 6,620,826.40 | 2.19 | .422 |

*Production of profitable mines of Hainaut.*

| Year. | Production. | Profit. | | Profit per ton. | |
|---|---|---|---|---|---|
| | *Tons.* | *Francs.* | | *Francs.* | |
| 1898 | 13,903,720 | 16,471,400 | $3,178,980.20 | 1.18 | $0.227 |
| 1899 | 14,973,670 | 25,406,100 | 4,903,377.30 | 1.17 | .328 |
| 1900 | 16,369,290 | 66,985,100 | 12,938,124.30 | 4.09 | .789 |
| 1901 | 14,798,770 | 36,574,700 | 6,059,227.10 | 2.47 | .507 |

*Export of coal, coke, and briquettes from Belgium to foreign countries during the year 1901.*

| Countries. | Coal. | Coke. | Briquettes. |
|---|---|---|---|
| | *Tons.* | *Tons.* | *Tons.* |
| Argentine Republic | 10,079 | | 4,350 |
| Australia | 8,000 | | |
| Brazil | 4,710 | | |
| Canada | 1,800 | | |
| Chile | 11,261 | | 2,852 |
| China | 4,650 | 1,200 | 5,900 |
| Congo Free State | 6,085 | | 9,920 |
| Denmark | 500 | | |
| Egypt | 7,040 | 900 | 2,050 |
| England | 36,827 | 800 | 6,975 |
| France | 3,832,231 | 547,296 | 449,538 |
| Germany | 304,032 | 98,385 | 44,327 |
| Grand Duchy of Luxemburg | 168,481 | 123,073 | 23,987 |
| Greece | | 1,700 | 1,300 |
| Holland | 255,735 | 32,790 | 9,067 |
| India | 7,560 | | |
| Italy | 2,390 | 6,560 | 2,980 |
| Japan | | | 700 |
| Norway | 410 | | |
| Portugal | | | 3,765 |
| Russia | 5,697 | | 8,560 |
| Spain | 11,714 | | 33,981 |
| Sweden | 4,120 | | |
| Switzerland | 84,403 | | 13,697 |
| Tunisia | | | 2,000 |
| Turkey | 4,760 | 2,610 | 4,650 |
| United States | 36,594 | 11,835 | 81,915 |
| Victoria colony | 800 | | |
| Other countries | 10,481 | 2,272 | 6,961 |
| Total | 4,820,300 | 829,421 | 714,455 |

*Export of coal and briquettes from the province of Namur to foreign countries during the year 1901.*

| Countries. | Coal. | | | Briquettes. | | |
|---|---|---|---|---|---|---|
| | Quantity. | Price per ton at frontier. | | Quantity. | Price per ton at frontier. | |
| | *Tons.* | *Francs.* | | *Tons.* | *Francs.* | |
| France | 154,380 | 19.80 | $3.82 | 33,320 | 22.79 | $4.40 |
| Germany | 12,770 | 24.97 | 4.82 | 9,115 | 23.17 | 4.47 |
| Grand Duchy of Luxemburg | 8,040 | 24.61 | 4.75 | 4,270 | 19.60 | 3.81 |
| Holland | 11,065 | 25.37 | 4.90 | 1,940 | 24.18 | 4.67 |
| Switzerland | 820 | 24.76 | 4.78 | 3,600 | 21.78 | 4.20 |
| Other countries | | | | 12,050 | 20.66 | 3.99 |
| Total, and average price | 187,075 | 20.71 | 4.01 | 64,295 | 22.22 | 4.29 |

STONE AND IRON.

*Quarries of Namur.*—The pro uct of quarries, although having decreased in 1901 as compared with 1900, which was a very prosperous year, gave the best results among mineral industries of this province. Work was carried on in 135 communes and included 162 underground and 254 open quarries, a total of 436. The value of the amount produced in 1901 was 10,439,050 francs ($2,014,736.65), a decrease of 1,151,700 francs ($222,278.10) as compared with 1900, which was the most prosperous year in the history of this industry; 6,690 workmen were employed, or 335 less than in 1900. The value of the production of quarries in the province of Namur for 1901 was:

| Product. | Value. | |
|---|---|---|
| | Francs. | U. S. equiv- alent. |
| Marble | 1,707,350 | $329,518.55 |
| Bluestone | 1,942,900 | 374,979.70 |
| Lime | 3,435,550 | 663,061.15 |

*Results of the quarries in the provinces of Hainaut and Namur in 1900 and 1901.*

| Year. | Hainaut. | | | Namur. | | |
|---|---|---|---|---|---|---|
| | Quar- ries. | Labor- ers. | Value of production. | Quar- ries. | Labor- ers. | Value of production. |
| | | | *Francs.* | | | *Francs.* |
| 1900 | 474 | 16,878 | 26,265,200   $5,069,183.60 | 406 | 6,965 | 11,590,750   $2,237,014.75 |
| 1901 | 505 | 16,312 | 24,565,900   4,741,218.70 | 436 | 6,660 | 10,439,050   2,014,736.65 |
| Decrease | | 66 | 1,699,300   327,964.90 | | 305 | 1,151,700   222,278.10 |
| Increase | 31 | | | 30 | | |

*Production of iron in the province of Namur during the years 1898, 1899, 1900, and 1901.*

| Year. | Produc- tion. | Value. | | Average price per ton. | | Laborers. | Average daily wages. | |
|---|---|---|---|---|---|---|---|---|
| | *Tons.* | *Francs.* | | *Francs.* | | | *Francs.* | |
| 1898 | 40,650 | 321,126.70 | $62,126.70 | 7.92 | $1.588 | 284 | 2.66 | $0.518 |
| 1899 | 32,400 | 304,400 | 58,749.20 | 9.40 | 1.814 | 278 | 2.73 | .529 |
| 1900 | 31,100 | 301,700 | 58,228.10 | 9.70 | 1.872 | 245 | 2.79 | .538 |
| 1901 | 19,300 | 173,400 | 33,466.20 | 8.96 | 1.783 | 128 | 2.82 | .544 |

*Iron and steel works in the province of Namur in 1901.*—Works working, 5; number of laborers employed, 142; production for 1901:

| Description. | Quantity. | Value. | |
|---|---|---|---|
| | *Tons.* | *Francs.* | |
| Wrought iron | 520 | 141,600 | $27,328.80 |
| Wrought steel | 200 | 122,000 | 23,546.00 |
| Total | 720 | 263,600 | 50,874.80 |

*Smelting furnaces in the province of Hainaut.*—Furnaces working, 10; shut down, 9; foundries working, 8; shut down, 2; number of laborers employed, 804; production for 1901:

| Description. | Quantity. | Value. |
|---|---|---|
| | *Tons.* | *Francs.* | |
| Cast iron, molding | 4,080 | 284,900 | $54,985.70 |
| Fine cast iron | 102,690 | 5,586,000 | 1,078,098.00 |
| Cast steel | 78,110 | 5,617,400 | 1,084,158.20 |
| Total | 184,880 | 11,488,300 | 2,217,241.90 |

*Iron works in the province of Hainaut.*—Number, 25; number of laborers employed, 7,464.   Production in 1901:

| Description. | Quantity. | Value. |
|---|---|---|
| | *Tons.* | *Francs.* | |
| Rough iron | 221,980 | 22,083,000 | $4,262,019.00 |
| Finished iron | 291,460 | 40,694,200 | 7,853,980.60 |
| Total | 513,440 | 62,777,200 | 12,115,999.60 |

*Steel works in the province of Hainaut.*—Working, 9; number of furnaces working, 3; converters working, 23; laborers employed, 2,362.   Production in 1901:

| Description. | Quantity. | Value. |
|---|---|---|
| | *Tons.* | *Francs.* | |
| Ingot steel (cast) | 108,065 | 10,744,600 | $2,073,707.80 |
| Ingots, blooms, and billets | 20,390 | 2,345,600 | 452,700.80 |
| Finished steel | 73,475 | 11,436,300 | 2,207,205.90 |
| Total | 201,930 | 24,526,500 | 4,733,614.50 |

## TRADE VIA BRUSSELS.

*Commercial movement through the Brussels custom-house with foreign countries during the year 1901.*

| Articles. | Imports. Quantity. Kilograms. | Imports. Quantity. Pounds. | Imports. Value. Francs. | Imports. Value. $ | Exports. Quantity. Kilograms. | Exports. Quantity. Pounds. | Exports. Value. Francs. | Exports. Value. $ |
|---|---|---|---|---|---|---|---|---|
| Alcoholic liquors, all kinds | 58,460 | 128,612 | 81,540 | $15,787.22 | 3,070 | 6,764 | 10,824 | $2,089.08 |
| Alimentary conserves | 896,102 | 1,975,824 | 603,826 | 116,588.42 | 6,130 | 13,488 | 7,986 | 1,531.66 |
| Almonds | 8,082 | 17,780 | 15,083 | 2,901.87 | | | | |
| Animals, live, for food, other than cattle | 105 | 231 | 525 | 101.37 | | | | |
| Animal matter, raw | 84,775 | 187,605 | 44,990 | 8,667.27 | 90,956 | 200,103 | 45,345 | 8,751.58 |
| Arms | 5,602 | 12,824 | 3,060 | 588.65 | | | | |
| Art, objects of | 6,189 | 13,616 | 11,665 | 2,251.84 | 7,616 | 16,755 | 32,762 | 6,323.07 |
| Ashes | 1,068,608 | 2,350,938 | 21,372 | 4,124.80 | | | | |
| Automobiles, including detached parts | 2,500 | 5,500 | 10,000 | 1,980.00 | 20,120 | 44,264 | 63,520 | 12,259.36 |
| Barley | 4,533,240 | 9,973,128 | 747,985 | 144,361.11 | 490 | 1,078 | 98 | 17.96 |
| Beans, peas, etc. | 249,288 | 548,324 | 47,166 | 9,101.11 | | | | |
| Beer | 2,388,252 | 5,276,154 | 789,981 | 152,456.68 | 125 | 276 | 1,100 | 212.30 |
| Bicycles, including detached parts | 227 | 499 | 1,055 | 203.61 | | | | |
| Boats of all kinds | 184,200 | 405,240 | 56,005 | 10,808.96 | | | | |
| Bread, ginger | 1,091 | 2,400 | 655 | 126.41 | | | | |
| Bread and sea | 65,768 | 122,690 | 22,307 | 4,305.25 | | | | |
| Butter, fresh and salted | 1,814 | 3,991 | 4,988 | 962.68 | | | | |
| Cacao | 184,311 | 409,884 | 313,329 | 60,472.50 | 3,600 | 7,920 | 6,120 | 1,181.16 |
| Cacao, butter | 66,998 | 147,396 | 227,789 | 43,964.05 | 2,370 | 7,414 | 8,058 | 1,555.19 |
| Candles | 19 | 42 | 31 | 5.98 | 23,285 | 51,227 | 16,425 | 3,170.02 |
| Carpets, wool | 1,724 | 3,814 | 9,494 | 1,882.34 | 100 | 220 | 500 | 96.50 |
| Carriages, all kinds, and detached parts | 389 | 856 | 397 | 76.62 | | | | |
| Cars, for trams and railways, iron and steel | 84 | 75 | 49 | 9.46 | | | | |
| Cement | 994 | 2,187 | 30 | 5.79 | | | | |
| Charcoal and turf | 850 | 770 | 7 | 1.85 | | | | |
| Cheese | 380,617 | 727,355 | 462,864 | 89,382.75 | 215,187 | 473,411 | 6,456 | 1,246.01 |
| Chemical products | 275,983 | 607,063 | 138,814 | 28,405.10 | 1,600 | 3,520 | 145 | 27.98 |
| Chocolate | 4,509 | 9,920 | 10,749 | 2,074.56 | 1,525 | 3,355 | 2,135 | 412.06 |
| Clothing of all kinds | 100,885 | 221,197 | 66,198 | 12,776.21 | 82,628 | 180,682 | 42,310 | 8,165.88 |
| Coal | 44,221,989 | 97,287,166 | 829,162 | 160,028.27 | 445,942 | 980,852 | 4,265,974 | 821,402.98 |
| Coffee | 685,156 | 1,287,343 | 655,374 | 126,487.18 | 14,821 | 31,506 | 269 | 51.91 |
| Coke | | | | | | | | |
| Cordage | 1,161 | 2,654 | 1,993 | 398.85 | 220,000 | 484,000 | 5,268 | 1,011.71 |
| Corn: | 110 | 242 | 13 | 2.51 | 8,585 | 7,777 | 4,242 | 818.71 |
| Cotton: Goods | 3,198 | 7,081 | 15,782 | 8,086.28 | 1,086 | 8,99 | 5,976 | 1,168.87 |
| Raw | 160 | 880 | 157 | 30.80 | 50 | 10 | 52 | 10.04 |
| Drugs | 187,702 | 302,944 | 179,012 | 34,949.82 | 4,650 | 10,230 | 6,045 | 1,166.68 |

| Article | | | | | | | | |
|---|---|---|---|---|---|---|---|---|
| Dyes and colors | | | | | | | | |
| Eggs | | | | | | | | |
| Fish: | | | | | | | | |
| Preserved | | | | | | | | |
| Other | | | | | | | | |
| Flour: | | | | | | | | |
| Wheat, spelt, and meslin | | | | | | | | |
| Buckwheat | | | | | | | | |
| Other | | | | | | | | |
| Fruits: | | | | | | | | |
| Fresh | | | | | | | | |
| Dried | | | | | | | | |
| Furniture | | | | | | | | |
| Glass: | | | | | | | | |
| Plate | | | | | | | | |
| Window | | | | | | | | |
| Broken | | | | | | | | |
| Common | | | | | | | | |
| Gloves | | | | | | | | |
| Glue | | | | | | | | |
| Gold and silver jewelry | | | | | | | | |
| Grains: | | | | | | | | |
| Of all kinds | | | | | | | | |
| Oleaginous | | | | | | | | |
| Grease | | | | | | | | |
| Groceries | | | | | | | | |
| Hay and forage | | | | | | | | |
| Hemp and flax | | | | | | | | |
| Hides and skins: | | | | | | | | |
| Raw | | | | | | | | |
| Tanned and prepared | | | | | | | | |
| Honey | | | | | | | | |
| Indigo | | | | | | | | |
| Instruments, musical | | | | | | | | |
| Iron: | | | | | | | | |
| Beams | | | | | | | | |
| Manufactures of | | | | | | | | |
| Nails | | | | | | | | |
| Cast, rough | | | | | | | | |
| Cast, manufactures of | | | | | | | | |
| did, with copper and nickel | | | | | | | | |
| Old map | | | | | | | | |
| Ore | | | | | | | | |
| Sheet | | | | | | | | |
| Lace | | | | | | | | |
| Lard | | | | | | | | |
| Lead | | | | | | | | |
| Lime | | | | | | | | |
| Macaroni, vermicelli, Italian pastes | | | | | | | | |
| Machines, implements, and tools | | | | | | | | |
| Manures | | | | | | | | |

Commercial movement through the Brussels custom-house with foreign countries during the year 1901—Continued.

| Articles. | Imports. Quantity. Kilograms. | Imports. Quantity. Pounds. | Imports. Value. France. | Imports. Value. | Exports. Quantity. Kilograms. | Exports. Quantity. Pounds. | Exports. Value. France. | Exports. Value. |
|---|---|---|---|---|---|---|---|---|
| Meal: | | | | | | | | |
| Corn | 1,500 | 8,300 | 218 | $42.07 | 98 | 216 | 14 | $2.70 |
| Oat | 6,444 | 14,177 | 1,159 | 223.69 | 4,150 | 9,180 | 747 | 144.17 |
| Meat, all kinds | 32,025 | 70,465 | 40,272 | 7,772.50 | 1,785 | 3,927 | 2,856 | 551.21 |
| Mercery and hardware | 97,300 | 214,060 | 121,684 | 23,895.01 | 684,545 | 1,175,999 | 1,752,979 | 338,324.96 |
| Milk and cream | 250 | | 39 | 7.58 | | | | |
| Mineral water | 33,247 | 73,143 | 19,690 | 3,800.17 | 87,856 | 82,188 | 15,120 | 2,918.16 |
| Mineral ore | 6,692,784 | 14,724,015 | 217,286 | 41,986.20 | 17,998 | 89,596 | 5,190 | 1,001.67 |
| Morocco leather | 29 | 64 | 183 | 26.67 | | | | |
| Mussels | 1,601,564 | 3,528,419 | 80,078 | 15,456.05 | | | | |
| Nickel and copper | 67,954 | 149,499 | 143,893 | 27,771.35 | 9,654 | 21,289 | 19,158 | 3,696.53 |
| Oats | 294,350 | 647,570 | 47,096 | 9,089.53 | | | | |
| Oleomargarine | 390,981 | 860,048 | 469,117 | 90,589.58 | 12,094 | 26,607 | 14,168 | 2,801.01 |
| Oil, vegetable: | | | | | | | | |
| Alimentary | 31,174 | 68,688 | 49,878 | 9,626.45 | | | | |
| Other | 703,900 | 1,548,600 | 436,188 | 84,852.62 | 1,058,198 | 2,328,086 | 666,644 | 128,666.15 |
| Oilcloth of all kinds | 170,200 | 374,440 | 176,624 | 34,068.48 | 287 | 631 | 490 | 94.57 |
| Paper of all kinds | 398,594 | 876,907 | 150,049 | 28,959.46 | 765,177 | 1,683,889 | 399,876 | 77,176.07 |
| Perfumery alcoholic and other | 146 | 321 | 695 | 184.18 | 16 | 41 | 50 | 9.65 |
| Petroleum, refined | 570 | 1,254 | 101 | 19.49 | 6,647 | 14,623 | 1,180 | 227.74 |
| Plants | 309 | 690 | 67 | 12.98 | 30 | 66 | 200 | 38.60 |
| Potatoes | 97,642 | 214,812 | 4,882 | 942.28 | 86,840 | 81,048 | 1,842 | 355.51 |
| Pottery, all kinds | 238,747 | 525,243 | 71,281 | 13,747.56 | 865 | 1,908 | 1,285 | 248.00 |
| Powder, gun | 4,673 | 10,482 | 5,487 | 1,058.99 | 220 | 484 | 440 | 84.92 |
| Poultry and game, fresh | 219 | | 547 | 105.57 | | | | |
| Products for industries | 15,180 | 33,396 | 17,305 | 8,889.36 | 764 | 1,681 | 4,820 | 883.76 |
| Rags | 851,969 | 774,332 | 123,189 | 28,775.48 | 122 | 288 | 43 | 8.30 |
| Rice | 580,006 | 1,276,018 | 130,501 | 25,186.69 | 88 | 194 | 20 | 8.86 |
| Rosin and bitumen | 991,529 | 2,181,384 | 247,852 | 47,841.28 | 260,689 | 578,516 | 65,172 | 12,678.20 |
| Rubber: | | | | | | | | |
| Crude | 5,569 | 12,290 | 86,183 | 6,973.67 | 6,025 | 13,266 | 39,162 | 7,558.27 |
| Manufactured | 15,888 | 34,988 | 72,609 | 14,013.04 | 1,300 | 2,860 | 6,000 | 1,158.00 |
| Salt, refined | 88,443 | 188,575 | 4,172 | 806.20 | | | | |
| Shoes | 27 | 59 | 175 | 33.77 | 160 | 550 | 1,200 | 231.50 |
| Scientific apparatus | 3 | 7 | 90 | 17.37 | 60 | 132 | 240 | 46.82 |
| Silk goods | 280 | 616 | 170 | 82.81 | 2 | 4 | 72 | 18.90 |
| Sirup and molasses | 144,000 | 316,800 | 57,600 | 11,116.80 | | | | |
| Soap | 132,289 | 290,992 | 49,446 | 9,543.08 | 55,038 | 121,064 | 118,792 | 21,961.86 |
| Soda, salt of | 962,080 | 2,116,466 | 86,599 | 16,713.30 | | | | |
| Sponges | 29,988 | 43,974 | 419,200 | 80,905.60 | 648 | 1,426 | 11,400 | 2,200.20 |
| Starch | 53,863 | 118,498 | 13,111 | 2,530.42 | | | | |

| | | | | | | | | |
|---|---|---|---|---|---|---|---|---|
| **Steel:** | | | | | | | | |
| Bars, sheet, etc | 9,416 | 20,716 | 1,601 | 306.99 | 164,288 | 389,324 | 10,025 | 1,994.82 |
| Manufactures of | 28 | 61 | 38 | 6.96 | | | | 162,884.87 |
| **Stone:** | | | | | | | | 105,687.46 |
| Rough and cut | 100 | 220 | 15 | 2.88 | 17,072 | 88,658 | 848,704 | 14,696.76 |
| Paving | | | | | 795,800 | 1,762,980 | 547,505 | |
| Polished | 24,929 | 64,844 | 12,738 | 2,458.05 | 8,045,980 | 6,701,090 | 78,149 | |
| Other | 350 | 770 | 21 | 4.05 | | | | 2.70 |
| **Sugar:** | | | | | | | | |
| Raw | 52,946 | 116,431 | 18,288 | 2,554.55 | 40 | 88 | 14 | 626.86 |
| Refined | 36,129 | 77,284 | 12,646 | 2,440.68 | | | | |
| Sulphur | 290 | 686 | 43 | 8.30 | 1,181 | 2,596 | 3,246 | |
| Tea | 12,580 | 27,546 | 84,467 | 6,649.20 | | | | 3,754.28 |
| Textiles, raw | 1,929 | 4,224 | 700 | 185.10 | | | | 618.18 |
| **Thread:** | | | | | | | | |
| Cotton | 9 | 20 | 23 | 4.25 | 8,456 | 18,608 | 19,452 | |
| Silk | 2 | 4 | 96 | 18.58 | 188 | 402 | 8,208 | 1,924.21 |
| Other | 50 | 110 | 310 | 59.88 | | | | |
| Files, all kinds | 9,760 | 21,450 | 341 | 65.81 | | | | |
| Tin, rough | 19,981 | 43,956 | 3,114 | 601.00 | 19,818 | 43,600 | 9,970 | 29.72 |
| Tissue, not specially mentioned | 1,623 | 3,571 | 6,658 | 1,284.99 | | | | |
| **Tobacco:** | | | | | | | | |
| Unmanufactured | 321,101 | 705,422 | 461,651 | 92,968.64 | 103 | 227 | 154 | 5.79 |
| Manufactured, cigars, cigarettes | 598 | 1,294 | 14,590 | 2,757.97 | | | | 3,256.49 |
| Manufactured, other | 38 | 84 | 128 | 24.70 | | | | |
| Type | 8 | 18 | 3 | 6.02 | 192 | 422 | 80 | 42.84 |
| **Typographic products:** | | | | | 5,287 | 11,681 | 16,873 | 125.45 |
| Newspapers | 25 | 55 | 60 | 11.58 | | | | 2,459.70 |
| Other | 14,458 | 31,807 | 86,700 | 7,160.47 | | | | |
| **Vegetables:** | | | | | 15,980 | 84,892 | 2,220 | |
| Preserved | 129,029 | 283,864 | 18,064 | 8,494.85 | 6,625 | 14,356 | 660 | |
| Substances | 228,863 | 508,499 | 29,950 | 6,780.35 | 9,825 | 21,616 | 12,900 | |
| Vehicles, other than automobiles | 665 | 1,463 | 1,040 | 200.72 | | | | |
| Vinegar | 4,382 | 9,646 | 501 | 96.89 | | | | 868.85 |
| Watch fitting and watches | 127 | 279 | 2,600 | 682.80 | 1,290 | 2,888 | 4,450 | 6,592.80 |
| Wax, raw | 6,135 | 13,497 | 21,166 | 4,066.04 | 209,555 | 461,021 | 84,167 | 6,247.22 |
| Wheat, spelt, and maslin | 365,100 | 796,550 | 69,185 | 11,422.70 | 13,494 | 29,687 | 82,389 | 16.02 |
| Wine | 219,688 | 458,308 | 145,810 | 27,658.88 | 490 | 1,078 | 88 | |
| Wire, iron | 800 | 1,760 | 188 | 26.25 | | | | |
| **Wood:** | | | | | | | | |
| Manufactures of | 78,012 | 167,226 | 17,761 | 8,425.94 | 351,602 | 809,604 | 99,623 | 19,207.76 |
| Oak and walnut | 18,000 | 39,600 | 3,107 | 569.65 | 425,250 | 985,660 | 36,485 | 6,844.74 |
| For building, other than oak and walnut | 3,197,482 | 7,084,460 | 763,995 | 147,451.28 | | | | |
| Wool | 4,070 | 8,964 | 7,728 | 1,462.47 | | | | |
| Woolen tissues | 2,025 | 4,467 | 5,457 | 1,049.84 | | | | |
| Yeast | 320 | 704 | 160 | 80.88 | | | | |
| Zinc | 2,005 | 4,411 | 580 | 160.19 | 826,923 | 719,281 | 149,088 | 28,768.87 |

*Declared value of exports from the consular district of Brussels (including Charleroi) to the United States for the fiscal years 1901 and 1902.*

| Articles. | Year ended June 30, 1901. | Year ended June 30, 1902. | Increase. | Decrease. |
|---|---|---|---|---|
| Aniline colors | $43,308.12 | $52,948.55 | $11,640.43 | |
| Automobiles | | 2,788.85 | | |
| Bagging | 580.86 | | | |
| Baskets | 2,564.28 | 1,689.76 | | $874.52 |
| Bleaching powder | | 5,475.97 | | |
| Books | 7,875.96 | 7,729.22 | | 146.75 |
| Braids: | | | | |
| Cotton and mohair | 877.37 | | | |
| Button stock | 207.17 | 311.04 | 108.87 | |
| Cotton | | 1,033.20 | | |
| Straw | 806.32 | | | |
| Bronze ornaments, statues, etc | 788.13 | | | |
| Cement | 309,043.68 | 301,780.01 | | 7,263.67 |
| Chemicals | 940.06 | 100.30 | | 839.73 |
| Church regalia | 166.29 | 317.68 | 151.98 | |
| Clay, fire | 1,019.92 | | | |
| Clocks | 649.67 | 780.60 | 80.63 | |
| Coke | | 14,031.00 | | |
| Corsets | 79,122.56 | 69,442.39 | | 9,680.17 |
| Diamonds | | 2,171.25 | | |
| Earthenware | 13,419.64 | 12,852.74 | | 566.90 |
| Enamel ware | | 4,715.97 | | |
| Fire bricks | 23,921.02 | 49,521.43 | 25,600.41 | |
| Fur, refuse | 25,570.20 | 22,018.38 | | 3,551.82 |
| Furniture | 2,829.45 | 1,799.59 | | 1,027.86 |
| Glass: | | | | |
| Plate | 845,688.06 | 825,576.24 | | 20,111.82 |
| Window | 705,128.27 | 1,692,119.13 | 986,990.86 | |
| Other | 5,204.96 | 10,454.15 | 5,249.98 | |
| Gloves | 192,798.61 | 121,24 | | 70,880.37 |
| Glue and glue stock | 14,271.81 | 16,918.37 | 2,387.56 | |
| Glycerin | 26,577.61 | 29,388.13 | 2,810.52 | |
| Hair, animal | 160.38 | 21,113.11 | 20,952.73 | |
| Hats: | | | | |
| Felt | 30,827.67 | 20,990.43 | | 9,837.24 |
| Straw | | 61.52 | | |
| Hatters' fur | 85,398.65 | 92,495.84 | 7,097.19 | |
| Horn strips | | 505.91 | | |
| Horses (stallions) | 32,172.14 | 57,089.39 | 24,917.25 | |
| Household goods and personal effects | 15,296.99 | 3,351.83 | | 11,945.16 |
| Instruments, musical | 1,393.91 | 1,790.97 | 397.06 | |
| Iron | 750.60 | | | |
| Iron, plate | 3,688.32 | | | |
| Iron and bronze articles | | 666.43 | | |
| Ironware | 586.48 | | | |
| Lace goods | 153,963.53 | 184,836.60 | 30,872.07 | |
| Laces, shoe | 21,331.92 | 10,697.05 | | 10,634.87 |
| Leather hatbands | 7,312.31 | 1,806.86 | | 5,505.45 |
| Linen goods | 399,279.45 | 418,098.23 | 18,828.78 | |
| Machinery, and parts of | 4,834.13 | 14,033.36 | 9,199.23 | |
| Marble | 18,294.36 | 14,952.52 | | 3,341.84 |
| Marble mosaic cubes | | 1,271.21 | | |
| Matches | 902.26 | 1,684.66 | 782.40 | |
| Metal coverings | 2,574.87 | 14,280.46 | 11,705.59 | |
| Millinery goods (spangled goods) | 48,351.10 | 17,740.31 | | 30,610.79 |
| Naphthaline | | 1,870.06 | | |
| Oil | 8,172.55 | 7,471.83 | | 701.72 |
| Oil, fusel | | 3,690.31 | | |
| Oxalic acid | | 1,141.63 | | |
| Paintings: | | | | |
| Oil | 3,071.82 | 691.91 | | 2,379.91 |
| Water colors | 260.55 | | | |
| Paper: | | | | |
| Old | 294.62 | | | |
| Parchment | 27,543.63 | 36,171.72 | 8,628.09 | |
| Paraffin, soft | 422.28 | 1,696.20 | 1,274.92 | |
| Phosphate of lime | 44,344.52 | 35,045.70 | | 9,298.82 |
| Plants | 951.63 | 2,980.63 | 2,029.00 | |
| Plants, medicinal | 11,553.88 | 10,544.13 | | 1,009.75 |
| Potash: | | | | |
| Salts of | | 1,905.91 | | |
| Sulphate of | | 38,047.78 | | |
| Potatoes | | 17,577.65 | | |
| Rags and new cuttings: paper stock | 23,218.71 | 27,211.85 | 3,993.14 | |
| Rattan | 1,217.18 | 2,501.06 | 1,284.90 | |
| Rubber toys | 12,842.27 | 22,434.38 | 9,592.11 | |
| Scales and weights | 571.49 | 1,304.37 | 782.88 | |
| Silk, artificial | 738.00 | 10,651.73 | 9,913.73 | |
| Skins: | | | | |
| Chamois | | 571.87 | | |
| Rabbit, sheep, and other | 300,148.05 | 570,748.68 | 270,600.63 | |
| Soap and perfumery | 334.66 | 299.90 | | 34.76 |

*Declared value of exports from the consular district of Brussels (including Charleroi) to the
United States for the fiscal years 1901 and 1902—Continued.*

| Articles. | Year ended June 30, 1901. | Year ending June 30, 1902. | Increase. | Decrease. |
|---|---|---|---|---|
| Soda: | | | | |
| Ferrocyanide | | $879.65 | | |
| Prussiate of | $9,191.17 | 8,432.68 | | $758.49 |
| Steel beams, billets, blooms, etc | | 344,119.15 | | |
| Stone | | 356.08 | | |
| Stone, flint | 7,510.35 | 6,208.43 | | 1,301.92 |
| Stones, precious | 1,494.75 | | | |
| Sugar, refined | 31,961.19 | 709.87 | | 31,251.32 |
| Sulphate of barytes | 1,470.00 | 4,450.98 | $2,980.98 | |
| Tiles | | 2,735.17 | | |
| Tin foil | 1,175.43 | 358.29 | | |
| Tools | | 609.91 | | |
| Vegetables, preserved | 16,607.46 | 26,986.00 | 10,378.54 | |
| Veils, cotton | 1,042.12 | 680.07 | | 362.05 |
| Wheels | | 513.78 | | |
| Wine | 4,780.01 | 937.01 | | 3,843.00 |
| Wire nails | 326.56 | | | |
| Yarn, cotton | 576.29 | 3,872.50 | 3,296.21 | |
| Sundries | 54,878.05 | 108,486.41 | 53,608.36 | |
| Total | 3,697,175.90 | 5,425,135.18 | 1,727,959.28 | |
| **EXPORTS TO PORTO RICO.** | | | | |
| Cars | | 3,045.54 | | |
| Earthenware | 672.94 | | | |
| Glass, window | 130.45 | | | |
| Glassware | 196.57 | | | |
| Iron pots | 1,483.95 | 787.93 | | 696.02 |
| Linen goods | 1,000.41 | | | |
| Marble | 260.55 | | | |
| Marble paving stones | | 323.08 | | |
| Paving tiles | | 445.06 | | |
| Tampons, iron and wood | | 228.89 | | |
| Wire nails | 329.86 | | | |
| General total | 3,701,250.63 | 5,429,965.68 | 1,728,715.05 | |

As will be observed by the foregoing table of declared exports, the
increase was in aniline colors, braids (button stock), church regalia,
clocks, fire bricks, glass (window), glass (other), glue and glue stock,
glycerin, hair (animal), hatters' fur, horses (stallions), instruments
(musical), lace goods, linen goods, machinery and parts of, matches,
metal coverings, paper, paraffin, plants, rags and new cuttings, rattan, rubber toys, scales and weights, silk (artificial), skins (rabbit,
sheep, and other), sulphate of barytes, vegetables (preserved), and
yarn (cotton).

### GLASS INDUSTRY.

*Imports into and exports from Belgium of plate and window glass during the first six
months of 1902.*

#### PLATE GLASS.

| Destination. | Imports. | Exports. | |
|---|---|---|---|
| | | *Francs.* | |
| Argentine Republic | | 191,264 | $36,913.95 |
| Australia | | 435,942 | 84,136.81 |
| Austria-Hungary | | 102,284 | 19,740.81 |
| Canada | | 194,492 | 37,586.96 |
| Denmark | | 80,195 | 15,477.63 |
| England | $134.13 | 6,293,281 | 1,214,603.23 |
| France | 4,488.41 | 335,780 | 64,795.89 |
| Germany | 313.05 | 137,622 | 26,561.05 |
| Holland | 3,265.13 | 617,320 | 119,142.76 |
| Japan | | 217,175 | 41,914.77 |
| Russia | | 4,460 | 860.78 |
| Spain | | 259,437 | 50,071.34 |
| Switzerland | | 101,537 | 19,596.64 |
| Turkey | | 100,742 | 19,443.21 |
| United States | | 1,289,790 | 248,917.89 |
| Other countries | 6.75 | 1,248,553 | 240,005.73 |
| Total | 8,207.71 | 11,604,764 | 2,239,719.45 |

*Imports into and exports from Belgium of plate and window glass during the first six months of 1902*—Continued.

WINDOW GLASS.

| Destination. | Imports. | | Exports. | |
|---|---|---|---|---|
| | *Francs.* | | *Francs.* | |
| Argentine Republic .......................... | .......... | .......... | 594, 647 | $114, 668. 87 |
| Australia .................................... | .......... | .......... | 555, 194 | 107, 152. 44 |
| Brasil ....................................... | .......... | .......... | 219, 640 | 42, 390. 52 |
| Canada ...................................... | .......... | .......... | 1, 702, 794 | 828, 639. 24 |
| Cape Colony ................................. | .......... | .......... | 133, 990 | 25, 860. 07 |
| Chile ........................................ | .......... | .......... | 182, 303 | 35, 184. 48 |
| China ....................................... | .......... | .......... | 2, 069, 919 | 398, 704. 37 |
| Denmark .................................... | .......... | .......... | 240, 639 | 46, 443. 33 |
| Egypt ....................................... | .......... | .......... | 162, 540 | 31, 370. 22 |
| England ..................................... | 6, 650 | $1, 288. 45 | 7, 989, 772 | 1, 542, 026. 00 |
| France ...................................... | 103, 087 | 19, 886. 14 | 228, 168 | 44, 086. 42 |
| Germany ..................................... | 9, 455 | 1, 824. 81 | 440, 923 | 85, 098. 14 |
| Greece ...................................... | .......... | .......... | 114, 374 | 22, 074. 18 |
| Hamburg .................................... | .......... | .......... | 193, 513 | 37, 048. 01 |
| Holland ..................................... | 8, 666 | 707. 54 | 1, 194, 373 | 230, 513. 99 |
| India ........................................ | .......... | .......... | 850, 574 | 164, 160. 78 |
| Italy ........................................ | .......... | .......... | 99, 680 | 19, 228. 59 |
| Japan ....................................... | .......... | .......... | 1, 456, 312 | 281, 068. 22 |
| Norway ..................................... | .......... | .......... | 54, 985 | 10, 612. 10 |
| Peru ........................................ | .......... | .......... | 46, 960 | 9, 061. 35 |
| Roumania ................................... | .......... | .......... | 281, 035 | 54, 239. 75 |
| Russia ...................................... | .......... | .......... | 52, 980 | 10, 215. 49 |
| Spain ....................................... | .......... | .......... | 97, 780 | 18, 871. 54 |
| Sweden ..................................... | .......... | .......... | 17, 605 | 3, 397. 76 |
| Switzerland ................................. | .......... | .......... | 363, 458 | 70, 146. 43 |
| Turkey ...................................... | .......... | .......... | 565, 899 | 110, 218. 51 |
| United States ............................... | .......... | .......... | 3, 287, 535 | 624, 846. 25 |
| Uruguay ..................................... | .......... | .......... | 85, 400 | 16, 482. 20 |
| Other countries ............................. | 1, 145 | 220. 96 | 695, 956 | 134, 319. 51 |
| Total ..................................... | 123, 953 | 23, 922. 93 | 23, 898, 833 | 4, 612, 474. 77 |

## BANKING.

*Statement of the National Bank of Belgium, August 28, 1902.*

| | Assets. | | Liabilities. | |
|---|---|---|---|---|
| | *Francs.* | | *Francs.* | |
| Capital .......................... | .......... | .......... | 50, 000, 000. 00 | $9, 650, 000. 00 |
| Gold and silver reserve, specie and bullion ..................... | 117, 459, 027. 99 | $22, 668, 592 | .......... | .......... |
| Bills and acceptances ............ | 491, 709, 195. 00 | 94, 899, 875 | .......... | .......... |
| Securities for current account .... | 8, 941, 590. 02 | 760, 727 | .......... | .......... |
| Bank notes in circulation ........ | .......... | .......... | 609, 000, 500. 00 | 117, 587, 096. 50 |
| Stocks (or public funds) .......... | 49, 913, 427. 50 | 9, 638, 292 | .......... | .......... |
| Reserve fund ..................... | 29, 104, 154. 89 | 5, 617, 101 | .......... | .......... |
| Reserve .......................... | .......... | .......... | 29, 111, 228. 72 | 5, 618, 467. 14 |
| Advances on Belgian public stocks | 50, 188, 752. 10 | 9, 686, 429 | .......... | .......... |
| Current account .................. | .......... | .......... | 66, 825, 307. 00 | 12, 800, 784. 25 |
| Real estate of the service, material, and furniture .............. | 13, 821, 875. 72 | 2, 667, 622 | .......... | .......... |
| Guaranty or realized values ...... | 4, 519, 922. 65 | 872, 345 | .......... | .......... |
| Public treasury: Bills and acceptances (stipulated circulation) ........... | 62, 929, 656. 85 | 12, 145, 424 | .......... | .......... |
| Statements of bills .............. | .......... | .......... | 62, 929, 656. 85 | 12, 145, 423. 77 |
| Deposited public funds ....... | 1, 779, 443, 844. 50 | 343, 432, 662 | .......... | .......... |
| Deposits in special and public funds ..................... | .......... | .......... | 1, 780, 433, 898. 10 | 343, 623, 741. 37 |
| Voluntary deposits ........... | 501, 857, 087. 58 | 96, 761, 918 | .......... | .......... |
| Depositors ................... | .......... | .......... | 501, 857, 087. 58 | 96, 761, 917. 89 |
| General account of the savings-bank and pension fund. | 225, 585, 112. 95 | 43, 528, 272 | .......... | .......... |
| General account and pension fund—statement of bills .... | .......... | .......... | 225, 585, 112. 95 | 43, 528, 276. 80 |
| Various ........................ | .......... | .......... | 5, 230, 861. 05 | 1, 009, 556. 18 |
| Total ...................... | 3, 829, 923, 647. 20 | 642, 675, 264 | 3, 829, 923, 647. 20 | 642, 675, 263. 90 |

Discounts and interests since June 15, 1901: Drafts accepted, 3 per cent; drafts unaccepted, 3¼ per cent; coupons, Belgian loans less than one hundred days, 3 per cent; purchase and sale of foreign securities, 3 per cent; advance on public funds, 3 per cent.

Uncovered deposits: Right to annually keep from 20 to 50 centimes (3.8 to 9.6 cents) per 1,000 francs ($193), according to nature of values.

Loans for the account of the savings-bank and pension fund, on designated value, 4 per cent.

GEO. W. ROOSEVELT, *Consul.*

BRUSSELS, *September 4, 1902.*

---

## BELGIAN MARITIME COMMERCE.

The following data, taken from statistics compiled by the department of finance and public works of Belgium for the year 1901, on the exterior commerce of the country show the importance of the international maritime traffic of this country.

### ANTWERP.

During the year 1901, goods entered at the port of Antwerp amounted to 7,534,226.8 tons, at a value of 1,676,984,002 francs ($323,657,912.39), of which 6,155,087 tons entered by sea and 1,379,139.8 tons by canals and rivers.

The quantities exported amounted to 5,464,578 tons, valued at 1,550,010,587 francs ($299,152,043.29), of which 4,145,405 tons were exported by sea and 1,319,173 tons by canals and rivers.

The principal countries contributing traffic to the port of Antwerp during the year 1901 were:

| Country. | Quantity. | Value. | |
|---|---|---|---|
| | | Francs. | U. S. currency. |
| | *Tons.* | | |
| United States | 1,562,634 | 365,889,447 | $70,616,663.27 |
| Germany | 1,223,155.9 | 104,898,527 | 20,245,415.71 |
| England | 878,533.2 | 282,794,891 | 54,579,413.96 |
| Roumania | 520,488.2 | 83,856,055 | 16,184,218.61 |
| Spain | 428,727.9 | 31,756,335 | 6,128,972.65 |
| Argentine Republic | 387,038.6 | 134,520,826 | 25,962,519.42 |
| Russia | 362,403.8 | 62,634,140 | 12,088,389.02 |
| Sweden | 339,857 | 32,710,516 | 6,313,129.59 |
| East Indies | 296,200.4 | 88,034,978 | 16,990,750.75 |
| Holland | 261,008.2 | 67,418,507 | 13,010,771.85 |
| France | 126,308 | 46,552,908 | 8,984,711.24 |
| Brazil | 126,146.2 | 57,002,902 | 11,001,560.09 |

The exportation of merchandise is classed and divided as follows:

| Country. | Quantity. | Value. | |
|---|---|---|---|
| | | Francs. | U. S currency. |
| | *Tons.* | | |
| England | 1,243,627 | 419,136,783 | $80,892,469.12 |
| Germany | 996,148.4 | 220,497,595 | 42,556,035.83 |
| United States | 459,400.5 | 188,413,502 | 36,363,805.89 |
| Holland | 452,117 | 79,772,505 | 15,396,093.46 |
| East Indies | 251,218.6 | 56,361,617 | 10,877,792.08 |
| Spain | 203,312.1 | 72,055,084 | 13,906,621.56 |
| Argentine Republic | 166,346.7 | 43,169,033 | 8,322,323.37 |
| France | 136,911.9 | 15,000,000 | 8,695,000.00 |
| China | 127,995.2 | 41,000,000 | 7,913,000.00 |

It may be observed that the above statistics show only goods recorded at the custom-house at Antwerp and do not include French articles, enormous quantities of which passed in transit through Belgium after having been recorded at the frontier offices, and reached Antwerp accompanied by duly legalized documents.

In a total of 1,411,211,208 francs ($272,363,763.14), representing the value of goods in transit through Belgium in 1901, France figures for 322,504,408 francs ($62,243,350.74). At least 130,000 to 150,000 tons—of which the greater part is brought by rail to be sent to England, the United States, South America, Australia, and other foreign countries—are shipped from Antwerp, generally via German or English steamers.

Germany figures in the importation of goods at Antwerp for 1,223,155.9 tons. The quantity imported by canals and rivers amounted to 1,093,356.4 tons. By these means of transport, France sent 13,056.9 tons and Holland 259,594.6 tons, against 1,413.6 tons sent by sea.

## OSTEND.

At Ostend, during the year 1901, the quantity of goods imported was 279,191.5 tons, representing a value of 59,926,260 francs ($11,565,768.18); the total weight of exportation was 45,095.9 tons, representing a value of 152,933,635 francs ($29,485,191.55). The principal countries concerned in the traffic of the port of Ostend were:

IMPORTS.

| Country. | Quantity. | Value. | |
|---|---|---|---|
| | | Francs. | U. S. currency. |
| | Tons. | | |
| England | 136,573.5 | 38,917,451 | $7,511,068.04 |
| Chile | 43,769 | 8,534,770 | 1,647,210.61 |
| Norway | 29,923.6 | 2,775,389 | 501,550.08 |
| Russia | 29,204.2 | 3,442,730 | 664,415.89 |
| Germany | 15,619.2 | 3,337,956 | 644,225.51 |
| France | 66.8 | 53,648 | 10,354.06 |

EXPORTS.

| | | | |
|---|---|---|---|
| England | 4,447 | 152,785,522 | $29,487,605.75 |
| France | 400 | 7,657 | 1,477.80 |

The exportation to other countries via Ostend was not of a sufficient importance to receive special mention.

## GHENT.

At Ghent, the quantity of goods imported represents a total weight of 775,438.7 tons and a total value of 148,086,320 francs ($28,580,659.76), of which 751,000 tons came by sea and 23,000 tons by land.

The quantity exported amounted to 468,719 tons, representing a value of 125,459,820 francs ($24,213,745.26), of which 401,000 tons were sent by sea and 67,000 tons by canals and river.

The principal countries sending goods via the port of Ghent were England, Russia, United States, Norway, Germany, Holland, and France.

## BRUSSELS.

Goods imported via the port of Brussels show a total quantity of 82,871.9 tons, representing a value of 15,783,999 francs ($3,046,311.80), of which 14,000 tons were imported by sea and 68,000 tons by canals and rivers.

Exportations amounted to 61,152.7 tons, representing a value of 21,048,975 francs ($4,062,452.17), of which 19,000 tons were exported by sea and 41,000 tons by canals and rivers.

The countries of origin were Germany, England, Holland, and France; countries of destination, Holland, England, Germany, and France.

## BRUGES.

At Bruges, the quantities of goods imported reached a total of 53,544.4 tons, valued at 1,869,155 francs ($360,746.91), of which 50,997.4 tons were imported by sea and 2,546.9 tons by canals and rivers.

The quantity exported amounted to 10.244.5 tons, valued at 344,444 francs ($66,477.69), of which 10,240 tons were sent by sea and the rest by canals and rivers.

The principal countries contributing to the traffic of the port of Bruges were the following:

IMPORTS.

| Country. | Quantity. | Value. | |
|---|---|---|---|
| | | Francs. | U. S. currency. |
| | *Tons.* | | |
| Germany | 184.2 | 16,985 | $3,268.45 |
| England | 45,386.8 | 1,042,964 | 201,292.05 |
| France | 605.2 | 99,857 | 19,272.40 |
| Norway | 4,422.7 | 530,385 | 102,364.30 |
| Holland | 2,546.9 | 120,871 | 23,328.10 |

EXPORTS.

| | Quantity. | Francs. | U. S. currency. |
|---|---|---|---|
| England | 10,106.3 | 335,614 | $64,773.50 |
| France | 134 | 3,350 | 376.55 |

Goods imported via Selzaete amounted to 256,891 tons, valued at 20,609,017 francs ($3,977,540.28), of which 15,454.8 tons were imported by sea and 241,436.2 tons by canals and rivers.

Exportations represented a total weight of 109,483.4 tons, valued at 5,714,073 francs ($1,102,816.08), of which 3,886 tons were exported by sea and 105.3 tons by canals and rivers.

Via Nieuport, the goods imported reached a total weight of 19,062.8 tons, valued at 1,037,670 francs ($200,270.31); exportations amounted to 3,835.9 tons, valued at 140,814 francs ($27,177.10).

GEO. W. ROOSEVELT, *Consul.*

BRUSSELS, *December 24, 1902.*

## GHENT.

Reports for East and West Flanders indicate a diminution in industry and commerce during 1901, caused, it is said, by the insurrection in China and the war in South Africa; although, in summing up the situation, the crisis was really a crisis of credit. Enormous losses were sustained by shareholders in numerous industrial enterprises, due to inflated returns in incorporated businesses. This has caused discussion in regard to reforming the law affecting incorporated societies, so that profits not actually realized can not be distributed. Food products decreased 4 per cent and raw materials for industrial purposes 8¼ per cent. The decline in merchandise is not important, as it is only a reflex of the real crisis of the stock exchange.

No public works have been projected in Ghent during the past year, but the museum of fine arts and the new telephone exchange building have been completed. Work has also been resumed on the new post-office. Although Ghent has a population of more than 163,000, there is no general sewage system nor municipal electric lighting plant. Baths are not obtainable, even in the hotels.

Work on the Terneuzen Canal, which connects Ghent with the sea, via the Schelde, is progressing slowly. At present, vessels of from 16 to 18 feet draft can enter, but when completed it will have a depth of about 37 feet, a width of 210 feet, and a length of 20½ miles. The harbor improvements at Ostend are assuming goodly proportions, and when finished this will be one of the best equipped ports in Belgium, and most easily accessible for ocean vessels, although it is problematical if it will equal Antwerp as a port of entry.

### TRADE WITH THE UNITED STATES.

The depressed trade conditions have had no appreciable effect on exports to the United States, as appears from the following table. The total increase over 1900 was $484,257.71, or 32 per cent more than was ever before exported from this consular district.

*Exports to United States, 1900 and 1901.*

| Quarter. | 1900. | | 1901. | | Increase or decrease. | |
|---|---|---|---|---|---|---|
| | Invoices. | Total value. | Invoices. | Total value. | Invoices. | Total value. |
| First | 307 | $441,232.24 | 274 | $529,581.35 | −33 | −$88,349.11 |
| Second | 331 | 374,669.06 | 367 | 525,382.97 | +36 | +150,713.91 |
| Third | 364 | 327,109.92 | 331 | 382,970.41 | −33 | − 55,860.49 |
| Fourth | 320 | 350,396.40 | 373 | 539,670.60 | +53 | +189,334.20 |
| Total | 1,322 | 1,493,347.62 | 1,345 | 1,977,605.83 | 23 | 484,257.71 |

This marked increase was due to the activity of American industries requiring raw materials from this district and to the demand for a large quantity of potatoes on account of a short crop in the United States. Potatoes are a new article of export.

*Exports to United States during first half of 1901 and 1902.*

| Quarter. | 1901. | 1902. | Increase. |
|---|---|---|---|
| First | $529,561.35 | $712,099.28 | $182,457.98 |
| Second | 525,882.97 | 694,901.21 | 169,518.24 |
| Total | 1,054,964.32 | 1,306,940.49 | 251,976.17 |

The declared exports for the first and second quarters of 1902, as shown by the preceding table, amount to $1,306,940.49, which, compared with the corresponding period of 1901, give an increase of $251,976.17. This increase was entirely due to shipments of potatoes—for the first time from this district—which amounted to $279,738.04. There were decreases in cement, cocoanut, and copra oils, flax, hatters' furs, and sprats.

The trade in the different articles of export in 1901 and 1900 is shown in the following table:

| Articles. | 1901. | 1900. | Increase. | Decrease. |
|---|---|---|---|---|
| Baskets | $602.59 | $6,814.74 | | $6,212.15 |
| Books | 409.91 | 188.18 | $221.73 | |
| Cement | 88,494.00 | 113,801.54 | | 25,307.54 |
| Chicory, granulated | 1,136.29 | 1,608.53 | | 472.24 |
| Chicory root | 7,875.58 | 6,284.33 | 1,141.20 | |
| Chicory seed | 267.30 | 646.98 | | 379.68 |
| Cordage | 952.43 | 4,004.77 | | 3,052.34 |
| Church regalia | 318.45 | | 318.45 | |
| Dogs | 61.76 | | 61.76 | |
| Earthenware | 114.42 | 815.91 | | 701.49 |
| Effects, household | 1,674.28 | 784.80 | 889.48 | |
| Flax | 485,044.74 | 273,217.64 | 211,827.10 | |
| Hatters' furs | 123,396.30 | 68,745.11 | 59,651.19 | |
| Horses | | 4,467.95 | | 4,467.95 |
| Jewelery | | 19.30 | | 19.30 |
| Jute goods | 348.91 | | 348.91 | |
| Lace | 22,050.40 | 13,950.54 | 8,099.86 | |
| Linen goods | 246,555.72 | 165,353.01 | 81,202.71 | |
| Matches | 2,189.98 | 16,654.98 | | 14,465.00 |
| Machinery | | 1,785.22 | | 1,785.22 |
| Marble busts | | 482.50 | | 482.50 |
| Naphthalene | | 1,188.60 | | 1,188.60 |
| Oil: | | | | |
| Cocoa | 59,775.91 | 50,358.01 | 9,417.90 | |
| Copra | 95,630.86 | | | 95,630.86 |
| Paintings, oil | 1,395.10 | 1,113.22 | 281.88 | |
| Palm nuts | | 411.48 | | 411.48 |
| Pictures, chromo | | 898.12 | | 898.12 |
| Pigeons | 170.42 | | 170.42 | |
| Plants | 187,126.14 | 181,064.43 | 6,063.71 | |
| Potatoes | 78,552.14 | | 78,552.14 | |
| Rabbit skins | 133,041.78 | 213,133.07 | | 80,091.29 |
| Rags and paper stock | 346,592.11 | 307,432.30 | 39,159.81 | |
| Sprats | 74,535.35 | 32,174.94 | 42,360.41 | |
| Sugar, granulated | 2,342.31 | 2,548.57 | | 206.26 |
| Thread, flax | 6,696.32 | 10,049.01 | | 3,352.69 |
| Tow | 10,017.26 | 15,059.39 | | 5,042.13 |
| Yarns: | | | | |
| Tow | 790.78 | 274.14 | 516.64 | |
| Jute | | 1,667.46 | | 1,667.46 |
| Flax | | 1,952.85 | | 1,952.85 |
| Total | 1,977,605.33 | 1,493,347.62 | 484,257.71 | |

During the month of May, in both 1901 and 1902, the cotton and flax spinning and weaving industries were much disturbed because of political agitation among the laboring class to secure "universal suffrage." When this measure was before the Chamber of Representatives in Brussels, there was daily rioting, and during certain hours, it required the presence of the police and troops to keep the peace. Little damage was done to property, but some factories were closed for several days. At that time, several manufacturers expressed the opinion that, for every day their employees "struck," they could afford to keep the factories closed for as many weeks, owing to the large stocks of manufactured products on hand and the poor demand. However, they kept the factories in operation on reduced capacity.

### JUTE INDUSTRY.

Generally speaking, prices were maintained and business was normal during the year. Competition from the Indies was hardly felt on the European markets, because of an understanding with the producers in the Calcutta district. However, the announcement of a good harvest and the canceling of contracts with mills in the Indies created considerable uneasiness.

The decrease in price of raw jute was the cause of a decrease in price of the woven article, but the uncertainty of purchasers produced the general crisis.

*Jute.*—The sowings of 1901 were made under better conditions and resulted in an abundant harvest, with a fiber considered, on the average, good. The total number of bales in 1901 was 2,223,500 bales, against 2,138,000 bales in 1900 and 1,526,000 bales in 1899.

*Thread.*—The decrease in price of raw jute produced a low price of thread. The importation of Scotch thread has completely ceased, as Scotland required all the thread spun to fill important orders received from the war office.

### FLAX AND TOW.

The flax harvest has been good in Belgium. The quantity sown was greater than in the preceding year. The plant grew well and did not suffer from hail or storms, thus rendering the fiber strong, which gave satisfaction to the spinners. Beet and chicory roots were grown under conditions which gave very poor results. For this reason, the probabilities are that the quantity of flax sown will remain considerable. Much of the raw flax used in this district is imported from Russia.

It is difficult to say whether the present crop will be a success or not. Opinions are divided on the subject. It is certain that the quantity sown is larger than last year, but in several districts the plants suffered on account of a prolonged drought. The retting has been done under most favorable conditions; so that if there is some doubt as to the quantity of flax Russia will furnish, there is no doubt as to the quality.

*Flax spinning.*—The year has been very trying for flax spinners. The price of raw material, already high at the end of 1900, increased more and more, and the price of thread attained such limits as almost to render it impossible for weavers to work, and consumption almost came to a standstill. For months, the sales of flax thread were nil, and spinners found orders decreasing to a minimum.

This was not the situation in Belgium alone, but in other countries as well. Poor sales were a general feature, and everywhere spinners had to reduce their production as a remedy against accumulation of stocks. In other centers, spinners agreed to decrease the working hours; here such an agreement was impossible. Large stocks were accumulated by manufacturers, which during the summer had to be sold at great loss.

During the latter part of the year, the arrival of flax of the new harvest somewhat relieved spinners. The harvest being exceptionally early in the retting districts, the flax came rapidly to market and prices soon decreased proportionately. This condition permitted, for the first time during the entire year, the production of flax thread at a small profit.

The tow industry was conducted under more favorable conditions. On the one hand, demands were numerous for all kinds of tow yarns, and on the other, the prices of the raw material were better than those for flax.

During the greater part of the year, the manufactories of tow yarns gave very satisfactory results. However, these two industries seem to-day to be in about the same position. The price of raw tow is exceedingly high (good qualities being hard to find), and the price of yarn does not increase in proportion.

The total declared value of flax shipped to the United States in 1901 amounted to $485,044.74, as against $273,217.64 in 1900, being an increase of $211,827.10, while the total value of tow shipped to the United States in 1901 was $10,017.26, as against $15,059.39 in 1900, being a decrease of $5,042.13.

## LINEN GOODS.

In this industry, 1901 was the worst year known for a long time, owing principally to high prices for thread, which stopped trade. Numerous weaving mills were compelled to shut down part of their machinery for the production of certain articles, chiefly furniture coverings. Many weavers were obliged to reduce their production by one-half to prevent accumulation of stocks.

Generally speaking, profits were nil, forced strikes having absorbed the small margin of benefit of the looms then running, and the fluctuations of the market having too much influence on the price of stocks on hand.

A good deal has been said about the influence of the South African war upon the general situation, but it has been proved, since hostilities ceased, that the crisis continues just the same, especially for the spinners.

## COTTON SPINNING.

Although the number of spindles was considerably increased, the number of active looms was lessened, as was the consumption of spun cotton, and the production of thread was in excess of the demand. The result was a reduction in price, to provide against disaster to the producers. Several spinners found it profitable not to work more than one or two days a week. A good understanding exists among the spinners, and with fewer hours of work it is hoped to reduce the stocks on hand so as to create a firm market, which is necessary at this time.

During 1901, the number of spinning spindles at Ghent was 623,120, as against 573,560 in 1900; increase, 49,560. The number of twisting spindles in 1901 was 93,088; in 1900, 83,110; increase, 9,978. In the remaining districts in Belgium there were, in 1901, 313,018 spinning spindles, and in 1900, 296,871; increase, 16,147. The number of twisting spindles was 83,336, against 80,224 in 1900; increase, 3,112, divided amond the following establishments:

| Establishments. | Spinning spindles. | Twisting spindles. | Establishments. | Spinning spindles. | Twisting spindles. |
|---|---|---|---|---|---|
| **IN GHENT.** | | | **OTHER LOCALITIES.** | | |
| Societe Gaud Zele Tubize.. | 156,896 | 27,000 | Omer Van Ham & Co ...... | 40,000 | 12,000 |
| Ferd Lousbergs ............. | 65,400 | 1,400 | Filature du Canal ........... | 80,000 | 1,580 |
| "La Louisiane" ............. | 52,896 | 12,098 | Soc. Gaud Zele Tubize .... | 20,104 | 9,804 |
| Jules de Hemptinne ....... | 48,112 | 24,000 | H. Van Hoegaerden ........ | 27,856 | 6,886 |
| Nouvelle Orleans............ | 47,600 | 2,280 | Vanderschueren & Co .... | 22,888 | 5,400 |
| "La Florida" .............. | 81,000 | 1,500 | Justin Van Ham ........... | 28,272 | 8,412 |
| Baertsven & Buysse........ | 28,020 | 760 | Motte Van Ham ........... | 24,000 | 6,216 |
| "Le Texas" ................ | 26,600 | 9,000 | Ed Van Hamme............. | 18,720 | 8,400 |
| Filature de Roygen......... | 18,000 | 9,000 | Filature & Teinturerie..... | 20,740 | 2,240 |
| De Smet Gueguier ......... | 17,584 | 8,130 | Ghislain freres.............. | 16,844 | 9,738 |
| Chas. Pipyu & fils.......... | 17,000 | ......... | Fr. Gerard ................. | 14,000 | 5,150 |
| J. J. Dierman................ | 15,000 | 500 | Ach. Dopchie................ | 13,892 | 8,250 |
| Chas. Van Loo ............. | 14,000 | ......... | Cotonniere Towmaisienne. | 12,794 | 8,220 |
| Vincent et Anger Vincent. | 13,716 | ......... | Van Coppernolle & Dupuis. | 8,208 | 8,000 |
| Van Acker-Vanden Brouck | 12,700 | 1,920 | Breuer & Co ................ | 7,200 | 8,040 |
| Diomede Vanderhaegen ... | 12,848 | 800 | | | |
| De Coster Rousseau........ | 10,500 | ......... | Total.............. | 966,188 | 176,424 |
| Motte freres................ | 10,000 | ......... | | | |
| Cotonniere de Ledeberg ... | 10,000 | 2,000 | | | |
| Cotonniere de Gaud ....... | 8,500 | 1,200 | | | |
| De Moor freres............. | 7,808 | ......... | | | |

## BREWERIES.

The brewing industry has undergone a slight crisis during the year 1901, which led to a small decrease in consumption. For the City of Ghent, 6,689 tons of materials were declared at the excise office, against 6,889 tons in 1900.

| Breweries in— | Number in activity. | Quantity of materials declared. | Excise duty. |
|---|---|---|---|
| | | *Tons.* | |
| Province of East Flanders ............................................. | 658 | 84,470 | $665,280.71 |
| Ghent.............................................................. | 75 | 6,668 | 129,090.81 |
| Gendbrugge........................................................ | 4 | 258 | 4,979.79 |
| Ledeberg .......................................................... | 8 | 148 | 2,767.91 |
| Mont St. Amand.................................................... | 8 | 550 | 10,628.59 |

The quality of the products used is becoming better and better. Since 1860, a brewery school has been established by the private initiative of the brewers. The benefits derived soon caused it to be placed under the protection of the provincial government and that of the city of Ghent.

The courses are divided into four sections: (1) Engineers for the industries of fermentation, comprising three years of study; (2) licentiates in brewing and distilling, two years of study; (3) master brewers or master distillers, one year of study; (4) workmen and foremen brewers, one year of study. The last-mentioned courses are gratuitous, and are given on Sunday mornings in French and Flemish.

## MALT.

This industry is at present undergoing an important change, due principally to the customs relations between Belgium and neighboring ountries.

The high duties imposed by France in 1892 and by Austria in 1894 practically prohibit the entry of the products of Belgium.

The use of malt in Belgium has been much reduced by the law of 1896, which decreased its employment in the manufacture of alcohol by two-thirds. France, by inaugurating a system of export premiums, has stimulated her industry, and of the 17,665 tons imported into Belgium in 1901 12,962 came from France. Germany has adopted a system which assures a profit to her maltsters, and Austria has decreased her transportation charges by 31 cents per 100 kilograms (220 pounds).

### HIDES AND LEATHER.

Prices were more steady in 1901 than in 1900. The supply was moderate. On account of the strong demand in England, because of the South African war, there was an increase of 5 per cent. Continental purchases were not important, on account of the poor situation of the tanning industry in Europe, particularly in Germany.

*Native hides.*—There was a good market throughout the year.

*Tanned leather.*—Prices were high, principally for heavy and exotic leather. The general situation is much influenced by duties imposed by Germany, which if persisted in will prohibit the entry of leather and precipitate a crisis.

### CEMENT.

*Ordinary.*—The manufacture is very active, which has caused production to exceed demands, producing low prices. The product is now manufactured in most countries of the world, to the detriment of the Belgian product, which was once much preferred.

*Portland.*—Prosperity reigns in this industry, due, it is claimed, to the superior quality of the product. Many workmen are given employment at satisfactory salaries. The total declared value of cement shipped from this district to the United States in 1901 was $88,494, as compared with $113,801.64 in 1900, showing a decrease of $25,307.64.

*Tiles and bricks.*—This is a very popular industry in Ghent, and porcelain and fancy-faced tiles are much used in interior decoration—wainscoting and floors. Eight hundred thousand square meters were produced in Ghent alone during 1901, and 1,250,000 square meters in the other cities of the country. About all of this stock is sold in Belgium, owing to high duties in other countries.

### LUMBER.

Since 1874, the lumber trade has not been so handicapped as during 1901. Most of the supply is from Norway and Sweden and Russia, which maintain services to the ports of Antwerp, Ghent, and Ostend. Shippers demanded such high freight rates that business was made possible only by keen competition. There were no consignments received direct from the United States, because there is no direct steamer service. Trouble is experienced in unloading in the port of Ghent, as no sheds are provided and the area at present available is too small. On account of exposure to the weather, the color of the pine soon changes.

The statistics of the importation of lumber for 1901 are:

| Kind. | 1900. | 1901. |
|---|---|---|
| | Cubic yds. | Cubic yds. |
| Oak logs | 17,463 | 24,498 |
| Oak, miscellaneous | 8,725 | 1,394 |
| Pitch-pine beams | 760 | 970 |
| Pitch-pine planks | 14,058 | 22,814 |
| Pine beams | 52,019 | 26,986 |
| Pine planks | 278,982 | 206,191 |
| Miscellaneous wood, trees, etc | 196,765 | 249,130 |
| Total | 563,772 | 531,983 |

The characteristics of the foregoing table are persistent increases in oak and pitch-pine timber, and perceptible decreases in pine beams, planks, and boards.

### BLEACHING AND DYEING.

The bleaching of flax thread was affected by disturbances in the general trade. The usual orders from Italy and Spain were materially reduced. Bleached cotton is being replaced more and more by the colored article.

### CHEMICAL INDUSTRY.

*Sulphate of ammonia.*—On account of a late agricultural season, the trade at first was poor. Later on, prices increased in harmony with nitrates, and the year closed at about the same as in the beginning. Importations from England tend to decrease; Germany, on the contrary, seems to be developing its trade.

*Nitrate of soda.*—An agreement between the manufacturers of Chile was put into force in March, 1901, and its principal objects—limitation of production and an understanding respecting the export trade—were conscientiously adhered to. The chief result of this measure was a gradual reduction of stocks with an advance in prices. General consumption also increased 60,000 tons.

*Sulphate of soda.*—After the strike in the glass industries, this product commanded good prices, but later large importations from England and Germany congested the market.

*Acetic acid.*—Acetic acid for table use is decreasing on account of the decline in price of vinegar. The export trade was important in spite of a sharp competition on the part of the German product. On account of the establishment of new factories in France, the exportation to that country decreased considerably.

The raw materials used in the manufacture of chemical products are almost wholly imported from South American countries.

### CEREALS.

*Wheat.*—The year was one of abundance in cereals.

North America again furnished the deficit in European markets, as did also, in smaller proportions, Argentina, India, Australia, and southern Russia.

*Corn.*—The shortages were made up partly by good crops in the Danube Valley, Russia, and the Plata. However, the price rose to rates heretofore unknown in Belgium. It was an easy matter to replace American corn for feeding cattle, but distilleries were obliged to buy better qualities than those ordinarily furnished by Europe and the Argentine Republic.

*Barley.*—The present situation of this trade is bad. Competition is so keen that profits are reduced to a minimum. For many years, Belgium has imported barley for brewing purposes from Asia, Syria, Russia, Danube Valley, Algeria, Tunis, United States, and Canada.

*Oats.*—Important purchases were made in Russia and shipped direct to Ghent or via Antwerp.

### SEEDS.

*Flaxseed and linseed—Oil cakes.*—This trade has been greatly developed with Russia, but a local authority says that if steamers were run direct from New York, Boston, Baltimore, or Philadelphia, much of these products would come from the United States.

*Flaxseed (for sowing).*—This is an important article of import into this district, because of the linen trade. Small crops generally made high prices. "Extra pink" sold at $7.14 per sack. The importations for 1901 amounted to 26,170 sacks, against 28,075 in 1900.

### HATTERS' FURS AND RABBIT SKINS.

During 1901, raw materials, especially rabbit skins, were less abundant and higher in price than the year before, and though the supply of hatters' furs could easily keep pace with the demand, prices averaged 6 to 7 per cent more than during 1900.

The bulk of the production of this city was exported to the United States.

As to dyed skins, in spite of the above-mentioned scarcity of raw skins, prices did not rise, the demand for this article having been very moderate.

The question has often been asked, Why do not Americans raise these rabbits and prepare the skins in the United States? It has been found on trial that, after a generation or two, the rabbits deteriorate rapidly—it is said on account of climatic conditions—and a secret process for the final preparation of rabbit skins is not generally available to the trade.

The declared exports of hatters' furs and rabbit skins from this consular district to the United States in 1901 were, respectively, $123,396.30 and $133,041.78 as compared with $63,745.11 and $213,133.07 in 1900

### HORTICULTURE.

This is an occupation peculiar to this consular district, and has become very important in recent years, on account of the increased export trade. The plants most largely exported to the United States are azaleas, palms, and bay trees. Only in two other localities is this culture profitably carried on—Dresden and Versailles, near Paris. Local nurserymen claim this is because of peculiarities of soil and climate, and some importers in the United States say they can purchase stocks in Europe cheaper than the plant can be cultivated in America.

H. Doc. 305, pt 2——7

During 1901, prices were about the same as in 1900. The demand was strong and the product good. Not so many small dealers are now entering this business, which has given greater stability to the market.

Exports to the United States in 1901 exceeded those of 1900 by $6,763.71.

### RAGS AND PAPER STOCK.

The situation was not materially changed during 1901. Although prices decreased about 15 per cent, the enlarged demand more than made up losses. The rapid development of the wood-pulp industry in America is making inroads on the rag business, because its products are cheaper.

This is one of the chief centers of the rag and paper-stock business, and most of the stocks are shipped to the United States.

The shipment of all kinds of rags and paper stock from this consular district to the United States was valued at $346,592.11 in 1901, as against $307,432.30 in 1900, showing an increase of $39.159.81.

### DECLARED EXPORTS.

*Value of declared exports from the consular district of Ghent to the United States during the year ended December 31, 1901.*

| Articles. | Quarter ending— | | | | Total. |
|---|---|---|---|---|---|
| | Mar. 31, 1901. | June 30, 1901. | Sept. 30, 1901. | Dec. 31, 1901. | |
| Baskets | | | | $602.59 | $602.59 |
| Books | $137.40 | $272.51 | | | 409.91 |
| Cement | 17,542.00 | 21,695.54 | $21,622.65 | 27,698.51 | 88,494.00 |
| Chicory, granulated | 366.70 | 377.86 | 391.73 | | 1,136.29 |
| Chicory root | 7,375.58 | | | | 7,375.58 |
| Chicory seed | 124.49 | 142.82 | | | 267.31 |
| Church regalia | | 318.45 | | | 318.45 |
| Cordage | | 462.82 | 489.61 | | 952.43 |
| Dogs | 61.76 | | | | 61.76 |
| Earthenware | 114.42 | | | | 114.42 |
| Effects, household | | 1,674.28 | | | 1,674.28 |
| Fertilizers | | 147.89 | | | 147.89 |
| Flax | 195,561.36 | 177,171.25 | 38,267.51 | 74,044.62 | 485,044.74 |
| Hatters' furs | 45,357.50 | 85,776.86 | 6,315.11 | 35,946.83 | 123,396.80 |
| Jute goods | | | | 348.91 | 348.91 |
| Lace | 7,278.54 | 4,312.81 | 6,860.49 | 3,608.60 | 22,050.44 |
| Linen goods | 77,424.27 | 38,973.75 | 57,953.41 | 72,204.29 | 246,555.72 |
| Matches | 472.66 | | 241.25 | 1,476.07 | 2,189.98 |
| Oil, cocoanut | 23,568.19 | 2,974.27 | 6,432.49 | 26,800.96 | 59,775.91 |
| Copra | 20,143.69 | 40,153.39 | 18,885.51 | 16,498.27 | 95,630.86 |
| Paintings, oil | | 410.80 | 996.05 | 48.25 | 1,395.10 |
| Paper stock and rags | 84,520.69 | 84,872.43 | 82,815.08 | 94,383.91 | 346,592.11 |
| Pictures, chromo | | | 196.00 | | 196.00 |
| Pigeons | | 81.46 | | 188.96 | 170.42 |
| Plants and bulbs | 1,879.67 | 63,808.72 | 74,833.01 | 47,306.74 | 187,828.14 |
| Potatoes | | | | 78,552.14 | 78,552.14 |
| Rabbit skins | 21,106.48 | 37,280.00 | 44,965.46 | 29,689.84 | 133,041.78 |
| Sprats | 25,049.18 | 8,736.84 | 14,511.86 | 26,237.97 | 74,535.35 |
| Sugar, granulated | | | | 2,342.21 | 2,342.21 |
| Thread, flax | 1,041.77 | 2,186.97 | 1,620.29 | 747.29 | 5,596.82 |
| Tow | | 3,325.75 | 5,672.87 | 1,018.64 | 10,017.26 |
| Yarns, tow | 454.78 | 336.00 | | | 790.78 |
| Total | 529,581.35 | 525,382.97 | 382,970.41 | 539,670.60 | 1,977,605.33 |

## MARITIME MOVEMENT OF BELGIAN PORTS DURING 1901.

### Shipping of port of Ghent.

| Flag. | Sailing vessels. | | Steamers. | | Total. | |
|---|---|---|---|---|---|---|
| | Number. | Tonnage. | Number. | Tonnage. | Number. | Tonnage. |
| English | 57 | 15,882 | 681 | 433,996 | 738 | 449,818 |
| German | 6 | 3,497 | 98 | 78,961 | 104 | 82,428 |
| Danish | 8 | 11,296 | 59 | 60,068 | 67 | 61,869 |
| Norwegian | 18 | 5,010 | 77 | 49,980 | 96 | 54,940 |
| Swedish | 5 | 1,817 | 32 | 22,270 | 37 | 28,587 |
| Belgian | 1 | 186 | 51 | 14,536 | 52 | 14,692 |
| Russian | 1 | 282 | 16 | 18,425 | 17 | 18,707 |
| Dutch | | | 16 | 11,558 | 16 | 11,558 |
| French | 4 | 294 | 3 | 2,004 | 7 | 2,296 |
| Spanish | | | 1 | 1,552 | 1 | 1,552 |
| Italian | 1 | 779 | | | 1 | 779 |
| Total | 101 | 28,433 | 1,082 | 688,290 | 1,188 | 716,728 |

### Merchandise arriving.

| Merchandise. | Sailing vessels. | | Steamers. | | Total. | |
|---|---|---|---|---|---|---|
| | Number. | Tonnage. | Number | Tonnage. | Number. | Tonnage. |
| Sundry merchandise | | | 606 | 392,470 | 606 | 392,470 |
| Wood, logs, and stanchions | 28 | 7,998 | 181 | 154,439 | 209 | 162,437 |
| Coal | | | 124 | 57,991 | 124 | 57,991 |
| Ballast | 5 | 1,931 | 60 | 27,246 | 65 | 29,177 |
| Phosphates | | | 20 | 19,852 | 20 | 19,852 |
| Pyrite | | | 18 | 11,180 | 18 | 11,180 |
| Nitrates | 10 | 9,609 | | | 10 | 9,609 |
| Flax | | | 8 | 7,620 | 8 | 7,620 |
| Petroleum | | | 5 | 7,255 | 5 | 7,255 |
| Cotton | | | 4 | 5,801 | 4 | 5,801 |
| Porcelain earth | 35 | 3,928 | | | 35 | 3,928 |
| Guano | 4 | 2,962 | | | 4 | 2,962 |
| Wood pulp | | | 5 | 2,308 | 5 | 2,308 |
| Barley | 9 | 1,234 | 1 | 220 | 10 | 1,454 |
| Wood and flax | | | 2 | 1,397 | 2 | 1,397 |
| Rafts | 1 | 67 | 2 | 689 | 3 | 756 |
| Sulphates | 6 | 482 | 1 | 177 | 7 | 659 |
| Ice | 1 | 136 | | | 1 | 136 |
| Herring | 2 | 86 | | | 2 | 86 |
| Total | 101 | 28,433 | 1,082 | 688,290 | 1,188 | 716,728 |

### Vessels according to tonnage.

| Tonnage. | Sailing vessels. | Steamers. | Total. | Tonnage. | Sailing vessels. | Steamers. | Total. |
|---|---|---|---|---|---|---|---|
| 1 to 100 tons | 30 | 2 | 32 | 1,001 to 1,100 tons | 3 | 22 | 25 |
| 101 to 150 tons | 24 | 9 | 33 | 1,101 to 1,200 tons | 1 | 39 | 40 |
| 151 to 200 tons | 10 | 24 | 34 | 1,201 to 1,300 tons | | 14 | 14 |
| 201 to 250 tons | 8 | 10 | 18 | 1,301 to 1,400 tons | | 8 | 8 |
| 251 to 300 tons | 3 | 12 | 15 | 1,401 to 1,500 tons | | 10 | 10 |
| 301 to 400 tons | 5 | 67 | 72 | 1,501 to 1,600 tons | | 6 | 6 |
| 401 to 500 tons | 4 | 111 | 115 | 1,601 to 1,700 tons | | 8 | 8 |
| 501 to 600 tons | 1 | 236 | 237 | 1,701 to 1,800 tons | | | |
| 601 to 700 tons | | 142 | 142 | 1,801 to 1,900 tons | 1 | | 1 |
| 701 to 800 tons | 7 | 75 | 82 | 1,901 to 2,000 tons | | | |
| 801 to 900 tons | 1 | 135 | 136 | | | | |
| 901 to 1,000 tons | 4 | 56 | 60 | Total | 101 | 1,082 | 1,133 |

*Arrivals of wood and logs.*

| Year. | With wood. | | With logs. | | Total. | |
|---|---|---|---|---|---|---|
| | Vessels. | Tonnage. | Vessels. | Tonnage. | Vessels. | Tonnage. |
| 1890 | 133 | 34,116 | 819 | 398,235 | 952 | 427,351 |
| 1891 | 104 | 28,217 | 911 | 465,581 | 1,015 | 493,798 |
| 1892 | 138 | 39,969 | 840 | 460,005 | 978 | 499,974 |
| 1893 | 130 | 31,735 | 800 | 452,655 | 930 | 484,390 |
| 1894 | 95 | 30,362 | 802 | 477,000 | 897 | 507,362 |
| 1895 | 89 | 28,437 | 773 | 480,880 | 862 | 509,317 |
| 1896 | 110 | 37,975 | 831 | 530,080 | 941 | 568,055 |
| 1897 | 106 | 36,590 | 873 | 566,772 | 979 | 603,362 |
| 1898 | 117 | 35,138 | 884 | 598,596 | 1,001 | 633,734 |
| 1899 | 101 | 30,383 | 851 | 586,893 | 952 | 617,276 |
| 1900 | 141 | 33,513 | 993 | 664,050 | 1,134 | 697,564 |
| 1901 | 101 | 28,433 | 1,082 | 688,290 | 1,183 | 716,723 |

*Vessels and tonnage arriving.*

| Month. | Sailing vessels. | | Steamers. | | Total. | |
|---|---|---|---|---|---|---|
| | Number. | Tonnage. | Number. | Tonnage. | Number. | Tonnage. |
| January | 5 | 1,272 | 77 | 51,070 | 82 | 52,322 |
| February | 8 | 2,377 | 63 | 42,117 | 71 | 44,354 |
| March | 9 | 2,531 | 90 | 55,602 | 99 | 58,133 |
| April | 9 | 4,616 | 78 | 19,491 | 87 | 54,107 |
| May | 7 | 1,188 | 87 | 56,985 | 94 | 58,173 |
| June | 9 | 3,203 | 84 | 58,948 | 93 | 62,151 |
| July | 10 | 3,308 | 80 | 57,974 | 90 | 61,282 |
| August | 6 | 979 | 95 | 64,498 | 101 | 65,477 |
| September | 8 | 1,074 | 95 | 63,942 | 103 | 65,016 |
| October | 10 | 1,883 | 98 | 66,917 | 108 | 68,800 |
| November | 11 | 1,528 | 94 | 61,203 | 105 | 62,731 |
| December | 9 | 4,594 | 91 | 59,543 | 100 | 64,137 |
| Total | 101 | 28,433 | 1,082 | 688,290 | 1,183 | 716,723 |

*Vessels and tonnage arriving, from 1891 to 1901.*

| Year. | Sailing vessels. | | Steamers. | | Total. | | Average tonnage per vessel. |
|---|---|---|---|---|---|---|---|
| | Number. | Tonnage. | Number. | Tonnage. | Number. | Tonnage. | |
| 1891 | 104 | 28,217 | 911 | 465,581 | 1,015 | 493,798 | 487 |
| 1892 | 138 | 39,969 | 840 | 460,005 | 978 | 499,974 | 512 |
| 1893 | 130 | 31,735 | 800 | 452,655 | 930 | 484,390 | 521 |
| 1894 | 95 | 30,362 | 802 | 477,000 | 897 | 507,362 | 566 |
| 1895 | 89 | 28,437 | 773 | 480,880 | 862 | 509,317 | 591 |
| 1896 | 110 | 37,975 | 831 | 530,080 | 941 | 568,055 | 604 |
| 1897 | 106 | 36,590 | 873 | 566,772 | 979 | 603,362 | 617 |
| 1898 | 117 | 35,132 | 884 | 598,596 | 1,001 | 633,734 | 634 |
| 1899 | 101 | 30,383 | 851 | 586,893 | 952 | 617,276 | 649 |
| 1900 | 141 | 33,514 | 993 | 664,050 | 1,134 | 697,564 | 616 |
| 1901 | 101 | 28,433 | 1,082 | 688,290 | 1,183 | 716,723 | 633 |

*Places of departure.*

| Country. | Sailing vessels. | | Steamers. | | Total. | |
|---|---|---|---|---|---|---|
| | Number. | Tonnage. | Number. | Tonnage. | Number. | Tonnage. |
| England | 50 | 6,428 | 672 | 398,508 | 722 | 404,936 |
| Russia | 4 | 1,918 | 164 | 156,306 | 168 | 158,224 |
| Sweden and Norway | 21 | 5,703 | 71 | 48,101 | 92 | 53,804 |
| North America | | | 24 | 34,694 | 24 | 34,694 |
| Germany | | 130 | 21 | 12,108 | 22 | 12,238 |
| South America | 12 | 11,390 | | | 12 | 11,390 |
| Holland | | | 19 | 10,811 | 19 | 10,811 |
| Portugal | | | 10 | 8,564 | 10 | 8,564 |
| Belgium | 4 | 556 | 29 | 7,643 | 33 | 8,199 |
| France | 7 | 1,128 | 16 | 5,901 | 23 | 7,029 |
| Algeria | | | 4 | 3,576 | 4 | 3,576 |
| Roumania | | | 1 | 1,294 | 1 | 1,294 |
| Africa | 2 | 1,251 | | | 2 | 1,251 |
| Spain | | | 4 | 788 | 1 | 788 |
| Total | 101 | 28,433 | 1,082 | 688,290 | 1,183 | 716,723 |

*Places of destination.*

| Country. | Sailing vessels. | | Steamers. | | Total. | |
|---|---|---|---|---|---|---|
| | Number. | Tonnage. | Number. | Tonnage. | Number. | Tonnage. |
| England | 69 | 15,265 | 924 | 608,828 | 998 | 624,008 |
| Belgium | 4 | 3,230 | 34 | 43,749 | 58 | 46,979 |
| Germany | 3 | 1,901 | 21 | 12,636 | 24 | 14,537 |
| Russia | 8 | 2,163 | 8 | 6,436 | 16 | 8,599 |
| Sweden and Norway | 11 | 3,376 | 4 | 2,217 | 15 | 5,593 |
| Holland | 2 | 172 | 9 | 5,263 | 11 | 5,435 |
| Denmark | | | 4 | 4,305 | 4 | 4,305 |
| France | 1 | 70 | 6 | 3,129 | 7 | 3,199 |
| North America | | | 2 | 2,837 | 2 | 2,837 |
| Total | 98 | 26,177 | 1,082 | 689,400 | 1,180 | 715,577 |

*Cargo of vessels departing.*

| Merchandise. | Sailing vessels. | | Steamers. | | Total. | |
|---|---|---|---|---|---|---|
| | Number. | Tonnage. | Number. | Tonnage. | Number. | Tonnage. |
| Sundry merchandise | | | 578 | 357,227 | 578 | 357,227 |
| Ballast | 36 | 15,956 | 353 | 288,068 | 389 | 304,024 |
| Potatoes | 8 | 1,545 | 48 | 19,360 | 56 | 20,905 |
| Phospha.tes | 31 | 4,986 | 28 | 12,479 | 59 | 17,465 |
| Cement | 19 | 2,709 | 9 | 2,815 | 28 | 5,524 |
| Sugar | | | 7 | 5,081 | 7 | 5,081 |
| Macadarn | | | 6 | 3,180 | 6 | 3,180 |
| Chalk | 1 | 136 | 2 | 733 | 3 | 869 |
| Briquet | | | 1 | 457 | 1 | 457 |
| Total | 98 | 26,177 | 1,082 | 689,400 | 1,180 | 715,577 |

During the year 1901 68 horses were exported from the port of Ghent.

*Arrivals at the docks of Avant Port of boats which have paid quay duties to the city.*

| Year. | Boats. | Tonnage | Year. | Boats. | Tonnage |
|---|---|---|---|---|---|
| 1880 | 2,312 | 221,441 | 1891 | 4,391 | 490,806 |
| 1881 | 2,080 | 194,864 | 1892 | 3,804 | 465,070 |
| 1882 | 2,010 | 179,972 | 1893 | 3,028 | 411,916 |
| 1883 | 2,422 | 201,342 | 1894 | 3,192 | 434,240 |
| 1884 | 2,390 | 231,330 | 1895 | 3,082 | 422,224 |
| 1885 | 2,778 | 265,055 | 1896 | 3,450 | 452,651 |
| 1886 | 2,808 | 288,109 | 1897 | 4,441 | 497,476 |
| 1887 | 3,486 | 370,246 | 1898 | 4,752 | 576,668 |
| 1888 | 3,275 | 396,469 | 1899 | 4,355 | 604,624 |
| 1889 | 3,642 | 418,496 | 1900 | 4,480 | 650,182 |
| 1890 | 4,426 | 508,182 | 1901 | 3,994 | 622,980 |

## MARITIME MOVEMENT OF BELGIAN PORTS DURING 1900.

*Arrivals and departures at the city by inland water courses.*

| Water course. | Arrivals. | | Departures. | |
|---|---|---|---|---|
| | Number. | Tonnage. | Number. | Tonnage. |
| Bas Escaut (Lower Scheldt) | 5,500 | 798,789 | 2,881 | 432,050 |
| Haut Escaut (Upper Scheldt) | 2,749 | 564,522 | 1,180 | 155,520 |
| Bruges Canal | 2,582 | 288,012 | 4,942 | 686,652 |
| Lys | 58 | 1,894 | 100 | 10,554 |
| Total | 10,889 | 1,648,217 | 9,103 | 1,284,776 |

*Statistics of merchandise imported and exported by the canal of Terneuzen.*

| Merchandise. | Im- ported. | Ex- ported. | Merchandise. | Im- ported. | Ex- ported. |
|---|---|---|---|---|---|
| | *Number.* | *Number.* | | *Tons.* | *Tons.* |
| Horses | 3,362 | 61 | Oil, cakes | 7,363 | |
| Other animals | 51 | 12,428 | Ore, iron | 14,710 | |
| | | | Potatoes | 222 | 63,909 |
| | *Tons.* | *Tons.* | Pepper | 65 | 17 |
| Apples | 11 | 8,562 | Plaster | 1 | 165 |
| Ammonia sulphates | 1,496 | | Porcelain, earth | 7,699 | |
| Biscuits | 29 | 46 | Paper stock and rags | 5,720 | 11,132 |
| Barley | 5,194 | | Phosphates | 25,365 | 32,707 |
| Baryta, sulphate of | | 2,813 | Petroleum | 9,873 | 230 |
| Coffee | 121 | | Plants | 22 | 922 |
| Coal | 244,659 | 6,066 | Rubber: | | |
| Cheese | 1,755 | | Raw | 64 | |
| Cordage | 84 | 175 | Manufactured | 4 | 211 |
| Chicory root | | 2,795 | Rice | 213 | 7 |
| Currants | 188 | 8 | Rabbit skins and furs | 2 | 141 |
| Cotton: | | | Raw animal materials, | | |
| Raw | 13,444 | 96 | miscellaneous | 87 | 104 |
| Waste | 860 | 85 | Resinous and bituminous, | | |
| Cement | 3 | 76,662 | substances | 759 | |
| Chalk | | 435 | Starch | 58 | 968 |
| Chemical productions, mis- | | | Salt: | | |
| cellaneous | 94 | 848 | Raw | 3,896 | 595 |
| Cotton goods | 797 | 1,762 | Refined | 2,616 | 505 |
| Dross | 7,185 | 54,165 | Sand washed | | 2,099 |
| Dyes and colors | 810 | 1,951 | Skins: | | |
| Eggs | | 1,272 | Raw | 1,669 | 763 |
| Earthenware | 1,008 | 3,799 | Manufactured | 7 | 256 |
| Furniture | 115 | 109 | Tanned | 106 | 180 |
| Flour | 318 | 19 | Stones | 15 | |
| Fish: | | | Soda: | | |
| Salted | 632 | 8 | Carbonate of | 529 | 21 |
| Dried | 222 | | Sulphate of | 2,369 | 4,764 |
| Flax: | | | Straw, etc | 55 | 554 |
| Raw | 21,629 | 12,500 | Sugar: | | |
| Waste | 94 | 3,229 | Beet | 595 | 54,440 |
| Glue | 161 | 3 | Cane | 492 | |
| Guano | 4,674 | | Soap | 173 | 17 |
| Glass: | | | Sirups and molasses | 157 | |
| Window | 5 | 1,750 | Seed: | | |
| Miscellaneous | 62 | 796 | Flax | 1,982 | 917 |
| Hemp, raw | 1,274 | 8 | Colza | 67 | 10 |
| Haberdashery | 158 | 3,272 | Miscellaneous | 343 | 646 |
| Iron and steel, drawn | 16,186 | 17,840 | Tow | 2,856 | 2,691 |
| Iron and steel nails | 7 | 5,223 | Tobacco | 360 | 5 |
| Miscellaneous | 135 | 2,005 | Vegetable substances | 447 | 1,280 |
| Old | 560 | | Wood | 275,878 | 1,298 |
| Cast | 2,658 | 8,093 | Wool: | | |
| Jute, raw | 12,661 | 161 | Raw | 8,853 | 15 |
| Liquids, alcoholic | 26 | 31 | Waste | 308 | 1 |
| Linen goods | 115 | 1,637 | Woolen goods | 663 | 74 |
| Machinery | 12,063 | 708 | Yarns: | | |
| Matches | | 2,043 | Hemp | | 414 |
| Marble | 2 | 1,176 | Cotton | 2,515 | 558 |
| Nitrates | 14,836 | | Tow | 84 | 1,999 |
| Oats | 2,100 | | Jute | 237 | 202 |
| Onions | 90 | 6,266 | Wool | 300 | 8 |
| Oranges and lemons | 2,086 | | Flax | 1,240 | 6,560 |
| Oil: | | | Miscellaneous | 6,912 | 42,583 |
| Colza | 42 | 2,595 | | | |
| Linseed | 57 | 1,020 | Total | 758,869 | 466,632 |
| Miscellaneous | 185 | 1,542 | | | |

*Arrivals and departures by the canal of Terneuzen.*

| | Number of boats. | Tonnage. |
|---|---|---|
| Arrivals | 3,358 | 369,281 |
| Departures | 3,349 | 400,904 |

## SHIPPING OF PORT OF OSTEND.

*Places of departure.*

| Place of departure. | Cargo. | | Ballast. | | Total. | |
|---|---|---|---|---|---|---|
| | Number. | Tonnage. | Number. | Tonnage. | Number. | Tonnage. |
| England | 806 | 895,784 | 1 | 50 | 807 | 895,834 |
| Germany | 21 | 10,249 | | | 21 | 10,249 |
| Norway | 57 | 19,460 | | | 57 | 19,460 |
| Sweden | 15 | 8,025 | | | 15 | 8,025 |
| Russia | 20 | 13,466 | 1 | 615 | 21 | 14,081 |
| America | 24 | 29,421 | | | 24 | 29,421 |
| France | 8 | 669 | 1 | 148 | 9 | 817 |
| Holland | | | 1 | 98 | 1 | 98 |
| Total | 951 | 417,074 | 4 | 911 | 955 | 417,985 |

*Places of destination.*

| Country. | Cargo. | | Ballast. | | Total. | |
|---|---|---|---|---|---|---|
| | Number. | Tonnage. | Number. | Tonnage. | Number. | Tonnage. |
| England | 586 | 252,399 | 311 | 146,013 | 899 | 398,412 |
| Germany | | | 5 | 2,960 | 5 | 2,960 |
| Norway | | | 31 | 9,572 | 31 | 9,572 |
| France | 5 | 525 | 5 | 1,411 | 10 | 1,996 |
| Belgium | 2 | 1,695 | 13 | 6,434 | 15 | 8,129 |
| Total | 593 | 254,619 | 365 | 166,390 | 958 | 421,009 |

## SHIPPING OF THE PORT OF BRUGES.

*Arrivals and departures.*

| Flag. | Arrivals. | | | | Departures. | | | |
|---|---|---|---|---|---|---|---|---|
| | Cargo. | | Ballast. | | Cargo. | | Ballast. | |
| | Number. | Tonnage. | Number. | Tonnage. | Number. | Tonnage. | Number. | Tonnage. |
| German | 1 | 153 | | | 1 | 153 | | |
| Belgian | 2 | 390 | | | 1 | 195 | 1 | 195 |
| Danish | 1 | 246 | | | | | 1 | 246 |
| English | 105 | 28,143 | | | 48 | 10,092 | 55 | 17,692 |
| French | 6 | 403 | | | 4 | 289 | 2 | 114 |
| Norwegian | 11 | 2,569 | | | | | 11 | 2,569 |
| Total | 126 | 31,904 | | | 54 | 10,729 | 70 | 20,816 |

*Imports and exports.*

### IMPORTS.

| | Tons. |
|---|---|
| Barley | 605 |
| Herring | 1,650 |
| Coal | 44,529 |
| Chemical fertilizers | 101 |
| Porcelain earth | 1,099 |
| Miscellaneous | 112 |
| Total | 48,096 |

## EXPORTS.

|  | Tons. |
|---|---:|
| Cement | 814 |
| Lime | 95 |
| Potatoes | 85 |
| Macadam | 7,517 |
| Chemical fertilizers | 1,390 |
| Chicory root | 187 |
| Straw | 21 |
| Miscellaneous | 94 |
| Total | 10,203 |

FRANK R. MOWRER, *Consul.*

GHENT, *September 27, 1902.*

## LIEGE.

The business and industrial interests of this consular district experienced during 1901 one of the dullest years for a decade. Many of the factories were working on half time and at reduced wages—which at the best are poor—and stocks and bonds declined sharply.

Prices of iron and steel fell sensibly, but the price of coal increased, owing to the strong coal combine that was then in existence, but has since gone to pieces in this city.

Crops were generally good, which relieved matters much, but taking everything into consideration, it was a very bad year.

### EXPORTS TO THE UNITED STATES.

The total value of exports to the United States from this consulate shows a marked increase, as indicated in the following table giving the declared exports for the fiscal years ended June 30, 1901 and 1902:

| Articles. | 1901. | 1902. | Increase. | Decrease. |
|---|---:|---:|---:|---:|
| Ammunition |  | $198.22 | $198.22 |  |
| Arsenic | $26,588.97 | 34,508.41 | 7,919.44 |  |
| Black salt |  | 2,068.01 | 2,068.01 |  |
| Card clothing | 1,140.15 | 2,444.62 | 1,304.02 |  |
| Cement | 3,702.60 | 8,564.80 | 4,862.20 |  |
| Clothing | 100.00 |  |  | $100.00 |
| Copper ingots |  | 4,652.26 | 4,652.26 |  |
| Electrical supplies | 112.10 |  |  | 112.10 |
| Degras |  | 7,618.99 | 7,618.99 |  |
| Firearms | 1,126,760.94 | 1,085,719.77 |  | 41,041.17 |
| Glassware | 140,255.09 | 167,755.80 | 27,500.71 |  |
| Gun barrels | 62,803.94 | 266,445.72 | 203,641.78 |  |
| Hones | 21,473.92 | 20,093.44 |  | 1,380.48 |
| Household goods |  | 13.40 | 18.40 |  |
| Lamp fixtures | 2,799.76 | 3,314.65 | 514.91 |  |
| Leather goods |  | 92.64 | 92.64 |  |
| Machinery | 15,238.80 | 11,072.02 |  | 4,166.78 |
| Old brass | 233.90 |  |  | 233.90 |
| Paper | 554.78 | 1,170.23 | 615.45 |  |
| Pictures |  | 38.60 | 38.60 |  |
| Potatoes |  | 2,131.76 | 2,131.76 |  |
| Returned American goods | 434.72 | 141.91 |  | 292.80 |
| Safety fuse |  | 8,630.27 | 8,630.27 |  |
| Salted sheepskins | 22,024.89 | 61,371.32 | 39,346.43 |  |
| Steel bars and angles |  | 25,880.63 | 25,880.63 |  |
| Steel rails |  | 45,663.21 | 45,663.21 |  |
| Steel wire | 391.30 | 1,938.47 | 1,547.17 |  |
| Straw goods | 7,442.70 | 1,085.50 |  | 6,357.41 |
| Sugar | 4,693.19 | 4,877.39 | 184.20 |  |
| Sundries |  | 54.90 | 54.90 |  |
| Superphosphates | 40,949.59 | 68,095.89 | 27,146.30 |  |
| Wool | 13.25 |  |  | 13.25 |
| Woolen goods | 155,418.24 | 229,444.17 | 74,025.93 |  |
| Zinc dust | 62,436.82 | 45,511.01 |  | 16,925.81 |
| Zinc sheets | 482.63 | 673.64 | 171.01 |  |
| Total | 1,696,212.19 | 2,111,271.65 |  |  |

As will be noted, there was a general increase amounting to $415,059.46, gun barrels being in the lead, with $203,641.78, steel products with $73,091.01, and woolen goods with $74,025.93.

The outlook indicates a much heavier export for the year ending June 30, 1903, especially along the line of steel rails and structural shapes. These two items showed a gain for the quarter ended September 30, 1902, of $100,242.35 over the same period of last year, and the indications are that for the quarter ended December 31, 1902, this will be raised to more than $250,000.

## IRON AND STEEL INDUSTRY.

The iron and steel industry of this consular district did a very fair business in 1901. During the year, 837,047 tons of iron ore were consumed by the furnaces, against 1,072,937 tons in 1900, that being the high-water mark for this district.

The following table shows the source of supply of iron ore for the years 1900 and 1901:

| Countries. | 1900. | 1901. | Countries. | 1900. | 1901. |
|---|---|---|---|---|---|
| | Tons. | Tons. | | Tons. | Tons. |
| Belgium | 86,954 | 82,874 | India | | 8,834 |
| Brazil | | 742 | Norway and Sweden | 56,784 | 58,131 |
| France and Algeria | 6,109 | 7,380 | Spain | 316,143 | 262,600 |
| Germany | 101,196 | 91,498 | Various | 41,103 | 45,080 |
| Grand Duchy of Luxemburg | 482,639 | 329,596 | Total | 1,072,937 | 837,047 |
| Greece | 24,009 | 1,165 | | | |

The value of pig iron fell from 92.65 francs (or $17.88) in 1900 to 65.13 francs (or $12.57) per ton in 1901, and steel billets from 116.97 francs (or $22.57) to 93.62 francs (or $18.07) per ton during the same time.

Since the first of the year 1902, business has been getting better, and now the mills are running on about full time, with orders coming in satisfactorily. The future promises well and prices are better, if not what they should be.

The increased demand for steel rails and structural shapes from the United States and Mexico has done much to improve business here. One order for 50,000 tons of steel rails for Mexico, and one of 27,000 tons and another of 50,000 tons from the United States, together with many smaller orders for rails and structural steel, have put the local industry on its feet.

## ZINC INDUSTRY.

This is one of the zinc industrial centers of the world, having had in operation during the year 1901, furnaces to the number of 483, with an average of 31,077 crucibles, consuming 285,157 tons of ore, of which Belgium produced only 6,870 tons. The product of the zinc works of this district was valued at 48,154,850 francs, or $9,293,886.05.

The following table shows the source of supply of the zinc ore consumed in this district during the year 1901:

| Countries. | 1900. | 1901. | Countries. | 1900. | 1901. |
|---|---|---|---|---|---|
| | Tons. | Tons. | | Tons. | Tons. |
| Italy and Sardinia | 65,177 | 78,908 | Greece | 9,693 | 3,557 |
| France | 33,186 | 22,556 | Australia | 21,999 | 15,098 |
| Sweden and Norway | 27,807 | 23,178 | England | 4,995 | 14,015 |
| Belgium | 10,178 | 6,870 | America | 21,978 | 28,458 |
| Germany | 14,912 | 17,348 | Other countries | 5,151 | 1,877 |
| Spain and Portugal | 45,517 | 50,514 | | | |
| Algeria and Tunis | 28,806 | 29,658 | Total | 279,221 | 285,157 |

This makes a fine showing for America, and compared with 1899, it is still better, for in that year only 9,385 tons were from that source. The outlook for 1902 is still brighter for the United States.

### COAL.

In the Liege coal basin, there were 71 coal shafts in operation during 1901, giving employment to 34,204 persons of all ages, at an average yearly wage of 1,253 francs, or $241.83, and producing 5,784,134 tons of all grades, valued at the mines at 15.58 francs or $3.01 per ton, against a production of 6,190,892 tons for 1900, valued at the mines at 17.36 francs or $3.28 per ton.

During 1901, according to official returns, there were mined in the world 762,702,000 tons of all kinds and grades of coal. Following are the countries producing the largest quantities during that time, with the number of tons mined and the average price per ton at the mines:

| Countries. | Tons mined. | Cost per ton at mine. |
|---|---|---|
| United States | 264,770,000 | $1.37 |
| England | 228,784,000 | 2.68 |
| Germany | 149,551,000 | 2.91 |
| Austria-Hungary | 39,704,000 | 1.64 |
| France | 33,400,000 | 3.18 |
| Belgium | 23,463,000 | 3.48 |
| Russia | 16,138,000 | 1.70 |

The local production for the first eight months of 1902 shows a slight increase, as well as a rise in price.

From the year 1831 to 1901, there were mined in Belgium 819,600,000 tons of coal, of which the Liege basin produced about 250,000,000 tons.

The new coal field lately discovered in the Province of Luxembourg, north of Liege, is much more extensive than was thought at first. It covers many square miles, and is one of the richest fields ever found on the Continent, the coal being of a fine quality. Soundings have been extensively made, and great things are promised for the future. At one point, at a depth of 1,485 feet, a vein of high-grade coal 16.5 feet thick has been discovered.

It is estimated this new field contains much more coal than the Liege basin, but its working will be more difficult and expensive than that of the other basins in Belgium, because of the greater depth and the presence of more water. It is thought, however, that this will be more than overcome by the thickness of the veins. Extensive preparations are being made to open up the field, and steps are being taken to have the Government provide the necessary canal and railway facilities.

This will offer a fine opportunity for the installation of up-to-date American coal-mining machinery, and now is the time to offer it.

### FIREARMS.

The firearms industry of Liege enjoyed a very good year during 1901, considering the general business depression. There was a constant increase in the number of machine-made guns shipped to the United States, and a reduction in price. There was also a great increase in the number of gun barrels in the rough shipped to the United States, very largely of what is known as the Damascus and Boston twist. These are successfully manufactured only in this consular district.

The Government proving station at Liege made 2,322,621 tests of firearms during 1901, which was the largest number ever made in one year in this city.

### WOOLEN INDUSTRY.

The woolen industry of this consular district, which is almost entirely confined to Verviers and its suburbs, gives employment to several thousand operators.

The industry in 1901 fell a little short of what it was in 1900, but since the beginning of 1902 it has been improving. The prospects for the future seem brighter, but it will be some time before it reaches the high-water mark of 1896 and 1897, when the United States was one of the heavy buyers. The business with the United States has shown quite a gain in 1902, but it is only a small fraction of what it was in 1897.

### SLAUGHTERHOUSE.

There were slaughtered during 1901, at the city slaughterhouse of Liege, 27,583 cattle, 41,578 sheep and goats, 32,069 hogs, and 1,211 horses, of which 460 were condemned by the inspection force as not fit for food. This is more than were ever killed here in a previous year. Horse meat is sold in a shop by itself. There is a very heavy penalty for offering it for sale in a shop where any other meat is sold.

### SCHOOL-CHILDREN'S SAVINGS BANK.

Of the 5,559 boys in the public schools in this city, 3,793 have deposited in the savings bank 85,913.23 francs, or $16,581.25; and of the 4,658 girls, 3,631 have deposited 81,077.34 francs, or $15,647.93. This is comparatively a new feature of the work, and it is taking well. It is hoped it will have a good effect on the rising generation.

### PUBLIC PAWN SHOP.

The city does the pawn-brokerage business in Liege, and it is not a small affair. During the year 1901, there were 132,553 articles pawned, on which the loans amounted to 175,281 francs, or $226,829.23; of these, 78,268 were for less than 4 francs, or 77 cents, and only 36 were for more than 800 francs, or $154.40. Of the whole number of articles pawned, 114,856 were redeemed for 981,214 francs, or $189,374.30, and 8,560 were sold for 78,175 francs, or $15,087.78.

## RIVERS AND CANALS.

The rivers and canals of Belgium play an important part in the transportation problem. The system of canals and slack-water river navigation is very complete, but extensive improvements are under consideration that will open the Antwerp-Liege Canal and the slack-water navigation of the Meuse River for all boats that now navigate the Rhine and its tributaries. The cost of these improvements is estimated at $10,300,000, and several years will be consumed in the work. When completed, boats of 800 and 900 tons can navigate these waterways in place of boats of only 350 tons, as at present.

## CROPS FOR 1902.

Crops in this consular district for the season of 1902 were in the main much above the average. Wheat was exceptionally fine, but potatoes were poor, owing to the rains in August and September, and the prices are higher than for several years. Last year, potatoes were quite extensively exported, but this year it will be necessary to import in order to supply the demand.

## UNIVERSAL EXPOSITION AT LIEGE.

The date for holding the Universal Exposition of Liege has been definitely settled for 1905, and the work of clearing and leveling the grounds for the buildings has been begun. This will require several months, since it necessitates the changing of the course of the Ourthe River for about 1 mile. Work has also been begun on a bridge over the Meuse River, which will connect the exposition grounds with the city proper.

A prize of 22,500 francs, or $4,342.50, has been offered to Belgian architects for plans for the three main exposition buildings, estimated to cost about $250,000.

This contest is to close January 1, 1903, and shortly thereafter bids will be solicited for the construction of the buildings, on which work can not be begun before May 1, 1904. They must be completed on or before October 1, 1904.

## AMERICAN GOODS IN BELGIUM.

The sale of American goods is increasing in this consular district. The consulate is often visited by parties soliciting addresses of reliable producers and manufacturers in the United States, in order that application may be made for goods direct from the producer, thus saving several commissions and putting the buyer in a position to compete with the European-made goods. The closer the American producer can get to the consumer the better. As it is now, quite a large proportion of the United States goods consumed in Belgium comes through England. The general agent in London gets a good commission, and he has a general agent for Belgium, and he in turn has subagents, all of whom must be paid, and usually, well.

The demand for machinery is on the increase, and especially is this true of farm machinery. One day last August, three wagon loads of American harvesting machinery passed the consulate, and a few days later, two more loads passed. Several persons who are getting ready for next season's trade have asked me for addresses of American manufacturers of farm machinery.

American exporters should join in opening salesrooms in the larger cities of Europe, and push business here as they do at home. If this were done, our exports could be doubled in three or four years.

CONDITIONS IN 1902.

Business and industrial conditions were very bad at the beginning of the year 1902, but they have been gradually getting better, until at this writing they are very greatly improved, and most of the industries are working on full time and are well supplied with orders. This is especially true of the steel mills.

For the first eight months of 1902, the imports amounted to $298,-961,400, an increase of $19,962,800 over the same period of 1901; and the exports to $234,360,400, a gain of $10,842,600.

The future promises well, and stocks and bonds are firmer. Confidence has been restored, and it is easier to finance undertakings.

ALFRED A. WINSLOW, Consul.

LIEGE, October 21, 1902.

---

# DENMARK.

In addition to my partial report on Danish trade for the year 1901 (published in Advance Sheets of Consular Reports, No. 1393, of July 16, 1902),[a] I would say that 1901 was a difficult year for trade in most parts of Europe. An industrial crisis was prevailing in Germany; and Great Britain was under the strain of the Boer war and suffering from the imposition of new taxes, a decreased volume of business, and an export duty of a shilling (24 cents) per ton on coal.

In the trade of Denmark, there was no advance. Money lenders were careful and scrutinizing. There was no increase in production; at times, it threatened to come to a standstill. The result in the lessened demand for labor was felt by the whole country. The harvest was disappointing as regards grain and hay, but in the southern portion, there was a good yield of clover, which led to a diminished import of feed stuffs (oil cake and Indian corn). It is estimated that the purchases of these decreased by about 2,000,000 kroner ($536,000).

The prices of agricultural products, especially of animal products, ruled high. Freighting on the longer routes was maintained at good prices.

The values of imports were:

| Articles. | Swedish currency. | U. S. currency. |
|---|---|---|
| MATERIALS USED IN PRODUCTION. | Million kroner. | |
| Fodder and seed | 13.8 | $3,698,400 |
| Textiles | 8.3 | 884,400 |
| Hair, feathers, skins, etc | 2.3 | 616,400 |
| Tallow, coal tar, oil, etc | 2.2 | 589,600 |
| Metals | 4.9 | 1,313,200 |
| Coal | 11.1 | 2,974,800 |
| LUXURIES AND NECESSARIES. | | |
| Animal food products | 14.7 | 3,939,600 |
| Field and garden products | 9.2 | 2,465,600 |
| Groceries | 5.4 | 1,447,200 |
| Wines and spirits | .6 | 160,800 |
| INDUSTRIAL PRODUCTS. | | |
| Draperies | 4.5 | 1,206,000 |
| Manufactures of hair and feathers | 1.6 | 428,800 |
| Manufactures of tallow and oil | .6 | 160,800 |
| Paper | .2 | 53,600 |
| Mineral products | .3 | 80,400 |

[a] Also in Consular Reports No. 264, September, 1902.

## CEREAL TRADE.

*Imports of cereals, in quantities and value.*

| Articles. | Total imports, 1901. | Home use. | | | | | |
|---|---|---|---|---|---|---|---|
| | | 1901. | 1900. | 1901 compared with 1900. | 1901. | 1900. | 1901 compared with 1900. |
| | *Mill. lbs.* | *Mill. lbs.* | *Mill. lbs.* | *Mill. lbs.* | | | |
| Barley .......... | 75.98 | 62.79 | 19.05 | + 43.64 | $758,440 | $238,520 | + $515,920 |
| Maize .......... | 680.70 | 601.00 | 815.83 | −214.83 | 15,005,320 | 8,768,980 | +6,236,380 |
| Oats............ | 59.07 | 55.20 | 57.51 | − 2.31 | 779,880 | 771,340 | + 8,040 |
| Bran .......... | 109.15 | 88.27 | 108.17 | − 19.95 | 959,440 | 1,208,680 | − 249,240 |
| Oil cake........ | 495.68 | 475.48 | 408.08 | + 72.40 | 6,683,920 | 5,778,080 | + 905,840 |
| Clover, grass, and garden seed.......... | 17.81 | 14.26 | 16.89 | − 2.63 | 1,307,840 | 1,583,880 | − 276,040 |
| Fertilizers: Natural..... | 2.86 | 2.86 | 10.43 | − 8.07 | } 1,262,280 | 970,160 | + 292,120 |
| Artificial.... | 161.88 | 158.60 | 118.94 | + 39.66 | | | |

*Imports and exports of cereals. by years.*

[Million pounds.]

| Articles. | 1899. | 1900. | 1901. |
|---|---|---|---|
| **IMPORTS.** | | | |
| Wheat ............ | 150 | 122.3 | 276 |
| Rye .............. | 179.7 | 186.9 | 199.7 |
| Barley ........... | 43.2 | 20.7 | 76 |
| Oats.............. | 27.4 | 59.4 | 59.1 |
| Maize ............ | 1,023.8 | 871.7 | 620.7 |
| Other kinds....... | 21.5 | 21.7 | 16.9 |
| Total........ | 1,455.6 | 1,282.7 | 1,248.4 |
| **EXPORTS.** | | | |
| Wheat ............ | 29 | 46 | 77.7 |
| Rye .............. | 13.2 | 7.6 | 8.2 |
| Barley ........... | 114.6 | 84.5 | 98.4 |
| Oats.............. | 4.2 | 6.9 | 3.9 |
| Maize ............ | 105.4 | 44.5 | 28.5 |
| Other kinds....... | 7.7 | 7.7 | 5.4 |
| Total........ | 274.1 | 197.2 | 217.2 |

### DETAILS OF EXPORTS.

*Butter.*—The total export of butter from Denmark in 1901 was 170 million pounds against 153 million in 1900. Of this, 162 millions went to England.

The export of butter in tins to the West Indian Islands and Brazil amounted to 4.2 million pounds, against 3.6 million in 1900. Prices for the year ruled low.

*Margarine.*—The consumption of margarine, from April, 1900, to April, 1901, was 41.5 million pounds against 36.6 million in the former year. Of this, 37 million were made in Denmark. Prices ruled higher.

*Eggs.*—An export of 31½ million dozen made 1901 a record year.

### DETAILS OF IMPORTS.

*Coal oil.*—The sales in 1901 were: American, 1,131,600 cwt.; Russian, 40,128.

*Coal.*—Three cargoes of American coal were delivered at Copenhagen during the year.

*Furniture.*—The trade in American furniture is steady. It has been impeded in the past by the caprice of American manufacturers, whose custom it was to change styles every six months. Now, this takes place once a year; but for the European trade, the custom is all wrong. When a style is approved by European buyers, no change should be made, and when a trade is once established, it should not be interfered with.

*Zinc.*—The trade in American zinc progresses well. Although the previous year was a good one, the trade in 1901 more than doubled.

*Corn.*—The falling off in the import of Indian corn, noted above, is of course accounted for by the lessened crop in the United States and the consequent high prices.

J. C. FREEMAN, *Consul.*

COPENHAGEN, *September 8, 1902.*

---

## DANISH TRADE IN 1902.

I submit the following report on Danish commerce and industries for the six months ended June 30, 1902:

The chief exports of Denmark, in order of quantities, are butter, pork, eggs, beef, horses, hides, and skins. None of these except the last can be exported to the United States, as the latter is itself a large exporter of the same products.

The approximate figures of the above exports for the six months ended June 30, 1902, are:

| | | |
|---|---|---:|
| Butter | tons.. | 44,000 |

(Of which 43,000 went to England. Of this, 35,000 was Danish product, the rest being principally imported from Russia and then exported.)

| | | |
|---|---|---:|
| Pork and bacon | tons.. | 33,000 |

(Of which 32,200 went to England. Of this 31,500 was Danish product.)

| | | |
|---|---|---:|
| Eggs | dozen.. | 6,000,000 |

(Almost all Danish product.)

| | | |
|---|---|---:|
| Beef | tons.. | 13,000 |
| Horses | head.. | 13,200 |
| Cattle | do... | 26,500 |

The chief imports include:

| | Tons. |
|---|---:|
| Bacon | 2,800 |
| Lard | 6,900 |
| Butter | 8,500 |
| Margarine | 4,000 |
| Unground cereals | 340,000 |
| Maize | 200,000 |
| Rye | 32,000 |
| Wheat | 37,000 |
| Barley | 88,000 |

### CEREALS.

Cereals exported amounted to only 44,000 tons; one-fourth of this was of Danish production. The imports of ground cereals were 25,000 tons; of this, wheat flour represented 15,000 tons. Ground cereals exported amounted to 2,700 tons, principally of Danish production (rye and barley flour).

The quantity of food stuffs imported into Denmark is in direct proportion to the results of the Danish harvests. If the grain is of excellent quality, one would suppose that the Danes would use it and would not be dependent on foreign countries for that year.   But the reverse is the case.   If the quality is good, the grain is sent to market and with the proceeds the farmers buy maize, bran, oil cake, etc., for their stock.

The season this year is very backward, and at the date of this writing (September 9) it is too early to say whether the Danish grain will be marketable and the farmers in a position to buy American food stuffs.

An element in the cereal trade of America and Denmark is, of course, the state of the harvests of other countries (England and Holland).   If the demand for American grain is strong there, the price may become too high for sales to Denmark.

### RUSSIAN MAIZE.

A feature in the trade of the past six months has been the unprecedented quantity of maize shipped to northern Europe from the Black Sea regions.   Southern Russia has shown herself a formidable competitor with America in supplying Europe with maize.   The small crop of maize in our country in 1901 of course led to this.   Russia showed herself equal to all demands.

### COTTON-SEED PRODUCTS.

Second in amount (next after maize) in American exports to Denmark are cotton-seed products.   The fall trade is slow, only about one-third of the usual orders having so far been placed.   The Danes are waiting to learn the condition of the American crop, and also to decide if they themselves will have funds to buy.

During a part of the year just closed, freights on cotton-seed cake from New Orleans to Copenhagen fell from 27 shillings ($6.57) per ton to 9½ shillings ($2.31), but the importers did a larger business at the higher rate than at the lower.

The prospects of the cotton-seed trade are good.

### UNITED STATES GOODS.

There are three obstacles in the way of promoting the sale of American machinery in Europe at the present time—the slowness of our makers in filling foreign orders, the lower prices of European manufacturers, and the longer credits given by the latter.   I know of "hurry orders" placed with Pittsburg producers nine months ago which are as yet unfilled.   No doubt, this arises from the activity of the trade in the home market.   It is understood here that some American companies have orders which will occupy them for the next four years.

Prices, particularly of German producers, range much lower than American rates.   Dealers in United States machinery find themselves obliged to carry German manufactures as a part of their stock, in order to reduce average selling prices.   They sell the German for the sake of their cheapness and the American for quality.

Shipments from America must be paid for by the Danish buyer before the goods leave New York.   The sending of the funds to New York and of the goods to Denmark takes about a month and a half.   The

Danish importer has to give his customers at least three months' credit. Some time will naturally elapse before his sales take place. Thus, he is out of the use of his money at least six months.

J. C. FREEMAN. *Consul.*

COPENHAGEN, *September 9, 1902.*

---

## FRANCE.

### REPORT FROM CONSULATE-GENERAL AT PARIS. ·

The trade of France for 1901 shows a slight increase in both imports and exports over the preceding year, which was a bad one, but the figures are lower than they were in 1899. It is satisfactory to note, however, that the returns for the first nine months of the current year show a very marked improvement. The figures for 1901 and 1900 were:

*Imports.*

| Class. | Value in 1901. | | Value in 1900. | |
|---|---|---|---|---|
| | Francs. | U. S. currency. | Francs. | U. S. currency. |
| Articles of food | 805,551,000 | $154,699,843 | 819,240,000 | $158,113,320 |
| Raw materials | 3,124,299,000 | 602,989,707 | 3,085,251,000 | 585,808,443 |
| Manufactured articles | 788,698,000 | 152,218,214 | 843,311,300 | 162,759,023 |
| Total | 4,714,548,000 | 909,907,714 | 4,697,802,000 | 906,675,786 |

Increase in 1901, 16,746,000 francs ($3,231,978).

Articles of food decreased by $3,413,977 and manufactured articles by $10,540,309, but this is more than balanced by the increase in raw materials, which was $17,186,964.

*Exports.*

| Class. | Value in 1901. | | Value in 1900. | |
|---|---|---|---|---|
| | Francs. | U. S. currency. | Francs. | U. S. currency. |
| Articles of food | 778,247,000 | $148,043,671 | 759,979,000 | $146,675,947 |
| Raw materials | 1,091,041,000 | 210,570,913 | 1,093,966,000 | 211,135,438 |
| Manufactured articles | 2,092,716,000 | 398,104,188 | 2,089,889,000 | 398,592,427 |
| Goods sent by parcels post (not included under above headings) | 284,161,000 | 45,196,173 | 215,415,000 | 41,575,095 |
| Total | 4,166,165,000 | 804,089,845 | 4,108,699,000 | 792,978,907 |

Increase, 57,466,000 francs, or $11,080,988.

It will be seen from the above figures that there has been an increase in all branches of exports, with the exception of raw materials, in which there was a comparatively small decrease, to the extent of $764,525. There is a very noticeable gain in the quantity of goods carried by parcels post, which no doubt is attributable to the fact that the rate for small parcels consigned to some foreign countries, notably England, has been lowered 25 per cent.

## TRADE OF FRANCE IN 1902.

The trade of France for the nine months ended September 30, 1902, as compared with the same period in the previous year, shows a considerable increase in exports and a very small increase in imports, as will be seen from the following tabulated statements:

*Imports.*

| Class. | Value in 1902. | | Value in 1901. | |
|---|---|---|---|---|
| | Francs. | U. S. currency. | Francs. | U. S. currency. |
| Articles of food | 565,783,000 | $109,196,119 | 559,799,000 | $108,041,207 |
| Raw materials | 2,130,707,000 | 411,226,351 | 2,134,393,000 | 411,937,849 |
| Manufactured articles | 572,731,000 | 110,537,063 | 574,523,000 | 110,882,939 |

It will be noticed that the importation of articles of food has increased by 5,984,000 francs ($1,154,912), which more than balances the decrease in raw materials (3,686,000 francs, or $711,498) and in manufactured articles (1,792,000 francs, or $345,856). Exactly the reverse will be found in the table of exports, food stuffs having diminished, while raw materials and manufactured articles have largely increased:

*Exports.*

| Class. | Value in 1902. | | Value in 1901. | |
|---|---|---|---|---|
| | Francs. | U. S. currency. | Francs. | U. S. currency. |
| Articles of food | 500,132,000 | $96,520,205 | 526,279,000 | $101,571,847 |
| Raw materials | 857,881,000 | 165,571,033 | 744,161,000 | 143,623,073 |
| Manufactured articles | 1,568,505,000 | 302,721,465 | 1,512,213,000 | 291,857,109 |

The exportation of articles of food has therefore decreased by $5,051,582, while that of raw materials has increased by $21,947,960, and of manufactured articles by $10,864,356. A sum of $33,473,829 was derived from the parcels post, showing an increase for the nine months of $1,438,815, as compared with 1901. The total increase in exports was 151,320,000 francs, equal to $29,204,760.

The countries from which France imported the most goods were:

| | |
|---|---|
| England | $128,802,796 |
| United States | 93,002,261 |
| Germany | 80,613,591 |
| Belgium | 74,540,846 |
| Argentine Republic | 69,240,294 |

The countries to which France principally exported were:

| | |
|---|---|
| England | $243,984,810 |
| Belgium | 115,128,553 |
| Germany | 89,028,198 |
| United States | 46,226,202 |
| Switzerland | 43,699,060 |

### FRENCH TRADE WITH THE UNITED STATES.

The total value of the goods imported into France from the United States during the first nine months of 1902 was $93,002,261, show-

ing a decrease, when compared with 1901, of $5,337,222. Exports to
the United States also decreased, the amount being $46,226,202, as
compared with $49,254,372 in 1901, or a falling off of $3,028,170.

On analyzing the returns, it is found that there has been an increase
in the imports from the United States in the following articles:

| Articles. | Total. | Increase. |
|---|---|---|
| Copper | $8,037,470 | $3,413,398 |
| Miscellaneous articles | 3,575,518 | 264,181 |
| Bran | 400,089 | 196,088 |
| Skins and raw hides | 434,688 | 176,981 |
| Oil cake | 445,611 | 138,381 |
| India rubber and gutta-percha | 827,521 | 92,254 |
| Heavy oil and petroleum residues | 547,155 | 67,938 |
| Coal | 149,961 | 20,265 |

There has also been a trifling increase of $16,000 in the importation
of cider apples, and of $5,600 in American tools, but both lines are
small at present. It should be noticed, moreover, that though the
importation of copper has increased by 50 per cent over last year's,
it is still inferior by nearly $1,000,000 to that of 1900.

The importations from the United States, in which there has been
the most serious falling off, are:

| Articles. | Total. | Decrease. |
|---|---|---|
| Cereals and flours | $554,108 | $4,861,800 |
| Cotton-seed oil | 1,690,487 | 1,280,555 |
| Tobacco | 8,307,827 | 987,581 |
| Fats (excluding fish oil) | 782,736 | 975,066 |
| Woods (ordinary) | 2,867,787 | 879,694 |
| Cotton in wool | 25,945,183 | 402,019 |
| Machinery | 4,180,959 | 354,927 |
| Canned meats | 597,528 | 298,746 |
| Millinery feathers | 157,874 | 239,809 |
| Agricultural seeds | 18,914 | 168,278 |

Unimportant diminutions may also be noted on whalebone, canned
lobster, dressed hides, coffee, rock oil, furniture, medicinal plants,
and chemical products.

Exports from France to United States diminished $254,374 during
the first nine months of this year, as compared with 1901, although
the following articles showed a considerable increase:

| Articles. | Total. | Increase. |
|---|---|---|
| Silks, silk embroideries, and ribbons | $8,515,546 | $1,660,765 |
| Cotton goods, embroideries, and ribbons | 4,190,802 | 1,274,958 |
| Millinery feathers | 1,322,436 | 341,224 |
| Wool in bulk | 345,470 | 208,440 |
| Furs of all kinds | 271,744 | 126,608 |
| Silks and silk wastes | 1,204,513 | 112,183 |
| Oils and essences | 777,404 | 66,199 |
| Perfumery | 142,820 | 18,528 |

On the other hand, there has been a considerable decrease in the exportation of the following articles:

| Articles. | Total. | Decrease. |
|---|---|---|
| Articles of dress | $505,660 | $433,272 |
| Artificial flowers | 1,299,253 | 439,461 |
| India rubber and gutta-percha (raw) | 211,914 | 410,511 |
| Skin or leather goods (not gloves) | 179,104 | 320,187 |
| Woolen cloths and trimmings | 2,481,980 | 307,256 |
| Gloves | 816,583 | 280,236 |
| Wine | 987,015 | 187,017 |
| Cream of tartar ....m | 899,380 | 182,576 |
| Millstones | 39,758 | 162,506 |
| Prepared skins | 332,346 | 154,979 |
| Fancy articles (fans, brushes, buttons, opera glasses, etc.) | 1,043,165 | 128,924 |
| Glycerin | 385,421 | 82,990 |

In some cases, these diminutions are ascribable to the ordinary fluctuations of commerce, but in others it seems evident that improved methods of American manufacture are rapidly destroying the foreign trade.

### THE BUDGET.

The minister of finance estimates that there will be a deficit of 207 million francs (nearly $40,000,000) in the budget for 1903. It is caused by diminished resources and increased expenses, except 41 million francs ($7,913,000), which will be lost by the lowering of the tax on sugar in conformity with the decision of the Brussels conference. All this deficit will be balanced by financial operations which affect only French interests, the sole exception being that a sum of 4 million francs ($772,000) is to be raised by increasing the price of Maryland tobacco. The contents of the ordinary packet have been reduced from 1⅔ to 1¼ ounces (from 50 grams to 40 grams), the price for the whole remaining the same. To what extent this will affect the importation of American tobacco it is as yet impossible to say, the change having only just come into operation.

### NAVIGATION.

The number of vessels entering French ports during the year 1901 was 25,508, of which 7,715 were French, and they brought 18,199,003 tons of goods. The tonnage exceeds that of 1899 by 1,111,000 tons, but is less than that of 1900 by 160,000 tons.

The number of vessels which cleared outward was:

| Nationality. | Vessels. | Tonnage. |
|---|---|---|
| French | 7,501 | 4,503,131 |
| Foreign | 13,152 | 8,622,599 |
| Total | 20,653 | 18,125,730 |

This shows an increase of 231,000 tons over the trade of 1900 and of 1,040,000 tons over 1899, though the number of vessels was slightly less than in either year.

### POSTAL RATES.

The only change of any importance that has been effected is the reduction in the price of the cards sent by pneumatic tube in Paris.

The fee was formerly 30 centimes (6 cents) for an open card and 50 centimes (10 cents) for a letter card. By a recent decree, the open card has been abolished and the postage of the closed-letter card reduced to 30 centimes (6 cents).

## RATE OF EXCHANGE.

The rate of exchange of the United States dollar during the year 1901 varied between 5 francs 20 centimes (September 18) and 5.15 francs (January, April, and November), the average rate for the whole year being 5.16⅝ francs. During the present year, it has fluctuated between 5.15 and 5.18 francs, the average for the nine months being 5.16¼ francs.

## PATENT LAWS.

The only changes in the patent laws are amendments regarding the specifications and drawings to be filed. There are to be no unnecessary repetitions in the specification, and the object of the invention must "be clearly stated in intelligible language." Several applications from American inventors have already been refused because this requirement was not complied with. A decree dated May 31, 1902, also stipulates that the specification shall not contain more than 500 lines of 50 letters each, nor must there be more than 10 sheets of drawings to each application. A second set of drawings, on bristol board, must accompany each application.

## LABOR LAWS.

A law was passed in March, 1900, that in all factories where women and children are employed along with men, the working hours should not exceed ten and one-half hours per day, exceptions being made in the case of small factories employing less than 20 hands or those handling perishable goods (fish, fruits, etc.), in which the time may be extended to twelve hours.

The law has given great dissatisfaction to employers, and last year there were 4,572 convictions for failure to comply with its regulations.

## FRENCH INVESTMENTS ABROAD.

From the reports of French consuls in various countries, it would appear that the total sum invested by French citizens abroad is 29,846,000,000 francs, equal to $5,760,278,000. Russia is the principal creditor, with nearly a quarter of the whole sum. Spain comes next with over a tenth, and Austria has nearly as much. French investments in the United States are estimated at 600 million francs ($119,-000,000). A great financial authority has, however, pointed out that the list is untrustworthy, all securities and shares having been returned at their nominal value, which often differs very widely from the price they would bring on the market.

## THE PARIS METROPOLITAN RAILROAD.

A large portion of the second branch of this railroad is now open, and several other lines, now in course of construction, will be opened in 1903. This rapid and convenient mode of transit is much appreciated by the public, and several lines of omnibuses and horse trams have already been suppressed.   The motive power is electricity, and much of the material is of American manufacture.

### AUTOMOBILES AND BICYCLES.

The value of the automobiles and bicycles exported last year was $4,098,526.   Eight years ago, it was only $850,323.

The automobiles and cycles imported into France were valued at $1,029,045, whereas in 1894 the sum reached $2,008,030.   French makers turn out excellent work at cheap rates, and many of their cars are purchased by foreign buyers.   It will be noticed that the exports have increased fivefold during the last seven years, while the imports are little more than half of what they then were.

### LICENSES FOR CARRYING ON BUSINESS.

In Paris, all trades people pay yearly a fixed sum, which varies according to the nature and extent of their business.   There are eight categories, and the sum payable ranges from 400 francs ($77.20) in the first class to 12 francs ($2.32) in the eighth class.   Certain professions—doctors, lawyers, architects, engineers, and a few others—are exempt from this tax.   In other parts of France, it varies according to the population of the town in which the business is established.   Bankers, stock brokers, etc., pay a fixed sum, plus a variable rate, according to the number of persons employed, and manufacturers according to the number of their workmen.

JOHN K. GOWDY,
*Consul-General.*

PARIS, October 28, 1902.

---

### BORDEAUX.

The commercial conditions of southwest France for the year 1902 show a lack of expansion, if not an actual decline, which is in remarkable contrast with the general spirit of the age.   The population hardly holds its own, though there is very slight emigration.   Agriculturally, there is little change in the character of production and practically none in the methods of culture.   Manufacturing seems at a standstill, while foreign commerce shows no marked increase.

These conditions are the natural result of many deplorable facts. Situated 70 miles from the sea, to which it has access only by the shallow and shifting channel of the Gironde, ships of but light draft, say 3,000 gross tonnage, can reach its wharves.   The result is that a steamer coming from the United States must lose three or four days, in comparison with Liverpool, Southampton, or even Antwerp and Hamburg.   On this account, it is impossible that any oceanic liners should make Bordeaux a port of call, like Cherbourg or Boulogne, and the great French lines, the Compagnie Generale Transatlantique and the Messageries Maritime, have ceased to maintain a regular service with this port, except that the former still runs a steamer once a month to the Antiles and the latter a supply line to its new terminal at La Pallice.   It is now about five years since the last passenger steamer left this port for the United States, and at the present time, there is not even a line of freight steamers plying between Bordeaux and any port of our country.   As a consequence, freight seeking the

United States from here must take the chance of a "tramp" going direct, or rely on transshipment in another port—Havre, Antwerp, Southampton, London, or Liverpool.

If shipped by Havre or Antwerp, goods may go either by rail or by a line of steamers which make the trip up the coast each week. These steamers connect with the French Line from Havre, and the Holland American Line and many tramps and sailing vessels from Antwerp. Many of the exports from southwest France to the Pacific coast of the United States and Hawaii are shipped via Antwerp.

There are two lines of steamers running from Bordeaux to English ports, where they connect with the great Atlantic lines. One of these is the General Steam Navigation Company. The boats run once a week to Southampton, where they connect with the American and Red Star lines from that port. Another is the Moss Line to Liverpool, also weekly, connecting with all the lines from that port to the United States. These are small boats (1,200 to 1,500 tons net) which carry passengers, but their accommodations are not of a kind to induce the traveler to take a three-day trip on the English Channel and the Bay of Biscay in addition to a week's ocean voyage. The result is that of the hundreds of thousands of American travelers who each year seek the Continent hardly one comes direct to Bordeaux. The port is losing the hold on American trade which it once had and might easily have retained. Bordeaux was the rival of Hamburg until the middle of the nineteenth century, when steam came to rule the sea.

### INTERNAL WATERWAYS.

There is at the present time a very decided sentiment throughout France in favor of extensive improvement of her internal waterways, some of which are expected to bring the products of the interior departments to this port. Rosy anticipations for the future prosperity of this city are based upon these improvements. The railroad system of southwest France, however, is very complete, reaching almost every little hamlet, and its service for both passengers and freight is very reasonable. Canals or improved riverways paralleling its lines may slightly reduce the cost of inland transport, but are not likely to so increase production as to have any considerable influence on the commercial prosperity of Bordeaux. The only hope that remains to her of recovering her former commercial prestige lies in providing a ship canal to the coast and establishing there a port which will invite ocean steamers of the largest tonnage to seek her wharves. American exporters should keep in mind the fact that the only means of cheap and direct shipment to this port is by "tramps" of moderate tonnage.

### A NEW SHIP CANAL.

A ship canal between the Atlantic and the Mediterranean has long been a favorite project of French statesmen, both as an economic and a strategic idea. Interest in this subject was revived by the action of the Parliament at its last session in instituting a special commission to report upon the practicability and desirability of such a work. The scheme necessarily embraces an available port on this coast, and would at once open to direct Atlantic trade and immensely stimulate the foreign commerce of the city. Up to the present moment, the House of Deputies has, I believe, taken no action in the matter.

The work would be a giant undertaking, its estimated length being

450 kilometers, or very nearly 300 miles, with 26 locks of 38 feet fall. It is estimated by the commission that a ship of war could pass through the canal at an average speed of 9 miles an hour with an added allowance of thirty-seven minutes for each lock, giving forty-six hours for the passage of the canal for ships of 5,000 tons and over. Such a canal, according to the report, would effect an average saving of about 700 miles for ships passing to and fro between ports on the English Channel and the principal Mediterranean ports over the route by Gibraltar. This allowance for difference of time between the open sea and the canal would mean an advantage of about three days for a fleet assembling in the British Channel from Toulouse via the canal, over one coming from Malta via Gibraltar. To merchant vessels making the same voyage it would mean a saving of three days' cost of steaming and of maintenance. Among other advantages to France, such a canal would wholly eliminate Gibraltar as a barrier between the Atlantic and the Mediterranean.

It is believed that such economy of time and steamer consumption would induce a large portion of the traffic between the ports of western Europe and the Mediterranean to take this route. It is also believed that a very large part of the traffic from America to central and southern Europe, which now takes the indirect northern routes through England and Germany, would be attracted to this route. Considering, however, only the commerce of western European ports with the Mediterranean littoral, it seems evident that the saving, even with a liberal system of tolls, would be such as to give an assured profit on the cost of construction, operation, and repairs.

The total cost of the canal is estimated at 1,400,000,000 francs, or about $300,000,000. This estimate omits, however, the cost of terminal harbors and of necessary crossings. It is believed that reasonable tolls upon the traffic which is sure to take this route would pay 3 per cent on the cost of construction over and above the expense of operation and repairs.

The conclusion of the commission, that a large augmentation of interior traffic would result from the construction of this immense waterway, seems hardly well based when one considers that the present Canal du Midi, which occupies substantially the route this is expected to take, is not taxed to anything like its capacity, and that the whole region through which it passes is already well served with railways, most of them belonging to the State, which carry freights at rates so low as to offer little hope of any great increase of production by the stimulation of lower rates by the canal.

### AGRICULTURE.

From an agricultural point of view, the year 1902 has been one of unusual prosperity in southwest France.

The wine crop, which is regarded as of more importance than all the others, is more than an average yield, and though less in quantity than that of 1901, is said to be of far better quality. The market seems to have recovered from its depressed condition, and prices for new wines, to be kept in stock until they have ripened and are fit for exportation, are higher than they have been for several years.

The only serious drawback in relation to the vintage of 1902 is the "brown rot," a disease which, if the statements of a noted writer upon viticulture are to be accepted as correct, seems likely to become no insignificant rival of phylloxera. The cause of this pest does not appear to be clearly established as yet, much less its cure. It is said to be akin to "mildew" of the leaf, but even the astonishing amount of "sulphurings," "mixtures," and doses of every kind, which are bestowed upon the vines of this region from the day the first leaf appears until the vintage begins, has been insufficient to discourage the microbe to which its ravages are said to be due. It seems, however, to be peculiarly adapted to exportation, being quite invisible except through a microscope magnifying from 600 to 800 diameters. It is not a new disease, and with its congener, the "mildew," is probably well known in the United States. If not, it soon will be, as many of our vineyardists are importing French vines—the result of hybridization with American vines, from which their resistant powers are derived—with the hope of avoiding the ravages of phylloxera. It would be much better if our vine growers turned their attention to protecting and developing their vines by studying local conditions and adopting or improving the methods by which the French have to a degree reconstituted and protected their vineyards. It is not true that they have developed varieties of the vine which are immune from attacks of phylloxera and kindred diseases, but they have adopted a system of treatment and devised remedies which are preventive rather than curative, by which vines that have received a certain resistant capacity from American stocks are enabled to withstand attacks of such diseases. It is a constant fight, however, and it is very rare to find a vineyard the leaves of which do not show through the summer months the unmistakable marks of frequent "treatments" and repeated "sulphurings." The conflict with the diseases of the vine in France has been a fight for life and this fight has been measurably successful because it has never been intermitted. Every year it is renewed. The California vineyardist would better rely on scientific warfare than an imported immunity.

I would again call attention to the action of the French Government in relation to plants and bulbs, including all sorts of nursery stock, grown in the United States. It absolutely excludes everything green that may be raised in the United States. Fruits, vegetables, flowers, trees, shrubs—plants of all kinds—are prohibited from landing and are even refused transport across French territory to any other country. I am informed that even the proposed reciprocity treaty does not revoke this law. Not an apple, a potato, or even an onion grown in the United States is admitted to French territory. At the same time, France is driving a lively trade in potatoes and other vegetables with Porto Rico and is shipping grape cuttings by the millions to California. This act excluding American products was passed in 1898, as soon as it was learned that certain hybrid vines had sufficient resistant quality to enable French vineyardists to dispense with American stocks in reconstructing their vineyards, and was extended to include all other plant products.

## OTHER CROPS.

The yield of wheat has been a fair average in quantity and could hardly have been excelled in quality. The same is true of rye, oats, and farm crops of all kinds. Perhaps the most noticeable fact in connection with the crop yield of this year is the greatly increased production of maize. The returns are not given in a form to give any conception of the yield of grain, as this is regarded generally as a forage crop and only the acreage is reported. It has ripened very well this year and will no doubt perceptibly reduce the deficit of wheat required for French consumption.   The Government and the exporters of the United States have expended no little energy in introducing into Europe, and especially into France, the use of corn in various forms as a food product.   Directly, the movement has not been a success. The French people have not taken to corn meal as a food.   One of the reasons is that it is regarded as a special food for domestic animals. Besides this, the Frenchman has no morning meal corresponding to our "breakfast," for which the many forms of "corn foods" are expressly adapted.   His "petit déjeuner" consists of a cup of coffee or chocolate with a piece of bread.   Many of the laboring classes eat nothing but a piece of bread until the noon meal, which is far too serious a matter for such light dishes.

It is these conditions which have chiefly prevented the introduction of Indian corn as an established feature of the food of any class of French society, despite its cheapness and unmistakable excellence. The increased cultivation of maize is not likely to greatly extend its use for culinary purposes, but only for fattening stock and the manufacture of alcohol.   As yet, the French growers have not learned to obtain the best results in its cultivation.   The seed is mostly the short-kerneled white Italian variety, and the yield per acre is rarely more than half our average production.   As a food for stock, either by itself or in combination with cotton-seed meal or oil cake, it is constantly growing in importance.   The strenuous efforts which France is making to increase her meat supply ought to open a market for such compounds in her borders if our American producers will take the trouble to study the market and not insist upon trying to make the purchaser buy what he does not want, instead of offering him what he desires in the form he prefers.

### EXPORTS.

The chief natural products exported from this port are wines, olive oil, skeepskins, goatskins, argols or tartar, prunes, and walnuts.   The effect of phylloxera and other diseases upon the wine production of California has caused an increased export of Bordeaux wines to our country.

*Argols.*—One of the most important exports from Bordeaux is bitartrate of soda, in its two crude forms of argols and wine lees, essential to the manufacture of baking powder, and is to be obtained only in wine-producing countries.   Nearly all baking powders are manufactured in the United States, which consequently consumes more of this product of vinous fermentation than all the rest of the world.

*Talc.*—Talc is produced in the Pyrenees, and is shipped in varying quantities to the United States.   It is a curious fact that it is one of the cheapest things in the world in its primitive form of a flaky ore. It is usually white or greenish-white color.   One of the most highly prized sorts is of a rosy hue, especially adapted to the manufacture of face powder.   Not infrequently the bags in which it is transported and the carriage to the railway constitute the greater part of the prime cost.

*Sheepskins without wool.*—Another export of no little importance is sheepskins without wool.   Most of these are imported from South America to Mazamet, a small city in the department of Tarn, whose waters are said to be peculiarly adapted to the treatment of the skins preparatory to removing the wool.   Here, they are macerated for some months, the wool taken off, and they are then shipped to the United States to be transformed into "morocco" leather.

*Hides.*—A very noticeable fact in the exports from this district during the past two years is the entire disappearance of any such thing as the hides of neat cattle. This was formerly a thriving and important business. Upon the arrival of the present consul here, he found the laws governing the disinfection of such hides very badly construed and practically not observed at all. The strict enforcement of the regulations on this subject soon reduced the trade to a nullity.

Two years ago, it became impossible to deny that, in more than half the departments of France, aphthous fever, the dreaded "hoof-and-mouth disease," was epidemic. This disease is almost impossible to eradicate. The French authorities forbade at once all commerce in cattle, sheep, and hogs between the infected departments and others. Little was done, however, to prevent the spread of the disease. After a time, interest in the matter died out and rumors began to prevail that the disease had ceased to exist at various points, in the hope that the disinfection regulations would be relaxed and the declaration of the exporter or of foreign officials that they had been complied with would be accepted by our consular officers. This consulate, however, refused to accept any evidence of disinfection unless done under personal supervision, believing any other certificate to be wholly illusory.

During the past summer, I made an extended tour through the various departments composing this consular district, visiting cattle fairs and markets wherever it was possible to do so. The result of this investigation was the most unmistakable evidence, not only of the existence of "hoof-and-mouth disease," but of universal apathy in regard to it. Cattle and sheep showing plainly the most striking symptoms of this disease were openly driven along the highways and through towns and villages without attracting any attention or causing any attempt at repression.

During all this time, the hides of neat cattle have been shipped to the United States. Disinfection, even if thorough, is a poor safeguard against this subtle disease.

Hides of neat cattle, glue stock, or sheepskins "with wool" from any country in which aphthous fever is known to exist should not be permitted to land in the United States unless they have passed through some process which essentially changes their character. Treatment so as to remove the wool of sheepskins or the hair and fleshy parts adhering to the hides of neat cattle would furnish an absolute protection against disease.

*Liqueurs.*—While Bordeaux is a city of varied and important manufactures, the chief business, except wine making, which is concerned with American trade is the concoction of liqueurs and the preparation of preserved foods. A liqueur, according to general commercial usage here, is a decoction consisting of a sirup flavored with the essential oils of certain herbs, to which is added more or less alcohol. According to the invoices of the past year, 39 varieties of liqueurs have been exported from this port to the United States, beginning with "absinthe" and ending with "vermuth." The essential principle of both these is the oil of wormwood, a peculiarly numbing and stupefying principle which seems to deprive the consumer of the power to appreciate the character and consequence of his acts.

The other varieties of liqueurs are intended chiefly as stimulants of appetite. They comprise "Eau d'Argent" (Silver Water), "Eau d'Or" (Water of Gold), "Eau de Noix" (Water of Walnuts), all of which are said to have achieved popularity in the United States. They are simply decoctions of alcohol, sugar, or glycerin, and unknown flavors.

*Comestibles.*—The food-preparing industries of Bordeaux are notable for their extent, variety, and daintiness of character. They embrace:

1. Fish of several varieties, such as sardines, anchovies, tunny-fish, mackerel, sprats, and others. All of these are shipped here from other points where they are caught, to be repacked either separately or in connection with other things.

2. Meats in various forms, but especially pâtés, purées, sausages, meat pies, and other forms of cooked or preserved delicacies.

3. Fruits, vegetables, jams, and extracts.

4. Pickles, sauces, and relishes in infinite variety.

5. Edible fungi, such as mushrooms, ceps, truffles.

These forms of comestibles are exported to all parts of the world. Except the edible fungi, none of the material has any special quality or distinctive excellence. The idea that French fruits and vegetables are better than those grown in the United States is entirely a mistake. In many cases, the reverse is true. Yet the skill with which they are treated enables the Bordeaux merchants to sell large quantities of their goods in the United States, in spite of our immense productiveness, our ingenuity, and unrivaled facilities for handling such articles. The reason for this lies in the indisputable fact that no people can compare with the French in the art of preserving and enhancing the appearance of everything they make. The fruits and vegetables of their conserves are so treated and arranged, the bottles and packages so ornamented and varied in form, as to capture the fancy and appeal to the appetite. Some of their preparations are too highly flavored for the American palate, and others are of a character quite at variance with our general preferences, yet they find their way into our hotels and kitchens, chiefly through the exquisite taste which makes them captivating to the eye.

In visiting the great "usines" where this infinite variety of comestibles is prepared, one is struck by nothing so much as the lack of what we know as the "factory air."

The packing is mostly done by girls. They work ten hours a day, with an hour for the midday meal. There is an entire absence of that hurried, rushing, wholesale method of work to which we are accustomed. In every room, there is abundance of light, good ventilation, and the utmost cleanliness, along with that sense of order which is peculiar to the French worker. There are as many chairs in each room as there are girls, and they sit or stand as they may prefer while at their work. Fruit and vegetables are prepared with the utmost nicety, and jars or bottles are filled, not according to routine, but so as to make pictures of them all. The pay is small; rarely, if ever, more than 2 francs (40 cents) a day, but it depends not merely upon the number of packages filled, but on the excellence and variety of packing. The work is individual rather than mechanical.

### IMPORTS FROM THE UNITED STATES.

In previous reports, I have noted the difficulty of giving reliable figures in regard to the importation of American products. It is impossible to determine from the French customs returns at this port the precise character of importations or their destination. The goods entered here are designated by the French classification according to their components, not according to their names and uses. A locomotive and a piano, a thrashing machine and a typewriter are in the same class, and one can never tell from the reports how many of each sort are imported.

Besides this, the French dealer does not advertise the fact that he sells American goods. He has a certain timidity about letting it be known that he sells foreign wares. The result is that no one could correctly answer the question so often asked by American manufacturers, "Who are the leading importers of American goods in Bordeaux?" The fact is not advertised in the papers nor in any other way. If one should walk the streets and read all the signs, he would hardly find a house which makes known the fact that it handles American goods of any kind.

*Agricultural implements.*—It is a matter of surprise to some of our American manufacturers of agricultural implements that their sales have not increased more in this portion of France. Many of our producers have been content to dump their wares on the French market and leave them to make their way without oversight or assistance, not reflecting that the French jobber has no special interest in pushing them. He is not a missionary of American commerce, nor is he greatly concerned in the excellence of the goods he handles. It is his business to sell the things his customers want, not to convince them that they ought to want something different. The demand in this market must always be created among those who use any specific article, not among the wholesale or retail dealers. For this reason, every American manufacturer who desires to push his wares in this part of France should arrange to have them under intelligent supervision by one having a personal interest in the matter. To achieve the best results, American energy should go with American goods.

Again, agricultural conditions here are entirely different from those at home. The small farms are not only much more numerous, but large ones are so rare that individual holdings average only about 6 acres each, and a man who owns 20 or 30 acres is regarded as a large proprietor. These small farms are worked by very cheap labor. Two francs a day, or 40 cents, would be a high average for the laborer who boards himself. A large portion of the farm work is done by women, while oxen and cows are the chief draft animals. An ordinary haying outfit is a wagon drawn by two cows, with two men, one to drive and load and two or three women to pitch and rake up the "scatterings." The plowing is mostly done by oxen. It is well done, too. It is very rare that one sees as good plowing in the United States. The cultivation of vines and other products grown in rows is mostly done with plows attached to long wooden beams like our old-fashioned cart tongues, drawn by a yoke of oxen. It is amazing what excellent work a French plowman will do with such an outfit. Many large proprietors, after trying our modern implements, have gone back to the old methods. Such farmers are not likely to be large purchasers of mowers, reapers, gang plows, and other farm-working machinery. A mowing machine drawn by oxen is sometimes seen. The small price paid to agricultural laborers tends to make the demand for labor-saving implements less than one familiar with such things in the United States would imagine. The large proprietors have mostly been supplied, and the small farmers do not require much machinery.

In common with other American devices, our agricultural machines are often unprotected by valid French patents. This is the fault only of the manufacturer, who should not be surprised to find his market after a time occupied by a lighter and less durable implement of the same general character, at a lower price. It is an irreparable mistake. If he failed to take out a patent within the time prescribed by law—that is, within seven months after the issue of his American patent—there is no remedy.

*Cash registers.*—The makers of the well known cash registers of Dayton, Ohio, are not only successful as a manufacturing concern, but have given an example of the application of common sense to their export trade which should be carefully considered by the makers of other American specialties. After having fully complied with the patent laws of France, they established a French branch under control of an agent thoroughly familiar with the cost and methods of manufacture. The result is not only a remarkable sale of these important instruments of retail trade, but a universal satisfaction with the company's methods. So much stress is often laid upon knowledge of the language of the country in which a salesman travels, that I feel compelled to say that a thorough knowledge of the business he represents is far more important. A little knowledge of a language goes a long way in trade, as the German salesman has demonstrated the world over.

*Prunes.*—The prune crop of southwest France was this season very light. This fact made it necessary for nearly all the merchants of this district to turn to the United States for a supply to fill their home orders, as well as for export to other markets. Large quantities of prunes were therefore imported from California and other prune-growing regions of the Pacific coast. While there was some dissatisfaction expressed with purchases made from the stock of old prunes before the crop of 1902 came into market, it is a gratifying fact that the purchases from the new crop were received with the liveliest approval, which even found expression in the public press—a very rare thing in France, where approval is especially reserved for home products. This is all the more gratifying from the fact that California prunes have hitherto been looked upon with a certain suspicion by Bordeaux dealers.

*Petroleum.*—The importation of American petroleum has greatly fallen off at this port during the past year. The exact amount of decrease can not be given, because the customs report is not obtainable until after the close of the year. The importer—for there is but one firm engaged in the business here—informs me that only a small quantity is now brought here, nearly the whole amount entered being Russian oil from Odessa. The reason assigned for this is the reduced cost of freight on the Russian article and more favorable duty granted on all Russian products.

*Fuel oils.*—Many tentative efforts have been made looking to the introduction of the products of the Texas wells for use as fuel. To use oil in this way would mean not only a change in the methods of application and regulation of heat, but the adoption of a new system of firing. The American producer must familiarize the foreign consumer with the practical methods of using liquid fuel before it will be possible to interest French capitalists in its exploitation.

Those who have written to this consulate on the subject have shown a lack of familiarity with the essential conditions of transportation.

All of them ask the cost of transport from New Orleans to Bordeaux. This is a question which can not possibly be decided from this end of the line. It is a variable quantity, depending chiefly on the number of "tramp" vessels there may be in the harbor of New Orleans. It is necessary to keep in mind three things:

1. That American ships rarely cross the Atlantic. It is now almost a decade since the American flag was seen in the port of Bordeaux. It is only foreign "tramps" that need be considered.

2. That the tonnage required to move American exports is always greatly in excess of that required to carry European exports to American ports, the former being usually heavy and bulky, and the latter of much less weight in comparison with their value.

3. That an oil-carrying vessel can rarely expect to obtain a return cargo to an American port, no matter what her character. The great steamship lines are practically sufficient to take all the exports to the United States, and are naturally preferred, even at higher rates, over oil and coal ships, which are not well-suited for the carriage of such freights as wines, silks, and various kinds of comestibles.

Those desiring to export petroleum or bituminous coal for use as fuel must therefore face the fact that it is necessary to provide the means of transport. No French importer will take any risks or share any responsibility of this kind.

*American shoes.*—American shoes have made their appearance in this market, which is one of the centers of the shoemaking art in Europe. The claim has always been made that the machine-made shoe of the United States could never compete with the articles produced by hand in southwest France in appearance, price, or durability. In appearance, the imported article far excels the native, because of the superior finish given by the perfected machinery. In price, it easily undersells the hand-made product. As to durability, time has not yet been given for an actual test, but the result of the competition ought not to be doubtful.

*Other goods.*—There are many varieties of American goods, such as typewriters, sewing machines, and phonographs, in which there is no competition. The trade in these goods is large. An attempt to introduce American stoves was not as successful as it deserved to be. This was chiefly because the American article did not fully meet the conditions required here. For instance, the gas range, a model of excellence for an American kitchen, did not appeal to the popular taste, because of the space and weight given to the oven. The fact that it baked well was of no consequence; the French cook never bakes anything. Boiling, frying, and roasting are the only things required of a cook stove in France—the bakers do the rest.

The attempt to introduce washing machines received a setback because of defective patents.

Several American business houses, or representatives of American houses, who have been established here for several years, and are both importers and exporters, inform me that their business has been exceptionally good during this year. There is no doubt that, with better shipping facilities to Bordeaux, the trade with the United States would greatly increase, to the advantage of both countries.

ALBION W. TOURGÉE, *Consul.*

BORDEAUX, *December, 1902.*

## CALAIS.

The city of Calais is important in only two respects: First, for its manufacture of machine-made lace, of which America is the principal buyer; and, second, as a port of embarkation and débarkation for passengers to or from England. The railway service between Calais and all parts of the continent is well organized to satisfy the demands of the traveling public, and, as a result, the route from Calais to Dover is one of the great highways of the world. The passenger service between Calais and Paris has been greatly improved in the past few years, and can now be said to rank among the very best. There are three fast trains each way daily, which enable passengers to make the trip between Calais and Paris, a distance of 186 miles, in three hours and twenty minutes. These trains are supposed to be the most rapid in the world for the distance traveled, yet in the nearly five years that I have resided in Calais, I have heard of no accident occurring. The French rapid train service between Calais and Paris is markedly superior to the corresponding service between Dover and London, especially in the comforts and conveniences of the coaches employed. There are also regular sleeping-car services between Calais and Marseilles and Calais and Brindisi, which enable travelers to the Orient to remain in London five or six days after the departure of the Peninsular and Oriental express boats, and yet overtake these boats at Marseilles or Brindisi.

A comparison of the trade of the fiscal year ended June 30, 1902, with the preceding twelve months shows an increase in the exportation of lace, pressed hay and straw, lumber, pig iron, iron ore, and coal, and an increase in the importation of wool.

The port trade with America is confined to petroleum from Philadelphia, pitch pine from Pensacola and Mobile, and chalk loaded in Calais and destined for Philadelphia and New York.

Only one American ship, the *Aryan*, has been in this harbor during the past year.

In the past year, Bigo & Co. have established a line of cargo boats between Calais and London. This makes two lines between these ports.

### QUARRIES.

About 12 miles southwest of Calais are marble quarries, whose output is becoming of increasing importance, due to the use of improved machinery for cutting and polishing. One quarry has a capacity of 50 French carloads a day. The product is worked into mantlepieces, monuments, facings, etc.

### ALCOHOL.

Distilleries of beet-root alcohol are passing through a crisis, on account of the recent increase of the tax on alcohol. It is claimed that this tax favors southern producers of wine and cider alcohol at the expense of northern manufacturers of alcohol from corn and beet root.

### SUBMARINE CABLES.

The plant for the manufacture of submarine cables was partially destroyed by fire last year, but has since been reconstructed. It recently completed a cable of 1,000 miles in length, which was ordered before the fire. This manufactory is expecting some legislation authorizing the laying of numerous government lines of submarine cables connecting France with her colonies.

## MOLDING.

There are a number of molding factories in Calais. One of these has a capacity of 100,000 yards a week.

### CYCLES AND AUTOMOBILES.

The high tax on foreign cycles and automobiles permits of a good market for Calais makers; and although prices are decreasing, the number of orders is greater. Brampton Brothers, manufacturers of separate pieces for automobiles and cycles, are meeting with good success.

### LAW ON MERCHANT MARINE.

The new law of April 7, 1902, enacted by the French Parliament, decreases the premiums on sailing vessels of the merchant marine and encourages the building of steamers.

### EXPORTS.

*Lace.*—The exportation of machine-made lace from Calais to the United States is increasing every year. For the twelve months ended June 30, 1901, it showed a growth in value amounting to $746,996 over the exports of the previous year. For the twelve months ended June 30, 1902, the increase over the preceding year was $917,845, or about 75 per cent.

The kinds of lace in favor on the American market are still Valenciennes and Chantilly.

The lace industry employs in its 400 factories the greater part of the population of Calais and surrounding towns and villages. There are also 8 factories for making embroidery laces of the Plauen type, which employ 300 men, women, and children.

*Sugar.*—Calais is especially equipped with facilities for storing sugar for exportation, having a number of large warehouses for this purpose. In the past fiscal year, 21,605 tons of sugar were exported from this port to England, which, however, is a decrease of 15,048 tons from the record for the preceding year. This decrease was due to the diminution of the premium awarded by the French Government, and this premium will be still further lessened this year.

*Pressed hay and straw.*—The South African war has required much hay and straw for use of horses of the English army, and as a result, the exportations of those products last year, 21,613 tons, show an increase of 9,765 tons over the figures for the preceding year.

*Fruits and vegetables.*—Large quantities of fruits and vegetables, packed in baskets and coming from the south of France, are shipped every night from Calais to London, where they arrive in time for the morning markets. In the past year, 3,538 tons of fruits and 1,759 tons of vegetables were exported.

*Wines.*—There has been no change in the wine trade. The exports last year amounted to 2,200 tons.

### IMPORTS.

*Lumber.*—Lumber is the most important import, many cargoes coming from the Baltic region and some, of pitch pine, from the

H. Doc. 305, pt 2——9

United States. The total quantity of lumber imported from all countries during the last fiscal year was 46,774 standards, or 6,741 standards less than the amount for the preceding year; 2,346 standards of pitch pine were received from the United States, which is 426 standards less than in 1901; 21,453 standards of pine were also received from Sweden. This is 2,241 standards less than was received last year; 20,063 standards were received from Russia, a decrease of 3,631 standards, and 2,732 standards from Norway, an increase of 1,477 standards.

*Pig iron.*—During the past fiscal year, 13,849 tons of pig iron were imported from England, or 13,672 tons less than in the preceding year.

*Iron ore.*—Four thousand two hundred and forty-five tons of iron ore were imported from Russia, a diminution of 11,793 tons compared with last year's record.

*Coal.*—Fifty-nine thousand four hundred and seventy-one tons of coal were imported from England, being 46,688 tons less than the preceding year. Five tons were imported from the United States.

*Wool.*—Twenty thousand four hundred and twenty-five tons of wool were imported, via England, from Australia, Argentine Republic, and Cape Colony. This is an increase of 7,425 tons over the preceding year.

*Petroleum.*—Twelve thousand seven hundred and twenty-seven tons of petroleum have been imported, a decrease of 4,601 tons from last year. The importations from the United States, however, were 8,391 tons, which is an increase of 1,968 tons. Four thousand three hundred and thirty-six tons also came from Russia, a decrease of 6,539 tons.

I know of no manufacturing plants or electric-railway lines owned or fostered by American capital in this consular district.

JAMES B. MILNER, *Consul.*

CALAIS, *November 5, 1902.*

———

## DIEPPE.

### MOVEMENT OF THE PORT.

The tonnage of vessels entering and leaving Dieppe during the year 1901 amounted to 902,882 tons, as against 948,656 in 1900. In 1878, the amount was 960,038; in 1880, 1,008,288; figures which seem to indicate that the port has made no gain in twenty years. The values of importations and exportations are a little more satisfactory; expressed in millions of francs, they amounted to 126 ($51,531,000) in 1867; 147 ($28,371,000) in 1878; 237 ($45,741,000) in 1880; 130 ($25,090,000 in 1885; 258 ($49,794,000) in 1898; 342 ($65,006,000) in 1899, and 370 ($71,410,000) in 1900. The number of vessels entering the port during the past year was 1,846, of which number 903 were French, with 135,621 tons; 851 English, with 294,272 tons; 20 Danish, with 5,887 tons; 9 Russian, with 3,272 tons; 25 Norwegian, with 10,105 tons; 2 Belgian, with 1,518 tons; 17 Swedish, with 11,434 tons; 4 Dutch, with 1,021 tons, and 15 German, with 7,809 tons. Of the 1,846 vessels entering, 67 were sailing vessels, with 13,917 tons.

The following shows the number, the tonnage, and the origin and destination of vessels entering and clearing during 1901:

| From and to— | Entered. | | | | Cleared. | | | | Total. | |
|---|---|---|---|---|---|---|---|---|---|---|
| | French. | | Foreign. | | French. | | Foreign. | | | |
| | No. | Tons. | No. | Tons. | No. | Tons. | No. | Tons. | No. | Tons. |
| Russia | | | 8 | 5,705 | | | 9 | 2,762 | 17 | 8,467 |
| Sweden | | | 19 | 12,433 | | | 1 | 185 | 20 | 12,618 |
| Norway | | | 8 | 2,857 | | | 2 | 369 | 10 | 3,226 |
| Denmark | | | | | | | 18 | 3,626 | 18 | 3,626 |
| England | 366 | 126,564 | 860 | 278,623 | 868 | 128,475 | 871 | 303,798 | 3,465 | 837,460 |
| Germany | | | | | | | 3 | 1,411 | 3 | 1,411 |
| Netherlands | | | 1 | 64 | | | 2 | 283 | 3 | 347 |
| Belgium | | | 3 | 502 | | | 3 | 830 | 6 | 1,389 |
| Spain | | | 1 | | 1 | 57 | 2 | 740 | 3 | 800 |
| Roumania | | | 1 | 1,209 | | | | | 1 | 1,209 |
| United States | 4 | 4,164 | 6 | 9,041 | 4 | 4,164 | 2 | 2,905 | 16 | 20,274 |
| Indies | | | 2 | 8,982 | | | | | 2 | 8,982 |
| Colombia | | | | | | | 1 | 299 | 1 | 299 |
| Holland-America | | | 1 | 571 | | | 1 | 535 | 2 | 1,106 |
| Algeria | 1 | 892 | | | | | | | 1 | 892 |
| Total | 871 | 131,620 | 909 | 314,987 | 874 | 132,756 | 914 | 317,743 | 3,568 | 897,106 |

## IMPORTS AND EXPORTS.

The importation of oil from the United States amounted in 1901 to 22,154 net tons, which was an increase of 5,994 tons over that of the previous year.

Sweden, Russia, the United States, and Norway, are the greatest exporters of timber to Dieppe, ranking in the order named. Last year, Sweden sent 22,110 tons; Russia, 11,506; the United States, 2,556; and Norway, 2,219. In the previous year the amounts were: Sweden, 23,614; Russia, 15,058; the United States, 2,800; and Norway, 1,835 tons.

Considerable English coal is imported. In 1901, the amount was 358,874 tons, as against 389,083 tons in 1900.

The imports and exports in 1901 were:

| Description of merchandise. | Imports. | Exports. | Description of merchandise. | Imports. | Exports. |
|---|---|---|---|---|---|
| | Metric tons. | Metric tons. | | Metric tons. | Metric tons. |
| Animals | 49 | 62 | Pottery, glass, and crystal. | 82 | 4,524 |
| Products and skins of animals | 601 | 9,918 | Thread | 2,085 | 1,721 |
| Fish | 466 | 97 | Tissues | 117 | 3,088 |
| Farinaceous food | 468 | 8,899 | Ready-made clothing | 1 | 78 |
| Fruit and seed | 13,389.6 | 6,097 | Paper | 128 | 502 |
| Colonial products | 920.6 | 10,018 | Hides and furs | 80 | 572 |
| Vegetable oils and juices | 130 | 46 | Jewelry, clocks | 2,447 | 1,495 |
| Medicinal goods | 4 | 128 | Weapons and ammunition | | 49 |
| Wood: | | | Furniture and musical instruments | 74 | 1,123 |
| Ordinary | 38,179 | 10 | Basket work, ropes, and esparto goods | 22 | 48 |
| Foreign | | | Miscellaneous articles | 82 | 2,329 |
| Fruit, roots, and fibers | 108 | 42 | Gold and silver | | 59 |
| Dyes and tannin | | 185 | | | |
| Produce and divers waste | 273 | 8,893 | | | |
| Beverages | 247 | 2,638 | Total | 454,594 | 119,241 |
| Stones, mineral combustibles, oil, etc. | 367,785 | 54,487 | International transportation | 29,805 | 18,825 |
| Metals | 8,060 | 684 | French salt | 339 | |
| Chemical products | 8,729 | 620 | Coasting, less the salt | 29,104 | 55 |
| Prepared dyes | | 72 | | | |
| Paints | 44 | 144 | Grand total | 513,842 | 138,121 |
| Divers compositions | 71 | 1,388 | | | |

## FISHERIES.

The products of the fisheries did not amount to as much as last year—1,940,767 francs ($374,568), as compared with 2,002,142 francs ($386,413). Fresh fish represented 1,790,107 francs ($345,491) and fresh and salted herrings 150,660 francs ($29,077). For the first time, salted mackerel did not figure in the fishing products.

## INDUSTRIES.

Besides being a terminal for the much-frequented Dieppe-Newhaven channel crossing, and a famous seaside resort, Dieppe has varied industries. In the district is an important paper factory, cotton and weaving factories, oil mills, clock manufactories, etc. No vessels are built here, except fishing boats.

The blue-flint pebbles from the beach are sent to England and Holland to be used in the manufacture of china. Spanish white is made from the chalk taken from the cliffs.

The soil of the district is very rich. Considerable rape is raised for oil. Rye, wheat, oats, and hay are the principal crops.

## PROJECTED IMPROVEMENTS.

The following is condensed from the deliberations of the Dieppe Chamber of Commerce at one of its sittings in 1901:

An account was given of the visit of the committee on cranes to Havre to examine the electric cranes at that port. The committee reported that these machines give excellent service, and recommended that a similar system be installed at Dieppe. An objection was raised to the effect that the conditions of commerce and the discharging of coal were not the same at the two cities, and that steam cranes would, perhaps, give better results at Dieppe.

The president of the chamber of commerce recalled the observations he had so often made concerning the importation of American coals, remarking that Dieppe should have as soon as possible a perfect system of cranes to be used for the discharging of large steamers, should American coal dealers suddenly choose Dieppe as a base for their operations.

The engineer of the port was asked to report on the question of expenses for a perfect installation of cranes.

### NEW TARIFF FOR CHARGING AND DISCHARGING VESSELS.

The new tariff for the use of the steam cranes at Dieppe went into effect April 1, 1901, and is as follows per 1,000 kilograms (2,204.6 pounds):

Charging or discharging merchandise of the first category, comprising coal, metals, minerals, plaster, flint, clay, earth, salt, sand, and ballast, 30 centimes (5.79 cents).

Charging or discharging merchandise of the second category, comprising resin, asphalt in rock, tar, briquettes, brick, wood, grain, wine, liquors in barrels, 40 centimes (7.72 cents).

Charging or discharging merchandise of the third category, comprising stone, coke, cotton, hemp, textiles, straw, provender, "articles de Paris," commodities, or others not named, 52.5 centimes (10.1325 cents).

If the merchandise is unweighed, the tariff will be applied according to the weight given at the custom-house.

Charging or discharging packages or merchandise the weight of which is unknown or which necessitate the use of one or more cranes less than half a day, 5 francs (96.5 cents) per hour and per crane. If the time is less than two hours, a supplementary tax is imposed for lighting and placing the crane in pressure, of 4 francs (77.2 cents) per crane.

THORNWELL HAYNES, *Consul.*

ROUEN, *October 27, 1902.*

## GRENOBLE.

Grenoble, like many French cities, is a commingling of the old and new. As far back as 122 B. C. a little settlement, tucked under the mountains on the banks of the river Isère and overlooking a broad and fertile plain, was taken by the Romans from the Allobroges, and, from its unique situation, given the name "Cularo." Afterwards, under the Emperor Gratian and in his honor because he raised it into a bishopric, it became "Gratianapolis," which name was subsequently reduced to its present form, Grenoble. The capital of the Dauphine, it has been identified with the history of this province, and this history is an interesting one from every point of view. A wealth of historic literature is to be found in its municipal library, one of the best in France. Among its 250,000 books and documents, there are two volumes of such precious value that the city keeps them covered by an insurance of $20,000 each.

The oldest quarter of the city is compactly built and presents a quaint appearance. At the same time, it is gradually changing to meet the necessities of modern life. Scattered in the old quarter, the streets of which are well paved with cement and kept in good condition, are modern structures of generous and pleasing architecture, while the wholly modern quarter, built up within the last twenty years, contains buildings of, in many instances, imposing proportions. New houses and manufacturing establishments are continually going up, and with the introduction of the water power from the torrents and glaciers of the Alps, and the general distribution of electrical force, there is promise of increasing prosperity. It is stated definitely that, for the past ten years or more, the business of the city as a whole has increased annually at the ratio of 10 per cent.

Grenoble is becoming known as one of the most attractive centers for excursions in the French Alps. Trolley lines are extending; an enthusiastic convention in the interest of more sanitary accommodations throughout this region has just been held; a thoroughly modern and well-appointed hotel has been opened in Grenoble, and a fine structure is to go up next season in the neighboring watering place of Uriage (much frequented by Americans); a second large department house will be finished next fall; the spacious structure of the chamber of commerce will soon be dedicated; the university, with its attendant lycées for younger scholars, is broadening its sphere, having now a special summer course in languages, attended by some 300 foreign students, of whom a score or more are Americans; while the presence of so many soldiers (this being the headquarters of the twenty-seventh division of the fourteenth army corps), together with military bands and local musical societies, makes this city bright and animated. It has a resident population of 70,000 within its walls, exclusive of troops, and there is a tributary population of some 200,000 people, which makes it a wholesale as well as a manufacturing center.

From this consular district, which represents the departments of the Isère, of Savoy, and of Upper Savoy, there have been exported to the United States during the year ended June 30, 1902, twenty different articles of merchandise, as shown below:

| Article. | Year ended— | |
|---|---|---|
| | June 30, 1901. | June 30, 1902. |
| Alimentary pastes | $4,397.66 | $4,868.15 |
| Automatic match distributers | | 669.53 |
| Bell ringing apparatus | 191.65 | |
| Chartreuse | 41,374.28 | 110,785.27 |

| Article. | Year ended— | |
|---|---|---|
| | June 30, 1901. | June 30, 1902. |
| Chlorate of potash | | $7,698.18 |
| Chlorate of soda | $2,946.98 | 1,378.86 |
| Church bells | 4,252.85 | |
| Dressed kid and lamb skins | 8,196.69 | 12,292.00 |
| Dried mushrooms | 367.28 | |
| Emery uncrushed | 2,129.90 | |
| Ferro-silicon | | 12,229.71 |
| Fromental | | 750.39 |
| Furniture | 8,906.95 | 418.81 |
| Gloves (kid and lamb skin) | 849,156.86 | 856,831.57 |
| Liqueurs | 1,275.72 | 2,390.80 |
| Machinery for combing silk waste | | 12,188.84 |
| Marble and stone | | 460.15 |
| Metal buttons | | 398.55 |
| Paper | 1,015.59 | 742.24 |
| Photographic paper | 156,143.23 | 165,370.25 |
| Rabbit-skin hair | | 563.40 |
| Tanning material | 1,266.72 | |
| Vermout | 666.51 | 861.76 |
| Walnuts (whole and shelled) | 280,432.02 | 266,049.73 |
| Wool | 3,883.58 | 20,236.80 |
| Total | 1,368,554.47 | 1,476,657.99 |

The figures show an increase over 1901 of $108,103.52, a large part of which ($66,729.24) is due to the one item of

### CHARTREUSE.

The increase is explained thus: Up to April 9, this article was forwarded by a business agent of the "Brothers Chartreux" to various selling houses in the United States (notably one in New York) in comparatively small invoices, averaging $3,000 to $4,000 each. Early this year, the exclusive right to sell this article in the United States was conceded to a French company formed expressly for its business exploitation. Accordingly, a central depot was established in New York to supply all future demands in America. There was invoiced through this consulate in April last one large consignment amounting to $84,219.78. None has been sent since that time. It is stated by some journals in the United States that the monks themselves have given up the making of the famous liqueur, but such is not the case. The monks who possess the "secret" prepare their specialty as heretofore; the only change has been that above stated.

The exportation of vermouth and other liqueurs made at Chambéry and La Côte St. André—not large in quantity—continues about the same from year to year.

### GLOVES.

By far the largest article of export in value, and the one for which the name of Grenoble is known the world over, is kid gloves. While the shipment of gloves from France has, for some years past, shown signs of decrease, because of rivalry from Germany, Belgium, and the United States, the loss from Grenoble has not been so marked, probably because these gloves are mainly made from the best quality of kid and lamb skins by work people who, it may be said, have inherited their skill through generations.

This year will doubtless show some falling off in the American demand, owing to changes in style or material and the favor shown to the "Mocha," to silk, linen, and other gloves made at Gloversville and Johnstown.

It may be mentioned that the figures here given do not include all the gloves that go to the United States from Grenoble. A large number are sent to the Paris representatives of United States houses who ship them from there. Some also go through buyers in Germany and London, so that it may be safely said that considerably over $1,000,000 worth of gloves find their way yearly from Grenoble to the United States. Nor does this by any means represent the entire output. More go to local markets than to America; twice as many go to Great Britain and her colonies, and one-half as many to other countries— such as Algeria, Russia, South Africa, etc. The total annual production is estimated at about $8,000,000.

## PHOTOGRAPHIC PAPER.

There are many paper mills in the department of the Isère, the water power being abundant, as well as the supply of wood. Much "Pâtes de Bois" is also made; that is, wood pulp bleached and compressed into cakes or blocks for easy handling and transportation to other paper factories. But the paper which passes this consulate is of the finest quality and is used mostly for photographic purposes. It is made at a very old and extensive establishment in Rives, which employs over 800 persons—men and women. The water used is remarkably fresh and limpid.

## WALNUTS.

The article of export second in importance is the well-known Grenoble walnut. Perhaps no better variety is produced anywhere than the kind known as the "pure mayettes."

There has been some transplanting of French walnuts to California, and it may be only a question of time when growers in that State will be able to control the American market. Not all the walnuts raised here are invoiced at Grenoble, a considerably quantity going through Marseille and some through Bordeaux. While a good annual average of shipments is maintained, the crop is always uncertain, owing to the uncontrollable factors of drought, moisture, and violent storms, especially of hail. In September of this year, two-thirds of the promising crop was destroyed by hail in thirty minutes.

## FERRO-SILICON AND CHLORATES.

These articles are relatively new to this office, the first appearing only in the past year. The chlorates come from Chedde in Upper Savoy, and the ferro-silicon from Bozel in Savoy. In view of the demand for these products for hydraulic and electrical work, etc., it is probable that the exportation will tend to increase.

## MACHINERY FOR COMBING SILK WASTE.

A large plant in Grenoble for making hydraulic and other special machinery—such as that for combing silk waste—has sent apparatus of this kind to America and other countries, and there is promise that it will continue to do so.

## OTHER INDUSTRIES.

Among other industries of Grenoble are the manufacture of metal buttons (sent to all parts of the world, some to the United States), silk weaving, paper making, metal working, typographic work, shipping anthracite from the mines of La Mure, manufacture of aluminum, acetylene, soda, carburet of calcium (in large quantities), carriages, automobiles and bicycles, linen (at Voiron), straw hats, and, on a vast scale, lime and cements (natural and artificial). Of cement, there is produced yearly about 200,000 tons, two-thirds of which is employed in France and one-third is sent to other countries—Switzerland, Italy, Algeria, Tunis, Spain, Turkey, Roumania, and South America. Lime is produced to the extent of about 150,000 tons yearly, most of which is employed in the Isère and southeastern France.

## WATER POWER.

A subject that is occupying much public attention at the present time is the utilization, for industrial, manufacturing, and transportation purposes, of the water power of the rapid torrents, lakes, and glaciers of the mountains. Millions of horsepower are locked in the glacial reservoirs of France. It is now beginning to be released, promising a new order of things in benefit to the people, and in supplying force at a minimum of cost. Many books have been written on the subject, and a monthly magazine is being published.

As the subject is not alone of local but of widespread interest, it has been thought best to devote a large part of this report to a description of this newly captured force, which is significantly termed in French.

## WHITE COAL.

An event marking a new era of prosperity for Grenoble and the region of the Dauphiné was the holding in September of this year of a "white coal" convention. More than 500 prominent men of science—engineers, polytechnists, mill owners, and manufacturers—from France and other countries assembled in the chamber of commerce building and devoted their time to a thorough discussion of the utilization of the water power of the glaciers and mountain streams of Alpine France. During the week, excursions were made in different directions within a radius of 50 miles to inspect the score or more of factories, where the water is already utilized for the generation of electricity, the making of paper, soda, aluminum, acetylene, and chemical products of various kinds, and in general for the distribution of force.

The railroads of France (25,000 miles) employ about 4,000,000 horsepower and the other industries about 2,500,000 horsepower—a total of 6,500,000 horsepower produced by steam. M. Bergès estimates the hydraulic forces of France in her mountainous regions to be 10,000,000 horsepower. Even at a much reduced estimate, the measure of industrial development possible can readily be seen.

The streams and cascades have been used to a certain extent for years, but not until recently, under the leadership of such enterprising men as Bergès and Joya and Desprez, has this water been "canalized"—conducted by huge pipes from vast heights down the mountain sides—and, with the aid of turbine wheels, made to develop tens of thousands of horsepower and to distribute energy, heat, and light in all directions.

It is a striking fact that the mighty energy cradled in the glaciers of the mountains and lying dormant through the centuries should be suddenly set free and made to turn the wheels of a hundred industries to meet the needs of man. The glaciers are a mine of "white coal" which, unlike the product of the earth, is inexhaustible, renewing itself from year to year. In 1863, it was deemed a bold achievement to bring water from a height of 260 feet, as at Uriage; but now M. Bergès has succeeded in canalizing a fall of 1,640 feet and another of 1,804 feet. At Epierre (Savoiè), M. Joya used a fall of 1,935 feet and at Chapareillan (25 miles from Grenoble) another of 2,040 feet—until this year said to be the highest single fall in the world.[a]

At Lancey, a few miles northeast of Grenoble, the water which gives power to mills of various kinds and to the electrical plant which lights the valley of the Graisivairdan and maintains its several tramway systems is brought by three successive falls whose total is 6,560 feet.

Light is furnished to the houses and farms of the vicinity at a very moderate cost. For example:

First lamp. 10 candlepower ................................ per year.. $4.82¼
Second lamp, 10 candlepower ............................... do..... 2.89¼
3 lamps of 5 candlepower each.............................. do..... 2.89¼

Total for 5 lamps, 35 candlepower ............................... 10.61¼

An average of $2.12 per lamp per year.

Starting from the little lake of Domènon, among the snows of the peak of the same name, the water is drawn by pipes which tap the lake at its bottom and is carried to a lake lower down the mountains, and from this still farther down to a third lake, whence the conduits bear it, always at a certain gradient, to the factories below, where it yields an equivalent of 10,000 horsepower.

As illustrating the enormous pressure of the water thus canalized, the pipes in many cases (as below) are as much as 3 meters 30 millimeters, or 10.83 feet, in diameter. The tunnel under the Thames at London has a diameter of about 11 feet, but this is for a distance of 30 meters, or 98½ feet only. The Société Hydro-Électrique de Fure et Morge at Grenoble, which utilizes the waters of the torrent Drac, near Vizille, has 4,600 meters, or 15,092 feet (of which 8,200 feet are in steel plates and 6,892 feet in wired cement), of piping with a diameter, as stated, of 10.83 feet.

This installation permits the distribution of force to the extent of 3,500 horsepower, under a tension of 26,000 volts, for a distance of 40 miles to factories in Moirans, Voiron, and Rives.

Grenoble will soon be lighted by electricity, the power being supplied by the Electro-Chemical Society of the Romanche, which has its works in the village of Livet (altitude 1,794 feet), 27 miles distant from this city. The valley of the Romanche was, until recent years, sparsely populated; to-day, within a distance of 12 miles, there are already installed six establishments for the making of paper, wood pulp, acetylene, aluminum, etc., and for the generation of electric force.

The stream itself is fed by the powerful glacial reservoirs of the

---

[a] The highest is at Vouvry, in Switzerland—3,018 feet.

Massifs of the Belledonne and the Peloux—ranges of mountains (in altitude from 9,800 to 13,000 feet) on either side of the valley; and in winter and summer alike, this water supply is unremitting and abundant.

With Grenoble thus lighted, as it were, by the melting snows, and furnished with a new motive force for turning its industrial wheels, it may well deserve its title of "the White Coal Capital."

C. P. H. NASON, *Consul.*

GRENOBLE, *December 4, 1902.*

### HAVRE.

Havre, like other commercial centers of France, in 1901, was still feeling in the reaction which took place after the exposition of Paris and suffered from the depression which existed throughout the metallurgic and other industries of Europe.

The wine crop, although not as large as that of the record year 1900, was above the average. Two unusually large yields coming together caused heavy stocks to accumulate, notwithstanding an increased consumption, and the prices fell to such a low level as to leave but little or no profit to the producers. As the production of wine is one of the largest industries of France, the crisis, which is still existing, has been far-reaching in its results, and has seriously affected the general trade conditions. The importations of Havre in 1901 fell off nearly 80,000 tons as compared with the previous year, and in the customs receipts of all kinds, the decrease was $1,242,174 in comparison with 1900, and $2,375,532 as compared with 1899.

Coal, which forms one-third of the total importations of Havre, showed a diminution of 95,000 tons as compared with 1900, when the imports were abnormally large, owing to the strikes in the French coal-mining regions. The falling off in the coal receipts was more than offset by the increase in the imports of cereals of 39,400 tons, of copper of 47,000 tons, and of cotton of 11,220 tons

Other articles showing a decrease in the imports were salt meats of 1,023 tons, hides of 8,617 tons, brandy and wine of 4,869 tons, animal fats of 2,690 tons, iron and steel of 1,302 tons, wood for cabinetmaking purposes of 3,946 tons, and machinery of 4,283 tons.

Among the products in which there was an increase in the imports in 1901 were common wood, coffee, cotton, cereals, oleaginous seeds, crude petroleum, wool, ores, pepper, sugar, and tobacco.

The lowering of the duties on coffee from 156 francs ($30.11) per 100 kilograms (220.46 pounds) to 136 francs ($26.25) had its influence upon the customs receipts.

As to the export trade of Havre, the conditions were somewhat more favorable than in 1900, the total exports being 47,071 tons in excess of those of the previous year and 82,123 tons greater than those of 1899.

The following articles showed an increase in the exports of 1901: Butter, cereals, and flour, cheese, steel, and iron, coal, fixed oils, artificial flowers, millinery, medicines, machinery, tools, chemical products, pepper, dried and salted fish, fabrics of all sorts, and oil cake.

Those in which there was a decrease in the exports were coffee, cocoa, copper, crude rubber, cotton, wine and brandy, raw wool, preserved vegetables, furniture, ores, hides and leather, pottery, glassware, bristles, sugar, and wines. In an annex to this report will be found tables showing the details of the imports and exports of Havre for the past three years.

A comparison of the customs receipts for the years 1899, 1900, and 1901 is given in the following table:

*Customs receipts of Havre.*

| Character. | 1899. | 1900. | 1901. |
|---|---|---|---|
| Customs duty | $15,268,178 | $14,159,010 | $12,911,662 |
| Statistic tax | 164,183 | 155,006 | 161,609 |
| Navigation tax | 288,574 | 278,936 | 274,058 |
| Auxiliary receipts | 98,204 | 87,808 | 89,349 |
| Salt tax | 41,595 | 36,441 | 38,457 |
| Total | 15,850,734 | 14,717,196 | 13,475,032 |
| Diminution in 1901 | 2,375,712 | 1,242,174 | ............ |

## TRADE IN 1902.

The customs receipts for the first six months of the present year, with the exception of the navigation tax, all show an increase in comparison with the corresponding period in 1901. The imports of coffee alone were 37,000 tons greater than during the first six months of 1900. Other articles in which there was an increase in the imports were hides, tallow, cereals, rice, cider apples, oleaginous seeds, cocoa, hard wood for cabinet-making purposes, brandy, coal, heavy oils, crude petroleum, and agricultural machinery.

Articles in which there was a decrease in the imports were salt and preserved meats, raw wool, lard, flour, dried vegetables, table fruits, sugar, wood for building purposes, cotton, wines, indigo, and nickel ore.

As to exports, the following showed an increase: Oil cake, butter, dye-wood extracts, ocher, silk and cotton fabrics, bonnets, and artificial flowers. Those in which there was a decrease were wine, medicines, white paper, furniture, prepared skins, etc.

In the following table are given the customs receipts for the first six months of the last three years, from which it may be seen that there was a decrease in 1902 of $1,044,145, as compared with the first six months of 1900, and an increase of $31,350 as compared with the same period of 1901:

*Customs receipts at Havre for the first six months of 1900, 1901, and 1902.*

| Character. | 1900. | 1901. | 1902. |
|---|---|---|---|
| Customs duties | $7,499,291 | $6,443,449 | $6,469,862 |
| Statistic tax | 84,435 | 73,977 | 85,200 |
| Navigation tax | 143,141 | 137,811 | 140,337 |
| Auxiliary receipts | 46,310 | 43,098 | 33,658 |
| Salt tax | 17,461 | 17,813 | 17,441 |
| Total | 7,790,638 | 6,715,143 | 6,746,493 |
| Increase or decrease in 1902 | −1,044,145 | +31,350 | ............ |

## COTTON.

Although the importations of cotton into Havre during the year 1901 were 187,408 bales more than in 1900, and, with the exception of the year 1899, the largest for the past ten years, the Havre cotton trade was not prosperous.  The increase in the imports was due to the fact that the stocks held by the spinners at the beginning of the year had been reduced to a minimum, and had to be replenished. The margin of profit was so small that many of the spinners, during the summer months, ran their mills on short time.  In fact, the profits both in the spinning and manufacturing trades were much smaller during 1901 than for the past three years.  This was to be expected, considering the general inactivity, amounting almost to a depression, which had prevailed since the exposition at Paris.

The price of cotton on January 1, 1901, was $12.11 per 50 kilograms (110.23 pounds).  It steadily fell to the end of May, when it was $9.46; then it rose till June 30, when it reached $10.91; then it fell again to $9.56 on August 17; then rose to $11.19 August 31; then steadily fell to the lowest price of the year, $9.02, at the end of November, and finished December 31 at $10.47.

In the following table are given the cotton statistics of Havre for the past ten years:

*Havre cotton statistics.*

| Year. | | Importations. | Sales. | Stocks on hand Dec. 31. |
|---|---|---|---|---|
| | | Bales. | Bales. | Bales. |
| 1892 | | 781,610 | 624,355 | 414,560 |
| 1893 | | 688,810 | 716,045 | 387,325 |
| 1894 | | 754,795 | 698,700 | 448,420 |
| 1895 | | 673,280 | 807,700 | 314,000 |
| 1896 | | 612,046 | 727,676 | 195,860 |
| 1897 | | 803,186 | 756,681 | 242,616 |
| 1898 | | 780,198 | 758,308 | 214,401 |
| 1899 | | 892,142 | 827,362 | 280,080 |
| 1900 | | 629,446 | 773,979 | 126,361 |
| 1901 | | 816,848 | 770,823 | 165,870 |

Of the importations of cotton, 767,656 bales came from the United States, 32,755 bales from India, and 16,436 bales from various countries.

British steamers, which heretofore have enjoyed the monopoly of the cotton-carrying trade between American ports and Havre, have met with considerable competition in the steamers of the Compagnie de Navigation Olazarri.  The latter is a Spanish line running monthly between Havre and New Orleans, via La Pallice, Bordeaux, Cuban and Mexican ports.

British steamers carried 493,574 bales of American cotton to Havre during 1901, which was only 4,979 bales more than in 1900.  When it is considered that the increase in the imports of American cotton amounted to 178,227 bales, the effect of the Spanish competition becomes apparent.

It is the general opinion of the cotton trade of Havre that the retrenchment of the last two years is having a beneficial effect, and that the prospects for a prosperous season are brighter.  One hears nowhere of accumulated stocks and ruinous prices.  There are almost no stocks of raw cotton at the mills, and the visible stocks at Havre are at a low figure.

By an inspection of the following table, showing the movement of the Havre cotton trade for the first nine months of 1900, 1901, and 1902, it will be seen that the importations were 55,089 bales less than in 1901, and 89,226 bales greater than in 1900. The sales, including exportations, were 889 bales less than in 1900. The visible stock on October 1 was 9,993 bales less than in 1901, and 14,340 bales greater than in 1900.

*Havre cotton statistics for the first nine months of 1900, 1901, and 1902.*

| Countries of origin. | Importations. | | | Sales. | | | Stock Oct. 1. | | |
|---|---|---|---|---|---|---|---|---|---|
| | 1900. | 1901. | 1902. | 1900. | 1901. | 1902. | 1900. | 1901. | 1902. |
| | *Bales.* | *Bales.* | *Bales.* | *Bales.* | *Bales.* | *Bales.* | *Bales.* | *Bales.* | *Bales.* |
| United States....... | 318,014 | 450,639 | 410,837 | 553,464 | 528,778 | 531,899 | 20,594 | 35,096 | 32,180 |
| India ................. | 11,048 | 32,069 | 16,780 | 13,091 | 20,080 | 21,155 | 3,637 | 14,978 | 7,114 |
| Other countries .... | 22,302 | 12,951 | 12,973 | 22,496 | 14,636 | 11,329 | 3,466 | 1,972 | 2,743 |
| Total........... | 351,364 | 495,679 | 440,590 | 589,051 | 563,494 | 564,383 | 27,697 | 52,030 | 42,037 |
| Increase or decrease in 1902............... | +89,226 | −55,089 | ......... | −24,668 | +889 | ......... | +14,340 | −9,993 | ......... |

### INDIA COTTON CROP, SEASON 1901-2.

According to the information furnished by the director-general of statistics of the government of India, there were 14,228,811 acres planted in cotton during the season 1901-2, against 14,267,645 acres in 1900-1901, which was an increase of 7 per cent over the average surfaces sown during the preceding five years. The crop is estimated at 356,826 tons against 385,450 tons in 1900-1901, a decrease of 7.4 per cent compared with the previous year, and a decrease of 2.4 per cent as compared with the average crops of the five last years. The provinces which produced the most cotton during the season were Bombay, 80,380 tons; provinces of the northwest and west, 48,277 tons; Berar, 44,449 tons, and central India, 40,741 tons. In Bengal and Burmah, the production was the smallest, 3,650 tons and 2,378 tons, respectively.

### ROUND BALES.

One of the cotton merchants in Havre, who is interested in the introduction of the round bale, writes me as follows:

We are still struggling manfully to get our ingenious way of packing cotton universally adopted. We are opposed strenuously by merchants at the ports because of interests. We have now determined to leave the ports alone, and to trade direct with spinners. The present season will go a long way toward showing whether this new policy is likely to be crowned with success. We may add that, owing to the competition of round bales, the shippers of square bales have improved their way of packing.

### HIDES.

There was no important change in the condition of the Havre hide market during the year 1901. The prices, which were low at the commencement of the year, varied but little till May, when there was a rise, particularly in the heavy hides, due to large purchases by the United States and England. These prices were maintained to the end of the year.

In 1901, there was a decrease in the importations of 370,841 pieces, as compared with 1900. The sales were 68,588 pieces less, and the stock in hand December 31 smaller by 101,977 pieces. In the follow-

ing table are given in detail the Havre hide statistics for the last three
years:

*Havre hide statistics.*

| Character. | Importations. | | | Sales. | | | Stocks, Dec. 31. | | |
|---|---|---|---|---|---|---|---|---|---|
| | 1899. | 1900. | 1901. | 1899. | 1900. | 1901. | 1899. | 1900. | 1901. |
| | *No.* | *No.* | *No.* | *No.* | *No.* | *No.* | *No.* | *No.* | *No.* |
| Plata and Rio Grande, dry .... | 33,946 | 65,575 | 48,973 | 67,184 | 43,933 | 53,667 | 584 | 21,226 | 16,582 |
| Plata, salted ....... | 235,450 | 325,797 | 308,539 | 312,421 | 287,054 | 352,740 | 6,276 | 65,019 | 20,818 |
| Rio Grande, salted. | 46,686 | 35,919 | 28,184 | 54,801 | 24,389 | 43,915 | 6,813 | 18,348 | 2,612 |
| Brazil ............. | 248,150 | 271,936 | 177,682 | 316,977 | 225,878 | 201,521 | 1,589 | 36,647 | 21,408 |
| South Pacific ...... | 163,875 | 153,531 | 148,811 | 188,156 | 129,668 | 166,424 | 14,112 | 36,348 | 19,075 |
| Various ............ | 338,525 | 591,592 | 361,820 | 354,506 | 562,092 | 366,159 | 10,291 | 39,791 | 34,952 |
| Total........ | 1,066,632 | 1,444,350 | 1,073,509 | 1,294,042 | 1,253,014 | 1,184,426 | 39,665 | 217,374 | 115,307 |
| Increase or decrease in 1901 .... | +6,877 | −370,841 | ........ | −109,616 | −68,588 | ........ | +75,782 | −101,977 | ....... |

There was a slight improvement in the Havre hide trade for the first
nine months of this year.

Although during the months of April and July the tanners bought
only to fill pressing wants, throughout the whole period there were
demands for exportation, which kept the market active. The prices
were firm, and in heavy hides they showed a tendency to rise.

There was an increase of 87,588 pieces in the exports for the first
nine months of 1902, as compared with the corresponding period of 1901;
the sales were about the same, and there was a decrease of 39,633
pieces in the stock on hand September 30.

In the following table are given the Havre hide statistics for the
first nine months of the last three years:

*Havre hide statistics for the first nine months of 1900, 1901, and 1902.*

| Character. | Importations. | | | Sales. | | | Stock, Dec. 31. | | |
|---|---|---|---|---|---|---|---|---|---|
| | 1900. | 1901. | 1902. | 1900. | 1901. | 1902. | 1900. | 1901. | 1902. |
| | *No.* | *No.* | *No.* | *No.* | *No.* | *No.* | *No.* | *No.* | *No.* |
| Plata and Rio Grande ........ | 30,422 | 84,790 | 19,491 | 23,998 | 36,451 | 33,381 | 7,008 | 19,585 | 2,722 |
| Plata, salted ..... | 245,276 | 256,952 | 269,274 | 195,133 | 300,021 | 271,620 | 56,407 | 31,900 | 18,487 |
| Rio Grande, salted ........... | 27,076 | 9,976 | 66,625 | 20,969 | 28,319 | 63,354 | 12,900 | 31,900 | 5,883 |
| Various ........... | 838,044 | 486,901 | 520,817 | 755,184 | 582,357 | 579,765 | 121,780 | 57,916 | 42,656 |
| Total........ | 1,140,818 | 788,619 | 876,207 | 995,304 | 947,148 | 948,070 | 198,095 | 109,381 | 69,748 |
| Decrease or increase, 1902..... | −264,611 | +87,588 | ........ | −47,234 | +922 | ........ | −123,347 | −39,633 | ....... |

As there are no large arrivals of hides in sight from the countries
of production, and there are great demands from the United States
and Great Britain, the indications are that the prices will still range
higher.

In the United States and in Great Britain, the prices of tanned
leather followed the rise in prices of the raw material, owing to the
increased consumption of the former in those countries, while in
France the prices of hides advanced, but those of leather did not
increase proportionately.

## WOOL.

The Havre wool market, owing to its excellent organization, passed through the serious crisis which was experienced in the French wool market in August, 1900, without being disastrously affected.

During 1901, the market resumed its normal condition, although the prices ruled comparatively lower than the average.

In January, there was a rise of about 10 per cent in the prices of fine wool as compared with the November prices of 1900. The large quantities of wool which were sold at the January sales in London, the low prices obtained, and the large stocks on hand caused the prices in the European markets to fall in February. The prices at the countries of production also declined, but the importers, after their experience of the previous year, hesitated to take advantage of the low market. The consequence was the imports were retarded, and the consumers having bought only for their pressing wants, the old stocks held over from 1900 were greatly reduced. This condition of affairs caused a sharp rise in April, and after a slight decline the prices remained firm till the close of the year.

The prices of ordinary wool were low during the whole year, closing at from 25 to 50 per cent, according to the quality, below the prices which were quoted at the end of 1900.

The imports of wool in 1901, the sales, and the stock on hand December 31 of that year were larger than during the previous season.

In the following table are given the Havre wool statistics in detail for the past three years.

*Havre wool statistics.*

| Countries of origin. | Importations. | | | Sales. | | | Stocks Dec. 31. | | |
|---|---|---|---|---|---|---|---|---|---|
| | 1899. | 1900. | 1901. | 1899. | 1900. | 1901. | 1899. | 1900. | 1901. |
| | *Bales.* | *Bales.* | *Bales.* | *Bales.* | *Bales.* | *Bales.* | *Bales.* | *Bales.* | *Bales.* |
| Buenos Ayres | 21,628 | 7,292 | 22,686 | 12,709 | 11,275 | 18,980 | | | |
| Montevideo and Rio Grande | 1,121 | 4,027 | 3,768 | 1,108 | 1,882 | 5,380 | | | |
| Peru and Chile | 6,877 | 5,501 | 2,895 | 7,462 | 2,082 | 5,024 | | | |
| Various | 748 | 150 | 805 | 883 | 371 | 180 | | | |
| Total | 30,374 | 16,970 | 30,154 | 22,157 | 15,510 | 24,404 | 12,596 | 14,056 | 19,806 |
| Increase (+) or decrease (−) in 1901 | −220 | +13,184 | | +2,247 | +8,894 | | +7,210 | +5,750 | |

During the past nine months of the present year, the prices of fine wool have advanced about 20 per cent and those of ordinary wool about 30 per cent.

As an indication of the present condition of the wool market, the result of the colonial wool auctions in London, which terminated October 2 last, shows that the sales have fallen off, the daily average being 11,741 bales, against 13,505 bales during the auction sales of the same period last year. Consumers only hold moderate stocks; larger orders are being received, and the chances are for a better trade.

During the first nine months of the present year, the imports of wool into Havre were 11,861 bales, as compared with 28,965 bales during the same period of 1901, a decrease of 17,104 bales; the sales were 17,661 bales, against 19,157 bales in 1901, a decrease of 1,496 bales, and the stock on hand September 30, 1902, 13,841 bales, against 23,864 bales in 1901, a decrease of 10,023 bales.

### COFFEE.

The importations of coffee in 1901 were the largest known in the history of the Havre market.    They were 2,065,898 bags, an increase of 811,792 bags over 1900 and 387,672 bags over 1899.    The increase was confined solely to Brazilian coffee, all the other coffees having fallen off in the receipts.    The imports of Brazilian coffee were 1,496,778 bags, an increase of 1,027,097 bags over 1900.

Exceptionally abundant crops in Brazil, following each other in two successive years, and the low prices resulting therefrom, stimulated the exports from that country to an unusual extent.

The great facilities for handling coffee at Havre, the moderate warehouse charges, the well-organized clearing-house system, and the low rates at which money can be borrowed on coffee from the local banks were the reasons why such large quantities of the Brazilian output found their way to this port.    The rate of interest fell as low as 2¾ per cent, while in other countries the rates were not lower than 4 per cent.

The buildings of the bonded warehouse company were found inadequate for storing the coffee, necessitating the renting of outside warehouses for bonded storage purposes.    There was also great difficulty experienced in obtaining insurance to cover the increased stock from the native and foreign insurance companies having agents in Havre, as their lines were full.    This fact was brought to the attention of American companies in a special report from this consulate,[a] but I have never heard of any action having been taken by them to secure a portion of the business.

The "Chargeurs Réunis," the French line of steamers having direct communication between the Brazilian coffee ports and 'Havre, was obliged to charter extra steamers to handle the increased imports.

Brazilian Santos is the only coffee sold on the terminal market of Havre.    Other coffees imported are those from Haiti, India, Central America, and the native and plantation Java.    In these coffees, there is a certain amount of speculation by those who do not wish to pay deposits or margins to the clearing house, as they would be required to do if they operated on the terminal market.

A large importer of Haitian products in Havre says:

I am of the opinion that the consumption of Haitian coffee in France is falling off.    The competition created by roasters is so keen and has increased to such an extent that they are bound in self-defense to buy cheaper qualities, which they find in Brazilian coffees.

In general, the coffee trade during the past year has been bad.  Reckless speculation in October and November, 1901, resulting from unfavorable reports on the growing crops in Brazil, succeeded in pushing prices to a dangerous level.  The inevitable smash came immediately after the beginning of the new year, with disastrous effects.

Haiti suffered severely, the bulk of the crop having been bought at high prices only to come to market at a considerably lower level.  In addition to this the quality was poor, an exceptionally prolonged rainy season having interfered with the drying before shipment.  Further, the crop was shorter than had been expected, the revolution which broke out early in May almost completely stopping deliveries. which, although generally small at that time of the year, would have otherwise been heavier.

In the following table is indicated the movement of the Havre coffee trade for the past three years.

---

[a] Consular Reports No. 258; Advance Sheets No. 1246.

*Havre coffee statistics.*

| Countries of origin. | Importations. | | | Sales. | | | Stocks Dec. 31. | | |
|---|---|---|---|---|---|---|---|---|---|
| | 1899. | 1900. | 1901. | 1899. | 1900. | 1901· | 1899. | 1900. | 1901.. |
| | *Bags.* | *Bags.* | *Bags.* | *Bags.* | *Bags.* | *Bags.* | *Bags.* | *Bags.* | *Bags.* |
| Brazil | 1,020,282 | 469,681 | 1,496,778 | 606,926 | 867,812 | 678,160 | 1,835,129 | 987,496 | 1,752,792 |
| Haiti | 237,850 | 271,736 | 270,147 | 268,100 | 238,500 | 246,688 | 98,458 | 131,689 | 160,094 |
| West Indies and Central America | 306,858 | 384,284 | 212,754 | 333,748 | 269,006 | 242,332 | 139,706 | 254,984 | 215,178 |
| East Indies | 78,568 | 99,450 | 70,357 | 61,881 | 70,268 | 79,530 | 58,937 | 88,119 | 79,980 |
| Various | 85,718 | 28,955 | 15,862 | 39,346 | 27,838 | 17,919 | 14,207 | 15,824 | 18,775 |
| Total | 1,678,296 | 1,254,106 | 2,065,898 | 1,310,001 | 1,472,424 | 1,259,629 | 1,646,432 | 1,428,114 | 2,221,764 |
| Increase (+) or decrease (−) in 1901 | +387,672 | +811,792 | | | −50,372 | −212,795 | | +575,332 | +798,650 | |

In the following table are given the importations, exportations, and
stocks on hand December 31 for the last ten years, in tons of 1,000
kilograms (2,204.6 pounds), for consumption in France or in transit to
other countries:

| Year. | Importations. | Exportations. | Stocks Dec. 31. | Year. | Importations. | Exportations. | Stocks Dec. 31. |
|---|---|---|---|---|---|---|---|
| | *Tons.* | *Tons.* | *Tons.* | | *Tons.* | *Tons.* | *Tons.* |
| 1892 | 116,957 | 46,391 | 22,705 | 1897 | 150,243 | 49,835 | 61,709 |
| 1893 | 114,901 | 60,599 | 18,489 | 1898 | 124,289 | 40,357 | 80,761 |
| 1894 | 100,442 | 50,432 | 24,367 | 1899 | 129,305 | 36,619 | 103,258 |
| 1895 | 122,175 | 50,590 | 26,408 | 1900 | 103,670 | 45,709 | 89,571 |
| 1896 | 100,807 | 42,259 | 21,794 | 1901 | 150,682 | 27,054 | 140,868 |

The price of good average Santos coffee per 50 kilograms (110.23
pounds) at the commencement of the year was 39 francs 25 centimes
($7.58). It slowly fell till the 1st of September, when it reached its
minimum, 33 francs 25 centimes ($6.42). The decline was due to the
Brazilian crops having been much larger than had been predicted,
causing stocks to accumulate all over the world. Toward the end of
September and in October, reports were sent out from Brazil stating
that, owing to the great and protracted drought, the buds were damaged
and that there would only be half a crop. The unfavorable news
caused heavy speculation, the prices rose rapidly, and on November
16 they reached their maximum of 49 francs 25 centimes ($9.51). The
reports of the injury to the growing crops were found to be exaggerated; the prices fell rapidly, the decline being assisted by the unloading of weak speculators, and in January of the present year, they
again reached the low level of 33 francs 50 centimes ($6.47). The
losses sustained by the speculators and by the coffee trade in general
were enormous.

The price quoted October 3, 1902, was 37 francs 50 centimes ($7.24).

H. Doc. 305, pt 2——10

In the following table are given Havre coffee statistics for the first nine months of 1900, 1901, and 1902:

*Havre coffee statistics for the first nine months of 1900, 1901, and 1902.*

| Countries of origin. | Importations. | | | Sales. | | | Stocks Oct. 2. | | |
|---|---|---|---|---|---|---|---|---|---|
| | 1900. | 1901. | 1902. | 1900. | 1901. | 1902. | 1900. | 1901. | 1902. |
| | *Bags.* | *Bags.* | *Bags.* | *Bags.* | *Bags.* | *Bags.* | *Bags.* | *Bags.* | *Bags.* |
| Brazil | 299,286 | 735,014 | 1,189,981 | 706,668 | 517,214 | 663,358 | 327,732 | 1,146,974 | 2,852,601 |
| Haiti | 241,568 | 216,562 | 228,251 | 187,641 | 184,737 | 188,781 | 152,380 | 168,460 | 197,857 |
| Antilles and Central America | 369,941 | 186,485 | 275,232 | 221,908 | 177,016 | 176,899 | 288,344 | 254,220 | 312,912 |
| India | 78,305 | 54,577 | 45,145 | 54,301 | 58,181 | 48,951 | 82,941 | 85,499 | 74,481 |
| Various | 26,285 | 11,765 | 22,880 | 22,257 | 13,156 | 16,098 | 18,235 | 14,441 | 20,117 |
| Total | 1,015,865 | 1,204,403 | 1,760,969 | 1,192,165 | 950,304 | 1,088,582 | 1,469,632 | 1,669,594 | 2,957,968 |
| Increase or decrease in 1902 | +745,574 | +556,586 | ........ | −108,583 | +133,278 | ........ | +1,488,836 | +1,288,874 | ........ |

By an inspection of the above table, it will be seen that the large importations of coffee into Havre during the year 1901 were continued during the first nine months of the present year.

The sales in that period and the stock on hand October 2, 1902, were also larger than in the corresponding months of 1901. The amount of coffee stored in the bonded warehouses of Havre to-day is probably the largest single stock in the world, being nearly 3,000,000 bags.

The visible stocks of the world have also been heavily increased; they were 447,810 tons on January 1, 1901, 639,010 tons on January 1, 1902, and 673,150 tons on July 1, 1902.

### INDIGO.

The imports of indigo into Havre during 1901 were the smallest for the past ten years, being 450 tons, as compared with 686 tons and 583 tons in 1900 and 1899, respectively. There were 2,314 cases received from Bengal, 80 cases from Madras, Bombay, and Kurpah, and 1,685 serons (baskets) from Guatemala. The indigo trade was unsatisfactory during the year, the natural product suffering keenly from the competition of the artificial dyes. The prices showed no recovery from the low figures of 1900. The absence of a commercial treaty between France and Guatemala, an indigo-producing country, tends to hamper the indigo trade between the two nations.

The following are the Havre indigo statistics for the past five years:

*Havre indigo statistics.*

| Year. | Importations. | Exportations. | Stock Dec. 31. | Year. | Importations. | Exportations. | Stock Dec. 31. |
|---|---|---|---|---|---|---|---|
| | *Tons.* | *Tons.* | *Tons.* | | *Tons.* | *Tons.* | *Tons.* |
| 1897 | 796 | 119 | 455 | 1900 | 686 | 110 | 419 |
| 1898 | 552 | 141 | 351 | 1901 | 450 | 191 | 311 |
| 1899 | 583 | 113 | 407 | | | | |

Of the total importations of indigo into France in 1900 (969 tons), 686 tons were received at Havre.

## COCOA.

There was no material improvement in the cocoa trade of Havre in 1901.

The prices at the end of the year were lower than for the past five years. The imports were 25,970 tons, a decrease of 1,360 tons as compared with 1900, and of 4,502 tons as compared with 1899.

In the following table are given the statistics for the past five years:

*Havre cocoa statistics.*

| Year. | Impor- tations. | Expor- tations. | Stock Dec. 31. | Year. | Impor- tations. | Expor- tations. | Stock Dec. 31. |
|---|---|---|---|---|---|---|---|
| | *Tons.* | *Tons.* | *Tons.* | | *Tons.* | *Tons.* | *Tons.* |
| 1897 | 17,364 | 10,227 | 3,842 | 1900 | 27,330 | 15,612 | 6,152 |
| 1898 | 25,513 | 12,506 | 4,943 | 1901 | 25,970 | 13,972 | 5,532 |
| 1899 | 30,472 | 14,870 | 7,961 | | | | |

The imports of cocoa into Havre for the first nine months of 1902 were the largest for several years. The sales and stock were also greater than during the same period of 1901.

Havre continues to be an important port for the reception of cocoa intended for consumption in the interior and for the use of the local manufacturers of chocolate. In 1900, the entire receipts of cocoa in France were 32,752 tons, of which 27,330 tons came to Havre.

In the following table are given the Havre statistics of cocoa for the first nine months of 1902, 1901, and 1900:

*Havre cocoa statistics for the first nine months of 1902, 1901, and 1900.*

| Countries of origin. | Importations. | | | Sales. | | | Stocks Sept. 30— | | |
|---|---|---|---|---|---|---|---|---|---|
| | 1902. | 1901. | 1900. | 1902. | 1901. | 1900. | 1902. | 1901. | 1900. |
| | *Bags.* | *Bags.* | *Bags.* | *Bags.* | *Bags.* | *Bags.* | *Bags.* | *Bags.* | *Bags.* |
| Para Maraguan | 25,643 | 11,766 | 8,598 | 18,125 | 11,875 | 9,140 | 10,590 | 4,612 | 4,821 |
| Trinidad | 76,147 | 42,909 | 68,096 | 66,064 | 42,760 | 56,480 | 21,962 | 18,559 | 24,463 |
| Cote Ferme | 88,918 | 56,411 | 65,731 | 72,060 | 50,932 | 65,600 | 32,419 | 21,418 | 19,389 |
| Bahia | 19,559 | 23,756 | 19,178 | 18,190 | 23,540 | 15,585 | 4,914 | 4,531 | 5,625 |
| Haiti and Domingo | 16,248 | 21,396 | 19,518 | 13,630 | 21,870 | 24,270 | 6,478 | 4,215 | 3,086 |
| Guayaquil | 92,685 | 85,188 | 60,519 | 88,850 | 80,200 | 68,480 | 31,162 | 32,306 | 24,058 |
| Martinique and Guadeloupe | 2,594 | 8,872 | 3,209 | 3,753 | 3,953 | 2,980 | 684 | 1,590 | 816 |
| Various | 103,270 | 61,527 | 66,602 | 78,080 | 53,790 | 60,975 | 32,544 | 16,288 | 23,501 |
| Total | 425,014 | 306,765 | 308,446 | 358,722 | 288,920 | 303,460 | 140,736 | 103,519 | 105,759 |
| Increase in 1902 | | 118,248 | 116,568 | | 69,802 | 55,262 | | 37,239 | 34,994 |

## PEPPER.

The importations of pepper into Havre in 1901 were 56,759 bags, as compared with 30,915 bags in 1900 and 23,807 bags in 1899. Of the imports in 1901, 25,296 bags were from Tellicherry and Alipee, Malabar Coast; 3,691 bags from Singapore, and 27,772 bags from the French possession of Saïgon. In the following table are shown the Havre pepper statistics for the last three years:

*Havre pepper statistics.*

| Origin. | Importations. | | | Sales. | | | Stocks Dec. 31— | | |
|---|---|---|---|---|---|---|---|---|---|
| | 1901. | 1900. | 1899. | 1901. | 1900. | 1899. | 1901. | 1900. | 1899. |
| | *Bags.* | *Bags.* | *Bags.* | *Bags.* | *Bags.* | *Bags.* | *Bags.* | *Bags.* | *Bags.* |
| Alipee and Telli-cherry | 25,296 | 4,948 | 4,623 | 22,594 | 23,532 | 23,598 | 48,425 | 45,723 | 59,351 |
| Singapore | 3,691 | 4,912 | 2,546 | 4,675 | 4,488 | 5,308 | 1,225 | 2,906 | 5,466 |
| Penang | | 143 | 60 | 23 | 90 | 178 | 36 | 59 | 1,742 |
| Saigon | 27,772 | 20,912 | 16,578 | 18,988 | 14,656 | 16,661 | 29,791 | 23,317 | 15,801 |
| Total | 56,759 | 30,915 | 23,807 | 46,280 | 42,861 | 45,740 | 80,177 | 72,005 | 82,360 |
| Increase or de-crease in 1901 | | +25,844 | +32,952 | | +3,369 | +490 | | +8,172 | −2,183 |

By an inspection of the above statistics, it will be seen that the receipts from Saïgon show a progressive increase.  This is due to the enactment of the French customs law by which pepper from the French colonies, up to 3,000 tons per year, is allowed to come into France upon the payment of half duty.

In the following table are shown the pepper statistics of Havre for the first nine months of 1902, 1901, and 1900.

*Havre pepper statistics for the first nine months of 1902, 1901, and 1900.*

| Origin. | Importations. | | | Sales. | | | Stocks Sept. 30— | | |
|---|---|---|---|---|---|---|---|---|---|
| | 1902. | 1901. | 1900. | 1902. | 1901. | 1900. | 1902. | 1901. | 1900. |
| | *Bags.* | *Bags.* | *Bags.* | *Bags.* | *Bags.* | *Bags.* | *Bags.* | *Bags.* | *Bags.* |
| Alipee and Telli-cherry | 1,200 | 24,905 | 4,111 | 21,327 | 14,357 | 13,056 | 27,561 | 56,271 | 55,868 |
| Singapore | 2,301 | 1,234 | 2,816 | 2,749 | 3,454 | 3,837 | 1,452 | 689 | 1,956 |
| Penang | 130 | | 143 | 42 | 16 | 58 | 129 | 43 | 91 |
| Saigon | 30,237 | 27,285 | 17,668 | 14,864 | 12,271 | 10,987 | 44,414 | 35,971 | 21,742 |
| Total | 33,868 | 53,424 | 24,738 | 39,582 | 30,098 | 27,438 | 73,556 | 92,974 | 79,657 |
| Increase or de-crease in 1902 | | −19,556 | +9,130 | | +9,484 | +12,144 | | −19,418 | −6,101 |

One of the largest importers of East India pepper at Havre writes to me as follows:

As far as East Indian pepper is concerned, the crop season 1901-2 was a very poor one, and very little business was done for export to Europe and America.

As regards Harve, this port has greatly lost its prestige as a large importing market for Tellicherry pepper, for the reason that prices have ruled high enough to preclude speculation.  You will see from the above table that the imports from January 1 to September 30, 1902, were only 1,200 bags, against 24,905 bags last year.

The fact of the matter is that the people interested in the article have manipulated the market in such a way as to prevent new imports.  Other European countries are appreciating more the quality of our staple article and the trade has become diverted.  Nowadays, we ship directly to ports which formerly consumed other kinds of pepper.

Stocks in Havre have been largely diminishing, owing to the fact that local prices have been kept below the values of producing countries, in consequence of which buyers were attracted and bought pepper in this market.  Good qualities have also been shipped to the United States.

Tellicherry pepper seldom enters into French consumption, owing to the increased production in the French colonies of Saïgon and Indo China.  As regards trade from the west coast of India to America, very little was done during the past season, owing to small crops in India and the relatively cheaper prices ruling in the Straits Settlements.  I think another obstacle to the trade between the west coast of India and America is the high rate of freight, as it is very seldom we can secure direct steamer shipments, which places us at a disadvantage as compared with Singapore.

## WOOD FOR CABINETMAKING PURPOSES.

The importations of hard wood of all kinds into Havre during 1901 were 22,735 tons, as compared with 24,843 tons in 1900 and 19,387 tons in 1899.

The imports of mahogany were 11,547 tons, against 10,382 tons in 1900 and 8,345 tons in 1899. Of the imports of mahogany for 1901, 2,067 tons were received from the island of Cuba. At the end of the year, the stock of mahogany was 4,698 tons. The hard-wood trade of Havre in 1901 was unsatisfactory. There were public sales in March and October, but the prices obtained and the amounts sold were not encouraging.

In the following table are given the Havre hard-wood statistics for the last four years:

*Havre hard-wood statistics.*

| Character. | 1898. | 1899. | 1900. | 1901. |
|---|---|---|---|---|
| | *Tons.* | *Tons.* | *Tons.* | *Tons.* |
| Mahogany | 8,673 | 8,345 | 10,382 | 11,547 |
| Pallisander | 1,872 | 1,655 | 2,108 | 667 |
| Mexican and other cedar | 433 | 558 | 614 | 699 |
| Espenille | 90 | 204 | 204 | 46 |
| Lignum vitae | 392 | 259 | 991 | 1,094 |
| Pencil cedar | 884 | 667 | 845 | 519 |
| Maple | 239 | 264 | 306 | 627 |
| Walnut | 780 | 364 | 914 | 301 |
| Box | 1,270 | 628 | 1,551 | 848 |
| Rosewood | 40 | 39 | 42 | 18 |
| Ebony | 1,363 | 1,006 | 1,496 | 1,980 |
| Various | 3,364 | 5,898 | 5,375 | 4,479 |
| Total | 19,300 | 19,387 | 24,843 | 22,735 |

Mahogany is bought by metric weight in the Havre market by English dealers, who will take a whole cargo, the good with the bad. It is sent to England, where the wood is assorted and choice logs sent to the United States to fill orders from American buyers; the poorer qualities being disposed of in England. It would seem as if the American dealer could save a middleman's profit by buying directly in the French market.

## DYEWOODS.

Over 90 per cent of the dyewoods received in France is imported into Havre. The wood is for the use of the large establishments engaged in the manufacture of dyewood extracts located in this city. The commerce is an extensive one, but is affected by the keen competition of the artificial dyes. The imports of dyewoods into Havre were the smallest for many years; those of logwood the smallest since 1875, and those of fustic smallest since 1878. The decline in the imports of 1901 is explained by the manufacturers by the general industrial depression which has existed in Europe through the wars in South Africa and China, but principally by the decreased demand for the natural products caused by the ever growing consumption of the aniline colors in the industrial arts.

There was also a decided falling off in the prices.

In the following table are given the details of the importations for the past five years:

*Havre dyewood statistics.*

| Character. | 1897. | 1898. | 1899. | 1900. | 1901. |
|---|---|---|---|---|---|
| | *Tons.* | *Tons.* | *Tons.* | *Tons.* | *Tons.* |
| Logwood | 61,995 | 45,970 | 64,500 | 60,465 | 48,935 |
| Fustic | 10,815 | 9,850 | 13,815 | 7,060 | 5,420 |
| Redwood | 970 | 470 | 1,690 | 840 | 925 |
| Quebracho | 8,960 | 10,595 | 18,500 | 23,075 | 11,050 |
| Total | 82,740 | 66,885 | 98,505 | 91,440 | 61,880 |

The bulk of the logwood received at Havre comes from Haiti, fustic from Central America and the West Indies, and redwood from Peru.

### WOOD FOR BUILDING PURPOSES.

There was a notable increase in the imports into Havre of wood for building purposes during 1901, especially in those of oak staves. All of the latter came from the United States.

During 1901, there were imported into the whole of France 202,815 tons of oak staves, 118,294 tons from Austro-Hungary, 55,702 tons from the United States, 13,194 tons from Russia, 433 tons from Germany, and 15,193 tons from other countries.

As has been mentioned several times in annual reports from this consulate, Havre is a good market for the sale of American wood, if our shippers will be careful in filling their orders according to the requirements of the French trade and if they will make prompt shipments. In my annual report for 1899,[a] under the subject of wood, there will be found information which will be useful to American wood exporters.

In the following table are given the Havre building-wood statistics for the past four years:

*Havre building-wood statistics.*

| Character. | 1898. | 1899. | 1900. | 1901. |
|---|---|---|---|---|
| | *Tons.* | *Tons.* | *Tons.* | *Tons.* |
| Oak, undressed, squared, or sawed in various dimensions. | 4,586 | 3,898 | 6,743 | 2,681 |
| Oak staves | 8,224 | 6,727 | 6,958 | 10,154 |
| Walnut, undressed, sawed or squared | 137 | 134 | 49 | 592 |
| Other woods, undressed, sawed or squared | 57,019 | 64,137 | 66,081 | 73,897 |
| Total | 69,966 | 74,891 | 79,776 | 87,324 |
| Increase in 1901 | 17,358 | 12,433 | 7,548 | |

### CRUDE RUBBER AND GUTTA-PERCHA.

There were increased imports of crude rubber and gutta-percha into Havre during the year 1901 as compared with previous years. They were 5,223 tons against 5,108 tons in 1900 and 5,037 tons in 1898. The exports showed a falling off, being 2,460 tons in 1901 as compared with 2,675 tons in 1900 and 2,824 tons in 1899. The value of the declared exports of crude rubber to the United States from this

---

[a] Commercial Relations, 1900, Vol. II.

consulate for the fiscal year ended June 30, 1902, was also less than in the previous year, being $62,919 against $155,884.

Rubber being a product in which there is much speculation, it is very sensitive to any change of values or conditions, and the current of trade is easily diverted. Besides, the United States last year imported largely increased quantities from the countries of production, thus requiring less from Europe.

Last season's crop having been a large one—the most abundant for many years—and the prospects of the coming crop also being favorable for another great yield, there has been a decline in the prices, aided by the industrial depression existing in Continental Europe.

In the following table are indicated the importations of crude rubber into Havre for the last four years and the countries of origin:

*Havre crude-rubber statistics.*

| Countries of origin. | 1898. | 1899. | 1900. | 1901. |
|---|---|---|---|---|
| | *Tons.* | *Tons.* | *Tons.* | *Tons.* |
| England | 333 | 446 | 346 | 509 |
| Germany | 37 | 208 | 201 | 145 |
| Holland | 59 | 30 | 11 | 29 |
| Belgium | 32 | 30 | 59 | 12 |
| Portugal | 282 | 50 | 15 | 42 |
| English India | 336 | 641 | 582 | 555 |
| United States | 200 | 230 | 276 | 176 |
| Colombia | 99 | 77 | 51 | 52 |
| Brazil | 1,736 | 1,714 | 2,167 | 2,090 |
| Venezuela | | | | 25 |
| Peru | | | 432 | 582 |
| English West Indies | | | | 148 |
| Haiti | | | | 23 |
| St. Thomas | | | | 29 |
| Dutch West Indies | | | | 45 |
| Other foreign countries | 771 | 800 | 195 | 37 |
| Senegal | 22 | 87 | 42 | 37 |
| West side of Africa | 230 | 434 | 432 | 407 |
| Nossi-Bé | 12 | 37 | 26 | |
| Madagascar | 72 | 148 | 131 | 66 |
| Other French colonies | | 80 | 150 | 283 |
| Total | 4,180 | 5,087 | 5,106 | 5,229 |

The increase in the receipts from England is due to the recent establishment of a terminal market for crude rubber at Liverpool. The rubber crop in Brazil for the season 1901–02 was 29,997 tons, against 27,640 tons in 1900–01, 26,693 tons in 1899–1900, 25,374 tons in 1898–99, and 22,257 tons in 1897–98.

## CEREALS.

France being an agricultural country in which large quantities of wheat are produced annually, the importation of foreign wheat depends almost entirely on the abundance of the local harvests. During 1901, the wheat crop of France, although but little below the average, was not sufficient to supply the native wants, and importation of foreign wheat was necessary. The imports into Havre of this cereal in 1901 were 61,824 tons against 41,800 tons in 1900 and 19,261 tons in 1899. Of the imports in 1901, 49,861 tons came from the United States.

As predicted in my last annual report, the imports of oats showed a decided increase, being 27,936 tons against 7,014 tons in 1900 and 21,725 tons in 1899. Of the 27,936 tons imported, 24,036 tons were American oats.

Owing to the short corn crop in the United States in 1901 and the high prices prevailing, the importations of that grain into Havre showed a decrease as compared with the previous year. They were 70,642 tons against 72,119 in 1900 and 67,074 tons in 1899.

This year's corn crop in America being a record breaker, it is thought that large quantities will be imported into France, both for fattening animals and for industrial purposes. Last year, the French distillers almost gave up the use of American corn, as its price was too high in comparison with that of alcohol.

Attention is again called to the condition in which cargoes of American corn arrive at Havre. In many cases the grain is heated, not having been properly dried before shipment. If more care were shown in preparing the corn for exportation, an increased trade abroad would result, there would be less loss to the French importer, and fewer complaints from the foreign consumer. Considering that but a small percentage of our corn crop is exported, enlarged foreign outlets would be desirable.

In the following table are given the importations of the principal cereals into Havre for the last ten years:

*Havre grain statistics.*

| Year. | Wheat. | Oats. | Corn. | Barley. | Total. |
|---|---|---|---|---|---|
| | Tons. | Tons. | Tons. | Tons. | Tons. |
| 1892 | 335,767 | 4 | 13,412 | 21 | 349,204 |
| 1893 | 228,998 | 8,330 | 16,929 | 15,497 | 269,749 |
| 1894 | 190,874 | 5,837 | 23,188 | 8,291 | 228,990 |
| 1895 | 62,417 | 5,345 | 28,894 | 4,253 | 100,909 |
| 1896 | 34,763 | 17,530 | 39,894 | 1,927 | 94,114 |
| 1897 | 127,165 | 38,555 | 61,148 | 5,238 | 232,106 |
| 1898 | 351,804 | 25,436 | 69,129 | 3 | 446,372 |
| 1899 | 19,261 | 21,725 | 67,074 | 1,759 | 109,819 |
| 1900 | 41,800 | 7,014 | 72,119 | 282 | 121,215 |
| 1901 | 61,824 | 27,936 | 70,642 | 709 | 161,111 |

Notwithstanding the efforts which were made by the United States Agricultural Department at the exposition in Paris in 1900, and are still being made by that Department, by our consular officers, and others to extend the use of American corn as an alimentary product in foreign countries, the sale of American corn preparations in France does not increase to any great extent. The local grocers inform me that they seldom have a call for corn goods, except from Americans or English.

The imports of corn flour into France, most of which came from the United States, were 1,031 tons in 1899, 724 tons in 1900, and 657 tons in 1901.

The law which was passed by the French Parliament January 29, 1902, modifying the system by which wheat was admitted temporarily into France, has curtailed the privileges enjoyed under the old law. Speculation in the custom-house receipts for wheat, which had attained large proportions, will now be rendered difficult. The conditions under which wheat may be imported temporarily, manufactured into flour, and reexported, are now so strict it is thought the importations will be greatly restricted.

The question of the increase of the duties on foreign corn to 5 francs (96½ cents) per 100 kilograms (220.46 pounds) will probably come up during this session of Parliament. It would be difficult to predict whether the measure will receive favorable consideration, as there is considerable opposition from the raisers of cattle and from the distillers.

The statistics of the imports of cereals into Havre for the present year are not available at this time, but according to the official customs returns there were 175,846 tons of wheat imported into France during the first nine months of 1902, for consumption in France (commerce spécial), against 114,843 tons in the same period of 1901. Of the former amount, 123,926 tons came from Algeria.

The imports of oats were 184,446 tons against 288,624 tons in 1901; barley, 113,900 tons against 123,720 tons, and corn, 189,921 tons against 241,406 tons.

### GRAIN CROP OF FRANCE IN 1901-2.

Now that the harvests are gathered, the minister of agriculture, the "Bulletin des Halles," and the "Marché Français" have published their estimates of the probable results of the wheat crop of France for the season 1901-2. The minister of agriculture, in the "Journal Officiel" of October 4, 1902, estimates the wheat crop at 124,296,601 hectoliters, or 352,753,754 bushels (a hectoliter being 2.838 bushels). The estimate of the "Bulletin des Halles" is 125,202,300 hectoliters, or 355,324,127 bushels, and that of the "Marché Français" 134,897,986 hectoliters, or 382,840,484 bushels. According to official statistics, the wheat crop of 1901 was 109,573,810 hectoliters, or 310,970,473 bushels.

It is the opinion of the "Bulletin des Halles" that, notwithstanding that the stocks of wheat on hand at the commencement of the present season were greatly reduced, the excess required to supply the wants of local consumption can be imported from Algeria and Tunis, the wheat from the latter countries coming into France without payment of duty.

The wheat crop this year, upon the basis of the estimate of the "Bulletin des Halles," will be 14,722,791 hectoliters, or 41,783,281 bushels, larger than the crop of last year, and 10,575,681 hectoliters, or 30,013,783 bushels, larger than the average crop for the last ten years.

Although the present wheat crop is a large one, there are doubts expressed as to its quality. Owing to the wet weather which prevailed in many regions of France during the harvest season, it is thought that much of the wheat will be unfit for milling purposes. Until it is definitely known what the exact condition of the new wheat is, the quantity to be imported will remain problematical.

### COAL.

The receipts of coal in France in 1901 were 13,775,560 metric tons, a decrease of 588,166 tons as compared with 1900, and an increase of 2,116,641 tons over 1899.

The decrease in the coal imports in 1901 is readily explained. During 1900 the imports were abnormally large, in fact the largest ever known, owing to the decreased production of native coal, caused by the general strike which took place in the mining regions of France. There was also an increased consumption during that year, as the country had not yet felt the effects of the reaction which took place after the Paris Exposition, and of the industrial depression which is now existing in continental Europe. The strikes having been settled, the native production became normal, and the demands for home consumption having decreased, the imports of foreign coal fell off.

Of the receipts in 1901, Great Britain sent 7,957,900 tons, Belgium 4,790,410 tons, Germany 782,460 tons, and the United States 228,930 tons.

The imports into Havre in 1901, all of which, except 1,900 tons, came from Great Britain, were 780,792 tons, a decrease of 94,854 tons as compared with 1900, but 80,000 tons greater than the average importations for the last five years.

The importation of American coal into northern France has practically ceased for the present, as the conditions are not favorable for the sale of the American combustible. Even before the great anthracite strike, which created scarcity of coal of all kinds in the United States and caused the prices to rise abnormally high, the prices at which British coal was selling left no margin of profit to the American shippers, notwithstanding the low rates of freights between American coal ports and those of northern France.

The two cargoes of American anthracite which were sent to Rouen last year unfortunately did not prove suitable for the French market, the coal being too hard for burning in French stoves. About 2,000 tons were left on the importer's hands, but on account of the scarcity and high prices of the American anthracite in the United States during the strike, the coal was recently sold in New York and shipped back to that port from Rouen at a profit, even after paying freight both ways and storage charges for nearly a year.

I am still of the opinion that there will be a favorable opening in France for American anthracite when the prices in the United States resume their normal level, if our anthracite miners will select a softer grade of coal for use in the French market.

### GERMAN COAL AT HAVRE.

German steam coal has made its appearance in Havre. The first shipment ever received in this port arrived some weeks ago. I have not been able as yet to ascertain the exact price paid for the coal, but I am informed that it can be sold cheaper than Cardiff small coal, the price of which at present, f. o. b. Havre, is 16 shillings ($3.89) per ton.

The German coal contains from 10 to 15 per cent of small pieces, the rest being dust, but the importers tell me that the results of the experiments they have made indicate that it is an economical steam producer. They are now making trials of larger sizes of German coal for household purposes.

I have also been told that one of the industrial establishments located in Havre has made a contract for 30,000 tons of the German coal. Cargoes have also been received at Rouen and Caen.

The coal, which came from the Westphalian mines, is loaded in large barges at Ruhrhort on the Rhine, then sent to Rotterdam, where it is put in steamers and shipped to the French ports.

Whether the trade in the German coal in the northern ports of France will be a permanent one, or if, when the demands for local consumption in Germany resume their normal proportions, the Westphalian syndicate will still continue their shipments, remains to be seen. The appearance of German coal in this part of France, however, indicates that the Germans are watching every opportunity of finding foreign outlets for their surplus production.

COAL PRODUCTION OF FRANCE FOR THE FIRST SIX MONTHS OF 1902.

According to the provisional statistics furnished by the minister of public works, the coal production of France for the first six months of the present year was 16,194,515 tons, of which 15,874,098 tons were anthracite and bituminous coal and 320,417 tons lignite. In comparison with the corresponding period of 1901, there was an increase of 448,562 tons in the output of anthracite and bituminous coal and a decrease of 21,178 tons in lignite, making a net increase of 427,384 tons.

### PETROLEUM AND HEAVY OILS.

The imports of crude petroleum into Havre for the year 1900 were 35,820 tons, 28,030 tons of which were received from the United States and 7,790 tons from Batum.

The imports of refined petroleum were 1,738 tons, all of which, with the exception of 4 tons, came from the United States.

The crude petroleum was imported for the use of the large refineries located at Havre.

The imports of heavy petroleum oils were 12,031 tons, of which 11,197 tons were from the United States, the remainder from Russia, England, and Germany.

In the following table are given the petroleum and heavy oil statistics for the past five years. Under the head of petroleum are included the receipts of the refined product:

*Havre petroleum and heavy oil statistics.*

| Character. | 1897. | 1898. | 1899. | 1900. | 1901. |
|---|---|---|---|---|---|
| | Tons. | Tons. | Tons. | Tons. | Tons. |
| Crude and refined petroleum | 19,108 | 37,008 | 37,189 | 35,708 | 37,558 |
| Petroleum heavy oils | 11,158 | 11,512 | 12,219 | 12,440 | 12,031 |

No action has yet been taken by the Parliament on the proposed legislation to impose a manufacturing tax of 1.50 francs (28.95 cents) per 100 kilograms (220.4 pounds) on crude mineral oils. The details of the measure were given in the last annual report of this consulate.

### NICKEL.

The nickel ore imported into Havre is for the use of the nickel-refining company (Société Anonyme Le Nickel), whose works are located in this city. The imports of ore, all of which came from New Caledonia, were 41,422 tons, against 17,681 tons in 1900 and 42,188 tons in 1899. Two hundred and fifty-three tons of nickel ingots were received from the United States.

In 1901, there were 27,926 tons of copper, pure and alloyed, imported into Havre and 3,149 tons of tin, pure or alloyed.

### WINES AND LIQUEURS.

The wine crop of 1901, although not so abundant as the record-breaking production of 1900, was a very large one, being 1,531,208,571 gallons, as compared with 1,779,466,000 gallons in 1900. Such large yields coming in two successive years checked the importation of wine for blending purposes. The exports were nearly the same as last year.

The importations into the whole of France in 1900 were: Ordinary wine, 101,508,221 gallons, and dessert wines, 10,189,195 gallons. Most of the former came from Algeria and the bulk of the latter from Spain. The exports of ordinary wine were 59,953,091 gallons, and dessert wines 2,526,892 gallons. The principal countries to which the wine was sent, in the order of their importance, were Switzerland, Germany, Belgium, and Holland.

The exports of champagne were 4,830,877 gallons, the principal countries receiving the wine being England, Belgium, United States, and Germany.

Havre imported during 1901, 30,905 barrels of rum and tafia, against 29,104 barrels in 1900 and 28,731 barrels in 1899. The rum trade of Havre during the year suffered a veritable crisis. Less than half the imports entered into consumption, and the prices fell from 60 francs ($11.58) to 27 francs ($5.21).

### TALLOW.

During 1901, there were 3,824 tons of tallow imported into Havre, as compared with 3,304 tons in 1900 and 5,696 tons in 1899.

Owing to the high prices of tallow prevailing in the United States, less was received from that country than for many years, while the imports from the Argentine Republic were more than doubled. Of the receipts in 1901, the United States furnished 1,106 tons and the Argentine Republic 2,435 tons.

The United States has this year imported large quantities of tallow and palm oil from Europe. Another feature of the trade has been the steady demand which has existed during the whole year for oleo stearine for shipment to our country, where the curtailed production of all beef fats and the large consumption of these products, which are used as a hardening fat in the manufacture of lard compounds from cotton oil, have kept the prices at an abnormally high figure.

During the first nine months of 1902, the imports of tallow into the whole of France for local consumption were 8,173 tons, against 12,896 tons and 9,841 tons during the corresponding periods of 1901 and 1900.

### LARD.

The imports of lard into France in 1901 were the lowest for many years, being 2,709 tons, against 5,952 tons in 1900 and 7,966 tons in 1899. The decline in the foreign lard trade was due to the high prices which prevailed in the United States, to the almost prohibitory duty of 25 francs ($4.825) per 100 kilograms (220.46 pounds), nearly 2.25 cents per pound, levied by the French Government on all foreign lard, to the increasing production of French compound lard, and to the low prices of French pure lard. The latter could be purchased at a third or a quarter less money than the American product. Since the 1st of January, 1902, the quantity of American lard which has passed into consumption in France is less than one-third of what was imported last year, and less than one-fifth of the consumption of 1900. The imports into the whole of France for the first nine months of 1902 were 1,838 tons, against 5,630 tons and 8,810 tons during the same periods of 1901 and 1900. The receipts from the United States were 1,472 tons, 5,262 tons, and 8,400 tons, respectively.

## SALT PROVISIONS.

The high prices prevailing in America for all food products caused the imports of salt provisions into Havre to again decline. They were, in 1901, 1,014 tons, against 1,846 tons in 1900 and 2,810 tons in 1899. Of the imports of 1901, 922 tons were hog meat and 92 tons beef products.

But little dry salted bacon was received during the year, as hams were comparatively cheaper than the bacon. Most of the foreign hams imported into France are shipped from Germany and England, and are often American hams which have been smoked and trimmed in these countries so as to resemble German and English products.

Of canned meats, almost the same quantity has been imported as for the last years. Of those received in France, the larger portion is reexported either to French colonies or used as ship stores for vessels fitting out in French ports. The amount of canned meats actually consumed in France itself keeps on declining steadily.

The imports of salt provisions into the whole of France for the first nine months of 1902 were 3,536 tons of salted pork products and 135 tons of salted beef, against 3,854 tons of salted pork products and 127 tons of salted beef during the same period in 1901, and 7,201 tons of salted pork products and 118 tons of salted beef during the first nine months of 1900.

## DRIED FRUITS.

In consequence of the monster cider production in France in 1900, and the decreased consumption of the beverage owing to the low price at which wine has been selling for the past two years, the imports of chopped apples into Havre in 1901 were much smaller than for several years. The receipts from the United States, the country from which the bulk of the chopped apples received in Havre is shipped, were 779 tons, against 1,705 tons in 1900 and 2,318 tons in 1899. The imports into the whole of France during the same periods were 1,265 tons, 5,208 tons, and 6,791 tons, respectively.

The French crops of nearly all kinds of fruit have been very poor this year, which has caused a largely increased demand for American products. The apple trees blossomed remarkably well, and everything seemed to point to one of the largest productions, but a cold and wet spring prevented the fruit from setting, and unfavorable weather during the summer caused much of the young fruit to fall. The crop is a very irregular one this year, and whereas in some districts there is a fair amount of fruit on the trees, in others the orchards are bare. Taking it all around, however, the crop will be a short one, and the season has opened at higher prices. American chopped apples have already commenced to arrive, and more business is likely to follow during the remainder of the season, unless prices in the United States should rule too high.

This year's wine crop will be smaller than those of 1901 and 1900, and prices have advanced somewhat; nevertheless, the lower grades of pure wine can still be bought at prices which, in some instances, are less than those at which good cider can be produced.

Under the existing internal-revenue regulations, farmers are permitted to distill apple and pear juice and convert it into alcohol free of excise duties for the use of their families and farm hands. They are not allowed to sell any of this alcohol, but the Government supervision is necessarily very difficult, and the privilege known under the

name of "Privilege des Bouilleurs de Cru" has been abused to such
an extent that the loss to the French treasury is estimated at not less
than 100,000,000 francs ($19,300,000) per annum. The Government
seems determined to put a stop to this abuse. Measures are to be
proposed during this session of Parliament, which opened October 14
last, for the purpose of materially curtailing the existing privilege.
It is thought that if the measure passes and becomes a law it may
result in a large supply of apples and pears being left on the hands
of the farmers which will be available for cider-making purposes.

I have had many complaints made to me both as regards the quality
of the chopped apples shipped from the United States and as to the
weights of the packages received. The trade in American chopped
apples would no doubt be larger, if more reliance could be placed in
the goods which the manufacturers send to the French market. Many
parcels have arrived in a fermented condition owing to defective packing, and in some cases to the fraudulent addition of water. The loss
to the importer on such goods is out of proportion to the profits he
can possibly expect to reap out of the business. Even when the
soaked apples are not fermented on arrival, they spoil shortly after.

Some dealers in the interior have given up handling American
chopped apples in consequence of the goods spoiling in their warehouses within a few weeks after receipt of the same; whereas when
the apples are properly prepared and packed, they should keep sound
and fresh during an entire season. There have also been cases of
false packing, cores and skins being found in the barrels, hidden by
layers of straight goods at the top, and also false indications of weight,
amounting, in some cases, to as much as 10 per cent. In all these
points, the careful and honest packers and shippers have to suffer
from the injury to their trade, which results from the actions of
unscrupulous competitors.

The imports of chopped apples into the whole of France for the first
nine months of 1902 were 2,009 tons, against 1,379 tons and 4,302 tons
during the same periods of 1901 and 1900.

### PRUNES.

The importation of prunes into the whole of France during 1901
was the smallest for many years, being 558 tons as compared with
1,874 tons in 1900 and 3,310 tons in 1899. The native crop this year
has been particularly bad, in fact, almost a complete failure. There
has already been a good trade in California prunes for delivery during
the coming autumn; considerable quantities of the old crop have been
brought forward, and it seems likely that the demand for California
prunes and apricots will continue until next season.

The packers in California can not have too urgently impressed
upon them the necessity of paying every attention to keeping up the
standard of quality of the goods they ship to France. A few complaints have reached me in this respect, also as to weights of the packages. These goods are packed in boxes of regular weights, and there
should never be the slightest suspicion in the buyer's mind as to the
10 kilo, or 12.5-kilo (22 lb. or 27 lb.) boxes of California prunes or
apricots containing a fraction less than what they are claimed to hold.

The large importation of these foreign fruits is sure to raise considerable outcry on the part of the growers of French plums and apricots. It would not be surprising if attempts were made to have the
duties on foreign fruits increased.

The shortness of the crop has induced some of the French packers to import the California fruit in bulk, repack them in boxes over here, and sell them as "California prunes packed in France."

The imports of prunes into the whole of France during the first nine months of 1902 were 1,432 tons, as compared with 20 tons and 1,830 tons during the corresponding periods of 1901 and 1900.

### OLEAGINOUS SEEDS.

The importations of oil-producing seeds into Havre in 1901 were 70,722 tons, against 61,159 tons in 1900, and 53,403 tons in 1899. The most notable increase was in the receipts of colza from India, 28,493 tons, against 6,301 tons in 1900. The details of the imports for the past four years are given in the following table:

*Imports of oleaginous seeds into Havre.*

| Character. | 1898. | 1899. | 1900. | 1901. |
|---|---|---|---|---|
| | *Tons.* | *Tons.* | *Tons.* | *Tons.* |
| Linseed | 16,457 | 14,160 | 6,700 | 7,976 |
| Sesame | 2,840 | 2,501 | 701 | 2,373 |
| European colza | | | 3,540 | 4,222 |
| Colza from India, Africa, and Japan | 29,273 | 22,056 | 6,301 | 28,493 |
| Rape seed | 108 | | 19,510 | 11,098 |
| Peanuts | 4,431 | 4,740 | 6,282 | 2,407 |
| Ravison | 5,300 | 2,900 | 5,000 | 1,100 |
| Cotton | 11,660 | 7,681 | 13,055 | 9,988 |
| Others | 361 | 134 | 70 | 8,070 |
| Total | 70,455 | 53,402 | 61,159 | 70,722 |

### PROPOSED DUTY ON OLEAGINOUS SEEDS.

Although no definite action has yet been taken on the bill to remove oleaginous seeds from the free list and to largely increase the present duties on vegetable oils imported into France, details concerning which were given in the last annual report of this consulate, it seems likely that fresh and determined efforts will be made during the present session of Parliament to pass the measure. This matter has been under discussion in the legislature for several years past, and until now it has been successfully opposed by the numerous industries which are interested in maintaining the status quo, but the agriculturists are well represented in the present houses, and any proposal tending to increase the protection on farm products is likely to meet with much favor.

### COTTON-SEED OIL.

The trade in cotton-seed oil has been seriously affected by the high prices ruling in America, and also by a largely increased home production of many kinds of vegetable oils. For instance, the imports from India of decorticated peanuts, the oil from which, owing to its inferior quality, is used exclusively for soap-making purposes, reached the large total of 106,000 tons during the first eight months of this year, against 40,000 and 21,000 tons, respectively, during the same periods in 1901 and 1900. As this seed yields about 40 per cent of oil, 106,000 tons represent nearly 250,000 barrels, which some years ago, when the supplies of these India peanuts had fallen to almost nothing, had to be replaced by cotton-seed oil. This oil, called arachide oil, has been selling at such low prices that some of it has even been shipped to the United States for the use of American soap makers.

While this low-grade peanut oil has been extremely abundant and cheap, the imports of peanuts in the shell, which come from the west coast of Africa, have fallen below those of last year. From these peanuts a very fine neutral edible oil is made, which is much appreciated in many parts of France. Owing to the decreased imports of unshelled peanuts the prices of the oil have ruled high throughout the year, which has enabled the best grades of American cotton-seed oil to be imported into France. But for this, the imports of the American oil would have been still more restricted, as the olive crop in this and most of the Mediterranean countries has been very bountiful.

The total imports of cotton-seed oil into France for the three years 1901, 1900, and 1899 were 48,226 tons, 54,070 tons, and 72,837 tons, respectively. Of these amounts, the United States furnished 45,200 tons, 49,057 tons, and 69,224 tons, respectively; 2,654 tons, 4,730 tons, and 3,082 tons, respectively, were received from England; the balance from various countries.

During the first nine months of 1902, the imports were 20,735 tons, against 35,089 tons and 39,032 tons during the corresponding periods of 1901 and 1900. The United States furnished 19,040 tons, 33,465 tons, and 36,302 tons, respectively. The custom-house statistics are given in gross weights, and include the weight of the barrel. In order to ascertain the net weight of oil, one-sixth should be deducted.

The prospects for the coming season are that moderate quantities of the better grades of edible cotton-seed oil will be taken by France, provided the prices are not too high in America, whereas a high range of values like those which prevailed last season would curtail the consumption considerably.

The prospects for the importation of American cotton-seed oil for soap-making purposes are not so bright. The supplies of arachide and sesame oil are still abundant and are selling even for future delivery at lower prices than those quoted for an equivalent quality of cotton-seed oil. The early reports as regards the new crops of peanuts and sesame seed in India, which are harvested during the fall and winter months, point to a fair yield; and as under the present customs regulations, oil seeds enter France free of duty, while cotton-seed oil is taxed 6 francs ($1.16) per 100 kilograms (220.46 pounds) on the gross weight (equal to 7.25 francs, or $1.40 on the net weight, i. e., 4.25 cents per gallon), there is little chance of foreign oils competing with the domestic article, so long as there is an abundant supply of the oil-producing seeds.

## OIL CAKE.

There has been an increased importation of oil cake from the United States during the past year. The French custom-house statistics do not furnish separate figures of each kind of cake, so that it is difficult to tell the quantities of each received. So far as I can learn, however, there has been a considerable increase in the demand for corn cake and a decrease in the imports of cotton cake and meal, whereas linseed cake has probably remained stationary.

The smaller takings of cotton cake and meal are to some extent due to the quality of last season's shipments, several lots having come forward which were decidedly inferior and gave rise to many complaints. The imports of corn cake would also have been larger had the quality of the goods been better. The consumer finds in some cases that it is more to his advantage to use the grain itself for fattening purposes.

The imports of oil cake into France during 1901, 1900, and 1899 were 116,964 tons, 111,860 tons, and 124,770 tons, respectively. The exports during the same periods were 111,429 tons, 98,531 tons, and 74,272 tons, respectively.

During the first nine months of 1902, 1901, and 1900, the imports were 80,364 tons, 80,250 tons, and 83,793 tons, respectively, and the exports 109,980 tons, 76,754 tons, and 66,719 tons.

The enormous production of domestic cake, as a result of the large imports of peanuts, sesame, and cotton seed, also affected the trade in foreign cake, and has naturally led to the great increase in the exports of the products from France, as shown by the above statistics.

The bulk of these exports went to Germany; 69,996 tons in the first nine months of 1902, against 48,440 tons in 1901 and 40,644 tons in 1900. The rest were divided between Great Britain and the Baltic ports. This large increase in the exportation of French cake must have affected to some extent the trade in American cake with Germany and other European countries which ordinarily draw their large requirements from the United States.

According to the United States Treasury statistics, the shipments of oil cake and oil-cake meal to Germany and Great Britain for the fiscal year ended June 30, 1902, show a falling off as compared with the previous fiscal year of 139,000,000 pounds and 29,000,000 pounds, respectively, a total decrease of 168,000,000 pounds. The exports to other European countries, however, were 71,000,000 pounds greater; the net decrease in the exports to the whole of Europe would therefore be 98,000,000 pounds, or about 43,700 tons.

## NAVIGATION.

Havre being one of the most important maritime gateways of northern Europe, the increase of the foreign commerce of France in 1901 was reflected in the improvement shown in the shipping industry of the port during last year. The total tonnage of vessels of all nationalities, loaded and in ballast, which cleared and entered Havre in 1901 was 5,983,638 tons, an increase of 236,573 tons as compared with 1900, and of 136,643 tons over 1899.

Taking into consideration that the imports of cereals were about the average of preceding years, and that the importations of coal were 94,000 tons less than in 1900, the improvement may be said to be encouraging.

The movement of navigation of the port for the last ten years, vessels loaded and in ballast, the entries and clearances combined, was as follows:

*General movement of navigation of the port of Havre since 1892.*

| Year. | Number of vessels. | Tonnage. | Year. | Number of vessels. | Tonnage. |
|---|---|---|---|---|---|
| 1892 | 12,505 | 5,678,125 | 1897 | 13,266 | 5,847,505 |
| 1893 | 12,924 | 5,729,411 | 1898 | 13,984 | 6,278,544 |
| 1894 | 13,818 | 6,129,740 | 1899 | 12,722 | 5,846,995 |
| 1895 | 12,888 | 5,602,712 | 1900 | 12,305 | 5,747,065 |
| 1896 | 12,832 | 5,564,750 | 1901 | 12,309 | 5,983,638 |

In 1901, the tonnage of French steam and sailing ships entering and leaving the port of Havre, engaged in the carrying trade open to the competition of all nations, was 1,084,671 tons, the tonnage of foreign vessels being 3,460,648 tons, making a total tonnage of 4,545,319 tons. The percentage secured by French vessels was 23.9 per cent, as compared with 23.7 per cent and 24 per cent in 1900 and 1899, respectively.

It is hoped by the framers of the measure for the improvement of the merchant marine of France, which became a law April 7 last and is now in operation, that the increased assistance granted to French vessels in the form of bounties, subsidies, etc., will enable them to obtain a larger proportion of the foreign trade of France.

By an inspection of a table in the annex to this report, which shows the navigation of the port by flag, it will be seen that, as for many years past, the greater part of the carrying trade is done in English bottoms; the French flag comes next; then follow, in the order of their importance, the German, Norwegian, Dutch, Swedish, and Spanish vessels.

It will be interesting to note the increase in the number of Spanish vessels which arrived in the port of Havre in 1901. There were 33 vessels, as compared with 7, 5, and 3 vessels in 1900, 1899, and 1898, respectively. The augmentation was due to the establishment of the Olazarri line of Spanish steamers, with regular monthly sailings to New Orleans via Cuban and Mexican posts, and to the increased number of Spanish tramp steamers which have entered into active competition with English vessels in the cotton-carrying trade between our Southern ports and the port of Havre.

Owing to the dullness of the dyewood trade, there was a large falling off in the shipping under the Norwegian and Swedish flags.

There was also a decline in the number of British vessels, but their tonnage was increased, which shows the tendency of modern times to transport merchandise in vessels of large proportions. Two large cargo boats visited the port of Havre last year, one 485 feet long and the other 470 feet. The British steamer *Mount Temple*, belonging to Elder, Dempster & Co., is expected shortly from New Orleans. Her cargo will consist of 3,176 tons of cotton, 1,500 tons of wheat, 240 tons of wood, and 397 tons of staves for Havre, and 2,785 tons of wheat, 140 tons of wood, and 25 tons of staves for Liverpool, a total of 8,268 tons. She is a steamer 485 feet long, 59 feet beam, and 30 feet deep.

The French coasting trade, which, as our own, is completely protected from foreign competition, showed a slight increase in 1901 in the number of vessels and in the tonnage.

The size of the local merchant fleet remained nearly stationary. There were added, either by construction or by purchase from foreign sources, 26 vessels, 16 sailing ships and 10 steamers, of which 4 steamers and 2 sailing vessels were foreign built.

The merchant shipping law of 1893 allowed no bounty or premium to vessels of foreign construction, but under the present law, vessels built in foreign shipyards and registered under the French flag are granted a subsidy called the shipping bounty (compensation d'armement). Although the bounty is not nearly as large as the subsidies given to vessels of home construction, yet, owing to the high cost of building ships in French dockyards and the great length of time required for delivery, there will certainly be an increase in the number of foreign vessels added to the French merchant marine.

## THE NEW FRENCH SHIPPING LAW.

The administrative regulations for the execution of the new shipping act[a] were published in the "Journal Officiel" of September 10, last. They form a document of considerable length, in 94 articles and occupying 28 columns of the Journal. It was from uncertainty as to the restrictions in the distribution of the bounties that might be introduced into the regulation that shipowners have hitherto deferred their purchases or orders for new ships.

Chapter I concerns the origin, age, measurement, and the loading of ships. It is stipulated that in order that the vessel may be entitled to the bounties provided for by the law of April 7, 1902, not only the hull, but also the engines and boilers must be built in France.

Chapter II designates the order in which vessels are to be admitted to the bounties prescribed by the new law. According to the law, the maximum tonnage for vessels which are or may be entitled to the bounties, in addition to those given to vessels prior to the promulgation of the law, is fixed at 500,000 gross tons for steamers and 100,000 tons gross for sailing vessels.

The global tonnage is divided as follows: French-built vessels, steamers, 300,000 tons; sailing vessels, 100,000 tons; foreign-built vessels, 200,000 tons.

The conditions under which vessels will take rank vary according to whether they are steam or sailing vessels of French construction, registered after the promulgation of the law of 1902, or foreign-built steamers, or French-built steamers registered before the promulgation of the law.

Chapter III is devoted to the question of speed trials. According to the conditions of the law, only steamers which on their speed trials, half loaded, make 12 knots per hour are entitled to the full bounty. If the speed exceeds 11 knots, but less than 12 knots per hour, when half loaded, the bounties are decreased 5 per cent.

If the speed, half loaded, is from 10 to 11 knots per hour only, the bounties are reduced 10 per cent.

No bounties are granted to steamers which, when half loaded, do not make at least 10 knots per hour on their speed trials.

In order that the tests of speed may be properly made, the regulations provide for the constitution in each maritime district of France, as well as in the French Colonies, of one or several commissions composed of the following members: A naval officer, a naval engineer, a naval constructor, appointed by the minister of marine; an engineer of Government docks, appointed by the minister of public works; a customs official, appointed by the minister of finance, and a member of one of the chambers of commerce of the district, appointed by the minister of commerce.

Chapter IV sets forth the manner in which are to be determined the distances from port to port which are to serve as a basis for the payment of the bounties.

Chapter V relates to the regulations and conditions imposed upon subsidized vessels for carrying the mail. According to the text of the law of 1902, the owners of these vessels are not only obliged to guarantee the carrying of the mail, but must also, if the Government exacts it, carry parcels sent by post.

---

[a] A special report on the French shipping law was published in Consular Reports No. 259, April, 1902, and a supplementary report in Consular Reports No. 262, July, 1902.

Chapter VI enters into the details of the formalities and conditions to obtain payment of the construction and navigation bounties. For the former, the declaration must specify whether the vessel is intended for a French owner or a foreign one. The bounty is the same in either case.

For the navigation and shipping bounties, the declaration required—in three copies—must state the name and domicile of the owner and captain, the name and port of the vessel, with the class to which it belongs, sail or steam, wood or iron; the place where the hull was built, that of the engine and boilers; the date of launching, if a foreign-built vessel; the place and date of registration in France; the gross and net tonnage; the maximum loading capacity, the speed, and the crew list. If the ship is foreign built, a declaration must be made that it is not mortgaged for more than one-half its value.

The final chapters refer to the deductions made from the bounties for the benefit of seamen's benevolent institutions, to the local dues, and to other details necessary for the execution of the law.

### NEW HARBOR WORKS AT HAVRE.

Work on the harbor improvements of the port of Havre has continued without intermission throughout the year, although but little progress has been made. The stonework of the new north jetty is about completed. In the month of September last, a contract was given for the construction of a mole in masonry to replace the old north jetty and for the demolition of the work north of the present entrance channel, to allow for the construction of the new entrance.

The riprapping for the south jetty is partly finished and work is proceeding on the new entrance gate. The construction of this portion of the work and the new channel of approach will make it necessary to dispense with the present channel. In order that the navigation of the port may not be interfered with, the new approaches will be finished, ready for service, before the final work of demolition of the south jetty, which would obstruct the present channel, is commenced. According to a report upon the condition of the new harbor works recently made to the Chamber of Commerce of Havre, it is thought that the new entrance to the basins and the new channel will be open to navigation at the end of 1904.

The lengthening of dry dock No. 4 was completed on December 16, 1901. It is capable of docking vessels 600 feet long. Its dimensions are as follows: Length, 656 feet; width of dock gates, 98¼ feet. The level of the sill is 33¼ inches below the zero of the marine charts of Havre, and the high level of the blocks is 29¼ inches below the aforesaid zero.

The new crane on the Quai de Madagascar, with a capacity of 120 tons, is finished and ready for service. Beside the above, there are 60 stationary cranes, ranging in capacity from 1¼ tons to 70 tons, and 13 floating cranes, from 1¼ to 10 tons.

Details concerning the improvement of the port of Havre were given in the last annual report of this consulate.

### EMIGRATION.

The official emigration statistics for the year 1901 show that the number of emigrants embarked at the port of Havre was the largest ever known, and the indications are that the emigration in 1902 will be still greater.

There were 35,478 steerage passengers whose destination was the United States and Canada, and 1,565 who went to Uruguay and the Argentine Confederation, making a total of 37,043; an increase of 4,826 as compared with 1900, of 13,099 with 1899, and of 20,366 with 1898.

The number of emigrants arriving in Havre since January 1 of the present year for transportation to the United States has been so great the Compagnie Générale Transatlantique has found it necessary to dispatch extra steamers.

The movement of passengers at the port of Havre, not including emigrants, for the past three years was as follows:

*Movement of passengers at Havre (emigrants not included) for the last three years.*

| Lines. | Departures. | | | Arrivals. | | |
|---|---|---|---|---|---|---|
| | 1899. | 1900. | 1901. | 1899. | 1900. | 1901. |
| Trans-Atlantic | 7,202 | 8,897 | 7,345 | 16,538 | 23,184 | 18,445 |
| Anglo-French | 12,547 | 17,092 | 13,832 | 18,946 | 15,834 | 14,724 |
| Coasting | 3,011 | 2,835 | 3,619 | 3,502 | 2,791 | 8,885 |
| Houfler, Trouville & Caen | 212,515 | 200,608 | 213,280 | 211,505 | 197,064 | 212,903 |
| Total | 235,275 | 229,437 | 237,976 | 245,486 | 238,873 | 249,907 |

## TRANS-ATLANTIC PASSENGER SERVICE AT CHERBOURG.

There was a falling off in the number of passengers who embarked and disembarked at Cherbourg during 1901, as compared with the previous year. The number of passengers carried by the different trans-Atlantic lines in 1900 was unusually large, owing to the exposition at Paris that year.

In the following table is shown the movement of the passenger service at Cherbourg for 1901 and 1900:

| Flag and line. | Steamers. | | Tonnage. | | Passengers. | |
|---|---|---|---|---|---|---|
| | 1901. | 1900. | 1901. | 1900. | 1901. | 1900. |
| **FRENCH.** | Number. | Number. | | | Number. | Number. |
| Havre to West Coast of Africa | 5 | 4 | 7,589 | 5,218 | | |
| Havre to Madagascar | 1 | | 1,200 | | | |
| **ENGLISH.** | | | | | | |
| St. Thomas to Southampton | 6 | 10 | 16,817 | 27,096 | 126 | 280 |
| Rio Janerio to Southampton | | 1 | | 3,369 | | 1 |
| Buenos Ayres to Southampton | 48 | 45 | 160,767 | 145,004 | 801 | 1,060 |
| New York to Antwerp via Cherbourg | 9 | | 56,600 | | 268 | |
| **GERMAN.** | | | | | | |
| New York to Hamburg and Bremen | 159 | 208 | 812,349 | 981,824 | 12,669 | 21,971 |
| Brazil to Hamburg | 20 | 30 | 48,042 | 102,694 | 70 | 243 |
| Buenos Ayres to Hamburg | 43 | 32 | 118,561 | 104,998 | 759 | 478 |
| Montevideo to Hamburg | 8 | 9 | 9,782 | 27,675 | 20 | 71 |
| Valparaiso to Hamburg | 1 | | 3,086 | | 16 | |
| **AMERICAN.** | | | | | | |
| Southampton to New York | 88 | 44 | 219,129 | 254,081 | 3,537 | 6,259 |
| Total | 388 | 378 | 1,453,852 | 1,651,874 | 18,266 | 30,313 |
| Decrease in 1901 | 1 | 45 | | 198,022 | | 12,047 |

## VITAL STATISTICS.

There were 4,036 births in the city of Havre during 1901, of which 2,049 were masculine and 1,987 feminine; an increase of 117 over 1900. Of the births, 591 were illegitimate.

There were 1,234 marriages; an increase of 42 as compared with 1900.

The deaths from all causes were 3,357; a decrease of 588 as compared with 1900, and a decrease of 116 as compared with the average of the past five years.

The death rate per 1,000 inhabitants was 25.7, against 33.1 in 1900, 32.2 in 1899, and 28.7 in 1898. The births exceeded the deaths by 688.

There was still a large mortality of children under 5 years of age, the deaths numbering 1,025, against 1,232 in 1900.

There were 70 deaths from typhoid fever, against 316 in 1900, and 653 deaths from consumption, as compared with 645 during the previous year.

## QUARANTINE MEASURES TO PREVENT THE INTRODUCTION OF BUBONIC PLAGUE IN FRANCE.

By the terms of the presidential decree of April 15, 1897, vessels arriving from a locality recognized as contaminated with plague, or carrying raw or manufactured wool, body linen used or unused, bedding used or unused, or green hides which have been brought from a plague-infected country, can enter France or Algeria only by the ports of Marseilles, Algiers, Pauillac, St. Nazaire, Havre, and Dunkirk. In 1900, the health office of Havre was authorized by the French Government to permit ships to discharge their cargoes at Rouen, after a partial disinfection at Havre, provided they did not carry any suspected merchandise, or goods which could not be disinfected by steam. Before allowing the vessel to proceed up the Seine, the health officer at Havre is obliged to make a special report to Paris on the sanitary condition of the ship, and receive permission from the Government health authorities.

According to the instructions from Paris of October 1, 1900, and the decree of September 26, 1901, it is rendered obligatory for the local health officer to disinfect clothes and effects used during the voyage, and also the parts of the ship occupied by the passengers and crew. Protective screens must be erected to prevent rats leaving the ship, and after the cargo is completely discharged, the hold must be hermetically sealed and fumigated with sulphur. The dead rats are afterwards either burnt or reserved for bacteriological examination. If, in the judgment of the health officer it is deemed necessary, he can disinfect the vessel and cargo by sulphur before the cargo is discharged. Before taking a new cargo, an inspection of the vessel should be made to determine whether the operation of disinfection has given satisfactory results, and if the vessel is in a good sanitary state.

When a foreign port is declared by the French Government to be contaminated with plague, the above regulations are put into force.

The local health officer informs me that up to the present time, there has been no cases of bubonic plague discovered in France outside of the quarantine stations.

## STREET CAR LINES OF HAVRE.

The results of the operations of the street-car lines and funicular railways of Havre during 1901 were:

*Société du Chemin de Fer de la Côte (Steam Funicular).*—Length, 1,125 feet; cost of installation up to December 31, 1901, $111,815; receipts, $15,338; expenses, $9,214; net profits, $6,124.

*Electric tramway from Havre to Montivilliers.*—Length, 8¼ miles; cost of installation up to December 31, 1901, $281,606; receipts, $56,909; expenses, $51,191; net profits, $5,718.

*Funicular de la Côte Sainte-Marie.*—Length, about five-eighths of a mile; cost of installation up to December 31, 1901, $114,448; receipts, $5,700; expenses, $5,644; net profits, $56.

*Compagnie Générale Française de Tramways.*—Length, 18¼ miles; total cost of installation, $1,403,475; receipts, $284,975; expenses, $185,571; net profits, $99,400. This company, which operates the principal tramway lines of Havre, also has street car systems in the cities of Marseilles, Nancy, Orleans, and Tunis. Its capital is $6,176,000.

## THE WESTINGHOUSE WORKS AT HAVRE.

One of the principal industrial establishments of Havre is that of the French Westinghouse Company (Société Anonyme Westinghouse). This company has an invested capital of 20,000,000 francs ($3,600,000), and was formed for the purpose of exploiting the Westinghouse interests in France.

The works, situated at Gravillé, just outside of the city limits, in convenient proximity to the Western Railway and to the docks, comprise an area of some 50,000 square yards, over 17,000 of which are covered by buildings. They are equipped with the most modern machinery, most of which is American, specially adapted for the rapid and economic production of electrical apparatus of every description.

The head offices are at Havre; but the company also owns large works at Freinville, a few miles from Paris, where is carried on the manufacture of the famous Westinghouse air brake. The company has agencies in Paris, Lyons Lille, Nancy, Toulouse, Brussels, Milan, Madrid, etc.

Business on the Continent being dull at present, the number of workmen employed at the Havre works is not more than 500; but it is expected in the near future to find employment for 1,200 or 1,500 men. The operatives are mostly French, with a few Belgians and Swiss. There is also a small number of American electrical engineers.

The French Westinghouse Company has proved by experience that the French workman is a good operative when working under American control and according to American methods and practice. The operative force, carefully trained by American foremen and engineers, has now reached a rapidity and excellence of production rarely met with on the Continent.

Labor is cheap in Havre, the skilled mechanics earning from 12 to 15 cents an hour, while the pay of the day laborer varies from 7 to 9 cents. Most of the skilled operatives, however, can earn up to 20 cents an hour at piecework.

The hours of labor are from 6.30 a. m. till noon, without any stop for breakfast, and from 1.30 p. m. till 6 p. m., making a ten-hour day.

As there is no Saturday afternoon closing, each man works sixty hours per week.

One of the head officers of the company writes me as follows:

The low wage rate of labor is counterbalanced to a great extent by the high cost of raw material, coal, etc.; but it is nevertheless certain that, given American management and methods and a proper training of the French operatives, the cost of production in France can, for the same output, be brought as low as in America. This fact should commend itself to the attention of the American manufacturer who finds his sales in Europe seriously handicapped by high shipping rates and prohibitive duties on American-made goods, which, by the way, are, for electrical apparatus imported from the United States into France, nearly twice as high as when imported from European countries. This is due to some extent to the fact that there exists no reciprocity treaty between France and the United States.

The discrimination against American-made electrical goods imported from the United States is even greater in some cases than that mentioned above. Take, for example, a dynamo weighing 5,000 kilograms (11,023 pounds) or over. The American machine would have to pay a duty of 30 francs ($5.79) per 100 kilograms (220.46 pounds) net if imported direct from the United States, while the duty on a German machine, imported direct, if 50 per cent of the material is cast iron, would only be 12 francs ($2.32) per 100 kilograms.

There are only three categories of duties for American dynamos, while there are seven for machines imported from European countries, which are entitled to the minimum tariff, as follows:

[Per 100 kilos (220.46 pounds) net.]

| | Francs. |
|---|---|
| Duties on dynamos imported into France from United States: | |
| Weighing 1,000 kilos (2,204.6 pounds) or more | 30=$5.79 |
| Weighing from 50 kilos (110.23 pounds) to 1,000 kilos | 45= 8.69 |
| Weighing from 10 kilos (22.05 pounds) and not more than 50 kilos | 100=19.30 |
| From countries enjoying the benefits of the minimum tariff: | |
| Weighing 5,000 kilos (11,023 pounds) or more and containing at least 50 per cent of cast iron | 12= 2.32 |
| Same, containing less than 50 per cent of cast iron | 20= 3.86 |
| Weighing from 2,000 kilos (4,409.2 pounds) to 5,000 kilos and containing at least 50 per cent of cast iron | 18= 3.47 |
| Same, containing less than 50 per cent of cast iron | 20= 3.86 |
| Weighing from 1,000 kilos to 2,000 kilos | 20= 3.86 |
| Weighing from 50 kilos (110.23 pounds) to 1,000 kilos | 30= 5.79 |
| Weighing from 10 kilos (22.05 pounds) to 50 kilos | 80=15.44 |

Small detached parts of electrical machines, weighing less than 1 kilo (2.2 pounds), and arc lamps imported from the United States pay a single duty of 100 francs ($19.30) per 100 kilos.

When imported from a favored nation the duties are:

| | Francs. |
|---|---|
| Small detached parts of electrical machines weighing less than 1 kilo when for machines weighing more than 2,000 kilos (4,409.2 pounds) | 35=$6.76 |
| Same, for machines weighing from 1,000 kilos (2,204.6 pounds) to 2,000 kilos | 40= 7.72 |
| Same, for machines weighing from 200 kilos (440.9 pounds) to 1,000 kilos | 45= 8.69 |
| Same, for machines weighing 1 kilo (2.2 pounds) to 200 kilos | 60=11.58 |
| Same, less than 1 kilo | 75=14.48 |
| Arc lamps | 60=11.58 |

It will be seen from the above it is very difficult for American electrical apparatus to compete in France with that made in European countries.

### TRADE RELATIONS OF HAVRE WITH THE UNITED STATES.

The value of the declared exports from Havre to the United States, including returned American goods for the fiscal year ended June 30,

1902, was $877,426.30, a decrease of $449,628.59 as compared with 1901, and a diminution of $1,293,537.40 in comparison with the fiscal year 1900, as shown in the following table, giving the values for each quarter:

*Values of declared exports from Havre, including returned American goods.*

| Quarter ending— | 1899–1900. | 1900–1901. | 1901–1902. |
|---|---|---|---|
| September 30 | $648,550.90 | $224,223.49 | $294,856.67 |
| December 31 | 729,376.60 | 365,127.69 | 246,766.84 |
| March 31 | 725,101.02 | 230,912.95 | 133,923.07 |
| June 30 | 167,985.18 | 596,790.76 | 202,380.32 |
| Total | 2,170,963.70 | 1,827,054.89 | 877,426.30 |
| Decrease in 1902 | 1,293,537.40 | 449,628.59 | |

The details of the declared exports to the United States from Havre for the last three fiscal years are given in a table annexed to this report.

The falling off in the declared exports from this consular district was due mostly to the decline in the shipments of copper and crude rubber, two products in which there is much speculation. The crisis which exists in the copper trade has so restricted the operations that the imports of American copper into Havre during 1901 were 16,300 tons less than in 1900, and the exports 1,720 tons less. The shipments of rubber to the United States were 3,850 tons less than in 1900. The decline in the rubber trade, besides the speculative operations in the product, was also due to the increased purchases of the United States in the countries of production. The values of the exports of hides and goatskins also showed a falling off in 1901-2 of $38,913 and $43,913, respectively, as compared with 1900–1901. The shipments of hides of neat cattle from Havre to the United States have become smaller each year for the past three years.

The regulations prescribed by the Department of Agriculture for the disinfection of French green hides destined for the United States are strictly enforced at this consulate, and as the steamship companies having direct or indirect communication with our country insist upon the production of a disinfection certificate, or a certificate declaring that the hides are dry salted or arsenic cured before receiving the goods on their steamers, it is very probable that the exportation is accomplished by shipping the hides to England and thence to the United States as English products.

Other articles in which there was a decline in the value of declared exports were ostrich and vulture feathers, benedictine, ocher, pepper, and wool.

The shipments of cocoa to the United States were considerably larger than for many years; there was also an increase in the exports of coffee, dyewood extracts, Percheron horses, nickel, cheeses, and pebbles. The latter are the sea flints (galets de mer) gathered along the shore from Havre to St. Valéry sur Somme, and are intended for grinding purposes and for making the cheaper grades of porcelain.

It is interesting to note the different kinds of food which are shipped from Havre every week to New York for the use, principally, of the French colony in that city. In season, there are sent fresh artichokes, beans, Brussels sprouts, cauliflowers, lentils, mushrooms, pease, potatoes, lettuce, shallots, various French cheeses, soles, and even fresh oysters.

Owing to its proximity to and its direct and indirect communications with the shipping ports of the United States, Havre is one of the most important centers in Europe for the reception and distribution of American products.

Its commerce with foreign countries and with the interior of France is carried on by means of 48 lines of steamers and sailing vessels, 26 of which are French and 22 foreign; by the Western Railway, which has a close connection with the Northern Railway; by the Tancarville Canal and River Seine, by which access is obtained to the great canal system of France.

Last year, the total imports declared at the Havre custom-house were nearly two millions of tons, 22 per cent of which were American-made goods. These figures do not indicate the whole volume of trade passing through the port, as large quantities of merchandise are received which are transported in bond to foreign countries or are entered for consumption in the custom-houses of the interior and do not appear in the local statistics.

If the value of goods is considered, the volume of trade of the port of Havre is even more important. For instance, while the weight of the imports into Havre during 1900 was $33\frac{1}{2}$ per cent less than that of the merchandise received at the port of Marseilles, the values of the imports into the two places were $223,000,000 and $233,000,000, respectively, a difference of less than 5 per cent in favor of the latter port.

The imports of American merchandise into Havre during 1901 were 430,448 tons, a falling off of 8,880 tons as compared with 1900. The diminution was due not only to the largely decreased imports of American copper, but also to the decrease in the receipts of nearly all of the American food products, owing to the high prices prevailing in the United States. A short corn crop in our country, like that of last year, curtailing as it does the production of so many products, has far-reaching effects upon trade in all parts of the world.

To form an idea of the many different varieties of American goods which are brought every week to Havre by the French Line, one has only to glance at the manifest of one of its steamers. The *Touraine*, on one of its recent voyages, landed the following merchandise, nearly all of which was of American production, viz: Dried apricots, dynamos and other electrical apparatus, typewriters, couplings, asbestos, silverware, household articles, photographic apparatus and materials, phonographs, oars, bicycles and parts, jewelry, refined oil, wheat, parquetry, cigar boxes, watch cases, watches, sausage cases, cocoa, coffee, picture frames, rubber, carbon, blacking, chairs, shoes, canned beef, canned soups, water meters, seashells, leather, electrotypes, ink, machine gears, cash registers, flour, steel and iron wire, insulated rubber wire, furs, air guns, grease, gilsonite, graphite, lubricating oils, printed matter, toys, newspapers, linen ware, books, sewing machines, other machines (including shoe-making machinery), motors, novelties, tools, gold, sandpaper, paper, paper pulp, perfumery, patterns, shovels, dried prunes, chopped apples and pears, spices, pumps, wood pulleys, printing and other presses, hardware, medicinal roots, springs, emery wheels, water turbines, wheels, ribbons, lard, soap, saws, silk goods, tobacco, pictures, drums, vaseline, glassware, bladders, clothing, preserved meats, vises, and whisky.

### UNITED STATES TRADE WITH FRANCE.

France is a larger importing nation than the United States. In 1901, the value of merchandise received in the former country was $910,-

000,000, against $823,000,000 imported into the United States. Of the French imports, $603,000,000 were raw materials, $155,000,000 alimentary products, and $153,000,000 manufactured goods. Of the latter, the United States furnished only $18,000,000, or a little less than 12 per cent.

The trade of our country with France is handicapped to some extent by the heavier freights and custom duties our shippers have to pay, in comparison with their German and English competitors, and no doubt, if the commercial agreement now existing between France and the United States were extended to cover other articles, the trade between the two countries would be materially increased. The question arises whether, under the present conditions, more of our manufactured goods could not be exported to this country? My answer would be in the affirmative, considering the good quality, the low price, and the efficiency of American-made products. The methods which American manufacturers use in introducing their goods in France, however, do not compare favorably with those they employ in their own markets. My views upon the subject are embodied in a letter I recently wrote to one of our large commercial institutions, extracts from which follow.

What the future of our export trade will be when our exporters have reduced the exploitation of their goods abroad to an exact science, as our German and English competitors have done, would be hard to forecast. In my opinion, the outlook is rosy.

Take France as an example of a country in which there is a good field for an increase in our trade in manufactured goods. I speak of manufactured goods, for the exportation of our food products, cereals, and raw materials must continue to augment proportionately to the development of our natural resources, to supply the normal increase in demand. According to the official French customs statistics, the total imports into France in 1901 were valued at $910,000,000, of which the United States contributed $93,000,000—a fraction over 10 per cent. We sent to France 15 per cent of her wood imports, 20 per cent of the machines and machinery imported, 5.5 per cent of the tools and hardware, 11.8 per cent of the lumber and woodwork, 7 per cent of the dressed skins, 1.25 per cent of the chemical products, 18.75 per cent of the oil cake, and 7 per cent of the rubber goods received. The imports of paper pulp, jewelry, watches, clocks, pottery, and glassware from the United States were so comparatively small that they were included under the general term of other articles. Now the question is whether the above percentage can be increased. I think it can.

I doubt very much if there are over 50 of our manufacturing concerns which are properly represented in France. I mean that there are not over the above number of American houses which have had agencies in Paris, with agents in the provincial cities who canvass their various districts to advertise their goods and to solicit orders.

Havre is a city of 130,000 inhabitants; but if one wished to buy American dairy machinery, he would not be able to do so without either going or writing to Paris. In that city, he would find the machines made by one or two American houses only, and sold by French concerns. On the other hand, in all the agricultural centers, French, Danish, and Swedish churns, centrifugal separators, butter workers, etc., are extensively advertised and kept in stock. There are few hotels, cafés, or restaurants in the farming districts of France in which posters are not displayed advertising American harvesting machinery and giving the name of the nearest resident agent. But I

have never seen—and I have traveled over a large portion of France—
an advertisement of a potato digger and sorter, or any of this class of
labor-saving machines which are so extensively used in the United
States.

American ice-cream freezers for family use can be bought in several
of the department stores of Havre; but if you wanted a household
refrigerator, the use of which is constantly increasing in France, you
would find one store which keeps them, but only one make, and that
not of the best. If you wanted an American base-burner stove, you
might, perhaps, find one or two French imitations on sale; but to have
the genuine article, if you happened to know the agents of American
stoves in Paris (for they are not advertised), you could write and
would receive a catalogue in reply, from which a selection could be
made. If the stove chosen was in stock, you would receive it in about
a week. If not on hand, you would have to wait at least six weeks.

Two of the best makes of American lawn mowers can be bought in
Havre. American-made shoes are being more extensively displayed in
the shop windows, but good assortments are by no means kept in stock.
I have never seen American fire and burglar proof safes on sale in
this city, nor have I ever heard of one being used.

American lathes and other machine tools, made by several of our
principal manufacturers, can be bought from the machinery dealers
of Havre. If the tool desired should not be on hand, the dealer can
easily get it from the agents in Paris, where large stocks are kept;
but if a builder wished to introduce into a house the American system of heating by hot water or steam, or to furnish bathrooms with
American specialties, he would find much trouble in doing so. Several of my friends have porcelain bath tubs and sanitary water-
closets, but they sent to England for them.

American building hardware, locks, etc., are also but little known
in the French provincial towns; neither are American sporting implements. In the past five years, outdoor sports have become very
popular in France. Formerly, football and tennis were confined to
Paris, where there is always a large colony of Americans and English, but now these games are extensively played in the provinces.
I have never seen American balls, rackets, nets, etc., used. In my
opinion, with proper methods, our trade with France in the following products could be materially increased: Steam fire engines;
printing presses; printing materials; hardware (including locks);
builders' hardware; hot-air and gas engines; chairs, desks, and other
office furniture; parlor organs; mechanical piano players; chemical
products, etc.

Spasmodic attempts to create foreign trade are never successful.
If our manufacturers really desire to secure outlets abroad for their
products, they should make systematic efforts, based on sound business methods, to do so. They should become conversant with the
needs and mode of life of the foreigners to whom they wish to sell
their wares, and then furnish goods which will be acceptable. Let
our exporters treat the foreigners courteously and kindly; make them
feel that they can get what they want and that they can always depend upon quick and complete shipments of their orders. The
principle that anything is good enough for foreigners will not increase
our export trade. They know what goods they can sell, and the
prices they can pay. Even more care and attention should be given
to filling foreign orders than those for the home markets, for mis-
takes are harder to rectify. Do not send too much or too little, but

execute the order exactly as it is given, or else vexatious delays are bound to occur, with possibly a refusal of the goods and a lawsuit, and certainly loss of future trade. One of the largest wood importers in France tells me that he is almost tempted to give up entirely the handling of American wood. He says he seldom receives a cargo which is according to order. Either the amount is in excess or it falls short, and often the quality is inferior to that which he expected to get. The American shipper, recognizing that the order is not properly filled, writes that the question of quantity and quality can be left to arbitration. This way of doing business is always unsatisfactory to the buyer, as he never knows what he may expect, and there is an unforeseen expense.

## METRIC SYSTEM.

The sooner American exporters learn the metric system of measurement, the better chance they will have of successfully meeting foreign competition in the French markets. For example: Austrian oak in France commands a higher price than American oak, and is used in preference, although in many cases the former is not as good as the American wood. The reason is that the Austrian shippers are careful in having their wood sawed to the metric dimensions called for by the French consumers, while the American shippers send their wood sawed to inches. There may not be much difference in the measurements, but there is enough to make the French cabinetmaker prefer the Austrian oak. The French customs law permits the free entry of certain woods if they are sawed to more than 2 decimeters (7.87 inches) square in the logs. If the logs measure even a small fraction under the above dimensions, they have to pay a duty of 1.50 francs (28.9 cents) per 100 kilograms (220.46 pounds). Frequently, owing to careless sawing and unfamiliarity with metric measurements, American shippers send logs to Havre which measure less than 7.87 inches, perhaps at one end only, which forces the consignee to pay the duty on the whole log.

At the present time, our country is enjoying wonderful prosperity. When the reaction takes place and there is a serious depression in our home markets, our manufacturers will realize that foreign trade is an important factor of our industrial life. Those who have kept up business relations with foreign consumers and have outside outlets for the sale of their goods will be the last to reduce their working force, to run on short time, or to sacrifice their overproduction by selling it at a loss on the home markets.

A. M. THACKARA, *Consul.*

HAVRE, *October 30, 1902.*

*Tonnage of vessels entering the principal ports of Europe.*

| Port. | 1890. | 1898. | 1899. | 1900. | 1901. |
|---|---|---|---|---|---|
| Marseilles | 4,785,277 | 6,005,880 | 6,806,964 | 6,164,431 | 6,531,780 |
| Havre | 2,877,458 | 3,164,448 | 2,917,606 | 2,874,828 | 3,045,486 |
| Bordeaux | 1,943,884 | 1,689,908 | 1,676,864 | 1,990,054 | 1,912,783 |
| Dunkirk | 1,457,196 | 1,709,487 | 1,648,622 | 1,613,770 | 1,678,968 |
| Rouen | 992,198 | 1,162,790 | 1,184,289 | 1,308,850 | 1,196,415 |
| Hamburg | 5,202,895 | 7,855,000 | 7,768,000 | 8,041,000 | 8,388,000 |
| Bremen | 1,783,809 | 2,464,800 | 2,406,748 | 2,494,059 | 2,389,382 |
| Rotterdam | 2,918,425 | 5,751,898 | 6,143,833 | 6,359,794 | 6,382,984 |
| Antwerp | 4,606,277 | 6,424,825 | 6,837,415 | 6,683,000 | 7,510,968 |
| Genoa | 8,859,782 | 4,560,795 | 4,557,430 | 4,830,882 | 5,080,671 |

*French and foreign navigation at Havre, not including vessels calling or engaged in French coasting trade.*

| Year. | French vessels. | Foreign vessels. | Total tonnage. | Year. | French vessels. | Foreign vessels. | Total tonnage. |
|---|---|---|---|---|---|---|---|
| 1892 | 1,263,232 | 3,096,853 | 4,300,085 | 1897 | 1,083,095 | 3,353,185 | 4,436,280 |
| 1893 | 1,167,665 | 3,065,279 | 4,232,944 | 1898 | 1,106,881 | 3,624,069 | 4,730,950 |
| 1894 | 1,059,249 | 3,508,443 | 4,562,692 | 1899 | 1,153,096 | 3,305,629 | 4,458,725 |
| 1895 | 968,768 | 3,121,103 | 4,089,871 | 1900 | 1,086,297 | 3,381,154 | 4,867,451 |
| 1896 | 1,081,396 | 3,154,370 | 4,235,766 | 1901 | 1,084,671 | 3,460,648 | 4,545,319 |

*Deep-sea navigation at Havre (entrances and clearances), not including vessels calling.*

| Year. | French vessels. | Foreign vessels. | Total tonnage. | Year. | French vessels. | Foreign vessels. | Total tonnage. |
|---|---|---|---|---|---|---|---|
| 1892 | 839,996 | 1,096,537 | 1,936,533 | 1897 | 676,018 | 1,166,282 | 1,842,300 |
| 1893 | 780,064 | 1,108,018 | 1,888,082 | 1898 | 667,457 | 1,356,254 | 2,023,711 |
| 1894 | 650,995 | 1,313,454 | 1,964,449 | 1899 | 703,956 | 1,188,804 | 1,892,760 |
| 1895 | 607,818 | 1,045,376 | 1,653,194 | 1900 | 642,083 | 1,100,328 | 1,742,411 |
| 1896 | 646,444 | 1,069,125 | 1,715,569 | 1901 | 666,976 | 1,223,883 | 1,890,859 |

*Navigation, by flag, at Havre—Statement showing the entrances and clearances, sail and steam, loaded, French coasting trade not included.*

ARRIVALS.

| Flag. | 1898. | | 1899. | | 1900. | | 1901. | |
|---|---|---|---|---|---|---|---|---|
| | Ships. | Tonnage. | Ships. | Tonnage. | Ships. | Tonnage. | Ships. | Tonnage. |
| French | 361 | 458,452 | 371 | 482,311 | 341 | 438,306 | 361 | 473,627 |
| German | 241 | 364,080 | 233 | | 221 | 356,267 | 224 | 304,134 |
| American | 2 | 3,249 | | | | | 1 | 2,125 |
| English | 1,375 | 1,207,694 | 1,276 | 1,025,495 | 1,342 | 1,063,740 | 1,263 | 1,106,893 |
| Austrian | 5 | 3,351 | 6 | 7,738 | | | 4 | 6,886 |
| Belgian | 7 | 1,631 | 1 | 455 | | | | |
| Danish | 25 | 19,990 | 22 | 19,894 | 18 | 13,187 | 13 | 12,547 |
| Spanish | 3 | 4,291 | 5 | 12,140 | 7 | 15,390 | 33 | 61,854 |
| Dutch | 85 | 46,576 | 75 | 44,359 | 78 | 47,308 | 81 | 49,884 |
| Italian | 12 | 8,191 | 25 | 14,192 | 26 | 15,972 | 19 | 14,638 |
| Norwegian | 138 | 89,196 | 164 | 97,716 | 162 | 98,540 | 114 | 72,085 |
| Portuguese | 4 | 6,083 | 13 | 27,341 | 5 | 10,980 | 1 | 307 |
| Russian | 9 | 4,871 | 8 | 4,196 | 9 | 5,012 | 14 | 11,400 |
| Swedish | 37 | 21,756 | 25 | 15,892 | 30 | 23,666 | 40 | 23,766 |
| Others | 8 | 19,017 | 5 | 7,873 | 5 | 8,345 | 5 | 5,209 |

DEPARTURES.

| Flag. | 1898. | | 1899. | | 1900. | | 1901. | |
|---|---|---|---|---|---|---|---|---|
| French | 461 | 592,214 | 423 | 595,698 | 389 | 585,181 | 364 | 530,751 |
| German | 223 | 349,676 | 221 | 353,919 | 208 | 348,543 | 214 | 388,161 |
| American | | | | | | | 1 | 1,658 |
| English | 609 | 470,951 | 634 | 465,991 | 622 | 454,341 | 668 | 533,490 |
| Austrian | 1 | 245 | 1 | 2,225 | | | 1 | 1,777 |
| Belgian | 2 | 358 | | | | | | |
| Danish | 36 | 19,315 | 20 | 13,933 | 37 | 19,060 | 35 | 22,586 |
| Spanish | | | 2 | 4,670 | 2 | 3,037 | 15 | 29,107 |
| Dutch | 76 | 44,553 | 76 | 46,680 | 83 | 55,180 | 78 | 55,283 |
| Italian | | | 6 | 2,683 | 2 | 1,397 | 5 | 4,680 |
| Norwegian | 51 | 28,897 | 39 | 24,037 | 42 | 19,485 | 38 | 26,077 |
| Portuguese | 2 | 4,668 | 12 | 27,524 | 2 | 3,317 | | |
| Russian | 15 | 9,495 | 5 | 2,169 | 9 | 7,284 | 7 | 11,584 |
| Swedish | 36 | 19,916 | 30 | 17,257 | 23 | 15,792 | 16 | 8,608 |
| Others | 8 | 17,761 | 8 | 7,168 | 2 | 4,923 | 1 | 1,415 |

*Number and tonnage of vessels which entered and cleared at Havre in the French coasting trade, laden and in ballast.*

| Year. | Number. | Tonnage. | Year. | Number. | Tonnage. |
|---|---|---|---|---|---|
| 1892 | 7,377 | 1,080,448 | 1897 | 8,212 | 1,107,896 |
| 1893 | 7,575 | 1,088,105 | 1898 | 8,701 | 1,220,334 |
| 1894 | 8,083 | 1,159,151 | 1899 | 7,704 | 1,018,396 |
| 1895 | 7,479 | 1,132,266 | 1900 | 7,194 | 980,219 |
| 1896 | 7,764 | 1,105,408 | 1901 | 7,458 | 967,097 |

*Number and tonnage of vessels belonging to the port of Havre.*

| Year. | Steamers. | | Sailing vessels. | | Total. | |
|---|---|---|---|---|---|---|
| | Number. | Tonnage. | Number. | Tonnage. | Number. | Tonnage. |
| 1895 | 204 | 143,040 | 192 | 21,912 | 396 | 164,962 |
| 1896 | 194 | 140,425 | 174 | 22,195 | 368 | 162,680 |
| 1897 | 195 | 134,539 | 181 | 28,683 | 376 | 163,222 |
| 1898 | 185 | 121,874 | 187 | 30,937 | 372 | 152,811 |
| 1899 | 194 | 122,748 | 194 | 48,344 | 388 | 171,092 |
| 1900 | 193 | 128,761 | 192 | 56,108 | 385 | 184,869 |
| 1901 | 195 | 137,715 | 196 | 60,403 | 391 | 198,118 |

*Vessels added to the merchant marine of Havre, either by construction or purchase.*

| Year. | French construction. | | | | Foreign construction. | | | | Total. | |
|---|---|---|---|---|---|---|---|---|---|---|
| | Steam. | | Sail. | | Steam. | | Sail. | | | |
| | No. | Tons. | No. | Tons. | No. | Tons. | No. | Tons. | No. | Tons. |
| 1895 | 1 | 76 | 4 | 294 | 8 | 3,533 | 4 | 1,053 | 17 | 4,956 |
| 1896 | 2 | 3,574 | 5 | 2,736 | 9 | 8,798 | 2 | 120 | 18 | 15,290 |
| 1897 | 8 | 19 | 11 | 7,069 | 5 | 1,630 | 6 | 453 | 18 | 9,171 |
| 1898 | 1 | 6 | 4 | 2,436 | 9 | 3,680 | 7 | 794 | 21 | 6,916 |
| 1899 | 6 | 2,316 | 16 | 19,534 | 12 | 6,180 | 6 | 2,646 | 40 | 30,676 |
| 1900 | 6 | 5,090 | 9 | 9,602 | 4 | 5,246 | 4 | 1,193 | 23 | 21,131 |
| 1901 | 6 | 8,312 | 14 | 5,782 | 4 | 5,686 | 2 | 702 | 26 | 20,482 |

*Merchandise received and exported at Havre.*

| Year. | Foreign commerce. | | | French coasting trade. | | | Total amount merchandise. |
|---|---|---|---|---|---|---|---|
| | Imports. | Exports. | Total. | Entries. | Clearances. | Total. | |
| | Tons. | Tons. | Tons. | Tons. | Tons. | Tons. | Tons. |
| 1892 | 1,820,894 | 581,497 | 2,402,391 | 204,373 | 402,069 | 606,442 | 3,008,833 |
| 1893 | 1,794,955 | 560,161 | 2,355,116 | 219,415 | 405,456 | 624,871 | 2,979,987 |
| 1894 | 1,822,482 | 599,611 | 2,422,093 | 226,549 | 411,282 | 637,831 | 3,059,924 |
| 1895 | 1,573,395 | 642,705 | 2,216,100 | 276,748 | 315,926 | 592,674 | 2,808,774 |
| 1896 | 1,594,158 | 602,508 | 2,196,081 | 275,374 | 441,621 | 716,995 | 2,913,656 |
| 1897 | 1,896,139 | 632,456 | 2,528,595 | 282,785 | 401,283 | 684,068 | 3,212,663 |
| 1898 | 2,154,973 | 625,108 | 2,780,081 | 313,870 | 498,975 | 812,845 | 3,592,926 |
| 1899 | 1,887,495 | 677,311 | 2,564,806 | 396,311 | 384,306 | 720,617 | 3,285,423 |
| 1900 | 2,052,450 | 711,015 | 2,763,465 | 333,577 | 362,461 | 696,038 | 3,459,508 |
| 1901 | 2,029,851 | 751,947 | 2,781,798 | ......... | ......... | ......... | ......... |

*General importations into Havre, for the years 1899, 1900, and 1901.*

| Articles. | 1899. | 1900. | 1901. |
|---|---|---|---|
| | *Tons.* | *Tons.* | *Tons.* |
| Baskets and cord work | 1,490 | 1,649 | 1,788 |
| Boats | 81,573 | 26,084 | 22,278 |
| Bones, hoofs, and horns of cattle | 9,730 | 11,718 | 5,196 |
| Brandy, spirits, and liqueurs | 9,648 | 8,629 | 8,780 |
| Camphor | 799 | 1,025 | 465 |
| Chemical products | 12,304 | 18,632 | 11,175 |
| Coal | 701,757 | 875,646 | 780,792 |
| Caoutchouc | 5,037 | 5,108 | 5,222 |
| Carriages | 302 | 2,248 | 183 |
| Cast iron and steel | 6,290 | 7,335 | 6,088 |
| Cereals and flour | 110,148 | 122,211 | 161,611 |
| Cocoa | 30,477 | 27,330 | 25,970 |
| Coffee | 129,312 | 108,672 | 150,682 |
| Copper | 38,805 | 45,548 | 29,451 |
| Cotton | 163,508 | 159,440 | 170,622 |
| Dyestuffs and tannin (crude) | | | 5,441 |
| Dyestuffs (manufactured) | | | 1,644 |
| Elephants' tusks and tortoise shells | 88 | 47 | 88 |
| Fruits (table) | 4,665 | 5,358 | 1,975 |
| Furniture and woodwork | 2,173 | 2,745 | 1,889 |
| Grain and oleaginous fruits | 44,019 | 68,090 | 70,714 |
| Grease: | | | |
|   Animal and other, excepting fish grease | 14,067 | 9,621 | 6,981 |
|   Fish | | | 1,549 |
| Hair | 319 | 559 | 182 |
| Hair (horse) | | | 184 |
| Indigo | 583 | 686 | 450 |
| Lead | | | 563 |
| Lobsters (fresh and canned) | 1,290 | 1,273 | 1,855 |
| Machines | 15,005 | 17,356 | 18,073 |
| Meat (fresh and salted) | 3,081 | 2,034 | 1,023 |
| Medicines | 1,259 | 955 | 766 |
| Minerals | 47,422 | 28,901 | 43,840 |
| Mother-of-pearl and shells | 2,115 | 2,980 | 2,144 |
| Nuts (gallnuts and filberts, broken or ground) | 1,148 | 3,183 | 2,817 |
| Oils: | | | |
|   Heavy and petroleum residues | 12,229 | 13,441 | 12,061 |
|   Volatile and essences | 80 | 69 | 68 |
|   Pure fixed | 14,224 | 10,285 | 11,726 |
|   Petroleum and schist | 87,189 | 85,717 | 87,626 |
| Oil cake | 13,969 | 24,686 | 17,811 |
| Pepper | 1,610 | 2,072 | 8,768 |
| Phormium, reeds, etc. | 7,503 | 7,894 | |
| Resinous products, excepting that of pine | 1,872 | 1,411 | 1,279 |
| Rice | 9,737 | 13,814 | 11,598 |
| Sago, salep, and other fecula | 5,655 | 3,749 | 3,618 |
| Skins and leather: | | | |
|   Undressed | 24,733 | 31,158 | 22,536 |
|   Dressed | 462 | 506 | 387 |
| Sugar | 28,680 | 15,835 | 21,056 |
| Tea | 454 | 663 | 779 |
| Textiles, blaid, and ribbons | 2,049 | 2,092 | 4,070 |
| Tin | 3,963 | 8,908 | 8,149 |
| Tobacco | 6,214 | 11,128 | 12,794 |
| Tools and manufactured metal | 2,470 | 3,125 | 2,278 |
| Vegetables (dry and flour of) | 16,212 | 13,782 | 12,318 |
| Vegetable fibers | | | 11,185 |
| Wax (animal) | 369 | 635 | 561 |
| Whalebone | 110 | 95 | 184 |
| Wines | 24,105 | 28,280 | 17,872 |
| Wood (common) | 75,459 | 80,709 | 88,040 |
| Wood (dyewood and cabinetmaking) | 117,711 | 122,525 | 88,065 |
| Wool | 9,421 | 8,876 | 12,745 |
| Zinc | 3,636 | 5,961 | 1,676 |
| Various articles | 68,349 | 64,896 | 48,088 |
|     Total | 1,876,274 | 2,051,760 | 1,978,380 |

*General exportations from Havre, for the years 1899, 1900, and 1901.*

| Articles. | 1899. | 1900. | 1901. |
|---|---|---|---|
| | *Tons.* | *Tons.* | *Tons.* |
| Boats | 8,856 | 9,208 | 9,874 |
| Brandy, spirits, and liqueurs | 4,418 | 4,320 | 8,139 |
| Butter | 2,908 | 1,958 | 2,095 |
| Caoutchouc | 2,824 | 2,675 | 2,460 |
| Carriages | 1,127 | 851 | 969 |

*General exportations from Havre, for the year 1899, 1900, and 1901*—Continued.

| Articles. | 1899. | 1900. | 1901. |
|---|---|---|---|
| | *Tons.* | *Tons.* | *Tons.* |
| Cereals (grain and flour) | 17,645 | 32,092 | 34,912 |
| Cheese | 1,388 | 1,505 | 1,811 |
| Chemicals | 12,191 | 11,985 | 18,487 |
| Coal | 287,101 | 291,473 | 307,924 |
| Cocoa | 14,870 | 15,613 | 13,972 |
| Coffee | 36,621 | 51,339 | 27,054 |
| Colors | 2,508 | 2,315 | 2,046 |
| Copper | 11,080 | 10,178 | 6,969 |
| Cotton | 5,605 | 10,636 | 4,020 |
| Dyewood extracts | 12,768 | | 9,530 |
| Fish (canned, salted, etc.) | 2,337 | 2,219 | 2,824 |
| Fruits (table) | 2,593 | | 2,502 |
| Furniture and woodwork | 9,937 | 10,907 | 4,725 |
| Glue | 1,346 | 1,198 | 1,051 |
| Hair | 498 | 543 | 471 |
| Indigo | 113 | 110 | 141 |
| Iron and steel (cast) | 5,200 | 7,653 | 8,458 |
| Machines | 6,115 | 4,764 | 5,748 |
| Medicines | 3,154 | 2,994 | 3,274 |
| Millinery | 2,171 | 1,473 | 1,945 |
| Millstones | 1,259 | 1,667 | 2,228 |
| Minerals | 3,282 | 1,850 | 474 |
| Oils: | | | |
| Fixed pure | 4,488 | 2,918 | 3,058 |
| Volatile and essences | 87 | 138 | 118 |
| Paper (cardboard, books, and engravings) | 7,728 | 6,239 | 6,399 |
| Pepper | 1,221 | 1,097 | 1,590 |
| Phormium, reeds, etc | 1,519 | 1,440 | 951 |
| Pottery, glass, and crystal | 14,666 | 14,325 | 13,358 |
| Seeds | 3,170 | 2,678 | 1,692 |
| Skins and leather: | | | |
| Undressed | 16,142 | 13,002 | 11,497 |
| Dressed | 2,696 | 2,450 | 1,916 |
| Sugar | 22,361 | 18,282 | 15,997 |
| Textiles | 31,731 | 27,663 | 28,331 |
| Tobacco | 1,561 | 1,370 | 1,945 |
| Tools and metal work | 14,814 | 11,574 | 13,815 |
| Vegetables (dry or canned) | 1,934 | 2,102 | 1,840 |
| Wine | 7,962 | 9,587 | 9,212 |
| Wood (foreign) | 7,208 | | 3,720 |
| Wool | 2,164 | 4,067 | 8,297 |
| Various articles | 88,426 | 104,464 | 159,596 |
| Total | 669,823 | 704,881 | 751,948 |

*Declared exports to the United States, fiscal years 1900, 1901, and 1902.*

| Articles. | 1900. | 1901. | 1902. |
|---|---|---|---|
| Albumen | | $597.54 | |
| Antiques | $3,019.48 | 1,284.04 | |
| Antimony | | 199.81 | |
| Arsenic | 3,997.80 | 1,505.92 | |
| Asphalt | 2,174.99 | | |
| Automobiles | | | $6,306.02 |
| Billiard cue tip | | 173.99 | 207.74 |
| Blacking | 43.68 | | |
| Bone chips | | 817.22 | 497.20 |
| Books | | 7,000.00 | |
| Brandy | | | 1,980.08 |
| Bristles | 10,478.95 | 10,329.94 | |
| Bronze | | 296.39 | |
| Brushes | 197.88 | | |
| Camphor | | 14,465.64 | |
| Caoutchouc | 666,899.72 | 155,884.06 | 62,949.26 |
| Caviar | 115.80 | | |
| Chalk | 162.12 | | |
| Cheese: | | | |
| Brie | | 19,718.11 | 349.90 |
| Camembert | 42,180.06 | 20,770.23 | 42,323.71 |
| Colommiers | | 188.49 | 115.80 |
| Gruyère | | 2,626.03 | 6,904.08 |
| Pont l'Evêque | | 135.09 | 191.60 |
| Port de Salut | | 382.05 | 1,006.24 |
| Roquefort | | 633.62 | 5,984.07 |
| Chemicals | | 26.41 | |
| Chessmen | 197.50 | 374.82 | 209.35 |

*Declared exports to the United States, fiscal years 1900, 1901, and 1902*—Continued.

| Articles. | 1900. | 1901. | 1902. |
|---|---|---|---|
| Church ornaments | | $281.49 | |
| Cocoa | $9,249.94 | 8,039.66 | $123,228.28 |
| Coffee | 180,105.20 | 1,415.85 | 32,223.06 |
| Confectionery | 259.02 | | |
| Copper | 758,140.08 | 446,482.91 | 33,512.18 |
| Cordage (old) | 10,463.10 | 12,002.19 | 11,778.75 |
| Carozo nuts | | 1,765.22 | |
| Cow hair | 19,754.94 | 6,427.84 | 4,174.62 |
| Currency | 20,265.00 | | |
| Dice | | | 173.51 |
| Dominoes | 802.83 | 950.36 | 451.91 |
| Dyewood extract | 70,698.11 | 39,162.64 | 47,715.56 |
| Emery | | | 292.76 |
| Feathers: | | | |
| Ostrich | | 59,110.68 | 18,775.85 |
| Vulture | 7,979.79 | | 18,766.57 |
| Figs | | | 110.97 |
| Flour | | 78.09 | |
| Flour pastes | | | 40.53 |
| Fruit (fresh) | 598.90 | 3.86 | |
| Furniture | | 165.02 | |
| Gelatin | 405.08 | | |
| Game | 114.80 | | |
| Glue | | | 706.65 |
| Glycerin | | 865.11 | 3,008.11 |
| Gum arabic | | | 1,171.25 |
| Hardware | 256.74 | | |
| Hats (fiber) | | | 212.30 |
| Hemp | | | 15,749.20 |
| Horses | 15,191.86 | 55,886.50 | 132,499.33 |
| Indigo | 4,606.68 | | |
| Ink | | 958.56 | 784.39 |
| Key rings | | 105.81 | |
| Lamp shades | | 99.88 | |
| Liqueur (benedictine) | 70,065.87 | 88,671.96 | 76,829.01 |
| Machinery | 119.82 | | |
| Marble | | | 236.17 |
| Mustard | 41.68 | 84.24 | 59.61 |
| Nickel | 61,059.29 | 41,578.02 | 49,032.15 |
| Ocher | 6,436.32 | 1,890.31 | 808.99 |
| Oils: | | | |
| Copra | 32,862.97 | 15,774.74 | 14,797.41 |
| Palm | | | 21,921.37 |
| Petigrain | | | 869.23 |
| Rape seed | | 787.88 | |
| Paintings | 442.94 | | 96.50 |
| Paper: | | | |
| Adhesive | 82.37 | 437.08 | |
| Tracing | | | 264.87 |
| Pâté de foie gras | | | 178.30 |
| Pearl (mother of) | 1,215.64 | 6,017.36 | 8,885.85 |
| Pebbles (flint) | 1,157.00 | 9,112.70 | 12,996.28 |
| Pens | 126.10 | 40.24 | 85.39 |
| Pepper | | 55,176.39 | 4,963.76 |
| Porcelain | | 77.61 | |
| Preserves (jam) | 1,933.98 | 1,428.50 | 723.76 |
| Raphia | | 175.65 | |
| Saddlery | 1,216.19 | 814.15 | |
| Saffron | 12,895.66 | 11,254.66 | 10,343.59 |
| Sausages | 542.83 | 601.20 | 794.88 |
| Seed (clover) | 1,329.53 | 2,429.25 | 2,081.98 |
| Senna | | 718.18 | |
| Silk goods | | | 109.06 |
| Skins: | | | |
| Calf | 87,989.89 | 77,255.79 | 38,343.11 |
| Deer | | | 1,965.29 |
| Goat | | 70,781.51 | 26,819.01 |
| Snails | 564.69 | 465.61 | 774.28 |
| Tea | 292.27 | | 140.02 |
| Tin | 14,272.14 | | 624.93 |
| Tin-plate advertisements | | | 4.03 |
| Tobacco | 188.18 | 168.74 | 188.20 |
| Tonka beans | | | 1,030.27 |
| Toothpicks | 960.67 | 2,908.92 | 1,775.45 |
| Tripe | | | 96.50 |
| Truffles | | | 114.10 |
| Vanilla | 3,847.54 | 1,205.13 | 5,431.97 |
| Vegetables: | | | |
| Artichokes | 26,784.23 | 3,351.84 | 4,654.50 |
| Beans | | 396.57 | 1,459.27 |
| Brussels sprouts | | | 375.55 |
| Cauliflower | | | 57.81 |
| Lentils | | | 195.51 |

*Declared exports to the United States, fiscal years 1900, 1901, and 1902—*Continued.

| Articles. | 1900. | 1901. | 1902. |
|---|---|---|---|
| Vegetables—Continued. | | | |
| Mushrooms | | | $145.73 |
| Peas | | | 93.41 |
| Potatoes | | | 37.95 |
| Salad | | | 9.36 |
| Shallots | | | 9.65 |
| Wine | $436.18 | $3,877.75 | 391.79 |
| Wood: | | | |
| Amaranth | | | 119.55 |
| Ebony | | | 3,940.63 |
| Fustic | | | 252.53 |
| Mahogany | 11,811.71 | 8,944.59 | 232.13 |
| Redwood | | | 724.42 |
| Rosewood | | | 2,553.93 |
| Walnut | | | 1,525.14 |
| Wood fiber | | 509.19 | |
| Wool | | 14,134.27 | 1,142.07 |
| Total | 2,161,955.46 | 1,284,363.03 | 874,812.16 |
| Returned American goods | 9,008.34 | 42,691.86 | 2,614.14 |
| Total | 2,170,963.80 | 1,327,054.89 | 877,426.30 |

## LIMOGES.

### EXPORTS.

The increase in the porcelain industry of this district during the
past year has been quite remarkable. There were so many orders left
over from 1901 that the factories could scarcely spare time to make
their annual inventories. The bright promise of a record year in
production, however, was seriously menaced by a long strike which
began about the 1st of April and continued for six weeks.

This strike was caused, not by demands for higher wages, but by
questions of factory government. The operatives claimed the right
to go out of or into the workshops whenever they chose. The manufacturers, on the other hand, declared that if any workman left the
building without permission he should forfeit the remainder of the
day. After a long and painful struggle, the operatives returned.

Since the strike, the manufacture of porcelain has been pushed forward as rapidly as possible; all the factories are working full time,
and orders are plentiful.

The prices of porcelain and raw materials remain about the same,
nor is there any marked change in wages. The United States continues to hold first rank among the countries importing this porcelain; fully 70 per cent of the output finds a market.
American taste is catered to and American buyers stimulate
the production.

### HUMAN HAIR.

The latest annual human-hair market, held in Limoges in June, 1902, was the largest for many years. A vast quantity of hair was disposed of, the reason for which is easily explained. The recent strikes in several industries and the unfavorable agricultural conditions of 1901 caused much suffering among the working classes, and the women and girls were willing to part with their hair for a little ready money. In very prosperous years, it is almost impossible to purchase human hair.

### GLOVES AND SKINS.

Two of the largest tanneries in France, where kid and lamb skins are tanned for gloves, are situated in this consular district. Glove makers in nearly every part of the world are supplied with skins prepared at these works.

Many glovers live in Limoges and adjacent villages, but the trade is practically in the hands of Parisian and London commission houses, which annually ship thousands of gloves to their customers in the United States.

### PAPER.

The paper-making industry of this part of France is of considerable importance. Most of the output is manufactured from straw. Of this kind of paper, there has been a large overproduction, and as a result, prices are low and some factories have either shut down or are working without profit. Manufacturers are trying to find new outlets for their goods, and recently, efforts have been made to open up a trade with Cuba.

### DYESTUFFS.

Central France is one of the largest producers of chestnuts in Europe. The wood of these trees, when old, is used very extensively in making dyes and tannic acid. Several large factories of this kind established in the Limoges district annually consume many tons of chestnut wood. They sell most of their output in France and Great Britain. One British firm buys, or receives on consignment, the entire ·production of the most important factories, and these shipments are, in turn, resold to the United States. French dyes and tannic acid are more highly esteemed by the trade than those of American manufacture, and sell at a lower price.

### CANNED GOODS.

The kinds of canned goods that are being exported from this section to America are undergoing a change; it is evident that Californian fruits are displacing the French product, not only in the United States, but also here in this country. The value of the goods shipped is about the same as in former years, but instead of vegetables and mushrooms, France is exporting, in increasing quantities, pâtés de foie gras, game, poultry, and walnuts. Great care and cleanliness are observed in the preparation of these products.

The canners state that their trade is prosperous, and that during the past year, they received orders from commission houses in Bordeaux, Havre, Paris, and even Hamburg, for goods to supply the American demand. Most of the canned vegetables is shipped to South

America, Great Britain, and the British colonies; the South American trade is especially large. The French market is, of course, the most important; the army and navy department take large quantities of all kinds of canned goods for the officers' mess.

## IMPORTS.

### AGRICULTURAL MACHINERY.

The quantity of agricultural machinery imported into this district is steadily increasing.

In a recent report to the Department of State,[a] attention is called to the change that is taking place in the rural districts of central France, viz, the replacing of cattle by horses as beasts of burden. This change is necessitated by the exodus of so many able-bodied peasants to the cities, who are drawn there by the apparently higher wages offered, the shorter hours of work, and the attractions of city life.

It is difficult for the "colons," stewards, and small proprietors to obtain enough laborers to work the soil. As a consequence, the demand for labor-saving machinery is, and must continue to be, on the increase. The flail is giving place to the thresher, the sickle to the reaper and binder, the scythe to the mower, and the ox and the cow to the horse. The change is gradual, but continuous.

British, German, and French implements are not as popular as the American, but those firms that have made the most careful study of the requirements of the French trade and have adapted their machinery to suit the peculiarities of the ground and people are being rewarded by larger orders than are the houses that try to force the sale of implements unadapted to the French market.

A thorough study of local conditions should be made by every manufacturer that desires to sell here. Capable representatives should visit the large "foires" (fairs) and "concours agricoles" which are held in the different cities of the provinces, and especially the "concours generals agricoles," which takes place in Paris during the spring. There, these agents can converse with the inhabitants and ascertain for themselves the requisites for success.

### SHOE MACHINERY.

Since the Paris exposition of 1900, there has been a complete revolution in the making of shoes.

Large shoe factories have been started all over France, and machine-made shoes are replacing the old-fashioned hand-made articles. The success of the American machines is remarkable.

American exporters have, in every instance, been wise enough to send over experienced American engineers or operators, who not only set up the machines properly, but also remain long enough to instruct the French machinists how to run them. As a consequence, many hundreds of our machines are now to be seen in France, and, indeed, in every other European country. The American operatives and engineers are, as a rule, a veritable revelation to the native workmen. The success of these machines, which have entirely revolutionized the

[a] See advance sheets No. 1397 (July 21, 1902).

shoe trade in France, is another proof of what has been repeatedly claimed in previous reports, viz, that American engineers and machinists should invariably accompany American machinery shipped abroad.

### TYPEWRITERS, CASH REGISTERS, ETC.

These machines are just finding their way into French offices, especially in the provinces.    The United States holds the lead in the manufacture of these classes of goods.    One reason that the sales have heretofore been so restricted is, that the agents employed by the exporting companies were not fully in sympathy with the enterprise that they had undertaken.    Now, however, live, intelligent men are coming over and are succeeding admirably in demonstrating the usefulness and practicability of their goods.

However, manufacturers who sell machines in foreign countries should establish depots where persons of intelligence and technical skill may be found to settle whatever questions may arise, and to make necessary repairs.    This advice holds true for all classes of American instruments, implements, and machines.    The lack of good repair shops has proven an effective barrier to sales.

### LOCOMOTIVES AND ENGINES.

The demand for American engines of all kinds is growing, in spite of the fact that there has been, on the part of French manufacturers and workmen, no little opposition to their introduction into this country. The importation of American machinery is discouraged as much as possible, but our locomotives have made their way by sheer force of merit.    It is to be regretted that American engineers have not always been employed to run them.

The fuel used in France is not the same as that employed in the United States, and this is another reason for some of the objections raised.    In many cases, a small alteration had to be made in the grates and flues to adapt them to the new kinds of coal.    This was not a fault of the machines themselves, but rather of the manufacturer, who did not familiarize himself with conditions in foreign countries. American locomotives have won for themselves, a good name, not only for power but also for endurance.

The demand for traction, stationary, and marine engines is increasing.    Greater attention should be given to this market, and every shipment should be accompanied by a practical engineer, to adapt the machines to the different uses to which they may be put.

### ELECTRICAL SUPPLIES.

Limoges has recently extended her system of electric street cars, and is now considering the laying of additional tracks.

Within the past few months, electric lighting has been introduced into the city.

Many of the manufacturers are using electric motors in their works. The systems principally employed are American, and a good deal of the supplies comes from the United States; but Germany, Switzerland, and Great Britain are active competitors, and it behooves the electrical workers in America to make strong efforts to retain their supremacy in this market.

## WOOD.

In view of the elimination of the forests, the demand for timber of all kinds for building, furniture, and other purposes is constantly growing, and the French market for American hickory and oak spokes, elm and lignum vitæ hubs, and staves is almost unlimited.

From the oak timber are constructed immense casks called "demimuids" and "foudres," the former holding 400 to 500 liters, and the latter any number of liters from 600 upward. These casks are usually mounted on railroad trucks, and are used for conveying wines, spirits, oils, etc. The imports of oak timber for this purpose is increasing constantly.

## PREPARED LEATHER.

United States "chrome" leather a few years ago found a good market in France and in Europe generally. The skins were prepared excellently and met with immense sales. Since that time, however, numerous imitations have appeared, all meeting with more or less success. These imitations, together with the fact that some American exportations have been exceedingly unsatisfactory, have so affected the French demand that sales have in some sections been reduced to almost nothing.

If the American tanner were as careful to maintain the standard of excellence set by him in former years as he is to compete in price with inferior productions, he could no doubt largely increase the sale of his goods.

## MEATS.

In spite of high duties and the general opposition, American meats are sold in this country in large and constantly increasing quantities. Owing to steep prices in the United States, the shipments were not so heavy last year; but while France and the rest of Europe are obliged to maintain large military and naval establishments, the demand for meats can not greatly decrease. It is well known that the French Government keeps on hand supplies of meat sufficient to meet the requirements of the army and navy for many months—a fact which American producers should not fail to bear in mind, for it means that there will always be a market here for their output.

The large provision stores throughout the country are all supplied, to a certain extent, with canned and preserved meats and fish from the United States. It is thought that large quantities of smoked salmon and the products of the Pacific fisheries and canneries could also be sold here.

The local retail price of codfish and other salted fish is nearly double that in America. If more attention were paid to this branch of the trade, and to American canned mackerel, herring, and salmon, the exportations would be larger.

There is also a strong probability that, if American canned clams and oysters, especially those from the southern waters, were properly introduced into France, there would be a large demand for them.

WALTER T. GRIFFIN,
*Commercial Agent.*

LIMOGES, *October 31, 1902.*

## LYONS.

### UNITED STATES TRADE.

There is nothing new in relation to the introduction of American manufactures into this part of France since my report on this subject one year ago. The same machines—cash registers, typewriters, sewing machines, wringers, ice-cream freezers, sausage grinders, meat choppers, bicycles, cider presses, and all kind of agricultural implements—are being imported from the United States, as they have been for the past five years or more. I do not believe any material increase will take place in the sales of American manufactures to France unless cheaper freight rates to Europe are obtainable, or unless reciprocal arrangements are entered into, by which lower rates of duty will be granted to certain classes of our manufactures in return for like concessions to certain products of France. Two-thirds or perhaps more of the business done in France is transacted through Paris. In pursuance of letters received from home, I have applied to business places here for data, and have invariably learned that application must be made to Paris. This suggests to me the propriety of creating the position of commercial attaché to our embassy at the French capital. This official should have absolutely nothing to do but to study the industry and commerce of the country, and to look out for openings for American products. I can see how such an official could easily open the way for a greatly increased consumption of our products in France.

Two years ago, a gentleman applied at this consulate for figures on steel blooms, saying that he would want to purchase perhaps 1,000,000 tons. I sent this query to a well-known firm in Cleveland, Ohio, and in the course of two months received a reply which had filtered through several agencies in the United States and a London office, stating that the entire product was absorbed by the home demand and that there was no surplus for export. I wrote back that the company should nurse such orders as these, as the time might come when the domestic demand would fall off and a foreign market be necessary to keep the men at work.

The French complain continually of our customs duties, but they never despair of selling us their goods. When the tariff bill of 1897 became a law, several Frenchmen immediately started silk mills in the United States, setting an example that Americans ought to follow. Our people would do well to establish many different lines of manufactures in the European countries. One of the important sources of the wealth of Great Britain is the extension of her varied lines of industry into her colonies and into the different nations of both the Old World and the New.

All nations are struggling, first, to protect their own markets against foreign competition; secondly, to gain possession of the markets of other countries. When two countries have equal advantages for production, the domination of the one over the other depends entirely upon cheapness of transportation. In all the great centers of Europe, there are colonial schools in which young men are taught everything relating to the markets of the colonies. One-half of the human race live in colonies, protectorates, and dependencies, and the wants of these people are supplied by the home nations. Great Britain, France, Germany, and Holland owe a large part of their prosperity to the constantly growing demand for supplies for their colonies and dependencies. The great nations are vieing with each other to gain cheap ocean freights. A distinguished English economist, Sir Robert Giffen, has suggested that Great Britain would do well to furnish free transportation of the purchases of her customers to any part of the world. This is on the principle that a wide-awake business house will send goods to its customers. Great Britain sells to Canada one-third more silk made in Lyons than the Lyonnese manufacturers and merchants themselves sell to the same country. The explanation of this is that Great Britain has lower freights to and preferential duties in her own colonies. The United States can surely have as cheap freight facilities. Our manufacturers could also build mills and workshops in all the nations of the world, and this would be a sure way to extend the demand for our manufactures.

Germany is manifesting an appreciation of this means of trade extension. Germans have started great chemical works or bought and remodeled old ones near this city, and to-day, they supply all the dyeing material to the great French establishments in Lyons. French chemical industries which, two years ago, were very prosperous have no business left them to-day, except in the line of perfumeries and pharmaceutics.

Wherever Germans or Englishmen build a plant in a foreign country they establish the nucleus of a market for their home products, besides sending to their own country the dividends earned. There is room in every country in Continental Europe for the establishment of American factories, and it would be a means of breaking down the barriers of protection, of opening a demand for American goods, and of increasing the market for American labor.

Americans visit Lyons quite often with samples of their goods, and I accompany them to dealers where I act as interpreter. In every instance, the Frenchmen express enthusiastic admiration for the goods shown and desire to become large purchasers. But after the high rates of duty in France are carefully considered, the Americans conclude that it is not worth while to attempt to establish an export trade with this country. The manufacturers of France never tire of complaining of our protective duties, but French duties shut most of our manufactures out of these markets.

People in the United States, however, have more money to spend, and a high duty will not keep them from buying a thing they want. The French, on the contrary, will hesitate long before making a purchase, and a very small saving will incline them to buy an inferior article. Reciprocity is not so necessary to France as it is to the United States, for the Frenchmen continue to sell to our people notwithstanding our high protective tariff, while the same duty shuts us entirely out of their market. If the United States could negotiate a reciprocity treaty with France, by which our manufactures of iron and steel could enter duty free, these articles would find a very rich market in this country.

I spent half of my last vacation in Spain, and found there on all sides evidences of the intense business activity of Germany, England, and France, especially of the first-named country. A Mr. Alexander, an enterprising Scotchman, who had been induced by our consul-general at Barcelona, Mr. Lay, to establish a warehouse for the exposition and sale of American manufactures, told me that he had been requested to name prices for American lathes, and that, while he was making every possible effort to get a big order, he expected that the Germans would underbid him. The latter own many of the electric

*General importations into Havre, for the years 1899, 1900, and 1901.*

| Articles. | 1899. | 1900. | 1901. |
|---|---|---|---|
| | *Tons.* | *Tons.* | *Tons.* |
| Baskets and cord work | 1,490 | 1,649 | 1,788 |
| Boats | 31,573 | 26,034 | 22,273 |
| Bones, hoofs, and horns of cattle | 9,730 | 11,718 | 5,198 |
| Brandy, spirits, and liqueurs | 9,648 | 8,629 | 8,760 |
| Camphor | 799 | 1,025 | 465 |
| Chemical products | 12,304 | 13,632 | 11,175 |
| Coal | 701,757 | 875,646 | 780,792 |
| Caoutchouc | 5,097 | 5,108 | 5,222 |
| Carriages | 802 | 2,248 | 183 |
| Cast iron and steel | 6,290 | 7,335 | 6,088 |
| Cereals and flour | 110,148 | 122,211 | 161,611 |
| Cocoa | 30,477 | 27,330 | 25,970 |
| Coffee | 129,312 | 108,672 | 150,682 |
| Copper | 38,805 | 45,548 | 29,451 |
| Cotton | 163,508 | 159,440 | 170,622 |
| Dyestuffs and tannin (crude) | | | 5,441 |
| Dyestuffs (manufactured) | | | 1,644 |
| Elephants' tusks and tortoise shells | 88 | 47 | 33 |
| Fruits (table) | 4,665 | 5,358 | 1,975 |
| Furniture and woodwork | 2,173 | 2,745 | 1,880 |
| Grain and oleaginous fruits | 64,019 | 63,090 | 70,714 |
| Grease: | | | |
|   Animal and other, excepting fish grease | 14,067 | 9,621 | 6,981 |
|   Fish | | | 1,549 |
| Hair | 319 | 559 | 182 |
| Hair (horse) | | | 184 |
| Indigo | 568 | 686 | 450 |
| Lead | | | 568 |
| Lobsters (fresh and canned) | 1,280 | 1,273 | 1,365 |
| Machines | 15,005 | 17,358 | 18,073 |
| Meat (fresh and salted) | 8,061 | 2,064 | 1,028 |
| Medicines | 1,259 | 955 | 766 |
| Minerals | 47,422 | 28,901 | 43,840 |
| Mother-of-pearl and shells | 2,115 | 2,980 | 2,144 |
| Nuts (gallnuts and filberts, broken or ground) | 1,148 | 8,188 | 2,317 |
| Oils: | | | |
|   Heavy and petroleum residues | 12,229 | 13,441 | 13,081 |
|   Volatile and essences | 89 | 69 | 68 |
|   Pure fixed | 14,224 | 10,285 | 11,736 |
|   Petroleum and schist | 37,180 | 35,717 | 37,626 |
| Oil cake | 13,989 | 24,686 | 17,811 |
| Pepper | 1,610 | 2,072 | 3,768 |
| Phormium, reeds, etc. | 7,508 | 7,894 | |
| Resinous products, excepting that of pine | 1,872 | 1,411 | 1,279 |
| Rice | 9,737 | 13,814 | 11,598 |
| Sago, salep, and other fecula | 5,655 | 8,749 | 8,613 |
| Skins and leather: | | | |
|   Undressed | 24,732 | 31,158 | 22,536 |
|   Dressed | 482 | 506 | 887 |
| Sugar | 23,660 | 15,835 | 21,056 |
| Tea | 454 | 668 | 779 |
| Textiles, blaid, and ribbons | 2,049 | 2,092 | 4,070 |
| Tin | 3,963 | 3,908 | 3,149 |
| Tobacco | 6,214 | 11,128 | 12,794 |
| Tools and manufactured metal | 2,470 | 8,128 | 2,273 |
| Vegetables (dry and flour of) | 16,212 | 13,782 | 12,213 |
| Vegetable fibers | | | 11,185 |
| Wax (animal) | 389 | 685 | 561 |
| Whalebone | 110 | 95 | 134 |
| Wines | 24,105 | 28,260 | 17,872 |
| Wood (common) | 75,459 | 80,709 | 88,040 |
| Wood (dyewood and cabinetmaking) | 117,711 | 122,525 | 88,035 |
| Wool | 9,421 | 8,376 | 12,745 |
| Zinc | 8,688 | 5,961 | 1,676 |
| Various articles | 68,349 | 64,896 | 48,088 |
| Total | 1,876,274 | 2,051,760 | 1,973,880 |

*General exportations from Havre, for the years 1899, 1900, and 1901.*

| Articles. | 1899. | 1900. | 1901. |
|---|---|---|---|
| | *Tons.* | *Tons.* | *Tons.* |
| Boats | 8,856 | 9,208 | 9,874 |
| Brandy, spirits, and liqueurs | 4,418 | 4,820 | 3,130 |
| Butter | 2,908 | 1,958 | 2,095 |
| Caoutchouc | 2,824 | 2,675 | 2,460 |
| Carriages | 1,127 | 851 | 989 |

*General exportations from Havre, for the year 1899, 1900, and 1901*—Continued.

| Articles. | 1899. | 1900. | 1901. |
|---|---|---|---|
| | *Tons.* | *Tons.* | *Tons.* |
| Cereals (grain and flour) | 17,645 | 32,092 | 34,912 |
| Cheese | 1,388 | 1,505 | 1,811 |
| Chemicals | 12,191 | 11,965 | 18,487 |
| Coal | 267,101 | 291,472 | 307,924 |
| Cocoa | 14,870 | 15,613 | 13,972 |
| Coffee | 36,621 | 51,339 | 27,054 |
| Colors | 2,598 | 2,315 | 2,046 |
| Copper | 11,080 | 10,178 | 6,909 |
| Cotton | 5,605 | 10,636 | 4,020 |
| Dyewood extracts | 12,768 | | 9,530 |
| Fish (canned, salted, etc.) | 2,337 | 2,219 | 2,834 |
| Fruits (table) | 2,563 | | 2,502 |
| Furniture and woodwork | 9,987 | 10,907 | 4,725 |
| Glue | 1,346 | 1,198 | 1,051 |
| Hair | 498 | 543 | 471 |
| Indigo | 113 | 110 | 141 |
| Iron and steel (cast) | 5,200 | 7,653 | 8,458 |
| Machines | 6,115 | 4,764 | 5,748 |
| Medicines | 3,154 | 2,994 | 3,274 |
| Millinery | 2,171 | 1,473 | 1,945 |
| Millstones | 1,259 | 1,667 | 2,226 |
| Minerals | 3,282 | 1,850 | 474 |
| Oils: | | | |
| Fixed pure | 4,488 | 2,918 | 3,058 |
| Volatile and essences | 87 | 138 | 118 |
| Paper (cardboard, books, and engravings) | 7,723 | 6,239 | 6,399 |
| Pepper | 1,221 | 1,097 | 1,590 |
| Phormium, reeds, etc | 1,519 | 1,440 | 951 |
| Pottery, glass, and crystal | 14,666 | 14,325 | 13,353 |
| Seeds | 3,170 | 2,678 | 1,692 |
| Skins and leather: | | | |
| Undressed | 16,142 | 13,002 | 11,497 |
| Dressed | 2,698 | 2,450 | 1,916 |
| Sugar | 22,331 | 18,262 | 15,997 |
| Textiles | 31,731 | 27,663 | 28,331 |
| Tobacco | 1,561 | 1,370 | 1,945 |
| Tools and metal work | 14,814 | 11,574 | 13,815 |
| Vegetables (dry or canned) | 1,934 | 2,102 | 1,840 |
| Wine | 7,962 | 9,587 | 9,212 |
| Wood (foreign) | 7,208 | | 3,739 |
| Wool | 2,164 | 4,007 | 3,297 |
| Various articles | 88,426 | 104,464 | 159,596 |
| Total | 669,823 | 704,881 | 751,948 |

*Declared exports to the United States, fiscal years 1900, 1901, and 1902.*

| Articles. | 1900. | 1901. | 1902. |
|---|---|---|---|
| Albumen | | $597.54 | |
| Antiques | $3,019.48 | 1,284.04 | |
| Antimony | | 199.81 | |
| Arsenic | 3,997.80 | 1,505.02 | |
| Asphalt | 2,174.99 | | |
| Automobiles | | | $6,306.02 |
| Billiard cue tip | | 173.90 | 207.74 |
| Blacking | 43.62 | | |
| Bone chips | | 817.22 | 497.20 |
| Books | | 7,000.00 | |
| Brandy | | | 1,390.08 |
| Bristles | 10,478.95 | 10,329.94 | |
| Bronze | | 226.39 | |
| Brushes | 197.83 | | |
| Camphor | | 14,465.64 | |
| Caoutchouc | 666,899.72 | 155,884.08 | 62,949.26 |
| Caviar | 115.80 | | |
| Chalk | 162.12 | | |
| Cheese: | | | |
| Brie | | 19,713.11 | 349.90 |
| Camembert | 42,180.06 | 20,770.23 | 42,823.71 |
| Colommiers | | 188.49 | 115.80 |
| Gruyère | | 2,626.03 | 6,904.69 |
| Pont l'Evêque | | 135.09 | 191.60 |
| Port de Salut | | 382.05 | 1,006.24 |
| Roquefort | | 633.62 | 5,064.67 |
| Chemicals | | 26.41 | |
| Chessmen | 197.50 | 874.82 | 262.35 |

H. Doc. 305, pt 2——12

*Declared exports to the United States, fiscal years 1900, 1901, and 1902—*Continued.

| Articles. | 1900. | 1901. | 1902. |
|---|---|---|---|
| Church ornaments | | $281.49 | |
| Cocoa | $9,249.94 | 8,039.66 | $123,228.28 |
| Coffee | 180,105.20 | 1,415.85 | 32,228.06 |
| Confectionery | 259.02 | | |
| Copper | 753,140.08 | 446,482.91 | 33,512.18 |
| Cordage (old) | 10,463.10 | 12,002.19 | 11,778.75 |
| Carozo nuts | | 1,765.22 | |
| Cow hair | 19,754.94 | 6,427.84 | 4,174.62 |
| Currency | 20,265.00 | | |
| Dice | | | 173.51 |
| Dominoes | 802.83 | 950.36 | 451.91 |
| Dyewood extract | 70,698.11 | 39,462.64 | 47,715.56 |
| Emery | | | 232.76 |
| Feathers: | | | |
| Ostrich | | 59,110.68 | 18,775.65 |
| Vulture | 7,979.79 | | 18,766.57 |
| Figs | | | 110.97 |
| Flour | | 73.09 | |
| Flour pastes | | | 40.53 |
| Fruit (fresh) | 598.30 | 3.86 | |
| Furniture | | 165.02 | |
| Gelatin | 405.05 | | |
| Game | 114.80 | | |
| Glue | | | 705.65 |
| Glycerin | | 865.11 | 3,008.11 |
| Gum arabic | | | 1,171.25 |
| Hardware | 256.74 | | |
| Hats (fiber) | | | 212.30 |
| Hemp | | | 15,749.20 |
| Horses | 15,191.86 | 55,386.50 | 132,499.33 |
| Indigo | 4,606.68 | | |
| Ink | | 358.56 | 784.39 |
| Key rings | | 105.81 | |
| Lamp shades | | 99.88 | |
| Liqueur (benedictine) | 70,085.87 | 88,671.96 | 76,829.01 |
| Machinery | 119.82 | | |
| Marble | | | 286.17 |
| Mustard | 41.68 | 84.24 | 59.61 |
| Nickel | 61,059.29 | 41,578.02 | 49,032.15 |
| Ocher | 6,436.32 | 1,800.31 | 808.99 |
| Oils: | | | |
| Copra | 32,862.97 | 15,774.74 | 14,797.41 |
| Palm | | | 21,921.37 |
| Petigrain | | | 369.23 |
| Rape seed | | 787.88 | |
| Paintings | 442.94 | | 96.50 |
| Paper: | | | |
| Adhesive | 82.37 | 437.08 | |
| Tracing | | | 264.87 |
| Pâté de foie gras | | | 178.30 |
| Pearl (mother of) | 1,215.64 | 6,017.35 | 8,885.85 |
| Pebbles (flint) | 1,157.00 | 9,112.70 | 12,996.28 |
| Pens | 126.10 | 40.24 | 85.39 |
| Pepper | | 55,176.39 | 4,963.76 |
| Porcelain | | 77.61 | |
| Preserves (jam) | 1,936.98 | 1,428.50 | 723.78 |
| Raphia | | 175.65 | |
| Saddlery | 1,216.19 | 814.15 | |
| Saffron | 12,895.66 | 11,254.66 | 10,343.59 |
| Sausages | 542.33 | 601.20 | 794.88 |
| Seed (clover) | 1,329.53 | 2,429.25 | 2,081.93 |
| Senna | | 713.18 | |
| Silk goods | | | 109.05 |
| Skins: | | | |
| Calf | 87,969.89 | 77,255.79 | 38,343.11 |
| Deer | | | 1,965.29 |
| Goat | | 70,781.51 | 26,819.01 |
| Snails | 564.69 | 465.61 | 774.28 |
| Tea | 292.27 | | 140.50 |
| Tin | 14,272.14 | | 624.93 |
| Tin-plate advertisements | | | 4.08 |
| Tobacco | 188.18 | 168.74 | 188.30 |
| Tonka beans | | | 1,030.27 |
| Toothpicks | 960.67 | 2,906.92 | 1,775.45 |
| Tripe | | | 96.50 |
| Truffles | | | 114.10 |
| Vanilla | 3,847.54 | 1,205.13 | 5,431.97 |
| Vegetables: | | | |
| Artichokes | 26,784.23 | 3,851.84 | 4,654.50 |
| Beans | | 396.57 | 1,459.27 |
| Brussels sprouts | | | 375.55 |
| Cauliflower | | | 57.81 |
| Lentils | | | 195.51 |

At the same time, legislation has been tending to interfere in the management of business concerns, to the detriment of both employers and employees. Producers, fearing unexpected demands for higher wages, and strikes, which would increase the cost of production, were afraid to undertake large contracts for future delivery or to negotiate for supplies ahead.

## THE SILK BUSINESS.

The principal business of Lyons during the past five hundred years has been the manufacture of silk. Notwithstanding the progress in this industry made in other great nations during the Nineteenth century, Lyons still maintains her place in the lead, almost every year seeing a slight increase in the quantity of silk made here and in the country tributary to this city.

In the year 1901, the condition house of Lyons conditioned 106,762 bales of raw silk, weighing 15,124,227 pounds, against 94,415 bales, weighing 13,291,878 pounds in 1900.

The year 1900 showed a decline as compared with the previous one. The year 1901, as compared with 1891, showed a progress of a little over 9½ per cent. The business of the condition house is a faithful barometer of the fluctuations in the silk industry of France.

But very little variation is recorded in the price or in the quantity of silk conditioned from month to month during the year 1901. The 28 condition houses now doing business in Europe registered, during the year 1901, 49,096,586 pounds of silk of all kinds. This is an excess of 6,824,589 pounds over the year 1900.

Of the total in 1901, 19,903,952 pounds were conditioned in the 12 houses of France, and 22,164,003 pounds in the 9 establishments in Italy.

I am informed that the condition house in London is closed and that the figures of its business for 1901 are not obtainable. More silk was conditioned in Milan than in any other city. The report of the chamber of commerce regrets that Lyons has lost its preeminence as the first market of Europe for raw silk, and attributes it to the protective duties that France imposed upon thrown silk in 1892. But this increase in business for Milan is not entirely at the expense of this city, as a number of silk dealers of Lyons have established houses in the Italian center and much of the business done there is in the interest of Lyonnese capital. France imported 15,138,420 pounds of raw silk in 1901. Of this, 5,087,280 pounds were exported to other countries.

The manufactures of silk in and around Lyons for the year 1901 were valued at $87,870,000, just $400,000 less than the product of 1900. Every loom in France was occupied during 1901, and if the value of the product was lower than in the former year, it was due to lower cost of cotton and wool, which permitted or necessitated lower prices of silk. The chamber of commerce gives statistical tables which prove that the volume of silk manufactures for 1901 was exceeded only twice—in 1899 and 1900. The report asserts that competition is so close that it is not unusual for manufacturers to sell the goods at cost, and that the work becomes more and more difficult with constantly diminishing profits.

The exports of manufactured silk from Lyons in 1901 amounted to $56,052,200, a higher figure than was reached at any time during the last decade, and an excess of $4,434,600 over 1900. The following table gives the countries to which goods were exported and the quantities:

| Country. | 1901. | 1900. | 1899. |
|---|---|---|---|
| England | $27,371,400 | $23,022,200 | $26,965,400 |
| Germany | 3,595,200 | 3,659,000 | 4,540,800 |
| Belgium | 2,326,200 | 2,467,200 | 2,101,800 |
| Switzerland | 3,099,800 | 2,204,200 | 1,736,000 |
| Russia | 159,800 | 161,000 | 173,800 |
| Italy | 1,001,200 | 591,800 | 528,600 |
| Austria | 452,400 | 279,400 | 331,400 |
| Spain | 1,197,200 | 1,136,200 | 2,015,600 |
| Turkey | 1,115,400 | 1,192,400 | 1,296,600 |
| United States | 10,306,000 | 10,299,200 | 10,613,600 |
| Brazil | 277,200 | 106,200 | 105,200 |
| Argentine Republic | 231,600 | 183,000 | 186,600 |
| Algiers | 66,400 | 101,200 | 172,600 |
| Other countries | 4,912,400 | 6,214,600 | ............ |
| Total | 56,052,200 | 51,617,600 | 50,768,000 |

Great Britain is credited with a larger share of French silk exports than she receives. The customs are in the habit of attributing to that country whatever is shipped in English bottoms, a large part of which is never discharged in England, or is merely transshipped there. If the above table were corrected, it is believed that it would stand thus:

| Year. | Exports. | |
|---|---|---|
| | To England. | To United States. |
| 1901 | $24,099,400 | $13,688,000 |
| 1900 | 23,022,200 | 10,299,200 |
| 1899 | 26,965,400 | 10,613,600 |

The importation of silk into France, which was $13,075,200 in 1899 and $12,402,000 in 1900, rose to $14,392,200 in 1901. The increase was almost entirely in Asiatic tissues, such as pongees, corahs, and tussahs, which amounted to $6,195,800 in 1901. It is held that these tissues really constitute a form of raw material, to be finished in the dyeing and printing houses of Lyons. The importations of silk from central Europe—that is to say, Switzerland and Germany—aggregated $6,017,800 in 1901, of which $3,963,400 was from Switzerland and $2,054,400 from Germany. From England, the imports of silk were $2,590,000, from Italy $261,600, and from Austria-Hungary $44,200. The imports from China in 1901 are not given, but they are believed to vary little from those of 1900, when the figures were $822,200. For Japan in the same year, they were $3,669,800.

JOHN C. COVERT, *Consul.*

LYONS, *September 18, 1902.*

---

## MARSEILLES.

The commercial tone of the Republic continues to be healthy, with a more buoyant note than heretofore. None of the gloomy predictions of foreign birth have been realized, and the country has passed through the most acute stage of the difficulties with the religious orders in a manner to indicate that however much political heat may have been engendered, fundamental institutions are not menaced. Money is plenty, especially in the center and north. France, with its resources in accumulated capital and natural wealth, is more inviting than ever as a field for the development of our foreign trade, and the surprising feature of the case is that so little, comparatively, of our enterprise turns hither. This backwardness is due in part to differences of language. Up to this time, our greatest successes have been registered in England, whose language is our own, and in Germany, whose language is spoken by millions of our people and taught in our schools. We have found it easier to turn our trade over to British and German commission houses than to take up and master the details of a direct trade with France. We have found it most easy of all to make New York the clearing house for our foreign trade, leaving the details of shipping, banking, and finding the actual consumer to foreigners who fatten off of our indifference and will desert us the moment they find an advantage in so doing. As a temporary condition, we are ourselves so marvelously prosperous at home as to be literally unequal to the task of seeking foreign markets in many cases, or uninterested in many more. The commercial organizations perhaps see the wisdom of expending a portion of present profits in establishing ourselves abroad, as an assurance against possible future stagnation, but I do not discover that the individual manufacturer cares to act practically upon this theory.

The ultimate supremacy in commercial fields abroad will not probably be determined by any foreign coalition against us, but by our own ability to organize and go forward as merchants with the same energy that we have demonstrated as producers. We are freely giving to our competitors the same tools with which we have learned to economize and perfect our manufacturing capacity, and we shall not be able to maintain a permanent monopoly of those advantages now distinctively American. In the meantime, we are doing nothing to advance ourselves as merchants. The time may be foreseen therefore when we shall lose ground where we are now strong unless we note the danger in time, and approach the consumer with our own sales agencies and in our own way, learning the peculiarities of each market and diminishing the number of commissions now being paid to middlemen.

To particularize, I may point out that, in Marseilles, there are but two or three established concerns now handling American machinery upon a large scale. I receive annually not one but hundreds of letters asking for local addresses of dealers in these lines. I am able to supply but these few established names, with the inevitable result that the American correspondent does not care to give over an agency to a house already representing his competitors, or that the Marseilles concerns do not care to enlarge their line. The American concludes that there is nothing in foreign trade for him, and the expansion of our commerce is slow. There are no resident American houses, few American commercial travelers appear, and I see business slipping from us that would be ours if we simply had the courage to open our own agencies and work by our own methods. The great successes in the sale of American goods have been made mainly by the firms that have set up for themselves, like the manufacturers of typewriters, for example, and have adapted themselves to French ways, while at the same time preserving their American individuality.

I shall not undertake to specify the particular classes of goods for which a market might be found in France.  I can best do that in my special reports, called for by correspondents or suggested by varying conditions.  It is sufficient here to point out that we are sending to France, roundly speaking, but one-tenth of the total imports, and we should send more.  Summarized, the situation stands thus:

*Imports and exports, by countries.*

| From or to— | Imports. | | Exports. | |
|---|---|---|---|---|
| | 1901. | 1900. | 1901. | 1900. |
| England | $128,801,700 | $130,208,900 | $243,984,800 | $236,927,200 |
| United States | 83,002,100 | 88,339,500 | 46,226,200 | 49,254,400 |
| Germany | 80,613,000 | 82,407,900 | 87,028,200 | 89,778,600 |
| Belgium | 74,540,800 | 81,432,500 | 114,128,600 | 115,463,600 |
| Argentina | 68,854,400 | 54,991,700 | 9,872,100 | 9,584,000 |
| Russia | 40,520,000 | 44,629,513 | 8,487,100 | 7,604,600 |
| Spain | 32,438,700 | 42,455,600 | 24,468,500 | 26,115,800 |
| Italy | 28,985,100 | 28,696,600 | | |
| Turkey | | | | 9,605,200 |
| Switzerland | 20,067,200 | 20,695,200 | 53,694,000 | 40,817,000 |
| Austria-Hungary | 16,102,300 | 17,019,100 | 4,108,800 | 3,511,000 |
| Brazil | 11,315,600 | 15,229,600 | 6,245,200 | 7,284,200 |
| Others | 287,133,600 | 269,767,900 | | |
| Total | 909,907,700 | 906,675,900 | 639,681,200 | 625,994,500 |

*Imports and exports, by articles.*

| Class. | Imports. | | Exports. | |
|---|---|---|---|---|
| | 1901. | 1900. | 1901. | 1900. |
| Food | $154,699,300 | $158,113,300 | $150,201,700 | $146,675,900 |
| Raw materials | 602,989,700 | 585,803,400 | 210,570,800 | 211,135,400 |
| Manufactured goods | 152,218,700 | 162,759,000 | 398,104,200 | 393,592,400 |
| Parcels post | | | 45,193,100 | 41,575,100 |
| Total | 909,907,700 | 906,675,700 | 804,069,800 | 792,978,900 |

| Class. | Imports for first eight months of— | | Exports for first eight months of— | |
|---|---|---|---|---|
| | 1902. | 1901. | 1902. | 1901. |
| Food | $94,614,800 | $94,859,900 | $95,796,600 | $91,474,100 |
| Manufactured goods | 98,332,900 | 99,506,700 | 257,620,900 | 258,674,000 |
| Raw materials | 375,044,400 | 374,524,200 | 146,148,300 | 128,054,300 |
| Parcels post | | | 29,761,000 | 28,910,800 |
| Total | 567,992,100 | 568,890,800 | 529,316,800 | 507,113,200 |

The commerce of the city of Marseilles gives these statistics:

| Year. | Exports. | | Imports. | |
|---|---|---|---|---|
| | Quantity. | Value. | Quantity. | Value. |
| | *Quintals.* | | *Quintals.* | |
| 1901 | 19,827,583 | $131,332,656 | 32,384,388 | $220,738,000 |
| 1900 | 20,710,553 | 165,857,618 | 30,029,522 | 216,565,724 |
| 1899 | 21,033,525 | 179,376,670 | 30,816,183 | 250,750,695 |
| 1898 | 18,818,086 | 152,511,379 | 31,958,671 | 224,105,597 |
| 1897 | 18,990,330 | 166,402,457 | 28,477,444 | 220,567,039 |

The following is the declared value of exports from Marseilles to the United States:

| | |
|---|---|
| 1902 | $5,125,774 |
| 1901 | 4,859,907 |
| 1900 | 5,414,536 |
| 1899 | 4,139,263 |
| 1898 | 3,458,853 |

## MARITIME TRADE IN FRANCE.

The advance of the lesser Mediterranean nations in commercial sea power, by which Great Britain and France have been the principal sufferers, continues steadily. Swept backward during the earlier years of steam navigation, probably through inability to control the capital necessary to the new form of navigation, they have now come forward again, either buying old, discarded ships in England or, as in the case of Italy, constructing new and modern fleets. With ample seafaring populations, low wages, and still lower cost of mainte-nance, they have acquired a position of great and growing importance. Capable of making money where British and French shipowners can not, it is a question how far they will succeed in going, especially as with increasing capital they will replace their old ships with those of recent construction. The apparent increase in British tonnage at Marseilles may be attributed almost exclusively to the use of this port as one of call for mails and passengers. British entries and clearances increased from 2,086,396 tons in 1896 to 3,264,998 tons in 1901, while the total increase in foreign tonnage devoted to long voyages was from 1,000,034 to 1,972,423. Since 1899, French and British tonnage have made no sensible progress at Marseilles, while the tonnage of other flags has increased 500,000 tons. In freight delivered and forwarded, which is the real test after all, France has been standing still since 1899, Great Britain has lost 9,201 tons, while the other foreign flags united have gained 188,005 tons. To what nations have these gains gone? This is the answer in tonnage arrived and cleared:

| Country. | 1901. | 1900. | 1899. | 1898. | 1897. |
|---|---|---|---|---|---|
| | Tons. | Tons. | Tons. | Tons. | Tons. |
| France | 6,573,573 | 6,448,554 | 6,736,221 | 6,332,051 | 6,248,055 |
| England | 3,264,998 | 3,082,564 | 3,081,470 | 2,987,057 | 2,164,700 |
| Germany | 310,048 | 170,853 | 185,385 | 146,082 | 168,310 |
| Spain | 595,309 | 568,512 | 609,976 | 623,206 | 624,982 |
| Italy | 767,066 | 700,268 | 642,206 | 673,759 | 509,257 |
| Greece | 423,285 | 309,328 | 375,701 | 264,190 | 207,940 |
| Austria-Hungary | 319,107 | 276,751 | 304,190 | 354,410 | 323,649 |
| Russia | 73,762 | 78,216 | 73,033 | 47,963 | 37,325 |
| Japan | 203,481 | 198,085 | 194,588 | 155,205 | 58,458 |
| Holland | 295,113 | 289,162 | 238,017 | 248,565 | 229,909 |
| Denmark | 84,834 | 48,643 | 41,690 | 26,904 | 29,882 |
| Turkey | 32,401 | 83,723 | 17,266 | 32,745 | 18,562 |
| Sweden and Norway | 94,277 | 76,207 | 81,408 | 100,878 | 67,407 |

From the foregoing details, the following summary may be made:

*Net tonnage of arrivals and clearances at Marseilles.*

| Flag. | 1901. | 1900. | 1899. | 1898. |
|---|---|---|---|---|
| | Tons. | Tons. | Tons. | Tons. |
| French | 6,578,573 | 6,448,554 | 6,736,221 | 6,179,620 |
| British | 3,264,998 | 3,082,564 | 3,081,470 | 1,672,803 |
| All other | 3,204,323 | 2,765,136 | 2,773,047 | 1,848,150 |
| Total | 13,042,894 | 12,296,254 | 12,590,788 | 9,700,573 |

As I have said before, however, it is the amount of freight actually carried which indicates the shifting of commercial power. This may be thus stated:

*Merchandise received and shipped from Marseilles.*

| Flag. | 1901. | 1900. | 1899. |
|---|---|---|---|
| | Tons. | Tons. | Tons. |
| French | 3,014,719 | 3,111,192 | 3,087,883 |
| British | 1,101,987 | 1,109,548 | 1,201,188 |
| Other | 1,733,301 | 1,479,335 | 1,545,396 |
| Total | 5,850,007 | 5,700,075 | 5,834,467 |

The proportion of tonnage entering and clearing at Marseilles is very much greater than that of any other Mediterranean port, although Genoa has latterly gained more rapidly than her French rival. Among French ports, this predominance is still greater, Marseilles doing double the trade of Havre, the second seaport of the Republic.

*Total navigation of France, coasting trade excluded, in tonnage, arrived and cleared.*

| Origin. | All France. | | Marseilles. | |
|---|---|---|---|---|
| | 1901. | 1900. | 1901. | 1900. |
| | Tons. | Tons. | Tons. | Tons. |
| French ships | 9,296,340 | 9,011,091 | 2,748,693 | 2,718,100 |
| Foreign ships | 22,028,398 | 22,243,649 | 6,469,321 | 5,847,700 |
| Total | 31,324,738 | 31,254,780 | 9,218,014 | 8,565,800 |

The presumption, certainly the hope, now is that a considerable increase will be registered in the French merchant marine in consequence of new and favorable legislation. Some local changes have already taken place, as, for example, the building and commissioning of two relatively fast steamers for the New York line of the Cyprien Fabre Company. These steamers, the *Roma* and *Germania*, are 476 feet long and have a displacement of 9,000 tons when loaded. Their speed is 15 knots and the horsepower 5,000. Each one is equipped to transport 2,000 immigrants.

Within the year, the "Compagnie de l'Est Asiatique Française" has been formed and engaged in trade with the Far East with new ships and others building. While the recent legislation is not precisely what the marine interests asked for, it has certainly stimulated the domestic shipbuilding industry. The famous Creusot firm of Schneider & Co., anticipating a marine revival, has erected large blast furnaces at Cette, for the avowed purpose of facilitating the equipment of new and extensive shipbuilding yards at that port.

In Marseilles, the improvement of the port progresses slowly but steadily. There is at present a project under study of enlarging the "old port" sufficiently to admit of its use by modern steamers. It is now available for light craft only.

The port is one of the most interesting in the world in extent and variety. At present, 36 foreign companies make Marseilles a regular port of call, and 18 local companies serving 60 regular routes make this their home port. In addition, there is an immense traffic by unattached steamers and sailing ships, both French and foreign. In former years, a very large coasting trade was served by many small steamers or sailing ships owned independently, but the tendency of the times has here again been manifested, these vessels for the most part having been lately taken over by one or two companies now giving regular and adequate service.

There is an opportunity here, in my opinion, for the sale of American loading and discharging lighters, which ought not to be missed.

The complaints of shippers of the indifference of transportation companies to their interests have resulted in agitation on the subject similar to that which preceded the passage of the Harter Act in the United States in 1893. Briefly, shippers have desired to prevent the navigation companies from evading responsibility for losses resulting from their own negligence and not due to faults of navigation. After preliminary discussion among themselves, they made it known to the transportation companies that they would demand an amendment of the law, and suggested that, if the transportation interests held aloof or antagonized the proposition, the proposed legislation might be much more drastic than the very reasonable demands of shippers themselves. They therefore extended an invitation to the transportation interests to join hands with them and aid them in preparing a bill to be presented to Parliament, which should be satisfactory to both sides. The invitation was accepted and a congress of representatives of both interests was held at Marseilles in the month of October. The work of the congress is contained in the following proposed addition to article 216 of the Code of Commerce, which is to be laid before both houses of Parliament:

Every proprietor of a ship transporting passengers and merchandise to or from a French port, may be relieved of responsibility for losses or damages resulting from faults or errors of navigation or management of the ship attributable to the captain. the pilot, the officers, or the crew.

It is forbidden to every captain, shipowner, their agents, brokers, and representatives, to insert in any charter party, bill of lading, note of recognition, transport paper, paper of embarkation, of whatever kind created in France, any clause, convention, or stipulation whatsoever, by the terms of which the persons above named may free themselves, in whole or in part, from losses or damages resulting from negligence. from over or under loading, trimming, proper care and delivery of legal merchandise confided to them, and this from the moment that the merchandise has been brought to them until it is actually delivered to the receiver.

Every evasion of the dispositions preceding exposes the persons above named jointly to a payment in favor of the shipper of the half of the freight agreed upon.

All conventions which are contrary to the dispositions which precede are null and void as regards shipping contracts created in France or those created in foreign lands. The proprietor of the ship, in proving that he has exercised all diligence to equip and provision his ship so as to render it from every point of view navigable before departure, may be able to relieve himself of responsibility arising from accident to the hull, machine, shafts, mechanical apparatus of the ship, such as the ordinary prudence of a good father of a family could not, before the departure, either foresee or prevent.

CEREAL CROPS IN FRANCE.

A short wheat crop in France means high prices everywhere. This year, average estimates place the total crop at 43,000,000 quarters, or about the annual consumption. It happens, however, that the granaries were empty at the beginning of the crop year, and heavy rains having fallen at the most unpropitious moment, a large amount of grain is out of condition and can not be used before two or three months. Farmers who are obliged to sell are now (September 20) obtaining from 6 to 8 cents less per bushel for damp grain than is. being paid for fair qualities. American wheat being now out of reach as far as Marseilles is concerned, it follows that for some months to come, Russian wheat must be imported to replace domestic or to mix with the latter.

Hard semolina wheat is being imported on a heavy scale at present, the demand for hard-wheat flour for export being very good. Russia seems to have a very large crop, generally good in quality, as have also Roumania and Bulgaria.

Imports of oats will be relatively small, France having a large crop. No corn has been purchased for over six weeks, there being a good local stock at prices much lower than ruling prices abroad. When corn reaches a certain level in France, further advance checks consumption materially.

For three years, I have repeatedly directed attention to the enormous and growing demand for a hard wheat suitable for the manufacture of macaroni and edible pastes generally. I have been interested in this subject primarily because I have felt that a macaroni industry of large proportions could be created at home if our farmers would grow the proper grain, and also because of a certain export market for a grain which can not be produced in French soil. During 1901, in a total importation by sea at Marseilles of 24,251,244 bushels of wheat, 5,814,944 consisted of hard or macaroni wheat, practically all of which came from Russia and Algeria. Of the total, 392,979 bushels are credited to New York and Baltimore, but I learn that it was really a hard Canadian wheat, very likely grown from Russian seed. Now, it should be understood that the difficulty in France is to find the proper grain, of which there is not enough, and in the absence of true macaroni wheat, the next best thing is employed. The development of the semolina and macaroni industries is arrested by the absence of a reliable supply of raw material. Our Department of Agriculture is doing all within its power to induce the cultivation of hard wheat in the United States, having sent its agents to France, Russia, and Algeria several times to secure seed and to study soil. A very satisfactory start has thus been made. Last year, I am told that the United States produced from 50,000 to 75,000 bushels of macaroni wheat, and the crop of 1902 should be twenty times greater. Thus far, four or five domestic milling companies have sought the wheat being grown, so that none has been placed on the European market. When we have fully solved all the problems connected with the manufacture of the semolina and the macaroni, I do not see why we should not become the greatest edible-paste consuming people in the world. With the already existing demand for so-called health foods, I do not see why an article of diet that is good, cheap, and nourishing should not become a staple and indispensable household article.

In respect to France, we shall probably have to content ourselves with selling the wheat, but elsewhere, the semolina could as readily be disposed of as the grain in bulk. I am prepared to put correspondents in touch with French buyers, upon request.

*Wheat supply of France.*

[In quintals of 220 pounds.]

| Year. | All France. | | Marseilles. | |
|---|---|---|---|---|
| | Crop. | Imports. | Crop. | Imports. |
| 1901 | 82,744,428 | 1,583,088 | 6,613,976 | a 284,430 |
| 1900 | 88,598,000 | 1,294,528 | 5,472,728 | |
| 1899 | 99,499,890 | 1,304,944 | 7,218,345 | |
| 1898 | 99,312,290 | 19,545,463 | 9,896,243 | |
| 1897 | 65,924,096 | 5,226,591 | 6,808,727 | |

a From United States.

*Miscellaneous imports of cereals, etc., at Marseilles during 1901.*

Oats ........................................ metric quintals.. 1,206,415
Rye .......................................... do ... 9,218
Barley ....................................... do ... 252,856
Corn ......................................... do ... 1,087,915
Flour ........................................ bales .. 116,866
Bran ......................................... sacks .. 213,347
Beans ...................................... metric quintals.. 170,972
Semolina .................................. bales ... 8,269
Carob beans ............................. metric quintals.. 46,754
Vetch ....................................... do ... 6,764

The carob beans mentioned above, or locust beans, are sold for horse feed, sometimes being fed in natural state, sometimes ground or chopped, and sometimes mixed with other feeds.

### COAL VERSUS WATER POWER AND PETROLEUM.

While coal retains its importance in industrial production, several things have happened worth noting. One is the increase in the annual output of coal in the department of Meurthe-et-Moselle from 100,000 to 5,000,000 tons within fifty years; a second is the rapid increase in the use of water power; a third is the preparation for the use of petroleum for steam navigation. In twenty years, France has seen the creation of installations for the conversion of water power into electricity with a present aggregate of more than 200,000 horsepower. I judge that Italy is even more active in this direction, having greater need for a substitute for coal. I have under my eye a circular from a firm of Genoese coal merchants in which they say:

It is well to know that within the last two years, manufacturers in the north of Italy are using hydraulic power to the extent of over 200,000 horsepower.

Thus far in France, the principal electrical power installations are in the Alps, and the work has progressed so rapidly that the companies interested have brought upon themselves the impossibility of disposing satisfactorily of their wares, and they have been holding meetings to determine upon a means of syndicating themselves. In the region about Grenoble, a number of immense works are under way, and the movement has provoked a national congress of engineers and questions as to the legal side of the utilization of streams for private profit. It is presumed that millions of horsepower are going to waste, and it is the dream of French engineers to prevent this waste of power, to transport it over great distances, and finally to employ it. The experiments under the head of electro-metallurgy are difficult to hear much about, but they are proceeding with feverish activity in both France and Italy. The day when the mountain torrents can be made to perform the present function of coal in the manufacture of steel will bring rich rewards to the countries now wholly or partially dependent upon other nations for their fuel.

The campaign for the greater use of petroleum in steam navigation is going on all over the world at the same time, for the very simple reason that until steamer owners are assured that they will be able to find fuel wherever they may go, they are unlikely to invest in petroleum-burning devices. That is why progress is apparently so slow. I am told, however, that in Marseilles the ground has been found for the erection of a proper storage plant for Texas petroleum, and it is announced that one local company, the Compagnie de l'Est Asiatique Française, has determined to adopt the new fuel. This is certainly very measurable progress since three years ago, when the captain of the port refused the pioneer steamer of the Shell Line the right to enter port, because of the presumed danger to other craft from a ship propelled by petroleum-generated power.

### COAL TRADE IN THE MEDITERRANEAN.

The importations of American coal into the Mediterranean have been much less this year than during 1901, when they reached 189,210 tons at Marseilles alone. It should be understood that the only reason why the statistical position of American coal in this region is less strong than last year is because our exporters declined to bid upon long-time c. i. f. contracts last fall, and not at all because there was anything in the foreign situation itself inimical to our combustible. I mention this because of systematic effort in certain directions, doubtless due to unfamiliarity with the trade, to create the idea that we have failed to satisfy our new buyers. Our capacity to ship coal to Europe and to meet foreign competition in every respect is already demonstrated. We have simply to begin to ship coal as soon as the domestic trade slackens and our miners feel the need of new outlets. The objection to this policy is that consumers forget their previous experience with our fuel, buyers get out of touch with our sellers, and much of the pioneer work has to be done anew. Freights have been favorable to us this year, but the stability of the low ruling rates, varying from $1.75 to $2, has been so ill assured that our shippers have not been interested. The conditions for trading abroad will always be unsteady and unsatisfactory until we possess a coal fleet prepared to care for our interests exclusively. The use of ocean-going barges will help our case wonderfully, especially as it is doubtful whether shipping people will ever dare to send out tugs with consorts from England through the rough water generally encountered in approaching the Mediterranean.

Much can be done for our foreign coal trade by our Navy, whose ships now go everywhere. The present Navy contract appears to have been drawn with special reference to guaranteeing that our vessels shall have coal wherever they may be at fair rates. In the development of this plan, it so happens that at Marseilles and Genoa, where American coal is fairly sure to be available at all times, British coal is specified in the contract and at prices which are sometimes higher than for American coal. I was at one time called upon to ascertain definitely what American coals could be had in the local market, with the immediate result that one local firm ordered a cargo of our coal on f. o. b. terms to be ready for eventualities, and procured consents from contract customers to accept American coal as a substitute for the British grades contracted for, at the option of the furnishing firm. I am informed by Messrs. Robert Bauer & Co., of Genoa, that during the first five months of the current year, 49,815 tons of American coal were landed at that point in a total importation of 1,014,608 tons. During this same period, many American war vessels visited Genoa for supplies and repairs, yet under the Navy coal contract, they must have taken aboard none but British fuel.

At Marseilles, the record of the first six months during recent years in regard to foreign coals has been:

| First half of— | British. | American. |
| --- | --- | --- |
| 1902 | 430,866 | 17,984 |
| 1901 | 389,308 | 97,622 |
| 1900 | 457,752 | 7,739 |

So long as coal retains its importance as navigation fuel, foreign supplies will be required, the native product lacking in the qualities desired. For industrial purposes, the domestic mines are annually responding more fully to domestic demands. Considerable deposits of lignite very near Marseilles have been worked for years, and further prospecting has revealed the existence of practically inexhaustible beds of similar coal in connection with a subterranean river which until now has prevented exploitation. Engineers took up the problem some years ago, with the result that a tunnel 14 kilometers (8.7 miles) in length will soon be completed between the coal beds and the city, which will drain the water and within which the coal will be transported by a gravity system to a profitable market. Incidentally, this underground canal will supply power and water for general purposes. It is a daring and comprehensive enterprise, deserving of more than the casual notice here given.

I subjoin national coal statistics for reference purposes:

| Year. | Production. | Consumption. | Imports. |
| --- | --- | --- | --- |
| | Tons. | Tons. | Tons. |
| 1901 | 32,301,757 | a47,500,000 | 13,929,120 |
| 1900 | 33,404,000 | 48,808,000 | 16,177,000 |
| 1899 | 32,862,712 | 45,228,000 | 11,897,544 |
| 1898 | 32,356,104 | 41,097,500 | 10,462,543 |
| 1897 | 30,797,629 | 40,088,800 | 10,457,254 |

a Estimated.

## THE OIL AND OIL-SEED TRADE.

The Marseilles oil and oil-seed market is followed so closely by American exporters, and has been reported by me with such frequency during the year (see Consular Reports Nos. 257, 259, 261, and 263, February, April, June, and August, 1902), that very little can be said in an annual report which will be interesting by the time such report reaches the public. The importation of American oils has fallen off heavily during the

nine months of the year, the net shortage of imports from the United
States during these nine months being 18,870 tons; but as imports from
other sources have increased slightly during the same period, the net
shortage for the port has been 18,189 tons.  This situation has been produced mainly by high prices prevailing in the United States, an exceptionally large and particularly good olive crop in Europe, and an increase
in receipts of oleaginous seeds at Marseilles.  There is some little
activity in cotton oil buying circles at present, but the year will be a
poor one, statistically speaking, the total receipts from all sources
having been 8,568 tons, as against 26,698 tons during the first nine
months of 1901.  Of the total imports, British mills supply 142 tons,
and other old-world mills 90 tons.  While it is dangerous to offer any
prophecy, still it may be said that the olive oil crop, which will come
into the market during the next nine months, will probably be considerably shorter than that of last season.  This is counterbalanced
to some extent in the minds of buyers by the excellent reports concerning the growing crop of sesame seed in India.

There is a feeling, based on no very definite data, that the local
market will be obliged to absorb greater quantities of American oil
during the coming twelve months.  The one important thought that
comes to my mind in connection with American cotton oils is the
desirability of arranging for the sale of the American comestible oils
on their own merits, under their own names, and labels.  Before the
business in the United States reached its present proportions, large
quantities of American oil were refined in Marseilles and put upon
the consuming market with foreign brands.  There are manufacturers
to-day who attempt to keep up the fiction of receiving American oil,
and of improving it by mixing it with their own.  The plain truth is,
however—and it is recognized as such by the best informed men in the
city—that the high grade American oils have no superior anywhere.
American manufacturers who cooperate knowingly with the foreign
refiners who buy their oil and subsequently sell it at higher prices
and under another name, simply delay the creation of a demand for
their own wares under their own names as a first-class American
product.

There appears to be a small decrease in the arrivals of copra from
various sources, although at time of writing, the market is a trifle
weaker than it has been earlier in the year.  This article is receiving
greater attention annually in all important oil manufacturing centers,
and Americans holding in their control the principal source of production in the Philippine Islands should keep themselves more in touch
with this product.  Marseilles, at the present time, is the only city in
which copra oil is refined in large quantities for comestible purposes.
Two manufacturers in this business have had great success, and one
has already organized a similar manufactory in Hamburg.  The oil is
relieved of its rancidity, packed attractively, and sold as a substitute
for butter, and seems to meet with success wherever offered.  The
principal mark is being advertised extensively in this city, and the
manufacturers are pushing it for exactly what it is—a refined product
of copra oil.  Thus far, none of this material has been shipped to the
United States.

Soap manufacturers have had the advantage of having plenty of
low-grade oils to draw upon during the year.  The total quantity of
oil seeds received during the nine months is 424 tons in excess of the
same months last year.  I learn that recently, a favored few of the
soap manufacturers have been offered American petroleum manipu-

lated in such fashion as to be available for their uses. This oil, partially saponified, has been offered in small quantities at 45 francs per 100 kilograms ($8.65 per 220 pounds), replacing a similar quantity of copra now selling at 69 francs ($13.31) per 100 kilograms. During the period that this oil has been on sale, it has averaged about 25 francs ($4.82) per 100 kilograms less than vegetable oils. My informants tell me that it can be used with advantage thus far in the manufacture of cheap oils only. These soaps, known in this market as "mi-cuit," are shipped to Algiers, Tunis, Tripoli, and the Levant markets in large quantities. When this petroleum was first offered it was used sparingly, but at the present time, as much as 5 per cent is regularly used in the factory of my informant, with good results. There seems to be some mystery about the name of the manufacturer, and no detailed information is at hand. About a year ago, a gentleman called at my office for information about American patents, and told me at that time that he believed he had perfected a method of treating Texas petroleum so as to convert it into a soap oil. He gave no name or additional information, but I am inclined to think that the furnisher of the material here mentioned and my visitor are the same. I judge that when the manufacturer is able to supply unlimited quantities of this material, there will be no difficulty in securing information through the regular channels. Certainly, if experience should demonstrate the possibility of converting Texas oils into soap, the trade will be revolutionized.

*Imports of oil seeds first nine months 1902 and 1901.*

|  | 1902. | 1901. |  | 1902. | 1901. |
|---|---|---|---|---|---|
|  | Tons. | Tons. |  | Tons. | Tons. |
| Sesame | 59,820 | 52,768 | Cotton | 11,964 | 11,369 |
| Arachides: |  |  | Copra | 62,712 | 62,437 |
|   Shelled | 102,816 | 54,166 | Palm kernels | 4,820 | 7,285 |
|   Unshelled | 58,242 | 68,368 | Mowrah seed, Illipe nuts | | |
| Linseed | 8,897 | 8,283 | Mafouraire, etc. | 4,697 | 5,477 |
| Rapeseed and ravisin | 2,470 | 7,278 | | | |
| Poppy seed | 2,903 | 2,602 | | 339,792 | 300,732 |
| Castor seed | 20,451 | 20,709 | | | |

## WOOL TRADE WITH THE UNITED STATES.

Symptoms are not wanting that American buyers of Levantine wools are finding it again advantageous to do so through Marseilles commission houses. The tariff act of 1897 influenced some buyers to seek the primary markets; but in addition to the difficulty of establishing satisfactory relations with orientals, due to differences of language and business methods, it was found that selling prices could be obtained only sufficiently low to enable the wool to clear the United States customs as class 3 wools, dutiable at 4 cents. By retiring from the market, the American buyers virtually forced the Levantine merchants to consign to Marseilles, where it became necessary to sell to Americans at the same price as that theretofore demanded in the primary market, in order to keep the merchandise in the class 3, 4 cent category. The advantage to the United States buyer was a lower freight than could be had from the Levant, and a more satisfactory class of dealers with whom to operate. The tariff act, then, has established 12 cents as the maximum price obtainable for low grade Syrian wools, and the variations from francs 1.32½ per kilogram, are very small.

Some acrimonious controversies have been caused during the
year by the invoicing of alleged Bagdad wools under names which
would permit them to be passed by the customs officers at 4 cents per
pound.   These difficulties have been adjusted upon the merits of
each case; but during the heat of debate, it has been claimed by
resident shippers that Bagdad wool has so degenerated of late years
that, as a commercial classification, the term has lost all significance.
It is true, indeed, that Bagdad wools may be had from time to time at
even less than the price of class 3 wools.   It is not true, however, that
the classification is merely geographical, as good Bagdad wool is frequently offered and bought because of its intrinsic merit as such.

The declared value of wool shipped from Marseilles to the United
States has been as follows during recent years: 1902, $398,504; 1901,
$146,634; 1900, $410,534; 1899, $165,380; 1898, $388,779.

## THE NEW FURNACES AT CETTE.

The last word has not yet been said in the matter of iron and steel
production, the erection of the new furnaces at Cette by Schneider &
Co., of Creusot, indicating a determination not only to adopt the most
modern and economical processes, but also to anticipate the opening
of mineral deposits in the Mediterranean countries.   The firm named,
one of the greatest in the world—certainly in France—has heretofore been hampered by the situation of its plant in the interior of the
country.   The construction of new works has doubtless been prompted
by many considerations.   It is fully expected that a considerable
development of the French marine will take place during coming
years, and quantities of iron will be required which, but for the Cette
works, would have to be shipped over long distances.   The domestic
coal supply is not always steady in the interior, and at Cette, both
Great Britain and the United States can be drawn upon if need be.
Finally, some remarkable deposits of iron ore have been found in
Algeria and Tunis, which will soon be worked on a large scale if all
promises are carried out, and Spain with its ore mines is always
within call.   Thus, in present and prospective advantages, Cette is
attractive as a site, and Schneider & Co. have quietly proceeded with
the erection of a new plant, the first furnaces of which were inaugurated in April last.   I translate the following description of the first
furnace, with which I have been favored by the consular agent at
Cette:

In building at Cette, Messrs. Schneider have had no thought of transporting thither their works at Creusot, which are really being enlarged
for the manufacture of their specialties.   The new works are the
complement of the old.   The furnace now in operation has a capacity
greater than any heretofore existing in France, accompanied by a
general economy under the head of labor, made possible by the use
of many new devices operated principally by electricity.   Other furnaces will be erected later, and the natural extension of the works
will lead to the creation of shipyards upon the seashore.

The general depot for raw materials occupies one side of a private
basin which forms an extension of the port of Cette and will have a
depth of 7.50 meters (about 23 feet).   Ample switching facilities are
provided for the handling of railway traffic.   Raw materials coming
by sea or canal are discharged by means of apparatus capable of
unloading 50 tons per hour, moved by electricity.   These devices, two
in number, are 472 feet long and can be moved with facility from

one part of the depot to another.   Three tunnels connect the depot with the furnace proper, the raw material being moved by electrical locomotives.   The furnace is capable of producing 200 tons of metal per day.   Four Cowper machines, each 30 meters (109 feet) in height and 6.50 meters (23 feet) in diameter, heat the blast to 800°, the blast being produced by two steam and three gas-blowing machines.   After leaving the furnace, the gases pass into a scouring apparatus, which prepares them for use in the gas motors and the Cowper machines.

There are 36 coke ovens, each 36 feet long.   The oven flames are utilized to heat the boilers whose steam generates the electricity.   The coal preparing department is so organized that electricity performs all the work of manipulating the fuel and charging it into the coke ovens.

The central electrical station contains three engines of 300 horse-power each.

Thus far only 1,500 tons of Greek ore have been imported for this plant, the department of the Pyrenees Orientales supplying the domestic ore now being used and mines near at hand the coal.

## STATISTICS OF MARSEILLES.

*Comparative table of exports from Marseilles in 1900 and 1901.*

| Article. | 1900. | 1901. | Article. | 1900. | 1901. |
|---|---|---|---|---|---|
| | Quintals.a | Quintals.a | | Quintals.a | Quintals.a |
| Animals, live............... | 21,695 | 14,544 | Chemical products...... | 742,338 | 775,764 |
| Animal products, including hides................ | 454,408 | 366,709 | Prepared dyes .......... | 11,253 | 9,139 |
| | | | Colors .................. | 190,529 | 180,918 |
| Fish....................... | 75,180 | 65,594 | Miscellaneous compositions.................. ...... | 276,329 | 277,784 |
| Drugs and medicinal products ............. | 4,310 | 2,508 | Potteries, glass, and crystals ............... | 509,458 | 567,129 |
| Hard materials for cutting or carving........ | 5,160 | 7,492 | Thread .................. | 25,507 | 35,498 |
| Farinaceous aliments... | 3,525,910 | 3,110,295 | Textile fabrics.......... | 288,473 | 265,626 |
| Fruits and grains ....... | 496,315 | 426,814 | Clothes ................. | 22,456 | 15,036 |
| Colonial products: | | | Paper ................... | 105,977 | 103,248 |
| Sugar ............... | 604,885 | 642,778 | Skins and furs, manufactured............. | 46,501 | 40,513 |
| Others ............. | 215,544 | 233,266 | | | |
| Vegetable oils........... | 508,670 | 455,557 | Jewelry and other goods in metals, including timepieces ........... | 338,384 | 283,908 |
| Wood: | | | | | |
| Common.............. | 175,759 | 153,177 | Furniture and similar objects ............. | 84,164 | 68,574 |
| Exotic .............. | 23,780 | 15,737 | Arms, powder, and ammunition............... | 33,911 | 19,115 |
| Fruits, stalks, and filaments for manufacturing purposes........... | 93,645 | 109,697 | Musical instruments.... | 2,767 | 3,098 |
| Dyes and tans......... | 14,002 | 18,534 | Mats and baskets, etc.... | 17,383 | 13,192 |
| Various products and waste .................. | 904,398 | 891,842 | Miscellaneous goods .... | 139,620 | 162,098 |
| Drinks.................... | 656,175 | 650,845 | Gold, silver, and bullion. | 4,996 | 3,793 |
| Stones, earths, and combustibles............... | 9,880,985 | 9,277,442 | Total ............... | 21,019,847 | 19,827,583 |
| Metals .................. | 461,057 | 490,118 | | | |

a Of 220 pounds.

*Statistics of principal imports of Marseilles during six months ended June 30, 1902.*

| Articles imported and country whence exported. | Quantity. | Total. |
|---|---|---|
| **ANIMAL MATTER.** | | |
| Animals, live: | | Head. |
| Cattle ......................................................... | ............ | 11,739 |
| Horses......................................................... | ............ | 281 |
| Pigs ......................................................... | ............ | 116 |
| Other, including fowls ......................................... | ............ | 874,000 |

*Statistics of principal imports of Marseilles during six months ended June 30, 1902*—Continued.

| Articles imported and country whence exported. | Quantity. | Total. |
|---|---|---|
| ANIMAL MATTER—continued. | *Tons.*ᵃ | *Tons.*ᵃ |
| Dairy products: | | |
| Butter | | 9 |
| Cheese— | | |
| Switzerland | 692 | |
| Other countries | 400 | |
|  | | 1,092 |
| Total | | 1,101 |
| Feathers | | 25 |
| Fibers, animal: | | |
| Silk | | 8,292 |
| Wool— | | |
| Australia | 6,160 | |
| Turkey | 1,752 | |
| Argentina | 7,042 | |
| Other countries | 5,895 | |
|  | | 20,849 |
| Glue | | 92 |
| Grease: | | |
| United States | 2,939 | |
| Other countries | 853 | |
|  | | 3,792 |
| Hides and skins: | | |
| Large— | | |
| Germany | 64 | |
| Brazil | 62 | |
| Other countries | 4,659 | |
|  | | 4,785 |
| Small— | | |
| Turkey | 1,223 | |
| Morocco | 541 | |
| Other countries | 2,458 | |
|  | | 4,222 |
| Honey | | 34 |
| Meat products: | | |
| Salt meat | 422 | |
| Charcuterie | 283 | |
| Canned meat | 145 | |
|  | | 850 |
| VEGETABLE MATTER, | | |
| Breadstuffs: | | |
| Wheat— | | |
| Russia | 10,507 | |
| Algeria | 5,812 | |
| United States | 300 | |
| Other countries | 2,127 | |
|  | | 18,736 |
| Oats— | | |
| Russia | 187 | |
| Algeria | 870 | |
| Tunis | 375 | |
| Other countries | 560 | |
|  | | 1,992 |
| Barley— | | |
| Algeria | 1,736 | |
| Other countries | 54 | |
|  | | 1,790 |
| Maize— | | |
| Russia | 1,700 | |
| Roumania | 1,629 | |
| Other countries | 702 | |
|  | | 4,031 |
| Wheat flour— | | |
| Algeria | 509 | |
| Other countries | 40 | |
|  | | 549 |
| Total breadstuffs | | 26,598 |
| Chocolate | | 30 |
| Cocoa: | | |
| Brazil | 142 | |
| Venezuela | 74 | |
| Other countries | 284 | |
|  | | 500 |
| Coffee: | | |
| Brazil | 10,649 | |
| British India | 957 | |
| Other countries | 2,983 | |
|  | | 14,589 |

ᵃ Of 2,205 pounds.

*Statistics of principal imports of Marseilles during six months ended June 30, 1902*—Continued.

| Articles imported and country whence exported. | Quantity. | Total. |
|---|---|---|
| VEGETABLE MATTER—continued. | | |
| Fibers, vegetable: | | |
| Cotton— | *Tons.* | *Tons.* |
| Turkey | 1,268 | |
| Egypt | 5,164 | |
| British India | 3,139 | |
| United States | 340 | |
| Other countries | 246 | |
| | | 10,157 |
| Hemp— | | |
| Italy | 1,929 | |
| Other countries | 469 | |
| | | 2,391 |
| Jute— | | |
| British India | 2,744 | |
| Other countries | 219 | |
| | | 2,963 |
| Ramie | | 178 |
| Total | | 15,689 |
| Fruits: | | |
| Lemons— | | |
| Spain | 2,863 | |
| Algeria | 1,069 | |
| Other countries | 1,268 | |
| | | 5,000 |
| Grapes | | 11 |
| Apples and pears | | 121 |
| Others | | 1,870 |
| Nuts: | | |
| Almonds— | | |
| Spain | 447 | |
| Italy | 322 | |
| Other countries | 227 | |
| | | 996 |
| Malt liquors: | | |
| Germany | 127 | |
| England | 10 | |
| Other countries | 50 | |
| | | 187 |
| Oil cake | | 4,721 |
| Oils, vegetable: | | |
| Olive— | | |
| Spain | 7,996 | |
| Algeria | 3,916 | |
| Tunis | 2,469 | |
| Other countries | 885 | |
| | | 15,266 |
| Palm | | 10,268 |
| Cotton— | | |
| United States | 10,814 | |
| England | 1,797 | |
| Other countries | 51 | |
| | | 12,162 |
| Rice | | 41,738 |
| Sugar | | 11,895 |
| Tea | | 419 |
| Tobacco: | | |
| United States | 866 | |
| Algeria | 516 | |
| Other countries | 1,042 | |
| | | 2,424 |
| Vegetables, dry: | | |
| Roumania | 20,013 | |
| Other countries | 5,015 | |
| | | 25,028 |
| Wines: | | |
| Ordinary— | *Liters.a* | *Liters.a* |
| Algeria | 26,844,000 | |
| Other countries | 1,735,000 | |
| | | 28,579,000 |
| Liqueur | | 2,016,000 |
| MISCELLANEOUS. | *Tons.* | *Tons.* |
| Chemical products | | 16,214 |
| Soap: | | |
| Scented | | 4 |
| Unscented | | 94 |

a 1 liter = 1.05 quarts.

*Statistics of principal imports of Marseilles during six months ended June 30, 1902—Continued.*

| Articles imported and country whence exported. | Quantity. | Total. |
|---|---|---|
| MISCELLANEOUS—continued. | | |
| Coal: | *Tons.* | *Tons.* |
| England | 454,800 | |
| United States | 12,300 | |
| Other countries | 2,200 | |
| | | 469,300 |
| Thread: | | |
| Cotton | | 1,051 |
| Hemp | | 116 |
| Textile fabrics: | | |
| Linen, hemp, or ramie | | 1,421 |
| Cotton— | | |
| England | 2,268 | |
| Other countries | 898 | |
| | | 3,161 |
| Wool— | | |
| England | 115 | |
| Belgium | 8 | |
| Germany | 4 | |
| Other countries | 7 | |
| | | 134 |

*Statistics of principal exports of Marseilles during six months ended June 30, 1902.[a]*

| Articles exported and country whence imported. | Quantity. | Total. |
|---|---|---|
| ANIMAL MATTER. | | |
| Animals, live: | | *Head.* |
| Cattle | | 500 |
| Horses | | 100 |
| Mules | | 100 |
| Sheep | | 2,700 |
| Pigs | | 13 |
| Total | | 3,413 |
| Dairy products: | *Tons.* | *Tons.* |
| Butter | | 812 |
| Cheese— | | |
| Algeria | 1,270 | |
| Other countries | 600 | |
| | | 1,870 |
| Milk (condensed) | | 83 |
| Total | | 2,265 |
| Feathers | | 2 |
| Fibers, animal: | | |
| Silk— | | |
| England | 242 | |
| Italy | 1,282 | |
| Other countries | 461 | |
| | | 1,985 |
| Glue: | | |
| England | 62 | |
| Belgium | 19 | |
| Other countries | 181 | |
| | | 262 |
| Grease | | 1,916 |
| Hair: | | |
| England | 45 | |
| United States | 63 | |
| Other countries | 68 | |
| | | 176 |
| Hides and skins: | | |
| Large— | | |
| England | 786 | |
| Italy | 1,049 | |
| Germany | 57 | |
| Belgium | 21 | |
| Other countries | 2,874 | |
| | | 4,787 |
| Small | | 2,173 |
| Total | | 6,940 |

[a] These are official French statistics. As respects the United States, there are many errors, merchandise destined for that country being frequently credited to the country of transshipment.

*Statistics of principal exports of Marseilles during six months ended June 30, 1902—Continued.*

| Articles exported and country whence imported. | Quantity. | Total. |
|---|---|---|
| ANIMAL MATTER—continued. | *Tons.* | *Tons.* |
| Honey | | 47 |
| Meat products: | | |
| Meat, fresh (beef) | | 220 |
| Salt meat, pork, ham, and lard | | |
| Charcuterie | | 157 |
| Tinned meat | | 360 |
| VEGETABLE MATTER. | | |
| Breadstuffs: | | |
| Barley— | | |
| England | 1 | |
| Other countries | 4 | |
| Wheat— | | 5 |
| Switzerland | 3 | |
| Other countries | 39 | |
| Oats— | | 42 |
| Switzerland | 12 | |
| Other countries | 4 | |
| | | 16 |
| Maize | | 28 |
| Flour (wheat)— | | |
| Switzerland | 106 | |
| England | 67 | |
| Belgium | 80 | |
| Other countries | 605 | |
| | | 858 |
| Chocolate | | 68 |
| Cocoa | | 254 |
| Coffee | | 9,586 |
| Fibers, vegetable: | | |
| Cotton | | 3,690 |
| Hemp | | 221 |
| Jute | | 1,304 |
| Total | | 5,215 |
| Fruits: | | |
| Lemons | | 204 |
| Grapes | | 6 |
| Apples | | 70 |
| Others | | 177 |
| Total fruits | | 457 |
| Nuts: | | |
| Almonds— | | |
| England | 139 | |
| United States | 18 | |
| Other countries | 1,056 | |
| | | 1,213 |
| Cocoanuts | | 4,484 |
| Malt liquors: | | |
| Algeria | 1,283 | |
| Other countries | 3,412 | |
| | | 4,695 |
| Oil cake | | 45,930 |
| Oils, vegetable: | | |
| Olive | | 5,266 |
| Palm | | 37 |
| Cocoanut | | 8,667 |
| Cotton | | 2,354 |
| Rice | | 12,516 |
| Sugar, refined: | | |
| Turkey | 6,782 | |
| Morocco | 8,439 | |
| Algeria | 4,749 | |
| Other countries | 9,089 | |
| | | 28,989 |
| Tea | | 439 |
| Tobacco | | 1,808 |
| Vegetables: | | |
| Fresh | | 638 |
| Salt | | 158 |
| Preserved | | 900 |
| Wines: | | *Liters.* |
| Champagne | | 464,000 |
| Ordinary— | | |
| Bottled | | 1,025,000 |
| Unbottled | | 13,848,000 |

*Statistics of principal exports of Marseilles during six months ended June 30, 1902*—Continued.

| Articles exported and country whence imported. | Quantity. | Total. |
|---|---|---|
| MISCELLANEOUS. | *Tons.* | *Tons.* |
| Coal | | 8 |
| Chemical products: | | |
| Total | | 26,940 |
| Glycerine | | 2,917 |
| Sulphate of soda | | 1,588 |
| Cream of tartar | | 2,138 |
| Ocher | | 8,263 |
| Soap | | 9,159 |
| Candles: | | |
| Algeria | 1,063 | |
| Other countries | 1,344 | |
| | | 2,407 |

## COMMERCE OF CETTE.

I am indebted to Consular Agent Hagelin, of Cette, for an excellent report upon trade and commerce at Cette. Especial attention is directed to his observations respecting staves.

Of merchandise interesting to the United States, there was imported during 1901:

| Articles. | Total imports. | From United States. |
|---|---|---|
| | *Tons.* | *Tons.* |
| Staves | 68,806 | 13,600 |
| Crude petroleum | 54,236 | 30,676 |
| Refined petroleum | 5,000 | 5,000 |
| Wood for building purposes | 41,280 | 2,370 |
| Natural phosphates | 29,208 | |

*Wine.*—All commerce in this district is dependent upon the wine business.

The wine production in all France in 1901, according to the official statistics, amounted to 57,963,514 hectoliters (1,530,236,770 gallons), which, in comparison with the previous year, shows a decrease of 9,389,147 hectoliters (247,873,481 gallons), but, as compared with the average of the past ten years, shows an increase of 18,005,372 hectoliters (475,341,821 gallons). To the above is to be added the production of Algeria, 3,563,032 hectoliters (94,064,050 gallons), and that of Corsica, 200,000 hectoliters (5,280,000 gallons), which gives a total of 63,710,514 hectoliters (1,681,957,570 gallons), this being a very respectable quantity. The prices to the growers ranged from 96 cents to $1.93 for inferior grades, and $2.31 to $3.80 for superior qualities, per hectoliter.

Wine growers ascribe the overproduction of the last few years as the cause of their bad situation. They now seem determined to avoid replanting in the future, and to be more sparing in the use of fertilizers. The total value of the wine crop is estimated at $179,919,606.

To the foregoing total of the wine crop of 1901, the departments in this consular district have contributed:

| | Hectoliters. | Gallons. |
|---|---|---|
| Aude | 5,230,815 | 138,093,516 |
| Hérault | 9,529,580 | 251,580,912 |
| Gard | 3,172,150 | 83,744,760 |
| Pyrénées Orientales | 2,280,491 | 60,204,962 |

*Staves.*—The commerce in staves has been very profitable, and the imports from the United States have increased from 6,519 tons last year to 12,600 tons this year, nearly one-fifth of the total imported, and will in the near future increase much more, considerable contracts of purchase having been concluded for deliveries up to end of next June. For four or five years, American staves have been worked in the same fashion as the Austrian, and they have made themselves felt more and more in the market. The sizes for casks of 500 to 600 liters (528 to 634 gallons), are 1¼ to 1½ inches thickness, 4 inches and more breadth, 40 to 44 inches length. The quality of the wood is perhaps not fully so good as the Austrian and Russian wood, but the price is a little lower, and our coopers buy now quite as much as of the Austrian wood. The following prices have been paid during the year:

| Quality. | Dimensions. | Price per 100. |
|---|---|---|
| Rough hogsheads | 1¼ to 1½ by 4 inches .. <br> 1 to 1¼ by 4 inches or more. | $17.37 <br> 15.44–16.40 |
| Dressed hogsheads | 1¼ or more by 4½ or more. | 18.34 |
| Bottom staves | 1 to 1¼ by 4 .......... <br> 1 to 1¼ by 4 to 6 inches | 16.96 <br> 18.51–14.47 |

Staves for casks of 225 liters (237 quarts) are not imported into Cette from the United States, but are employed at Bordeaux. These prices have been firm up to the present, but show a downward tendency. At Bordeaux, prices have already declined.

*Coal.*—The fever in the coal market last year has passed away, and prices have become normal. The imports for Cette, from 104,986 tons last year, have declined to 63,878 tons. No American coal has been sold in the market. The imports consist for the most part of English gas coals for the towns of Cette, Montpellier, Narbonne, Nimes, Beaucaire, Baziers, etc.

The prices of gas coals are quoted at 24 to 26 francs ($4.63 to $5.02) per 100 kilos (220 lbs). French coal for steamers' use, first quality, is equal to best Cardiff, 29 to 32 francs ($5.60 to $6.18).

*Natural phosphate.*—There have been no imports from the United States, against 19,500 tons last year. The manufacture of chemical manure has decreased this year, owing to bad times. Wine growers generally have no power to buy, for the reason cited above.

*Petroleum.*—The total imports during 1900–1901 were 54,832 tons, and during 1901–2, 54,235 tons. In this sum the United States figures for about 35,676 tons, against 38,138 tons in the year 1901, showing a decrease of 2,462 tons.

Most of the petroleum imported into Cette is employed by the refinery at Balaruc, a few kilometers from Cette, belonging to Messrs. Pluchi & Co., of Paris. The price of refined oil sold to dealers has been 28.50 francs ($5.50) to 31.50 francs ($6.08) per 100 liters (105 quarts).

H. Doc. 305, pt 2——14

*Imports and exports at Cette during the fiscal year ended June 30, 1902.*

| Articles. | Imports. | Exports. |
|---|---|---|
| Ale........................................gallons.. | 38,760 | ............. |
| Alcohol...............................do.... | 80,018 | 178,712 |
| Bark for tannery.................metric tons.. | 1,258 | ............. |
| Bauxite..............................do.... | ............. | 8,594 |
| Bone black..........................do.... | ............. | 29 |
| Cattle (sheep)......................head.. | 47,420 | ............. |
| Carting iron.....................metric tons.. | ............. | 8,272 |
| Cement..............................do.... | ............. | 496 |
| Chemical manure..................do.... | ............. | ............. |
| Codfish..............................do.... | ............. | 507 |
| Corn: | | |
|     Wheat..........................do.... | 6,941 | ............. |
|     Oats...........................do.... | 3,598 | ............. |
|     Barley.........................do.... | 6,027 | ............. |
|     Maize..........................do.... | 2,431 | ............. |
|     Wheat flour.................do.... | 1,611 | ............. |
| Cork.................................do.... | 1,982 | ............. |
| Coals................................do.... | 63,878 | ............. |
| Coal tar.............................do.... | 27,648 | 5,584 |
| Fruits, fresh: | | |
|     Oranges and lemons.........do.... | 1,676 | ............. |
|     Carobs and grapes..........do.... | 5,415 | ............. |
| Fruits, dry.........................do.... | 1,272 | ............. |
| Hemp................................do.... | 198 | ............. |
| Hides................................do.... | 28 | ............. |
| Iron ore.............................do.... | 1,500 | ............. |
| Kaolin...............................do.... | 983 | ............. |
| Lead ore............................do.... | 91 | ............. |
| Lime superphosphates............do.... | ............. | ............. |
| Lime.................................do.... | ............. | 11,472 |
| Lobsters.............................do.... | 41 | ............. |
| Marble..............................do.... | 577 | ............. |
| Nitrate of potash..................do.... | ............. | ............. |
| Phormium..........................do.... | 993 | ............. |
| Phosphate, natural.................do.... | 29,203 | ............. |
| Petroleum: | | |
|     Crude.......................gallons.. | 14,327,689 | ............. |
|     {........................do.... | 1,294,325 | ............. |
|     Refined {.................do.... | ............. | 1,312,582 |
| Pyrites..........................metric tons.. | 14,760 | ............. |
| Potatoes............................do.... | 778 | ............. |
| Rice.................................do.... | 3,481 | ............. |
| Salt..................................do.... | ............. | 2,618 |
| Soap.................................do.... | ............. | 4,430 |
| Staves...............................do.... | 68,805 | ............. |
| Sumach..............................do.... | 477 | ............. |
| Sulphur..............................do.... | 22,143 | 425 |
| Sulphur, sublimated................do.... | ............. | 28,596 |
| Tallow...............................do.... | 1,444 | ............. |
| Wine............................gallons.. | 16,197,084 | 2,501,770 |
| Wool.............................metric tons.. | 2,142 | ............. |
| Wood................................do.... | 41,280 | 6,244 |
| Vegetables..........................do.... | 790 | ............. |
| Sulphate of copper.................do.... | 2,928 | ............. |

## TRADE IN CORSICA.

Consular Agent Damiani submits the following report concerning the island of Corsica:

From the 1st of January, 1901, to the 30th of June, 1902, there have been imported from the United States and annexed Territories:

| | | |
|---|---|---|
| Coffee.........................................metric tons.. | 14 |
| Leaf tobacco.................................do.... | 54 |
| Coal...........................................do.... | 200 |
| Petroleum....................................gallons.. | 182,809 |
| Ink, rope, and chain.......................metric tons.. | 0.2 |
| Household articles...........................do.... | 41 |
| Chocolate....................................do.... | 6 |

The last citron crop was medium in quantity, and was sold at a very low price. It was estimated at about 1,600 tons, but as about 400 tons had been carried over from the preceding year, the market had to take up about 2,000 tons. Of that quantity, only 253 tons were exported to the United States, the balance going to England, Germany, and (the greater portion) to Belgium.

The annual imports of flour from France, shipped from Marseilles, are about 300,000 bags, of 122½ kilograms (270 lbs.) each, sold at an average of 40 francs ($7.72) per bag, wholesale price. Said flour pays a custom duty of 10½ francs ($2) per bag. As communication between New York and Marseilles is sufficiently rapid, I think that millers in America would find this a good market. I am at the entire disposal of those interested in the development of the trade for any supplementary details in regard to it. The best plan would be to create a depot at Bastia, in order to be able to promptly furnish the trade of the island at any moment.

MINING.

Lack of capital and initiative have prevented a proper development of Corsica's great mineral wealth up to this time. Coal (anthracite and lignite) is found in the department, but the production remains stationary and almost insignificant. The only mines in operation are the Osani and the Francardo. The product is a low-grade anthracite, and the veins are 6 feet in thickness. The opening of new workings would be profitable.

The copper-ore mining industry is developing in an active manner. Among the many copper workings are included the following important mines: Altiani, Focicchia, Erbayolo, Castineta, Vezzani, and Morosaglia. All bearings discovered up to the present are clean, rich, and continued veins. The ores yield 33 per cent of copper.

Latterly there has been a steady extraction of the ores of antimony, which are of an incomparable richness. The most famous are those situated on the territory of the communes of Meria and Ersa, in the region of the Cap-Corsica. There are also found in the country ores of iron, manganese, arsenic, zinc, lead (rich in silver), sulphur, and, to a small extent, gold quartz. All these require only to be worked on large scale. Metallurgic works are to be created for the smelting of these ores and for the manufacture of iron and steel.

The production of the quarries, so numerous in the island, deserves special mention. The extracted substances can be divided into five groups:

*Construction.*—Soft and tough freestone, millstone, heavy limestone, roofing slate, brick clay, sand, and gravel.

*Industrial.*—Limestone, silex, white gypsum, fire clay, sand for glass.

*Agriculture.*—Phosphate of lime, marl, lime.

*Paving, etc.*—Granite and porphyry blocks, flag and curb stones, ballast of marble.

*Miscellaneous.*—Mosaic stones, heavy slate, whetstones, chalk, asbestos, granite, and porphyry.

The marble industry is very active. Among the decorative species it is important to mention the marble "Verde Stella," of Ersa, spangled silver of remarkable beauty, the white marble of Corte, and the marble of Oletta.

The department of Corsica also comprises salt marshes, the product of which is sent in part to France and Italy. Chlorine of sodium is extracted from the sea water.

Ore prospecting is very active in the department. In the districts of Bastia and Corte, diggings and borings continue, for the most part under favorable conditions, and have resulted in discoveries of important bearings in copper, antimony, and sundry ores. I would also call attention to the quest after arsenic in Belgodere (a ward of Calci), two rich and parallel veins cropping out at the surface.

In Corsica, there are numerous springs or sources of sulphurous and ferruginous waters, remarkable, even famous, for their valuable medicinal properties. The flow is, in all known springs, continuous, abundant, and without depreciations of constituents, but at least 99 per cent is allowed to run to waste, which could be very profitably used for the export market.

In summing up the foregoing general information I am bound to express, most energetically, the opinion that Corsica affords excellent opportunities for mineral industries, and above all for metallurgical works. It is needless to remark that the more or less recently founded works for extraction of gallic acid in the woodlands of Corsica, by their remarkable success, fully confirm this opinion. Those settled upon the streams utilize the natural water power most advantageously.

## TRADE AT TOULON.

Consular Agent Jouve reports as follows:

No ships are being constructed in the Government dockyards; I give below the list of works at the Chantie de la Mediteranée at La Seyne (one of the largest shipyards in France).

The new French law upon the merchant marine has been good for builders, on account of the number of ships ordered. The opinion in general is that the premium is too high, comparatively, for any profit which the country may realize from it.

*List of principal vessels constructed or in course of construction at the Forges et Chantiers de la Seyne during the year 1902.*

| | Length. | Breadth. | Height. | Mean draft. | Displacement. | Tonnage, net. | Horsepower. | Destination. |
|---|---|---|---|---|---|---|---|---|
| | *Meters.a* | *Meters* | *Meters.* | *Meters.* | *Tons.* | | | |
| Albatros, ferryboat. | 28 | 5.8 | 1.8 | 1.1 | 81.5 | 94 | 135 | Societé des Batcaux à vapeur de la Seyne at Toulon. |
| 2 float cofferdams | 29 742 | 3.3 | 11.975 | 8.35 | 480 | b184 | ........ | Arsenal of Sidi Abdallah at Bizerte. |
| Caobang, packet boat | 135 | 14.38 | 12.4 | 6.405 | 8,055 | 6,800 | 4,000 | Cie Nationale de Navigation. |
| Patrie, man-of-war. | 133.8 | 24.25 | 14.75 | 8.2 | 14,870 | 9,572 | 17,500 | French Government. |
| Bonneveine, 3 masted bark. | 79.55 | 12.35 | 9.59 | 6.594 | 4,700 | 2,700 | ........ | Societé Anonyme Marseillaise de Voiliers. |
| Joliette, 3-masted bark. | 79.55 | 12.35 | 9.59 | 6.594 | 4,700 | 2,700 | ........ | Do. |
| 4 small boats..... | 18 | 4.9 | 1.9 | 1.5 | 78.2 | 38.5 | ........ | French marine at Bizerte. |
| Justice, man-of-war. | 133.8 | 24.25 | 14.75 | 8.2 | 14,870 | 9,572 | 18,000 | French Government. |
| 2 buoys for depths of 8,000 meters. | c2.5 | ........ | d2.4 | ........ | ........ | ........ | ........ | Submarine cable factory at La Seyne. |

a 1.09 yards.    b Each.    c Diameter.    d Height.

The bulb prices for hyacinths are about $14.47 to $15.44 for 1,000. The bulbs are in bad condition and very small, so that many sellers will not be able to furnish the number they are already engaged to sell.

I supplement Mr. Jouve's brief reference to the bulb business with the following facts, brought to my attention. Growers of flower bulbs in the vicinity of Ollioules, a suburb of Toulon, claim that no other soil in the world has been found thus far capable of producing the bulbs successfully cultivated in that region. The plants are cultivated entirely by hand, and require close attention. A mild, even temperature, and a light sandy soil are requisite to success. Extreme heat, cold, or humidity are fatal. The bulbs are cultivated for two or three years before they are shipped. The United States consumes about two-thirds of the total output. A few years ago, the average price was about 30 francs ($5.79) per 1,000, the cultivators then claiming that they could not make any money, and to a considerable number, turning their land into vineyards. This proved as bad a speculation as the other and since that time, the farmers having in the meantime formed themselves into a syndicate embracing fully three-fourths of the total acreage, prices have been put up to a very profitable figure, 75 to 80 francs ($14.47 to $15.44) per 1,000, this year.

ROBERT P. SKINNER,
*Consul-General.*

MARSEILLES, *October 23, 1902.*

---

### NANTES.

In the absence of any definite statistics, it may be stated in a general way that the year 1902 has not been a satisfactory one in the great industrial region of which Nantes is the center. This region, it should be understood, is geographically and commercially known as Basse-Loire—i. e., the Lower Loire. In this territory, there are some 300 manufactories of various sorts, consuming annually about 800,000 tons of coal and employing some 31,000 laborers. Iron, steel, brass, and copper foundries, shipyards, and manufactories of chemical products are in a state of advanced development. Nantes is also famous as the center of the sardine industry. The most important exporting and jobbing houses for this trade are located here. Another industry in a high state of development is that of canning vegetables, such as peas, beans, asparagus, and mushrooms. These products of Nantes are famous the world over, and are exported to all countries.

### SHIPBUILDING.

The first and most important industry of the region, however, is shipbuilding. There are several important yards here and at St. Nazaire, employing between them some 6,000 skilled workmen. At present, all these yards are virtually doing nothing, and as a consequence 5,000 workmen are idle. This condition has existed for some months, and has had a depressing influence on the whole commerce of the Lower Loire. It is the result of the rapid construction of the past several years, which was stimulated by the action of the Government in offering liberal cash compensation to shipbuilders for merchant vessels. The shipyards of Nantes are especially organized for the building of sailing vessels, and having constructed so rapidly as to exhaust their quota of the Government's allowance for 1902 for the construction of sailing vessels, were compelled some time ago to shut down. The result, as stated above, has been bad for the commerce of Nantes. Some of the yards are now increasing their facilities for the construction of steam vessels, and it is believed that the year 1903 will be a busy one throughout.

## FAILURE OF THE SARDINE CATCH.

The almost complete failure of the sardine catch this year was due principally to the large size of the sardines and to the parsimonious use of bait by the fishermen at the outset of the season. One of the principal dealers told me the other day that he had been unable to meet 10 per cent of the demand for sardines from the United States. Incidentally, it may be stated that, in view of this shortage, some of the French exporters are supplying their customers in Central Europe and the United States with Portuguese sardines.

## BAIT FOR SARDINE FISHERMEN.

In this, connection, it is probably worth while for American fishermen to study the opportunity of supplying fish eggs for bait to French sardine packers. Sardine bait is locally known here as "la rogue." It consists of the eggs of codfish preserved in brine, and reaches this market principally from Norway and Sweden. The price of "la rogue" varies from 30 to 120 francs ($5.79 to $23.16) the barrel. This year it opened at 120 francs, but the fishermen bought so sparingly that, at the end of the season, the price had dropped to 40 francs ($7.72). The "rogue," or bait, of Newfoundland is also known here, and has indeed found a market to a small extent, but is not so popular as the Norway product for the reason that the entrails and other parts of the fish are mixed with it, thus diminishing the quantity of eggs and the quality of the bait. There is generally a big demand for "la rogue" from the 1st of May to the 1st of August, and if American . exporters can meet the prices of the shippers of northern Europe, there is no reason why they should not do business here.

The principal sardine packing factories of the French coast are at Concarneau and Douarnenez. They belong almost exclusively to exporting firms of Nantes and Bordeaux. The most important ones at Nantes are:

Amieux frères, suc. Amieux & Cie.; Arsène Saupiquet Company; Philippe & Canaud, Lechat Philippe & Benoît, successeurs; Gustave Doré, Litchery, successeur; Lemarchand; Chancerelle frères, and others, all at Nantes. Rodel & fils, frères, Bordeaux; Verdeau frères, Bordeaux.

The only ones located exclusively at Concarneau and Douarnenez are Gustave Penauvos, les frères Penauvos; and Chancerelle Joseph, Chancerelle Pierre, Chancerelle frères.

The French customs duty on fish eggs is 80 centimes (16 cents) per 100 kilograms (220 pounds); mimimum, 60 centimes (12 cents). If, however, the product arrives via any English port—no matter what its origin—there is an additional duty of 3 francs and 50 centimes (60 cents) per 100 kilograms.

## THE PAPER INDUSTRY.

The manfacture of paper is one of the thriving industries of Nantes, and the great mills of the Société Anonyme des Papeteries Gouraud, which are located here, have had a busy year, although I am informed that, in order to meet constantly growing competition, the company has found it necessary to reduce prices this season and sacrifice a considerable percentage of profits. Much of the white paper on which the daily newspapers of Paris are printed is manufactured by this company.

### SUGAR, PHOSPHATES, AND VEGETABLES.

After shipbuilding, the most important industry of Nantes is sugar refining. There are noted refineries here, and their products are not only sold all over France, but are exported in considerable quantities to England, Belgium, Portugal, and other countries. It was to a refinery of Nantes that the Universal Exposition of 1900 awarded the first prize. One company here, known as the "Raffinerie de Chantenay," has a capital of 2,000,000 francs ($380,000). The present year has not been a busy one for these great sugar refiners. They are overstocked and do not find it easy to get rid of the surplus.

Nantes is the home of the petits pois (little peas) of commerce, and the canning factories have had a fairly good year, though their exports to the United States have fallen off.

The manufacture of phosphates for fertilizing purposes is also a growing industry, and during the past few years it has assumed large proportions. Natural or raw phosphates are imported from the United States, Tunis, Algeria, Belgium, Chile, and the Antilles. The United States heads the list this year.

### AMERICAN PRUNES AND DRIED APPLES.

The French prune crop is almost a complete failure, and, as a consequence, there is an unusually large demand not only for California prunes, but also for dried apples and peaches. These products, already well known here, are now being imported in larger quantities than ever before. This is particularly true of American prunes. The trouble is that they can not get here fast enough to satisfy the importers, some of whom claim that they may lose business on account of the tardy arrivals. American chopped apples are also finding a considerable market. They are used largely for making cider. Referring again to the failure of the prune crop, it may be stated that this has been followed by very high prices for that favorite article. No prunes worth eating can be bought at retail for less than 1 franc (19.3 cents) a pound. Better qualities are much dearer.

### AMERICAN AGRICULTURAL IMPLEMENTS.

It is an old story to call the attention of American exporters to the fact that the only way to do business in Europe is to send out traveling salesmen with samples, just as is done at home. This necessity is more marked in France than in almost any other European country, for the reason that Frenchmen are very well satisfied with their own goods and are not to be easily convinced that any other country can produce better articles. It is necessary to show them in a practical way that they are wrong. No amount of literature will convince them. They must have object lessons. Thus, for example, an American reaper in a grainfield, or even an exhibition in a store window, would be worth more than all the circulars that could be distributed in a lifetime.

Nantes is the center of a great agricultural region. It is also a center of commerce and manufacture, and would be an excellent city in which to make an exhibit of American agricultural machines, such as reapers, mowers, and wheeled hay rakes. I have made inquiry and can find no trace of any representatives of our great manufacturing concerns having been here this year. Only to-day, however, an importer of American dried fruits called at the consulate and asked me to furnish him with the addresses of some of our manufacturers of agricultural machinery. He tells me that he will write to them with the idea of establishing an agency here, and will ask that a practical man be sent over to aid him.

### OTHER IMPORTS FROM THE UNITED STATES.

The most important imports at Nantes from the United States for the ten months of 1902 ended October 31 were phosphates of a declared value of $300,000; lumber, $50,000, and dried fruits, $60,000. These figures, however, must not be understood as in any manner indicating the volume of business. There is, unfortunately, no line of ships direct from Nantes or its seaport, St. Nazaire (30 miles distant, at the mouth of the Loire), to the United States. Consequently, nearly all the American goods intended for this market reach it by way of Havre or Bordeaux. For this reason I do not give the statistics of the Nantes custom-house, which would be entirely misleading.

### GENERAL TRADE.

The principal articles imported at Nantes are the following: Coal (almost exclusively from England); rice straw from the British and Chinese Indies; rice in large quantities from Indo-China; tapioca from the British Indies; raisins from Turkey and Spain; cotton seed from Egypt; dried fruits from the United States and Germany; coffee from Haiti, Brazil, and the Dutch and British Indies; copra from Oceania and Indo-China; olive oil from Italy, Spain, and Algeria; natural phosphates from the United States, Tunis, Algeria, Belgium, and Chile; aolin from England; paper pulp from Norway, Sweden, Germany, and Belgium; pyrites from Portugal and Spain; pitch-tar from England; bitumen from the United States and England; drawn iron from Sweden and Belgium; lead pigs from Spain, England, and Belgium; pewter from England and the East Indies; oats from Algeria, Bulgaria, and Turkey; nitrate of soda from Chile; lumber for building from Russia, Sweden, Norway, the United States, Germany, and Canada; wine from Spain and Algeria; guano from Peru; canned meats from England and Australia; barley from Algeria; corn from Bulgaria; asphalt from Trinidad, the United States, and England; cotton seed from Egypt.

The principal exports from Nantes are: Boneblack to England; undressed skins, tallow, sugar, sardines, and the fish in oil to all countries; buckwheat to Belgium; sweetened crackers and biscuits to all countries; honey and butter to Belgium and England; slate tiles to England; oil cake for animal food, and raw zinc to England and Belgium.

### COAL.

I regret to have to report that no American coal has been received at Nantes since last April, when the steamer *Guild Hill* brought a cargo of 4,000 tons from Philadelphia, of which the Orleans Railway Company took 2,100 tons and the Western Railway Company 1,500.

The coal ran large and clean, and appeared to resemble in many respects good "Durham" steam. In regard to the outlook for American coal in this region, Mr. Thomas Sankey, an important importer of Welsh coal at St. Nazaire, said to me yesterday:

> The present low prices of coal in Wales and the low freights ruling will make it difficult for American coal to compete, and I do not think that the coal to suit this market has yet been sent. The great difficulty is the size of the boats that come across. Merchants who would risk a small cargo of 1,000 tons hesitate about taking 2,500 or 3,000 tons of a coal which they do not know, which may not suit their clients. The average size of the colliers received here is about 2,000 tons. There would be an opening for good pitch in small cargoes of, say, 1,000 to 1,200 tons.

Mr. Sankey also tells me that the year 1902 has shown a falling off in the coal imports at St. Nazaire, which is the seaport of Nantes.

The chief point of interest has been the first appearance of Westphalian coking coals, some 20,000 tons having been purchased by the Trignac Iron Works at St. Nazaire. These coals are shipped at Rotterdam and have been sold at a trifle over 15 francs ($2.90) c. i. f. St. Nazaire. They are of a bituminous nature, appear to be clean, and contain about 10 per cent of large. Some three-fourths cargoes of this coal have also been sold to the Gouraud Paper Mills at Nantes.

The bulk of the coal sent to this region is Welsh. Some 250,000 tons of colliery smalls for the railway companies and about 300,000 tons of large steam are imported by the coal merchants at St. Nazaire alone. The coal, as a general rule, is of second quality, known as "dry." The big industries consume either small or "thro and thro," a steam coal containing about 50 per cent of large at shipment.

Some 8,000 tons of Scotch coal are also received, but it is of inferior quality, such as "Ayrshire" Mains or "Fife."

A large trade is done at St. Nazaire in patent fuel, which is made on the spot, there being four fuel works. The fuel is manufactured with coal dust and about 8 per cent of pitch. This latter article is becoming very scarce, and the value has increased 25 to 30 per cent, the present price being 80 francs ($15.44) at St. Nazaire, while at this date last year it was only worth about 60 francs ($11.58). More than 100,000 tons of patent fuel is manufactured at St. Nazaire every year. The present price is about 28 francs ($5.40) per ton. The cost of making the fuel is close upon 10 francs ($1.93) per ton, as it is necessary to use 8 per cent of pitch to obtain the cohesion. The present prices of Welsh coals are—

|  | s. | d. |  |
|---|---|---|---|
| Best steam, colliery screened | 16 | 0 | = $3.55 |
| Second colliery | 13 | 0 | = 3.22 |
| Forge thro and thro | 12 | 6 | = 3.08 |

Colliery smalls, according to quality, 7 to 8 shillings ($1.70 to $1.96) f. o. b. Cardiff, all with the export tax of 1 shilling (24 cents) not included. Anthracite nuts, 26 to 28 shillings ($5 to $5.48) f. o. b. Swansea.

These prices show a fall of about 50 cents a ton from the prices ruling a year ago. The freight for St. Nazaire is 4½ francs (89 cents) per ton, of which sum the steamer pays 1 franc (19 cents) per ton for discharging the coal. There has been very little variation in the freights during the year. They have been exceptionally low, and will average less than 5 francs (96 cents).

WIDENING AND DEEPENING THE LOIRE.

The enterprising chamber of commerce of Nantes is making all possible speed with the project of widening and deepening the Loire from St. Nazaire to Nantes, in order to permit ships of the heaviest draft and burden to come direct to the docks in this city. The chamber of deputies has already voted the appropriation of 22,000,000 francs ($4,246,000) for putting this work into effect, and it is certain that the senate will confirm this appropriation next month. The work, which all the engineers agree can be easily and quickly accomplished, will be commenced at once, and it is confidently believed that the end of two years will see it completed. A direct line of steamships of heavy burden from Philadelphia or New York to Nantes would mean a great deal to the United States in the extension of its commerce with France, and it seems to me that the matter is well worth the attention of the International Mercantile Marine Company or of the great coal and petroleum companies of Pennsylvania.

It should be remembered that Nantes occupies a privileged situation on the ocean. In fact, it is one of the nearest and most accessible points to the American coast, and at the same time, its continental position gives it an especial advantage with regard to the interior.

If we take, for example, the distances from Paris, we find that Nantes is the most-favored port on the Atlantic, being only some 240 miles, while its two rivals, Bordeaux and La Palice, are 360 and 300 miles, respectively, from Paris. The study of the authorized time table of the railways shows that the shortest routes from Geneva and Lyons, as well as Basel, to the ocean terminate in Nantes. The region itself is of sufficient industrial importance to justify the importation of 1,500,000 tons of English coal. In the Basse-Loire, there are 300 manufactories, employing some 31,000 workmen. The shipyards and the metallurgical and chemical factories are now in full development. The statistics of the departments in the immediate vicinity of Nantes for the year 1899 give the following consumption of coal:

| | Tons. | | Tons. |
|---|---|---|---|
| Loire-Inférieure | 800,000 | Tarthe | 119,000 |
| Morbihan | 126,000 | Maine and Loire | 175,000 |
| Ille and Vilaine | 192,000 | Vendée | 117,000 |
| Mayenne | 105,000 | | |

These departments, whose total consumption of coal amounts to more than 1,600,000 tons (and this must certainly have increased since 1899), can be supplied directly by water: The departments of Morbihan and the Ille and Vilaine, by the canal from Nantes to Brest and the canalized Vilaine; the Maine and Loire, by the Loire, which will soon be navigable as far as Angers; The Mayenne and the Sarthe, by the two rivers of the same name, which are both navigable and flow into the Loire at Angers; and by the Loire, an admirable natural canal which with little expense could be made into a waterway to the Loire and Cher.

From the point of view of railways, Nantes is the center of three great systems, the Orleans, the West, and the State, which are all three thinking of enlarging their coal depots as soon as the new organization will permit, that is to say, within a short space of time. This situation will certainly allow an increase in the field of action and bring the city within reach of other departments. As for the facilities of access and unloading offered by the port of Nantes, the project above referred to will enable ships drawing from 24 to 25 feet to proceed straight to the wharves, even during the lowest tides, without delay and without passing any locks.

The State Railways have already decided to make Nantes their great port on the ocean, and are carrying on works costing 5,000,000 francs. ($965,000), which will enable them to handle an eventual traffic in their principal station of from 5,000,000 to 6,000,000 tons. Meanwhile, the chamber of commerce is preparing a modern and powerful equipment for the half mile of new wharves, which will be in use next year. In looking for places adapted to the location of large depots of petroleum, few will be found as suitable as Nantes. On the left bank of the river, below Nantes, there are a number of isolated fields which could easily be joined by a branch line to the State Railways and where one could build as many petroleum warehouses as might be necessary, without fear of either troubling or being troubled by the neighbors.

In less than ten years, the total commerce of Nantes has increased from 350,000 tons to more than a million, and the increase continues. The new industries established give every reason to suppose that this advance will become even more rapid. Thus it seems certain that Nantes is the most desirable port for the establishment of a line of heavy cargo steamers between central Europe and Pennsylvania, and for the founding of a great distributing center of solid and liquid combustibles.

BENJ. H. RIDGELY, *Consul.*

NANTES, *December 11, 1902*

---

## NICE.

The last census gives a population to this city of 127,027, as against 108,227 in 1895. These figures do not comprise the garrison nor the veritable crowds of tourists living in the place during the winter and spring. This consular district is about 96 kilometers (59.65 miles) square, with 75 kilometers (46.6 miles) of coast line, and has a population of about 293,213, of whom 67,835 are aliens.

### PUBLIC HEALTH.

As compared with other cities having a more or less agglomerated population and subject to the arrival of large numbers of strangers, the public health has been about normal. During the past few years, the questions of improved sewerage and other innovations in the interest of hygiene have been receiving attention from the local authorities. The authorities appreciate the importance of such measures to a town dependent upon the influx of visitors for its prosperity, and the near future will witness important progress in this respect.

### LOCAL INDUSTRY.

There is not much to be reported under this head. Some of the local companies have been overcapitalized, and the initial expenditure has been disproportionate to the earning capacity. The monopoly of the gas and electric-light company expires in 1913, and the question of its renewal is a source of preoccupation for its shareholders.  The new electric-power company will play an important part in the future of this industry.  Building is fairly active, new houses of all classes going up in various parts of the town and the suburbs.  The extension of the electric tramways to Mentone is giving an impetus to building on the admirable sites between Nice and Mentone, notably at La Turbie and in the new section overlying the principality of Monaco, known as Monte Carlo Supérieur.

### RAILWAYS AND ELECTRIC LINES.

As foreshadowed by me in previous annual reports, certain difficul-ties have arisen in connection with the proposed railway from Nice to Cuneo.  It has been hinted that the Paris, Lyons and Mediterranée Railway, which has the exclus've right to build the portion leading to the Italian frontier, is not particularly anxious to burden itself with a new line that may not pay.  The desire of the people of Nice for the realization of the scheme has, however, induced the deputies of Nice to push matters in Paris, and only the other day, the Government decree calling for a line from Nice to Sospel and thence to the Italian frontier was published.  In Italy, however, much opposition exists, and powerful influences are at work for a line from Cuneo to Venti-miglia, partly or wholly upon Italian territory.  In the former case, permission to cross a part of its territory would hardly be obtained from the French Government, and in the latter, the cost of the line would be tremendously increased by technical difficulties.  It may safely be stated that the near future will not see the problem solved. In a discussion which occurred the other day in Italy, it was stated that the line between Turin and Savona no longer sufficed for the traffic and that the building of a new line was imperative.  The casual observer fails to comprehend how lines having a monopoly and gov-ernment aid (thus fearing no competition) and large traffic pay so little.  A line from Nice through Piedmont to Turin would seem to the average railroad expert to be very profitable.

Propositions for various lines of electric tramways in the valleys of what may be called the "hinterland" of this consular district are in a preliminary stage.

An electrical engineer (a British subject, but whose career began in the United States) has obtained a concession for fifty years for an electric line over the famous Cornice road, from Nice to La Turbie. This historical route is one of the objective points of tourists, and the line will render it easily accessible.  In order not to mar the road for carriages, he has decided to adopt a new system, whereby he will be enabled to run comfortable cars over any part of the width of the road without using rails.  His purpose is to use a type of car, designed by himself, which will be the nearest approach possible to a conve-nient and luxurious "observation car."  I am informed that he cal-culates the entire cost of the line, if his plans and specifications are carefully carried out, at not more than $300,000.

No projects for additional high roads are to be recorded.  It must be noted that this entire consular district boasts of roads that, in point of fact, leave nothing to be desired.

## HARBORS OF NICE AND MONACO.

The first steps have been taken in the enlargement of the existing harbor at Nice.

The "Coal Quai" has been deepened and the "West Quai" given an increase of frontage. The harbor itself will be enlarged, but if the railway line to Piedmont is built, the harbor will, nevertheless, be found inadequate. I think it necessary to repeat that, for the present, ships entering this harbor should not be of over 2,500 tons burden, nor draw more than 18 feet of water. This detail was overlooked during the year in the case of a cargo of British coal, causing considerable inconvenience to both consignor and consignee.

Work on the harbor of Monaco has begun. It is calculated that it will require some four years for completion, and the consulate has taken steps to place the contractors in communication with American firms for the furnishing of machinery of various kinds.

### TRADE WITH THE UNITED STATES.

Referring to the direct trade which this consulate has aimed to create and promote, I am happy to be able to submit the following table, handed to me by the custom-house authorities. I do not place it among the others, as it refers to new conditions.

*Merchandise imported into Nice directly from the United States during 1901.*

| | | | | |
|---|---|---|---|---|
| Flour | pounds | 7,044 | Printing machines pounds | 5,832 |
| Pickles and preserves | do | 406 | Tools do | 870 |
| Cotton-seed oil | do | 4,304 | Stoves and heaters do | 4,546 |
| Essences | do | 1,110 | Cast-iron work do | 1,190 |
| Sawed wood | tons | 532 | Chairs do | 340 |
| Dried vegetables | pounds | 227 | Other furniture do | 4,974 |
| Residue of petroleum | do | 1,254 | Casks (empty) do | 710 |
| Perfumery, without alcohol, pounds | | 1,900 | Organs or harmoniums do | 610 |
| | | | Bicycles do | 306 |

It should be remembered that these figures represent only such goods as have arrived on through bills of lading. They do not represent in any sense the real quantity of American goods that have come to this market through second and third hands. I have personal knowledge of direct importations during the present year of lamps, paper-cutting machines, patented articles, lamp suspensions, grates, petroleum stoves, and bath cabinets, not to mention naphtha launches, and this for the first time in the history of this harbor. Now that the wedge has entered, buyers here, I am confident, will see the immense advantages of importing direct, and our own manufacturers will recognize the importance of opening up relations of this kind. I look for a very marked increase in trade during the present year.

### OCEAN FREIGHTS.

I have ascertained that through bills of lading from New York to Nice have been executed at the rate of from 27s. 6d. to 32s. 6d. per ton, weight or measurement, at the choice of the ship. Shippers in the United States should try to obtain the lowest possible rates. I think 25s. an ample figure, and as direct shipments to this harbor are at present experimental, the reduction of ocean freights, as well as of other charges, is important.

## GENERAL EXPORTS AND IMPORTS.

The declared value of articles manufactured in this consular district and exported to the United States, as taken from the consular invoice book, has been:

| Article. | 1901. | 1900. |
|---|---|---|
| Confectionery | $6,379.02 | $5,921.50 |
| Meal (almond) | 649.15 | 733.39 |
| Oil: | | |
| Almond | 11,509.92 | 14,209.70 |
| Olive | 89,809.44 | 70,437.57 |
| Perfumery | 604,138.09 | 568,577.09 |
| Total | 711,985.62 | 659,879.25 |

The value of exports from the consular district of Nice for the year 1901 was:

| Article. | Value. | Countries whither exported. |
|---|---|---|
| Bricks | $2,058 | Italy. |
| Coal | 24,848 | Do. |
| Flour | 4,500 | Do. |
| Hides | 81,600 | Do. |
| Olive oil | 174,600 | Germany, Austria, United States. |
| Perfumery | 400,000 | Italy, United States. |
| Plaster | 8,000 | Italy. |
| Pottery | 7,120 | Do. |
| Wool | 61,200 | Do. |
| Total | 718,926 | |
| Silk (raw) | 1,260,000 | In transitu Marseille to Italy. |

The value of imports[a] for the consular district of Nice for the year 1901 was:

| Article. | Value. | Countries whence imported. |
|---|---|---|
| Bran | $83,640 | Italy, Russia. |
| Carobs | 102,090 | Turkey, Spain. |
| Charcoal | 90,340 | Italy. |
| Coal | 670,110 | England. |
| Flour | 66,900 | Austria, Italy. |
| Lumber | 229,040 | Roumania, Russia, Italy, Austria. |
| Maize | 12,428 | Italy. |
| Malt | 9,250 | Germany, Austria. |
| Oats | 170,160 | Algiers, Turkey. |
| Olive oil | 900,600 | Tunis, Spain, Italy. |
| Rice | 1,860 | Italy. |
| Stockfish | 11,400 | Norway. |
| Wheat | 78,320 | Russia, Algiers. |
| Wines | 367,300 | Spain, Italy, Algiers. |
| Total | 2,796,838 | |

[a] The United States excluded. The amount of duties collected was $285,730.

## SHIPPING.

*Aggregate number and tonnage of vessels engaged in foreign trade entered at the ports of the consular district of Nice, with cargo or in ballast, during the year 1901.*

| Ports. | Number of vessels. | | | Tonnage. | | |
|---|---|---|---|---|---|---|
| | Cargo. | Ballast. | Total. | Cargo. | Ballast. | Total. |
| Nice | 254 | 6 | 260 | 87,924 | 260 | 88,184 |
| Antibes | 7 | 93 | 100 | 823 | 4,889 | 5,212 |
| Cannes | 25 | .......... | 25 | 9,821 | .......... | 9,821 |
| Golfe Juan | 5 | .......... | 5 | 250 | .......... | 250 |
| Menton | 18 | .......... | 18 | 3,568 | .......... | 3,568 |
| Monaco | 37 | .......... | 37 | 6,445 | .......... | 6,445 |
| Villefranche | 5 | .......... | 5 | 5,872 | .......... | 5,872 |
| Total | 351 | 99 | 450 | 114,703 | 4,649 | 119,252 |

*Aggregate number and tonnage of vessels engaged in foreign trade, cleared as above, during the year, 1901.*

| Ports. | Number of vessels. | | | Tonnage. | | |
|---|---|---|---|---|---|---|
| | Cargo. | Ballast. | Total. | Cargo. | Ballast. | Total. |
| Nice | 102 | 136 | 238 | 36,634 | 50,613 | 87,247 |
| Antibes | 98 | 1 | 99 | 4,590 | 568 | 5,158 |
| Cannes | 7 | 8 | 15 | 965 | 4,643 | 5,608 |
| Golfe Juan | 6 | 1 | 7 | 349 | 35 | 384 |
| Menton | 1 | 8 | 9 | 30 | 2,489 | 2,519 |
| Monaco | 1 | 33 | 34 | 793 | 5,179 | 5,972 |
| Villefranche | 4 | .......... | 4 | 7,839 | .......... | 7,839 |
| Total | 219 | 187 | 406 | 51,200 | 63,527 | 114,727 |

No American vessels entered or cleared.

HAROLD S. VAN BUREN, *Consul.*

NICE, *July 31, 1902.*

## SUPPLEMENTARY.

There has been during the past year further evidence of a desire to purchase American articles direct. Each month witnesses the appearance of new goods in the shops, and with concerted action on the part of our manufacturers and local firms, the consumption of such products is bound to increase in proportion to the diminution in the cost resulting from direct dealings. The annexed table of direct importations sufficiently indicates the trend of this trade.

### INDUSTRIES OF NICE.

The only addition to the incorporated companies of this district since my last report has been one that has taken over the "Casino Municipal," the "Jetée Promenade," and the "Cercle Massena," all of which will be run by this company. Changes have been made in the former building, and it is stated that an authorization has been obtained by the company to operate an open game of "baccarat." A new hotel is being built at La Mantega, a suburb in the northwestern portion of the town. Building operations continue on a moderate scale and the price of land is steady. I annex a list of incorporated companies in the district which were not included in the table accompanying my report of October 22, 1898,[a] which figure in an official review just issued.

NEW LINES OF COMMUNICATION.

The Hamburg-American Steamship Line has announced that in December it will inaugurate a triweekly passenger service to and from Genoa. This will supply a want that has been felt for many years, and will afford a remarkably pleasant and rapid means of reaching the latter city and there making connections with various parts of Italy. The elimination of the delay at the custom-house of Ventimiglia will of itself recommend the new line to travelers.

The work on the electric tramway to Menton is being actively prosecuted. As I write, I am informed that London capitalists are looking into the matter of the concession for an electric line over the Cornus road, mentioned in my last annual report.

The question of the Nice-Coni route is still being discussed, and the complicated problems of frontier lines and of conflicting interests are being considered.

The lines that are planned wholly upon Italian territory are expensive, owing to long tunnels which are inevitable, some being 7 miles in length. The shortest and most direct route would cost but $5,440,000, but it would pass over about 10 miles of French territory on its way to Ventimiglia from Vievola. It is evident that the question is destined to remain for a considerable time in the domain of international discussion.

In the month of April last, the conseil-général adopted a report recommending the building of the following lines of tramways in this district: (1) Gueydan to Guillaumes; (2) La Mescla to St. Sauveur; (3) Pont-Charles-Albert to Roquesteron; (4) Vésubie to St.-Martin-Vésubie; (5) Le Loup to Thorenc; (6) Nice to Levens; (7) Cagnes to Vence; (8) Villeneuve-Loubet to Grasse; (9) Menton to Sospel. No concessions have yet been obtained for these lines. Subventions are to be asked from the Government, and they are expected to be delivered to the public at the end of 1905.

THE OLIVE CROP.

There are evidences that the olive crop will mature early this season. Present indications point merely to a good average crop, but as the activity of the keiroun or olive worm is the element that decides the quantity and quality of the crop, it is too early at present to know, the ravages of the fly causing the worm to become evident only when the fruit is approaching maturity. Rumors are current here that considerable damage has accrued from this cause to the southern Italian crop. I can not report that any organized efforts are being made to combat the maladies that for years have been decimating the crops in this district.

PUBLIC HEALTH.

An isolation hospital for contagious diseases has been opened at St. Pons, on the Paillon Stream. Work is being continued on the new system of sewers decided upon two years ago. The question of the cremation of garbage and refuse is receiving attention, and the law making vaccination compulsory is expected to become operative in February next.

_a Commercial Relations, 1898, Vol. II._

## COMMERCE.

I submit the following tables:

*Direct importations of merchandise from the United States to the port of Nice during the first six months of 1902.*

| Article. | Quan-tity. | Article. | Quan-tity. |
|---|---|---|---|
| | *Pounds.* | | *Pounds.* |
| Flour | 2,876 | Candied fruits | 684 |
| Fruit in sirup | 120 | Coffee | 402 |
| Cotton | 550 | Dried vegetables | 585 |
| Glassware | 343 | Lamp chimneys | 60 |
| Cut glass | 55 | Glass in panes | 78 |
| Small machinery | 2,790 | Grates | 2,340 |
| Lamps | 600 | Zinc work | 250 |
| Nickel work | 80 | Furniture | 200 |
| Bicycles | 105 | Sewing machines | 820 |
| Small agricultural tools | 125 | Patent medicines | 65 |
| Perfumes | 18 | Varnish for dynamos | 40 |
| Extract of meat in cakes | 62 | Preserved fish | 30 |
| Leaf tobacco | 110 | Kitchen utensils | 90 |
| Various glassware | 60 | Sulphur | 25 |
| Imitation jewelry | 8 | Clothing | 60 |
| Sirup | 65 | Various small articles | 160 |

*Declared value of articles manufactured in this district and exported to the United States for the first six months of 1902.*

[Taken from the consular invoice books.]

| | 1902. | 1901. | | 1902. | 1901. |
|---|---|---|---|---|---|
| Almond meal | $261.49 | $385.35 | Oil, almond | $5,899.41 | $4,317.09 |
| Confectionery | 200.92 | 487.09 | Oil, olive | 45,898.67 | 46,171.43 |
| Lace | 289.50 | | Perfumery | 329,617.01 | 230,081.58 |
| Linen | 2,754.18 | 6,145.99 | | | |
| Marble work | 154.40 | | Total | 380,005.58 | 277,566.58 |

Increase in 1902, $102,417.

*Value of exports from the consular district of Nice for the first six months of 1902.*

| Description. | Value. | Countries whither exported. |
|---|---|---|
| Bricks and clay | $3,676 | Italy. |
| Casks | 900 | Do. |
| Fruits | 600 | Do. |
| Oil, olive | 24,900 | Italy, United States, Austria. |
| Perfumery | 212,000 | Italy, United States. |
| Plaster | 672 | Do. |
| Pottery | 2,476 | Italy, Greece, Turkey, United States. |

*Value of imports for same period.*

| Bran | $42,160 | Italy, Russia. |
|---|---|---|
| Carobs | 41,970 | Spain, Turkey. |
| Charcoal | 42,840 | Italy. |
| Coal | 290,061 | England. |
| Flour | 28,600 | Austria, Italy. |
| Lumber | 109,780 | Austria, Roumania, Russia, Italy. |
| Maize | 22,568 | Italy. |
| Malt | 4,050 | Austria, Germany. |
| Oats | 53,670 | Algiers, Turkey. |
| Oil, olive | 227,200 | Tunis, Italy, Spain. |
| Stockfish | 2,180 | Norway. |
| Wheat | 95,920 | Russia, Algiers. |
| Wines | 138,400 | Algiers, Spain, Italy. |

*List of incorporated companies in the district of the Alpes-Maritimes not included in table accompanying report of October 22, 1898.[a]*

| Name of company. | City. | Capital. | Last dividends. | | Par value. | Last quota- tion. |
|---|---|---|---|---|---|---|
| | | | 1898. | 1899-1900. | | |
| Terminus Hotel | Nice | $142,000.00 | $6.25 | | $100.00 | |
| Palace Splendide Hotel | do | 60,000.00 | | | 100.00 | |
| Grand Hotel de Cimiez | do | 270,000.00 | | | 100.00 | |
| Excelsior Hotel Regina | do | 300,000.00 | | | 100.00 | |
| Belvedere Hotel | do | 44,000.00 | | | 100.00 | |
| Tramways Nice and Littoral | do | 3,000,000.00 | | (a) | 100.00 | 110.00 |
| Union des Propriétaires | do | 100,000.00 | 14.00 | $15.00 | 75.00 | 300.00 |
| Société des Huiles d'Olive | do | 110,000.00 | 5.20 | 5.80 | 100.00 | 100.00 |
| Raffineries d'Huile d'Olive | do | 150,000.00 | | 7.00 | 100.00 | 100.00 |
| Société Maison A. Gal | do | 400,000.00 | 70.00 | 90.00 | 1,000.00 | |
| Société Jetée Promenade | do | 201,100.00 | | | 100.90 | |
| Cercle de la Méditerranée | do | 120,000.00 | | | 200.00 | |
| Société des Courses de Nice | do | 2,000.00 | | | 100.00 | |
| Société du Trotting du Littoral | do | 1,000.00 | | | 50.00 | |
| Banque Populaire de Nice | do | 53,740.00 | .90 | .90 | 20.00 | 20.00 |
| Société des Bazars du Littoral | do | 80,000.00 | 6.50 | 6.95 | 100.00 | |
| Magasins de la Place Clichy | do | 170,000.00 | | | 1,000.00 | |
| Verreries de Nice | do | 60,000.00 | | | 100.00 | |
| Société d'Alimentation du Littoral | do | 36,000.00 | | | 100.00 | |
| Docks et entrepôts de Nice | do | 250,000.00 | | | 100.00 | |
| Brasserie de Nice | do | 150,000.00 | | (b) | 100.00 | |
| Imprimerie des Alpes Maritimes | do | 10,000.00 | | (c) | 20.00 | |
| La Mantega | do | 140,000.00 | | | 100.00 | |
| Gaz de Villefranche | do | 114,400.00 | | | 100.00 | |
| Bains de Mer de Monaco | Monaco | 6,000,000.00 | 55.00 | 44.00 | 100.00 | 700.00 |
| Halles et Marchés de Monaco | do | 100,000.00 | 14.96 | 15.00 | 100.00 | 300.00 |
| **Société Monegasque d'Electricité** | do | 135,000.00 | 5.00 | 7.00 | 100.00 | |
| **Grand Hotel Monte Carlo Limited** | do | 350,000.00 | | | 5.00 | |
| Panification Franco Viennoise | do | 140,000.00 | | | 100.00 | |
| **Glacières de Monaco** | do | 60,000.00 | | | 100.00 | |
| **Chemin de Fer à Crémaillère** | Turbie | 320,000.00 | | | 100.00 | |
| Campagnie du Littoral | do | 400,000.00 | | | 20.00 | |
| Forces Motrices de Monte Carlo | do | 200,000.00 | | | 100.00 | 80.00 |
| Banque Populaire de Menton | Menton | 85,400.00 | 1.00 | 1.00 | 20.00 | |
| Halles et Marchés de Menton | do | 20,000.00 | 1.40 | 1.51 | 20.00 | 25.00 |
| Compagnie Pompes Funèbres | do | 130,000.00 | | | 20.00 | |
| Céramique Saïssi | do | 40,000.00 | | | 100.00 | |
| Hotel des Iles Britanniques | do | 200,000.00 | | | 100.00 | |
| Tramways de Cannes | Cannes | 530,000.00 | | .40 | 20.00 | |
| Société d'Eclairage Electrique | do | 220,000.00 | 1.00 | 1.11 | 37.00 | |
| Station Climatérique | do | 60,000.00 | | | 50.00 | |

   *a* Commercial Relations, 1898, Vol. II.    *b* 5 per cent.    *c* 7 per cent.

HAROLD S. VAN BUREN, *Consul.*

NICE, *October 29, 1902.*

---

## RHEIMS.

The exports to the United States from the consular district of Rheims for the fiscal year ended June 30, 1902, were the following:

| | | |
|---|---|---|
| Rheims | | $5,212,592.16 |
| Troyes | | 802,075.56 |
|  Total | | 6,014,669.72 |
| Year ended June 30, 1901: | | |
|  Rheims | $4,462,787.40 | |
|  Troyes | 744,161.85 | |
| | | 5,205,948.75 |
|  Increase for 1902 | | 808,720.97 |

The following table lists all articles of export amounting to $10,000 or over, and comprises a little less than 97 per cent of the whole:

| Articles. | 1902. | 1901. | Increase ( + ) or decrease ( − ) |
|---|---|---|---|
| Bleaching powder | $57,985.04 | | |
| Chloride of lime | 53,776.92 | | |
| Caoutchouc | 14,089.29 | 9,890.99 | + 4,816.30 |
| Crockery | 18,633.67 | 1,554.55 | + 17,079.12 |
| Glassware | 21,229.32 | 3,239.72 | + 17,989.60 |
| Hosiery | 327,201.79 | 315,923.24 | + 11,278. |
| Kid gloves | | | |
| Machinery | | | |
| Steel billets | 108,707.37 | | |
| Steel manufactures | 49,087.80 | 570.19 | |
| Straw hats | 41,822.04 | 18,609.68 | |
| Spun waste silk | 65,822.01 | 6,219.95 | |
| Wine champagne | | | |
| Cotton goods | 71,646.68 | 76,824.07 | − |
| Glass for mirrors | 16,559.57 | 20,082.04 | |

### CHAMPAGNE WINE TRADE.

The exports to the United States from this consular district have increased in value 50 per cent during the last four years, in round numbers, from $4,000,000 to $6,000,000. Of this amount, $1,500,000 is represented by champagne wine. Over 314,000 cases, of 1 dozen bottles each, were exported during the last fiscal year.

The champagne wine business has been increasingly prosperous. This year, however, will be exceptional. The summer and early fall have been very cold and wet, and the grapes have not ripened. The quality of the juice will be inferior, and the manufacturers, who have large quantities of wine on hand from the vintages of previous years, will buy very little. The loss will fall heavily upon the growers of the grapes, and indirectly it will be severely felt by the tradesmen of the city.

### EXPORTS OF STEEL AND IRON.

While the exportation of champagne has increased nearly $500,000 during the past year, there have been notable gains in other articles. The most remarkable are the exports of steel and pig iron.

During April, May, and June, 1902, the "Société Anonyme des Michéville," near Nancy, department of Meurthe et Moselle, exported to New York, via Antwerp, over $100,000 worth of Bessemer steel billets. The price, delivered free on board at Antwerp, was about $20 per metric ton (2,204 pounds).

In March, 1901, a firm engaged in manufacturing files, cutlery, and other steel goods at Nancy, commenced sending to the United States manufactures of steel invoiced as steel bars. The exportation for the fiscal year ended June 30, 1901, amounted only to $570.19; but during the year just ended another house has taken up the exportation of the same kind of goods, and the shipments have increased to nearly $50,000.

These steel bars were shipped principally to New York and New Orleans and were invoiced at from 25 to 40 cents a pound. The material is used, probably, for making files and cutlery.

During the last quarter, several shipments of pig iron were sent from Longwy, department of Vosges, to San Francisco, and Portland, Oreg. These exportations continue in increased quantities, and are now being sent to the Atlantic coast, also.

## SPUN SILK.

Two years ago, a company entitled "La Société Industrielle de la Schappe," doing business in Germany, France, and Switzerland, with headquarters at Basel, established a branch at Rheims for carding and spinning silk. The raw material is silk from cocoons, which have been damaged by the holes made in them by the escaping insects, kept for propagation. It has been combed and prepared for spinning in the southern part of France. The finished product is called spun silk, and $65,000 worth was exported last year to the United States. Large quantities are shipped to Lyons and Calais for the silk and lace industries there.

The operatives of the factory are women (at present 300 in number), who receive 40 to 50 cents a day of ten and a half hours. The factory is furnished with the most approved machinery, is well managed, and has lost no time since it started.

## STRAW HATS.

The exportation of straw hats for the fiscal year amounted to $41,-822, an increase of over $23,000. These goods are not all of French origin, nor are they all really made of straw. The hats called Panama are imported from Central and South America, put through certain processes to give them color and form, and reexported. They are invoiced at from $40 to $80 a dozen. The business with the United States is divided among six firms, located at or near Nancy.

## WOOLEN TISSUES.

The manufacture of woolen goods in Rheims during the past year has not been profitable, and yet during the month of April last there was a strike of the operatives. This was caused by a new law reducing the number of working hours in a day from eleven to ten and a half. The working people demanded the same wages for the shorter day, which the employers refused. It was settled finally in favor of the employees, for the mills had orders which had to be filled. Business now is in a very depressed condition, and most of the mills are working on three-quarter time. The exports to the United States for 1901 and 1902 were only $2,504.79.

## KID GLOVES AND HOSIERY.

Ninety-eight per cent of the exports to the United States from the consular agency at Troyes is composed of kid gloves and hosiery (stockings and knit underwear).

Hosiery has about held its own during the last four years, but kid gloves have increased over $150,000. The gain for the last year was nearly $46,000. The kid gloves are all exported by a single firm, located at Chaumont in the Department of Haute-Marne. The goods are of excellent quality.

## THE SUBURBAN RAILROADS OF RHEIMS.

The suburban railroads centering at Rheims are of narrow gauge, and are owned and controlled by a stock company. The motive power is steam, but the locomotives are small and very slow time is made. All the trains carry both passengers and freight.

During the last year, a line has been constructed from Rheims to Fismes, and a branch is now being built from Bouleuse to Dormans. There are now three lines: From Rheims to Ambonnay, 23½ miles; time of transit, two hours and twenty minutes; fare, first class, single, 72 cents; excursion, $1.18; fare, second class, single, 43 cents; excursion, 72 cents. From Rheims to Cormicy, 13¾ miles; time of transit, one hour and twenty-two minutes. From Rheims to Fismes, about 25 miles; time of transit, three hours.

## TELEPHONE SERVICE.

The telephone service is conducted by the Government. Rheims can communicate with Paris and most of the large cities in France; also with Geneva, Berlin, Frankfort, Metz, and several cities in Belgium.

There are at present about 750 subscribers in this city. Each one pays, first, for the installation of a double wire, at the rate of 20 francs ($3.86) for each 100 meters (about 325 feet) of distance between his residence or place of business and the central office; second, for the appurtenances, which become the property of the subscriber; third, 200 francs a year for the service.

Subscribers are entitled to the use of the telephone at any time, day or night. For all places outside of the city limits, the regular charge is added. The long distance tariff is very cheap; for example, the distance to Paris is 97½ miles, and the charge for the service is 10 cents for a conversation of three minutes.

Rheims has communication, locally, with the capitals of all the cantons in the Department of Marne.

## GAS AND ELECTRICITY.

The "Compagnie du Gaz" of this city has the monopoly of furnishing light and heat by gas. For this privilege it pays the city $4,000 a year. The price of gas, which is of poor quality, is 24 centimes the cubic meter—about $1.30 per 1,000 cubic feet.

In 1900, this company was authorized to furnish electricity for light, heat, and power for the term of twenty-seven years. The wires are to be placed underground, but the mayor may authorize overhead wires in certain streets.

The maximum price for electric energy is 0.063 franc ($0.012) per hectowatt hour for light, and 0.045 franc ($0.0086) for power. This price is to be reduced from 1 to 15 per cent according to the amount consumed by the purchaser. The city is to be furnished at half rates, and is to receive for the privileges granted the company $1,000 for the first year, $2,000 for the second, and an increase of $200 for each and every year thereafter.

The city is to receive also a percentage of the gross receipts, as follows:

Ten per cent of the gross receipts for light, less 450,000 francs ($86,850).

Five per cent of the gross receipts for power, less 150,000 francs ($28,950).

The company, after paying to the stockholders from the net receipts 5 per cent upon the capital invested, is to divide 5 per cent of the remainder among those employees of the company who receive a salary of $600 or less per year.

The city reserves the right to purchase the plant at a stated price after fifteen years. At the end of the concession, all the conduits, wire, poles, etc., are to become the property of the city, gratis; but the city is to pay for the power houses and material. If the price can not be agreed upon, it is to be left to three experts, one to be named by the city, one by the company, and the third by the judge of the court of common pleas.

### PUBLIC AUCTIONEERS.

There are three public auctioneers licensed by the city. All public sales are conducted by one or more of these persons. They receive 20 per cent commission, which expense is divided equally between the purchaser and the seller.

These positions are very lucrative, and each incumbent can sell his office to another person, subject to the approval of the city. The positions sell readily for from 90,000 to 100,000 francs ($17,370 to $19,300). The city receives 18,000 francs ($3,474) a year from each auctioneer for his exclusive privilege.

### COAL.

Coal for steaming purposes is quoted at present at 21 francs ($4.15) the metric ton (2,205 pounds), but a general strike of the operatives in all of the coal mines in France has just begun, and unless this can be speedily adjusted, prices will rise. Most of the mills have stocks on hand sufficient to last until spring. Semibituminous coal for heating and cooking purposes is selling at retail at 46 to 48 francs ($8.88 to $9.26) the metric ton.

### COST OF LIVING.

Living is expensive at Rheims, as may be seen by the following table of prices:

| | | |
|---|---|---|
| Flour | per pound | $0.04 to $0.08 |
| Sugar | do | .09 to .11 |
| Tea | do | .60 to 2.00 |
| Coffee | do | .60 to .80 |
| Rice | do | .08 to .12 |
| Macaroni | do | .08 to .12 |
| Fish | do | .14 to .60 |
| Beef | do | .12 to .50 |
| Pork | do | .18 to .22 |
| Mutton | do | .16 to .30 |
| Ham | do | .24 to .30 |
| Bacon | do | .16 to .24 |
| Rabbit | do | .14 to .20 |
| Potatoes | do | .01 to .02 |
| Beans, dry | per quart | .06 to .10 |
| Peas, dry | do | .06 to .10 |

Fruit is very dear, as the season has been very unfavorable. Prices are—

| | | | |
|---|---|---|---|
| Apples for the table | per pound.. | $0.04 to | $0.10 |
| Apples for cooking and cider | per 220 pounds.. | 3.20 to | 3.60 |
| Pears for the table | per pound.. | .06 to | .12 |
| Oranges | per dozen.. | .45 to | .60 |
| Lemons | do.... | .20 to | .30 |
| Bananas | per pound.. | .16 to | .35 |

## UNITED STATES TRADE.

The depression in the woolen industry and the failure of the grape crop in the champagne district make business of all kinds very dull in this city; but business is booming at Nancy, the center of the iron and steel trade.

Trade with the United States is increasing rapidly. This consular district is not only selling more goods to the United States every year, but it is also buying more from that country.

The agricultural implement stores, particularly, are full of American goods. I received a letter recently from the Paris agent of an American furniture house stating that American desks are now on sale at one of the large department stores in Rheims. American bicycles, carpet sweepers, glassware, meat grinders, sewing machines, typewriters, etc., are seen in the show windows.

These goods are not bought directly. General agencies have been established at important trade centers, usually at Paris. This mode of procedure has not only reduced the cost of transportation, because importations are made in large quantities, but it has also brought the agent into direct communication with the purchaser. This consular district has no port of entry; the merchants are not familiar with customhouses, and make very few, if any, direct importations. They wish to see the articles offered for sale and to know just what they will cost, in French money, delivered at their stations.

There will be a good opportunity to exhibit all kinds of American goods at the Grand Industrial Fair to be held at Rheims from May to September, 1903. This city is the largest in this part of France. There will be no other exposition in France in 1903, and the attendance will certainly be heavy. All letters on the subject should be addressed to "Monsieur Vige, Administrateur de l'Exposition Industrielle, Rheims, France."

WM. A. PRICKETT, *Consul.*

RHEIMS, *October 28, 1902.*

---

## ROUBAIX.

Trade in the consular district of Roubaix during the past year has been far from satisfactory. The causes are many, the principal ones being the long war in South Africa, which diminished trade with England, continued strikes, reduction of the hours of labor, increased foreign competition, and stagnation following the activity produced by the Paris Exposition of 1900.

WOOL DRESS GOODS.

The production and sale of dress goods have been relatively small, owing to the causes enumerated above. Manufacturers have realized very little profit. This condition of affairs has affected salaries, not so much by decreasing the price of labor, as by diminishing the output, factories being frequently closed on account of there being no demand for their products.

The future is regarded with apprehension. For many years, at least one half of the woolen manufactures of France were made for exportation. During 1901, foreign competition has increased to such an alarming extent in America, Belgium, Germany, Spain, and Italy, that these countries not only buy less in France, but are conquering trade in other markets, particularly in England, Denmark, and Sweden. The English market is the only one offering a fair profit at present to Roubaix goods, and the sales will shortly be more restricted, as Bradford is manufacturing Roubaix styles with success.

The French manufacturer is handicapped in competing for foreign trade by the increase in the price of production, caused by new taxes on industry, and accident laws. He is also menaced in the near future with a workman's pension, the cost of which will be imposed principally upon him.

On April 1, the law limiting the laborer's day to ten and one-half hours went into effect. The result has been a decrease in production and such loss to the manufacturers that several have established factories just over the border in Belgium to evade high taxes and restrictive laws. Owing to the temporary admission act, they can have their goods dyed and finished in France, thus creating a formidable competition in foreign markets with goods manufactured exclusively in this place.

WOOL.

The wool trade, the principal industry of Roubaix-Tourcoing, while not good, was not as unfavorable as was feared at the beginning of the season. A noticeable feature of the year was the comparative stability of prices. Merino wool advanced in value and was more in favor than crossbred. This class decreased from 25 to 30 per cent, and reached an extremely low level.

The terminal wool market shows a marked decrease in its operations, falling from 79,005 tons in 1900 to 17,745 tons in 1901, the smallest amount in the last ten years. Two thousand three hundred and ninety-one tons of combed wool passed through the conditioning house for the terminal market in 1901, against 4,049 tons in 1900. The general conditioning, however, increased from 51,390 tons in 1900 to 52,060 in 1901.

The following table will show the fluctuation in prices each month during 1900 and 1901.

|  | 1900. | 1901. |  | 1900. | 1901. |
|---|---|---|---|---|---|
|  | Francs. | Francs. |  | Francs. | Francs. |
| January | 6.19 | 4.00 | August | 4.4725 | 4.825 |
| February | 5.98 | 3.8725 | September | 3.83 | 4.4195 |
| March | 5.67 | 4.08 | October | 3.8325 | 4.205 |
| April | 5.04 | 4.3475 | November | 3.78 | 4.185 |
| May | 4.3225 | 4.3125 | December | 4.115 | 4.19 |
| June | 4.9435 | 4.2975 |  |  |  |
| July | 4.74 | 4.24 | Mean average | 4.79 | 4.1985 |

The mean decimal quotations are:

|  | Francs. |
|---|---|
| 1888-1897 | 4.72¼ |
| 1889-1898 | 4.68¼ |
| 1890-1899 | 4.67¼ |
| 1891-1900 | 4.55¼ |
| 1892-1901 | 4.45 |

### COTTON.

The past year has been fairly profitable to manufacturers of cotton, especially towards its close, when manufacturers were reported to be busier than usual, on account of large orders for future delivery.

Business in upholstery goods has remained normal in spite of the unsatisfactory state of textiles.

### METALLURGY, IRON AND STEEL.

The situation in this industry has not been so critical since the years 1879–80. All machine makers have been forced to reduce the number of workmen and the hours of labor, and the difficulty in securing orders is such that prices too low to be remunerative must be accepted.

The production of pig iron in France during 1900 was 2,400,240 metric tons, a decrease of 314,058 tons compared with 1900. The department of the north produced the second largest amount, viz, 266,570 tons. In the production of iron rails, sheet iron, etc., the northern department leads with 217,173 tons out of a total of 554,309 tons for all France. There was a decrease of 153,965 tons in this industry.

The decrease in the steel industry was marked. The whole of France yielded 1,151,170 tons, against 1,226,537 tons in 1900, a loss of 75,367 tons. The department of the north was again second on the list, with 226,602 tons.

The brass industry has also decreased. Three important establishments have shut down, on account of the entire loss of their capital. It is reported that the production was only one-half that of 1885 and 1898, and only one-third or even one-fourth that of 1899–1900.

### ALCOHOL.

The application of industrial alcohol to lighting, heating, and motive power is developing largely in this consular district, where most of the alcohol is produced. This alcohol pays no duty if sufficiently denatured to make it unfit for consumption. The operation is subject to special regulations, and the cost of the alcohol is about 2.10 francs per hectoliter.

The annual production is valued at 2,000,000 hectoliters and is stated as follows: Denatured alcohol, 30 francs per hectoliter (16 cents per proof gallon); ordinary alcohol, 28 francs (15 cents); alcohol made from molasses, 26 francs (14 cents); f. o. b. Dunkirk.

It is now being extensively used for lighting, and, when used in a Bunsen burner, gives a light perfectly free from carbon. At the above prices it yields the same result as coal gas at 20 cents per cubic meter, equal to $1.08 per 1,000 cubic feet.

The amount of alcohol produced in the department of the north was only 226,728 hectoliters in 1901, against 428,990 in 1900. The principal reasons for this decrease are, the rise in duty on industrial alcohol—viz, from 150 to 220 francs per hectoliter—and the decrease in price from 31 to 29 francs. The price in former years was about 35 francs.

### COAL AND COKE INDUSTRY.

The coal-mining industry was most unsatisfactory during the past year in comparison with conditions in 1900. Out of 10 companies in this department, only 4 show an increase in production. This state may be justly attributed to continued strikes and the unsettled condition of labor, as well as to stagnation in trade. One of the principal demands of the strikers is that miners at the age of 50 years, or after twenty years' service, irrespective of age, shall be allowed a pension at the rate of 700 francs per annum. This demand of course created great dissension, and for several months, a general strike was feared. The agitation has not entirely ceased.

Until the port of Dunkirk (the only port in this consular district) shall have had its facilities increased, there will be very little chance for the importation of American coal.

The annexed table will show the quantity of coal and coke produced, also the increase and decrease in the different mines.

### CANAL IMPROVEMENTS.

It is proposed to make several improvements in this consular district—viz, a canal from the river Escaut to the Meuse, the Chiero canal, and the Northern canal.

The proposed canal from the Escaut to the Meuse is to be 146.360 kilometers long, and the estimated cost is 88,000,000 of francs.

The Chiero canal, a continuation of the one above named, will be 95 kilometers long, and cost about 43,000,000 francs; and the Northern canal, which will comprise 3 sections (Arleux to Perronne, Perronne to Ham, and Ham to Noyon), will be about 94½ kilometers long, and is estimated to cost 60,000,000 francs.

### NEW INDUSTRIES.

There is very little to report with regard to new industries. The general stagnation of trade has not induced manufacturers to build new mills or to remodel old ones, although a few cotton and flax makers have enlarged their mills and put in modern machinery in order to hold their own against formidable competition.

A new conditioning house opened its doors January 1, 1902. It is fitted with the latest improvements, the old system of hot-air ovens giving heat of 120° to 130° having been abandoned for steam coils giving a temperature of 110°. The variations in heat in any part of the oven are thus not more than 1° or 2°, whereas under the old system the difference was often 12° to 15°.

A boot and shoe manufacturer of Valenciennes, after thoroughly testing an American boot-making machine, was so impressed with its speed and the finish of the boots that he has had his old machinery removed and replaced by American apparatus.

### AMERICAN MACHINERY.

There is a large field in this district for all kinds of American machinery, as well as for produce. Labor-saving machinery especially is in demand; also hardware, office supplies, bicycles, type-writers, motor cars, farming implements, buggies, etc. In order to facilitate sale of these goods, however, a thoroughly competent agent, understanding the language and something of the system of doing business in this country, should make personal solicitations, as catalogues, even though they be in the language of the country, are very often never read.

## REPORTS FROM CONSULAR AGENCIES.

### CAUDRY.

The principal industries at this agency consist of the manufacture of laces, mosquito and other nets, and embroideries, weaving, and beet-root sugar.

#### LACES AND TULLES.

This, the principal industry of Caudry, has passed through a grave crisis, which has deprived many workmen of work. Three years ago, there was a general strike of such proportions that, out of 1,500 hands employed in the manufacture of lace, only about 100 continued to work. Two hundred were not members of the union, but as a rule, they made common cause with union men.

The strike lasted three months, the men receiving financial aid to the amount of 120,000 francs from union men at Calais and St. Quentin, towns where similar industries exist, so that in the end manufacturers were compelled to grant their demands.

The manufacture is divided into several branches: (1) Machine-made lace (principal branch); (2) Plain net, tulle grec and point d'esprit; and (3) Curtain lace.

For the past year, there has been a large manufacture in the first branch of silk lace flounces 45 centimeters wide and galloon insertions, the value of which may be estimated at about 9,000,000 of francs. More than half of this was bought by the United States.

In the second branch, the sale of plain nets and tulle grecs, flourishing two years ago, has decreased to such an extent that manufacturers have little profit. Point d'esprit is still in demand and brings remunerative prices, but the manufacture is limited, as there are only ten machines in Caudry. The machines are too costly to be in general use. They are worth 45,000 francs each.

The third branch, curtain, lace, or bobbinet, has been less prosperous during the two past years than ever before. There is strong competition and tulle grec is also largely used for curtains.

Machinery is being changed. Factories are increasing their apparatus in order to fill orders more rapidly, and altering them for the manufacture of round mesh, the square mesh having fallen into disfavor.

Before the close of the year, the machinery at Caudry will be increased at least one-tenth. Commercial transactions with the United States are also on the point of change. American firms are abandoning intermediate commission houses and establishing offices, with employees of their own. Messrs. Wilson & Son, Levi Sondheimer & Co., Marshall Field & Co., Goldenberg Brothers, the Claflin Company, limited, Sidenberg & Co., and Vom Baur have had agencies here for several years past.

Although Caudry goods to the amount of $1,000,000 have been exported to the United States, not more than $13,361 worth has been invoiced at Caudry. The greater part was packed in Calais, and many goods were packed in Caudry and invoiced elsewhere. Not one meter of plain or mosquito net or spot net is made or finished in Calais, and yet these articles are constantly exported to the United States as from that place.

### EMBROIDERIES.

Thread embroidery seems to have fair prospects, and many sales have already been made to the United States.

### BEET-ROOT SUGAR.

Beet-root sugar manufacture, one of the most important industries in the north of France, is declining. Beet roots with a density of 7° that once commanded from 28 to 30 francs ($5.40 to $5.79) per thousand kilos (2,204 pounds) will be sold for 15 francs ($2.90) during the present year. Cultivators have consequently planted less than one-half the usual quantity, and have replaced beets by wheat and oats.

### TRANSPORTATION.

Changes are to be made in transportation methods, principally for coal. The facilities of the canal uniting the Oise to the Escant from above St. Quentin to Douai have been doubled, and to compete with this line the Northern Railway is laying a double track from Douai to St. Just.

There is also a proposition to build a new canal between the basin of the Escant and the Sambre from Valenciennes to Landrecies, thus permitting the workshops of the north to compete more advantageously with the metal industry of Hautmont and coal of Belgian origin.

### DUNKIRK.

The annexed statistics for the last year show that the traffic at this port continues to progress favorably, the registered tonnage being higher than ever before. This is due to the development of the regular lines between Dunkirk and the Argentine Republic and Indo-China, referred to in my report of last year.

The reduction in harbor dues for the regular lines will still further promote traffic, and it is expected that new lines to the west coast of Africa and to Russia will soon be established.

Parliament has not yet definitely adopted the bill for new dock works, but it is to be hoped that it will be voted this year, as the need of extension of the docks is more obvious every year.

There are no new industries and none can be looked for until after the removal of the fortifications.

Dunkirk is a sanitary station with a lazaret, where sick seamen are cared for. The quarantine quay is one of the docks, and the chamber of commerce has called the attention of the Government to the necessity of transferring the sanitary buildings to the east of the channel. This will have the double advantage of permitting the present quarantine quay to be used for loading and discharging ships and of isolating the said buildings and giving more security for the public health. The cost of constructing a special tidal quay to be used for this purpose has been estimated at 1,200,000 francs, half of which will be included in the general expenses for the improvement of the harbor and the other half paid through a loan raised by the chamber of commerce, redeemable within sixty years and guaranteed by proceeds of the tonnage dues.

## LILLE.

Lille, the commercial and industrial center of the Department of the North and Calais, has a population of 250,000.

Financial, industrial, and commercial conditions for 1901 were disastrous. Since 1879–80, the state of affairs has never been so precarious. The overproduction of 1900 and foreign competition are considered the causes of this general crisis.

The local manufacturer, according to the annual report of the Lille Chamber of Commerce, is handicapped by increasing taxation, and is unable, therefore, to compete successfully with the English, Belgian, and German manufacturers. This great industrial center is utterly lacking in modern machinery and tools, and can not for this reason turn out good work at a profit. The necessity of modernizing the workshop has been recognized. The moment is propitious for the introduction of American machinery and tools. No district of France offers a larger and more varied field than this. The following statistics speak for themselves:

| Industry. | Establishments. | Steam boilers. | Horsepower. |
|---|---|---|---|
| Mines, quarries, etc | 802 | 820 | 49,058 |
| Iron works | 485 | 1,300 | 58,384 |
| Agriculture, etc | 449 | 599 | 4,074 |
| Industry, alimentary | 1,851 | 2,110 | 85,519 |
| Chemical works, etc | 246 | 458 | 11,579 |
| Textile | 946 | 2,584 | 187,208 |
| Wood turning, furniture making, etc | 126 | 135 | 1,478 |
| Paper mills, printing | 40 | 77 | 3,299 |
| Electrical production | 25 | 50 | 3,299 |
| Building enterprises | 473 | 584 | 8,244 |
| Public works | 24 | 56 | 942 |
| Total | 4,567 | 8,722 | 357,994 |

### COTTON AND LINEN.

The cotton industry for the moment is prosperous. The district of Lille has 150 factories, with over 1,000,000 spindles, and 60,000 in course of construction. A large proportion of the cotton goods exported from France is produced here. The consumption of cotton for 1899 was about 500,000,000 pounds, much of which came from America. France imported 713,684 bales from America this year against 703,695 bales a year ago. Brokers assure me that American cotton would have a greater sale here if our merchants would give more attention to the packing of the bales, and guarantee their contents. It is suggested that American merchants should establish responsible agencies here in order to guarantee the buyer against fraud. The confidence of the spinner gained, American cottons would soon gain the ascendency over Egyptian. Egyptian brokers always sell their cotton at American prices.

The linen industry in Lille is renowned. There are 60 mills, with 250,000 spindles and 15,000 hands, and conditions are prosperous.

Attention is also given to this industry in Amentieres, Gorgue, Bailleul, Hazebrouck, and other neighboring towns.

The annual consumption of flax for the linen industry amounts to 20,000,000 pounds grown in this department and 140,000,000 pounds imported from Russia. The annual output of spun flax is valued at 50,000,000 francs, or about $10,000,000. One hundred cloth factories produce yearly 160,000,000 pounds of linen cloth and canvas. The production of the neighboring towns is estimated at the same total.

The exportation of fancy cotton and linen goods to the United States is important. The invoices for various reasons are not legalized at this consular agency. American buyers, according to the testimony of a prominent manufacturer, prefer to do business with large exporting houses situated outside the district of manufacture. These houses, it is said, invoice goods at a lower price than is demanded by the manufacturer.

### EXPOSITION.

The International Exposition at Lille offers an opportunity to study the commerce and products of this department. The gallery of machines contains English, Belgian, and German exhibits. The agricultural department comprises almost all the products of temperate regions. Three hundred thousand persons are employed in this portion of France in cultivating the soil. The last wheat returns show that this department produced 40 hectoliters (113 bu.) for every hectare (2,471 acres), or a total of 7,000,000 hectoliters (19,859,000 bu.) of wheat, the same quantity of oats, 700,000 hectoliters (1,985,900 bu.) of barley, and 600,000 (1,702,200 bu.) of rye. Potatoes and beet root for fodder take up 55,000 hectares (135,905 acres), and give a result in weight of 12,000,000 hundredweight.

Beet root for sugar is planted in 80,000 hectares (197,680 acres), and furnishes 25,000,000 hundredweight of root to about 100 sugar factories. The cultivation of flax of excellent quality is steadily increasing, and at present covers 5,000 hectares (12,355 acres).

American farming implements are much used. Machinery for creameries would have a large field and an excellent sale.

The grounds and buildings of the exposition are almost entirely illuminated by acetylene gas. Much money is being expended to render acetylene popular. The people who have largely promoted the exposition are the manufacturers of acetylene gas and industrial alcohol.

The great distilleries of the north, owing to the enormous taxation on spirits, are now producing denatured or sterilized alcohol for industrial purposes. This effort has received the support and encouragement of the minister of agriculture. The distilleries are capable of producing annually 180,000,000 to 210,000,000 gallons of alcohol.

All the attractions of the exposition are of American origin, and are under the management of Mr. Kiralfy, of New York.

W. P. ATWELL, *Consul.*

ROUBAIX, *July 18, 1902.*

*Principal imports and exports of the consular district of Roubaix during the year 1901.*

| Articles. | Value. | Articles. | Value. |
|---|---|---|---|
| **IMPORTS.** | | **EXPORTS.** | |
| Cereals | $12,186,126 | Caoutchouc | $1,173,070 |
| Chemicals | 8,168,411 | Cereals | 81,840 |
| Chicory | 254,508 | Chalk | 20,147 |
| Coal | 72,818 | Chemicals | 6,269,465 |
| Copper | 3,498,263 | Chicory | 40,655 |
| Cotton | 5,186,276 | Coal | 232,796 |
| Cotton tissues | 276,106 | Copper | 1,147,161 |
| Dyes | 323,051 | Cotton | 1,850,027 |
| Flax | 4,665,508 | Cotton tissues | 665,711 |
| Grease | 480,897 | Dress goods | 5,005,885 |
| Hemp | 736,873 | Drills | 2,600,675 |
| Hops | 408,000 | Flax, combed, waste, etc | 570,179 |
| Iron and steel | 928,637 | Grease | 271,319 |
| Iron, cast | 192,878 | Iron and steel | 3,457,041 |
| Jute | 2,394,962 | Iron, cast | 21,154 |
| Lead | 20,384 | Machinery | 2,197,760 |
| Lumber | 1,577,696 | Malt | 580,259 |
| Machinery | 5,454,880 | Oils | 347,370 |
| Nitrate of soda | 8,100,457 | Paper, cardboard, etc | 957,296 |
| Oil cake | 558,762 | Pottery | 558,869 |
| Oils: | | Spirits and liqueurs | 775,451 |
|    Heavy | 2,296,970 | Skins | 1,792,186 |
|    Petroleum | 971,221 | Tools | 264,795 |
| Paper and cardboard | 887,177 | Upholstery goods | 1,877,919 |
| Pottery | 2,737,982 | Wool | 789,999 |
| Skins | 775,808 | Wool, combed | 2,099,431 |
| Tools and accessories | 424,258 | Wool waste | 6,190,765 |
| Wool | 45,762,343 | Yarns of all kinds | 3,600,213 |
| Wool waste | 32,581 | Zinc | 1,091,721 |
| Yarns of all kinds | 1,594,089 | All other articles | 167,736,089 |
| Zinc | 28,918,818 | | |
| All other articles | 203,034,185 | | |
|    Total | 317,138,606 |    Total | 213,876,698 |

*Exports declared for the United States from the consular district of Roubaix for the fiscal year ended June 30, 1902.*

| Articles. | Value. | Articles. | Value. |
|---|---|---|---|
| Baskets | $589 | Lace goods | $7,743 |
| Bleaching powder | 9,275 | Leather goods | 729 |
| Bluing | 298 | Linen goods | 589 |
| Chemicals | 80,376 | Machinery | 70,795 |
| Colors, aniline | 2,570 | Parchment | 855 |
| Cotton goods | 7,372 | Pease | 91 |
| Cotton thread | 4,973 | Perfumery | 833 |
| Cotton waste | 1,484 | Pitch | 1,601 |
| Dogs, bull | 613 | Plain nets | 808 |
| Dress goods | 483,216 | Potash | 88,013 |
| Flax | 74,768 | Potatoes | 5,233 |
| Flax, combed | 1,955 | Rope, manila | 9,558 |
| Flax thread | 4,082 | Sateen | 4,087 |
| Flax and tow | 10,195 | Seeds | 8,776 |
| Flax waste | 43,591 | Soap lyes | 9,953 |
| Glycerin | 9,679 | Sheepskins | 82,840 |
| Grease | 52,643 | Stonework | 1,775 |
| Hair, cow | 2,007 | Table covers | 11,617 |
| Hardware | 388 | Upholstery goods | 317,308 |
| Hides, goat | 2,458 | Vestings and linings | 1,567 |
| Hosiery goods | 899 | Wool waste | 8,063 |
| Indigotin | 788 | Wool yarns | 4,788 |
| Jacquard cards | 149 | | |
| Jute yarns | 883 |    Total | 1,850,315 |

*Coal and coke production in the consular district of Roubaix during the year 1901.*

| Name of mine. | 1901. | 1900. | Increase. | Decrease. | Number of pits. |
|---|---|---|---|---|---|
| **COAL.** | *Tons.* | *Tons.* | *Tons.* | *Tons.* | |
| Ansin | 2,881,750 | 8,105,501 | ............ | 228,751 | 20 |
| Aniche | 1,150,785 | 1,161,952 | ............ | 11,167 | 9 |
| Douchy | 352,605 | 395,028 | ............ | 42,423 | 4 |
| Vicoigne | 122,892 | 140,414 | ............ | 17,522 | 1 |
| Crespin | 76,009 | 71,416 | 4,958 | ............ | 1 |
| Marly | 18,307 | 18,600 | ............ | 298 | 1 |
| Azincourt | 106,206 | 108,055 | 8,151 | ............ | 1 |
| Thivencelles | 138,744 | 138,479 | 265 | ............ | 3 |
| Escarpelle | 716,574 | 750,858 | ............ | 84,284 | 7 |
| Flines-les-Raches | 138,681 | 132,221 | 6,410 | ............ | 2 |
| Total | 5,692,508 | 6,007,524 | 14,419 | 329,440 | 49 |
| **COKE.** | | | | | |
| Aniche | 152,458 | 172,497 | ............ | 20,099 | ......... |
| Ansin | 204,660 | 290,025 | ............ | 85,365 | ......... |
| Azincourt | 36,901 | 77,552 | ............ | 40,651 | ......... |
| Douchy | 123,755 | 147,147 | ............ | 23,392 | ......... |
| Escarpelle | 80,543 | 101,866 | ............ | 21,323 | ......... |
| Total | 598,317 | 789,087 | ............ | 190,770 | ......... |

## DUNKIRK.

*Principal articles of import and export during the year 1901.*

### IMPORTS.

| Articles. | Quantity. | Articles. | Quantity. |
|---|---|---|---|
| | *Tons.* | | *Tons.* |
| Wool | 130,544 | Olive oil | 661 |
| Tallow | 2,271 | Palm oil | 3,170 |
| Wheat | 41,995 | Coal | 186,984 |
| Barley | 156,325 | Manganese | 18,978 |
| Oats | 57,404 | Ore: | |
| Oleaginous seeds | 175,344 |   Iron | 178,404 |
| Molasses | 264 |   Zinc | 40,415 |
| Wood: | |   Lead | 5,510 |
|   For buildings | 69,377 |   Copper | 10,113 |
|   For dyeing | 980 | Cast iron | 5,731 |
|   Spars, etc | 10,626 | Lead | 759 |
| Flax and tow | 35,490 | Nitrate of soda | 182,483 |
| Jute | 35,249 | Maize | 78,915 |
| Hemp | 5,532 | Rice | 18,000 |
| Cotton | 22,155 | Machines for agriculture | 1,187 |
| Oil cake | 42,326 | Hides, large, dry, or fresh | 557 |
| Pyrite | 85,759 | Sheepskins, small, and others | 710 |
| Bitumen | 2,134 | Guano | 812 |
| Petroleum | 51,813 | Manure | 8,626 |

### EXPORTS.

| Articles. | Quantity. | Articles. | Quantity. |
|---|---|---|---|
| | *Tons.* | | *Tons.* |
| Tallow | 2,187 | Cement | 14,518 |
| Wool | 2,307 | Coal | 49,446 |
| Flax and tow | 597 | Block chalk | 8,010 |
| Flour | 18,456 | Potash | 1,718 |
| Linseed | 1,097 | Glycerin | 158 |
| Sugar: | | Chicory | 554 |
|   Refined | 5,106 | Starch | 791 |
|   Brown | 247,347 | Stearin candles | 501 |
| Hay and straw | 13,967 | Glue | 534 |
| Bran | 80 | Hardware | 498 |
| Rags | 2,459 | Glass: | |
| Oil cake | 3,362 |   Polished | 802 |
| Phosphate | 16,377 |   Window | 790 |
| Slates | 2,285 |   Empty bottles | 5,000 |

*Principal articles of import and export during the year 1901—Continued.*

EXPORTS—Continued.

| Articles. | Quan- tity. | Articles. | Quan- tity. |
|---|---|---|---|
| Jute: | *Tons.* | Rails: | *Tons.* |
| Yarn | 2,362 | Iron | 819 |
| Tissues | 261 | Steel | 31,322 |
| Sacks | 118 | Champagne wines | 577 |
| Linen tissues | 396 | Spirits of all sorts | 2,585 |
| Empty barrels | 1,785 | Steel, in bars | 2,624 |
| Oil: | | Iron bars, or rounds | 14,797 |
| Linseed | 1,518 | | |
| Ground nuts | 1,260 | | |
| Colza | 173 | | |

*Principal articles in trade with the United States during the year 1901.*

IMPORTS.

| Articles. | Quan- tity. | Articles. | Quan- tity. |
|---|---|---|---|
| | *Tons.* | | *Tons.* |
| Machines for agriculture | 1,156 | Wood for building purposes | 7,498 |
| Machines (electro-dynamos) | 6 | Cotton in bales | 4,840 |
| Machinery | 68 | Oil cake | 4,044 |
| Maize | 12,313 | Natural phosphate | 24,801 |
| Wheat | 81,606 | Petroleum (crude) | 34,818 |
| Oats | 3,835 | Mineral oil | 4,850 |
| Cotton seed | 17 | Copper in bars, etc | 5,392 |
| Cotton oil | 246 | Pyrolignite of lime | 47 |

EXPORTS.

| Articles. | Quan- tity. | Articles. | Quan- tity. |
|---|---|---|---|
| | *Tons.* | | *Tons.* |
| Sardines (preserved) | 83 | Block chalk | 1,500 |
| Grease (animal) | 16 | Soap lyes | 89 |
| Rags | 189 | Glycerin | 55 |

BENJAMIN MOREL, *Consular Agent.*

## ROUEN.

The general trade conditions of the port of Rouen during the year 1901 were not good, and during the first half of the present year there has been no improvement. The custom-house receipts show a considerable diminution.

*Customs receipts at Rouen.*

| Character. | 1899. | 1900. | 1901. |
|---|---|---|---|
| Customs duties | $7,849,430 | $7,790,482 | $6,668, |
| Navigation tax | 87,626 | 106,258 | 93,839 |
| Salt tax | 12,567 | 11,998 | 17,668 |
| Total | 7,949,628 | 7,908,788 | 6,744,245 |

The traffic of this port during the year 1901 and the first half of this year has also been very much less than that of preceding years. During 1900, there entered 2,031 vessels with 2,302,743 tons, and 2,018 vessels cleared with 231,474 tons. During 1901, there entered 1,758 vessels with 1,984,818 tons, and 1,762 vessels cleared with 270,902 tons. For the first months of this year, traffic has been very dull, the quays at times almost deserted, and the workmen circulating petitions for help. During last month (September, 1902), 127 vessels entered with 146,881 tons (4,000 of which were discharged by two vessels at Croisset), and 128 vessels cleared with 11,879 tons. During the corresponding month of last year, 212,204 tons entered and cleared. Since the beginning of this year—that is, until the end of September—1,436,554 tons have entered, against 1,691,125 for the same period in 1901.

The principal imports of this port are coal, timber, and wine, and during the past year these three imports, from three distinct, but temporary causes, have decreased. The number of tons of coal fell in twelve months from 1,264,108 tons to 944,587 tons, on account of the Transvaal war and the depressed state of the continental metallurgic industry; the amount of timber in the same length of time decreased from 352,449 to 318,146 tons, because of the demolition following the world's fair, and the import of wine, which usually comes from Spain and Algeria, fell from 220,360 to 155,752 tons, because of the abundant harvests in middle and southern France.

The inactivity of this port, however, has a deeper cause than those above mentioned. Industrial and commercial questions are gradually giving way to political ones, not only in Normandy—where the privileges of private distillers (bouilleurs de cru) are threatened by the Government, and the alcoholic industry has already been virtually destroyed by the new régime of drinks, and where the agreements stipulated at the Brussels sugar conference threaten the ruin of the sugar-beet industry—but all over France.

Since the last issue of Commercial Relations, the Republic has undergone many changes. A new ministry has come into power; a new chamber has been elected; important diplomatic and prefectural changes have been made; the new law of ten and one-half hours' labor has come into effect, causing thousands of workmen to quit work; customs receipts have steadily diminished and public expenses increased to such an extent that a loan of 130,000,000 francs ($25,900,000) is spoken of as the only remedy to relieve the financial embarrassment of the Government.

### FRANCE'S PUBLIC EXPENSES.

In 1874, after the liquidation of the war of 1870, the ordinary expenses of the Government amounted to 2,554,000,000 francs ($492,-922,000). For 1900 they were 3,537,000,000 francs ($682,641,000)—an augmentation of 983,000,000 francs ($189,719,000) in twenty-six years of peace. The average augmentation of the ordinary expenses from 1874 to 1898 was 36,000,000 francs ($6,948,000) annually. The increase of 1899 over 1898 is 43,000,000 francs ($8,299,000), and 1900 is superior to 1899 by 60,000,000 francs ($11,580,000). This country supports the greatest budget of the world. Its public debt at present is more than 30,000,000,000 francs ($5,790,000,000). The net interest upon its debt in 1874 amounted to 985,000,000 francs ($190,105,000), since which time, by the transformation of stocks, it has been lessened 108,000,000 francs ($20,844,000). To-day, however, instead of being 108,000,000 francs ($20,844,000) less, it is actually more than 1,152,-000,000 francs ($222,336,000). Naturally, the wheels of industry turn slowly beneath the burden of taxes which such an interest demands. There is a rent tax, a dog tax, a land tax, a vehicle tax, a door and window tax, besides two kinds of customs duties on all food—one on foreign imports, another on consumption.

## GOVERNMENT REVENUE.

By examining the different branches of receipts, it is seen that the amount for the first seven months of this year, 341,500,000 francs ($65,909,500), is 10,500,000 francs ($2,026,500) less than the Government's estimate. For the first seven months of the present year, the revenue derived from exchange transactions was 333,000 francs ($64,269) less than the Government's estimate. The tax on personal property, which perhaps more than anything else testifies to the progress or stagnation of a country, has amounted to 59,185,000 francs ($11,422,705), being only 41,500 francs ($8,900) less than the Government's estimate, but 2,202,000 francs ($424,986) less than the receipts during the first seven months of last year. In uniting the four branches of revenue which show more than all others the industrial and commercial activity of the French, viz—registration, postal, tax on bank operations, and personal property tax—there is found to be a deficit of 7,000,000 francs ($1,351,000).

The amount of customs duties for the first seven months of this year has been 212,352,000 francs ($40,984,946); that is, 32,000,000 francs ($6,366,000) less than the Government's estimate, and 8,900,000 francs ($1,717,700) less than the receipts for the corresponding seven months of last year. Customs receipts are much greater, of course, when there is a bad home harvest of wheat or of wine, especially wheat.

Internal-revenue receipts—sugar, salt, and monopolies not included—are 24,232,000 francs ($4,676,776) less than the estimate, and 28,608,000 francs ($5,522,344) less than in the seven months of last year. It is always alcohol which shows the greatest deficiency. On this article, in the single month of July last, the deficit was 6,500,000 francs ($1,254,500) as compared with the estimate, and 2,000,000 francs ($386,000) as compared with last year. Despite the 50 per cent augmentation of the tax on alcohol, which was intended to lessen the consumption of this article and to increase the consumption of home-raised wine, the tax on alcohol produces no more than before 1901, when the lower tax was in vogue. So far, it has produced less. For the first seven months of 1902, it amounted to 172,923,000 francs ($33,374,139), whereas during the same period in 1900 it amounted to 175,857,000 francs ($33,940,401), or 3,000,000 francs ($579,000) more.

As to the revenue on salt, it is somewhat more constant, being only 87,000 francs ($16,791) less than the estimate, and 366,000 francs ($70,638) less than that of last year.

But sugar shows an enormous deficiency. The amount for the first seven months of this year is 81,284,000 francs ($15,689,812), which is 8,877,000 francs ($1,713,261) less than the estimate, and 4,028,000 francs ($777,404) less than last year. Some years, the tax on sugar has produced 200,000,000 francs ($38,600,000), and even more.

In counting the supplementary credits, the expenses of guaranteed interests defrayed by emission of bonds, there is found to be a deficit greater than 200,000,000 francs ($38,600,000).

It must not be forgotten that the fiscal system of France has not the support of an increasing population. In England, there are 400,000 and in Germany 800,000 new producers and consumers and taxpayers annually.

## FRANCE'S FOREIGN INVESTMENTS.

The French do not emigrate, but under existing conditions, their capital does. A Rouen merchant, one evening not long since, left his funds in his office preparatory to carrying them to the bank on the morrow. They were stolen. An ordinary theft usually passes unnoticed, but this one points a lesson. Years ago, half the value of a theft of 20,000 francs ($3,860) would have been represented by Government bonds; the other half by French railway and industrial stock. Foreign investment would have been insignificant. In the theft spoken of, however, the 20,000 francs were all represented by foreign bonds.

An examination of probated wills in France shows that values represented by Russian, Swiss, Hungarian, Swedish, Norwegian, Danish, and Dutch State and industrial bonds are exceedingly abundant—investments that years ago were never made.

Some time ago, the minister of foreign affairs addressed to the French diplomatic and consular officers a circular, as follows:

State if there exists in your district—
1. Any French commercial houses? Under what form are they established? At how much do you estimate the value of their property, real and personal? In what business are they engaged, and do they trade mostly with France and the country in which they are established? Do they carry on any important operations with other countries?
2. French real estate—its value?
3. French agricultural interests—their nature, extent, and income?
4. French credits open to commercial, industrial, or agricultural enterprises—under what form have they been opened? Are they guaranteed or not?
5. French banks—their field of operation?
6. Vessels flying the French flag plying at that port?
7. French capital engaged in maritime or fluvial navigation enterprises?
8. French railroad investments—their income?
9. French capital invested in mines and quarries—nature of the latter? How much capital have they absorbed? What is their income?
10. French capital invested in industry—their nature, capital, and income?
11. French agricultural establishments—their regulation? Are they run by Frenchmen?
12. Do there exist other French interests belonging to anyone domiciled in your district, or to any Frenchman living in France or another country? What is their value, extent, and income?

From the reports in answer to this circular, it is found that France's foreign investments in the five parts of the world amount to about 30,000,000,000 francs ($5,770,000,000), a figure, by a singular coincidence, equaling the country's debt. Of this amount, Europe naturally has the majority. Russia and Spain first; England, Austria, Turkey, Belgium, and Roumania following in order. In Africa, the greatest amounts are invested in Egypt and the Transvaal; in Asia, in China and Asiatic Turkey; in America, in the United States, Mexico, the Argentine Republic, and Colombia. The total for Europe is 21,000,000,000 francs ($3,983,000,000); for Asia, 1,121,000,000 francs ($216,353,000); for Africa, 3,693,000,000 francs ($712,749,000); for North America, 1,058,000,000 francs ($204,194,000); for Central America, 290,000,000

francs ($55,970,000); for South America, 2,624,000,000 francs ($506,-
432,000); for Oceania, 57,000,000 francs ($11,000,000).   These figures
give a grand total of 29,855,000,000 francs ($5,762,015,000).   It must
be remembered, however, that this is still not the total amount, as those
making the reports left out all figures which they could not verify as
exact.   To stop this emigration of capital, to balance the budget, to
lessen expenses and increase receipts, are problems which, together
with the specter of depopulation stalking in upon every census sheet,
necessarily occupy the public mind to the neglect of ordinary commercial and industrial questions.

### IMPORTATIONS AND EXPORTATIONS.

The reverse side of the medal is the recent small increase of importations.   According to the customs statistics, the value of importations for the first eight months of the present year amounts to 2,942,-
964,000 francs ($567,992,052) and the exports to 2,742,626,000 francs
($529,326,718).
Importations have been less by 13,657,000 francs ($2,635,801) than
in the corresponding eight months of 1901.   On the contrary, exportations during the first eight months of this year have exceeded by a
value of 115,101,000 francs ($22,214,493) those of the corresponding
period of last year.

### IMPORTS AT ROUEN.

*Coal.*—The imports of this article at Rouen have greatly increased
within the last few years.   In 1894, the British consul at this place
said in his annual report: "Rouen appears to require from 500,000
to 600,000 tons of coal annually."   In 1896, there entered 547,895 tons;
in 1897, 563,396; in 1898, 562,246; in 1899, 707,270; in 1900, 1,264,108;
and in 1901, 1,040,362.   The sudden augmentation of the last three
years is due mostly to the strikes in French coal regions.
The proximity of the northern coal fields to this port would seem to
indicate that considerable French coal is brought here; but the
amount is very little—about one-eighth.   The quantity coming from
Belgium is infinitesimal.   England furnishes nearly all, perhaps
because of better quality, and the excellent water transportation
facilities at Rouen.   If the latter did not exist, the import of coal
would be about one-half of what it is at present.   For example, of the
1,040,362 tons brought here last year, 682,704 tons were transshipped.
Seagoing vessels moored here discharge from one side onto the quay
for Rouen consignment, and at the same time, unload from the other
side into lighters for canal delivery at Paris and other fluvial ports of
the Seine.
The only cargo of American coal ever landed on the Rouen quays
was brought by the British vessel *Westgate* last year.   It appears
impossible, however, for American coal to enter northern France in
foreign bottoms, when English, Belgium, and German coal fields have
the advantage of proximity.   Strikes present no real opportunity for
the American product.   A strike is an abnormal condition which can
be only temporarily considered.   But apart from all such conditions,
it must be admitted, as our consul at Havre, who has studied the
question thoroughly, says, that "the most important factor in the creation of a permanent export trade in American coal is the solution of
the question of cheap ocean transportation."   The American article

can not hope to enter northern France until this question is solved. British vessels for American coal means British coal for France, at least this part of it.

*Grain and flour.*—For the last five years, the imports of oats, wheat, rye, etc., and flour at Rouen have been:

| Years. | Entered. | Cleared. |
|---|---|---|
| | *Tons.* | *Tons.* |
| 1897 | 238,041 | 252,292 |
| 1898 | 371,486 | 442,868 |
| 1899 | 253,162 | 183,546 |
| 1900 | 227,835 | 208,567 |
| 1901 | 320,852 | 332,223 |

It will be seen that, taken as a whole, the clearances and entrances are about the same, this being due to the great agricultural resources of this district. Occasionally, a shipload of wheat and oats comes here from the United States, but the cargo is invariably consigned to Paris or some other inland destination. In the table given above, oats figure for by far the greatest quantity, being 202,334 tons of the total 320,852 tons entering in 1901. A few tons of hard Hungarian wheat come here for mixing purposes.

*Wine.*—The greatest import next to coal is wine, but, unlike other agricultural imports, it nearly all remains here. Most of it comes from Spain and Bordeaux. The former is generally used for mixing with native wine to give body and color. It is said to be mixed with a spirit strength as high as possible within the limits prescribed for wine, and the alcohol has generally been furnished to Spain by Germany, where the free admission of corn permits cheap distillation. The last four years show that the movement of the product has been as follows:

| Year. | Entered. | Cleared. |
|---|---|---|
| | *Tons.* | *Tons.* |
| 1898 | 244,672 | 8,826 |
| 1899 | 299,016 | 10,228 |
| 1900 | 220,360 | 22,648 |
| 1901 | 155,752 | 8,545 |

*Timber and wood.*—Because of its bulky character, timber will always form one of the main imports of an inland port like that of Rouen. The greater part of the imports of timber here consists of white and red pine from the Baltic ports of Russia and Sweden. Some oak also comes from Austria, and a little walnut from Spain. For the last four years, the quantity of lumber entering and leaving here has been as follows:

| Year. | Entered. | Cleared. |
|---|---|---|
| | *Tons.* | *Tons.* |
| 1898 | 323,017 | 264,106 |
| 1899 | 335,587 | 256,060 |
| 1900 | 352,449 | 304,078 |
| 1901 | 318,146 | 282,082 |

From the above, it will be seen that about 90 per cent of the lumber brought here is transshipped by the fluvial basin to Paris and ports in middle and southern France.

*Petroleum.*—The imports of raw petroleum at Rouen increase yearly. For the four years previous to 1894, they kept between 45,000 and 50,000 tons. The average for the triennial period 1894–1896 was 93,000 tons. In 1897, the imports were 111,000 tons; in 1898, 120,339 tons; in 1899, 117,000 tons; in 1900, 139,614 tons; in 1901, 145,773 tons. This more than treble increase in less than ten years is partly accounted for by the enlargement of refineries on the banks of the petroleum basin, and partly by the additional accommodation provided for petroleum vessels frequenting this port. It has been remarked that no import at Rouen has had a more vigorous expansion than this, and it is instructive to note that it is one of the very few products on which the customs duties have been reduced since the tariff of 1892. Fifteen months after the new tariff went into effect, a special commercial convention with the United States and Russia reduced the former duties of 18 francs ($3.474) and 25 francs ($4.825) per 100 kilograms (220.46 pounds) to 9 francs ($1.737).

The fiscal burdens on this product have regularly diminished. In 1871, raw petroleum was taxed 20 francs ($3.86) per 100 kilograms (220.46 pounds) on entry, and refined 32 francs ($6.176). Every change since then has removed a restriction and lightened the burden. French agriculturists are at present insisting that the Government should stop the annual payment of 50,000,000 francs ($9,650,000) to America for oil by raising the tariff, thus increasing the use of homemade alcohol.

The director of the oil company here showed me a few days ago samples of oil stoves he had received from headquarters in America, which the company intends to put upon the French market. They probably will bring no profit, or very little, but they consume oil and plenty of it.

### INDUSTRIAL SITUATION OF ROUEN.

Rouen, surrounded by a most fertile agricultural country, producing wheat, the finest vegetables, the famous Norman apples, the Percheron horses, and excellent breeds of cattle, but no cotton, is, strange to say, a great cotton manufacturing center. Cotton is imported here in British bottoms via Liverpool, and reshipped to America in the form of cloth. Cheap labor, economy of manipulation, utilization of by-products, etc., go largely to explain this movement.

*Spinning and weaving.*—The spinning and weaving industries of Rouen have been in a state of more or less marked depression during the last twelve months. During the first part of last year, under the double influence of a reduced stock and high prices, business was brisk, but the low prices which followed, and the tendency of buyers to hold off, in the general belief of a large American cotton crop, contributed to the depression. In December, however, reports from the United States indicating a short crop relieved matters to some extent, and sales began to increase, and at present conditions are better.

*Rouennaries and handkerchiefs.*—Business during 1901 was not good.

In Algeria, the high prices asked caused buyers to order only from day to day in the hope of ameliorated rates. During the last six months, business with Algeria has been better.

Trade with Indo-China and Madagascar has not been animated because of high prices.

*Printed goods.*—For the first nine months of 1901, business was dull because of high prices. The last three months of the year were somewhat better, but customers were still very prudent.

Business with Algeria has not been good, and with Indo-China and Madagascar almost nothing.

*Leather.*—The tanned leather trade has not been prosperous. Sales have been difficult, even at 5 per cent discount. Prices of raw hides, on the other hand, have remained good. This abnormal situation results from important purchases on the part of America and England, both from the countries of production and from European importing markets.

Some tanneries near here have lately gone into liquidation, a condition which naturally renders importers very careful.

*Chemicals.*—Coal, which constitutes such an important factor in the price of chemicals, was somewhat cheaper last year, but the depression under which this industry labored was not greatly relieved. The prospect at present is that the price of coal will advance very materially in the near future.

The acids and sodas are now demanding nearly their normal price. The chlorines feel the effect of the sharp competition of the electric process.

Chemical fertilizers are more and more employed in culture, but sales are scarcely remunerative because of Belgian and English importations.

Nitrate of soda is increasingly employed each year by agriculturists, but prices are high. The reason of this is the understanding between Chilean producers, the strikes, and the diplomatic difficulties between Chile and the Argentine Republic, all of which, of course, limited the production.

### SHIPBUILDING.

Rouen possesses especial advantages for a dockyard. It has been asserted that, while the investments of a shareholder in a shipbuilding yard at Havre or Marseilles could be reduced to ashes in twenty-four hours by the shells of a hostile fleet, no such misfortune could overtake them here. Rouen is secure from the attack of a hostile fleet, for none will ever ascend the Seine. Moreover, a tranquil, natural basin is afforded by the river, and when shipbuilding began here, land suitably placed was to be had for little more than its agricultural value. Every encouragement that nature and a protective government could give favored the construction of a dockyard at Rouen, and promised its financial success.

Accordingly, as far back as 1892, a dozen or more of the richest and most influential men determined to start the enterprise. It was decided at first to construct only sailing ships. The profits over and above those gained by a British shipbuilder would, it was computed, work out approximately thus: The cost of building an iron or steel vessel of 2,000 tons, for example, would be about $70,000 in England. The construction bounty alone on a vessel of this tonnage built in France would be $26,000. According to some, the gain of the shipbuilders would be more than this, for they could demand of the owners a certain proportion of the navigation bounty to be gained by the ship. However this may be, circumstances seemed very favorable to such a scheme, but for many months, it was found nearly impossible to find 200 men, out of Rouen's 160,000, willing to subscribe the necessary capital, $200,000. It was finally done, but from some unaccountable reason, the business has never succeeded. The loss on some of the vessels amounted to as much as 140,000 francs ($27,020). In 1897, conditions became so bad that something had to be done. An issue had already been made of bonds secured upon · the property of the yard, and it was impossible to raise more money in this manner. Nothing was left but to form a new company, and enough capital to finish the four vessels remaining on the stocks was secured only by an issue of shares, which were almost entirely taken up by the shipowners to whom these vessels were to have been delivered. The original shareholders were allowed, in the new company, shares to the value of one-fifth of their original investment, thus losing four-fifths of their capital. With the fresh capital thus raised, the four ships then on the stocks were completed, but for a time, all the slips were vacant and work was practically stopped. Efforts were made to induce foreign capital to take the matter in hand, but doubts were expressed as to whether the bounty on construction would be paid if the yard were in the hands of foreigners. Although the prefect, the mayor of Rouen, and the president of the chamber of commerce waited upon the minister of commerce at Paris and obtained from him an affirmation on this point, no foreign capital was induced to invest. Little was done until March, 1901, when the works were bought by the Chantier of St. Nazaire, which began operations in November of the same year. To all appearances, work now progresses successfully. Since November, 1901, until the end of September, 1902, the present director tells me they have finished and delivered six steel sailing ships of 3,200 tons. Two similar vessels are being prepared for delivery at the end of November. They have also in process of construction two torpedo-boat destroyers and one other vessel for the French navy.

## ALCOHOL AND WINE.

The distillers of grain throughout Normandy have felt severely the effect of the law on drinks. One of the distilleries near here is in liquidation, and another has been compelled to shut down on account of a lack of orders. It is impossible for this industry to struggle against the competition of thousands of gallons of alcohol upon which no tax is paid. Some say that the bounty of 14 per cent on the treacle should be suppressed. This.would be good for beet-root distillers, but it seems nothing can relieve the situation for all, unless the industrial uses of alcohol (lighting, heating, motor force) are increased by law.

The wine trade is not good because of the bad quality and abundant quantity, and the competition of the "bouilleurs de cru," or private distillers.

*Bouilleurs de cru.*—These are the farmers or proprietors who distill wine and cider from cherries or plums from their own harvest. This designation is used to distinguish them from the professional distillers, or those who distill any fruit by whomsoever grown. Bouilleurs de cru are exempt from taxes if they do not retail their product. They are also exempt from declaring their establishments, vessels, etc., which the regular distillers must do. They are exempt from inspection by the employees of the administration of taxes, and they do not have to declare the quantity of brandy or spirits in their possession. According to the law of 1816, these private distillers do not pay the general-consumption tax on wine, spirits, etc., for their own domestic use or for that of their servants or employees. They pay only upon that portion of the product which they sell. The principal object of the law of 1816 was to allow the bouilleurs de cru to place upon the receiver or buyer the burden of the tax on the brandy, etc., which they sold. Except in the exemption from license and bond, the position of the bouilleurs de cru is exactly the same as that of wholesale wine and liquor dealers.

*Legislation of bouilleurs de cru.*—The privileges accorded these private distillers having caused some abuses, the national assembly, by the law of 1872, restricted them by placing them, with certain exceptions, in the same category as professional distillers. This brought forth so many protests, however, that in 1875 the bouilleurs were given the privileges they had enjoyed before and have enjoyed ever since.

The new régime of drinks of January 1, 1901, which placed a heavier tax upon alcohol, was an effort at temperance, in trying to decrease the consumption of alcohol, and an economic measure in attempting to augment the revenue and afford an outlet for the bountiful production of home-raised wine. Neither object has been gained, because the privileges of the bouilleurs de cru allow the new law to be evaded.

The revenue income from drinks during the year 1901 was inferior to that of 1900 by 100,000,000 francs ($19,300,000). It appears that the deficit this year will be still greater. In a comparison of the alcoholic production in 1901 and 1900, published under the direction of the internal revenue, it is found that, from 1900 to 1901, the quantity of alcohol submitted to tax at the homes of the professional and private distillers diminished 300,000 hectoliters (7,925,100 gallons). This astonishing decrease in the production of taxed alcohol is due for the most part to the augmentation of frauds. The minister of finance stated last week that he would urge the Chambers in their coming meeting to regulate the privileges of the bouilleurs de cru, for it is only through these privileges, he is convinced, that such a quantity of taxable product escapes the payment of taxes. It is true that the bouilleurs de cru can sell the alcohol which comes from their own distilled harvest at 400 francs ($77.20) the hectoliter (26.417 gallons), while the cost of production is hardly more than 25 or 30 francs ($4.825 or $5.79).

Opposition to abolishing the privileges of these private distillers comes from those who assert that it is an invasion of personal liberty to prevent a producer from exercising a right over his own production; and that the consumption of alcohol and the damages resulting therefrom will not be less when the cultivator is prohibited from distilling for his own uses, for he will then buy at the wine shop an adulterated alcohol.

### A PROJECTED CROSSING OF THE SEINE.

One serious hindrance to the commercial improvement of this district is the lack of any bridge or means of crossing other than by boat between Rouen and Havre. This inconvenience has for years been a drawback to trade between the two cities, each of which seems disinclined to look with favor upon the other's betterment. Many years ago, both were agreed upon a subterranean passage of the railway line from Havre to Pont-Audemer, and the project was embraced in the law of 1883. Soon after, however, Havre pronounced itself for a viaduct, and held out for it as uncompromisingly as Rouen did for the tunnel. A month ago, the project was seriously taken in hand, and a solution now seems probable. The eminent French engineer, M. Berlier, has expressed an opinion before the chambers of commerce of Rouen and of Havre on the feasibility of a tunnel under the Seine, near Tancarville. He instanced submarine tunnels constructed under the same conditions, such as under the St. Clair, the Hudson, the Clyde, and the Blackwall tunnel under the Thames near Greenwich, which connects the two counties of Middlesex and Kent. The latter he mentioned for two reasons, he said: First, because it is serviceable for foot passengers; secondly, because it is the most recent tunnel constructed. He asserted that when the English wished to communicate with the other side of their principal navigable artery, they invariably preferred the subterranean passage.

After listening attentively to the explanations of Mr. Berlier the Chambers of Commerce voted 10,000 francs ($1,930) each, to defray the cost of supplementary studies which the engineer wished to make before pronouncing the project unqualifiedly sure of success.

The plan of Mr. Berlier, if carried out, will, it is thought, cost from 20,000,000 to 25,000,000 francs ($3,860,000 to $4,825,000).

### IMPROVEMENT OF THE PORT OF ROUEN.

The deepening of the Seine by dredging between Rouen and the sea continues. The project for the amelioration of French ports, adopted by the Chambers of Deputies last January, provides 11,500,000 francs ($2,219,500) for Rouen. The general council of the lower Seine, in its meeting at Rouen last August, proposed that this amount be expended for the following works, to be finished within a period of twelve years:

1. The lengthening of the quays on both sides of the maritime basin, and the uniting of the waterwings of the petroleum basin.
2. Construction of a graving dock and of embankments and waterways at the entrance.
3. Construction of quays on the river south of the wood basin.

The general council, at the same meeting, decided to accord a departmental subsidy of 937,500 francs ($180,937) for improvements in the port of Havre, and 1,191,916 francs ($230,040) in the port of Rouen.

The question of making Paris a seaport, or making a maritime waterway of the Seine between Rouen and Paris, has always occupied public attention to a greater or less extent. When the parliamentary commission, elected to report upon it in 1897, declared it "to be of public utility," much embarrassment was felt among shipping interests at Rouen. But a reassuring note, both to Rouen and Havre, was struck in the Chamber of Deputies the first of this year by the then minister of public works, who said:

The expense of this project exceeds the revenues of the State, and I can not, for my part, agree to a proposition which will increase the burden of taxes.

The minister of public works who has since been appointed has not to my knowledge expressed an opinion, but doubtless will at the coming meeting of the Chambers.

The execution of such a work, if it is ever carried out, will be disastrous to the shipping interests of Rouen, which look unfavorably upon the development of Paris as a seaport, much in the manner that Havre regards the development of the port of Rouen.

## LABOR CONDITIONS.

Like Tennyson's brook, the labor problem in France goes on forever. That it has gained such tremendous proportions seems due to the many laws and restrictions to which labor is subjected. On April the first last, when the new law of ten and one-half hours came into effect, strikes immediately occurred, labor contending for the same rate paid when the law allowed eleven hours.

The law, applying to all workmen, appeared especially unfavorable to those engaged in building. Regardless of the season, all engaged in mining, manufacturing, etc., can work ten hours and a half a day all the year round, but during the short days of winter, masons, carpenters, and all outdoor laborers can put in only seven or eight hours. The question is, Why should these outdoor workmen be limited to ten hours and a half in summer when it is possible to work for twelve hours? If nature handicaps them during winter, why should the Government do so during summer? The employers and employees engaged in the building industries of the city and arrondissement of Rouen, responding to an appeal of the general building syndicate, met some weeks ago and formulated a strong appeal to the Government against the law.

## OCTROI OF ROUEN.

For the month of last August, the octroi duties amounted to 311,300 francs ($60,081), and for the first eight months of the year, to 2,550,000 francs ($486,150), which, compared with the corresponding period of last year, shows a loss of 76,000 francs ($14,668). This falling off has been mostly in duties upon beverages and provender.

There is considerable discussion in Rouen over the advisability of suppressing the octroi, as has been done at Lyons and more recently, at Rheims. Those who favor the change would replace the deficiency by a property tax. The objectors say that such a proceeding would impose upon the Rouennais population alone the payment of the tax, which by the octroi is paid by a floating population, viz, provisioners, buyers, drummers, tourists, etc.; in fact, all who stop at hotels, restaurants, cafés, etc., many of whom have horses with them. They say that the influence of this consumption, considering the receipts of the octroi, is undeniable. Last year, the comparative receipts were:

| Articles. | Receipts. | United States currency. |
|---|---|---|
| | *Francs.* | |
| Drinks and liquids | 1,192,689 | $230,189 |
| Comestibles | 1,190,345 | 229,737 |
| Combustibles | 575,443 | 110,080 |
| Provender | 272,523 | 52,597 |
| Materials | 344,382 | 66,466 |
| rs objects | 97,420 | 18,802 |
| Total | 3,672,802 | 708,851 |

It is thus seen that more than two-thirds of the product of the octroi comes from three sources: Drinks and liquids, comestibles, and provender—a part of which all visitors, travelers, etc., necessarily pay for. On the other hand, the partisans of the suppression of the octroi say that the number of foreign individuals who pass through Rouen represent not more than one out of every 75 inhabitants, and that it is unjust to tax 75 for fear that one will escape.

### FINANCES, RAILWAYS, AND STREET CARS OF ROUEN.

The results of the operations of the Rouen street car lines and funicular railways during 1901 were:

Rouen to Petit-Quevilly (Maletra Society): Receipts, 55,424 francs ($10,697); expenses, 54,607 francs ($10,539); net profit, $158. During the year 1900, the receipts were 64,685 francs ($12,484); expenses, 63,627 francs ($12,280), and net profits $204.

Funicular from Rouen-Eauplet to Bonsecours: This line was suspended in 1901, but began operations four months ago. During 1900, the receipts were 13,899 francs ($2,683); expenses, 20,708 francs ($3,997); loss, $1,314.

Rouen to Bonsecours and Mesnil-Esnard: Receipts, 192,946 francs ($37,239); expenses, 121,276 francs ($23,406); net gain, $13,833. During 1900, the receipts were 174,846 francs ($33,745); expenses, 159,827 francs ($30,847); net gain, $2,897.

Rouen Tramway Company (first line): Receipts, 2,017,239 francs ($389,327); expenses, 1,153,288 francs ($222,585); gain, $166,742. During 1900, the receipts were 1,936,937 francs ($373,829); expenses, 1,088,754 francs ($210,130); profit, $163,699.

Rouen Tramway Company (second line): Receipts, 200,219 francs ($38,642); expenses, 287,923 francs ($55,569); total loss, $16,927. During 1900, the receipts were 194,091 francs ($37,460); expenses, 263,804 francs ($50,914); net loss, $13,454.

THORNWELL HAYNES, *Consul.*

ROUEN, *October 8, 1902.*

---

### MOVEMENT OF THE PORT OF ROUEN.

During the month of December, 1902, 153 vessels discharged on the Rouen quays 156,273 tons of merchandise, and 149 embarked 21,235 tons. During the corresponding month of 1901, the arrivals and departures combined amounted to 162,192 tons, being 25,316 tons more in December, 1902.

The total amount for the year 1902 has been 3,218 vessels, with 2,103,309 tons. In 1901 it was 3,520 vessels, with 1,255,720 tons.

The merchandise discharged during last December was as follows: Coal, 76,347 tons; liquids, 32,209 tons; grains, 4,928 tons; timber, 8,555 tons; billets of wood, 1,100 tons; oil, 11,273 tons; wood fiber (for paper making), 4,300 ton; metals and minerals, 3,341 tons; divers, 11,270 tons.

THORNWELL HAYNES, *Consul.*

ROUEN, *January 5, 1903.*

## FRENCH BUDGET FOR 1903.

In the autumn session of the French Chamber of Deputies, the minister of finances submitted the following budget for 1903:

| Description. | Francs. | U. S. currency. |
|---|---|---|
| Diminution of resources | 124,000,000 | $23,962,000 |
| Augmentation of expenses | 42,000,000 | 8,106,000 |
| Loss in reducing sugar tax to 25 francs | 41,000,000 | 7,913,000 |
| Initial deficit | 207,000,000 | 39,951,000 |

| Details. | Francs. | Total francs. | U. S. currency. | Total U. S. currency. |
|---|---|---|---|---|
| **RESOURCES.** | | | | |
| Conversion of the 3½ per cents | 32,000,000 | | $6,176,000 | |
| Half-quarter of the new 3 per cents | 26,000,000 | | 5,018,000 | |
| Suppression of the redemption of the 560 million francs ($108,080,000) of the savings banks | 22,000,000 | | 4,246,000 | |
| Chinese indemnity | 11,100,000 | | 2,142,300 | |
| Suppression of the annuity of the school fund | 3,700,000 | 94,800,000 | 714,100 | $18,296,400 |
| **NEW RECEIPTS.** | | | | |
| Bouilleurs de cru | 50,000,000 | | 9,650,000 | |
| Tobacco zones | 19,000,000 | | 3,667,000 | |
| Extension of the 4 per cent tax on life annuity | 3,700,000 | | 714,100 | |
| Revision of the mortmain tax on built property | 3,000,000 | | 579,000 | |
| Augmentation of the price of tobacco | 4,000,000 | 79,700,000 | 772,000 | 15,382,100 |
| Sexennial bonds for guarantee of interests | | 44,000,000 | | 8,492,000 |
| Aggregate | | 218,500,000 | | 42,170,500 |

| | Francs. | U. S. currency. |
|---|---|---|
| Excess of resources | 11,500,000 | $2,219,500 |
| Employment of the excess, redemption of the sexennial bonds | 11,000,000 | 2,123,000 |
| Excess of the budget | 500,000 | 96,500 |

From the above, it is seen that there is a deficit of 207,000,000 francs ($39,951,000), as follows: Sixty-four million francs ($12,352,000), representing treasury bonds issued to assure the balance of the budget of 1902; 60,000,000 francs ($11,580,000), resulting from the deficit in the receipts of 1901—receipts which serve as a basis for the calculations of 1903; 41,000,000 francs ($7,913,000), resulting from the lowering of the revenue on sugar—a sacrifice made in favor of agriculture, to develop home consumption; 42,000,000 francs ($8,106,000), resulting from the increased expenses necessary for the execution of law and of treasury engagements.

To obtain these 207,000,000 francs ($39,951,000), no new taxes can be imposed. The minister of finances has resource to the reduction of expenses in the different ministerial departments, to the conversion of the 3½ per cents, to a revision of the arrangement made in 1901 with the "Caisse des Dépôts et Consignations," and to a suppression of the annuity to teachers. Also, the treasury will be very much benefited in 1903 by the arrears of a half-quarter of the new 3 per cents. The new minister, in trying to stop the leakage in the present fiscal system, proposes to regulate the privileges of the "bouilleurs de cru" (private distillers), to lessen the extent of the zones in which tobacco is sold at a reduced price, and to revise the tax on built property. These modifications, he thinks, will produce about 79,700,000 francs ($15,382,100). This, together with the 94,800,000 francs ($18,296,400) mentioned above as resources, will give 174,500,000 francs ($33,678,500), to which should be added the 44,000,000 francs ($8,492,000) due from the railroads for the guarantee of interests, making a total of 218,500,000 francs ($42,170,500), a figure superior by 11,500,000 francs ($2,219,500) to that of the expenses.

THORNWELL HAYNES, *Consul.*

ROUEN, *October 17, 1902.*

## ST. ETIENNE.

### TRADE OUTLOOK.

The advance in the importation of American products has been marked, and the list of our manufactures now offered for sale on this market is long and steadily increasing. But there is one important and profitable line that has not received attention in this region. I refer to agricultural implements and farm machinery. All agricultural machinery builders, however, should bear in mind that oxen almost exclusively are used on the farms here, and consequently, the gears of mowers, reapers, seeders, etc., should be adjusted to the slow pace of these animals.

The plows and harrows, with few exceptions, are of primitive style. Grass is cut only with scythes and grain with sickles; raking is done with hand rakes, seeds are sown broadcast, thrashing is accomplished by small hand flails or in some cases by tramping, and winnowing is often effected by means of a rustic sieve and a fresh breeze.

Improved agricultural machinery could be sold here, if possible buyers were properly solicited and then taught how to use it. A central depot for supplies and repairs would also be a necessity. Success, however, would depend on the efforts of practical agents, who should call on the farmers at their homes and demonstrate in the small villages the utility and economy of their goods. In a word, they should work on the same lines as they would were they introducing their wares in an isolated American farming community.

Agents in this business would need to enlist young farmers to aid them, especially as many of the rural population do not speak Parisian French, but a "patois," which it is often difficult for a city Frenchman even to understand and which he can not speak.

### IMPORTS FROM UNITED STATES.

The imports from the United States to this region may be classed under two heads—direct and indirect—the latter being much more important than the former. Among the direct imports may be mentioned machine oil, fishing tackle and accessories, nickel-plated hardware, machines for boring guns, countersinks, mechanical razors, bicyclettes, carriages, harness. The indirect importation covers a large field of varied articles—locks, patent door springs, perfume, sewing machines, medicines, comestibles (tinned), fountain pens, hardware, machine tools, etc.

## INDUSTRIES.

The fact that there are not less than 30,000 looms in use in this district, on silk ribbons, cotton goods, braids, elastics, etc., may suggest that there may be a demand for machinery of improved pattern.   There have been recent inquiries on this subject from American makers having in view the introduction of some recently invented loom accessories.

The output of this industry in 1901 gave a total of 94,472,694 francs, or nearly 19 million dollars.   Of this amount, a little more than half was exported to different countries.

An American company is at present making, in the interests of French coal operators, exhaustive explorations in the department of the Puy-de-Dome to locate and define that coal field.

## RAILWAYS AND TRAMWAYS.

The most important item is the extension of the line which, when completed, will place this city in direct communication with the departments lying to the south.   Also, a new steam railway has been put in operation, connecting St. Etienne with St. Heand and St. Chamond, nearby towns.

Tramway improvements consist chiefly in the complete abolition of horse cars and in the granting of concessions for new electric lines to connect with St. Genest Lerpt and Rochetaille, towns 3 or 4 miles distant.

## CROPS.

A cold wet spring damaged potatoes and vegetables to the extent that prices ranged unusually high during the summer.   Late vegetables suffered because of prolonged drought.   Fruit crops were also greatly injured and can be marked as a half yield in the district. Walnuts will be a total failure in many sections.  .

Hay and forage are below the average, which accounts for the prevailing high prices of meat and butter.

Wheat and other grain crops gave unequal yields in the same localities and even on individual farms, and viewed as a whole the return is considerably below the average in quantity and quality.

Grapes will show a serious falling off from earlier prospects, having recently suffered from hail storms, drought, and disease.   The prospective vintage is officially rated "mediocre."

## FIREARMS.

Though the general condition of manufacturing remains about average, the capacity of the Government factory has been reduced by the discharge of some 500 skilled workmen, for lack of Government orders.   In the proving house at St. Etienne, the number of gun barrels presented to the proof, in 1901 was 76,000, of which 72,000 received the proof mark.   The number for the previous year was only 55,000.

## COAL MINERS.

A congress of the coal miners of all France will be held at Commentry in the last week of this month (September) and it is anticipated that a general strike will immediately follow, as there is no likelihood that the demands for an eight-hour day, increase of wages, etc., will be acceded to.

In the basin of the Loire, which is the second in importance of the coal districts of France, a referendum has resulted in a decision to strike immediately, without waiting for the action of the national federation in a few days; but the facts that only 3,300 out of over 19,000 miners voted at the referendum, and that the majority was less than 1,000, would seem to indicate the existence of a strong sentiment in favor of awaiting the opportunity for united action with the other regions after the congress of Commentry, rather than entering upon a partial strike, in which the segregated local miners would be foredoomed to defeat.

The German export bounty on coal has recently, it is said, enabled German shippers to offer steam coal f. o. b. at Lyons at 26 francs (\$5) per ton. Local miners complain that the cost of mining increases year by year on account of the greater depth of mines, which entail more and larger machinery for pumping and hoisting. It is also estimated that at least 2 francs (\$0.40) per ton is required to indemnify property owners above and near the mines, whose buildings or fields suffer from broken walls or crevasses.

Official figures for the first six months of 1902 give the total production of coal, bituminous and anthracite, in the department of the Loire as 1,770,410 tons, and in the department of the Rhone as 12,730 tons.

### NEW INVENTIONS.

The French public, at least, seem to have arrived at a high appreciation of the United States consular reports, judging from the recent efforts of many inventors to have mention made therein of divers articles in which they wish to interest Americans. Among the most important of these may be mentioned:

Petroleum briquettes, M. B. Gonnet, rue Parmentier 11 St. Etienne. Machine for blowing bottles and window glass, P. B. Maussier, Ingenieur, St. Galmier (Loire). Detonating device for coal mining, M. Aubert, Rue St. Jean, St. Etienne. Centrifugal coal and gold washer, M. Paul, Rue Buisson, 8 St. Etienne. Combination screwdriver and nippers for watchmakers and others using small screws, M. F. W. Mercer, Faubourg Poissonniere 64, Paris.

### POPULATION.

The corrected census returns credit the city of St. Etienne with a population of 146,559. Of this number 1,563 are foreigners, there being Italians, 991; Swiss, 195; Belgians, 102; Germans, 77; Spanish, 66; Alsace-Lorraine, 44; Russians, 28; Swedes and Norwegians, 20; Austrian, 17; English and Irish, 11; Americans, 6; Danish, 1; Hollander, 1; Haitian, 1; Egyptian, 1, and Turk 1.

HILARY S. BRUNOT, *Consul.*

ST. ETIENNE, *September 18, 1902.*

H. Doc. 305, pt 2——17

# GERMANY.

## REPORT FROM CONSULATE-GENERAL AT BERLIN.

The period of industrial reaction and financial depression in Germany, which began during the summer of 1900, has continued, with varying and often suddenly fluctuating conditions, throughout 1901 and down to the date of the present report.   It is true that certain branches of manufacture, notably the textile industry, have during the past eight months shown encouraging signs of recovery, and there were apparent at the close of 1901 various indications that the worst of the crisis was past, and that the process of recovery, however slow it might prove, had been definitely begun.   Since then, however, those favorable prognostics have been only measurably confirmed, and but for an active, well-sustained foreign trade, it is difficult to say wherein the general economic situation of this country is improved since the early autumn of 1901.   It is not too much to say that the steady increase in exports from year to year, and especially the strong and sustained demand for German manufactures in the markets of the United States, now form the brightest spot on the commercial horizon of the fatherland.   The total values of Germany's foreign trade during the nine years which ended with 1901 were the following:

| Year. | Imports. | Exports. | Total foreign trade. |
|---|---|---|---|
| 1893 | $996,908,660 | $772,205,756 | $1,766,114,416 |
| 1894 | 1,019,956,854 | 726,252,246 | 1,746,209,100 |
| 1895 | 1,010,574,418 | 814,977,450 | 1,825,551,868 |
| 1896 | 1,088,480,624 | 874,287,702 | 1,962,768,326 |
| 1897 | 1,150,228,058 | 906,335,178 | 2,056,563,236 |
| 1898 | 1,303,680,224 | 952,415,548 | 2,256,095,772 |
| 1899 | 1,376,508,464 | 1,039,681,342 | 2,416,184,806 |
| 1900 | 1,438,234,000 | 1,131,214,000 | 2,569,448,000 |
| 1901 | 1,420,150,046 | 1,132,738,866 | 2,552,888,912 |

In quantity, the exports were 318,252 tons less in 1901 than in 1900, but there was, notwithstanding this, an increase of $1,524,866 in value, and this indicates an increased proportion of higher grade merchandise in the shipments of the year.

In respect to imports, the most notable falling off was 1,064,244 tons of coal, 582,445 tons of iron, and 545,974 tons of lumber, and the diminished demand for these staple materials of manufacture has been in close and direct relation to the stagnation which prevailed in most branches of industry.

## LEADING CLASSES OF IMPORTED AND EXPORTED MERCHANDISE.

The following summary of twenty-four leading articles of import and export during the year 1901, grouped in the order of their respective values, shows the relative importance of raw materials and manufactured products in each category:

*Imports during 1901.*

| Articles. | Value. | | Per cent of total. |
|---|---:|---:|---:|
| Cotton, raw | 200,000 | $70,495,000 | 5.2 |
| Wheat | 700,000 | 67,282,000 | 5 |
| Wool | 600,000 | 55,120,800 | 4.1 |
| Coffee, raw | | 35,152,000 | 2.6 |
| Gold coin | | 32,510,800 | 2.4 |
| Gold bullion | | 28,607,000 | 2.1 |
| Corn | 119,800,000 | 28,512,400 | 2.1 |
| Tobacco, raw | 112,300,000 | 26,727,400 | 2 |
| Lard and other fats | 106,700,000 | 25,410,000 | 1.9 |
| Silk, raw | 105,500,000 | 25,109,000 | 1.8 |
| Barley | 105,400,000 | 25,085,200 | 1.8 |
| Eggs, and yolks of | 104,800,000 | 24,942,400 | 1.8 |
| Coal | 92,200,000 | 21,943,600 | 1.6 |
| Chile saltpeter | 90,000,000 | 21,420,000 | 1.6 |
| Rye | 85,100,000 | 20,253,800 | 1.6 |
| Wood and lumber | 87,000,000 | 20,706,000 | 1.5 |
| Copper, raw | 85,100,000 | 20,253,800 | 1.5 |
| Cattle hides | 84,500,000 | 20,111,000 | 1.5 |
| Woolen yarn | 82,900,000 | 19,730,200 | 1.5 |
| Horses | 78,600,000 | 18,706,800 | 1.4 |
| Brown coal (lignite) | 75,400,000 | 17,945,200 | 1.3 |
| Petroleum | 71,300,000 | 16,969,400 | 1.2 |
| Iron ores | 69,700,000 | 16,588,600 | 1.2 |
| Machinery | 64,300,000 | 15,303,400 | 1.1 |
| All other imports | | | 51.3 |

*Exports during 1901.*

| Articles. | Value. | | Per cent of total. |
|---|---:|---:|---:|
| | *Marks.* | | |
| Cotton goods | 219,800,000 | $52,312,400 | 4.9 |
| Woolen goods | 212,600,000 | 50,598,800 | 4.7 |
| Mineral coal | 209,700,000 | 49,908,600 | 4.6 |
| Sugar | 202,800,000 | 48,266,400 | 4.5 |
| Machinery | 200,700,000 | 47,866,680 | 4.4 |
| Iron manufactures, coarse | 144,500,000 | 34,272,000 | 3.2 |
| Silk goods | 137,300,600 | 32,677,400 | 3 |
| Clothing of all kinds | 116,600,000 | 27,750,800 | 2.6 |
| Engravings, etchings, etc | 89,900,000 | 21,396,200 | 2 |
| Aniline and other colors | 79,600,000 | 18,944,800 | 1.8 |
| Books, maps, and music | 79,400,000 | 18,897,200 | 1.8 |
| Iron manufactures, fine | 77,900,000 | 18,540,200 | 1.7 |
| Gold and silverware | 60,900,000 | 14,494,200 | 1.3 |
| Woolen yarn | 56,300,000 | 13,399,400 | 1.2 |
| Leather | 54,800,600 | 13,042,400 | 1.2 |
| Toys | 53,100,000 | 12,637,800 | 1.2 |
| Coke | 52,200,000 | 12,423,600 | 1.2 |
| Porcelain | 45,200,000 | 10,757,600 | 1 |
| Furs and skins | 44,400,000 | 10,567,200 | 1 |
| Wrought-iron bars | 34,800,000 | 8,358,600 | .8 |
| Sheet iron and tin | 34,700,000 | 8,258,600 | .8 |
| Angle and structural iron | 34,600,000 | 8,234,800 | .8 |
| Cattle hides | 34,400,000 | 8,187,200 | .8 |
| Iron wire | 33,100,000 | 7,877,800 | .7 |
| Pianos | 29,900,000 | 7,116,200 | .7 |
| Wood, manufactures of | 29,900,000 | 7,116,200 | .7 |
| Leather goods, fine | 29,700,000 | 7,068,600 | .7 |
| Copper and brass manufactures | 29,400,000 | 6,997,200 | .6 |
| Cotton yarn | 28,500,000 | 6,783,000 | .6 |
| All other exports | | | 45.5 |

Among the notable surprises in the foregoing statistics is the fact
therein revealed that the exports of engravings, etchings, etc., exceed
in value those of aniline and other colors, leather, or porcelain, all of
which are leading products of this country, and that the imports of
corn exceed in value those of raw silk, tobacco, or coal. The imports
of eggs are more valuable than those of lumber and timber, copper,
petroleum, iron ores, or machinery.

## GEOGRAPHICAL DISTRIBUTION OF GERMANY'S FOREIGN TRADE.

In respect to the origin of merchandise imported into this country last year, the United States again heads the list with a total, according to German statistics, of 1,042,100,000 marks ($248,009,800), or 18.2 per cent of the entire bulk of imports, as against $242,950,400, or 16.9 per cent, in 1900.   The distribution for the year presents the following interesting exhibit:

*Imports by countries during 1901.*

| Countries. | Value. | Per cent of total. |
|---|---:|---:|
| | *Marks.* | |
| United States | 1,042,100,000 | $248,009,800 | 18.2 |
| Russia and Finland | 729,500,000 | 173,621,000 | 12.8 |
| Austria-Hungary | 687,800,000 | 165,005,400 | 12.1 |
| Great Britain | 657,800,000 | 156,556,400 | 11.5 |
| France, Algeria, etc | 289,200,000 | 68,829,000 | 5 |
| British East Indies | 214,800,000 | 51,122,400 | 3.8 |
| Netherlands | 203,800,000 | 48,504,400 | 3.6 |
| Argentine Republic | 200,800,000 | 47,790,400 | 3.5 |
| Belgium | 186,500,000 | 44,387,000 | 3.3 |
| Italy | 182,600,000 | 43,458,800 | 3.2 |
| Switzerland | 154,200,000 | 36,699,600 | 2.7 |
| Brazil | 113,900,000 | 27,108,200 | 2 |
| British Australia | 100,900,000 | 24,014,200 | 1.9 |
| Chile | 100,700,000 | 23,966,600 | 1.8 |
| Dutch East Indies | 96,700,000 | 23,014,400 | 1.7 |
| Sweden | 84,300,000 | 20,063,400 | 1.5 |
| Spain | 78,300,000 | 18,635,400 | 1.4 |
| Denmark | 68,300,000 | 16,255,600 | 1.2 |
| Roumania | 47,800,000 | 11,376,400 | .8 |
| China | 44,700,000 | 10,538,600 | .8 |
| Central America | 25,400,000 | 6,045,200 | .6 |
| Egypt | 32,100,000 | 7,639,800 | .7 |
| Turkey | 30,100,000 | 7,163,800 | .7 |
| British South Africa | 22,000,000 | 5,236,000 | .4 |
| Norway | 21,600,000 | 5,140,800 | .4 |
| Free port of Hamburg | 20,300,000 | 4,831,400 | .4 |
| Japan | 19,800,000 | 4,712,400 | .3 |
| Portugal | 18,100,000 | 4,307,800 | .3 |
| Uruguay | 14,500,000 | 3,451,000 | .3 |
| Cuba and Porto Rico | 12,400,000 | 2,951,200 | .2 |
| Mexico | 10,800,000 | 2,570,400 | .2 |
| Venezuela | 9,400,000 | 2,237,200 | .2 |
| Greece | 9,200,000 | 2,189,600 | .2 |
| Ecuador | 8,600,000 | 2,046,800 | .1 |
| Dominica | 6,100,000 | 1,451,800 | .1 |
| Haiti | 2,200,000 | 523,600 | |
| Servia | 7,500,000 | 1,785,000 | .1 |
| Bolivia | 7,400,000 | 1,761,200 | .1 |
| British North America | 7,400,000 | 1,761,200 | .1 |
| Peru | 7,200,000 | 1,713,600 | .1 |
| Siam | 6,700,000 | 1,594,600 | .1 |
| British West Africa | 30,900,000 | 7,354,200 | .7 |
| Portuguese West Africa | 6,600,000 | 1,570,800 | .1 |
| All other countries | 67,400,000 | 16,041,200 | 1.2 |
| **Total** | **5,710,300,000** | **1,359,051,400** | **100** |

*Exports by countries during 1901.*

| Countries. | Value. | Per cent of total. |
|---|---:|---:|
| | *Marks.* | |
| Great Britain | 916,400,000 | $218,108,200 | 20.3 |
| Austria-Hungary | 491,500,000 | 116,977,000 | 10.9 |
| United States | 385,800,000 | 91,820,400 | 8.5 |
| Netherlands | 379,000,000 | 90,202,000 | 8.4 |
| Russia and Finland | 345,900,000 | 82,024,200 | 7.7 |
| Switzerland | 264,300,000 | 62,908,400 | 5.9 |
| France, Algeria, etc | 250,800,000 | 59,690,400 | 5.6 |
| Belgium | 236,000,000 | 56,168,000 | 5.2 |
| Italy | 127,200,000 | 30,273,600 | 2.8 |
| Denmark | 118,000,000 | 28,094,000 | 2.6 |

*Exports by countries during 1901*—Continued.

| Countries. | Values. | | Per cent of total. |
|---|---|---|---|
| | *Marks.* | | |
| Sweden | 111,400,000 | $26,513,200 | 2.5 |
| British East Indies | 79,500,000 | 18,921,000 | 1.8 |
| Free port of Hamburg | 73,300,000 | 17,445,400 | 1.6 |
| Norway | 65,000,000 | 15,470,000 | 1.4 |
| Argentine Republic | 54,200,000 | 12,839,000 | 1.2 |
| Australia | 52,200,000 | 12,423,000 | 1.2 |
| Spain | 50,000,000 | 11,900,000 | 1.1 |
| China | 47,500,000 | 11,305,000 | 1 |
| Japan | 45,500,000 | 10,829,000 | 1 |
| Turkey | 37,300,000 | 8,877,400 | .8 |
| Brazil | 35,740,000 | 8,449,000 | .8 |
| Chile | 34,000,000 | 8,052,000 | .8 |
| Roumania | 34,000,000 | 8,052,000 | .8 |
| British North America | 25,000,000 | 6,092,800 | .6 |
| Mexico | 26,000,000 | 6,188,000 | .6 |
| Dutch East Indies | 26,000,000 | 6,000,000 | .6 |
| British South Africa | 20,000,000 | 4,000,000 | .4 |
| Portugal | 19,000,000 | 4,200,000 | .4 |
| Egypt | 16,500,000 | 3,000,000 | .4 |
| German West Africa | 11,400,000 | 2,000,000 | .2 |
| Peru | 11,000,000 | 2,618,000 | .2 |
| Cuba and Porto Rico | 10,500,000 | | .2 |
| Uruguay | 9,600,000 | 2,284,800 | .2 |
| Servia | 7,200,000 | 1,713,000 | .2 |
| Philippines | 7,000,000 | 1,666,000 | .2 |
| Venezuela | 7,000,000 | 1,666,000 | .2 |
| Greece | 6,500,000 | 1,547,000 | .1 |
| Central America | 5,900,000 | 1,404,200 | .1 |
| Bulgaria | 5,900,000 | 1,404,200 | .1 |
| Free port of Bremerhaven | 8,900,000 | 2,118,200 | .2 |
| British West Africa | 7,600,000 | 1,808,800 | .2 |
| Portuguese Africa | 1,800,000 | 428,400 | |
| All other countries | 42,800,000 | 10,186,400 | 1 |
| Total | 4,512,600,000 | 1,073,998,800 | 100 |

It is thus shown by German statistics that the imports from the United States into Germany during 1901 were valued at $248,009,800, while German exports to our country reached a total valuation of $91,820,000, leaving the formidable balance of $156,189,800 in favor of the United States. It is to be remarked, however, that the foregoing import figures include the vast bulk of American merchandise landed at Hamburg and Bremen for transit to Russia, Austria-Hungary, and Switzerland, which did not, therefore, belong to Germany at all. On the other hand, official valuations of German exports are estimated—not absolute—and are not, therefore, always exact. The sum of values of exports declared at United States consulates throughout Germany, which certainly do not err on the side of overvaluation, was $99,616,731.93, and these did not include the large quantity of miscellaneous merchandise bought and taken home by American tourists or exported hence by package-post in quantities valued at less than $100, which do not require a consular invoice, and therefore pass unrecorded at consulates. But, making full allowance for all possible errors in statistics, the excess of German imports from, over exports to, the United States is enormous and steadily growing, the adverse balance having increased from $138,391,800 in 1900 to $156,189,800 in 1901.

### FOREIGN TRADE OF THE, 1902.

The record for the first six months of 1902 shows that the exports of Germany to all countries reached a total of 18,895,185 tons, valued at 2,286,000,000 marks ($571,500,000), as compared with 17,862,857 tons, valued at 2,136,000,000 marks ($508,368,000), during the same period in 1901. The net increase for the six months was, therefore, 1,032,328 tons in bulk and $63,132,000 in value. Imports for the same period were 23,869,407 tons, valued at 2,840,000,000 marks ($710,000,000), against 25,119,077 tons, valued at 2,752,000,000 marks ($688,000,000) during the first half of the preceding year. For reasons that have been explained in previous reports of this series, this sustained increase in exports, although a favorable indication, is subject to the qualification that some at least of the exported goods have been sold abroad at prices which yielded to the exporters very meager profits, and in some cases none at all. For example, the exports of iron and steel during the first six months of 1902 rose to 1,503,742 tons, against 994,404 tons for the same period in 1901 and 744,224 tons in 1900; but there can be no doubt that much of all this vast export was marketed abroad at prices which barely covered the cost of production.

As a test of the degree to which the present industrial situation in Germany, the pending tariff legislation, and the influence of the meat-inspection law and other legislation have collectively exerted upon the importations of raw materials and food products from the United States, there is given in the following table a few leading items from the record of the six months—January 1 to June 30—as compared with that of the corresponding period for 1901 and 1900.

*Imports from the United States for the first six months of 1900, 1901, and 1902.*

| Article. | 1900. | 1901. | 1902. |
|---|---|---|---|
| | Met. tons. a | Met. tons.a | Met. tons. a |
| Raw cotton | 155,706 | 142,808 | 165,054 |
| Cotton waste | 6,667 | 5,724 | 6,905 |
| Wheat | 256,208 | 389,940 | 566,989 |
| Rye | 14,793 | 15,079 | 20,172 |
| Oats | 26,730 | 44,478 | 2,090 |
| Corn | 546,662 | 571,104 | 43,995 |
| Raw tobacco and stems | 6,433 | 5,800 | 6,397 |
| Hides and skins | 3,963 | 2,149 | 1,412 |
| Lumber, timber, and staves | 131,655 | 107,109 | 168,164 |
| Meats of all kinds | 8,659 | 7,086 | 9,065 |
| Petroleum and products | 367,495 | 374,128 | 429,455 |
| Pig iron | 5,787 | 9,309 | 309 |
| Cotton-seed oil | 9,188 | 10,918 | 7,705 |
| Copper | 33,762 | 28,195 | 35,780 |
| Electrical machinery | 232 | 232 | 102 |

a 1 metric ton=2,204 pounds.

Especially noticeable in this exhibit is the heavy increase in wheat imports and the important falling off in corn, due mainly to its high price in America, which permitted the corn of Russia, Roumania, Hungary, Argentine Republic, and Servia to compete, although there was a decline in the total import of corn from 831,451 tons during the first six months of 1901 to 592,087 tons during the same period in 1902. Cotton, lumber, petroleum, and tobacco imports from our country show a steady, normal increase; even meats, in spite of all restrictions, rather more than held their own. Copper shows a satisfactory increase, while the import of pig iron dropped to a bagatelle of 309 tons, and was replaced by an export of 7,465 tons of German pig iron to the United States. The imports of agricultural machinery declined from 19,214 tons in the first half of 1900 to 17,162 and 11,028 tons, respectively, for the corresponding periods in 1901 and 1902. The importation of American machinery into Germany, which reached its climax in 1900, has since then steadily declined, the aggregate imports in all classes—viz, sewing machines, agricultural implements, machine tools, pumps, and other machinery—having been valued at 10,800,000 marks ($2,570,400) in 1898, 17,500,000 marks ($4,165,000) in 1899, 31,800,000 marks ($7,568,400) in 1900, and 19,200,000 marks ($4,269,600) in 1901. The machine tools imported from America two and three years ago have been employed to make Germany a producer of machinery for export at prices with which the American makers, rushed and driven as they are by demands at home, find it difficult to compete.

### THE METAL AND MINING INDUSTRIES.

It is a recognized principle in national economics that the ratio of consumption of pig iron is an approximately accurate measure of the prevailing degree of prosperity among an industrial people. Accordingly, the relapse which came upon industrial Germany in the summer of 1900 is accurately reflected in the declining product of its mines and iron mills during the subsequent year. Thus the production of coal, which rose from 70,000,000 tons in 1890 to 109,290,237 tons in 1900, dropped back to 108,417,029 tons, a decrease of 870,000 in 1901. It is true the decrease was only four-fifths of 1 per cent, but it was sufficient to show that the high-water mark of activity had been passed and the period of contraction begun. Similarly, the output of iron ores fell from 18,964,294 tons in 1900 to 16,570,258 tons—a loss of 2,400,000 tons—in 1901, while the production of pig iron showed a corresponding decline from 8,494,852 to 7,835,204 tons, a loss of 660,000 tons, or 7.8 per cent. Equally significant is the fact that while the average value of pig iron fell from $15.38 in 1900 to $14.85 in 1901, the price of coal—at the mouth of the mine—advanced from $2.10 to $2.23 per ton during the same period. Prices of coal in Germany are governed by the decrees of the syndicate that controls practically the entire native supply, so that the higher rates which prevailed in 1901 were the result, not of increased demand for consumption, but of a restricted output and cleverly manipulated selling arrangements. The stubbornly maintained price of coal was, indeed, one of the factors which contributed to increase the embarrassment of the iron and steel industries, and serious complaints were heard from the owners of furnaces and rolling mills, who, having no coal mines of their own, were dependent upon purchased supplies and were either bound by fuel contracts made in prosperous times, or, what was worse, were forced to either shut down or pay the still higher prices which were maintained after the depression in iron and steel interests had come. Meanwhile, the iron and steel makers, deprived of their previous insatiable home market by the paralysis that had overtaken so many branches of manufacture, gave their best energies to extending their exports, with such success that the exports of iron and steel, which had amounted to 744,224 tons during the first six months of 1900, rose to 994,404 tons during the first six months of 1901 and 1,503,742 tons during the same period in 1902. These were by far the largest exports in that class ever recorded in Germany. But while the increase in quantity from 1901 to 1902 was 51.2 per cent, the increase in values was only 22.7 per cent, and this revealed the fact—well known to those in the trade—that much of the iron and steel exported from Germany during the past year has been sold on the basis of a clearing-out sale, for what it would bring, and for prices which yielded little, if any, profit to the exporters.   However, the large export served to clear out accumulated stocks, and by keeping the mills and workmen measurably employed, helped to palliate some of the worst effects of the crisis. So timely was the relief thus obtained that a powerful special syndicate was formed during the summer of 1902 for the purpose of paying bounties on exports of iron and steel.   This combination includes the coal, coke, pig-iron, and semiproduct syndicates, the wire-drawers' association, and the syndicates of sheet metal, girders, and structural iron, respectively, and has its central office at Cologne.   The purpose of the combination is to pay to such of its members as export all or part or their product a bonus equal to the difference between the current price of the merchandise in the German market and the price actually obtained for it abroad; in other words, to sustain exports at the expense of the home consumers of steel and iron.

### SOME EFFECTS OF SYNDICATED MANAGEMENT.

It is but natural that a period of industrial depression like that through which Germany is now passing should furnish a supreme test of the efficiency of consolidated management, for which so much had been promised and expected.   Unquestionably, some of the more important German syndicates served a good purpose by preventing sudden and undue advances in prices of products during the years of great prosperity.   It had been promised for them that they would "serve as a parachute to let manufacturers gently down to solid ground" when the time of reaction and contraction should come. That they have done this to some extent and thus perhaps saved the country from a worse crisis is conceded, but there is a growing number of thoughtful men in Germany who begin to question whether the cost of such a system is not unduly great for the domestic consumer. In connection with the discussion thus inspired, some curious facts have been revealed.   It was shown in evidence produced before a court at Godesberg that the coke syndicate had sold to three large iron companies in Austria blast-furnace coke for $1.97 per ton, while the price to German furnace men was held stiff at 17 marks ($4.04), or more than double the export rate.   The girder syndicate mills are charged with having taken foreign orders at from 89 to 92 marks ($21.18 to $21.89) per ton, while maintaining a home rate of 120 marks ($28.56).   The rail syndicate sold rails abroad for 30 marks ($7.14) per ton below the inland price, the wire mills cut their home rate of 150 marks ($35.70) down to 105 marks ($25) for export, and the rollers of plates and other shipbuilding material pursued a similar policy until the shipbuilders of the Lower Rhine made formal complaint that they could not compete with the Dutch and Belgian shipyards which derived their metal supplies from Germany.   Whatever may be the result, the fact is that the industries of Germany are now more thoroughly and largely syndicated than ever before, and a movement is taking shape to provide a system of closer and more exacting Government supervision over such combinations.

Aside from the metal·and mining industries, the other leading branches of manufacture seem to have weathered the adverse wind and tide, at least down to the close of 1901, reasonably well.   While it is difficult to be exact in a study of this kind, the average dividends paid by joint-stock and limited-liability companies during the two past years may be taken as a nearly correct key to the real situation. The comparison, based upon trustworthy published reports, is as follows:

| Description. | Dividends. | |
|---|---|---|
| | 1900. | 1901. |
| | Per cent. | Per cent. |
| Earthenware, glass, and porcelain | 13.64 | 12.41 |
| Chemical manufactures | 11.24 | 10.41 |
| Breweries and distilleries | 10.09 | 9.39 |
| Paper mills | 10.96 | 8.13 |
| Textile manufactures | 4.58 | 3.18 |
| Electrical machinery and supplies | 9.55 | 5.79 |

As might have been expected, the worst showing in this brief list is made by the electrical manufacturers, whose situation and the causes which led to it have been so fully described in previous reports of this series (Advance Sheets No. 1429, August 27, 1902[a]) as to render superfluous any further extended reference to the subject. In a word, the electrical manufacturing capacity of Germany was enormously overfinanced and overexpanded. It has suffered a serious relapse and heavy losses, but is now pluckily trying to get back to solid ground. Meanwhile, it is turning out large quantities of machinery and materials, which, except for certain Government contracts, are being sold at little or nothing above cost, by way of keeping the factories open and the trained workmen together and employed until brighter days may come.

### UNDERLYING CAUSES OF DEPRESSION.

No analysis of the existing situation in Germany can be discriminating or just which does not take into account certain basic and inherent conditions, which are beyond governmental or corporate control, and reach backward and down to the vital foundations of the Empire.

Germany was in 1871 a nation of 39,119,000 inhabitants, of whom 60 per cent were engaged in agricultural pursuits. In December, 1900, it had grown to an empire of 57,793,000 souls, of whom 35 per cent derived their support from agriculture and 65 per cent—nearly two-thirds—were engaged in professional pursuits or some form of industry or trade. This transformation from agriculture to industries and commerce took place mainly during the period from 1880 to 1895. During those fifteen years, the increase of working population was 17.8 per cent, of which agriculture gained only 0.7 per cent, while manufactures, mining, and the building trades were augmented by 29.5, and commerce by 48.9 per cent. It was a time when young men by hundreds of thousands left their native farms and villages, and flocked to mines, factories, and to industrial cities and towns. In 1881, 486 persons out of every 100,000 of the population emigrated, mainly to the continent of America. In 1899, the number of emigrants per 100,000 had fallen to 44. The Empire was by this time increasing in population at a rate of nearly 800,000 per annum. As late as 1895, 20,104 men were engaged in shipbuild-

[a] Consular Reports No. 265 (October, 1902).

ing, but five years later their numbers had increased to 40,808—more than doubled.  Trade unions multiplied rapidly and trebled their membership within five years, and strikes increased in number from 73 in 1892 to 967 in 1899.  Wages in all departments increased slowly, but employment was steady, many mechanics and operatives worked overtime, the condition of the laboring classes improved, their wants increased, and there was a general advance in respect to their dwellings, food, clothing, and standard of living.

There could be but one sequel to all this, and the inevitable happened.  The enormous transfer of productive labor from agriculture to industries changed the whole economic balance of the Empire, and the result was a vast overproduction of many kinds of merchandise, but an underproduction of food materials.  While the population of the Fatherland had increased 36 per cent during the twenty-eight years from 1872 to 1900, coal production had increased 260 per cent, pig iron production by nearly 330 per cent, shipping by 500 per cent, railway earnings 400 per cent, and exports, although rapidly developing, had increased only 100 per cent.  Inevitably, such conditions entailed overproduction, and the accumulation of surplus products for which there was no adequate and natural market at home or abroad.  This was not noticed so long as the general prosperity continued.  There was an abundance of money for everything.  Banks of high repute and vast resources took to financing industrial enterprises to an extent never perhaps seen in any other country.  In many cases, bankers urged electrical and other manufacturers to enlarge their plants or build new ones and equip them with the most perfect modern machinery.  Any industrial enterprise with a plausible prospectus could obtain all the money it needed for construction and working capital; and so the productive capacity of the nation outran the demand for its products, rival companies competed for what legitimate trade there was by cutting prices, and when that failed, began buying orders by organizing and taking stock in new companies which would purchase their products.

The result is written in the history of the two critical years since May, 1900, when the zenith of prosperous activity was passed and the period of reaction and depression began.  The losses through depreciation of industrial securities were so great as to radically change the financial status of hundreds of thousands of people.  The stocks of 21 of the principal electrical manufacturing companies, whose shares were valued on January 1, 1899, at 443,550,000 marks ($105,564,900), had fallen in December, 1901, to an aggregate valuation of 270,810,000 marks ($64,452,780), an average loss of 61 per cent.  The failure of the Leipziger and other important banks, through reckless management, added to the public distrust, and people hastened to get their money out of banks and industrial enterprises and into safe and solid public securities.  The imperial loan went from 92 to above par, good municipal and State securities rose in proportion, and the Russian loan offered in Germany was oversubscribed a hundred times.  The meaning of it all was that most intelligent men realized that Germany had, during the past twenty years, been following new paths, the outcome of which was not yet clear; that in the transformation from an agricultural to an industrial state, new conditions had been created which would require time, good management, and skillful legislation to harmonize, adjust, and solidify into the basis of permanent national prosperity.  Meanwhile, they preferred solid securities bearing low rates of interest to speculative enterprises.

## TARIFF REVISION.

To this already difficult situation is added the uncertainty entailed by the long and strenuous discussion of the new tariff act, the uncertainty of its enactment by the present Reichstag, and the renewal of the commercial treaties on which the export trade of Germany so largely depends, which latter must have as a basis the revised tariff law that should take effect at the beginning of 1904.[a] The present state of suspense throws its shadow across the industrial and commercial revival which has been so hopefully awaited during the past year.

Another element in the problem which must be taken into account is the fact that the population of Germany is increasing at the rate of 800,000 a year. There is a steady, rapid growth in the number of persons to be sheltered, employed, clothed, and fed. Certain food materials, especially meats, have recently grown abnormally scarce and dear. How far this is due to the inability of the farmers to raise sufficient swine and cattle for the food of the people, and how far this circumstance is aggravated by the new difficulties laid in the way of importing animals by the meat-inspection law, or whether the higher prices are due rather to the greed of butchers and meat dealers, are disputed points concerning which public opinion is divided and excited. Add to this the far-reaching effect of the pending abolition of sugar-export bounties by the Brussels conference, and it will be apparent that the task of adjusting a governmental policy in all its details to the needs of the German Empire of to-day and the future is one which calls for the exercise of the highest attributes of statesmanship. No one doubts that the German people, with their highly trained intelligence, their industry, enterprise, and energy will in due time surmount all difficulties and reach a basis of solid, enduring prosperity.

The vitality which still exists in the iron and steel trades, machinery, and other leading industries is fully attested by the exposition at Düsseldorf, which was opened on May 1. Although representing only the manufactures of the Rhenish-Westphalian provinces, the exposition is conceded to have been one of the most important and interesting of its class ever held in any country. American and English expert electricians, engineers, and machinists, who visited it in large numbers, are unanimous in saying that it gave a new and impressive picture of Germany's high position among industrial nations and her power to meet on equal terms the competition of Great Britain and the United States in the markets of the world.

FRANK H. MASON, *Consul-General.*

BERLIN, *September 27, 1902.*

---

## AIX LA CHAPELLE.

The woolen-cloth industries have been depressed, but the home demand is improving, and the outlook for next year is encouraging. The Aix la Chapelle Chamber of Commerce, in a recent report, advises the woolen-cloth manufacturers to act in unison, especially for the abatement of long credits and other abuses that impede business.

[a] The new tariff law was passed by the Reichstag December 14, 1902. See Advance Sheets No. 1558, January 30, 1903.

The automobile and electric factories are filled with orders. The pin industry, since the manufacturers have fixed prices of labor and amount of sales, has been remunerative to all concerned, and I am informed that the organization is to be continued for another year.

Owing to the American demand for steel billets and beams and structural iron, the larger mills as well as the small ones in Aix la Chapelle and the Grand Duchy of Luxembourg are busy, and anticipate working to their full capacity for the ensuing year.

There is a decided increase in the quantities of American goods found in shops, and in the consumption of pork products, lumber, and furniture; but no statistics on these lines are available. Aix la Chapelle is fertile ground for American products adapted to the needs of the country, and should not be overlooked in considering German markets. This office will be pleased to answer any questions in regard to placing American products, and must repeat its former advice, "Show goods and send reliable agents."

More American farm machinery would be sold if manufacturers would locate a competent mechanic to make repairs; and the same applies to all American machines.

The following gives the amounts and character of exports to the United States for the year ended June 30, 1902:

| Articles. | September quarter, 1901. | December quarter, 1901. | March quarter, 1902. | June quarter, 1902. |
|---|---|---|---|---|
| Automobiles | | | | $409.36 |
| Agate buttons | $4,450.22 | $7,760.92 | $5,695.84 | 7,993.11 |
| Chemicals | 33,180.59 | 42,579.28 | 59,929.85 | 47,552.10 |
| Ladies' coats | 208.15 | | | |
| Church effects | 97.58 | 640.23 | | 142.80 |
| Earthenware | 95.81 | 1,213.08 | | |
| Felt | | | 490.41 | |
| Glassware | 3,541.11 | 896.64 | 3,801.03 | 13,251.99 |
| Hooks and eyes | 874.73 | 687.86 | 470.07 | 1,254.75 |
| Ironware hooks | | 101.87 | | |
| Iron | | | 8,483.86 | |
| Lead | | | | 668.14 |
| Lin mesh | 19,700.71 | 21,886.74 | 12,818.16 | 25,933.67 |
| Leather aprons | | 470.46 | | |
| Machinery | | 8,390.82 | | |
| Needles and pins | 32,894.86 | 28,846.21 | 31,786.85 | 33,296.39 |
| Natural mineral water | 2,885.71 | 8,609.00 | 1,252.66 | 4,665.74 |
| Paper | 98,242.45 | 74,672.56 | 57,982.78 | 67,296.54 |
| Silk, artificial | 13,434.22 | 16,694.79 | 20,135.19 | 29,733.48 |
| Skins | 11,969.46 | 12,591.62 | 12,224.63 | 10,731.66 |
| Steel | | | | 288,548.16 |
| Shears | 179.63 | | | 47.36 |
| Steel cards | 229.28 | 72.71 | | |
| Wine | | 126.14 | | 426.08 |
| Woolen cloth | 147,832.95 | 112,226.42 | 180,011.37 | 98,583.32 |
| Yarn | 59.74 | | | |
| Total | 369,396.62 | 328,382.34 | 345,089.70 | 580,524.60 |
| Increase | 32,523.42 | 23,680.04 | 102,995.91 | 814,537.81 |

FRANKLIN BRUNDAGE, *Consul.*

AIX LA CHAPELLE, *August 19, 1902.*

---

## ANNABERG.

The trade and industries of this consular district have undergone no material change during the past twelve months. Dress trimmings, laces, and kid gloves, the leading articles of manufacture here, have met with good demand in the markets of the world, and manufacturers and exporters have had no special reason to complain of lack of orders, although their expectations in every respect were not fully realized.

The glove industry of Johanngeorgenstadt continues in a prosperous condition.

Eibenstock has had a favorable year. Laces are in good demand, and the manufacturers of that town have been busily employed.

The dress-trimming industry of Annaberg can not be said to be in a prosperous condition. The constant changes of fashion render it difficult for the manufacturers to keep pace with the capricious demand for this peculiar line of goods.

## IMPORTS AND EXPORTS.

This consular district is situated far in the interior of Germany, and consequently the local merchants obtain their foreign goods through wholesale houses in Hamburg, Bremen, Leipzig and Chemnitz. It is therefore impossible to secure reliable data in regard to the amount of imports received from the United States.

Through the courtesy of the Chamber of Commerce of Chemnitz, I am enabled to give some statistics of interest relative to the amount and value of exports of the leading article of manufacture of this district—dress trimmings (passementerie)—to the leading countries of the world for the years 1900 and 1901. They are:

| Countries. | 1901. | 1900. | Countries. | 1901. | 1900. |
|---|---|---|---|---|---|
| Great Britain | $375,000 | $325,000 | Belgium | $80,000 | $77,000 |
| United States | 475,000 | 500,000 | Spain and Portugal | 95,000 | 85,000 |
| France | 85,000 | 80,000 | Italy | 74,000 | 72,000 |
| Russia | 70,000 | 65,000 | South America | 73,000 | 65,000 |
| The Orient | 95,000 | 90,000 | Austria-Hungary | 105,000 | 95,000 |
| Sweden and Norway | 45,000 | 40,000 | | | |

The consumption in the German Empire of dress trimmings, manufactured in this district, amounted to $150,000 in 1900, as against $165,000 consumed in 1901.

These statistics furnish some idea of the importance of this special line of industry in Annaberg and its vicinity.

The following tables show in detail the declared value of exports from the consular district of Annaberg and its agency at Eibenstock to the United States during the year ended December 31, 1901, as compared with 1900; also for the half years ended June 30, 1901 and 1902, respectively.

*Declared value of exports from Annaberg to the United States during the year ended December 31, 1901.*

| | |
|---|---|
| Buttons | $13,467.94 |
| Corks | 777.09 |
| Cotton, fringes, yarn, hosiery | 2,275.89 |
| Linen goods | 26,382.84 |
| Miscellaneous | 1,624.64 |
| Musical goods | 1,971.88 |
| Paperware | 22,016.29 |
| Tinsel goods | 543.98 |
| Toys | 51,266.71 |
| Trimmings | 398,769.20 |
| Wooden ware | 2,671.41 |
| Total for 1901 | 521,767.37 |
| Total for 1900 | 548,223.29 |
| Decrease | 26,455.92 |

*Declared value of exports from Eibenstock to the United States during the year ended December 31, 1901.*

| | |
|---|---:|
| Baskets | $9,973.76 |
| Brushes | 3,725.13 |
| Chemical colors | 7,926.78 |
| Cotton hosiery | 555,571.23 |
| Gloves, leather | 260,946.41 |
| Hair lace | 577.60 |
| Laces | 56,285.10 |
| Lace curtains | 30,165.90 |
| Linen goods | 18,045.37 |
| Metal goods | 67,717.19 |
| Miscellaneous | 21,882.18 |
| Paper, colored | 78,840.43 |
| Toys | 9,114.82 |
| Trimmings | 210,980.53 |
| | |
| Total for 1901 | 1,326,251.93 |
| Total for 1900 | 1,490,756.25 |
| | |
| Decrease | 164,504.32 |

*Declared value of exports from Annaberg to the United States during the half year ended June 30, 1902.*

| | |
|---|---:|
| Buttons | $14,785.31 |
| Linen goods | 18,070.79 |
| Paper ware | 6,667.12 |
| Toys and wooden ware | 20,863.58 |
| Trimmings | 136,963.80 |
| Miscellaneous | 8,846.75 |
| | |
| Total | 195,147.35 |
| Total for same period of 1901 | 206,499.14 |
| | |
| Decrease | 11,351.79 |

*Declared value of exports from Eibenstock to the United States during the half year ended June 30, 1902.*

| | |
|---|---:|
| Cotton hosiery | $388,240.31 |
| Gloves, leather | 140,225.20 |
| Laces and lace curtains | 36,841.16 |
| Machinery and metal goods | 28,672.03 |
| Paper, colored | 28,056.18 |
| Trimmings | 95,933.25 |
| Miscellaneous | 28,235.88 |
| | |
| Total | 745,704.01 |
| Total for same period of 1901 | 530,508.72 |
| | |
| Increase | 215,195.29 |

The total amount of exports from the consular district of Annaberg to the United States for the year 1901 was $1,847,919.30, as against $2,038,979.54 for 1900, showing a decrease of $191,060.24 in 1901.

The total amount of exports from this district to the United States for the half year ended June 30, 1902, was $940,851.36, against $737,007.86 for the first half of the year 1901, or an increase of $203,843.50 for the first six months of 1902.

JNO. F. WINTER, *Consul.*

ANNABERG, *October 30, 1902.*

## BAMBERG.

Commerce and industry in this district during the year 1901 suffered by continuation of the trade reaction which had set in at the beginning of 1900, and there seems to be little improvement up to this time. The crisis in the banking business last summer and the breaking down of several large mercantile institutions so strained conditions that, for a while, it was feared a most serious catastrophe was inevitable. To make matters worse, the publication, last fall, of the contemplated increase in the tariff created consternation among the merchants and manufacturers.

The most important manufacturing plant of this city, the cotton mills, has perhaps suffered most, but in the whole district there is hardly an industry whose business was not less profitable this year than last.

With all these unfavorable conditions, it is remarkable that so large a majority of the German mercantile and banking institutions weathered the storm, and apparently with little damage. It certainly shows that most of them are built upon solid foundations.

### EXPORTS TO UNITED STATES.

The United States imports from this district are principally china ware—mostly of the cheapest kind—basket ware, and hops.

#### CHINA WARE.

The trade in china ware showed a marked increase in comparison with that of last year. That this should be, in the face of a tariff of 60 per cent, can be accounted for only by the cheapness of manufacture, due to the very low wages paid.

#### BASKET WARE.

The basket-ware industry held its own against the record of former years, but manufacturers admit that the trade with the United States was the only redeeming feature in the general stagnation of business here and in other countries.

#### HOPS.

The hop trade fell off considerably, owing principally to very poor local crops last year and to the very good ones elsewhere, the United States included. As my special report on hops [a] shows, the trade in this article will in the coming year probably more than make up for last year's shortcoming, and a good deal of the exports will be to the United States.

#### BEER.

The export of beer from this district to the United States has been very much reduced, in comparison with former years; other articles, such as steel balls, acetic acid, chemicals, and dyestuffs, have also suffered a large reduction in the volume of their business with America.

The following table shows the exports from the Bamberg consular

---

[a] See Advance Sheets of Consular Reports, No. 1454, September 26, 1902.

district for the first six months in 1902, as compared with those for the same period in 1901:

| Articles. | 1901. | 1902. |
|---|---|---|
| Basket ware | $106,109.13 | $110,868.97 |
| Beer | 5,747.26 | 7,047.85 |
| China ware | 179,577.86 | 201,996.58 |
| Hops | 33,477.72 | 50,430.36 |
| Piano wire | 2,288.61 | 3,015.70 |
| Sundries | 8,981.87 | 6,082.29 |
| Total | 336,188.45 | 379,391.75 |

Increase for first six months in 1902, $43,208.30.

## AMERICAN GOODS.

Cotton for textile purposes is about the only article that, as a rule, reaches this city by direct importation. In view of the habitual disinclination of the German manufacturer to disclose details of his business, it is impossible to tell how much American cotton is used here. It is safe to say, however, that at least 25,000 bales are imported at Bamberg and elsewhere in this district.

I understand that several large snuff factories in Bamberg work up considerable quantities of American tobacco, all of which comes through importers at Bremen, Hamburg, and other ports.

Owing to the general stagnation of every branch of business, the import of American goods into this district has not increased during the last twelve months. Such articles as agricultural implements, machinery, household goods, rubber goods, tools, and thread are in demand here, but there seems no systematic attempt to increase the trade. If properly handled, no doubt it could be greatly enlarged. Our exporters should not neglect this market; too often the sale of their goods is trusted to German dealers who, for various reasons, fail to do justice to American manufactures.

The greater neatness and cheapness of most of the American articles mentioned above, as compared with similar goods made here, are so striking that the consumer will not hesitate to buy if such articles are properly brought to his attention.

WM. BARDEL, *Commercial Agent.*

BAMBERG, *September 20, 1902.*

## BARMEN.

Commerce and industry throughout Germany during the past year have not been at all active. In this consular district, where are located many kinds of manufactories, 1901 has been a record of small profits and increased business risks. But it can not be denied that, owing to the manifold interests represented here, this section of Germany has suffered less, perhaps, than any other. Its working classes have been able to find employment at all times, often at the expense of the manufacturers, who preferred to increase their stocks of goods rather than bring suffering to their workmen by closing down, knowing that the latter had little or no chance of securing positions elsewhere.

The exports of manufactures from this consular district to the United States during the calendar year 1901 show an increase of $356,595.67 in value, although the shipments of textiles were less than in the preceding twelve months. This increase is due principally to an unusually large demand for chemicals, drugs, and dyes, which demand continued the year round.

The continental trade in textiles has been very dull. Some branches of this industry, however, have been quite busy and prosperous, especially during the first six months of 1902. The unsatisfactory results of last year's business were due partly to the South African war and partly to the troubles in China. Still another cause of the general depression is the too rapid development of the German iron industry in the last decade.

The iron mills have another unsuccessful year to record. Orders have been limited and sales of most products profitless. In the fierce competition and high rates for raw material, lies the explanation for this depression.

Boiler makers were rather busier, but even they labored under the same difficulties.

Machine factories had on their books a number of old orders from the preceding year, but new ones came in slowly. Only in those factories building machines for mining purposes—the working of mines not having experienced any retrogression—was activity manifested.

Tool manufacturers during the first months of the year were kept busy on old orders, but both business and prices fell off toward the latter part of 1901. Sincethe beginning of the current year, there has been a livelier call for goods, from various quarters.

The demand and prices for bicycles continued to decrease. Business in this line is unprofitable, owing chiefly to both European and American competition. Orders from foreign countries for parts of bicycles were plentiful. Automobile factories were also busily engaged.

On the other hand, depreciation in value of investments—banking as well as industrial—has brought on such losses to all classes of people that restoration of confidence will be slow.

Although slight improvement in certain manufacturing districts can already be felt, uncertainty as to the fate of the tariff schedule now being considered in the Reichstag is a decided handicap to swifter progress in that direction.

The condition of the different branches of trade represented in this consular district are illustrated by the following statement:

## YARNS.

The trade in cotton yarns during 1901 yielded no profits. The price of cotton showed a downward tendency, the supply being greater than the demand. Only since the beginning of the present year have prices begun slowly to advance.

Turkey-red yarns were depressed until about the end of November, when, in company with prices for cotton yarns, their quotations increased some. Dealers and manufacturers bought from hand to mouth; and one of the results of this policy is that the dyeing establishments have been unable to work full force.    The exports of Turkey red remained small and unprofitable.

The quotations for wool yarns have never been so low as in 1901. Stocks of raw wool were heavy out of all proportion, while consumption continued unusually light.

All cotton-yarn factories in this district during these hard times kept their workmen employed only at a great sacrifice.    The export trade, on account of keen foreign competition, also greatly decreased.

### SILK.

Dealers in raw silk are now obliged to keep on hand stocks of the many different grades of silk (titres) used, the manufacturers—even the larger ones—buying only what they actually need.

Trade in silk and half-silk goods during the past year was rather slow, and owing to the great change in the variety and quality of the articles, their manufacture has become more complicated.

Raw silk from Asia maintained its usual price, due, no doubt, to the 5,000,000 or 6,000,000 kilograms purchased by the United States. Italian silk also was steady.    The demand for dyed piece goods of silk and half-silk material was backward compared with previous years, dyed-yarn materials having the preference.

Trade in silk, half-silk, and wool cloakings in the German market was dull, on account of fashion's demand for only plain material.    Fancy designs are almost entirely out of date.    Vestings of piqué, wool, and half silk were in fair demand in this country, but exports were limited.

### DYEING INDUSTRY.

Silk-dyeing establishments say 1901 was the poorest season in ten years.    Despite the fact that they had to pay higher prices for their chemicals and other materials—such as soaps, cateshu, metallic preparations, etc.—used by them, the rates for dyeing silks, owing to outside competition, have fallen constantly.

Establishments for dyeing wool yarns and other fabrics also complain of a most unsatisfactory trade, a natural consequence of the general dullness in the textile industry.    The substitution of artificial silk for mohair and genappe has also affected the dyeing business unfavorably.

Cotton-yarn and piece-goods dyers consider last year even worse than 1900.

### WOOLEN AND COTTON DRESS GOODS.

The sale of half-wool and all-cotton dress goods suffered from the decline of cotton and cotton-yarn prices resulting from overproduction.

Men's woolen goods, although low in prices, were bought only to complete stocks.    Toward the end of the year, however, the increasing demand induced manufacturers to again start up their looms.

### ITALIAN CLOTHS.

The trade in Italian cloths and similar goods, which at the end of 1900 showed slight signs of recovery, failed to continue to improve and remained unsatisfactory throughout last year.    Profits were even lower than during the preceding twelve months. The Allgemeine Deutsche Zanella convention in April, 1901, reduced the prices of Italian cloths from 8 to 10 per cent, intending to again advance these rates in the fall. This idea, however, could not be successfully carried out, and prices dropped continually until the end of the year.

### UPHOLSTERY GOODS.

Business in these goods was very slow during 1901, owing to French competition, which flooded this market with furniture coverings and almost crippled the local manufacturer. German makers hope that the new tariff will give better protection to this industry.

The export of plushes suffered considerably by the South African war. England, usually a large buyer, showed no desire last year to order more than it actually needed. The export of mohair plushes to the United States, extensive in former years, has dwindled down to only a few cases of high-pile goods. All the other grades, which a quarter of a century ago were shipped by thousands of cases, are to-day manufactured in America. Two of the largest factories in Elberfeld, after trying in vain to keep in touch with their old customers abroad, have lately gone into liquidation.

### BRUSSELS AND TOURNAY CARPETS.

The home trade, although far from satisfactory, was more profitable than the business with other countries, and for this reason local manufacturers were in a position to keep their force of workmen more or less actively employed.

### CLOAK MATERIALS.

The competition of ladies' cloak materials manufactured in France, has seriously affected the production of these fabrics in Germany. The cheaper grades from Saxony are the only kinds that have not suffered from this cause.

### BUTTONS AND METAL WARE.

Metal buttons continued in fashion and the demand for them so increased that manufacturers were obliged to engage many new hands. Clasps for ladies' belts are also in good demand.

### ALPACA BRAIDS AND VELOURS BORDERS.

The former article is still being made here, but its manufacture does not yield satisfactory profits. Competition of Austria and Italy, where wages are much lower, is so seriously felt that German manufacturers will finally be completely forced from the field.

The competition in velours borders has greatly increased, and prices are down to below the actual cost of manufacture. There appears to be no chance for improvement this year, the present demand for these goods being even less than was felt last winter.

### TRIMMINGS.

Metal woven trimmings met with fair sales during the first six months of 1901, but when artificial silk tresses became the fashion, the demand suddenly almost ceased.

Artificial silk cords and soutaches at the beginning of last year were extensively used in Berlin, but since that times, tresses for ladies' trimmings have been receiving the preference and are expected to remain in good demand.

Of Nottingham, Torchon, fine-threaded Valencienne laces, the report is favorable. Their consumption is increasing.

White and colored cotton labels and trimmings were somewhat neglected in 1901. Prices were below cost of production, but toward the end of the year a slight improvement was noticed.

Linen and cotton tapes were rather lively at the opening of 1901, but fell off in March and April, and have not since recovered.

### HATBANDS.

Hatbands for men's hats sold slowly and with little profit, owing to enormous competition. The recently adopted credit system in this branch of manufacture gives the following terms of sales: Five per cent discount for cash, which, however, means payment within three to four months on notes.

### PAPERS.

Fancy papers, chromo papers, etc., which during 1901 were rather quiet, showed a slight temporary improvement later. The exports were far behind those of the preceding year.

### IRON YARN, SHOELACES, ETC.

The year 1900 closed with but poor prospects for these lines, and 1901 brought no improvement. The rise in the price of American and Egyptian cotton during 1900 has also had a depressing effect. Yarn prices were lower last year and stocks of the finer grades heavy.

In the winter months of 1900, the factories making either hat braids or shoelaces were continually busy, but in the spring and summer of the following year the production had again to be reduced. At present, there is a better feeling, and most factories are fully engaged. They complain, however, that although quotations for raw yarn have been advanced about 6 per cent, the prices received for shoelaces remain extremely low.

### CHEMICALS AND COAL-TAR COLORS.

Business during the greater part of 1901 was unsatisfactory. Production remained about the same as in the preceding year. The depression of the textile industry caused dyers to use a much smaller amount of colors and dyes. Besides this, the usually large export of dyes to China came almost to a standstill during the greater part of the year, while the trade with England, on account of her African war, was also greatly reduced. All these troubles naturally had a bad effect on prices. A slight improvement in this industry has been felt within the past few weeks, but whether this change for the better will be continued yet remains to be seen.

Glycerin was in lively demand, and consequently prices of the raw product were somewhat higher. This increased sale of raw glycerin has had no effect on the selling price of the manufactured article, and it will apparently be some time before higher rates are quoted.

## COAL AND IRON.

Owing to the general industrial depression in this district, the demand for these combustibles during 1901 was considerably less than in the preceding year. The consumption of coal averaged fairly well, but the sale of coke could not be pushed even at greatly 1educed figures.

Trade in iron and steel goods was not satisfactory; competition continually increased, new orders were slow in coming in, and selling prices went lower and lower.

## CEMENT.

Without exception, all the cement works in the Westphalian districts have made a very poor showing. The syndicate which a few years ago was formed for the protection of this industry was dissolved at the end of 1901, and since that time, prices have been reduced continually. There is not one of the many cement works that does not complain of heavy losses throughout the year. This industry suffers principally from overproduction, and it is hard to say whether it will ever be able to fully recover from the present crisis. The output of cement in Germany is reported to have increased tenfold, while, on the other hand, the exports of last year constantly decreased.

MAX BOUCHSEIN, *Consul.*

BARMEN, *August 14, 1902.*

---

## BREMEN.

Bremen, one of the free Hanseatic cities, and the second most important port of Germany, has 186,822 inhabitants. The shipping interests naturally predominate; other leading industries are rice mills, oil mills, manufactories of jute and hemp, and linoleum, etc.

## SHIPBUILDING.

There are altogether about sixty shipyards in Germany, large and small, of which five are located in this consular district. All of the latter were very busy during the first six months of the current year, and have orders ahead for some time to come, as will be seen from the following:

| Company. | Completed. | | | | Lighters. | Under construction. | | | |
|---|---|---|---|---|---|---|---|---|---|
| | Sailboats. | | Steamers. | | | Sailboats. | | Steamers. | |
| | Number. | Gross tons. | Number. | Gross tons. | | Number. | Gross tons. | Number. | Registered tons. |
| Joh. C. Tecklenborg (Actien-Gesellschaft), Bremerhaven........ | 1 | 5,200 | .......... | .......... | .......... | 1 | 8,000 | 6 | 27,510 |
| Rickmers Reismuehlen, Rhederei, and Schiffbau (Actien-Gesellschaft), Bremerhaven.................. | 1 | 3,242 | 1 | 1,700 | .......... | .......... | .......... | 3 | 6,100 |
| G. Seebeck (Actien-Gesellschaft), Bremerhaven............ | .......... | .......... | 7 | 4,000 | .......... | .......... | .......... | 11 | 6,500 |
| Bremer Vulkan, Vegesack.............. | .......... | .......... | 6 | .......... | .......... | .......... | .......... | 17 | 60,000 |
| Actien-Gesellschaft Weser, Bremen...... | .......... | .......... | 3 | 5,160 | 2 | a 1 | 270 | 2 | 5,800 |
| Total ............. | 2 | 8,442 | 17 | 10,860 | 2 | 2 | 8,270 | 39 | 104,910 |

*a* Fire ship.

IMPORTS FROM THE UNITED STATES.

While the export from Bremen to the United States, though steadily increasing, is comparatively light, the import from the United States is not inconsiderable. Next to Liverpool, Bremen is the principal cotton port of Europe, and many millions of dollars' worth of this staple is entered here every year. Some 185,957 tons of American cotton was landed during the first six months of the current year.

The following table gives the exact quantities of the leading articles imported at and exported from Bremen from January 1 to June 30, 1902:

| Articles. | Imported. | | Exported. | |
|---|---|---|---|---|
| | 1901. | 1902. | 1901. | 1902. |
| | Tons. | Tons. | Tons. | Tons. |
| Coal | 421,289 | 440,209 | 246,937 | 254,273 |
| Cotton | 182,766,185 | 183,589,541 | 179,013,754 | 189,971,216 |
| Flour | 15,589,281 | 14,547,752 | 16,627,551 | 17,658,185 |
| Grain | 272,572 | 188,563 | 262,495 | 142,546 |
| Honey | 299,941 | 1,031,488 | 234,994 | 1,002,440 |
| Lard | 5,353,136 | 5,717,971 | 5,041,843 | 5,397,589 |
| Linseed | 10,935,029 | 14,411,274 | 1,907,034 | 3,902,242 |
| Lumber | 108,472 | 102,477 | 73,935 | 75,261 |
| Margarin | 1,377,009 | 1,657,579 | 529,198 | 613,161 |
| Oil cake | 4,581,389 | 7,319,367 | 11,094,368 | 13,996,202 |
| Petroleum and naphtha | 34,880,018 | 37,252,012 | 27,733,437 | 26,323,449 |
| Rice | 98,262,920 | 172,036,361 | 88,706,068 | 107,693,910 |
| Tobacco | 29,865,143 | 26,554,209 | 25,860,510 | 23,878,021 |
| Wool | 41,889,678 | 55,980,832 | 41,368,308 | 56,089,991 |

LUMBER.

Touching the import of lumber, attention should again be called to the complaints which have been current here, viz, that American saw-millers and lumber dealers frequently do not cut the timber exactly as the German market demands. If this were done, the export of American lumber would doubtless be much increased. There are a number of American firms which have taken pains to closely investigate conditions here and to meet requirements, and are now doing a large and lucrative business. Only about 7 per cent of the lumber imported into Germany comes from the United States, while Austria supplies approximately 43 per cent, Russia 28 per cent, and Sweden 11 per cent. There is, however, one great difficulty under which American shippers of timber and lumber work, and that is, that, according to the rules of the German railroads, American pitch pine, yellow pine, hickory, and black walnut must pay a higher rate for inland transportation than wood from other countries.

FACTORY SITES.

It is important to note that the State of Bremen recently bought considerable tracts of land on the left bank of the river Weser. When these tracts are provided with ample railway connections, they will for years to come offer excellent sites for the establishment of factories. The object of this scheme is to reduce the cost of tranportation as much as possible, and in view of the fierce competition in nearly every branch of industry and of the prevailing low prices, is expected that manufacturing enterprises will not be slow in taking advantage of the inducements offered.

With its extensive railway connections, and with the abundant facilities of the free harbor—to which another, much larger and better equipped, is soon to be added—Bremen offers to manufacturers, exporters, and importers every advantage for transportation.

HENRY W. DIEDERICH, *Consul.*

BREMEN, *October 29, 1902.*

## BRESLAU.

The decline in the industrial prosperity of Germany, which began a couple of years since, continued during 1901, at times almost paralyzing activity. The brilliant expansion of German industries during the last half decade of the century just ended had led to an extravagant overestimate, especially in the iron industries, of the power of absorption of the home market; to feverish extension of the old and the erection of new factories, and, in consequence of a seemingly insatiable demand, to a tremendous rise in the price of leading raw materials. This latter condition was a serious obstacle to export sales, especially to countries where the cost of production was less than in Germany.

In addition to the glutted home markets, very bad harvests in eastern Germany in 1901 greatly reduced the purchasing capacity of the most extensive agricultural district of the Empire, with attendant unfavorable effect upon the industrial situation.

This condition of things has emphasized the fact that commercial solidity rests heavily upon the acquirement of foreign markets, and this question continues to arouse increasing interest in Germany. Everything possible is done to encourage and develop the export trade, and to prevent any disturbing element from affecting the commercial treaties in force between Germany and other nations.

### DECLARED EXPORTS.

The declared exports from this consular district during the fiscal year ended June 30, 1902, showed a considerable growth, the total amounting to $1,345,738.29, being an increase of $130,534.25 over the preceding year and a gain of $97,900.38 over the export to the United States from this district for the same period in 1900.

There was an increase in most of the leading exports, particularly porcelain, paper, and woolen goods, leather gloves being the only article showing any considerable decline.

The declared exports for the three months ended September 30, 1902, continued to advance, and amounted to $421,348.23, being $53,854.77 over the same quarter in 1901 and $86,087.11 over the same period in 1900. The gain was in the same goods as in the fiscal year ended June 30, 1902, viz, paper and porcelain, while leather gloves showed even a proportionately larger decrease.

### PAPER.

No improvement in the situation of the paper manufacturers of this district took place during this year. The large number of new factories in Silesia and other parts of Germany produced more paper than could be disposed of to advantage. In finding a foreign market, heavy competition was encountered with Sweden, Norway, and Finn-land, as well as with the United States. The English market had long since been lost, and export to Russia and Austria was no longer possible, owing to the fact that these countries have an export duty on rags, while Germany has none, which has had the effect of developing the paper industry in Russia and Austria to such a degree that it would be difficult for Germany to catch up with them, even under an altered tariff.

The overproduction of paper manufactured here at a high cost, and the stagnation in sales, even when made at a loss, affected this industry seriously.

Cromo-lithographs and art prints are not sent to the United States in as large quantities as formerly, owing, it is said, to the high development attained in these branches in America, where such wares can be produced and delivered in large numbers more advantageously than the German goods can be imported.

### KID GLOVES.

This has been a bad year for the kid-glove factories of this district, the export to the United States having decreased very considerably, partly because of the scarcity and high price of lambskins.

The home demand has also lessened on account of the lower prices of Bohemian and Italian gloves, with which it is difficult for the German manufacturers to compete, so long as the supply of skins used here continues limited, and, therefore, costly. These are for the most part lambskins, which come from the Orient, Russia, and Italy, and stand at a high figure, so that this once flourishing industry has greatly fallen off, without any encouraging signs for the immediate future.

### AMERICAN GOODS.

Imports of American goods, as far as can be judged from the exhibits of retail dealers, seem not only to have held their own here in spite of hard times, but also to be actually on the increase; particularly shoes, office furniture, and easy chairs. These importations are indirect, as American goods are usually purchased from large houses in the seaport cities. The merchants who handle them here purchase in too small quantities to import direct.

*Shoes.*—Although there is in this city a large shoe factory, with an American manager and a number of American workmen, that turns out shoes which are made in so-called American styles, the number of stores selling genuine American shoes has increased to five. One of the dealers here told me that he had some difficulty in disposing of his first investment, owing to the comparatively broad toes, and generally comfortable lines of the shoe, which are sacrificed here to the idea of trimness and elegance associated with a sharp pointed toe and a medium high heel. But there seems to be a growing appreciation of the greater ease and the superior make of American shoes.

*Furniture.*—American office furniture and easy chairs attract attention here, and sell on their great merits, but I understand that their plain finish is objected to by the people in this district who prefer something on the lines to which they are accustomed. Desks and cabinets are made in architectural shapes and ornamented with columns and pilasters glued to, and hampering the movements of, the doors, drawers, and other portions, and making the furniture heavy and cumbersome.

*Fruits.*—American dried fruits enjoy great favor here, and during the summer of 1901, when the prospects of the German apple crop seemed dubious, American evaporated apples were eagerly sought at very high prices. The ring-sliced evaporated apple is the favorite, the halved and cored fruit not meeting with the same appreciation.

American dried apricots are also largely sold here, but a report has lately spread through the press, that many shipments have been held up by the police authorities, on account of containing sulphuric acid, and that the Dusseldorf Chamber of Commerce has said that American apricots as a rule have to be subjected to a sulphurizing process in order to preserve them, and there is no telling what the effect on the market may be.

Aside from the fact that the interests of American manufacturers are represented here by Germans only, one of the greatest obstacles in the way of more extensive sales of our goods is the desire of dealers to obtain the same prices they have been accustomed to getting for goods of tedious and costly production. For instance, they expect to sell inexpensive machine-made furniture, knocked down for cheap transportation and readily put together again, at the same price as the laboriously constructed and ornamented furniture made here. If our manufacturers would investigate the methods practiced by Germans in introducing their goods into the United States, they would no doubt find valuable precedents and examples which could be followed in Germany with equally good results.

ERNEST A. MAN, *Consul.*

BRESLAU, *October 21, 1902.*

---

### CHEMNITZ.

The general industrial laxity of Germany is prevalent in Chemnitz as elsewhere, with a slight tendency toward improvement at the present time. The complaints heard all over the Empire are not wanting in this city, although Chemnitz has apparently not suffered as severely as most of the other industrial centers, as the American import trade has, on the whole, been good, especially during the last half year. Those business interests that are dependent mainly on home trade and local consumption are still at a great disadvantage, and continue to struggle under the ban of hard times.

A brief review of the present and past export trade from Chemnitz to the United States will serve to show the tendencies of our commercial relations with this industrial center, and will at the same time throw side lights upon local business in its most important branches.

#### COTTON HOSIERY.

As is well known, it is in the manufacture of hosiery that American industry comes most prominently in contact with the business world of Chemnitz. Marked changes have, during the last decade, been obtaining in this branch of foreign trade. In the export of hosiery of all

kinds from Chemnitz to the United States, there has been a constant
decline.  The trade is being more and more confined to the finer grades
of fancy and embroidered hosiery, the plainer varieties being supplied in rapidly increasing quantities by the prospering hosiery industry of America.  The export of cotton hosiery from Chemnitz to the
United States during the first six months of the present year amounted
to $2,125,828.85.  For the entire year—that is, from July 1, 1901, to
June 30, 1902—it amounted to $3,778,126.47, while for the preceding
year the figures were $3,917,213.20.  The export for the past year
was only about one-half of what it was in the year 1889–90, when the
American market was supplied with $6,103,848.58 worth of cotton
hosiery.  From the above figures, it will be seen that the export for the
first half of the year 1902 was comparatively large, but it must be
remembered that this is the cotton goods export season; and while the
figures for the present year exceed those for the first six months of
1901 by about $85,000, the advance will not be large and will be due
to the increased demand in America for higher-priced hosiery.

WOOLEN HOSIERY.

The woolen hosiery export for the first six months of the present
year amounted to $24,224.59, as against $20,697.91 for the same period
in 1901.  This points toward a slight increase for the entire current year.  For the full year 1901–2 the export of woolen hosiery
amounted to $64,044.37.  Here again, as in the case of cotton hosiery,
there has been a decided decrease in the export for the last fifteen years
or more, as the tables given below indicate.  The heaviest export
occurred in the year 1896–97, when $253,144 worth was sent across
the ocean, exceeding even the extraordinary year of 1889–90.  In
1897–98, there was a sudden drop from $221,634.28 to $53,036.58.

SILK HOSIERY.

The silk hosiery export for the first six months of 1902 was $38,939.42,
as against $23,366.60 during the same period of 1901, thus also indi-
cating better prospects for the German manufacturer for the coming
year.  The export for the entire year 1901–2 was $61,729.36, while
for the preceding year it was $42,723.86.  During the last four or five
years, the American market for German silk hosiery has recovered
slightly, but only very slightly, due, undoubtedly, to the increasing
demand for the high-grade lace and embroidered product.  On the
whole, however, the German silk hosiery export shows a marked
decline, the total amount bought by the United States during the last
year being not even one-half of what was purchased in 1895 and less
than one-fourth of what was purchased in 1889–90.  This must be
accounted for largely by the phenomenal development of the silk
industry in America, as a result of which our production is now within
70 per cent of the entire consumption.
By taking a large view of the hosiery exports to America, the following facts stand out most prominently: An unusually heavy export
during the years clustering around the banner year 1889–90; a subsequent decline, followed by a partial recovery, in 1894–95, and
again a rapid and continued decline up to the present year.  There
seems to be another slight recovery at the present time, but the

American industry appears to be taking permanent possession of its home hosiery market, as the following figures indicate:

| Year. | Exports of— | | |
|---|---|---|---|
| | Cotton hosiery. | Woolen hosiery | Silk hosiery. |
| 1889–90 | $6,108,348.58 | $225,374.63 | $275,611.81 |
| 1890–91 | 5,118,409.73 | 116,045.12 | 185,007.75 |
| 1891–92 | 4,494,150.26 | 141,179.21 | 158,672.46 |
| 1892–93 | 4,865,061.48 | 118,414.45 | 176,754.09 |
| 1893–94 | 4,108,368.20 | 56,186.34 | 60,438.19 |
| 1894–95 | 5,366,991.75 | 143,704.67 | 149,537.83 |
| 1895–96 | 4,302,430.00 | 253,144.00 | 63,189.00 |
| 1896–97 | 4,324,159.47 | 221,634.28 | 40,258.73 |
| 1897–98 | 3,223,864.84 | 53,036.56 | 52,530.90 |
| 1898–99 | 3,177,825.00 | 90,206.00 | 37,443.00 |
| 1899–1900 | 3,515,001.29 | 66,418.42 | 41,785.20 |
| 1900–1901 | 3,917,213.20 | 56,499.30 | 42,723.86 |
| 1901–2 | 3,778,126.47 | 66,187.58 | 61,729.36 |

During the months of July, August, and September, just passed, the export of hosiery, as compared with the same months of the preceding year, has been unusually heavy, so that an increase in trade will undoubtedly be recorded for the coming fiscal year.

### GLOVE EXPORT.

During the first six months of the present year, $555,731.66 worth of cotton gloves was exported to the United States from Chemnitz. This is a most pronounced increase over the export for the same period of the year, 1901, when $345,498.89 worth was exported. The entire year, from July 1, 1901, to June 30, 1902, shows a remarkable export, amounting to $764,812.28, as against $622,663.66 for the preceding twelve months. In general, there was a decline in the glove as well as in the hosiery export trade from the year 1889 (the year of uniformly heavy exports in all branches of textiles) until 1897. From 1897 to the present time, there has been a continued increase in the glove trade which developed into the phenomenal traffic of the six months just passed. The coming year promises even more remarkable figures, as the export for the first half of 1902 exceeds that of any entire year from 1890 to 1900.

### WOOLEN GLOVES.

. The same expansion in the market is shown in the woolen glove trade. The export in this article for the first six months of the present year was $174,813.86, as against $65,845.32, for the same period of the preceding year. The export for the entire year 1901–2, was $419,528.08, while in the preceding year it was but $118,212.22. Here, also, is a remarkable gain, the export being equal to four times that for the preceding year.

### SILK GLOVES.

Silk gloves were exported to the extent of $68,783.19 during the first six months of 1902, as against $50,912.73 for the first half year of 1901. For the entire year, the figure stood at $91,647.13, while for the preceding year it was $96,621.11. The decrease in the export of silk gloves and silk hosiery has been by far more pronounced than in any other branch of the textile trade.

As a result of the extreme activity now manifest in the glove and
hosiery trade, owing to the great popularity of the finer grades of
fancy, embroidered, jacquard hose in the United States, Chemnitz
manufacturers have considerably increased the productive capacity of
their factories by installing new machines. Some factories are so
overcrowded with orders that they do not expect to execute them for
months ahead. Wages in the textile branch have as a result gone up
slightly. This, coupled with the fact that yarn prices also advanced, has
occasioned a rise in the cost of the finished product which is at present,
in some cases embarrassing American importers by forcing the payment of a higher duty through the operation of the price limit incorporated in our tariff.

The following table demonstrates the trade changes which have been
obtaining in the glove export from Chemnitz to the United States
during the last twelve years:

| Year. | Exports of— | | |
| --- | --- | --- | --- |
| | Cotton gloves. | Woolen gloves. | Silk gloves. |
| 1889–90 | $465,690.69 | $686,171.22 | $681,652.85 |
| 1890–91 | 359,806.34 | 263,590.25 | 501,820.64 |
| 1891–92 | 319,639.98 | 344,081.10 | 472,213.93 |
| 1892–93 | 470,823.33 | 461,642.04 | 530,913.55 |
| 1893–94 | 223,491.28 | 200,807.21 | 145,300.58 |
| 1894–95 | 248,800.08 | 164,274.49 | 374,358.07 |
| 1895–96 | 256,637.00 | 381,456.00 | 271,493.00 |
| 1896–97 | 233,107.95 | 293,881.58 | 115,450.53 |
| 1897–98 | 244,887.81 | 36,161.63 | 112,390.28 |
| 1898–99 | 320,701.00 | 134,285.00 | 147,775.00 |
| 1899–1900 | 420,522.43 | 108,875.72 | 111,568.21 |
| 1900–1901 | 622,668.66 | 118,212.22 | 96,621.11 |
| 1901–2 | 764,812.28 | 419,528.08 | 91,647.13 |

### MACHINE EXPORT.

Next in importance to hosiery and gloves in the export to America
ranks machinery, represented mainly by textile machinery and sewing
machines. The export trade in this line has been continually increasing. In 1896, $56,000 of machinery was exported to America; in 1899,
$73,000; in 1900, $91,000; in 1901, $125,000; and in 1902, $158,000.
These figures would probably be much larger were it not that the
machine manufacturing industry is still suffering from the general
trade depression. Wages have been reduced, men are unemployed,
and orders are coming in but slowly. Especially is this reported to be
true of factories making weaving and spinning machines. English
orders for knitting machines driven by motors are reported to be
decreasing. Crochet machines are reported to be in but slight request.
The export of German textile machinery to neighboring States is
considerably hampered by high protective tariffs. Bobbin machines
are in demand. Spool, cord, chenille, lace, and other haberdashery
machines are weak in the market.

### INTERNATIONAL TRADE IN TEXTILE MACHINERY.

The English and German textile and trade journals from time to
time devote space to discussions bearing upon the foreign trade in textile machinery. The German papers deplore the fact that, in spite of
the excellent machinery which Germany furnishes for the home

industry, only a small quantity, comparatively, is exported. British papers go even further in speaking of the unsatisfactory condition of trade in this line, by publicly paying tribute to the superiority of the American makes over the home products, and admitting the progress made by Germany in this branch of the machine industry. One English textile journal, in referring to the seamless knitting machines, says:

Unfortunately, a very large proportion of the machinery used in the Leicester district is of American or German manufacture, but still, it is better to use the most modern machinery, even if of foreign build, than to work on the old lines with old-fashioned machines, and allow the trade to drift away into more enterprising districts.

The question as to the extent to which American textile machinery is actually employed in British factories is a matter of considerable controversy. It is claimed that in but one branch of the hosiery trade is it necessary for the Englishman to come to the American for new ideas, namely, in machinery for the manufacture of seamless hosiery. But even of this class of machinery, only a limited number are of American make, because, since the seamless machine was introduced into England from America in 1891, by a firm of Nottingham machinists, there have been thousands of machines built in England. Attention is also called to the fact that numerous improvements have also been upon the seamless machine by English machinists and manufacturers, such as plating and openwork appliances, and the application of a ribbing attachment for making ribbed hose with plain foot bottom, and for footing fashioned and circular ribbed hose.

Statistics, however, show that there has recently been a marked decrease in Great Britain's foreign trade in textile machinery, due, as English papers seem to admit, to the fact that the English machines are not as up to date as those built in America. The total foreign trade of England in textile machinery dropped from $16,200,000 in 1900 to $10,200,000 in 1902. A very notable falling off is found in the export to Russia, which country took $1,900,000 less in 1902 than in 1900. Germany took $954,000 less; France, $560,000 less; Holland, $275,000 less; the United States, $610,000 less. These figures show that a change of considerable significance is obtaining in the international trade in textile machinery, in which the United States appears to be a good gainer.

### UNDERWEAR EXPORT.

In underwear, the export to the United States shows a slight recovery at the present time, but, in general, there has been a decline in the demand for this article on the part of the American buyers. In 1896, $159,000 of underwear was exported to the United States. In 1901, this figure had gone down to $117,000, and for 1902 renewed activity in the market is demonstrated by the declared export of $142,000. On the whole, the condition of the Chemnitz industry in this branch is extremely unsatisfactory, and complaints from the manufacturers are numerous.

### UPHOLSTERY EXPORT.

The export of upholstery goods, including furniture stuffs of all varieties, fell off considerably during the last fiscal year. In 1896, this item amounted to $67,000; in 1901, it was $188,000, and in 1902, $86,000. Undoubtedly the development of the plush and velvet industry of the United States is largely responsible for the retrogressive tendencies.

The South African war reduced the export of German upholstery goods, including fantasy stuffs, cotelins, moquettes, plushes, divan covers, portierres, etc., to England. In the Orient, the trade suffered considerably from Italian competition. A large quantity of these goods was sent to Sweden, Norway, and Denmark. High protective tariffs in Russia, Austria, Italy, France, Spain, Portugal, and the United States make the exportation of upholstery by German manufacturers extremely difficult.

### SPINNING INDUSTRY.

The cotton-spinning industry, especially where American or Indian cotton is used, is reported to be in a most unsatisfactory condition. The country is suffering from an extreme overproduction because of the installation of a large number of spindles, especially in the Rhine country and in Westphalia, on the Holland border. An attempt was made to restrict the production through the cooperative action of all spinning mills, but it failed because of the varied conditions under which the spinners in different parts of the country were operating. During the months from August to October, 1901, spinning mills were running at a loss of from one-half to 1½ per cent per pound. The total number of cotton spindles in Saxony is 1,044,800. Wages in this branch are reported as having gone up some 4 per cent, but working hours have been reduced, and some unemployed are registered. As a result of the rise in the price of coal, the Saxon spinners have found it exceedingly difficult to compete with the other great spinning centers.

In flax spinning, the same extreme depression is observed. The continued bad harvests of flax in Russia have raised the price about 80 per cent. German production of flax is inconsiderable in relation to the amount annually consumed in the Empire, and most of the crop is said to have been exported. To aggravate the situation, the successful competition of cotton yarn with linen yarn caused the price of the latter to sink. In general, the spinning industry is declared to be in worse condition at present than at any time in the past.

### THREAD INDUSTRY.

The German thread industry finds itself in a similarly depressed condition. Overproduction, heavy competition, fall in prices, characterize the situation. Vain attempts have been made to stifle the intense competition which is forcing prices down to a loss. At present, English competition is feared, because of the consolidation of the Coats Company with the English Sewing Company, representing a capital of about $75,000,000, and now practically controlling the world's market. Germany's main thread markets, aside from the large home trade, are Austria, Switzerland, Denmark, Sweden, Norway, and Russia. English competition is reported to have been so severe in many cases as to force German manufacturers to sell at a loss in order to hold the market.

### RAILROADS.

During the last eight or ten years, there has been an unusual activity in the construction of railroads and in the building or remodeling of depots in all parts of Saxony. Since 1894, some $19,000,000 has been devoted to the extension of new lines, and about $4,250,000 for the purchase of old ones. More extraordinary still are the figures that represent the expenditures for the construction or rebuilding of depots, which, for the last six years, amount to a total of about $36,500,000.

The greater part of this immense sum was used upon the depots of Dresden and Chemnitz. The total investment in railroads, which in 1888 amounted to $160,250,000, has been increased by 25 per cent.

It is a significant fact that, almost without exception, the final cost of construction greatly exceeded the original estimate submitted to the Saxon Government, and sanctioned by it. The following table shows the estimated cost of the work as submitted to the Government, and the amount by which the final cost exceeded the original estimate:

| Name of depot. | Final cost. | Excess over estimate. | Name of depot. | Final cost. | Excess over estimate. |
|---|---|---|---|---|---|
| Borsdorf | $214,000 | $28,250 | Borna | $373,650 | $132,400 |
| Chemnitz (Hilbersdorf) | 3,640,000 | 1,186,000 | Mittweida | 298,500 | 37,500 |
| Dresden | 16,068,500 | 7,601,000 | Wuestenbrand | 363,500 | 47,850 |
| Freiberg | 1,225,250 | 563,250 | Auerbach | 100,925 | 83,050 |
| Plaeun | 307,250 | 63,850 | Hohenstein-Ernstthal | 465,500 | 115,500 |
| Schwarzenberg | 300,000 | 125,000 | Herlasgruen | 55,000 | 25,500 |
| Radebeul | 246,750 | 84,250 | Werdau | 587,500 | 225,000 |

In the construction of new lines, the following mistaken estimates were made:

| Name of line. | Final cost | Excess over estimate. | Name of line. | Final cost. | Excess over estimate. |
|---|---|---|---|---|---|
| Koenigsbrueck - Schwepnitz | $395,725 | $70,725 | Chemnitz-Wechselburg | $2,007,500 | $673,875 |
| | | | Reichenbach | 276,500 | 42,250 |
| Zwoenitz-Scheibenberg | 1,290,500 | 236,500 | Chemnitz-Kleritzsch | 1,274,250 | 500,000 |
| Johannesgeorgenstadt | 195,425 | 95,500 | Schwarzburg-Zwickau | 748,740 | 188,750 |

Local papers call attention to the fact that the enormous expenditures for railroads have almost reached the danger point. However, it is said that no more heavy outlays will be necessary for a considerable time, as the transportation facilities are now sufficient to meet all demands, even with a strong revival of industrial activity. Most of the improvements were begun during the period of great prosperity in the last decade.

Of great local significance is the new Chemnitz Thalbahn. After twenty years of preparation and three years spent in construction, this new railroad running down the Chemnitz Valley was opened on July 1, 1902. It was a great industrial need which called the road into existence. The many small villages and cities clustering along the Chemnitz River have been rapidly developing their textile and other industries. Better facilities for the transportation of raw material as well as of the manufactured products were desired by the manufacturers. The importance of this new line to the American manufacturer lies largely in the fact that it increases the competitive ability of the local textile and machine industry by providing more rapid and cheaper means of communication with the immediate shipping centers.

### FREIGHT RATES ON SAMPLE TRUNKS.

The Traveling Salesmen's Association of Germany recently petitioned the Prussian minister of public works for a reduction of 50 per cent in the freight rates on the sample trunks carried by traveling agents. Austria-Hungary and other foreign countries are cited as having granted such reductions. In France, the Syndicate of Commercial

Travelers has made a request for the transportation of 50 kilograms (110 lbs.) free of charge. Four railroads have granted the privilege, and hopes of general concessions are entertained. It is held that, at present, mercantile travelers tend to reduce the number of samples carried, thereby diminishing their chance of sales.

## FREIGHT AND PASSENGER SERVICE.

During the year 1901, 910,957 tons of freight were received at Chemnitz and 252,156 tons were sent out. The passenger service report shows that 1,633,915 persons left or took trains at the Chemnitz depots during the year 1901.

## COAL CONSUMPTION.

The total quantity of coal consumed in the Chemnitz district, as shown by the amount received at the different coal depots, was, for the year 1900:

| Where mined. | Tons. | Where mined. | Tons. |
|---|---|---|---|
| Stone coal: | | Brown coal: | |
| Zwickau | 173,899 | Altenburg in Saxony | 131,968 |
| Dresden | 23,303 | Thuringia | 91,431 |
| Silesia | 14,407 | Bohemia | 691,808 |
| Westphalia | 30,599 | | |
| | | Total | 915,207 |
| Total | 242,008 | | |

The price of coal went up considerably during the middle of the year 1901, but has since fallen. At present, coal dealers report a fairly steady market. One lowry (100 centners or 22,000 pounds) is quoted at 117 marks, or $27.85, for the ordinary grade of local coal. English anthracite is quoted at 5.50 marks, or $1.31, per hectoliter, which is at the rate of about $12.60 per ton.

## POPULATION.

In 1895, the population of Chemnitz was 161,017; in 1899, 180,813, and in 1901, 207,156.

## POSTAL AND TELEGRAPH SERVICE.

The number of letters (letters, postal cards, printed matter, and samples) received at the local post-office in 1901 was 21,053,006; the number sent was 20,069,998. The number of packages (value- not stated) received was 1,059,948; sent, 1,404,488. With value stated, the number of packages was: Received, 20,654; sent, 80,638. The number of letters, value stated, received was 63,509; sent, 80,638. Money orders were received to the amount of $13,411,110, and sent to the amount of $10,654,675. The number of telegrams received was 10,296; sent, 71,113. Postage charges, including telegrams, amounted to $549,590.

## MEAT MARKET.

The meat crisis is rapidly growing worse in Chemnitz, as in all other parts of Germany. The high protective tariff is an effective barrier against the importation of live stock, while Germany herself is unable to furnish sufficient meat for her people. As a result, meats of all kinds are rapidly rising in price. In Chemnitz, pork is predicted to reach the 25-cent per pound limit by October 1. The poorer people must now look upon it as a luxury. Complaints are numerous and bitter. Appeals are made to those in authority by organizations and clubs of all kinds, while newspapers everywhere are outspoken for the opening of the borders to foreign live stock. The following are the current prices of meats upon the retail market: Beef, $0.166; veal, $0.166; pork, $0.214; mutton, $0.166; bacon, $0.214; ham, $0.2856; sausages range all the way from $0.238 to $0.381.

## LEATHER AND SHOE TRADE.

Manufacturers of leather report that the trade was fairly satisfactory in 1901 and the first half of 1902; but complaints are made that the heavy exportation of hides to the United States is causing a rise in price, thereby reducing the profits of the trade. During the year 1901–2, $75,467.89 worth of calfskins were exported from this consular district to America.

The shoe trade is still suffering from the general industrial depression, as a result of which a large amount of stock was carried over from 1901 to 1902. American shoes, however, continue to find an expanding market, as illustrated by the pronounced success of the American stores in Berlin and Frankfort-on-the-Main. The American shoe is superior in style and finish, and is put upon the market at a lower price than the German article of the corresponding class. Owing to the extensive introduction of American shoemaking machinery, competition with the imported article is developing.

## SOAP TRADE OF SAXONY.

The soap industry of Saxony is in an unsatisfactory condition. This is due to the general trade depression and to the extreme rise in the price of all soap fats. The increasingly bad condition of the working classes and the cold weather during the past year have greatly reduced the demand for soaps. In spite of this, however, prices have gone up because of the scarcity of lard.

It seems that there might be an opportunity for American manufacturers of substantial soaps to enter the German market to a greater extent than at present, if care is taken to cater to the peculiar taste of the German in this article.

## NEW BUILDINGS.

A project that is hailed with joy by the people of Chemnitz is that for a large city hospital, the plan of which was recently submitted to the city authorities for approval. The building itself will occupy a ground space of 30,000 square yards and will be located on a lot of some 150,000 square yards. The plans contain provisions for all the

H. Doc. 305, pt 2——19

modern and most approved arrangements, permitting of the isolation and independent treatment, in some cases in separate buildings, of the various contagious and infectious diseases. There will be room for the accommodation of 1,017 patients. The medical force is to consist of 1 head doctor, 18 regular assistants, and 10 voluntary physicians. Besides this, there is to be a kitchen, a special heating plant, several disinfection rooms, an extensive bathing establishment, convalescent quarters, and adjacent rooms for nurses, attendants, superintendents, and a director. The foundation is to be made of heavy stone and the rest of the building of brick.

In spite of the widespread industrial stagnation, there has been considerable activity in the construction of buildings in Chemnitz during the past year. In the central part of the town, and abutting upon the newly opened street, a number of large business houses and a hotel have gone up. Many concerns also remodeled their interiors or built additions. In the residence portion of the town, costly and luxurious dwellings have been erected.

### ANIMAL CREMATORY.

On August 15, 1902, the new crematory was opened. The erection of this plant marks a distinct advance in the hygienic and sanitary conditions of the city. The offensive odors and poisonous gases which spread in the vicinity of the former dumping grounds (located in a forest on the outskirts of the town) were a source of great annoyance to tourists and residents near that quarter. Now, dead animals of all kinds, large and small, and heavy garbage are quickly and thoroughly disposed of by the process of cremation, taking the form of hot-air disintegration. The bone and glue products are utilized and furnish a source of income to the establishment.

The following schedule of fees is established by the city council for cremation:

1. Large animals (horses, cattle, asses, etc.):
    When not afflicted with contagious disease and hide in uninjured condition, owner to receive 10 marks ($2.38)............................ Free.
    When afflicted with contagious disease and hide to be destroyed....... Free.
2. Smaller animals (hogs, goats, sheep, dogs, and larger game):
    When delivered by owner to the crematory........................... Free.
    When sent for by crematory, hide intact............................. $0.238
    When without hide ................................................ .476
3. Smallest animals (cats, small game, fowls):
    When delivered.................................................... Free.
    When not delivered (first one)...................................... .119
    For every succeeding one .......................................... .0238
4. Cremation of parts of animals:
    When delivered at crematory ....................................... Free.
    When not delivered, for first 10 kilograms (22 pounds) .............. .119
    For every succeeding kilogram (2.2 pounds)......................... .0238
5. Killing of animals outside of crematory:
    Large animals..................................................... .238
    Smaller animals................................................... .119
6. Feeding and care of—
    Large animals (per day)............................................ .476
    Smaller animals (per day).......................................... .119
7. Sending for the same:
    Large animals..................................................... .952
    Small animals..................................................... .476
8. Redeeming and delivery of stray dog................................. .714
9. Use of slaughter rooms, apparatus, and assistance:
    For killing of large animal (and dissection)........................ .476
    For small animals ................................................ .238

The crematory authorities reserve the right to make additional charges in case of special and unusual inconveniences connected with the delivery or cremation of animals.

## WOOD TRADE.

The principal hard woods found upon the local market come from Saxony, Thuringia, Silesia, Prussia, and America. Soft woods are reported to have been drawn almost exclusively from Saxony itself. The Hungarian market, which has in the past furnished the bulk of the hard wood for the local traffic as well as for the general German trade, is now in a precarious condition, owing to the scarcity of the supply. The replanting of the cut areas has been neglected, and it is reported that the present supply will be exhausted in about a decade, while no new supply from the areas that are covered by young wood can be expected for twenty years or more. The exhaustion of the Hungarian forests will create a splendid opportunity for American shippers of hard woods to enter the German market to a greater extent than at present. Full advantage of the situation can, of course, not be obtained unless special pains are taken to cut slabs intended for the manufacture of barrel staves and keg bottoms so as to conform to the requirements of German keg and barrel sizes. In the shipment, also, care is requisite to prevent the sea air from affecting the dark pigment of the grain in the wood, as it is reported that chemical changes are apt to occur which render certain constituents of the wood cells soluble, thereby injuring the quality of the contents of barrels and kegs made of such wood.

## GENERAL.

In conclusion, it may be said that the encouraging aspects of the situation in the local industrial world, as suggested on the early pages of the report, are apparent only in those branches of industry that enjoy a large foreign trade, for those dependent upon local consumption and the home trade are still depressed. Dividends have been considerably reduced during the past year, and in some lines of industry, reports show that factories have been operating at a loss. The condition of the working classes is worse. Lack of employment, reduction in hours, fall in wages, together with a pronounced rise in price of meats and food stuffs in general, are causing much misery. Stocks have gone down, and financial reports show that discounts have been increased. The intense international commercial strife adds to the straitened conditions.

J. F. MONAGHAN, *Consul.*

CHEMNITZ, *September 25, 1902.*

---

## COBURG.

### TRADE WITH UNITED STATES.

The Thuringian States would have suffered greatly in the last fiscal year had not the merchants of the United States blessed them so plentifully with orders for goods. Business with other foreign countries amounted to practically nothing, while the demands of the home market were exceedingly slight.

A great mistake has been made by most American buyers in the past two or three years in ordering goods from the little makers in the mountains who accepted larger contracts than they could hope to fill. Consequently, when delivery time came, the goods were not completed, or, if completed, were wholly unlike original samples. The lack of money and experience on the part of the small manufacturer engendered a feeling of dissatisfaction that could lead to but one result; buyers from the United States have been compelled to go back to doing business through large and reliable merchants in the different Thuringian cities, in that way getting not only a better class of goods, but also having their purchases shipped correctly and in time to supply the demands of the different seasons in their home market.

For the fiscal year ended June 30, 1902, the exports from this district were $115,209.37 in excess of those for the preceding twelve months, which had been considered the banner year; and little Thuringia had shipped $3,564,315.28 worth of its dolls, toys, china, glassware, etc., over the ocean to the United States. During the last three months, the exports increased by $51,077.60 over those for the corresponding period of last year.

### MISCELLANEOUS EXPORTS.

The better kinds of toys and dressed dolls were very much more in demand now than in previous years. The export of slate pencils nearly doubled; that of basket ware, on the other hand, decreased some. The export of the celebrated product of the "Coburg Brewery" has increased markedly, while the shipments of the bitter waters, "Friederichshalle," once so well known and used in America, have almost entirely ceased. These bitter waters are among the best of the world, and are a true product of nature, unlike so many others that are "natural" in name only.

### WOOL-SPINNING INDUSTRY.

The German wool-spinning factories did a much better business last year than in 1900, the general improvement in the weaving centers at Greiz, Gera, Meran, and other localities reacting beneficially on the spinning mills, and causing prices to increase at a steady though slow rate. Cheaper fuel and an easier labor market also contributed to the general betterment of conditions. The tariff changes now under discussion in the German Reichsrath will not affect this industry.

As regards raw wool, sheep breeding is decreasing rapidly in Germany, the acreage under pasture is being reduced gradually, and cheap ocean freights have enabled Argentine, Australian, and South African breeders to underbid home-grown wool. The fate of German sheep breeding is sealed.

### COTTON-SPINNING INDUSTRY.

The cotton-spinning industry was in rather a bad way. Out of 41 joint-stock companies, 25 are said to have paid no dividends, and only 6 yielded more than 6 per cent profit. The majority of spinners, I am informed, are now working at a loss of 1¾ to 2½ cents on the pound.

This industry also is not likely to be affected by the new tariff. The reductions on counts under 30 will have no effect, and on coarse counts German spinners can compete without protection. It is even likely that the duty would be entirely abolished but for fear of the market being swamped with imported yarns.

### SILK WORMS AND SILK SPINNING.

The numerous attempts to cultivate the silk worm (started in 1830) have failed completely, owing to the climate being too severe for growing the mulberry tree.

The prices for silk cocoons in northern Italy ruled, on the average, higher than those paid last year. The quantity of the harvest, however, was not less, but the quality in most districts left much to be desired. German spinners demand, therefore, an advance of from 1 to 2 francs (19 to 38 cents) for silk of the new harvest, and have raised the prices of their stock on hand from one-half to 1 franc (9 to 19 cents). The manufacturers have negotiated for the new silk, but seem unwilling to pay the high prices asked. Chinese and Canton silks, in which the German market is greatly interested, have risen in price considerably, and an attempt is now being made to substitute for them silks from other districts.

But in spite of the high price of raw silk, many orders have been accepted at a loss simply to keep the looms and operatives busy. Work is very slack; in fact many factories are running on three-fourths time only, especially the velvet makers, and manufacturers are utilizing the present quiet times to make up their new collections of samples. Scotch patterns have found good sale, in cloth as well as in velvet, especially those with blue and green ground colors, and fine white stripes. In silk goods, all kinds of Moiré patterns, notably Moiré rayé on satin stripes or figures, seem to have the call. The following prices are at present quoted for raw silk:

| | Marks. | |
|---|---|---|
| Mail organdie: | | |
| Extra class, 17 to 19 threads.......per kilogram.. | 47½ to 48 = | $11.30 to $11.42 |
| Class, 17 to 19 threads..................do........ | 46 | 10.95 |
| Turkish organdie, extra class, 21 to 23 threads .................................do........ | 46 | 10.95 |
| Japanese organdie, extra twisted, 22 to 24 threads.................................do........ | 45 | 10.71 |
| Mail trame, class 34 to 38 threads, treble.....do........ | 42½ | 10.12 |
| Japanese trame, twisted extra, 36 to 40 threads...............................do........ | 43 | 10.23 |
| Canton trame, twisted class, 36 to 40 threads, treble............................do........ | 33 | 7.85 |

### CERAMICS.

The second most important industry in this district is ceramics; and in order to review correctly the state of affairs during the fiscal year ended July 1, 1902, and to consider carefully the outlook for the future, it is necessary to take into consideration the present general condition of the trade.

Many trade journals seemed inclined to paint the outlook at the beginning of 1902 in colors too rosy. These hopeful views were justified only in so far as the last few months have not changed the situa-

tion for the worse. Trade is still rather slow, and it will be some
time before the disastrous consequences of 1901 are overcome. In
Thuringen, most of the potteries are engaged in the export trade, and
as the United States has been an especially good customer, they were
fairly busy. The trade with America is of vital interest to them,
especially at the present time when the home market is just recovering from the recent crisis. England is the next most important buyer,
but even the end of the Boer war has not yet brought so stimulating
an influence to bear on the exports from here to that country as was
hoped for. On the other hand, much coronation ware, such as cups
and saucers, tumblers, etc., have been made in this district and shipped
to England. Yet these extraordinary purchases can hardly be regarded
as regular trade, and as the postponement of the coronation ceremonies
has undoubtedly caused immense loss to London dealers, they will naturally be very cautious buyers in the coming fall. It is not to be
expected that conditions will be decidedly improved in the near future.
Evidently, American buyers are taking advantage of the situation, and
prices for crockery are lower now than for some years past. However, combinations have been instrumental in preventing the cutting
of quotations too much. A good deal has been said and done against
these combinations, but in spite of this fact, they seem to be rather
successful. The idea of forming trade combinations seems to appeal
to the Germans. The Central Union of German Industries especially
is advocating vigorously the cause of syndicates, but so far without
practical results. In the manufacture of pottery ware, the success of
the Coburger Einkaufsvereinigung is significant—54 factories combined in order to buy at the cheapest wholesale rates as much as possible of their raw materials, especially fuel. From a small beginning,
this combination has grown to considerable size. It is partly due to
the Coburg Union that, in this district, the prices of coal went down as
far as they did. On the other hand, it must be granted that the abnormally high rates for this commodity of the previous year could not prevail in a period of general depression like that of the present. The
coal syndicates, however, made every attempt to keep up the abnormal
prices and to reduce production by working shorter hours and discharging many of their men. Following are some of the prices per 10
tons for coal used in this district: The Sächsische Steinkohle, from the
Von Arnim mines, 175 to 185 marks ($41.65 to $44.03); Bohemian coal,
from the Sulkow mines, reduced from 162 to 142 marks ($38.66 to
$33.80); from the Paucraz mine, from 150 to 138 marks ($35.70 to
$32.84); from the Boghead mine, from 150 to 130 marks ($35.70
to $30.94); the very light brown coal from the Britannia mines, from
61 to 53 marks ($14.52 to $12.61). Other independent mines reduced
their price in the same proportion. Of the raw materials necessary in
the manufacture of crockery or china, clay is the most important. The
standard china clay of Germany and Austria is that of Zettlitz, which is
not only exceedingly pure but is also more plastic than the English china
clay which is sometimes used. There are still old practical potters who
claim it impossible to make good hard spar porcelain without using
Zettlitz clay, and this explains why the syndicate that controls the output of the Zettlitz mines has been able to keep up a price of 570 to 580
marks ($135.66 to $138.04) in spite of the fact that there are white
kaolins, such as the kaolin of Hirschau, which can be bought f. o. b.
factory in Thuringia at 208 marks ($49.50). There is rather an abun-

dance of kaolins in Germany, but plastic clays that burn white are very scarce, and there is not one that could compare favorably with some of our Indiana, Florida, Georgia, or Texas clays.

## GOVERNMENT INSURANCE DUES.

Laboring under the burden of expensive fuel and with very few advantages in regard to the most essential raw materials, the German manufacturer is burdened with taxes for Kranken, Invaliden, Alters, and Unfallversicherung (Government insurance for sickness, age, and accident), which have to be paid, no matter what may be the conditions of trade and which annually draw from the industry millions of marks. In looking over the transactions of meetings of manufacturers held within the last few months, one is astonished to note how much of their time was occupied in the consideration of such questions as accident and other insurance. Social reform is undoubtedly an excellent thing; but when a nation that, for its commercial development, is dependent upon the international market goes so much farther than the rest of the world in such reforms, it must face the danger of seriously handicapping its own industries. It would be disastrous to German industry should the German manufacturer finally spend more time in studying social problems than in advancing technical progress or in improving methods that have become antiquated. Thuringia has ceramic factories, where the slip house is 2 or 3 miles from the works to which the clay has to be transported by wagon; plants where the decorator has a ten-minute walk from his shop to carry his work to the kiln—and it would be easy to enumerate many such cases.· Of course, there are factories equipped with every modern device, but the majority find it much easier to cut down the wages of the workingman than to change their method of manufacture.

The labor paper of the operative potters describes the condition in one porcelain factory as follows: A jiggerman in four and one-half days' work produced 500 cups, for which he was paid 22 pfennigs (5.24 cents) per hundred, or a total of 11 marks ($2.62). From this sum there was deducted: for clay, 2.04 marks (48.5 cents) (one wedge of clay weighing 20 kilograms (44 pounds), costing 4 pfennig (0.9 cents); for kranken und invaliden insurance, 55 pfennig (13 cents); so that the man actually received for four and one-half days' labor 8.40 marks, or, in round figures, $2.10. Another instance cited is that of an apprentice boy, who in six days made 1,600 saucers, at 18 pfennig (4.2 cents) per 100, or 2.88 marks. From this amount there was deducted 0.80 mark (19 cents) for clay and 0.17 mark (4 cents) for insurance, leaving him 1.91 marks, or 48 cents, for the week's work. But even if the factory had been in operation only four days a week, the amount of work turned out would still be very small in comparison with that produced by American workmen. We have to take into consideration the German system, which expects the jiggerman to do many things for which cheap help would be employed in the States. In the cases mentioned by the labor paper, probably the lowest figures are given. In other instances, jiggermen are reported to earn as much as 2.50 marks (60 cents) per day. The earnings of decorators seems to vary a great deal. Some shops report wages of 11 marks ($2.62), 14 marks ($3.33), 16 marks, ($3.81), 20 marks ($4.76), and even 30 marks ($7.14) per week— all piecework. The owners of these plants also claim to have other men at work who earn in the same time 40 marks ($9.52). 45 marks ($10.71), 50 marks (11.90), 56 marks ($13.33), or 60 marks ($14.28). The average of both statements is probably the truth.   Laborers receive from 1.50 to 1.75 marks (36 to 42 cents) per day.

Outside of paying low wages, the German factories deduct on account of bad workmanship, for every piece that comes defective from the kiln, in some cases, three to four times the amount paid for making the ware.   Until recently, it was a general custom for all pieceworkers to furnish their own light, or, in cases where the working room was lighted by electricity, to pay a certain amount to the firm for light. This system, however, has been abolished in Bavaria within the last year, on account of a decision by the Government, and for the same reason, the custom is also gradually disappearing in other parts of Germany.   The reduction of wages amounted during the last year, on an average, to from 5 to 15 per cent.   In some factories, the decrease was even greater; others paid at the old rate, but did not run full time or else increased the number of hours in a day's work.   Very few firms were able to keep up the same conditions as before.   But notwithstanding these facts, there was no serious labor trouble, the men being well aware of the state of affairs and the general trend of the trade.

The best illustration of the foregoing remarks is given in the annual reports of the Töpfereiberufsgenossenschaft, the Verband Keramischer Gewerke, and of other stock companies, that are forced by law to publish yearly statements of their business.

### POTTERY.

The Töpfereiberufsgenossenschaft comprises all the ceramic plants of Germany.   At its meeting at Berlin (June 5, 1902), it was stated that the number of ceramic plants had increased by 18 during the last year.   The Berufsgenossenschaft has a membership of 1,014 concerns, with a total of 76,132 workingmen insured against accidents.   The general depression of the trade did not, however, allow a great increase in the number of hands employed.   Compared with 1900, we find only 372 more persons working in ceramics, and this slight increase was caused by the starting of the 18 new firms mentioned above.   Among the new establishments are 5 porcelain factories, 1 white granite factory, 3 stoneware plants, 6 factories making tiles, and 3 firms manufacturing common earthenware.

The Verband Keramischer Gewerke Deutschlands, once the foremost potters' association of this country, has 106 members.   Upon being asked to give their experience during the past year, only 57 of the 106 responded, and of these, 25 said that the amount of business transacted by them decreased, 23 said it remained about the same, and only 9 could report an increase of trade.   The decrease in business naturally varies.   Some porcelain manufacturers talk about losing anywhere from 15 per cent to 33⅓ per cent of their trade, while the white granite factories report an average decrease of 10 per cent.

Following are the dividends of some porcelain factories, as published in the trade journals:

Increased: Porzellanfabrik Triptis, 8 per cent (1900, 5 per cent); Porzellanfabrik Tirschenreuth, 5 per cent (1900, 4 per cent); Unger & Schilde, Porzellanfabrik Roschutz, 5 per cent (1900, 3½ per cent); Porzellanfabrik Rauenstein, 7 per cent (1900, 5 per cent).

Same as last year: Porzellanfabrik Kahla, 30 per cent; Porzellanfabrik Unterweisbach, 12 per cent; Philipp Rosenthall-Selb, 10 per cent; Porzellanfabrik Limbach, 8 per cent.

Decreased: Porzellanfabrik Kloster Veilsdorf, 10 per cent (1900, 12½ per cent); Ilmenauer Porzellanfabrik, 9 per cent (1900, 11 per cent); Porzellanfabrik Schönwald, 7 per cent (1900, 9 per cent); Sitzendorfre Porzellanfabrik, loss $7,000 (last year, 4½ per cent dividend).

In regard to white granite factories, business was best with those firms that make kitchen implements and other articles, such as the Wachtersbacher Steingutfabrik. Unfortunately, however, these concerns did not publish their statements, although I find that the Norddeutsche Steingutfabrik Grohn paid 11 per cent (last year, 10 per cent); O Titel, Kunsttöpferei, 2 per cent (last year, 1 per cent), and Steingutfabrik Sörnewitz, 7 per cent (last year, 7 per cent).

All other branches of the trade in stoneware were fairly prosperous. The concerns making tiles were, however, very much handicapped by the increasing import of French, Bohemian, and, of late, Italian tiles; and those plants engaged in the manufacture of fireproof products had a very poor year.

Thonwaarenfabrik Neufahrn sustained a loss of nearly $30,000; Annawerk Oeslau, near Coburg, declared 6 per cent (1900, 10 per cent); Theo. Neizert, Beudorf, lost $5.960 (1900, 4 per cent dividend); Grossalmeroder Thonwerke, 2 per cent (1900, 5 per cent); Pfälzische Chamotte & Thonwerke Grünstadt, 4 per cent (1900, 10 per cent); Deutsche Steinzougfabrik Friedrichsfeld, 19 per cent (1900, 19 per cent); Ernst Feichert, Sächsische Ofenfabrik (Fayence), 10 per cent (1900, 15 per cent); Schorn & Bourdois, in Düsseldorf, loss $14,989 (last year, $4,061 profit); Didier, Stettin, 10 per cent (1900, 25 per cent); Thonindustrie Klingenberg, loss 32,994 marks ($7,853); Theo. A. Markowsky, Meipen, loss 76,739 marks ($18,264); Chamottefabrik Münsterberg, 8 per cent (1900, 11 per cent); Greppiner Werke, 7½ per cent (1900, 8¼ per cent.)

Of course, this is not a complete list, as actually only a small number of firms give out public statements. I trust, however, that even these few examples will, better than a lengthy article on that subject, demonstrate the condition of the pottery trade in Germany.

### AUTOMOBILES.

Automobiles of American make have never been introduced into this part of Germany, and owing to the high prices asked, I doubt whether there would be much sale for them. If a depot run by a local American house were started, something might be done, but all dealers here are very much opposed to the introduction of automobiles and bicycles from the United States, even going so far as to warn the public in the daily newspapers against using our machines, and branding them inferior to the article " made in Germany."

### OYSTERS.

Fresh oysters have had considerable sale here during the past winter months. They are shipped to this city via Hamburg, and are received in very fair condition.

### RUBBER GOODS.

American rubber goods are excellent sellers, and if a little more effort were made to market our rubber overshoes, a big business might also be built up in that class of merchandise. Russian rubbers, which are rather heavy and clumsy, at present lead all other kinds in the amount sold.

### STOVES.

Our cooking and heating stoves have a virgin field open to them in this part of the world, and the man who has pluck enough to introduce properly the genuine American furnace will no doubt reap a rich harvest.

### EXPORT OF DOLLS.

The last fiscal year has been a very poor one for this trade in Thuringia; in fact, it has come almost to a standstill.

With Great Britain, business has been the dullest in many years. The class of goods exported thither has also been of a very inferior quality, owing largely to the Boer war. The many small doll and toy factories, which have sprung up in England itself recently, and which will no doubt in time fully supply the demand there, have also seriously affected the Thuringian industry.

The demand of Canada for the cheaper grades of dolls and toys from this district has remained steady.

Australia buys most of her Thuringian goods through London agents of local houses and has sent in some quite extensive orders. This trade is on the increase.

With other British colonies, no direct business is done; hence it is hard to judge how much their trade is worth. I imagine, however, from conversations with local merchants, that it is hardly worth figuring out.

The doll trade with Austria-Hungary is epitomized by a well-posted merchant as follows: "On account of the high import duties and the very arbitrary interpretation of the customs laws and rules, what used to be a very important business for us is now reduced to a minimum." And I am told that these remarks apply equally well to France.

With Italy, trade has decreased year by year, and there are no prospects for improvement in the near future.

There never has been much demand for Thuringian dolls in Spain and Portugal, and the present outlook for business with those countries is no brighter than heretofore.

As the duty on dolls, toys, etc., in Switzerland is only 20 francs ($3.86) per 100 kilos (220.46 pounds), considerable business is done with that country, and in return the Swiss send quite a number of their watches, musical boxes, boots and shoes, etc., to supply the local demand for these articles.

The business with Holland and Belgium is considerable, but consists mostly of cheap-grade goods. The high tariffs of Denmark and Sweden and Norway prohibit trade with those countries.

The Argentine Republic, owing to its high duties on such articles as are manufactured in Thuringian, is gradually ceasing to import goods from this district.

Brazil and the west coast of South America have never been large purchasers of Thuringian dolls and toys. What few are bought are of a very cheap grade.

Mexico was once a very big buyer of local products, but of late years has not been so, owing to her increased import duties, which prohibit the low-priced articles being sold at a profit.

Before the Spanish-American war, Cuba was a good consumer for the better grades of toys, dolls, china, etc., but during the past few years, this trade has fallen off greatly.

Trade with Central America is not at all lively at the present time, and shows no signs of becoming so in the near future.

With the Far East, very little business is done direct, this trade being in the hands of London buyers.

## CATALOGUES.

I wish to again call the attention of our manufacturers to the fact that the sending of catalogues printed in English to Germany is simply a waste of time and money. If they want to advertise their goods abroad, they should first get their advertising matter translated into the language of the country whose trade they seek; then, there would be much less risk of its being consigned to the waste-paper basket. Not only must our exporters pay more attention to details such as this, but they must also overcome certain national prejudices (and the latter is no small consideration) before they can hope to see the sale of their goods established firmly in this market. The thrift and shrewdness that have gained for them the patronage of their own country should not be abandoned when they seek the trade of others.

## BOOTS AND SHOES.

An American boot and shoe concern has invaded the German market during the last two years by opening large stores at Berlin and Frankfort, and by prompt business methods and excellent goods, has done more than anything else to make American footwear popular in this country. If others of our manufacturers would follow the example set by this plucky firm—that of importing and selling its own goods and not allowing them to get into the hands of competing German houses—the so-called "American commercial invasion" would be much more serious and far-reaching than it is or ever will be under present methods.

## DRIED FRUITS.

The American dried-fruit business is not increasing as rapidly as it should. Although a "compot" (dried, preserved, or stewed fruit) loving nation, the Germans, especially of central and southern Germany, consume very little of the finer classes of our dried fruit. No German dinner is complete without its dish of "compot," and one would think that the United States, with its splendid fruit products, would be a keen competitor for this trade. But such is not the fact. It would be a good idea for a number of our large fruit-drying and fruit-growing concerns to jointly place a number of cases, filled with

the best specimens of their products, in some twelve or fifteen stores
in as many different cities of the interior.   Our exporters are paying
too much attention to the coast cities and far too little to the good
markets inland.   This is, indeed, a fact that can not be too thoroughly
looked into by anyone interested in promoting our trade with all parts
of Germany.

### HARDWARE AND AGRICULTURAL IMPLEMENTS.

American hardware and agricultural implements have, I am happy
to state, made good strides forward in this district, though there is
still plenty of room here for up-to-date representatives of our agricultural machinery to make profitable sales.   Such agents might
exhibit their goods at the country cattle fairs, to attract the attention
of the real users of farm machinery—the small farmers.   And this is
where illustrated catalogues printed in German would prove valuable,
for it is only after talking the matter over all winter that the village
elders determine what shall be bought for the common use of their
community.
The sales of American coal during the past year have amounted to
but little.   Coal importers are not pushing this trade as they should.
What samples were sent here gave satisfaction, but I am told by local
manufacturers that, owing to the difficulty of getting our coal when
needed, no regular business has been established.

### HORSES.

I wish once more to call the attention of American horse shippers to
the good market for carriage horses in this and neighboring districts.
Horses raised in the Eastern States get along better here than those
brought from the West—a fact probably due to the stony character of
this part of Germany.

### FIRE ENGINES.

Chemical fire engines, if not too expensive, would be good sellers in
all the small towns and villages which possess only the old-fashioned
hand pumps.

### FLOUR.

Wheat flour is beginning at last to be recognized as a good food
product in this part of Germany and is selling well.   The bakers,
however, have been hard to convince of its value.

### PINEAPPLES.

Pineapples, preserved whole or cut up, are a good selling article
here.   A very inferior variety of this fruit put up in tins at Singapore is in greatest demand.   In my opinion, our excellent home article
could compete successfully with the Singapore product in the German
markets.

*Value of declared exports from the consular district of Coburg to the United States of America during the year ending June 30, 1902.*

| | | | |
|---|---|---|---|
| Artificial glass eyes | $1, 338. 11 | Porcelain and stone ware. | $1, 390, 237. 95 |
| Baskets | 11, 612 39 | Slate pencils and slates | 20, 965. 95 |
| Cotton textures and yarns. | 36, 563. 90 | Steel and iron ware | 14, 576. 76 |
| Dolls and toys | 1, 806, 322. 87 | Whetstones | 6, 721. 98 |
| Drugs, chemicals, paints, | | Wine, beer, brandies | 23, 323. 69 |
| colors | 11, 647. 94 | Wooden ware | 2, 364. 09 |
| Glassware | 122, 071. 26 | Woolens | 23, 971. 27 |
| Glove leather | 2, 897. 13 | Sundries | 2, 005. 65 |
| Guns | 23, 700. 25 | | |
| Hardware | 3, 715. 87 | Total in U. S. gold. | 3, 564, 315. 28 |
| Marbles: | | Previous year | 3, 449, 105. 91 |
| China | 16, 202. 03 | | |
| Glass | 14, 259. 02 | Increase | 254, 857. 05 |
| Masks | 9, 103. 11 | | |
| Mineral waters | 352. 84 | Decrease | 139, 647. 68 |
| Paintings on china | 6, 927. 42 | Total increase for | |
| Paper ware | 11, 745. 02 | fiscal 1901-2 | 115, 209. 37 |
| Papier-maché ware and | | | |
| fancy goods | 1, 688. 78 | | |

OLIVER J. D. HUGHES,
*Consul-General.*

COBURG, *July 1, 1902.*

## COLOGNE.

There has been no material change in the industrial condition of this part of Germany since my last annual report. Business, which began to decline about the middle of 1900, according to official statements, has been growing steadily worse.

Overproduction, together with the closing of certain foreign markets to German manufactures, are probably the principal reasons for the general trade reaction. Money is scarce, prices have tumbled, and many firms that had purchased raw material at high rates have been forced to sell their manufactured products at a loss, discharge large numbers of their employees, and reduce wages.

To take care of the many men thrown out of employment on account of hard times, German officials have ordered extensive public improvements in the cities most seriously affected by the depression. For example, the city of Cologne has expended more money for improvements during the past year than in any two previous years, and many persons unable to secure employment at their trade have been given work by the various municipal departments.

### IRON AND STEEL.

Iron and coal, the chief industries of this district, have been affected most seriously by the depression; and although, during the past few months, many iron manufacturers have secured from American firms large orders for spiegel iron and steel bars, it is claimed that the prices received have been exceedingly low. But even at no profit at all, the mills prefer to operate and await better times rather than shut down completely.

The following table shows the exports of iron and steel during 1900, 1901, and the first six months of 1902:

| | Iron. | Steel. | | Iron. | Steel. |
|---|---|---|---|---|---|
| Quarter ended— | | | Quarter ended— | | |
| March 31, 1900 ........ | $5,508.35 | $12,688.73 | June 30, 1901.......... | $5,193.06 | $26,203.91 |
| June 30, 1900 .......... | 8,173.12 | 20,478.76 | September 30, 1901... | 5,879.35 | 33,236.65 |
| September 30, 1900 .... | 21,173.56 | 17,098.88 | December 31, 1901 ... | 237,433.19 | 190,761.30 |
| December 31, 1900..... | 6,557.36 | 22,354.44 | March 31, 1902 ....... | 124,907.25 | 322,224.20 |
| March 31, 1901 ........ | 6,437.47 | 17,356.00 | June 30, 1902.......... | 58,578.03 | 344,127.66 |

## PORT STATISTICS.

There was a noticeable decrease in traffic at the port of Cologne during the past year, as will be seen from the following table:

| | 1900. | | 1901. | |
|---|---|---|---|---|
| | Ships. | Tons. | Ships. | Tons. |
| ARRIVALS. | | | | |
| Upstream.................................................... | 2,438 | 398,585 | 2,415 | 384,678 |
| Downstream................................................ | 3,405 | 192,976 | 2,924 | 112,075 |
| DEPARTURES. | | | | |
| Upstream.................................................... | 3,353 | 135,723 | 2,852 | 107,263 |
| Downstream................................................ | 2,290 | 131,077 | 2,279 | 120,350 |

Concerning the industrial prospects for the future, it may be said that a slight improvement has recently been noticed, and a further increase may be expected, providing production is limited to a reasonable degree.

CHAS. E. BARNES, *Consul.*

COLOGNE, *August 28, 1902.*

---

## CREFELD.

Industrial conditions in this district show no decided change from the preceding twelve months; the general business depression which began in 1900 still continues. The chief industries—silk and velvet—however, suffered less from the unfavorable conditions than did other branches.

The total sales have not materially diminished, but prices could not be advanced, and there is a decided lack of activity in most industries. The South African war has also been instrumental to no small extent in decreasing the total trade of the Empire. The exports and imports of Germany during the last two calendar years have been:

| Year. | Million marks. | United States currency. |
|---|---|---|
| EXPORTS. | | |
| 1900 ................................................... | 4,611.4 | $1,097,513,200 |
| 1901 ................................................... | 4,431.4 | 1,054,673,200 |
| Decrease of ..................................... | 180.0 | 42,840,000 |
| IMPORTS. | | |
| 1900 ................................................... | 5,765.6 | 1,372,212,800 |
| 1901 ................................................... | 5,421.2 | 1,290,245,600 |
| Decrease of ..................................... | 344.4 | 81,967,200 |

## SILK.

The general depression of the past year has not been so distinctly felt in the silk industry. Most of the factories have been reasonably busy, but in some, periods of idleness could not be avoided. The demand for silks does not, on the whole, appear to have decreased, although prices are lower. But as these goods are continually growing in popularity, a return of normal conditions would warrant a hopeful view of the future welfare of this industry.

Business with England has in the main been satisfactory; however, the influence of the South-African war and the competition of France, Switzerland, and Italy were felt. The immense business of former years with the United States, because of the high tariffs and the tremendous progress made by the factories of that country, has been reduced to scarcely more than the supplying of special articles.

The raw-silk trade of the past year may be considered as satisfactory. Although profits were not large, they were better than were expected, considering the unfavorable political and financial conditions. Prices at the beginning of the year were very low. It was generally believed that the stocks of raw silk, particularly in Yokohama, were large; early in the year, however, an increased demand stimulated prices. The heavy purchases by America were especially significant. In June, prices showed material advances, and under the influence of a steady world demand, continually went upward. The year closed with the raw-silk business in a healthy condition.

The first half of the year was unfavorable to the spun-silk trade; the price fell about 11 cents per pound. With the beginning of the second half of the year, however, there was a change for the better.

There was a good demand for spun silk for both velvet and silk goods. The loss in price has not only regained, but also advanced to beyond that of the preceding January. The largest demand was for the cheaper qualities.

### VELVETS.

The past year did not again witness the severe slump in raw materials which in 1900 resulted so disastrously to the velvet trade. The price of silk, schappe, and cotton yarn went below even the low prices of December, but in May and June, the quotations for silk schappe began to pick up, continuing to advance irregularly until the highest price of January was reached and exceeded. On the other hand, the price of cotton yarn remained at the low point reached in June. The downward tendency of the prices of raw material so affected the trade that only with difficulty was the fall business closed at profitable prices.

### FINISHERS' STRIKE.

A strike occurred among the velvet finishers, lasting from the latter part of July until the middle of September, 1901. It was caused by about 300 velvet shearers demanding a 20 per cent increase of pay and certain modifications of the wage scale. Their places were filled by workmen from the other branches of the industry, and the factories suffered only a small loss. Very few of the strikers have as yet returned to their places.

## DYEING.

Business with the silk and velvet factories has been quite good.  The amount of silk and schappe colored was about the same as last year. The coloring of schappe for the velvet factories was especially satisfactory.

The business for cotton velvet was very good for the first half of the year, but decreased during the last half.  Very little cotton for cloth was colored.  Despite the low prices of 1900, they were still further reduced in 1901.  Piece dyeing was very unsatisfactory.  The dyehouses have established uniform prices, which has somewhat improved conditions.

The total paid for dyeing amounted to 10 million marks.

## COTTON-SPINNING MILLS.

The hope for improvement in the cotton-spinning industry in Germany, during the year 1901, was not realized.  A report of the incorporated companies of Germany (numbering 44 concerns, with a total of about 2 million spindles and a combined capital of about $10,472,000, or, including loans, $20,700,000) says that only 11 companies will be able to declare a dividend, and that some of the mills have been operated at a loss.

Under steadily declining prices and altogether unsatisfactory conditions, the cotton-spinning industry in 1901 went from bad to worse, and the year closed with a situation amounting to a real crisis.  The unfortunate results in this industry during the past year would seem to be due not so much to the lack of demand for cotton goods as to the fluctuating and generally declining price of raw cotton.

The improvements in the Krefelder Spinnerei have been completed. Its capacity has been enlarged from 45,111 spindles to 53,250 spindles for spinning and 1,760 spindles for twisting.  The plant is now equipped with up-to-date machinery.

The difficulty in securing skillful operators has not yet been fully overcome, but as the efforts being made to educate workmen for the purpose are meeting with a fair degree of success, the management hope for better results in the coming year.

The Uerdingen Spinnerei, also in the Crefeld district, reports a production, in 1901, of 2,494,963 pounds of yarn of an average No. 20, as against 2,079,166 pounds of an average No. 20.6 in 1900.

## VELVET AND SILK INDUSTRIES.

The following statistics are taken from the report of the Crefeld Chamber of Commerce:

*Factories in operation during the past two years.*

| Year. | Velvet. | Silk and part silk. | Silks and velvets. | Dye. houses. |
|---|---|---|---|---|
| 1900 | 26 | 84 | 7 | 39 |
| 1901 | 29 | 85 | 8 | 37 |

*Average number of looms in operation during 1900 and 1901.*

| For— | 1900. | | 1901. | |
|---|---|---|---|---|
| | Hand looms. | Machine looms. | Hand looms. | Machine looms. |
| Velvet | 846 | 2,076 | 649 | 1,961 |
| Velvet ribbons | 221 | 276 | 234 | 365 |
| Silk | 5,834 | 7,151 | 5,410 | 7,783 |
| Ribbons | 262 | 151 | 258 | 159 |

The following is the value of silk and velvet products of the Crefeld factories during the past two years:

| Year. | Velvet. | Silk. | Total. |
|---|---|---|---|
| 1900 | $5,800,000 | $13,750,000 | $19,550,000 |
| 1901 | 5,650,000 | 13,710,000 | 19,360,000 |

The number of pounds of raw material used was as follows:

| Year. | Silk. | Schappe. | Cotton. | Wool. |
|---|---|---|---|---|
| | *Pounds.* | *Pounds.* | *Pounds.* | *Pounds.* |
| 1900 | 1,336,000 | 696,000 | 3,411,000 | 336,900 |
| 1901 | 1,383,000 | 680,000 | 3,000,000 | 267,000 |

### SILK AND VELVET DYEHOUSES.

The quantity of raw material colored in 1901 was:

| In Crefeld factories: | Pounds. | Outside of Crefeld: | Pounds. |
|---|---|---|---|
| Silk | 1,096,000 | Silk | 1,431,000 |
| Schappe | 612,000 | Schappe | 423,500 |
| Cotton | 2,480,000 | Cotton | 1,512,000 |
| Wool | 197,000 | Wool | 19,000 |

The average number of workmen employed in this industry during the year was 2,646.

### EXPORTS.

The total value of declared exports to the United States from this consulate for the year ended June 30, 1902, was as follows:

| | | | |
|---|---|---|---|
| Cotton goods | $73,744.31 | Silk | $65,980.07 |
| Cotton velvets | 94,797.04 | Spun silk | 685,266.19 |
| Dyestuffs | 208,490.22 | Sundries | 130,134.38 |
| Half silks | 328,082.03 | Velvet | 726,053.49 |
| Paper ware | 54,264.71 | | |
| Ribbons | 271,281.68 | Total | 2,638,094.12 |

The total value of declared exports for the five years 1896–1900 was: 1896, $3,104,914.74; 1897, $1,865,429.93; 1898, $2,065,027.21; 1899, $2,846,165.17; 1900, $2,684,629. The exports of velvet and silk were:

| Goods. | England. | France. | Austria. | Other European countries. | Outside of Europe. | Domestic trade. |
|---|---|---|---|---|---|---|
| Velvet | $1,800,000 | $305,000 | $55,000 | $304,000 | $1,850,000 | $2,500,000 |
| Silk | 2,900,000 | 630,000 | 420,000 | 810,000 | 780,000 | 8,400,000 |

H. Doc. 305, pt 2——20

The total values of both export and domestic trade are about the same as for the year 1900.

## PUBLIC BUILDINGS.

The new chamber of commerce building was formally opened on November 8, 1901, in the presence of the State, city, and board of trade officials and representatives of the various business interests of the district.

The building provides ample and convenient office rooms and assembly hall for the board and in addition contains "The Kaufmann Schule" (merchants' school). The purpose of this school is to prepare young men and women for business life. Shorthand, typewriting, and general account work, including banking, are taught; also commercial correspondence in the German, English, and French languages. Last term, 352 pupils were enrolled in this school, which is under the management and control of the chamber of commerce.

THOMAS R. WALLACE,
Consul.

CREFELD, October 24, 1902 ·

## DRESDEN.

According to the last estimate made by the bureau of police, the population of Dresden is 405,600.

## ECONOMIC CONDITIONS.

The era of hard times in Saxony, referred to in my last report, still continues, but the people are economical and thrifty and will soon work out of their difficulties. The depression throughout the country is largely due to an overproduction in manufactured goods, particularly in electrical machinery and appliances, in the production and use of which the German is abreast of the times. Several electrical roads were built and equipped between points where traffic did not warrant the enormous expenditure, and the result was failure not only to the enterprises in question, but also to the banks which largely furnished the means.

During the spring and summer of 1901, the financial storm culminated in the failure of the Actien Gesellschaft Electricitaetswerke, vorm. A. L. Kummer & Co., causing the Creditanstalt fuer Industrie und Handel at Dresden, with its numerous branches, to suspend payment. This created a panic among the depositors in all the banks in Dresden, and several of the latter were forced to close their doors; but the Dresden Bank met all demands promptly and came out of the storm with increased credit. Closely following this, the Leipziger Bank, founded in 1839, and one of the oldest and most trusted moneyed institutions of Saxony, failed, resulting in a loss to depositors and stockholders of some 80,000,000 marks ($19,040,000). An examination of the books of the bank developed great irregularity on the part of the directors, who were all men of prominence. One of the directors committed suicide, one fled to America, while a number have recently been sentenced to several years' imprisonment.

During the prosperous years of manufacturing, real estate largely appreciated in value, and when the reverse was felt, the values of real estate dropped to a low figure in comparison. As a result, several savings banks in this city failed, and this proved a great disaster, as the depositors were mainly among the poorer classes.

These financial difficulties severely affected many manufacturing interests, compelling them to reduce their force or shorten working hours. Wages were reduced about 10 per cent, but only a few strikes occurred, among which the glass workers' strike was the most prominent, resulting in defeat of the workmen.

In the face of this deplorable condition, the Government levied an increase of 25 per cent in the city and state taxes, and made a similar advance in court costs, to continue at least during the current year. The total taxes in Dresden, on all incomes amounting to 400 marks ($95.20) annually and over, are about 6$\frac{1}{2}$ per cent.

While the situation here is not cheerful, it would be much worse but for the fact that orders for goods from the United States and other export countries continued, the volume to America showing an increase of 30 per cent over the traffic in 1900. Exports to England and South Africa have suffered somewhat because of the war, and to Russia a reduction may be expected if the proposed new tariff, and especially if the proposed agricultural customs duties, are placed in effect; but the people are fairly well satisfied with the foreign trade, and believe it has prevented a more widespread depression among the manufacturing interests in Saxony.

### COMMERCE.

The total value of declared exports from this consular district to the United States of America during the fiscal year ended June 30, 1902, was $1,390,923.32, an increase of $253,429.53 over the preceding fiscal year. Artificial flowers have advanced again from $271,535.98 last year to $444,790.14, while tobacco has dropped from $144,788.70 to $24,992.10, for reasons stated in my last report.

Direct imports from the United States into this consular district are limited, and while American manufactured goods are exposed for sale in many stores, they are purchased in most cases from the large importing houses in Hamburg and Bremen.

Some machinery, patent medicines, and boots and shoes are purchased direct from the manufacturers, but it seems impossible to ascertain to what extent. The customs duties are directed by the Imperial German Government, and whenever I have sought information on the subject, I have been referred to the authorities at Berlin.

I am convinced that American exporters can increase their trade with this consular district, but it can not be accomplished by correspondence or by sending circulars printed in English. It must be done by agents who speak the language and have time and patience to deal with a slow, cautious people. Tardy results must be expected, but if our manufacturers will study the requirements of the market, as has been done with bicycles and some kinds of machinery, and make the goods to suit, I am satisfied the outcome will prove satisfactory.

### GENERAL TRAFFIC.

(a) *Railroads.*—The Royal Saxon railroads during 1901 carried 66,270,743 passengers and 37,926 tons of passenger baggage, besides

23,608,609 tons of merchandise. The total receipts, including freight traffic, amounted to 114,293,765 marks ($27,201,916), showing a decrease of 4.70 per cent since the preceding year. It is proposed to withdraw the forty-five-day return tickets and issue instead only single tickets, at reduced rates. The average wages of all the workmen in the government railroad shops were 2.85 marks (68 cents) a day.

(b) *Street cars.*—The two electric street car companies in Dresden carried, in 1901, 78,534,176 passengers, against 72,280,129 in 1900. The total receipts were 7,198,454 marks ($1,713,232). The total length of track was 109 kilometers (67.7 miles). Both companies operated 854 cars, of which 509 were motor cars.

NOTES.

The number of transients in this city was 284,073, against 351,905 in 1900.

So far as I can learn, considerable interest is felt by the people here in the St. Louis Exposition, and if business conditions improve during the remainder of this and the coming year, as may be expected, I believe a number of the manufacturers in this district will send exhibits.

CHAS. L. COLE, *Consul-General.*

DRESDEN, *August 15, 1902.*

DÜSSELDORF.

The situation of the iron and steel industry, which, in conjunction with the mining of coal and ore and the production of coke and other fuel, is the most conspicuous trade in this consular district, is described by a thoroughly informed manufacturer as follows:

The present time is by no means the worst which the German iron and steel industries have had to endure, but it never was so difficult to give a correct opinion of the general commercial situation of this district as is the case now. The wars in China and South Africa, to which the general decline which set in two years ago had been attributed, are over, but it can not be said that this gratifying fact has had any favorable effect on the present market condition. The truth is that while those political events may have contributed to the aggravation of the situation, they were certainly not the cause of the decline, but the latter was brought about by the immense overspeculation and overproduction in all branches of the iron and steel industries. The remedy must therefore not be expected to come from outside, but from within, and this requires much time.

COAL.

Before the beginning of the general decline in the prominent trades of this district, the consumption of fuel had reached an enormous height, and had caused an extraordinary demand upon the productiveness of the Rhenish-Westphalian coal mines. The consequence was that mine owners enlarged their plants to the best of their abilities, and new shafts were sunk and additional coal fields made accessible. Even as late as 1900 and 1901, over 30 new mining plants were added to the establishments belonging to members of the Rhenish-Westphalian coal syndicate, and equipped with the most modern improvements and appliances. In 1900, the said syndicate (a combine comprising almost 90 per cent of all coal-producing concerns of Western Germany and regulating and controling their entire output and sale) was still in a position to refer orders for coal to its several members, to the full extent of the production allowed to each by the administration of the trust.    This was no longer the case in 1901, and a general reduction in coal production of 3.20 per cent was agreed upon by the members of the syndicate.    This reduction has steadily advanced until it is now 28.6 per cent.

The entire production of coal in the Kingdom of Prussia amounted to 101,966,158 metric tons[a] during 1900; during 1901 it was 101,203,-807 tons, thus showing a decline of 762,351 tons or 0.75 per cent.    In these figures, the production of the eastern districts is included, with 24,829,284 metric tons in 1900 and 25,251,943 in 1901 (increase 1.70 per cent).    The production of the western or Ruhr district was 60,119,-378 metric tons in 1900 and 59,004,609 tons in 1901.    These figures include the production of the aforementioned syndicate—52,080,898 tons in 1900 and 50,411,926 in 1901.

The decline in the consumption of coal on the domestic market has prompted the managers of the syndicate to pay more attention to the export business, and they succeeded fairly well in increasing the same, though not at the rate expected nor at satisfactory prices, their British competitors being very active, because their domestic market, like the German, is unable to take up the entire home production.

About 16¼ per cent of the coal shipped by the members of the syndicate in 1901 went outside of Germany, or 3.45 per cent more than during the previous year.

The following table shows the quantities of coal ready for consumption in Germany, taking into account the production, imports, and exports of coal for the past five years:

[1 kilogram = one one-thousandth of a metric ton.]

| Years. | Production of coal in German Empire. | Percentage of increase (+) or decrease (−) against previous year. | Imports. | Percentage of increase (+) or decrease (−) against previous year. | Total. | Percentage of increase (+) or decrease (−) against previous year. |
|---|---|---|---|---|---|---|
| | *Metric tons.* | *Per cent.* | *Metric tons.* | *Per cent.* | *Metric tons.* | *Per cent.* |
| 1897 | 91,054,982 | +6.26 | 6,072,080 | +10.87 | 97,127,012 | +6.54 |
| 1898 | 96,309,652 | +5.77 | 5,820,332 | − 4.15 | 102,129,984 | +5.15 |
| 1899 | 101,639,758 | +5.53 | 6,220,489 | + 6.88 | 107,860,242 | +5.61 |
| 1900 | 109,290,237 | +7.53 | 7,384,049 | +18.71 | 116,574,236 | +8.17 |
| 1901 | 108,417,029 | −0.80 | 6,297,389 | −14.72 | 114,714,418 | −1.68 |

| Years | Exports. | Percentage of increase (+) or decrease (−) against previous year. | Consumption. | Percentage of increase (+) or decrease (−) against previous year. | Per capita of the population. | Percentage of increase (+) or decrease (−) against previous year. |
|---|---|---|---|---|---|---|
| | *Metric tons.* | *Per cent.* | *Metric tons.* | *Per cent.* | *Kilogram.* | *Per cent.* |
| 1897 | 12,389,907 | + 6.82 | 84,737,105 | +6.50 | 1,577 | +4.92 |
| 1898 | 13,989,223 | +12.91 | 88,140,761 | +4.02 | 1,618 | +2.60 |
| 1899 | 13,943,174 | − 0.33 | 93,917,068 | +6.55 | 1,700 | +5.07 |
| 1900 | 15,275,805 | + 9.56 | 101,398,481 | +7.97 | 1,800 | +5.88 |
| 1901 | 15,266,267 | − 0.06 | 99,448,151 | −1.92 | 1,765 | −1.94 |

[a] Of 2,205 pounds.

## IRON AND STEEL.

At the beginning of last year, the producers of pig iron and the manufacturers of the various shapes in which iron and steel are brought on the market had their books filled with orders, and were at the same time bound by contracts to take up large quantities of raw materials at high prices. But the purchasers of finished articles were unable to call for the goods they had taken, nor could they pay the old prices. In many cases, the works gave the goods to the bailiff for public auction for account of the parties who had purchased the wares.

In order to avoid an accumulation of stocks, and to keep their laborers employed, manufacturers began again to cultivate the export business, which had been somewhat neglected under the pressure of the demand from the domestic market. Assisted by export premiums from the syndicates, they succeeded in getting rid of considerable quantities, the present flourishing conditions in the United States proving of great benefit to the German industry, and enabling the latter to dispose of huge consignments of pig iron, steel billets, joists, beams, girders, rails, etc.

The value of ferro manganese declared at this office for export to the United States during the year ended December 31, 1901, amounted to $133,034.16, and from January, 1902, to the present day, $129,573.03. In these figures are not included the exports of this article from the United States consular agency at Essen, which began in the middle of last year and have up to this time reached $167,306.62.

The exportation of steel in the various shapes above enumerated commenced during the first quarter of the current year, and, up to this date, has aggregated $927,086.29 from Duesseldorf and vicinity, and $404,466.03 from the agency at Essen.

Thus, the United States industry has relieved the foundries and steel works of this consular district of $429,913.81 worth of pig iron and $1,331,552.32 of steel, altogether $1,761,466.13. The exports of both pig iron and steel have apparently not yet come to an end.

## MACHINES AND MACHINE TOOLS.

German manufacturers of most classes of machines and machine tools are complaining bitterly about the present poor business, and say they are suffering severely from lack of orders and also from the unsatisfactory prices they receive for their work. This is very natural, as in all branches manufacturers are trying to get along with old machines, and they actually do get along, as there is no inducement for them to increase their output. There are only a few establishments that recognize that this is a good time for replenishment, in order to be in a position to meet all exigencies when business revives.

## UNITED STATES TOOLS.

The importation of American machine tools and other machinery used in iron and steel works and in mines, which was a paying business a few years ago, naturally suffered severely under the business depression, and many machines that had been imported and laid in stock for sale were returned to the United States during the past and the current year, because there was no way of disposing of them in this country.

While it will require a long time for this trade to revive, there are still specialties in other lines, such as sewing machines, agricultural machines, automatic cutters, and apparatus for clay working and ceramic establishments, which are preferred for their superiority in construction and finish, and find a comparatively ready sale.

The exportation of machinery from this district to the United States is confined to specialties used in the manufacture of sugar and to some textile machines and machinery parts. For the year ended June 30, 1902, $190,144.38 worth of machinery and parts were declared for export to the United States at this office, which .figure includes considerable shipments of sugar machinery for Cuba.

### IRON AND STEEL STRUCTURES.

This branch of business is of considerable importance in this district. As long as the business of mining companies, steel works, rolling mills, blast furnaces, and machine shops was flourishing, they had work for the constructors of iron and steel framing, and even now, while those industries can no longer be relied upon as customers, the demand from State and municipal authorities and railroad administrations has not ceased. Constructors also obtain orders from outside of Germany, and are thus busy enough. The prices, however, are complained of as very low at present, and so inadequate that many firms prefer not to undertake any large jobs, but to reduce their operations to the smallest possible scale. While at the beginning of 1901, the erection of large steel structures was still paid for at the rate of from 250 to 300 marks (=$59.50 to $71.40) per metric ton, at the end of the same year, when competition was invited for the erection of railroad bridges, there were offers submitted to the railroad authorities at the rate of 190 marks ($45.22) per ton, inclusive of freight and everything.

Constructors complain also of the proceedings of German manufacturers of joists and other structural iron and steel, who offer their products in the foreign markets at considerably lower prices than at home, and thereby enable foreign constructors purchasing their material in Germany to work at less rates than their German competitors, and render the latter's foreign business even more difficult than under ordinary circumstances.

### EXPOSITION.

The industries above alluded to being the leading trades in this consular district, its commercial condition is dependent on their prosperity, and consequently all other trades are suffering severely under the general depression.

This depression has not, however, prevented Rhenish and Westphalian manufacturers and producers from displaying the results of their abilities, resources, and energies in a splendid exhibition, held at this city during the present season, which tends to show that there are still considerable reserves at their disposal. The exposition, in which the mining of coal and ore, the production of iron and steel, the manufacture of guns, shipbuilding, the construction of all sizes, kinds, and descriptions of machinery, and electricity, are most prominent, but in which all other trades, arts, and crafts of these provinces, as well as their social, sanitary, and educational institutions, are represented, has proved a success in every respect and has excited the unanimous admiration of some 3,000,000 visitors from all parts of the world, among them a good many from the United States. The undertaking has also proved self-sustaining. About $200,000 has been contributed by the exposition toward the erection of an art palace, and any other surplus will likewise be devoted to the promotion of fine arts.

P. LIEBER, Consul.

DÜSSELDORF, <i>September 30, 1902.</i>

----

## FRANKFORT-ON-THE-MAIN.

The business depression of Germany, which set in about two years ago, is still felt very keenly in many branches of industry. Owing to the severe losses sustained through bank failures, the collapse of manufacturing establishments and other commercial enterprises, the German people have been forced to economize, and consequently, the home demand for goods of all kinds has been greatly lessened; wages have decreased, workingmen have been discharged, and hours of labor reduced. This has had the result, also, of diminishing imports. Fortunately, however, for German manufacturers, and especially for German labor, the export trade has not suffered, at least not in quantity. The export to the United States shows an increase of over 30 per cent in value for the third quarter of the present year, compared with the same period of 1901, rising from $24,722,767.06 to $32,399,526.49.

While German manufacturers have undoubtedly sold their industrial products in many instances at very low prices, still German labor has been benefited by being kept busy for foreign markets, and this has alleviated the situation to a very marked degree.

The latest official statistics of the German Federal Government at my disposal are those for the first eight months of the current year. For the purpose of comparison of the imports and exports, I have in the following tables compared the first eight months of 1902 with the corresponding periods of preceding years.

The total imports and exports of Germany for these periods (expressed in metric tons of 2,204.6 pounds) were:

| IMPORTS. | | EXPORTS. | |
|---|---|---|---|
| 1902 | 27, 830, 094 | 1902 | 22, 029, 385 |
| 1901 | 29, 854, 879 | 1901 | 20, 785, 476 |
| 1900 | 29, 215, 675 | 1900 | 21, 386, 857 |

The imports for the first eight months of 1902 were 1,524,785 tons less than for the same period of 1901, and 1,385,581 tons less than for 1900, while the exports for 1902 are 1,243,909 tons in excess of the same period of 1901, and 642,528 tons over 1900.

The excess of imports over exports was—

| | Tons. |
|---|---|
| 1902 | 5, 800, 709 |
| 1901 | 8, 569, 403 |
| 1900 | 7, 828, 818 |

A decrease of imports for the first eight months of 1902 was shown in the following articles, compared with the same period of 1901:

Tons.
Waste ........................................................ 125, 713
Iron, and wares of iron ....................................... 117, 750
Earths, ores, precious metals, asbestos ....................... 388, 158
Cereals and other agricultural products ....................... 180, 224
Woods and goods of, and other carved articles ................. 491, 167
Coal, coke, and peat .......................................... 318, 890

A noticeable increase of exports for the first eight months of 1902 occurred in the following articles:

Tons.
Waste ........................................................ 31, 291
Iron, and wares of ........................................... 680, 437
Earths, ore, precious metals, asbestos ....................... 138, 889
Groceries and confectionery .................................. 153, 290
Coal, coke, and peat ......................................... 121, 729

In the table below, I have noted a number of articles imported into Germany from the United States during the first eight months of 1902, 1901, and 1900, showing more or less fluctuation:

| Article. | 1902. | 1901. | 1900. |
|---|---|---|---|
| | Metric tons. | Metric tons. | Metric tons. |
| Bran | 5,506 | 18,266 | 27,415 |
| Malt | 10,125 | 12,348 | 9,227 |
| Waste, not specified | 46,185 | 54,007 | 42,032 |
| Rags | 706 | 468 | 490 |
| Lead, raw | 7,694 | 12,906 | 16,377 |
| Oils, ethereal, not specified | 23 | 27 | 82 |
| Blacking | 83 | 47 | 58 |
| Lime, carbide of | 768 | 85 | 117 |
| Logwood | .8 | 478 | 608 |
| Extracts, for tanning | 322 | 496 | 850 |
| Wood alcohol | 1,441 | 1,138 | 1,149 |
| Lime, wood acetate of | 12,343 | 11,687 | 6,216 |
| Magnesia, carbonate of, artificial | 11 | 83 | 14 |
| Sugar of milk, lactic acid | 48 | 40 | 80 |
| Quercitron | 338 | 680 | 578 |
| Oil of turpentine | 13,722 | 15,693 | 18,671 |
| Blue vitriol | 1,212 | 680 | 1,166 |
| Zinc ash and zinc, white | 82 | 60 | 434 |
| Chemicals for technical purposes, not specified | 280 | 588 | 142 |
| Pharmaceutical preparations | 110 | 51 | 38 |
| Iron, raw | 380 | 9,859 | 10,177 |
| Iron, goods of, coarse | 2,556 | 2,182 | 2,116 |
| Wrought-iron pipes | 5,915 | 4,542 | 6,995 |
| Iron, wares of, not lacquered, zinc coated, etc | 2,083 | 2,687 | 1,896 |
| Tools, of iron, not specified | 53 | 65 | 98 |
| Iron: | | | |
| Goods of, fine | 210 | 174 | 216 |
| Wrought, goods of | 219 | 200 | 177 |
| Sewing machines without frames, and parts of | 886 | 912 | 1,038 |
| Bicycles, and parts of | 84 | 74 | 107 |
| Typewriters and calculating machines | 70 | 58 | 82 |
| Asbestos | 309 | 549 | 762 |
| Graphite | 359 | 325 | 299 |
| Earths, not specified, borax, lime, etc | 1,583 | 1,288 | 1,189 |
| Ores of copper and pyrites of copper | 5 | | 266 |
| Ores, zinc | 7,767 | 7,812 | 5,728 |
| Gold, coined | .97 | 6.44 | 8.96 |
| Gold, in bars, plates | 5.05 | 5.9 | 2.29 |
| Precious metals, not specified | .39 | .10 | 17 |
| Asbestos, goods of, not specified | .2 | 1 | .3 |
| Manila hemp, from Philippines | 1,116 | 2,168 | 1,638 |
| Wheat | 659,490 | 656,250 | 343,446 |
| Rye | 25,711 | 24,983 | 1,166 |
| Oats | 2,191 | 46,226 | 38,779 |
| Buckwheat | 2,431 | 8,162 | 8,088 |
| Barley | 2,841 | 7,687 | 53,472 |
| Cotton seed | 4,643 | 3,258 | 2,805 |
| Linseed | 11,498 | 14,767 | 5,577 |
| Corn | 47,403 | 728,937 | 778,335 |
| Plants, bulbs of flowers | 86 | 109 | 92 |
| Grass seed and timothy | 878 | 227 | 1,726 |

| Article. | 1902. | 1901. | 1900. |
|---|---|---|---|
| | *Metric tons.* | *Metric tons.* | *Metric tons.* |
| Seed, clover, lucern, etc. | 1,380 | 561 | 4,982 |
| Fruit, fresh, excepting grapes and tropical fruits. | 214 | 543 | 595 |
| Seeds, not specified. | 101 | 95 | 51 |
| Feathers, for beds. | 77 | 96 | 130 |
| Bristles. | 70 | 49 | 96 |
| Hair, horse. | 69 | 45 | 40 |
| Hides: | | | |
|   Cow, limed and dry. | 256 | 297 | 598 |
|   Horse, green and salted. | 71 | 59 | 120 |
|   Goat. | 430 | 843 | 302 |
| Hides and pelts, for furs; also bird skins. | 220 | 156 | 172 |
| Shells, raw. | 40 | 92 | 98 |
| Timber: | | | |
|   Raw, for building and carpentering, hard. | 15,816 | 5,414 | 15,695 |
|   Soft. | 6,560 | 4,642 | Not stated. |
|   Staves, oak. | 8,968 | 8,552 | 10,861 |
|   Hewn, hard. | 2,877 | 3,097 | 6,318 |
|   Hewn, soft. | 2,809 | 3,104 | Not stated. |
|   Boxwood, mahogany, etc., raw. | 4,020 | 7,215 | 2,269 |
|   Sawed, hard. | 42,083 | 58,078 | 150,907 |
|   Sawed, soft. | 120,189 | 109,220 | Not stated. |
|   Of boxwood, mahogany, sawed. | 11 | 44 | 326 |
| Cooper goods, coarse. | 24 | 38 | 38 |
| Furniture, and parts of, of hard wood and veneered. | 334 | 390 | 470 |
| Pianos. | 11 | 4.4 | 7.2 |
| Zithers. | .8 | 13.7 | 18 |
| Locomotives and locomobiles. | 9 | 90 | 154 |
| Wagons, for rails, in connection with motors. | 98 | 31 | Not stated. |
| Sewing machines, with frames in the main of cast iron. | 289 | 367 | 509 |
| Sewing machines, with frames in the main of wrought iron. | 11 | 9 | 10 |
| Agricultural machines. | 11,484 | 17,553 | 19,780 |
| Milling machines. | 14 | 20 | 170 |
| Electrical machines. | 115 | 255 | 251 |
| Engines. | 62 | 56 | 178 |
| Tool machines. | 445 | 965 | 3,670 |
| Transmissions. | 16 | 10 | 28 |
| Pumps. | 116 | 172 | 216 |
| Machines for cutting and perforating metals. | 11 | 34 | 55 |
| Hoisting machines. | 39 | 37 | 529 |
| Machinery, other, for industrial purposes. | 394 | 990 | 2,092 |
| Rubber, boots and shoes of. | 71 | 48 | 85 |
| Hose of hemp, belting, etc., in combination with rubber. | 2 | 3 | 6 |
| Clothing and millinery goods of textiles in connection with rubber. | 18 | 15 | 13 |
| Aluminium, pure. | 155 | 192 | 137 |
| Copper: | | | |
|   Raw. | 40,340 | 30,614 | 45,102 |
|   Coins of, scrap and waste. | 62 | 36 | 48 |
| Brass and tombac. | 6 | 36 | 43 |
| Nickel. | 82 | 233 | 272 |
| Metals, not precious, not otherwise specified, and alloys of. | 9 | 5 | 79 |
| Copper alloys, not plated. | 142 | 218 | 260 |
| Teeth, artificial. | 1.42 | 1.16 | .12 |
| Watch cases, other than of gold. | .1 | 26 | 27 |
| Leather: | | | |
|   Not specified. | 99 | 154 | 166 |
|   Sole. | 9 | 23 | 85 |
| Shoes, leather, fine. | 48 | 48 | 24 |
| Books, charts, music, and periodicals. | 161 | 157 | 108 |
| Chromos, engravings, photographs, etc. | 35 | 48 | 48 |
| Paintings, drawings. | 4.5 | 5.3 | 6.3 |
| Beer, in bottles. | 7.1 | 5.2 | 5.9 |
| Wine and must, in barrels. | 243 | 280 | 350 |
| Butter, fresh and salted. | 11 | 197 | 38 |
| Beef (also veal), simply prepared. | 1,688 | 1,228 | 1,064 |
| Pork. | 2,492 | 2,208 | 2,663 |
| Ham. | 707 | 730 | 960 |
| Bacon. | 5,109 | 5,527 | 4,314 |
| Sausages. | | 1.7 | 2,387 |
| Meat, in boxes. | 22 | 5 | 2,673 |
| Beef extract, etc. | 8 | 8 | 27 |
| Fish, salted and smoked. | 1,194 | 570 | 459 |
| Honey, natural and artificial. | 195 | 101 | 142 |
| Fruit, dried, baked, and boiled down. | 11,981 | 12,060 | 16,014 |
| Dextrin. | 13 | 2 | 3 |
| Rice starch. | 2.5 | 2.1 | 1.6 |
| Starch, other than rice. | 202 | 278 | 299 |
| Cereals and legumes, prepared. | 1,057 | 2,106 | 1,998 |
| Flour: | | | |
|   Wheat. | 6,388 | 7,770 | 7,286 |
|   Of corn, rice, etc. | 431 | 409 | 858 |
| Tobacco leaves. | 5,850 | 6,236 | 7,040 |
| Tobacco sauces. | 393 | 329 | 283 |
| Chewing tobacco. | 2.5 | 3.6 | 2.8 |
| Glucose, maltose, etc. | | 3.6 | 9.3 |

| Article. | 1902. | 1901. | 1900. |
|---|---|---|---|
| | *Metric tons.* | *Metric tons.* | *Metric tons.* |
| Cotton-seed oil: | | | |
| In barrels | 18,250 | 18,561 | 10,871 |
| In barrels, officially denaturized | 8,430 | 18,765 | 11,419 |
| Oleic acid and oily refuse | 1,413 | 2,388 | 2,017 |
| Oils, fatty, for technical purposes | 469 | 440 | 325 |
| Oil cakes | 121,120 | 158,833 | 132,101 |
| Oleomargarine | 12,012 | 15,166 | 12,511 |
| Lard | 53,482 | 61,108 | 64,045 |
| Fatty substances, artificial, for table use | 1,802 | 1,543 | 1,266 |
| Steric and palmetic acid, paraffin, etc | 3,225 | 2,303 | 2,481 |
| Tallow | 6,090 | 6,226 | 7,968 |
| Animal fats and refuse fats, not otherwise specified | 174 | 1,296 | 1,878 |
| Beeswax and other wax of insects | 16 | 16 | 96 |
| Cellulose, straw, and other fiber pulps | 1,040 | 1,176 | 806 |
| Packing paper, exclusive of straw paper | 40 | 73 | 101 |
| Paper, leather board, etc | 98 | 83 | 81 |
| Packing papers, smoothed (also oilcloth papers) | 181 | 483 | 290 |
| Paper and goods of, not specially specified: | | | |
| Without other materials | 50 | 40 | 29 |
| With other materials | 53 | 37 | 39 |
| Petroleum, refined abroad | 416,595 | 426,227 | 416,718 |
| Oils, mineral: | | | |
| For lubricating purposes | 32,299 | 29,505 | 30,399 |
| For other than lubricating purposes | 1,104 | 1,304 | 1,402 |
| Exclusive of coal-tar oils, for refining and distilling | 25,470 | 21,967 | 22,539 |
| Soap, soft, etc., in barrels | 174 | 110 | 21 |
| Precious stones | .28 | 1.59 | .1 |
| Half-precious stones | 11.5 | 16.6 | .186 |
| Anthracite coal | 4,810 | 317 | 70 |
| Asphaltum, resin, and wood cement | 1,580 | 709 | 1,913 |
| Resin of turpentine | 49,203 | 69,082 | 59,415 |
| Resins, not specified | 171 | 189 | 16 |
| Bladders, guts, and stomachs for technical purposes | 4,241 | 5,522 | 5,295 |
| Sponges | 18 | 26 | 24 |
| Horses: | | | |
| Heavy draft mares .................... number | | 108 | |
| Studs and geldings ............... do | | 288 | |
| Hair, animal, not specified ............. tons | 567 | 207 | 185 |
| Wool, raw ............ do | 142 | 208 | 208 |
| Zinc, raw ............ do | 160 | .1 | 52 |
| Tin, raw, also scrap ........... do | 17 | 4.5 | 16 |

The following table shows the goods exported from Germany to the United States for the first eight months of 1902, 1901, and 1900, noting more or less fluctuation:

| Article. | 1902. | 1901. | 1900. |
|---|---|---|---|
| | *Metric tons.* | *Metric tons.* | *Metric tons.* |
| Rags | 12,389 | 6,807 | 13,794 |
| Cotton: | | | |
| Waste | 1,089 | 268 | 195 |
| Yarn | 108 | 107 | 108 |
| Textiles | 304 | 193 | 179 |
| Velvet | 78 | 55 | 57 |
| Passementerie goods of | 281 | 380 | 408 |
| Gloves | 166 | 80 | 78 |
| Hosiery | 1,912 | 1,845 | 2,502 |
| Loose textiles, bleached, colored, printed | 49 | 47 | 29 |
| Laces | 183 | 127 | 106 |
| Embroideries | 122 | 76 | 82 |
| Brush maker goods, coarse | 19 | 13 | 25 |
| Brushes, cloth and hair, fine | 58 | 104 | 55 |
| Oils, ethereal, not specified | 44 | 31 | 26 |
| Potash: | | | |
| Prussiate | 11 | 21 | 30 |
| Cyanide | 723 | 676 | 522 |
| Caustic | 396 | 535 | 506 |
| Soda, prussiate | 78 | 86 | 101 |
| Lime, chloride | 7,444 | 6,298 | 5,404 |
| Glue | 147 | 207 | 285 |
| Matches | 88 | 129 | 235 |
| Potash, bicarbonate | 3,021 | 3,506 | 3,107 |
| Alizarin | 2,061 | 1,944 | 1,398 |
| Alkaloids, and salts of (santonin, cocaine, etc., exclusive of quinine) | 12 | 3 | 5 |
| Ammonia, carbonate and muriate; aqua ammoniæ | 627 | 360 | 482 |
| Aniline, oil and salts of | 2,650 | 2,312 | 2,540 |
| Aniline, and other coal-tar colors | 3,796 | 3,294 | 3,588 |
| Arsenic combinations | 337 | 384 | 268 |

| Article. | 1902. | 1901. | 1900. |
|---|---|---|---|
| | *Metric tons.* | *Metric tons.* | *Metric tons.* |
| Baryta salts, not specified .................................... | . 424 | 870 | 855 |
| Benzoic acid ................................................ | 111 | 74 | 103 |
| Cantharides ................................................. | 1 | 8.1 | 8.5 |
| Quinine ..................................................... | 25 | 43 | 34 |
| Potassium, chlorate ......................................... | 15,567 | 25,677 | 26,627 |
| Chrome alum ................................................ | 504 | 270 | 172 |
| Indigo....................................................... | 800 | 400 | 352 |
| Indigo, carmine ............................................. | 2.7 | 4.9 | 6.4 |
| Potash and potash magnesia, sulphate of ..................... | 12,354 | 10,840 | 6,900 |
| Carbolic acid................................................ | 284 | 862 | 192 |
| Lacquer colors .............................................. | 284 | 170 | ⌐ 80 |
| Manganese, preparations of .................................. | 149 | 181 | ⌐ 77 |
| Red lead .................................................... | 316 | 251 | 271 |
| Mineral water............................................... | 1,408 | 1,172 | 1,422 |
| Soda, sulphite, and hyposulphite............................. | 537 | 413 | 1,477 |
| Archil, extract of, persio, litmus....: | .3 | 6.7 | 6.9 |
| Salicylic acid, soda, salicylate of .......................... | 70 | 67 | 50 |
| Saccharine, dulcin, etc ..................................... | .4 | .7 | 15 |
| Zinc, ash of, zinc white..................................... | 896 | 587 | 653 |
| Lithopone................................................... | 345 | 868 | 746 |
| Colors for printing .......................................... | 26 | 21 | 18 |
| Dyeing and tanning articles .................................. | 88 | 78 | 118 |
| Preparations, raw, for technical or medicinal purposes, not otherwise specified ............................................. | 234 | 324 | 289 |
| Chemicals for technical purposes, not specified .............. | 1,048 | 965 | 615 |
| Pharmaceutical preparations ................................ | 157 | 172 | 134 |
| Strontia, preparations of ................................... | 224 | 165 | 236 |
| Iron: | | | |
| Raw ..................................................... | 20,662 | 104 | .......... |
| Bars, etc................................................. | 11,912 | 878 | 826 |
| Rails of.................................................. | 40,012 | 115 | 7.6 |
| Wrought, in bars, etc .................................... | 5,745 | 291 | 240 |
| Ingots, etc .............................................. | 51,789 | | .......... |
| Wire of, raw ............................................. | 2,072 | 2,184 | 206 |
| Wire of, tin coated, copper coated, polished .............. | 105 | 169 | 894 |
| For railroad axles, wheels, etc ........................... | 3,184 | 2,468 | 2,670 |
| Wares of, not finished, nor lacquered, nor zinc coated ....... | 1,116 | 641 | 784 |
| Enameled ironware .......................................... | 1,481 | 646 | 279 |
| Ironware, polished, lacquered, zinc coated, etc .............. | 638 | 584 | 441 |
| Iron, goods of, fine.......................................... | 49 | 57 | 150 |
| Cutlery, tailors' instruments, fine........................... | 272 | 246 | 212 |
| Guns, and parts of, for hunting.............................. | 6.4 | 4.4 | 1.7 |
| Needles, sewing, darning, embroidery, and for sewing machines.. | 66 | 86 | 29 |
| Fertilizing salts............................................. | 98,476 | 192,919 | 119,026 |
| Pumice stone................................................ | 144 | 92 | 54 |
| Cement, hydraulic, lime..................................... | 140,949 | 78,850 | 155,873 |
| Kaoline, feldspar, fireproof clay ............................ | 6,213 | 7,747 | 7,129 |
| Barytes..................................................... | 3,557 | 2,374 | 2,124 |
| Earths, not specified, borax, lime, etc....................... | 814 | 2,148 | 1,476 |
| Ores, not specified ......................................... | 80 | 6 | 19 |
| Oakum ..................................................... | 797 | 428 | 715 |
| Millet ...................................................... | 20 | | 15 |
| Anis, fennel, coriander, caraway seeds ...................... | 14 | 28 | 8 |
| Plants, living, flower bulbs.................................. | 22 | 9 | 11 |
| Grass and timothy seed ..................................... | 24 | 140 | 57 |
| Potatoes.................................................... | 6,584 | 294 | 289 |
| Clover, esparcet, lucern seed, etc ........................... | 95 | 130 | 48 |
| Seeds, not otherwise specified ............................... | 1,433 | 842 | 977 |
| Glass: | | | |
| Common ................................................. | 1,899 | 1,599 | 1,413 |
| Optical .................................................. | 160 | 138 | 85 |
| White ................................................... | 740 | 842 | 1,311 |
| Colored, not specified.................................... | 91 | 101 | 75 |
| Bristles..................................................... | 227 | 208 | 164 |
| Hair, horse ................................................. | 20 | 47 | 18 |
| Feathers, ornamental ....................................... | 36.54 | 17.79 | 9.23 |
| Skins of hares and rabbits................................... | 490 | 628 | 497 |
| Hides: | | | |
| Calf, green and salted .................................... | 1,721 | 1,088 | 1,087 |
| Limed and dry ...................................... | 1,151 | 891 | 440 |
| Cattle, green and salted................................... | 773 | 1,227 | 1,546 |
| Limed and dry ...................................... | 102 | 152 | 59 |
| Horse, green and salted .................................. | 602 | 345 | 45 |
| Limed and dry ...................................... | 74 | 18 | 162 |
| Sheep, raw .............................................. | 97 | 62 | 145 |
| Goat, raw ............................................... | 481 | 848 | 802 |
| Raw for tanning, not specified .......................... | 28 | 41 | 63 |
| Hides and skins: | | | |
| For manufacture of furs, not from fur animals............. | 63 | 53 | 50 |
| From fur animals; also bird skins........................ | 408 | 868 | 241 |
| Amber, raw................................................. | 6.2 | 4.5 | 8.9 |
| Ivory ...................................................... | 10.7 | 16.9 | 14.4 |
| Cane, for chairs, raw........................................ | 350 | 164 | 242 |
| Wooden ware, fine .......................................... | 56 | 89 | 30 |
| Baskets, etc., fine........................................... | 168 | 48 | 58 |

| Article. | 1902. | 1901. | 1900. |
|---|---|---|---|
| | *Metric tons.* | *Metric tons.* | *Metric tons.* |
| Goods, carved, of animal and vegetable material, not specified... | 201 | 170 | 303 |
| Hops | 209 | 279 | 336 |
| Violins | 41 | 72 | 75 |
| String instruments, not otherwise specified | 5.6 | 7.9 | 7.9 |
| Other musical instruments | 266 | 163 | 87 |
| Instruments, astronomical, optical, mathematical, chemical, physiological | 21.3 | 17.7 | 12.3 |
| Instruments, surgical | 20.6 | 23.5 | 17.8 |
| Agricultural machines | 28 | 8 | 48 |
| Machines for cotton spinning | 42 | 45 | 86 |
| Machines for weaving | 170 | 313 | 297 |
| Steam engines | 168 | 57 | 21 |
| Machines for working wool | 169 | ........ | 147 |
| Caoutchouc and gutta-percha | 2,395 | 1,722 | 1,561 |
| Caoutchouc, threads of, spun over | 17 | 28 | 26 |
| Textiles in connection with rubber and gutta-percha (exclusive of wearing apparel, millinery, and parts of bicycles) | 6 | 10 | 12 |
| Clothing, millinery, underwear: | | | |
| Of silk | 2.3 | 1.2 | 1.4 |
| Half silk | 1.7 | 2.7 | 3.7 |
| Dresses, women's of cotton, linen, wool | 11.5 | 27.9 | 40.1 |
| Corsets | 32.2 | 18.7 | 28.3 |
| Underwear, cotton and linen | 15 | 21 | 19 |
| Artificial flowers | 62 | 52 | 44 |
| Copper, raw | .3 | 152 | ........ |
| Copper coins, scraps of copper | 521 | 235 | 157 |
| Brass and tombac | 244 | 127 | 60 |
| Copper: | | | |
| Alloys in bars, etc. | 14 | 16 | 75 |
| Wire of, plated | 30 | 18 | 9 |
| Wares of copper, brass, etc., nickel plated, fine | 43 | 33 | 27 |
| Jewelry | 2.90 | 1.64 | 1.71 |
| Goods of amber, ivory, mother-of-pearl; also artificial teeth | 6.1 | 11.2 | 6.8 |
| Goods of celluloid | 9.2 | 12.6 | (a) |
| Goods, textile, in connection with other materials, not otherwise specified | 81 | 208 | 211 |
| Leather, not otherwise specified | 46 | 36 | 28 |
| Shoes, fine, of leather or in connection therewith (exclusive of rubber) | .6 | 3.3 | 2.1 |
| Leather goods, fine (exclusive of shoes): | | | |
| Albums and bookbinders' goods | 14.3 | 13.1 | 34.2 |
| In connection with other materials, albums and bookbinders' goods, of fine or imitation leather | 35 | 39 | 291 |
| Gloves, leather | 121 | 124 | 187 |
| Leather, cut for gloves | 1.7 | 13.2 | (a) |
| Textiles of linen, jute, manila, hemp, etc. | 28 | 30 | 14 |
| Do | 305 | 266 | 329 |
| Passementerie goods | 14 | 11 | 6 |
| Chromos, engravings, photographs | 737 | 651 | 546 |
| Paintings, drawings | 20 | 13 | 23 |
| Beer, in barrels | 4,172 | 3,709 | 3,565 |
| Whisky, in bottles | 139 | 81 | 94 |
| Sparkling wines | 102 | 83 | 67 |
| Cacao, butter and oil of | 130 | 65 | 25 |
| Vegetables, fine | 29 | 43 | 9 |
| Chicory | 109 | 163 | 252 |
| Seeds and vegetables, dried, powdered, boiled, or salted | 51 | 13 | 47 |
| Chocolate | 18 | 16 | 76 |
| Confectionery, in whole or in part of chocolate | .8 | ........ | 92 |
| Cacao, powdered | 9 | 8.5 | 26 |
| Dextrin | 1,669 | 1,407 | 1,547 |
| Starch of potatoes and flour of potatoes | 2,357 | 715 | 447 |
| Cereals and legumes, prepared | 18,518 | 12,085 | 6,815 |
| Flour of corn, rice, and legumes | 431 | 409 | 358 |
| Rice | 3,582 | 4,152 | 3,791 |
| Sugar, raw | 59,294 | 106,726 | 187,470 |
| Sugar, in loaves | 1,403 | 4,457 | 1,162 |
| All other sugars | 69 | 663 | .5 |
| Palm oil, cocoanut oil, and other vegetable tallow | 1,594 | 212 | (a) |
| Rape-seed oil, in barrels | 177 | 225 | 100 |
| Oils, not otherwise specified, for medicinal use | 1.8 | 1.2 | .9 |
| Lanoline | 15 | 30 | 47 |
| Ozocerite | 138 | 61 | 112 |
| Cellulose, straw and fiber pulp | 4,689 | 2,013 | 3,079 |
| Packing paper, also oilcloth paper | 870 | 724 | 540 |
| Photographic paper | 33 | 41 | 18 |
| Paper, colored, gold, silver, etc | 688 | 796 | 1,175 |
| Writing paper, etc. | 180 | 115 | 141 |
| Printing paper, also colored | 485 | 542 | 483 |
| Drawing paper | 103 | 85 | 50 |
| Paper, not otherwise specified, painters' cardboard, colored cardboard | 57 | 83 | 30 |
| Covers of comptulikon, linoleum, korticium | 140 | 241 | .6 |
| Wall paper | 141 | 173 | 114 |

a Not stated.

| Article. | 1902. | 1901. | 1900. |
|---|---|---|---|
| | *Metric tons.* | *Metric tons.* | *Metric tons.* |
| Pelts of sheep, not covered, unfinished furs | 90 | 90 | 149 |
| Coal-tar oils, heavy | 462 | 592 | 488 |
| Silk, colored, combed, also spun | 10.4 | 4.2 | 2.7 |
| Raw silk, colored and once threaded | 32 | 20 | 1.1 |
| Passementerie goods, half silk | 4 | 3 | 1.5 |
| Laces, with metal threads, etc., of half silk | .1 | .5 | .2 |
| Hosiery, half silk | 14.1 | 5.3 | 2.5 |
| Shawls, etc., half silk | 19 | 8 | 6 |
| Laces, without metal threads; embroideries, half silk | 10 | 5 | 5 |
| Goods, half silk, silk without metal threads | 138 | 117 | 221 |
| Button-makers' goods, half silk | 24 | 15 | 19 |
| Soap, fancy | 54 | 45 | 46 |
| Perfumery | 2.1 | | 3.4 |
| Precious stones and corals, pearls, not set | .203 | 58 | .86 |
| Lithographic stones | 1,069 | 626 | 464 |
| Coke | 8,162 | | 4,707 |
| Ozocerite, raw | 420 | 518 | 394 |
| Bladders, guts, stomachs, for technical purposes | 116 | 87 | 90 |
| Earthenware | 513 | 170 | 110 |
| Clay wares, painted, gilded, etc | 1,074 | 718 | 651 |
| China ware: | | | |
| White | 298 | 407 | 503 |
| Gilded, and in connection with other materials | 8,054 | 6,855 | 5,463 |
| China: | | | |
| De luxe | 645 | 555 | 700 |
| Not otherwise specified | 29 | 49 | 26 |
| Stud-horses, for breeding purposes ................number.. | 84 | 73 | |
| Alpaca, llama, camel, etc., wool and hair ..............tons.. | 76 | 88 | 83 |
| Hair of hares, rabbits, greavers, etc | 18 | 45 | 5 |
| Hair, of animals not otherwise stated | 754 | 355 | 947 |
| Wool: | | | |
| Of sheep, raw | 79 | 149 | 97 |
| Washed, bleached, etc | 61 | 29 | 52 |
| Combings | | .42 | |
| Woolen yarn: | | | |
| Raw | 27 | 47 | 27 |
| Bleached or colored | 3.2 | 5 | 14.4 |
| Threaded thrice or more | 9.7 | 13.9 | 19.5 |
| Felt, and wares of | 47 | 19 | 15 |
| Woolen hosiery | 145 | 91 | 100 |
| Woolen passementerie goods | 18 | 28 | 103 |
| Woolen cloth, printed | 44 | 98 | 95 |
| Zinc: | | | |
| Raw | 76 | 180 | 304 |
| Plates, etc | 129 | 229 | 154 |
| Tin, raw | 108 | 82 | 57 |
| Tin, goods, of fine | 57 | 32 | 19 |

*Declared values of exports to the United States from the consular districts included under the Frankfort consulate-general for the first three quarters of 1902, 1901, and 1900.*

| | 1902. | 1901. | 1900. |
|---|---|---|---|
| Frankfort | $5,764,795.30 | $5,309,762.96 | $4,598,412.60 |
| Aix la Chapelle | 2,150,196.96 | 881,277.20 | 961,859.36 |
| Bamberg | 727,368.39 | 576,035.45 | 504,176.46 |
| Barmen | 5,169,903.41 | 3,480,083.96 | 3,456,824.12 |
| Cologne | 2,788,327.08 | 1,456,506.76 | 1,782,083.71 |
| Crefeld | 2,062,351.48 | 2,026,182.21 | 2,214,134.42 |
| Dusseldorf | 2,637,031.01 | 875,091.85 | 869,931.12 |
| Freiburg | 805,292.95 | 850,406.16 | 967,467.60 |
| Kehl | 2,139,489.91 | 1,276,312.37 | 987,126.91 |
| Mayence | 1,723,079.81 | 1,459,839.70 | 1,366,693.67 |
| Mannheim | 3,479,397.70 | 3,172,456.91 | 3,655,284.97 |
| Nuremberg | 2,813,671.64 | 2,781,018.21 | 2,770,122.70 |
| Solingen | 1,228,601.34 | 1,087,450.26 | 1,057,791.02 |
| Stuttgart | 890,772.32 | 793,629.73 | 687,747.67 |
| Weimar | 934,873.82 | 817,164.21 | 715,845.54 |
| Total | 35,315,153.07 | 26,843,217.94 | 26,535,451.87 |

Being an increase for 1902 of $8,471,935.13, or over 31 per cent, over 1901, and $8,779,701.20, or over 33 per cent, over 1900.

The principal articles of export from the Frankfort consular district were:

| Article. | 1902. | 1901. | 1900. |
|---|---|---|---|
| Coal-tar colors............................................ | $1,257,345.01 | $1,175,909.50 | $1,286,289.87 |
| Hair, cattle.............................................. | 151,400.99 | 153,686.08 | 255,278.42 |
| Platinum............................................... | 715,459.69 | 508,862.44 | 457,143.52 |
| Skins: | | | |
| Cattle.............................................. | 308,437.00 | | |
| Goat............................................... | 496,231.40 | 1,404,344.03 | 801,250.08 |
| Hare............................................... | 387,753.84 | | |
| Wool.................................................. | 174,406.18 | 99,357.83 | 119,481.25 |

Other articles of export were: Drugs and chemicals, blue clay, leather and leather goods, nickel, optical wares, paper, artificial silk, silverware, and wine.

The increase of exports was not confined to any one particular class of goods, but was especially marked in the case of platinum, leather, optical wares, artificial silk, and silverware.

The large increase of exportation from Aix la Chapelle, Barmen, Cologne, Dusseldorf, Kehl, and Mayence in 1902 was chiefly due to abnormally large sales of iron and steel. Other articles showing a considerable increase were:

Aix la Chapelle: Paper, artificial silk, linen mesh, and chemicals. Bamberg: China ware and hops. Barmen: Hatbands and ribbons and aniline colors. Cologne: Aniline colors and potash. Crefeld: Silks and velvets. Dusseldorf: Ferro-manganese and machinery. Freiburg: Cotton goods. Mayence: Agate wares. Mannheim: Rags and wood pulp. Solingen: Hardware and hatbands. Stuttgart: Woolen goods. Weimar: Gloves, machinery, and woolen goods.

*Declared values of exports from all of Germany to the United States, by consular districts, during the third quarter of 1901 and 1902.*

| From— | Third quarter, 1901. | Third quarter, 1902. | Gain (+) or loss (−). |
|---|---|---|---|
| Aix la Chapelle............................... | $369,396.62 | $1,224,632.66 | + $855,236.04 |
| Annaberg ................................... | 671,906.04 | 817,469.98 | + 145,563.94 |
| Bamberg ................................... | 239,847.00 | 347,976.54 | + 108,129.54 |
| Barmen ................................... | 1,101,652.69 | 1,841,307.26 | + 739,654.51 |
| Berlin ...................................... | 2,222,805.70 | 2,652,195.58 | + 429,389.88 |
| Bremen .................................... | 731,478.12 | 665,705.03 | − 66,043.09 |
| Breslau .................................... | 367,993.46 | 421,848.23 | + 53,854.77 |
| Brunswick ................................. | 512,613.42 | 540,445.70 | + 27,832.28 |
| Chemnitz................................... | 1,274,223.44 | 1,952,408.48 | + 678,185.04 |
| Coburg .................................... | 1,572,175.50 | 1,533,101.00 | − 39,073.00 |
| Cologne ................................... | 651,566.19 | 1,153,757.83 | + 502,191.64 |
| Crefeld .................................... | 738,106.23 | 789,815.31 | + 56,709.08 |
| Dresden ................................... | 442,234.74 | 322,729.00 | − 119,505.00 |
| Dusseldorf.................................. | 303,448.31 | 1,150,358.54 | + 846,910.23 |
| Frankfort on Main .......................... | 1,868,614.66 | 2,014,513.41 | + 145,898.75 |
| Freiburg ................................... | 236,660.29 | 222,779.05 | + 13,881.24 |
| Glauchau................................... | 160,665.65 | 183,512.15 | + 22,846.50 |
| Hamburg ................................... | 2,298,765.89 | 3,307,893.69 | +1,009,127.80 |
| Hanover.................................... | 177,337.25 | 323,863.89 | + 146,526.64 |
| Kehl ....................................... | 350,067.77 | 1,002,222.50 | + 652,154.73 |
| Leipzig .................................... | 1,357,705.30 | 1,835,473.81 | + 477,768.51 |
| Magdeburg................................. | 1,826,120.70 | 1,431,844.22 | − 394,276.48 |
| Mannheim .................................. | 911,522.44 | 1,241,479.04 | + 329,956.60 |
| Mayence ................................... | 492,089.06 | 588,258.56 | + 96,169.50 |
| Munich..................................... | 302,794.25 | 461,008.25 | + 158,214.00 |
| Nuremberg ................................. | 1,100,962.66 | 1,185,320.55 | + 84,367.89 |
| Plauen .................................... | 896,052.93 | 1,038,331.94 | + 142,279.01 |
| Solingen ................................... | 421,578.28 | 461,938.25 | + 40,359.01 |
| Stettin..................................... | 199,003.78 | 608,803.35 | + 409,799.57 |
| Stuttgart .................................. | 261,828.10 | 315,539.17 | + 53,711.07 |
| Weimar .................................... | 382,141.61 | 436,115.17 | + 53,973.56 |
| Zittau ..................................... | 284,481.98 | 326,878.85 | + 42,459.37 |
| Total ................................. | 24,722,767.06 | 32,399,526.49 | .............. |

Increase third quarter, 1902, $7,676,759.43 = 32,242,389 marks.

The following table shows the relative value of the German imports from and exports to the five principal countries for the last ten years:

IMPORTS.

| Country. | 1901. | 1900. | 1899. | 1898. | 1897. | 1896. | 1895. | 1894. | 1893. | 1892. |
|---|---|---|---|---|---|---|---|---|---|---|
| | Per ct. | Per ct. | Per ct. | Per ct. | Per ct. | Per ct. | Per ct. | Per ct. | Per ct. | Per ct. |
| United States ...... | 18.2 | 16.9 | 15.7 | 16.1 | 13.5 | 12.8 | 12.1 | 12.4 | 11.1 | 74.5 |
| Russia .............. | 12.8 | 12.1 | 12.4 | 13.5 | 14.6 | 13.9 | 13.4 | 12.7 | 8.5 | 9.1 |
| Austria-Hungary... | 12.1 | 12.0 | 12.6 | 12.2 | 12.3 | 12.7 | 12.4 | 13.6 | 14.0 | 13.6 |
| Great Britain ...... | 11.5 | 13.9 | 13.4 | 15.2 | 13.6 | 14.2 | 13.6 | 14.2 | 15.9 | 14.7 |
| France.............. | 5.0 | 5.2 | 5.3 | 4.9 | 5.1 | 5.1 | 5.4 | 5.0 | 5.8 | 6.2 |

EXPORTS.

| Country. | 1901. | 1900. | 1899. | 1898. | 1897. | 1896. | 1895. | 1894. | 1893. | 1892. |
|---|---|---|---|---|---|---|---|---|---|---|
| | Per ct. | Per ct. | Per ct. | Per ct. | Per ct. | Per ct. | Per ct. | Per ct. | Per ct. | Per ct. |
| United States ...... | 8.5 | 9.2 | 8.6 | 8.3 | 10.5 | 10.2 | 10.8 | 8.9 | 7.4 | 7.4 |
| Russia .............. | 7.7 | 7.6 | 10.0 | 11.0 | 9.8 | 9.7 | 6.5 | 6.4 | 5.7 | 7.6 |
| Austria-Hungary... | 10.9 | 10.7 | 10.7 | 11.8 | 11.5 | 12.7 | 12.7 | 13.2 | 13.0 | 12.0 |
| Great Britain ...... | 20.3 | 19.2 | 19.5 | 20.0 | 18.5 | 19.0 | 19.8 | 20.8 | 20.7 | 20.3 |
| France.............. | 5.6 | 5.9 | 5.0 | 5.1 | 5.6 | 5.4 | 5.9 | 6.2 | 6.3 | 6.4 |

From the foregoing table, it will be seen that Germany in 1901 bought from the United States a larger percentage of her total imports than during any preceding year, while the United States in 1901 bought from Germany a lesser percentage of Germany's total exports than in 1900, 1899, 1897, 1896, 1895, and 1894.

The balance of trade between Germany and the five countries named in the two foregoing tables, based upon the percentage of Germany's total commerce with these countries, was:

| Country. | 1901. | 1900. | 1899. | 1898. | 1897. | 1896. | 1895. | 1894. | 1893. | 1892. |
|---|---|---|---|---|---|---|---|---|---|---|
| United States ...... | +9.7 | +7.6 | +6.9 | +7.8 | +3.0 | +2.6 | +1.3 | +3.5 | +3.7 | +7.1 |
| Russia .............. | +5.1 | +4.5 | +2.4 | +2.5 | +4.8 | +4.2 | +6.9 | +6.3 | +2.8 | +1.5 |
| Austria-Hungary... | +1.2 | +1.3 | +1.1 | +0.9 | +0.8 | 00 | −0.3 | +0.4 | +1.0 | +1.6 |
| Great Britain ...... | −8.8 | −5.3 | −6.1 | −4.8 | −4.9 | −4.8 | −6.2 | −6.6 | −4.8 | −5.6 |
| France.............. | −0.6 | −0.7 | +0.3 | −0.2 | −0.5 | −0.3 | −0.5 | −1.2 | −0.5 | −0.2 |

These figures make an excellent showing for the United States, and it is ardently hoped that the relations now existing between these two great commercial countries will continue, and that both may prosper and mutually contribute to each other's welfare.

### EXPORT DEPOT.

The export-sample depot of this city, whose object is to find new markets for German exports, is doing excellent work. During the last year, a large number of new catalogues, containing advertisements of the German firms represented, was sent to all parts of the globe. The management furnishes to customers free information concerning every phase of the export trade, sources of supply of raw materials, conditions and customs in foreign markets, duties, etc. During 1901, the depot was visited by many exporters from Hamburg, Bremen, Berlin, Nuremberg, Furth, Elberfeld, and other German cities, and from the following foreign centers: Adelaide, Alexandria, Auckland, Basel, Batavia, Belgrade, Belize, Bergen, Birmingham, Bombay, Boston, Brussels, Bukharest, Buenos Ayres, Cairo, Calcutta, Cape

Town, Chicago, Constantinople, Durban, Fez, Florence, Genoa, Geneva, Glasgow, Hankau, Hongkong, Johannesburg, Copenhagen, Lemberg, Lisbon, Liverpool, London, Lucerne, Madras, Madrid, Milan, Manchester, Melbourne, Mexico, Milwaukee, Montevideo, Moscow, Naples, New York, Odessa, Padang, Paris, Philadelphia, Prague, Pretoria, Providence, Rangoon, Rio de Janeiro, Rotterdam, San Francisco, Sao Paulo, Setubal, Shanghai, Sidney, Singapore, Soerabaya, Stockholm, St. Gall, St. Petersburg, Tokyo, Toronto, Valencia, Valparaiso, Verviers, Warsaw, Vienna, Yokohama, and Zurich.

The German Commercial Museum of Frankfort was visited during 1901 by about 2,800 callers.

## AMERICAN ENTERPRISES.

With reference to manufacturing plants and other business enterprises conducted by Americans in the Frankfort consular district, I addressed letters to Mr. Adolf Barthman, the Brecht Automobile Company, the Brecht Butchers' Supply Company, the Deutsche Vereinigte Schuhmaschinen Gesellschaft (German United Shoe Machine Company), the International Reece Buttonhole Sewing Machine Company, the Vaughn Machine Company, Keats Shoe Machine Manufacturing Company, and the Mergenthaler Typesetting Company. I append the answers that have been received.

RICHARD GUENTHER,
*Consul-General.*

FRANKFORT, *October 13, 1902.*

### LETTER FROM ADOLF BARTHMAN.

In answer to your note, I wish to state that we opened on April 6, at 60 Friedrich street, Berlin, an American shoe store for the exclusive sale of American shoes; the second store was opened in Frankfurt a M., Rossmarkt 19, on February 27, this year; the third store will be opened in Hamburg about October 15, at Jungfernsteig 25. When finished, it will not alone be one of the handsomest shoe stores in Europe, but the equal of any in the world.

The amount of capital invested in the three stores will exceed $100,000, and I am pleased to say that the two already opened are meeting with great success, especially the Berlin store, which is daily improving, and running away ahead of all expectations.

We employ in the three stores in the neighborhood of 40 persons; of these, 3 are Americans and the balance Germans, with whom I have had good results, but I find a great difference between them and the American clerks, in that the American is an independent workman, while the German clerk requires a master, in a majority of cases.

The hours of business, as well as the lunch hours, differ entirely from the American, especially as business here is conducted not only late into the evenings (about 9) but also on Sundays. The large dry goods houses close on Sundays, but remain open evenings until 8. The salaries of the different clerks run considerably lower than they do in America, and living is higher, especially for the working man, as the necessities of life are so expensive in this country.

The clerks in our establishment report mornings at 8 and are allowed a half hour for lunch, two hours for dinner, and remain in the store until closing time, namely, 8 on week days and 9 on Saturdays.

### LETTER FROM BRECHT AUTOMOBILE COMPANY.

This company ships its product to Germany partly finished; capital invested, $25,000. We employ German workmen; average wages, 30 marks ($7.14) per week; working hours per day, nine and one-half. Our venture has been successful.

H. Doc. 305, pt 2——21

### LETTER FROM GUS. V. BRECHT BUTCHERS' SUPPLY COMPANY.

This company does not manufacture anything on this side, but all goods are manufactured by us in the States and sent over here finished.

We employ a capital of $150,000 for our European business.

Our venture has been successful. We do not employ any Americans.

### LETTER FROM DEUTSCHE VEREINIGTE SCHUHMASCHINEN GESELLSCHAFT.

I fear that I can only give you information as far as the questions apply to the Deutsche Vereinigte Schuhmaschinen Gesellschaft (German United Shoe Machine Company), of this city.

(1) This company is incorporated here as a German concern. It imports from America, and also manufactures here. The manufacture in this country is being steadily increased, and would have been increased much more rapidly in the past if considerable delay had not been involved in procuring the necessary plant and setting it up in this country. The machinery which the company builds and leases, or sells, is chiefly of American invention.

(2) The authorized capital of the parent company in America is $25,000,000. The authorized capital of this offspring company is 2,500,000 marks ($595,000).

(3) We employ, as a rule, about 100 hands. At the present moment, there are only seven or eight Americans employed as expert operators, or instructors, on our machines. The latter having had more experience, and having made the operating of certain machines a specialty, are the best that can be procured; but as far as the manufacture of machines is concerned, we have found Americans of special benefit only in getting the plant set up and in giving instructions to others. We have not found American workmen of general advantage in permanent employment here.

(4) The working hours are from 7 a. m. till 6 p. m., with an interval of one hour at midday, and the wages vary from 16 to 50 marks ($3.80 to $11.90) per week for German workmen. Americans receive higher remuneration, their engagement being generally only of a temporary nature.

(5) Establishments similar to our own in Germany are not conducted by Americans.

(6) We do not know of any Americans who have received contracts from or are employed by the German Government.

### LETTER FROM VAUGHN MACHINE COMPANY.

Our firm, the Vaughn Machine Company, G. m. b. H. Frankfort on Main, is the European selling agency of the Vaughn Machine Company, Peabody, Mass., manufacturers of tanners' machinery of every description.

We have storehouses and repair shops at Frankfort on Main, at Vienna, Austria, and at Leicester, England.

The capital invested in the stock of goods we carry in Europe may be put down as $150,000 to $200,000. In spite of a keen competition by European manufacturers, which competition is growing more active every day, we so far have been able to steadily increase our business from year to year.

Our annual sales amount to $300,000 to $350,000. We are employing at our various shops 20 hands, all told, and we have an office force of 18, including our traveling salesmen and managers. Among the latter number are 5 Americans, who, on account of their special training, can not as yet be duplicated by any European help.

At our repair shops, we work nine hours a day. The average pay is about $1 a day.

There are no other establishments in our line in Germany conducted by Americans.

I do not know of any Americans who have received contracts from or are employed by governments or corporations in this country.

### LETTER FROM FELIX LEVY, AGENT OF MERGENTHALER TYPESETTING COMPANY.

For four and one-half years, I have had the general agency of the Mergenthaler typesetting machine for about half the territory of Germany. At first, I sold the American machines known as "linotype." Later on, the German company for the sale of linotypes—the Mergenthaler Typesetting Machine Company, of Berlin—made a contract with the Berliner Maschinenbau Actien Company, to the effect that the linotype machines were henceforth to be built in Germany. The Berlin company building these machines still imported from the United States machine parts, especially the types composed of brass. But even these have of late been made in Germany and supplied by the type foundry of D. Stempel, which company has the right to make the linotype types in Germany, Austria-Hungary, and Switzerland.

It was a difficult matter to introduce these machines into Germany, because the German publishers are slow to adopt new modes. In the beginning, they were also rather mistrustful. In addition, there was not sufficient consideration given to the style of type required in Germany, but this want was afterwards filled by the two-lettered linotype, which at one and the same time casts two styles of lettering. This improvement stimulated, in an extraordinary manner, the sale of the machines. To-day, there are about 700 linotype machines in use throughout Germany, Austria-Hungary, and Switzerland, whereas, at the close of the year 1898, hardly 100 were in operation.

Owing to the general depression of business existing for the last two years, the sale of these machines has declined, but an improvement now appears noticeable. However, it can not be expected that the sales will compare with those in the United States. While the American publisher keeps ready a large number of these machines to give the reader a paper containing the latest news, the German publisher (even of the leading papers) wants to make the utmost use of each machine by running the same day and night. American printers keep them going only five to seven hours per day.

Thus it happens that a large publishing concern in New York will employ 60 to 70 linotypes, whereas a German concern of equal extent has not the sixth of these machines.

Other typesetting machines, lower in price, are more widely used than the linotype in Germany, but the larger publishing firms prefer the last named, on account of its greater working capacity and more solid construction.

For six months, I also have had the agency for the sale of the Harris automatic printing press, which is made at Niles, Ohio. But after next month, these machines will also be made at Zweibruecken, in Germany, the rights having been purchased by German machine-building companies.

At present, no decided opinion can be given as to the successful sale of these machines, though they possess immense advantages over printing presses now used in Germany.

## HAMBURG.

Although unfavorable signs were noticeable during the latter part of 1900, these were not considered in commercial circles as indicating a decrease or stagnation of business. The chamber of commerce of Hamburg, in its report for 1900, expressed the hope that business would improve during the coming year, which expectation, however, has not been realized. Disturbances, which at that time occurred only sporadically, developed during last year into a general depression. This unfavorable situation was principally due to over-production and to the high prices of the most essential raw materials, coal and pig iron. Moreover, a number of financial disasters alarmed the market considerably; however, Hamburg itself did not suffer as much as the interior of Germany, for the reason that those branches of industry affected—i. e., iron and steel manufactures, textiles, etc.—are not represented in this city.

On the other hand, in shipbuilding, one of the principal industries of Hamburg, considerable business was transacted, and numerous orders from abroad, were filled.

A good idea of the variety of business in Hamburg can be obtained by a study of the principal articles of trade.

### COFFEE.

Although business was dull on account of the dropping of prices until about July, 1901, in the second half of that year it improved considerably, and prices rose again to a higher figure than at the beginning of the year. This rise was chiefly caused by exaggerated speculation and was, therefore, not of long duration; nevertheless, it is hoped that, in expectation of a smaller crop from Brazil, business will become and remain firm and favorable.

*Imports of coffee at port of Hamburg for years 1900 and 1901.*

| From— | 1900. | | 1901. | |
|---|---|---|---|---|
| | Bags. | Million pounds. | Bags. | Million pounds. |
| Santos | 1,572,855 | 188.7 | 1,870,125 | 224.4 |
| Rio | 232,730 | 27.9 | 419,086 | 50.6 |
| Bahia | 27,386 | 3.3 | 88,569 | 10.6 |
| La Guaira | 162,080 | 21.1 | 62,946 | 8.2 |
| Santo Domingo | 96,109 | 13 | 13,224 | 1.8 |
| Maracaibo and Savanilla | 12,051 | 1.4 | 13,224 | 1.6 |
| Central America | 683,827 | 89.8 | 599,570 | 77.9 |
| Porto Rico | 2,250 | .4 | 2,200 | .4 |
| East Indies | 12,748 | 1.6 | 13,330 | 1.7 |
| Africa | 61,855 | 7.4 | 34,572 | 4.2 |
| Miscellaneous | 209,978 | 26.2 | 227,493 | 28.4 |
| Total | 3,073,869 | 379.9 | 3,344,289 | 409.8 |

### SUGAR.

In the first half of 1901, an extensive export business was transacted, partly to the United Kingdom, on account of the expected sugar-duty bill (which afterwards, in April, went in force), and partly to Japan, because of the tax to be imposed on this article. As both countries had supplied themselves for a long time, and as the United States imported only a comparatively small quantity of beet sugar, because of the increased demand for cane sugar, business became so dull toward the end of the year that the German beet-sugar industry seemed to be endangered.

*Estimated European sugar production.*

| Country. | 1900–1901. | 1899–1900. | 1898–1899. |
|---|---|---|---|
| | Tons. | Tons. | Tons. |
| Germany | 1,970,000 | 1,798,630 | 1,721,718 |
| Austria | 1,095,000 | 1,108,007 | 1,051,290 |
| France | 1,170,000 | 977,850 | 830,132 |
| Russia | 890,000 | 910,000 | 776,066 |
| Belgium | 340,000 | 304,000 | 244,017 |
| Holland | 180,000 | 171,029 | 149,763 |
| Other countries | 375,000 | 258,929 | 209,015 |
| Total | 6,020,000 | 5,523,445 | 4,982,000 |

### RUBBER.

An interesting change took place in this line. Only two years ago, it was feared that it would be impossible to produce sufficient rubber to supply the demand. Several scientific expeditions were sent out with a view to discovering new fields. The demand has since decreased so much that the price of rubber has dropped about 30 per cent.

### GRAIN.

Although a poor crop was expected in the northern parts of Germany, the result was better than was anticipated. In some sections,

the crop of rye and summer grain was quite good, and the importers
of foreign cereals of that kind were at a disadvantage, having over-
rated the domestic demand and imported an excess from abroad. The
imports of corn, on account of the poor crop in the United States,
were light, and for the same reason, very small quantities of other
feed stuffs were imported therefrom.

*Average prices of grains per 1,000 kilos (2,205 pounds) at Hamburg on December 31, 1900 and 1901.*

| Cereal. | 1900. | 1901. |
|---|---|---|
| **Wheat:** | | |
| German | $34.87 | $42.95 |
| Foreign, transit | 31.89 | 32.76 |
| **Rye:** | | |
| German | 32.13 | 34.51 |
| Foreign, transit | 25.59 | 25.59 |
| **Barley:** | | |
| German fine malt | 46.41 | 42.84 |
| Austrian fine malt | 39.87 | 38.06 |
| Russian, Danube, feeding | 23.80 | 24.04 |
| **Oats:** | | |
| German | 32.73 | 37.37 |
| Foreign, transit | 25.59 | 32.13 |
| **Corn:** | | |
| North American mixed, transit | 20.59 | 28.92 |
| Round River Plate, Russian, Danube, and Turkish, transit | 20.59 | 26.18 |

## TOBACCO.

Because of the unfavorable condition in the German industrial districts and a decrease, therefore, of the demand, business was considerably
affected during last year. The cigar manufacturers of Hamburg did
not suffer to the same extent as those in the interior, for the reason
that only superior qualities of cigars are manufactured here.

*Imports of tobacco at port of Hamburg during years 1900 and 1901.*

| | 1900. | 1901. | | 1900. | 1901. |
|---|---|---|---|---|---|
| | Packages. | Packages. | | Packages. | Packages. |
| Habana | 13,000 | 20,000 | Rio Grande | 1,100 | 3,200 |
| Yara and Guiza | 7,000 | 600 | Paraguay | 4,500 | 900 |
| Cuba | 7,000 | 1,100 | Mexico | 12,000 | 5,700 |
| Santo Domingo | 158,000 | 96,000 | Java and Sumatra | 38,400 | 30,500 |
| Porto Rico | 2,800 | 12,800 | Esmeralda | 350 | |
| Varinas | 50 | 100 | Seedleaf | 500 | 8,600 |
| Colombia | 24,000 | 48,000 | Kentucky, Virginia, Ohio, etc. | 4,400 | 4,500 |
| Cumana, etc | | | Turkish and Greek | 27,000 | 30,000 |
| Brasil | 130,000 | 161,000 | | | |

## HIDES.

Local business was in a very unfavorable condition on account of
the industrial depression in Germany, which also affected the tanning
industry considerably. The imports of valonia, divi-divi, myrobolans,
and other tanning materials, with the exception of quebracho wood,
were comparatively small.

## RICE.

Of great importance for the rice business was the amalgamation of
all German rice mills, including those of Hamburg, into a combine,

with its seat at Bremen. In competition with this enterprise, a mill was established in the free port of Hamburg, principally for the purpose of importing, shelling, and reexporting rice.

*Imports of rice at port of Hamburg during year 1901.*

|  | | Imports. | Stock, Dec. 31, 1901. |  | | Imports. | Stock, Dec. 31, 1901. |
|---|---|---|---|---|---|---|---|
| Carolina | barrels.. | 11 | ......... | Saigon | bags.. | 629,841 | 110,000 |
| Java | bags.. | 29,186 | 100 | Moulmein | do.... | 87,793 | 4,000 |
| Japan | do.... | 46,284 | 3,500 | Italian | do.... | 261 | ......... |
| Bengal | do.... | 50,769 | 250 | Raree, Ballam, etc | do.... | .......... | .......... |
| Rangoon | do.... | 340,732 | 50,000 | Miscellaneous | do.... | 225,205 | 114,650 |
| Bassein | do.... | 50,909 | 2,500 |  | | | |
| Arracan and Larong | do.... | 135,637 | 15,000 | Total | | 1,788,002 | 330,000 |
| Siam | do.... | 191,385 | 30,000 |  | | | |

### EVAPORATED APPLES.

Business was not as good in 1901 as in former years. Offers for products of the new crop began at 33 marks per 50 kilograms ($7.85 per 110 pounds), c. i. f. Hamburg, for October shipments. The demand, however, was weak until it was ascertained that only a small crop was to be expected in the eastern districts of Europe.

A new competition with goods from the eastern parts of the United States appeared last year in the shape of California apples. The manner of preparing evaporated apples in California has greatly improved lately. Two years ago, California apples were refused because of their bad appearance, but last year, they easily conquered the market, being very similar in appearance to the Eastern States apples. The difference in price between California and Eastern apples, which at first amounted to 8 marks per 50 kilograms ($1.90 per 110 pounds), decreased rapidly to 5 marks ($1.19), and at the end of the year, the prices were 46.50 and 44.50 marks ($11.07 and $10.59), respectively.

### LUMBER.

*American maple.*—But little of the stock remained unsold; prices were not high and the demand for this perishable article was small.

*Dogwood and persimmon.*—An increase of imports could be noted in 1901. As these woods mostly arrive under contract, there is little to report about the market.

*American oak.*—The imports of this article have grown considerably and prices rose. Cut woods and squares were in constant demand.

*American hickory.*—Logs were in steady demand, but on account of the increased imports, not all the shipments could be disposed of, so that at the end of last year some stock remained unsold. Partly manufactured articles are more in demand now than the raw material.

*American walnut.*—The demand during the entire year was not a large one, but sufficient to dispose of the shipments arriving, particularly for better classes. Inferior qualities remained unsold for a long period, thereby considerably increasing the stock on hand.

*American poplar and whitewood.*—Business was very good and high prices were obtained. The imports were larger in 1901 than in the preceding year. A few blocks of cottonwood were sold; however, they did not seem to be desirable.

## PHOSPHATE.

The total imports (estimated) of phosphate into Hamburg and Harburg amounted to—

| | Tons. | | Tons. |
|---|---|---|---|
| 1898 | 114,500 | 1900 | 106,200 |
| 1899 | 168,800 | 1901 | 111,600 |

Price quotations at the end of December, 1901, were the following:

| For— | Quotations. | |
|---|---|---|
| | Pence. | U. S. equivalent. |
| Florida hard rock, 76 to 80 per cent | 7¼ to 7½ | $0.14.6 to $0.14.8 |
| Florida land pebble, 68 to 78 per cent | 5¼ | 11.1 |
| Florida Peace River, 58 to 63 per cent | 5¼ | 11.1 |
| Tennessee, 78 to 80 per cent | 6¼ | 12.6 |
| Christmas Island, 80 to 85 per cent | 7¼ | 15.2 |
| Algiers, 63 to 70 per cent | 5¾ | 11.6 |
| Algiers, 57 to 63 per cent | 5¼ | 11.1 |

## COAL.

The attempts to import American coal were continued in 1901. On account of the prevailing low freight rates, it was possible to bring a number of shipments to Hamburg; these, however, did not amount to much, a more favorable business being done with Mediterranean ports. Undoubtedly, American coal will eventually become a rival in Germany to the domestic and English product, with which industrial and commercial circles will have to count.

Prices on December 31, 1901, for English coals, free lighter or barge in the port of Hamburg, per 40 hectoliters (about 3 tons), were:

West Hartley:
  Steam coal ... $11.90–$12.38
  Unscreened ... 10.95  11.42
  Small ... 7.38  7.85
Gas and coking coal ... 11.90  12.38
Sunderland:
  Steam coal, unscreened ... 11.19  11.42
  Double-screened nuts ... 12.61  12.85
Yorkshire:
  Steam coal ... 11.42  12.85
  Double-screened nuts ... 11.19  12.61
Scotch:
  Household coal, prime large ... 11.42  12.14
  Steam coal ... 10.71  11.42
  Double-screened nuts ... 10.00  10.71

## HARBOR TRAFFIC.

In 1901, there was again an increase in the tonnage of vessels arrived. In 1899, 7,165,000, and in 1900, 8,037,000 net register tons were entered. By November, 1901, the number amounted to 7,844,000 tons, compared with 7,448,000 tons during the same period of the preceding year. There was, however, a decrease in the number of vessels compared with 1899, when the highest figure was reached, with 13,312 vessels, while in 1900 this figure was reduced by 210, thereby showing an increase in the average capacity of each vessel. Compared with competing seaports, Hamburg has held its leading position in

the increase of tonnage, with the exception of Rotterdam, where a
faster growth of tonnage took place, as shown in the following statistical schedule:

| Vessels arrived. | 1895. | | 1900. | |
|---|---|---|---|---|
| | Vessels. | 1,000 tons. | Vessels. | 1,000 tons. |
| Hamburg | 9,443 | 6,254 | 13,102 | 8,087 |
| Without coastwise | 6,596 | 5,682 | 8,419 | 7,323 |
| Bremen | 4,063 | 2,182 | 3,843 | 2,493 |
| Rotterdam | 5,199 | 4,177 | 7,268 | 6,589 |
| Antwerp | 4,710 | 5,822 | 6,420 | 6,842 |
| Liverpool | 19,457 | 8,675 | 20,309 | 9,315 |
| Without coastwise | 3,716 | 5,598 | 3,503 | 6,001 |
| London | 53,916 | 14,991 | 25,814 | 15,553 |
| Without coastwise | 10,212 | 8,435 | 11,118 | 9,580 |

SHIPPING BUSINESS.

The mercantile marine of Hamburg shows a very satisfactory development, for besides the deep-sea fishing fleet, it consisted of—

| Class. | 1900. | | 1901. | |
|---|---|---|---|---|
| | Number. | Net registered tonnage. | Number. | Net registered tonnage. |
| Steamers | 437 | 638,007 | 486 | 748,435 |
| Sailing vessels | 286 | 218,832 | 307 | 240,419 |

On January 1, 1902, the number was increased to 521 steamers, of
842,966 net register tons, and 333 sailing ships, of 242,765 net register
tons. The growing number of the latter class is remarkable, and its
ability to compete with steamers has been aided by high prices of
coal. Among the sailing ships there are at present 115 sea lighters, of
34,582 tons.

In 1900, good financial results were obtained, as shown by the published statements of the various steamship companies. While the
prospects for 1901 were equally good, and a lively movement in emigration and other passenger business was expected, the unfavorable
able business situation in Germany and several foreign countries made
itself felt by a decrease in available cargoes. Besides, a great number
of newly built vessels entered the freight market, and rates took a
downward movement, which became still more conspicuous when the
steamers used as transports for troops from China were again available for freight-carrying purposes. This movement was furthered
by the small corn crop in the United States, and a fall of 30 to 40 per
cent in rates took place.

In order to facilitate coaling of steamers in foreign seas, coal depots
were established in Algiers on account of Hamburg and Bremen firms,
and, as this arrangement has proved successful, a similar depot will
also be opened at Suez, from which the Imperial German Navy will
draw its supplies.

The present shipping business situation will be aggravated by the
proposed new tariff, which is now under consideration in Germany,
and German shipowners have good reason to look with apprehension
upon the consequences to be expected from a tariff hostile to free
international trade movements.

## NEW GERMAN CUSTOMS TARIFF.

On this subject, the Hamburg Chamber of Commerce writes, in its report for the year 1901, as follows:

After the various committees nominated to consider a new tariff had filed their reports, their suggestions were submitted to a conference of delegates from the various German governments. As foreign trade will be chiefly affected by the new tariff, it was expected that representatives of the Hanseatic cities—Hamburg, Bremen, and Lubeck—would be called to participate in this conference, and the fact of this not being the case made it evident that commercial interests were not to be properly considered. The proposed new tariff submitted to the various governments was to be kept secret, and even the views of the several chambers of commerce were not to be heard. Through an indiscretion, the project was published, and its stipulations surpassed all previous apprehensions in regard to its agrarian protective tendencies. From all parts, vigorous protests were raised against the extraordinary increase of import duties on all kinds of grain and provisions. Agricultural interests in Germany are based more upon the raising of cattle and pigs than upon grain culture, and in the end they will be more impaired by an artificial rise in feed stuffs than they will be benefited by a high duty on cereals. On the other hand, industrial enterprises, the exports of the products of which in all branches surpass the imports to a large extent, are not interested in a protective tariff, but, on the contrary, look for a moderation of foreign duties and lasting favorable commercial treaties. In commercial and industrial circles, it is generally admitted that the now existing treaties, which have brought about the prosperous development of Germany, should be renewed for a period of ten to fifteen years, and that, on the same basis, similar treaties with other countries, especially with the United States, would be most desirable. It is of mutual interest to both countries to avoid any tariff war, and, if Germany admits American goods at low rates of duty, it is only fair to expect an equal treatment from the United States. American industry has made such wonderful progress that it hardly stands in need of a high protective tariff, and it is to be hoped that ways and means will be found to compensate the interests of both countries on the basis of mutual advantages.

## TELEPHONE SERVICE.

In 1901, several cities were connected by direct wires with Hamburg. The Breslau Chamber of Commerce has taken steps to secure direct telephone connection with this city, but, although the importance of direct communication between these places is fully recognized, the matter has not been settled.

Although Hamburg has telephone connection with Paris, but little use is made of the service, for the reason that conversations have to pass through Frankfort on the Main, and are, therefore, not sufficiently distinct. Besides, connections can not be made promptly enough.

Night telephone service was established last year. For each conversation, an extra fee of 20 pfennigs (about 5 cents) is charged. Long-distance conversations at special rates can also be held during the night with Berlin. Cologne, Frankfort on the Main, Paris, and Copenhagen.

## KAISER WILHELM CANAL.

While in the opening year, 1896, the traffic through the canal amounted to but 19,960 vessels, measuring 1,848,000 tons, it increased in 1898 to 25,816 vessels of 3,177,000 tons and in 1900 to 29,045 vessels of 4,282,000 tons. The respective receipts were, marks 1,016,000, 1,634,000, 2,174,000 ($241,808, $388,892, $517,412); so that, exclusive of the tug service, the expenses of which surpassed the receipts to the extent of marks 395,000, ($94,010) a surplus of about marks 80,000 ($19,040) would have been reached.

### HARBOR AND QUAYS OF THE HAMBURG-AMERICAN LINE.

A very spacious new harbor has been completed on the southern bank of the Elbe, especially for the service of the Hamburg-American Line, at an expense of about 32,000,000 marks ($7,616,000). This harbor will accommodate a large fleet of steamships of deep draft, and all facilities for loading and discharging cargoes are provided. A new harbor for colliers has also been built near by, thus giving more space on the river for other seagoing vessels.

The Hamburg-American Line has arranged to dispatch its express steamers from Cuxhaven, and an increase of the receipts for tonnage dues will take place at that port; also, certain changes in the regulations about entry certificates of goods, in order to facilitate correct statistical records of imports, have been made.

*Arrivals of seagoing vessels.*

| From— | 1901. | |
| --- | --- | --- |
| | Ships. | Registered tonnage. |
| German ports | 4,570 | 759,067 |
| Great Britain (colliers) | 1,615 | 1,119,868 |
| Great Britain (with other cargo) | 2,344 | 1,451,715 |
| Other European ports | 2,706 | 1,488,595 |
| America | 1,117 | 2,597,588 |
| Africa | 203 | 287,881 |
| Asia and Australia | 292 | 729,200 |
| | 12,847 | 8,383,365 |
| In cargo | 9,449 | 7,620,267 |
| In ballast | 3,398 | 763,098 |
| Sailing vessels | 4,103 | 847,419 |
| Steamships | 8,744 | 7,535,946 |
| Average tonnage: | | |
| Sailing vessels | .......... | 207 |
| Steamships | .......... | 862 |
| Percentage: | | |
| Sailing vessels | 31.9 | 10.1 |
| Steamships | 68.1 | 89.9 |

*Departures of seagoing vessels.*

| To— | 1901. | |
| --- | --- | --- |
| | Ships. | Registered tonnage. |
| German ports | 4,049 | 678,826 |
| Great Britain and Ireland | 4,351 | 3,299,207 |
| Other European ports | 3,035 | 1,143,566 |
| America | 864 | 2,172,919 |
| Africa | 233 | 366,257 |
| Asia and Australia | 291 | 691,042 |
| | 12,823 | 8,351,817 |
| In cargo | 9,647 | 5,918,135 |
| In ballast | 3,176 | 2,433,682 |
| Sailing vessels | 4,096 | 844,615 |
| Steamships | 8,727 | 7,507,202 |
| Percentage: | | |
| Sailing vessels | 31.9 | 10.1 |
| Steamships | 68.1 | 89.9 |

*Hamburg merchant marine in 1901.*

| Class. | Ships. | Registered tonnage. |
|---|---|---|
| Full rigged ships | 41 | 69,609 |
| Barks and schooner barks | 89 | 134,291 |
| Schooner brigs and schooners | 9 | 287 |
| Three-masted schooners | 4 | 1,022 |
| Galleys | 14 | 674 |
| Galliots, gaff schooners | 15 | 1,118 |
| Other small sailing craft | 164 | 36,133 |
| Steamships | 532 | 843,460 |
| Total | 868 | 1,086,594 |

*Emigration via Hamburg.*

| To— | Ships. | Emigrants. |
|---|---|---|
| Great Britain | 324 | 9,855 |
| Other European countries | 7 | 47 |
| The United States of America | 94 | 73,980 |
| British North America | 6 | 2,845 |
| Mexico, Central America, and West Indies | 74 | 269 |
| Brazil and Rio de la Plata States | 133 | 2,968 |
| Other South American States | 21 | 448 |
| Africa | 96 | 1,587 |
| Asia | 17 | 169 |
| Australia and Polynesia | ...... | 4 |
| Total | 772 | 92,172 |

*Quotations of exchange at Hamburg in 1901.*

### AVERAGE EXCHANGE OF NEW YORK DRAFTS.

#### [Per $1 gold.]

| Month. | Short sight. | Sixty days from date. | Month. | Short sight. | Sixty days from date. |
|---|---|---|---|---|---|
| | *Marks.* | *Marks.* | | *Marks.* | *Marks.* |
| January | 4.17 | 4.14 | July | 4.16 | 4.13 |
| February | 4.18 | 4.14 | August | 4.17 | 4.14 |
| March | 4.17 | 4.13 | September | 4.19 | 4.14 |
| April | 4.16 | 4.13 | October | 4.18 | 4.12 |
| May | 4.17 | 4.12 | November | 4.17 | 4.12 |
| June | 4.16 | 4.12 | December | 4.17 | 4.13 |

### AVERAGE EXCHANGE OF UNITED STATES MONEY.

| Month. | Eagle. | Bank notes. | Month. | Eagle. | Bank notes. |
|---|---|---|---|---|---|
| | *Marks.* | *Marks.* | | *Marks.* | *Marks.* |
| January | 20.85 | 4.16 | July | 20.85 | 4.14 |
| February | 20.86 | 4.17 | August | 20.85 | 4.15 |
| March | 20.86 | 4.17 | September | 20.87 | 4.16 |
| April | 20.85 | 4.17 | October | 20.90 | 4.16 |
| May | 20.85 | 4.15 | November | 20.82 | 4.16 |
| June | 20.85 | 4.14 | December | 20.84 | 4.16 |

HUGH PITCAIRN, *Consul.*

HAMBURG, *October 31, 1902.*

## LEIPZIG.

While it may be said that the commercial and industrial conditions of this section—which consists of the territory covered by the chambers of commerce of Leipzig, Altenburg, Gera, and Halle on the Salle, respectively—were better during the year ended June 30, 1902, than they were in 1900-1901, and perhaps even in the year before that, at the same time one would hardly be justified in saying that in all branches of trade a satisfactory state of affairs exists.

The business depression, which already made itself noticeable at the beginning of 1900, has been felt in all sections of the German Empire, more in some places, of course, than in others. Leipzig was perhaps one of the worst sufferers, for, in addition to the general depression, it was the scene of several failures of more than ordinary importance, one of which, that of the Leipziger Bank, June 26, 1901, will go down in history as one of the largest and most disastrous business suspensions of the twentieth century.

Nevertheless, Leipzig has been undoubtedly one of the first districts to show signs of recovery. This is largely due to the great export business that local merchants and manufacturers have been engaged in building up during the past ten years. In 1900 and 1901—when the home trade was at a standstill—a number of manufacturers were able to keep their factories running only by orders received from abroad. But within the last few months, the German market has revived, and the outlook for the future is promising.

As to the exact condition of the different industries, it is, of course, hard to obtain accurate information; but it may be said with confidence that, while the business of the iron foundries, machine factories, and the color and soap manufactories, as well as the millers' and the brewers', could be very much improved, on the other hand, the fur trade, the textile, china ware, paper, toy, doll, musical instrument, and hardware industries have greatly increased their output—indeed, some factories have already begun to work overtime.

### MONEY PRICES.

The price of money has been, if anything, easier than last year, when the Reichsbank's average discount rate was 4.099 per cent as against 5.333 per cent in 1900.

### STOCK COMPANIES.

The law passed in 1898 forbidding the watering of stock has been of great benefit to the public, in that it has served as a protection to persons wishing to invest money against placing their funds in paper companies. Another good feature about the law is that, in almost every instance, the minimum par value of a share is fixed at 1,000 marks (about $250). This, of course, has not only a tendency to restrain the poorer classes from putting their savings into this sort of investment, which is more or less uncertain, but, at the same time, it also decreases materially the swarm of margin speculators.

The number of new stock companies in Germany, according to the Deutscher Oekonomist, is:

| Year. | Stock companies. | Capital. |
|---|---|---|
| 1898 | 329 | $110,432,000 |
| 1899 | 364 | 129,710,000 |
| 1900 | 261 | 80,920,000 |
| 1901 | 156 | 37,604,000 |

It is believed that the number of companies which will be started in 1902 will far exceed that of last year.

### POPULATION.

The estimated population of the city of Leipzig was, on July 1, 1902, 473,910, and on July 1, 1901, 461,519, an increase of 12,391. Not only is this city increasing in the number of its inhabitants, but Halle on the Salle, and Gera, Reuss, also show large gains.

### CITY IMPROVEMENTS.

Work upon the Leipzig Central Railroad station has at last begun. When completed, it will be one of the finest stations in Germany. It is estimated that the work in connection with the erection of this station will cost between $20,000,000 and $25,000,000, it being necessary to take up and relay a large number of car tracks in and about the city.

The new city hall, which was commenced in 1899, will be finished next spring. The Leipzig Central Theater, a large theater, restaurant, and concert hall combined, costing $500,000 or more, has just been completed. Several new streets have been opened up and others have been widened. New parks have been laid out and the old ones beautified.

The building operations, however, showed the effect of the adverse industrial conditions. The total number of building permits issued during the year 1901 was 961—against 983 in 1900—of which 503 were for the erection of houses upon vacant lots.

### IMPORTS.

The value and quantity of every article imported into Germany is, of course, known, but it is extremely difficult to even approximate the amounts of foreign goods which are consumed in the different consular districts.

A very good way of getting an idea of the imports into this section is by applying to the importing houses and forwarding agents, and data gathered from them would indicate that the imports from Russia, North and South America, Austria-Hungary, and Australia, most of which are raw products, have increased in some lines and fallen off in others.

The shipments from Spain, Portugal, England, France, etc., have remained about the same, except that certain drugs from the last-mentioned country may have been imported in larger quantities than formerly.

## EXPORTS.

Certainly, no fault can be found with the exports from this section; they have never been so large as during the year ended June 30, 1902.

The Central American States have purchased in larger quantities than last year, as have also the Argentine Republic, Brazil, China, Japan, the Philippines, Australia, Canada, England, France, Russia, South America, and Mexico—indeed, the shipments to all countries have materially increased. A Leipzig firm only recently received a contract for the construction of a rope haulage plant for South America, to cost about $375,000.

### TRADE WITH THE UNITED STATES.

*Imports.*—The usual large quantities of raw products have been consumed here during the past year. In some lines of manufactured goods, such as shoes, typewriters, etc., there seems to have been a decided increase.

*Exports.*—The following table gives the articles, and the value of each, which have been exported from this district during the last five fiscal years:

*Exports from consular district of Leipzig during the five years ended June 30, 1902.*

| Articles. | 1897-98. | 1898-99. | 1899-1900. | 1900-1901. | 1901-2. |
|---|---|---|---|---|---|
| Accordions | | | | | $6,331.98 |
| Antiquities | | | | | 242.11 |
| Artificial flowers | $2,949.84 | $1,225.48 | | | 247.74 |
| Artists' canvas | | | | $143.87 | 817.66 |
| Beet seeds | | 65,010.02 | $68,768.72 | 55,961.84 | 26,121.11 |
| Bleached cotton | | | | 583.10 | 1,142.07 |
| Bleaching powder | | | | 70,041.43 | 217,453.17 |
| Books, periodicals | 411,017.77 | 384,555.72 | 423,360.33 | 448,390.48 | 453,258.18 |
| Brass ware | | | | | 838.39 |
| Bristles | 498,580.91 | 620,968.41 | 666,754.89 | 632,338.15 | 772,950.06 |
| Bulbs and roots | | | | | 1,326.32 |
| Carpets | | | | 193.96 | 414.85 |
| Capsules | | | | | 437.02 |
| Carbonate of potash | | | | | 6,496.43 |
| Caustic potash | | | | 36,689.30 | 105,042.02 |
| Chemicals | 244,681.63 | 213,504.87 | 235,898.21 | 220,823.45 | 77,686.40 |
| Chinaware | | | | 367.00 | 826.71 |
| Chromolithographs | 66,201.72 | 66,586.70 | 86,119.97 | 61,689.69 | 58,712.52 |
| Cocoa butter | 8,527.72 | | | | |
| Colored paper | | | | 4,328.28 | 10,285.48 |
| Colors | | | | 6,457.97 | 18,143.10 |
| Cotton gloves | | | | 8,501.88 | |
| Cotton laces | | | | | 1,824.71 |
| Cyanide of potassium | | | | 63,668.93 | 121,026.98 |
| Drugs | | | | 7,750.00 | 38,025.71 |
| Earthenware | | | | 2,139.74 | 792.18 |
| Eis-wool squares | | | | 1,199.66 | |
| Electrotypes | | | | | 621.68 |
| Essential oils | 68,565.98 | 154,733.51 | 97,172.07 | 139,891.99 | 129,982.98 |
| Fancy boxes | | | | 3,486.17 | 11,357.16 |
| Fennel seeds | | | | 163.86 | |
| Foot rules | | | | 2,489.70 | 3,569.54 |
| Fruit juice | 14,662.36 | 9,840.98 | 11,149.33 | 6,112.40 | 4,002.92 |
| Furs and skins | 1,613,205.68 | 2,348,133.86 | 2,889,109.31 | 2,151,232.18 | 4,166,311.28 |
| Glassware | | | | 1,198.10 | 2,859.29 |
| Hardware | | | | | 162.73 |
| Head models | | | | | 211.80 |
| Hides | 1,375.62 | | 68,359.51 | 63,788.78 | 171,592.88 |
| Household goods | | | | 4,762.52 | 4,885.06 |
| India rubber goods | | | | 8,531.53 | 8,808.85 |
| Iron sand | | | | | 366.66 |
| Lace goods | | | | 958.05 | 574.77 |
| Leather gloves | | 9,714.51 | 18,943.36 | | |
| Linen goods | | | | | 960.11 |
| Machinery | 34,299.21 | 75,586.63 | 95,208.71 | 11,241.49 | 29,298.97 |
| Magnesium powder | | | | | 4,780.04 |

*Exports from consular district of Leipzig, etc.*—Continued.

| Articles. | 1897–98. | 1898–99. | 1899–1900. | 1900–1901. | 1901–2. |
|---|---|---|---|---|---|
| Mexican antiquities............ | | | | | $716.52 |
| Musical instruments ........... | $38,618.08 | $19,637.50 | $15,979.50 | $12,495.02 | 4,130.37 |
| Oil of roses ................. | | | | | 32,631.45 |
| Oil paintings ................ | | | | | 1,545.91 |
| Oxalic acid.................. | | | | | 13,148.23 |
| Oxide of cobalt.............. | | | | | 16,224.62 |
| Penholder tips............... | | | | 257.08 | 1,342.85 |
| Pepto-mangan................ | | | | 57,748.37 | 106,680.04 |
| Permanganate of potash ...... | | | | | 3,575.05 |
| Piano felt .................. | | 22,045.10 | 51,879.47 | 51,464.85 | 64,359.28 |
| Piano hammers .............. | | | | | 659.94 |
| Plows ...................... | | | | | 614.65 |
| Polishing extract ........... | | | | | 8,273.99 |
| Potatoes.................... | | | | 166.74 | 169.12 |
| Printed music ............... | 61,229.48 | 69,506.41 | 69,641.68 | 75,168.41 | 83,988.29 |
| Scientific instruments......... | 651.74 | 8,361.16 | 6,524.70 | 7,296.08 | 8.473.42 |
| Sugar (beet)................. | | | | 86,308.62 | |
| Table covers................. | | | | | 4,971.37 |
| Toothpicks.................. | | | | | 196.40 |
| Toys....................... | | | | 3,946.72 | 7,507.44 |
| Wafers..................... | | | | 1,038.19 | 1,454.18 |
| Wall paper ................. | | | | 8,604.13 | 15,124.86 |
| Watches.................... | | | | | 192.92 |
| Woolen goods ............... | 62,127.66 | 83,583.39 | | 39,963,59 | 10,896.77 |
| Wool grease ................ | | | | 5,007.38 | 17,069.59 |
| Worsted yarns............... | | | | | 2,640.08 |
| Wooden patterns............. | | | | | 152.32 |
| Wine ...................... | | | | | 281.37 |
| All other articles............. | 34,421.43 | 55,586.78 | 47,125.91 | 19,042.70 | |
| Total .................... | 3,161,066.78 | 4,208,150.98 | 4,905,882.38 | 4,378,623.38 | 6,863,525.45 |

From the above table, it will be seen that this year's exports have
increased 50 per cent over last year's and more than 100 per cent over
the record of five years ago. The principal articles shipped abroad
are, as usual, furs and skins, which alone show an increase over
1900–1901 of more than $2,000,000.

From present indications, this district will make larger shipments
to the United States in the year 1902–3 than it has ever done before.

BRAINARD H. WARNER, Jr., *Consul.*

LEIPZIG, *November 26, 1902.*

---

## MAGDEBURG.

The consular district of which Magdeburg is the most important
business and trade center comprises that portion of the Kingdom of
Prussia which was segregated from Saxony proper by the treaty of
1815, and embraces within its borders one of the most fertile and productive agricultural sections in the German Empire.

The land is held in larger areas than is the case in many other sections of the country, and nowhere else are advanced and up-to-date
methods of cultivating the soil more apparent, nor is there any other
region where the earth is made to yield more abundant crops to the
acre. This result is attained by careful, painstaking preparation of
the ground before seeding it. Magdeburg's location, in the center of
so productive a region, has made it one of the most enterprising and
prosperous cities in Prussia, if not in Germany, its exports to the
United States almost equaling those of any other consulate in the
Empire.

It has become a manufacturing city of the first class, and its varied industries embrace enormous plants located in the suburbs, as well as in the city proper. The active business methods of the citizens are more akin to the American than to the typical German. Competition in every branch of business is evidenced by generous advertising, and in spite of the general business depression, the city is growing rapidly in inhabitants and wealth, its population now approximating 250,000.

Tariff agitation has had much to do with the depression in all kinds of business, not alone in this city, but throughout the consular district, and this will continue until the question is finally determined.

The uncertainty of the result of this tariff agitation has doubtless had its effect in curtailing importations from the United States, and it is therefore difficult to suggest the kind of articles that could be profitably introduced into this district.

### FRUITS.

I have, however, made inquiry of some of the largest grocers and dealers in fruits here, and am persuaded that there is a chance to establish a fairly good trade in California and other American canned goods of the best grades, if pains are taken to send only such fruits as are known to keep well, and proper care is bestowed on their packing and shipment.

Dried fruits from California are highly favored here, but only thoroughly dried ones should be sent, as the others mold in this moist climate.

I have no doubt that a large trade could be built up in apples also, if fruit of the best quality were selected and great care observed in their packing. I am informed that, several years ago, an effort was made to introduce American apples into this market, but on account of their poor quality and careless packing, they arrived in such a damaged condition and the loss was so great that any further attempt to deal in them was abandoned.

If our shippers would give but a tithe of the attention to selecting and packing that is bestowed on an inferior grade of fruit brought to this market from Italy, the South Tyrol, and elsewhere, there would be no doubt about the success of the undertaking. Fruit of all kinds is sold by weight, at exorbitant rates when compared with prices in America.

### WHEAT.

The trade in wheat was fairly good in the spring of 1901, but later became dull, influenced by the fear of the enactment of an unfavorable tariff on cereals. Domestic wheat touched its highest price—$42.84 per metric ton (2,205 pounds)—on the 30th of April, 1901, and fell to $41.41 on the 31st of December.

Of foreign wheat, American was the favorite, and on the 30th of April brought $43.81 per ton, falling to $42.16 in January, 1902. Domestic wheat averaged $39.41 for the year 1901 and American $41.65 for the same period.

### MAIZE AND OATS.

In the first few months of the year, on account of ice, the river Elbe was closed to navigation and little was done in maize; but in the spring, when the river became navigable, prices rose from $26.89 to $29.98 for American. Oversupply, however, soon reduced the price to $27.13. Later, discouraging crop reports from America, coupled with scant supplies on hand, caused active speculation, and prices ruled very high in spite of heavy importations of Argentina maize. This attracted Russian, Galician, and even Roumanian maize to north Germany, and these being cheaper, notwithstanding exorbitant railroad rates, deals in American maize practically ceased.

The average for the year 1901 was: American, $30.46; Argentine, $28.79 per ton.

American oats were but little dealt in. The average price for the year was: American, $33.08; Russian, $33.32; German, $34.98.

### EXPORTS.

The principal exports from this consular district consist of leather gloves, glove leather, enameled iron ware, kanit, machinery, metals and type metal, carbonate, muriate, sulphate, and cyanide of potash, salt, manure, earthenware, chloride of ammonium, seeds, cement, raw and refined sugars.

The value of exports for the last six months of the year 1901 amounted to $4,449,568.93, against $1,896,747.74 for the first six months of 1902, being a decrease of $2,552,821.19, largely in sugar.

### UNITED STATES TRADE.

I regret that I have been unable to procure reliable statistics of the value of imports into this consular district for the period embraced in this report. The boards of trade of Magdeburg and Halberstadt have not as yet made their reports for the first six months of 1902, and are not likely to do so for some time. They furnish, when published, the fullest and most reliable information obtainable.

An American firm, under the name of "The Nationale Radiator Gesellschaft," has in course of construction at Schoenebeck (half an hour distant by railroad) a very large plant for the manufacture of radiators, but it is not yet completed.

There is no place in the district that I know of where American-made shoes are sold, but there is one place in this city where a German who has worked in the United States advertises to make shoes in the American as well as in the German style. Within the past week, a drummer exhibited here samples of German shoes closely resembling those made in our country. They were evidently machine-made, and though lacking to some extent in the style and finish of the American shoe, they were very good imitations and could be palmed off upon the inexperienced as shoes manufactured in the United States.

I regret that I can not make a fuller presentation of the trade conditions in this district, but I only assumed charge of the consulate at Magdeburg on the 16th of September last.

WILLIAM A. McKELLIP, *Consul.*

MAGDEBURG, *October 20, 1902.*

H. Doc. 305, pt 2——22

## MAINZ.

The expectations that the year 1901 would again restore confidence to the commercial undertakings of Germany, and that commerce and industries would recover from the setback experienced in 1900, have not been realized. A sign of the times was that, in December, 1901, there were 240.6 applicants for every 100 vacant positions, against 177.9 in the month of December, 1900, as the labor statistics show. Furthermore, the number of business failures greatly increased in 1901, official statistics showing an increase of 23 per cent above the year 1900.

### NEW COMPANIES.

The general business depression in Germany also greatly influenced the formation of new industrial corporations. The number of new corporations organized, which reached high-water mark in 1899, with 364 corporations and a combined capital of $129,564,820, and in 1900 had already fallen to 261 corporations with a combined capital of $81,029,480, experienced another shrinkage in 1901, only 158 new corporations being formed in that year, with a combined capital of $37,663,500.

### COAL AND IRON.

An exception to the general depression was found in the coal mining and iron and steel industries, these having made contracts far ahead for the disposal of their products, thus forcing the other industries dependent upon these materials to take the quantities contracted for, even though they did not require them. The output of the German coal mines for the last four years has been: 1898, 96,300,000 long tons; 1899, 101,600,000 long tons; 1900, 109,300,000 long tons; and 1901, 107,800,000. The production of pig iron for the last three years has been: 1899, 8,100,000 long tons; 1900, 8,500,000 long tons; and 1901, 7,800,000 long tons. In order to find markets for this overproduction, the manufacturers of the finished wares sought outlets in foreign countries, and it frequently happened that manufacturing concerns belonging to syndicates (and thereby forced to sell at certain high prices within the country) took export orders at almost half the home rates. For this reason, supporters of the syndicate system would very much like to see the export business regulated in a similar manner as at home.

### RAILWAYS.

On the whole, the receipts of the German railways have decreased, as was to be expected. Nevertheless, this decrease was not so large as was feared. Those railroads whose fiscal year terminates with the 31st day of March (and these embrace the majority) showed receipts for the period of April 1 to December 31, 1901, in the freight department, of $79,095,000, against $84,711,800 for the same period the year previous, and in the passenger traffic of $82,919,200, against $84,228,200 in 1900; while those railroads whose fiscal year ends with the calendar year showed receipts for 1901 in the freight department of $33,034,400, against $35,152,600 for the calendar year 1900, and in the passenger traffic of $18,564,000, against $18,802,000 in 1900.

A noteworthy innovation in the passenger traffic was the order extending the validity of return tickets to forty-five days.

## POSTS AND TELEGRAPHS.

In the division for posts and telegraphs, the new system of telephone rentals caused an increase of subscribers to the extent of 26.7 per cent. Notwithstanding the lower telephone rentals and lower postal charges, the receipts of the department of posts and telegraphs showed an increase.

## STOCKS.

The dealings on the exchange are of especial value in gauging the industrial activity of a country. Of course, such dealings do not portray the actual state of the various industries, but rather in a great measure the public feeling regarding industrial undertakings. During the period of prosperity, industrial values were forced up beyond reasonable figures, and during the depression of the past year, the reverse was the case. This was further augmented, toward the middle of the year, by the failure of a number of banking institutions which had hitherto been considered sound beyond the shadow of a doubt. The values of even prime undertakings dropped in a manner to cause almost national alarm. This caused the banking institutions to become wary in giving credit, and the calamity might have become overwhelming had not the Imperial Bank stepped into the breach and granted credits where possible, so that, during the critical months of June, July, and August, 1901, the amount loaned on notes and other paper by the Imperial Bank exceeded by about $125,000,000 that of the previous year. Considering the circumstances, the discount rate of the Imperial Bank was rational throughout. At the beginning of the year, the rate was 5 per cent, and it was reduced to 4½ per cent on February 26, and to 4 per cent on April 22. It was further reduced to 3½ per cent on June 18, and it was not until September 23 that the rate was again raised to 4 per cent, at which figure it remained for the balance of the year.

To sum up, it may be said that the period of industrial depression, which began in 1900, continued throughout the past year, involving in a greater or less degree almost every branch of German industry. The main cause for this may be sought in the overproduction which had taken place in almost every industry, causing the accumulation of finished products. This condition was augmented by the trusts keeping prices high for the necessary raw materials, the difficulty in securing credits, owing to the failure of a number of industrial enterprises and banking institutions, and the uncertainty of the outcome of pending political questions, such as the new customs tariff and the new commercial treaties.

The following is a résumé of the commerce and industries of this consular district, in some of the more important branches:

## RIVER TRANSPORTATION.

Owing to the general industrial depression, this business was very unsatisfactory, especially as the importations of raw materials and grains were rather light.

The freight tonnage arriving in Mainz during the year 1901 was as follows: From the sea and Lower Rhine, 935,021 tons; from the Upper Rhine, 509,958 tons.

## TRAMWAYS.

The tramways of this city (population 85,000) carried 2,769,767 passengers in 1901, as against 2,413,329 in 1900. The total receipts for the year were $66,468.88, against $59,569.25 for the previous year. Profits have again increased, a dividend of 6.6 per cent having been declared, as against 5.5 per cent the year previous. The tramway company owns 101 horses, at an average value of $137.56 per horse. The average work performed by a horse per day was 14.34 miles. The average cost of feed per horse per day was 35 cents, against 33 cents for the previous year.

## WINE TRADE.

The vintage of 1901 yielded about one-half to three-fourths of a normal return. The spring and early summer months were favorable, but September set in cool and rainy, so that the development of the grapes was greatly checked. In order to save the crop from rotting, the grapes were, to a large extent, picked before they were entirely ripe, and consequently the must showed a high percentage of acidity.

The general business depression also made itself felt in the wine trade, and dealers bought only what they absolutely needed. The export of wine dropped off slightly. The export of wine in casks amounted to 283,613 hundredweight, a decrease of 27,071 hundredweight as compared with the foregoing year; still wine in bottles to 177,043 hundredweight, a decrease of 642 hundredweight, and sparkling wine to 43,098 hundredweight, a decrease of 1,892 hundredweight. This decrease was chiefly in the export trade to Belgium, France, Great Britain, Scandinavia, and Switzerland. The export trade to the United States, Netherlands, and China showed an increase.

On the whole, the manufacturers of sparkling wine had a fair year. Their output increased, and they were able to purchase a good quality of still wines for their requirements, especially in France, at very reasonable prices.

## CANNING INDUSTRY.

This industry was favored by a good harvest of both fruits and vegetables, at normal prices. However, sales of canned goods were difficult to effect, due in a great measure to the general business depression as well as to the very mild winter.

## HOPS: BREWING.

At the beginning of 1901, prices for the better qualities of German hops ranged from $20 to $27 per hundredweight, but toward the end of June they declined $5 or $6. As, however, during the month of July the new crop suffered from drought, prices for the crop of 1900 rapidly advanced from $5 to $7.50. Toward the end of July, however, rains set in, and prices sank again, and when, in September, the new crop came on the market, it was almost impossible to sell any of the former year's crop.

The German hop crop of 1901, according to official statistics, amounts to only about 250,000 hundredweight, as against 530,000 hundredweight in 1900, while quality and color are also not up to the standard.

The brewing business was satisfactory, and the consumption has increased. The average selling price, however, has declined somewhat. Wages averaged $22.50 per month, with free board and lodging.

### GROCERY TRADE.

The general business depression was also felt in this trade. As a rule, the workingman's wages were curtailed and he was obliged to live more economically.

Owing to successively large coffee crops, the price of coffee was low. The sugar business was rather unsatisfactory, due to the frequent changes of prices by the sugar trust.

High prices were maintained for lard throughout the year, reaching $24 per hundredweight at the end of December. The consumption of cocoa increased, while that of tea dropped off.

Spices maintained their prices, except nutmegs, which dropped suddenly in the spring.

### LUMBER TRADE.

The lumber business was not satisfactory, owing to the general business depression, which checked building operations. As a rule, prices declined. Swedish and American lumber could also be bought more cheaply, owing to reduced ocean and river transportation rates.

The oak cask stave trade is always in a great measure dependent upon the result of the vintage, and as the one of 1901 was rather moderate, the stave trade was also dull. Nevertheless, higher prices were realized.

### CORK STOPPERS.

Prices for cork wood again increased, owing to the greater demand for stoppers of the better qualities, while the production of cork wood does not keep pace with the requirements. On the whole, the business was satisfactory.

### CEMENT.

This business was rather unsatisfactory during 1901, because of reduced building activity and overproduction in the industry. Furthermore, the export business is growing poorer from year to year, and the markets of the United States, especially, will soon be lost entirely to German cement manufacturers.

### JEWELRY AND SILVERWARE.

During the first half of the year, the manufacturers of these articles were busy and the sales were satisfactory, while, during the last half, business dropped off appreciably. The demand was for designs of the ultramodern style.

STATISTICS.

I append table of exports declared from the consular district of Mainz for the calendar years 1899, 1900, and 1901, and a table of the chief imports at the port of Mainz for the same years.

WALTER SCHUMANN, *Consul.*

MAINZ, *August 28, 1902.*

*Declared exports from the consular district of Mainz.*

| Articles. | 1899. | 1900. | 1901. |
|---|---|---|---|
| Agate ware, jewelry, and imitation jewelry.................. | $759,430.17 | $572,299,26 | $656,778.13 |
| Aniline and other colors......................... | 120,460.19 | 4,980.34 | 7,420.91 |
| Black (printing ink and powder) ......................... | ................. | ................. | 739.78 |
| Capsules and tin foil.......................... | 3,632.15 | ................. | ................. |
| Cement (Portland)........................ | 56,378.86 | ................. | ................. |
| Chemicals and drugs......................... | 820,324.66 | 341,892.46 | 422,882.68 |
| Earthen and glass ware ......................... | 24,787.30 | 28,250.81 | 35,752.41 |
| Glue........................ | 41,831.69 | 22,368.02 | 16,401.36 |
| Hops ......................... | 70,971.85 | 119,084.23 | 120,448.25 |
| Household and personal effects......................... | ................. | ................. | 8,546.20 |
| Jewelry cases......................... | ................. | ................. | 910.82 |
| Leather ......................... | 25,716.41 | 44,579.84 | 86,516.70 |
| Linen and woolen goods ......................... | 1,196.54 | 445.77 | 420.56 |
| Mineral water (natural)......................... | 4,170.36 | 30,351.11 | 47,219.96 |
| Oil and varnish......................... | 1,309.08 | 491.62 | ................. |
| Oil paintings ......................... | 6,988.87 | 726.04 | 938.96 |
| Preserved fruits and vegetables......................... | 16,571.34 | 15,855.14 | 17,793.80 |
| Printed books and charts......................... | 478.98 | ................. | 1,232.39 |
| Printed music ......................... | 2,315.97 | 3,088.69 | 354.80 |
| Saws, tools, etc ......................... | 8,122.42 | 10,980.27 | 9,345.96 |
| Seeds ......................... | 5,377.87 | 37,214.78 | 29,582.25 |
| Sundries......................... | 7,360.05 | 8,375.12 | 8,789.05 |
| Tiles (glazed and unglazed)......................... | 9,876.56 | 4,938.76 | 6,780.29 |
| Wall paper ......................... | ................. | ................. | 752.92 |
| Wine ......................... | 658,514.46 | 668,722.81 | 710,357.12 |
| Total ................................ | 2,145,765.77 | 1,914,595.07 | 2,134,945.30 |

*Chief imports entered at the port of Mainz.*

[Expressed in hundredweights avoirdupois.]

| Articles. | 1899. | 1900. | 1901. |
|---|---|---|---|
| Wheat and rye ......................... | 168,894 | 157,506 | 214,566 |
| Oats......................... | 86,264 | 52,005 | 96,356 |
| Legumes ......................... | 26,780 | 23,185 | 89,485 |
| Barley......................... | 32,150 | 8,621 | 18,563 |
| Rape seed ......................... | 43,403 | 51,869 | 70,677 |
| Indian corn ......................... | 48,230 | 29,077 | 41,417 |
| Malt......................... | 690 | 446 | 449 |
| Cedar and mahogany wood......................... | 98,335 | 47,735 | 122,604 |
| Oak barrel staves......................... | 11,387 | 11,893 | 4,730 |
| Cork stoppers......................... | 4,700 | 4,897 | 6,996 |
| Sheepskins ......................... | 12,876 | 11,387 | 5,894 |
| Brandy, rum, and arrack......................... | 2,965 | 5,430 | 1,841 |
| Wine, still and sparkling......................... | 33,614 | 37,296 | 49,487 |
| Spices of all kinds......................... | 1,709 | 1,641 | 1,859 |
| Salted herrings......................... | 12,432 | 12,872 | 10,452 |
| Coffee ......................... | 31,282 | 34,597 | 29,121 |
| Dried fruits, prunes, etc......................... | 40,801 | 35,545 | 27,947 |
| Flour, farina, etc......................... | 3,623 | 2,574 | 1,531 |
| Rice ......................... | 31,706 | 22,921 | 23,456 |
| Sugar, raw and refined......................... | 5,055 | 6,406 | 18,385 |
| Oil, olive, linseed, palm, and cocoanut......................... | 8,595 | 3,731 | 5,843 |
| Lard......................... | 16,880 | 13,483 | 15,932 |
| Fish oil......................... | 1,762 | 3,192 | 1,659 |
| Tallow ......................... | 3,714 | 1,001 | 878 |
| Petroleum......................... | 376,079 | 317,567 | 274,848 |
| Lubricating oil (mineral)......................... | 26,688 | 51,555 | 79,200 |
| Eggs of poultry......................... | 122,098 | 129,978 | 126,970 |

## MANNHEIM.

The general trade conditions of this consular district do not differ materially from those of a year ago. Business depression has continued and in some lines increased. With but few exceptions, factories have kept in operation; in some cases, however, with a much-reduced force of employees. The dull condition of the home market has led to special efforts to sell abroad, and these sales have, in some measure, relieved the stress of hard times. The exports of manufactured articles to the United States from this district during the last fiscal year have, with few exceptions, increased both in volume and variety. The shipment, in recent months, of large quantities of pig iron, steel blooms, steel beams, etc., has afforded some relief to the greatly depressed local iron and steel trade. Small concerns engaged in the manufacture of paper, yarn, metal ware, stone and glass ware, linoleum and other products for the home market have sought trade in other countries, and have thus been able to keep in operation.

Nevertheless, the general business condition is unfavorable and the outlook for the near future is not at all bright. As the development of business for some years previous to 1900 was startlingly rapid, so, too, the period of reaction promises to be correspondingly long and discouraging. This is especially true of the manufacture of electrical machinery and supplies, of gas engines, automobiles, bicycles, steel and iron working machinery and allied industries. Many concerns in these and other lines, which even last year continued to be fairly prosperous, are now paying practically no dividends at all.

The number of unemployed has increased over that of last year. Instead of a phenomenally rapid increase of population in this city, as has been the case for several years past, an actual falling off is shown during the last twelve months, mainly by departures of single men and women engaged in factories. Thus, the estimated population of Mannheim at the end of July, 1902, was 864 less than at the end of the January preceding, while during the corresponding six months of 1901 there was an estimated increase of 3,426.

Crops, fortunately, have been fairly good throughout Germany in the past two years, so that the cost of living, outside of the item of meat, has not increased.

From this cursory view, it is not to be understood that all branches of manufacturing have been equally affected, or that a wholly pessimistic view prevails among German business men. Several new factories have been started in the district within the past eighteen months, and extensive additions have been made to a number of plants already established. No recent disastrous failure has occurred here, except that of the Actien Gesellschaft für Chemische (Corporation for the Chemical Industry). This failure is not to be ascribed to the stringency of the times, as it is now apparent that, at no time in its history of fifteen or sixteen years, has the enterprise been on a paying basis.

### CHEMICAL INDUSTRY.

The chemical industry, including the manufacture of dyestuffs, in which this district is largely engaged, has probably, upon the whole, suffered less from the general business depression than any other single branch, which is accounted for by the large export trade and the preeminent position which Germany holds in this field.  Complaint is heard, however, as to the low prices obtained for the manufactured product, and the growing competition on both sides of the ocean. Statistics from the latest United States census showing the growth of chemical manufacture in that country have been published in the German commercial journals, which freely admit the growing importance of America in this trade.

The German manufacturer, to retain his supremacy in this branch of industry, relies strongly upon his long experience and upon the large body of trained chemists that the German technical schools are constantly supplying.  These men leave the schools, generally with the degree of doctor of philosophy, and enter the factory as a distinct professional class.  They are always addressed as "doctor," are accorded a certain distinction by the other employees, and are generally well equipped for original investigation.  To them, as a class, are largely due the important discoveries that have given Germany preeminence in this branch of manufacturing.  As these discoveries are made, they are patented in all countries where patent laws exist, an assignment of the patent being usually taken in the name of the employing firm.  Thus, one concern in this consular district, employing from 150 to 160 of these professional chemists, has already taken out about 400 patents in the United States and a corresponding number in the different countries of Europe.

The German chemical manufacturer would doubtless concede that, if the United States had as large a body of well-trained chemists as it has of electrical and mechanical engineers and mining experts, its chemical products would soon take first place in the world's markets.  He would also acknowledge that the kindred industries of tanning, soap making, bleaching, dyeing, metal working, etc., would be gainers thereby.

The exports of chemical products from the Empire for the years 1900 and 1901 were the following, the values being given in dollars and the volume in metric tons of 2,204 pounds:

| Year. | Metric tons. | Value. |
|---|---|---|
| 1900 | 749,500 | $83,095,000 |
| 1901 | 789,300 | 86,394,000 |

## PATENT LEATHER.

The patent-leather industry has long been of great importance in this district.  The value of exports of this product to the United States has for many years past amounted to about $1,000,000 annually, but in the fiscal year ended June 30, 1902, it dropped to $688,548.28, as against $1,023,586.66 for the preceding twelve months.  No other single item of export from the district has shown so great a change.

## AGRICULTURAL IMPLEMENTS, WIRE CABLE, ETC.

The largest manufactory of agricultural machinery, traction engines, etc., in Germany is located at Mannheim.  While this business has, like many others, suffered greatly from the general depression, it has received material assistance from the good crops that have been gathered.

On the other hand, the falling off in the manufacture of electrical machinery and supplies has seriously affected the extensive wire and cable works located here. These works also manufacture hemp cord and rope, Mannheim being one of the three largest customers for hemp in the Empire. Of this material, from 40,000 to 50,000 bales are used annually in Germany, the supply coming through London dealers who import from the Philippines. Arrangements, however, have recently been made, it is said, to have the hemp brought direct from those islands to Bremen and Hamburg, without the intervention of the English dealer.

## PORTLAND CEMENT.

The Portland cement industry has been one of the chief sufferers in Germany during the past few years. A large amount of capital is invested in this business, and the tendency has been toward great overproduction. Various efforts have been made to reduce the output and to maintain prices, but without success. In 1890, an average dividend of 15 per cent was paid on the capital invested; in 1900 it had dropped to 11 per cent, while in 1901 the average rate paid was only 4 to 5 per cent, several large concerns paying no dividend at all. It is said that, in 1902, the business will not pay as much as 2 per cent. The total production of the German cement factories in 1901 was about 30,000,000 barrels, while the sales, including the export trade, amounted to but 21,000,000 barrels, leaving 9,000,000 barrels unsold.

In this industry, this consular district has been affected in common with other parts of the Empire. The cement produced is of superior quality and has been quite largely exported. The exports to the United States have risen rapidly within the past few months.

## MISCELLANEOUS MANUFACTURES.

This district has important sugar producing and refining interests which, with a fairly good beet crop, insure fair returns. Large amounts of capital are also invested in the manufacture of sewer pipe and stoneware, automobiles, bicycles, steam engines and boilers, printing presses, furniture, celluloid, asbestos, plate and bottle glass, rubber goods, oils, wood pulp, brick and tile, fertilizers, sewing machines, pianos, tobacco and cigars, and in brewing of beer. In all of these industries, not excepting the last-named, there is a feeling of concern as to the future. Indeed, it may be said truthfully that all the different branches of manufacture here are affected more or less seriously by existing trade conditions.

## CUSTOMS AND FREIGHT STATISTICS.

Mannheim is an important distributing point for grain, petroleum, lumber, and other products. General business conditions are reflected somewhat by the following figures compiled from the customs statistics of the city for the year ended June 30, 1902, as compared with the preceding twelve months. These figures do not include the statistics of the Bavarian city of Ludwigshafen, on the opposite side of the

Rhine, whose trade in some of the items is nearly as important as that of Mannheim.  The amounts are given in metric tons:

|  | 1901. | 1902. |  | 1901. | 1902. |
|---|---|---|---|---|---|
| Wheat | 347,224 | 391,380 | Lumber | 79,125 | 56,809 |
| Rye | 5,567 | 7,750 | Raw coffee | 8,287 | 3,210 |
| Oats | 15,828 | 10,489 | Raw tobacco | 2,226 | 2,234 |
| Barley | 11,771 | 17,654 | Petroleum | 78,222 | 69,986 |
| Corn | 44,458 | 41,655 |  |  |  |

Freight statistics show that the amounts of freight shipped to and from Mannheim by water and by rail during the first six months of the year 1902 do not differ materially from the shipments for the corresponding months of 1901.  The totals were as follows: For the first six months of 1901, 2,581,000 tons; for the first six months of 1902, 2,626,000 tons.

### BUILDING AND OTHER IMPROVEMENTS.

Building and other improvements have been continued uninterruptedly in all parts of the district.  The electric lines of Mannheim have been much extended, and a complete system has also been recently put into operation at Heidelberg.  The river harbors, noted as the finest on the Rhine, have been further improved.  The Mannheim Stock Exchange recently completed and took possession of a handsome four-story stone building erected at large cost.  Three fine, new churches are nearing completion, as are also a new post-office building, city music hall, and many private business blocks.

### EXPOSITION OF THE GERMAN AGRICULTURAL SOCIETY.

The most important local industrial event of the current year was the annual exposition of the German Agricultural Society (Deutsche Landwirtschaftliche Gesellschaft), held in Mannheim in June.  The exposition was the sixteenth given by the society and was the first to be held in Baden.  The exhibits included nearly 2,000 head of live stock and a vast array of agricultural machinery of all kinds.  The principal American harvesting machine companies were well represented, the superiority of this class of American machinery being amply demonstrated.  The German exhibits of agricultural implements and machines, including traction and portable engines, gasoline engines for feed cutting, etc., threshers, creamery and other dairy appliances, were highly creditable, and showed that the German agriculturist is awake to the value of better tools than he has had heretofore.  A similar trend of improvement was shown in an industrial exposition (Gewerbe Austellung), held in this city during the past summer, where special prominence was given to house furnishings.  The exhibits of modern bath tubs, sanitary plumbing of improved types, gas and petroleum stoves for cooking and for use in bathrooms attracted much attention.

### ART EXHIBITION.

The importance of Carlsruhe, the capital of Baden, as an art center was shown by a creditable art exhibition, which remained open for several months during the past summer. The exhibit was well housed in an attractive building erected for the purpose, and was one of the features of the semicentennial jubilee in honor of Grand Duke Friedrich of Baden. The exposition was well attended, the Emperor being among the prominent visitors.

### AMERICAN PRODUCTS.

This district being at the head of the more important Rhine navigation, is an important center of trade in coal, grain, lumber, petroleum, flour, etc. In each of the items named, except coal and perhaps lumber, the United States holds by far the most important. place; but statistics showing the amount and value of these imports for the past fiscal year are not now obtainable. The relative amounts of American grain and flour handled in the local markets do not vary greatly from year to year. The business is, for the most part, conducted by old well-established houses with ample capital and facilities for handling and storing.

The petroleum trade in this city and in Ludwigshafen is very large, amounting to about 500,000 barrels annually. American oil is far in the lead, although Russian, Roumanian, and Galician oils come into this market. The Russian agency has recently increased its facilities for storage by building two 18,000-barrel tanks, and has put wagons on the streets. It would be difficult to ascertain what proportion of the trade is held by American oil. It certainly amounts to at least two-thirds of the trade in the district and perhaps considerably more. As is well known, oils other than American receive certain preferences in Germany that aid greatly in their introduction. Much newspaper criticism has recently been evoked by a movement on the part of the Standard Oil interests to establish in the more important towns small storage tanks capable of holding a few carloads of oil and furnish retail dealers direct, and thus eliminate the middleman who has heretofore bought oil in barrels and furnished the retailer as his trade demanded. Chambers of commerce, state railway management, and other powers have been appealed to to prevent the carrying out of the plan. In some cases, the relief has been granted; in others refused.

To the American imports above named must be added cotton and cotton seed, raw copper, agricultural and other machinery, hog and cattle casings, cash registers, typewriters, office furniture, hardware, California dried fruits, oatmeal, cornstarch, shoes and rubbers, and a variety of less important items.

As touching the cotton trade in Germany, it is interesting to note that, in the year 1900, the Empire imported 25,212 metric tons of Egyptian cotton to the value of $7,616,000. Of this amount, nearly one-fourth came direct to Hamburg as a result of that wise German foresight which is furnishing a steamship line to every foreign port whose commerce will warrant it.

The phenomenal sales of American cash registers, typewriters, sewing machines, and harvesting machinery in all parts of Germany have been due perhaps not more to the merit of the goods themselves than to the consummate skill and energy with which they are placed on the market. It is no accident, for example, that American cash registers are now in all the more important stores of every city in this district, that nearly 1,500 American typewriters are in use here, and that a single harvester company has, within the past eighteen months, sold machines running far up into the hundreds in South Germany, a region which, for grass and grain growing, is of minor importance.

### AMERICAN AND OTHER FOREIGN MANUFACTURING INTERESTS.

Four important manufacturing concerns backed by foreign capital are located in or near this city. · Each has a large and well-equipped factory. Of these enterprises, one is American, engaged in the manufacture of matches; one is English, engaged in the manufacture of soap, and two are French, one manufacturing rubber goods of all kinds, including rubber shoes, and the other, plate glass and mirrors. The French concerns are old and well established, and are understood to be profitable. The rubber works has for many years had an American manager. In all of the four factories mainly German workmen are employed. The salesmen also are German.

The American and English concerns are newer, but each is having a measure of success. Legal and other restrictions undoubtedly make factory management more difficult here than in the United States. Wages paid are much lower than for the same class of work in America. Those having experience in both countries say that this difference of wages is offset to a considerable extent by losses of time due to the shutting down of a plant both in the forenoon and afternoon to enable employees to take lunch, by the frequent holidays in Germany, and by the smaller amount of work German operatives as a class perform in a day. Girls employed in factories have, in many cases, been accustomed to work in the fields or even in brickyards, and are much less skillful and capable than American factory girls. The same is true of boys and men doing piecework or employed in feeding machines.

Factory construction and repair is said to cost quite as much as or even more than in the United States.

An American manager, upon his arrival, usually decides that he will change some things merely matters of local custom, but in the end, he is apt to yield to the established ways of the people.

In this connection, it should be noted that Europeans are a good deal more set in their trade methods than are the people of the United States, and persons wishing to do business here should carefully study these customs, which involve not only the goods themselves, but also the manner of selling, the terms of payment, the business correspondence, the intercourse with the dealer, and, indeed, every part of the transaction.

An illustration of this fact was recently seen in the effort of a large concern manufacturing matches in Germany to sell its product put up in small paper boxes instead of in boxes made of thin wood covered with paper, which is the characteristic German match box. The paper boxes were of the same size as the wooden boxes and were of the exact form. In the United States it is not likely that the matter would have been even noticed. But after a very thorough trial, it was found that the effort would have to be abandoned, which was done at no small inconvenience. The German trade wished the wooden box and would have no other.

The German is, as a rule, a student of the peculiar demands of the trade of any field into which he goes. This has been one secret of his commercial success. If a particular style, color, or quality of ware is desired, he sets about supplying that demand.  In a large factory of this city are made an endless variety of combs, beads, and other articles of personal adornment.  Among these goods are combs of huge size and grotesque shapes, and beads almost or quite as large as walnuts, made expressly for the trade in certain of the East India islands.  The managers of the concern, or their agents, make as careful a study of the latest fashions of the Borneo dames as a local milliner might be supposed to make of the Paris fashions.

## DECLARED EXPORTS.

The following statement shows the values of the twelve principal articles of export to the United States from this consular district during the fiscal year ended June 30, 1902:

| | |
|---|---|
| Chemicals and drugs | $1, 582, 150. 78 |
| Colors and dyestuffs | 1, 074, 434. 85 |
| Patent leather | 688, 548. 28 |
| Rags, cuttings, etc | 217, 017. 48 |
| Lambskins | 190, 404. 69 |
| Wines | 174, 412. 69 |
| Wood pulp | 141, 463. 23 |
| Portland cement | 47, 680. 26 |
| Hops | 37, 032. 44 |
| Glue | 36, 797. 97 |
| Corks | 29, 004. 42 |
| Gelatin | 27, 057. 44 |
| Other articles variously classified | 179, 716. 26 |
| Total | 4, 225, 720. 89 |

Total declared exports from the district to the United States for the
ten years ended June 30, 1902 ................................... 42,984,370. 12

H. W. HARRIS, *Consul.*

MANNHEIM, *November 11, 1902.*

## MUNICH.

The year in Germany has shown continued depression in business. Many manufacturing concerns were compelled to work at a loss.  Trade was aided, however, by the great prosperity of the United States.  The extraordinary development of the iron and steel trades there made it possible for the German firms engaged in this industry to dispose of their surplus product in America and England.  Coke also found an excellent market in the United States.  Had it not been for this opening across the sea, Germany could hardly have escaped a serious crisis within the last two years.

In all branches of trade, there have been liquidations which must result in placing the business condition of Germany upon a sounder basis.  This change has been mainly effected by an absorption of the weaker concerns, when salvage seemed possible, by the stronger and well-financed concerns.  The Deutsche Bank of Berlin has perhaps been the best financial agent toward restoring order and confidence, and it would now seem as if trade and industry were slowly recovering.

In September, 1902, a convention of the leading jurists and professors of economics was held in Germany, and the question of management and supervision of trusts was made the special subject of con sideration.    The convention adjourned, however, without reaching any conclusion as to the best methods of controlling the organizations of the Empire.    At the present moment, a commission, consisting of three of the most eminent university economists, has been convened at Berlin by the ministry of the interior to formulate, if possible, a line of legislation that will prove practicable.

As to conditions in this particular district, Augsburg, which is a manufacturing center for yarns, cotton goods, paper, cloth, machinery, and mechanical instruments, has felt the business depression in a superlative degree.    A great increase in the number of spindles, the low prices for yarns and other products, and the unfavorable condition of the raw-material market have resulted in curtailed production and low prices, yielding in a large number of the spinning mills no profit, and in others but a limited return for the capital invested.    In other branches of manufacturing, want of confidence, lack of enterprise, and unfavorable relations between the cost of raw materials and the market price of the manufactured product have led to similar results.

Munich, which is only slowly developing as a manufacturing point, continues to prosper as an art and educational center and as a resort for travelers.    By the opening of the Prince Regent Theater for the production of Wagnerian operas with the same accuracy and perfection as at Bayreuth, an increased number of Americans have been attracted hither, and by liberal purchases have largely augmented the export of special products of the art industry of Munich.    In other departments of manufacturing, the increased cost of labor, brought about by the expense of living and the high prices of raw materials, has rendered it increasingly difficult for the producers to compete with their American competitors.    In the metal, paper, kid glove, and stained glass industries the trade has been very quiet and the profits nominal.

### HIDES.

One important item, which formerly appeared in the list of exports, continues to be produced here, but finds its way to the United States without figuring in the statistics of this consulate.    I refer to raw hides, in which · certain specialties are produced at Munich.    Among the largest and finest cattle in the world are those that are raised in the provinces of Austria bordering on Bavaria, and stall-fed principally for the Munich market.    The hides are very large and of even thickness, and particularly adapted to the production of continuous belts for electric and other machinery.

Another class of hides largely handled here consists of salted and air-dried calfskins.    The province of Algaeu in Bavaria is a fertile dairy country, famous throughout Germany for its products, and stocked with herds of fine cattle.    The dairy farmers devote their attention to bringing their calves to market as early and in as good condition as possible, and as veal is an important article of Bavarian diet, a large number of these calves find their way to Munich.

### UNITED STATES GOODS.

As far as can be ascertained, there has been only a slight increase in the exports from the United States to this consular district.    American

shoes are winning their way to popular appreciation, on account of
their price and quality, notwithstanding the fact that shoes are being
manufactured on American lasts in Germany. The trade in American
bicycles has declined, owing to the extremely low price of German
machines, and to the greater facility for repairing and for obtaining
duplicate parts of the latter. American typewriters and mimeo-
graphs and supplies for same are being extensively introduced, and
are holding their ground against domestic competition. The same
holds true of photographic goods of all kinds.

Canned goods, especially canned fruits, are growing in favor and a
good trade could be established, if there were a general depot here,
from which stocks could be replenished without delay. American cut
and pressed glass has been introduced everywhere, and on account of
its comparative low price, finish, and brilliancy, defies domestic competition.

American furniture manufacturers should cultivate this field. As
yet, but little has been accomplished, because a good trade is possible
only with the assistance of an emporium exhibiting the various styles.
Dining and rocking chairs have already secured a fair market. Manufacturers should omit all pressed ornamentations, these offending the
taste of the wealthier German classes, and being subject to a duty
similar to that on carvings. Picture moldings are also being introduced,
but this trade will continue restricted until the suggestion for the establishment of a depot for this class of manufactures is carried out.

Mechanical and machine tools and agricultural implements are seen
in the market, but have thus far been bought from the North German
agents, and therefore, the reduced profit offers no special inducement
to the dealer to favor this trade.

The cereal trade is only just developing, and goods introduced here
find favor. Persistent and liberal advertising would no doubt be productive of good results. This is also true of baking powders. The
presence of so many American families is slowly but surely convincing
the Germans of the practicability and healthfulness of these food
products. The recent marked advance in the price of meats favors
their introduction, and the advertiser should make this a point in his
offer to the consumer.

James H. Worman,<br>
Consul-General.

Munich, *October 20, 1902.*

---

### NUREMBERG.

Germany is still laboring under a great depression which influences
nearly all industries. What I stated in my report last year still holds
good at the present time.

### TOYS.

The toy trade, one of the chief industries in this consular district, is
by no means as actively engaged in as before the year 1900. The United
States, Canada, Mexico, the Argentine Republic, and especially Australia, were and still are willing buyers, but business with England,
India, and also with Brazil, is unsatisfactory.

### LEAD PENCILS.

This business, another chief factor of Nuremberg's trade, is suffering from low prices. Competition, not only foreign, but also local,
is said to account for this. The competition of American goods is
now met with in all markets of the world, and is a special cause of
complaint by the Nuremberg factories.

### METAL PAPER.

As in other local industries, the production of metal paper was about
the same as last year, but the profit has been much lessened, owing to
the rise in the price of some of the raw material, especially silver leaf.
On account of a strike, the price of silver leaf was raised from 10 to
12 per cent.

### BRONZE POWDER.

The production was the same as in 1900, or even larger, but prices,
owing to competition, were greatly depressed.

### HAIR PENCILS.

The depression prevailing for the past two years has not been felt
so much in this industry, as the greater portion of the production is
exported, and the export business continues satisfactory. Trade with
the United States has even increased.

### DECALCOMANIA OR TRANSFER PICTURES.

Some factories have been fully occupied; others have had to reduce
the number of their workmen, though not to such an extent as in other
industries. Export to the United States is still satisfactory. Orders
are plentiful, but prices are depressed owing to competition. A good
business with South Africa is expected, as inquiries are received daily
from that country. The prices of some of the raw materials, which
had risen enormously during the last three years, have of late fallen
again.

### CHROMOS, PICTURE BOOKS, CHRISTMAS CARDS.

Business, both home and export, is complained of. The export trade
with England is still very bad, and, on the whole, prospects are not
bright at present.

### GLASS PLATES, WINDOW GLASS.

Trade on the whole, both for home and export, was unsatisfactory.
In fact, the home trade was even less than last year's.
The export to the United States has again diminished. The ship-
ments to Austria-Hungary, too, show a decrease.

### GOLD LEAF.

This is one industry which, owing to a strike in the United States, is
doing, at present, a profitable business. For years, the manufacturers

of genuine gold leaf have not been able to export their goods to the United States, because of the high tariff on this class of merchandise and also because our home production was able to satisfy the demand; but a strike having occurred in a Philadelphia firm, which, I understand, is the largest American manufacturer of genuine gold leaf, the Nuremberg makers are now able to export this merchandise and to obtain a fair price.

### UNITED STATES TRADE.

The exports from this consular district to the United States for the fiscal year ended June 30, 1902, were about the same as in the preceding year, namely:

1901 ................................................................. $3, 860, 933. 43
1902 ................................................................. 3, 859, 801. 15

United States imports into this country are rising rapidly from year to year. As I frequently receive inquiries from my countrymen in regard to the establishment of agencies or depots in this consular district, I would mention that Nuremberg lies too far inland to be a good place for such establishments.

The better plan is to open agencies at German seaports, like Bremen or Hamburg, and at cities like Berlin, Cologne, Frankfort-on-the-Main, or even Mannheim, which have better connection by river or rail with the continental seaports. From these agencies, the other cities in the German Empire could be visited. I have found that American manufacturers, after trying other methods, finally adopt this plan, which I think is the best one.

GEORGE E. BALDWIN, *Consul.*

NUREMBERG, *September 10, 1902.*

### PLAUEN.

The fiscal year ended June 30, 1902, has been most satisfactory to manufacturers of laces and embroideries in the consular district of Plauen.

The general advance in exports to the United States is 43.4 per cent over last year. Of this amount, the lace and embroidery industry claims 61.3 per cent, holding, as usual, the lead in exports to the United States from this district.

### WOOLEN INDUSTRY.

The manufacturers of woolen goods and of goods made of worsted yarns have not found the sale for their products they expected. The importation of such goods by Germany, however, has not been large, amounting to only 1,779,140 pounds, valued at $1,362,857, for the first six months of 1902, against 1,818,740 pounds, valued at $1,380,238, for the same period in 1901, a decrease in value of 1.2 per cent in favor of 1901.

The export of German woolen dress goods amounted to 23,025,860 pounds, valued at $17,676,190, in the first six months of 1902, while for the same period in 1901, Germany exported 22,028,820 pounds, valued at $16,868,095, or a gain for 1902 of 4.8 per cent.

The principal importer was England, which bought 21.7 per cent of the output of the German mills. The United States, which formerly bought so largely, is now in the sixth place, with only 4.4 per cent; Holland took 9.3 per cent, Switzerland 8.4 per cent, Denmark 6.9 per cent, and Belgium 4.8 per cent.

### MUSICAL INSTRUMENTS.

The consular agency of Markneukirchen shows, during the past fiscal year, a decrease of 6.6 per cent in its exports to the United States The principal decrease was in harmonicas, accordians, strings, and shell goods. In violins, on the other hand, there was an advance of $31,433.84. Thus, the claim made by the American manufacturers of musical goods " that they manufacture, with the exception of violins, better and cheaper instruments and all that are required for the home trade," would seem to be sustained.

### TOGO COTTON.

Industrial Germany is much interested in an experiment made with Togo cotton, grown in German West Africa. The experiment in weaving was made by the firm Brandls, of Müchen-Gladbach, and the result was exhibited at the Düsseldorf exhibition of 1902 and found most satisfactory. The manufacturer says: " The cotton has a good staple. The fiber is strong and of rough and woolly character, and is certainly of as good a quality as the common American cotton, and for many purposes preferable. It spins and takes dye well, and if it can be delivered in Germany at the same price as the American cotton, there is a great future for it."

### EXPORTS AND IMPORTS.

From the Royal Statistical Bureau of Berlin, I gather the following statistics for the year ended December 31, 1901, regarding the export and import trade between Germany and the United States.

Germany received from the United States, cotton, wheat, corn, lard, copper, oil for lamps, gold, oilcakes, oleomargarine, machines, cottonseed oil, building and joiners' wood, meat, kali, rosin oil, bladders, turpentine gum, tobacco, lubricating oil, and tallow.

The United States imported from Germany sugar, china, half-silk stuffs, aniline dyes, toys, lithographic plates, engravings, etchings, laces, calfskins, chemical salts, books, and woolen goods.

Up to 1898, the United States was Germany's best customer; now it holds second place. The United States exported to Germany $248,100,000 worth of goods, while Germany imported from the United States $91,857,000 worth. The heaviest shrinkages in the German export to the United States were in sugar, which amounted to something over $11,900,000, cotton hosiery, rubber, cement, and half-silk goods.

### AGRICULTURAL LOAN ASSOCIATION.

I reported on this association in my dispatch of April 14, 1896,[a] giving its rules and regulations and advocating the adoption of something of the same nature in the United States. The association has done so well, and has been of such wonderful help to the farmers and landholders of the country, that I think its latest statement will be of interest. In 1900, the loans made by the association amounted to 261,546,383 marks ($62,248,039); in 1901, they were 270,890,665 marks ($64,491,978). Of this amount, 33,436,550 marks ($7,957,899) was at 4 per cent, 200,749,850 marks ($47,778,464) at 3½ per cent, and 27,352,700 marks ($6,519,943) at 3 per cent. All these loans were issued on the average total value of the property, and on this total value only 44.79 per cent is given in loan.

In 1901, the association made a clear profit of 492,623 marks ($117,244), which allowed a dividend of 4 per cent to its 15,041 members.

Without this mutual association, it would be impossible for the German landowner and farmer to compete with the outside agricultural world.

Just now, the agriculturists are much encouraged by the hope that the new German tariff will give them such protection that good times will return to them.

The fact is, land values are too high; the land can not support the one or two mortgages with which it is weighted and at the same time give a good income to its owner. The new tariff may do temporary good to the farmer, at the expense of the manufacturer and working people, but the benefit can not last. At least, this is the opinion of many in Germany, and among them are some of the most intelligent farmers and landowners.

The food question is the all-important one. Prices are very high, as the following table for dressed meats will show:

PRICE OF MEATS.

|  | Per pound. |
|---|---|
| Beef: | |
| First quality | $0.1357 |
| Second quality | .1326 |
| Third quality | .1231 |
| Fourth quality | .1133 |
| Veal: | |
| First quality | .0969 |
| Second quality | .0914 |
| Third quality | .0850 |
| Fourth quality | .0827 |
| Mutton: | |
| First quality | .0686 |
| Second quality | .0653 |
| Third quality | .0583 |
| Pork: | |
| First quality | .1403 |
| Second quality | .1356 |
| Third quality | .1301 |

The above are all supposed to be sold in 110-pound lots.

---

[a] See Consular Reports, No. 192, September, 1896.

### CONDITION OF LABOR.

From the statistics collected by the German Employment Journal, it would seem that the condition of labor in Germany is far from favorable. The Journal says: "It was hoped in the spring that the business conditions would so improve that there would be an active demand for labor; this, however, does not seem to be the case."

In May, 1901, for every 100 positions offered there were 145 applicants; in May, 1902, for every 100 positions offered there were 172 applicants, and for every 100 positions offered in which men only were required there were 224 applicants, against 177 in 1901.

The above statistics apply to all Germany. Plauen, on account of its great activity in the lace business, has a steady demand for labor, both in mechanical and building branches.

### GENERAL PROSPERITY OF PLAUEN.

The prosperity of the Plauen district is shown by the advance in the taxable value of property, from 362,000,000 marks ($86,156,000) in 1901 to 372,000,000 marks ($88,536,000) in 1902, divided as follows: Land, 41.28 per cent; interest on money, 34.34 per cent; labor, 181.13 per cent; general business, 115.57 per cent. This is a total increase of 2.53 per cent over the value of 1901.

### SAVINGS BANKS.

The thirty-five savings banks from which these figures are taken show an increase in deposits of 9.31 per cent over the year 1901, which, considering the condition of other sections of the country, is very good.

### AMERICAN ARTICLES.

On this important question, I can only reiterate what I have written in former dispatches: Our manufacturers, if they wish to compete with the Germans, must have active agents—agents who understand the people, their wants, and methods of doing business; and I think it would be more to our advantage were the agents Americans.

I can quite understand that it might be too expensive for one manufacturer alone to try the experiment, but a number might pool their interests, say for a year. I am quite sure that this scheme would work better than selling through German agents.

I find that the German agent who purchases goods at his own risk and for his own account is apt to ask too high a price for them. In his hands, the simplest American article becomes a luxury, to be purchased only by the favored few.

American agents visiting every local town with their samples and having a main supply depot either in Hamburg or Bremen would be sure to do a far greater business than that done by the ordinary agent. They would get to know the people and understand their wants and requirements, and, returning to the United States, would carry with them a fund of valuable information that can not be collected in any other manner. It is possible that the first year might not be so profitable as expected, but the next and the next after that would prove what could be done, and would, I am sure, mark a brilliant increase in our exports.

THOMAS WILLING PETERS, *Consul.*

PLAUEN, *September 12, 1902.*

## SOLINGEN.

The business depression which set in about the middle of 1900 continued throughout the following year. . Production was largely in excess of the demand, and as a result, prices were lower, stocks increased, and buyers hesitated to make their usual purchases, hoping by delay to secure still more favorable terms when they should enter the market.

### IRON INDUSTRY.

The crucible steel industry, owing to keen foreign competition, especially from Austria and Sweden, has suffered most severely. Greatly reduced profits in the production of cast steel are also to be recorded; in some cases, even losses are reported. Throughout the year, many iron foundries and rolling mills have suffered from lack of orders. Nor was tool steel for saws, files, cutlery, etc., in much demand.

In addition to the general local depression, it is claimed that American competition is also greatly responsible for the present condition of the iron and steel trade. This is said to be true especially in regard to the tool industry, which finds in the United States its closest competitor; and it is this knowledge that has impelled the German manufacturer to seek to have raised the import duties on saws, files, knives, mowing machines and parts, hammers, axes, hatchets, hoes, pitchforks, garden utensils, meat choppers, chisels, planes, etc., which, in some cases, are sold at prices so low that he can successfully compete only at a loss. Recognizing the excellence of design of many of the American articles—for instance, pitchforks, spades, garden utensils—manufacturers here do not hesitate to copy them; some, indeed, going so far as to reproduce even the labels.

### CUTLERY.

In the manufacture of cutlery, the chief industry in this consular district, business was but little better than that of the preceding twelve months.

This was true especially of the home trade, the depression throughout Germany having caused a lack of larger orders. Factories, in order to keep their hands employed, were obliged to overstock to a considerable extent. Selling prices, however, dropped only when the scarcity of raw materials was at an end.

The export trade relieved to some extent the slackness of the home market. The United States particularly showed an increased willingness to buy, although its purchases were mostly the cheaper kinds of goods.

Not all branches of the cutlery industry, however, suffered alike; for instance, the trade in razors and saws showed, as a whole, satisfactory results. The manufacture of firearms, which has been nearly at a standstill for a number of years, has revived somewhat, owing to Government orders having been received by three of the larger local firms.

The export of cutlery to the United States from the Solingen consular district for the fiscal years ended June 30, 1901 and 1902, was as follows:

|  | 1901. | 1902. | Increase (+). Decrease (—). |
|---|---|---|---|
| First quarter | $313,133.06 | $347,140.47 | +$34,007.41 |
| Second quarter | 255,969.12 | 283,200.49 | + 27,231.37 |
| Third quarter | 245,197.16 | 253,733.58 | + 8,536.42 |
| Fourth quarter | 316,182.88 | 314,667.63 | — 1,515.25 |
| Total | 1,130,482.22 | 1,198,742.17 | + 68,259.95 |

The total increase of exports over 1901 was $210,053.47. The total export of German cutlery and cutting instruments, exclusive of surgical instruments, was 134,398 hundredweight, of which the following countries respectively received: '

|  | Cwt. |
|---|---|
| Russia | 21,863 |
| British West Africa | 15,340 |
| United States | 8,593 |
| Austria-Hungary | 8,461 |
| Netherlands | 7,213 |
| France | 5,599 |
| Belgium | 5,297 |
| German West Africa | 4,888 |
| Spain | 3,722 |
| Switzerland | 3,716 |
| British India | 3,650 |
| Argentina | 3,300 |
| Brazil | 3,161 |
| Great Britain | 2,574 |

### SMALL IRON WARES.

The trade in umbrella frames was good until the fall of 1900. After that time, it showed a decided decline, both as to the amount of business done and the selling prices.

Manufacturers of corset stays and springs, as well as of malleable cast and small iron wares, on account of lack of orders, were obliged to reduce the number of their employees.

The demand for chains improved somewhat toward the end of the year, but that for seamless tubing and bicycle parts grew worse.

### LASTING AND SATEEN INDUSTRY.

The weaving of colored and plush goods, as well as the dyeing of Turkish red yarns, cotton and silk-mixed goods, showed great inactivity.

### WOOD-PULP AND PACKING-PAPER INDUSTRY.

Trade was satisfactory, both as to sales and prices, until summer. Sharp foreign competition and the depressed business conditions in general then caused an all-around decline, which may still be increased in 1902. Many printing-paper syndicates, in order to keep their machines running, went into the wall-paper line, causing selling prices for this article to drop so far as to barely pay the cost of manufacture.

### BRICK ROOF AND GROOVE TILES.

Owing to the lack of activity in the building trades, these works were compelled to reduce their output about half, and selling prices declined to such an extent as to barely cover the cost of production.

The export trade prospects for 1902 are not favorable, on account of closer competition and decreased demands in the markets of foreign countries.

### PIG IRON AND HALF STUFF.

The following data cover the first six months of 1902 compared with the first half of the last three years, the pig iron and half stuff trade being as follows (figures given being in tons):

| Description. | 1902. | 1901. | 1900. |
|---|---|---|---|
| **IMPORT.** | *Tons.* | *Tons.* | *Tons.* |
| Pig iron | 79,262 | 175,994 | 390,624 |
| Half stuff | 524 | 807 | 1,367 |
| Total | 79,786 | 176,801 | 391,991 |
| **EXPORT.** | | | |
| Pig iron | 150,316 | 62,657 | 67,495 |
| Half stuff | 288,743 | 53,090 | 11,509 |
| Total | 439,059 | 115,747 | 79,004 |

It is to be noted that the imports and exports in raw products of the iron industry have exchanged places during the last two years. Of the 390,000 tons imported during the first half of 1900, England alone furnished 376,000 tons, while during the six months just passed it furnished only 66,000 tons.

Of the exports during the latter period England received 187,000 tons; Belgium, 99,000; Netherlands, 55,000; America, 44,000; France, 22,000.

Following is a more detailed table of exports:

| Articles. | 1902. | 1901. | 1900. |
|---|---|---|---|
| | *Tons.* | *Tons.* | *Tons.* |
| Bar iron | 190,318 | 149,969 | 90,261 |
| Angle iron, etc | 200,362 | 182,766 | 116,228 |
| Iron rails | 164,639 | 88,596 | 83,763 |
| Tin | 145,288 | 129,377 | 85,736 |
| Wire | 84,658 | 78,797 | 52,075 |
| Wire (coppered, etc.) | 46,020 | 43,708 | 44,518 |

### ENAMELED WARE.

The export of this ware increased somewhat. England received nearly one-quarter of the total export. The export to the United States is fourfold what it was two years ago.

### TOOLS AND TOOL MACHINERY.

The export of tools decreased, being affected greatly by the lack of orders from Russia. From the United States, 44 tons of tools were imported.

A surprising fact is the decrease of the import of tool machinery from the United States. The first six months of 1900 showed an import of 3,231 tons, against 328 tons for the same period of 1902, or about one-tenth of what it was two years ago. Germany supplied Spain with more tool machinery than Germany imported from the United States, the figures being 9,092 and 747 tons, respectively.

### BICYCLES.

The reaction from the too rapid growth of the bicycle trade has not yet been overcome. Nevertheless, Germany exported to each of nine countries more bicycles than it imported from the United States (which imports amounted to 77 tons); one of these countries receiving triple and four twice this amount.

JOSEPH J. LANGER, *Consul.*

SOLINGEN, *August 21, 1902.*

## STETTIN.

In my last annual report, I made the statement that Germany had reached her highest point in trade and commerce during the calendar year 1900, and that it was unreasonable to expect a repetition of that year's trade for at least three years.

Imperial statistics for the year 1901 show a decrease of $79,301,600 in the total import, and $57,120,000 in the export; in each case, about 5 per cent.

The imports for 1901 show a decrease of $14,042,000 in wool and the same amount in iron; copper import decreased $9,282,000, and wood $7,616,000. These are four of the most important materials for manufacture. An increase of $26,180,000 in the import of grains, of $2,856,000 in live stock, and of $3,332,000 in groceries and other food products, as compared with 1900, show Germany's dependence upon foreign countries for the necessaries of life, upon which, in the pending tariff, the import duty is to be materially increased.

Commercial securities have not recovered from the reaction from the overproduction of 1900–1901; as a consequence, Government bonds have been steady, and for the past six months, have not fluctuated 1 mark, a fact that has not occurred within the past four years in the case of Prussian consols. To-day, Prussian consuls are quoted at 102.20; in 1900, they went as low as 92.30.

### IMPORTS.

Official statistics for the year 1901 show a total import of 2,400,136 tons, as compared with 2,463,876 tons for the year 1900, or a decrease of 63,740 tons.

The greater part of this loss is in iron ore and raw iron for ship-launching purposes, and can be explained by the fact that the local shipbuilding yards made heavy importations, during 1900, for vessels that were launched in 1901. Russian rye shows a heavy decrease, due to the good German crop of 1901. Clover, ammonia, sulphur, phosphate, Russian wheat, herring, wood pulp, and hard coal show an increase, and coals show a gain of 92 tons. The United States is credited with an importation of 658 tons in this line.

The following table shows the leading articles of import into Stettin (direct and transshipped) from the United States, expressed in metric tons: [a]

*Direct imports from the United States to Stettin for the fiscal year ended June 30, 1902.*

| | Tons. | | Tons. |
|---|---|---|---|
| Aluminum | 17 | Oil cake | 200 |
| Bacon, sides of | 312 | Oleomargarine | 39 |
| Beef | 69 | Paraffin | 485 |
| Bran | 130 | Phosphate | 25,420 |
| Coal | 1,726 | Rosin | 882 |
| Copper | 357 | Seed, grass | 11 |
| Copper plates (1,263 pieces). | | Steam | 10 |
| Fruits, dried (plums and apples) | 7 | Tallow | 14 |
| Guts | 105 | Wheat | 5,979 |
| Lard | 2,459 | Wine | 15 |
| Lime, acetic | 23 | | |
| Machinery (343 cases) | 114 | Total tons | 45,790 |
| Maize | 6,973 | Total cases | 1,175 |
| Miscellaneous (832 cases) | 8 | Total pieces | 1,263 |
| Oil: | | | |
|    Cotton | 226 | | |
|    Mineral | 209 | | |

[a] Of 2,205 pounds.

## EXPORTS.

The total exports from this port for the year 1901 amounted to 813,279 tons, against 817,013 tons for the preceding year, showing a decrease of 3,734 tons. To the United States, 53,851 tons were exported, or a decrease of 24,584 tons. In value, the export for the fiscal year 1901-2 amounted to $903,326.09, against $2,991,720.69 for 1900-1901, a decrease of $2,088,394.60.

The total export from this consulate and the agencies at Danzig, Koenigsberg, and Swinemünde amounted to $2,126,615.56, a decrease of $3,162,249.14 compared with 1900-1901, which is partly accounted for by the falling off of $2,280,348.56 in raw sugar. Cement, chemicals, glue stock, and seeds also show a decrease, while hides, animal hairs, potato flour, pig iron, and refined sugar show a gain in the export to the United States.

The declared values of the principal articles exported from Stettin to the United States for the fiscal year 1901-2 were:

| | Value. | | Value. |
|---|---|---|---|
| Amber goods | $8,152.52 | Oil, of fusel | $6,608.37 |
| Cement | 26,033.28 | Oil, of rape | 12,837.15 |
| Dextrin | 29,825.78 | Pig iron | 267,316.74 |
| Fire-clay goods | 8,962.80 | Potato flour | 43,271.38 |
| Glue stock | 51,918.06 | Rags and old jute baggings | 2,529.10 |
| Goose meats | 2,489.50 | Seed | 2,070.89 |
| Hair, animal | 7,115.76 | Sugar: | |
| Herrings | 6,374.47 | Raw | 403,748.40 |
| Hides | 2,647.39 | Refined | 6,410.89 |

## IMPORTS.

Imports from the United States for the year 1901 show an increase of 32,598 tons as compared with 1900. Shipments from the United States via Hull, England; Copenhagen, Denmark; or Hamburg are not credited to the United States, but to England and Denmark. For instance, in the local official statistics of imports and exports, Denmark is credited with an export to Stettin of 1,117 tons, and England with 3,890 tons of lard. It is safe to say that four-fifths of this 5,000 tons comes from the United States.

*Florida phosphate*, of which almost 20,000 tons were imported, is threatened by the serious competition of Christmas Island phosphate, a rock of superior quality. Within the past few months, a trial cargo from "Ocean Island" was imported, and if the sample represents the average of the island phosphate, the Florida product will be shut out of the local market.

*Lard.*—The high price for German lard and butter increased the demand for American lard, in face of the fact that there was also a continual advance in the cost of the American article.

*Seeds.*—The import was not as extensive as in 1900, due to the favorable spring. The proposed increase of the duty on clover and grass seeds would seriously cripple the import business.

*Cereals.*—Throughout the Empire, the winter wheat crop was 2,500,000 tons less than in 1900, and winter rye 1,400,000 tons less, while the potato crop of 1901 showed an increase of 8,100,000 tons. Local imports of American grain were dull, and by no means satisfactory to the Stettin merchants.

*Coals.*—The importation of coal and coke for the year 1901 (by sea) amounted to 1,035,856 tons, as against 900,200 in 1900.   Of this quantity, 5,842 tons were of American origin, the greater part coming from England.

*Iron and metals.*—Last year was the slowest since 1892 in imports for the iron and metal industries.   The decline in this branch since was due to overproduction, added to the collapse of several banks, entailing an enormous loss.   Forced sales have put a great quantity of merchandise into the retail market at less than cost prices.

*Herring.*—The advance in the cost of meats has created an increased demand for fish.   The import will show a gain of about 500,000 barrels.

In the matter of tonnage, the United States ranks third among the countries importing to Stettin.   England is first and Sweden second. Coals form the bulk in weight of England's imports, while iron ore forms the bulk from Sweden.

The following table is a list of the principal articles of import into Stettin from the United States:

*The principal articles imported from the United States into Stettin.*

| | Metric tons. | | Metric tons. |
|---|---|---|---|
| Bacon, sides of | 1,430.2 | Machinery, agricultural | 567.9 |
| Bran | 565.8 | Maize | 44,523.7 |
| Clover seed | 112.3 | Oil: | |
| Corn oil cake, etc. | 593.2 |    Cotton | 1,771.5 |
| Coal | 658.4 |    Mineral | 798.9 |
| Flour, of wheat | 82.9 |    Turpentine and rosin | 271.5 |
| Fruits, dried | 187.8 | Petroleum, refined | 79,031 |
| Iron, raw | 1,523.8 | Refuse, lubricating | 1,268.3 |
| Lard | 13,995.4 | Rosin | 3,209.1 |
| Lime: | | Rye | 8,383.9 |
|    Acetic | 462.9 | Stearin and palmitic acid | 582.4 |
|    Phosphate of | 17,111 | Tallow | 975.7 |
| Lumber: | | Tanning material | 62.2 |
|    Hard wood, and timber | 106.4 | | |
|    Soft wood | 688.8 | | |

### GENERAL.

Stettin needs a waterway to Berlin and a change in the present scale of port dues, which are higher than those of any other Prussian port. A magnificent free harbor, finished some four years ago, has not had the expected result of hastening the canal project.

Shipbuilding is not booming; one yard has passed into the hands of a receiver.   The largest yard, the Vulcan, is fairly busy and will launch on the 11th of this month the *Kaiser Wilhelm II* for the North German Lloyd, a vessel which is expected to exceed everything afloat in the way of speed.   In addition, this yard has contracts for several small steamers and for three war ships.

The export of cement to the States is rapidly passing into history, because of the excellent quality of our own production.

Foreign vessels flying the American flag on the foremast, and loaded down with heavy cargoes can be seen on an average of once a week; American vessels, with the American flag on the afterdeck staff, can be seen at this port on an average of once every fifteen years, and then it is a steam yacht.   These facts are not due to the isolation of Stettin or to want of proper port facilities, but to the lack of an American merchant marine.

JOHN E. KEHL, *Consul.*

STETTIN, *July 28, 1902.*

## WEIMAR.

The fear entertained last year, that 1901 would witness a further considerable decline in the commerce and industries of this consular district, has been realized. The metal industry was the greatest sufferer from the crisis, especially the manufacture of machines. The electric industry, as well as the manufacture of lamps, which is a specialty in this district, also suffered severely. The china, glass, hose, and toy industries were less affected, but could work only at reduced profits.

Especially heavy were the losses on goods that had been bought at high prices. The great decrease in the value of these goods led either to the failure of many firms or to a considerable reduction of their profits. Some lines, however, look upon 1901 as at least satisfactory, and these include the growing of seeds and plants, and the manufacture of ladies' cloaks, linen, and shoes. Wages of workmen were in many instances cut to correspond to the depressed state of the markets.

### SEEDS AND PLANTS.

Owing to the unsettled weather in 1901, the results of seed growing vary extremely. The flower-seed crop was an average one, but vegetable seeds, with a few exceptions, such as beans, cucumbers, peas, and onions, were less favorable.

Dried flowers, leaves, and grasses found a good market abroad and at home, but low prices admitted of only a small profit. Imports of leaves and flowers were about the same as last year, while the artificial-flower trade was no livelier.

### LADIES' CLOAKS.

Business was, as a whole, satisfactory. The sales, yearly increasing, again exceeded the figures for the previous year. Generally, the cheap articles find purchasers most easily. The workshops were fully occupied all the year. Good hands could not always be procured in sufficient number, in spite of the high wages offered.

### FANCY GOODS.

Woolen fancy goods suffered, owing to increased production, which, under present circumstances, could not be easily got rid of. Consequently, they commanded lower prices. The present custom duties of foreign countries preclude export to a great extent, and better conditions in this respect are eagerly sought for.

### SHOES.

The shoe manufacturers that used mostly German leather were not so much affected as others by the depression. Their establishments, however, were not fully provided with orders, and, as a rule, concessions in prices had to be made to effect sales. American shoes imported into Germany showed in 1901 a considerable increase, viz, $201,000 worth, as against $142,000 worth in 1900. On the other hand, the imports of American leather in the same period decreased in value from $201,600 to $142,000.   The contemplated customs tariff provides for a higher duty on footwear of foreign manufacture, but the Erfurt Shoe Manufacturers Union does not consider the increase sufficient.

### AGRICULTURAL MACHINES.

The supply of agricultural machines exceeded the demand, which resulted in decreased prices.

### TRADE WITH THE UNITED STATES.

The export trade of the Weimar consular district with the United States continues to show a steady increase.   The value of goods exported thither during the calendar year 1901 was $1,073,416.02, as against $971,640.65 in 1900, an increase of $101,775.37.   The exports for the first six months of 1902 were $497,758.65, as against $425,022.60 in 1901, an increase of $72,736.05.   The most noticeable increases were in chinaware, dyes, fancy goods, and machinery, as shown by the following tables:

*Exports from the Weimar consular district to the United States during the calendar years 1900 and 1901.*

| Articles. | 1900. | 1901. |
|---|---|---|
| China | $247,301.98 | $307,054.27 |
| Cotton goods | 27,177.24 | 25,982.48 |
| Dyes | 35,566.26 | 55,229.46 |
| Fancy goods and toys | 318,539.21 | 364,954.96 |
| Gloves | 183,200.00 | 141,364.24 |
| Hair | 9,861.67 | 17,110.26 |
| Machines | 8,559.13 | 16,950.84 |
| Minerals | 9,216.89 | 8,534.88 |
| Optical goods | 30,991.26 | 43,945.85 |
| Pipes, smoking | 6,844.62 | 5,180.67 |
| Seeds and plants | 58,392.90 | 51,395.48 |
| Woolen goods | 32,111.25 | 29,969.34 |
| Sundry goods | 3,878.29 | 5,243.89 |
| Total | 971,640.65 | 1,073,416.02 |

*Exports from the Weimar consular district to the United States during the first six months of 1901 and 1902.*

| Articles. | 1901. | 1902. |
|---|---|---|
| China | $131,654.15 | $158,998.87 |
| Cotton goods | 16,183.66 | 6,349.95 |
| Dyes | 23,834.32 | 23,839.33 |
| Fancy goods and toys | 130,131.76 | 152,649.91 |
| Gloves | 58,045.44 | 50,100.05 |
| Hair | 7,456.15 | 3,068.86 |
| Machinery | 4,718.86 | 22,004.29 |
| Minerals | 3,247.72 | 28,581.69 |
| Optical goods | 21,758.37 | 16,781.28 |
| Pipes, smoking | 3,256.40 | 1,781.20 |
| Seeds and plants | 12,143.50 | 9,023.59 |
| Woolen goods | 15,457.98 | 20,955.82 |
| Sundry goods | 2,134.29 | 3,628.81 |
| Total | 425,022.60 | 497,758.65 |

WEIMAR, *September 11, 1902.*

THOS. EWING MOORE, *Consul.*

## ZITTAU.

The recently issued report of the Zittau Chamber of Commerce for the calendar year 1901 contains interesting information relative to the industrial, financial, and agricultural conditions of this district, some of which may be of sufficient general importance to justify a brief review.

The limits of the commercial district in question slightly exceed those of this consular district, but for the present purposes, they will be treated as identical. Considerations of thoroughness regularly delay the issue of these reports beyond the time when they might be regarded as contemporaneous, yet it may be safely assumed that industrial conditions hereabouts have not materially changed during the first half of the current year, and I shall endeavor to adapt the statistics to the existing status.

### MANUFACTURING.

This district has an area of a little less than 1,600 square miles, being (according to the census of December, 1900) inhabited by 405,173 people. When it is stated that the largest city in the district contains but 32,000 souls, it will be observed how thickly settled is this territory. In fact, every valley appears to the eye as one continuous village. These valleys are dotted with 2,636 manufacturing establishments, giving employment to 60,935 laborers, of whom 37,424 are males and 23,511 females. Industrial labor by children under 14 years of age has almost entirely ceased, owing to interdiction by recent laws of Saxony. Some 60 per cent of all industrial laborers—to wit, 36,987—are employed in the 371 textile establishments of the district, but this number by no means embraces all the people engaged in weaving, as well nigh every home in and about these villages still contains its handloom, operated by some members of the family. No separate statistics of this home production are kept, and in fact, most of the latter is rendered possible only through plant owners furnishing thread to the weavers and afterwards disposing of the finished product for them.

The change from hand power to steam power in all textile branches has been most rapid, there having been an increase of 72 per cent in steam plants between the years 1895 and 1901. The average of wages in textile branches (for men, women, and children) in 1901 was 530 marks ($126.14) per annum for each person employed, and while the greater part of the work is paid for by the piece, yet it is unusual to find any one skillful enough to earn above 75 cents per day. The earnings of hand workers are more difficult to estimate, but it may be assumed that they range lower still. All wages have declined slightly during the year 1901, owing principally to the shortening of hours made necessary by decreased business. When it is remembered that the prices of victuals here have for years exceeded those which obtain under similar conditions in the cities of our own country, and that these prices are now experiencing still further and sharp advances, it will be understood that the lot of the industrial laborer in this country is a hard one. The captains of industry are still complaining of general lethargy in business, and when they contemplate the efforts of those countries that have heretofore been large consumers of their products to gain commercial independence through the establishment

of manufacturing plants of their own (notably the States of South
America and the provinces of Russia), they are disinclined to report
brighter prospects for the future.

### LINENS

Linen products, however, have here a firmer trade foundation than
other textile fabrics, showing less overproduction and meeting a readier
sale, both at home and abroad.  In this branch, also, most plants manufacture mainly upon direct orders, and thus avoid the evil effects of overproduction.  The many ages during which the inhabitants of this
section have followed the occupation of weaving and producing high-
class damask linens have served to evolve a people that possesses peculiar expertness in this direction, and the principal textile centers have
wisely aided this natural capacity through the establishment of excellent weaving schools in which theoretical training is imparted to a
large number of apprentices.  Combining, as they do, skilled labor
with the advantage of easily secured raw material, it is likely that the
local manufacturers of high-class linen products will be able to compete
in the markets of the world for an unlimited time.  Not so with the
producers of other textile fabrics.

### COTTON GOODS.

The local manufacturers of cotton goods, in common with those of
other districts in Germany, feel the effects of depression in home
markets and the ever-increasing virility of foreign competition.  An
alarming number of cotton spinneries have for a number of years been
conducted without profit, and it is openly predicted that a considerable
proportion of these will soon cease operations entirely.  Some blame
for present conditions is placed upon fluctuations in the prices of raw
cotton, but the real causes may be sought in a decreasing market for
the finished product.

### MOHAIR.

One specialty in this district is the fabric known by the general
designation of mohair or alpaca (here commonly called "orleans").
It is claimed that American competition and tariff duties have practically destroyed a once favorable market for this product, and as no
fully equivalent outlets have as yet been found elsewhere, this branch
also complains of insufficient employment.

### CLOTHS AND SILKS.

Woolen cloths and silk goods are also produced in considerable
quantities in this district, but neither branch seems to possess a direct
market in our country.

### OTHER PRODUCTS EXPORTED.

Artificial flowers, metal leaf and cigar labels are also manufactured
here in large quantities, and a not inconsiderable proportion reaches
the United States; but no change, as compared with previous years,
can be noted, and all other exports are overshadowed by those of linen

goods, which are steadily increasing and constitute 90 per cent of the total annual export of over a million dollars from this district to the United States.

## COAL.

Much impetus is imparted to the manufacturing industries of this district by the prevalence of so-called "brown coal." Although of low calorific quality, it is easily mined, twelve out of the thirty-eight mines within this district being surface mines. These furnished employment to some 785 miners during the past year, producing 392,374 metric tons[a], which sold at an average price of 2.84 marks (68 cents) per ton. The average yield for each miner was 533 metric tons, while the average wages paid were 781.33 marks ($185.88) per annum. Of the entire output, about 75 per cent is consumed by manufacturing plants in this district. A harder and much more valuable coal is obtained from the adjacent districts of Silesia, and is largely mixed with brown coal in firing.

## CROPS, ETC.

Agricultural conditions in this district during the year 1902 have, in the main, been very favorable. Grain was heavy, and while constant rains may have in places affected the quality, there can be, on the whole, no just cause for complaint. Oats and hay are most abundant, and one explanation of the universally deplored scarcity in meats may well be found in the fact that the agrarians can this year afford to hold back their cattle.

This district being principally industrial in character, the rural classes can not, in any event, produce adequate food stuffs to satisfy the demands of its entire population. Prices (and chances) of labor having in general declined, and the cost of victuals having, in consequence of a rigid exclusion of imports, soared to almost unheard of heights, the lot of the laboring classes is gloomy indeed.

Fruit, which at the beginning of the year promised but poorly on account of an abnormally late spring, has exceeded all expectations, and more than an average crop will be harvested. Notwithstanding this abundance, however, American apples and dried fruit have even here obtained a foothold, and would doubtless conquer more of this market were it not for inimical legislation.

## MACHINERY.

But little American machinery is seen in this region, except in the agricultural branches. Several makes of American reapers and mowers are used upon the larger farms, though these are mostly of the older varieties, and self-binders are rare. The rising prosperity of the agricultural classes should insure a larger trade in this class of machinery for the future.

HUGO MUENCH, *Consul.*

ZITTAU, *September 27, 1902.*

---

[a] Of 2,204.6 pounds,

# GREECE.

## ATHENS.

Since my last annual report, there has been no marked change in the commerce and industries of this consular district. The prosperous condition of the past four years still continues, as is evident from the number of new business blocks and private residences in the course of erection in Athens and Piræus, and from the augmented value of both the imports and exports of the Kingdom, the former showing an increase of $2,055,568 and the latter of $270,630 over last year.

### STEAMSHIP LINE TO THE UNITED STATES.

The trade of Greece with the United States increases rather slowly; but last March, a direct line of steamships was established between New York and the ports of the Black Sea and of the eastern Mediterranean, and we may see in the near future a more rapid growth in this commerce. The new line, as previously reported, is known as the Deutsche Levant Line, and runs at present four steamships, which carry both passengers and freight. These vessels touch at Grecian ports about once a month; but it is hoped American shippers will patronize the line so well that in another year, the service will be greatly increased. The agents of the line in the United States are the Hamburg American Line, 37 Broadway, New York; Funch, Edye & Co., Produce Exchange, New York, and D. J. Donavan, 240 Lasalle street, Chicago.

American exporters to Greece should ship by this line, as one of the reasons given by Greek exporters for not dealing more extensively in American products has been the roundabout routes, through European countries, over which freight from the United States had to be shipped and the consequent vexatious delays and losses. The greater part of the imports from the United States still comes over those old routes; but it is hoped that, before the end of another year, the direct line will carry a larger percentage of all this freight.

A line of steamers between Greece and the United States is something this consulate has worked long and persistently to have established, and it is hoped that American exporters will not let it lapse for want of patronage. By shipping direct, the charges of middlemen and of reshipment at foreign ports, with the consequent losses and long delays, are avoided. Shipments through Europe should not be made. Heretofore, American shippers have lost freight and patronage by the unreliability of the roundabout routes to the Levant, and they should endeavor to not only maintain the direct line but also to encourage the establishment of others, until there is at least a weekly arrival of a steamship laden with American products. The Greeks want American goods. They consider them in most cases far superior to the manufactures of other countries, and prefer to import them if they can be delivered here without great delay, in good condition, and on terms that will compete with the products of other lands. It is certain that a direct line of transportation can deliver freight in the shortest time, in the best condition, and—if properly patronized—for the least cost.

## HINTS TO EXPORTERS.

One of the principal drawbacks to American trade with Greece is the custom of American exporters in demanding cash payments, while their competitors give credits. Many British, German, and other European exporters to Greece keep reliable agents here to deliver their goods, collect payments, and look after their interests generally. American exporters to whom I have written this fact say, "We can not afford to send an agent to Greece; our trade is not large enough." The European exporters can not, alone, stand the expense of keeping an agent here; but for that purpose, they combine with other exporters from the same country, and in time, the trade of each increases sufficiently to justify a separate agency.

Without a reliable agent on the ground, time payments can not be given except at risk of great loss, and without time payments, it will be a very difficult matter to work up a large trade in the face of the competition in this market.

## COLLECTION OF PAYMENTS.

Many complaints have been made to this consulate by American exporters, that they are unable to collect payments for goods shipped to Greece; but in nearly every case, the American exporter had either a native agent here or no agent at all. This very rarely happens to the foreign exporter who has a capable and reliable agent in Greece. I have advised for years the sending of trusted men here, and some American firms have followed this advice, with profit to themselves, while others who can not afford to keep agents in Greece, have had their European agents visit the country once or twice a year to look after their trade.

## TRADE WITH UNITED STATES.

In the statistics included in this report is shown the value of the imports and exports of Greece, by countries, for the years 1899 and 1900, the latest data obtainable. It will be seen by these figures that the United States still occupies eighth place, and that, although I have asserted our trade with Greece is increasing, the direct imports into this country from the United States during 1900 were valued at only $718,545, or $89,489 less than in 1899, and $263,464 less than in 1898; while the value of the exports to the United States in that year was $1,494,560, or $307,493 more than in 1899 and $689,753 more than in 1898. All the direct imports from the United States, up to the establishment of the through line of vessels last March, were brought to Greece by tramp steamships coming over for currants, magnesite, emery stone, iron ore, etc. The indirect imports from the United States came through other European countries, and were transshipped to Greece as the products of Germany, Great Britain, Italy, etc., the United States thus losing credit for goods that amount in value to four or five times the value of the imports that were credited to it. Therefore, this table does not show the true standing of the United States in the commerce of Greece, as far as imports are concerned.

H. Doc. 305, pt 2——24

The principal imports into Greece from the United States during the year ended June 30, 1902, were the following:

### Machinery.

Boring machines.
Churns and cream separators.
Cotton gins.
Fanning mills.
Feed mills.
Flour mills.
Gas motors.
Harvesters.
Ice-making machines.
Ironing machines.
Mowers.
Paper-cutting machines.
Printing presses.
Pumps, steam and hand.

Plows.
Steam engines.
Spinning machines.
Sewing machines.
Sausage machines.
Straw cutters.
Seeders.
Thrashing machines.
Typewriters.
Turning lathes.
Turbines.
Wine presses.
Windmills.

### Hardware.

Agricultural tools.
Building iron.
Coal stoves.
Candlesticks.
Door locks.
Gas and other piping.
Harness and saddle hardware.
Kitchen utensils.
Knives.

Oil stoves.
Railroad material.
Revolving-chair irons.
Razors.
Saws.
Sheet iron.
Tubing.
Wire, telegraph, etc.
Various other small articles.

### Food stuffs.

Butter.
Corn.
Corn meal.
Coffee.
Cinnamon and other spices.
Cod and other cured fish.

Chestnut meal.
Nuts.
Oatmeal.
Pepper.
Rice.
Rice meal.

### Miscellaneous.

Bags and bagging.
Belting.
Bicycles and bicycle sundries.
Blue vitriol.
Books.
Carriages.
Chemical products.
Clocks.
Cloth, cotton and woolen.
Coal.
Cotton.
Dress trimmings.
Drugs.
Furniture and furniture ornaments.
Firearms.
Fly paper.
Glassware.
Green hides.
Handcarts.
Jewelry.
Kodaks and kodak sundries.

Lamps, kerosene and acetylene.
Lamp chimneys.
Lithographs and engravings.
Leather.
Lumber.
Linoleum and oilcloths.
Medicinal plasters.
Optical apparatus.
Paraffin.
Pharmaceutic products.
Paints.
Photographic apparatus.
Petroleum.
Patent medicine.
Railway coaches.
Sacks and sacking.
Stepladders.
Toilet articles.
Veneering woods.
Watches.
Writing utensils.

Allow me to repeat the advice to American exporters to Greece that is given annually in these reports: (1) Do not burden the mails with catalogues printed in the English language, as few of the Greek merchants read English; French is more common. (2) Send American agents here; do not depend upon native agents or upon residents of other nationalities. (3) Ship only your best goods. Many exporters ruin their trade by sending inferior wares. (4) Pack goods securely. (5) Ship by most direct lines or routes. Numerous complaints reach this consulate of the carelessness of American exporters as regards the packing and shipping of their goods or products. The American exporter should never lose sight of these details. Some of our leading manufacturers have heeded the above advice, with profit to themselves.

The exports to the United States invoiced in this consular district during the year ended June 30, 1902, and their values, were:

| | | | |
|---|---|---|---|
| Sponges | $54,241.10 | Caviare | $1,307.20 |
| Hematite iron ore | 36,698.13 | Tobacco | 961.20 |
| Marble | 33,247.92 | Sausage casings | 579.15 |
| Magnesite | 22,934.81 | Figs | 566.97 |
| Cheese | 16,023.41 | Almonds | 458.68 |
| Goatskins | 14,034.84 | Polypus | 438.50 |
| Olives | 11,036.03 | Other articles | 3,357.23 |
| Olive oil | 8,704.30 | | |
| Whetstones | 6,424.80 | Total value | 224,670.33 |
| Oriental rugs | 4,706.37 | Total value for year | |
| Cognac | 3,869.80 | ending June 30, 1901. | 199,198.92 |
| Household effects | 2,151.74 | | |
| Currants | 1,577.02 | Increase | 25,471.41 |
| Wine | 1,331.13 | | |

## FREIGHT RATES.

There have been during the year no important changes in freight rates between the United States and Greece. Freight rates on coal from Great Britain are from $1.23 to $1.85, and from the United States from $3.85 to $4.25 per ton.

## MERCHANT MARINE: SHIPPING.

No report of the condition of the Greek merchant marine has been published this year. The latest published was in 1900. It showed that 112 steamers, valued at $9,732,201, were owned in this Kingdom at the close of that year, a gain of 29 over 1899.

There are no Grecian laws that discriminate against American vessels, but as shown by the tables in this report which give the movement of foreign shipping in Greek ports, the flag of the United States has not appeared during the year on a single merchant vessel in Grecian waters.

## DRY DOCKS AND OTHER IMPROVEMENTS.

So far as I have been able to learn, there have been during the year no changes in port regulations and none in wharfage, dockage, or other port dues. The work on the two large dry docks now in process of construction at Piræus is nearing completion. It is expected that both docks will be finished within a few months. The construction of the new breakwater that is being built to enlarge the harbor at Piræus is going forward rapidly. When finished, it will nearly double the present size of the harbor.

As will be seen by reference to one of the statistical tables of this report, the number of manufactories at Piræus has been increased during the year. One of the new industries established is a large electric-power house, which is to furnish power for the Piræus-Athens railway as soon as new cars and outfit are received.

### RAILWAYS.

Work has been resumed on the railway which is to run from Athens north through Larissa. It is expected that the line will be completed to the latter place by the end of 1903. A railway from Pyros to Kyparissia, in the Peloponesus, was completed during the year. So far as can be learned, the tramway from Athens to Piræus via Phalerum, which is now using steam, has done nothing toward providing the electric power called for by its charter. The street-railway company of Athens has made no extensions of its lines during the year; horses are still its motive power.

There have been no extensions of the postal or telegraph lines of the Kingdom, but during the year, the postal and telegraph departments of Athens were moved into new, well-fitted offices.

### TAXES, ETC.

There have been no changes in tariff rates and customs rules, and none in patent, copyright, and trade-mark laws since my last report. There are no laws, regulations, taxes, or licenses affecting commercial travelers any more than any other travelers, nor is there any law or rule requiring goods to be marked so as to show country of origin.

### ·GENERAL IMPORTS OF GREECE.

*Value of Greek imports for the three years ended December 31, 1899, 1900, and 1901.*

| Articles. | 1901. | 1900. | 1899. |
|---|---|---|---|
| Cereals | $6,825,900 | $6,485,587 | $7,014,349 |
| Cotton and woolen goods | 3,760,114 | 3,182,399 | 4,165,551 |
| Coal and other crude minerals | 3,550,825 | 2,886,734 | 1,782,090 |
| Lumber and wood | 1,703,118 | 2,151,119 | 1,828,339 |
| Metals | 1,481,462 | 1,089,670 | 1,248,138 |
| Cod and other cured fish | 1,413,900 | 1,190,406 | 1,326,221 |
| Druggists' materials and chemical products | 879,936 | 808,871 | 760,738 |
| Live animals | 801,489 | 650,763 | 1,113,556 |
| Green hides | 717,900 | 644,566 | 548,323 |
| Sugar | 608,600 | 496,008 | 584,880 |
| Paper | 537,909 | 559,465 | 546,102 |
| Coffee | 501,500 | 530,614 | 496,746 |
| Glass crystals, and pottery | 462,720 | 390,182 | 428,040 |
| Dyes | 417,090 | 249,877 | 188,580 |
| Rice | 360,068 | 317,110 | 378,607 |
| Leather and worked bone | 227,457 | 282,303 | 275,839 |
| Butter and cheese | 214,859 | (a) | ........... |
| Vegetables | 119,250 | (a) | ........... |
| Wine and liquors | 59,880 | (a) | ........... |
| Hats | 58,788 | (a) | ........... |
| Other articles | 2,451,698 | 3,174,238 | 2,584,586 |
| Total | 27,149,408 | 25,098,835 | 25,617,181 |

a Not reported.

## GENERAL EXPORTS OF GREECE.

*Value of Greek exports for the three years ended December 31, 1899, 1900, and 1901.*

| Articles. | 1901. | 1900. | 1899. |
|---|---|---|---|
| Currants | $9,956,015 | $10,210,529 | $7,601,590 |
| Crude minerals | 3,654,890 | 4,017,383 | 4,760,002 |
| Olives and olive oil | 987,381 | 506,961 | 707,664 |
| Tobacco | 796,237 | 688,193 | 565,374 |
| Figs | 608,391 | 469,067 | 487,754 |
| Nutgall | 408,500 | 312,760 | 325,991 |
| Wine | 364,712 | 928,894 | 1,296,184 |
| Sponges | 280,048 | 170,791 | 264,006 |
| Silk | 189,164 | 178,158 | 188,011 |
| Cognac | 180,560 | 117,704 | 289,777 |
| Cocoons | 159,642 | 59,613 | 170,068 |
| Emery stone | 116,888 | 122,217 | 93,567 |
| Tanned hides | 102,468 | 37,296 | 85,847 |
| Soap | 76,270 | 36,202 | 68,538 |
| Fruit | 73,861 | 55,575 | 52,061 |
| Soil of Santorini | 72,575 | 35,030 | 82,231 |
| Gunpowder | 67,955 | 116,834 | 124,360 |
| Live animals | 60,989 | 24,040 | .......... |
| Butter and cheese | 43,820 | 105,592 | 21,601 |
| Marble | 26,279 | 18,491 | 9,340 |
| Other articles | 1,752,285 | 1,441,798 | 1,731,173 |
| Total | 19,979,030 | 19,708,400 | 18,983,122 |

Imports exceed exports, 1901, $7,170,373; 1900, $5,385,485; 1899, $6,684,059.

*Value of Greek imports for the six months ended June 30, 1902.*

| Articles. | Value. | Articles. | Value. |
|---|---|---|---|
| Cereals | $3,342,882 | Coffee | $237,455 |
| Cotton and woolen goods | 1,621,644 | Dyes | 164,023 |
| Coal and other crude minerals | 1,112,484 | Rice | 163,565 |
| Lumber and wood | 796,800 | Glass, crystals, and pottery | 151,955 |
| Metals | 770,445 | Leather and worked bone | 117,048 |
| Cod and other cured fish | 412,672 | Butter and cheese | 47,116 |
| Druggists' materials and chemical products | 409,708 | Vegetables | 32,310 |
| Sugar | 288,320 | Hats | 21,314 |
| Live animals | 285,100 | Wines and liquors | 18,140 |
| Green hides | 268,700 | Other articles | 854,548 |
| Paper | 258,745 | Total | 11,874,968 |

*Greek exports for six months ended June 30, 1902.*

| Articles. | Value. | Articles. | Value. |
|---|---|---|---|
| Currants | $1,306,888 | Butter and cheese | $45,364 |
| Minerals | 2,049,478 | Tanned skins | 37,922 |
| Olives and olive oil | 1,038,036 | Soap | 36,645 |
| Tobacco | 379,106 | Gunpowder | 29,289 |
| Wine | 330,793 | Live animals | 27,008 |
| Nutgall | 197,525 | Cocoons | 21,913 |
| Silk | 166,156 | Soil of Santorini | 19,490 |
| Sponges | 188,847 | Marble | 1,320 |
| Figs | 70,798 | Other articles | 5,086,347 |
| Emery stone | 59,780 | | |
| Cognac | 55,048 | Total | 11,146,962 |
| Fruit | 48,209 | | |

*Value of Greek imports and exports, by countries, for the years 1899 and 1900.*

| Countries. | 1900. | | 1899. | |
|---|---|---|---|---|
| | Imports. | Exports. | Imports. | Exports. |
| Great Britain .......................................... | $5,395,435 | $7,417,030 | $5,022,957 | $5,191,265 |
| Russia ................................................. | 6,450,865 | 157,500 | 6,548,518 | 276,670 |
| Austria-Hungary .................................... | 3,029,355 | 1,640,825 | 2,971,702 | 1,760,812 |
| Germany............................................... | 2,457,985 | 1,998,315 | 1,872,322 | 988,117 |
| France.................................................. | 2,442,215 | 1,368,213 | 1,904,517 | 2,200,094 |
| Turkey ................................................ | 2,112,060 | 720,367 | 3,111,180 | 1,340,981 |
| Italy.................................................... | 1,156,330 | 835,415 | 1,197,647 | 780,415 |
| United States......................................... | 718,545 | 1,494,580 | 808,084 | 1,187,067 |
| Belgium ............................................... | 624,495 | 1,656,965 | 644,849 | 1,949,661 |
| Holland ............................................... | 210,205 | 1,353,630 | 212,756 | 1,367,711 |
| Roumania ............................................. | 118,610 | 98,060 | 127,482 | 143,545 |
| Egypt................................................... | 109,240 | 522,610 | 71,108 | 662,820 |

*Movement of foreign shipping at Piræus during the years 1900 and 1901.*

| Flag. | 1901. | | | | 1900. | | | |
|---|---|---|---|---|---|---|---|---|
| | Entered. | | Cleared. | | Entered. | | Cleared. | |
| | Number. | Tons. | Number. | Tons. | Number. | Tons. | Number. | Tons. |
| Austrian ..................... | 121 | 146,399 | 109 | 148,548 | 149 | 179,722 | 145 | 174,728 |
| Italian ........................ | 148 | 214,046 | 153 | 215,863 | 167 | 234,442 | 162 | 183,330 |
| French........................ | 100 | 168,633 | 99 | 167,385 | 116 | 170,788 | 125 | 181,858 |
| British ........................ | 162 | 139,779 | 182 | 156,073 | 158 | 169,494 | 112 | 117,258 |
| Turkish ....................... | 339 | 97,352 | 350 | 131,432 | 237 | 87,984 | 218 | 82,725 |
| Russian ....................... | 67 | 156,649 | 68 | 164,084 | 64 | 125,577 | 73 | 167,364 |
| German ....................... | 58 | 113,251 | 53 | 94,306 | 56 | 70,652 | 47 | 50,456 |
| Dutch......................... | 26 | 23,448 | 28 | 29,057 | 27 | 28,169 | 27 | 28,169 |
| Scandinavian................ | 8 | 26,369 | 8 | 26,369 | 2 | 1,660 | 1 | 934 |
| Belgian ....................... | 14 | 25,758 | 11 | 14,774 | 4 | 5,374 | 3 | 4,530 |
| Samian ........................ | 9 | 1,229 | 9 | 1,229 | 5 | 1,756 | 6 | 1,906 |
| Cretan ........................ | 10 | 1,221 | 17 | 2,338 | 4 | 498 | 6 | 736 |
| Bulgarian..................... | 1 | 735 | 1 | 735 | .......... | .......... | .......... | .......... |
| Danish......................... | 1 | 1,920 | 1 | 1,920 | .......... | .......... | .......... | .......... |
| Spanish ....................... | 2 | 2,412 | 2 | 2,412 | .......... | .......... | .......... | .......... |

*Movement of foreign shipping at Syra during the years 1900 and 1901.*

| Flag. | 1901. | | | | 1900. | | | |
|---|---|---|---|---|---|---|---|---|
| | Entered. | | Cleared. | | Entered. | | Cleared. | |
| | Number. | Tons. | Number. | Tons. | Number. | Tons. | Number. | Tons. |
| Austrian ..................... | 120 | 134,249 | 134 | 193,278 | 63 | 73,922 | 82 | 99,498 |
| Italian ........................ | 110 | 117,070 | 81 | 104,960 | 21 | 23,712 | 11 | 11,977 |
| French........................ | 3 | 4,324 | 11 | 15,518 | 18 | 27,156 | 25 | 38,747 |
| British ........................ | 72 | 98,930 | 74 | 95,896 | 84 | 92,860 | 66 | 77,270 |
| Turkish ....................... | 509 | 70,643 | 341 | 49,105 | 417 | 15,938 | 413 | 24,137 |
| Russian ....................... | 2 | 8,186 | 3 | 4,958 | .......... | .......... | .......... | .......... |
| German ....................... | 2 | 4,492 | 8 | 18,989 | .......... | .......... | .......... | .......... |
| Dutch......................... | 1 | 1,530 | 4 | 3,419 | 1 | 941 | .......... | .......... |
| Roumanian .................. | 1 | 134 | 4 | 804 | 1 | 1,426 | 1 | 1,426 |
| Spanish ....................... | 1 | 1,725 | 1 | 1,725 | .......... | .......... | .......... | .......... |

*Movement of foreign shipping at Corfu during the years 1900 and 1901.*

| Flag. | 1901. | | | | 1900. | | | |
|---|---|---|---|---|---|---|---|---|
| | Entered. | | Cleared. | | Entered. | | Cleared. | |
| | Number. | Tons. | Number. | Tons. | Number. | Tons. | Number. | Tons. |
| Austrian | 284 | 272,633 | 270 | 265,931 | 267 | 256,057 | 271 | 281,433 |
| Italian | 135 | 108,480 | 139 | 117,742 | 150 | 140,598 | 156 | 141,425 |
| British | 11 | 11,469 | 10 | 10,782 | 7 | 7,382 | 7 | 7,382 |
| Turkish | 260 | 21,474 | 257 | 20,867 | 177 | 13,861 | 199 | 15,273 |
| German | 1 | 1,964 | 1 | 1,964 | 3 | 3,240 | 1 | 1,151 |
| Samian | 1 | 1,253 | 1 | 1,253 | ........ | ........ | ........ | ........ |

*Movement of foreign shipping at Patras during the years 1900 and 1901.*

| Flag. | 1901. | | | | 1900. | | | |
|---|---|---|---|---|---|---|---|---|
| | Entered. | | Cleared. | | Entered. | | Cleared. | |
| | Number. | Tons. | Number. | Tons. | Number. | Tons. | Number. | Tons. |
| Austrian | 3 | 6,246 | 6 | 9,823 | 4 | 4,343 | 4 | 4,343 |
| Italian | 11 | 12,226 | 11 | 12,226 | 25 | 3,470 | 26 | 4,267 |
| French | 1 | 1,869 | 1 | 1,869 | 1 | 870 | 1 | 870 |
| British | 25 | 25,647 | 20 | 15,506 | 24 | 18,156 | 24 | 21,719 |
| Turkish | 9 | 1,128 | 9 | 1,128 | 1 | 278 | 5 | 713 |
| German | 6 | 9,269 | 8 | 10,522 | 6 | 6,785 | 5 | 7,753 |
| Dutch | 1 | 718 | 1 | 718 | ........ | ........ | ........ | ........ |
| Danish | 1 | 940 | 2 | 2,134 | 2 | 1,848 | 1 | 927 |
| Swedish | 6 | 3,130 | 1 | 760 | 2 | 2,879 | 1 | 1,876 |
| Belgian | 2 | 2,689 | 6 | 5,589 | ........ | ........ | ........ | ........ |

*Movement of foreign shipping at Cephalonia during the years 1900 and 1901.*

| Flag. | 1901. | | | | 1900. | | | |
|---|---|---|---|---|---|---|---|---|
| | Entered. | | Cleared. | | Entered. | | Cleared. | |
| | Number. | Tons. | Number. | Tons. | Number. | Tons. | Number. | Tons. |
| Austrian | 3 | 3,500 | 3 | 3,500 | 7 | 7,445 | 9 | 9,845 |
| German | 3 | 3,505 | 1 | 1,059 | 1 | 868 | 2 | 2,463 |
| Italian | 6 | 779 | 4 | 660 | 3 | 385 | 2 | 247 |
| Dutch | 4 | 2,687 | 1 | 710 | 3 | 2,344 | 5 | 4,694 |
| Swedish | 1 | 259 | 1 | 259 | ........ | ........ | ........ | ........ |

*Movement of foreign shipping at Volo during the years 1900 and 1901.*

| Flag. | 1901. | | | | 1900. | | | |
|---|---|---|---|---|---|---|---|---|
| | Entered. | | Cleared. | | Entered. | | Cleared. | |
| | Number. | Tons. | Number. | Tons. | Number. | Tons. | Number. | Tons. |
| Austrian | 25 | 27,736 | 43 | 47,421 | 35 | 27,286 | 49 | 54,212 |
| German | 10 | 12,793 | 10 | 12,793 | 1 | 1,045 | 1 | 1,045 |
| Italian | 3 | 1,329 | 3 | 1,032 | 1 | 679 | 1 | 679 |
| Swedish | 1 | 1,022 | 1 | 1,022 | ........ | ........ | ........ | ........ |
| British | 15 | 18,909 | 18 | 29,112 | 2 | 2,423 | 16 | 22,039 |
| Turkish | 34 | 6,715 | 28 | 7,281 | 47 | 9,540 | 58 | 11,111 |
| Samian | 2 | 77 | 1 | 33 | 1 | 216 | ........ | ........ |

Movement of foreign shipping at Kalamata during the years 1900 and 1901.

| Flag. | 1901. | | | | 1900. | | | |
|---|---|---|---|---|---|---|---|---|
| | Entered. | | Cleared. | | Entered. | | Cleared. | |
| | Number. | Tons. | Number. | Tons. | Number. | Tons. | Number. | Tons. |
| Austrian | 12 | 7,196 | 11 | 6,120 | ...... | ......... | 1 | 1,075 |
| Italian | 17 | 1,828 | 9 | 595 | ...... | ......... | 13 | 1,791 |
| Belgian | 1 | 1,347 | 7 | 7,660 | | | | |
| British | 5 | 3,753 | 1 | 1,327 | 3 | 4,185 | 8 | 4,185 |
| Turkish | 2 | 704 | 2 | 704 | 6 | 1,939 | 6 | 1,939 |
| Swedish | | | 1 | 1,110 | 1 | 1,110 | | |
| French | 2 | 2,334 | 1 | 1,631 | 4 | 6,423 | 4 | 6,423 |

Movement of foreign shipping at Zante during the years 1900 and 1901.

| Flag. | 1901. | | | | 1900. | | | |
|---|---|---|---|---|---|---|---|---|
| | Entered. | | Cleared. | | Entered. | | Cleared. | |
| | Number. | Tons. | Number. | Tons. | Number. | Tons. | Number. | Tons. |
| Austrian | 3 | 3,865 | 4 | 4,104 | 10 | 9,876 | 3 | 2,370 |
| Italian | 15 | 2,498 | 14 | 2,085 | 29 | 4,611 | 19 | 2,717 |
| British | 9 | 8,180 | 7 | 6,148 | 9 | 12,744 | 3 | 5,444 |
| Turkish | 5 | 809 | 6 | 767 | 5 | 459 | 10 | 1,725 |
| German | 1 | 923 | 2 | 2,196 | 1 | 987 | | |
| Swedish | | | 1 | 1,113 | | | | |
| Samian | | | 1 | 193 | 2 | 386 | 4 | 619 |
| Montenegrian | 1 | 159 | 1 | 159 | | | | |

Movement of foreign shipping at other Greek ports during the years 1900 and 1901.

| Flag. | 1901. | | | | 1900. | | | |
|---|---|---|---|---|---|---|---|---|
| | Entered. | | Cleared. | | Entered. | | Cleared | |
| | Number. | Tons. | Number. | Tons. | Number. | Tons. | Number. | Tons. |
| British | 67 | 88,907 | 62 | 87,916 | 64 | 69,787 | 60 | 73,551 |
| Italian | 55 | 80,737 | 74 | 29,491 | 100 | 49,831 | 79 | 30,236 |
| Turkish | 329 | 22,811 | 260 | 17,010 | 198 | 24,623 | 189 | 18,187 |
| Austrian | 20 | 19,343 | 23 | 25,086 | 40 | 26,896 | 37 | 34,719 |
| Belgian | 11 | 12,708 | 8 | 9,637 | 16 | 28,276 | 19 | 32,701 |
| Swedish | 9 | 11,844 | 15 | 18,326 | 82 | 37,475 | 25 | 27,309 |
| French | 7 | 7,369 | 9 | 9,198 | 15 | 5,390 | 20 | 7,865 |
| Spanish | 4 | 4,792 | 2 | 3,731 | 8 | 11,791 | 9 | 13,187 |
| German | 3 | 3,619 | 3 | 3,619 | 12 | 6,728 | 12 | 6,728 |
| Dutch | 2 | 1,486 | 2 | 1,468 | 5 | 7,870 | 6 | 8,790 |
| Russian | 1 | 1,176 | ...... | ......... | 1 | 2,500 | 5 | 10,004 |
| Danish | 1 | 1,087 | 2 | 1,813 | 15 | 18,796 | 9 | 14,707 |
| Samian | 5 | 640 | 3 | 420 | 6 | 480 | 5 | 420 |
| Cretan | 5 | 390 | 6 | 490 | 3 | 370 | 6 | 560 |

Receipts of the Greek Government from its monopolies, revenues, etc., during the years 1898–1901.

| Source | 1901 | 1900. | 1899 | 1898. |
|---|---|---|---|---|
| Taxes on customs privileges | $3,573,800 | $3,372,230 | $2,255,740 | (a) |
| Stamped paper | 1,934,140 | 1,665,640 | 1,023,220 | ...... |
| Tobacco wrappers | 1,534,210 | 1,728,740 | 84,130 | ...... |
| Hacking or cutting tobacco and snuff | 1,073,130 | 1,067,870 | 930,040 | $889,090 |
| Petroleum | 796,290 | 796,060 | 716,620 | 639,660 |
| Cigarette paper | 534,710 | 312,860 | 366,840 | ...... |
| Salt | 350,380 | 350,980 | 310,140 | 305,490 |
| Stamps | 327,610 | 309,880 | 127,400 | ...... |
| Matches | 172,640 | 166,150 | 155,220 | 142,170 |
| Naxos emery stone | 120,370 | 130,140 | 58,040 | ...... |
| Playing cards | 40,020 | 38,960 | 38,980 | 37,990 |
| Total | 10,757,300 | 9,939,410 | 6,068,370 | 2,017,400 |

a Not reported.

*Postal orders issued and paid by the Greek Government during the years 1898–1901.*

| Year. | Issued. | | Paid. | |
|---|---|---|---|---|
| | Number. | Value. | Number. | Value. |
| 1901 ................................................. | 8,876 | $110,485 | 18,146 | $323,249 |
| 1900 ................................................. | 7,826 | 90,077 | 15,335 | 263,383 |
| 1899 ................................................. | 6,860 | 79,250 | 12,173 | 224,210 |
| 1898 ................................................. | 5,863 | 60,383 | 9,049 | 137,070 |

*Manufactories in operation at Piræus, in 1902.*

| Industry. | Number. | Industry. | Number. |
|---|---|---|---|
| Distilleries (mostly cognac) ............ | 27 | Rope factories............................ | 3 |
| Chair factories ........................ | 20 | Dynamite factories..................... | 3 |
| Steam flour mills ...................... | 14 | Glass factories.......................... | 3 |
| Cloth and cotton mills................. | 10 | Ice factories............................ | 3 |
| Machine shops and foundries.......... | 9 | Paper mills............................. | 2 |
| Macaroni factories...................... | 9 | Tanneries............................... | 2 |
| Dyeing works............................ | 8 | Shipyards .............................. | 2 |
| Soap factories........................... | 5 | Match factories ........................ | 1 |
| Nail factories ........................... | 3 | Electric power house................... | 1 |

*Average rate of exchange in Greek paper money during the years 1899–1902.*

| Month. | 1902. | | 1901. | | 1900. | | 1899. | |
|---|---|---|---|---|---|---|---|---|
| | Value in paper drachmas of 1 gold franc. | Value in paper drachmas of 1 U. S. dollar. | Value in paper drachmas of 1 gold franc. | Value in paper drachmas of 1 U. S. dollar. | Value in paper drachmas of 1 gold franc. | Value in paper drachmas of 1 U. S. dollar. | Value in paper drachmas of 1 gold franc. | Value in paper drachmas of 1 U. S. dollar. |
| January ............ | 1.668 | 8.64 | 1.705 | 8.83 | 1.674 | 8.61 | 1.545 | 8.01 |
| February ........... | 1.661 | 8.60 | 1.695 | 8.78 | 1.682 | 8.71 | 1.55 | 8.03 |
| March .............. | 1.644 | 8.52 | 1.695 | 8.78 | 1.638 | 8.48 | 1.56 | 8.06 |
| April ............... | 1.634 | 8.46 | 1.69 | 8.75 | 1.63 | 8.44 | 1.585 | 8.21 |
| May................. | 1.603 | 8.30 | 1.625 | 8.42 | 1.644 | 8.51 | 1.545 | 8.01 |
| June ................ | 1.58 | 8.18 | 1.58 | 8.18 | 1.66 | 8.59 | 1.508 | 7.81 |
| July................. | 1.578 | 8.17 | 1.598 | 8.08 | 1.684 | 8.72 | 1.51 | 7.82 |
| August.............. | 1.588 | 8.19 | 1.60 | 8.29 | 1.616 | 8.37 | 1.515 | 7.83 |
| September .......... | 1.634 | 8.46 | 1.653 | 8.56 | 1.553 | 8.04 | 1.568 | 8.12 |
| October ............. | 1.648 | 8.53 | 1.69 | 8.75 | 1.61 | 8.33 | 1.62 | 8.39 |
| November .......... | 1.639 | 8.49 | 1.69 | 8.75 | 1.654 | 8.56 | 1.623 | 8.40 |
| December........... | | | 1.67 | 8.65 | 1.684 | 8.72 | 1.65 | 8.55 |

ATHENS, *December 20, 1902.*

DANIEL E. McGINLEY,
*Consul.*

## PATRAS.

The conditions which have prevailed throughout the Kingdom of Greece during the past eighteen months are probably different from any which have obtained for many years hitherto, and are in the main of a very favorable nature. Capital has gathered a good deal of courage during this period and promises, in general, many changes, some of which are destined to place the country in an entirely new relation to the Continent proper, and all of which are calculated to add materially to its development. While it is true that a large proportion of this capital comes from abroad, and that the country can not reap the full benefit accruing from its employment, it is at least encouraging to find so much willingness on the part of foreigners to invest in local enterprises. Even as it is, much good will be gained by the people in the increased facilities which these enterprises assure.

## THE PIRÆUS-LARISSA RAILROAD.

The principal financial undertaking of this period is unquestionably the commencement of construction of the long-projected railway from Piræus to Larissa, through the rich sections of central and northern Greece, which have remained isolated from their less rich but more fortunate neighbors, and the eventual junction of the line with the transcontinental railway in Turkish territory. Particulars of this project have already appeared in the Consular Reports[a] and need not be repeated here. Greece has not had a very great hand in the formation of the new company—less than she probably would have had under the former agreement—nor has she subscribed heavily to the first loan of $4,283,520, which has already been issued; but the Government has retained an interest both in the capital and in the supervision of the road, so that Greek influence will be largely felt in the organization.

## THE ELECTRIC POWER PLANT AT NEW PHALERON.

Another merger of capital which promises much to the section centering about Athens is the great power plant of the Greek Electric Company, which is now nearing completion, and is intended not only to furnish electric power for the light, street, and suburban service of the three or four cities clustered in that section, but also to solve the fuel question—the most knotty problem of the country aside from the currency—and ought to add much to the manufacturing interests of the Attican plain. The same company has also recently installed an electric street railway system in Patras, which has not proved in any sense a disappointment in the six months of its existence; and in many other sections of the country, new industries have arisen which have added much to the capital, employment, and convenience of their particular districts, notably the progressive sections in the Peloponnesus which center about the inland cities of Pyrgos and Tripolis.

## EXTENSION OF THE PELOPONNESUS RAILROAD.

A matter of great interest which has not received as much attention as it deserves, largely for the reason that it has been an extension of capital rather than a new organization of it, and because the work has been pushed gradually and unostentatiously for a number of months, is the completion of the Peloponnesus Railway as far as Calamota on the southwestern coast of the Peloponnesus. The new line was opened for traffic a few weeks ago. With the extension of this railway from Pyrgos to Cyporissia, and thence to Meligala, where it joins the line already constructed to Calamota, including the branch from Pyrgos to Cotocolo, the other port of West Peloponnesus, practically all sections of the Peloponnesus have been brought within immediate touch with one another, and the whole district with the rest of the country

---

[a] See Advance Sheets, No. 1328, April 29, 1902.

and with the outside world. The section of country penetrated and connected by the new line is peculiarly rich in agricultural and fruit products, its difference in climate from that of northern Peloponnesus enabling it to grow in abundance a variety of things especially suited for export, such as currants, figs, olives, etc.

## THE GREAT CURRANT CROPS OF 1901 AND 1902.

Of equal importance with these combinations of capital, and in a certain sense responsible for many of them, are the two great currant crops which the Peloponnesus has experienced in successive years, the gross yield for the seasons of 1901 and 1902 reaching little short of 784,000,000 gross pounds (350,000 tons). Being the principal export, this one product is, in a measure, the keystone to the commercial arch of the entire Kingdom. So many of the smaller landholders throughout Southern Greece and the contiguous islands are engaged exclusively in the raising of currants, that a failure of this crop necessarily shakes to its foundations the economic structure of more than half the country. Correspondingly, therefore, a yield such as was experienced in 1900–1901, following as it did a year of disastrous failures, instilled much-needed life into business investments; and the phenomenon—for it is little short of one—of a second and successive enormous crop for the present season, 1901–1902, has naturally added even more confidence, although it has, or had at the opening of the season, caused a glut in the currant market which promised not a few ill consequences.

## EXCHANGE.

But the country, in spite of these favorable signs of financial extension, which are in detail more numerous than I have here mentioned, is facing some problems which, in the light of general prosperity, are somewhat paradoxical. Gold has been at a premium of not less than 60 per cent over currency during the past year; a part of that time has seen it 5 per cent higher, and the disastrous fluctuation in money rates has been strikingly apparent. Exporters are reaping a harvest from the exchange, which the Government can ill afford to lose. More than once during the past year, the directors of the different banking houses of the country have conferred upon the subject, but no adequate solution of the problem is yet forthcoming. At this date, the pound sterling, which should be worth about 25 drachmas (gold), is bringing 41.65 drachmas (currency), and has but recently dropped from 42.20.

## THE PROBLEM OF EMIGRATION.

Another subject of vital interest to the country is the matter of emigration. I need not say that the stream of emigration is westward, since it is a well-known fact that few large centers in the United States are without a Greek colony. But other countries are receiving their quotas also, especially South Africa, which, since the cessation of hostilities, has drawn some thousands of the inhabitants of the Ionian Islands. The numbers departing for the United States during the year have been exceptionally large. This steady efflux of the working classes is placing the country in a difficulty which bids fair to become chronic, whatever truth there may be in the widely prevalent opinion that only with difficulty do Greeks become expatriated. Work in all parts of the country has been more plentiful than workmen; wages have risen in many sections 100 per cent. But despite this fact, there is no apparent staying of the migratory movement, and the currant-growing districts have been obliged to import laborers from the adjoining islands and even from Turkey. Favorable as these signs would be under ordinary circumstances, they have for this section a significance quite the reverse, since a decrease in the number of workmen rather than an increase in the amount of work is responsible for these evidences of unusual prosperity, and the paucity of workmen is directly traceable to the inroads of emigration.

But however sinister these conditions appear, they are not likely to produce an immediate crisis and their settlement may be looked for at no distant date. The country has more conveniences, more miles of railways, more harbors, better shipping facilities, and better connections with the foreign centers of trade than it has ever before enjoyed. Capital is becoming organized along various industrial lines; labor is tending toward increased wages. Through the agricultural stations and schools, new life is being infused into farming, and the outlook for trade both home and abroad is becoming more and more favorable.

### THE EXPORT TRADE.

Shipments to foreign countries have naturally been large, in view of the great currant industry which is wholly centered in this district, but the export figures for the country as a whole show a loss for the year 1901 of $1,600,000 from those for 1900, and since this loss is principally concerned with the currant and wine industries, it is set down against this district. The figures, however, are a trifle misleading, since the first half of the year 1901 is shouldered with the disastrous crop failures of 1900, while the year 1900 is greatly bolstered by the enormous currant yield of the preceding year. So that, if the years are compared with respect to their actual productions, the year 1901 must considerably outstrip the preceding twelve months, and the present year will establish probably a still higher record. An increase in exports for this district is shown for figs, olives, and olive oils. During the year, several oil refineries have been erected in the district, the principal one in this immediate vicinity being that of G. Topali & Co., which has a capacity to reduce 50,000 pounds of olives and to produce about 8,000 pounds of oil per day. The refining of oil is an installation of the period under review. Crude oils have long been made in large quantities, but hitherto it has never occurred to anyone that they ought to be refined for export. It is natural that some difficulty should be met in competing with the oils of other countries, such as those of France and Italy, which have a long-established reputation, although it has been pretty well shown that oils of a superior grade can be made from Greek olives, and it is further said that olives of this section are freer from the inroads of *Mosca Olearia* than are those of either France or Italy, owing to the quickness with which the fruit in this part of the Peloponnesus reaches maturity.

The export trade in currants remains, as it has been for many years past, the most lucrative that this district enjoys, as well the most intricate in its nature. The problem of battling with the *Peronosporus*, the American blight which has consumed a reported average of one-third to one-half of each alternate crop for many years, is apparently solved. Sulphate of copper and various chemical products and chemically prepared soaps are used in such quantities as to combat the disease unquestionably in its earlier stages. The new problem arises forthwith as to the disposition of the increased production at reasonable prices. The retention law, which calls for a retention of as much as 20 per cent of each crop, while manifestly working on a wrong economic basis, has undoubtedly accomplished its purpose so far, but apparently at some sacrifice in certain quarters; and it is very questionable whether it has not reached its limit of usefulness in the present season, since it has been applied to its limit of retention without materially affecting prices. There is naturally, therefore, extraordinary activity among exporters in finding new markets and in finding new ways of increasing old markets. The termination of hostilities in South Africa has turned attention thither, but so far no creditable showing has been made, nor could such showing be expected at this early date. Attempts are also being made to regain a portion of the trade once enjoyed in this product with Russia, but here also success is uncertain. In fact, it seems more than likely that the solution of the problem will be confined principally and most effectively to an extension of old markets. The cheapness of the fruit for the present and previous seasons has naturally increased the consumption in countries where the currant is already known, so that, should the supply continue large, it is not improbable that the demand will remain sufficiently firm to insure the sale of all fruit at marginal figures. England has up to date taken an exceptionally large quantity of this season's fruit; Germany is finding it profitable, owing to the low prices, to import large quantities for the manufacture of wine, and it is confidently believed that France will come to the aid of the years' surplus, in view of her own fruit failures. As to the possibilities of the American market, they are constantly before the local exporters. A syndicate, in fact if not in name, has been recently organized and chartered to extend the currant trade, and expressly to extend it throughout the United States. I have already outlined the scope of this company in a special report upon the subject.[a] More capital has come into the project than was first reported, and the National Bank of Greece has joined with the Currant Bank and other stockholders in placing the company on a very sound financial basis, but thus far, the organization has not taken an active part in the market. I give elsewhere a table of currant exports for the past decade, as well as for the shipments of the present season to date, from which it will be noticed that the quantity purchased by the United States last year was, with one exception, the greatest of the period, and that the present season's figures are in advance of those of last year, so that the efforts made from this quarter are not without marked results.

---

[a] See Advance Sheets 1427, August 25, 1902.

## OTHER EXPORTS.

While the currant is the chief product exported to the United States, it is by no means the only one worthy of attention nor the only one in which an increase is noticeable. During the last two years, there has been a marked increase in the shipments of olives, olive oil, cheese, wine, figs, and the various other products of southern Peloponnesus. This growth is partly due to the increase in Greek immigration to America, since the black olives, the white cheese, and the products generally which find favor with the Greeks at home are in even greater demand abroad; and partly due, I should say, to the energy of many Greek merchants, in New York especially, who press these articles upon emigrants from other parts of the world, particularly from Italy. There is also an especial demand this season for the Calamota fig, which, while inferior in quality to the Smyrna variety, seems to be considered a fair substitute at a reasonable price.

## AMERICAN IMPORTS.

As indicated in the subjoined table of imports, the usual injustice is done to the American market, since the latter is not credited with many of the articles which belong to it, while it has confused with it all the imports from South American states. However, the truth is not distorted so much as to prevent us from seeing the insignificant part we are yet playing in this market, which last year purchased $27,000,000 worth of foreign goods. We continue to supply Greece with refined petroleum, but it is questionable whether this trade can be kept in our hands, since both Russia and Roumania are endeavoring to secure it, and political reasons may reach the point where they will influence commercial ones. We have placed about $50,000 worth of copper sulphate in this port early in 1902, in addition to what appears in the tables, and have furnished the rolling stock for the electric street railway of this city. We are also beginning to furnish directly a number of articles, such as metal ware, musical instruments, cheap watches, machines, etc. I say directly, since unquestionably many American products are sold here through German and English houses. In fact, it is not infrequently true that articles purchased at the local stores have the American mark of origin, although they are not known or considered as American goods.

The possibilities for increasing the trade of the United States with this district are more promising than they have been, for a number of reasons. There is now a direct line of steamships plying between New York and Greek ports, so that the question of transportation is less complicated than it was a year ago. There is also a greater willingness on the part of this market to try American products, and from all indications, a greater inclination on the part of American exporters to consider the trade here as worthy of attention, so that two fundamental difficulties of doing business have been largely removed. There are, nevertheless, some further obstacles which need to be taken away; otherwise, our progress will be slow and uncertain. We must secure men on the field, or send men to the field, who will show the goods. This is the way we do with other people, and this is the way other people are doing with Greece, which accounts for our success elsewhere and for their success here. I scarcely believe any other tactics will work.  Merchants like to see and handle the goods, and to expect them to purchase from catalogues or from mere representations is asking more than they are disposed to give.  We must also solve the payment question somehow, either by proving that cash against shipping bills is the best policy for the buyer as well as for the seller, or by creating such a demand for our goods that buyers will prefer them for cash to other goods on credit; or we must do as other countries trading with this market persist in doing—give a discount for cash or a credit of three or four months.  If we can not do either of the former, and are not inclined to favor the latter, the market, in spite of favorable conditions, will remain for us practically what it is at present—undeveloped.

As I have already suggested, we ought to make special efforts to catch a large part of the copper-sulphate trade, since it is one of the most remunerative yearly purchases of the Peloponnesus, reaching the possible figures of almost $1,000,000.  We opened the annual market last spring by bidding in the first order of the Currant Bank at prices which no companies of Europe could better or equal.  The trade, in consequence, should have been ours, if our supplies had been nearer this market.  As it was, however, the demand for this material, a demand which is largely regulated by weather conditions, was heaviest when the season was well advanced, and when ten days time at the farthest had to find the new shipments in hand for distribution to the growers.  Naturally, therefore, with our source of supplies almost thirty days distant, American exporters had to stand aside while the very countries which were unable to compete for the opening order hurried forward tons of sulphate at prices practically of their own making.  In my last annual report, I anticipated a considerably larger trade in this commodity on the part of American shippers, from the success of the small shipment of that year, and comparatively this prediction is fulfilled, as the figures mentioned indicate; but actually, for the reason above stated, it is far from being the case.  So far as I am able to learn, the matter of time was and is the only drawback, and if some place in Europe were made a distributing center, or, more to the point, if a supply sufficient to meet the needs of the Peloponnesus were kept on hand at this port, I see no reason why this very creditable part of the trade of this district should not all be turned our way.  But to accomplish any results for the coming year, steps ought to be taken immediately, or another year may find us looking at the matter from the same point of view, since the season opens early in the spring of each year, and is of short duration.

There are other markets meriting but not yet receiving much attention, possibly for the reason assigned by a Boston journal in commenting upon a recent report from this consulate—that the demands of the home market are such as to center our interests there along certain lines.  Greece is much less fortunate; her demand for the things she produces in greatest quantities are relatively slight, and her need for the things she is unable to produce comparatively great.  Her markets, consequently, are always open to a variety of goods.  Her trade in coal, iron and steel, steel wire, machines, cotton and woolen goods, lumber, heating and lighting apparatus, the cereals, especially wheat, and many things additional, is entirely in the hands of foreign countries, and as soon as American exporters care to turn their attention seriously to it, a share in all this trade will come as naturally and as easily to them as it now flows elsewhere.

In conclusion, I am impelled to add one additional import in which the United States may be considered a heavy contributor, i. e., the import of gold. It is probably true that a stream of American gold, continuous if not large, is pouring into this country from the numerous Greek subjects who are looking for and not infrequently finding fortune in the Western world; and with even more certainty it may be said that a good deal of this precious metal finds its way here by means of the crowds of tourists who annually visit the classic shrines of the Kingdom. Statistics ignore the part which these archæological points of interest play in the economic history of each year, but the annual revenue from this source is noteworthy, both because of its size and because of its wide distribution among the working classes. And the United States may well be proud of the fact that if her imports in other lines are insignificant in comparison with certain European countries, in this respect she properly stands at or near the head of the list.

FRANK W. JACKSON, *Consul.*

PATRAS, *October 31, 1902.*

*Imports at Patras in 1901.*

| | Textures. | Raw metal and metal wares. | Spirits. | Un-dressed lumber. | Mineral water and soft drinks. | Fish, conserves, etc. | Leather and hides. | Wax candles, etc. | Hats, etc. | Arms and ammunition. |
|---|---|---|---|---|---|---|---|---|---|---|
| England | $832,300 | $151,070 | $187 | | $33,637 | $155,411 | | $7,188 | $103 | |
| Germany | 17,590 | 54,775 | 14 | | 17,785 | | $2,351 | 34 | | $222 |
| Austria | 10,638 | 18,186 | 165 | $77,143 | 5,179 | 11,182 | 211 | 3,991 | 340 | 1,355 |
| Italy | 4,354 | 3,984 | 127 | 3,671 | 2,187 | 15,981 | 92 | 856 | 3,017 | 564 |
| Belgium | 2,178 | 77,123 | | | 363 | | 1,290 | | | 264 |
| France | 14,464 | 8,608 | 867 | | 13,847 | 2,679 | 4,218 | 945 | 443 | 600 |
| Switzerland | 1,614 | | | | | | | | | |
| Turkey | 1,209 | | | | 44,452 | 3,832 | | | | |
| Holland | | | | | | | | | | |
| Roumania | | | | | 1,758 | | | | | |
| Bulgaria | | | | | 32,170 | | | | | |
| Russia | | | | | 623,161 | 2,729 | | | | |
| United States | | | | | | | 20,323 | | | |
| All others | | 263 | | | | | | | | |
| Total | 384,347 | 314,009 | 1,360 | 80,814 | 774,539 | 191,314 | 28,485 | 13,014 | 3,903 | 3,005 |

*Imports at Patras in 1901.*

| | Sugar. | Rice, fruits, etc. | Coffee. | Coal. | Copper sulphate and chemical products. | Glass, colonial, and wooden wares. | Oils, etc. | Paper and writing materials. | Divers. | Total. |
|---|---|---|---|---|---|---|---|---|---|---|
| England | $11 | $14 | | $37,500 | $166,174 | $3,923 | $11,662 | $1,210 | $5,976 | $906,366 |
| Germany | | 500 | | | 505 | 8,019 | 344 | 3,110 | 8,057 | 113,306 |
| Austria | 67,076 | 20,324 | | | 2,561 | 13,329 | 896 | 9,874 | 17,033 | 259,483 |
| Italy | 20 | 8,245 | | 72,453 | 2,074 | 1,587 | 110 | 801 | 16,569 | 136,642 |
| Belgium | | | | 26,945 | | 6,211 | | | | 114,374 |
| France | | | | | | 8,215 | 1,852 | 356 | 17,430 | 74,524 |
| Switzerland | | 121 | | | | | | | 2,280 | 4,015 |
| Turkey | | 5,429 | | | | 383 | 226 | | 10,077 | 65,108 |
| Holland | | | | | | 511 | | | 482 | 993 |
| Roumania | | 277 | | | | | | | | 2,035 |
| Bulgaria | | 217 | | | | | | | | 32,387 |
| Russia | | 116 | | | | 152 | | | | 626,158 |
| United States | | | $40,988 | | 8,453 | | | | | 69,764 |
| All others | | 500 | 698 | | | 4,997 | | | 1,486 | 7,943 |
| Total | 67,107 | 35,743 | 41,686 | 136,898 | 179,767 | 47,277 | 15,090 | 15,351 | 79,389 | 2,413,098 |

*Exports from Patras in 1901.*

| | Currants. | Valonia bark. | Figs. | Wine. | Spirits cognac. | Cheese. | Olive oil. | Olives. | Tobacco. | Sundries. | Totals. |
|---|---|---|---|---|---|---|---|---|---|---|---|
| England............. | $1,823,559 | $388 | $978 | $2,365 | $2,457 | | $200 | | $377 | $377 | $1,830,701 |
| United States........ | 662,969 | | | | | $852 | 450 | $1,918 | | 98 | 666,287 |
| France............. | 38,127 | 246 | | | | 60 | 50 | 188 | 27 | 13,782 | 52,480 |
| Germany........... | 834,674 | 7,169 | | 15,615 | | | 1,364 | | 872 | 3,529 | 863,223 |
| Holland............ | 469,773 | | | | | | | | | 84 | 469,857 |
| Australia.......... | 212,751 | | | | | | | | | | 212,751 |
| Austria............ | 92,925 | 16,538 | 796 | 7,233 | 766 | 636 | 950 | 155 | | 63,828 | 183,827 |
| Italy ............. | 8,727 | 14 | | 2,427 | | 2,028 | | 418 | | 13,318 | 26,982 |
| Turkey............. | 9 | 324 | 20 | | 103 | | | 78 | | | 534 |
| Russia............. | 139 | | | 26 | | | | | | | 165 |
| Egypt............. | 238 | | | 181 | | 63 | | 110 | | | 592 |
| Other countries ...... | 1,378 | | | | | 138 | | 10 | | 253 | 1,779 |
| Total........... | 4,145,269 | 24,679 | 1,794 | 27,847 | 3,326 | 3,777 | 3,014 | 2,877 | 1,276 | 95,269 | 4,309,128 |

*Declared exports to the United States for the fiscal year ended June 30, 1902.*

| | |
|---|---|
| Cheese ................................................ | $975.53 |
| Citrons................................................ | 2,728.68 |
| Cognac ................................................ | 249.77 |
| Cordial................................................ | 82.99 |
| Currants............................................... | 1,190,541.21 |
| Figs .................................................. | 4,192.37 |
| Goatskins.............................................. | 97.33 |
| Grapes, sirup of ....................................... | 163.01 |
| Laurel leaves.......................................... | 1,613.73 |
| Licorice root.......................................... | 253.06 |
| Olives ................................................ | 36,123.24 |
| Olive oil ............................................. | 2,576.95 |
| Pepper (red).......................................... | 43.80 |
| Sage leaves........................................... | 1,185.63 |
| Soap ................................................. | 583.25 |
| Vinegar .............................................. | 7.16 |
| Wine................................................. | 885.30 |
| Total....................................... | 1,242,303.01 |

*Exports of currants, seasons 1891-92 to 1901-2.*

| Destination. | 1891-92 | 1892-93 | 1893-94 | 1894-95 | 1895-96 | 1896-97 | 1897-98 | 1898-99 | 1899-1900 | 1900-1901 | 1901-2 |
|---|---|---|---|---|---|---|---|---|---|---|---|
| United Kingdom ..... | 83,500 | 74,000 | 84,200 | 81,000 | 70,000 | 69,000 | 68,300 | 76,200 | 71,500 | 38,200 | 70,500 |
| United States........ | 17,500 | 16,000 | 28,200 | 10,500 | 15,700 | 13,500 | 13,800 | 15,800 | 17,700 | 5,600 | 20,300 |
| North of Europe...... | 21,400 | 19,000 | 34,500 | 28,000 | 37,400 | 34,000 | 27,000 | 43,250 | 45,800 | 8,000 | 37,600 |
| Australia ............ | 1,300 | 1,500 | 900 | 1,300 | 2,100 | 3,200 | 3,700 | 6,000 | 6,800 | 4,100 | 5,800 |
| Canada (direct) ...... | 1,300 | 1,200 | 1,500 | 1,400 | 1,400 | 1,400 | 1,700 | 1,900 | 2,000 | 500 | 1,600 |
| France .............. | 11,500 | 19,500 | 7,800 | 19,500 | 28,000 | 6,700 | 2,400 | 6,850 | 4,500 | 350 | 1,400 |
| Russia .............. | 500 | 500 | 10,500 | 30,600 | 25,400 | 19,500 | | | | | |
| Trieste, Venice, etc .. | 3,000 | 3,300 | 4,400 | 2,700 | 4,500 | 4,700 | 3,100 | 3,500 | 1,700 | 150 | 2,000 |
| Total gross tons. | 170,000 | 135,000 | 172,000 | 175,000 | 184,500 | 152,000 | 120,000 | 153,500 | 140,000 | 56,900 | 138,900 |

*Currant exports from Patras.* a

| Destination. | From commencement of season to December 31— | |
|---|---|---|
| | 1902. | 1901. |
| | *Gross tons.* | *Gross tons.* |
| United Kingdom | 63,500 | 60,400 |
| United States | 12,900 | 15,600 |
| Continent | 26,000 | 24,000 |
| Australia | 4,100 | 3,700 |
| Canada | 2,100 | 1,600 |
| Trieste, etc | 2,350 | 1,700 |
| France | 1,250 | 500 |
| Total | 112,200 | 107,500 |

a At the time this report was made (October 31, 1902) the quantity of currants purchased by the United States for 1902 exceeded that for 1901. This year's sales have since fallen behind the sales of last year for the same period.

*Maritime movement at port of Patras in 1901.*

| Flag. | Number of vessels. | Tonnage. | Personnel. | |
|---|---|---|---|---|
| | | | In. | Out. |
| Sailing vessels: | | | | |
| Greek | 2,897 | 69,796 | 8,976 | 8,947 |
| Italian | 278 | 11,092 | 1,641 | 1,640 |
| Turkish | 11 | 1,300 | 56 | 56 |
| English | 6 | 746 | 35 | 35 |
| Cretan | 6 | 120 | 24 | 24 |
| Austrian | 2 | 63 | 11 | 11 |
| Danish | 1 | 89 | 5 | 5 |
| Samoan | 1 | 206 | 8 | 8 |
| Total | 3,202 | 83,412 | 10,756 | 10,726 |
| Steamers (cargo): | | | | |
| English | 55 | 58,498 | 1,173 | 1,172 |
| German | 17 | 14,827 | 334 | 334 |
| Norwegian | 9 | 6,662 | 166 | 166 |
| Austrian | 7 | 10,403 | 183 | 183 |
| Greek | 4 | 2,880 | 76 | 76 |
| Italian | 2 | 3,458 | 58 | 58 |
| French | 2 | 1,281 | 39 | 39 |
| Belgian | 1 | 1,362 | 25 | 25 |
| Danish | 1 | 940 | 18 | 18 |
| Dutch | 1 | 713 | 23 | 23 |
| Total | 99 | 96,019 | 2,095 | 2,094 |
| Mail steamers: | | | | |
| Greek | 1,374 | 415,672 | 32,628 | 32,562 |
| Austrian | 213 | 291,569 | 10,348 | 10,346 |
| Italian | 146 | 190,109 | 6,883 | 6,883 |
| English | 54 | 79,834 | 1,696 | 1,696 |
| Turkish | 45 | 35,610 | 1,279 | 1,279 |
| French | 31 | 48,830 | 1,563 | 1,563 |
| German | 24 | 26,537 | 606 | 606 |
| Belgian | 6 | 7,261 | 183 | 183 |
| Dutch | 3 | 2,776 | 66 | 66 |
| Total | 1,896 | 1,098,198 | 55,201 | 55,123 |

# ITALY.

### REPORT FROM CONSULATE-GENERAL AT ROME.

The value of merchandise imported into Italy during the first six months of 1902 amounted to 922,556,087 lire ($178,053,325), and the value of exports during the same period was 689,512,554 lire $133,075,923). The first shows an increase of 44,574,699 lire ($8,602,917) and the second an increase of 23,839,710 lire ($4,601,064) over the corresponding period of 1901.

From the preceding figures are excluded precious metals and currency, imports of which amounted to 2,952,800 lire ($569,890) and exports to 5,455,600 lire ($1,052,931), with a decrease of 3,344,800 lire ($645,546) in imports and a decrease of 2,111,500 lire ($407,520) in exports. It is well to remark that there has been an increase in the imports of cotton of 18,000,000 lire ($3,474,000); of coal, 17,000,000 lire ($3,281,000); of horses, 7,000,000 lire ($1,351,000); of wool, 6,500,- 000 lire ($1,254,500); of silks, 15,000,000 lire ($2,895,000); of sugar, etc., 3,000,000 lire ($579,000); and a decrease of 13,000,000 lire ($2,509,000) in wheat and 13,000,000 lire ($2,509,000) in corn.

In the exports, there has been an increase of 6,500,000 lire ($1,254,500) in lemons; of 6,000,000 lire ($1,158,000) in olive oil; of 4,000,000 lire ($772,000) in jute; of 3,000,000 lire ($579,000) in almonds, etc.; and a decrease of 4,700,000 lire ($907,100) in eggs and 3,000,000 lire ($579,000) in manufactured silks.

The above figures are very encouraging, and show a decided revival in the commerce and industries of the country.

The receipts of the Government have also considerably increased during the first six months of the year, and prove beyond doubt a notable improvement in the economic condition of the nation.

HECTOR DE CASTRO, *Consul-General.*

ROME, ITALY, *July, 1902.*

---

## CASTELLAMARE DI STABIA.

I inclose statement of exports to the United States in the year 1901, and in the six months ended June 30, 1902; return of shipping in this district for the year 1901; and return of exports and imports for the year 1901. These last returns are compiled from the records of the custom-houses of Castellamare, Sorrento, and Torre Annunziata—the only ports of commercial importance in this consular district.

The business of this year shows a distinct increase over that of last year. California wheat continues to be imported in increasing quantities and seems to have gained a footing in the market. American coal is not in demand, and though several cargoes were imported in the year 1900, none was received here in 1901, or has been received so far this year, to my knowledge.

During the past summer, there were many more visitors to Castellamare than in 1901, most of them Italians, who come to take the baths and drink the mineral waters for which the place is noted.

Public health is generally good, though there are a few cases of typhoid fever in town.

C. S. CROWNINSHIELD, *Commercial Agent.*

CASTELLAMARE DI STABIA, *October 10, 1902.*

*Exports to the United States, 1901.*

| Articles. | Value. | Articles. | Value. |
|---|---|---|---|
| Bologna sausage | $471.54 | Mosaic | $253.54 |
| Beans | 4,995.76 | Olive oil | 6,306.27 |
| Chick-peas | 833.51 | Oranges | 50,053.45 |
| Cheese | 99,656.64 | Potatoes | 537.82 |
| Chestnuts | 12,440.55 | Salt pork | 1,006.09 |
| Figs | 1,607.61 | Sulphur oil | 180.37 |
| Filberts | 5,050.81 | Semolina | 226.83 |
| Garlic | 3,959.04 | Sundry articles | 3,590.60 |
| Ham | 2,400.31 | Tomato paste | 873.27 |
| Lemons | 111,072.22 | Walnuts | 77,032.52 |
| Long peppers | 873.10 | Wine | 4,239.07 |
| Lupines | 454.88 | | |
| Macaroni | 592,867.68 | Total | 980,483.48 |

*Exports to the United States for the six months ended June 30, 1902.*

| Articles. | Value. | Articles. | Value. |
|---|---|---|---|
| Beans | $184.74 | Sausages | $1,508.26 |
| Cheese | 51,322.84 | Seed | 119.86 |
| Filberts | 1,854.67 | Sundry articles | 781.70 |
| Garlic | 1,544.87 | Tomato paste | 1,528.67 |
| Hams | 2,960.55 | Walnuts | 9,647.80 |
| Lemons | 23,376.69 | Wine | 2,486.17 |
| Macaroni | 322,146.48 | | |
| Mosaic | 106.89 | Total | 535,389.18 |
| Olive oil | 18,306.76 | Total for same period of 1901 | 327,389.51 |
| Oranges | 102,810.63 | | |
| Peppers | 216.60 | Increase | 207,999.67 |

*Shipping in the consular district of Castellamare di Stabia for the year 1901.*

ENTERED.

| Nationality. | Sailing vessels. | | Steam vessels. | | Total. | |
|---|---|---|---|---|---|---|
| | No. | Tonnage. | No. | Tonnage. | No. | Tonnage. |
| British | 1 | 148 | 74 | 99,960 | 75 | 100,108 |
| Italian | 5 | 3,236 | 26 | 34,226 | 31 | 37,462 |
| Greek | | | 39 | 42,635 | 39 | 42,635 |
| German | | | 10 | 13,863 | 10 | 13,863 |
| Dutch | | | 9 | 7,092 | 9 | 7,092 |
| Spanish | | | 3 | 4,688 | 3 | 4,688 |
| French | | | 4 | 3,508 | 4 | 3,508 |
| Norwegian | | | 2 | 2,267 | 2 | 2,267 |
| Swedish | | | 3 | 2,963 | 3 | 2,963 |
| Other nations | | | 6 | 6,082 | 6 | 6,082 |
| Total | 6 | 3,384 | 176 | 217,284 | 182 | 220,668 |

CLEARED.

| | | | | | | |
|---|---|---|---|---|---|---|
| British | 1 | 148 | 74 | 99,960 | 75 | 100,108 |
| Italian | 3 | 1,906 | 26 | 34,226 | 29 | 36,132 |
| Greek | | | 39 | 42,635 | 39 | 42,635 |
| German | | | 10 | 13,863 | 10 | 13,863 |
| Dutch | | | 9 | 7,092 | 9 | 7,092 |
| Spanish | | | 3 | 4,688 | 3 | 4,688 |
| French | | | 4 | 3,508 | 4 | 3,508 |
| Norwegian | | | 2 | 2,267 | 2 | 2,267 |
| Swedish | | | 3 | 2,963 | 3 | 2,963 |
| Other nations | | | 6 | 6,082 | 6 | 6,082 |
| Total | 4 | 2,054 | 176 | 217,284 | 180 | 219,338 |

*Imports and exports in the consular district of Castellamare di Stabia during the year 1901.*

| Articles. | Quantity. | Value. | Articles. | Quantity. | Value. |
|---|---|---|---|---|---|
| **IMPORTS.** | *Tons.* | | **EXPORTS.** | *Tons.* | |
| Coal...................... | 133,150 | $642,448.75 | Building and paving | | |
| Wheat.................... | 63,746 | 3,075,744.50 | stones ................. | 5,250 | $12,665.62 |
| Old rails and scrap iron.. | 8,868 | 149,758.35 | Macaroni................. | 12,217 | 1,178,940.50 |
| Fire bricks................ | 225 | 2,171.25 | Green fruit.............. | 4,500 | 217,125.00 |
| Pipe clay................. | 250 | 1,008.60 | Dry fruit ............... | 500 | 72,375.00 |
| Timber and shooks........ | 5,490 | 52,978.50 | Potatoes ................ | 3,556 | 34,315.40 |
| Cheese.................... | 100 | 19,300.00 | Olive oil................. | 276 | 53,268.00 |
| | | | Wine ................... | 6 | 463.20 |
| | | | Cheese.................. | 460 | 88,780.00 |
| Total ............... | ........ | 3,943,404.95 | Total ............... | ........ | 1,657,932.72 |

## CATANIA.

With the exception of citrus fruits, trade in this district in 1901 was active; crops were large and good prices were realized. The statistics appended show an increase of exports amounting in value to $605,190.68 and a decrease in imports of $204,259.81. It is gratifying to note that the United States did not share in this loss, but on the contrary its shipments to Catania increased over those of 1900 by $97,755.66.

### SULPHUR.

Exports to America show a gain of $125,159.15. This increase is caused almost entirely by the shipments of brimstone—the first shipments from this port in six or seven years—the amount being valued at $112,371.32. It is very probable that large exports of brimstone will be made from Catania in the future—new mines are being opened that are nearer to Catania than Girgenti or Licata, and the difficulty of loading at the latter ports during the winter months will give Catania much of this trade.

The continuation of the contracts with the sulphur mine owners and lessees under the options held by the Anglo-Sicilian Sulphur Company has kept this important industry in a flourishing condition; prices remain firm, and notwithstanding the large decrease of exports this year from those of 1900—93,540 tons—and the increase of stock on hand—291,600 tons, against 219,700 tons the previous year—the company continues to hold the market well in hand.

The greater part of the decrease of exports was to the United States, France, and Italy, amounting to 77,479—29,836, 30,154, and 17,489 tons, respectively.

The menace to the continued prosperity of the sulphur industry is the large stock—nearly 300,000 tons—which the Anglo-Sicilian Company is compelled to carry to sustain the market. Should the export again attain the amount of 1900—550,160 tons—which exceeded production, and should this continue until the end of present contracts—July 31, 1906—the company could leave the field without any stock on hand, or at least with so little that the market would not be seriously affected.

Should the company, at the termination of the period of contract, discontinue business, either by its own wish or by the refusal of the mine owners to renew contracts, and still have so enormous a quantity of sulphur on hand (which of necessity it would be compelled to throw on the market), a crisis would result from which the industry could not recover for years.

## TRADE IN 1902.

### ALMONDS.

The almond crop of this consular district is estimated at about 26,000 bags (shelled) of 100 kilograms. Prices are higher than last season, shelled almonds shipped this year averaging at $19.75 per 100 kilograms (220.46 pounds), as against $14.45 last season. Freight rates were $6.17 per metric ton (2,204 pounds), as against $5.02 last year.

### FILBERTS.

The decrease in exports this year is about one-third from last season, the whole being placed at 18,000 bags of 220 pounds, against 25,000 bags in 1901; but good crops in other parts of Sicily have kept prices from advancing to any appreciable extent. Prices rule at about $11.50 per bag f. o. b. Catania; freight rates 85 cents per bag to New York, as against 48.3 for last year.

### LEMONS AND ORANGES.

The winter crop of lemons is far from being an average one; the quantity will be a third less, and the quality is poor. The lack of rains has caused the decline. No rain fell for a period of nearly five months.

There is every prospect for a large crop of oranges, but at this date it is too early to make an estimate of the size.

### WINE.

The production of wine will be about one-half of last season's crop, which was an unusually large vintage. The estimate for this season is 2,250,000 hectoliters (59,438,250 gallons). The quality will be much superior to that of last season, the long drought and hot summer being especially beneficial to the production of good wine.

### NEW STEAMSHIP LINES.

Commencing this month, the Deutsche Levante-Linie and A. O. De Freitas & Co., both of Hamburg, have inaugurated fortnightly services for Catania; the former to Black Sea and Danubian ports, and the latter to Adriatic ports.

ALEXANDER HEINGARTNER, *Consul.*

CATANIA, *November 6, 1902.*

*Export of sulphur.*

[Expressed in tons of 13 cantars (2,275 pounds).]

| To— | From Catania. | | Total for Sicily. | |
|---|---|---|---|---|
| | 1901. | January 1 to October 1, 1902. | 1901. | January 1 to October 1, 1902. |
| America | 6,860 | 4,817 | 142,509 | 127,367 |
| England | 9,474 | 6,978 | 22,422 | 21,009 |
| Belgium | 1,308 | 3,326 | 7,735 | 8,413 |
| Netherlands | 8,038 | 5,354 | 9,530 | 6,972 |
| Germany | 13,997 | 14,498 | 24,234 | 18,581 |
| Sweden, Norway, and Denmark | 8,325 | 8,114 | 21,882 | 18,886 |
| Russia | 2,178 | 4,843 | 17,064 | 16,735 |
| Spain | 3,140 | 807 | 3,460 | 807 |
| Portugal | 5,458 | 8,532 | 11,331 | 10,577 |
| France | 4,912 | 1,216 | 75,894 | 40,073 |
| Austria | 13,621 | 9,356 | 19,377 | 15,107 |
| Greece and Turkey | 19,641 | 21,208 | 21,582 | 21,280 |
| India | 1,816 | 1,603 | 1,816 | 1,603 |
| Sundries | 2,648 | 4,144 | 6,489 | 11,657 |
| Italy | 54,008 | 24,385 | 71,778 | 37,267 |
| Total | 155,414 | 119,176 | 456,573 | 356,334 |
| Stock on hand | 53,846 | 43,615 | 291,600 | 298,500 |

*Quantity of sulphur exported from Sicily during the last ten years.*

[Expressed in cantars of 75 pounds.]

| Year. | Whence exported. | | | | | Total. | Total in tons of 2,275 pounds. |
|---|---|---|---|---|---|---|---|
| | Girgenti. | Licata. | Catania. | Termini. | Palermo. | | |
| 1892 | 1,700,433 | 799,702 | 1,536,009 | | | 4,036,144 | 310,473 |
| 1893 | 1,990,344 | 936,186 | 1,598,078 | | | 4,524,608 | 348,047 |
| 1894 | 2,271,918 | 777,683 | 1,445,565 | | | 4,495,166 | 345,782 |
| 1895 | 2,152,096 | 789,164 | 1,567,017 | | | 4,508,277 | 346,791 |
| 1896 | 2,236,787 | 970,546 | 1,741,690 | | 49,231 | 4,998,254 | 384,481 |
| 1897 | 2,245,955 | 1,166,666 | 1,603,547 | 108,263 | 242,546 | 5,366,977 | 412,844 |
| 1898 | 2,619,778 | 1,284,869 | 1,658,865 | 55,914 | 159,159 | 5,779,585 | 444,583 |
| 1899 | 2,733,383 | 1,338,393 | 1,989,856 | 83,627 | 138,221 | 6,283,480 | 479,498 |
| 1900 | 3,194,002 | 1,421,191 | 2,266,406 | 81,029 | 189,473 | 7,152,101 | 550,161 |
| 1901 | 2,520,997 | 1,171,716 | 2,020,387 | 52,367 | 169,966 | 5,935,433 | 465,572 |

*Export of asphalt from Sicily.*

[Expressed in tons of 2,240 pounds.]

| Destination. | Port of shipment. | | | | | |
|---|---|---|---|---|---|---|
| | Mazzarelli. | | Syracuse. | | Catania. | |
| | 1901. | Jan. 1 to Oct. 31, 1902. | 1901. | Jan. 1 to Oct. 31, 1902. | 1901. | Jan. 1 to Oct. 31, 1902. |
| Amsterdam | | | | | 3,420 | 2,500 |
| Antwerp | | | | 1,000 | | |
| Boston | 4,800 | | | | | |
| Bremen | 1,000 | 800 | | 700 | | |
| Fiume | | | 1,030 | 300 | | |
| Frankfort | | | | | | 500 |
| Galats | | | | 100 | | |
| Hamburg | 17,360 | 14,006 | 5,500 | 2,500 | 1,050 | 1,900 |
| Leipzig | | | | | | 350 |
| London | 3,600 | 4,100 | 4,600 | 2,835 | | 507 |
| Marseille | | | 1,760 | 370 | 100 | |
| New York | 1,500 | 3,200 | 5,620 | 1,140 | 456 | 50 |
| Pescara | | | | 470 | | |
| Rotterdam | | | 3,050 | 2,300 | 500 | |
| Rouen | | | 4,150 | | | |
| Trieste | 320 | 300 | 460 | 600 | 1,062 | |
| All other ports | | | | | 558 | 163 |
| Total | 28,580 | 22,406 | 26,170 | 12,315 | 7,146 | 5,970 |

Total 1901 ............ 61,896
Total January 1 to October 31, 1902 ............ 40,691

*Movement of vessels to and from the port of Riposto during the year 1901.*

| Nationality. | Sailing vessels. | | | | Steamers. | | | | Total. | | | |
|---|---|---|---|---|---|---|---|---|---|---|---|---|
| | Number. | Tonnage. | | Crew. | Number. | Tonnage. | | Crew. | Number. | Tonnage. | | Crew. |
| | | Registered. | Merchandise. | | | Registered. | Merchandise. | | | Registered. | Merchandise. | |
| **ENTERED.** | | | | | | | | | | | | |
| Italian.......... | 93 | 2,175 | 1,453 | 466 | 311 | 181,374 | 807 | 7,464 | 404 | 183,549 | 2,260 | 7,930 |
| Austrian-Hungarian ........ | | | | | 60 | 55,548 | 13 | 1,645 | 60 | 55,548 | 13 | 1,645 |
| German. | | | | | 1 | 503 | ........ | 14 | 1 | 503 | ........ | 14 |
| British.......... | | | | | 13 | 19,324 | ........ | 353 | 13 | 19,324 | ........ | 353 |
| Total..... | 93 | 2,175 | 1,453 | 466 | 385 | 256,749 | 820 | 9,476 | 478 | 258,924 | 2,273 | 9,942 |
| **CLEARED.** | | | | | | | | | | | | |
| Italian.......... | 95 | 2,231 | 437 | 474 | 311 | 181,374 | 10,612 | 7,464 | 406 | 183,605 | 11,049 | 7,938 |
| Austrian-Hungarian ........ | | | | | 60 | 55,548 | 5,451 | 1,645 | 60 | 5,548 | 5,451 | 1,645 |
| German.......... | | | | | 1 | 503 | 62 | 14 | 1 | 503 | 62 | 14 |
| British.......... | | | | | 13 | 19,324 | 1,797 | 353 | 13 | 19,324 | 1,797 | 353 |
| Total..... | 95 | 2,231 | 437 | 474 | 385 | 256,749 | 17,922 | 9,476 | 480 | 258,980 | 18,359 | 9,950 |

*Movements of vessels to and from the port of Catania during the year 1901.*

| Nationality. | Steamers. | | | Sailing vessels. | | | Total. | | |
|---|---|---|---|---|---|---|---|---|---|
| | Number. | Tonnage. | | Number. | Tonnage. | | Number. | Tonnage. | |
| | | Registered. | Merchandise. | | Registered. | Merchandise. | | Registered. | Merchandise. |
| **ENTERED.** | | | | | | | | | |
| Italian ............. | 901 | 734,162 | 64,685 | 1,949 | 71,336 | 53,594 | 2,850 | 805,498 | 118,259 |
| Austrian-Hungarian .............. | 172 | 136,203 | 5,631 | 1 | 182 | ........ | 173 | 136,385 | 5,631 |
| Belgian ............. | 1 | 876 | ........ | | | | 1 | 876 | ........ |
| Danish ............. | 5 | 3,959 | | | | | 5 | 3,959 | ........ |
| Greek ............. | 29 | 31,377 | 28,677 | 53 | 9,536 | 3,150 | 82 | 40,913 | 31,827 |
| French ............. | 2 | 2,820 | | | | | 2 | 2,820 | ........ |
| German ............. | 76 | 87,165 | 9,708 | | | | 76 | 87,165 | 9,708 |
| British ............. | 140 | 176,243 | 46,711 | | | | 140 | 176,243 | 46,711 |
| Montenegrian ...... | | | | | | | | | |
| Norwegian ......... | 28 | 22,379 | 13,508 | | | | 28 | 22,379 | 13,508 |
| Hollandish ......... | 34 | 23,204 | 683 | | | | 34 | 23,204 | 683 |
| Turkish ............ | | | | 5 | 705 | 115 | 5 | 705 | 115 |
| Roumanian ......... | | | | | | | | | |
| Russian ............ | 5 | 8,370 | | | | | 5 | 8,370 | ........ |
| Grecian Archipelago | | | | 4 | 746 | 90 | 4 | 746 | 90 |
| Spanish ............ | 2 | 3,435 | ........ | 1 | 168 | ........ | 3 | 3,603 | ........ |
| Swedish ............ | 8 | 6,816 | 25 | | | | 8 | 6,816 | 25 |
| Total ......... | 1,403 | 1,237,009 | 169,628 | 2,013 | 82,673 | 56,929 | 3,416 | 1,319,682 | 226,557 |
| **CLEARED.** | | | | | | | | | |
| Italian ............. | 900 | 732,102 | 83,876 | 1,949 | 70,511 | 65,528 | 2,849 | 802,613 | 149,404 |
| Austrian-Hungarian .............. | 171 | 135,825 | 27,312 | 1 | 182 | 270 | 172 | 136,007 | 27,582 |
| Belgian............. | 1 | 876 | 1,832 | | | | 1 | 876 | 1,832 |
| Danish ............. | 5 | 3,959 | 1,602 | | | | 5 | 3,959 | 1,602 |
| Greek ............. | 28 | 30,376 | 1,729 | 51 | 9,092 | 13,820 | 79 | 39,468 | 15,549 |
| French ............. | 2 | 2,820 | 350 | | | | 2 | 2,820 | 350 |
| German ............. | 75 | 86,184 | 19,870 | | | | 75 | 86,184 | 19,870 |
| British ............. | 140 | 176,243 | 22,291 | | | | 140 | 176,243 | 22,291 |
| Montenegrian ...... | | | | 1 | 278 | 400 | 1 | 278 | 400 |
| Norwegian ......... | 27 | 21,657 | 13,954 | | | | 27 | 21,657 | 13,954 |
| Hollandish ......... | 34 | 23,204 | 7,419 | | | | 34 | 23,204 | 7,419 |
| Turkish ............ | | | | 5 | 705 | 110 | 5 | 705 | 110 |
| Roumanian ......... | | | | 1 | 134 | 230 | 1 | 134 | 230 |
| Russian ............ | 5 | 8,370 | 1,662 | | | | 5 | 8,370 | 1,662 |
| Grecian Archipelago | | | | 5 | 874 | 775 | 5 | 874 | 775 |
| Spanish ............ | 2 | 3,435 | 3,220 | 1 | 168 | 83 | 3 | 3,603 | 3,303 |
| Swedish ............ | 8 | 6,816 | 1,791 | | | | 8 | 6,816 | 1,791 |
| Total ......... | 1,398 | 1,231,867 | 186,908 | 2,014 | 81,944 | 81,216 | 3,412 | 1,313,811 | 268,124 |

*Imports and exports of Catania, by articles, for the year 1901.*

| Articles. | Imports. | United States equivalent. | Exports. | United States equivalent. |
|---|---|---|---|---|
| | *Lire.* | | *Lire.* | |
| Spirits, beverages, oils............... | 644,019 | $124,296 | 2,414,625 | $466,023 |
| Colonial goods, groceries, tobacco ............... | 200,669 | 38,729 | 366,337 | 70,703 |
| Chemicals, medicines, rosins, perfumes ............ | 1,145,428 | 221,067 | 1,214,610 | 234,520 |
| Dyestuffs, tanning products ...................... | 265,837 | 51,307 | 26,537 | 5,122 |
| Hemp, jute, cordage ............................. | 49,955 | 9,641 | 8,943 | 1,726 |
| Cotton, manufactures of ......................... | 592,955 | 114,440 | 52,398 | 10,113 |
| Wool, manufactures of ........................... | 424,013 | 81,835 | 38,580 | 7,446 |
| Silk, manufactures of............................ | 39,717 | 7,666 | ............ | ............ |
| Wood and straw.................................. | 1,998,750 | 385,759 | 85,305 | 16,464 |
| Paper and books................................. | 99,201 | 19,146 | 4,395 | 848 |
| Hides and leather................................ | 1,598,751 | 307,594 | 254,332 | 49,066 |
| Minerals, metals, manufactures of................ | 1,290,589 | 249,074 | 10,573 | 2,041 |
| Stone, earthen, glass, and crystal wares.......... | 2,352,052 | 453,946 | 11,715,267 | 2,261,047 |
| Cereals, flour, etc............................... | 5,946,554 | 1,147,685 | 18,121,617 | 3,497,472 |
| Animal products................................. | 601,831 | 116,153 | 199,866 | 33,574 |
| Other articles................................... | 160,124 | 30,903 | 408,335 | 78,809 |
| Total........................... | 17,435,390 | 3,359,241 | 34,921,720 | 6,739,994 |

*Trade of Catania with the United States for the year 1901.*

| Articles. | Imports. | United States equivalent. | Exports. | United States equivalent. |
|---|---|---|---|---|
| | *Lire.* | | *Lire.* | |
| Spirits, beverages, oils ...................... | 416,405 | $80,366 | 196,941 | $38,012 |
| Colonial goods, groceries, tobacco ............... | 129,564 | 25,004 | 49,423 | 9,539 |
| Chemicals, medicines, perfumeries ............... | 10,831 | 2,090 | 60,796 | 11,734 |
| Cotton, manufactures of ......................... | 93 | 18 | ............ | ............ |
| Wool, manufactures of ........................... | 85 | 16 | ............ | ............ |
| Wood and straw ................................. | 212 | 40 | ............ | ............ |
| Hides and leather ............................... | 10,874 | 2,099 | ............ | ............ |
| Fruits and nuts.................................. | ............ | ............ | 1,392,704 | 268,792 |
| Asphalt, sulphur................................ | ............ | ............ | 621,795 | 120,006 |
| Minerals, metals, manufactures of ............... | 1,210 | 234 | ............ | ............ |
| Animals and their products ..................... | 277,762 | 53,608 | 24,813 | 4,789 |
| Total........................... | 847,026 | 163,475 | 2,346,482 | 452,872 |

*Imports and exports of Catania, by countries, for the year 1901.*

| Countries. | Imports. | United States equivalents. | Exports. | United States equivalents. |
|---|---|---|---|---|
| | *Lire.* | | *Lire.* | |
| Austria-Hungary .............................. | 2,867,525 | $253,432 | 9,147,589 | $1,765,484 |
| France........................................ | 453,558 | 87,536 | 1,726,170 | 333,150 |
| Germany ...................................... | 922,070 | 177,959 | 4,668,344 | 900,990 |
| Great Britain ................................. | 3,447,547 | 665,376 | 3,530,522 | 681,394 |
| Greece ........................................ | 519,617 | 100,286 | 1,922,286 | 870,991 |
| United States ................................. | 847,026 | 163,476 | 2,346,470 | 452,872 |
| Holland....................................... | 306,514 | 59,157 | 3,728,396 | 719,580 |
| Turkey ....................................... | 429,508 | 82,895 | 859,189 | 165,823 |
| Spain ......................................... | 4,432 | 855 | 493,565 | 95,258 |
| Russia ........................................ | 5,519,272 | 1,065,219 | 2,075,619 | 400,594 |
| Other countries............................... | 2,088,361 | 403,050 | 4,423,620 | 853,758 |
| Total........................... | 17,435,330 | 3,359,241 | 34,921,720 | 6,739,994 |

*Italy's exports of citrus fruits, 1892 to 1901.*

| Years. | Quantity. | Years. | Quantity. |
|---|---|---|---|
| | *Metric tons.* | | *Metric tons.* |
| 1892 ................................. | 170,462.8 | 1897.................................. | 224,280.6 |
| 1893 ................................. | 197,813.4 | 1898.................................. | 197,055.0 |
| 1894 ................................. | 214,801.1 | 1899.................................. | 239,215.5 |
| 1895 ................................. | 220,687.0 | 1900.................................. | 200,498.2 |
| 1896 ................................. | 237,236.9 | 1901.................................. | 244,432.4 |

*Italy's exports of citrus fruits, by countries, for the years 1900 and 1901.*

| | 1900. | 1901. | | 1900. | 1901. |
|---|---|---|---|---|---|
| | Tons. | Tons. | | Tons. | Tons. |
| Austria-Hungary | 53,428.7 | 67,174.1 | Russia | 17,605.2 | 27,305.6 |
| Belgium | 1,180.6 | 1,454.7 | Norway and Sweden | 2,019.3 | 1,286.9 |
| Denmark | 771.3 | 1,889.8 | Turkey | 4,928.7 | 2,644.4 |
| France | 2,485.4 | 2,774.9 | North America | 44,973.8 | 54,693.9 |
| Germany | 19,604.9 | 20,595.2 | Australia | 2,784.6 | 2,411.1 |
| Great Britain | 37,529.8 | 46,453.9 | Other countries | 4,581.9 | 5,883.9 |
| Malta | 1,854.3 | 2,435.8 | | | |
| Holland | 6,849.7 | 7,428.8 | Total | 200,498.2 | 244,432.5 |

## FLORENCE.

### EXPOSITIONS.

*Horticulture.*—The Royal Tuscan Horticultural Society, aided by the General Government, will hold, in the month of May, 1903, a large national horticultural show, with international sections. The prospectus announces that there will be 286 competitions, of which 191 are national and 95 international, embraced in the following classes:

| Description. | National. | Inter-national. | Description. | National. | Inter-national. |
|---|---|---|---|---|---|
| Plants for conservatories | 70 | 36 | Fresh flowers | 4 | |
| Plants for open air | 70 | 21 | Art and industries pertain- | | |
| Plants for decorations | 25 | | ing to horticulture | | 32 |
| Plants, fruit, etc | 19 | | Horticultural literature | 3 | |

Twenty-two gold medals and some 500 others are to be awarded as prizes.

*Aviculture.*—Connected with the horticultural is to be the avicultural exhibition, including 274 competitions, distributed in 15 classes, viz: Fowls, 63; peacocks, 4; turkey cocks, 7; pharaoh chickens, 7; pheasants (partridges), 32; pigeons, 59; doves, 42; web footed, 44; parrots, 5; foreign birds in cage, 1; Italian birds, 5; foreign birds for parks, 1; stuffed birds, 1; incubation machinery; implements. Applications for space in the expositions are to be made by January 31, 1903.

A limited exposition of pigeons, parrots, etc., was held in May, 1902, with encouraging results.

*Cheese.*—At Reggio-Emilia, an exposition of cheese will be held from the 17th to the 31st of May, 1903. The principal agrarian institutions and the provincial chambers of commerce will confer prizes to promote cheese making. It will be divided into five distinct sections, of which the only international one is intended for the exhibition of machinery, implements, and tools relating to the product of cheese making. The national sections will cover processes by which milk is centrifugalized, and the interprovincial machinery for creameries and products of cheese.

### ORRIS ROOT.

The "Iris Florentina" threatens to become the cause of a crisis in Tuscan industry. The decrease in prices is such as to leave no profit in its culture. Farmers and exporters agree in saying that the actual price, viz, 43 lire per quintal ($8.29 per 220.46 pounds) covers only the expense of production. Ten years ago, the price of orris root was as high as 300 lire per quintal ($57.90 per 220.46 pounds). Orris was a staple production in those days, the yield being from 400 to 1,000 tons. Essence of violet, then produced only from orris roots, is now displaced to a large extent by proprietary preparations. A resident of Carmignano suggests the floating of a company for extracting the orris essence in Florence.

### EXPORTS.

The returns of exports from Florence for 1900–1901 are $1,419,944, against $1,305,986 for the previous year, showing an increase of $113,958.

The exports are steadily advancing, and in the quarter ended September 30, 1902, they were $83,979 above the corresponding quarter of last year. Majolica ware and antiquities are in great demand. Modern paintings are no longer sought after. The trade in salted hides is increasing in importance, and, to a limited extent, that in tallow. Olive oil is now sent to New York more than heretofore.

### IMPORTS.

"American shirtings," so called, are sold in Florence, but the goods are in many cases the output of factories at Bergamo, in Lombardy. The manufacturers consider their product an excellent specimen, but it is not equal to the genuine "American shirtings," which might be introduced into the Italian market.

Two linotypes have been imported by leading firms, and prove very satisfactory. Tools, implements, and machinery from the United States are much appreciated.

In order to compete with European manufacturers, exporters from the United States should remember that it is not so much a question of quality as of terms of payment. The consignee on this side has no opportunity of presenting himself at Genoa or Naples for the clearance of goods ordered. When these goods are not sent in bond to an inland place (which does not often occur, on account of the additional expense), the clearance takes place at a seaport, whence the goods are usually dispatched, by slow conveyance, to the destination. The consignee is prepared to settle at once the expense of transportation, but not to pay for the goods. He should have a fortnight's grace in which to exhibit the goods, and to advertise them if necessary; then he will duly honor the draft. Responsible merchants in Italy prefer this method of transacting business, although the moment the draft is due they are prepared to honor it. Of course, among persons ordering goods from the other side, there are those who would take advantage of the exporter; but merchants with references should have more favorable terms.

The quantity of coal imported in 1901 exceeds that of 1900 by 100,000 tons; that of cotton oil by over $1,300,000, and of timber by over $1,000,000. Imports of tobacco leaves, sulphate of copper, agricultural implements, and firearms are all increasing. Decreases are quoted in canned meats (ham products excepted), cast iron, machinery, and railway cars.

## FEMALE AND CHILD LABOR.

The law enacted June 19, 1902, raises the minimum age for child labor in manufactories, mines, and quarries not underground, to 12 years. Children not under 10, who were already at work previous to the promulgation of this law, are to be allowed to continue their occupation. To prevent trouble, the chambers of commerce are authorized to prohibit the admission of children between 9 and 10 years of age for day work and of those under 15 for night work.

## STRAW TRADE.

The German consul in Florence has reported to his Government that, during the last two years, the straw industry has shown a large development, especially with regard to fancy hats. The cheapest style is generally preferred. Chip, silk chip, bast, and silk laces are the materials most in vogue. Through Marseilles, Hamburg, and Bremen, there are imported barks from Madagascar, Japan, and Reunion as substitutes for the Bohemian bark formerly used. The principal markets for straw goods are North America, Great Britain, France, and Germany.

## IMPORTS AND EXPORTS OF ITALY.

The value of merchandise imported into Italy during the calendar year 1901 was 1,717,592,768 lire ($331,405,404), exceeding by 17,357,103 lire ($3,349,921) that of the year 1900; and the value of goods exported was 1,374,524,896 lire ($265,283,305), an increase of 36,278,643 lire ($71,001,809) over 1900.

The notable increases in imports were 46 million lire ($8,878,000) in wheat, 24 million ($4,632,000) in Indian corn, 23 million ($4,439,000) in silk, 6 million ($1,158,000) in cotton, 9 million ($1,737,000) in combed wool, 4 million ($772,000) in silk tissues, and 3¼ million ($675,500) in jute.

The decreases were 57 million lire ($11,001,000) in coal (partly on account of diminished cost), 16 million ($3,088,000) in machinery, 13 million ($2,509,000) in rough and cast iron, 6 million ($1,158,000) in olive oil, 3 million ($579,000) in iron manufacture, and 3 million ($579,000) in sulphate of copper.

Exports increased as follows: 50 million lire ($9,650,000) in silk materials, 16 million ($3,088,000) in almonds, 13 million ($2,509,000) in olive oil, 8 million ($1,544,000) in silk products, 4 million ($772,000) in grapes and fresh fruits, 3 million ($579,000) in cotton goods, and 2 million ($386,000) in lemons; while there was a decrease of 20 million lire ($3,860,000) in wine, 9 million ($1,737,000) in hemp, 6 million ($1,158,000) in sulphur, 4 million ($772,000) in oxen, 3 million ($579,000) in poultry, and 2½ million ($482,500) in eggs.

## SUGAR AND COFFEE.

In the year 1899, there were four sugar mills in Italy, producing 59,724 quintals (13,166,713 pounds) of "second quality sugar." In the year following, there were thirteen mills, with a production of 231,158 quintals (50,961,292 pounds). In 1901, they increased to twenty-eight, giving 601,254 quintals (132,552,456 pounds), upon which a "fabrication tax" of 67.20 lire per quintal ($12.13 per 220.46 pounds) was assessed. For the year 1902, the production is estimated at 745,000 quintals (164,242,300 pounds).

The Bologna district began with seven factories, with an aggregate of 231,000 quintals (50,926,460 pounds), thus distributed:

| Locality. | Facto-ries. | Quintals. | Pounds. |
|---|---|---|---|
| Bologna | 2 | 102,000 | 22,486,900 |
| Ferrara | 3 | 76,000 | 16,755,160 |
| Ravenna | 2 | 53,000 | 11,684,400 |
| Total | 7 | 231,000 | 50,926,460 |

This represents almost one-third of the entire Italian production.

The quantity of sugar imported in 1901 was 399,635 quintals (88,-103,132 pounds), at an average cost of 27 lire ($5.21) per quintal (220.46 pounds), to which should be added 88 lire ($16.98) duty, making 115 lire ($22.19) per quintal; it was retailed at 1.50 ($0.29) and 1.60 lire ($0.31) per kilo (2.2046 pounds).

The aggregate income from sugar (duty and tax) during 1900–1901 was 75,641,000 lire ($14,598,713).

The quantity of coffee imported in 1900–1901 was 154,377 quintals (34,033,913 pounds), with a duty of 115 lire ($22.19) per quintal, making a revenue of 20,204,310 lire ($3,899,432). The coffee itself was calculated at a value of 130 lire ($25) per quintal, plus the tax, and was retailed at from 4 to 5 lire ($0.77 to $0.96) per kilo, according to the brand.

The population of Italy in 1900 is reported to have been 32,449,774. The yearly consumption of sugar is estimated at 3.023 kilos (6.6645 pounds) per head, and of coffee, 0.475 kilo (1.0472 pounds). The raw sugar imported in 1900–1901, as stated, amounts to 399,636 quintals (88,102,642 pounds), and after adding the native product of 601,254 quintals (132,552,456 pounds), the total amounts to 1,000,880 quintals (220,654,048 pounds), on which there is a duty of 88 lire ($16.28) per quintal.

### AGRICULTURE.

Florence was the first Italian province to start peripatetic lessons and lectures for suppressing plant diseases, destructive insects, etc., with the object of aiding agriculture. Circulating agrarian libraries are now being established in every district. The country looks prosperous in every direction. Farmers are in more comfortable circumstances, perhaps, than in any other part of Italy, therefore contributing but a small contingent to emigration.

The wheat crop has been an average one; the vintage was inferior in quantity, but superior in quality, compared with 1901; the olives do not promise well, as the spring was too wet and the summer too dry.

Small agricultural implements of American manufacture are appreciated here, but agricultural machines are not considered suitable for Tuscan hills, although a few are used on level ground. Oil presses and the like are produced by large manufactories in Florence and Bologna.

## COAL.

The Adriatic Railway Company, with its offices in Florence, spent in 1901 more than $3,000,000 for coal, mostly for American anthracite. The coal consumed yearly by Italian railways and industries involves an expenditure of from 36 to 40 million dollars, 15 millions of which are required by the navy. This sum is said to represent above 5,000,000 tons.

The cost of the American coal is about equal to that of Cardiff in Italian markets, owing to the English export tax. It is well known that good Pennsylvania coal is by no means inferior to the best English kinds. The only fault with American coal, if there be any, is its friability and the dense smoke it emits when used in the same way as Cardiff coal.

It is only a question of time when American coals will displace those of other countries. The trade has progressed remarkably during the past five years, and it is now equal to that of other countries which have been fifty years in this field.

## STRIKES.

The "Pignone Foundry," of Florence, ranks as one of the first Italian industrial establishments of the kind. It gives work to 230 hands. During last summer, there were fewer orders to be executed than usual, and 20 workmen had to be dispensed with for the time being. Grievances were laid before the Chamber of Industry (Trades Union) on the ground that experienced hands were discharged as unfit for work. The attention of the municipal authorities was called to the matter, but in spite of many interviews and conferences, no settlement was made; a strike of all the foundry hands was ordered, and soldiers were called out to watch the premises. After a few days, the workmen, reconsidering the situation and finding they had only the support of the Chamber of Industry to count upon, tried to extend the strike to the metal workers and printers. It spread to cab and tramway hands; provisions were stopped at the gates; bakers and firemen were obliged to cease work. Steps were taken by the municipality, the prefect, and the commander of the army corps for the protection of the city; the artillery, cavalry, and infantry, which were absent at the annual maneuvers, were recalled, and troops were stationed at the various gates of the city. Armed soldiers patrolled the streets. The population was calm and no serious disturbances occurred. The street cars were accompanied by gendarmes, and traffic in the city was resumed.

## THE LOUISIANA PURCHASE EXPOSITION.

The committee of the Louisiana Purchase Exposition has established in Florence headquarters for the encouragement of an Italian exhibit. The following resolutions were adopted by a meeting of the Commercial Association, recently held here:

The Congress of the International and Commercial Associations of Italy, gathered in Florence, being convinced that the market of the United States is most advantageous for the exportation of our artistic and industrial products, therefore of great benefit to the Italian arts and industries; convinced also that the international expositions in the United States are a great means of facilitating and increasing our exports to that prosperous country, invites this Government to recede from its refusal to take part officially in the exposition of St. Louis, and to find, on the contrary, the best means of having Italy represented in the widest and most dignified manner.

E. C. CRAMER, *Consul.*

FLORENCE. *October 14, 1902.*

## GENOA.

### COTTON MANUFACTURING IN ITALY.

I have received from the ministry of agriculture, industry, and commerce an exhaustive report on the cotton-milling industry of the Kingdom, from which I have compiled the following statistics.

The importation of cotton in recent years has increased as follows:

|  | Tons. |
|---|---|
| 1870 | 14,695 |
| 1880 | 47,254 |
| 1890 | 101,736 |
| 1900 | 122,690 |

It is seen that in the past three decades, the imports of cotton have increased from 60,000 bales to 536,000 bales. The imports came mainly from the following countries:

|  | Tons. |
|---|---|
| United States | 93,459 |
| British India | 14,399 |
| Egypt | 6,929 |

The United States furnishes four-fifths of the cotton consumed by Italian mills. The number of operatives in the mills in 1900 was 135,198, classified as follows:

| Description. | Males. | Females. |
|---|---|---|
| Adults | 34,738 | 82,932 |
| Under 15 years of age | 4,358 | 13,170 |

The total number of operatives in 1876 was 53,000. The following table gives other data:

| Description. | 1876. | 1900. |
|---|---|---|
| Power employed: | | |
| Steam...................horsepower.. | 2,990 | 39,245 |
| Water power...................do.... | 9,703 | 33,590 |
| Mills...................number.. | 647 | 727 |
| Spindles...................do.... | 764,862 | 2,111,170 |
| Looms...................do.... | 27,000 | 78,306 |

The value of the output in 1876 was 51,000,000 lire ($9,843,000); in 1900 it was 304,000,000 lire ($58,672,000).

The principal increase in the industry has taken place in Lombardy and Piedmont, and especially around the cities of Milan, Turin, Novara, Como, and Bergamo, which enjoy the triple advantage of abundant and constant water power, cheap labor, and excellent climate.

*Average wages per day.*

| Description. | Amount. | |
|---|---|---|
| | *Lire.* | *Cents.* |
| For men | 2.20 | 42 |
| For women | 1.70 | 33 |
| For children | .80 | 16 |

Labor is still cheaper in southern Italy and in Sicily, but the population in those parts of the Kingdom is not as industrious as that of Liguria, Piedmont, and Lombardy.

It is natural that the best water power in Italy should be found along the streams from the lakes which are fed by the rains and melting snows of the Alps. The water courses which have their sources in the Apennines either diminish greatly in volume or dry up entirely in the summer, because there is no snow even on the highest peaks during eight months of the year, while the eternal beds of snow on the Alps furnish an abundant supply of water for the lakes of northern Italy in the driest and hottest season. Some of these lakes are 1,000 feet deep and 25 miles long, and they lie at varying elevations above the sea, the smaller ones sending their overflow into Maggiore, Como, and Garda, which in turn find outlets into the Po. In location, volume, and constancy, this water power is simply ideal, and goes far to compensate Italy for the absence of coal; in fact, it gives her what the French call "houille blanche," or white coal.

### WATER SUPPLY OF GENOA.

It would be difficult to imagine a more perfect supply of drinking water than that furnished to the city of Genoa. Since the introduction of pure water, there has been a marked improvement in the health of the city. Owing to the peculiar situation of Genoa—lying, as it does, in a kind of shell, sloping seaward from the Apennines to the Mediterranean—and on account of the dense population living along the two streams which run into the sea on the east and west of the city, the water supply was found to be rapidly deteriorating, and a new source was recognized as necessary. The problem was surrounded by physical obstacles which seemed insuperable, but its solution was as successful as it was bold and costly. A reservoir on the sea slope of the mountains being out of the question, the new company, composed of enterprising Belgians, determined to bring the water from the other side of the range, and for this purpose they purchased an extensive area of land on the north and west slopes of the Apennines. This land was wild and sparsely settled at the time, and is now absolutely uninhabited, not even sheep or cattle being allowed to range upon the watershed. Two enormous dams of granite were constructed to catch and confine the water, and then a tunnel, nearly 2 miles in length, was built through the heart of the mountain to conduct the water by gravitation to the Genoa side of the range. The work is a monument to the engineer, Mr. Nicolo Bruno. The first cost is practically the only cost, and the water is entirely pure. It yields about 10,000,000 gallons daily and is used exclusively for drinking purposes, the supply for other uses coming from the two old aqueducts leading from the streams above mentioned.

## THE SIMPLON RAILWAY.

I have recently made a visit to the Simplon, in order to ascertain the character and progress of this stupendous undertaking, whose success or failure means so much for the future of Genoa.

In my report of last March,[a] upon the authority of an American engineer, I stated that such serious obstacles had been encountered in the south side of the tunnel that no progress was being made, and that the location of the line would probably have to be changed.

My examination, on the spot, removed all doubts on this score. The work is progressing rapidly in the tunnel on both sides of the Alps; about 4,000 workmen are employed in the tunnel, and not less than 6,000 on the Italian section of the road between Isella, at the mouth of the tunnel, and Arona, the present terminus of the railway running north from Milan. It is now practically certain that the road will be completed within the estimated time—that is to say, by July 1, 1905— as nearly two-thirds of the tunnel was finished on July 1, 1902, and the worst obstacles have already been met and mastered. The greatest of the impediments was the ever-increasing heat in the tunnel, caused by the growing volume of water, which, although it starts at the summit of the mountain, 6,000 feet above the line of railway, after percolating through beds of limestone, becomes almost boiling hot and flows into the tunnel at a temperature of from 112° to 140° F., rendering not only work but life impossible without resort to artificial means of refrigeration. The engineer, by turning cold air on hot air and cold water on hot water, has reduced the temperature in the tunnel from 140° to 70° F.

The volume of water flowing out of the south end of the tunnel is over 15,000 gallons per minute, and furnishes motive power sufficient not only to work the refrigerating apparatus, but to compress the air by which the drills are operated.

This tunnel, when completed, will be the largest in the world, to wit, 14 miles long, or twice the length of the Mont Cenis and 5 miles longer than the St. Gotthard. The cost of the tunnel alone will be 70,000,000 francs ($13,510,000), an average of nearly $1,000,000 per mile.

### EXCHANGE.

Italian paper currency is steadily approaching par with gold, the depreciation now being only about one-half of 1 per cent. The fluctuations in the relative value of paper and gold now depend largely upon the manipulations of bankers.

### ITALIAN VINTAGE OF 1902.

The gathering of the grapes is now in full progress. Reports from all parts of the Kingdom indicate that the crop is abundant and of exceptional excellence.

I have recently made excursions among the vineyards of Liguria, Piedmont, and other provinces. The abundance, size, and perfection of the grapes are notable.

---

[a] See Commercial Relations, 1901, VII.

## STEAMSHIP LINES.

Communication between Genoa and the United States is not only easy, but frequent. Eight distinct lines of passenger steamers have regular schedules between this city and New York and Boston.

In addition to these passenger steamers, an indefinite number of freight steamers, varying according to the trade conditions and the seasons of the year, ply between Genoa and Pensacola, Norfolk, Baltimore, Philadelphia, New Orleans, Galveston, San Juan, Porto Rico, and San Francisco.

The regular passenger lines are:

| Name of the company. | Flag. | Sailings. |
|---|---|---|
| North German Lloyd | German | Weekly. |
| Navigazione Generale Italiana | Italian | Twice a month. |
| La Veloce | ....do | Do. |
| Hamburg-American | German | Do. |
| Dominion Line | British | Do. |
| Prince Line | .....do | Do. |
| Compania Transatlantica of Barcelona | Spanish | Do. |
| Anchor Line | British | Do. |

The number of bills of health issued from this consulate is second only to the number issued from Hamburg for vessels sailing from the continent of Europe to ports in the United States, and the number of bills of health measures approximately the volume of ocean traffic.

### TRADE.

*Exports declared from the consular district of Genoa to the United States during the year ended June 30, 1902.*

Quarter ending—

| | |
|---|---|
| September 30, 1901 | $210, 437. 01 |
| December 31, 1901 | 254, 183. 83 |
| March 31, 1902 | 193, 333. 61 |
| June 30, 1902 | 245, 653. 65 |
| | |
| Total for year | 903, 608. 10 |
| Total for preceding year | 717, 328. 48 |
| | |
| Increase | 186, 279. 62 |

*Principal articles of export from the consular district of Genoa to the United States during the last two years.*

| Articles. | Year ended June 30— | |
|---|---|---|
| | 1901. | 1902. |
| Cheese | $48,802.26 | $61,981.35 |
| Cotton waste | 27,677.55 | 73.517.60 |
| Gloves | 58,595.40 | 59,420.25 |
| Glycerin | 101,046.28 | 99,809.23 |
| Olive oil | 118,963.42 | 140,342.77 |
| Rice | 60,851.45 | 42,280.86 |
| Wine | 28,235.93 | 45,099.91 |
| Tin sheets | 15,940.21 | 83,363.79 |
| Total | 460,112.50 | 605,765.76 |

*Tonnage and customs receipts of the port of Genoa at end of past three decades.* a

| Year. | Vessels arrived. | | Merchandise discharged. |
|---|---|---|---|
| | Number steamers. | Number sailing vessels. | |
| | | | *Tons.* |
| 1880 | 1,998 | 5,675 | 1,155,763 |
| 1890 | 3,062 | 3,260 | 4,170,383 |
| 1900 | 3,714 | 3,229 | 5,203,201 |

a Obtained from the mayor's office.

Of the imports into Italy from the United States, amounting annually to about $35,000,000 in value, three-fourths are landed in Genoa; 30 per cent for consumption in and near the city and 70 per cent in transit to Lombardy, Piedmont, Switzerland, and southern Germany.

Of the exports from Italy to the United States, amounting annually to about $25,000,000 in value, one-half is shipped from Genoa, and about 92 per cent of this total originates in Lombardy, Piedmont, and other provinces of northern Italy outside of this consular district.

The relative importance of the port of Genoa, as compared with all the other ports of Italy combined, is measured and illustrated by the following table:

| Year. | Customs receipts at Genoa. | | Year. | Customs receipts at all other Italian ports. | |
|---|---|---|---|---|---|
| | Amount. | U. S. currency. | | Amount. | U. S. currency. |
| | *Lire.* | | | *Lire.* | |
| 1870 | 19,220,449 | $3,709,547 | 1870 | 54,001,868 | $10,422,361 |
| 1880 | 38,827,535 | 7,493,714 | 1880 | 86,758,696 | 16,744,428 |
| 1890 | 84,116,515 | 16,234,487 | 1890 | 172,234,586 | 33,241,275 |
| 1900 | 90,551,181 | 17,476,378 | 1900 | 158,746,555 | 30,638,085 |

This shows that Genoa pays nearly one-half of all the customs duties collected at some 80 ports of entry in the Kingdom.

*Exports from Genoa by ocean steamers during the year 1900.*

| Flag. | Tonnage. | Flag. | Tonnage. |
|---|---|---|---|
| Italian | 251,202 | German | 101,408 |
| British | 42,483 | Greek | 1,968 |
| French | 29,965 | Dutch | 6,461 |
| Spanish | 26,311 | Danish | 1,306 |
| Austrian | 11,071 | Norwegian | 750 |

It will be remarked that the imports, in weight, exceed the exports in the ratio of ten to one, and that the imports from Great Britain exceed in weight the exports to Great Britain in the ratio of thirty to one. This great disparity is due to the fact that most of the coal brought into Genoa comes from England, and many coal steamers are obliged to return empty. The same is true of boats bringing cotton and lumber from the United States.

*Imports from ocean steamers at the port of Genoa during the year 1900.*

| Flag. | Tonnage. | Flag. | Tonnage. |
|---|---|---|---|
| British | 1,476,821 | Norwegian | 107,383 |
| Italian | 1,378,112 | Austrian | 84,791 |
| Spanish | 255,826 | Danish | 67,165 |
| Greek | 196,744 | Dutch | 59,052 |
| German | 160,795 | French | 39,901 |

## OPENINGS FOR AMERICAN ENTERPRISE IN ITALY.

*Coal.*—It is certain that the American firm which first establishes itself in Genoa in the coal trade, and handles the business even at a very narrow margin of profit, will in time make money. Four years ago, the importation of our coal here amounted to only 20 tons; the next year the quantity imported was 28,000 tons; the next year 78,000 tons; while in the first half of the current year, notwithstanding the strikes, the imports of American coal have exceeded 65,000 tons. This port requires 2,000,000 tons per annum now, and the demand increases every year. The greater part goes to the interior, to the mills in Lombardy, Piedmont, and Switzerland. Ninety-five per cent of the coal imported here comes from Wales and England.

*Cotton.*—Another field for American enterprise is the establishment of an agency here to import cotton direct from the Gulf and South Atlantic ports. Genoa requires 500,000 bales of American cotton annually. Much of this goes to Liverpool or Havre, where it has to be rehandled and transshipped to Genoa. It goes without saying that direct trade, avoiding intermediaries, would save money for the shipper.

*Elevators.*—American elevators, if once introduced here and elsewhere on the Continent, would quickly and surely supplant the cumbrous, uncertain, and inefficient machines turned out by the factories in Milan and in various parts of France. The houses in this city average seven stories in height. Elevators are greatly needed; the few that are installed were purchased in Milan, and the contrivances are almost comically defective. They take passengers upstairs at a snail's pace, and can not bring them down at all.

*Mill machinery.*—There is a most promising field here for American cotton-mill machinery. Three-fourths of the mills now in operation are equipped with old-fashioned machinery made in France.

*Bath tubs.*—American plumbing supplies, especially modern bath tubs and water-closets, are gaining a foothold on the Continent, mostly in the large hotels. An American commercial traveler tells me that his house has just installed 24 porcelain-lined bath tubs in a new hotel at Stuttgart. This fact alone assures the patronage of American tourists.

*Locks.*—American door locks and keys ought to supplant the grotesque and ponderous concerns found everywhere on the Continent. The key to this consulate is nearly 8 inches long and weighs about half a pound. The transportation of this quaint implement on the person would require a specially constructed pocket, and the key itself might easily be mistaken for a deadly weapon.

RICHMOND PEARSON, *Consul.*

GENOA, *September 23, 1902.*

## LEGHORN.

### GENERAL TRADE STATISTICS.

The value of Leghorn's foreign trade during the year 1901 was $28,865,493, exports amounting to $9,609,167, and imports to $19,256,326. The total is an increase of $3,634,007 over the year 1900. Exports declined slightly, but importations reached a very high point—nearly four million dollars over that of the previous year. The heavy importations of wheat, due to the partial failure of the crop in Italy, account in a large measure for this result.

### TRADE WITH THE UNITED STATES.

In nearly all the more important and usual articles of export to the United States from here, an advance was made during the year 1901 over the figures of 1900. The increase was $247,539.78, in a total exportation of $1,665,532.47. The improvement would be more marked, were it not that, during 1900, the exportations declined far below the normal for several years previous, and the increase in 1901 is simply a return, with a slight addition, to the figures of these years. It is gratifying to note that the importations, which in 1900 had reached a total more than double that of 1899, have still further advanced. It was hardly expected that such would be the case, as it was observed that some of the more important articles of importation from the United States had shown a decided falling off. The large receipts of grain, however, more than offset this decline. A detailed statement of exportations and importations between Leghorn and the United States is given in the tables annexed.

### MARBLE EXPORTS FROM CARRARA.

The declared value of marble shipped from Carrara to the United States in 1901 reached the highest point on record, amounting to $761,812.50, an increase of 30 per cent over the year previous. I am enabled for the first time to give a detailed statement of the quantity and value of marble exports to all the principal countries during 1900 and 1901. From this, it appears that the United States was during the latter year much the largest buyer, purchasing nearly 27 per cent, in value, of the total exported. It is to be noted also that a certain portion of the amount represented as being sold in Italy finds its way to the United States as a manufactured article—statuary, etc. During the first six months of the present year, exportations to the United States have still further increased, amounting to $488,399, and as at present writing, there is no diminution in the shipments, the total for this year may be expected to reach the million-dollar mark. It must be said, however, that this increase is in value rather than quantity, an advance of from 15 to 20 per cent in the price of block and other marble having been made. This rise in price, without considering the large demand, is due mainly to the higher wages now paid in all the different branches of the industry. In the early part of the present year, a strike among the Carrara workmen took place. It at one time threatened to assume serious proportions, but a compromise was fortunately reached on the basis of an average of 8 hours' work per day and an increase in wages of 15 per cent.  Quarrymen now receive from 64 to 71 cents per day; laborers, from 46 to 56 cents; cutters, from 59 to 72 cents; sawyers, from 59 to 68 cents; sculptors, from $1.35 up.  It is generally believed that, because of the concession made, no further trouble will take place for some time.

### MARBLE QUARRIES OF GARFAGNANA.

It has been known for a long time that in the region called "Garfagnana," on the opposite slope of the Carrara mountains, there existed a vast deposit of marble.  The difficulty of access and lack of communication have until now stood in the way of the development of this property.  A Roman company, however, having obtained a concession for nearly all of these deposits, has recently undertaken the excavation of the marble, and several hundred tons have already been quarried and distributed among the various markets.  The quality of the marble is of the finest, the larger percentage being pure white and fully equal in grade to the well-known "Bianco P." of Carrara.  The smaller portion, which is less white, is said to be superior in quality to the "white ordinary" of Carrara, a marble which it resembles closely. The marble is very sound, and blocks of extra large dimensions can be procured.  Some 300 tons have already been sent to the United States, but it is perhaps too soon to judge with what favor this marble will eventually be received there.  The producers are confident that they will be able to compete successfully with the marble of Carrara.  The lack of railway facilities is the most serious drawback to their plans, the nearest accessible shipping point being the Bagni di Lucca, 28 miles distant from the quarries, to which place the blocks must be hauled by ox team.  A branch line from the Bagni di Lucca to Aulla, passing through the Garfagnana region has, however, been authorized by the Government, and once constructed, the quarry owners will be able to place their product on the market more extensively and at a lower price.  The firm of Pisani & Figli, of Carrara and New York, controls the sale of this marble in the United States.

### OLIVE CROP.

Olive oil forms the chief article of export from this district to the United States.  The crop last season throughout Italy was fairly favorable, both as regards quality and quantity.  In Tuscany, where the finest quality of oil is produced, the yield was abundant, but the constantly increasing demand for "Lucca oil" kept prices up, and they were but little if any lower than the previous year, when the yield was more limited.  The southern provinces produce by far the largest quantity of oil, but the quality is not as good as in the north, and much of it is used for industrial purposes.  The total yield in Italy for 1901 is estimated at 159,350 tons, divided among the provinces as follows:

| | Tons. |
|---|---|
| Lombardy | 250 |
| Venetia | 400 |
| Liguria | 10,550 |
| Emilia | 420 |
| Umbria | 12,030 |
| Tuscany | 19,300 |

|  | Tons. |
|---|---|
| Romagna | 6,700 |
| Bari | 33,100 |
| Naples | 30,600 |
| Sicily | 42,500 |
| Sardinia | 3,450 |
| Total | 159,350 |

Olive oil to the value of $1,084,616 was exported from Leghorn during 1901, of which $624,796.26, or 57 per cent, went to the United States. France, which is Italy's best customer for this article, supplies itself largely from the Riviera.

## COAL.

There were received here during 1901, from all sources, 365,815 tons of coal, of which 97 per cent was English; but 5,708 tons came from the United States. The latter amount is less by 4,000 tons than in the previous year. With a difference of about $1 per ton in freight, our producers are evidently not able, under normal conditions, to compete successfully in this market with the English product. The abnormally high prices for Cardiff coal ruling in 1900 enabled them to secure a foothold, but it has not been maintained.

### EXPORTS FOR THE FIRST SIX MONTHS OF 1902.

The declared value of exports to the United States for the first six months of the present year was $836,195.91, a slight decrease from the amount for the corresponding period of the previous year. I regret that I am unable as yet to procure statistics of importation for this period.

JAS. A. SMITH, *Consul.*

LEGHORN, *September 13, 1902.*

---

*Principal articles imported and exported at Leghorn from all countries during the years 1900 and 1901.*

| Articles. | 1900. | | 1901. | |
|---|---|---|---|---|
| | Quantity. | Value. | Quantity. | Value. |
| **IMPORTS.** | | | | |
| Carbonate of soda............cwt.. | 69,819 | $78,151 | 95,450 | $70,427 |
| Coal and coke............tons.. | 364,134 | 2,230,312 | 365,815 | 2,923,729 |
| Coffee............cwt.. | 11,763 | 104,590 | 12,532 | 142,276 |
| Cotton: | | | | |
| Raw............do... | 6,598 | 11,305 | 7,182 | 87,275 |
| Yarn and threads............do... | 270 | 19,631 | 315 | 23,894 |
| Ribbons............do... | 1,395 | 64,334 | 975 | 51,010 |
| Fish, cured............do... | 196,065 | 1,079,398 | 214,642 | 1,323,049 |
| Hides and skins, raw............tons.. | 2,351 | 931,887 | 2,065 | 841,281 |
| Iron, pig and scrap............do... | 7,631 | 163,577 | 9,387 | 219,663 |
| Jute, raw............do... | 1,645 | 120,275 | 1,628 | 138,301 |
| Mineral oils............do... | 3,553 | 157,913 | 3,055 | 135,847 |
| Sugar............cwt.. | 4,069 | 10,993 | 2,972 | 8,029 |
| Sulphate of copper and zinc............tons.. | 3,177 | 395,461 | 4,027 | 517,128 |
| Tobacco, leaf............do... | 11,032 | 3,176,963 | 9,295 | 2,350,786 |
| Wheat............do... | 26,345 | 984,166 | 78,995 | 3,148,697 |
| Wool: | | | | |
| Washed and unwashed............cwt.. | 10,164 | 273,073 | 7,216 | 208,063 |
| Yarns............do... | 161 | 11,368 | 314 | 21,135 |
| Tissues............do... | 961 | 67,059 | 788 | 46,761 |

*Principal articles imported and exported at Leghorn from all countries during the years 1900 and 1901—*Continued.

| Articles. | 1900. | | 1901. | |
|---|---|---|---|---|
| | Quantity. | Value. | Quantity. | Value. |
| **EXPORTS.** | | | | |
| Boracic acid..............................tons.. | 1,692 | $123,686 | 2,010 | $146,815 |
| Borax.....................................do... | 286 | 22,643 | 85 | 3,129 |
| Candied fruit..............................cwt.. | 46,910 | 741,479 | 32,192 | 516,778 |
| Coral, worked..........................pounds.. | 29,453 | 458,190 | 30,136 | 429,269 |
| Eggs.....................................cwt.. | 5,313 | 68,223 | 4,062 | 56,183 |
| Hemp, raw...............................tons.. | 10,643 | 1,588,109 | 6,761 | 1,162,139 |
| Hides and skins, raw......................do... | 4,412 | 1,227,277 | 4,717 | 1,298,314 |
| Marble and alabaster: | | | | |
| Blocks.................................do... | 16,013 | 179,603 | 15,337 | 182,220 |
| Worked ...............................do... | 11,979 | 498,898 | 12,884 | 521,829 |
| Mercury...................................cwt.. | 5,016 | 223,764 | 5,801 | 343,852 |
| Olive oil..................................do... | 62,721 | 748,430 | 89,358 | 1,084,616 |
| Pumice stone, limestones, etc ............tons.. | 862 | 4,257 | 537 | 3,182 |
| Rags, mixed..............................do... | 2,429 | 219,356 | 1,516 | 119,346 |
| Siena earth...............................do... | 1,159 | 22,896 | 1,172 | 126,012 |
| Straw hats..............................number.. | 380,882 | 148,267 | 278,520 | 106,488 |
| Wax......................................cwt.. | 2,787 | 77,162 | 2,362 | 69,994 |
| Wine: | | | | |
| In barrels............................gallons.. | 139,850 | 33,651 | 111,237 | 147,343 |
| In flasks and bottles...................number.. | 613,553 | 184,780 | 659,438 | 198,767 |

*Total value of imports and exports at the port of Leghorn, during the years 1900 and 1901.*

| Years. | Value. | | |
|---|---|---|---|
| | Imports | Exports. | Total value. |
| 1900............................................ | $15,347,053 | $9,884,433 | $25,231,486 |
| 1901............................................ | 19,256,326 | 9,609,167 | 28,865,493 |
| Increase ................................... | .............. | .............. | 3,634,007 |

*Value of declared exports from the consular district of Leghorn to the United States during the years ended December 31, 1900 and 1901.*

| Articles. | Value in U. S. gold. | |
|---|---|---|
| | 1900. | 1901. |
| Alabaster work ............................................. | $12,449.80 | $14,794.57 |
| Anchovies ................................................. | 10,534.11 | 12,645.55 |
| Antimony.................................................. | 13,750.40 | 50,940.31 |
| Aniseed ................................................... | 71.45 | .............. |
| Argols..................................................... | 181,757.83 | 116,170.18 |
| Beans..................................................... | 49,269.75 | 82,592.30 |
| Beeswax................................................... | 3,841.60 | 1,969.87 |
| Books ..................................................... | 2,208.45 | 872.13 |
| Boracic acid ............................................... | 17,388.64 | 22,250.05 |
| Brier wood................................................. | 39,862.20 | 48,490.55 |
| Castor oil ................................................. | 288.52 | .............. |
| Chalk ..................................................... | 168.74 | |
| Cheese .................................................... | 140,891.85 | 178,859.96 |
| Citron; | | |
| Candied.............................................. | 6,839.32 | 15,061.62 |
| In brine.............................................. | 10,391.45 | 3,481.68 |
| Fruits (dry)............................................... | 14,791.66 | 15,549.12 |
| Furniture.................................................. | .............. | 2,944.08 |
| Glue ...................................................... | 326.80 | |
| Glycerin .................................................. | 17,017.80 | 30,195.65 |
| Herbs (dry)................................................ | 3,644.13 | 5,465.53 |
| Hemp...................................................... | 33,041.41 | 29,885.26 |
| Hides: | | |
| Dry................................................... | 490.20 | 9,470.10 |
| Salted................................................ | 243.18 | 2,580.22 |
| Iron ore................................................... | 53,001.66 | .............. |
| Juniper berries ............................................ | 5,516.21 | 8,338.96 |
| Laurel leaves .............................................. | .............. | 122.79 |
| Liquors ................................................... | 229.47 | 324.33 |
| Macaroni .................................................. | 4,592.16 | 3,879.34 |

*Value of declared exports from the consular district of Leghorn to the United States during the years ended December 31, 1900 and 1901—Continued.*

| Articles. | Value in U.S. gold. | |
|---|---|---|
| | 1900. | 1901. |
| Marble: | | |
| Blocks | $25,907.49 | $7,815.85 |
| Worked | 155.85 | ............ |
| Slabs. | 575.92 | ............ |
| Cubes | 120.63 | ............ |
| Medicines | 257.41 | 1,516.98 |
| Mushrooms | 3,891.44 | 2,971.56 |
| Olive oil | 410,364.60 | 624,796.26 |
| Olive nuts | 2,673.82 | 7,320.40 |
| Orris root | 19,678.44 | 18,213.33 |
| Paintings | 1,157.32 | 73.15 |
| Pumice stone | 11,336.67 | 7,004.11 |
| Rags | 67,358.24 | 40,461.95 |
| Rice | 2,096.13 | 2,236.15 |
| Sausages | 1,358.30 | 548.19 |
| Siena earth | 6,080.79 | 8,084.93 |
| Soap | 160,457.56 | 164,334.53 |
| Soap stock | 51,692.42 | 88,237.64 |
| Talc | 417.10 | ............ |
| Umber earth | 11,448.76 | 12,108.74 |
| Wool | 598.52 | 257.59 |
| Wine | 15,363.77 | 20,571.73 |
| Miscellaneous | 2,452.72 | 2,075.74 |
| Total | 1,417,992.69 | 1,665,582.47 |

Increase, $247,539.78.

*Imports at the port of Leghorn from the United States during the years 1900 and 1901.*

| Articles. | 1900. | | 1901. | |
|---|---|---|---|---|
| | Quantity. | Value. | Quantity. | Value. |
| Bicycles .....................Number.. | 7 | $405.30 | 1 | $48.25 |
| Cotton-seed oil.................kilos.. | 1,224,154 | 166,734.05 | 1,478,756 | 202,683.93 |
| Copper, brass, and bronze.............do... | 1,769,647 | 659,073.42 | 649,730 | 213,480.81 |
| Coal.............do... | 9,749,207 | 78,832.40 | 5,708,000 | 84,150.96 |
| Corn.............do... | 1,928,834 | 44,652.48 | | |
| Greases.............do... | 166,075 | 22,856.56 | 59,960 | 8,125.54 |
| Gum and resins .............do... | | | 156,219 | 4,311.86 |
| Hides.............do... | 9,443 | 10,488.96 | | |
| Lard .............do... | 3,818 | 921.00 | | |
| Lead .............do... | | | 106,287 | 6,564.28 |
| Medicines.............do... | | | 24,634 | 7,837.61 |
| Mineral phosphates.............do... | 11,151,167 | 129,128.58 | 3,300,000 | 35,029.50 |
| Meats, salted and smoked .............do... | 2,664 | 1,259.62 | | |
| Machinery .............do... | 65,909 | 18,852.76 | 65,099 | 14,428.62 |
| Olive oil.............do... | 2,375 | 467.44 | 2,972 | 690.81 |
| Oxide of lead .............do... | 20,730 | 1,880.39 | 15,162 | 1,755.77 |
| Optical instruments.............do... | 713 | 4,128.27 | 89 | 515.31 |
| Oats .............do... | 842,706 | 29,250.08 | | |
| Petroleum.............do... | 1,541,758 | 65,570.97 | 1,875,894 | 76,840.57 |
| Paraffin .............do... | 883,091 | 149,983.95 | 962,930 | 104,831.83 |
| Sulphate of copper.............do... | 978,074 | 125,401.36 | 1,582,163 | 167,946.60 |
| Staves.............do... | 208,236 | 8,028.80 | | |
| Tobacco.............do... | 11,207,721 | 2,768,755.41 | 9,434,290 | 2,494,520.62 |
| Varnishes .............do... | 12,857 | 3,722.00 | 10,996 | 3,183.34 |
| Wood in the log .............do... | 175,000 | 2,026.50 | 2,838,600 | 71,220.48 |
| Wood, squared and sawed .............do... | 4,802,250 | 8,341.07 | 227,250 | 39,473.33 |
| Wheat.............do... | 1,463,213 | 61,790.88 | 26,841,776 | 939,758.46 |
| Wheat flour .............do... | | | 29,550 | 1,653.92 |
| Miscellaneous.............do... | | 9,525.63 | | 23,317.79 |
| Total | ............ | 4,367,077.78 | ............ | 4,452,320.19 |

Increase, $85,242.41.

*Value of declared exports from the consular district of Carrara to the United States during the years 1900 and 1901.*

| Articles. | Value in United States gold. | |
|---|---|---|
| | 1900. | 1901. |
| Alabaster works | $4,339.75 | $1,947.15 |
| Breccia blocks | 5,119.35 | 5,294.40 |
| Bronzes | 57.90 | 463.20 |
| Furniture | 260.55 | 182.00 |
| Machinery | | 1,051.35 |
| Mushrooms | | 623.30 |
| Marble: | | |
| Blocks | 460,246.20 | 596,995.75 |
| Worked | 23,500.10 | 19,699.30 |
| Statuary | 41,220.55 | 47,465.00 |
| Slabs | 41,246.25 | 60,998.80 |
| Tiles | 1,420.40 | 12,341.30 |
| Cubes | 8,073.15 | 12,804.70 |
| Chippings | 682.10 | 324.75 |
| Dust | 14.50 | |
| Waste | | 580.80 |
| Olive oil | 19.60 | 14.50 |
| Pumice stone | 386.00 | 656.20 |
| Ropes | 38.50 | 94.20 |
| Wine | | 280.80 |
| Miscellaneous | 90.70 | |
| Total | 586,715.60 | 761,812.50 |

Increase, $175,096.90.

*Shipping at the port of Leghorn during the year 1901.*

### ENTERED.

| Nationality. | Sailing. | | Steam. | | Total. | |
|---|---|---|---|---|---|---|
| | Number. | Tons. | Number. | Tons. | Number. | Tons. |
| British | 10 | 1,167 | 327 | 451,315 | 337 | 452,482 |
| Italian | 3,003 | 171,772 | 1,067 | 947,156 | 4,070 | 1,118,928 |
| Austro-Hungarian | 4 | 933 | 9 | 13,988 | 13 | 14,921 |
| Dutch | | | 43 | 34,820 | 43 | 34,820 |
| French | 2 | 796 | 161 | 103,674 | 163 | 104,469 |
| German | | | 54 | 57,863 | 54 | 57,863 |
| Greek | 7 | 2,345 | 21 | 26,669 | 28 | 29,014 |
| Norwegian | 5 | 522 | 23 | 20,431 | 28 | 20,953 |
| Swedish | | | 18 | 17,009 | 18 | 17,009 |
| Other countries | | | 60 | 59,371 | 60 | 59,371 |
| Total | 3,031 | 177,534 | 1,783 | 1,782,356 | 4,814 | 1,909,890 |
| Total, 1900 | 2,962 | 156,565 | 1,785 | 1,684,389 | 4,747 | 1,839,954 |

### CLEARED.

| Nationality. | Sailing. | | Steam. | | Total. | |
|---|---|---|---|---|---|---|
| | Number. | Tons. | Number. | Tons. | Number. | Tons. |
| British | 9 | 1,030 | 328 | 450,677 | 337 | 451,707 |
| Italian | 3,007 | 159,717 | 1,089 | 983,583 | 4,096 | 1,143,300 |
| Austro-Hungarian | 3 | 399 | 9 | 13,988 | 12 | 14,387 |
| Dutch | | | 43 | 34,820 | 43 | 34,820 |
| French | 2 | 796 | 161 | 103,674 | 163 | 104,469 |
| German | | | 54 | 57,863 | 54 | 57,863 |
| Greek | 7 | 2,345 | 21 | 26,669 | 28 | 29,014 |
| Norwegian | 4 | 404 | 23 | 20,431 | 27 | 20,835 |
| Swedish | | | 18 | 17,009 | 18 | 17,009 |
| Other countries | 6 | 1,769 | 34 | 42,856 | 40 | 44,625 |
| Total | 3,038 | 166,459 | 1,780 | 1,751,630 | 4,818 | 1,918,089 |
| Total, 1900 | 2,955 | 155,401 | 1,796 | 1,694,108 | 4,751 | 1,849,509 |

*Exchange at Leghorn for the years 1900 and 1901.*

| 1900. | Value United States gold dollars in currency. | Value Italian currency lire in gold. | 1901. | Value United States gold dollars in currency. | Value Italian currency lire in gold. |
|---|---|---|---|---|---|
| January 31 ............... | 107.15 | 18.00 | January 31............... | 105.85 | 18.02 |
| February 28............... | 106.58 | 18.01 | February 28............... | 105.40 | 18.08 |
| March 31.................. | 106.98 | 18.00 | March 31.................. | 105.50 | 18.02 |
| April 30 .................. | 106.13 | 18.01 | April 30.................. | 105.40 | 18.08 |
| May 31 ................... | 106.08 | 18.01 | May 31.................... | 105.40 | 18.08 |
| June 30 .................. | 105.98 | 18.02 | June 30 .................. | 104.45 | 18.04 |
| July 31 .................. | 106.63 | 18.00 | July 31 .................. | 104.43 | 18.04 |
| August 31................. | 106.38 | 18.01 | August 31 ................ | 104.10 | 18.05 |
| September 30 ............. | 106.73 | 18.00 | September 30 ............. | 103.10 | 18.07 |
| October 31................ | 105.63 | 18.02 | October 31 ............... | 102.68 | 18.08 |
| November 30 ............. | 105.58 | 18.02 | November 30.............. | 102.10 | 18.09 |
| December 31 ............. | 105.38 | 18.03 | December 31 ............. | 101.45 | 19.00 |

*Exports from the port of Leghorn to the United States, for the first six months of the years 1901 and 1902.*

| Articles. | Value. 1901. | 1902. | Articles. | Value. 1901. | 1902. |
|---|---|---|---|---|---|
| Alabaster works .......... | $4,446.05 | $3,981.59 | Macaroni................ | $3,326.75 | $108.99 |
| Anchovies ................. | 379.55 | 1,186.99 | Marble: | | |
| Aniseed .................... | | 80.87 | Blocks............... | 2,902.12 | 10,070.25 |
| Antimony ................. | 20,857.24 | 15,438.50 | Worked ............ | | 66.00 |
| Argols .................... | 80,702.92 | 69,044.46 | Medicines ............. | 1,154.58 | 1,063.25 |
| Beans .................... | 31,092.11 | 11,050.00 | Mushrooms............. | 1,867.74 | 612.10 |
| Beeswax .................. | 1,062.97 | 2,088.17 | Olive oil.............. | 355,330.00 | 364,086.71 |
| Books..................... | 346.15 | 1,170.49 | Olive nuts............. | 2,064.89 | 4,324.12 |
| Boracic acid .............. | 9,232.99 | 14,014.80 | Orris root............. | 7,089.79 | 19,132.89 |
| Brier wood ............... | 26,890.66 | 34,823.58 | Paintings............. | 73.15 | |
| Cheese ................... | 53,727.64 | 64,820.25 | Pumice stone.......... | 5,786.22 | 3,171.54 |
| Citron: | | | Rags.................. | 14,623.33 | 35,153.25 |
| Candled ............... | 2,603.04 | 7,112.47 | Rice.................. | 1,050.50 | 690.60 |
| In brine .............. | 3,441.44 | | Sausages.............. | 80.48 | 625.55 |
| Fruits (dry) .............. | 6,626.98 | 5,730.48 | Sienna earth .......... | 2,881.68 | 6,803.88 |
| Furniture ................. | 2,099.45 | 2,204.17 | Soap.................. | 76,328.85 | 91,992.07 |
| Glue ...................... | | 250.57 | Soap stock............ | 57,579.59 | 20,669.82 |
| Glycerin .................. | 18,956.14 | 10,852.13 | Umber earth .......... | 6,697.99 | 6,294.85 |
| Herbs (dry)............... | 2,283.43 | 2,144.59 | Wool ................. | 158.22 | |
| Hemp..................... | 28,104.86 | 4,114.92 | Wine ................. | 7,931.35 | 15,567.68 |
| Hides (dry) ............... | 2,580.22 | | Miscellaneous .......... | 577.48 | 2,790.85 |
| Juniper berries ........... | 1,796.04 | 1,862.12 | | | |
| Laurel leaves.. ........... | 122.79 | | Total ............. | 843,030.83 | 836,195.91 |
| Liquors .................. | 179.20 | 100.26 | | | |

Decrease, $6,834.92.

*Exports from Carrara to the United States for the first six months of the years 1901 and 1902.*

| Articles. | Value. 1901. | 1902. | Articles. | Value. 1901. | 1902. |
|---|---|---|---|---|---|
| Alabaster statuary ....... | $562.10 | .......... | Machinery ............. | $288.60 | .......... |
| Breccia blocks ........... | 1,698.40 | $1,586.43 | Macaroni............... | .......... | $76.00 |
| Bronze works ............ | 463.20 | .......... | Mushrooms............. | 623.30 | .......... |
| Furniture ................ | 182.00 | .......... | Olive oil............... | 14.50 | .......... |
| Marble: | | | Pumice stone........... | 656.20 | .......... |
| Blocks................ | 256,356.25 | 390,080.50 | Ropes ................. | 49.20 | 37.80 |
| Chips................. | 324.75 | .......... | Wine ................. | 145.70 | 191.00 |
| Cubes .. ............. | 4,682.80 | 5,004.57 | | | |
| Slabs................. | 25,078.70 | 54,647.10 | Total .............. | 325,247.40 | 488,399.00 |
| Statuary.............. | 22,666.60 | 22,604.10 | | | |
| Tiles.................. | 4,557.20 | 2,553.00 | | | |
| Worked ...... ...... | 6,897.90 | 11,618.50 | | | |

Increase, $163,151.60.

*Quantity and value of marble exported from the districts of Massa and Carrara during the years 1900 and 1901.*

| Countries. | Blocks. | Slabs. | Worked. | Total. | Value in United States currency. |
|---|---|---|---|---|---|
| **1900.** | *Tons.* | *Tons.* | *Tons.* | *Tons.* | |
| France and colonies............ | 25,894 | 5,709 | 3,773 | 35,376 | $530,640 |
| England and colonies............ | 7,555 | 17,302 | 11,617 | 36,474 | 688,980 |
| Germany............ | 17,535 | 6,072 | 559 | 24,166 | 363,200 |
| Switzerland............ | 1,791 | 868 | 41 | 2,700 | 36,300 |
| Sweden and Norway............ | 58 | 1,060 | 41 | 1,159 | 17,350 |
| Holland............ | 2,031 | 1,357 | 134 | 3,522 | 52,830 |
| Belgium............ | 6,586 | 1,207 | 447 | 8,240 | 112,200 |
| Austria-Hungary............ | 3,673 | 4,487 | 199 | 8,359 | 125,400 |
| Russia............ | 1,882 | 1,993 | 329 | 4,204 | 63,000 |
| Denmark............ | 112 | 1,473 | 15 | 1,600 | 24,000 |
| Spain............ | 2,740 | 270 | 87 | 3,097 | 35,600 |
| Portugal............ | 130 | 388 | 4 | 522 | 7,800 |
| United States............ | 27,375 | 12,268 | 2,253 | 41,896 | 586,715 |
| Greece............ | ...... | 95 | 12 | 107 | 1,600 |
| Turkey and dominions............ | 223 | 1,783 | 869 | 2,875 | 46,000 |
| Central and South America............ | 212 | 2,900 | 984 | 4,136 | 62,000 |
| Other countries ............ | 243 | 319 | 348 | 910 | 13,600 |
| Total foreign exportations............ | 98,040 | 59,641 | 21,662 | 179,343 | 2,767,195 |
| Italy............ | 32,791 | 22,948 | .......... | 55,739 | 580,500 |
| Total............ | 130,831 | 82,589 | 21,662 | 235,082 | 3,347,695 |
| **1901.** | | | | | |
| France and colonies............ | 29,922 | 5,384 | 2,102 | 37,418 | 523,900 |
| England and colonies............ | 5,045 | 16,805 | 8,414 | 30,264 | 465,500 |
| Germany............ | 20,187 | 8,360 | 447 | 28,994 | 423,000 |
| Switzerland............ | 1,087 | 511 | 22 | 1,620 | 24,500 |
| Sweden and Norway............ | 56 | 120 | 424 | 600 | 9,200 |
| Holland............ | 2,254 | 1,110 | 178 | 3,542 | 52,000 |
| Belgium............ | 8,208 | 1,635 | 291 | 10,184 | 136,000 |
| Austria-Hungary............ | 3,576 | 2,933 | 109 | 6,618 | 92,600 |
| Russia............ | 679 | 1,453 | 66 | 2,198 | 31,200 |
| Denmark............ | 128 | 270 | 47 | 445 | 6,200 |
| Spain............ | 6,196 | .......... | 55 | 6,251 | 70,000 |
| Portugal............ | 510 | 80 | 8 | 598 | 9,000 |
| United States of America............ | 34,458 | 7,673 | 1,510 | 43,641 | 761,812 |
| Greece............ | .......... | 2 | 1 | 3 | 58 |
| Turkey and dominions............ | 88 | 462 | 63 | 563 | 8,000 |
| Central and South America............ | 1,171 | 6,201 | 939 | 8,311 | 125,000 |
| Other foreign countries ............ | 11 | 30 | 189 | 230 | 3,500 |
| Total to foreign countries............ | 113,526 | 53,029 | 14,875 | 181,430 | 2,741,470 |
| Italy............ | 21,735 | 19,815 | .......... | 46,550 | 492,730 |
| Total............ | 140,261 | 72,844 | 14,875 | 227,980 | 3,234,200 |

## MILAN.

Milan is often described by Italians as the "moral capital" of Italy. Its claims to the title arise from the fact of its being the commercial and industrial center of the kingdom. It is certainly nothing if not active, industrious, and enterprising; so much so, in fact, that there is little here to remind a visitor of Italian life as found in other parts of Italy.

In comparison with certain cities of the United States, Milan may fall somewhat short of the standard, but if the comparison be made with European cities or other Italian cities, then its progress becomes very marked indeed. The public services are conducted in a more progressive spirit than formerly; here and there is noticeable amelioration.

The railway services furnish a striking illustration of the good and bad; the new lines, with their respective rolling stock, forming a remarkable contrast to the old. Street lighting also has recently been improved by a considerable augmentation in the number of street lamps, which, from first to last, are now furnished with incandescent burners.

Tap water supply is extending, doing away almost entirely with the pump system, and within a prescribed period all houses, including those in the old parts of the city, must be provided with the good water from the city mains. These old houses, at least the exteriors, must be kept in a state of repair, and one sees many blocks which have been, in accordance with municipal orders, whitewashed and generally trimmed up.

All new houses are being built with modern improvements, including bath rooms, better sanitary arrangements, electric lights, and lifts. A great number of large tenement blocks are being erected in the suburbs, and, divided into well-appointed apartments, form very attractive residences.

A new street, which has just been opened for public traffic, has proved a great acquisition to the city, providing a short and much desired means of communication between the two busiest parts of the town.

## THE MILAN EXPOSITION OF 1904.

The preparations for this important exposition seem to be in abeyance. Even committee work appears to have been suspended, so that it is not possible, at this date, to give any outline of what has been done. The project was to hold an international industrial and art exhibition in the year 1904, in celebration of the completion of the new tunnel from Isella (Italian side) to Brigue (Swiss side). This tunnel is to form part of the new railway route from Italy to the north.

It was anticipated that the excavation work would be finished by that time, inasmuch as the boring from both ends had been carried on successfully. However, obstacles have arisen on account of the unexpected presence of large quantities of water, and for this reason, the work of excavation will require more time.

It is therefore a question whether the exposition will not be postponed until 1905. The matter is causing much dissension in this city. However it may result, there is at present no tangible evidence of any preparation being made for this important exposition, which is planned to be the best ever held in Milan.

## A NEW ELECTRIC RAILWAY.

In September, after several months' delay on account of defects which only became patent when put into actual service, the new electric railway between Lecco-Sondrio-Chiavenna was successfully inaugurated for passenger and freight service.

This new electric service, on the overhead-wire system, is run on the existing rails of the Adriatic Railway Company. The line has been selected only on account of the presence of hydraulic force with which to generate the necessary electric energy, as the road itself presents a combination of technical difficulties almost insuperable. The numerous tunnels, sudden and narrow curves, and awkward declivities which make up this road along the lake shore, and through the valleys known as the "Valtellina" as far as Chiavenna, have provided a field for experiment of no mean order.

The alternating normal current produced is 20,000 volts, which is rendered operative, and at the same time less perilous, by fixed transformers at 9 under-stations along different parts of the line. These transformers, of 450 kilowatt each, were built by Ganz & Co., of Budapest, as were also the several groups of powerful generators of 2,000 horsepower each.

The cars used on the new line are built with every comfort and luxury, and are well adapted to carry passengers of the tourist class, who frequent this route throughout the season.

The rolling stock consists of 5 cars for fast service, 5 for slow service, and 2 locomotives for freight cars. Each passenger car is divided into smoking and nonsmoking compartments, with baggage and toilet rooms.

The speed established for the through cars is 37 miles an hour and that for the slow or local service 18½ miles.

The success of this new venture, following so soon on that of the electric railway between Milan and Porto Ceresio, on the Lake of Lugano, which is on the third-rail system, has encouraged the company to commence work on a scheme for extending the Lecco line as far as Milan. Such a work will present much less technical difficulty, and would prolong the distance now covered, which is something like 94 miles, to a total distance from Chiavenna to Milan of 130 miles.

### MUNICIPAL FINANCE.

A brief notice of the receipts and disbursements of the city of Milan for the year 1901 may be of some interest. The total receipts resulting from all local taxation amounted to $4,926,420. The most remunerative of these taxes is the entrance tax, which is levied on articles of consumption passing in through the tollgates or the customs boundaries of the city. Within recent years, these boundaries have been extended to embrace most of the suburbs, so that receipts have correspondingly increased.

Among other important sources of revenue are the tramways, the gas consumption, and the habitation tax. The tax paid by the tramways alone was $245,000.

Of the above-mentioned sum of $4,926,420, the following amounts (extraordinary expenditures) have been disbursed on city improvements:

| | |
|---|---:|
| Continuation of city drainage | $159,849 |
| Laying down tap water in parts of city | 73,678 |
| Slaughterhouse improvements | 65,335 |
| Public laundries | 6,815 |
| Sanitary building | 9,650 |
| Street expenditure | 188,298 |
| Cooperation in excavation of Simplon Tunnel | 39,047 |
| New elementary schools | 159,473 |
| Improvements, advanced schools | 41,890 |
| New furnishings of schools | 12,547 |
| Total | 756,582 |

## LOCAL STRIKES.

The trades union of Milan, called the "Camera del Lavoro" (chamber of labor), has lately issued its Moral and Financial Relations, and Balance for the year 1901. From this publication, I extract the following summary of strikes during the said year:

| Month. | Number of strikes. | Number of strikers. | Result of strikes. | | | Losses caused by strikes. | | | Annual aggregate gains. | |
|---|---|---|---|---|---|---|---|---|---|---|
| | | | Favorable. | Compromised. | Unfavorable. | Number of days. | Wages. | Subsidies. | Hours. | Lire. |
| | | | | | | | *Lire. a* | *Lire.* | | |
| January...... | 7 | 860 | 1 | 3 | 3 | 18,112 | 46,386 | 1,040 | 24,327 | 18,510 |
| February .... | 4 | 74 | 3 | 1 | ...... | 140 | 282 | .......... | .......... | 495 |
| March ....... | 2 | 170 | 2 | ...... | ...... | 1,370 | 3,782 | .......... | .......... | 19,455 |
| April......... | 3 | 671 | 3 | ...... | ...... | 2,102 | 5,694 | .......... | 90,000 | 882 |
| May.......... | 5 | 12,634 | 4 | ...... | 1 | 252,884 | 495,991 | 50,562 | .......... | 1,438,940 |
| June ......... | 6 | 175 | 2 | 3 | 1 | 1,417 | 3,743 | 808 | 8,700 | 5,400 |
| July ......... | 9 | 2,946 | 8 | 1 | ...... | 27,527 | 61,432 | 1,810 | 33,600 | 230,882 |
| August....... | 8 | 2,916 | 5 | 2 | 1 | 16,548 | 43,233 | 1,008 | 480,000 | 227,040 |
| September ... | 15 | 2,043 | 12 | 2 | 1 | 14,745 | 35,696 | 4,094 | 73,800 | 176,487 |
| October...... | 11 | 3,811 | 4 | 4 | 3 | 27,803 | 64,610 | 3,771 | 94,200 | 179,645 |
| November ... | 10 | 5,649 | 8 | ...... | ...... | 60,456 | 138,547 | 38,562 | 1,006,500 | 7,002,345 |
| December.... | 12 | 1,826 | 6 | ...... | 2 | 11,670 | 24,158 | 11,027 | 14,790 | .......... |
| Total... | 92 | 33,706 | 58 | 16 | 12 | 434,768 | 923,549 | 112,682 | 1,825,917 | 3,300,081 |

*a* The value of a lire is 19.3 cents.

## EXPORTS.

The exports to the United States from Milan for the quarter ended September 30, 1902, were valued at $2,610,330.64, or more than those for any other corresponding quarter in the history of this consulate; and the exports for the three quarters of the calendar year 1902 amounted in value to $8,035,906.39, which is also a record.

The following table shows the value of exports to the United States for the first three quarters of each calendar year for the last ten years:

| Year. | Quarter ending— | | | Total. |
|---|---|---|---|---|
| | March 31. | June 30. | September 30. | |
| 1893 | $1,994,020.92 | $1,367,747.31 | $666,369.85 | $4,028,138.08 |
| 1894 | 1,632,146.20 | 1,230,831.62 | 1,137,617.94 | 4,000,595.76 |
| 1895 | 1,290,852.25 | 1,780,295.00 | 1,523,155.65 | 4,594,302.90 |
| 1896 | 1,118,848.99 | 602,169.25 | 552,320.10 | 2,273,338.34 |
| 1897 | 1,089,029.53 | 1,031,172.12 | 1,408,131.06 | 3,478,332.71 |
| 1898 | 1,977,260.66 | 1,689,552.72 | 1,847,444.19 | 5,464,257.57 |
| 1899 | 2,888,862.64 | 2,684,990.53 | 1,735,810.36 | 7,259,663.53 |
| 1900 | 3,846,950.80 | 2,520,372.94 | 1,477,506.52 | 7,844,830.26 |
| 1901 | 2,094,628.55 | 2,375,465.86 | 2,286,355.16 | 6,756,449.57 |
| 1902 | 2,783,003.87 | 2,642,571.88 | 2,610,330.64 | 8,035,906.39 |

## IMPORTS.

In regard to the importation from the United States into this consular district, I have heretofore been unable to obtain any reliable statistics, and only now have I succeeded in getting the following information, through the courtesy of the director of the Milan customs, in regard to the amount—in weight alone—imported into the city of Milan from January 1 to September 30, 1902, which, although very incomplete, will serve as a basis for future comparison. Many goods are not included in this list, and I presume that the articles enumerated are only some of the more important ones.

| Articles. | Kilos. | Pounds. |
|---|---|---|
| Pepper | 180 | 286 |
| Chemical products | 306 | 674 |
| Rubber and rubber resin | 484 | 1,067 |
| Colors | 500 | 1,102 |
| Varnishes | 500 | 1,102 |
| Hides cured | 61 | 134 |
| Iron waste and iron and steel filings | 38,240 | 84,304 |
| Scrap iron | 643 | 1,418 |
| Iron plates | 334 | 736 |
| Copper, brass, and bronze: | | |
| Ornamental works | 39 | 86 |
| Unclassified works | 549 | 1,210 |
| Machines, boilers, and parts of machines | 8,255 | 18,199 |
| Instruments, physical, surgical, and precision | 4,237 | 9,341 |
| Watches | 287 | 633 |

The articles which are cleared at the customs at the ports of arrival do not figure in this list.

### FOREIGN ADVERTISEMENTS IN LOCAL JOURNALS.

Local technical journals contain many full-page and half-page advertisements of foreign manufacturers relating to machinery of all kinds. The majority of these are of German and Swiss houses which are represented here, but there are other foreign concerns which advertise their goods direct from headquarters.

I have recently seen a novel advertisement which appeared in a popular daily paper of Milan. In a space of 7 by 7½ inches were grouped 100 names and addresses (with brief references to class of goods) of German manufacturers and commercial houses. There were 63 head lines arranged in alphabetical order, classifying the trades under which the trade addresses appear. Over the space was printed in large type "Table of addresses of reliable manufacturers and commercial firms. Please keep this list." The cost of such an announcement can not be much, while in itself it forms a comprehensive guide.

### SALES OF AMERICAN GOODS.

How to facilitate sales of American goods is a subject which should be well studied by manufacturers who wish to supply the foreign markets.

With practical buyers, the difficulties of calculation in varying measurements and weights have possibly been removed by experience, but facilities for transport have not yet been found. It is not impossible to obtain an estimate of the freight from an American seaport to an Italian one, but Italian shipping agents are usually able to make a quotation only after correspondence with their American agents, and for each fresh shipment the same ground has to be gone over again, as the agent will not establish a precedent. Even with the experienced buyer, this proves an obstacle which might be lessened by exporters quoting their goods f. o. b. Genoa, when dealing with Milan firms. For an inexperienced buyer or small purchaser, the undertaking is a serious one, and he is usually amazed to find how much the transportation expenses have increased the cost of his small import.

The most objectionable and at the same time apparently unnecessary expense is that which arises from the goods passing through so many hands, thus multiplying the attendant costs at each port until the sum to be paid is out of all proportion to the value of the goods received. For this reason, goods sold to Milan should be sent through a shipping agent who is in a position to handle the matter straight through, and if this were arranged by the American seller, he would be conferring a benefit on the Italian buyer which the latter would know how to appreciate. In this connection, it might be mentioned that several American export journals, in quoting approximate freights from New York to Genoa, give figures which they suggest can be taken by the foreign purchaser as a basis of calculation. These figures are so much below the price paid here that, were they accepted by a prospective buyer, he would be greatly misled.

It is when dealing with small articles or samples that this annoyance is most manifest. A merchant wishing to import requires samples. He is not unwilling to pay for these when of value, but the extra cost incurred in freight and the handling by different forwarding agents brings up the price far beyond anything ever contemplated. On the next occasion, he seems to prefer getting his samples from a European country, within a few days, at very little expense, and with possibly a prompt visit from a traveler anxious to make a deal with him and ready to give him every encouragement.

The credit question is also worthy of attention. Business here is not done on a cash basis, and if we insist too strenuously on trying to introduce it, other countries will continue to take the orders. The system among merchants here is that of credit, and bills at three to twelve months are readily accepted. For a first order, it is usual to pay cash, but when relations are established, customers expect facilities and if these are not accorded, they are forced, even against their will, to place their orders elsewhere. Great precaution should be exercised as to whom credit can be given, but when once the financial standing of a firm is satisfactorily established, orders can be obtained and business done which otherwise must inevitably be lost.

WM. JARVIS, *Consul.*

MILAN, *October 28, 1902.*

---

## NAPLES.

Statistics recently published show that the exports from Naples to the United States for the year 1901 exceeded those of 1900 by $251,491, and the imports from the United States for the year 1901 exceeded those of 1900 by $2,044,962. The following table, showing the total value of all articles exported from and imported to Naples in the trade with foreign countries during the year 1901, is submitted:

| Countries. | Exports. | Imports. |
|---|---|---|
| United Kingdom | $3,181,995 | $5,870,902 |
| France | 1,641,957 | 1,788,041 |
| United States | 1,678,782 | 5,463,634 |
| South America | 455,206 | 449,601 |
| Egypt | 518,936 | 212,291 |
| Belgium | 207,381 | 531,539 |
| Austria-Hungary | 372,842 | 1,146,659 |
| Germany | 288,462 | 1,197,996 |
| Africa | 191,930 | 93,286 |
| Turkey | 707,331 | 418,407 |
| Spain | 86,231 | 189,813 |
| Holland | 154,531 | 445,908 |
| Greece | 38,538 | 94,653 |
| Switzerland | 97,666 | 56,583 |
| Russia | 20,804 | 2,833,924 |
| Roumania | 21,057 | 4,175,637 |
| Norway and Sweden | 16,989 | 138,369 |
| Other countries | 112,820 | 441,207 |
| Total | 9,773,458 | 25,498,450 |

The following is the return of the principal articles of export and import from and to Naples for the year 1901:

*Exports and imports, 1901.*

| Articles. | Exports, 1901. | | Imports, 1901. | |
|---|---|---|---|---|
| | Quantity. | Value. | Quantity. | Value. |
| Wine, oil, and spirits............galls.. | 1,465,657 | $487,609 | 2,946,811 | $700,957 |
| Drugs, colonials, and tobacco......tons.. | 749 | 94,537 | 3,296 | 806,637 |
| Chemicals, medicines, and perfumery........do... | 3,382 | 476,912 | 12,583 | 1,415,694 |
| Colors and dyes .............................do... | 5 | 6,496 | 6,305 | 427,843 |
| Hemp, flax, and manufactures of............do... | 4,714 | 1,005,867 | 1,138 | 218,510 |
| Cotton, and manufactures of...............do... | 1,386 | 518,565 | 9,027 | 2,249,895 |
| Wool, hair, and manufactures of............do... | 685 | 252,810 | 322 | 490,232 |
| Silk, and manufactures of.................do... | 33 | 326,109 | 18 | 143,314 |
| Timber and straw.......................do... | 2,703 | 134,009 | 25,351 | 532,663 |
| Paper and books .........................do... | 6,057 | 407,019 | 3,985 | 322,114 |
| Curriery................................do... | 644 | 535,787 | 3,144 | 1,649,456 |
| Metals................................do... | 610 | 192,324 | 23,616 | 2,269,030 |
| Stone, earthenware, and glass ...............do... | 7,041 | 86,906 | 294,893 | 2,531,118 |
| Cereals ...................................do... | 34,356 | 2,200,145 | 254,400 | 9,711,377 |
| Live animals and animal produce............do... | 1,319 | 2,912,422 | 9,324 | 1,788,366 |
| Sundries ................................do... | 23 | 105,957 | 280 | 209,148 |
| Precious metal and specie ...............pounds.. | .......... | .......... | .......... | 18,818 |
| Total................................ | .......... | 9,773,474 | .......... | 25,488,172 |

I regret my inability to furnish statistics for the six months ended June 30, 1902, as these returns are prepared annually and are not made public until 1903. However, I append a list of declared export returns to the United States during that period:

| Articles. | Value. | Articles. | Value. |
|---|---|---|---|
| Argols ...................... | $603.43 | Earthenware...................... | $1,033.52 |
| Artichokes..................... | 1,395.39 | Filberts ..................... | 12,180.56 |
| Billiard chalk.................. | 138.96 | Furniture ..................... | 6,166.45 |
| Ball woolen goods ............. | 405.65 | Garlic ..................... | 12,167.56 |
| Bronzes..................... | 4,243.07 | Gloves ..................... | 28,884.16 |
| Books..................... | 147.48 | Goatskins ..................... | 15,799.25 |
| Carpets..................... | 8,313.62 | Glycerin ..................... | 14,666.54 |
| Carpet wool..................... | 13,194.66 | Hams ..................... | 5,354.38 |
| Coral..................... | 1,956.92 | Haricot beans ..................... | 1,861.56 |
| Cheese..................... | 75,519.65 | Hazelnuts..................... | 162.89 |
| Chestnuts..................... | 1,137.22 | Hemp..................... | 41,629.97 |
| Cotton yarn..................... | 26.14 | Household effects..................... | 119.58 |
| Drawings..................... | 386.00 | Human hair ..................... | 10,191.73 |
| Decorated earthenware............. | 331.31 | Jewelry ..................... | 1,324.27 |

| Articles. | Value. | Articles. | Value. |
|---|---|---|---|
| Lard ..................... | $772.10 | Sausages..................... | $7,523.79 |
| Licorice.................. | 2,795.91 | Seeds ..................... | 156.73 |
| Lupins................... | 3,143.06 | Shirtings................... | 200.84 |
| Majolica................. | 4,778.08 | Silk ..................... | 12,043.20 |
| Macaroni................. | 2,261.08 | Snuff..................... | 1,113.60 |
| Marble................... | 424.60 | Soap..................... | 397.71 |
| Medicine specialties..... | 139.54 | Soapstock ................. | 51,539.56 |
| Miscellaneous ........... | 17,019.21 | Sulphur oil ............... | 37,405.75 |
| Musical instruments...... | 1,611.81 | Statue................... | 193.00 |
| Oil ..................... | 5,740.15 | Salt fish................. | 499.87 |
| Oil paintings............ | 1,121.61 | Sculpturing machine ...... | 996.65 |
| Olive oil ............... | 20,987.06 | Shoes ................... | 308.80 |
| Olives................... | 430.64 | Skins ................... | 12,953.38 |
| Onions................... | 5,808.98 | Tartar ................... | 194,741.69 |
| Oriental rugs ........... | 140.82 | Tomato paste.............. | 2,674.19 |
| Paste.................... | 6,802.28 | Tapestries ............... | 1,362.77 |
| Pastels.................. | 807.44 | Terra cotta............... | 629.09 |
| Paintings................ | 218.76 | Wall paper................ | 252.42 |
| Picture.................. | 982.37 | Walnuts .................. | 936.05 |
| Personal effects ........ | 1,618.93 | Water colors .............. | 1,861.38 |
| Peppers.................. | 657.65 | Wine..................... | 22,035.14 |
| Preserves ............... | 5,276.24 | Works of art ............. | 705.22 |
| Returned American goods.. | 131.24 | | |
| Scrap iron .............. | 199.95 | Total.................... | 689,277.11 |

As of interest in considering the imports and exports, 1 give a return
of the shipping of the port of Naples for the year 1901:

| Nationality. | Sailing vessels. | | Steam vessels. | | Total. | |
|---|---|---|---|---|---|---|
| | Number. | Tonnage. | Number. | Tonnage. | Number. | Tonnage. |
| ENTERED. | | | | | | |
| British ..................... | 10 | 968 | 372 | 706,668 | 382 | 707,626 |
| Italian .................... | 3,248 | 128,824 | 1,419 | 1,221,256 | 4,667 | 1,350,080 |
| French ..................... | 8 | 233 | 214 | 241,221 | 222 | 241,454 |
| German..................... | 3 | 305 | 244 | 289,306 | 247 | 289,611 |
| Norwegian.................. | 4 | 859 | 37 | 35,609 | 41 | 36,468 |
| Danish..................... | 2 | 357 | 11 | 9,776 | 13 | 10,133 |
| Other nationalities.......... | .......... | .......... | 318 | 569,538 | 318 | 569,538 |
| Total.................... | 3,275 | 131,536 | 2,615 | 3,073,374 | 5,890 | 3,204,910 |
| Total 1900 ................. | 3,480 | 150,835 | 2,644 | 3,185,070 | 6,124 | 3,335,914 |
| CLEARED. | | | | | | |
| British ..................... | 8 | 723 | 367 | 694,558 | 375 | 695,281 |
| Italian .................... | 3,245 | 128,584 | 1,423 | 1,220,875 | 4,668 | 1,349,459 |
| French ..................... | 8 | 233 | 214 | 241,221 | 222 | 241,454 |
| German..................... | 3 | 305 | 243 | 288,035 | 246 | 288,340 |
| Norwegian.................. | 3 | 550 | 37 | 35,609 | 40 | 36,159 |
| Danish..................... | 2 | 357 | 11 | 9,776 | 13 | 10,133 |
| Other nationalities.......... | 1 | 89 | 314 | 565,848 | 315 | 565,937 |
| Total.................... | 3,270 | 130,841 | 2,609 | 3,055,922 | 5,879 | 3,186,763 |
| Total 1900 ................. | 3,411 | 145,562 | 2,635 | 3,175,709 | 6,046 | 3,321,271 |

A table of the highest and lowest monthly rate of exchange on
London, and of premium on gold during the year 1901 follows:

| Month. | Rate of exchange. | | Premium on gold, per cent. | |
|---|---|---|---|---|
| | Highest. | Lowest. | Highest. | Lowest. |
| | Lire. | Lire. | Lire. | Lire. |
| January ..................... | 26.54 | 26.30 | 5.97 | 5.42 |
| February .................... | 26.70 | 26.57 | 6.00 | 5.38 |
| March ...................... | 26.58 | 26.53 | 5.50 | 5.85 |
| April....................... | 26.54 | 26.51 | 5.42 | 5.32 |
| May ........................ | 26.54 | 26.46 | 5.42 | 5.34 |
| June ....................... | 26.53 | 26.31 | 5.42 | 4.43 |
| July ....................... | 26.33 | 26.25 | 4.64 | 4.30 |
| August...................... | 26.30 | 26.24 | 4.45 | 4.14 |
| September ................... | 26.24 | 25.98 | 3.74 | 3.06 |
| October ..................... | 25.97 | 25.65 | 3.30 | 2.20 |
| November ................... | 25.81 | 25.62 | 2.80 | 2.11 |
| December.................... | 25.66 | 25.50 | 2.09 | 1.45 |

### LABORATORY.

Importers of wines and spirits will be glad to hear that a laboratory is about to be established in connection with the Naples custom-house to test the wines and spirits imported into this harbor, so that the duty may be assessed upon them here instead of having a sample bottle sent to Rome. The delays incurred by sending samples to Rome have been exceedingly vexatious to importers, and it is a matter of much congratulation that they will be done away with.

### NICKEL CURRENCY.

Another change has been made in the Italian coinage. This time a 25-centesimo nickel piece has been issued in place of the 20-centesimo nickel piece, which is to be withdrawn. A 10-centesimo nickel piece will also be coined. It is hoped thus to decrease the circulation of copper, which, owing to its weight and size, is a source of considerable inconvenience.

### STEAMSHIP LINES.

At present, there are seven lines of steamships having a regular service between Naples and New York—North German Lloyd, Hamburg-American, Navigazione Generale Italiana, La Veloce, Anchor, Fabre, and Prince. A new departure has been made by the Dominion Line in instituting a service between Naples and Boston.

A. H. BYINGTON, Consul.

NAPLES, *August 28, 1902.*

---

## PALERMO.

### IMPORTS.

The total of imports from various countries during 1901 was $5,729,446, against $5,000,156 in 1900, an increase of $729,290, most of which should be put to the credit of the United States. In fact, it may be observed that the total amount of merchandise imported from the United States alone during 1901 was $1,415,107, against $775,761 imported during 1900, an increase of $639,346.

This increase is derived principally from tobacco, which in 1901 amounted to $987,920, while in 1900 it was only $467,405, and wheat, which in 1901 amounted to $86,310, while none was imported during 1900.

The other articles which are usually imported into Palermo from the United States amounted to the following in 1901: Petroleum, $121,814 (in 1900, $106,176); timber, $96,480 (in 1900, $92,820); lard, $52,825 (in 1900, $55,844); dry or smoked fish, $17,259 (in 1900, $10,470).

### EXPORTS.

The total of goods exported to various countries during 1901 was $5,893,993, against $5,470,780 in 1900, an increase of $423,213.

The countries to which goods were exported during 1901 in a greater quantity than in the preceding year were the United States, with an increase of $534,548; England, $387,090, and France, $335,907; while the countries to which merchandise was consigned in a smaller amount than in 1900 were Austria, with a decrease of $677,624, and Germany, of $131,667.

The increase to the United States was principally caused by green fruit, sumac, and olive oil, the value of which in 1901 amounted to $758,309, $254,629, and $226,796, respectively, while in 1900 it was only $548,030, $194,145, and $59,808.

The increase to England was principally caused by sumac, green fruit, tartar, and essence (oil of orange and lemon), the value of which in 1901 amounted to $603,519, $398,296, $183,532, and $111,680, respectively, while in 1900 it was only $467,813, $170,884, $147,370, and $96,880, respectively.

The increase to France was principally due to sumac, olive oil, and dry fruits (almonds, nuts, etc.), the value of which in 1901 amounted to $442,190, $117,651, and $101,106, respectively, while in 1900 it was only $337,625, $42,648, and $23,554.

The decrease to Austria was exclusively due to wine, the value of which in 1901 amounted only to $652,638, while in 1900 it was $1,340,458.

The decrease to Germany was caused by sumac, which in 1901 amounted only to $79,763, while in the preceding year it amounted to $237,285. The decrease in the total of goods exported to that country continues, although there were exported in 1901 dry fruits (almonds, nuts, etc.), for a value of $102,276, while the same goods exported in 1900 amounted only to $27,254.

I would call attention to the difference in the values of the several goods exported to the United States, as given in this statement, from those given in the table of declared exports.

JAMES JOHNSTON, *Consul.*

PALERMO, *September 5, 1902.*

---

*Principal articles imported into Palermo, and value thereof, by countries, in 1901.*

| Articles. | Austria. | England. | France. | Germany. | United States. | Other countries. | Total. |
|---|---|---|---|---|---|---|---|
| *Spirits, oils, and drinkables.* | | | | | | | |
| Water, mineral.............. | $1,302 | .......... | $644 | .......... | .......... | .......... | $1,946 |
| Wine, common: | | | | | | | |
|   In casks.............. | 18 | .......... | 306 | $6 | .......... | a $11,418 | 11,748 |
|   In bottles.............. | .......... | $348 | 5,742 | 290 | .......... | .......... | 6,380 |
| Beer: | | | | | | | |
|   In casks.............. | 42 | .......... | .......... | .......... | .......... | .......... | 42 |
|   In bottles.............. | 1,955 | 212 | .......... | 2,021 | .......... | .......... | 4,188 |
| Spirit: | | | | | | | |
|   Pure, in casks.............. | 945 | .......... | .......... | 117 | .......... | 90 | 1,152 |
|   Sweetened, in casks...... | .......... | 239 | 310 | 287 | .......... | 95 | 931 |
|   Sweetened, in bottles ..... | 243 | 194 | 1,944 | 48 | .......... | .......... | 2,429 |
| Oil: | | | | | | | |
|   Fish, raw.............. | .......... | .......... | 44 | .......... | .......... | 99 | 143 |
|   Olive.............. | .......... | .......... | .......... | .......... | .......... | b 3,529 | 3,529 |
|   Flaxseed .............. | .......... | 11,037 | 73 | .......... | .......... | .......... | 11,110 |
|   Heavy, mineral .............. | .......... | 220 | 3,616 | 400 | .......... | c 7,236 | 11,836 |
| Petroleum.............. | .......... | .......... | 22 | .......... | 121,814 | d 3,088 | 124,924 |
| Essence of clove.............. | 900 | 300 | .......... | 900 | .......... | .......... | 2,100 |
| Total.............. | 5,405 | 12,550 | 12,701 | 4,069 | 122,178 | 25,555 | 132,458 |

a Turkey, $9,498; Greece, $1,373.     c Russia.
b Spain, $3,060; Tunis, $469.     d Russia, $3,062.

*Principal articles imported into Palermo, and value thereof, by countries, in 1901*—Cont'd.

| Articles. | Austria. | England. | France. | Germany. | United States. | Other countries. | Total. |
|---|---|---|---|---|---|---|---|
| *Colonials, groceries, and tobacco.* | | | | | | | |
| Coffee ......................... | $7,654 | $2,967 | $3,013 | $1,058 | .......... | a $58,374 | $73,066 |
| Chicory, ground............... | 20 | | | | | | 20 |
| Sugar....................... | 6 | 756 | | | | 80 | 842 |
| Glucose, liquid ............... | | | | 84 | | | 84 |
| Sweets..................... | | 648 | 291 | | $32 | 32 | 1,003 |
| Condensed milk............ | 40 | | | | | 200 | 240 |
| Tea biscuits ................ | | 292 | | | | | 292 |
| Milk flour ................. | | | | 80 | | 440 | 520 |
| Cocoa, in pieces............. | | 1,892 | | | | 1,877 | 3,769 |
| Cinnamon................... | | 170 | | 147 | | 2,738 | 3,055 |
| Cloves..................... | | 242 | | | | | 242 |
| Pepper and pimento ........ | | 6,412 | 896 | | | b 15,288 | 22,596 |
| Tea........................ | | 255 | | | | | 255 |
| Mustard in powder.......... | | | 75 | | | | 75 |
| Tobacco, leaf............... | | | | | 987,920 | | 987,920 |
| Cigars ..................... | | | | | | 90 | 90 |
| Total ..................... | 7,720 | 18,634 | 4,275 | 1,369 | 987,952 | 79,119 | 1,094,069 |
| *Chemical products, drugs, resin, and perfumes.* | | | | | | | |
| Acids........................ | 111 | 37 | 148 | 279 | | | 575 |
| Ammonia .................... | | 220 | | 40 | | | 260 |
| Potash and caustic soda, impura............. | | 12,955 | 811 | 643 | | 3,835 | 18,244 |
| Salts of quinine ............. | | 2,400 | | | | | 2,400 |
| Oxide ....................... | | 108 | | 909 | | 2,133 | 3,150 |
| Carbonate................... | | 19,852 | 1,504 | 4,822 | | 7,744 | 33,922 |
| Chlorides................... | | 344 | 3,156 | 6,152 | | | 9,652 |
| Nitrate ..................... | | 1,440 | 2,429 | 864 | | | 4,733 |
| Borax ...................... | | 90 | | | | | 90 |
| Sulphate ................... | | 86,567 | 16 | 6,617 | 3,263 | 1,336 | 97,799 |
| Tartar...................... | 665 | | | | | 147 | 147 |
| Cream of tartar ............. | 665 | | | | | | 665 |
| Bromine and iodine.......... | | 450 | | | | | 450 |
| Ammoniacal salts........... | | 254 | | 98 | | 13 | 360 |
| Paraffin .................... | | 18,040 | | 721 | 10,047 | 457 | 29,265 |
| Chemical products not named. | 396 | 756 | 1,062 | 360 | | 558 | 3,132 |
| Gunpowder ................. | | | | | 480 | | 480 |
| Licorice roots ............... | | | | | | 2,754 | 2,754 |
| Herbs, medicinal, cassia and tamarinds................ | | 345 | | 950 | | | 1,296 |
| Manna ..................... | | | | 300 | | | 300 |
| Lemon juice, crude .......... | 33 | | | | | | 33 |
| Medicinal articles not named . | | 252 | 216 | 180 | | 216 | 864 |
| Medicaments, compounded, wines...................... | | | 200 | | | | 200 |
| Gums....................... | 288 | 2,291 | 6 | 22 | 1,414 | | 4,021 |
| Soap........................ | 550 | 700 | 600 | 900 | | 1,000 | 3,750 |
| Perfumes................... | | 240 | 1,080 | 120 | | | 1,440 |
| Total ..................... | 2,043 | 147,341 | 11,228 | 23,972 | 15,204 | 20,193 | 219,981 |
| *Colors and materials for dyeing and tanning.* | | | | | | | |
| Woods, roots, and herbs for dyeing and tanning........ | 7,655 | | 6,370 | | | c 158,280 | 172,305 |
| Colors ...................... | | 1,476 | 85 | 2,011 | | d 2,824 | 6,396 |
| Varnish ..................... | 160 | 4,040 | 120 | 120 | | d 1,160 | 5,600 |
| Pencils ..................... | | | | 126 | | | 126 |
| Ink ........................ | | | 480 | 176 | | | 656 |
| Blacking, shoe, of bone, not named...................... | 210 | | 60 | 180 | | | 450 |
| Total ..................... | 8,025 | 5,516 | 7,115 | 2,613 | | 162,264 | 185,533 |
| *Hemp, linen, jute, and other fibrous vegetables, excluding cotton.* | | | | | | | |
| Hemp, linen, vegetable hair, raw....................... | | 1,264 | 7,836 | | | e 36,182 | 45,282 |
| Cordage and ropes........... | | | | | | f 360 | 360 |

a Brazil, $57,776.
b Brazil, $7,672; British India, $7,616.
c Of which $152,360 was for lentisk from Tunis used for the adulteration of sumac.
d Holland.
e Tunis, $31,384; Switzerland, $4,191; Belgium, $607.
f Belgium.

*Principal articles imported into Palermo, and value thereof, by countries, in 1901*—Cont'd.

| Articles. | Austria. | England. | France. | Germany. | United States. | Other countries. | Total. |
|---|---|---|---|---|---|---|---|
| *Hemp, linen, jute, and other fibrous vegetables excluding cotton*—Continued. | | | | | | | |
| Yarns of hemp and linen...... | $840 | $2,100 | ......... | $168 | ......... | ......... | $3,108 |
| Textures of jute, velvety...... | 112 | ......... | ......... | ......... | ......... | ......... | 112 |
| Textures of flax, bleached, dyed, smooth, worked....... | 1,480 | 1,480 | $5,772 | 1,110 | ......... | ......... | 9,842 |
| Bags, sewed ................ | 2,240 | 2,672 | 656 | 400 | $400 | $3,632 | 10,000 |
| Other sewed articles........... | 360 | 6,000 | 240 | 480 | ......... | ......... | 7,080 |
| Total ................ | 5,032 | 13,516 | 14,504 | 2,158 | 400 | 40,174 | 75,784 |
| *Cotton.* | | | | | | | |
| Cotton yarns................ | ......... | 400 | ......... | 400 | ......... | ......... | 800 |
| Yarns, llama ................ | 240 | ......... | ......... | ......... | ......... | ......... | 240 |
| Tissues: | | | | | | | |
| Bleached, dyed, stamped, smooth, worked, muslin. | 3,712 | 22,156 | 2,784 | 8,584 | 4,176 | 580 | 41,992 |
| Waxed .................... | ......... | 3,024 | ......... | ......... | 3,024 | 144 | 6,192 |
| Polished ................. | ......... | 96 | ......... | 1,440 | ......... | ......... | 1,536 |
| Velvets, dyed, printed, common and fine ............... | 1,570 | 5,181 | 471 | 2,041 | ......... | ......... | 9,263 |
| Knit goods ................ | ......... | 89 | ......... | ......... | ......... | ......... | 89 |
| Laces and tulles............. | ......... | 540 | ......... | 540 | ......... | ......... | 1,080 |
| Galloons and ribbons......... | ......... | ......... | ......... | 102 | ......... | ......... | 102 |
| Cotton tissues, mixed with silk or wool........ | 4,356 | 1,980 | 396 | 4,752 | ......... | ......... | 11,484 |
| Sewed goods ................ | 584 | 1,460 | 292 | 1,168 | 584 | 292 | 4,380 |
| Total ................ | 10,462 | 34,926 | 3,943 | 19,027 | 7,784 | 1,016 | 77,158 |
| *Wool and hair.* | | | | | | | |
| Bristled hair ............... | ......... | ......... | ......... | 156 | ......... | ......... | 156 |
| Animal hair, raw............ | ......... | ......... | ......... | ......... | ......... | a 1,760 | 1,760 |
| Tissues of wool, carded, combed, printed ............ | 27,712 | 40,875 | 26,673 | 31,002 | 1,039 | 519 | 127,820 |
| Blankets .................. | ......... | ......... | ......... | 164 | ......... | ......... | 164 |
| Carpets.................... | 800 | 4,800 | 1,900 | 3,100 | ......... | ......... | 10,600 |
| Sewed articles.............. | 330 | 1,980 | 660 | 1,320 | 330 | 330 | 4,950 |
| Total ................ | 28,842 | 47,655 | 29,233 | 35,742 | 1,369 | 2,609 | 145,450 |
| *Silk.* | | | | | | | |
| Tissues: | | | | | | | |
| Silk, black, colored, plain, worked.................. | 1,500 | ......... | 6,000 | 1,500 | ......... | ......... | 9,000 |
| Mixed, black, colored, plain, worked ........... | 1,600 | ......... | 2,400 | 4,800 | ......... | ......... | 8,800 |
| Velvets: | | | | | | | |
| Silk ...................... | ......... | ......... | 3,500 | ......... | ......... | ......... | 3,500 |
| Mixed .................... | 1,920 | 960 | ......... | 960 | ......... | ......... | 3,840 |
| Laces and tulles............. | ......... | ......... | 2,240 | ......... | ......... | ......... | 2,240 |
| Galloons and ribbons......... | ......... | ......... | 940 | ......... | ......... | ......... | 940 |
| Sewed articles.............. | ......... | 1,450 | 2,900 | 1,450 | ......... | ......... | 5,800 |
| Total ................ | 5,020 | 2,410 | 17,980 | 8,710 | ......... | ......... | 34,120 |
| *Wood and straw.* | | | | | | | |
| Timber..................... | 203,355 | 925 | 250 | ......... | 96,840 | b 21,825 | 322,835 |
| Roots for brushes........... | ......... | ......... | ......... | ......... | ......... | c 112 | 112 |
| Cork, raw .................. | ......... | ......... | ......... | ......... | ......... | 60 | 60 |
| Casks with iron hoops........ | 3,792 | ......... | ......... | ......... | ......... | ......... | 3,792 |
| Furniture .................. | 14,490 | 2,988 | 547 | 1,245 | 547 | ......... | 19,817 |
| Utensils, wood ............. | 42 | 126 | 70 | 42 | 168 | ......... | 488 |
| Mercery of wood ........... | 160 | 480 | 240 | 560 | ......... | ......... | 1,440 |
| Bicycles (22 in number) ...... | 120 | 120 | 360 | 600 | 120 | ......... | 1,320 |
| Automobiles (8 in number) ... | ......... | ......... | 7,560 | ......... | ......... | d 1,000 | 8,560 |
| Reeds and rushes ........... | ......... | ......... | ......... | 240 | ......... | 440 | 680 |
| Basket-makers' works......... | 312 | ......... | 117 | 975 | ......... | 273 | 1,677 |
| Rope of esparto............. | ......... | ......... | 732 | 552 | ......... | 168 | 1,452 |
| Total ................ | 222,271 | 4,639 | 9,876 | 4,214 | 97,315 | 23,878 | 362,193 |

a Tunis.  b Roumania.  c Greece.  d Tunis.

*Principal articles imported into Palermo, and value thereof, by countries, in 1901*—Cont'd.

| Articles. | Austria. | England. | France. | Germany. | United States. | Other countries. | Total. |
|---|---|---|---|---|---|---|---|
| *Books and paper.* | | | | | | | |
| Paper: | | | | | | | |
| White, ruled or not ruled, in envelopes | $39 | $960 | $392 | $58 | $58 | .......... | $1,507 |
| Colored, guilded, wall | 704 | 1,184 | 2,272 | 2,976 | .......... | .......... | 7,136 |
| Wrapping | .......... | .......... | .......... | 532 | .......... | .......... | 532 |
| Blanks, lithographs, and labels | 2,600 | 600 | 600 | 1,000 | .......... | .......... | 4,800 |
| Pasteboards, ordinary | 9,834 | .......... | 9 | 768 | .......... | .......... | 10,611 |
| Paper and pasteboard articles. | 1,400 | 1,500 | 1,000 | 1,900 | 100 | $400 | 6,300 |
| Books of any kind | .......... | 100 | 1,500 | 300 | .......... | 100 | 2,000 |
| Total | 14,577 | 4,344 | 5,778 | 7,534 | 158 | 500 | 32,896 |
| *Hides, skins, and furs.* | | | | | | | |
| Skins or hides: | | | | | | | |
| Crude, dry, ox and cow ... | 205 | 9,512 | 12,751 | 3,444 | 5,166 | a 35,834 | 66,912 |
| Calf, goat, tanned, varnished | 2,100 | 840 | 5,880 | 87,860 | 210 | 210 | 96,600 |
| Gloves, skin | .......... | 360 | .......... | .......... | .......... | .......... | 360 |
| Boots and shoes | .......... | .......... | .......... | 560 | 700 | .......... | 1,260 |
| Belting | .......... | 360 | .......... | .......... | .......... | .......... | 360 |
| Articles of leather not named. | .......... | 252 | 126 | 126 | .......... | .......... | 504 |
| Valises | .......... | .......... | .......... | 330 | .......... | .......... | 330 |
| Total | 2,305 | 11,324 | 18,757 | 91,820 | 6,076 | 36,044 | 166,326 |
| *Minerals, metals, and articles thereof.* | | | | | | | |
| Scoriæ | .......... | 1,154 | 255 | .......... | .......... | 379 | 1,788 |
| Iron scraps | 12 | 107 | 8 | .......... | .......... | 50 | 177 |
| Cast iron: | | | | | | | |
| In pigs | .......... | 18,052 | .......... | 122 | .......... | .......... | 18,174 |
| Wrought | 1,100 | 12,254 | 3,058 | 726 | .......... | b 19,052 | 36,190 |
| Iron: | | | | | | | |
| In bars and rods | 3,410 | 5,250 | 243 | 4,770 | .......... | 7,080 | 20,703 |
| In sheets | .......... | 10,550 | .......... | 767 | .......... | c 10,158 | 21,475 |
| In rails | .......... | 800 | .......... | 15,332 | .......... | d 82,160 | 98,292 |
| In pipes | .......... | 4,944 | .......... | 216 | .......... | e 5,724 | 10,884 |
| Forged | .......... | 272 | .......... | 7,288 | 1,176 | .......... | 8,736 |
| Of second manufacture.... | 1,647 | 10,727 | 4,335 | 24,378 | 1,360 | f 34,748 | 77,195 |
| Steel springs | .......... | 11 | .......... | 139 | .......... | 174 | 324 |
| Iron, sheets of, covered with tin | .......... | 40,920 | .......... | .......... | .......... | .......... | 40,920 |
| Usual utensils and instruments | 216 | 2,160 | 456 | 2,904 | .......... | 1,008 | 6,744 |
| Iron utensil, burnished | .......... | .......... | .......... | 220 | .......... | 132 | 352 |
| Needles and pins | .......... | .......... | .......... | 400 | .......... | b 5,600 | 6,000 |
| Brass, copper, bronze, worked | 4,340 | 14,012 | 1,488 | 16,244 | 372 | 620 | 37,076 |
| Metallic tissues | .......... | .......... | .......... | 144 | .......... | .......... | 144 |
| Nickel in cubes and worked .. | 8,960 | .......... | 140 | 280 | .......... | 420 | 9,800 |
| Lead: | | | | | | | |
| In pigs | .......... | 1,073 | .......... | .......... | .......... | .......... | 1,073 |
| In type | .......... | .......... | .......... | 512 | .......... | .......... | 512 |
| Pewter | 1,330 | 210 | 490 | 1,890 | .......... | .......... | 3,920 |
| Zinc: | | | | | | | |
| In pigs | .......... | .......... | .......... | 756 | .......... | .......... | 756 |
| Worked | 134 | 537 | 100 | 2,956 | .......... | b 13,540 | 17,267 |
| Guns, complete | .......... | .......... | 1,200 | 528 | 1,284 | g 5,724 | 8,735 |
| Revolvers | .......... | .......... | 60 | 464 | 368 | 160 | 1,052 |
| Boilers and supplies | 11,460 | 59,820 | 1,320 | 11,290 | 3,900 | 7,830 | 95,610 |
| Apparatus for warming, distiling, etc. | .......... | 966 | 368 | .......... | .......... | 782 | 2,116 |
| Scientific instruments | 13,600 | 2,400 | 4,800 | 5,200 | 800 | 400 | 27,200 |
| Railway cars | .......... | .......... | .......... | .......... | .......... | 1,020 | 1,020 |
| Silver articles | .......... | 2,400 | .......... | .......... | .......... | .......... | 2,400 |
| Watches and clocks | .......... | .......... | .......... | 400 | 1,600 | .......... | 2,000 |
| Total | 46,209 | 188,619 | 18,321 | 97,916 | 10,860 | 196,711 | 558,636 |

a British India, $20,623; Africa, $7,790; Argentine Republic, $3,731, etc.
b Holland.
c Holland, $9,671: Belgium, $487.
d Belgium, $78,840; Holland, $3,320.
e Belgium, $5,644.
f Belgium, $13,175; Holland, $21,573.
g Belgium.

*Principal articles imported into Palermo, and value thereof, by countries, in 1901—Cont'd.*

| Articles. | Austria. | England. | France. | Germany. | United States. | Other countries. | Total. |
|---|---|---|---|---|---|---|---|
| *Stones, earth, pottery, glass, and crystal.* | | | | | | | |
| Colored earths .............. | $19 | $14 | $127 | $33 | ........... | ........... | $193 |
| Lithographic stones .......... | ........ | ........ | ........ | 98 | ........... | ........... | 98 |
| Stones and earths, other ..... | ........ | 2,096 | 8 | ........ | ........... | $5 | 2,109 |
| Cement and chalk, hydraulic. | ........ | ........ | 10,380 | ........ | ........... | ........... | 10,380 |
| Bricks........................ | ........ | 2,714 | ........ | ........ | ........... | ........... | 2,714 |
| Coal ......................... | 25 | 815,453 | ........ | ........ | ........... | 1,680 | 817,158 |
| Terra cotta of all other kinds . | 162 | 399 | 693 | 18 | ........... | ........... | 1,272 |
| Iron clay (grès) ............. | ........ | 6 | 12 | 18 | ........... | 36 | 72 |
| Majolica, white ............. | ........ | 257 | ........ | ........ | ........... | ........... | 257 |
| Earthenware, white and colored ..................... | 435 | 495 | 240 | 300 | ........... | ........... | 1,470 |
| Porcelain, white and colored.. | 1,860 | 150 | 360 | 1,770 | ........... | ........... | 4,140 |
| Plates of glass and crystal.... | ........ | 217 | 392 | 965 | ........... | 2,545 | 4,119 |
| Works of glass and crystal.... | 4,012 | 1,105 | 3,264 | 11,821 | ........... | 68 | 20,270 |
| Bottles, common ............. | 771 | 72 | 747 | 375 | ........... | ........... | 1,965 |
| Demijohns ................... | ........ | ........ | 8 | ........ | ........... | ........... | 8 |
| Glasswork (cut as gems) ..... | 96 | ........ | ........ | ........ | ........... | ........... | 96 |
| Total .............. | 7,380 | 822,978 | 16,231 | 15,398 | ........... | 4,334 | 866,321 |
| *Cereals, flour, paste, and vegetable products.* | | | | | | | |
| Wheat........................ | ........ | ........ | ........ | $46,310 | a1,180,452 | 1,266,762 | |
| Oats......................... | ........ | ........ | ........ | ........ | b6,620 | 6,620 | |
| Maize, yellow ............... | ........ | ........ | ........ | ........ | c51,168 | 51,168 | |
| Dry legumes................. | 32,338 | ........ | ........ | ........ | d36,366 | 68,704 | |
| Other grains................. | ........ | ........ | ........ | ........ | 744 | 744 | |
| Canary seed ................. | ........ | ........ | ........ | ........ | 2,304 | 2,304 | |
| Potatoes..................... | 338 | ........ | ........ | ........ | ........... | 338 | |
| Wheat flour ................. | ........ | ........ | 93 | ........ | ........... | 93 | |
| Macaroni.................... | ........ | ........ | 24 | ........ | 16 | 40 | |
| Feculas...................... | ........ | 5,568 | 324 | 60 | 4,224 | 10,176 | |
| Starch, in boxes............. | 78 | 65 | 156 | 858 | 2,379 | 3,536 | |
| Dates........................ | ........ | ........ | ........ | ........ | e13,992 | 13,992 | |
| Walnuts ..................... | ........ | ........ | 330 | ........ | 420 | 750 | |
| Preserved vegetables......... | ........ | ........ | 504 | ........ | 22 | 526 | |
| Sesame seed................. | 320 | ........ | 4,160 | ........ | 2,457 | 6,937 | |
| Seeds, not oleaginous ........ | 20,736 | 108 | ........ | ........ | 117 | 20,961 | |
| Palm oil..................... | ........ | ........ | 264 | ........ | ........... | 264 | |
| Other vegetable products .... | 54 | ........ | 390 | ........ | 264 | 708 | |
| Total ............... | 53,864 | 5,741 | 6,245 | 918 | 86,310 | 1,301,545 | 1,454,623 |
| *Animals, and products thereof.* | | | | | | | |
| Horses, mules, and asses (15 in number)................ | ........ | ........ | ........ | ........ | ........... | 1,660 | 1,660 |
| Oxen, cows, bulls, and calves (350 in number)............ | ........ | ........ | ........ | ........ | ........... | 9,602 | 9,602 |
| Cattle (29 in number) ........ | ........ | ........ | ........ | ........ | ........... | 81 | 81 |
| Swine of more than 20 kilograms (125 in number)...... | ........ | ........ | ........ | ........ | ........... | 1,000 | 1,000 |
| Meat, salted or smoked....... | ........ | ........ | ........ | 245 | 7,479 | ........... | 7,742 |
| Fowls, alive................. | ........ | ........ | ........ | ........ | ........... | 1,144 | 1,144 |
| Intestines, salt ............. | ........ | ........ | ........ | ........ | ........... | 176 | 176 |
| Fish: | | | | | | | |
| Fresh..................... | ........ | ........ | ........ | ........ | ........... | 3,960 | 3,960 |
| Dry and smoked .......... | ........ | 21,351 | ........ | ........ | 17,259 | ........... | 38,610 |
| Salted.................... | ........ | ........ | ........ | ........ | ........... | 2,980 | 2,980 |
| Preserved in tins ......... | ........ | ........ | 1,176 | ........ | ........... | ........... | 1,176 |
| Cheese ...................... | ........ | ........ | ........ | 560 | ........... | f41,132 | 41,692 |
| Eggs of fowls................ | ........ | ........ | ........ | ........ | ........... | 8,232 | 8,232 |
| Lard......................... | 400 | 225 | ........ | ........ | 52,825 | ........... | 53,450 |
| Stearic acid ................. | 792 | 8,442 | 90 | 2,052 | ........... | 8,100 | 19,476 |
| Oleic acid (oleina) ........... | ........ | ........ | 18,656 | ........ | ........... | ........... | 18,656 |
| Stearic candles .............. | ........ | ........ | 2,295 | 486 | ........... | ........... | 2,781 |
| Wax, white, worked ..... ... | 540 | ........ | 270 | 180 | ........... | ........... | 990 |
| Glue· | | | | | | | |
| Strong..................... | 195 | ........ | ........ | ........ | ........... | ........... | 195 |
| Fish ..................... | 780 | 720 | 300 | 1,200 | ........... | ........... | 3,000 |
| Sponges, common, raw....... | ........ | ........ | ........ | ........ | ........... | g12,000 | 12,000 |
| Fertilisers................... | ........ | 48 | 23 | ........ | ........... | 20 | 91 |
| Total ............... | 2,707 | 30,786 | 22,810 | 4,723 | 77,581 | 90,087 | 228,694 |

a Russia.
b Turkey.
c Turkey, $19,152, Russia, $32,016.

d Russia, $25,384; Roumania, $7,676, etc.
e Tunis.

f Russia, $34,188
g Greece.

*Principal articles imported into Palermo, and value thereof, by countries, in 1901*—Cont'd.

| Articles. | Austria. | England. | France. | Germany. | United States. | Other countries. | Total. |
|---|---|---|---|---|---|---|---|
| *Sundry articles.* | | | | | | | |
| Mercery, common and fine, toys | $5,760 | $2,560 | $3,840 | $10,560 | $1,920 | .......... | $24,640 |
| Fans, fine and ordinary ...... | | | | 800 | | | 800 |
| Pianos, upright ............... | 3,900 | .......... | 910 | 9,750 | .......... | $390 | 14,950 |
| India rubber in ribbons ...... | 330 | | 660 | 660 | | 990 | 2,640 |
| Isolated electric threads and cords ..................... | | | | | | 308 | 308 |
| Caps........................... | | | 78 | .......... | | | 78 |
| Hats: | | | | | | | |
|   Ladies' .................... | | | 795 | | | | 795 |
|   Men's .................... | | 725 | | .......... | | | 725 |
| Umbrellas, silk .............. | .......... | | .......... | 278 | .......... | .......... | 278 |
| Total .................. | 9,990 | 3,285 | 6,283 | 22,048 | 1,920 | 1,688 | 45,214 |

*Comparison of imports, by countries, for the years 1901 and 1900.*

| Total imports from— | | 1901. | 1900. | Decrease. | Increase. |
|---|---|---|---|---|---|
| Austria ........................................ | | $431,852 | $385,866 | .......... | $45,985 |
| England ........................................ | | 1,349,264 | 1,231,475 | .......... | 117,789 |
| France.......................................... | | 205,275 | 238,201 | $32,926 | .......... |
| Germany........................................ | | 342,231 | 432,756 | 90,525 | .......... |
| United States ................................. | | 1,415,107 | 775,761 | .......... | 639,346 |
| Other countries, viz: | | | | | |
|   Russia ............................... | $1,284,274 | | | | |
|   Tunis .............................. | 214,351 | | | | |
|   Belgium ............................ | 132,668 | | | | |
|   Holland............................. | 109,443 | | | | |
|   Brazil.............................. | 68,071 | | | | |
|   Turkey............................. | 53,660 | | | | |
|   Roumania .......................... | 40,431 | | | | |
|   British colonies.................... | 30,737 | | | | |
|   Greece ............................. | 16,596 | | | | |
|   Switzerland........................ | 12,628 | | | | |
|   Other countries .................... | 22,858 | | | | |
| | | 1,965,717 | 1,936,097 | .......... | 49,620 |
| Total................................... | | 5,729,446 | 5,000,156 | .......... | 729,290 |

*Principal articles exported from Palermo, and value thereof, by countries, in 1901.*

| Articles. | Austria. | England. | France. | Germany. | United States. | Other countries. | Total. |
|---|---|---|---|---|---|---|---|
| *Spirits, oils, and drinkables.* | | | | | | | |
| Wine: | | | | | | | |
|   Marsala, in casks.......... | $2,928 | $6,000 | $2,464 | $6,000 | $2,032 | .......... | $19,424 |
|   Common, in casks......... | 649,650 | 120 | 1,236 | 2,052 | 6,600 | $840 | 660,498 |
|   Common, in bottles ...... | 60 | 480 | 120 | 60 | 450 | 540 | 1,710 |
| Oil: | | | | | | | |
|   Sulphur, or soap stock..... | .......... | 34,347 | .......... | .......... | 45,170 | .......... | 79,517 |
|   Olive ..................... | 446 | 248 | 117,651 | 16,541 | 226,796 | a 7,439 | 369,121 |
|   Of orange ................. | 16,640 | 8,000 | 56,000 | 7,040 | .......... | b 17,600 | 105,280 |
|   Of lemon ................. | .......... | 111,680 | .......... | .......... | 14,080 | .......... | 125,760 |
| Total ...... ......... | 669,724 | 160,875 | 177,471 | 31,693 | 295,128 | 26,419 | 1,361,310 |
| *Colonials, groceries, and tobacco.* | | | | | | | |
| Must, concentrated............ | .......... | .......... | .......... | 3,531 | .......... | .......... | 3,531 |
| Mustard seed ................. | .......... | .......... | 8,527 | .......... | .......... | .......... | 8,527 |
| Tomato paste................. | 225 | 945 | 3,888 | 1,060 | 32,112 | c 47,587 | 85,837 |
| Snuff ......................... | | | | | 3,360 | | 3,360 |
| Total .................. | 225 | 945 | 12,415 | 4,611 | 35,472 | 47,587 | 101,255 |

a Holland.        b Belgium.        c Tunis, $23,670, Malta, $16,146; Belgium, $3,177, etc.

*Principal articles exported from Palermo, and value thereof, by countries, in 1901*—Cont'd.

| Articles. | Austria. | England. | France. | Germany. | United States. | Other countries. | Total. |
|---|---|---|---|---|---|---|---|
| *Chemical products, drugs, resin, and perfumes.* | | | | | | | |
| Carbonate of sodium ......... | ......... | ......... | ......... | $506 | ......... | ......... | $506 |
| Tartar or dregs of wine...... | ......... | $183,532 | $30,635 | ......... | ......... | a $38,097 | 252,264 |
| Citrate of lime ............... | $960 | 26,400 | ......... | 10,812 | $15,336 | ......... | 53,508 |
| Licorice roots ............... | ......... | ......... | 180 | ......... | ......... | ......... | 180 |
| Licorice juice ............... | ......... | 8,192 | 2,112 | ......... | 640 | ......... | 10,944 |
| Manna ....................... | 5,500 | 10,900 | 15,800 | 23,500 | 5,800 | b 24,300 | 85,800 |
| Orange peel .................. | ......... | 935 | 1,290 | 465 | ......... | 770 | 3,460 |
| Lemon juice, crude .......... | ......... | 998 | 10,017 | ......... | 957 | ......... | 11,972 |
| Gums, indigenous, raw ....... | 108 | ......... | ......... | ......... | ......... | ......... | 108 |
| Soap, perfumed .............. | ......... | ......... | ......... | ......... | ......... | 480 | 480 |
| Perfumes, not alcoholic ..... | ......... | ......... | ......... | ......... | ......... | 320 | 320 |
| Total ................ | 6,568 | 230,957 | 60,034 | 35,283 | 22,733 | 63,967 | 419,542 |
| *Colors and materials for dyeing and tanning.* | | | | | | | |
| Sumac: | | | | | | | |
| Leaf..................... | 17,100 | 90,817 | 240,442 | 38,469 | 45,185 | c 114,336 | 546,349 |
| Ground.................. | 29,409 | 512,702 | 201,748 | 41,294 | 209,444 | d 71,341 | 1,065,938 |
| Total ................ | 46,509 | 603,519 | 442,190 | 79,763 | 254,629 | 185,677 | 1,612,287 |
| *Hemp, linen, and jute.* | | | | | | | |
| Textures, waxed ............. | ......... | ......... | ......... | ......... | ......... | e 210 | 210 |
| Sewed articles (bags)........ | ......... | ......... | ......... | ......... | ......... | e 90 | 90 |
| Total ................ | ......... | ......... | ......... | ......... | ......... | 300 | 300 |
| *Cotton.* | | | | | | | |
| Yarns ....................... | ......... | ......... | ......... | ......... | ......... | e 832 | 832 |
| Textures: | | | | | | | |
| Raw, bleached, dyed, printed ................ | ......... | ......... | ......... | ......... | ......... | e 9,025 | 9,025 |
| Tarred.................. | ......... | ......... | ......... | ......... | ......... | e 208 | 208 |
| Total ................ | ......... | ......... | ......... | ......... | ......... | 10,065 | 10,065 |
| *Wool and hair.* | | | | | | | |
| Wool, natural, raw ........... | 1,680 | 8,400 | ......... | ......... | ......... | ......... | 10,080 |
| Hair, animal, raw ........... | ......... | 2,376 | ......... | ......... | ......... | ......... | 2,376 |
| Total ................ | 1,680 | 10,776 | ......... | ......... | ......... | ......... | 12,456 |
| *Wood and straw.* | | | | | | | |
| Timber ...................... | ......... | ......... | ......... | ......... | ......... | 31 | 31 |
| Cork, raw ................... | 2,544 | ......... | 13,712 | ......... | ......... | f 5,864 | 22,120 |
| Furniture ................... | ......... | 60 | ......... | ......... | ......... | e 120 | 180 |
| Utensils of wood, raw ....... | ......... | ......... | ......... | ......... | ......... | e 100 | 100 |
| Mercery of wood ............. | ......... | ......... | ......... | ......... | ......... | e 400 | 400 |
| Bicycles..................... | ......... | ......... | 140 | ......... | ......... | ......... | 140 |
| Carriages of two wheels ..... | ......... | ......... | ......... | ......... | ......... | e 1,120 | 1,120 |
| Carriages of more than two wheels................. | ......... | ......... | ......... | ......... | ......... | e 2,640 | 2,640 |
| Basket-maker's works........ | ......... | ......... | ......... | ......... | ......... | e 216 | 216 |
| Total ................ | 2,544 | 60 | 13,852 | ......... | ......... | 10,491 | 26,947 |
| *Books and paper.* | | | | | | | |
| Rags, vegetable ............. | ......... | ......... | 93 | ......... | ......... | ......... | 93 |
| Paper, white, not ruled ..... | ......... | ......... | ......... | ......... | ......... | 90 | 90 |
| Blanks and lithographs ...... | ......... | ......... | ......... | ......... | 600 | 400 | 1,000 |
| Books, printed in Italian language................... | ......... | ......... | 420 | ......... | 84 | 756 | 1,260 |
| Music, printed, bound........ | ......... | ......... | 770 | ......... | ......... | ......... | 770 |
| Total ................ | ......... | ......... | 1,283 | ......... | 684 | 1,246 | 3,213 |

a Belgium.
b Belgium, $8,900, Turkey, $6,700: Holland, $5,600, etc.
c Belgium, $52,251; Russia, $51,078; Holland, $10,575, etc.
d Holland, $42,835; Belgium, $17,774, etc.
e Tunis.
f Russia.

*Principal articles exported from Palermo, and value thereof, by countries, in 1901—Cont'd.*

| Articles. | Austria. | England. | France. | Germany. | United States. | Other countries. | Total. |
|---|---|---|---|---|---|---|---|
| *Hides and skins.* | | | | | | | |
| Skins or hides: | | | | | | | |
| Ox and cow, crude, dry ... | | | $30,429 | | | | $30,429 |
| Lamb, crude, dry............ | | | 9,408 | | | | 9,408 |
| Kid, crude, dry............. | | | 4,'33 | | | | 4,433 |
| Horse, crude, dry........... | | | | $4,457 | | | 4,457 |
| Harness ..................... | | | | | | $500 | 500 |
| Total ................. | | | 44,270 | 4,457 | | 500 | 49,227 |
| *Minerals, metals, and articles thereof.* | | | | | | | |
| Cast iron, in pigs ............. | | | | | | 33 | 33 |
| Iron of second manufacture.... | | | | | | 50 | 50 |
| Sheets of iron covered with tin. | | $612 | 348 | | | 420 | 1,380 |
| Copper or brass scraps......... | | 579 | | | | | 579 |
| Copper or brass in works not named.... | | | | | | 1,122 | 1,122 |
| Lead, in pigs................. | | 88 | | | | | 88 |
| Zinc: | | | | | | | |
| In pigs ...................... | | 129 | | | | | 129 |
| In works not named.......... | | | | | | 416 | 416 |
| Machines and supplies ........ | $84 | | | | $2,289 | 273 | 2,646 |
| Total ................. | 84 | 1,406 | 348 | | 2,289 | 2,314 | 6,443 |
| *Stones, earth, pottery, glass, and crystal.* | | | | | | | |
| Marble ........................ | | | | | 72 | 4,896 | 4,968 |
| Stones and earth, other ...... | | | | 6 | | a5,854 | 5,860 |
| Cement........................ | | | | | | 493 | 493 |
| Bricks........................ | | | | | | 41 | 41 |
| Brimstone..................... | 154 | 102 | 828 | | 137,406 | b110,466 | 248,456 |
| Bituminous solids............. | | 4,001 | | | | | 4,001 |
| Terra-cotta of common use.... | 39 | | | | 205 | 3,615 | 3,859 |
| Earthenware, white and colored.... | | | | | | 3,390 | 3,390 |
| Porcelain, colored............ | | | | | | 78 | 78 |
| Total ................. | 193 | 4,103 | 828 | 6 | 137,683 | 128,883 | 271,146 |
| *Vegetable products.* | | | | | | | |
| Wheat......................... | | | | | 208 | | 208 |
| Legumes, dry ................. | | | 5,845 | | 2,967 | c99,588 | 108,400 |
| Chestnuts .................... | | | 858 | | | 231 | 1,089 |
| Potatoes...................... | | | | | | 26 | 26 |
| Flour of other grain (not of wheat)...... | | | | | 92 | | 92 |
| Macaroni...................... | 16 | 12,836 | 16 | 168 | 27,664 | 88 | 40,288 |
| Oranges and lemons ........... | 8,802 | 398,296 | 2,329 | 108,581 | 756,309 | d82,322 | 1,356,139 |
| Fruits: | | | | | | | |
| Fresh, not named ........... | | | 48 | 276 | 2,268 | a8,544 | 11,136 |
| Dry (almonds, nuts, figs, etc.)..... | 8,280 | 15,732 | 101,106 | 102,276 | 6,048 | e22,518 | 255,960 |
| Preserved (under vinegar, salt, oil)..... | | | 4,312 | 638 | | 63,272 | 3,168 | 71,390 |
| Seeds: | | | | | | | |
| Oleaginous .................. | | | | 19 | | 140 | | 159 |
| Not oleaginous ............. | 48 | 112 | 64 | 16 | 160 | | 400 |
| Vegetable products not named. | | | | | 2,691 | 42 | 2,733 |
| Pistachio .................... | 9,180 | 13,260 | 9,180 | 7,820 | | | 39,440 |
| Total ................. | 25,826 | 444,048 | 120,103 | 219,187 | 863,819 | 216,527 | 1,889,460 |
| *Animals and products thereof.* | | | | | | | |
| Fish: | | | | | | | |
| Fresh....................... | | | | | 1,416 | | 1,416 |
| Salted ..................... | 4,676 | 560 | | | 5,992 | 2,226 | 13,454 |
| Caviar...................... | | | | | 1,760 | | 1,760 |
| Cheese...................... | | 3,276 | | | 27,096 | 336 | 30,708 |
| Human hair, raw ............ | 25,200 | | | | 30,000 | 16,800 | 72,000 |
| Horns and bones, raw........ | | | 660 | | | | 660 |
| Fertilizers................. | 235 | 8 | | | | 920 | 1,163 |
| Total ................. | 30,111 | 3,844 | 660 | | 66,264 | 20,282 | 121,161 |

a Tunis.
b Portugal, $23,382; Spain, $25,314; Russia, $24,801, etc.
c Spain, $68,456; Portugal, $21,414; Tunis, $8,815, etc.
d Holland, $71,589; Russia, $6,690, etc.
e Holland, $3,550, etc.

*Principal articles exported from Palermo, and value thereof, by countries, in 1901—Cont'd.*

| Articles. | Austria. | England. | France. | Germany. | United States. | Other countries. | Total. |
|---|---|---|---|---|---|---|---|
| *Sundry articles.* | | | | | | | |
| Mercery, common and fine ... | ............ | 140 | ............ | ............ | 980 | 1,120 | 2,240 |
| Caps.................. | ............ | ............ | ............ | ............ | ............ | *a* 551 | 551 |
| Objects of collection .......... | 1,120 | 620 | 420 | 320 | 3,840 | 70 | 6,390 |
| Total ................ | 1,120 | 760 | 420 | 320 | 4,820 | 1,741 | 9,181 |

*a* Tunis.

*Comparison of exports, by countries, for the years 1901 and 1900.*

| Total exports to— | | 1901. | 1900. | Decrease. | Increase. |
|---|---|---|---|---|---|
| Austria ................................. | | $784,584 | $1,462,208 | $677,624 | ............ |
| England................................. | | 1,461,295 | 1,074,205 | ............ | $387,090 |
| France ................................. | | 873,374 | 587,467 | ............ | 335,907 |
| Germany................................. | | 375,270 | 506,937 | 131,667 | ............ |
| United States ......................... | | 1,683,521 | 1,148,973 | ............ | 534,548 |
| Other countries, viz: | | | | | |
| Holland.................... | $147,616 | | | | |
| Belgium .................... | 140,869 | | | | |
| Spain .................... | 93,770 | | | | |
| Russia .................... | 89,791 | | | | |
| Tunis .................... | 79,702 | | | | |
| Portugal .................... | 50,296 | | | | |
| British colonies.................... | 29,549 | | | | |
| Other countries.................... | 84,356 | | | | |
| | | 715,949 | 740,990 | 25,041 | ............ |
| Total.................................. | | 5,898,993 | 5,470,780 | ............ | 423,213 |

*Total trade of Palermo during 1901.*

| Countries. | Imports. | Exports. | Total. | Increase. | |
|---|---|---|---|---|---|
| | | | | Imports. | Exports. |
| United States.................. | $1,415,107 | $1,683,521 | $3,098,628 | ............ | $268,414 |
| Austria ......................... | 481,852 | 784,584 | 1,216,436 | ............ | 352,732 |
| England......................... | 1,349,264 | 1,461,295 | 2,810,559 | ............ | 112,031 |
| France ......................... | 205,275 | 873,374 | 1,078,649 | ............ | 668,099 |
| Germany......................... | 842,231 | 375,270 | 717,501 | ............ | 33,089 |
| Russia ......................... | 1,284,274 | 89,791 | 1,374,065 | $1,194,483 | ............ |
| Tunis............................ | 214,351 | 79,702 | 294,053 | 134,649 | ............ |
| Belgium......................... | 132,668 | 140,869 | 273,537 | ............ | 8,201 |
| Holland......................... | 109,443 | 147,616 | 257,059 | ............ | 38,173 |
| Other countries ............... | 244,981 | 257,971 | 502,952 | ............ | 12,990 |
| Total......................... | 5,729,446 | 5,898,993 | 11,628,439 | ............ | 164,547 |

*Declared exports from the port of Palermo to the United States during the year ended December 31, 1901, in comparison with the preceding year.*

| Articles. | 1901. | 1900. | Articles. | 1901. | 1900. |
|---|---|---|---|---|---|
| Almonds .................. | $16,472 | $15,510 | Olives.................... | $2,880 | $1,669 |
| Beans .................... | 1,665 | 1,760 | Olive oil.................... | 45,956 | 22,653 |
| Brimstone.................. | 76,936 | 157,889 | Oil of lemon and orange. | 8,605 | 12,196 |
| Cheese .................... | 35,781 | 24,279 | Oranges.................... | 16,968 | 21,407 |
| Citrate of lime ............ | 110,883 | 61,587 | Orange and lemon peel.. | 797 | 1,168 |
| Cork, raw.................. | 72,762 | 26,611 | Pistachio .................... | 510 | ............ |
| Cosmetics.................. | 447 | 458 | Preserved vegetables (to- | | |
| Filberts .................. | 1,134 | 26,831 | mato paste, artichokes, | | |
| Fish, salted or preserved | | | etc.).................... | 60,459 | 34,215 |
| (sardines, anchovies, | | | Snuff.................... | 2,905 | 1,288 |
| etc.).................... | 6,385 | 3,303 | Soap stock, or sulphur oil. | 93,202 | 24,950 |
| Garlic .................... | 6,083 | 5,093 | Sumac .................... | 226,258 | 240,008 |
| Human hair................ | 28,780 | 16,600 | Tartar, or dregs of wine.. | 13,880 | 35,350 |
| Lemons .................... | 2,073,217 | 2,541,586 | Wine..................... | 8,218 | 9,968 |
| Lemon juice .............. | 3,269 | 4,700 | Walnuts .................... | 191 | 692 |
| Macaroni.................. | 62,636 | 54,900 | Sundries .................... | 7,490 | 3,822 |
| Manna.................... | 9,029 | 9,336 | | | |
| Mustard seed............. | 1,570 | | Total................ | 2,990,318 | 3,360,311 |

*Value of declared exports from the port of Palermo to the United States during the six months ended June 30, 1902, in comparison with the six months ended June 30 of the preceding year.*

| Articles. | First six months of— | | Articles. | First six months of— | |
|---|---|---|---|---|---|
| | 1902. | 1901. | | 1902. | 1901. |
| Almonds .................. | $9,565 | $2,525 | Olives..................... | $1,426 | $1,161 |
| Brimstone ............... | 18,643 | 52,386 | Olive oil ................. | 34,676 | 27,300 |
| Cheese.................... | 17,143 | 16,980 | Oranges.................. | 44,023 | 16,677 |
| Citrate of lime.......... | 24,708 | 87,609 | Orange and lemon peel.. | 708 | 505 |
| Cork, raw............... | 34,946 | 42,672 | Pistachio ................ | 498 | ............ |
| Essence (oil of lemon and | | | Preserved vegetables (to- | | |
| orange)................. | 9,356 | 7,021 | mato sauce, artichokes, | | |
| Filberts.................. | 2,753 | ............ | etc.) ................... | 35,964 | 21,193 |
| Fish, salted or preserved | | | Snuff...................... | 1,978 | 1,883 |
| (sardines, anchovies, | | | Soapstock, or sulphur oil. | 43,961 | 51,838 |
| tunny) ................. | 2,021 | 752 | Sumac .................... | 100,393 | 106,736 |
| Garlic ................... | 1,102 | 1,101 | Tartar, crude, or dregs of | | |
| Human hair.............. | 19,753 | 12,469 | wine ................... | ............ | 13,880 |
| Lemons .................. | 1,907,110 | 1,569,475 | Wine..................... | 5,195 | 2,712 |
| Lemon juice ............. | 3,181 | 3,269 | Sundry articles .......... | 2,548 | 1,610 |
| Macaroni................. | 32,722 | 33,243 | | | |
| Manna ................... | 212 | 3,096 | Total............... | 2,354,585 | 2,079,663 |
| Mustard seed............. | ............ | 1,570 | | | |

*Navigation of the port of Palermo during the year 1901.*

| Flag. | Steamers. | | Sailing vessels. | | Total. | |
|---|---|---|---|---|---|---|
| | No. | Tons. | No. | Tons. | No. | Tons. |
| **ENTERED.** | | | | | | |
| Italian .................... | 1,285 | 967,211 | 1,776 | 93,929 | 3,061 | 1,061,140 |
| English .................... | 297 | 415,693 | 2 | 224 | 299 | 415,917 |
| Austrian ................... | 128 | 128,589 | ............ | ............ | 128 | 128,589 |
| German.................... | 73 | 92,544 | ............ | ............ | 73 | 92,544 |
| French..................... | 66 | 63,157 | ............ | ............ | 66 | 63,157 |
| Hollander ................. | 33 | 23,364 | ............ | ............ | 33 | 23,364 |
| Grecian ................... | 22 | 24,826 | 2 | 378 | 24 | 25,204 |
| Norwegian................. | 12 | 12,442 | 1 | 74 | 13 | 12,516 |
| Russian ................... | 5 | 6,017 | ............ | ............ | 5 | 6,017 |
| Swedish................... | 5 | 4,228 | ............ | ............ | 5 | 4,228 |
| Spanish ................... | 3 | 4,732 | ............ | ............ | 3 | 4,732 |
| Roumanian ............... | 2 | 2,878 | ............ | ............ | 2 | 2,878 |
| Danish.................... | 2 | 2,093 | ............ | ............ | 2 | 2,093 |
| Belgian ................... | 1 | 738 | ............ | ............ | 1 | 738 |
| Tunis ..................... | ............ | ............ | 6 | 208 | 6 | 208 |
| Turkish ................... | ............ | ............ | 2 | 319 | 2 | 319 |
| United States ............. | ............ | ............ | 1 | 1,284 | 1 | 1,284 |
| Total.................. | 1,934 | 1,743,512 | 1,790 | 96,416 | 3,724 | 1,839,928 |
| **CLEARED.** | | | | | | |
| Italian..................... | 1,274 | 967,726 | 1,797 | 98,188 | 3,071 | 1,065,914 |
| English .................... | 299 | 421,552 | 2 | 245 | 301 | 421,797 |
| Austrian.................... | 127 | 124,833 | ............ | ............ | 127 | 124,333 |
| German..................... | 73 | 92,223 | ............ | ............ | 73 | 92,223 |
| French..................... | 67 | 67,216 | ............ | ............ | 67 | 67,216 |
| Hollander ................. | 33 | 23,728 | ............ | ............ | 33 | 23,728 |
| Grecian ................... | 22 | 25,692 | 2 | 389 | 24 | 26,081 |
| Norwegian................. | 13 | 13,511 | 1 | 82 | 14 | 13,593 |
| Russian ................... | 5 | 6,019 | ............ | ............ | 5 | 6,019 |
| Swedish................... | 5 | 4,318 | ............ | ............ | 5 | 4,318 |
| Spanish ................... | 3 | 4,682 | ............ | ............ | 3 | 4,682 |
| Roumanian ............... | 2 | 2,899 | ............ | ............ | 2 | 2,899 |
| Danish.................... | 2 | 2,217 | ............ | ............ | 2 | 2,217 |
| Belgian ................... | 1 | 738 | ............ | ............ | 1 | 738 |
| Tunis ..................... | ............ | ............ | 7 | 196 | 7 | 196 |
| Turkish ................... | ............ | ............ | 2 | 273 | 2 | 273 |
| United States ............. | ............ | ............ | 1 | 1,379 | 1 | 1,379 |
| Total.................. | 1,926 | 1,756,854 | 1,812 | 100,752 | 3,738 | 1,857,606 |

## TURIN.

This consular district is constituted by the territory included in the province of Piedmont, which is the northwestern part of Italy. Piedmont is composed of two words, pied, meaning foot, or base, and mont, meaning mountain, hence the word means at the foot of the mountain, and very appropriately, as the territory is bounded by the Alps on the north, west, and southwest.

Its leading cities are Turin, Novara, Alessandria, Cueno, and Pinerolo.

Turin is one of the most modern and progressive cities in Italy. Its people are intelligent, its system of public schools is admirable and thorough, and education of the young is compulsory. It is said that 92 males and 87 females out of every 100 can read and write. The city has numerous and important industries, and exports and imports a vast quantity of goods, as will be seen farther on. The population is claimed to be 350,000, but many put it as high as 385,000.

Novara, in the northeastern part of the province, has a population of about 45,000, is in the midst of the great rice garden of Italy, and is an historic city, having been the scene of terrible battles.

Alessandria is located in the southeastern part of the district, and has a population of about 75,000. Its citadel is pronounced one of the strongest in Europe. It sends considerable goods to the United States.

Cuneo is situated in the southwestern part of the district, and has a population of nearly 30,000. It contributes its share of exports to the United States.

Pinerolo is located in the western part of the district, and has a population of about 19,000. It is quite a center of industry, and sends a considerable quantity of goods to our country.

There are many other towns in this province, and its total population, it is claimed, is nearly 3,600,000.

### SILK.

This is the great silk district of Italy, producing nearly as much silk as all the rest of the country, as the following official figures for 1901 indicate:

| Provinces. | Markets. | Cocoons. |
|---|---|---|
| | | *Pounds.* |
| Piedmont | Turin | 13,237,880 |
| Lombardy | Milan | 2,879,844 |
| Veneto | Venice | 3,651,780 |
| Liguria | Genoa | 44,440 |
| Emilia | Bologna | 4,898,212 |
| Marche-Umbria | Ancona | 1,591,612 |
| Tuscana | Florence | 3,106,730 |
| Lazio | Rome | 61,600 |
| Elsewhere in Italy | | 1,284,760 |

I am informed that the crop this year is estimated to be about the same as that of last.

Although this is the great silk-producing center of Italy, the greater part of the silk exported to the United States reaches there in some roundabout way, because for the six months ended June 30, 1902, the total of raw silk sent to the United States from here amounted in value to only $210,323. The actual quantity sent was several times that amount. I am at a loss to account for this.

I have secured eleven samples of cocoons of this season's product, which I send herewith.[a]

### RICE.

Piedmont is also noted for being one of the best rice-producing districts of the world. The rice fields are watered with ease, the supply of water being secured from the Alpine regions and the necessary canals having been built at the cost of millions. Great care is taken in its culture. Hundreds of men and women may be seen in the fields, with water up to their knees, removing weeds and other unwelcome materials.

A well-informed Italian, who has had much experience in the rice trade, has told me that the rice raised in this district is largely taken to Genoa, and in the free port there is mixed with Japanese and Indian rice. The Indian rice is called "Rangoon," and is very inferior. The resultant product is sent to the United States as pure Italian rice.

### OTHER EXPORTS.

The raising of chestnuts is an important industry in this province, large quantities being shipped to the United States, the exports for the past season amounting to over $20,000.

Another industry for which this locality is specially noted is the production of vermouth. Many firms are engaged in this business, and immense fortunes have been reaped. The value of the vermouth shipped to the United States during the six months ended June 30, 1902, was $114,623, and for the year, $229,000.

Pickled sheepskins are sent to the United States from this consular district in large quantities, the shipments for the period indicated above amounting to $51,221. During the same six months there were shipped: Glycerin, $38,340; plumbago, $14,209; and human hair, $22,175.

The last item is worthy of mention, the amount for the six months ended June 30, 1902, being $10,571.

Wood carving has a very high reputation in this city, but not much of it is shipped to the United States.

### AMERICAN ENTERPRISE.

A new industry has been started by an American from Detroit. The plant is capitalized at $400,000, of which $40,000 is American capital. The manager informs me that they expect to be in full operation in a few weeks, and to employ 400 men, the wages averaging 60 cents per day. The principal articles to be made are glue, gelatine, fertilizers, and sulphuric and hydrochloric acids. The quantity of cattle horns and bones used every twenty-four hours will be 21 tons, these coming largely from South America and the United States. Three tons of hide cuttings per day will be used, and Tennessee phosphate will be employed to the amount of 4,000 tons per year. The management expects this plant to reach a high degree of efficiency, and to sell a good portion of its products in the markets of the United States.

---

[a] Transmitted to the Department of Agriculture.

## RAILWAYS.

The roadbeds and tracks of the leading railway lines from Turin to Genoa, Pisa, Florence, Bologna, Venice, and Milan are first class, and the trains make good time, but the passenger coaches and the freight cars are inferior to those of the chief American lines.

Freight cars and many passenger cars here have but two wheels under each end, while American coaches have never less than four and often six, which enables the cars to move much more smoothly. I have noticed, however, that on all the lines on which I have traveled in Italy, there is a system of gates and watchmen at grade crossings which renders accidents of very rare occurrence. Watchmen also do not allow pedestrians to walk on the railway tracks when trains are expected within ten minutes. Such precautions are to be commended.

## AMERICAN GOODS.

The radical advance in the price of American coal, and the high freight necessary to get it here, are fatal to its sale in this market, especially as the transport cost of English coal is only about half as much, or $1.12 against $2.30 per ton from the United States.

I have personally visited and interviewed agents for the sale of American goods, such as cash registers, typewriting machines, tools, machinery, bicycles, and sewing machines, and all report increase of sales, the responses of some being quite enthusiastic.

## CEMENT.

I wish to make special mention of the cement industry in this consular district. It is made in great quantities, is pronounced equal to the Portland, and is used in façading and finishing the exteriors as well as the interiors of buildings. I am informed that the builders erect a support of lumber; on it they put cement, with certain portions of gravel, then smooth the surface. In a few days, the temporary support is removed, the ceiling is frescoed and the floor is complete, all in one piece, as if made of one stone. I am told that this cement becomes even harder than stone. A bridge for pedestrians near the city, over 20 feet long and 10 wide, is made in that way and all in one piece. A proposition has also been made to the city to build a cement bridge over the Po River.

## WAGES IN IRON INDUSTRY.

Iron is extensively made in this district, the machinery employed being either American or copied after our patterns. There is a large plant near this city, and I am informed skilled employees receive about $1 per day and laborers 40 or 60 cents per day. Mechanics in this city are paid from 60 to 70 cents per day, while laborers get 40 or less. Motormen and conductors on street cars, who are required to be on duty fourteen hours per day, and furnish their own suits, are paid from 50 to 60 cents per day.

H. Doc. 305, pt 2——28

## FINANCES.

The financial condition of Italy has materially improved during the past few years, the paper lire being valued within 1 per cent of gold.

PIETRO CUNEO, *Consul.*

TURIN, *September 20, 1902.*

TRANSLATION OF LETTER FROM CHAMBER OF COMMERCE IN TURIN.

From inquiries made, it appears that the rice crop of 1901 in Piedmont was 2,500,000 hectoliters (6,092,500 bushels).

It also appears that 1,351,000 quintals (399,922,000 pounds) of raw cotton was imported, of which 956,000 quintals (212,232,000 pounds) came from the United States.

We have no statistics showing the raw cotton consumed in Piedmont, but we know that there were, in 1901, about 1,900,000 spindles in Italy, of which 550,000 spindles were in Piedmont.

As American cotton is much more consumed in this than in other provinces of Italy, we can say that about 250,000 quintals (55,000,000 pounds) of raw cotton imported from the United States is spun here each year.

## VENICE.

In the past year, the increasing importance of Venice as a commercial port has been emphasized, and according to reliable authorities this city holds the second place among the commercial ports of the Kingdom, the total tonnage being more than two millions. With the improved economic situation in Italy, there seems to be no reason why this progress should not continue.

The work of improving the Stazione Marittima, which connects the sea traffic with the railway, has gone on uninterruptedly. The grain elevator with its storehouses, known as the Magazzini Sylos, is in active operation. At the Sylos quay, three vessels can discharge at the same time, and, as the depth of the water is 8½ meters (9.2 yards), the largest-sized freight steamers can lie alongside the dock. Two thousand tons of grain can be unloaded from a ship's hold per day, and owing to an excellent system of electric lighting, the work can be carried on by night. The total capacity of the warehouse is about 30,000 tons. The motive power used in running the elevators is supplied by a special electric station, having a force of 700 horsepower, and the grain in the vessels can be either discharged into trucks on the docks—passing previously through automatic weighing machines—or into lighters, or directly into the warehouse. The president of this company is Baron Albert Treves, the head of a large banking house in Venice. It is presumed that the operation of this warehouse will divert to this port large shipments of American wheat which at present pass through Genoa.

### FREIGHT RATES.

Freight rates from New Orleans, Savannah, Galveston, and Pensacola, for sulphate of copper, phosphate, lumber, and rosin have fallen about 25 per cent; that is, from 19s. to 15s. ($4.62 to $3.65) per ton.

Freights from New York on the usual imports, such as cotton-seed and mineral oils, bales of cotton, paraffin, machinery, etc., have dropped about 20 per cent, or from 40s. to 32s. ($9.73 to $7.79). The importations of the above-mentioned articles have largely increased, especially cotton from New Orleans, Savannah, and Galveston, and phosphates from Port Tampa and Pensacola. It is believed that, during the coming year, Venice will receive large shipments of cotton which up to the present time have gone to Genoa.

For exports from this district to New York and Boston, which consist principally of hemp, glycerine, furniture, marble, and glassware, freight rates have fallen from 5 to 10 per cent.

### SHIPPING.

ᴀ have not yet received from the chamber of commerce statistics regarding the movement of shipping at this port. From my registry of bills of health, I find that sailings to the United States have decidedly increased. The total number of steamers leaving this port for the United States in the year 1901 was 22, while from January 1 of the present year, the number has already reached 28. These sailings were principally to New York, and by steamers of the New York and Mediterranean Steamship Company—operated by Phelps Brothers, of New York—which line does most of the direct carrying trade between Venice and the United States.

The Austro-American Navigation Company has established an agency and begun a regular freight service between Venice and New York, Philadelphia, Savannah, New Orleans, and Galveston, with monthly sailings, and once every two months a steamer is to leave for the Gulf of Mexico.

A royal commission has recently been looking into the question of renewing a line from Venice to Calcutta, which service some time ago was performed by the Peninsular and Oriental Steamship Company, under a subsidy from the Government. It appears, however, that this was not remunerative for the company, and at the expiration of its contract, this service was discontinued, and since then, there has been no regular line to India. Several Italian steamship companies have made bids for the route, among them being the Navigazione Generale and a Venetian company known as the Societa Veneta. It is probable that, within the course of a few months, the new service will be in operation.

### EXPORTS.

The exports from this consulate during the fiscal year ended June 30, 1902, considerably exceeded those of the preceding year. The total value of exports for the year 1900–1901 amounted to $508,522.49, while the exports during the year 1901–2 reached a total of $574,451.09, showing an increase of $65,928.60. For the present fiscal year, the exports will in all probability be still greater. The shipments of hemp are constantly on the increase, and owing to the growing number of Americans who visit this city, the amount of carved marble, Venetian glass, furniture, and so-called antiquities exported to our country is steadily advancing. Trade is much more active than it was a few years ago; the Italian lira, after fifteen years' depreciation, has again arrived at par, and the general economic progress of the entire kingdom is shown notably in this district.

### IMPORTS.

It is impossible at this date to obtain the total value of the exports and imports for the last year at this port. I have, however, succeeded in procuring statistics of the imports from the United States for the first six months of the current year, which are:

[Quintal = 220.4 pounds.]

| Description. | Quantity. | Value. | Description. | Quantity. | Value. |
|---|---|---|---|---|---|
| | *Quintals.* | | | *Quintals.* | |
| Lumber ................. | 8,129 | $9,413.38 | Paraffine............... | 6,580 | $12,699.40 |
| Coal .................... | 65,000 | 37,635.00 | Petroleum ............. | 40,000 | 165,980.00 |
| Coffee .................. | 480 | 1,158.00 | Phosphate ............. | 215,870 | 249,977.46 |
| Cotton.................. | 69,855 | 1,145,971.27 | Metals ................. | 1,035 | 8,389.71 |
| Oil: | | | Rosin ................. | 45,930 | 106,373.88 |
| Cotton-seed......... | 7,921 | 107,012.71 | Sulphate of copper..... | 16,049 | 173,457.59 |
| Mineral ............ | 810 | 5,471.55 | Sundries............... | 1,022 | 2,761.44 |

### WATER POWER.

The work of utilizing the water power from the river Celina, referred to in my last annual report, is progressing satisfactorily, and it is thought that, within a space of two years, Venice can be lighted by electricity derived from this source. There are, however, serious legal difficulties which must be overcome by the municipality before a new system of illumination can be put into operation, as the present contract for lighting by gas, made some fifty years ago, is for a period of ninety years. The town is at present very badly illuminated, the quality of the gas being poor and the price probably in excess of that of any other large city in Italy.

Considerable interest has been taken of late in the question of developing the immense water power which is available in this region. It is estimated by a celebrated engineer of Udine, Mr. Tonini, that the water courses reaching the plains of Friuli alone could be made to produce something like 500,000 horsepower at the most favorable season. This great power is at the present time lying idle simply for the want of necessary capital, which it seems to me would be well invested in organizing and fostering such an important undertaking.

### LOCAL IMPROVEMENTS.

There has been little done in Venice in the way of building during the past year. Since the fall of the Campanile of San Marco on July 14, a great deal of anxiety has been felt for the safety of other towers and lofty buildings here, and steps have been taken by the Government to avoid fresh disasters of this sort.

The dredging of the Grand Canal from its head at the railway station to the basin of St. Mark has been completed, and dredging operations are at present under way in the Canal of the Giudecca and in other parts of the lagoon.

### TRADE OPPORTUNITIES.

With the exception of a relatively small quantity of agricultural machinery, American manufactured products do not figure largely among the imports of this district; but it seems to me that, if properly pushed, there are exceptionally good opportunities for the introduction of our goods. The rapid improvement in economic conditions throughout the kingdom appears especially to favor the present moment. There is a decided tendency to adopt the various products of modern industrial activity, in which the United States is preeminent, which have heretofore found little favor among the inhabitants of this region.

*Electrical appliances, stoves, etc.*—With the probable introduction into the city, within a relatively short time, of electricity at a low cost for lighting and various domestic uses, a chance is presented to our manufacturers of electrical appliances, and they would do well to give the matter immediate attention. The demand for all sorts of household utensils and conveniences is already quite large and is steadily increasing, most of the modern articles sold under this head being of American invention. If the genuine American article is no longer found in the market, it is simply because a successful imitation has been made of it in Europe, principally in Germany. The need of modern stoves, cooking ranges, every description of heating apparatus, and plumbers' supplies is at last realized, and I believe that a large sale could be found for this class of goods. There is also a fairly good market here for stationery, printing machines, druggists' supplies, patent medicines, etc.

*Shoes.*—I have been requested on various occasions by shoe manufacturers to furnish information as to the opportunities in this district for the sale of American footwear. I believe there is little hope in this line, either in this part of Italy or anywhere in the kingdom. A cheap grade of shoes is manufactured at Milan, which seems to satisfy the popular demand, and although very inferior to the low-priced shoe sold in our country, retails for something like $1 per pair.

*Motor boats.*—In former reports, I have called attention to the opening for the introduction of a cheap but well-built motor boat of some sort, and I have endeavored personally to interest an American firm in the matter. The great trouble about introducing anything of that kind here is that nobody is willing to buy an article upon catalogue representations only. Intending purchasers wish to inspect samples before committing themselves, and our manufacturers make little headway in this market, as they do not seem disposed to satisfy this requirement by seeking reliable agents for the sale of their merchandise, and by furnishing samples free of charge. American goods will undoubtedly find an opening in this market in time, in spite of the lack of exertion on the part of manufacturers, but unless greater efforts are made to satisfy the local demands than at present, I fear that it will not be at an early date.

I again take this occasion to call the attention of those seeking to open up trade in this district to the waste of time and money involved in trying to advertise by means of elaborate catalogues and printed matter in the English language. These publications, with rare exceptions, are consigned to the rubbish heap, unread. They can serve no purpose whatever. The inhabitants of this region avoid advertising matter, even when it is in their native tongue, so it is easy to imagine what publications in a foreign language can expect.

H. ALBERT JOHNSON, *Consul.*

' VENICE, *November 15, 1902.*

## MALTA.

For the past three or four years, in my annual reports on trade conditions in Malta, I have been able to show that traffic between the United States and this island has been increasing. From year to year, also, the favorable predictions as to a still further increase have been fully justified by results. This year will prove no exception, and it is gratifying to be able to state that there was a still further advance in the value and variety of goods of American origin imported.

### IMPORTS.

This increase, however, was not as large as it might have been had our business houses paid a little more attention to the requirements of this island. Malta is now easily reached by direct transport from New York, and the great drawback—lack of direct communication,— which existed for so many years, has been removed. Malta produces very little and manufactures practically nothing, so that she must import nearly everything needed. Manufactured goods, with the exception of a few food products, pay no duty on entering this port; for this reason, it is impossible for me to give a complete list of the articles in demand here, inasmuch as records are compiled only on the basis of articles paying duty. The usual Government statistics for last year are not yet published, but the following tables, made up from other sources, may prove of interest; the one below shows the principal articles subject to duty released from bond for consumption during the year 1901, exclusive of similar articles consumed by the fleet and garrison, on which no duty is levied:

| Articles. | Quantity. | Articles. | Quantity. |
|---|---|---|---|
| Wheat..................bushels.. | 491,968 | Cotton-seed oil..............pounds.. | 1,957,891 |
| Corn.......................do.... | 1,624 | Potatoes...................do.... | 14,246,898 |
| Barley......................do.... | 32,392 | Chick pease ................bushels.. | 178,884 |
| Saggina....................do.... | 102,088 | Beans.....................do.... | 188,586 |
| Flour...................pounds.. | 29,987,578 | Other seeds ...................do.... | 25,120 |
| Semola....................do.... | 281,538 | Carob beans................pounds.. | 8,661,952 |
| Biscuits ...................do.... | 225,034 | Cotton seed.................do.... | 9,081,334 |
| Oatmeal...................do.... | 54,631 | Petroleum ...................gallons.. | 832,462 |
| Wine ....................gallons.. | 3,464,072 | Mules .....................heads.. | 47 |
| Spirits.....................do.... | 155,268 | Sugar .......................pounds.. | 2,757,538 |
| Beer.......................do.... | 1,638,989 | Tobacco: | |
| Vinegar ....................do.... | 7,296 | Plug .........................do.... | 2 |
| Cattle and meat.............pounds.. | 14,827,748 | Cut .........................do.... | 2,366 |
| Horses .....................heads.. | 476 | Raw .........................do.... | 15,365 |
| Olive oil....................pounds.. | 998,487 | Cigars and cigarettes ..........do.... | 7,520 |

The foregoing figures show, on the whole, an increase over those of the preceding year. Recent augmentation of the fleet and garrison would warrant a greater enlargement. The quantity of wheat for local consumption on which duty was paid again showed a decrease, but was compensated for by the quantity of flour used. The cumbersome and expensive methods still obtaining here in handling wheat sweep away whatever advantages local millers would derive from the difference in duty between the raw and the manufactured article; and the by-products of wheat, on account of the reduced quantity now being ground here, command what would under other conditions be very remunerative prices; in fact, bran is imported not infrequently from near-by countries. Notwithstanding this, a recent attempt to work up a trade in American bran did not meet with success.

## WHEAT AND FLOUR.

No American wheat was imported here during the year 1901, and none has come thus far during 1902, and the quantity of Canadian received by way of New York was smaller than in previous years. This wheat is not taken by the local trade, although it comes as near as possible to satisfying requirements. It is used only by the commissariat of the British troops garrisoning these islands. A tender for the supply of some 12,000 bushels of wheat, preferably Canadian, recently called for by the army authorities, was secured on a sample of Russian hard Black Sea wheat at a lower figure than that for the Canadian. I fear there is no hope of our soft or even hard wheats finding a market here for the present. Local millers do not seem to be equipped to handle them, and are, moreover, prejudiced in favor of the very hard wheat from Black Sea ports, which they say answers their requirements. Imported flour is, moreover, gradually killing the local milling industry. In the absence of figures, official or otherwise, I am unable to give the precise quantity of American flour imported during the year 1902. I am, however, sure that the proportionate rank gained last year has not only been maintained, but increased. Maltese merchants are now drawing their supplies of American flour directly from some of the principal milling concerns in the United States. Several brands of flour coming from Liverpool, Newcastle, and Bristol, England, however, maintain their wide sale in these islands. In seeking to discover why American flour does not preponderate, I have been told that the standard of several brands has not been kept up, and that, consequently, the latter have gained a bad reputation. It takes a long time to introduce a new brand in substitution. Another complaint is that American flour is not obtainable on more favorable terms than the British. A supply of the latter reaches this port from Liverpool in two weeks from date of cable, whereas American flour ordered at the same time occupies about six weeks in reaching this port. Ocean freights from New York to Malta by the direct line were very low during the past summer; in fact, they were at times lower than those from Liverpool to Malta, and I fully expected to see a heavy import of American flour in consequence; but when the cost at this port of American and British was compared, no difference was to be found in favor of the former.

## UNITED STATES TRADE.

By watching the discharge of the steamships of the direct line, I have observed the introduction of some new article on nearly every arrival from New York. These new lines have in general consisted of domestic and other cotton goods, picture-frame stock, safes, photographer's supplies, wooden and brass goods, wire and wire nails, cold water paint, white lead, zinc, and linseed oil, and quite a number of other kinds of goods. The importation of many other lines has become practically steady. During the past year, American wickless cooking oil stoves have taken quite a hold here, notwithstanding their much higher price compared with that of the old-fashioned wick stoves imported from other countries. The market is now well stocked for the coming season, and oil heating stoves of American origin appear for the first time. Although an undoubted change has been wrought in the last few years by the advent of the Phelps line from New York (which, by bringing merchandise direct, permits the goods to be credited to our country, and thus proves a valuable advertisement), there is plenty of room for improvement in the import trade. European drummers visit Malta regularly, and few go away without sufficient orders to warrant another call. I have frequently pointed out the desirability of our exporters meeting their competitors on these lines. One merchant here has very expressively remarked to me: "Price lists and catalogues do not talk." Another prominent business man says:

Your manufacturers and exporters advertise their goods well, and I have no doubt their circulars, price lists, and trade journals reach every part of the world. We are frequently attracted by plausible advertisements of American firms, but as often as not find it impossible to do business with them on account of the conditions which they impose; such conditions, for instance, as "carload lots, spot cash quotations" for goods placed free on board cars at some town at a considerable distance from New York, etc. Your manufacturers appear to imagine that Europeans have been sitting around all this time waiting for American houses to discover us and to send us their goods. There is no doubt that your country will hold sway in certain lines of goods. We can not, for instance, turn elsewhere for Kentucky or Virginia tobacco, if we want to continue to smoke the kind of cigars we have become accustomed to, but in manufactured goods in general our side of the globe is not behind yours. Some of your firms have overcome the carload lot and spot cash nonsense, but it is one of the greatest difficulties to get them to quote rates c. i. f. Malta, or at least f. o. b. New York. Often, when instructed to make a shipment on trial, the firms. have left the matter of transportation in the hands of railway or forwarding agents, with the result that these charges figured so high as to preclude repetition of orders. Again, your concerns, and even some shipping agents, show a lack not only of geographical knowledge but even of the proper lines of steamships. I can quote you instances where New York agents sent goods by an indirect line, incurring more freight, when they should have known there were steamships direct for this port, by which a considerable freight saving would have been made, without subjecting the goods to the tumbling about incidental to transshipment. Some of your firms don't seem to know what to do with an ocean bill of lading. It is filed away instead of being mailed to the consignee, and when the consignee has finally sent for and obtained it, it has arrived unindorsed, although delivery was made out to "order." We all have a general liking for things American and would be happy to extend our trade to you, but you must remember that we work for profit and must place our orders with your manufacturers more advantageously than we do nearer home.

### TOBACCO.

The tariff on raw and manufactured tobacco imposed here last fall caused a cessation of imports, the markets having been supplied fully in anticipation of its imposition. The stocks of plug tobacco having gradually been worked off, small fresh importations are beginning to arrive. The duty imposed (18 cents per pound) restricts the consumption. There is still a good supply of free raw tobacco here, but the higher prices now asked for the American product, and the duty to which importations are subject, prevent any new business until the stock becomes exhausted, which, I am given to understand, will not be for some months.

### EMIGRATION.

If the present tide of emigration to the United States is kept up, I am told that Malta will become a port of departure for emigrants brought here from Black Sea, Greek, and other eastern Mediterranean ports, to be forwarded to New York.

During the past year, Malta has gained a second direct connection with New York, the steamers of the Dutch Levant Line now calling here both to and from New York. Harbor and other improvements mentioned in my former annual reports are still in progress. Banking and postal facilities continue amply to meet requirements.

I have recently been requested to obtain information relative to American wood-working machinery. Any printed matter upon this subject that may be received at this consulate will be handed to the right parties. Straw hats are worn here about nine months in the year, and yet—although I have often stated that there is a wide field in Malta for our goods of this line—no American manufacturer has essayed to gain the trade. There is also a good market for our fly paper. Cash registers of American manufacture are beginning to appear, while our typewriters are being more and more used. American bicycles are popular. Cheap cutlery, to compete with the German, would find a market.

There seems to be a growing demand in the United States for Maltese lace goods, as during the last three months I find that more were shipped to our country than in any similar period for many years. Formerly, much cummin and fennel seed was exported to the United States, but this has recently fallen off. Parcels post facilities would benefit trade.

### SHIPPING.

The following tables show the marine movement for the year 1901:

#### GOVERNMENT VESSELS.

| Nationality. | Arrived. | Sailed. | Nationality. | Arrived. | Sailed. |
|---|---|---|---|---|---|
| British | 348 | 344 | Dutch | 2 | 2 |
| United States | 13 | 13 | French | 1 | 1 |
| Greek | 7 | 7 | Portuguese | 1 | 1 |
| German | 5 | 5 | | | |
| Italian | 3 | 3 | Total | 382 | 378 |
| Austro-Hungarian | 2 | 2 | | | |

#### STEAM AND SAILING YACHTS.

| Nationality | Arrived | Sailed | Nationality | Arrived | Sailed |
|---|---|---|---|---|---|
| British | 21 | 21 | German | 1 | 1 |
| United States | 4 | 4 | Greek | 1 | 1 |
| Belgium | 2 | 2 | | | |
| Austro-Hungarian | 1 | 1 | Total | 31 | 31 |
| French | 1 | 1 | | | |

#### MERCHANT STEAMSHIPS.

| Nationality. | Arrived. | Sailed. | Tonnage. | Nationality. | Arrived. | Sailed. | Tonnage. |
|---|---|---|---|---|---|---|---|
| British | 1,470 | 1,472 | 2,484,367 | Russian | 20 | 20 | 23,478 |
| Austro-Hungarian | 456 | 455 | 321,195 | Greek | 20 | 20 | 22,407 |
| German | 198 | 198 | 280,997 | Belgian | 18 | 18 | 24,146 |
| Italian | 165 | 168 | 172,871 | Swedish | 14 | 14 | 14,075 |
| French | 60 | 60 | 49,233 | Danish | 12 | 12 | 9,931 |
| Norwegian | 32 | 32 | 37,664 | Ottoman | 3 | 3 | 1,935 |
| Dutch | 30 | 30 | 20,817 | | | | |
| Spanish | 23 | 25 | 38,167 | Total | 2,321 | 2,527 | 3,501,283 |

NOTE.—In the case of Austria-Hungary, the figures include the arrival and departure of the daily mail boat, of 514 tons, to and from Syracuse, Sicily.

#### MERCHANT SAILING VESSELS.

| Nationality | Arrived | Sailed | Tonnage | Nationality | Arrived | Sailed | Tonnage |
|---|---|---|---|---|---|---|---|
| British | 71 | 69 | 8,260 | Samos | 10 | 9 | 562 |
| Greek | 140 | 134 | 11,505 | Montenegro | 5 | 4 | 1,048 |
| Ottoman | 44 | 45 | 2,923 | Italian | 1,045 | 1,056 | 39,913 |
| Tunesian | 41 | 37 | 2,036 | | | | |
| Spanish | 21 | 19 | 1,652 | Total | 1,377 | 1,373 | 67,899 |

STEAMSHIPS PASSED IN SIGHT OF THE ISLANDS.

| Nationality. | Number. |
|---|---|
| British | 551 |
| German | 75 |
| United States | 5 |
| French | 3 |
| Others | 71 |
| Total | 705 |

COAL IMPORTATIONS.

| | Tons. |
|---|---|
| Welsh steam coal | 411,816 |
| North country and Mersey | 54,838 |
| United States | 21,015 |
| Belgian | 500 |
| Total | 488,169 |

JOHN H. GROUT, *Consul.*

MALTA, *October 14, 1902.*

## SUPPLEMENTARY REPORT.

I have just received copies of Trade Statistics for 1901, prepared by the local customs authorities. The publication of this report is over six months behindhand. I had hoped, in preparing my annual report on the commerce and industries of this island, to be able to incorporate figures issued by the local government, but for the above reason was obliged finally to relinquish all hope of doing so. Trade Statistics, however, contains many interesting facts. First of all, by consulting the table that follows, it will be seen that, in value of imports, the United States now occupies fifth place, whereas in the previous year it ranked seventh, and in the year before that ninth. Owing to the fact that the authorities here keep no record of the values of articles except such as may be dutiable, manufactured goods are not included, and their valuation is unknown. For this reason, the figures given in the table apply only to the dutiable goods that arrived here. Could the value of the nondutiable articles be ascertained, I am sure it would have the effect of sliding the United States still higher up the list. Again, large quantities of flour from the United States arrived here through transshipment in England and Germany, all of which is accredited to those two countries instead of to America. If the port of origin were given, the figures would also help to better the showing of our trade. As things are, however, it is known that the United States has gone up two points at least over the year 1900, and that its trade with Malta is increasing slowly but surely.

### PETROLEUM.

Unfortunately, statistics as to petroleum have not this year been given. The imports from some countries are mentioned, it is true, but no total amounts have been stated that would give one an idea of the quantities consumed.

## GENERAL COMMERCE.

The following table shows the values of imports and exports of Malta for the year 1901 as compared with those of 1900:

| Countries. | 1901. | | 1900. | |
|---|---|---|---|---|
| | Imports. | Exports. | Imports. | Exports. |
| United Kingdom ........................ | $2,070,029.03 | $5,763.96 | $1,484,331.16 | $5,153.16 |
| Russia ................................. | 752,321.96 | 1,148.62 | 799,600.01 | 1,484.28 |
| Italy .................................. | 704,722.73 | 13,095.75 | 803,045.23 | 47,375.37 |
| Barbary ............................... | 671,594.73 | 217,761.27 | 395,446.92 | 97,685.25 |
| United States ......................... | 384,453.50 | 700.77 | 170,205.83 | 291.99 |
| Turkey ................................ | 380,341.30 | 11,577.40 | 367,717.60 | 3,275.15 |
| Tunis ................................. | 330,605.67 | 51,010.65 | 137,532.15 | 19,631.46 |
| Spain ................................. | 273,628.69 | 34.06 | 75,421.01 | 53.53 |
| Australia ............................. | 184,927.00 | 34.06 | 166,069.31 | .............. |
| Austria-Hungary ...................... | 176,799.94 | 2,593.84 | 111,759.17 | 866.23 |
| France ................................ | 146,593.57 | 15,129.94 | 227,508.87 | 15,071.55 |
| Greece ................................ | 89,684.72 | 1,561.62 | 70,457.18 | 1,722.74 |
| Germany .............................. | 67,746.54 | 773.77 | 8,813.23 | 160.59 |
| Morocco .............................. | 36,304.09 | .............. | 93,128.79 | .............. |
| Cyprus ................................ | 17,572.93 | 19.46 | 939.23 | 199.52 |
| Belgium and Holland .................. | 16,137.31 | 116.79 | 7,129.42 | 214.12 |
| British war ships ..................... | 13,485.07 | 58,398.00 | 4,808.23 | 37,549.91 |
| Egypt ................................. | 2,004.99 | 9,771.98 | 1,506.61 | 3,406.55 |
| Gibraltar ............................. | 889.32 | 613.17 | .............. | .............. |
| Algiers ............................... | 141.12 | 107.06 | 1,046.29 | 472.05 |
| India ................................. | .............. | 1,494.12 | .............. | 2,301.85 |

From the above table, it will be seen that Germany has dropped from thirteenth to fourteenth place, while France has dropped from sixth to eleventh place. On the contrary, Spain has gone up from the twelfth to the eighth position. Italy has changed places with Russia, to the latter's advantage. It will be observed that, in the case of England, there was a large increase. This was due to the augmentation of the fleet and garrison as well as to goods transshipped through English ports.

In point of articles of greatest value, England contributed beer, flour, and cotton-seed oil; Australia, frozen beef and mutton; Austria-Hungary, spirits, flour, pulse, and sugar. Belgium and Holland also sent large quantities of sugar. The contribution of France consisted of flour, olive and cotton-seed oil; of Germany, flour and manufactured tobacco; of Greece, wine, tobacco, and seeds; of Italy, olive oil, pulse, seeds, and wines; of Russia, large quantities of wheat; of Spain, olive oil; of Turkey, cigarettes, and wine; of Barbary, olive oil and large numbers of cattle. Tunis also sent large numbers of cattle. The principal article imported from the United States was flour.

The following table shows the duties collected upon imports from the United States during 1901, comparison being made with the preceding year:

| Articles. | Total amount of duties received. | |
|---|---|---|
| | 1901. | 1900. |
| Cattle (preserved meats) ........................................ | $9.73 | $34.06 |
| Wheat .......................................................... | 11,251.34 | 3,649.87 |
| Flour .......................................................... | 37,886.64 | 23,962.64 |
| Flour, damaged ................................................. | 4.86 | 9.73 |
| Cotton-seed oil ................................................ | 8,219.51 | 3,756.93 |
| Pulse .......................................................... | 9.73 | .............. |
| Spirits ........................................................ | 408.78 | 9.73 |
| Total ..................................................... | 57,790.59 | 31,422.96 |

The total value of exports from Malta during the year is given as £8,683,126 ($42,256,433). This would seem a remarkably large amount, until one discovers that at least £8,000,000 ($38,932,000) worth, and perhaps more, of these goods was never landed here at all, but were forwarded in the same ship that brought them. The local export figures are so arranged that it would be perfectly useless to try to give the actual values of goods and the countries of destination. It is known, however, that beer, flour, potatoes, spirits, and wine to the value of £144, or $700.77, were shipped to the United States. In looking over the records of this office, I find that to this amount may also be added cummin seed, $3,682.33, and lace goods, $1,962.44, making an apparent total of $6,345.54.

It is impossible to ascertain the value of agricultural products actually raised on these islands and exported, but they consisted of not large amounts of potatoes, onions, oranges, cummin seed, and orange peel. There was also a fairly large export of stone.

### TONNAGE DUES.

The amount received from tonnage dues was $33,762.98, which is a slight increase over the previous two years. Tonnage dues are levied at this port as follows: Upon each steam vessel not exceeding 400 tons, $4.86; exceeding 400 tons, but not over 800, $9.73; exceeding 800 tons, $14.59; sailing vessels, per ton, 72 cents.

### PORT REVENUE.

The total revenue of the port department for the year amounted to $1,099.72, and was made up from receipts from duties upon imports, from tonnage dues, store rent, and office fees. This sum is quite a material increase over that produced in any one of the past ten years, and is due largely to the fact that the old duties were increased and new duties placed for the first time upon certain articles.

JOHN H. GROUT, *Consul.*

VALLETTA, *December 20, 1902.*

# NETHERLANDS.

## AMSTERDAM.

The speech from the throne at the opening of the chambers on September 16, 1902, stated that the crisis which had arisen elsewhere had not been without its effect upon the Dutch shipping trade; but commerce and industry remained in a satisfactory condition while agriculture had yielded not unfavorable results. In the field of labor, encouraging signs were visible, but there was still much room for improvement. The bad harvests in some parts of Java had rendered substantial assistance from the Government necessary.

Among the bills announced were measures for extending facilities for intermediate and higher education, for developing technical education, for restricting compulsory vaccination, and making better provision for granting pensions to teachers in private schools and the widows of teachers in general. Bills would also be submitted for amending the labor law, for regulating lotteries, and for abolishing the State lottery. Other measures would be introduced dealing with labor contracts, the amendment and extension of the sugar law, the reform of the national bank, the telegraph and telephone systems, river legislation, irrigation, and the exploitation of minerals by the State.

A royal commission would be appointed to codify the various educational laws. Parliament would also be asked at an early date to ratify the recent convention on private international law.

As soon as the Government of Surinam had taken the necessary steps, a proposal would be submitted for the construction by the State of a railway to the territory of the Lawa.

FINANCIAL.

The budget for the year 1903, as recently presented to the chambers, places the receipts at 156,504,260 florins ($62,914,712.52), and the expenditures at 164,574,169 florins ($66,158,815.94), leaving a deficit of 8,069,909 florins ($3,244,103.42).

Following are the heads of the budget:

|  | Amount. | |
| --- | --- | --- |
|  | Florins. | U. S. equivalent. |
| 1. Household of the queen | 800,000 | $321,600 |
| 2. High colleges and cabinet of the queen | 689,402 | 277,139 |
| 3. Foreign affairs | 1,136,148 | 456,781 |
| 4. Justice | 6,356,369 | 2,555,260 |
| 5. Home affairs | 18,636,108 | 7,491,713 |
| 6. Navy | 16,512,820 | 6,638,153 |
| 7. National debt | 34,783,842 | 13,963,004 |
| 8. Finances | 25,783,131 | 10,845,120 |
| 9. War | 25,202,456 | 10,131,387 |
| 10. Waterways, etc. | 33,104,918 | 13,308,177 |
| 11. Colonies | 1,617,979 | 650,427 |
| 12. Miscellaneous expenses | 50,000 | 20,100 |
| Total | 164,574,168 | 66,158,811 |

The estimated deficit in the previous fiscal year was 13,331,884 florins, or $4,359,416.36.

Under existing conditions, the projected draining of the Zuider Zee will not be realized in the near future.

The total amount of receipts and expenditures of the municipality of Amsterdam for the year 1903 are estimated at 26,797,251 florins ($10,752,494.90), against 25,311,835 florins ($10,175,357.67) for the year 1902.

The increased expense occurs mainly under the following heads:

|  | Amount. | |
| --- | --- | --- |
|  | Florins. | U. S. equivalent. |
| For schools, increase | 452,000 | $181,704 |
| For the poor, increase | 194,000 | 77,988 |
| Interest and amortization of loans | 573,000 | 230,346 |

There is a decrease in care of the streets of 166,199 florins ($66,812).

The Netherlands was a silver-standard country up to 1875, and silver is still the money in general circulation, the act of 1875 authorizing the unlimited coinage of 10-guilder gold pieces and suspending indefinitely the coinage of silver.

There is no State bank, and the bank of the Netherlands is a private institution, but it is the only bank that has the privilege of issuing bank notes. This was granted for a period of twenty-five years in 1863, and extended for fifteen years in 1888, with a further extension of ten years in case the contract is not broken by one of the parties before the expiration of the time extended. The Netherlands Bank must have a reserve to protect paper money in circulation up to two-fifths of the amount.

The capital of the bank is 20,000,000 florins ($8,040,000), and the reserve fund 5,500,000 florins ($2,211,000). The bank is the Government depository and receives the cash of the Postal Savings Bank. It has 5 per cent of the net profits, the remainder being divided between the bank and the Government.

The following data is taken from the report of the officers of the Netherlands Bank, made to the stockholders on May 13, 1902:

The number of stockholders of the bank is 4,355.

The average operating capital, which was 120,283,824 florins ($48,354,097.25), for the year 1900–1901, was 111,827,388 florins ($44,954,609.98) for the year 1901–2.

Subtracting the foreign paper from the operating capital, it consisted in the year 1900–1901 of 109,365,941 florins ($43,964,108.28); 1901–2, of 100,625,679 florins ($40,451,522.96).

During the last ten years the average amount of operating capital was:

|  | Amount. | |
| --- | --- | --- |
|  | Florins. | U. S. equivalent. |
| 1892–93 | 98,629,471 | $39,649,047.34 |
| 1893–94 | 98,747,503 | 39,696,496.21 |
| 1894–95 | 92,690,900 | 37,261,741.60 |
| 1895–96 | 101,246,049 | 40,721,011.70 |
| 1896–97 | 108,964,945 | 43,799,887.80 |
| 1897–98 | 113,827,671 | 45,758,723.74 |
| 1898–99 | 111,220,225 | 44,710,530.45 |
| 1899–1900 | 121,059,560 | 48,665,943.12 |
| 1900–1901 | 120,283,824 | 48,354,097.25 |
| 1901–2 | 111,827,388 | 44,954,810.98 |

The discount rate of the bank in 1901, compared with that of several other State banks, was:

|  | Per cent. |
| --- | --- |
| Netherlands Bank | 3.23 |
| Bank of England | 3.72 |
| Bank of France | 3 |
| National Bank of Belgium | 3.28 |
| Deutsche Bank | 4.10 |

The amount of discounts in 1901–2 was 268,813,718 florins ($107,063,114.64), against 327,075,537 florins ($131,484,365.87) in 1900–1901.

The amount loaned on securities during the year 1901–2 was 188,536,150 florins ($75,791,523.30), or 15,302,500 florins ($6,151,605) less than in 1900–1901.

The amount loaned on merchandise was 37,304,950 florins ($14,996,589.90), or 3,351,800 florins ($1,347,423.60) less than during the preceding year.

The average amount of bank notes in circulation in the year 1900–1901 amounted to 222,742,592 florins ($89,542,521.98) against 227,848,909 florins ($91,595,261.42) during 1901–2.

Bank checks were issued as follows:

| | Number. | Value. | |
|---|---|---|---|
| | | Florins. | U. S. currency. |
| 1895–96 | 35,396 | 256,170,992 | $102,980,738.78 |
| 1896–97 | 36,507 | 242,717,090 | 97,572,270.02 |
| 1897–98 | 38,463 | 253,865,535 | 102,053,943.07 |
| 1898–99 | 40,820 | 272,246,786 | 109,459,287.97 |
| 1899–1900 | 43,597 | 296,060,773 | 118,622,470.75 |
| 1900–1901 | 45,692 | 311,355,218 | 125,164,797.64 |
| 1901–2 | 46,677 | 317,691,251 | 127,711,882.90 |

The average amount of bank notes, checks, and credit balances of accounts current during the year 1901–2 was 236,220,559 florins ($94,960,664.72), against 232,099,776 florins ($93,304,119.95) in 1900–1901.

Dr.

*Balance sheet of the Netherlands Bank on March 31, 1902.*

Cr.

| | Florins. | | | Florins. | |
|---|---|---|---|---|---|
| Inland bills of exchange | 42,259,919.23½ = | $16,988,487.53 | Capital | 20,000,000.00 = | $8,040,000.00 |
| Foreign bills of exchange | 11,281,366.88 = | 4,535,109.28 | Reserve fund | 5,351,780.00 = | 2,148,355.46 |
| Loans | 46,161,175.00 = | 18,556,792.35 | Bank notes in circulation | 222,031,660.00 = | 89,256,727.32 |
| Overdrawn account current | 6,531,461.23½ = | 2,625,647.43 | Bank checks | 1,521,196.55¼ = | 611,521.01 |
| Cash | 104,461,888.85 = | 41,998,679.32 | Accounts current | 4,660,812.17¼ = | 1,833,446.49 |
| Bullion | 33,024,765.80 = | 13,275,961.83 | Interest on national exchanges | 147,819.63¼ = | 59,423.49 |
| Securities account | 9,304,553.23 = | 3,740,430.40 | Interest on foreign exchanges | 18,496.92 = | 7,435.76 |
| Buildings and furniture of the bank | 752,000.00 = | 302,304.00 | Expense account | 1,000.00 = | 402.00 |
| Interest on securities | 69,121.16½ = | 27,786.71 | | | |
| Interest on loans | 218,036.34½ = | 87,650.61 | | Florins. | |
| Interest on overdrawn accounts current | 45,242.20¼ = | 18,187.36 | Dividend account | 1,000,000.00 | |
| Commission account | 3,340.19 = | 1,342.76 | Unclaimed dividends | 21,468.00 | |
| Foreign correspondents | 1,411,653.06 = | 567,484.53 | Profits at disposal of the general meeting | 1,021,468.00 = | 410,680.14 |
| | | | | 890,329.46 = | 357,912.44 |
| | 255,624,512.74½ = | 102,720,854.11 | | 255,624,512.74½ = | 102,720,854.11 |

*Coin in the Netherlands.*

SILVER.

| December 31— | Total. | | In the bank. | | In circulation. | |
|---|---|---|---|---|---|---|
| | Florins. | U. S. currency. | Florins. | U. S. currency. | Florins. | U. S. currency. |
| 1892 | 140,692,000 | $56,678,184 | 85,160,000 | $34,224,220 | 55,532,000 | $22,323,964 |
| 1893 | 142,483,000 | 57,278,164 | 84,390,000 | 33,900,660 | 58,163,000 | 23,377,506 |
| 1894 | 141,610,000 | 56,927,221 | 82,722,000 | 33,254,244 | 58,888,000 | 23,672,976 |
| 1895 | 139,659,000 | 56,142,917 | 82,239,000 | 33,060,078 | 57,420,000 | 23,062,84 |
| 1896 | 139,638,000 | 56,134,47 | 82,507,000 | 33,167,814 | 57,131,000 | 22,966,662 |
| 1897 | 139,659,000 | 56,152,91 | 81,897,000 | 32,920,94 | 57,762,000 | 23,220,404 |
| 1898 | 140,251,000 | 56,380,90 | 81,449,000 | 32,742,498 | 58,802,000 | 23,638,804 |
| 1899 | 132,802,000 | 53,386,464 | 71,886,000 | 28,878,072 | 60,986,000 | 24,508,332 |
| 1900 | 129,787,000 | 52,174,371 | 67,491,000 | 27,131,382 | 62,296,000 | 25,042,992 |
| 1901 | 139,356,000 | 56,021,11 | 76,615,000 | 30,799,280 | 62,741,000 | 25,221,882 |

GOLD.

| December 31— | Total. | | In the bank. | | In circulation. | |
|---|---|---|---|---|---|---|
| | Florins. | U. S. currency. | Florins. | U. S. currency. | Florins. | U. S. currency. |
| 1892 | 47,489,000 | $19,068,578 | 23,816,000 | $9,573,032 | 23,773,000 | $9,450,746 |
| 1893 | 47,581,000 | 19,127,562 | 23,987,000 | 9,642,774 | 23,594,000 | 9,484,788 |
| 1894 | 47,581,000 | 19,127,562 | 23,910,000 | 9,611,820 | 23,671,000 | 9,515,742 |
| 1895 | 47,581,000 | 19,127,562 | 23,927,000 | 9,618,654 | 23,654,000 | 9,508,908 |
| 1896 | 46,891,000 | 18,850,182 | 23,899,000 | 9,607,394 | 22,992,000 | 9,242,784 |
| 1897 | 46,856,000 | 18,836,112 | 23,847,000 | 9,596,594 | 23,009,000 | 9,219,618 |
| 1898 | 47,063,000 | 18,919,326 | 23,811,000 | 9,572,022 | 23,252,000 | 9,347,304 |
| 1899 | 46,923,000 | 18,883,046 | 23,748,000 | 9,546,696 | 23,175,000 | 9,316,850 |
| 1900 | 46,914,000 | 18,869,425 | 23,615,000 | 9,498,230 | 23,299,000 | 9,366,196 |
| 1901 | 47,905,000 | 19,257,810 | 23,590,000 | 9,483,180 | 24,315,000 | 9,774,630 |

The condition of Dutch finances was not unsatisfactory during the year 1901, though no improvement took place. The receipts during the first eleven months of 1901 nearly equaled those of the preceding year. A considerably smaller amount was collected for succession taxes, which, however, was counterbalanced by higher receipts from other sources. The Goverment made no call on the money market during the year 1901.

The large municipalities continued to emit loans. In the month of March, Rotterdam placed 5,000,000 florins ($2,010,000) 4 per cent bonds at 100¼ per cent; Haarlem, 2,000,000 florins ($804,000) 4 per cent bonds at 100¼ per cent. In order to pay off the 3½ per cent bonds of the Amsterdam Street Car Company, which had been taken over by the city, Amsterdam issued, in May, 5,000,000 florins ($2,010,000) 4 per cent bonds at 101 per cent.

Dutch railway companies called for 4 per cent loans to a considerable amount. The Dutch India Railway Company placed on the market during the month of April 4,000,000 florins ($1,608,000) at 100¼ per cent; the Dutch Central Railway Company in June, 2,000,000 ($804,000) 4 per cent bonds at 99 per cent; the Deli Railway Company, in November, 2,000,000 ($804,000) 4 per cent bonds at 99¼ per cent; and the company for the exploitation of State railways, in December, 7,000,000 ($2,814,000) 4 per cent bonds at 100½ per cent.

### AMERICAN SECURITIES.

The following statement of the holdings of American securities in Holland has been courteously prepared by Mr. H. Swain, of the banking house of Adolph Boissevain & Co., of Amsterdam and New York:

I believe the statement given below represents fairly accurately the market value of American securities at present held in Holland.

| | | | |
|---|---|---|---|
| State, county, and municipal bonds | $4,000,000 | Banking and commerce | $4,000,000 |
| Railroad bonds | 90,000,000 | Real estate and real estate mortgages | 10,000,000 |
| Stocks and income bonds | 100,000,000 | | |
| Manufacturing and mining securities | 15,000,000 | Total | 223,000,000 |

A striking feature is that although Holland is continually selling stocks on every rise, and thereby reducing holdings as regards face value, the market value of what she still holds, owing to the heavy appreciation, is very slightly changed, compared with two years ago.

The course of the Amsterdam market following so closely that of London or New York, does not require detailed treatment. The largest operation in American securities during the year was the Grand Trunk deal, involving about $6,000,000. It was conducted through the banking house of Wertheim & Gompertz, of this city. Ten million dollars of Southern Pacific stock were placed in this market by Teixeira de Mattos & Co. In the recent rise, Dutchmen have made a great deal of money in American securities; London, on the other hand, as in 1873, 1893, 1896, and 1899, having scored stupendous losses.

The rate of money is so high here, and money is so plentiful at home, that there is not now the same opportunity to place American investments as formerly.

PETROLEUM COMPANIES.

| | Dividends paid. | | Shares quoted at— | |
|---|---|---|---|---|
| | 1899. | 1900. | Jan. 2, 1899. | Dec. 29, 1900. |
| | Per cent. | Per cent. | Per cent. | Per cent. |
| Elsasser | 5 | 5 | 83 | 97 |
| Schibaleff | 13 | 15 | 158½ | 147½ |
| Russian Fuel | 20 | 50 | 230 | 305 |
| Hannover Oil Springs | 1 | 1½ | 50 | 89 |
| Amsterdam Roumenian | | | 60 | 68 |
| Holland Roumenian | | | 56 | 30 |
| Netherland Roumenian | | | 40 | 23 |
| International Roumenian | | | | 85 |
| Royal Petroleum Springs | 6 | 6 | 276 | 337 |
| Sumatra Palembang | | | 84 | 73 |
| Moeara Enim | | | 135 | 150 |
| Dordrecht Petroleum Co | 7 | 9 | 122 | 128 |
| Java Petroleum Co | | | 75 | 43 |

BANKS.

| | Dividends paid. | | Shares quoted at— | |
|---|---|---|---|---|
| | 1899. | 1900. | Jan. 2, 1899. | Dec. 29, 1900. |
| | Per cent. | Per cent. | Per cent. | Per cent. |
| Netherland Trading Co | 7½ | 8⅝ | 147½ | 151½ |
| Netherland Indian Commercial Bank | 4½ | 5 | 84½ | 85½ |
| Trading Company "Amsterdam" | 8 | 9 | 115 | 122 |
| Colonial Bank | | | 52 | 49 |
| Colonial Bank, preferred shares | | | 68½ | 69 |
| Cultivation Society "Vorstenlanden" | 2½ | 2 | 64 | 55 |
| Cultivation Society "Vorstenlanden," preferred shares | 7½ | 7 | 138 | 135 |
| Java Cultivation Society | 5 | 9 | 102 | 98 |
| Sentanen Lor | 8 | 8 | 128 | 114 |

TOBACCO COMPANIES.

| | Dividends paid. | | Shares quoted at— | |
|---|---|---|---|---|
| | 1899. | 1900. | Jan. 2, 1899. | Dec. 31, 1900. |
| | Florins. | Florins. | Per cent. | Per cent. |
| Deli Company | 38 | 27 | 416 | 430 |
| Senembah Co | 43 | 22 | 412 | 399 |
| | Per cent. | Per cent. | | |
| Amsterdam Deli Co | 92½ | 72 | 680 | 629 |
| Rotterdam Deli Co | | 14½ | 219 | 232 |
| Deli Batavia Co | 43 | 10 | 325 | 384 |
| Amsterdam Sumatra Cultivation | 11½ | | 124 | 100 |
| Deli Plantage | | 2 | 78 | 86 |
| Franco Deli | | | 60 | 56 |
| Langkat Cultivation A | 10½ | 8½ | 134 | 120 |
| Padang Tobacco | 6 | 5 | 180 | 131 |
| Namoe Djawi | 6 | | 85 | 94½ |
| Netherland Asahan, preferred shares | | | 143 | |
| New Asahan | | | | 123½ |

TRANSPORTATION COMPANIES.

The fear of strong competition in freight rates, already expressed in the preceding year, continued during 1901. Although coal prices fell, the expenses necessary to stand competition were large.

The following Dutch steamer companies emitted new loans:

The Royal Packet Company placed, in January, 1901, with its shareholders 1,000,000 florins ($402,000) new shares, at 149 per cent.

The steamer company Oostzee placed, in February, 500,000 florins ($201,000) 4½ per cent bonds, at 98 per cent.

The Holland-America Line placed, in April, 1,000,000 florins ($402,000) 4 per cent bonds, at 98⅜ per cent.

The Royal West Indian Mail Service placed, in July, 500,000 florins ($201,000) 4 per cent bonds, at 99 per cent.

The General Navigation Company (Wm. H. Muller & Co.), at Rotterdam, placed, in November, 1,400,000 ($562,800) 4 per cent bonds, at 95 per cent.

The Netherlands Lloyd, a company established by the Rotterdam-American Petroleum Company, offered in September, by inscription, 651,000 florins ($261,702), in shares.

Many of the Dutch tramway companies can boast of a moderate improvement in the receipts per day-kilometer.

During the month of September, 1901, the Dutch Tramway Company placed 400,000 florins ($160,800) 4 per cent bonds, at 98¼ per cent, and the Dutch Westphalian Steam Tramway Company 250,000 florins ($100,500) 4 per cent bonds, at 99 per cent.

The committee of accountants have delivered to the court at Amsterdam their report upon the application of the Netherlands South African Railway for suspension of payment (surséance van betaling), which was granted on October 30, 1902, for eighteen months, by the district court of Amsterdam.

The possessions of the company in Africa and the claims which may be made for destruction of property, or damages thereto, amount 103,956,702 florins ($41,790,594.20), represented by:

|  | Amount. | |
|---|---|---|
|  | Florins. | U. S. currency. |
| Reserve.................................................................. | 7,582,565 | $3,048,191.13 |
| Railways ................................................................ | 65,827,783 | 26,462,768.77 |
| Tramway Krugersdorp Springs................................................ | 4,858,520 | 1,953,025.04 |
| Line Klerksdorp.......................................................... | 8,368,618 | 8,364,184.44 |
| Inventory................................................................ | 1,556,486 | 625,707.39 |
| Locomotives............................................................. | 4,187,996 | 1,683,574 39 |
| Rolling stock............................................................ | 6,710,926 | 2,697,792.25 |
| Warehoused goods........................................................ | 1,050,116 | 422,146.68 |
| Goods which could not be entered into the Republics..................... | 474,972 | 20ᶜ,184.74 |

The damages arising out of the war can not be stated at present. The English gave checks on the Imperial Military Railway to the amount of 2,500,000 florins ($1,005,000).

The seat of this company is at Amsterdam, where it was organized in 1887, for a period of ninety-nine years, with a capital of 14,000,000 florins or $5,600,000.

On December 1, 1897, the line consisted of 717 miles.

### POSTAL SAVINGS BANK.

The Postal Savings Bank was established by law in 1880 and began operations in 1881. The institution has thus been in operation twenty years, and has an accumulated experience entitled to consideration.

The principal office is at Amsterdam.

The governing power consists of one director and a board of five members appointed by the Crown, under control of the minister of waterstaat, etc.

The number of employees April 1, 1901, was 142, of whom 104 were male and 38 female, against 5 employees on April 1, 1881. On April 1, 1881, there were 353 offices, against 1,322 on April 1, 1901. In 1881 there were 22,831 depositors, with 858,622.85 florins ($345,166,39), against 838,716, with 86,522,207.88 florins ($34,781,927.57) in 1900.

In 1881, one house was rented at Amsterdam. In 1887, this building was extended. In 1892, a second house was rented. In 1894, a far larger one was used, while in 1898 another was rented also. In 1892, it was concluded to erect an office building for the bank. In 1898, the building was begun, and it will be ready at the end of July, 1901.

Deposits may be made at any post-office, and postmasters and numerous special agents are empowed to receive them.

Applications are made on printed form. A post book is then issued free, and in it amounts of deposits must be entered, in words and figures, with the date. Postmasters receive 5 Dutch cents (2 cents United States currency) for every new account opened, and 1½ Dutch cents (three-fifths of a cent United States currency) for each entry. For the convenience of the personnel of the navy, most of which is stationed in the colonies or in foreign countries, 767 pass books were issued in 1899 against 762 in 1898.

There was deposited by them a total of 161,070.45 florins ($64,750.32), against 133,336.07 florins ($53,601.10) in 1898.

Money deposited with the Netherlands Postal Savings Bank or the Belgian General Savings and Pension Bank (Caisse d'Epargne et de Retraite) can be transferred from one institution to the other without expense on the request of parties interested.

Payments can also be made in either country of money deposited in the other. Requests for transfers and disbursements are accepted in both countries at all post-offices or designated agencies.

Deposits may be made by the mail carrier for people who reside at a distance of over twenty minutes from a recognized depository. Anyone may make a deposit, including minors and married women; deposits can be withdrawn only by the depositor himself or by a regularly authorized agent.

On receiving the little pass book, the depositor signs a form obligating himself to obey the law and rules, existing and prospective, relating to depositors in Government postal savings banks.

Deposits may be made and withdrawn in post-offices other than the one in which the first entry in the depositor's book was made. Deposits of less than 25 cents Dutch currency (10 cents United States currency) are not accepted, but for the encouragement of small savings, forms for a guilder (40 cents United States currency) are provided free of expense, with 20 blank spaces, each blank space being intended for the attachment of a 5-cent ($0.02) postage stamp. When this sheet is filled, it may be presented with the pass book, and the depositor's account is credited with a guilder, the receiver canceling the stamps and filling the blank form. Inmates of orphan asylums and school children may receive blank forms with 100 spaces to be filled with 1-cent stamps, which may be finally also entered in the pass book on deposit at the value of a florin.

The receivers of deposits report every five days to the minister of waterstaat, trade, and industry the amount of receipts and disbursements, and every ten days balances are struck by the transfer of such other funds as they are required to transmit. From the ten-day reports, the main office at Amsterdam sends to the director a statement of the amount of money to the credit of the bank. The memoranda of receipts and disbursements are transmitted to the bank, where the individual accounts are kept. These accounts are balanced every ten days, and must agree with the statements of the general post-office. A statement is also sent to the depositor at certain periods.

Interest is reckoned on the 1st and 16th of each month. Deposits made during the first half of the month begin to draw interest on the 16th of the month and those made subsequently from the 1st of the following month. The rate of interest has been fixed at 2.64 per cent. This figure, besides being determined for business reasons as the highest amount that the bank could pay, is convenient also, since it is an exact multiple of 24, the number of interest-periods of a year.

Thus, on every 1,000 guilders ($402) the interest is 11 Dutch cents (4 cents United States currency) for a single period.

The Crown reserves the right to fix by royal decree another rate of interest, provided it does not exceed 2.64 per cent.

The Netherlands Bank is the treasurer of the Postal Savings Bank. The director and the council determine the amount to be invested in public funds, designated by law. The Government guarantees the deposits as well as the repayments and interest.

Forms used are free of stamp duty, and correspondence between the bank, post-offices, and depositors is free of postage; in return, the banks pay the treasury 10 cents Dutch ($0.04) annually for each depositor.

In case the book is lost, another will be issued, if applied for within six weeks; it costs 25 cents Dutch ($0.10).

No interest is paid on deposits of individuals above 1,200 guilders, nor to societies and corporations on more than 2,400 guilders.

The statement of the bank for the month of September, 1902, was:

The deposits that month amounted to 3,746,821.06 florins ($1,506,222.07) and there was paid out 3,161,888.37 florins ($1,271,079.12), of which 21,492.32 florins ($8,639.91) were for purchase of inscriptions in the grootboek of funds and certificates of inscription, so that there was an excess of disbursements of 584,932.68 florins ($235,142.94). At the end of August, 1902, there were deposits of 98,084,774.34 florins ($39,430,079.28), so that on September 30, 1902, the balance amounted to 98,669,707.02 florins ($39,665,222.22).

In the course of the month, 8,658 new pass books were issued and 3,204 taken up, so that at the end of the month there were 951,065 in circulation.

Since the vinculation between the Postal Savings Bank of the Netherlands and Belgium is so close, I think it advisable to add the official statistics of the Belgium Government Savings Bank as transmitted to the Department of State by Consul Roosevelt, of Brussels, April 24, 1901. (See Consular Reports No. 250, July, 1901.) Official statistics concerning the Government savings bank show that on December 31, 1900, the number of books was 1,762,434 (against 1,647,263 in the previous year) and the amount of deposits 660,249,447.57 francs ($127,428,143.38), an increase during the year of $7,200,144. The capitalized interest amounted to 17,942,178.42 francs ($3,462,840.43), which, added to the amount represented in depositors' books, made a grand total of 678,191,625.99 francs ($130,890,983.82), belonging almost exclusively to the working class.

*Savings-bank statistics.*

| Year. | Deposits. | | | Disbursements. | | | Depositors, Dec. 31. | | |
|---|---|---|---|---|---|---|---|---|---|
| | Number. | Amount. | Average amount. | Number. | Amount. | Average amount. | Number. | Amount. | Average amount. |
| | | *Florins.* | *Florins.* | | *Florins.* | *Florins.* | | *Florins.* | *Florins.* |
| 1881... | 86,023 | 1,126,961.96 | 13.10 | 7,405 | 276,622.38½ | 37.35½ | 22,831 | 868,622.85½ | 37.61 |
| 1891... | 562,549 | 13,558,868.79 | 24.10½ | 207,031 | 11,367,454.62 | 54.90½ | 319,016 | 24,013,724.49½ | 75.25 |
| 1899... | 1,172,966 | 38,253,542.11½ | 32.61½ | 460,854 | 31,825,422.06 | 69.05½ | 764,201 | 78,344,636.72 | 102.51½ |

*Number of depositors for each province per 1,000 inhabitants.*

| December 31— | North Brabant. | Gelderland. | South Holland. | North Holland. | Zeeland. | Utrecht. | Friesland. | Overysel. | Groningen. | Drente. | Limburg. | Total, country. |
|---|---|---|---|---|---|---|---|---|---|---|---|---|
| 1881 | 6.7 | 5.4 | 7.3 | 6.2 | 8.2 | 6.3 | 3.5 | 4.1 | 2.4 | 2.2 | 4.7 | 5.7 |
| 1882 | 11.4 | 11.0 | 14.0 | 13.2 | 14.3 | 11.1 | 6.8 | 8.8 | 3.9 | 4.4 | 11.0 | 11.1 |
| 1883 | 17.0 | 16.6 | 21.1 | 22.8 | 20.7 | 17.0 | 9.5 | 12.3 | 5.8 | 6.7 | 16.5 | 13.9 |
| 1884 | 22.2 | 20.9 | 24.7 | 28.2 | 25.5 | 23.3 | 11.6 | 15.6 | 6.6 | 8.6 | 22.0 | 21.2 |
| 1885 | 27.0 | 25.6 | 30.9 | 36.0 | 31.1 | 29.1 | 13.7 | 18.3 | 7.6 | 10.1 | 27.0 | 26.3 |
| 1886 | 33.4 | 31.9 | 38.3 | 46.8 | 37.2 | 35.3 | 15.8 | 23.0 | 9.6 | 12.4 | 32.9 | 32.7 |
| 1887 | 40.4 | 38.5 | 45.2 | 57.8 | 44.8 | 42.0 | 18.6 | 27.7 | 11.6 | 15.2 | 40.7 | 39.5 |
| 1888 | 48.8 | 45.9 | 52.9 | 70.6 | 51.8 | 51.1 | 21.8 | 32.7 | 13.8 | 17.5 | 48.4 | 47.2 |
| 1889 | 58.0 | 53.8 | 61.8 | 86.6 | 59.2 | 61.7 | 26.4 | 40.0 | 17.2 | 20.6 | 58.1 | 56.4 |
| 1890 | 64.5 | 59.0 | 66.2 | 93.4 | 64.2 | 63.5 | 30.0 | 46.7 | 20.1 | 23.0 | 63.1 | 62.0 |
| 1891 | 72.0 | 65.4 | 73.3 | 102.8 | 71.4 | 77.7 | 33.1 | 52.0 | 20.9 | 25.6 | 71.2 | 69.1 |
| 1892 | 79.8 | 73.2 | 82.2 | 117.4 | 78.3 | 89.5 | 35.6 | 57.2 | 25.2 | 28.9 | 79.5 | 77.6 |
| 1893 | 88.5 | 81.1 | 89.8 | 129.5 | 87.2 | 102.6 | 39.9 | 63.3 | 27.9 | 32.1 | 88.2 | 85.9 |
| 1894 | 97.9 | 90.0 | 98.2 | 141.0 | 95.1 | 115.2 | 44.0 | 69.1 | 31.4 | 37.8 | 101.8 | 94.8 |
| 1895 | 108.2 | 100.0 | 107.6 | 154.5 | 105.0 | 123.2 | 43.4 | 76.8 | 34.9 | 43.8 | 107.9 | 104.3 |
| 1896 | 119.9 | 111.3 | 118.5 | 170.0 | 117.6 | 144.7 | 54.7 | 86.3 | 40.0 | 49.5 | 119.0 | 115.6 |
| 1897 | 130.7 | 132.9 | 130.5 | 183.9 | 131.5 | 159.7 | 62.0 | 97.1 | 45.6 | 58.0 | 131.4 | 127.3 |
| 1898 | 140.5 | 134.0 | 140.8 | 199.8 | 143.5 | 174.2 | 69.5 | 107.3 | 51.4 | 63.9 | 148.6 | 138.5 |
| 1899 | 151.3 | 145.1 | 152.0 | 216.8 | 155.2 | 187.5 | 78.7 | 118.2 | 58.0 | 70.0 | 157.8 | 150.6 |

The number of investments during the year 1899 amounted to 257, representing a nominal capital of 215,800 florins, divided as follows:

|  | | Florins. |
|---|---|---|
| a. | Nominal inscriptions on the public ledger of the national debt, 2½ per cent. | 25,500 |
| b. | Nominal inscriptions on the public ledger of the national debt, 3 per cent.. | 44,500 |
| c. | Government bonds to bearer, 3 per cent. | 104,800 |
| d. | Certificates national debt, 2½ per cent | 16,300 |
| e. | Certificates national debt, 3 per cent | 24,700 |

*a* 215.800

*Depositors during the year 1899.*

| Occupation. | Number of depositors. | Depositors living at Amsterdam. | Occupation. | Number of depositors. | Depositors living at Amsterdam. |
|---|---|---|---|---|---|
| Industry | 32,635 | 7,076 | Workmen | 6,546 | 849 |
| Commerce | 22,096 | 4,944 | Resigned officers without profession | 10,264 | 1,701 |
| Agriculture | 11,327 | 250 | | | |
| Hunting and fishing | 571 | 31 | Minors living in a charity house | 212 | 11 |
| Liberal professions, education, different professions | 11,127 | 1,969 | Different associations | 626 | 72 |
| Servants | 9,865 | 1,497 | | | |

*Population and number of persons enjoying the right of suffrage on account of their deposits at the postal savings bank.*

| In— | Population on Dec. 31, 1898. | Number per 1,000 electors. | In— | Population on Dec. 31, 1898. | Number per 1,000 electors. |
|---|---|---|---|---|---|
| Municipalities of over 50,000 inhabitants. | 512,989 309,309 | 3.11 5.33 | Provinces: | | |
| | | | South Holland | 1,125,875 | 4.18 |
| Amsterdam | 199,285 | 2.69 | North Holland | 966,713 | 2.66 |
| Rotterdam | 100,066 | 5.05 | Zeeland | 215,330 | 5.66 |
| The Hague | 64,921 | 3.42 | Utrecht | 248,140 | 7.26 |
| Utrecht | 63,689 | 2.75 | Friesland | 341,622 | 1.63 |
| Groningen | 56,422 | 1.61 | Overysel | 329,099 | 6.27 |
| Haarlem | 53,915 | 3.13 | Groningen | 299,658 | 2.23 |
| Arnhem | | | Drente | 147,839 | 2.82 |
| Leiden | | | Limberg | 285,185 | 3.84 |
| Provinces: | | | | | |
| North Brabant | 553,392 | 1.28 | | | |
| Gelderland | 572,323 | 7.98 | Total, country | 5,084,476 | 4.07 |

*a* Equivalent to $86,751.60 United States currency.

*Amount of deposits and percentage of yearly increase for the years 1881, 1891, and 1899.*

| Year. | Amount of deposits at end of year. | Yearly increase. |
|---|---|---|
| | *Florins.* | *Per cent.* |
| 1881 .......................................................................... | 858,622.85½ | .......... |
| 1891 .......................................................................... | 24,013,724.49½ | 13 |
| 1899 .......................................................................... | 78,344,636.72 | 11.9 |

*Number of books in circulation and the percentage of yearly increase.*

| Years. | Number of books in circulation at end of year. | Yearly increase. | Years. | Number of books in circulation at end of year. | Yearly increase. |
|---|---|---|---|---|---|
| | | *Per cent.* | | | *Per cent.* |
| 1881 ........................ | 22,831 | .......... | 1891 ........................ | 319,106 | 13.2 |
| 1882 ........................ | 46,242 | 102.5 | 1892 ........................ | 358,483 | 12.3 |
| 1883 ........................ | 67,922 | 46.8 | 1893 ........................ | 401,046 | 11.9 |
| 1884 ........................ | 90,798 | 83.6 | 1894 ........................ | 448,581 | 11.9 |
| 1885 ........................ | 112,306 | 23.6 | 1895 ........................ | 499,963 | 11.5 |
| 1886 ........................ | 139,989 | 24.6 | 1896 ........................ | 561,989 | 12.4 |
| 1887 ........................ | 169,027 | 20.7 | 1897 ........................ | 627,409 | 11.6 |
| 1888 ........................ | 201,768 | 19.8 | 1898 ........................ | 693,228 | 10.5 |
| 1889 ........................ | 241,175 | 19.5 | 1899 ........................ | 764,201 | 10.2 |
| 1890 ........................ | 281,870 | 16.9 | | | |

The postal savings bank has assumed a leading place among the institutions of the Netherlands.

The site, and the new building opened in August, 1901, have been paid for by the bank, and are kept separately from Government properties, although the bank is closely connected with the Government. The building cost 600,000 florins ($240,000), while the land was bought from the municipality for 120,000 florins ($48,000); total cost, 720,000 florins ($288,000).

The building for account-current books is made exclusively of cement and iron, and is separated from the main building by iron doors. The account-current books are placed on racks. In the cellars there are also racks on which the pass books, correspondence, old receipts, etc., are kept, so that any paper of any year may be procured promptly.

### NEW BOURSE.

The city council voted on October 7, 1896, to build a new exchange. The work was begun in 1898 and is still under way. The building is to cost 1,300,000 florins ($520,000). It will be, when completed, one of the most spacious exchanges in Europe. The exterior dimensions are: West side, 467 feet; south side, 117; east side, 470; and north side, 167 feet. The tower is 125 feet in height.

The new bourse has three principal divisions. From the entrance at the south end of the building, the visitor passes at once into the main exchange, whose dimensions are 150 by 75 feet. A passage, on the left of which is the shipping exchange, leads on the right to the stock exchange and on the left to the grain exchange. The dimensions of the stock exchange are 125 by 62½ feet, and of the grain exchange

125 by 62½ feet. To the left of the grain exchange is the restaurant. The cellars are used for safes, etc., while the upper floor is provided with office rooms, which are to be rented to merchants.

The following description of the original bourse, erected in Amsterdam in the years 1608–1611, has been taken by the writer from the classic Wagenaar, published in the year 1765, Volume III, Book I, Chapter II:

From a regulation of July 29, 1592, it appears that the merchants were accustomed to meet at the east end of the new bridge for the transaction of business. Here stood the so-called "Paelhuiske," where they congregated daily from 11 to 12 a. m. In the year 1586, the authorities decided that merchants should meet at "St. Olofs Kapel," and later on in the "Old Church."

In 1607, the authorities adopted a resolution to establish a separate bourse. Two plans were made and the less ambitious of the two carried out. On May 29, 1608, the first stone was laid by Henrik Hooft, son of the Burgomaster Cornelis Pieterszoon Hooft, and brother of the celebrated historian, Pieter Corneliszoon Hooft, called by Motley "the Dutch Tacitus." The work continued regularly, and on August 1, 1613, the first meeting was held. The building was 200 feet long and 124 feet broad. Ships could pass under the middle arch with masts down, but after 1622 it was prohibited for ships to remain there during the night, as a result of the discovery of a plot to blow up the bourse. The attempt was detected by a city orphan boy, who being asked by the burgomaster what reward he wanted, only asked the privilege for the Amsterdam boys to beat the drum at the bourse during Kermess time (in the month of September), which privilege has remained in force up to the present.

After an existence of about fifty-five years, the bourse was extended. The exchange, established in the "rokin," was a long, square building, built on five arches—one large one in the middle and two smaller ones at each side. The place where the merchants met was surrounded by a broad gallery, which rested on 23 arches with 46 pillars. Those pillars were numbered, so that the merchants, who all had their fixed place, were easily to be found. In winter a wooden floor was laid on the stone one for the comfort on the merchants.

In the beginning, the bourse was held twice per day, viz., from 11 to 12 a. m., and during the months of May, June, July, and August from 6.30 to 7.30 p. m. and during the other months half an hour before the ringing of the gate bell. Later, in the year 1667, the bourse opened but once a day, at 12 o'clock. Those who wished to enter after the closing of the bourse gates had to pay 0.30 florin ($0.12), while the brokers had to pay a higher penalty to the municipal poor. But this regulation has been neglected.

For more than two centuries, the original bourse was the pride of Amsterdam, but at the beginning of the nineteenth century, it appeared that the building was getting old and rather dangerous. In consequence, it was closed in the year 1836, and a wooden building was temporarily put into requisition. After several plans were canceled, a plan for a new bourse was adopted in 1840, and in 1845, the building was opened with great festivities in the presence of King William II.

But nobody was content with the new building. Visitors complained of the draft, so that in the year 1848 the authorities adopted a plan to cover the middle court, where the merchants used to meet, which plan caused an extra expense of 57,000 florins ($22,800). But after that, the ventilation was not sufficient, and agitation for a new bourse began. Another commanding argument was that the bourse was too small, and that a surface of at least 6,000 square meters was required, while the existing one possessed only 2,833 square meters. A number of plans were made, and at last, in 1898, that of Mr. H. P. Berlage Nzn. was adopted, and the new bourse is now in course of construction. It is expected that it will be opened on May 1, 1903.

The present membership of the bourse consists of about 4,000 members. The dues are 20 guilders, or $10, annually. In the main exchange, all the staple articles of modern commerce are dealt in, tobacco and other tropical products holding a commanding place. Amsterdam is the second market for American flour, hence the grain exchange is an important branch.

In the stock branch, American securities are largely dealt in, as well as stocks and bonds of most of the leading nations of the world, both government and private.

The bourse is treated very seriously here. Members are expected to be present for forty-five minutes daily, whether they have business or not, and to be seen in their place in the exchange daily.

I give below translation of the regulations:

### Regulations of the bourse at Amsterdam.

ARTICLE 1. The bourse at Amsterdam shall be open from 1.30 p. m. to 3.30 p. m. Doors shall be opened at 1 o'clock p. m. The exchange bell shall be rung from 1.30 to 1.45 p. m., at which time doors shall be closed. They shall be reopened at 2.30 p. m. The bourse closes at 3.30 p. m. It shall not be opened on Sundays, on generally recognized Christian holidays, or upon those days designated by burgomaster and aldermen.

ART. 2. There shall be a board of commissaries for the bourse of Amsterdam, consisting of three members, to be appointed and dismissed by burgomaster and aldermen. Commissaries shall give their opinion to the burgomaster and aldermen with respect to trade, and if necessary, make propositions to the municipality.

ART. 3. It is prohibited to peddle goods on the steps of the bourse or in the bourse itself during exchange hours.

ART. 4. Smoking is prohibited in the bourse between 1 and 2.45.

ART. 5. It is prohibited to disturb good order, to cause anyone trouble in carrying on his business or to obstruct anybody.

ART. 6. The maintenance of good order in the bourse shall be intrusted to seven exchange policemen, one of whom has the title of chief; these are appointed and dismissed by burgomaster and aldermen.

### Regulations for the levying and collecting of dues for the use of the bourse and corn exchange at Amsterdam.

ARTICLE 1. For the use during bourse hours of the rooms of the bourse or of the corn exchange, to be designated by burgomaster and aldermen, or both, before the opening of the bourse during bourse hours, or after the closing of the doors, the following dues shall be paid:

A. Everyone to whom the use of the rooms is granted, per year, 25 florins ($10).

B. Everyone not paying under "A" shall pay each session 0.25 florin ($0.10).

C. Everyone who wishes to enter during bourse hours after the closing of the doors shall pay an extra fee per session of 0.25 florin ($0.10).

Merchants can also get tickets, described under "A," for their employees.

ART. 2. The year for dues shall begin on January 1. The dues shall be prepaid every year. Levied as a yearly tax, the full amount must be paid for the current year, except when one enters during the last six months of the year. In this case, only half of the tax shall be paid. Under extraordinary circumstances, the burgomaster and aldermen may grant that the dues shall only be paid at the rate of 3.50 florins ($1.40) per month.

ART. 3. After having paid the tax, according to provisions of 1A, members receive tickets. Those tickets are given out by name, and strictly nontransferable. Merchants can indorse the ticket issued in the name of one of their employees to another employee without paying dues again.

Tickets must be shown on application to the persons to be appointed by the burgomaster and aldermen.

ART. 4. In the tax described in article 1 are not included dues for the use of separate rooms, chairs, tables, sample cases, etc.

## MERCHANT MARINE.

The latest figures respecting the merchant marine of the Netherlands are:

| Year. | Number of ships. | Tonnage. | Year. | Number of ships. | Tonnage. |
|---|---|---|---|---|---|
| 1902 | 933 | 576,751 | 1889 | 649 | 313,942 |
| 1901 | 628 | 588,152 | 1888 | 654 | 309,315 |
| 1900 | 570 | 443,382 | 1887 | 685 | 318,682 |
| 1899 | 578 | 374,213 | 1886 | 723 | 349,170 |
| 1898 | 574 | 362,893 | 1885 | 736 | 347,403 |
| 1897 | 550 | 373,387 | 1884 | 732 | 345,228 |
| 1896 | 570 | 386,187 | 1883 | 768 | 352,432 |
| 1895 | 576 | 384,066 | 1882 | 825 | 338,401 |
| 1894 | 577 | 380,123 | 1881 | 897 | 330,587 |
| 1893 | 615 | 378,102 | 1880 | 1,006 | 330,115 |
| 1892 | 652 | 378,888 | 1879 | 1,100 | 308,066 |
| 1891 | 643 | 344,890 | 1878 | 1,111 | 242,266 |
| 1890 | 686 | 371,160 | 1877 | 1,190 | 156,614 |

*Shipping companies in the Netherlands.*

| Name of company. | Plying to— | Number of ships. | Tonnage. | Number of ships in construction. | Tonnage. |
|---|---|---|---|---|---|
| Maatschappy "Nederland" | Java | 18 | 62,520 | | |
| Nederlandsche Stoomboot Maatschappy. | Several directions | 3 | 2,923 | | |
| Holland-Amerika-Line | New York | 6 | 43,369 | 5 | 49,000 |
| | Newport News | | | 1 | 5,600 |
| Rotterdamsche Lloyd | Java | 14 | 43,982 | | |
| Maatschappy "Ocean" | do | 11 | 28,422 | | |
| West-Indische Mail | West India | 8 | 13,390 | | |
| Koninklyke Pakketvaart Maatschappy. | Between different East Indian ports. | 36 | 47,044 | 2 | 2,800 |
| Zuid Amerika Lyn | La Plata River | 3 | 12,510 | 1 | 4,170 |
| Koninklyke Nederlandsche Stoomboot Maatschappy. | London, Baltic, Mediterranean. | 28 | 25,748 | 2 | 2,253 |
| P. A. van Es & Co. | Hamburg | 3 | 1,571 | | |
| Burger & Zoon | Bergen, Norway | 2 | 1,481 | 1 | 900 |
| Boutmy & Co. | Leith | 4 | 4,120 | | |
| Smith & Co. | Bordeaux | 2 | 1,366 | | |
| Hollandsche Stoomboot Maatschappy. | London, Hull, etc | 8 | 7,656 | 1 | 1,200 |
| C. Balgurie & Co. | Havre | 1 | 528 | | |
| Maatschappy "Zeeland" | Flushing Queensborough. | 8 | 13,931 | | |
| Hollandsche Scheepvaart Maatschappy. | Hull | 2 | 1,564 | | |

The Java-China-Japan Steamship line was established September 15, 1902, and authorized by Royal resolution of September 10, 1902.

The capital is 6,000,000 florins ($2,412,000), divided into five series. The first series, amounting to 2,000,000 florins ($804,000), divided into shares of 1,000 florins ($402), was opened to subscription on September 23, 1902, at the rate of 100 per cent. The first payment of 30 per cent took place on October 1, while 25 per cent must be paid on November 15, 1902; 25 per cent on February 16, 1903, and 20 per cent on May 15, 1903.

The company has made an agreement with the Netherlands Trading Company by which the latter agrees to pay 3 per cent interest on the paid up capital up to October 1, 1903.

The Netherlands Government will pay the following subsidy: During the first five years, 300,000 florins ($120,600); during the next five years, 250,000 florins ($100,500); during the next five years, 200,000 florins ($80,400), beginning with the first voyage from Java.

The company will establish a monthly service with three steamers of about 5,000 tons, starting September, 1903, on the following route: Batavia, Samarang, Soerabaya to Hongkong, Shanghai, Kobé, and Yokohama, and return via Amoy and Hongkong.

The steamers will be fitted for transport of goods, for steerage passengers, and for a few cabin passengers.

Sugar, tin, arrack, hides, guns, timber, indigo, cinchona bark, kapok, copra, coffee, and rattan will form the freight from Java. Coal will be carried from Japan and all products of Japanese and Chinese industries.

The transport of steerage passengers from southern China to India will probably increase regularly.

During 1901, the steamers of the Holland-America Steamship Line made 51 round trips to New York and 5 round trips to Newport News and Norfolk. Besides, 21 round trips were made by chartered steamers. In 1901, a fourth double-screw steamship, the *Ryndam*, was added to the fleet, and the freight steamers *Soestdyk* and *Amsteldyk* were put on the Newport News service. Since then, a fifth double-screw steamer, the *Noordam*, has been added, and a third freight steamer, the *Sloterdyk*, plies to Newport News.

To pay for the three new freight steamers, the capital of the company was increased by a new issue of 2,000,000 florins ($804,000), and 4 per cent bonds of 1,000,000 florins ($402,000) were floated.

The profit and loss account of the company for 1901 was:

*Profit and loss account of the Holland-America Line on December 31, 1901.*

| Dr. | | | Cr. | | |
|---|---|---|---|---|---|
| | *Florins* | | | *Florins* | |
| Management and office expenses | 89,874.69 = | $36,129.62 | Balance of preceding year | 1,798.77 = | $723.11 |
| Advertising expenses | 26,814.35 = | 10,779.37 | Exploitation account | 1,670,874.34 = | 671,691.48 |
| Interest account | 22,036.06 = | 8,858.49 | Bills of exchange | 9,714.50 = | 3,905.23 |
| Writing off: | | | Mail carrying | 8,104.14 = | 1,247.96 |
|   *Florins* | | | Sale of steamer Spaarndam | 63,783.03 = | 25,620.64 |
|   Materials ... 799,786.82 | | | | | |
|   Buildings, etc. ... 138,738.97 | | | | | |
|   Reserve boiler and repairing fund ... 153,459.74 | 1,091,985.53 = | 438,978.18 | | | |
| Dividends, 16,000 shares, at 30 florins ... 480,000.00 | | | | | |
| Taxes, 2½ per cent ... 12,000.00 | 492,000.00 = | 197,784.00 | | | |
| Gratifications according to article 38 of the by-laws | 21,343.08 = | 8,579.92 | | | |
| Balance to new account | 5,171.08 = | 2,078.74 | | | |
| | 1,749,224.79 = | 708,188.82 | | 1,749,224.79 = | 708,188.82 |

*Balance sheet of the Holland-America Line on December 31, 1901.*

| Dr. | | | Cr. | | |
|---|---|---|---|---|---|
| | *Florins* | | | *Florins* | |
| Material | 9,449,508.00 = | $3,798,702.22 | Capital | 8,000,000.00 = | $3,216,000.00 |
| Steamers in construction | 2,846,087.16 = | 1,144,127.04 | Loan of 1888, with interest up to December 31, 1901 | 254,952.50 = | 102,490.90 |
| Buildings, etc. | 364,001.00 = | 146,328.40 | Loan of 1890, with interest up to December 31, 1901 | 1,006,666.67 = | 404,680.00 |
| Cash and cashier | 1,157,096.26 = | 465,152.70 | Loan of 1899, with interest up to December 31, 1901 | 2,315,333.38 = | 930,764.00 |
| Bills of exchange | 332.83 = | 133.80 | Loan of 1901, with interest up to December 31, 1901 | 1,006,666.67 = | 404,680.00 |
| Securities | 515,842.34 = | 207,368.62 | Repairing and boiler fund | 800,000.00 = | 321,600.00 |
| Prepaid year premium | 263,502.09 = | 105,927.84 | Insurance fund | 205,462.40½ = | 82,596.89 |
| Equipment current voyage | 72,820.86 = | 29,273.78 | Fund for the employees | 152,565.42 = | 61,331.30 |
| Debtors | 379,355.84½ = | 152,501.05 | Creditors | 809,727.81 = | 325,510.53 |
| | | | Dividend, 1901, and taxes | 492,000.00 = | 197,784.00 |
| | | | Profit and loss account | 6,171.08 = | 2,078.78 |
| | 15,048,545.88½ = | 6,049,515.45 | | 15,048,545.88½ = | 6,049,515.45 |

I regret to say that the Cosmopolitan Line discontinued its service between Amsterdam and Philadelphia in August, 1901, on account of low freights.

Not a single ship under our flag entered or cleared at Amsterdam during the year.

The Royal West Indian Mail Steamship Company, of this city, extended its fleet during the year by building a new steamer—the *Prins der Nederlanden.* This ship was built by the firm of Blohm & Voss, of Hamburg.

It has a length of 298 feet, breadth of 38 feet, and measures 2,150 tons. It is provided with triple-expansion engines of 1,600 horse-power, with 3 boilers, one of which is a reserve, and develops a speed of 13¼ miles by 85 revolutions.

There is provision for only 40 first-class and 8 second-class passengers.

### FISHERIES.

The proceeds of the herring fishery (one of the primary industries of the Netherlands) have been:

| | Value. | | | | Value. | |
|---|---|---|---|---|---|---|
| | Florins. | U. S. currency. | | | Florins. | U. S. currency. |
| 1896 | 4,924,879 | $1,979,801.86 | 1899 | | 5,626,068 | $2,261,679.34 |
| 1897 | 5,567,756 | 2,238,237.91 | 1900 | | 7,339.275 | 2,950,388.55 |
| 1898 | 6,370,532 | 2,560,953.86 | 1901 | | 7,390,345 | 2,970,918.69 |

The Netherlands Government has allowed the following number of young salmon to pass into the Upper Rhine:

| | | | | |
|---|---|---|---|---|
| 1891 | 327,000 | 1898 | | 1,790,000 |
| 1892 | 1,017,500 | 1899 | | 2,050,000 |
| 1893 | 1,132,900 | 1900 | | 1,750,000 |
| 1894 | 1,621,200 | 1901 | | 1,959,200 |
| 1895 | 1,510,450 | 1902 | | 1,868,000 |
| 1896 | 1,894,200 | | | |
| 1897 | 1,429,000 | Total during 12 years | | 18,350,850 |

Expenses in this work have been: 4.42 florins ($1.78) per 1,000.

### LABOR.

The chambers of labor established in 1897 are in operation in the following trades: (1) building; (2) metals and wood; (3) wearing apparel; (4) the diamond industry; (5) articles of nutriment; (6) tobacco; (7) printing.

The number of members of each is 10.

An old-age and invalid-pension act was unfavorably reported by a committee of the Dutch Parliament in 1898.

Wages are low for farm laborers. Formerly, no money wages were paid; at present a suit of clothes, a pair of boots, some linen, and about $60 a year is the usual remuneration for the hired man. Day labor in the fields is paid at the rate of 80 Dutch cents, or 32 American cents. Farm laborers are scarce, the higher wages in Germany and the industrial works of Belgium attracting the Dutch peasant.

Wages in towns are low, also, from an American standpoint, a carpenter, blacksmith, or painter earning about $5 a week. Factory wages are small, and children after attaining the age of 12 are permitted to work twelve hours per day.

There are 24 schools for technical education, that at Amsterdam having been established in 1861 and the last at Nymegen in 1900.

There are 450 benefit funds in the Netherlands, half being burial funds and half burial and sickness funds, divided among 150 towns.

The canal population is estimated at 50,000 souls, of whom about 30,000 are children. Until the compulsory education act (leerpligt wet) of March, 1900, these children received little regular schooling; an improvement is now expected.

## LABOR INSURANCE.

The accident law which passed the Dutch Parliament on January 2, 1901, providing indemnification to workmen for the pecuniary loss arising out of accidents occurring while in the prosecution of their trades, is the most important labor legislation ever enacted in the Netherlands. The idea underlying this legislation was that such accidents may be classed as inevitable, notwithstanding every precaution, and in consequence the loss caused thereby is a part of the necessary cost of production, and as the risk is inherent in the work of production, it must be charged to it. By its terms, the workman is secure in his indemnification, independently of the good will or the financial resources of the employer, the State obliging itself to pay the workman or his family the indemnity provided by the law. To carry the provisions of the act into operation, the Government insurance bank has been created. The premium rather than the mutual system of insurance was decided upon, a tariff being established fixing the percentage of danger for every guilder of wages, thus enabling the employer to add to the cost of production a certain amount to cover accident insurance. The law, though maintaining the tariff system for the employers connected with the Government insurance bank, at the same time offers to them an opportunity to meet their obligations in another way. After obtaining the sanction of the Queen, and under sufficient guarantee, they may take upon themselves the risk of accident insurance of their workmen or transfer the risk to a stock company or other lawfully authorized association. In case the employer stands the risk himself, he must pay to the Government insurance bank the indemnifications, so far as they do not consist of life interests; also the installments of provisional interests, paid by the bank in case of an accident to a workman insured by the employer at his own risk, and if the interest is fixed, the cash amount of that interest, to be determined by the managers of the Government insurance bank. If the risk has been transferred to some company or association, then that company or association must pay, with the difference that instead of paying the cash amount of the interest, it will give a bond, the value of which shall be equivalent to the cash amount. When the employer has paid to the bank the cash amount of the fixed interest, the bank has no further claim on him, even in case the workman dies afterwards, leaving a family which is entitled to indemnification, or when his widow remarries, or if the interest is afterwards revised.

The Government insurance bank, however, holds a claim on the insurance company or association which stood the risk, and settlement must be made.

In case of transfer of the risk to an insurance company, or an association, the parties are at liberty to make a contract regulating the manner in which the employer has to meet his obligations toward the company.

Of the two systems of insuring the workmen, the collective and the individual, the former has been selected.

It is assumed, as has been said, that industry has to pay for its accidents, and industry consists of employers and workmen.

The maximum life interest—viz, the interest which will be paid to the party concerned, in case of being wholly unfit for work—amounts to 70 per cent of his daily wages; in case of partial unfitness, the interest will be fixed at a proportionate rate. This fixed interest goes into effect on the forty-third day after the accident, but he will receive up to that day, or on an earlier recovery, as long as his unfitness for work lasts, beside medical assistance, a periodical payment from the day following the accident.

This periodical payment shall amount to 70 per cent of the daily wages of the party concerned, for every day, not counting Sundays and official holidays, and will be paid in case he is not fit for work on the third day following the accident.

Every employer requiring accident insurance, independently of his being connected with the Government insurance bank, must keep a list of wages according to a prescribed form. These lists shall be used as a basis for the indemnifications, and for fixing the premium to be paid by the employers connected with the Government bank.

All the trades stipulated by law shall be divided into sections, according to the danger involved. No fixed percentage has been stipulated in case of loss of certain limbs.

The enforcing of the law is entrusted to the management of the Government insurance bank, which management shall consist of three members. These members, the actuary and the subordinate officers, shall be appointed by the Queen. In some cases, the managers can command the assistance of the Government or municipal police.

The government post offices shall also be agents of the bank. In certain cases, they shall be the intermediaries between the management of the bank on one side and the employer or the workman on the other. They take charge of notices from the trades requiring accident insurance, of notices of discontinuation of trades, of payments of the premiums by the employers, of the share of the noninsured employers in the expenses of administration, of indemnifications not consisting of life interests, of the installments of provisional interests due, and of the notices of accidents; and payment to the parties insured is made through them.

The managers of the bank decide upon the notices to the employers, the classification of the dangers and the percentages of dangers, the premiums to be paid, and the indemnifications to be paid to the workmen or their families.

The bank must investigate the condition of the workman to whom the accident has happened, and must also keep an eye upon his condition after the settlement of the interest.

In case the risk is transferred to a stock company or an association, the bank takes care of the settlement of the stocks deposited with it as a bond, after the cash value, which is to be paid, has been fixed.

The managers of the bank have the care of moneys received, in cooperation with a board of survey, to be appointed afterwards. The Netherlands Bank is the cashier of the Government insurance bank.

The managers of the bank shall compile yearly statistics of accidents, and shall draw every five years a balance sheet. As they are responsible to the minister of waterways, commerce, and industry for all their acts, not only concerning the management, but also as to the fixing of indemnifications, the supervision of the bank is entrusted to a special committee.

That committee, the board of survey, shall be appointed by the Queen, who will choose a third of them from employers, and another third from among the workmen. Employers are bound to furnish the necessary information to agents of the bank in order to enable them to perform their duties.

The municipal committee shall, besides entering appeals in cases where the law authorizes them, investigate if it is necessary to revise the already fixed interests, and hear the workmen to whom an accident happened, when ordered by the bank so to do.

When the law goes into effect, employers whose trades require an accident insurance shall be furnished with blank forms, in duplicate, which they will have to fill and deliver at the local post-office. These notices shall be forwarded to the managers of the Government insurance bank. By these blank forms, the bank will be posted as to, 1, the requirement of the insurance; 2, the danger connected with the trade, taking into consideration the working hours; 3, the number of workmen employed and wages paid.

The managers of the bank shall classify every trade requiring accident insurance, and shall fix the percentages of danger. The employer shall be informed by official letter of advice of the classification of his trade, and furnished with a tariff. This will enable him immediately to calculate the amount he has to pay for the insurance, as the tariff states the premium for every percentage of danger and for every guilder of wages paid. If the employer does not accept the classification of his trade or the percentage of danger, he has the right of appeal. The employer is obliged, in case of an accident happening in his trade to an insured workman, to call at once for medical assistance. Within twenty-four hours after the medical examination, and in every case within forty-eight hours after the accident, a duplicate notice of the accident shall be delivered at the post-office, which forwards same to the bank.

This notice must state the name and residence of the attending surgeon, as also the time the party concerned will be unfit for the work, according to his opinion. If it is shown that the insured workman died in consequence of the accident, or presumably will die, or that he will not be able to perform his ordinary work during more than two days, the officers of the bank make a report stating, 1, the cause and kind of the accident; 2, name and residence of the party concerned; 3, his wages; 4, a description of the physical damage caused by the accident; 5, in case of his death, name of the family left by him, who according to law are entitled to indemnification. In case of his death, the indemnification will be fixed as soon as possible.

Indemnifications will be paid weekly at the post-offices located in the district where the workman lives.

LIST OF TRADES REQUIRING ACCIDENT INSURANCE, ACCORDING TO THE LAW PASSED JANUARY 2, 1901.

1. Every trade using motive power.
2. Every trade using steam or gas, whereof the tension is higher than prescribed by general rules.
3. Every trade using explosive substances, or substances the vapors of which, mixed with the air, form explosive mixtures, in larger quantities than prescribed by general rules.
4. Every trade manufacturing, transporting, or warehousing explosive substances.
5. Every trade in substances mentioned in 3, having a larger stock than prescribed by general rules.
6. Boating, as also canal and river traffic.
7. Packet boating.
8. Fishing on canals and rivers.
9. Shipbuilding and taking ships apart.
10. Ship tackling.
11. Salvaging of ships and cargoes.
12. Exploitation of dry docks.
13. Attending locks and movable bridges.
14. Railway, tramway, omnibus, carriage and saddle horse enterprises.
15. Ballasting, loading and discharging ships, weighing, measuring, transporting of merchandise.
16. Making, repairing, and taking up railways or tramways, canal locks, ports, docks, bridges, dikes, or other waterworks.
17. Diving.
18. Constructing, repairing, and examining of sewers, conduits, electric cables, or lightning rods.
19. Digging in the ground, pile driving, dredging, and pit boring.
20. Turf making.
21. Iron and stone mining.
22. Exploitation of stone quarries.
23. Manufacturing of diamonds and precious stones.
24. Building and taking down houses.
25. Constructing, repairing, and examining roofs.
26. Painting and glazing.
27. Paper hanging and upholstering.
28. Plastering and whitewashing.
29. Cleaning of windows, buildings, and fronts of buildings.
30. Chimney sweeping.
31. Glass manufacturing.
32. Working in metals, stone, wood, cork, and reed.
33. Manufacturing straw in trades using machines.
34. Manufacturing glass, earthenware, lime, brushes, leather, articles made from caoutchouc or paper, paper boxes, flax, rope, sailcloth, and soap.
35. Basket making.
36. Tanning.
37. Shoemaking in trades using machines.
38. Manufacturing bricks and tiles.
39. Manufacturing cement iron.
40. Printing and bookbinding.
41. Refining of salt.
42. Apothecaries and manufacturing chemicals.
43. Laboratories for scientific or technical investigations, also for the use of schools.
44. Slaughter houses, butcher shops, and manufacturing meat.
45. Manufacturing canned goods or fruit juices.
46. Drying, smoking, and salting fish.
47. Beer brewing and manufacturing vinegar.
48. Distilling and manufacturing gin and liqueurs
49. Malting.
50. Manufacturing mineral waters.
51. Manufacturing coffee sirup and chicory.
52. Manufacturing butter by centrifugal machines.
53. Melting of grease.
54. Boiling of oil and varnishes.
55. Manufacture of sealing wax.

56. Packing of yeast.
57. Tobacco cutting.
58. Assorting of rags.
59. Street-lamp lighting.
60. Fire brigade.
61. Cleaning of roadways, streets, markets, sewers, closets, collecting of ashes and garbage, and manufacturing fertilizer.

## THE DIKING OF THE ZUIDER ZEE.

By the diking, the Zuider Zee will become a lake with a superficies of 356,820 hectares (881,727 acres), which, after deducting the four polders,[a] will be reduced to a surface of 145,000 hectares (358,295 acres). These four polders will consist of: Northwest polder, total surface, 21,700 hectares (53,620 acres), of which 18,700 hectares (46,207 acres) will be fertile land. Southwest polder, total surface, 31,520 hectares (77,886 acres), of which 27,820 hectares (68,742 acres) will be fertile land. Southeast polder, total surface, 107,760 hectares (266,275 acres), of which 98,900 hectares (143,382 acres) will be fertile land. Northeast polder, total surface, 50,850 hectares (125,650 acres), of which 48,900 hectares (119,832 acres) will be fertile land. Total surface, 211,830 hectares (523,232 acres), of which 194,410 hectares (479,687) will be fertile land.

The expenses of the diking will amount to—

| For— | Amount. | |
|---|---|---|
| | Florins. | U. S. currency. |
| Northwest polder | 12,700,000 | $5,105,400 |
| Southeast polder | 61,850,000 | 24,863,700 |
| Southwest polder | 22,850,000 | 9,185,700 |
| Northeast polder | 32,500,000 | 13,065,000 |
| Total | 129,900,000 | 52,219,800 |

Time estimated in completing the work: Dike shutting off the lake from the ocean, completed in the ninth year; northwest polder, completed in the fourteenth year; southeast polder, completed in the twenty-fourth year; southwest polder, completed in the twenty-eighth year; northeast polder, completed in the thirty-third year.

The total estimated cost of the entire work is 189,000,000 florins ($75,978,000), of which 40,500,000 florins ($16,281,000) is for the dike, and 148,500,000 florins ($59,697,000) for all the other work, while the net number of hectares of reclaimed useful ground will be 194,410 (479,687 acres), and the duration of the work will occupy thirty-three years.

From the seventeenth year up to the thirty-sixth year, 10,000 hectares (24,710 acres) can be yearly delivered.

---

[a] Land reclaimed by drainage.

*Statement showing the yearly cost of the work during the thirty-three years of the construction.*

| Years. | Cost of the work. | | Value in the 36th year. | |
|---|---|---|---|---|
| | *Guilders.* | | *Guilders.* | |
| 1 | 6,500,000 | $2,613,000 | 18,838,800 | $7,573,197.60 |
| 2 | 6,000,000 | 2,412,000 | 16,883,100 | 6,787,006.20 |
| 3 | 7,000,000 | 2,814,000 | 19,123,300 | 7,687,566.60 |
| 4 | 7,000,000 | 2,814,000 | 18,566,300 | 7,463,652.60 |
| 5 | 7,500,000 | 3,015,000 | 19,313,100 | 7,763,866.20 |
| 6 | 7,000,000 | 2,814,000 | 17,500,000 | 7,035,200.00 |
| 7 | 5,500,000 | 2,211,000 | 13,349,900 | 5,366,659.80 |
| 8 | 7,250,000 | 2,911,500 | 17,085,100 | 6,868,210.20 |
| 9 | 5,250,000 | 2,110,500 | 12,011,600 | 4,828,663.20 |
| 10 | 4,000,000 | 1,608,000 | 8,885,100 | 3,571,810.20 |
| 11 | 7,000,000 | 2,814,000 | 15,096,100 | 6,068,832.20 |
| 12 | 8,000,000 | 3,216,000 | 16,750,200 | 6,733,580.40 |
| 13 | 9,000,000 | 3,618,000 | 18,295,100 | 7,354,680.20 |
| 14 | 8,000,000 | 3,160,000 | 15,788,700 | 6,347,057.40 |
| 15 | 6,000,000 | 2,412,000 | 11,496,600 | 4,621,633.20 |
| 16 | 5,000,000 | 2,010,000 | 9,301,500 | 3,739,203.00 |
| 17 | 5,000,000 | 2,010,000 | 9,030,500 | 3,630,261.00 |
| 18 | 4,500,000 | 1,809,000 | 7,890,800 | 3,172,101.60 |
| 19 | 4,000,000 | 1,608,000 | 6,803,700 | 2,737,499.40 |
| 20 | 4,000,000 | 1,608,000 | 6,611,400 | 2,657,782.80 |
| 21 | 6,000,000 | 2,412,000 | 9,628,200 | 3,870,536.40 |
| 22 | 6,500,000 | 2,613,000 | 10,126,800 | 4,070,973.60 |
| 23 | 7,500,000 | 3,015,000 | 11,311,400 | 4,560,448.80 |
| 24 | 6,500,000 | 2,613,000 | 9,545,500 | 3,837,291.00 |
| 25 | 6,500,000 | 2,613,000 | 9,268,400 | 3,725,896.80 |
| 26 | 6,000,000 | 2,412,000 | 8,305,400 | 3,338,770.80 |
| 27 | 6,000,000 | 2,412,000 | 8,063,500 | 3,241,527.00 |
| 28 | 6,000,000 | 2,412,000 | 7,828,600 | 3,147,097.20 |
| 29 | 5,000,000 | 2,010,000 | 6,333,800 | 2,546,187.60 |
| 30 | 5,000,000 | 1,206,000 | 3,689,600 | 1,483,219.20 |
| 31 | 2,500,000 | 1,005,000 | 2,985,100 | 1,200,010.20 |
| 32 | 2,000,000 | 804,000 | 2,318,500 | 973,770.00 |
| 33 | 2,000,000 | 804,000 | 2,251,000 | 904,902.00 |
| Total | 189,000,000 | 75,978,000 | 370,816,200 | 148,867,112.40 |

The estimated price at which the recovered land may be sold is 950 florins ($381.90) per hectare (2.471 acres); thus, the 10,000 hectares (24,710 acres) of recovered land would bring yearly to the Government 9,500,000 florins ($3,819,000).

The twelfth province will be divided in eight municipalities of five villages each.

### NORTH SEA CANAL AND PORT OF AMSTERDAM.

The following invaluable technical account of the North Sea Canal, the Ymuiden Locks, and the port of Amsterdam, appeared in Engineering, of London, in January and February, 1902:

The Netherlands are so much the country of canals and of reclaimed land that it requires a huge scheme to excite public attention. Such a scheme was the draining of the Zuyder Sea, under which term several projects, notably Mr. Lely's, of 1892, were known. What he in reality proposed was to close the northern part of the bay by a huge dike 25 miles in length, and to transform a portion of the shallow basin thus reconverted into an inland lake (which it had been up to the thirteenth century) into four large polders, together of an area of 750 square miles. The dike was to cross from the peninsula of North Holland over to Friesland, not by way of Enkhuyzen-Kampen, however, a route often marked on maps, but farther to the north, via the island of Vieringen, over to Piaam. A canal was to be cut through this island more than half a mile wide, to provide an outlet for the Yssel, Vecht, and other rivers which discharge their waters into the Zuyder Sea. The work was to be carried out within a period of about thirty years. Although Mr. Lely, the chief originator of this project, has meanwhile been minister of public works at The Hague, the scheme has not yet been submitted to the Netherlands Parliament. The fact that the many fisher folk who dwell on the shores of the Zuyder Sea and on its islands would not readily submit to their being converted into farmers may have proved one of the greatest obstacles. Some day, however, the project may be executed.

Meanwhile, another enterprise has matured without attracting the attention it deserves. The city of Amsterdam has become a seaport, and that means a great deal more than the construction of the North Sea Canal, which was opened in 1876.

Amsterdam, though not the official seat of the Government (which is at The Hague), is, with its population of 500,000 inhabitants—503,300 in 1898—the first town of the country. More a town of commerce than a transit port, Amsterdam regards its navigation only as one of the chief sources of its prosperity, a prosperity which must not be measured simply by the extent of its shipping. Yet it could not maintain its place at the head of the Netherlands trade and its rank among the great emporiums of the Continent, with its situation on the bay of the shallow Zuyder Sea, called the Y, on account of its shape, without having better connections with the open sea.

The rise of Amsterdam is said to date back to the ruin of Antwerp, which, weakened by Alva's massacre of 1576, succumbed to Alexander Farnese, of Parma, in 1585, after a heroic defense. Antwerp has once more developed into a great port. Rotterdam has known how to make the best of its splendid situation on the Rhine, the most important river-trade route in existence, and Amsterdam has finally attained its ambition of being admitted into the ranks of the seaports. The North Holland Canal, finished in 1825, which joins Amsterdam to the Helder and the Nieuwe Diep at the northern extremity of North Holland, and thus to the North Sea, lost much of its importance when large steamers were more and more replacing sailing craft. It is not a small canal by any means; from 100 to 130 feet wide and 20 to 23 feet deep, it can accommodate large vessels. But a canal 52 miles in length, leading to a terminus, not a thoroughfare offering shorter passages on international high roads, can satisfy modern requirements only under exceptional circumstances. The North Sea Canal took the shorter route straight west. It has a length of 15 miles only, reckoned from Amsterdam to Ymuiden on the North Sea. The Y was partly dredged and partly filled up, and the narrow isthmus separating the Y from the North Sea was cut at the spot where the fishing village of Ymuiden has since risen. The eastern Amsterdam extremity of the new canal had to be closed against the Pampus, the southwestern marshy portion of the Zuyder Sea, which often threatened Amsterdam with inundation. The port of Amsterdam had to be improved to accommodate the largest seagoing vessels, and an outlet by water, direct canal connection with the Rhine, has been provided for—the Rhine-Merwede Canal, which starts at the eastern end of the port of Amsterdam. These are the tasks with which the Government and the city of Amsterdam had to deal.

## I.—THE NORTH SEA CANAL.

The construction of the 24 kilometers (15 miles) of canal did not involve any particular difficulties. Outside the city, there were no towns nor industrial properties of especial value blocking the way, no rivers to be crossed, and only three bridges—two railway bridges and one road bridge—to be built or maintained. As over a large portion of the northeast sea canal in Holstein, the canal had to be cut through open shallow water and soft, marshy ground. It meant, essentially, dredging, creating firm banks, and filling up, draining, and utilizing the reclaimed land. Nor did the original locks at Ymuiden cause exceptional trouble. There were three locks for draining and for locking large and small boats. Boats of 443 feet length, 52 feet beam, and 23 feet draft could pass through the large middle lock. Each of the two shipping locks was provided with three pairs of flood gates (or pairs of gate leaves, rather) and two ebb gates. The mean tidal range is only 1.65 meters (5 feet, 5 inches), though heavy, high seas are by no means rare.

It was the outer harbor and the moles which taxed the skill of the engineers and contractors severely. The harbor has a length of 1,555 meters (nearly 5,100 feet), and the moles converge, leaving a clear inner basin about 850 feet across. The false work was severely damaged the day after it was finished, and was totally destroyed two years afterwards—in 1869. At first thought that the beton blocks could be laid directly upon the sand. That did not answer, however, and a grounding of basalt, 3½ feet in thickness and 115 feet in width, was put down. On this base of granite rest the huge concrete blocks of 10 tons, and over these a layer of concrete has been cast. The crown is slightly inclined toward the harbor; the breast wall is simply brickwork. Below the low-water line the concrete blocks are not cemented, but clamped together by iron rods from 4 feet to 7 feet long, bent over at the ends and fixed by means of oak wedges. Huge blocks of concrete have further been piled up in front of the moles, forming a protective belt about 15 feet wide on the sea side to break the force of the waves.

In spite of the severe gales, which are certainly not less common there than on other shores of the North Sea, the entrance to and the exit from the harbor are exceptionally easy and safe. Only two accidents occured during the first eight years. In this respect, the work has been remarkably successful. It resulted, however, that the distance from the harbor entrance to the old lock gates, 2,500 meters (8,220 feet), was not always sufficient to allow the vessels to slacken down completely after having effected their entrance at good speed. This point had to be considered when the question of larger locks forced itself upon the authorities.

The canal was originally built with a bottom width of 27 meters (87.7 feet), a batter of 2:1, and the depth carried down to 7.5 A. P. The normal canal level is about 0.5 meter below the Amsterdam datum A. P., so that the available depth was 7 meters (23 feet). A gradual enlargement of the section was contemplated. The canal was opened in 1876, and the traffic proved from the commencement that the advocates of this waterway had not been misled by optimistic expectations. Ships of an aggregate burden of 500,000 cubic meters [a] were locked at Ymuiden in 1876, and of 4,000,000 cubic meters burden in 1877. It soon became clear that larger locks would have to be constructed for the largest ocean vessels. The new locks would have been built to the south of the old locks if the new community of Ymuiden—a very neat modern hamlet with streets running at right angles—had grown less quickly. The locks had hence to be placed farther north, and they were put farther back, lengthening the passage from the harbor entrance by 600 yards.

The new locks, then the largest in existence as to length, though not in other respects—they have since been surpassed by the locks of the Canadian Ship Canal, Sault Ste. Marie, Lake Huron, which are also worked by electric motors, the power being derived from turbines—could be excavated and built in the dry. The piers have a length of 282 meters (925 feet). Three pairs of gates divide the locks into a small outer chamber 73 meters useful length, and a large inner chamber 144 meters in length, giving a total available length of 225 meters (738 feet). The width is 25 meters (82 feet), and the sill is at 10 meters—that is, the lock has a depth of 9.5 meters (31.5 feet). The outer end of the canal at the locks has its bottom at 15 meters, the inner end at 13.6 meters. The dimensions will suffice for the largest steamers that might call at Amsterdam. In each pier runs a culvert 3.2 meters high and 2 meters wide (10 feet 7 inches by 6 feet 7 inches). We shall have more to say about the locks in the next section. There was no necessity for an emergency lock to prevent flooding of the country in case the gates should be crushed. The gates afford ample protection, and if they should fail, the waters would find plenty of polder area to spread upon before they would reach districts where they could do much damage to life and property.

The new locks were opened in December, 1896. When they had been completed the widening and deepening of the canal was taken up more energetically again, and a new grant was made by the Government in July, 1899, especially for this purpose, and further for substituting more suitable roads for the bridges at present crossing the canal. The actual cross section is: Width at bottom, 119 feet; depth of water, 28 feet; batter, 2:1. The distance of the embankments from center to center is 470 feet. It is thus possible to enlarge the section to a bottom width of 165 feet; in curves, 200 feet, and a depth of 32 feet, with a batter of 3:1 without removing the embankments. A foreshore 16 feet wide will be left, washed by 4 inches of water, and bordered by a stone pitching of basalt. The cost for dredging and laying this stone pitching is estimated at $1,215,000. The outer harbor at Ymuiden, which now has a depth of 26 feet at low water and of 34 feet at high water, will also be deepened, so that 32 feet of water will be available at low tide and 38 feet at high tide. These operations will add $142,155 to the cost for enlarging the canal section, allowing about $58,320 for unforeseen expenses. A railway and road bridge crosses the canal at Velsen, on the southern bank of the canal, not far from Ymuiden, with which Velsen is connected by rail. Passengers coming from Ymuiden change at Velsen to proceed either north or south to Haarlem, on the way to Amsterdam or Rotterdam. There is no railway skirting the northern canal bank at all. Near Amsterdam, the railway to Zaandam passes over the canal. The actual railway swing bridges have a span of 63 feet only, and they will be replaced by swing bridges leaving a clear waterway 180 feet in width, allowing two ships to cross between the piers The pivot pier has its foundations in the slope of the one embankment, and the two bridge arms will be of equal length. The Zaandam bridge will not have to be operated for small vessels, as the lower member is 36 feet above water level in mid-channel. At Velsen this height will be 25 feet only; the difference is connected with the local conditions. The absence of any towns on the canal banks—Velsen is some distance from the

---

[a] 1 cubic meter=35.3 cubic feet.

southern bank—makes the canal simply the high road to Amsterdam. There is, so far, no regular steamer connection between Ymuiden and Amsterdam, and in fact no local traffic to speak of. There are, however, a few factories on the northern bank near the Velsen railway bridge.

Each railway bridge will be worked by two electric motors of 25 horsepower each. The operation is to take two and one-half minutes. The Velsen road bridge, the only road bridge leading over the canal, is being replaced by a steam ferry to convey passengers and carts and tramway locomotives and carriages. This project is complicated by the fact that the canal is apt to freeze in winter. The Government always maintains open water for the canal shipping free of charge, and the ice breakers have proved well suited for their work. As regards this cross traffic, two landing stages are being built on either bank, for the summer and for the winter service, the latter stages being pushed farther out into the water. Connection with the shore will be effected by means of girder bridges, hinged at the shore end to be lowered on to the ferry with other end, as is done with the railway ferries plying between the Danish isles. The boats will have a length of 122 feet, sufficient to accommodate a tramway engine and three cars; longer trains will be divided into two sections, and shunted on parallel tracks on the ferry. The ferries will be paddled steamers, with two engines, indicating 200 horsepower each, and two rudders.

The grant of July, 1899, which we mentioned above, provides the sum of $249,075 for two ferries and the landing stages. The swing bridges near Velsen and near Zaandam are estimated to cost $607,500 and $1,093,500, respectively, and nearly $97,200 will have to be paid as an indemnity to the railway companies, which will remain in charge of the swing bridges. Together with the items previously stated for dredging, etc., the canal improvements will require a capital of $3,402,000. The State bears the main expense, the city of Amsterdam will contribute one-tenth of the total. The improvements are to be completed within a period of ten days.

The Zuyder Sea end of the canal, or of the Y, was closed by a dam, leaving communication through the Orange Locks. The great pumping station is situated on this dam. Before this dam was constructed, there had been no difficulty in maintaining a tidal flow in the Y inlet, which kept a deep-water channel, though it silted other parts of the Y up. After the erection of this dam, the approach to Amsterdam through the Pampus, from the Zuyder Sea side, became difficult. A dike has therefore been drawn from the Orange Locks in an easterly direction, with a branch stretching back toward the great dam to the south of the main dike. The dike, which thus also resembles the letter Y, has a length of 5,000 yards. The navigable channel, 9 feet deep, is to north of the dike; to the south of it the dredged soil is being deposited, and this part will in the course of time become cultivable. The bottom of the Zuyder Sea, whose depth nowhere exceeds 20 feet, is very soft, and firm sand and clay are only met with at a depth of about 36 feet. Vast bulks of sand had hence to be deposited for the construction of the dike, the crown of which is convex and paved.

All canal and harbor dues (except the State pilot dues) at Ymuiden were abolished in 1890. The ice breakers, which clear the canal of ice free of charge, are provided by the State, the province and the city of Amsterdam. •

The fishing harbor at Ymuiden, a fine tidal basin, 270 meters long and 120 meters wide (1,215 by 395 feet), has recently been deepened to 5.6 meters (18.3 feet).

## II. THE ELECTRIC WORKING OF THE YMUIDEN LOCKS.

In deciding upon the question of motive power for the large lock, the Government proceeded with great and commendable caution. Hydraulic power was applied almost everywhere, and worked satisfactorily, yet there were some undeniable drawbacks, among which must be reckoned the difficulty of keeping the machinery in good order during severe winters. Glycerin will not freeze, and glycerin is used therefore in the hydraulic pipes, but it is more expensive than water. Electricity was recommended, but nobody could point to any example of important locks being worked by electric motors, and this problem concerned the largest lock in existence. In June, 1893, the minister for "waterstaat, handel, and nyverheid" (waterways, commerce, and industry) invited projects for operating the locks. Thirteen plans were submitted to the committee, and four premiums—two of $486 and two of $388.80— were awarded to four schemes, two of which were hydraulic and two electric. The successful competitors were at the same time invited to make certain alterations. After reexamination of the improved schemes, the joint tenderers of the electric design to which the higher prize had been awarded, Messrs. Figee Brothers, of Haarlem, manufacturers of hoisting machinery, and Messrs. P. H. ter Meulen & Company, electrical engineers, representatives of the Elektricitäts-Actien-Gesellschaft, vormals

Schuckert & Company, of Nuremberg, were asked to make preliminary experiments at Ymuiden. These two firms soon afterwards amalgamated to the Haarlemsche Maschinenfabriek, voorheen Gebroeders Figee, whose works, considerably extended and refitted in thorough modern fashion, have borne the brunt of this inauguration of electric lock operation. For that it was an inauguration, and that it meant very hard and anxious work for many months, need hardly be emphasized. It fell particularly on Mr. Hulswit and Mr. Dufour, underdirectors under Mr. Figee, and on the electrician, Mr. Lohr, who had come over from the Schuckert Works.

The preliminary experiments proved that the opening of a gate within eighty seconds against a waterhead of 4 inches required an electric motor of 45 horsepower. The minister first contracted with the Haarlem Engine Works for a plant to operate 2 gates, 2 sluices, and 2 capstans. After a successful trial period extending over ten months, the full contract was intrusted to the Haarlem firm, and the whole plant is now—the approbation period being over—the property of the Government. When we consider that a breakdown in the great lock would shut out the large ocean steamers from the canal and from the port of Amsterdam, which has made special exertions for the accommodation of the largest vessels, we can only approve of the wise caution exercised by the Government.

The large locks are fitted with 3 pairs of flood gates and 3 pairs of ebb gates, comprising 12 gate leaves. They form floating boxes, built up of steel plates and angle irons, and contain adjustable water-ballast chambers. The Holtenau and Brunsbüttel locks of the Northeast sea canal, were the last example of big gates of this type to which we have referred. It was, of course, the designers of the Holstein gates who had the benefit of the experience gained at Ymuiden, and not vice versa. The largest Ymuiden gates have a height of 15 meters (49.2 feet), a width of 77.5 feet, and weigh 140 tons each; the smaller gates are 13 meters (42.7 feet) high.

The contract specified that the large gates should be moved, opened, or closed within ninety seconds, against a water-level difference of 4 inches, and that the culvert sluices should be operated in sixty seconds against a water head of 2 meters (6.7 feet) and a water current of 4 meters (13 feet) per second. The movements were to be simultaneous for the two leaves of a gate and the two sluices, and to require only one attendant. The whole machinery, except the capstan, was to be placed underground, so as to leave the piers unobstructed. The capstans are provided for operating the gates in cases of emergency and for assisting vessels through the lock. As neither case has proved to be frequent, only two of the 12 capstans are driven by electricity, the other ten being turned by hand. For the former case, the contract stipulated a force of 5 tons and a circumferential speed of 20 centimeters (8 inches) per second; for the latter, double the force at half the speed.

THE OPERATION OF THE GATES.

We proceed now to a description of the machinery which is placed in chambers within the lock walls. There are 12 such chambers, each containing the machinery for one gate leaf and for one sluice; two further chambers contain each the machinery for one capstan. The ceilings are beton, strengthened by iron wire, arranged in Monnier fashion; the floor is 8 feet below the quay edge. Descending into one of these chambers, which are high enough to allow the attendant to stand erect, we notice three doors. The door in front of us gives access to the machinery for opening the gate, which requires a long movement. On our right we have the sluice gear and the capstan, on our left the switch chamber. The electric motor is a series-wound machine designed for 360 revolutions, slightly compounded for speed regulation. The motor is placed in a separate room, to which we ascend by a few iron steps, the top of the staircase being 4 inches above the highest water level ever observed; water-tight doors would, moreover, keep out any water. This room is at the back of the long passage, and the continuation of the motor shaft passes through a stuffing box in the partition wall. The coupling between the motor shaft and its continuation is elastic. The shaft bears two worms, one right-handed and one left-handed, to counterbalance any endwise thrust. The corresponding worm wheels—bronze, with cast-steel centers—run in oil boxes. The pinions engage with two large gear wheels, each consisting of two parts—a cast-steel center, keyed to the shaft, and a cast-steel rim, which would slip but for the downward pressure of 12 screws bearing against six blocks.

The object of the friction coupling is to protect the whole machinery in case the resistance offered by the gates should be excessive. In that case, the rim would simply slip. To the shafts, which are provided with steel roller bearings, are keyed chain sheaves, two for each shaft, which when turned in either direction pull four heavy endless chains fastened to a carriage of cast steel. The carriage runs with four wheels on two rails, and is further guided by two pairs of horizontal wheels on each side. The long boom which connects the carriage is built up of four profile irons and is doubly hinged at both ends, as it has to describe a radial path and must be able to adapt itself to small variations in the level. The pull on the chains is balanced by means of equalizing beams, hinged to the carriage. In fastening the chains to the carriage, care is taken that severe shocks, caused by waves striking the gates, should not affect the machinery. The far ends of the chain attachments bear against heavy steel springs. At the outer end of the passage, the chains are slung round four guide sheaves on two shafts. Although these sheaves are provided with pockets to prevent any bending of the chain links, the strain on the chains might still not be perfectly balanced. Hence, one of the sheaves on each of the other shafts has been made loose.

When the motor starts, the carriage will be pulled inward or outward according to the direction in which the motor, and with it the winch, are turned, and the boom will push or pull the gate. Cut-out contacts have been located on the extremities of the carriage travel. Their action is instantaneous, and the gate will hardly budge by an inch, as soon as the current is cut off. If the cut-out should fail to act, the gate would strike against the brickwork or against the sill; but the springs, which are inserted in the chain fastenings, and the friction coupling of the winch rims would yield, and the motor might spin on without causing any serious damage. If, on the other hand, the motor should for some reason fail to move, then the couplings on the main shaft could be loosened by hand, thus disconnecting the chain-wheel shaft from the winch, and the upper shaft could be turned by hand from the capstan; special gear wheels enable the lower shaft to participate in this motion.

### CULVERT SLUICES.

The sluices are built up of wood and sheet metal, fixed in strong iron framing. The frame terminates in a yoke, which is amply braced and pivoted above. The two endless Gall chains, by which the sluice is suspended, are fixed to the ends of the yoke, and rest on a horizontal shaft above, through which they receive their motion, and are further carried round a secondary winding shaft half way down the pit. They are equally stretched by means of turnbuckles, with right and left handed threads, and the pull is further equalized by the aid of the yoke. The transmission of power from the motor, which is placed in a separate chamber at a safe level behind a partition wall, through which the shaft continuation is carried, is of the type already described, and the machinery comprises an elastic coupling, worm and helical gear, and a winch. The motor develops 17 horsepower when running at 270 revolutions; it is fitted with an electromagnetic brake, and interruption of the current short-circuits the armature. The end thrust is taken up by steel balls. The weight of the sluice is partly balanced by a counterweight, which is attached to the chain end, and which glides on two rods provided with collars bearing against strong helical springs.

Damage to the machinery in case of failure of action of the contact cut-outs, located at the extremity of the sluice travel, is prevented in the manner previously explained. The helical springs referred to play a part in this safety device. This is, moreover, a second contact, which breaks the main current in case of overwinding. The emergency mechanism for raising and lowering the sluice with the aid of the capstan comprises a vertical shaft and bevel gearing. The sluice travels 10 feet per minute. The sluice bars the flow in one direction only; there are, therefore, an ebb and a flood sluice in each pier head.

### CAPSTANS.

Only two of the capstans are fitted for electrical power, as we stated already, and they are all of a simple construction. The cast-iron drum contains a sun and planet gearing. For manual operation, eight poles can be inserted, and 16 men be put to the work. When thus driven indirectly, the circumferential speed is only half of the 8 inches per second realized in the case of direct driving by the electric motor. The coupling and the chain wheel under the drum are for the emergency cases when the gates and sluices have to manipulated from the capstan. The gearing of the electric motor consists of toothed wheels, contershaft, bevel wheel, and a large crown wheel on the capstan shaft. The electric motor is designed for 21 horsepower at 270 revolutions.

### AUTOMATIC SWITCHES AND STARTING DEVICES.

As there were twelve chambers or systems of chambers, and as the manifold operations are to be controlled from switch pillars on the pier heads, of which there are only six altogether, intermediate switch arrangements of a special kind will obviously be required. Their objects will, however, better be understood if we first consider which operations the locking of a big vessel involves.

We will assume that a ship of the largest dimensions wishes to enter the canal at high water outside, and that the lock has accidentally not been left, after the preceding locking, in a condition which would facilitate matters. The full length of the two combined basins being needed, the middle gates have first to be opened. We begin by equalizing the water level in the two basins. Then we have to reduce the level of the water inclosed between the flood and the ebb gate of the outer pier head. For this purpose, small sluices in the gates themselves need only be raised. We can then open the ebb-culvert sluices and the ebb-gate leaves. A level difference between the high water outside and the water in the combined basin will now become apparent; that is adjusted by operating the fluid sluices in the culverts. The attendant further raises small sluices in the flood gates, and watches until the lighter sweet water of the lock basin begins to pass outside through the sluices just mentioned, which lie at a higher level than the culvert sluices. That outward flow tells him that the level differences have been equalized, and he can proceed to open the flood gate. The ship may then steam into the lock. The next step is to close the flood sluices, the secondary gate sluices, and the flood gates. The lock keeper now walks over to the third inner pier head, in order to balance the lock chamber and canal level and to open the lock gates.

Some of these movements are always simultaneous, apart from emergency cases, and others, fortunately, must necessarily be consecutive. The task is difficult enough, anyhow. Simultaneously are moved from either pier the two leaves of a gate, two corresponding culvert sluices, two corresponding capstans. Corresponding parts are opposite one another on the north and south piers. As noncorresponding movements are not called for at the same time, one starting gear will suffice for the three motors of one chamber. All the motors are reversible. The reversing could not be effected in the keeper's switch pillars without complicating the arrangements too badly, and each motor has, therefore, been provided with its own reversing switch. That means three reversing switches for the chambers where electric capstans have been put up and two in the others.

ELECTRIC POWER AND LIGHT.

The temporary installation consisted of two boilers, one steam engine driving a dynamo of 90 horsepower, and a high-speed vertical engine of 25 horsepower actuating two light generators. The permanent power station, which the Haarlem Engine Works completed last year, supplies the power and gives light to the new as well as the old locks, and further to the fishery harbor. The locks are worked day and night without interruption. The plant, which lies to the south of the old locks, comprises three boilers, each of 480 square feet heating surface, two steam engines, each of 110 horsepower, and dynam' s of 75 kilowatts, one set being reserved, and a battery of 124 cells, in addition to the high-speed engine and dynamos already mentioned. Light is supplied on the three-wire system, power on the two-wire plan, at 350 volts. The 12 arc lamps of 10 amperes on the piers are suspended on very strong masts, to be able to resist the violent storms which sweep the flat country. Reflectors throw the light down upon the locks, leaving the country behind in comparative darkness. Two of the arc-lamp posts further bear colored glow lamps indicating whether the lock is free. Two other electric lights tell the approaching vessel which lock it is to pass through—the old or the new. The way is shown by flashlights consisting of two groups of five incandescent lamps, fixed above the arc lamps on their poles at the entrance to the lock. A clockwork-driven switch in the power house, with arc extinguisher, closes the circuit of these lamps for two seconds, and then breaks it for eight seconds. The incandescent lamps number 500

The cables are all placed underground or under water. The land cables are protected with a double lead sheath; the water cables are insulated with okonite, and have one lead sheath and a fourfold iron armor. The cables rested parallel on cross boards laid over two pontoons. A girder was built up of gas pipes and deal boards, and suspended from floating sheers, the distancing pieces between the cables being attached to the girder by wires. Girder and cables were then lowered between the two pontoons down into their trench and the attachment wires cut by divers; the girder could then be raised again.

A new pair of floating sheer legs for loads of 20 tons has been built for Ymuiden. It is fitted with oil motors and two propellers.

### III.—The Port of Amsterdam.

The hinterland of the Netherlands is Germany, and a very considerable portion of her trade by rail and by water is with Germany A trip round the magnificent port of Rotterdam impresses that fact upon the visitor. There are fine docks all round, but many of the large liners throw anchor in the deep stream and take their cargo from or deliver it into the lighters which have come down the Rhine or are going up the Rhine. Most of the Rotterdam coal comes from the Ruhr Basin, either by rail—the railway connection is ample—or down the Rhine; and in the trade with the United Kingdom, Holland plays in some instances a more important part than is really due to her, because the British custom-house authorities generally credit the merchandise to the country from which it was shipped direct to our ports. If Amsterdam wished to become a seaport, a further outlet from the new Sea Canal, better connection with the great trade artery, the Rhine, was necessary. That the great scheme of the Rhine-Elbe Canal is for the present shelved is a question in which Amsterdam is indirectly interested. Since 1892, Amsterdam has been directly joined to the Rhine by the so-called Rhine Canal, which was built by the State and which is continued as the Merwede Canal. There are several Rhines, but the chief outlets by which the Rhine finally discharges its water into the North Sea bear different names. A short geographical recapitulation may not be out of place.

The Rhine divides as soon as it enters into the Netherlands. The right arm takes the name of Nether Rhine, and sends almost at once the Yssel and later, near Utrecht, the Vecht to the Zuider Zee. The name Nether Rhine is changed into Crooked and Old Rhine; and as Old Rhine, the Rhine ends below Leiden—rather ingloriously, sentimentalists lament, because this branch certainly does not recall the majestic Rhine. Before reaching Utrecht, the Nether Rhine has sent the Lek straight on to Rotterdam. The left main arm is known as the Waal, which at Woudrichem receives from the left the powerful Maas, or Meuse. At Gorinchem, only a little way below Woudrichem, the Linge, a branch intermediate between the Nether Rhine and Waal, is taken up, and the united streams—that is, most of the Rhine and the whole Maas—proceed westward as the Merwede, which almost immediately divides again. The southern branches unite with the outlets of the Scheld, or Escaut; the Old Maas continues in a westerly course, but the North Maas, a short branch, joins the Lek a little above Rotterdam, and Rotterdam is said to be situated, not on the Lek, but on the New Maas.

The Rhine Canal now joins the Lek at Vreeswyk, some miles south of Utrecht, and the Merwede, the main river, at Gorinchem, or Gorkum. The canal has a length of 47 kilometers (29 miles) to the Lek and of 70 kilometers (43 miles) to the Merwede, a width of 20 meters (66 feet) at the bottom and of 35.2 meters (107 feet) on the water line, and is provided with locks 120 meters long and 12 meters wide (395 by 39.5 feet). The depth is 3.3 meters (10⅔ feet). The protection of the polders on both sides of the canal route was supposed to require especial measures, which the Government adopted, yielding to the remonstrances of the landowners against the advice of some experts. A trench was dug along either embankment line and filled with good clay. No tolls are levied on this Rhine Canal for the through traffic. Amsterdam, which lies at the extremity of this free canal, is thus also a free port. The exemption is subject to certain conditions, to which we shall refer later on; but lock and bridge dues which might have been exacted within the city boundaries are refunded for Rhine vessels. By this canal route via the Lek River the distance from Amsterdam to Ruhrort, one of the chief Rhine ports for the coal trade, is reduced to 216 kilometers (104 miles); the distance to Cologne to 308 kilometers (192 miles). With Emmerich, on the Rhine, German territory is reached at 145 kilometers (90 miles). As the North Sea Canal has a length of 24.5 kilometers (15.23 miles), the port of Amsterdam a length of 9.5 kilometers (5.9 miles), the total distance from the North Sea via Amsterdam to the German frontier by this water route is 178 kilometers (111 miles).

The absence of tides and the constancy of the water level, which is regulated by means of the locks—chiefly the Ymuiden locks in the west and the Orange locks in the east—much facilitate the docking and clearing arrangements in the port of Amsterdam, and have kept many a cost item at a reasonable figure. The necessity of basing all foundations on hundreds of piles unfortunately counterbalances this advantage. Lighter ships can be brought up to the big vessels in the deep canal water, where they can be moored to more than 60 pollards and buoys situated in front of the commercial quay in the old east and west docks. In some of these basins, a water depth of 8.5 meters (9.3 feet) is available, and this will partly be increased to 9.5 meters (10.3 feet). There are many quays. The New Vaart, which adjoins the goods stations of the Dutch Railway Company, is the usual terminus for boats from the Levant, the Mediterranean, and the north and east seas. The railway basin is placed between a multitude of tracks of the Dutch Railway Company and the State railways. The commercial quay, which has a length of 6,650 feet, is provided with a pair of steam sheer legs of 80 tons capacity and hydraulic cranes of a maximum capacity of 30 tons. Steamers from Asia and Great Britain frequent this quay particularly. The municipal sheds alone cover an area of 7,500 square meters (1.9 acres). In the Amsterdam entrepôt docks, the municipality owns warehouses covering an area of 140,000 square meters (35 acres). The large granary, which has a storage capacity of 17,000 tons, is the property of a private company. Private companies also own sheds and warehouses of considerable dimensions in various parts—the Blauwhoeden Veem, for instance, two stores, 300 yards long, on the commercial quay.

The timber dock has an area of 125 hectares (308 acres), and comprises, as already mentioned, three basins, styled the Minerva Harbor and the new and old timber harbors, for seagoing ships. These basins occupy about a third of the total area. The rest of the area is taken up by the floating timber basin, the transit harbor, and the slips and timber yards. In the transit harbor, logs and baulks may be kept free of charge for three months. Timber which is bound for Germany enjoys reduced rates.

The petroleum dock forms a fine basin of horseshoe shape, 910 meters (nearly 3,000 feet) long, the width from shore to the central island being 760 feet, with a total water surface of 28 hectares (69 acres), and a storage area on shore of 12 hectares (30 acres). The basin is entered by two channels 30 meters (98 feet) wide. Since 1895, the municipality has seven large tanks of its own on the western shore. The respective municipal body undertakes all the duties of a dock company and the transport of petroleum, and lets space and tanks; the American Petroleum Company, for instance, has put up three tanks of 60,000 barrels.

The extensions of the docks, to which allusion has already been made, were only resolved upon after long debates in the city council. The controversy concerned, however, only the manner in which further accommodation was to be provided; the necessity of the extensions was generally acknowledged. The work has been executed to the plans of the then director of public works of Amsterdam, Mr. Lambrechtsen van Ritthem, and of the dock engineer, Mr. P. W. C. de Graaf. Mr. van Ritthem retired at the beginning of 1900, leaving the completion of the work to his successor, Mr. J. van Hasselt. The extensions were formally opened by Queen Wilhelmina at the end of April, 1900. The erts kade (ore quay) forms an eastward continuation of the commercial quay, and has a length of 300 meters (983 feet), with a water depth of 8.5 meters (26 feet). It is built chiefly for discharging coal and ores into railway trucks. The old steam cranes have been replaced by six hydraulic cranes, which can lift 3 tons, and have ranges varying between 5.5 and 14.75 meters (17 and 49 feet). The hydraulic pipes come from the pump station, situated at the end of the inner harbor basin.

The Y kade was created by widening a dyke which had been drawn parallel to the commercial quay to shelter it against the wash from the north. The Y has a very considerable width at its eastern end. Along the southern bank of the new quay a deep channel, 330 feet wide, has been, or will be, dredged to — 10 A.P. giving an available depth of 9.5 meters (31 feet 2 inches). This channel has, so far, a length of 1,850 feet; there are the moorings already mentioned. Two of the sheds were completed by 1900. The railway crosses over from the commercial quay. This quay is served by seven electric cranes of 2 tons capacity, with a range of 13.5 meters (51 feet). Six of these cranes are of the old type first, we believe, adopted at Mannheim and Rotterdam; a seventh, which is to have several successors, represents a new type of the Haarlem Engine Works, which also supplied the hydraulic cranes. The electric current is generated in a building adjoining the hydraulic power station on the commercial quay. The concentric cables were furnished by Felten & Guillaume, of Mühlheim-on-the-Rhine. They are provided with double-lead sheaths and are armored with steel wires; joints are further protected by spherical sleeves.

The new entrepôt dock has been built by the municipality on reclaimed ground. The channel is being excavated to a depth of 8.5 meters (26 feet), and the basin is in connection with the inner canal system. The quay length is at present 350 meters (1,150 feet), and two bonded warehouses, covering an area of 53,000 square meters (13.5 acres), have so far been erected. There is ample space for very large magazine extensions on both banks of the basin, which communicates with the outer basin of the Rhine-Merwede Canal. The completed dock will form a basin of 5¼ acres area, with a quay length of 5,600 feet. Nine hydraulic 1.5-ton cranes of a range of 9 meters (30 feet) have been put up in front of the warehouses. In the warehouses are twelve hydraulic lifts of 1 ton capacity. The electric motors of the pumping station contain four radial poles within a field ring made up of two pieces, and drive the pumps by toothed gearing.

It had originally been contemplated to lay down a special hydraulic station, with boilers and engines, for the entrepôt dock. As an electric-power central station—the one already mentioned—was needed in any case, it was afterwards decided to drive the hydraulic pumps by electric motors. This has been done, and we find thus a curious combination of steam plant, electric generators, underground cables, electric motors, nydraulic pumps, and hydraulic cranes, and, further, dynamos and electric cranes. The pumping station of the entrepôt dock is situated at the inner end of the basin. Two Worthington pumps, each giving 360 liters (80 gallons) of water per minute under a maximum pressure of 50 kilograms (110 lbs.), and an accumulator have been erected on a common foundation, together with their motors. As the accumulator rises, the pumps move slower and slower; when it has reached its highest position the pumps are stopped; when it sinks again the pumps are restarted. As the cables cross many rail tracks, they had, of course, to be buried.

The electric power house on the commercial quay is a fine hall, quite as roomy and neat as we now expect to find electric power centrals. Two Sulzer horizontal condensing engines, each of 200 horsepower, drive each by ropes two four-pole continuous dynamos of the Schuckert Company, of Nüremberg, yielding 75 kilowatts. One of these dynamos, supplying a constant current of 95 amperes at tensions up to 800 volts, feeds the motors of the just-mentioned Worthington pumps. The other dynamo furnishes currents of 550 volts and 140 amperes maximum to the electric cranes on the Y kade. The electric light is supplied by two dynamos, each of 120 amperes and 250 volts, actuated by compound engines. The main switchboard consists of two large wings, united at an obtuse angle and placed in one of the corners of the hall. There are further to be mentioned a battery of Tudor accumulators, a Crossley gas engine of 35 horsepower, and hydraulic pumps of Armstrong and of Smulders, Utrecht. Some buoys—so far five—have been fitted with electric flashlights. Within a strong iron cage a glass lantern contains two electric incandescent lamps, whose cables are joined to the main cables on the commercial quay. To distinguish these lights from the many fixed lights, the current is switched on for eight seconds and then interrupted for eight seconds. This is done by means of an electric motor and a switch placed on shore. The machinery is made by the Netherlands Tool and Railway Material Works, of Amsterdam; the electric dynamos and motors were supplied by the Elektricitäts-Aktien Gesellschaft, late Schuckert & Co., of Nüremberg, and the hydraulic and electric cranes and lifts by the Haarlem Engine Works, late Figee Brothers.

A few remarks on the revolving cranes. The old type of electric cranes rests on two high portals, diagonally braced, and the cab is at the same time the motor house, containing the motors, haulage drum, and gearing, all of which have to revolve together with the machinist. The new type of the Haarlem Engine Works, late Figee Brothers, resembles in outer appearance closely their hydraulic cranes. The cab is stationary. The attendant has nothing but his levers in his hut, and the crane standard and the jib revolve alone about an axis which is on the very edge of the quay. The construction is especially suitable for narrow quays, and allows of using jibs of large overhang on such quays, as there is no danger of obstruction. The attendant is, moreover, not disturbed by the noise made by the gearing. The type has evidently found favor, as a number of these cranes have already been supplied to Rotterdam. Each crane is fitted with an electric cable drum and 25 yards of cable for making connection to posts on the quay.

Pile driving was, of course, a very important feature in these dock extensions. All Amsterdam is built on piles. Long experience must have sufficiently taught the people of the Netherlands how to perform this work, and it is, on the whole, no doubt well done, though one can not help noticing occasionally that a warehouse floor, generally paved in wood, is not exactly level. The erection of the 460 meters (1,500 feet) of quay wall and the sheds on the newly created island on the Y (on the Y quay) required 6,922 piles, and the piling engines were at work there for sixteen weeks, not always working continuously, however. The tough ground suggested recourse to hydraulic jets for softening the earth into which the pile was forcing its way. The piles had a length of 14 meters (46 feet) and measured about 1 foot in diameter at the top. One or two hydraulic pipes descended with the pile under the blows of a monkey weighing 15 hundredweight, which was allowed a considerable fall. The maximum number of such machines at work at a time was eight, but they did only ninety-one days of work altogether. The average number of piles fixed per day was 134; the average number per machine per day about 12, varying between 5 and 20, according to the difficulties of the soil.

The arrangement of the piles was designed by Mr. Lambrechtsen van Ritthem. In front of a shed there should, in his opinion, be room for two rail tracks; behind, room for three tracks, and between the first and second of the latter for a roadway. The different sheds must not be too close to one another, and after every fourth shed a quay length of 80 meters (260 feet) should be left free for facilitating shunting operations and for providing some emergency free space. An ample provision of turntables and traveling platforms would permit of reducing that distance. The front of a shed consists entirely of sliding doors; at the back doors are put in every 9 meters (30 feet). These doors have an iron frame covered by corrugated sheets.

The sheds themselves are essentially built in woods and roofed with wooden boards, over which shingles of galvanized iron are fixed. Corrugated iron roofs have not been applied, because the heat becomes oppressive under them and the condensation of moisture unpleasant. Only the partition walls are in corrugated iron. The interior is illuminated by low-power incandescent lamps, from 0.8 to 1.5 candlepower being allowed per square meter (10 square feet) of floor space. The pitchpine flooring, 4.5 centimeters (1.8 inches) in thickness, rests on longitudinal beams and crossbeams 0.14 by 0.22 meter and 0.25 by 0.26 meter (5.5 by 8.7 and 10 by 10.2 inches), respectively, supported by rows of piles 17 meters (60 feet) long. These figures refer to the sheds on the commercial quay, which have a length of 100 meters and a width of 22.5 meters (328 by 74 feet).

## WAREHOUSES.

Four kinds of dock magazines are distinguished in the Netherlands—free public entrepôts, owned by the State or the municipality; private free entrepôts, fictive entrepôts, and particular entrepôts. They do not differ much, however, as to the regulations. The first two are under continuous observation by the custom-house authorities. Both dutiable and free merchandise may be stored in them, but articles like sugar, wines, spirits, etc., which are subject to duties on a higher scale, can only be received in the second class. In the last two classes, the control by the customs officials is occasional. The stores of the third class are generally confined to one article. The municipal petroleum stores and tobacco warehouses belong to this class. The fourth class accepts all kinds of goods against negotiable documents. The respective companies, which are known as "veems," charge themselves with storage and transport. As to construction, these magazines are all buildings of five or six stories. On the water side, room is left in front for a crane path and for a platform 2.50 meters (8 feet) in width at the level of the first floor. Two tracks will not, as a rule, be required in front at Amsterdam, because much of the merchandise arrives or leaves again by boat, while at the back three tracks and a roadway 8 meters (26 feet) in width are at least necessary; there are four tracks in the case we speak of. The iron skeleton of the building is embedded in about an inch of cement, and the long warehouses are divided by fireproof walls in bulkhead fashion, without any doors, in order to reduce the dangers from fire. The lifts and stairways are outside the real house walls and connect the balconies. The width of the buildings is 30 meters (98 feet). Larger buildings would be too dark. The warehouses are, like the sheds, illuminated by electric incandescent lamps. Each floor of the building can support a load of 2 tons per square meter (10 feet). At the back of these warehouses are, first, the tracks and roadway we have spoken of, then a public street and cattle market and slaughterhouses. These buildings have their fronts on the quay of the New Vaart.

It need not be emphasized that all these improvements and extensions, among which we should further mention the new floating dock *Königin Wilhelmina*, which can take boats of 10,000 tons burden, have involved very heavy expenditure. The improvements on the ore quay and Y quay were estimated to cost $311,040. The entrepôt dock extension involved an outlay of $364,500. The expenses have been borne by the State and by the city of Amsterdam.

In order to complete the description of the port of Amsterdam, I cull from a report recently forwarded to the Department[a] an account of the "veems" or warehouses:

During the reign of the counts of Holland, it had already become necessary to establish a weigh-house in order to guarantee to merchants correct weighing by means of weights controlled by the city authorities. Weighing dues were paid to those counts. It is supposed that as early as the year 1275, such a weigh-house existed on the dam at Amsterdam. It can not be exactly stated at what time the privilege of the weigh-house was transferred to the city. It is claimed that Count Albrecht of Bavaria awarded this privilege to the city of Amsterdam in the year 1389.

During the seventeenth century, the period during which the East India Company and the West India Company flourished so extraordinarily, every merchant, before delivering goods, was compelled to have them weighed in the city weigh-house (stadewaag). The city of Amsterdam possessed four of these weigh-houses, managed by weighmasters, employing weighers.

Merchants brought their wares to the city weigh-house and employed weigh-house carriers (waagdragers) to place their goods upon the scales of the weigh-house and

---

[a] See Special Consular Reports, "Stored goods as collateral for loans."

to deliver them on board ship. These waagdragers formed corporations called "veems," and in order to show to what "veem" they belonged wore hats of different forms and colors. The names of the principal of these "veems" were: "Vriesseveem," "Blaauwhoedenveem," "Groenhoedenveem," "Zwarthoedenveem," "Withoedenveem," etc.

The "veems" were under the direction of four to five chiefs or "bosses" (bazen) and four trustees chosen from among the leading merchants. These directors employed laborers to perform the work. When the city abolished the municipal weighhouses, the waagdragers took a city oath, and were then called "sworn weighers" and "werkers van den handel" (workers for the trade). Their work consisted of receiving goods from on board ship, weighing same, and either warehousing or delivering same.

Now and for a long period—perhaps forty or fifty years—the "veems" issue "cedullen" (warrants) to bearer for the goods stored by them in their warehouses. .

These warrants are accepted by the Netherlands Bank and also by private bankers and banking institutions as collateral for loans.

In consequence of the increase of trade and of the extension of warehouses, the "veems" of late years have been transformed into stock companies, each having a capital of from 1,000,000 to 3,000,000 florins ($402,000 to $1,206,000).

The following circular of the Blaauwhoedenveem (blue hat warehousemen) may answer as a sample of all the "veems":

*Blaauwhoedenveem (Joint Stock Company, Limited), forwarding agents, sworn city weighers, lightermen, wharfingers, stevedores. Established A. D. 1616.*

Offices: Amsterdam, Singel 206-208; Rotterdam, Leuvehaven 227.

Managers: Amsterdam—Mr. C. H. Klyn, Mr. W. J. van Haren Noman, jr., Mr. P. van Nop. Rotterdam—Mr. J. C. A. Hol, Mr. H. H. van Dam, A. C. zn.

Board of directors: Amsterdam—Mr. M. C. Calkoen, Mr. E. H. Crone, Mr. A. J. de Bordes. Rotterdam—Mr. C. H. van Dam, Mr. Herman Kolff.

Share and debenture capital fully paid, 2,710,000 florins ($1,098,400), D. C.

The Naamlooze Vennootschap Blaauwhoedenveem is fully equipped for the forwarding, handling, and warehousing of all kinds of merchandise.

Steamers and vessels loaded and discharged. Warrants issued for all goods stored in the company's warehouses, on which bankers pay advances as well as against shipping documents.

Commercial establishments, docks, and wharves managed for either own or joint account.

All kinds of business conducted in connection with above-mentioned branches, such as surveying, delivering, superintending the weighing of goods.

### AMSTERDAM.

The Naamlooze Vennootschap Blaauwhoedenveem owns two capital warehouses, situated on the principal quay (de Handelskade). These establishments are divided into five separate premises, called Europa, Azie, Afrika, Amerika, Australie, consisting of 323,000 square feet floor space and equipped with all modern facilities, as hydraulic cranes, lifts, etc., and electric light. Private piers and railroad sidings in connection with the Dutch railroads.

### ROTTERDAM.

The Naamlooze Vennootschap Blaauwhoedenveem possesses here three spacious warehouses. The first is situated on the Wilhelminakade, opposite the pier of the Netherlands-American Steam Navigation Company. This establishment has been divided into three separate premises, called Scheepvaart (navigation), Handel (commerce), Nyverheid (industry), which are provided with electric elevators and lifts, and are lighted by electricity. There is a private pier, length 403 feet, and railroad sidings, in connection with the State and Dutch railways. There are three fire and waterproof cellars, containing 6,000 barrels each.

The second building, "Santos," is specially constructed for the storage of coffee, with cool cellars for margarin, oil, wine, etc., and lies between the Rhine and Maas harbors.

The third establishment, "Nederlandsche Indië," Leuvehaven, in the center of the town, is for local goods, adjoining the newly constructed coffee-peeling establishment, "Blaauwhoedenveem Cy."

## ELECTRIC PLANT.

The city council of Amsterdam voted a credit of 6,500,000 florins ($2,613,000), and afterwards a second credit of 2,900,000 florins ($1,165,800), for building a plant to furnish electricity for lighting and motive power, for changing the track of the horse tramway for electric traffic, and to buy the required electric street cars.

The building of the electric plant was given to home people. The steam engines, dynamos, and the full installation of the plant will be furnished by the Algemeine Electricitäts Gesellschaft, of Berlin, in cooperation with the Koninklyke Fabriek voor Stoomwerktuigen en Spoorwegmateriaal, of this city, Gebroeders Stork & Co., of Hengelo, and some German manufacturers.

The trolley wire will be furnished by the firm of Siemens & Halske, of Berlin, and the electric street cars by the Ungarische Maschinen und Waggon Fabrik. One hundred and seventy kilometers (27.2 miles) of electric cables will be required for lighting and motive power, and 70 kilometers (11.2 miles) of cables for the electric street cars.

The description and particulars of the 240 kilometers (148 miles) of electric cables were published on July 1 last, and bids for same were delivered September 1, 1902.

The following are the bids for the cables, as published:

| Company or corporation. | Location. | Value of bid. | |
|---|---|---|---|
| | | Florins. | U. S. currency. |
| Deutsche Kabelwerken (Actien Gesellschaft). | Berlin, Rummelsburg | 773,400.20 | $310,906.88 |
| Simon Bros., Limited | London | 946,060.55 | 380,316.34 |
| Western Electric Co | do | 759,925.75 | 305,490.15 |
| Société Française des cables électriques | Lyons | 1,001,957.60 | 402,786.92 |
| Kabelfabrik Actiengesellschaft | Vienna | 778,130.06 | 311,602.28 |
| W. F. Henley's Telegraph Works Co., Limited | London | 845,087.15 | 339,725.03 |
| British Insulated Wire Co., Limited | Prescot | 938,781.00 | 377,349.96 |
| Dr. Casserer & Co | Charlottenburg | 865,752.60 | 348,032.54 |
| Land und Seekabelwerke (Actien Gesellschaft) | Cologne | 901,306.25 | 362,325.11 |
| Kabelwerk Rheydt (Actien Gesellschaft) | Rheydt | 1,000,396.38 | 402,561.34 |
| Siemens & Halske (Actien Gesellschaft) | Berlin | 949,218.75 | 381,585.94 |
| St. Helens Cable Co., Limited | Warrington | 817,794.70 | 328,753.47 |
| Felten & Guillaume, Carlswerk | Mühlheim on the Rhine | 941,777.50 | 378,694.55 |
| Société Industrielle des Téléphones | Paris | 999,451.66 | 401,779.57 |
| Algemeine Electricitäts Gesellschaft | Berlin | 915,145.75 | 367,888.59 |
| Callender Cable and Construction | London | 813,853.50 | 327,169.11 |
| W. F. Glovers & Co., Limited | Manchester | 812,354.00 | 326,566.31 |

This office is compelled with chagrin to report that, after considerable preliminary investigation, no American company succeeded in securing orders for material for this electric plant. The only American bid for cars was very high, and extracts from a letter from an officer of one of our great cable companies, who it was hoped would furnish at least a part of the wires, exhibit the situation:

Referring to the duplicate copies of specifications and descriptions of electric cables required by the city of Amsterdam, we beg to advise that we have given the matter our most careful investigation and consideration, and regret to have to advise you that the conditions surrounding the prospective bidding and letting of this order are such as to make it extremely unlikely, and, indeed, quite improbable, that the city could give consideration to any bid which did not contemplate the complete installation in manner described by them. You will understand, without our giving any particular reasons therefor, that American practice in lines pertaining to electric transmission is materially different in points of detail from the European practice. It is also true that the methods of installation prescribed in the case of the city of Amsterdam involve the use of accessories and devices which are not used in this country. The whole matter is also so complicated in its details that, in the time at our disposal, it would have been practically impossible to prepare the bid in the form required and to submit the samples and detailed drawings which are called for.

## WATERWORKS.

Water for the city of Amsterdam is supplied by three waterworks, viz: The Dune waterworks, with a yearly capacity of about 8,000,000 cubic meters (282,640,000 cubic feet); the Vecht (name of the river) waterworks, established between the years 1884–1888, having a yearly capacity of fully 14,000,000 cubic meters (494,620,000 cubic feet), and the spring waterworks, with a yearly capacity of, at the highest, 1,500,000 cubic meters (52,995,000 cubic feet).

The supplies being, however, insufficient for the needs of the city, which has been largely extended during the last twenty-five years, the city council of Amsterdam appropriated on January 20, 1897, the amount of 25,000 florins ($10,500)—increased February 8, 1900, to 50,000 florins ($20,100)—in order to make examination respecting the establishment of a reservoir east of Hilversum, in the province of North Holland, and as to the condition of the water of the River Lek, near Amerongen, in the province of Utrecht. The average quantity of drinking water furnished at Amsterdam, per capita and per day, during the years 1896, 1897, 1898, and 1899 was 85, 80, 81, and 83 liters (22.45, 21.13, 21.398, and 21.92 gallons).

The following table shows the average quantity of water used per capita and per day in some of the largest cities on the Continent of Europe for the years 1898 and 1899:

| Cities. | Inhabitants. | Liters. | Gallons. |
|---|---|---|---|
| Hamburg | 668,700 | 184 | 48.6 |
| Breslau | 408,133 | 80 | 21 |
| Stockholm | 287,568 | 100 | 26.4 |
| Charlottenburg | 478,000 | 69 | 18.25 |
| Copenhagen | 349,000 | 81 | 21.3 |
| Leipzig | 422,000 | 67 | 17.9 |
| Frankfort on the Main | 224,500 | 171 | 45 |
| Dresden | 366,000 | 101 | 26.7 |
| Cologne | 334,000 | 108 | 28.5 |
| Prague | 252,850 | 112 | 29.6 |
| Hannover | 280,000 | 66 | 17.4 |
| Munich | 436,000 | 198 | 52.3 |
| Christiania | 220,055 | 120 | 31.7 |
| Glasgow | 840,000 | 225 | 59.4 |
| Liverpool | 798,853 | 129 | 34 |
| St. Petersburg | 960,000 | 150 | 39.6 |
| Rotterdam | 303,870 | 162 | 42.8 |

The director of the sanitary service of the city of Amsterdam states that the water required for household use, per day and per capita, in Great Britain and Germany, is as follows:

| Description | Great Britain. | | Germany. | |
|---|---|---|---|---|
| | Liters. | Gallons. | Liters. | Gallons. |
| Drinking water | 1.5 | 0.39 | | |
| Cooking | 3.5 | 0.90 | 30 | 7.9 |
| Toilet | 22.5 | 5.94 | | |
| Housecleaning | 13.5 | 3.56 | | |
| Washing | 13.5 | 3.56 | 15 | 3.96 |
| Bath (once a week) | 18 | 4.75 | 50 | 13.2 |
| Closets | 27 | 7.10 | 6 | 1.58 |
| Waste of water | 12.5 | 3.3 | 12.5 | 3.3 |
| Total | 112 | 29.5 | 113.5 | 29.9 |

The existing water supply in Amsterdam fell short of the demand, for maximum daily use, 53,750 cubic meters (1,881,250 cubic feet); for average daily use, 27,500 cubic meters (962,500 cubic feet).

The projected waterworks must be able to furnish, in the year 1925, for maximum daily use, 98,750 cubic meters (3,456,250 cubic feet), and for average daily use, 57,500 cubic meters (2,012,500 cubic feet).

To illustrate the foregoing, the following comparative table shows the number of baths and closets connected with the waterworks in different cities for the years 1898 and 1899:

| Cities. | Inhabitants. | Baths. | Closets. |
|---|---|---|---|
| Zurich | 153,000 | 3,600 | 22,500 |
| Frankfort on the Main | 224,500 | 12,919 | 53,544 |
| Dresden | 366,000 | 6,852 | 21,394 |
| Cassel | 87,240 | 1,540 | 12,215 |
| Wiesbaden | 79,000 | 2,849 | 20,516 |
| Rotterdam | 303,870 | 1,769 | 15,229 |
| Amsterdam | 523,743 | 2,785 | 5,919 |

The production of the collecting reservoir of the Dune waterworks was:

| Years. | Rainfall of— | Quantity of water per year. | |
|---|---|---|---|
| | | Cubic meters. | Cubic feet. |
| | *Millimeters.* | | |
| 1888 | 668 | 8,134,727 | 284,715,445 |
| 1889 | 837 | 7,193,711 | 251,779,885 |
| 1890 | 445 | 7,687,120 | 269,049,200 |
| 1891 | 855 | 8,343,816 | 292,033,560 |
| 1892 | 918 | 8,114,440 | 284,005,400 |
| 1893 | 714 | 8,700,777 | 304,527,195 |
| 1894 | 848 | 8,839,493 | 309,381,255 |
| 1895 | 774 | 9,009,202 | 315,322,070 |
| 1896 | 622 | 8,919,226 | 312,172,910 |
| 1897 | 799 | 8,671,776 | 303,512,160 |
| 1898 | 883 | 8,335,718 | 291,750,130 |
| 1899 | 634 | 8,590,202 | 300,657,070 |
| Average | 746 | 8,378,350 | 293,242,250 |

*Estimate of cost of the projected waterworks of the city of Amsterdam.*

[Heath waterworks of a full capacity, viz. an approximate daily capacity of 77,000 cubic meters (2,695,000 cubic feet) to be reached in 1914 to 1917.]

| Description. | Florins. | U. S. currency. |
|---|---|---|
| Purchase of ground and special indemnifications | 890,000 | $357,780.00 |
| Works for the reservoir foundations, artificial works, springs, air, and pressure pumps, etc | 2,874,798 | 1,155,668.80 |
| Primary pumping station buildings and steam pumping engines, secondary pumping stations, buildings, and steam pumping engines, pressure pipes in the reservoir, sundry pipe lines for the stations, and plants to extract the iron from the water, central pits, filters, and pure-water tanks | 3,411,017 | 1,371,208.83 |
| Central pumping station, buildings, worksteads, large reservoirs, steam pumping engines, and sundry engines | 1,336,500 | 537,273.00 |
| Main pipe lines, 76,000 meters (82,840 yards), to Amsterdam | 3,781,894 | 1,520,321.39 |
| Telephone and telegraph, transportation means, railway tracks, laboratory, laborers' houses, houses for employees and engineers | 639,100 | 256,918.20 |
| Projecting expenses, expenses during building and survey of works, etc | 816,691 | 328,309.78 |
| Estimate of cost | 13,750,000 | 5,527,480.00 |

*Estimate of cost of the projected waterworks of the city of Amsterdam*—Continued.

[Lek River waterworks of full capacity, viz., a maximum daily capacity of 100,000 cubic meters (3,500,000 cubic feet) to be reached in the year 1925.]

| Description. | Florins. | U. S. currency. |
|---|---|---|
| Purchase of grounds and special indemnifications ............................ | 58,300 | $23,436.60 |
| Works of the collecting reservoir foundation, artificial works, reservoir pipe lines, pits, and pumping station, with electric motor pumps......... | 973,132 | 391,199.06 |
| Settling reservoir, filters, pure-water tanks, and pipe lines................. | 3,548,068 | 1,426,319.32 |
| Pumping-station buildings, engines, and institution for sand washing .... | 1,471,254 | 591,444.11 |
| Main pipe line, 154,000 meters (167,860 yards) to Amsterdam................ | 10,843,685 | 4,158,161.37 |
| Telephone and telegraph, railway, laboratory, houses for laborers, employees, and engineers................................................. | 438,900 | 176,437.80 |
| Projecting expenses, expenses during course of building, and survey of work ..................................................................... | 1,096,671 | 440,861.74 |
| Estimate of cost ............................................... | 17,930,000 | 7,207,860.00 |

[Extension of Dune waterworks by means of irrigation, of full capacity, viz., a maximum daily capacity of 100,000 cubic meters (3,500,000 cubic feet) to be reached in the year 1925.]

| | Florins. | U. S. currency. |
|---|---|---|
| *A. Gain of water (average per day, 60,000 cubic meters), 2,100,000 cubic feet.* | | |
| Purchase of grounds and special indemnifications ............................ | 242,000 | $97,284.00 |
| Works of the collecting reservoir foundations, pipe lines, supply pumping station with electric motor pumps and artificial works .................... | 714,000 | 287,028.00 |
| Settling reservoirs ..................................................... | 761,200 | 306,002.40 |
| Pumping stations, buildings, engines, and pipe lines........................ | 1,170,379 | 470,492.36 |
| Main pipe line to the dunes, 70,000 meters (76,300 yards) ................. | 5,390,000 | 2,166,780.00 |
| Telephone and telegraph laboratory, houses for laborers, employees, and engineers ............................................................. | 333,300 | 133,986.60 |
| Projecting expenses, expenses during course of building, survey of works.. | 489,121 | 196,626.64 |
| Estimated cost of Works A............................................ | 9,100,000 | 3,658,200.00 |
| *B. Irrigation, average per day 60,000 cubic meters (2,100,000 cubic feet).* | | |
| Purchase of ground and special indemnification ............................ | 595,000 | 198,990.00 |
| Works on the existing reservoir ......................................... | 862,723 | 346,814.65 |
| Houses for laborers and employees ....................................... | 48,400 | 19,456.80 |
| Projecting expenses, expenses during course of building and survey of works ..................................................................... | 100,877 | 40,552.55 |
| Estimated cost of Works B............................................ | 1,507,000 | 605,814.00 |
| *C. Filters at Leiduin for 40,000 cubic meters (1,400,000 cubic feet) daily.* | | |
| Purchase of ground...................................................... | 5,500 | 2,211.00 |
| New filters and renewing of existing filters and pipe lines................. | 771,872 | 310,292.54 |
| Projecting expenses, expenses during course of building and survey of works ..................................................................... | 58,628 | 23,568.46 |
| Estimated cost of Works C............................................ | 836,000 | 336,072.00 |
| *D. Pumping station at Zandvoort for a maximum daily capacity of 85,000 cubic meters (2,975,000 cubic feet).* | | |
| Purchase of ground and special indemnification ............................ | 102,300 | 41,124.60 |
| Works of the collecting reservoir foundations, artificial works, second basin, and pipe lines.................................................... | 178,577 | 71,787.95 |
| Pumping station, buildings and engines .................................. | 1,133,000 | 455,466.00 |
| Filters, pure water cellars, pipe lines, sand washing plant, and works for the delivery of water ................................................ | 2,525,103 | 1,015,091.41 |
| Main pipe line, 25,000 meters (27,250 yards), to Amsterdam ................ | 1,872,409 | 752,708.42 |
| Telephone, telegraph, laboratory, houses for laborers, employees, and engineers................................................................ | 262,900 | 105,685.80 |
| Projecting expenses, expenses during course of building, survey of works.. | 415,711 | 167,115.82 |
| Estimated cost of Works D............................................ | 6,490,000 | 2,608,980.00 |
| *Recapitulation.* | | |
| Works A ............................................................... | 9,100,000 | 3,658,200.00 |
| Works B ............................................................... | 1,507,000 | 605,814.00 |
| Works C ............................................................... | 836,000 | .............. |
| Works D ............................................................... | 6,490,000 | 2,608,980.00 |
| Total estimate of cost................................................ | 17,933,000 | 7,209,066.00 |

*Estimate of cost of the extension of the pumping station near Amsterdam, of full capacity, being a maximum capacity per hour of 1,200+5,063 cubic meters (42,000+177,205 cubic feet).*

| Description. | Florins. | United States currency. |
|---|---|---|
| Purchase of ground........................................................ | 142,000 | $57,486.00 |
| Extension of the existing engine capacity, boilers, and pipe lines.......... | 107,800 | 43,335.60 |
| Additional pumping station, buildings, engines, pipe lines, and low reservoir................................................................ | 1,494,020 | 600,596.04 |
| Sundries, houses, etc...................................................... | 134,200 | 53,948.40 |
| Projecting expenses, expenses during course of building, survey of works.. | 144,980 | 58,281.96 |
| Estimate of cost............................................... | 2,024,000 | 813,648.00 |
| The estimated cost is represented as follows: | | |
| Heath waterworks......................................... | 13,000,000 | 5,226,000.00 |
| Extension of pumping station near Amsterdam...................... | 2,024,000 | 813,648.00 |
| Sufficient to 1914–1917................................................. | 15,024,000 | 6,039,648.00 |
| Lek River waterworks....................................... | 17,930,000 | 7,207,860.00 |
| Extension of pumping station near Amsterdam...................... | 2,024,000 | 813,648.00 |
| Sufficient to 1925................................................. | 19,954,000 | 8,021,508.00 |
| Irrigation of existing dune waterworks ........................ | 17,933,000 | 7,209,066.00 |
| Extension of pumping station near Amsterdam...................... | 2,024,000 | 813,648.00 |
| Sufficient to 1925................................................. | 19,957,000 | 8,022,714.00 |

## POPULATION.

The following statement shows the increase of the population of the different provinces of the Netherlands during the year 1901:

| Location. | January 1— | | Increase. | Per cent. |
|---|---|---|---|---|
| | 1901. | 1902. | | |
| North Brabant............................................. | 559,301 | 566,550 | 7,249 | 1.3 |
| Gelderland ............................................... | 572,805 | 580,724 | 7,919 | 1.4 |
| South Holland............................................. | 1,171,437 | 1,194,465 | 23,027 | 2.1 |
| North Holland............................................. | 983,828 | 1,001,798 | 17,970 | 1.8 |
| Zeeland................................................... | 217,332 | 219,832 | 2,500 | 1.1 |
| Utrecht................................................... | 254,867 | 259,834 | 4,967 | 1.9 |
| Friesland ................................................ | 342,274 | 345,004 | 2,730 | .8 |
| Overysel ................................................. | 338,411 | 343,924 | 5,513 | 1.6 |
| Groningen ................................................ | 302,681 | 305,676 | 2,995 | 1.0 |
| Drente ................................................... | 150,364 | 153,281 | 2,917 | 1.9 |
| Limburg .................................................. | 285,828 | 292,072 | 6,244 | 2.2 |
| Total............................................... | 5,179,128 | 5,263,159 | 84,031 | 1.6 |

The estimated population of the city of Amsterdam is now 537,023 (October, 1902).

### STEAM ENGINES.

The report of the chief engineer states that during the year 1901, 12,034 boilers and 1,573 steam engines were in use in the Netherlands. The number of boilers had increased 553, and that of steam engines 333, compared with 1900.

Of the total number of boilers examined during the year 1901, 0.78 per cent showed direct danger, 2.70 per cent indirect danger, and 48.71 per cent small defects, whereas 47.80 per cent proved to be in a fully satisfactory condition. The percentages of the year 1900 were respectively 0.86, 4.50, 44.65, and 49.96.

## CREAMERIES.

In nearly every village of the provinces of Friesland and North Holland, from three to four cooperative and other creameries, either worked by steam or hand power, may be found. The daily output of the creameries is from 500 to 1,500 gallons, and it is calculated that the prices for the milk average from 5 to 6 cents ($0.02 to $0.025) per liter (1.05 quarts).

There are no prospects for new enterprises in this line, on account of the present decrease in the prices of cheese. The Government has encouraged the industry by the establishment in every province of a government council of advisers, whose services are at the disposal of the public, free of charge. The duty on dairy machinery, when not imported as agricultural machinery, is 5 per cent ad valorem; agricultural machinery is admitted free of duty.

The Laval system is nearly everywhere used for separators; these are manufactured by the Laval factory at Stockholm, which has a branch house at New York.

## INDUSTRIES OF TWENTE.

The cotton industry remained during the year 1901 in an unfavorable condition, the fall in the prices of the raw material causing a decrease in prices of manufactured goods, which was to the disadvantage of goods consigned before that time, as these were manufactured of materials commanding higher prices.

Spinning suffered largely on account of the unfavorable condition of spinneries in Germany, whereby German yarns, which are admitted duty free, found a market here.

The trade in dry goods decreased in Java, Celebes, and Sumatra, and the population of British India lacked cash on account of the failure in the rice crop. Of course, no business has been transacted in South Africa.

Although the metal industry could not boast of being in a favorable condition, there was no reason for complaint.

The exports from Enschede to the Dutch East Indies amounted to 4,133,150 florins ($1,661,526.30) during the year 1901, against 4,121,450 florins ($1,656,822.90) in 1900. The home consumption amounted to 6,861,000 florins ($2,758,122) in 1901, against 7,605,287 florins ($3,057,325.37) in 1900.

Exports to foreign countries amounted to 2,769,800 florins ($1,113,459.60) in 1901, against 1,897,920 florins ($762,963.84) in 1900. The total amount of exports was 13,763,950 florins ($5,533,107.90) in 1901, against 13,624,552 florins ($5,477,071.91) in 1900.

Lieutenant-General den Beer Poortugal, in a brochure "Nederland and Duitschland," is authority for the statement that in the last eight years, the output of certain textile factories in the Twente district has increased from 50 to 60 per cent. It is said that the textile industry here has a great advantage over Germany, where, on account of protective duties, machinery, petroleum, oils, leather, and factory supplies are dearer.

On January 1, 1901, there were in the manufacturing district of Twente 297,338 spindles and 21,261 looms for cotton alone, and on January 1, 1902, approximately 317,000 and 22,000, respectively. The

factory at Hengelo is exporting to British India, to Africa, to the
Philippines, to Siam, etc., and employs at present 868 steam looms.
The Twente colored cotton goods factory (Bontwevery) uses 304 power
looms.

### DEVENTER RUGS.

The rugs made at Deventer attract the favorable notice of visitors to
Holland.  The establishment dates from 1776, and its present capital
is 230,000 florins ($92,460).
The director has recently written this office:

We have no agency in the United States, but a collection of our designs and samples have often been sent to the New York houses, on which we have received many
orders of importance.  As we are overloaded with orders for Holland, we have not
seen our way to place an agency in the United States, but we now intend to attempt
to extend our trade.  It will be some years, however, before we have more trained
people, as our carpets are all made by hand, and it is not easy to learn the work.
For that reason, we do not expect to exhibit at St. Louis, as it would be of no use,
since we could not execute the orders we might receive.

### MINING IN DUTCH COLONIES.

The gold-mining industry in the Dutch colonies improved somewhat,
but up to the present it has not yielded much return, on account of the
difficulties due to a tropical climate.  The Guiana Gold Placer Company offered for inscription in the month of June 600,000 florins
($241,200) shares of the Mindrinetti Exploitation Company at 120 per
cent, which were quoted at 156 per cent at the end of December, 1901.
The Singkep Tin Company gave fair results.  The Dutch India
Mining Company was compelled to emit a loan of 800,000 florins
($321,600).  The inscription for 7,000 10 per cent mortgage bonds of
100 florins ($40.20) at 106 per cent took place in December, 1901.

### DIAMOND TRADE OF AMSTERDAM.

Mr. Louis Tas, one of the largest dealers of this city, has written
this office as follows on the diamond trade of Amsterdam:

Although during 1901 many contradictory statements were circulated concerning
the diamond market, still that year may be looked upon with satisfaction.
The year started very well for the diamond manufacturers, the demand for rough
and polished diamonds having been so large during the first four months that the
syndicate considered the time propitious to raise the prices of the rough material.
This rise in prices, instead of checking, increased the demand, whereto continued
rumors of other rises and the scarcity of rough diamonds largely contributed.
The great prosperity prevailing in the United States and. as a natural result, the
increasing demand for luxuries was largely responsible for this state of affairs.
It was claimed that the market had become inflated, that prices had reached the
highest point, and that as soon as America would stop buying, the high prices could
not be maintained.  Some parties even thought that if the demand from the United
States should stop, the strongly constructed foundations of the syndicate might break,
in which case hundreds of thousands of pounds of rough material would have accumulated and would have lain uncalled for in the safes of the syndicate, as there was
no demand from other countries, Germany suffering under the most serious of financial and industrial panics, and the business in France and Russia being at a standstill.,
As American dealers had overstocked themselves during the spring to such an
extent that they could carry on their business without any necessity of making new
purchases, the demand fell largely during some months, principally during July and
August.  If ever the time was favorable to produce a change, as had been predicted
by some parties, surely it was in those months.

The surprise of those pessimists, however, was great when, instead of seeing a fall in prices, another advance of 7½ per cent took place during the month of October. Dealers here are convinced that the syndicate will keep its prices up, as it is claimed that the production of rough diamonds has largely decreased.

The same gentleman, in addition to the above statement made in December, 1901, writes, at the end of October, 1902:

The diamond business since spring has undergone a radical change. It will be remembered that the strike of the diamond workers, which caused a scarcity of polished goods, was amicably settled and all hands are working to their full capacity now. Business on the Continent, which had suffered greatly up to that time, has revived steadily, so that the demand from European nations for diamonds has become fully as keen as that in the United States. The mere fact that nearly all the manufacturers are completely sold out offers the best guarantee for this statement. The rough material is but scantily distributed among them, and the very things which at one time were plentiful have become the most desired articles. Manufacturers are compelled to shut down occasionally, owing to the fact of not receiving enough raw material from the syndicate to keep their men busy. Here, as well as in all the diamond markets, the same conditions exist, the demand being greatly in excess of the supply, so much so that the situation has really become acute.

The syndicate, which receives its weekly shipments from the Cape, has more than its share of troubles in trying to meet the demand, but is unable to cope with the difficulty of satisfying all hands. As soon as polished goods are finished, there is any number of prospective buyers waiting for them, and as long as this situation prevails there is not the slightest doubt that prices will remain very firm and that the tendency will be toward an increase in values. The United States has not been a very prominent factor in the diamond market during the last two months, as most of the American houses had put in a supply earlier in the season and are fully provided; but how the market will be affected when America starts in buying again, this or next month, it is hard to say; but even the most sanguine bear will admit that it will once for all establish the stability of the market, and that it will no longer be a question of lower prices, but more a question of how much more prices will have to be raised in order to curtail the demand for goods which is growing from day to day, and which is entirely out of proportion to the supply.

## PETROLEUM TRADE.

Messrs. P. & G. C. Calkoen state the following:

The petroleum trade being monopolized by certain parties, the trade was very calm. There was no chance for speculation, as prices in the United States and in this country remained stationary during the year 1901.

During the first eleven months, 31 tank steamers discharged in the petroleum harbor, 2 of these carrying Russian oil, which for the greater part was intended for transit.

The imports of American petroleum at Amsterdam amounted to 15,701,000 gallons during the year 1901, against 16,181,615 gallons in 1900; at Rotterdam, 46,626,500 gallons in 1901, against 40,960,350 gallons in 1900.

The price quoted at the beginning of the year was 10.30 florins ($4.14), rising to 10.65 florins ($4.28) during the month of March, closing, however, at the end of the year at 9.55 florins ($3.84).

## TOBACCO.

Tobacco planters in Sumatra followed the advice of the Dutch dealers and paid more attention to quality, instead of quantity. On account thereof, and also in consequence of the favorable condition of the weather, the crop of 1900 brought higher prices. During the year 1901, 223,730 bales of the 1900 Sumatra crop were sold, at an average price of 111½ cents ($0.448) per half kilogram (1.1 pounds), against 263,978 bales in the former year, at an average price of 82 cents ($0.3296) per half kilogram (1.11 pounds).

With the sale of October 17, the 1902 season for Sumatra and Borneo tobacco came to its close. The average price realized for the

Sumatra crop compares poorly with that for 1901. The average price of the Borneo crop shows, on the other hand, a distinct advance.

The crop brought to market this year from Sumatra was undoubtedly inferior in quality to that of last year, and other causes, such as the commercial depression in Germany (one of the largest customers for this class of leaf) and some alteration in the fashion as regards the appearance and color of the tobacco in demand, united to keep prices lower than might have been expected to rule. It is noteworthy that not a single bale of either the Sumatra or Borneo crop is returned as unsold, a healthy sign for the opening of the new campaign in 1903.

While the general state of the market was similar for both Sumatra and Borneo tobacco, the crop from the latter island suited better the market taste of the year than did that from Sumatra.

### TIN TRADE.

Mr. F. Joosten, tin broker of this city, has furnished me with the following statement as to the tin trade:

The trade in tin at Amsterdam was very satisfactory during the year 1901. At the end of that year, the London market suffered severely by the failure in business of one of the large brokers who for a long time manipulated tin. Our market, however, was not affected by it.

The steadily increasing shipments of Banka tin from here to the United States were favorable to this market, showing that this seems to be attracting the same attention it held some eight or nine years ago. The revival of the trade with the United States is well deserved, as no such difficulties as to delivery exist here as in London.

Though the London market used to be much larger than this one, on account of dealings in Straits tin, whereof the supplies are enormously larger than of Banka tin, the Amsterdam market of late showed by the deliveries that it was the larger one. The deliveries during the year 1901 amounted at London to 14,756 tons and at Amsterdam to 16,993 tons.

The year 1901 witnessed a sharp advance in prices. The prices, however, clearly showed that the condition was fictitious, as there was no real ground whatever for such an advance as was witnessed at the end of the month of June, 1901, when 78 florins ($31.35) was paid for spot Banka.

### GERMAN—DUTCH CABLE.

In July, 1901, a telegraph convention was signed between Germany and Holland, and the Dutch Government has brought a bill embodying its main provisions into the Chambers at The Hague for their approval.

The plan furnishes the two signatory powers with the requisite authority to establish new telegraphic communication between Germany and Holland on the one hand and their Asiatic possessions on the other, by means of cables, which shall be under the joint control of the two powers and independent of the British cable companies concerned. It is proposed to accomplish this end by the formation of a German-Dutch cable company, the seat of which will probably be at Cologne. This company is to obtain the exclusive concession for laying telegraph cables from Menado, the chief place of northern Celebes, to the island of Guam, and from Guam to Shanghai. At Guam, these cables will connect with the American Pacific cable between San Francisco and the Philippines. The Dutch Government having undertaken to lay a cable between Menado and Balik Papan, in Borneo, where telegraphic communication already exists with Java, the result of the whole scheme, when completed, will be the establishment of an independent German-Dutch cable communication with the colonies of the two States in Asia, and with China, by way of San Francisco.

The German-Dutch cable company will receive during a period of (at most) twenty years an annual subsidy which, in the case of Germany, will amount to about £50,000 ($243,325) and in the case of the Netherlands to about £14,000 ($68,131). But 90 per cent of the receipts of the company will be used for the purpose of reducing the annual subventions. The joint control of the two powers will be exercised by an international directorate, one-fourth of the directors being German subjects and one-fourth Dutch subjects. Of the two managing directors, one must be a German, the other a Netherlander. The two Governments will, moreover, be represented on the board of the cable company. The convention, as far as its contents are known, contains one important proviso: In case of disputes concerning its interpretation, the signatory powers agree to invoke and abide by the decision of the International Court of Arbitration at The Hague.

## PARCELS POST.

The following is a statement from the director of the post-office at Amsterdam concerning the parcels-post system to the United States (in translation):

From March 1, 1901, parcels post may be forwarded to the United States of America by the intermediary of the German and Swiss postal administrations, according to the convention of Washington of July 15, 1897, the service being carried out according to the regulations made by the post and telegraph department at The Hague, in cooperation with the respective administrations.

The following are the main points of the said regulations:

### A. GENERAL REGULATIONS.

Parcels must be provided with as full an address as possible, mentioning, besides the name of the addressee, the place of destination, the street, and the house number, the district, and the State where the place of destination is situated.

Each parcel must be accompanied by one address card, three customs declarations (in postal form), and an invoice for the custom-house, stating the same value as the customs declarations.

If the parcel is over 500 francs ($96.50) in value, the invoice must be legalized by a United States consul.

### B. TARIFFS.

| Locality. | Up to 1 kilogram (2.2 pounds). | | From 1 to 3 kilograms (6.6 pounds). | | From 3 to 5 kilograms (11 pounds). | |
|---|---|---|---|---|---|---|
| | Florins. | U. S. currency. | Florins. | U. S. currency. | Florins. | U. S. currency. |
| New York, Brooklyn, Hoboken, Jersey City | 1.50 | $0.60 | 1.87½ | $0.75 | 2.25 | $0.90 |
| All other places except Alaska | 2.00 | .80 | 3.50 | 1.41 | 5.00 | 2.01 |
| Alaska (only Juneau, Sitka, and Wrangell) | 5.00 | 2.01 | 7.00 | 2.81 | 9.00 | 3.62 |

For registered parcels, there is further due for every 300 francs ($57.90)—

New York, Brooklyn, Hoboken, Jersey City ................florins.. 0.70=$0.28
All other places except Alaska ..................................do.:. .90= .36
Alaska (only Juneau, Sitka, and Wrangell) ......................do. 1.05= .42

For C. O. D. parcels there is levied, besides the postage stated in the three foregoing groups, a fixed rate of 1 per cent of the value, with a minimum of 0.10 florins ($0.04).

### C. GENERAL REMARKS.

1. Notices of receipt of parcels are not allowed; on parcels free of postage and duties and express parcels they are allowed; for these, an extra postage of 0.25 florins ($0.10) is charged.

2. Parcels which can not be delivered, on account of departure or death of the addressee, or on account of his being unknown, or of refusal to accept parcels, are returned, the duties paid not being refunded.

3. Parcels are not accepted containing: (*a*) Eatables and beverages detrimental to health. (*b*) Wine containing over 24 per cent of alcohol. (*c*) Cigars and cigarettes of a quantity of less than 3,000 pieces (cigarettes must be packed in boxes of 10, 20, 50 thousand or 100 pieces). (*d*) Adulterated provisions. (*e*) Articles bearing factory marks of American firms.

The following are the rates between Amsterdam and Hawaii:

Parcels up to 1 kilogram (2.2 pounds)...........................florins.. 2.00 =$0.80
Parcels from 1 to 3 kilograms (2.2 to 6.6 pounds)...............do.... 4.12½= 1.66
Parcels from 3 to 5 kilograms (6.6 to 11 pounds).................do.... 6.25 = 2.51

*Imports and exports of the Netherlands during the year 1901.*

IMPORTS.

| Articles. | Kilograms. | Pounds. | Increase. | | Decrease. | |
|---|---|---|---|---|---|---|
| | | | Kilograms. | Pounds. | Kilograms. | Pounds. |
| **FROM BELGIUM.** | | | | | | |
| Bark..................... | 8,948,000 | 19,685,600 | ............ | ............ | 3,140,000 | 6,908,000 |
| Barley.................. | 52,770,000 | 116,094,000 | 10,859,000 | 23,889,800 | ............ | ............ |
| Beers, malt extract...... | 128,000 | 281,600 | ............ | ............ | 54,000 | 118,800 |
| Brimstone............... | 849,000 | 1,867,800 | ............ | ............ | 66,000 | 145,200 |
| Butter.................. | 25,000 | 55,000 | 4,000 | 8,800 | ............ | ............ |
| Cattle............head.. | 1,606 | ............ | ............ | ............ | 124 | ............ |
| Coal.................... | 450,741,000 | 991,630,200 | ............ | ............ | 176,946,000 | 389,281,200 |
| Coffee.................. | 6,700,000 | 14,740,000 | ............ | ............ | 578,000 | 1,271,600 |
| Cotton-seed oil......... | 3,436,000 | 7,559,200 | 747,000 | 1,643,400 | ............ | ............ |
| Crockery ware and porcelain................. | 186,522,000 | 410,348,400 | ............ | ............ | 28,076,000 | 61,767,200 |
| Distilled liquors ....... | 5,013,000 | 11,028,600 | ............ | ............ | 71,000 | 156,200 |
| Drugs, dyestuffs, and chemicals.............. | 105,824,000 | 232,812,800 | 8,324,000 | 18,312,800 | ............ | ............ |
| Dry goods............... | 8,775,000 | 19,305,000 | ............ | ............ | 1,828,000 | 4,021,000 |
| Flax and hemp......... | 4,001,000 | 8,802,200 | 1,027,000 | 2,259,400 | ............ | ............ |
| Flour, wheat............ | 31,792,000 | 69,942,400 | 7,970,000 | 17,534,000 | ............ | ............ |
| Glass and glassware ....' | 37,414,000 | 82,310,800 | 6,104,000 | 13,428,800 | ............ | ............ |
| Hides, skins, and leather | 12,664,000 | 27,860,800 | 856,000 | 1,883,200 | ............ | ............ |
| Indian corn............. | 125,327,000 | 275,719,400 | ............ | ............ | 69,562,000 | 153,036,400 |
| Lumber, timber for ships | 60,188,000 | 132,413,600 | ............ | ............ | 18,841,000 | 41,450,200 |
| Lumber, dyewood....... | 11,676,000 | 25,687,200 | 2,129,000 | 4,683,800 | ............ | ............ |
| Manure................. | 157,446,000 | 346,381,200 | 18,836,000 | 41,439,200 | ............ | ............ |
| Margarin .............. | 2,501,000 | 5,502,200 | ............ | ............ | 378,000 | 831,600 |
| Meat................... | 2,316,000 | 5,095,200 | ............ | ............ | 491,000 | 1,080,200 |
| Mercery ware .......... | 2,775,000 | 6,105,000 | ............ | ............ | 34,000 | 74,800 |
| Metals ................. | 188,064,000 | 413,740,800 | ............ | ............ | 28,919,000 | 63,621,800 |
| Metal ware............. | 48,240,000 | 106,128,000 | 854,000 | 1,878,800 | ............ | ............ |
| Oats.................... | 27,703,000 | 60,946,600 | ............ | ............ | 5,887,000 | 12,885,400 |
| Palm oil ............... | 38,837,000 | 85,441,400 | ............ | ............ | 2,106,000 | 4,683,200 |
| Palm seeds.............' | 313,000 | 688,600 | ............ | ............ | 461,000 | 1,014,200 |
| Paper................... | 6,772,000 | 14,898,400 | ............ | ............ | 355,000 | 781,000 |
| Petroleum .............. | 22,467,000 | 49,427,400 | ............ | ............ | 1,772,000 | 3,898,400 |
| Potash ................. | 38,074,000 | 83,762,800 | 4,700,000 | 10,340,000 | ............ | ............ |
| Potato flour............ | 4,606,000 | 10,133,200 | 694,000 | 1,526,800 | ............ | ............ |
| Rice ................... | 8,701,000 | 19,142,200 | ............ | ............ | 2,141,000 | ............ |
| Rye .................... | 29,456,000 | 64,803,200 | 6,167,000 | 13,567,400 | ............ | ............ |
| Sesame oil............. | 745,000 | 1,639,000 | 300,000 | 660,000 | ............ | ............ |
| Steam agricultural engines................. | 14,713,000 | 32,368,600 | ............ | ............ | 2,388,000 | 5,253,600 |
| Stone .................. | 654,298,000 | 1,439,455,600 | 60,977,000 | 134,149,400 | ............ | ............ |
| Sugar. | | | | | | |
| Raw ............... | 52,209,000 | 114,859,800 | 1,558,000 | 3,427,600 | ............ | ............ |
| All other............ | 12,402,000 | 27,284,400 | 1,572,000 | 3,458,400 | ............ | ............ |
| Tallow, soot, etc........ | 8,550,000 | 18,810,000 | 874,000 | 1,988,800 | ............ | ............ |
| Tar and pitch.......... | 505,000 | 1,111,000 | ............ | ............ | 7,515,000 | 16,533,000 |
| Tobacco and cigars ..... | 5,533,000 | 12,172,600 | 2,011,000 | 4,424,200 | ............ | ............ |
| Wheat ................. | 543,306,000 | 1,195,273,200 | 181,568,000 | 399,449,600 | ............ | ............ |
| Wine, hogsheads........ | 2,866,000 | 6,305,200 | 542,000 | 1,192,400 | ............ | ............ |
| Wine, bottled ..... .... | 2,148,000 | 4,725,600 | ............ | ............ | 3,000 | 6,600 |
| Wool................... | 13,594,000 | 29,906,600 | 1,284,000 | 2,824,800 | ............ | ............ |
| Yarns.................. | 11,179,000 | 24,593,800 | ............ | ............ | 2,442,000 | 5,372,400 |

*Imports and exports of the Netherlands during the year 1901*—Continued.

IMPORTS—Continued.

| Articles. | Kilograms. | Pounds. | Increase. | | Decrease. | |
|---|---|---|---|---|---|---|
| | | | Kilograms. | Pounds. | Kilograms. | Pounds. |
| **FROM GREAT BRITAIN.** | | | | | | |
| Beers, malt extract ..... | 505,000 | 1,111,000 | | | 201,000 | 442,200 |
| Coffee.................. | 9,837,000 | 21,641,400 | 3,529,000 | 7,763,800 | | |
| Cotton ................. | 5,981,000 | 13,158,200 | | | 1,895,000 | 4,169,000 |
| Cotton-seed oil......... | 5,710,000 | 12,562,000 | | | 1,786,000 | 3,929,200 |
| Crockery ware and por- celain.................. | 14,886,000 | 32,749,200 | | | 5,516,000 | 12,135,200 |
| Distilled liquors........ | 566,000 | 1,245,200 | 51,000 | 112,200 | | |
| Drugs, dyestuffs, and chemicals.............. | 20,046,000 | 44,101,200 | | | 5,256,000 | 11,563,200 |
| Dry goods.............. | 15,408,000 | 33,897,600 | | | 3,275,000 | 7,205,000 |
| Fish................... | 3,740,000 | 8,228,000 | | | 512,000 | 1,126,400 |
| Fish oil................ | 900,000 | 1,980,000 | | | 270,000 | 594,000 |
| Flax and hemp......... | 33,412,000 | 73,506,400 | 6,366,000 | 14,005,200 | | |
| Flour, wheat........... | 160,000 | 352,000 | | | 174,000 | 382,800 |
| Fruits................. | 2,502,000 | 5,504,400 | 1,027,000 | 2,259,400 | | |
| Glass and glassware.... | 2,698,000 | 5,935,000 | | | 873,000 | 1,920,600 |
| Hides, skins, and leather | 7,670,000 | | | | 1,217,000 | 2,677,400 |
| Lard.................. | 528,000 | 1,161,600 | | | 287,000 | 631,400 |
| Lumber: | | | | | | |
| Cabinet wood....... | 3,888,000 | 8,553,600 | 90,000 | 198,000 | | |
| Dyewood .......... | 521,000 | 1,146,200 | 383,000 | 842,600 | | |
| Manure .............. | 12,567,000 | 27,647,400 | | | 1,001,000 | 2,202,200 |
| Margarin ............. | 133,000 | 292,600 | | | 14,000 | 30,800 |
| Meat................. | 493,000 | 1,984,600 | | | 370,000 | 814,000 |
| Metals .............. | 257,560,000 | 566,632,000 | | | 345,349,000 | 759,767,800 |
| Metal wares.......... | 16,448,000 | 36,185,600 | | | 6,830,000 | 15,026,000 |
| Palm oil ............. | 27,459,000 | 60,409,800 | 3,357,000 | 7,385,400 | | |
| Potash .............. | 6,704,000 | 14,748,800 | | | 1,953,000 | 4,296,600 |
| Potato flour......... | 361,000 | 794,200 | | | 48,000 | 105,600 |
| Salt ................. | 16,924,000 | 37,232,800 | | | 1,024,000 | 2,252,800 |
| Seeds ............... | 3,992,000 | 8,782,400 | | | 5,660,000 | 12,452,000 |
| Sesame oil .......... | 290,000 | 638,000 | | | 256,000 | 563,200 |
| Spices............... | 926,000 | 2,037,200 | | | 628,000 | 1,381,600 |
| Steam and agricultural engines............. | 20,225,000 | 44,495,000 | | | 7,640,000 | 16,808,000 |
| Stone ............... | 25,363,000 | | | | 3,273,000 | 7,200,600 |
| Sugar, raw........... | 2,855,000 | 6,281,000 | | | 1,196,000 | 2,631,200 |
| Sirup and molasses .... | 686,000 | 1,509,200 | | | 736,000 | 1,619,200 |
| Tallow, suet, etc...... | 28,801,000 | 63,362,200 | 4,781,000 | 10,518,200 | | |
| Tea ................. | 2,406,000 | 6,293,200 | | | 313,000 | 688,600 |
| Tobacco and cigars .... | 2,404,000 | 5,288,800 | 1,565,000 | 3,443,000 | | |
| Wine, hogsheads ...... | 637,000 | 1,401,400 | | | 265,000 | 583,000 |
| Wool ................ | 19,247,000 | 42,343,400 | 6,726,000 | 14,797,200 | | |
| Yarns................ | 26,842,000 | 59,052,400 | | | 5,217,000 | 11,477,400 |
| **FROM GERMANY.** | | | | | | |
| Bark ................. | 215,000 | 473,000 | | | 22,000 | 48,400 |
| Barley .............. | 31,523,000 | 69,350,600 | 6,008,000 | 13,217,600 | | |
| Beer and malt extract.. | 14,988,000 | 32,973,600 | 810,000 | 1,782,000 | | |
| Brimstone ........... | 396,000 | 871,200 | | | 60,000 | 132,000 |
| Buckwheat .......... | 8,000 | 17,600 | | | 1,000 | 2,200 |
| Butter .............. | 93,000 | 204,600 | 7,000 | 15,400 | | |
| Cattle............head. | 17 | | 1 | | | |
| Coal ................ | 5,494,692,000 | 12,088,322,400 | 283,349,000 | 623,367,800 | | |
| Coffee............... | 4,960,000 | 10,912,000 | 866,000 | 1,905,200 | | |
| Cotton .............. | 16,501,000 | 36,302,200 | | | 7,980,000 | 1,758,600 |
| Crockery ware and por- celain.................. | 73,505,000 | 161,711,000 | 3,051,000 | 6,712,200 | | |
| Distilled liquors ...... | 10,220,000 | 22,484,000 | | | 3,824,000 | 8,412,800 |
| Dyestuffs, drugs, and chemicals.............. | 183,434,000 | 403,554,800 | 12,970,000 | 28,534,000 | | |
| Dry goods............ | 38,548,000 | 84,805,600 | | | 1,503,000 | 3,306,600 |
| Flax and hemp........ | 2,963,000 | 6,518,600 | | | 522,000 | 1,148,400 |
| Flour: | | | | | | |
| Wheat ............. | 16,984,000 | 37,364,800 | 306,000 | 673,200 | | |
| Rye ............... | 35,289,000 | 77,635,800 | | | 6,406,000 | 14,093,200 |
| Fruits, fresh......... | 1,627,000 | 3,689,400 | | | 164,000 | 360,800 |
| Glass and glassware .... | 37,419,000 | 82,321,800 | 1,486,000 | 3,269,200 | | |
| Hides, skins, and leather | 14,079,000 | 30,973,800 | 1,968,000 | 4,329,600 | | |
| Lard ................ | 113,000 | 248,600 | | | 20,000 | 44,000 |
| Lumber: | | | | | | |
| Timber for ships .... | 234,160,000 | 515,152,000 | 26,372,000 | 58,018,400 | | |
| Cabinet wood....... | 2,006,000 | 4,413,200 | 847,000 | 1,863,400 | | |
| Dyewood .......... | 682,000 | 1,500,400 | 4,000 | 8,800 | | |
| Margarin ............ | 1,164,000 | 2,560,800 | 486,000 | 1,069,200 | | |
| Meat................ | 408,000 | 897,600 | 13,000 | 28,600 | | |
| Mercery ware......... | 35,619,000 | 78,361,800 | | | 2,097,000 | 4,613,400 |

*Imports and exports of the Netherlands during the year 1901*—Continued.

IMPORTS—Continued.

| Articles. | Kilograms. | Pounds. | Increase. | | Decrease. | |
|---|---|---|---|---|---|---|
| | | | Kilograms. | Pounds. | Kilograms. | Pounds. |
| **FROM GERMANY—c't'd.** | | | | | | |
| Metals | 647,390,000 | 1,424,258,000 | 252,694,000 | 555,926,800 | | |
| Metal wares | 484,859,000 | 1,066,689,800 | 120,151,000 | 264,332,200 | | |
| Oats | 13,928,000 | 30,641,600 | | | 5,676,000 | 12,487,200 |
| Palm oil | 25,914,000 | 57,010,800 | | | 1,713,000 | 3,768,600 |
| Paper | 61,016,000 | 134,235,200 | | | 12,355,000 | 27,181,000 |
| Petroleum | 587,000 | 1,291,400 | 227,000 | 499,400 | | |
| Potash | 24,217,000 | 53,277,400 | 768,000 | 1,689,600 | | |
| Potato flour | 26,785,000 | 58,927,000 | | | 645,000 | 1,419,000 |
| Rye | 27,973,000 | 60,540,600 | 12,923,000 | 28,430,600 | | |
| Salt | 77,070,000 | 169,554,000 | 7,474,000 | 16,442,800 | | |
| Seeds | 18,197,000 | 40,033,400 | 5,958,000 | 13,107,600 | | |
| Sesame oil | 4,229,000 | 9,303,800 | 320,000 | 704,000 | | |
| Sheep........head. | '81,958 | | 19,783 | | | |
| Spices | 390,000 | 858,000 | | | 328,000 | 721,600 |
| Steam and agricultural engines | 53,597,000 | 117,913,400 | 1,836,000 | 4,039,200 | | |
| Stone | 1,220,314,000 | 2,684,690,800 | | | 61,374,000 | 135,022,800 |
| Sugar: | | | | | | |
| Raw | 23,638,000 | 52,000,300 | | | 17,981,000 | 39,558,200 |
| All other | 30,488,000 | 67,073,600 | 3,231,000 | 7,108,200 | | |
| Tallow, suet, etc | 2,246,000 | 4,941,200 | | | 273,000 | 600,600 |
| Tar and pitch | 306,000 | 673,200 | | | 84,000 | 184,800 |
| Tobacco and cigars | 10,924,000 | 24,032,800 | 1,993,000 | 4,384,600 | | |
| Wheat | 17,881,000 | 39,338,200 | | | 39,262,000 | 86,376,400 |
| Wine: | | | | | | |
| Hogsheads | 17,173,000 | 37,780,600 | | | 1,190,000 | 2,618,000 |
| Bottles | 13,683,000 | 30,102,600 | 794,000 | 1,746,800 | | |
| Wool | 3,608,000 | 7,937,600 | | | 307,000 | 675,400 |
| Yarns | 10,210,000 | 22,462,000 | 896,000 | 1,971,200 | | |
| **FROM FRANCE.** | | | | | | |
| Coffee | 6,317,000 | 13,897,400 | | | 3,459,000 | 7,609,800 |
| Cotton | 363,000 | 798,600 | | | 771,000 | 1,696,200 |
| Cotton-seed oil | 39,000 | 85,800 | | | 29,000 | 63,800 |
| Crockery ware and porcelain | 874,000 | 1,922,800 | 786,000 | 1,729,200 | | |
| Distilled liquors | 2,365,000 | 5,203,000 | 39,000 | 85,800 | | |
| Drugs, dyestuffs, and chemicals | 17,353,000 | 38,176,600 | | | 3,003,000 | 6,606,600 |
| Dry goods | 92,000 | 204,600 | 9,000 | 19,800 | | |
| Fruits: | | | | | | |
| Fresh | 3,574,000 | 7,862,800 | | | 566,000 | 1,245,200 |
| All other | 1,238,000 | 2,723,600 | | | 1,636,000 | 3,599,200 |
| Hides, skins, and leather | 1,165,000 | 2,563,000 | | | 142,000 | 312,400 |
| Lard | | | | | 16,000 | 35,200 |
| Lumber: | | | | | | |
| Cabinet wood | 301,000 | 662,200 | 235,000 | 517,000 | | |
| Dyewood | 35,000 | 77,000 | 26,000 | 57,200 | | |
| Mercery ware | 363,000 | 798,600 | | | 83,000 | 182,600 |
| Metal wares | 138,000 | 303,600 | | | 221,000 | 486,200 |
| Palm oil | 630,000 | 1,386,000 | 11,000 | 24,200 | | |
| Sesame oil | 647,000 | 1,423,400 | | | 61,000 | 134,200 |
| Steam and agricultural engines | 141,000 | 310,200 | 53,000 | 116,600 | | |
| Sugar: | | | | | | |
| Raw | 10,445,000 | 22,979,000 | 6,782,000 | 14,920,400 | | |
| All other | 521,000 | 1,146,200 | 194,000 | 426,800 | | |
| Tobacco and cigars | 540,000 | 1,188,000 | 203,000 | 446,600 | | |
| Wine: | | | | | | |
| Hogsheads | 9,324,000 | 20,512,800 | | | 1,280,000 | 2,816,000 |
| Bottles | 692,000 | 1,522,400 | 68,000 | 149,600 | | |
| **FROM ITALY.** | | | | | | |
| Brimstone | 5,907,000 | 12,995,400 | | | 8,380,000 | 18,436,000 |
| Drugs, dyestuffs, and chemicals | 2,253,000 | 4,956,600 | | | 330,000 | 726,000 |
| Fruits: | | | | | | |
| Fresh | 11,127,000 | 24,479,400 | | | 4,017,000 | 8,837,400 |
| All other | 1,814,000 | 3,990,800 | | | 1,353,000 | 2,976,600 |
| Stone | 10,797,000 | 23,753,400 | 3,526,000 | 7,757,200 | | |
| **FROM AUSTRIA.** | | | | | | |
| Barley | 4,326,000 | 9,517,200 | | | 6,689,000 | 14,715,800 |
| Drugs, dyestuffs, and chemicals | 363,000 | 798,600 | | | 179,000 | 393,800 |
| Fruits | 448,000 | 985,600 | | | 716,000 | 1,575,200 |

*Imports and exports of the Netherlands during the year 1901*—Continued.

IMPORTS—Continued.

| Articles. | Kilograms. | Pounds. | Increase. | | Decrease. | |
|---|---|---|---|---|---|---|
| | | | Kilograms. | Pounds. | Kilograms. | Pounds. |
| **FROM RUSSIA.** | | | | | | |
| Barley ............... | 170,790,000 | 375,738,000 | 20,241,000 | 44,530,200 | | |
| Buckwheat ......... | 5,443,000 | 11,974,600 | ............. | ............. | 731,000 | 1,608,200 |
| Flax and hemp ..... | 540,000 | 1,188,000 | ............. | ............. | 36,000 | 79,200 |
| Indian corn.......... | 19,671,000 | 43,276,200 | ............. | ............. | 506,000 | 1,113,200 |
| Lumber, timber for ships | 681,191,000 | 1,498,626,800 | 16,033,000 | 35,272,600 | | |
| Oats................. | 266,389,000 | 586,055,800 | ............. | ............. | 42,939,000 | 94,465,800 |
| Petroleum ............. | 10,950,000 | 24,090,000 | 2,672,000 | 5,878,400 | | |
| Potash ............... | 15,000 | 33,000 | ............. | ............. | 6,000 | 13,200 |
| Rye ................ | 362,844,000 | 798,256,800 | ............. | ............. | 62,020,000 | 136,444,000 |
| Seeds ............... | 25,850,000 | 56,870,000 | ............. | ............. | 47,314,000 | 104,090,800 |
| Tar and pitch.......... | 2,157,000 | 4,745,400 | ............. | ............. | 2,236,000 | 4,919,200 |
| Wheat ............... | 340,799,000 | 749,757,800 | 139,926,000 | 307,837,200 | ............. | ............. |
| **FROM SPAIN.** | | | | | | |
| Wine in hogsheads ..... | 8,646,000 | 19,021,200 | 1,238,000 | 2,723,600 | ............. | ............. |
| **FROM PORTUGAL.** | | | | | | |
| Fruits: | | | | | | |
| Fresh ............... | 646,000 | 1,421,200 | 131,000 | 288,200 | ............. | ............. |
| All other........... | 1,684,000 | 3,704,800 | 266,000 | 585,200 | ............. | ............. |
| Palm oil, etc........ | ............. | ............. | ............. | ............. | ............. | ............. |
| Salt ................. | ............. | ............. | ............. | ............. | 35,000 | 77,000 |
| **FROM TURKEY.** | | | | | | |
| Fruits................. | 12,438,000 | 27,363,600 | | | 4,374,000 | 9,622,800 |
| **FROM ROUMANIA.** | | | | | | |
| Barley ............... | 55,778,000 | 122,711,600 | 30,380,000 | 66,836,000 | ............. | ............. |
| Indian corn.......... | 66,750,000 | 146,850,000 | 42,751,000 | 94,052,200 | ............. | ............. |
| Oats.... ............. | 10,009,000 | 22,019,800 | 9,508,000 | 20,917,600 | ............. | ............. |
| Rye ............. | 102,930,000 | 226,446,000 | 51,409,000 | 113,099,800 | ............. | ............. |
| Wheat . ............. | ............. | ............. | ............. | ............. | ............. | ............. |
| **FROM NORWAY.** | | | | | | |
| Lumber, timber for ships. | 59,156,000 | 130,143,200 | ............. | ............. | 16,512,000 | 36,326,400 |
| **FROM SWEDEN.** | | | | | | |
| Metals .. ............. | 12,892,000 | 28,362,400 | ............. | ............. | 8,074,000 | 17,762,800 |
| Tar and pitch.......... | 733,000 | 1,612,600 | 160,000 | 352,000 | ............. | ............. |
| **FROM BRITISH INDIES.** | | | | | | |
| Cotton ................. | ............. | ............. | ............. | ............. | 69,000 | 151,800 |
| Rattan ................. | 88,000 | 193,600 | ............. | ............. | 836,000 | 1,839,200 |
| Rice ................. | 128,099,000 | 281,817,800 | 14,795,000 | 32,549,000 | ............. | ............. |
| **FROM DUTCH EAST INDIES.** | | | | | | |
| Coffee................. | 24,207,000 | 53,255,400 | ............. | ............. | 16,144,000 | 35,516,800 |
| Distilled liquors ........ | 1,981,000 | 4,358,200 | 732,000 | 1,610,400 | | |
| Drugs, dyestuffs, and chemicals............. | 18,252,000 | 40,154,400 | 3,210,000 | 7,062,000 | ............. | ............. |
| Hides, skins, and leather | 5,733,000 | 12,612,600 | 891,000 | 1,960,200 | ............. | ............. |
| Lumber, dyewood..... . | 65,000 | 143,000 | 50,000 | 110,000 | ............. | ............. |
| Rattan ................. | 3,983,000 | 8,762,600 | ............. | ............. | 924,000 | 2,032,800 |
| Rice................... | 22,811,000 | 50,184,200 | ............. | ............. | 11,201,000 | 24,642,200 |
| Spices ............... | 3,066,000 | 6,745,200 | ............. | ............. | 329,000 | 723,800 |
| Sugar, raw ............. | 1,003,000 | 2,206,600 | ............. | ............. | 4,020,000 | 8,844,000 |
| Tea ................. | 6,336,000 | 13,939,200 | ............. | ............. | 44,000 | 96,800 |
| Tobacco ............... | 26,344,000 | 57,956,800 | ............. | ............. | 14,872,000 | 32,718,400 |
| **FROM JAPAN.** | | | | | | |
| Rice ............... | 2,250,000 | 4,950,000 | 1,350,000 | 2,970,000 | ............. | ............. |
| **FROM HAITI.** | | | | | | |
| Lumber, dyewood ...... | 1,330,000 | 2,926,000 | ............. | ............. | 1,481,000 | 3,258,200 |
| **FROM CURAÇAO.** | | | | | | |
| Coffee................. | 38,000 | 83,600 | 26,000 | 57,200 | ............. | ............. |

*Imports and exports of the Netherlands during the year 1901*—Continued.

IMPORTS—Continued.

| Articles. | Kilograms. | Pounds. | Increase. | | Decrease. | |
|---|---|---|---|---|---|---|
| | | | Kilograms. | Pounds. | Kilograms. | Pounds. |
| **FROM SURINAM.** | | | | | | |
| Coffee.................... | 22,000 | 48,400 | .............. | .............. | 597,000 | 1,313 400 |
| Sugar ................... | 700,000 | 1,540,000 | .............. | .............. | 270,000 | 594,000 |
| **FROM SOUTH AMERICA.** | | | | | | |
| Coffee.................... | 61,607,000 | 135,535,400 | 15,688,000 | 34,513,600 | .............. | .............. |
| Drugs, dyestuffs, and chemicals............. | 50,313,000 | 110,688,600 | .............. | .............. | 8,762,000 | 19,276,400 |
| Indian corn............. | 50,622,000 | 111,368,400 | 22,556,000 | 49,623,200 | .............. | .............. |
| Manure................... | 2,650,000 | 5,830,000 | .............. | .............. | 2,509,000 | 5,519,800 |
| **FROM UNITED STATES.** | | | | | | |
| Ashes .................... | 55,000 | 121,000 | .............. | .............. | 123,000 | 270,600 |
| Cotton .................... | 14,715,000 | 32,373,000 | 2,144,000 | 4,716,800 | .............. | .............. |
| Cotton-seed oil........... | 42,785,000 | 94,127,000 | 5,738,000 | 12,623,600 | .............. | .............. |
| Flour, wheat.......... | 117,109,000 | 257,639,800 | 12,194,000 | 26,826,800 | .............. | .............. |
| Fruits.................. | 5,252,000 | 11,564,400 | .............. | .............. | 4,658,000 | 10,247,600 |
| Indian corn............. | 267,298,000 | 588,055,600 | .............. | .............. | 250,765,000 | 551,683,000 |
| Lard..................... | 27,628,000 | 60,781,600 | .............. | .............. | 2,145,000 | 4,719,000 |
| Lumber: | | | | | | |
|   Cabinet wood...... | 9,088,000 | 19,993,600 | 1,676,000 | 3,687,200 | .............. | .............. |
|   Dyewood ........... | 5,266,000 | 11,585,200 | 2,514,000 | 5,530,800 | .............. | .............. |
| Margarin ............... | 40,970,000 | 90,134,000 | .............. | .............. | 3,238,000 | 7,123,600 |
| Meat..................... | 10,464,000 | 23,020,800 | .............. | .............. | 944,000 | 2,076,800 |
| Petroleum .............. | 412,978,000 | 908,551,600 | 39,799,000 | 87,557,800 | .............. | .............. |
| Seeds .................... | 12,398,000 | 27,275,600 | .............. | .............. | 17,379,000 | 38,233,800 |
| Tallow, suet, etc........ | 5,503,000 | 12,206,600 | .............. | .............. | 1,454,000 | 3,198,800 |
| Tobacco.................. | 12,722,000 | 27,988,400 | .............. | .............. | 713,000 | 1,568,600 |
| Wheat ................... | 626,421,000 | 137,812,620 | 410,409,000 | 902,899,800 | .............. | .............. |

EXPORTS.

| Articles. | Kilograms. | Pounds. | Increase. | | Decrease. | |
|---|---|---|---|---|---|---|
| | | | Kilograms. | Pounds. | Kilograms. | Pounds. |
| **TO BELGIUM.** | | | | | | |
| Barley .................. | 69,615,000 | 153,153,000 | .............. | .............. | 766,000 | 1,685,200 |
| Butter .................. | 5,281,000 | 11,618,200 | 2,758,000 | 6,067,600 | .............. | .............. |
| Cattle...........head.. | 43,938 | .............. | .............. | .............. | 9,374 | .............. |
| Cheese .................. | 10,549,000 | 23,207,800 | .............. | .............. | 785,000 | 1,727,000 |
| Coffee................... | 8,440,000 | 18,568,000 | .............. | .............. | 56,000 | 123,200 |
| Cotton .................. | 3,748,000 | 8,245,600 | .............. | .............. | 683,000 | 1,502,600 |
| Cotton-seed oil.......... | .............. | .............. | .............. | .............. | 209,000 | 459,800 |
| Distilled liquors........ | 6,708,000 | 14,757,600 | .............. | .............. | .............. | .............. |
| Drugs, dyestuffs, and chemicals............. | 63,079,000 | 138,773,800 | 4,434,000 | 9,754,800 | .............. | .............. |
| Fish oil .................. | 1,078,000 | 2,371,600 | .............. | .............. | 144,000 | 316,800 |
| Flax and hemp........ | 32,746,000 | 72,041,200 | 6,849,000 | 15,067,800 | .............. | .............. |
| Flour, wheat............ | 1,445,000 | 3,179,000 | .............. | .............. | 2,963,000 | 6,518,600 |
| Fruits: | | | | | | |
|   Fresh .............. | 2,317,000 | 5,097,400 | .............. | .............. | 854,000 | 1,878,800 |
|   All other............ | 3,796,000 | 8,351,200 | 373,000 | 820,600 | .............. | .............. |
| Hides, skins, and leather | 7,000,000 | 15,400,000 | .............. | .............. | 223,000 | 490,600 |
| Hogs..............head.. | 4,473 | .............. | 1,338 | .............. | .............. | .............. |
| Indian corn............. | 8,223,000 | 18,090,600 | .............. | .............. | 2,124,000 | 4,672,800 |
| Lumber: | | | | | | |
|   Cabinet wood...... | 50,000 | 110,000 | .............. | .............. | 502,000 | 1,104,400 |
|   Dyewood ........... | 666,000 | 1,465,200 | 405,000 | 891,000 | .............. | .............. |
| Margarin ............... | 3,577,000 | 7,869,400 | .............. | .............. | 155,000 | 341,000 |
| Margarin butter........ | 635,000 | 1,397,000 | 423,000 | 930,600 | .............. | .............. |
| Manure ................. | 58,819,000 | 129,401,800 | .............. | .............. | 973,000 | 2,140 600 |
| Mercery ware........... | 6,929,000 | 15,243,800 | 255,000 | 561,000 | .............. | .............. |
| Metals .................. | 351,118,000 | 772,459,600 | 74,716,000 | 164,375,200 | .............. | .............. |
| Oats.................... | 12,410,000 | 27,302,000 | 5,490,000 | 12,078,000 | .............. | .............. |
| Paper ................... | 21,379,000 | 47,033,800 | 1,528,000 | 3,361,600 | .............. | .............. |
| Petroleum .............. | 19,941,000 | 43,870,200 | 2,543,000 | .............. | .............. | .............. |
| Rags .................... | 16,152,000 | 35,534,400 | .............. | .............. | 2,028,000 | 4,461,600 |
| Rice .................... | 15,549,000 | 34,207,800 | 429,000 | 943,800 | .............. | .............. |
| Rye ..................... | 3,452,000 | 7,594,400 | .............. | .............. | 72,000 | 158,400 |
| Salt .................... | 43,087,000 | 94,791,400 | 3,151,000 | 6,932,200 | .............. | .............. |
| Seeds ................... | 3,810,000 | 8,382,000 | 169,000 | 371,800 | .............. | .............. |
| Sesame oil ..... ....... | 223,000 | 490,600 | .............. | .............. | 250,000 | 550,000 |
| Sheep and lambs. head.. | 66,346 | .............. | .............. | .............. | 3,050 | .............. |
| Steam and agricultural engines ............... | 23,095,000 | 50,809,000 | 2,361,000 | 5,194,200 | .............. | .............. |

*Imports and exports of the Netherlands during the year 1901*—Continued.

EXPORTS—Continued.

| Articles. | Kilograms. | Pounds. | Increase. Kilograms. | Pounds. | Decrease. Kilograms. | Pounds. |
|---|---|---|---|---|---|---|
| **TO BELGIUM—cont'd.** | | | | | | |
| Stone .............. | 228,364,000 | 502,400,800 | .......... | .......... | 53,223,000 | 117,090,600 |
| Sugar: | | | | | | |
|   Raw .......... | 5,496,000 | 12,091,200 | .......... | .......... | 70,000 | 154,000 |
|   All other.......... | 4,364,000 | 9,600,800 | 2,058,000 | 4,527,600 | .......... | .......... |
| Sirup and molasses .... | 464,000 | 1,020,800 | .......... | .......... | 7,276,000 | 16,007,200 |
| Tallow, suet, etc ...... | 5,967,000 | 13,127,400 | .......... | .......... | 815,000 | 1,793,000 |
| Tar and pitch.......... | 14,330,000 | 31,526,000 | .......... | .......... | 716,000 | 1,575,200 |
| Tea .............. | 66,000 | 145,200 | .......... | .......... | 10,000 | 22,000 |
| Tobacco and cigars .... | 5,253,000 | 11,556,600 | .......... | .......... | 605,000 | 1,331,000 |
| Wheat .............. | 102,631,000 | 225,788,200 | .......... | .......... | 16,391,000 | 36,060,200 |
| Wine ......hogsheads.. | 2,627,000 | 5,779,400 | .......... | .......... | 438,000 | 963,600 |
| Wool.............. | 9,408,000 | 20,697,600 | 3,240,000 | 7,128,000 | .......... | .......... |
| **TO GREAT BRITAIN.** | | | | | | |
| Bark .............. | 44,000 | 96,800 | 44,000 | 96,800 | .......... | .......... |
| Barley .............. | 2,552,000 | 5,614,400 | .......... | .......... | 2,231,000 | 4,908,200 |
| Brimstone ............ | | | | | | |
| Butter .............. | 13,279,000 | 29,213,800 | 220,000 | 484,000 | .......... | .......... |
| Cattle.......head.. | 1 | | | | 1 | |
| Cheese.............. | 18,005,000 | 39,611,000 | 1,126,000 | 2,477,200 | .......... | .......... |
| Coal .............. | 1,789,000 | 3,935,800 | .......... | .......... | 3,610,000 | 7,942,000 |
| Distilled liquors ...... | 6,084,000 | 13,384,800 | 585,000 | 1,287,000 | .......... | .......... |
| Drugs, dyestuffs, and chemicals.......... | 31,563,000 | 69,438,600 | 111,000 | 244,200 | .......... | .......... |
| Dry goods.............. | 19,350,000 | 42,570,000 | .......... | .......... | 73,000 | 160,600 |
| Fish oil .............. | 115,000 | 253,000 | 3,000 | 6,600 | .......... | .......... |
| Glass and glassware .... | 36,575,000 | 80,465,000 | 9,373,000 | 20,620,600 | .......... | .......... |
| Hides, skins, and leather | 9,526,000 | 20,957,200 | 1,918,000 | 4,219,600 | .......... | .......... |
| Margarin .............. | 795,000 | 1,749,000 | .......... | .......... | 309,000 | 679,800 |
| Margarin butter ....... | 635,000 | 1,397,000 | 413,000 | 908,600 | .......... | .......... |
| Meat.............. | 50,422,000 | 110,928,400 | 1,696,000 | 3,731,200 | .......... | .......... |
| Mercery ware.......... | 12,968,000 | 28,529,600 | .......... | .......... | 2,376,000 | 3,027,200 |
| Metals .............. | 120,139,000 | 264,305,800 | 75,434,000 | 165,954,800 | .......... | .......... |
| Metal wares.......... | 90,533,000 | 199,172,600 | .......... | .......... | 1,031,000 | 2,268,200 |
| Oats.............. | 4,422,000 | 9,728,400 | .......... | .......... | 4,004,000 | 8,808,800 |
| Palm oil, etc ..... ..... | 9,007,000 | 19,815,400 | 725,000 | 1,595,000 | .......... | .......... |
| Paper .............. | 107,678,000 | 236,891,600 | 1,033,000 | 2,272,600 | .......... | .......... |
| Rice .............. | 23,825,000 | 52,415,000 | .......... | .......... | 3,106,000 | 6,833,200 |
| Seeds .............. | 5,466,000 | 12,025,200 | .......... | .......... | 697,000 | 1,533,400 |
| Sheep and lambs.head.. | 6 | | .......... | .......... | 24 | |
| Spices.............. | 1,400,000 | 3,080,000 | 127,000 | 279,400 | .......... | .......... |
| Steam and agricultural engines .............. | 5,930,000 | 1,304,600 | 1,824,000 | 4,012,800 | .......... | .......... |
| Sugar: | | | | | | |
|   Raw .............. | 18,815,000 | 41,393,000 | .......... | .......... | 7,188,000 | 15,813,600 |
|   All other.......... | 143,233,000 | 315,112,600 | 24,196,000 | 53,231,200 | .......... | .......... |
| Tallow, suet, etc........ | 1,238,000 | 2,723,600 | 90,000 | 198,000 | .......... | .......... |
| Tea .............. | 3,167,000 | 6,967,400 | .......... | .......... | 11,000 | 24,200 |
| Tobacco and cigars .... | 2,828,000 | 6,221,600 | .......... | .......... | 483,000 | 1,062,600 |
| Wine: | | | | | | |
|   Hogsheads.......... | 3,219,000 | 7,081,800 | 220,000 | 484,000 | .......... | .......... |
|   Bottled ............ | 5,077,000 | 11,169,400 | 145,000 | 319,000 | .......... | .......... |
| Wool.............. | 1,021,000 | 2,462,000 | 137,000 | 301,400 | .......... | .......... |
| Yarns.............. | 1,836,000 | 4,039,200 | .......... | .......... | 432,000 | 950,400 |
| **TO GERMANY.** | | | | | | |
| Bark .............. | 491,000 | 1,080,200 | 285,000 | 627,000 | .......... | .......... |
| Barley .............. | 179,826,000 | 395,617,200 | 25,437,000 | 55,961,400 | .......... | .......... |
| Brimstone .............. | 8,834,000 | 19,434,800 | .......... | .......... | 10,593,000 | 23,304,600 |
| Buckwheat .......... | 10,139,000 | 22,305,800 | 2,460,000 | 5,412,000 | .......... | .......... |
| Cattle.......head.. | 302 | | 194 | | .......... | .......... |
| Cheese .............. | 9,070,000 | 19,954,000 | .......... | .......... | 38,000 | 83,600 |
| Coal.............. | 329,701,000 | 725,342,200 | .......... | .......... | 701,878,000 | 1,544,131,600 |
| Coffee .............. | 59,605,000 | 131,131,000 | .......... | .......... | 2,533,000 | 5,572,600 |
| Cotton .............. | 40,499,000 | 89,097,800 | 1,023,000 | 2,250,600 | .......... | .......... |
| Cotton-seed oil.......... | 30,389,000 | 66,856,800 | 3,490,000 | 7,678,000 | .......... | .......... |
| Distilled liquors ...... | 13,240,000 | 29,128,000 | .......... | .......... | 4,755,000 | 10,461,000 |
| Drugs, dyestuffs, and chemicals.......... | 226,197,000 | 497,633,400 | .......... | .......... | 4,709,000 | 10,359,800 |
| Dry goods.............. | 9,084,000 | 19,984,800 | .......... | .......... | 1,968,000 | 4,829,600 |
| Fish .............. | 48,635,000 | 106,997,000 | 3,342,000 | 7,352,400 | .......... | .......... |
| Fish oil .............. | 4,402,000 | 9,684,400 | .......... | .......... | 71,000 | 156,200 |
| Flax and hemp .......... | 24,812,000 | 54,586,600 | 14,408,000 | 31,697,600 | .......... | .......... |
| Flour: | | | | | | |
|   Wheat .............. | 8,546,000 | 18,801,200 | .......... | .......... | 518,000 | 1,139,600 |
|   Rye .............. | 25,781,000 | 56,718,200 | .......... | .......... | 6,479,000 | 14,253,800 |

*Imports and exports of the Netherlands during the year 1901*—Continued.

EXPORTS—Continued.

| Articles. | Kilograms. | Pounds. | Increase. | | Decrease. | |
|---|---|---|---|---|---|---|
| | | | Kilograms. | Pounds. | Kilograms. | Pounds. |
| TO GERMANY—cont'd. | | | | | | |
| Fruits: | | | | | | |
| Fresh .............. | 37,301,000 | 82,062,200 | .............. | .............. | 2,588,000 | 5,693,600 |
| All other.......... | 26,098,000 | 57,415,600 | .............. | .............. | 6,134,000 | 13,494,800 |
| Hides,skins,and leather. | 17,797,000 | 39,153,400 | .............. | .............. | 65,000 | 143,000 |
| Indian corn............ | 214,230,000 | 471,306,000 | .............. | .............. | 77,088,000 | 169,593,600 |
| Lard .................. | 21,635,000 | 47,597,000 | 864,000 | 1,900,800 | .............. | .............. |
| Lumber: | | | | | | |
| Ship timber........ | 630,925,000 | 1,388,035,000 | .............. | .............. | 45,983,000 | 101,162,600 |
| Cabinet wood...... | 10,574,000 | 23,262,800 | 4,713,000 | 10,368,600 | .............. | .............. |
| Dyewood .......... | 42,018,000 | 92,439,600 | .............. | .............. | 200,000 | 440,000 |
| Margarin .............. | 16,627,000 | 36,579,400 | 1,434,000 | 3,154,800 | .............. | .............. |
| Margarin butter ....... | 850,000 | 1,870,000 | .............. | .............. | 363,000 | 798,600 |
| Manure................ | 171,405,000 | 377,091,000 | 4,981,000 | 10,958,200 | .............. | .............. |
| Meat.................... | 13,224,000 | 29,092,800 | 6,957,000 | 15,305,400 | .............. | .............. |
| Mercery ware........... | 3,183,000 | 7,002,600 | .............. | .............. | 2,421,000 | 5,326,200 |
| Metals ................. | 300,613,000 | 661,414,600 | .............. | .............. | 370·051,000 | 814,112,200 |
| Metal wares . ......... | 42,932,000 | 94,450,400 | .............. | .............. | 3,410,000 | 7,502,000 |
| Oats.................... | 289,400,000 | 636,680,000 | .............. | .............. | 43,786,000 | 96,329,200 |
| Palm oil, etc .......... | 92,450,000 | 203,390,000 | .............. | .............. | 3,031,000 | 6,668,200 |
| Palm seed ............. | 22,432,000 | 49,350,400 | .............. | .............. | 2,859,000 | 6,289,800 |
| Paper .................. | 6,862,000 | 15,096,400 | .............. | .............. | 2,740,000 | 6,028,00C |
| Petroleum ............. | 272,326,000 | 599,139,200 | 10,651,000 | 23,432,200 | .............. | .............. |
| Rags ................... | 36,120,000 | 79,464,000 | 14,349,000 | 31,567,800 | .............. | .............. |
| Rice ................... | 27,889,000 | 61,355,800 | .............. | .............. | 2,287,000 | 5,031,400 |
| Rye .................... | 288,307,000 | 634,275,400 | .............. | .............. | 38,790,000 | 85,338,000 |
| Salt .................... | 2,531,000 | 5,574,800 | 576,000 | 1,267,200 | .............. | .............. |
| Seeds................... | 203,600,000 | 447,920,000 | 9,964,000 | 21,920,800 | .............. | .............. |
| Sesame oil ............. | 10,797,000 | 23,753,400 | .............. | .............. | 1,091,000 | 2,400,200 |
| Spices.................. | 2,826,000 | 6,217,200 | .............. | .............. | 58,000 | 127,600 |
| Steam and agricultural engines .............. | 24,903,000 | 54,786,600 | .............. | .............. | 8,907,000 | 19,595,400 |
| Stone................... | 131,338,000 | 288,943,600 | 31,494,000 | 69,286,800 | .............. | .............. |
| Sugar: | | | | | | |
| Raw ............... | 8,287,000 | 18,231,400 | .............. | .............. | 27,651,000 | 60,832,200 |
| Refined ........... | 36,140,000 | 79,508,000 | .............. | .............. | 4,597,000 | 10,113,400 |
| Tallow, suet, etc........ | 18,000,000 | 39,600,000 | .............. | .............. | 490,000 | 1,078,000 |
| Tar and pitch........... | 68,927,000 | 151,639,400 | .............. | .............. | 4,871,000 | 10,716,200 |
| Tea .................... | 1,547,000 | 3,403,400 | 95,000 | 209,000 | .............. | .............. |
| Tobacco and cigars ..... | 31,908,000 | 70,197,600 | .............. | .............. | 415,000 | .............. |
| Wheat .................. | 1,378,379,000 | 3,032,433,800 | 435,159,000 | 957,349,800 | .............. | .............. |
| Wine: | | | | | | |
| Hogsheads ......... | 23,454,000 | 51,598,800 | .............. | .............. | 78,000 | 171,600 |
| Bottles.............. | 5,008,000 | 11,017,600 | 1,395,000 | 3,069,000 | .............. | .............. |
| Wool................... | 21,438,000 | 47,163,600 | 3,958,000 | 8,707,600 | .............. | .............. |
| Yarns.................. | 20,245,000 | 44,539,000 | .............. | .............. | 3,857,000 | 8,485,400 |
| TO FRANCE. | | | | | | |
| Cheese ................. | 3,412,000 | 7,506,400 | 38,000 | 83,600 | .............. | .............. |
| Coffee ................. | 119,000 | 261,800 | .............. | .............. | 13,000 | 28,600 |
| Cotton ................. | 7,000 | 15,400 | 7,000 | 15,400 | .............. | .............. |
| Distilled liquors ....... | 177,000 | 389,400 | .............. | .............. | 14,000 | 30,800 |
| Dry goods.............. | .............. | .............. | .............. | .............. | .............. | .............. |
| Fish oil ............... | 1,181,000 | 2,598,200 | 94,000 | 206,800 | .............. | .............. |
| Hides, skins, and leather | 436,000 | 959,200 | .............. | .............. | 19,000 | 41,800 |
| Metal wares............ | 213,000 | 468,600 | 22,000 | 48,400 | .............. | .............. |
| Paper .................. | 146,000 | 321,200 | 29,000 | 63,800 | .............. | .............. |
| Rice ................... | 2,002,000 | 4,404,400 | .............. | .............. | 663,000 | 1,458,600 |
| Sugar, raw ............. | .............. | .............. | .............. | .............. | .............. | .............. |
| Wine: | | | | | | |
| Hogsheads .......... | 37,000 | 81,400 | 13,000 | 28,600 | .............. | .............. |
| Bottles.............. | 22,000 | 48,400 | 2,000 | 4,400 | .............. | .............. |
| TO RUSSIA. | | | | | | |
| Cheese ................. | 145,000 | 319,000 | 61,000 | 134,200 | .............. | .............. |
| Metal wares............ | 2,883,000 | 6,342,600 | 363,000 | 798,600 | .............. | .............. |
| TO ITALY. | | | | | | |
| Metal wares............ | 2,506,000 | 5,513,200 | 707,000 | 1,555,400 | .............. | .............. |
| TO NORWAY. | | | | | | |
| Margarin .............. | 342,000 | 752,400 | .............. | .............. | 373,000 | 820,600 |
| Margarin butter ........ | 233,000 | 512,600 | 195,000 | 429,000 | .............. | .............. |
| Metal wares ............ | 3,617,000 | 7,957,400 | 522,000 | 1,148,400 | .............. | .............. |

*Imports and exports of the Netherlands during the year 1901*—Continued.

EXPORTS—Continued.

| Articles. | Kilograms. | Pounds. | Increase. | | Decrease. | |
|---|---|---|---|---|---|---|
| | | | Kilograms. | Pounds. | Kilograms. | Pounds. |
| **TO DENMARK.** | | | | | | |
| Coffee | 3,552,000 | 7,814,400 | 426,000 | 937,200 | | |
| Fruits | 36,000 | 79,200 | | | 66,000 | 145,200 |
| Tobacco and cigars | 942,000 | 2,072,400 | | | 3,000 | 6,600 |
| **TO SWEDEN.** | | | | | | |
| Coffee | 2,643,000 | 5,814,600 | 675,000 | 1,485,000 | | |
| Cotton | 834,000 | 1,834,800 | 834,000 | 1,834,800 | | |
| Cotton-seed oil | 191,000 | 420,200 | 24,000 | 52,800 | | |
| Distilled liquors | 1.123,000 | 2,470,600 | 47,000 | 103,400 | | |
| Sugar, refined | 46,000 | 101,200 | 2,000 | 4,400 | | |
| Tallow, suet, etc | | | | | | |
| **TO PORTUGAL.** | | | | | | |
| Sugar, refined | 741,000 | 1,630,200 | | | 1,472,000 | 3,238,400 |
| **TO TURKEY.** | | | | | | |
| Sugar, refined | 156,000 | 343,200 | 77,000 | 169,400 | | |
| **TO BRITISH INDIES.** | | | | | | |
| Dry goods | 245,000 | 539,000 | | | 55,000 | 121,000 |
| Tar and pitch | | | | | 4,000 | 8,800 |
| **TO DUTCH EAST INDIES.** | | | | | | |
| Beer and malt extract | 4,608,000 | 10,137,600 | 74,000 | 162,800 | | |
| Butter | 862,000 | 1,896,400 | | | 146,000 | 321,200 |
| Cheese | 305,000 | 671,000 | | | 4,000 | 8,800 |
| Coal | 5,430,000 | 11,946,000 | 2,369,000 | 5,211,800 | | |
| Crockery ware and porcelain | 9,336,000 | 20,539,200 | | | 2,233,000 | 4,912,600 |
| Distilled liquors | 2,439,000 | 5,365,800 | 46,000 | 101,200 | | |
| Drugs, dyestuffs, and chemicals | 5,162,000 | 11,356,400 | 1,015,000 | 2,233,000 | | |
| Dry goods | 12,706,000 | 27,953,200 | | | 670,000 | 1,474,000 |
| Glass and glassware | 1,481,000 | 3,258,200 | | | 435,000 | 957,000 |
| Hides, skins, and leather | 94,000 | 206,800 | | | 110,000 | 242,000 |
| Margarin butter | 220,000 | 484,000 | 93,000 | 204,600 | | |
| Meat | 545,000 | 1,199,000 | 100,000 | 220,000 | | |
| Mercery ware | 3,601,000 | 7,922,200 | | | 2,003,000 | 4,406,600 |
| Metals | 18,918,000 | 41,619,600 | | | 5,267,000 | 11,587,400 |
| Metal wares | 39,166,000 | 86,165,200 | | | 1,269,000 | 2,791,800 |
| Paper | 3,201,000 | 7,042,200 | 927,000 | 2,039,400 | | |
| Steam and agricultural engines | 8,148,000 | 17,925,600 | | | 2,386,000 | 5,249,200 |
| Stone | 640,000 | 1,408,000 | | | 204,000 | 448,800 |
| Sugar, refined | 168,000 | 369,600 | 17,000 | 37,400 | | |
| Tar and pitch | 1,243,000 | 2,734,600 | 378,000 | 831,600 | | |
| Vinegar | 108,000 | 237,600 | 13,000 | 28,600 | | |
| Wine: | | | | | | |
| Hogsheads | 259,000 | 569,800 | 60,000 | 132,000 | | |
| Bottles | 1,132,000 | 2,490,400 | 110,000 | 242,000 | | |
| Yarns | 512,000 | 1,126,400 | | | 98,000 | 204,600 |
| **TO SURINAM.** | | | | | | |
| Beer and malt extract | 1,265,000 | 2,783,000 | | | 35,000 | 77,000 |
| Butter | 146,000 | 321,200 | | | 26,000 | 57,200 |
| Distilled liquors | 749,000 | 1,647,800 | 80,000 | 176,000 | | |
| Dry goods | 723,000 | 1,590,600 | 9,000 | 19,800 | | |
| Mercery ware | 196,000 | 431,200 | 9,000 | 19,800 | | |
| Rice | 4,169,000 | 9,171,800 | 568,000 | 1,249,600 | | |
| Vinegar | 33,000 | 72,600 | 1,000 | 2,200 | | |
| **TO AFRICA (WEST COAST).** | | | | | | |
| Beer and malt extract | 43,000 | 94,600 | 19,000 | 41,800 | | |
| Distilled liquors | 8,839,000 | 19,445,800 | 229,000 | 503,800 | | |
| Dry goods | 331,000 | 728,200 | | | 228,000 | 501,600 |
| Mercery ware | 60,000 | 132,000 | | | 28,000 | 61,600 |
| Metal wares | 1,137,000 | 2,501,400 | 696,000 | 1,529,000 | | |
| Oils | 8,000 | 17,600 | | | 350,000 | 770,000 |
| Petroleum | | | | | 2,000 | 4,400 |
| Sugar, refined | 46,000 | 101,200 | | | 235,000 | 517,000 |

H. Doc. 305, pt 2——32

*Imports and exports of the Netherlands during the year 1901*—Continued.

EXPORTS—Continued.

| Articles. | Kilograms. | Pounds. | Increase. | | Decrease. | |
|---|---|---|---|---|---|---|
| | | | Kilograms. | Pounds. | Kilograms. | Pounds. |
| TO UNITED STATES. | | | | | | |
| Coffee.................... | 1,067,000 | 2,347,400 | .............. | .............. | 300,000 | 660,000 |
| Distilled liquors ........ | 1,028,000 | 2,261,600 | .............. | .............. | 143,000 | 314,600 |
| Spices.................... | 2,337,000 | 5,141,400 | 96,000 | 211,200 | .............. | .............. |
| Sugar, refined........... | 10,276,000 | 22,607,200 | .............. | .............. | 1,649,000 | 3,627,800 |
| Wine: | | | | | | |
| Hogsheads .......... | 3,486,000 | 7,669,200 | 125,000 | 275,000 | .............. | .............. |
| Bottles............. | 2,025,000 | 4,455,000 | 439,000 | 965,800 | .............. | .............. |

*Imports and exports of the Netherlands during the first half year 1902.*

IMPORTS.

| Articles. | Kilograms. | Pounds. | Increase. | | Decrease. | |
|---|---|---|---|---|---|---|
| | | | Kilograms. | Pounds. | Kilograms. | Pounds. |
| FROM BELGIUM. | | | | | | |
| Bark..................... | 4,375,000 | 10,725,000 | .............. | .............. | 1,180,000 | 2,596,000 |
| Barley................... | 34,597,000 | 76,113,400 | 5,264,000 | 11,580,800 | .............. | .............. |
| Beer and malt extract.. | 92,000 | 202,400 | 26,000 | 57,200 | .............. | .............. |
| Brimstone ............. | 411,000 | 904,200 | 291,000 | 640,200 | .............. | .............. |
| Butter ................. | 12,000 | 26,400 | 4,000 | 8,800 | .............. | .............. |
| Cattle...........head.. | 1,560 | | 6,991 | | .............. | .............. |
| Coal .................... | 232,196,000 | 510,831,200 | 47,096,000 | 103,611,200 | .............. | .............. |
| Coffee................... | 3,402,000 | 7,484,400 | 969,000 | 2,131,800 | .............. | .............. |
| Cotton-seed oil.......... | 1,316,000 | 2,895,200 | .............. | .............. | 1,092,000 | 2,402,400 |
| Crockery and porcelain. | 118,366,000 | 260,405,200 | 15,096,000 | 33,211,200 | .............. | .............. |
| Distilled liquors ....... | 2,926,000 | 6,437,200 | 706,000 | 1,553,200 | .............. | .............. |
| Drugs, dyestuffs, and chemicals............. | 66,294,000 | 145,846,800 | 13,089,000 | 28,795,800 | .............. | .............. |
| Dry goods............... | 3,624,000 | 8,072,800 | .............. | .............. | 1,515,000 | 3,333,000 |
| Flax and hemp.......... | 2,571,000 | 5,656,200 | 33,000 | 72,600 | .............. | .............. |
| Flour, wheat............ | 20,314,000 | 44,690,800 | 6,500,000 | 14,300,000 | .............. | .............. |
| Fruits, fresh ............ | 3,193,000 | 7,024,600 | .............. | .............. | 1,560,000 | 3,482,000 |
| Glass and glassware .... | 23,704,000 | 52,148,800 | 7,460,000 | 16,412,000 | .............. | .............. |
| Hides,skins, and leather | 6,160,000 | 13,552,000 | .............. | .............. | 846,000 | 1,861,200 |
| Indian corn............. | 36,447,000 | 80,183,400 | .............. | .............. | 23,551,000 | 51,812,200 |
| Lard ................... | 2,274,000 | 5,002,800 | .............. | .............. | 55,000 | 121,000 |
| Lumber: | | | | | | |
| Timber for ships .... | 30,331,000 | 66,728,200 | 3,016,000 | 6,635,200 | .............. | .............. |
| Cabinet wood ...... | | | | | | |
| Dyewood ........... | 3,824,000 | 8,412,800 | .............. | .............. | 1,774,000 | 3,902,800 |
| Manure................. | 139,935,000 | 307,857,000 | 54,952,000 | 120,894,400 | .............. | .............. |
| Margarin ............... | 64,000 | 140,800 | 47,000 | 103,400 | .............. | .............. |
| Meat.................... | 946,000 | 2,081,200 | .............. | .............. | 152,000 | 334,400 |
| Mercery ware........... | 1,289,000 | 2,835,800 | .............. | .............. | 103,000 | 226,600 |
| Metals ................. | 107,113,000 | 235,648,600 | 12,810,000 | 28,182,000 | .............. | .............. |
| Metal wares............ | 28,181,000 | 61,998,200 | 3,460,000 | 7,616,000 | .............. | .............. |
| Oats.................... | 15,189,000 | 33,415,800 | .............. | .............. | 1,510,000 | 3,322,000 |
| Palm oil................ | 19,705,000 | 43,351,000 | 2,743,000 | 6, ,600 | .............. | .............. |
| Palm seeds............. | 683,000 | 1,392,600 | 415,000 | 834,000 | .............. | .............. |
| Paper................... | 3,624,000 | 7, 2,800 | 442,000 | 972,400 | .............. | .............. |
| Petroleum ............. | 11,367,000 | 25,007,400 | 438,000 | 963,600 | .............. | .............. |
| Potash ................. | 16,141,000 | 35,510,200 | 1,463,000 | 3,218,600 | .............. | .............. |
| Potato flour............ | 2,549,000 | 5,607,800 | 520,000 | 1,144,000 | .............. | .............. |
| Rice.................... | 5,730,000 | 12,606,000 | 1,353,000 | 2,976,600 | .............. | .............. |
| Rye..................... | 24,713,000 | 54,368,600 | 10,490,000 | 23,078,000 | .............. | .............. |
| Sesame oil ............. | 808,000 | 1,777,600 | 478,000 | 1,051,600 | .............. | .............. |
| Steam and agricultural engines ............... | 3,642,000 | 8,012,400 | .............. | .............. | 5,641,000 | 12,410,200 |
| Stone .................. | 299,023,000 | 657,850,600 | .............. | .............. | 25,235,000 | 55,517,000 |
| Sugar: | | | | | | |
| Raw ............... | 19,872,000 | 43,718,400 | 9,808,000 | 21,577,600 | .............. | .............. |
| All other......... | 4,658,000 | 10,247,600 | .............. | .............. | 2,163,000 | 4,758,600 |
| Tallow, suet, etc......... | 4,944,000 | 10,876,800 | 874,000 | 1,822,800 | .............. | .............. |
| Tar and pitch........... | 2,790,000 | 6,138,000 | 2,431,000 | 5,348,200 | .............. | .............. |
| Tobacco and cigars ..... | 2,942,000 | 6,472,400 | .............. | .............. | 444,000 | 976,800 |
| Wheat ................. | 314,159,000 | 691,149,800 | 66,270,000 | 145,794,000 | .............. | .............. |
| Wine: | | | | | | |
| Hogsheads.......... | 1,589,000 | 3,495,000 | 15,000 | 33,000 | .............. | .............. |
| Bottles............. | 875,000 | 1,925,000 | 40,000 | 88,000 | .............. | .............. |
| Wool................... | 13,040,000 | 28,688,000 | 4,576,000 | 10,067,200 | .............. | .............. |
| Yarns.................. | 5,829,000 | 12,823,800 | 84,000 | 184,802 | .............. | .............. |

*Imports and exports of the Netherlands during the first half year 1902*—Continued.

IMPORTS—Continued.

| Articles. | Kilograms. | Pounds. | Increase. | | Decrease. | |
|---|---|---|---|---|---|---|
| | | | Kilograms. | Pounds. | Kilograms. | Pounds. |
| **FROM GREAT BRITAIN.** | | | | | | |
| Beer and malt extract.. | 259,000 | 569,800 | | | 2,000 | 4,400 |
| Coffee.................... | 1,804,000 | 3,968,800 | | | 2,483,000 | 5,462,600 |
| Cotton................... | 2,997,000 | 6,593,400 | 129,000 | 283,800 | | |
| Cotton-seed oil.......... | 6,853,000 | 15,076,600 | 4,333,000 | 9,532,600 | | |
| Crockery ware and porcelain............... | 7,502,000 | 16,504,400 | | | 613,000 | 1,348,600 |
| Distilled liquors........ | 179,000 | 393,800 | | | 51,000 | 112,200 |
| Drugs, dyestuffs, and chemicals............ | 9,731,000 | 21,308,200 | 124,000 | 272,800 | | |
| Dry goods................ | 9,195,000 | 20,229,000 | 1,169,000 | 2,571,800 | | |
| Fish .................... | 1,086,000 | 2,389,200 | | | 493,000 | 1,084,600 |
| Fish oil................. | 709,000 | 1,559,800 | 364,000 | 800,800 | | |
| Flax and hemp.......... | 21,252,000 | 46,754,400 | 2,451,000 | 5,392,200 | | |
| Flour, wheat ........... | 98,000 | 215,600 | 41,000 | 90,200 | | |
| Fruits .................. | 276,000 | 607,200 | | | 1,225,000 | 2,695,000 |
| Glass and glassware .... | 922,000 | 2,028,400 | | | 336,000 | 737,000 |
| Hides,skins,and leather | 3,773,000 | 8,300,600 | | | 167,000 | 367,400 |
| Lard.................... | 228,000 | 501,600 | | | 169,000 | 371,800 |
| Lumber: | | | | | | |
| Cabinet wood...... | 1,130,000 | 2,486,000 | | | 1,010,000 | 2,222,000 |
| Dyewood .......... | 55,000 | 121,000 | | | 79,000 | 173,800 |
| Manure ................. | 12,348,000 | 27,165,600 | 4,847,000 | 10,663,400 | | |
| Margarin ............... | 45,000 | 99,000 | 3,000 | 6,600 | | |
| Meat.................... | 596,000 | 1,311,200 | 210,000 | 462,000 | | |
| Metals .................. | 96,902,000 | 213,184,400 | | | 42,761,000 | 94,074,200 |
| Metal wares ............ | 7,455,000 | 16,401,000 | | | 552,000 | 1,214,400 |
| Palm oil ................ | 10,427,000 | 22,939,400 | | | 2,674,000 | 5,882,800 |
| Potash ................. | 3,461,000 | 7,614,200 | 39,000 | 85,800 | | |
| Potato flour............ | 252,000 | 554,400 | 87,000 | 191,400 | | |
| Salt..................... | 8,033,000 | 17,672,600 | | | 57,000 | 125,400 |
| Seeds ................... | 3,334,000 | 7,334,800 | 1,796,000 | 3,951,200 | | |
| Sesame oil .............. | 235,000 | 517,000 | 35,000 | 77,000 | | |
| Spices................... | 386,000 | 849,200 | | | 105,000 | 231,000 |
| Steam and agricultural engines ............... | 8,230,000 | 18,106,000 | | | 1,564,000 | 3,440,800 |
| Stone ................... | 9,894,000 | 21,766,800 | | | 8,106,000 | 6,833,200 |
| Sugar, raw.............. | 655,000 | 1,441,000 | | | 519,000 | 1,141,800 |
| Sirup and molasses .... | 283,000 | 622,600 | | | 20,000 | 44,000 |
| Tallow, suet, etc ....... | 11,176,000 | 24,587,200 | | | 4,218,000 | 9,279,600 |
| Tea ..................... | 1,403,000 | 3,086,600 | 178,000 | 391,600 | | |
| Tobacco and cigars .... | 770,000 | 1,694,000 | | | 73,000 | 160,600 |
| Wine.......hogsheads.. | 346,000 | 761,200 | 65,000 | 143,000 | | |
| Wool.................... | 11,425,000 | 25,135,000 | 2,714,000 | 5,970,800 | | |
| Yarns................... | 13,129,000 | 28,883,800 | | | 39,000 | 85,800 |
| **FROM GERMANY.** | | | | | | |
| Bark .................... | 146,000 | 321,200 | 72,000 | 158,400 | | |
| Barley .................. | 13,176,000 | 28,987,200 | 7,439,000 | 16,365,800 | | |
| Beer and malt extract.. | 6,735,000 | 14,817,000 | 152,000 | 334,400 | | |
| Brimstone .............. | 203,000 | 446,600 | | | 4,000 | 8,800 |
| Buckwheat ............. | 700,000 | 1,540,000 | 694,000 | 1,526,800 | | |
| Butter .................. | 26,000 | 57,200 | | | 29,000 | 63,800 |
| Cattle.............head. | .......... | .......... | | | 12 | |
| Coal.................... | 3,321,214,000 | 7,306,670,800 | 827,297,000 | 1,820,053,400 | | |
| Coffee................... | 2,176,000 | 4,787,200 | 182,000 | 400,400 | | |
| Cotton.................. | 12,199,000 | 26,837,800 | 4,162,000 | 9,156,400 | | |
| Crockery ware and porcelain................. | 34,967,000 | 76,927,400 | | | 98,000 | 215,600 |
| Distilled liquors ....... | 5,154,000 | 11,338,800 | | | 1,000 | 2,200 |
| Dyestuffs, drugs, and chemicals.............. | 95,024,000 | 209,052,800 | 15,306,000 | 33,673,200 | | |
| Dry goods............... | 18,737,000 | 41,221,400 | 1,717,000 | 3,777,400 | | |
| Flax and hemp.......... | 1,289,000 | 2,835,800 | | | 148,000 | 325,000 |
| Flour: | | | | | | |
| Wheat .............. | 6,182,000 | 13,600,400 | | | 1,707,000 | 3,755,400 |
| Rye................. | 11,250,000 | 24,750,000 | | | 6,368,000 | 14,009,600 |
| Fruits, fresh ........... | 271,000 | 596,200 | 43,000 | 94,600 | | |
| Glass and glassware .... | 17,941,000 | 39,470,200 | | | 504,000 | 1,108,800 |
| Hides, skins, and leather | 490,000 | 1,078,000 | 228,000 | 501,600 | | |
| Lard.................... | 123,000 | 270,000 | 78,000 | 171,600 | | |
| Lumber: | | | | | | |
| Timber for ships.... | 101,475,000 | 223,245,000 | | | 112,000 | 246,400 |
| Cabinet wood....... | 809,000 | 1,779,800 | | | 563,000 | |
| Dyewood .......... | 490,000 | 1,078,000 | 228,000 | 501,600 | | |
| Margarin ............... | 35,000 | 77,000 | 1,000 | 2,200 | | |
| Meat.................... | 234,000 | 514,800 | | | 39,000 | 85,000 |
| Mercery ware........... | 15,165,000 | 33,363,000 | 351,000 | 860,200 | | |
| Metals .................. | 418,699,000 | 921,137,800 | 182,295,000 | 401,049,000 | | |
| Metal wares ............ | 289,446,000 | 636,781,200 | 91,653,000 | 201,636,600 | | |

*Imports and exports of the Netherlands during the first half year 1902*—Continued.

IMPORTS—Continued.

| Articles. | Kilograms. | Pounds. | Increase. Kilograms. | Pounds. | Decrease. Kilograms. | Pounds. |
|---|---|---|---|---|---|---|
| **FROM GERMANY—c't'd.** | | | | | | |
| Metals | 418,699,000 | 921,137,800 | 182,295,000 | 401,049,000 | | |
| Metal wares | 289,446,000 | 636,781,200 | 91,653,000 | 201,636,600 | | |
| Oats | 19,163,000 | 42,158,600 | 15,396,000 | 38,871,200 | | |
| Palm oil | 15,115,000 | 33,253,000 | 7,388,000 | 16,253,600 | | |
| Paper | 38,131,000 | 83,888,200 | 9,800,000 | 20,460,000 | | |
| Petroleum | 263,000 | 578,600 | | | 142,000 | 312,400 |
| Potash | 11,244,000 | 24,736,800 | 1,137,000 | 2,501,400 | | |
| Potato flour | 11,227,000 | 24,699,400 | 1,845,000 | 4,059,000 | | |
| Rye | 13,883,000 | 30,542,600 | 376,000 | 827,200 | | |
| Salt | 31,722,000 | 69,788,400 | | | 355,000 | 781,000 |
| Seeds | 4,224,000 | 9,292,800 | | | 949,000 | 2,087,800 |
| Sesame oil | 3,011,000 | 6,624,200 | 1,715,000 | 3,773,000 | | |
| Sheep........head.. | 56,907 | | | | 17,000 | |
| Spices | 191,000 | 420,200 | 42,000 | 92,400 | | |
| Steam and agricultural engines | 26,862,000 | 59,096,400 | 2,418,000 | 5,319,600 | | |
| Stone | 626,832,000 | 1,379,030,400 | 2,007,000 | 4,415,400 | | |
| Sugar: | | | | | | |
| Raw | 49,608,000 | 109,137,600 | 35,291,000 | 77,640,200 | | |
| All other | 8,628,000 | 18,981,600 | | | 7,204,000 | 15,848,800 |
| Tallow, suet, etc. | 1,794,000 | 3,946,800 | 1,072,000 | 2,358,400 | | |
| Tar and pitch | 167,000 | 367,400 | 25,000 | 55,000 | | |
| Tobacco and cigars | 5,930,000 | 13,046,000 | 467,000 | 1,027,400 | | |
| Wheat | 1,132,000 | 2,490,400 | | | 15,000,000 | 33,000,000 |
| Wine: | | | | | | |
| Hogsheads | 9,306,000 | 20,473,200 | 1,044,000 | 2,296,800 | | |
| Bottled | 6,240,000 | 13,728,000 | 54,000 | 118,800 | | |
| Wool | 2,252,000 | 4,954,400 | 641,000 | 1,410,200 | | |
| Yarns | 5,304,000 | 11,668,800 | 960,000 | 2,112,000 | | |
| **FROM FRANCE.** | | | | | | |
| Coffee | 4,316,000 | 9,495,200 | 1,676,000 | 3,687,200 | | |
| Cotton | 22,000 | 48,400 | | | 134,000 | 294,800 |
| Cotton-seed oil | 5,000 | 11,000 | | | 23,000 | 50,600 |
| Crockery ware and porcelain | 35,000 | 77,000 | | | 35,000 | 77,000 |
| Distilled liquors | 1,038,000 | 2,283,600 | | | 12,000 | 26,400 |
| Drugs, dyestuffs, and chemicals | 6,844,000 | 15,056,800 | | | 842,000 | 1,852,400 |
| Dry goods | 45,000 | 99,000 | | | 9,000 | 19,800 |
| Fruits: | | | | | | |
| Fresh | 1,137,000 | 2,501,400 | | | 1,267,000 | 2,787,400 |
| All other | 249,000 | 547,800 | | | 600,000 | 1,320,000 |
| Hides, skins, and leather | 802,000 | 1,764,400 | 333,000 | 782,600 | | |
| Lard | 7,000 | 15,400 | 7,000 | 15,400 | | |
| Lumber: | | | | | | |
| Cabinet wood | 600,000 | 1,320,000 | 338,000 | 748,600 | | |
| Dyewood | 59,000 | 129,800 | 59,000 | 129,800 | | |
| Merceryware | 168,000 | 369,600 | | | 4,000 | 8,800 |
| Metal wares | 59,000 | 129,800 | | | 14,000 | 30,800 |
| Palm oil | 339,000 | 745,800 | 50,000 | 110,000 | | |
| Sesam oil | 187,000 | 411,400 | | | 234,000 | 514,800 |
| Steam and agricultural engines | 24,000 | 52,800 | | | 104,000 | 228,800 |
| Sugar: | | | | | | |
| Raw | 376,000 | 827,200 | | | 7,352,000 | 16,174,400 |
| All other | 51,000 | 112,200 | | | 294,000 | 646,800 |
| Tobacco and cigars | 178,000 | 391,600 | | | 65,000 | 143,000 |
| Wine. | | | | | | |
| Hogsheads | 535,000 | 1,177,000 | 681,000 | 1,498,200 | | |
| Bottled | 213,000 | 468,600 | | | 59,000 | 129,800 |
| **FROM ITALY.** | | | | | | |
| Brimstone | 3,480,000 | 7,656,000 | 1,710,000 | 3,762,000 | | |
| Drugs, dyestuffs, and chemicals | 995,000 | 2,189,000 | | | 159,000 | 349,800 |
| Fruits: | | | | | | |
| Fresh | 6,255,000 | 13,761,000 | | | 1,108,000 | 2,437,600 |
| All other | 929,000 | 2,043,800 | | | 233,000 | 512,600 |
| Stone | 4,968,000 | 10,929,600 | | | 1,502,000 | 3,304,400 |
| **FROM AUSTRIA.** | | | | | | |
| Barley | 2,846,000 | 6,261,200 | 298,000 | 655,600 | | |
| Drugs, dyestuffs, and chemicals | 243,000 | 534,600 | | | 33,000 | 72,600 |
| Fruits | 667,000 | 1,467,400 | 292,000 | 642,400 | | |

*Imports and exports of the Netherlands during the first half year 1902*—Continued.

IMPORTS—Continued.

| Articles. | Kilograms. | Pounds. | Increase. | | Decrease. | |
|---|---|---|---|---|---|---|
| | | | Kilograms. | Pounds. | Kilograms. | Pounds. |
| **FROM RUSSIA.** | | | | | | |
| Barley .................. | 65,922,000 | 145,028,400 | 13,126,000 | 28,877,200 | .......... | .......... |
| Buckwheat ............. | 1,712,000 | 3,766,400 | 161,000 | 354,200 | .......... | .......... |
| Flax and hemp ........ | 308,000 | 677,600 | .......... | .......... | 130,000 | 286,000 |
| Indian corn............. | 116,349,000 | 255,967,800 | 110,452,000 | 242,994,400 | .......... | .......... |
| Lumber,timber for ships | 142,221,000 | 312,886,200 | .......... | .......... | 25,756,000 | 56,663,200 |
| Oats.................... | 87,561,000 | 192,634,200 | .......... | .......... | 40,740,000 | 89,628,000 |
| Petroleum ............. | 11,118,000 | 24,459,600 | 8,346,000 | 18,361,200 | .......... | .......... |
| Potash ................. | 169,000 | 371,800 | 163,000 | 359,600 | .......... | .......... |
| Rye .................... | 127,048,000 | 279,505,600 | .......... | .......... | 38,299,000 | 84,257,800 |
| Seeds................... | 4,504,000 | 9,908,800 | .......... | .......... | 8,683,000 | 19,102,600 |
| Tar and pitch .......... | 549,000 | 1,207,800 | .......... | .......... | 96,000 | 211,200 |
| Wheat ................. | 256,932,000 | 565,250,400 | 122,342,000 | 269,152,400 | .......... | .......... |
| **FROM ROUMANIA.** | | | | | | |
| Barley ................. | 23,749,000 | 52,247,800 | 7,722,000 | 16,988,400 | .......... | .......... |
| Indian corn............. | 50,981,000 | 112,048,200 | 25,922,000 | 57,028,400 | .......... | .......... |
| Oats.................... | 3,664,000 | 8,060,800 | 3,049,000 | 6,707,800 | .......... | .......... |
| Rye .................... | 29,757,000 | 65,465,400 | .......... | .......... | 6,624,000 | 14,572,000 |
| Wheat ................. | 59,236,000 | 130,319,200 | 33,953,000 | 74,696,600 | .......... | .......... |
| **FROM NORWAY.** | | | | | | |
| Lumber,timber for ships | 38,526,000 | 84,757,200 | 4,944,000 | 10,876,800 | .......... | .......... |
| **FROM SWEDEN.** | | | | | | |
| Metals ....... .......... | 7,150,000 | 15,730,000 | 3,468,000 | 7,629,600 | .......... | .......... |
| Tar and pitch.......... | .......... | .......... | .......... | .......... | 1,000 | 2,200 |
| **FROM SPAIN.** | | | | | | |
| Wine ................... | 5,749,000 | 12,647,800 | 732,000 | 1,610,400 | .......... | .......... |
| **FROM PORTUGAL.** | | | | | | |
| Fruits: | | | | | | |
| Fresh .............. | 321,000 | 706,200 | 100,000 | 220,000 | .......... | .......... |
| All other. ........... | 11,000 | 24,200 | .......... | .......... | 2,000 | 4,400 |
| Palm oil, etc.......... | .......... | .......... | .......... | .......... | .......... | .......... |
| Salt.................... | 13,290,000 | 29,238,000 | .......... | .......... | 462,000 | 1,016,400 |
| **FROM TURKEY.** | | | | | | |
| Fruits................... | 5,317,000 | 11,697,400 | 1,864,000 | 4,100,800 | .......... | .......... |
| **FROM BRITISH INDIES.** | | | | | | |
| Rattan.................. | 130,000 | 286,000 | 42,000 | 92,400 | .......... | .......... |
| Rice ................... | 123,246,000 | 271,141,200 | 40,256,000 | 88,563,200 | .......... | .......... |
| **FROM DUTCH EAST INDIES.** | | | | | | |
| Coffee.................. | 10,315,000 | 22,693,000 | .......... | .......... | 1,669,000 | 3,671,800 |
| Distilled liquors ....... | 1,323,000 | 2,910,600 | 146,000 | 321,200 | .......... | .......... |
| Drugs, dyestuffs, and chemicals............. | 7,336,000 | 16,139,200 | .......... | .......... | 1,745,000 | 3,839,000 |
| Hides,skins,and leather. | 2,149,000 | 4,727,800 | .......... | .......... | 483,000 | 1,062,600 |
| Lumber, dyewood ..... | 28,000 | 61,600 | .......... | .......... | 16,000 | 35,200 |
| Rattan.................. | 2,507,000 | 5,515,400 | 305,000 | 671,000 | .......... | .......... |
| Rice ................... | 5,432,000 | 11,950,400 | .......... | .......... | 2,128,000 | 4,681,600 |
| Spices.................. | 2,594,000 | 5,706,800 | 801,000 | 1,762,200 | .......... | .......... |
| Sugar, raw............. | 213,000 | 468,600 | 212,000 | 466,400 | .......... | .......... |
| Tea .................... | 3,539,000 | 7,785,800 | 58,000 | 127,600 | .......... | .......... |
| Tobacco ............... | 23,053,000 | 50,716,600 | 4,753,000 | 10,456,600 | .......... | .......... |
| **FROM JAPAN.** | | | | | | |
| Rice ........ .......... | 7,130,000 | 15,686,000 | 4,880,000 | 10,736,000 | .......... | .......... |
| **FROM HAITI.** | | | | | | |
| Lumber, dyewood ..... | .......... | .......... | .......... | .......... | 1,330,000 | 2,926,000 |
| **FROM CURAÇAO.** | | | | | | |
| Coffee.................. | 33,000 | 72,600 | .......... | .......... | 4,000 | 8,800 |
| Lumber, dyewood ..... | .......... | .......... | .......... | .......... | .......... | .......... |

*Imports and exports of the Netherlands during the first half year 1902*—Continued.

IMPORTS—Continued.

| Articles. | Kilograms. | Pounds. | Increase. | | Decrease. | |
|---|---|---|---|---|---|---|
| | | | Kilograms. | Pounds. | Kilograms. | Pounds. |
| **FROM SURINAM.** | | | | | | |
| Coffee................... | 13,000 | 28,600 | ............ | ............ | 9,000 | 19,800 |
| Sugar................... | 208,000 | 457,600 | ............ | ............ | 150,000 | 330,000 |
| **FROM SOUTH AMERICA.** | | | | | | |
| Coffee................... | 34,324,000 | 75,512,800 | 9,818,000 | 21,599,600 | ............ | ............ |
| Drugs, dyestuffs, and chemicals.......... | 30,561,000 | 67,234,200 | 5,831,000 | 12,828,200 | ............ | ............ |
| Indian corn............ | 5,203,000 | 11,446,600 | ............ | ............ | 1,923,000 | 4,230,600 |
| Manure................. | 1,930,000 | 4,246,000 | ............ | ............ | 720,000 | 1,584,000 |
| **FROM THE UNITED STATES.** | | | | | | |
| Ashes.................. | 28,000 | 61,600 | 3,000 | 6,600 | ............ | ............ |
| Cotton................. | 2,622,000 | 5,768,400 | ............ | ............ | 8,275,000 | 18,205,000 |
| Cotton-seed oil......... | 23,425,000 | 51,535,000 | ............ | ............ | 7,148,000 | 15,725,600 |
| Flour, wheat........... | 42,547,000 | 93,603,400 | ............ | ............ | 10,694,000 | 22,426,800 |
| Fruits................. | 3,015,000 | 6,633,000 | ............ | ............ | 155,000 | 341,000 |
| Indian corn............ | 24,309,000 | 53,479,800 | ............ | ............ | 176,237,000 | 387,721,400 |
| Lard.................. | 14,321,000 | 31,506,200 | ............ | ............ | 704,000 | 1,548,800 |
| Lumber: | | | | | | |
| Cabinet wood....... | 5,416,000 | 11,925,200 | 1,572,000 | 3,458,400 | ............ | ............ |
| Dyewood.......... | 6,979,000 | 15,353,800 | 1,713,000 | 3,768,600 | ............ | ............ |
| Margarine ............. | 13,392,000 | 29,462,400 | ............ | ............ | 6,439,000 | 14,165,800 |
| Meat.................. | 4,174,000 | 9,182,800 | ............ | ............ | 1,142,000 | 2,512,400 |
| Petroleum ............. | 171,785,000 | 378,927,000 | ............ | ............ | 30,071,000 | 66,156,200 |
| Seeds................. | 8,237,000 | 18,121,400 | 8,098,000 | 17,815,600 | ............ | ............ |
| Tallow, suet, etc ....... | 2,909,000 | 6,399,800 | ............ | ............ | 423,000 | 930,600 |
| Tobacco............... | 4,766,000 | 10,485,200 | ............ | ............ | 907,000 | 1,995,400 |
| Wheat................. | 92,547,000 | 203,603,400 | ............ | ............ | 144,694,000 | 318,326,800 |

EXPORTS.

| | | | | | | |
|---|---|---|---|---|---|---|
| **TO BELGIUM.** | | | | | | |
| Barley................. | 34,091,000 | 75,000,200 | ............ | ............ | 1,489,000 | 3,275,800 |
| Butter................. | 1,179,000 | 2,593,800 | ............ | ............ | 140,000 | 308,000 |
| Cattle............head.. | 21,973 | ............ | 2,458 | ............ | ............ | ............ |
| Cheese................ | 5,538,000 | 12,183,600 | 1,392,000 | 3,062,400 | ............ | ............ |
| Coffee................. | 4,450,000 | 9,790,000 | 306,000 | 673,200 | ............ | ............ |
| Cotton................. | 4,615,000 | 10,153,000 | 1,722,000 | 3,788,400 | ............ | ............ |
| Cotton-seed oil......... | 134,000 | 294,800 | ............ | ............ | 7,000 | 15,400 |
| Distilled liquors ....... | 3,375,000 | 7,425,000 | 194,000 | 426,800 | ............ | ............ |
| Drugs, dyestuffs, and chemicals............ | 33,322,000 | 73,308,400 | 5,508,000 | 12,117,600 | ............ | ............ |
| Fish oil ............... | 414,000 | 910,800 | 21,000 | 46,200 | ............ | ............ |
| Flax and hemp......... | 24,096,000 | 53,011,200 | 6,524,000 | 14,352,800 | ............ | ............ |
| Flour, wheat........... | 819,000 | 1,801,800 | ............ | ............ | 106,000 | 233,200 |
| Fruits: | | | | | | |
| Fresh .............. | 686,000 | 4,509,200 | 29,000 | 63,800 | ............ | ............ |
| All other........... | 2,235,000 | 4,917,000 | 1,101,000 | 2,422,200 | ............ | ............ |
| Hides, skins, and leather. | 4,021,000 | 8,846,200 | 603,000 | 1,326,600 | ............ | ............ |
| Hogs..............head.. | 1,147 | ............ | ............ | ............ | 1,706 | ............ |
| Indian corn............ | 14,001,000 | 30,802,200 | 8,369,000 | 18,411,800 | ............ | ............ |
| Lumber: | | | | | | |
| Cabinet wood....... | 295,000 | 649,000 | 252,000 | 554,400 | ............ | ............ |
| Dyewood.......... | 363,000 | 798,600 | ............ | ............ | 222,000 | 488,400 |
| Margarin ............. | 1,374,000 | 3,022,800 | ............ | ............ | 220,000 | 484,000 |
| Margarin butter ....... | 424,000 | 932,800 | 150,000 | 330,000 | ............ | ............ |
| Manure............... | 31,385,000 | 69,047,000 | 10,018,000 | 22,039,600 | ............ | ............ |
| Mercery ware.......... | 2,435,000 | 5,357,000 | ............ | ............ | 596,000 | 1,311,200 |
| Metals................ | 191,978,000 | 422,351,600 | 35,223,000 | 77,490,600 | ............ | ............ |
| Oats.................. | 6,271,000 | 13,796,200 | 1,933,000 | 4,252,600 | ............ | ............ |
| Paper................. | 13,575,000 | 29,865,000 | 3,880,000 | 8,536,000 | ............ | ............ |
| Petroleum ............ | 11,618,000 | 25,559,600 | 4,551,000 | 10,012,200 | ............ | ............ |
| Rags.................. | 7,783,000 | 17,122,600 | ............ | ............ | 262,000 | 576,400 |
| Rice ................. | 11,957,000 | 26,305,400 | 5,309,000 | 11,679,800 | ............ | ............ |
| Rye .................. | 1,705,000 | 3,751,000 | ............ | ............ | 421,000 | 926,200 |
| Salt ................. | 18,028,000 | 39,661,600 | 404,000 | 888,800 | ............ | ............ |
| Seeds ................ | 2,753,000 | 6,056,600 | ............ | ............ | 24,000 | 52,800 |
| Sesame oil ............ | 134,000 | 294,800 | ............ | ............ | 7,000 | 15,400 |
| Sheep and lambs..head.. | 37,384 | ............ | 10,037 | ............ | ............ | ............ |
| Steam and agricultural engines.............. | 10,787,000 | 23,731,400 | ............ | ............ | 297,000 | 653,400 |

*Imports and exports of the Netherlands during the first half year 1902*—Continued.

EXPORTS—Continued.

| Articles. | Kilograms. | Pounds. | Increase. | | Decrease. | |
|---|---|---|---|---|---|---|
| | | | Kilograms. | Pounds. | Kilograms. | Pounds. |
| TO BELGIUM—continued. | | | | | | |
| Stone | 79,503,000 | 174,906,600 | | | 24,419,000 | 53,721,800 |
| Sugar: | | | | | | |
| Raw | 1,384,000 | 2,984,800 | | | 760,000 | 1,672,000 |
| All other | 906,000 | 1,993,200 | | | 1,243,000 | 2,734,600 |
| Sirup and molasses | 404,000 | 888,800 | 213,000 | 468,600 | | |
| Tallow, suet, etc | 2,397,000 | 5,273,400 | | | 461,000 | 1,014,200 |
| Tar and pitch | 7,069,000 | 15,551,800 | | | 1,036,000 | 2,279,200 |
| Tea | 26,000 | 57,200 | | | 10,000 | 22,000 |
| Tobacco and cigars | 2,182,000 | 4,800,400 | | | 442,000 | 972,400 |
| Wheat | 60,132,000 | 132,290,400 | 16,127,000 | 35,479,400 | | |
| Wine ......hogsheads. | 1,680,000 | 3,696,000 | 280,000 | 616,000 | | |
| Wool | 4,932,000 | 10,850,400 | 559,000 | 1,229,800 | | |
| TO GREAT BRITAIN. | | | | | | |
| Bark | 107,000 | 235,400 | 101,000 | 222,200 | | |
| Barley | 16,000 | 35,200 | | | 989,000 | 2,175,800 |
| Butter | 6,277,000 | 13,809,400 | | | 359,000 | 789,800 |
| Cattle ......head. | 3 | | | 2 | | |
| Cheese | 7,833,000 | 17,232,600 | | | 453,000 | 996,600 |
| Coal | 642,000 | 1,412,400 | 18,000 | 39,600 | | |
| Distilled liquors | 2,583,000 | 5,682,600 | | | 223,000 | 490,600 |
| Drugs, dyestuffs, and chemicals | 18,325,000 | 40,315,000 | 4,170,000 | 9,174,000 | | |
| Dry goods | 17,000 | 37,400 | | | 24,000 | 52,800 |
| Fish oil | 51,000 | 112,200 | 14,000 | 30,800 | | |
| Glass and glassware | 21,317,000 | 46,897,400 | 3,469,000 | 7,631,800 | | |
| Hides, skins, and leather | 4,240,000 | 9,328,000 | | | 242,000 | 532,400 |
| Margarin | 149,000 | 327,800 | | | 152,000 | 334,400 |
| Margarin butter | 22,738,000 | 50,023,600 | 2,607,000 | 5,735,400 | | |
| Meat | 24,897,000 | 54,773,400 | 1,457,000 | 3,205,400 | | |
| Mercery ware | 6,080,000 | 13,376,000 | 805,000 | 1,771,000 | | |
| Metals | 71,720,000 | 164,384,000 | 34,720,000 | 76,384,000 | | |
| Metal wares | 46,313,000 | 101,888,600 | 1,985,000 | 4,367,000 | | |
| Oats | 3,919,000 | 8,621,800 | 2,358,000 | 5,187,600 | | |
| Palm oil, etc | 3,291,000 | 7,240,200 | | | 581,000 | 1,278,200 |
| Paper | 60,441,000 | 132,970,200 | 4,095,000 | 9,009,000 | | |
| Rice | 14,069,000 | 30,951,800 | 1,063,000 | 2,338,600 | | |
| Seeds | 2,930,000 | 6,446,000 | 534,000 | 1,174,800 | | |
| Sheep and lambs. head. | | | | | 4 | |
| Spices | 879,000 | 1,933,800 | 45,000 | 99,000 | | |
| Steam and agricultural engines | 3,754,000 | 8,258,800 | 1,529,000 | 3,363,800 | | |
| Sugar: | | | | | | |
| Raw | 14,576,000 | 32,067,200 | 2,937,000 | 6,461,400 | | |
| All other | 68,484,000 | 150,664,800 | | | 3,503,000 | 7,706,600 |
| Tallow, suet, etc | 716,000 | 1,575,200 | 307,000 | 675,400 | | |
| Tea | 2,444,000 | 5,376,800 | 936,000 | 2,059,200 | | |
| Tobacco and cigars | 1,817,000 | 3,997,400 | 425,000 | 935,000 | | |
| Wine: | | | | | | |
| Hogsheads | 1,995,000 | 4,389,000 | 395,000 | 869,000 | | |
| Bottled | 2,526,000 | 5,557,200 | | | 72,000 | 158,400 |
| Wool | 382,000 | 840,400 | | | 287,000 | 631,400 |
| Yarns | 715,000 | 1,573,000 | | | 323,000 | 710,600 |
| TO GERMANY. | | | | | | |
| Bark | 50,000 | 110,000 | | | 27,000 | 59,400 |
| Barley | 81,689,000 | 179,715,800 | 17,183,000 | 37,802,600 | | |
| Brimstone | 4,920,000 | 10,824,000 | | | 123,000 | 270,600 |
| Buckwheat | 1,839,000 | 4,155,800 | | | 1,762,000 | 3,876,400 |
| Cattle ......head. | 44 | | | | 32 | |
| Cheese | 3,769,000 | 8,291,800 | 17,000 | 37,400 | | |
| Coal | 162,281,000 | 357,018,200 | | | 383,000 | 842,600 |
| Coffee | 28,936,000 | 63,659,200 | 1,826,000 | 4,017,200 | | |
| Cotton | 24,034,000 | 52,874,800 | | | 3,574,000 | 7,862,800 |
| Cotton-seed oil | 15,572,000 | 34,258,400 | 1,500,000 | 3,300,000 | | |
| Distilled liquors | 6,790,000 | 14,938,000 | | | 47,000 | 103,400 |
| Drugs, dyestuffs, and chemicals | 120,136,000 | 264,299,200 | 19,153,000 | 42,136,600 | | |
| Dry goods | 5,435,000 | 11,957,000 | 1,279,000 | 2,813,800 | | |
| Fish | 14,941,000 | 32,870,200 | 3,842,000 | 8,452,400 | | |
| Fish oil | 2,529,000 | 5,563,800 | 864,000 | 1,900,800 | | |
| Flax and hemp | 17,760,000 | 39,072,000 | 3,126,000 | 6,877,200 | | |
| Flour: | | | | | | |
| Wheat | 3,233,000 | 7,112,600 | | | 432,000 | 950,400 |
| Rye | 15,189,000 | 33,415,800 | | | 7,511,000 | 16,524,200 |

*Imports and exports of the Netherlands during the first half year 1902*—Continued.

EXPORTS—Continued.

| Articles. | Kilograms. | Pounds. | Increase. | | Decrease. | |
|---|---|---|---|---|---|---|
| | | | Kilograms. | Pounds. | Kilograms. | Pounds. |
| TO GERMANY—cont'd. | | | | | | |
| Fruits: | | | | | | |
| Fresh ............... | 12,916,000 | 28,415,200 | ............ | ............ | 223,000 | 490,600 |
| All other........... | 14,616,000 | 321,552,000 | 4,768,000 | 10,489,600 | ............ | ............ |
| Hides, skins, and leather | 9,496,000 | 20,891,200 | ............ | ............ | 708,000 | 1,557,600 |
| Indian corn ............ | 103,128,000 | 226,881,600 | ............ | ............ | 31,453,000 | 69,196,600 |
| Lard ..................... | 10,202,000 | 22,444,400 | ............ | ............ | 468,000 | 1,029,600 |
| Lumber: | | | | | | |
| Ship timber........ | 192,608,000 | 423,737,600 | ............ | ............ | 65,410,000 | 143,902,000 |
| Cabinet wood...... | 4,450,000 | 9,790,000 | ............ | ............ | 2,029,000 | 4,463,800 |
| Dyewood .......... | 19,300,000 | 42,473,200 | ............ | ............ | 7,298,000 | 16,055,600 |
| Margarin ................ | 6,463,000 | 1,421,860 | ............ | ............ | 1,762,000 | 3,876,400 |
| Margarin butter ....... | 141,000 | 310,200 | ............ | ............ | 47,800 | 105,160 |
| Manure ................. | 130,385,000 | 286,847,000 | 51,060,000 | 112,332,000 | ............ | ............ |
| Meat.................... | 7,673,000 | 16,880,600 | 2,875,000 | 6,325,000 | ............ | ............ |
| Mercery ware........... | 1,327,000 | 2,919,400 | 236,000 | 519,200 | ............ | ............ |
| Metals .................. | 151,342,000 | 332,952,400 | ............ | ............ | 4,531,000 | 9,968,200 |
| Metal wares ............ | 16,846,000 | 37,061,200 | ............ | ............ | 646,000 | 1,421,200 |
| Oats.................... | 124,154,000 | 273,147,600 | ............ | ............ | 18,254,000 | 40,158,800 |
| Palm oil, etc............ | 48,294,000 | 106,246,800 | 6,390,000 | 14,058,000 | ............ | ............ |
| Palm seed ............. | 10,223,000 | 22,490,600 | 2,635,000 | 5,797,000 | ............ | ............ |
| Paper................... | 6,206,000 | 13,653,200 | 159,000 | 349,800 | ............ | ............ |
| Petroleum ............. | 118,652,000 | 261,034,400 | ............ | ............ | 11,740,000 | 25,828,000 |
| Rags ................... | 15,321,000 | 33,706,200 | ............ | ............ | 1,967,000 | 4,327,400 |
| Rice ................... | 15,336,000 | 33,739,200 | 590,000 | 1,298,000 | ............ | ............ |
| Rye ................... | 110,823,000 | 243,810,600 | ............ | ............ | 35,690,000 | 78,518,000 |
| Salt.................... | 1,338,000 | 2,943,600 | 300,000 | 660,000 | ............ | ............ |
| Seeds .................. | 105,160,000 | 231,352,000 | 1,393,000 | 3,064,600 | ............ | ............ |
| Sesame oil ............. | 7,970,000 | 17,534,000 | 3,436,000 | 7,559,200 | ............ | ............ |
| Spices.................. | 1,212,000 | 2,666,400 | 74,000 | 162,800 | ............ | ............ |
| Steam and agricultural | | | | | | |
| engines ............... | 9,946,000 | 21,881,200 | ............ | ............ | 6,974,000 | 15,342,800 |
| Stone .................. | 49,831,000 | 109,628,200 | ............ | ............ | 6,682,000 | 14,700,400 |
| Sugar: | | | | | | |
| Raw ............... | 31,904,000 | 70,188,800 | 28,391,000 | 62,460,200 | ............ | ............ |
| Refined ........... | 6,391,000 | 14,060,200 | ............ | ............ | 16,261,000 | 35,774,200 |
| Tallow, suet, etc........ | 8,035,000 | 17,677,000 | 676,000 | 1,487,200 | ............ | ............ |
| Tar and pitch........... | 30,276,000 | 66,607,200 | ............ | ............ | 8,167,000 | 17,967,400 |
| Tea ................... | 726,000 | 1,597,200 | ............ | ............ | 221,000 | 486,200 |
| Tobacco and cigars ..... | 15,747,000 | 34,643,400 | ............ | ............ | 713,000 | 1,568,600 |
| Wheat ................. | 616,035,000 | 1,335,277,000 | 19,638,000 | 43,203,600 | ............ | ............ |
| Wine: | | | | | | |
| Hogsheads.......... | 14,505,000 | 31,911,000 | 636,000 | 1,399,200 | ............ | ............ |
| Bottled ............. | 2,445,000 | 5,379,000 | 22,000 | 48,400 | ............ | ............ |
| Wool................... | 17,883,000 | 39,342,600 | 5,869,000 | 12,911,800 | ............ | ............ |
| Yarns.................. | 10,863,000 | 23,898,600 | 827,000 | 1,819,400 | ............ | ............ |
| TO FRANCE. | | | | | | |
| Cheese .................. | 1,529,000 | 3,363,800 | ............ | ............ | 1,000 | 2,200 |
| Coffee .................. | 20,000 | 44,000 | ............ | ............ | 49,000 | 107,800 |
| Cotton ................. | 13,000 | 28,600 | 6,000 | 13,200 | ............ | ............ |
| Distilled liquors ........ | 97,000 | 213,400 | ............ | ............ | 1,000 | 2,200 |
| Fish oil ................. | 178,000 | 391,600 | ............ | ............ | 97,000 | 213,400 |
| Hides, skins, and leather | 276,000 | 607,200 | ............ | ............ | 13,000 | 28,600 |
| Metal wares ............ | 119,000 | 261,800 | 47,000 | 103,400 | ............ | ............ |
| Paper .................. | 175,000 | 385,000 | 91,000 | 200,200 | ............ | ............ |
| Rice ................... | 790,000 | 1,738,000 | ............ | ............ | 218,000 | 479,600 |
| Wine: | | | | | | |
| Hogsheads.......... | 5,000 | 11,000 | ............ | ............ | 6,000 | 13,200 |
| Bottled ............. | 10,000 | 22,000 | ............ | ............ | 2,000 | 44,000 |
| TO RUSSIA. | | | | | | |
| Cheese .................. | 109,000 | 239,800 | 28,000 | 61,600 | ............ | ............ |
| Metal wares............. | 1,034,000 | 2,274,800 | 40,000 | 88,000 | ............ | ............ |
| TO ITALY. | | | | | | |
| Metal wares ............ | 2,129,000 | 4,683,800 | 1,156,000 | 2,543,200 | ............ | ............ |
| TO NORWAY. | | | | | | |
| Margerin ............... | 201,000 | 442,200 | 103,000 | 226,600 | ............ | ............ |
| Margerin butter ........ | 69,000 | 151,800 | ............ | ............ | 1,000 | 2,200 |
| Metal wares ............ | 2,933,000 | 6,452,600 | 1,372,000 | 3,018,400 | ............ | ............ |
| TO DENMARK. | | | | | | |
| Coffee................... | 1,303,000 | 2,866,600 | ............ | ............ | 135,000 | 297,000 |
| Fruits................... | 47,000 | 103,400 | 47,000 | 103,400 | ............ | ............ |
| Tobacco and cigars..... | 477,000 | 1,049,400 | 101,000 | 222,200 | ............ | ............ |

*Imports and exports of the Netherlands during the first half year 1902*—Continued.

EXPORTS—Continued.

| Articles. | Kilograms. | Pounds. | Increase. | | Decrease. | |
|---|---|---|---|---|---|---|
| | | | Kilograms. | Pounds. | Kilograms. | Pounds. |
| **TO SWEDEN.** | | | | | | |
| Coffee................... | 853,000 | 1,876,600 | .......... | .......... | 4,000 | 8,800 |
| Cotton ............. | 294,000 | 646,800 | .......... | .......... | 154,000 | 338,800 |
| Cotton-seed oil.......... | 42,000 | 92,400 | .......... | .......... | 15,000 | 33,000 |
| Distilled liquors ....... | 270,000 | 594,000 | .......... | .......... | 81,000 | 178,200 |
| Sugars, refined.......... | 14,000 | 30,800 | 5,000 | 11,000 | .......... | .......... |
| Tallow, suet ........... | | | | | | |
| **TO PORTUGAL.** | | | | | | |
| Sugar, refined.......... | 353,000 | 776,600 | 102,000 | 224,400 | .......... | .......... |
| **TO TURKEY.** | | | | | | |
| Sugar, refined.......... | 122,000 | 268,400 | 73,000 | 160,600 | .......... | .......... |
| **TO BRITISH INDIES.** | | | | | | |
| Dry goods............. | 38,000 | 83,600 | .......... | .......... | 56,000 | 123,200 |
| Tar and pitch ......... | | | | | | |
| **TO DUTCH EAST INDIES.** | | | | | | |
| Beer and malt extract.. | 2,642,000 | 5,812,400 | 259,000 | 569,800 | .......... | .......... |
| Butter ............... | 396,000 | 871,200 | 13,000 | 28,600 | .......... | .......... |
| Cheese ............... | 127,000 | 279,400 | 1,000 | 2,200 | .......... | .......... |
| Coal.................. | 1,155,000 | 2,541,000 | .......... | .......... | 2,332,000 | 5,130,400 |
| Crockery ware and porcelain.............. | 4,158,000 | 9,147,600 | .......... | .......... | 824,000 | 1,812,800 |
| Distilled liquors ....... | 1,131,000 | 2,488,200 | .......... | .......... | 69,000 | 151,800 |
| Drugs, dyestuffs, and chemicals............ | 1,922,000 | 4,228,400 | .......... | .......... | 459,000 | 899,800 |
| Dry goods............. | 5,157,000 | 11,345,400 | .......... | .......... | 1,212,000 | 2,666,400 |
| Glass and glassware..... | 588,000 | 1,293,600 | .......... | .......... | 188,000 | 413,600 |
| Hides, skins, and leather. | 183,000 | 402,600 | 144,000 | 316,800 | .......... | .......... |
| Margarin butter........ | 97,000 | 213,400 | 33,000 | 72,600 | .......... | .......... |
| Meat................. | 328,000 | 721,600 | 51,000 | 112,200 | .......... | .......... |
| Mercery ware.......... | 1,527,000 | 3,359,400 | .......... | .......... | 313,000 | 688,600 |
| Metals ............... | 12,540,000 | 27,588,000 | 2,539,000 | 5,585,800 | .......... | .......... |
| Metal wares........... | 22,193,000 | 48,824,600 | 1,725,000 | 3,795,000 | .......... | .......... |
| Paper ................ | 1,606,000 | 3,533,200 | .......... | .......... | 231,000 | 508,200 |
| Steam agricultural engines................ | 3,673,000 | 8,080,600 | .......... | .......... | 399,000 | 877,800 |
| Stone ................ | 493,000 | 1,084,600 | 184,000 | 294,800 | .......... | .......... |
| Sugar, refined ........ | 79,000 | 173,800 | .......... | .......... | 9,000 | 19,800 |
| Tar and pitch ......... | 490,000 | 1,008,000 | .......... | .......... | 67,000 | 147,400 |
| Vinegar .............. | 34,000 | 74,800 | .......... | .......... | 11,000 | 24,200 |
| Wine: | | | | | | |
| Hogsheads.......... | 85,000 | 177,000 | .......... | .......... | 70,000 | 154,000 |
| Bottled ............ | 521,000 | 1,146,200 | .......... | .......... | 11,000 | 24,200 |
| Yarns................ | 291,000 | 640,200 | 67,000 | 147,400 | .......... | .......... |
| **TO SURINAM.** | | | | | | |
| Beer and malt extract.. | 606,000 | 1,333,200 | .......... | .......... | .......... | .......... |
| Butter ............... | 72,000 | 158,400 | .......... | .......... | .......... | .......... |
| Distilled liquors ....... | 330,000 | 726,000 | .......... | .......... | 95,000 | 209,000 |
| Dry goods............. | 53,000 | 116,600 | .......... | .......... | 47,000 | 103,400 |
| Mercery ware.......... | 309,000 | 679,800 | .......... | .......... | 44,000 | 96,800 |
| Rice ................. | 2,811,000 | 6,184,200 | 509,000 | 1,119,800 | .......... | .......... |
| Vinegar............... | 14,000 | 30,800 | .......... | .......... | 2,000 | 4,400 |
| **TO AFRICA (WEST COAST).** | | | | | | |
| Beer and malt extract.. | 19,000 | 41,800 | .......... | .......... | 11,000 | 24,200 |
| Distilled liquors ....... | 5,062,000 | 11,136,400 | 844,000 | 1,856,800 | .......... | .......... |
| Dry goods............. | 93,000 | 204,600 | .......... | .......... | 59,000 | 129,800 |
| Mercery ware .......... | 56,000 | 123,200 | 33,000 | 72,600 | .......... | .......... |
| Metal wares........... | 887,000 | 1,951,400 | 658,000 | 1,447,600 | .......... | .......... |
| Oils ................. | 5,000 | 11,000 | 2,000 | 4,400 | .......... | .......... |
| Petroleum ........... | .......... | .......... | .......... | .......... | .......... | .......... |
| Sugar, refined.......... | 14,000 | 30,800 | .......... | .......... | 2,000 | 4,400 |
| **TO UNITED STATES.** | | | | | | |
| Coffee ............... | 1,209,000 | 2,659,800 | 531,000 | 1,168,200 | .......... | .......... |
| Distilled liquors ....... | 508,000 | 1,117,600 | .......... | .......... | 56,000 | 123,200 |
| Spices................ | 923,000 | 2,030,600 | .......... | .......... | 325,000 | 715,000 |
| Sugar, refined ......... | 318,000 | 699,600 | .......... | .......... | 7,498,000 | 16,495,600 |
| Wine: | | | | | | |
| Hogsheads .......... | 1,640,000 | 3,608,000 | 76,000 | 167,200 | .......... | .......... |
| Bottled............. | 891,000 | 1,960,200 | 40,000 | 88,000 | .......... | .......... |

*Statement showing the declared exports from the consular district of Amsterdam to the United States during the fiscal years ended June 30, 1898, 1899, 1900, 1901, and 1902.*

| Articles. | 1898. | 1899. | 1900. | 1901. | 1902. |
|---|---|---|---|---|---|
| Aniline colors | $32,076.19 | $16,092.78 | $17,160.34 | $24,107.91 | $13,220.52 |
| Antiquities | 11,641.02 | 15,251.04 | 18,437.25 | 33,101.30 | 30,204.37 |
| Books | 15,596.72 | 18,325.21 | 20,684.77 | 14,850.12 | 23,949.67 |
| Bulbs and plants | 22,210.78 | 17,443.19 | 15,544.16 | 24,096.91 | 40,239.33 |
| Canary seed | | | 7,968.91 | | |
| Caraway seed | 55,848.11 | 55,013.74 | 56,577.07 | 60,518.77 | 72,512.30 |
| Cassiavera | 68,673.48 | 30,800.18 | 100,520.14 | 33,940.28 | 4,889.07 |
| Cheese | 54,509.46 | 62,861.21 | 68,496.51 | 63,678.61 | 67,277.23 |
| Chromos | | | | 3,064.85 | |
| Cinchona bark | 202,599.03 | 234,088.38 | 437,291.72 | 627,505.89 | 490,766.10 |
| Cloves | 1,718.19 | 6,225.22 | 77,245.71 | 74,744.39 | 52,283.80 |
| Cocoa | 217,819.02 | 284,365.22 | 289,875.35 | 271,327.51 | 291,978.12 |
| Cocoa beans | 104,474.79 | 117,879.52 | 143,677.65 | 160,223.39 | 119,059.18 |
| Cocoa butter | 313,285.35 | 332,646.61 | 415,875.00 | 558,910.08 | 390,605.47 |
| Coffee | 237,971.30 | 344,279.24 | 249,744.28 | 172,576.24 | 227,569.74 |
| Cubebs | | | 720.60 | 6,341.84 | |
| Diamonds | 2,413,618.81 | 3,964,617.42 | 3,884,870.06 | 6,041,160.04 | 5,802,655.73 |
| Earthenware | | | | 527.71 | |
| Eau de Cologne | | | | 282.28 | |
| Garden seeds | 25,942.94 | 30,702.89 | 54,238.49 | 41,374.35 | 68,750.28 |
| Glassware | | | | | 577.49 |
| Glycerin | | | 18,405.42 | 11,013.87 | 36,658.95 |
| Goatskins | 17,440.51 | | | | |
| Gold in bars | 90,166.82 | 50,235.65 | | | 10,234.28 |
| Gum damar | 8,166.09 | 7,307.41 | 9,934.88 | 6,215.97 | 6,965.28 |
| Hair combs | | | | 2,573.62 | 3,322.97 |
| Hemp and flax | | | | | 306,067.56 |
| Hides and skins | 195,284.32 | 290,045.70 | 484,355.21 | 318,353.61 | 2,257.23 |
| Household effects | | | 3,216.00 | 3,312.08 | |
| Indigo | 27,759.92 | 20,003.83 | 2,849.17 | | |
| Kapok | | | 24,260.35 | 64,502.97 | 53,809.15 |
| Liqueurs and gins | 18,326.63 | 27,661.66 | 31,823.24 | 33,986.87 | 44,461.23 |
| Mace | 8,322.54 | 21,503.29 | 13,352.08 | 24,958.33 | 12,870.56 |
| Madder | | 590.07 | 893.01 | 474.66 | 1,919.56 |
| Metallic capsules | 3,076.11 | 7,007.54 | 8,541.69 | 7,660.22 | 5,031.99 |
| Nutmegs | 42,832.80 | 86,422.41 | 60,432.77 | 122,860.06 | 40,214.46 |
| Oils, Haarlem, etc | 26,605.02 | 23,625.28 | 29,114.96 | 29,306.07 | 38,456.79 |
| Old copper | | | | | 5,911.62 |
| Paintings | 38,713.40 | 27,997.44 | 40,512.61 | 53,956.12 | 94,801.08 |
| Paper | 1,772.22 | 2,569.30 | 4,455.02 | 5,454.04 | 5,723.54 |
| Pepper | 62,217.65 | 18,084.75 | 28,340.76 | 252,283.79 | 92,859.62 |
| Plate glass | 8,287.25 | | | 877.37 | |
| Poppy and other seeds | | | | | 17,333.17 |
| Potatoes | | | | | 7,573.06 |
| Quinine | | | 13,296.63 | 40,790.71 | 5,223.91 |
| Rags and cotton tares | 25,909.43 | 21,104.32 | 46,595.98 | 16,110.97 | 30,961.68 |
| Rattan | | | 1,452.01 | 22,271.17 | |
| Rice | 195,069.66 | 72,374.99 | 55,335.45 | 19,623.84 | 25,838.35 |
| Rubber | 5,999.12 | 2,244.38 | 417.26 | 768.44 | 314.64 |
| Sardelles | 5,795.92 | 5,729.99 | 6,386.27 | 6,346.15 | 4,277.36 |
| Strawboards and straw covers | 13,149.14 | 11,335.19 | 24,549.85 | 16,363.56 | 11,756.22 |
| Sugar, refined | 908,499.36 | 177,874.12 | 28,717.92 | 770,832.50 | 107,223.91 |
| Tapioca flour | | | | 468.13 | 2,270.33 |
| Tea | 132,072.98 | 144,030.78 | 508,657.53 | 457,850.39 | 409,887.52 |
| Tin, Banka and Straits | 3,714,420.20 | 3,591,678.06 | 4,789,695.74 | 5,520,134.24 | 4,783,864.12 |
| Tobacco, Sumatra | | | | 756.17 | |
| Tortoise shells | | | | | |
| Turf litter | 9,852.48 | 2,676.68 | | 3,176.68 | 751.77 |
| Vanila beans | | | | 8,817.34 | 28,011.95 |
| Vegetables in brine | 9,068.08 | 9,116.06 | 19,896.73 | 1,667.91 | 34,297.94 |
| Wool | | | 2,090.83 | | |
| Sundries | 16,611.40 | 26,086.01 | 26,328.75 | 22,274.40 | 11,334.88 |
| Total | 9,363,303.74 | 10,177,896.85 | 12,837,784.95 | 16,051,891.74 | 13,988,978.52 |

The above returns show that diamonds and Sumatra leaf tobacco made up in 1902 over 75 per cent of Amsterdam's exports to the United States, and that the only other large items—of half a million dollars or above—were cinchona bark, hides and skins, sugar, and tin.

An interesting item is that of books in the Dutch language, which amount to about $50,000 per year. These go, for the most part, to the region about Grand Rapids, Mich., and to Iowa.

Paintings ran up to about $100,000 last year, the works of the present vigorous school of Dutch painters—Mesdag, the Marises, and, most of all, Israels—finding patronage in the United States. Most of the paintings invoiced here are the products of American artists residing at Laren or Egmond; the best-known names being those of Hitchcock and Melchers.

The exports to our new possessions from January 1 to November 1, 1902, have been, according to invoices authenticated in this office: Cheese, Hawaii, to Honolulu, 450 florins ($180.90); Porto Rico, to San Juan, Ponce, and Mayaguez, 50,627.83 florins ($20,352.39).

To Cuba, also, during the same period, there were exported: Santiago de Cuba, cheese, 2,218 florins ($892.02); Brazos de Santiago, candles, 916.25 florins ($368.33); Manzanillo, cheese, 739.39 florins ($297.23).

## UNITED STATES TRADE.

Great and increasing interest is taken here in things American. Our illustrated publications are found in the popular cafés and reading rooms, and our standard authors and even late novels are sold at all leading book stores.

While the most friendly feeling prevails toward American enterprises, it will be difficult to awaken interest in the exposition at St. Louis. The writer, who is brought into close contact with the leaders of trade, industry, and finance at Amsterdam, has sounded sentiment on this subject quietly for some months past, and finds a feeling very prevalent, and in some cases rooted, that practical benefits have not accrued from expositions in the past.

The number of American visitors has increased probably 25 per cent over last year, or about 20,000. Dividends of the hotel companies rest on this patronage. The Amstel and the Bible hotels have increased their facilities for accommodation, while a new American hotel has been erected upon the site of the old. The tide of English visitors, formerly reckoned upon, has disappeared altogether.

I have received during the year various letters on our trade methods, and inasmuch as they all bear on that most vital question, viz, How to sell American goods abroad, I quote from certain of them:

### TEXTILES.

With respect to textiles, the following extracts are taken from a letter written to a firm in the United States:

I beg to acknowledge receipt of your favor, and regret to see that you can not accept the terms asked by myself, re agency.

You say that this trade has always been done through "intermediary" houses in America, which I will readily accept; but I venture to give my opinion that I do not think this will be possible for your trade with our colonies, as I fear that the many commissions to be paid will increase the cost of the goods too much.

American staples will have to compete against the Dutch and the Manchester goods in the Dutch colonies, and as it is greatly a question of chops, established long ago, I think that it will take at least some time to get American goods "in."

Of course, in the beginning, suppliers on your side will have to sacrifice something, either by consigning or by making small allowances. Now, it seems quite natural to me that commission houses will not assist our shippers as well as the mills themselves, for if you stick to your "spot-cash terms," such commission houses will have to bear heavy outlays for trial shipments on consignments. Therefore I think that the mills, being the first hands, ought to grant these facilities.

Now, there is the question of competition.

*Dutch textiles.*—The mills are in direct communication with the shipping houses in Holland, so there are no commissions to be paid to anyone. Payments are made generally at thirty days.

*Manchester goods.*—The various English mills in the cotton district sell the cloth to the merchants, who attend to the shipping and, as a rule, give cost, insurance, and freight quotations via Southampton net cash, viz, remittance from the Dutch house one week after receipt of documents.

There are several other arrangements as regards financing, one month remittance, three and even six months' bills, etc., but those are not usual.

Manchester merchants have on the spot an agent, who looks after the business and gets a small commission.

You only deliver the goods "free alongside" and "spot cash," so that I should want for the forwarding of the goods some representative, against say 1 per cent commission. For the payment of the goods, I should either want to appoint the same representative, or make arrangements with bankers, for opening banking credit, which I understand from my bank here would cost about three-fourths per cent. Then my own commission and small traveling expenses, etc., would come to another 1 per cent.

The freight from New York on through bill via Amsterdam-Rotterdam would be higher than from Southampton direct; also the insurance, and as shippers would have to pay interest on the bills from date of payment by the bank in your city up to date of their payment here, I think that you will find my fears just—that too many commissions and heavier expenses may perhaps upset everything.

There is a second side to the question. In case you do not wish to give way, I should have to look out for a commission house which must be A1, and also must understand thoroughly the dry goods trade, for otherwise it would not be of any use to our shippers here, for almost everything depends on the good outturn of the goods and the character of the mills which produce them.

Moreover, such a commission house would not stick to your mills, but could buy from others too. And would you be willing to supply this commission house with your goods for the Java trade exclusively through my hands? Unless I could get such assurance, the agency would not be of any use to me.

I hope you will have the kindness to mention a good house with which you have long-established connections and to which you are selling your goods regularly for other markets.

I myself still think that if your house could ship these goods and quote cost and insurance Java ports, and I could make arrangements with my bankers for payment against those bills of lading in New York, all further trouble could be avoided; you paying me a certain commission on the turnover.

I may mention that another manufacturer of American hammocks is willing to adopt this system. and I trust you will follow suit.

Another party has written the office that there is a good demand for American goods, but that there will be no chance to do business if America insists on cash terms. Woven fancies, linings, sateens, drills, and prints are in greatest demand.

The same gentleman informs me this week that letters received accord more liberal terms as regards cash payments.

### CLOCKS.

Some time ago, this office received the following letter:

As we wish to begin exporting and intend to send a representative to Europe, we would like to know what is the duty on American clocks imported into the Netherlands, and would be pleased to have your opinion on the outlook for them in that country. We manufacture low-priced articles exclusively—alarms, gilt and china clocks, watches and movements. Any information you will be kind enough to give us on the condition of the market will be highly appreciated.

The following reply, illustrating some of our methods, was received by the firm here which was good enough to write the people in the United States:

We are in receipt of your favor of September 28, and have noted same carefully. Beg to state that we are at present fully occupied with our domestic trade. There are certain times of the year, mid-winter and mid-summer, when we are in a position to export clocks, and our recent inquiries of the American consul were only in preparation for any exporting we might be able to do later on.

Under separate cover, we are sending you our catalogue. Any quotation we would make would be f. o. b. cars New York, and our terms would be draft attached to bills of lading on your New York office, or whatever firm you indicated in New York to handle your shipments; all sample orders to be paid for at the regular price.

### FURNITURE, MACHINES, PAPER, ETC.

The American Trading Company, which has recently been converted into a joint-stock company with 500,000 florins ($200,000) capital and is engaged in Dutch-American import business, has furnished me the following:

*Furniture.*—There is an extended business to be done in the different kinds of American furniture, especially cheap grades. The better class of work, especially hand-carved, is made more cheaply in Holland. American manufacturers, however, would find a larger market for their goods if they would allow themselves to be advised by Dutch importers, and would make the designs desired without regard to the American shapes. The Holland people like their own designs, which can be imitated cheaply in America.

Especial attention should be given that all goods be furnished knocked down, only the wooden parts carved and planed, and boxed for export. The fittings have to be put together in special factories here.

In this way, an enormous business could be done throughout Europe, because American prices are far cheaper than European. The American finish is not liked in Holland, therefore all articles should be sent in the white.

*Office desks.*—The American model is introduced everywhere, but must also be furnished in the white.

*Wooden ware and household goods.*—The demand is increasing; wooden specialties as well as small ironware are well known everywhere, but the delivery is slow, owing to lack of goods for export in the factories.

*Paints and varnishes.*—Quantities of dry paints, and especially varnishes, are sent to the Continent. The export would increase if delivery were quicker. During the last twelve months, the average monthly shipment of paints and varnishes to Holland alone has been $4,602.

*Prairie-grass carpets.*—These are asked for more and more in this country, but there seems to be no competition in the United States.

*Organs.*—Holland is one of the countries using, proportionately, the largest number of house organs and harmoniums. Most houses in the countryside have a small instrument.

*Ironware, hammers, tools, etc.*—America is producing a first quality, which is very good, but too expensive; and a third quality, which is cheap, but not durable enough for the professional workman.

Germany is producing a medium quality, which is sufficient, and far cheaper than the American first quality. American manufacturers should make such a medium quality, and they would be successful in export business. First and second qualities are forged; third, cast.

*Locks and padlocks.*—All kinds are good articles for export, but the cheaper kinds especially have to meet German competition.

*Stoves.*—These are of special design, furnished by European importers, as prices are far lower in America, but the patterns are quite different. In parts of stoves, a large business could be done if the iron-plate goods were made in America, the tin parts here, and the stove put together here.

*Agricultural goods.*—Heavy machinery is used here very much. The exporters would find it profitable to keep samples in Holland, as heavy machinery will not be bought from drawings or catalogues.

*Machinery.*—In the past three to four years, a large quantity of American machinery has been exported to Holland, and has been received with open arms by the people who use it. To-day, the export of American machinery is small, and the only reason is that Germany can imitate the American inventions more cheaply than the Union can furnish the goods.

*Paper for printing.*—Notwithstanding Swedish, German, and Dutch competition, it is possible to export American paper, as very cheap offers have been made by American manufacturers, and some trial orders from Holland printers have been very successful. However, as soon as the American manufacturers found a market for their product in their own country, they stopped exporting and did not even carry out their contracts. When they could no longer place their manufactures in the United States, they tried again to export their paper, but everybody was then afraid to import it. If contracts could be made, or better, if stock could be laid down in Europe, success would not fail.

*Paper packings.*—There would be a good market here for the American manufactures, especially boxes for soap, confectionery, chocolate, cocoa, tea, starch, etc. These boxes must be furnished flat, to save freight.

*Flint and sand paper.*—For a few years past, flint and sand paper has been imported from America in large quantities.

*Oilcloth.*—The export of American oilcloth has been increasing of late, but there seem to be only a few manufacturers who make the article for export. If there were more to compete with the English product, they would have good results, as oilcloth is an article of importance in this country. The average shipment during the last months has been: From America, $4,200; from England, $12,500.

*Drugs.*—We have had frequent demands for American drugs, but this trade can only become of importance if manufacturers are willing to spend some money in advertising. In that case, these goods could be imported with good results.

*Plumbing materials.*—These are asked for and used here on all new buildings. American water-closets, especially, will become a great article if manufacturers are willing to exhibit samples. American sanitary plumbing material is known as the best in the world.

*Benzine (gasoline) and turpentine.*—There is a good demand for these articles, as they are known as the cheapest on the market. We advise manufacturers to send offers.

*Canned fruits.*—These are imported in large quantities, notwithstanding the duty. If the fruits were cooked only in pure water, without the addition of any sugar, the duty would only be 5 per cent. American exporters should try to supply them in this way, as other European countries have similar rates.

*Meat preserves.*—Large quantities are sent by well-introduced firms. For other manufacturers, however, there would also be a market here if the goods were properly advertised.

*Cottons and dry goods.*—As soon as American manufacturers are ready to compete with the English Manchester and Oxford goods, especially in cottons and linings, there will be a large field here. Importers are anxious to get American dry goods at the same prices as British manufactures, because the British makers are going round in Holland to sell to retailers.

*Hats.*—We have lately seen the American flag in many hat stores in Holland. That is the best sign that the people like American hats and ask for them.

*Motor boats.*—Some manufacturers have agents here. There is a market for motor boats at a reasonable price, Holland being a country of water and boats being in continual demand.

*Notes.*—Americans excel in the manufacture of goods for their own use. Some of these goods are very well received here; others are not wanted at all, owing to the strange models, or their finish. It is very hard to make American manufacturers understand that they must make other patterns for other countries.

Furthermore, Americans should be more liberal in their way of doing business. They generally ask payment against shipping documents, even if they know that they are dealing with a first-class firm. In their own country, they give credits from six to nine months. Everything received from America must be accepted, whether delivered according to order and in good condition or not.

It has happened that a manufacturer has sent a different kind of goods from those ordered and paid for in New York, and they were not fitted for the purpose of the receiver; however, he had to accept them.

It would be advisable to have some good firms here represent American manufacturers, and, if possible, have stock on hand.

Another drawback to American export is that shipping agents sometimes overcharge freight rates.

American manufacturers should take care in shipping their goods, and not be satisfied merely with receiving the money, or they will not obtain a second order.

The United States is known as a country of the greatest industry and of the highest exporting power; its goods are wanted in Europe; but American manufacturers must not hesitate to make present sacrifices in the interest of future trade.

### SHOES.

Lately, there has been a growing demand for American shoes, in men's as well as in women's styles. Some manufacturers have introduced these goods here with a moderate degree of success, especially in the finer grades. The retail selling prices vary from 4.50 florins ($1.80) to 25 florins ($10) per pair. There is no prejudice against American shoes. The local factories confine themselves for the most part to the manufacture of the cheaper and inferior grades, though in some cases fine shoes are also turned out. The cost of production varies from 2.50 florins ($1) to 7.50 florins ($3) per pair. Some of the local factories are fitted out, in a measure, with American machinery, principally that of "The Goodyear Welt Company." The success of this machinery is, however, indifferent, owing largely to the fact that it is operated by inexperienced hands.

The entrance duty is 5 per cent on all grades and the tare is from 3 to 3½ per cent. It is advisable to duplicate the German lasts, for the American are not, as a rule, suited to Dutch feet. While payments are often tardy, if proper precautions are used, losses rarely occur. A certain amount of good can be done by sending representatives, but at the same time it will be found necessary to have a permanent local representative.

Germany and Austria supply the largest quantity of shoes sold in Holland. It is difficult to compare these goods with those of American make, other than to say that the American shoe is far superior in material and workmanship, but it is also much more costly. One great drawback to trade has been the long delay in filling small orders which have been sent to complete numbers which have been sold out. The only remedy for this would be the establishment here of a whole-sale distributing station, which would greatly develop the sale of the American shoe.

This office could dispose of advertising matter, if sent; it would be advisable to have it printed in the Dutch language, and it would also be desirable to advertise in the trade journals moderately, though the latter would not be of much use unless a show room and distributing station were established here.

### BICYCLES AND AUTOMOBILES.

The bicycle trade is good and promises to remain so for some time to come. The interest in cycling is now about what it was in the United States five to eight years ago.

The trade is not, however, so large in regular goods as in "special offerings" made, from time to time, by the American manufacturer, including frames, stripped wheels, and sundries. The reason for this is that the majority of dealers prefer to do their own assembling, and by taking advantage of these special lots—usually offered at the beginning or end of the year—they can put up a good wheel under their own name much more cheaply than they can buy the American stand-ard makes. Another reason is that American wheels can not be repaired at all places on the continent, owing to the difference in size of threads and fittings.

There is at present no American automobile trade here. While American makes are somewhat higher in price than those of conti-nental manufacture, it can not be said that this would prove a serious drawback. One objection is, however, the model. The style of machine most preferred seems to be the one known as the "Duc," and is something like an open wagonette, with one wide seat in front, and two side seats in rear, with room, as a rule, for six persons. The fuel used is benzine; the tires are all double tubes, on the Dunlop or continental system, while the machine itself is much heavier.

American manufacturers will do more business in motorcycles just now than in automobiles; here, however, the price is a consideration. A first-class motorcycle of continental manufacture can be purchased by the wholesaler for 225 florins ($90) f. o. b. here, while comparatively the same machine, American make, will cost f. o. b. vessel, New York, from $130 to $150. This is, however, the field for several years to come, and the motorcycle, being far more popular here than in the Union—coming as it does within the reach of so many more persons—it is bound to have a sale far larger than that of the automobile.

The manner of introduction is exceedingly important, and in order to gain this trade, the manufacturer must change his present method radically. He must make up his mind at the start that there are two sides to the question, and instead of demanding "cash against documents in New York" he must be willing to give his agent some assistance and treat him in the same manner that he would were he placing the same agency in the United States. There is no more risk in doing that here than there, if proper precautions are used.

The manufacturer who will appoint a reliable firm with an established trade, give a machine in consignment, and agree to fill orders on the basis of one-third with order and two-thirds on receipt and examination of goods on this side, will get the business.

The following figures show the extent to which bicycles are used here, the amount of the tax and the number of machines for 1899 and 1900 being given:

| Description. | Tax. | | Number. | |
|---|---|---|---|---|
| | Florins. | U. S. currency. | 1899. | 1900. |
| Bicycles for one person | 0.50 | $0.20 | 20,589 | 27,363 |
| Do | 1.00 | .40 | 25,277 | 31,464 |
| Do | 2.00 | .80 | 40,325 | 45,379 |
| Bicycles for more than one person | 4.00 | 1.60 | 474 | 477 |
| Bicycles of letters | 1.50 | .60 | 3,146 | 3,254 |
| Bicycles of sellers | 1.00 | .40 | 4,614 | 5,291 |

The field for automobiles is now held by French and Belgian makers. The Dion, Panhard, Peugeot, Mors, and Darracq are the best known French, and the Dechamps and Herstal, Belgian machines.

Manufacturers in the United States have been making efforts to compete in steam automobiles, but these are thought to be too lightly built and of too complicated mechanism.

Only in a few cities are there opportunities for filling the accumulators, which restricts for the present the use of electric machines. Prospects for the steam mobiles seem more favorable, but manufacturers must deliver the machines with detachable tires or rims suited for European tires, and they must, under no circumstances, use single tubes, as these do not sell on the Continent. Up to the present, no steam mobiles have been used in the Netherlands. It will be necessary to send a sample first, as every automobile must have a license here, and this is not granted until the machine has been examined by a Government officer.

Prices must be not higher than 2,000 florins ($804) retail. The import duty is 5 per cent ad valorem.

## HATS.

Dunlap and Stetson hats are now sold here. I am told that although prices are high from a Dutch standpoint—12 guilders ($4.80) for a Dunlap derby and 10 guilders ($4) for a Stetson of same style—sales are satisfactory.

The leading English and German makes are also sold. The ordinary price for derby hats is 4 or 5 guilders ($1.60 to $2).

## COAL.

Although nearly 7,000,000 tons of coal are imported into the Netherlands annually, none at all has come from the United States during the year. Special Consular Reports, Foreign Markets for American Coal, contain about all that can be said upon this topic. Freight rates forbid business at this time.

## CASH REGISTERS.

Mr. Cord. H. van Erk, resident agent of the National Cash Register Company, of Dayton, Ohio, writes this office:

As in all other countries, the business in cash registers is nearly exclusively in our hands. Now and then, other cash registers of German, English, or Dutch manufacture are offered for sale, but none can get a trade on a paying basis.

The business of the National Cash Register Company, however, is increasing steadily. A few years ago, sales amounted to only one machine a week; now there is about one machine every day, and 1902 shows an increase over 1901 of about 45 per cent.

Except England, Germany, and Denmark, there is no country in Europe where the cash register is more in use than here.

Prices range from $14 up to $400. The machines mostly sold are either cheap autographics or high grade registers of $300 and upward.

*List of firms importing goods from the United States.*

| Name of firm. | Articles. | Name of firm. | Articles. |
|---|---|---|---|
| **AMSTERDAM.** | | **AMSTERDAM—cont'd.** | |
| M. Adler | Bicycle parts. | Figee & de Kruyff | Machinery. |
| P. de Bruyne | Tobacco. | Goldschmit & Sohn | Lard. |
| Bulsing & Heslenfeld | Flour. | M. G. van Genderingen | Bicycles. |
| Van den Berg & Co | Hardware and agricultural implements. | G. E. Gude | Flour. |
| Gustav Briegleb | Vaseline. | J. C. Grootjan | Do. |
| B. & W. Birnbaum | Flour. | H. Glessen | Do. |
| A. J. H. van Beusichem | Flour, bacon, and lard. | G. Gompen | Shoe pegs and leather. |
| J. J. Bolten & Zoon | Flour. | J. J. Nye | Flour. |
| G. Bruning & Zoon | Do. | H. F. Osleck | Do. |
| H. C. de la Rey | Do. | Oldenboom & Lely | Essential oils and extracts. |
| J. Beuns & Zoon | Leather. | | |
| Brusse & Gransberg | Tobacco. | Peck & Co | Machinery and tools. |
| M. Breebaart | Organs. | Gebroeders Peters | Feathers. |
| C. C. Bender | Do. | Pitlo & Lageman | Staves. |
| G. H. F. Benier | Typewriters and desks. | Pharmac. Handels-vereeniging. | Chemicals, roots, and essential oils. |
| J. van den Berg Wzn | Cocoa beans and coffee. | Pardow & Rust | Coffee. |
| J. Buys Wzn | Flour. | J. Rose & Co | Varnish and paint. |
| Calkoen & Zoon | Cotton. | E. Rinkel | Flour. |
| Kampen & Co | Apples and dried fruit. | Gebrs. Rikkers | School slates and crayon. |
| F. van den Corput | Cigars. | | |
| J. B. Claus Huis & Zoon | Casing and lard. | Oscar Rohte & Jiskoot | Tobacco. |
| Van Dam & Co | Cotton. | A. J. Reynvaan | Cigars. |
| Henri Dentz | Tobacco. | Reyffert & Stilz | Tobacco. |
| J. B. Dievelaar & Co | Bacon, hams, sausages, and lard. | Fred. Stieltjes & Co | Typewriters, school furniture, regulators, valves. |
| G. H. van Erk | Cash registers. | | |
| J. A. van Eernien | Flour and sirup. | G. Stronk | Beef. |
| Wed. Joh. van Elden | Clothespins and washboards, general importers. | Smidt & Amesz | Flour. |
| | | F. C. Stahle | Do. |
| | | Singer Mfg. Co | Sewing machines. |

*List of firms importing goods from the United States—Continued.*

| Name of firm. | Articles. | Name of firm. | Articles. |
|---|---|---|---|
| **AMSTERDAM—cont'd.** | | **AMSTERDAM—cont'd.** | |
| Schaap & Van Veen ... | Tobacco. | P. C. Vis & Co .......... | Flour, oil cake, etc. |
| L. Salomonson .......... | Cigars. | W. Ankersmit & Zoon.. | Tobacco. |
| Stoffers & Co ........... | Ashes, dyewood extracts. | Jacob Ankersmit & Zoon. | Do. |
| Th. W. Sanders......... | Dyewood extracts. | Perry & Co............. | Soap, inkstands, etc. |
| | Sausages and canned meat. | American Trading Co . | Furniture. |
| H. G. Scholten & Co.... | | Kuyk & Abas ........... | Sail cloth. |
| J. H. L. Salts & Co ...... | Machinery and tools. | A. van Ardenne......... | Beef and lard. |
| J. Tas Ezn.............. | Flour and dried apples. | Gebrs. Catz............. | Fruits. |
| E. E. Visser & Zoon .... | Lard and honey. | Gebrs. Sickesz.......... | Honey and sirup. |
| J. & J. Vinke ........... | Beef. | G. J. Smit & Co......... | Tobacco. |
| H. van der Velden&Co. | Do. | Van Gelder Zonen ..... | Wood pulp and paper. |
| J. T. Visser ............. | Flour. | Gebauer & Menges .... | Lard, sirup, honey. |
| Worthington Pump Co. | Pumps and machinery. | J. H. A. Gebing......... | Tobacco. |
| M. Witsenburg, jr ....... | Flour. | G. Herlema ........... | Do. |
| Wed. W. Wieffering .... | Lard and sirup. | E. Rosenwald Bros..... | Do. |
| J. Witmondt .......... | Bicycles. | H. L. Rosenfeld ....... | Do. |
| A. P. van de Water & Zoon. | Flour. | Amst. Tabak Handel Co. | Do. |
| G. S. Goldschmeding ... | Organs. | F. & E. Cranz........... | Do. |
| Geveke & Co........... | Machinery. | H. Oldenkott & Zoon ... | Do. |
| J. G. Gaveel ........... | Hams, lard, and beef. | Ronge & Drost........ | Sirup. |
| Gunters & Meusers .... | Hardware. | D. Schumacher ........ | Coffee. |
| H. van de Grient....... | Hams and bacon. | Gebr. Warendorff...... | Dried fruits. |
| Höweler & Co.......... | Hardware. | B. W. de Jong & Co.... | Tobacco. |
| G. van der Horst & Zoon | Grain. | Driessen & Van Ommen & Co. | Do. |
| L. Hoyack & Co ........ | Do. | | |
| Hes & Co................ | Flour. | **EDAM.** | |
| Hay & Biller............ | Do. | A. Banning ............ | Flour. |
| Heybroek & Co ........ | Coffee. | | |
| Hausemann & Hütte .. | Hardware, general merchandise. | **KOOG AAN DE ZAAN.** | |
| Holcombe & Co ........ | General merchandise. | T. Crok ................ | Flour. |
| Wed. de Jonge ......... | Flour. | | |
| Arnold de Jong ........ | Hides. | **HAARLEM.** | |
| G. F. Jusjaans .......... | Organs. | Grippeling & Verkley.. | Flour. |
| H. R. Jurjans........... | Oatmeal and matzena. | Hunk Wefers & Bettink | Hardware. |
| Joh. Koopmans & Co... | Bicycles, flour, and scales. | **HILVERSUM.** | |
| J. & B. H. Klasen....... | Beef and pork. | J. G. Lasonder ......... | Wine. |
| P. E. Kupfer & Zoon ... | Flour and oil cake. | | |
| J. A. Kluytenaar ....... | Tobacco. | **DE RYP.** | |
| G. Kettner ............. | Organs. | Groothandel ........... | Flour. |
| Kirberger & Co ....... | Fruits. | | |
| H. van der Kaay & Co . | Oatmeal. | **ALKMAAR.** | |
| Kirberger & Kesper.... | Books. | T. S. Ohmstede ........ | Washboards and Clothes pins. |
| J. H. Kruse............. | Tobacco. | | |
| Landré & Glinderman . | Machinery. | **WORMERVEER.** | |
| M. Luchsinger & Co.... | Flour. | H. S. Pieper Zoon...... | Dyewoods and extracts. |
| M. Levenbach ......... | Leather. | | |
| S. de Leeuw & Zoon.... | Do. | **KROMMENIE.** | |
| Linther & Cokart ...... | Tobacco. | Alb. Schut ............. | Flour. |
| C. Moerbeek .......... | Flour, honey, and sirup. | Verwers Vernis Fact... | Machinery. |
| My. voor Meel en Broodfabrieken. | Flour. | **ZAANDAM.** | |
| B. H. Manus............ | Tobacco. | P. Verkade & Co....... | Flour. |
| P. C. Muller & Co....... | Machinery. | Klaas Blans............ | Flour and starch. |
| S. H. van Minden & Zoon. | Tobacco. | W. Lenselink & Zoon.. | Flour. |
| W. G. and K. de Wit .... | Machinery. | **BEVERWYK.** | |
| Willems & Morel....... | Scythestones. | P. Verhagen Pzn. & Co. | Flour. |
| A. Witmondt & Co ..... | Gas stoves. | | |
| W. F. Weyntjes ........ | Hardware. | **LEIDEN.** | |
| D. van der Zee, jr ...... | Flour. | J. N. van der Heyden.. | Flour. |
| Van der Zee & Grippeling. | Do. | | |
| Beerbrewery de Valk.. | Corn flour. | | |
| Delibrewery ........... | Do. | | |
| Glasener & Zoon....... | Flour. | | |
| Ch. van Messel........ | Typewriters. | | |
| Schade van Westrum .. | Lard. | | |
| Royal Candle Factory . | Wax. | | |
| N. V. Koelit............ | Hides. | | |
| Louis Hirsch........... | Fruits. | | |
| Leopold Herz.......... | Do. | | |
| Gerhard Polak......... | Flour. | | |

## NETHERLANDS CHAMBER OF COMMERCE IN NEW YORK.

In concluding this report, it is with the liveliest gratification that I am able to chronicle the fact, just given to the press here, of the establishment of a Netherlands Chamber of Commerce at New York.

The preliminary meeting at New York was presided over by Baron Gevers, minister of the Netherlands, and the following gentlemen have consented to enter the executive board: Col. John Jacob Astor, Mr. Stuyvesant Fish, Mr. W. Bayard van Rensselaer, Mr. Cornelius Vanderbilt.

To represent the present generation of Hollanders, the following are the members of the executive board: Mr. D. G. Boissevain, Mr. John F. Praeger, Mr. J. Schimmel, Mr. J. Ripperda Wierdsma. The secretary is Mr. A. van de Sande Bakhiuzen.

From the inception of the project, in cooperation with Mr. E. G. de Clercq., secretary of the Netherlands Society for the Extension of Industry, of Haarlem, this office has done all in its power to aid in the establishment of the chamber, believing that it will be a powerful agency in promoting the interests of the two great commercial nations.

FRANK D. HILL, *Consul.*

AMSTERDAM, *November 1, 1902.*

---

## ROTTERDAM. [a]

The wholesale and retail trade in the Netherlands has, generally speaking, not been satisfactory so far this year. This is to some extent to be ascribed to the overproduction of the two staple commodities, sugar and coffee, which greatly influence general trade in this country; further, to the less favorable industrial position of the great purchaser from the Netherlands, Germany, and also largely to the smallness of last year's corn crop in the United States. Owing to the above conditions, ocean and river traffic has decreased somewhat. At Rotterdam, the decrease in ocean traffic for the first nine months of this year amounted to 314 vessels and 143,110 net registered tons. The decrease in traffic with Germany may be best illustrated by mentioning that some months ago, more than 500,000 tons of Rhine barge capacity was lying idle at this port. In this country, where cattle raising is an important industry, the highness of corn prices, caused by the small American crop, has been much felt, and although beef rose in unison with the price of corn and other cattle food, the advance was not sufficient to allow the beef and pork raisers any profits.

The trade outlook, however, is improving. Good grain crops, according to an old maxim, cause prosperity, and good grain crops are reported from the supplying countries. This will cause ocean freights, which have been low all the year, to rise again somewhat, and a rise in ocean freight rates acts beneficially on all branches of the transit trade, the most important trade of this country.

Crops in the Netherlands have turned out fairly satisfactory, as far as quantity is concerned, but the quality of most of the cereals and seeds has suffered more or less from this summer's inclement weather. Hay is plentiful and of first-class quality. The rapeseed crop is

---

[a] See also Appendix.

larger than the average of former years.  The oat crop is also larger than usual, as much beet-root land has lately been planted to oats.

Those engaged in horticulture have, as a rule, not found this year profitable.  Pears are very scarce and apples far from plentiful. Early fruits ripened very late, and all suffered from want of sunshine.

In the following pages, I submit such detailed information on the commerce and industries of the Netherlands and Rotterdam for 1901 as was not contained in my last annual report, besides such details as I have been able to obtain for 1902.

### IMPORTS AND EXPORTS.

The importation of merchandise, excepting chalk, coal, and stone, was (in tons of 1,000 kilograms, or 2,205 pounds):

| Year. | In the Netherlands. | At Rotterdam. | Share of Rotterdam in total imports. |
|---|---|---|---|
| | | | Per cent. |
| 1891 | 9,370,891 | 3,904,765 | 41.66 |
| 1892 | 9,491,995 | 3,934,564 | 41.45 |
| 1893 | 9,976,690 | 4,624,528 | 46.35 |
| 1894 | 11,262,137 | 5,358,349 | 47.56 |
| 1895 | 11,431,440 | 5,819,158 | 50.91 |
| 1896 | 13,392,458 | 7,057,642 | 52.69 |
| 1897 | 14,668,113 | 7,939,861 | 54.13 |
| 1898 | 15,487,658 | 8,449,529 | 54.55 |
| 1899 | 16,591,297 | 9,163,260 | 55.22 |
| 1900 | 16,420,644 | 9,286,792 | 56.55 |

*Total imports at Rotterdam.*

| Articles. | 1898. | 1899. | 1900. | 1901. |
|---|---|---|---|---|
| | Pounds. | Pounds. | Pounds. | Pounds. |
| Ammunition | 872,872 | 1,124,543 | 1,298,686 | 1,086,818 |
| Animal charcoal | 3,759,789 | 3,725,911 | 3,251,509 | 3,484,188 |
| Ashes | 30,338,580 | 28,273,777 | 28,788,663 | 25,714,981 |
| Bark | 1,186,977 | 1,713,582 | 1,565,056 | 2,858,559 |
| Beans and pease | 83,888,317 | 78,644,548 | 73,801,664 | 88,936,445 |
| Beer and malt extract | 12,801,518 | 14,756,852 | 15,800,121 | 17,297,381 |
| Bran | 43,998,782 | 67,983,177 | 46,977,007 | 78,324,415 |
| Bread, biscuits, etc | 7,861,641 | 7,278,924 | 6,149,790 | 6,855,790 |
| Butter | 2,590,980 | 2,168,848 | 1,155,931 | 1,661,605 |
| Cattle food | 207,671,733 | 263,968,248 | 250,451,417 | 298,678,349 |
| Cereals: | | | | |
| Wheat | 2,071,120,735 | 1,818,203,308 | 2,009,616,052 | 2,659,925,646 |
| Rye | 815,834,985 | 763,019,992 | 928,779,001 | 974,101,086 |
| Barley | 731,705,808 | 628,252,489 | 491,532,711 | 575,377,436 |
| Corn | 1,334,964,092 | 1,354,824,314 | 1,050,558,744 | 766,728,316 |
| Oats | 504,022,429 | 596,149,834 | 783,412,318 | 231,815,834 |
| Buckwheat | 58,783,406 | 38,568,042 | 20,461,011 | 29,498,137 |
| Rice | 149,472,517 | 140,782,140 | 121,253,024 | 185,585,463 |
| Other kinds | 24,835,382 | 35,647,484 | 60,751,175 | 44,265,927 |
| Chalk, raw and ground | 879,034 | 487,098 | 1,500,935 | 730,965 |
| Cheese | 401,229 | 367,849 | 487,648 | 735,060 |
| Coal | 1,130,494,754 | 1,592,845,443 | 2,579,558,252 | 1,262,496,908 |
| Coffee | 182,590,133 | 185,640,673 | 175,437,759 | 207,013,169 |
| Cotton, raw | 40,201,278 | 57,521,356 | 45,051,736 | 45,825,624 |
| Drapers' ware | 43,717,428 | 45,271,644 | 43,286,071 | 36,815,469 |
| Drugs, dyestuffs chemicals | 476,677,641 | 500,694,263 | 539,959,132 | 487,815,924 |
| Earthenware and tiles | 68,724,748 | 70,366,888 | 63,585,266 | 58,343,714 |
| Engines and machinery | 67,881,273 | 81,878,372 | 92,527,066 | 82,683,405 |
| Fish | 22,592,583 | 22,732,827 | 21,037,091 | 28,362,326 |
| Fish oil | 13,163,960 | 15,046,755 | 11,415,700 | 14,391,430 |
| Flax and hemp | 45,399,765 | 31,277,398 | 31,977,541 | 45,684,549 |
| Flour | 246,889,588 | 276,585,978 | 213,653,824 | 292,867,905 |
| Fruits | 105,825,773 | 121,135,505 | 112,329,149 | 99,057,545 |
| Glass and glassware | 34,694,350 | 36,711,668 | 42,306,363 | 46,187,546 |
| Gold | 2,620 | 3,980 | 3,929 | 1,505 |
| Ground nuts | 33,897,470 | 31,806,006 | 37,426,650 | 41,048,980 |
| Hides, skins, and leather | 36,352,299 | 37,753,866 | 36,065,356 | 40,702,183 |

*Total imports at Rotterdam*—Continued.

| Articles. | 1898. | 1899. | 1900. | 1901. |
|---|---|---|---|---|
| | *Pounds.* | *Pounds.* | *Pounds.* | *Pounds.* |
| Hops | 1,179,629 | 1,179,944 | 989,287 | 1,232,607 |
| Lard | 78,992,791 | 83,506,104 | 68,282,388 | 68,764,628 |
| Lime | 1,629,661 | 2,429,126 | 17,244,698 | 22,088,266 |
| Manganese | 1,328,230 | 686,976 | 640,319 | 3,742,825 |
| Manure | 253,564,876 | 338,122,906 | 237,961,660 | 224,497,095 |
| Margarin: | | | | |
| Butter | 628,724 | 543,756 | 445,394 | 511,683 |
| Raw | 96,413,751 | 95,325,824 | 100,811,819 | 102,832,924 |
| Meat | 40,797,493 | 29,048,254 | 26,832,390 | 26,023,554 |
| Mercury | 33,178,422 | 43,302,307 | 52,648,944 | 51,453,184 |
| Metal: | | | | |
| Articles | 228,853,072 | 265,564,862 | 279,244,449 | 328,096,701 |
| Raw | 789,261,924 | 1,199,392,819 | 1,408,994,059 | 842,514,849 |
| Mineral spring water | 80,945,787 | 54,020,850 | 36,976,663 | 40,766,974 |
| Oils: | | | | |
| Ground nut | 3,170,006 | 4,475,570 | 4,433,157 | 4,439,855 |
| Cotton seed | 83,925,842 | 85,825,791 | 91,709,556 | 118,122,332 |
| Sesame | 20,216,608 | 19,258,173 | 15,334,341 | 13,607,205 |
| Petroleum | 688,795,738 | 662,478,001 | 583,729,890 | 685,745,144 |
| Palm and other | 121,036,040 | 123,055,988 | 152,361,543 | 156,753,496 |
| Ores | 5,854,325,424 | 6,896,241,273 | 6,943,837,441 | 7,504,189,680 |
| Palm nuts | 48,779,227 | 47,194,374 | 55,419,147 | 51,405,651 |
| Paper | 65,732,982 | 70,992,163 | 86,799,176 | 76,482,212 |
| Potato flour and its products | 51,067,317 | 59,947,716 | 56,563,610 | 54,852,701 |
| Rags | 40,188,210 | 40,249,084 | 51,231,136 | 55,056,208 |
| Rattans | 1,401,757 | 1,643,343 | 2,820,489 | 2,743,455 |
| Ropes | 6,098,712 | 5,826,263 | 7,336,421 | 6,860,779 |
| Resin | 73,450,137 | 61,545,519 | 57,909,069 | 67,677,707 |
| Salt | 26,921,218 | 23,617,713 | 32,875,414 | 35,316,290 |
| Seeds | 201,010,788 | 360,785,289 | 413,432,455 | 363,641,936 |
| Sirup | 31,255,252 | 27,912,355 | 26,830,531 | 26,832,980 |
| Spices | 6,779,804 | 10,741,989 | 7,925,874 | 7,254,271 |
| Spirits | 28,058,788 | 33,509,043 | 19,353,363 | 17,137,450 |
| Stone | 96,762,162 | 92,203,982 | 160,817,693 | 187,351,289 |
| Sugar: | | | | |
| Raw | 45,881,741 | 48,955,163 | 85,899,268 | 81,556,595 |
| All other | 61,984,943 | 67,062,884 | 76,872,169 | 72,909,001 |
| Sulphur | 7,608,093 | 1,969,752 | 6,820,061 | 5,863,749 |
| Tallow, suet, etc | 54,152,160 | 55,729,502 | 63,608,952 | 68,402,006 |
| Tar and pitch | 10,321,699 | 10,302,525 | 17,835,536 | 8,633,742 |
| Tea | 6,539,103 | 6,412,908 | 6,195,880 | 6,518,919 |
| Tobacco and cigars | 68,132,256 | 76,583,195 | 77,011,858 | 74,041,279 |
| Vinegar | 2,060,956 | 2,245,731 | 2,218,335 | 1,893,398 |
| Wine | 66,483,197 | 78,041,330 | 76,757,072 | 79,186,564 |
| Wood: | | | | |
| For ship building and timber | 1,425,191,167 | 1,494,496,405 | 1,417,765,382 | 1,402,659,575 |
| Dyewoods | 61,483,396 | 54,179,564 | 62,580,606 | 63,138,308 |
| Hard woods | 82,419,818 | 37,750,783 | 52,944,581 | 98,334,337 |
| Wool | 11,662,341 | 17,421,386 | 17,316,708 | 24,395,147 |
| Yarns | 65,648,315 | 67,126,063 | 56,630,075 | 50,604,627 |
| Miscellaneous | 215,992,842 | 136,578,884 | 157,667,467 | 147,358,358 |
| Total | 19,881,312,363 | 21,846,951,348 | 23,188,564,208 | 22,447,544,779 |

*Imports and exports of principal articles from January 1 to June 30, 1902.*

| Articles. | Imports. | | Exports. | |
|---|---|---|---|---|
| | At Rotterdam. | In the Netherlands. | From Rotterdam. | From the Netherlands. |
| | *Pounds.* | *Pounds.* | *Pounds.* | *Pounds.* |
| Ashes | 12,898,600 | 69,627,800 | 5,801,400 | 41,173,000 |
| Bark | 888,800 | 11,884,400 | 987,800 | 8,808,800 |
| Beer and malt extract | 7,211,600 | 16,577,000 | 7,466,800 | 25,297,800 |
| Butter | 473,000 | 719,400 | 833,800 | 22,187,000 |
| Cereals: | | | | |
| Wheat | 978,595,200 | 1,710,066,400 | 842,338,200 | 303,913,400 |
| Rye | 337,785,800 | 534,963,200 | 204,188,600 | 247,566,000 |
| Barley | 236,374,600 | 300,127,600 | 140,538,200 | 254,753,400 |
| Corn | 417,709,600 | 539,228,800 | 151,786,800 | 257,697,000 |
| Oats | 249,132,400 | 288,382,600 | 233,882,000 | 300,792,800 |
| Buckwheat | 11,587,400 | 14,687,200 | 2,596,000 | 4,169,000 |
| Rice | 143,061,600 | 330,089,600 | 50,769,400 | 121,477,400 |
| Other kinds | 4,072,200 | 5,231,600 | | |
| Cheese | (a) | (a) | 19,905,600 | 46,120,800 |
| Coal | 402,646,200 | 8,599,597,600 | 514,599,800 | 2,783,052,800 |

a No statistics.

*Imports and exports of principal articles from January 1 to June 30, 1902—*Continued.

| Articles. | Imports. | | Exports. | |
|---|---|---|---|---|
| | At Rotterdam. | In the Netherlands. | From Rotterdam. | From the Netherlands. |
| | *Pounds.* | *Pounds.* | *Pounds.* | *Pounds.* |
| Coffee | 101,453,800 | 132,029,000 | 48,831,200 | 99,672,000 |
| Cotton, raw | 13,582,800 | 81,769,600 | 5,572,600 | 66,882,200 |
| Drapers' wares | 20,229,000 | 72,382,200 | 23,081,600 | 63,481,600 |
| Drugs, dyestuffs, and chemicals | 250,610,800 | 545,465,800 | 187,550,000 | 440,968,000 |
| Earthenware | 29,739,600 | 354,866,600 | 21,019,600 | 111,469,400 |
| Engines and machinery | 38,860,800 | 97,918,400 | 26,435,200 | 67,317,800 |
| Fish | 5,814,600 | 18,598,800 | 25,121,000 | 85,826,400 |
| Fish oil | 9,034,800 | 6,465,800 | 4,644,200 | 7,308,400 |
| Flax and hemp | 26,665,200 | 57,888,600 | 19,078,400 | 99,864,600 |
| Flour | 94,162,000 | 187,882,200 | 19,239,000 | 30,217,000 |
| Fruits | 72,547,200 | 132,419,200 | 46,620,400 | 76,093,600 |
| Glass and glassware | 20,649,200 | 93,827,800 | 23,328,800 | 79,710,400 |
| Ground nuts | 42,361,000 | 41,796,400 | 15,692,800 | 13,930,400 |
| Hides, skins, and leather | 18,414,000 | 47,680,600 | 18,865,000 | 47,003,000 |
| Lard | 33,415,800 | 38,260,200 | 13,684,000 | 23,751,200 |
| Manure | 100,423,100 | 550,853,600 | 91,668,200 | 450,908,800 |
| Margarine: | | | | |
|   Butter | 184,800 | 360,800 | 45,784,200 | 54,956,000 |
|   Raw | 34,557,600 | 42,620,600 | 8,927,600 | 18,464,600 |
| Meat | 10,808,600 | 13,882,000 | 25,081,600 | 75,297,200 |
| Mercury | 21,661,200 | 43,225,600 | 18,464,600 | 32,467,600 |
| Metal: | | | | |
|   Articles | 151,140,000 | 729,350,600 | 170,306,400 | 542,572,800 |
|   Raw | 405,169,600 | 1,446,537,400 | 497,888,600 | 1,208,648,600 |
| Oils: | | | | |
|   Ground nut | 2,010,800 | 2,112,000 | 2,290,200 | 3,154,800 |
|   Cotton seed | 65,238,800 | 70,116,200 | 33,969,400 | 37,842,200 |
|   Sesame and other edible | 13,123,000 | 18,629,600 | 14,491,400 | 19,192,800 |
|   Palm and other | 83,518,600 | 138,758,400 | 73,385,400 | 136,903,800 |
|   Petroleum | 272,437,000 | 428,322,400 | 216,825,400 | 288,307,500 |
| Palm nuts | 18,337,000 | 21,016,600 | 12,529,000 | 22,490,600 |
| Paper | 41,624,000 | 101,356,200 | 66,051,600 | 192,330,600 |
| Potato flour and its products | 25,836,800 | 35,145,000 | 27,526,400 | 79,752,200 |
| Rags | .......... | .......... | 38,796,600 | 80,264,500 |
| Rattans | .......... | 6,250,200 | 1,942,600 | 5,031,400 |
| Salt | 18,873,800 | 120,025,400 | .......... | 13,527,000 |
| Seeds | 136,087,600 | 395,062,800 | 60,126,000 | 253,089,600 |
| Spices | 8,289,000 | 8,696,600 | 3,416,600 | 8,470,000 |
| Spirits | 10,122,200 | 24,138,400 | 29,002,600 | 40,244,800 |
| Stone | 2,088,699,800 | (*a*) | 94,800,200 | 438,957,200 |
| Sugar: | | | | |
|   Raw | 71,462,600 | 171,045,600 | 70,738,800 | 105,283,200 |
|   All other | 23,663,200 | 45,463,000 | 19,665,800 | 170,783,800 |
| Sulphur | 8,040,400 | 9,053,000 | 4,875,200 | 11,288,200 |
| Sirup | 11,968,000 | 17,287,600 | 10,111,200 | 26,670,200 |
| Tallow suet, etc | 36,031,600 | 54,709,600 | 13,252,800 | 31,273,000 |
| Tar and pitch | 3,429,800 | 59,562,800 | .......... | 86,896,600 |
| Tea | 3,691,600 | 11,096,800 | .......... | 7,913,400 |
| Tobacco and cigars | 103,941,200 | 40,213,800 | 21,194,800 | 61,094,000 |
| Vinegar | .......... | .......... | 600,600 | 14,764,200 |
| Wine | 44,849,200 | 78,454,200 | 41,927,600 | 66,519,200 |
| Wood: | | | | |
|   For shipbuilding and timber | 457,327, | 1, ,965,200 | 293,235,800 | 645,042,200 |
|   Dyewoods | 25,610, | ,206,600 | 35,534,400 | 44,435,600 |
|   Hard woods | 30,489, | ,846,800 | 6,446,000 | 11,490,600 |
| Wool | 13,703,200 | 139,866,200 | 8,342,400 | 54,872,400 |
| Yarns | 25,513,800 | 88,093,600 | 15,037,000 | 29,909,000 |

*a* No statistics.

' The following statement gives the amount of the principal articles imported at Rotterdam from the United States for the years 1895–1901. A list of all articles was not to be had.

[In thousand pounds.]

| Articles. | 1895. | 1896. | 1897. | 1898. | 1899. | 1900. | 1901. |
|---|---|---|---|---|---|---|---|
| Wheat | 111,800 | 162,057 | 425,295 | 722,089 | 877,328 | 467,912 | 1,497,833 |
| Rye | 1,767 | 28,737 | 110,696 | 139,285 | 45,558 | 10,331 | 9,064 |
| Barley | | 5,026 | 38,365 | 7,193 | 40,844 | 70,499 | 15,869 |
| Corn | 129,500 | 564,182 | 792,774 | 1,093,900 | 1,871,227 | 894,810 | 463,412 |
| Oats | | 57,822 | 130,183 | 219,600 | 220,701 | 75,363 | 88,535 |
| Buckwheat | 11,170 | 37,708 | 46,910 | 54,371 | 24,312 | 10,628 | 16,749 |

[In thousand pounds.]

| Articles. | 1895. | 1896. | 1897. | 1898. | 1899. | 1901. | 1902. |
|---|---|---|---|---|---|---|---|
| Beans and peas | 19 | 244 | 500 | 476 | 108 | 2 | 13 |
| Coffee | 305 | 371 | 253 | 1,872 | 472 | 1,452 | 517 |
| Margarine | 55,000 | 73,864 | 79,921 | 94,127 | 88,499 | 97,275 | 96,906 |
| Ores | 3,130 | 53 | 26,528 | 141,453 | 319,770 | 63,239 | 470,721 |
| Metals: | | | | | | | |
|   Manufactured | 51,020 | 4,707 | 8,134 | 19,310 | 27,540 | 24,750 | 23,756 |
|   Raw | ...... | 80,859 | 157,018 | 122,665 | 155,163 | 204,945 | 86,995 |
| Cotton-seed oil | 51,940 | 31,078 | 60,856 | 73,826 | 78,851 | 79,858 | 102,881 |
| Sesame oil | 67 | 23 | 13 | 50 | 22 | 2 | 11 |
| Petroleum | 478,200 | 591,778 | 584,000 | 667,292 | 638,396 | 565,059 | 684,222 |
| Lard | 25,270 | 32,721 | 62,806 | 68,402 | 74,556 | 65,346 | 66,673 |
| Tobacco | 24,600 | 29,218 | 34,944 | 27,711 | 28,588 | 29,060 | 27,859 |
| Tallow, suet, etc | 643 | 1,145 | 4,109 | 13,373 | 11,462 | 14,903 | 12,921 |
| Seeds | 263 | 28,114 | 13,657 | 36,700 | 36,623 | 65,512 | 46,928 |

*Statement showing quantity of principal articles imported at Rotterdam from the United States in 1901, and also the quantities of such articles imported from other countries of importance.*

[In thousand pounds.]

| Countries. | Wheat. | Rye. | Barley. | Corn. | Oats. | Buckwheat. | Beans and peas. | Coffee. | Margarine. |
|---|---|---|---|---|---|---|---|---|---|
| United States | 1,497,883 | 9,064 | 15,869 | 463,412 | 38,535 | 16,749 | 18 | 517 | 96,906 |
| Algeria | | | | | | | | | |
| Australia | 7,555 | | | | | | | | |
| Belgium | | | 112 | | | | | 1,439 | 227 |
| India | 16,474 | | | 2 | 667 | | 22 | | |
| France | | 1 | 308 | | | 2,893 | 48 | 11,271 | 521 |
| Greece | | | 57 | | 1 | | 75 | | |
| Great Britain | 713 | | 2,204 | | 20 | | 156 | 16,243 | 1,252 |
| Germany | 45,250 | 10,278 | 59,573 | 42 | 17,501 | 15 | 49,007 | 7,977 | 4,387 |
| Italy | | | 297 | | | | 101 | 90 | |
| Java | | | | | | | | 24,284 | |
| Norway | | | | | | | | 11 | 31 |
| Portugal | | | | | | | 1 | 6,360 | 24 |
| Russia | 786,153 | 729,995 | 341,651 | 50,640 | 589,505 | 9,354 | 30,232 | 1 | |
| Spain | | | | | | | 1 | | |
| Turkey | 9,865 | 8,513 | 7,022 | 9,493 | 748 | | 357 | 20 | |
| Sweden | | | 830 | | | | | 4 | |
| Denmark | | | 7,612 | | | 486 | | | |
| Countries on Danube | 198,670 | 221,232 | 121,506 | 151,384 | 24,339 | | 7,003 | | |
| South America | 262,414 | 15 | | 92,411 | | | | 138,699 | 6,499 |
| Austria | | | 18,834 | | | | 838 | | |
| Africa | | | | | | | | 97 | |
| Canada | | | | | | | | | |
| Malta | | | | | | | | | |

| Countries. | Ores. | Metals, manufactured. | Metals, raw. | Cotton-seed oil. | Sesame oil. | Petroleum. | Lard. | Tobacco. | Tallow, suet, etc. | Seeds. |
|---|---|---|---|---|---|---|---|---|---|---|
| United States | 470,721 | 23,756 | 86,995 | 102,881 | 11 | 684,222 | 66,673 | 27,859 | 12,921 | 46,928 |
| Algeria | 557,069 | 2 | | | 24 | | | 86 | | |
| Australia | 26,717 | | | | | | | | | |
| Belgium | 66 | 22,462 | 17,670 | 4,446 | 548 | 1,228 | 618 | 2,209 | 2,066 | 211 |
| India | 21,956 | | | | | | | | 1,514 | 4,004 |
| France | 202,972 | 194 | 3,522 | 90 | 1,234 | | | 1,232 | 5,573 | 163 |
| Greece | 290,071 | | 20 | | 1,962 | | | 1,852 | 11 | 2,504 |
| Great Britain | 16,619 | 16,463 | 414,308 | 9,522 | 506 | 211 | 1,188 | 2,633 | 38,295 | 7,249 |
| Germany | 8,945 | 2,500 | 278,747 | 1,184 | 4,891 | 84 | 287 | 10,556 | 6,085 | 16,229 |
| Italy | 122,791 | 4 | 295 | | 8,672 | | | 167 | 77 | 46 |
| Java | 1,379 | 18 | 19,719 | | | | | 26,811 | 1,331 | 123 |
| Norway | 85,639 | 852 | 636 | | | 2 | | 2 | 15 | |
| Portugal | 187,565 | | 251 | | 46 | | | | | |
| Russia | 274,542 | 15 | 97 | | | | | 123 | | 52,483 |
| Spain | 3,345,065 | 9 | 1,516 | | | | | | | |
| Turkey | 4,380 | 61 | | | 711 | | | 398 | | 1,641 |
| Sweden | 1,885,418 | 312 | 17,266 | | | | | | | |
| Denmark | | | | | | | | 4 | 852 | |
| Countries on Danube | | | | | | | | | | |
| South America | 2 | 15 | 37 | | | | 4 | 20 | 2 | 62,878 |
| Austria | | 352 | 20 | | | | | 84 | 158 | 152,957 |
| Africa | | 7 | 1,415 | | | | | | | 108 |
| Canada | | | | | | | | | | 40 |
| Malta | | | | | | | | 4 | | 16,064 |

11

*Value of declared exports to the United States of America from the consular district of Rotterdam for the fiscal years 1896 to 1902.*

| Articles. | 1896. | 1897. | 1898. | 1899. | 1900. | 1901. | 1902. |
|---|---|---|---|---|---|---|---|
| Bulbs and plants | $293,588.77 | $314,072.28 | $268,405.21 | $302,354.97 | $366,852.42 | $397,210.61 | $399,805.04 |
| Cheese | 64,758.79 | 62,123.48 | 54,102.82 | 185,137.04 | 61,154.96 | 68,595.75 | 58,791.74 |
| Cocoa: | | | | | | | |
| Beans | | | | | | 11,183.33 | 25,925.95 |
| Butter | | | 2,422.03 | 2,509.71 | 3,673.02 | 66,178.99 | 92,147.77 |
| Coffee | 194,809.09 | 189,970.18 | 128,979.42 | 65,519.35 | 56,658.80 | 27,695.21 | 54,652.70 |
| Earthenware | 18,990.16 | 13,025.91 | 11,838.76 | 13,132.19 | 13,771.20 | 13,484.71 | 27,516.34 |
| Flax and tow | 57,642.10 | 71,073.10 | 46,145.91 | 79,486.65 | 95,827.87 | 154,904.33 | 163,401.29 |
| Gin and spirits | 107,535.74 | 118,671.08 | 38,227.54 | 51,738.67 | 72,287.51 | 80,768.67 | 65,570.48 |
| Glycerin | 57,338.14 | 27,047.41 | 42,887.46 | 11,114.76 | 104,256.60 | 78,376.02 | 77,655.03 |
| Herring, mackerel, etc. | 641,543.26 | 508,772.95 | 490,525.44 | 422,172.37 | 752,892.22 | 588,725.12 | 744,102.88 |
| Indigo | 5,796.24 | 13,943.53 | 61,256.97 | 46,736.87 | 17,309.12 | 5,011.15 | 6,148.67 |
| Madder | 10,843.24 | 10,227.85 | 10,486.21 | 8,137.06 | 5,983.52 | 9,683.68 | 6,988.34 |
| Mineral water | 21,887.02 | 27,843.68 | 1,686.00 | 6,174.32 | 4,214.09 | 7,219.60 | 4,504.55 |
| Oils | 5,193.81 | 8,747.81 | 3,756.54 | 6,709.89 | 3,058.60 | 4,526.56 | 3,606.44 |
| Oleo stearin | | | | | | | 31,884.50 |
| Paper | | | | | 24,368.06 | 44,031.10 | 81,658.93 |
| Peat moss | 85,836.94 | 54,084.87 | 31,370.77 | 44,845.52 | 86,885.60 | 3'',998.89 | 46,767.70 |
| Potatoes | | | | | | | 36,241.28 |
| Potato starch | | | | | | | 23,044.20 |
| Rags and paper stock | 63,169.08 | 68,416.71 | 56,333.48 | 50,344.46 | 73,590.50 | 78,623.02 | 135,087.83 |
| Rattans | | | | | | 32,944.01 | 5,114.88 |
| Rubber | 182,754.27 | 74,107.10 | 84,393.88 | 118,093.75 | 109,683.98 | 114,704.28 | 166,372.19 |
| Seeds | | | | | 35,196.49 | 34,596.47 | 133,138.22 |
| Silverware | 33,308.09 | 28,739.26 | 24,490.27 | 31,255.93 | 35,486.78 | 42,364.61 | 58,948.26 |
| Skins and hides | 14,407.11 | 10,234.72 | 120,175.27 | 485,017.63 | 438,902.68 | 617,412.88 | 680,353.99 |
| Spices | 37,783.06 | 19,315.92 | 11,684.52 | 3,419.76 | 21,897.97 | 200,168.48 | 117,915.89 |
| Stearin pitch | | | | | 11,066.22 | 20,626.26 | 82,802.46 |
| Straw covers | 4,923.52 | 8,145.76 | 607.82 | 1,358.92 | 4,062.90 | 15,782.55 | 23,913.38 |
| Sugar | 107,106.18 | 195,005.57 | 13,812.48 | | | | |
| Tin | 30,863.75 | 135,624.13 | 190,830.18 | 243,753.56 | 721,916.52 | 421,443.77 | 479,946.04 |
| Tobacco | 223,035.95 | 389,002.93 | 171,136.99 | 91,808.59 | 144,421.18 | 50,357.81 | 45,867.87 |
| Miscellaneous | 175,781.69 | 180,284.28 | 151,091.64 | 213,624.22 | 194,499.66 | 269,514.47 | 305,392.23 |
| Total | 2,332,885.80 | 2,467,429.96 | 1,996,647.64 | 2,484,445.72 | 3,442,817.98 | 3,443,432.82 | 4,081,217.02 |

## TRAFFIC ALONG THE NORTH SEA-ROTTERDAM WATERWAY.

Thirteen thousand seven hundred and eighty-five steamers and 626 sailing vessels, together 14,411 ships, with a capacity of 12,867,664 registered tons, entered and cleared from the new waterway in 1901, against 14,519 steamers and 683 sailing vessels, together 15,202 ships, with a capacity of 12,793,367 registered tons, in 1900. Besides, 4,730 fishing smacks entered and cleared in 1901, against 4,517 in 1900.

The waterway was navigated by 3,982 vessels drawing 16 feet or more.

The following table shows the traffic for the last three years:

| Description. | 1899. | | 1900. | | 1901. | |
|---|---|---|---|---|---|---|
| | Number. | Tonnage. | Number. | Tonnage. | Number. | Tonnage. |
| INWARD. | | | | | | |
| Steamers | 6,843 | 6,099,875 | 7,266 | 6,238,482 | 6,875 | 6,247,362 |
| Sailing vessels | 397 | 218,412 | 349 | 185,041 | 318 | 170,197 |
| Total | 7,240 | 6,318,287 | 7,615 | 6,423,523 | 7,193 | 6,417,559 |
| OUTWARD. | | | | | | |
| Steamers | 6,835 | 6,175,536 | 7,253 | 6,277,604 | 6,910 | 6,283,290 |
| Sailing vessels | 371 | 211,372 | 334 | 178,240 | 308 | 166,815 |
| Total | 7,206 | 6,386,908 | 7,587 | 6,455,844 | 7,218 | 6,450,105 |

In 1901, 422 ships less than in 1900, and 47 less than in 1899, entered the new waterway from the sea. The average tonnage, however, increased.

From January 1 to September 30, 1902, 5,055 vessels, measuring 4,795,386 net registered tons, entered the new waterway to Rotterdam, against 5,369 vessels, measuring 4,938,496 net registered tons during the same period in 1901, showing a decrease in traffic of 314 vessels and 143,110 net registered tons.

### NAVIGATION AT DUTCH PORTS.

*Statement showing vessels entered and cleared at the principal Dutch ports in 1900 and 1901.*

| Port. | Inward. | | | | | | Outward. | | | | | |
|---|---|---|---|---|---|---|---|---|---|---|---|---|
| | 1900. | | | 1901. | | | 1900. | | | 1901. | | |
| | Steamers. | Sailing vessels. | Total. | Steamers. | Sailing vessels. | Total. | Steamers. | Sailing vessels. | Total. | Steamers. | Sailing vessels. | Total. |
| Brouwershaven............ | 3 | 8 | 8 | 7 | 1 | 8 | 3 | 2 | 5 | 4 | ...... | 4 |
| Goerée Estuary............ | 145 | 48 | 193 | 113 | 30 | 143 | 148 | 43 | 191 | 118 | 28 | 146 |
| New Waterway............ | 7,307 | 296 | 7,603 | 6,909 | 274 | 7,183 | 7,318 | 287 | 7,605 | 6,870 | 306 | 7,187 |
| Ymuiden ................ | 2,164 | 84 | 2,252 | 2,199 | 59 | 2,258 | 2,161 | 93 | 2,254 | 2,188 | 77 | 2,265 |
| Nieuwediep................ | 43 | 6 | 49 | 64 | 24 | 88 | 38 | 3 | 41 | 47 | 9 | 56 |
| Vlie.................... | 381 | 90 | 471 | 361 | 60 | 421 | 378 | 88 | 466 | 374 | 79 | 453 |
| Zierikzee ................ | ...... | 41 | 41 | 2 | 49 | 51 | ...... | 43 | 43 | 1 | 51 | 52 |
| Flushing................ | 895 | 21 | 916 | 870 | 20 | 890 | 901 | 24 | 925 | 873 | 19 | 892 |

### NAVIGATION AT ROTTERDAM.

Six thousand eight hundred and eighty-one ocean vessels (foreign tug boats and fishing smacks not included), with an aggregate tonnage of 6,382,934 net tons, entered Rotterdam by sea from foreign countries in 1901. The number of entrances at Rotterdam and in the Netherlands since 1850 has been as follows:

| Year. | At Rotterdam. | | In the whole Kingdom. | | Percentage share of Rotterdam in the whole. | |
|---|---|---|---|---|---|---|
| | Number. | Capacity. | Number. | Capacity. | Number. | Capacity. |
| | | *Tons.* | | *Tons.* | | *Tons.* |
| 1850 ................ | 1,940 | 316,180 | 6,961 | 967,710 | 27.9 | 35.77 |
| 1855 ................ | 2,247 | 452,295 | | | 27.2 | 37.12 |
| 1860 ................ | 2,449 | 592,978 | 8,714 | 1,458,894 | 28.1 | 40.64 |
| 1865 ................ | 2,459 | 751,036 | 8,550 | 1,660,762 | 28.76 | 45.25 |
| 1870 ................ | 2,973 | 1,026,348 | 8,351 | 2,037,491 | 35.60 | 50.37 |
| 1875 ................ | 3,390 | 1,411,828 | 7,921 | 2,624,520 | 42.3 | 53.80 |
| 1880 ................ | 3,456 | 1,681,650 | 8,164 | 3,434,083 | 42.53 | 48.91 |
| 1885 ................ | 3,724 | 2,120,347 | 8,021 | 4,137,064 | 46.55 | 51.01 |
| 1890 ................ | 4,535 | 2,918,125 | 9,475 | 5,116,158 | 48.24 | 53.58 |
| 1895 ................ | 5,199 | 4,177,478 | 9,600 | 6,778,127 | 54.15 | 61.67 |
| 1896 ................ | 5,904 | 4,951,560 | 11,085 | 7,890,694 | 53.67 | 62.75 |
| 1897 ................ | 6,213 | 5,409,417 | 11,235 | 8,513,620 | 55.37 | 63.53 |
| 1898 ................ | 6,373 | 5,751,398 | 11,067 | 8,634,297 | 57.93 | 66.15 |
| 1899 ................ | 6,890 | 6,523,072 | 11,803 | 9,450,386 | 58.38 | 66.90 |
| 1900 ................ | 7,268 | 6,326,501 | 12,307 | 9,450,710 | 59.01 | 66.94 |
| 1901 ................ | 6,881 | 6,382,934 | 11,698 | 9,336,897 | 58.86 | 68.36 |

*Number of ocean ships entered at Rotterdam from the various countries, and their percentage of the total tonnage entered for the last five years.*

| Country. | 1897. | | 1898. | | 1899. | | 1900. | | 1901. | |
|---|---|---|---|---|---|---|---|---|---|---|
| | Num-ber. | Ton-nage. | Num-ber. | Ton-nage. | Num-ber. | Ton-nage. | Num-ber. | Ton-nage. | Num-ber. | Ton-nage. |
| | | *Per ct.* | | *Per ct.* | | *Per ct.* | | *Per ct.* | | *Per ct.* |
| France.................. | 242 | 1.76 | 245 | 1.87 | 227 | 1.50 | 286 | 1.56 | 261 | 1.70 |
| Great Britain and Ireland ... | 2,587 | 29.82 | 2,514 | 28.44 | 2,911 | 29.50 | 3,284 | 31.66 | 2,704 | 26.40 |
| Hanseatic Towns ............ | 298 | 2.20 | 317 | 2.28 | 348 | 2.41 | 357 | 8.47 | 406 | 4.88 |
| Prussia.................. | 336 | 2.90 | 396 | 3.18 | 488 | 3.18 | 474 | 2.70 | 421 | 2.71 |
| Portugal................. | | | | | | | 68 | ........ | 77 | ........ |
| Russia .................. | 673 | 16.07 | 681 | 12.71 | 514 | 9.59 | 611 | 11.11 | 641 | 11.60 |
| Spain .................. | 636 | 10.10 | 596 | 10.70 | 600 | 11.08 | 592 | 10.49 | 682 | 10.34 |
| Ports on the Danube........ | | | | | | | 96 | ........ | 129 | ........ |
| Sweden and Norway........ | 472 | 7.65 | 459 | 7.10 | 473 | 6.84 | 461 | 6.67 | 497 | 7.66 |
| French colonies............ | 43 | .88 | 47 | .98 | 83 | 1.74 | 104 | 2.16 | 92 | 1.96 |
| Argentine Republic......... | 17 | .19 | 47 | 1.06 | 98 | 2.67 | 147 | 2.54 | 89 | 2.53 |
| Brazil.................. | | | | | | | 39 | ........ | 36 | ........ |
| United States of America .... | 473 | 15.78 | 580 | 19.48 | 599 | 19.58 | 441 | 14.86 | 540 | 18.41 |
| Dutch colonies............. | 33 | .96 | 33 | .88 | 34 | .92 | 33 | .93 | 83 | .92 |
| Divers countries ............ | 502 | 11.69 | 508 | 10.82 | 515 | 10.99 | 830 | 11.85 | 323 | 10.89 |
| Total.............. | 6,212 | 100 | 6,873 | 100 | 6,890 | 100 | 7,268 | 100 | 6,881 | 100 |

*Number of ships of each nationality entering the port of Rotterdam in 1901.*

| Nationality. | Sailing vessels. | | Steamers. | | Total. | |
|---|---|---|---|---|---|---|
| | Number. | Gross ca-pacity in cubic meters. | Number. | Gross ca-pacity in cubic meters. | Number. | Gross ca-pacity in cubic meters. |
| Belgian............. | | | 33 | 199,785 | 33 | 199,785 |
| Danish................. | 4 | 1,366 | 208 | 1,029,034 | 212 | 1,030,400 |
| British............... | 53 | 112,564 | 3,193 | 12,965,644 | 3,246 | 18,078,208 |
| French............... | 3 | 16,068 | 76 | 123,089 | 79 | 139,147 |
| Grecian............. | | | 29 | 196,599 | 29 | 196,599 |
| Italian............. | 8 | 21,280 | 28 | 264,389 | 86 | 285,669 |
| Japanese............. | | | 2 | 29,625 | 2 | 29,625 |
| Dutch................. | 71 | 64,264 | 1,138 | 5,207,757 | 1,209 | 5,272,021 |
| German................. | 20 | 66,381 | 1,177 | 5,382,690 | 1,197 | 5,399,071 |
| Norwegian............. | 49 | 79,949 | 254 | 1,006,042 | 303 | 1,085,991 |
| Austrian............. | | | 28 | 204,419 | 28 | 204,419 |
| Roumanian ............ | | | 24 | 152,439 | 24 | 152,439 |
| Russian................. | 10 | 10,983 | 22 | 111,013 | 32 | 121,996 |
| Spanish................. | | | 273 | 1,669,858 | 273 | 1,669,858 |
| Uruguayan ............. | 1 | 2,154 | | | 1 | 2,154 |
| Swedish................. | 8 | 13,381 | 169 | 720,162 | 177 | 733,543 |
| Total.............. | 227 | 338,380 | 6,654 | 28,212,490 | 6,881 | 29,600,870 |

*Arrivals of ocean vessels at Rotterdam compared with those at other European ports.*

| Port. | 1900. | | 1901. | |
|---|---|---|---|---|
| | Number. | Tonnage. | Number. | Tonnage. |
| London ..................... | 25,814 | 15,558,001 | 26,421 | 15,952,453 |
| Liverpool .................. | 20,300 | 9,315,674 | 20,100 | 9,704,160 |
| Cardiff..................... | 14,966 | 9,480,252 | 14,695 | 9,290,785 |
| Hamburg ................... | 13,102 | 8,036,000 | 12,847 | 8,883,000 |
| Glasgow .................... | 10,750 | 3,583,985 | 10,899 | 3,757,271 |
| Marseille................... | 8,543 | 6,164,431 | 8,228 | 6,581,780 |
| Rotterdam.................. | 7,268 | 6,326,901 | 6,881 | 6,382,934 |
| Hull ....................... | 6,592 | 3,417,916 | 6,057 | 3,102,869 |
| Antwerp.................... | 5,244 | 6,691,791 | 5,225 | 7,488,579 |
| Bremen..................... | 3,843 | 2,494,059 | 4,024 | 2,717,633 |
| Dunkirk ................... | 2,698 | 1,613,770 | 2,577 | 1,669,906 |
| Amsterdam................. | 2,110 | 1,812,528 | 2,213 | 1,869,151 |
| Havre...................... | 2,263 | 2,106,659 | 2,191 | 2,248,645 |

To show the importance of Rotterdam, in comparison with the competing ports Hamburg and Antwerp, the following table of entrances for the last ten years is given:

| Year. | Hamburg. | | Antwerp. | | Rotterdam. | |
|---|---|---|---|---|---|---|
| | Number. | Tonnage. | Number. | Tonnage. | Number. | Tonnage. |
| 1892 | 8,569 | 5,638,483 | 4,321 | 4,500,091 | 4,423 | 3,120,698 |
| 1893 | 8,792 | 5,886,378 | 4,418 | 4,692,211 | 4,631 | 3,566,170 |
| 1894 | 9,165 | 6,223,821 | 4,640 | 5,008,963 | 5,109 | 4,413,403 |
| 1895 | 9,443 | 6,255,718 | 4,653 | 5,363,569 | 5,199 | 4,177,478 |
| 1896 | 10,477 | 6,445,000 | 4,961 | 5,820,669 | 5,904 | 4,951,560 |
| 1897 | 11,173 | 6,708,000 | 5,106 | 6,215,550 | 6,212 | 5,409,417 |
| 1898 | 12,523 | 7,355,000 | 5,198 | 6,415,501 | 6,373 | 5,715,393 |
| 1899 | 13,312 | 7,768,000 | 5,420 | 6,842,163 | 6,890 | 6,323,072 |
| 1900 | 13,103 | 8,041,000 | 5,244 | 6,691,791 | 7,268 | 6,326,901 |
| 1901 | 12,847 | 8,383,000 | 5,225 | 7,488,579 | 6,881 | 6,382,934 |

The increase and decrease of ocean traffic in 1901 as compared with 1900, at Hamburg, Antwerp, Amsterdam, and Rotterdam, has been:

| Port. | Number of ships. | | Per cent. | | Tonnage. | | Per cent. | |
|---|---|---|---|---|---|---|---|---|
| | Increase. | Decrease. | Increase. | Decrease. | Increase. | Decrease. | Increase. | Decrease. |
| Hamburg | | 256 | | 1.9 | 342,000 | | 4.2 | |
| Antwerp | | 19 | | .3 | 796,788 | | 11.2 | |
| Amsterdam | 103 | | 4.9 | | 56,623 | | 3.1 | |
| Rotterdam | | 387 | | 5.3 | 56,033 | | .8 | |

The average tonnage, per ship, entered in the three ports was:

| Years. | Hamburg. | Antwerp. | Rotterdam. |
|---|---|---|---|
| 1892 | 658 | 1,041 | 705 |
| 1893 | 669 | 1,062 | 757 |
| 1894 | 679 | 1,079 | 797 |
| 1895 | 662 | 1,152 | 808 |
| 1896 | 615 | 1,182 | 838 |
| 1897 | 600 | 1,217 | 870 |
| 1898 | 587 | 1,234 | 902 |
| 1899 | 583 | 1,262 | 917 |
| 1900 | 613 | 1,276 | 906 |
| 1901 | 652 | 1,433 | 927 |

The quantity of merchandise imported at the ports of Rotterdam and Antwerp, in tons of 1,000 kilograms (2,205 pounds), was:

| Years. | Rotterdam. | Antwerp. |
|---|---|---|
| 1892 | 4,278,849 | 4,042,237 |
| 1893 | 4,936,896 | 4,302,142 |
| 1894 | 5,686,320 | 4,742,696 |
| 1895 | 6,102,419 | 5,100,139 |
| 1896 | 7,519,066 | 5,822,736 |
| 1897 | 8,484,789 | 5,961,534 |
| 1898 | 9,008,114 | 6,337,454 |
| 1899 | 9,930,296 | 7,298,469 |
| 1900 | 10,540,256 | 7,023,791 |
| 1901 | 10,203,429 | 7,510,938 |

Five hundred and forty ships, with a capacity of 5,551,294 cubic meters, entered Rotterdam from the United States in 1901, against 441 ships, with a capacity of 4,323,688 cubic meters[a] in 1900, and 599 ships, with a capacity of 5,423,944 cubic meters, in 1899. Two hundred and eighty ships cleared from Rotterdam to the United States, against 294

[a] 1 cubic meter=35.3 cubic feet.

ships in 1900 and 335 ships in 1899. Among this number were the combined passenger and freight steamers of the Holland-America Line, which ply weekly between Rotterdam and New York, and the steamers of the regular freight lines from Rotterdam to Newport News, Baltimore, Philadelphia, and Boston.

The fleet of the Holland-America Line consists at present of the following steamers: Combined passenger and freight steamers; twin-screw steamers—*Noordam*, *Ryndam*, and *Potsdam*, each with a tonnage of 12,500 tons; *Statendam*, 10,320 tons; *Rotterdam*, 8,302 tons; and the screw steamer *Amsterdam*, with a tonnage of about 4,000. Freight steamers: *Soestdyk*, *Amsteldyk*, and *Sloterdyk*, with a tonnage of about 8,100 each.

The Holland-America Line in 1901 carried the following number of passengers:

| Passengers. | To New York from— | | From New York to— | |
|---|---|---|---|---|
| | Rotterdam. | Boulogne-sur-Mer. | Rotterdam. | Boulogne-sur-Mer. |
| Saloon | 3,938 | 1,571 | 3,339 | 1,424 |
| Steerage | 22,343 | 3,464 | 5,896 | 388 |
| Total | 26,281 | 5,035 | 9,235 | 1,812 |

Rotterdam has at present the following direct ocean steamship connections:

| To— | Schedule. | To— | Schedule. |
|---|---|---|---|
| Aberdeen | Every 10 days. | Leith, Edinburgh, Glasgow. | Every Tuesday and Friday. |
| Antwerp | Daily, except Monday. | Lisbon | Every 2 weeks. |
| Archangel | Monthly. | Liverpool | Wednesday and Saturday. |
| Algiers, Venice, Abcona, Bari, and Taranto. | Every 2 weeks. | London (Netherlands Steamship Co.). | Daily. |
| Baltimore | Weekly. | London (General Steam Navigation Co.). | Tuesday, Thursday, and Saturday. |
| Bergen, Stavanger | Every Wednesday. | London (via Harwich) | Daily. |
| Belfast, Dublin | Every Friday. | London (Rotterdam-London Steamship Co.). | Wednesday and Saturday. |
| Bremen | Weekly. | Liege | Thursday and Sunday. |
| Bilbao and Santander | Every 2 weeks. | Malta, Piræus, Salonica, Smyrna, Constantinople, Odessa, and Batum. | Monthly. |
| Bordeaux | Do. | | |
| Brussels | Every Wednesday. | | |
| Boston | Every 2 weeks. | | |
| Bristol | Every 10 days. | | |
| Cardiff | Every 2 weeks. | | |
| Christiania | Every 8 days. | | |
| Christiansand | Every 2 weeks. | Malta, Pireus, Smyrna, Constantinople, Alexandria, Jaffa, Beirut, Alexandretta, Messina, Odessa, Batum. | Every 2 weeks. |
| Constance, Sulina, Galatz, and Braila, and sometimes Constantinople. | Every 2 or 3 weeks. | | |
| Cork | Every 2 weeks. | Manchester (Cork Steamship Co.). | Every Friday. |
| Danzig and Neufahrwasser. | Every 8 or 10 days. | Marseilles (Rotterdam Lloyd). | Every 2 weeks. |
| Drontheim | Every 3 weeks. | Marseilles, Genoa, Leghorn. | Every 2 or 3 weeks. |
| Dunkirk | Every Wednesday. | | |
| Dundee | Every Saturday. | Middlesborough-on-Tees and Stockton-on-Tees. | Weekly. |
| Fiume and Trieste | Every 2 weeks. | | |
| Ghent | Every Wednesday. | Montreal | Every 2 weeks. |
| Glasgow-Grangemouth | Tuesday and Friday. | Newcastle-on-Tyne | Tuesday and Friday. |
| Gloucester | Every 8 days. | New York | Every Thursday. |
| Grimsby | Tuesday and Saturday. | Newport News | Monthly. |
| Goole | Do. | Oporto | Every 2 weeks. |
| Gothenburg | Weekly. | Philadelphia | Every 3 weeks. |
| Hamburg | Twice a week. | St. Petersburg | Weekly. |
| Havre | Every Friday. | Plymouth | Every 10 to 14 days. |
| Hull | Tuesday, Wednesday, Thursday, and Saturday. | Reval (only in winter) | Every 10 days. |
| | | Riga | Weekly. |
| Java and Sumatra | Every other Saturday. | Penang, Singapore, China, and Japan. | Twice per month. |
| Kiel and Lubeck | Every 10 days. | | |
| Kings-Lynn | Every Saturday. | Stettin | Weekly. |
| Konigsberg-Pillau | Every 8 or 10 days. | Swansea | Every 10 or 12 days. |
| Copenhagen | Every 8 days. | West Africa | Weekly. |

The following shows the river steamship connections between Rotterdam and the interior of the Netherlands, and the number of trips annually made:

| Place of destination. | Number of trips per year. | Place of destination. | Number of trips per year. |
|---|---|---|---|
| Alkmaar | 194 | Maastricht | 202 |
| Amsterdam | 660 | Meppel | 106 |
| Arnhem | 438 | Middelburg | 290 |
| Apeldoorn | 96 | Middelharnis | 910 |
| Bergambacht | 41 | Nieuwenhoorn | 52 |
| Bodegrave | 354 | Nymegen | 459 |
| Breda | 148 | Oosterhout | 312 |
| Breskens | 52 | Ouderkerk on the Yssel | 465 |
| Old Beyerland | 600 | Pernis | 1,290 |
| Bommel | 260 | Puttershoek | 104 |
| Brielle and Hellevoetsluis | 2,242 | Schoonhoven | 995 |
| Culemborg | 342 | Sneek | 304 |
| Delft | 2,550 | Streefkerk | 48 |
| Deventer | 144 | Stellendam | 300 |
| Dokkum | 50 | Tholen | 52 |
| Dordrecht | 856 | Tiel | 475 |
| Doesburg | 100 | Tricht | 100 |
| Edam | 52 | Utrecht | 610 |
| Eindhoven | 150 | Venlo | 199 |
| Gorinchem | 2,721 | Vlaardingen | 2,420 |
| Goes | 52 | Veghel | 102 |
| Gouda | 1,263 | Waalwyk | 130 |
| Groningen | 112 | Willemstad | 337 |
| Great Ammers | 46 | Wageningen | 50 |
| Haarlem and Haarlemmer Meer | 460 | Wyk and Driel | 52 |
| Helder | 50 | Woerden | 52 |
| S'Hertogenbosch | 770 | Ysselmonde | 2,380 |
| Heusden | 680 | Zaandam | 300 |
| Hoorn | 52 | Zierikzee | 485 |
| Helmond | 164 | Zwolle | 175 |
| Hook of Holland | 1,340 | Zutphen | 145 |
| Leerdam | 275 | Zuidland | 170 |
| Lekkerkerk | 700 | Zwyndrecht | 402 |
| Leeuwarden | 152 | | |
| Maassluis | 810 | Total | 33,449 |

## PORT CHARGES.

Quay dues, pilotage rates, and tonnage charges or harbor dues are given in Commercial Relations, 1899, volume 2, pages 562 and 563. All dues are moderate. There are no landing charges.

The harbor dues received at Rotterdam during the last ten years amounted to:

| Year. | River and inland vessels. | Seagoing vessels. | Total. |
|---|---|---|---|
| 1892 | $61,179 | $197,878 | $259,057 |
| 1893 | 64,874 | 232,213 | 297,087 |
| 1894 | 71,786 | 277,869 | 349,655 |
| 1895 | 77,505 | 283,808 | 361,313 |
| 1896 | 92,361 | 339,646 | 432,007 |
| 1897 | 101,493 | 375,978 | 477,471 |
| 1898 | 108,548 | 399,268 | 507,816 |
| 1899 | 116,436 | 433,395 | 549,831 |
| 1900 | 120,898 | 455,250 | 576,148 |
| 1901 | 122,070 | 456,289 | 578,359 |

## RIVER TRAFFIC.

Rotterdam is connected by a large number of canals with the principal towns of the interior of the Netherlands, and also with the chief waterways of Germany, Switzerland, Belgium, and France. The total length of the network of canals covering the Netherlands is about 2,943 miles.   More than 100,000 river ships and boats, with a capacity in the aggregate of more than 15,000,000 cubic meters (529,740,000 cubic feet), enter Rotterdam from the interior of the Netherlands, Germany, and Belgium annually.

### RHINE FREIGHTS AND TRAFFIC.

The average Rhine freight charges in 1901 for cargoes of 600 to 700 tons, towage included, were:

| Articles. | Per 1,000 kilograms (2,205 pounds). | | | |
|---|---|---|---|---|
| | First quarter. | Second quarter. | Third quarter. | Fourth quarter. |
| | *Cents.* | *Cents.* | *Cents.* | *Cents.* |
| For ore and other crude materials from Rotterdam to Ruhrort Duisburg, Hochfeld, Alsum, Rheinhausen............ | 22–24 | 20–22 | 22–24 | 22–24 |
| For ore, saltpeter, and phosphates to the Middle Rhine, (Cologne, Deutz, Porz, Mülheim, Neuwied, Mühlhofen) ... | 34–38 | 34–38 | 36–40 | 32–34 |
| For ore (copper ore, phosphates, etc.), to the Upper Rhine and towns on the main....................................... | 60–64 | 66–68 | 60–64 | 60–64 |
| For grain by cargoes of ± 400 tons— | | | | |
| To the Lower Rhine........................................ | 26–28 | 24–26 | 26–28 | 28–30 |
| To the Middle Rhine....................................... | 44 | 44 | 46 | 42 |
| To the Upper Rhine (lighterage not included)........... | 64–68 | 74–76 | 70–72 | 64–68 |

The Rhine freight charges per 2,000 kilograms (about 4,410 pounds) for ore, excluding charges for towage, were:

| Destination. | 1897. | | 1898. | | 1899. | | 1901. | | 1902. | |
|---|---|---|---|---|---|---|---|---|---|---|
| | High-est. | Low-est. | High-est. | Low-est. | High-est. | Low-est. | High-est. | Low-est. | High-est. | Low-est. |
| To the Ruhr: | | | | | | | | | | |
| First quarter......................... | $0.50 | $0.20 | $0.50 | $0.20 | $0.36 | $0.20 | $0.48 | $0.22 | $0.64 | $0.30 |
| Second quarter........................ | .48 | .22 | .44 | .22 | .40 | .28 | .40 | .22 | .56 | .24 |
| Third quarter......................... | .88 | .38 | 1.00 | .28 | .80 | .28 | .68 | .28 | .32 | .24 |
| Fourth quarter........................ | 1.04 | .30 | 1.10 | .36 | .96 | .48 | .76 | .30 | .32 | .24 |
| To the Middle Rhine:* | | | | | | | | | | |
| First quarter......................... | .40 | .28 | .60 | .32 | .50 | .28 | .56 | .36 | .68 | .36 |
| Second quarter ....................... | .44 | .28 | .48 | .32 | .56 | .30 | .52 | .34 | .48 | .28 |
| Third quarter......................... | .84 | .38 | 1.20 | .40 | 1.00 | .60 | .98 | .54 | .40 | .32 |
| Fourth quarter ....................... | ...... | ...... | 1.80 | .60 | 1.12 | .72 | 1.06 | .68 | .38 | .36 |

The following statement shows the quantity of dutiable merchandise arriving by Rhine boats from Germany at the principal Dutch Rhine stations:

| Port. | 1901. | 1900. | Port. | 1901. | 1900. |
|---|---|---|---|---|---|
| | *Tons.* | *Tons.* | | *Tons.* | *Tons.* |
| Rotterdam ................... | 875,054 | 669,805 | Tiel ...... .................. | 18,592 | 20,592 |
| Amsterdam .................. | 160,693 | 154,224 | Arnhem ................... | 16,575 | 15,590 |
| Dordrecht................... | 85,840 | 69,985 | Gorinchem .................. | 23,871 | 24,678 |
| Nymwegen................... | 138,973 | 118,489 | | | |

There were shipped to Germany from the principal Dutch Rhine stations:

| Port. | 1901. | 1900. | Port. | 1901. | 1900. |
|---|---|---|---|---|---|
| | *Tons.* | *Tons.* | | *Tons.* | *Tons.* |
| Rotterdam ............... | 6,860,253 | 7,176,239 | Nymwegen.............. | 855 | 550 |
| Amsterdam .............. | 275,145 | 292,613 | Tiel ...................... | 8 | ............ |
| Dordrecht............... | 40,215 | 100,811 | Arnhem.................. | 449 | 477 |

The tota¹ Rhine traffic at the principal stations was:

| Port. | 1901. | 1900. | Port. | 1901. | 1900. |
|---|---|---|---|---|---|
| | Tons. | Tons. | | Tons. | Tons. |
| Rotterdam ................. | 7,735,307 | 7,845,544 | Arnhem ................. | 17,024 | 16,067 |
| Amsterdam ............... | 435,838 | 446,837 | Gorinchem ............. | 23,871 | 24,678 |
| Dordrecht ................. | 126,065 | 170,796 | | | |
| Nymwegen ................. | 139,828 | 119,038 | Total .............. | 8,496,518 | 8,643,492 |
| Tiel ....................... | 18,595 | 20,592 | | | |

The share of Rotterdam in the Rhine traffic of the Netherlands with Germany was: In 1892, 84 per cent; 1893, 86 per cent; 1894, 1895, 1896, 1897, and 1898, 89 per cent; 1899, 89½ per cent; 1900, 90 per cent; and 1901, 91 per cent.

Besides the traffic at the principal Rhine stations of the Netherlands, the following was received and shipped from different points:

| Description. | 1901. | 1900. |
|---|---|---|
| | Tons. | Tons. |
| Received .................. | 1,772,807 | 1,751,333 |
| Shipped ................... | 59,722 | 81,694 |
| Total ................... | 1,832,529 | 1,833,027 |

This makes the total Rhine traffic between Germany and the Netherlands:

|  | Tons. |
|---|---|
| 1900 ................... | 10,476,579 |
| 1901 ................... | 10,329,047 |
| Decrease ........... | 147,532 |

The Rhine traffic between Germany and Belgium was:

|  | Tons. |
|---|---|
| 1901 ................... | 2,757,330 |
| 1900 ................... | 2,605,632 |
| Increase ........... | 151,698 |

The Rhine traffic of Rotterdam, Amsterdam, and Belgium was:

| Years. | Rotterdam. | Amsterdam. | Belgium. |
|---|---|---|---|
| | Tons. | Tons. | Tons. |
| 1892 ................... | 2,461,495 | 211,740 | 1,447,016 |
| 1893 ................... | 3,290,048 | 199,686 | 1,310,033 |
| 1894 ................... | 4,130,074 | 237,109 | 1,430,759 |
| 1895 ................... | 3,989,827 | 242,315 | 1,571,765 |
| 1896 ................... | 5,272,513 | 308,760 | 1,940,728 |
| 1897 ................... | 5,914,008 | 339,498 | 1,982,566 |
| 1898 ................... | 6,449,375 | 464,093 | 2,469,306 |
| 1899 ................... | 6,947,164 | 504,809 | 2,657,764 |
| 1900 ................... | 7,845,544 | 446,837 | 2,605,632 |
| 1901 ................... | 7,735,307 | 435,838 | 2,757,330 |

At Lobith, the Dutch frontier station, there passed to and from Germany—

| Year. | Number of ships. | Under Dutch flag. | Year. | Number of ships. | Under Dutch flag. |
|---|---|---|---|---|---|
| 1892 ................... | 38,174 | 30,251 | 1897 ................... | 51,424 | 37,749 |
| 1893 ................... | 41,427 | 33,280 | 1898 ................... | 58,546 | 42,456 |
| 1894 ................... | 44,439 | 35,472 | 1899 ................... | 57,259 | 40,634 |
| 1895 ................... | 40,633 | 31,284 | 1900 ................... | 56,680 | 39,186 |
| 1896 ................... | 48,072 | 36,205 | 1901 ................... | 56,288 | 40,067 |

The total Rhine traffic, including traffic between German Rhine stations and Belgian points, and Germany and Dutch Rhine stations, and points along the Rhine in Germany, amounted (in thousand tons) to: 1891, 19,685; 1892, 20,793; 1893, 21,337; 1894, 24,629; 1895, 23,434; 1896, 30,251; 1897, 31 579; 1898, 35,063; 1899, 37,295; 1900, 41,326.

*Railroad freight traffic at Rotterdam.*

[In tons of 1,000 kilograms, or 2,205 pounds.]

|  | 1897. | 1898. | 1899. | 1900. | 1901. |
|---|---|---|---|---|---|
| GOODS SHIPPED. | | | | | |
| State Railway | 650,659 | 646,368 | 644,278 | 498,372 | 511,048 |
| Holland Railway Co | 163,254 | 177,529 | 204,229 | 319,020 | 346,486 |
| Total | 813,913 | 823,897 | 848,502 | 812,392 | 857,534 |
| GOODS ARRIVED. | | | | | |
| State Railway | 615,247 | 859,915 | 813,607 | 745,054 | 837,146 |
| Holland Railway Co | 148,076 | 289,694 | 201,246 | 217,265 | 237,702 |
| Total | 763,323 | 1,149,609 | 1,014,853 | 962,319 | 1,074,848 |
| Total freight movement | 1,577,236 | 1,973,506 | 1,863,355 | 1,774,738 | 1,932,382 |

## EMIGRATION.

| Emigrants. | 1897. | 1898. | 1899. | 1900. | 1901. |
|---|---|---|---|---|---|
| Dutch starting from Rotterdam: | | | | | |
| Men | 323 | 395 | 619 | 883 | 895 |
| Women | 162 | 191 | 303 | 466 | 504 |
| Children | 126 | 160 | 305 | 505 | 392 |
| Total | 611 | 746 | 1,227 | 1,854 | 1,791 |
| Foreign starting from or passing through Rotterdam: | | | | | |
| Men | 2,665 | 5,596 | 8,063 | 15,152 | 14,460 |
| Women | 2,279 | 4,018 | 6,107 | 9,912 | 9,884 |
| Children | 1,450 | 2,199 | 3,565 | 6,463 | 6,770 |
| Total | 6,394 | 11,813 | 17,735 | 31,527 | 31,114 |
| Grand total | 7,005 | 12,559 | 18,962 | 33,381 | 32,905 |

| Destination. | 1897. | 1898. | 1899. | 1900. | 1901. |
|---|---|---|---|---|---|
| The United States: | | | | | |
| Per direct steamer from Rotterdam | 5,972 | 10,167 | 13,985 | 22,121 | 22,300 |
| Via Liverpool | 549 | 1,235 | 2,472 | 6,759 | 6,069 |
| Via Antwerp | 122 | 71 | 162 | 143 | 172 |
| Via London | 249 | 519 | 1,617 | 3,081 | 2,725 |
| Via Glasgow | 113 | 555 | 726 | 1,277 | 1,619 |
| Total | 7,005 | 12,599 | 18,962 | 33,381 | 32,905 |

## PORT IMPROVEMENTS.

The new harbor, "Maashaven," 1¼ miles long and 1,050 feet wide, has been completed. There are now about 25 miles of quays at Rotterdam, which, besides the buoys in the river Maas (1,200 feet wide) and in the large harbors "Maashaven," "Rynhaven," and "Schiehaven," provide mooring places for ocean and river vessels. Vessels with a draft of 30 feet can navigate the river Maas and enter the principal harbors.

The large wooden shed, 492 feet long and 65 feet wide, mentioned in my report in Commercial Relations for 1901 (vol. 2), has been completed, and several new sheds and warehouses for storage companies are in course of construction, in anticipation of a renewed increase in traffic. The storage sheds and warehouses on the left bank of the river, with those in course of construction, cover an area of about 2,000,000 square feet. All the sheds and warehouses are connected by rail with the railroad freight yards of the city.

The Royal Netherlands Company, for the exploitation of petroleum wells in the Dutch Indies, has established its first depot in Europe at Rotterdam. Tanks and a benzine refinery are being constructed on the company's grounds, which cover 5 acres and are situated on the river Maas near the tanks of the four other petroleum companies, viz, the American Petroleum Company, the Pure Oil Company, the German-American Petroleum Company, and Pakhuismeesteren.

There are 24 steam, 13 hydraulic, and 29 electric cranes in the commercial establishments on the left side of the river Maas at Rotterdam; the total number of cranes belonging to the city is 78, with a lifting capacity of from 1,500 to 66,000 pounds. Besides, the city owns a large number of capstans and windlasses, with a capacity of from 1,100 to 4,400 pounds. The railroad companies have 12 cranes, and private parties also own considerable hoisting machinery.

The third coal tip has gone into use. The three coal tips together worked, in 1901, three hundred and forty-seven days and one hundred and eighty-one nights, accommodating 190 vessels, while the two old coal tips worked, in 1901, three hundred and five days and one hundred and twenty nights, accommodating 183 vessels.

The aggregate work done by the coal tips was: In 1892, 90,562 tons; in 1893, 113,909; 1894, 114,598; 1895, 109,809; 1896, 213,660; 1897, 120,110; 1898, 346,847; 1899, 259,297; 1900, 139,784, and in 1901, 191,260 tons.

The coal tips move 20 carloads, or 200 tons, of coal per hour, at a cost of 4 cents per ton.

The steam, hydraulic, and electric cranes (66) together worked five thousand three hundred and seventy-two days and seven hundred and seventy-nine nights in 1901, against five thousand nine hundred and ninety-three days and one thousand and thirty-three nights in 1900. That they worked less in 1901 than in 1900 is due to the smaller cargoes of general merchandise that arrived.

With the 2½-ton electric ore cranes, 95,377 tons of ore were hoisted in 1901, against 74,796 in 1900.

### DRY DOCKS.

There are at Rotterdam three large floating dry docks. The largest is 335 feet in length, and has a lifting power of 17 tons per running foot. The other two docks have a length of 275 and 146 feet, respectively, and a lifting power of 14 tons per foot. The docks are 84 feet wide, and are capable of different combinations with each other. Two still larger docks, of sufficient size to accommodate ships of 12,500 tons, are now in course of construction. Besides the docks mentioned, ship builders and repairers own many small floating docks.

H. Doc. 305, pt 2——34

MERCHANT MARINE.

The following table shows the number of ocean-going vessels belonging to Rotterdam and towns in the vicinity on January 1, 1902:

| Location. | Sailing vessels. | | Steamers. | | Total. | |
|---|---|---|---|---|---|---|
| | Number. | Tonnage. | Number. | Tonnage. | Number. | Tonnage. |
| Alblasserdam ........................ | 2 | 2,828 | 7 | 562 | 9 | 3,390 |
| Dordrecht............................ | 51 | 3,682 | ......... | ......... | 51 | 3,682 |
| Krimpen on the Lek................. | 6 | 8,960 | ......... | ......... | 6 | 8,960 |
| Maassluis ........................... | ......... | ......... | 2 | 103 | 2 | 103 |
| Rotterdam .......................... | 11 | 5,354 | 101 | 171,699 | 112 | 177,053 |
| Schiedam ........................... | 4 | 268 | ......... | ......... | 4 | 268 |
| Total...................... | 74 | 21,092 | 110 | 172,364 | 184 | 193,456 |

*Number of vessels belonging to Rotterdam and vicinity during the last ten years.*

| Year. | Sailing vessels. | | Steamers. | | Total. | |
|---|---|---|---|---|---|---|
| | Number. | Tons. | Number. | Tons. | Number. | Tons. |
| January 1— | | | | | | |
| 1893 ............................. | 61 | 40,067 | 83 | 131,462 | 144 | 175,549 |
| 1894 ............................. | 53 | 35,565 | 85 | 141,321 | 139 | 176,876 |
| 1895 ............................. | 56 | 43,123 | 83 | 104,317 | 139 | 147,440 |
| 1896 ............................. | 48 | 40,073 | 83 | 108,670 | 131 | 148,743 |
| 1897 ............................. | 44 | 34,808 | 88 | 111,760 | 132 | 146,569 |
| 1898 ............................. | 37 | 27,810 | 86 | 111,301 | 123 | 139,111 |
| 1899 ............................. | 95 | 25,876 | 87 | 122,032 | 182 | 147,908 |
| 1900 ............................. | 87 | 24,826 | 90 | 129,691 | 177 | 154,517 |
| 1901 ............................. | 84 | 22,402 | 101 | 145,522 | 185 | 167,924 |
| 1902 ............................. | 74 | 21,092 | 110 | 172,364 | 184 | 193,456 |

The figures for Antwerp and Hamburg, Rotterdam's great competitors for the last ten years, were:

| Year. | Antwerp. | | | | Hamburg. | | | |
|---|---|---|---|---|---|---|---|---|
| | Sailing vessels. | Steamers. | Total. | | Sailing vessels. | Steamers. | Total. | |
| | | | Ships. | Tons. | | | Ships. | Tons. |
| 1893 ........................... | 2 | 42 | 44 | 68,391 | 292 | 326 | 618 | 591,096 |
| 1894 ........................... | 2 | 46 | 48 | 74,195 | 295 | 335 | 630 | 613,339 |
| 1895 ........................... | 1 | 48 | 49 | 79,033 | 286 | 349 | 635 | 658,173 |
| 1896 ........................... | 1 | 53 | 54 | 87,576 | 284 | 357 | 641 | 668,084 |
| 1897 ........................... | 1 | 52 | 53 | 85,977 | 291 | 377 | 668 | 677,463 |
| 1898 ........................... | 1 | 54 | 55 | 86,469 | 294 | 381 | 675 | 717,509 |
| 1899 ........................... | 1 | 60 | 61 | 92,871 | 296 | 392 | 688 | 767,186 |
| 1900 ........................... | 3 | 69 | 72 | 113,356 | 289 | 436 | 725 | 856,716 |
| 1901 ........................... | 1 | 73 | 74 | 120,176 | 307 | 486 | 793 | 988,854 |
| 1902 ........................... | 2 | 64 | 66 | 109,808 | 205 | 526 | 731 | 1,051,593 |

The Netherlands merchant fleet consisted of:

| Year. | Steamers. | | Sailing vessels. | | Total. | |
|---|---|---|---|---|---|---|
| | Number. | Tons. | Number. | Tons. | Number. | Tons. |
| December 31— | | | | | | |
| 1901 ............................. | 235 | 306,694 | 417 | 75,408 | 652 | 382,102 |
| 1900 ............................. | 212 | 268,205 | 425 | 78,577 | 638 | 346,783 |
| Increase or decrease ......... | 22 | 38,489 | 8 | 3,169 | 14 | 35,319 |

*Vessels condemned and sold abroad.*

| Year. | Steamers. | | Sailing vessels. | | Total. | |
|---|---|---|---|---|---|---|
| | Number. | Tons. | Number. | Tons. | Number. | Tons. |
| 1901 ................................ | 14 | 23,019 | 46 | 8,152 | 60 | 311,171 |
| 1900 ................................ | 8 | 12,742 | 31 | 9,052 | 39 | 21,794 |

*Vessels registered for the first time.*

| Year. | Steamers. | | Sailing vessels. | | Total. | |
|---|---|---|---|---|---|---|
| | Number. | Tons. | Number. | Tons. | Number. | Tons. |
| 1901 ................................ | 36 | 64,495 | 38 | 5,633 | 74 | 70,128 |
| 1900 ................................ | 29 | 47,779 | 24 | 3,628 | 53 | 51,407 |

*Vessels built on wharves in the Netherlands.*

| Year. | Steamers. | | Sailing vessels. | | Total. | |
|---|---|---|---|---|---|---|
| | Number. | Tons. | Number. | Tons. | Number. | Tons. |
| 1901 ................................ | 17 | 16,344 | 38 | 5,633 | 55 | 21,977 |
| 1900 ................................ | 14 | 20,818 | 20 | 1,616 | 34 | 22,434 |
| Increase or decrease ......... | 3 | 4,474 | 18 | 4,017 | 21 | 457 |

*Vessels built abroad for Dutch account.*

| Year. | Steamers. | | Sailing vessels. | | Total. | |
|---|---|---|---|---|---|---|
| | Number. | Tons. | Number. | Tons. | Number. | Tons. |
| 1901 ................................ | 19 | 48,151 | .......... | .......... | 19 | 48,151 |
| 1900 ................................ | 15 | 29,961 | 4 | 2,012 | 19 | 28,973 |
| Increase or decrease ......... | 4 | 21,190 | 4 | 2,012 | .......... | 19,178 |

*Composition of the Dutch merchant marine.*

| Year. | Steamers. | | Sailing vessels. | | Total. | |
|---|---|---|---|---|---|---|
| | Number. | Tons. | Number. | Tons. | Number. | Tons. |
| 1892 ................................ | 447 | 121,391 | 150 | 169,142 | 597 | 290,533 |
| 1893 ................................ | 442 | 116,426 | 154 | 176,171 | 596 | 292,597 |
| 1894 ................................ | 424 | 108,679 | 157 | 181,385 | 581 | 291,064 |
| 1895 ................................ | 405 | 100,392 | 162 | 188,820 | 567 | 289,212 |
| 1896 ................................ | 440 | 96,560 | 172 | 196,938 | 612 | 293,498 |
| 1897 ................................ | 441 | 95,100 | 171 | 200,728 | 612 | 296,828 |
| 1898 ................................ | 429 | 88,183 | 176 | 213,742 | 605 | 301,925 |
| 1899 ................................ | 432 | 84,268 | 192 | 235,840 | 624 | 320,108 |
| 1900 ................................ | 425 | 78,577 | 213 | 268,206 | 638 | 346,783 |
| 1901 ................................ | 417 | 75,408 | 235 | 306,694 | 652 | 382,106 |

## POST-OFFICE AT ROTTERDAM.

From the interior of the Netherlands there were received in 1901 7,510,175 letters, against 7,158,159 in 1900, and 3,892,234 postal cards, against 3,767,894 in 1900. From abroad, 1,765,686 letters were received, against 1,746,755 in 1900, and 661,076 postal cards, against 570,193 in 1900.

There were also received 5,523,359 packages of newspapers, against

5,078,727 in 1900, and 3,006,692 packages of other printed matter, against 2,993,194 in 1900; 128,089 samples were received from the interior and 102,830 from abroad, against 131,389 and 84,916, respectively, in 1900.

From the city of Rotterdam and the interior of the Netherlands, there were received 122,365 registered letters, representing a value of $3,079,344, and 97,288 from abroad, representing a value of $983,908.68; while the figures for 1900 were, from the interior, 117,965, representing a value of $4,956,584.87, and from abroad, 92,321, representing a value of $1,495,405.81.

From the Rotterdam post-office, there were sent abroad 89,078 registered letters, representing a value of $664,376.40, against 95,260 letters, with a value of $826,299, in 1900.

The number of registered and other letters sent and received from abroad does not include letters handled at railroad post-offices.

To the interior, there were forwarded per parcel post 224,916 parcels, and there were received 169,472 parcels, against 216,792 and 164,654 parcels, respectively, in 1900. To foreign countries, there were sent 32,725 parcels, and there were received from foreign countries 92,767, against 34,446 and 88,110 parcels, respectively, in 1900.

Postal money orders to the number of 168,200, amounting to $1,700,236.95, were dispatched, and 254,665, amounting to $2,365,254.26, were paid at the Rotterdam post-office. In 1900, 172,227 money orders, to the value of $1,654,240.93, were dispatched, while 236,948, to the value of $2,220,850.48, were paid. In 1901, postal checks to the amount of $6,268.60 were paid, while checks to the amount of $7,422.40 were issued from the office. In 1900, checks to the amount of $6,431.40 were issued, while checks to the amount of $8,479.60 were paid.

The post-office collected checks for individuals to the amount of $586,101.10 and paid to depositors $2,298,667.62, while in 1900 checks were collected to the value of $540,038.60 and $2,027,134.78 was paid out to depositors.

## TELEGRAPH AND TELEPHONES.

At the Government telegraph offices at Rotterdam there were handled, in 1901, 3,116,026 telegrams, against 2,983,711 in 1900 and 2,886,362 in 1899.

The number of people at Rotterdam connected by city telephone was on December 31, 1896, 1,151; 1900, 2,352, and 1901, 2,730.

The average number of daily connections in the city was 25,591, against 21,690 in 1900; the average number of connections during the night was 480, against 404 in 1900; on Sundays, 2,926, against 2,605 in 1900.

The number of conversations with the interior of the Netherlands was 341,659, against 298,926 in 1900.

The number of international conversations was, with Germany, 10,910, and with Belgium, 10,498; total, 21,408.

## COIN.

The following amount of new coin was delivered for circulation by the mint of the Netherlands:

For the colonies, 200,085 10-florin gold pieces.

For the Netherlands, 13,900,000 brass 1-cent and half-cent pieces.

The amount of coin in circulation in the Netherlands was estimated as follows:

| Description. | December. | |
|---|---|---|
| | 1899. | 1900. |
| | *Florins.* | *Florins.* |
| 10-florin gold pieces | 46,923,580.00 | 46,914,380.00 |
| Silver standard coin | 124,123,799.50 | 120,581,324.50 |
| Other silver | 8,678,488.05 | 9,206,000.15 |
| Bronze coin | 2,158,500.00 | 2,297,500.00 |
| Total | 181,884,317.55 | 178,999,204.65 |

## DISCOUNT RATES.

The following fluctuations took place in 1901 and 1902 in the rates of the Bank of the Netherlands:

| Description. | Jan. 1, 1901. | June 15, 1901. | Jan. 1, 1902. |
|---|---|---|---|
| | *Per cent.* | *Per cent.* | *Per cent.* |
| For bills | 3½ | 3 | 3 |
| For promissory notes | 4 | 3½ | 3½ |
| On home stocks | 4 | 3½ | 3½ |
| On foreign stocks | 4½ | 4 | 4 |

## RATES OF EXCHANGE.

The following were the highest and lowest rates of exchange on the five principal European countries in 1901:

| Market. | Lowest. | Highest. |
|---|---|---|
| London (£1): | *Florins.* | *Florins.* |
| Short | 12.04 | 12.13 |
| Three months | 11.90 | 12.08 |
| Paris (100 francs): | | |
| Short | 47.80 | 48.17½ |
| Three months | 47.45 | 47.70 |
| Germany (100 reichsmarks): | | |
| Short | 58.80 | 59.25 |
| Three months | 58.20 | 58.70 |
| Vienna (100 crowns), three months | 49.30 | 49.90 |
| St. Petersburg (1 ruble), three months | 1.25 | 1.26 |

*Rate of exchange in 1902.*

| Market. | Lowest. | Highest. |
|---|---|---|
| London (£1): | *Florins.* | *Florins.* |
| Short | 12.08 | 12.14½ |
| Three months | 11.97 | 12.04 |
| Paris (100 francs): | | |
| Short | 48.05 | 48.30 |
| Three months | 47.67½ | 47.85 |
| Germany (100 reichsmarks): | | |
| Short | 59.10 | 59.25 |
| Three months | 58.60 | 58.80 |
| Vienna (100 crowns), three months | 49.85 | 49.90 |
| St. Petersburg (1 ruble), three months | 1.25½ | 1.26½ |

## PUBLIC REVENUE OF THE NETHERLANDS.

The following table shows the amounts derived from the public revenues in 1900 and 1901:

| Description. | 1900. | | 1901. | |
|---|---|---|---|---|
| *Direct taxes.* | *Florins.* | $5,064,577.508 | *Florins.* | $5,134,609.522 |
| Land tax | 12,661,443.77 | $5,064,577.508 | 12,836,523.805 | $5,134,609.522 |
| Personal tax | 8,829,328.675 | 3,581,729.47 | 8,847,016.315 | 3,538,806.526 |
| Trades and professions | 6,356,248.755 | 2,542,499.502 | 7,188,830.795 | 2,875,532.318 |
| Property tax | 7,381,502.14 | 2,952,600.856 | 7,547,515.405 | 3,019,006.162 |
| Mining royalties | 11,253.796 | 4,501.518 | 26,158.46 | 10,463.384 |
| Total | 35,239,772.135 | 14,095,908.854 | 36,446,044.78 | 14,578,417.912 |
| *Import duties.* | | | | |
| Import duties | 9,668,617.765 | 3,867,447.106 | 9,899,296.655 | 3,959,718.662 |
| Officially stamped paper | 19,025.325 | 7,610.18 | 18,738.90 | 7,495.56 |
| Total | 9,687,643.09 | 3,875,058.286 | 9,918,035.555 | 3,967,214.222 |
| *Excise.* | | | | |
| Sugar | 14,156,893.735 | 5,662,757.494 | 15,543,024.49 | 6,217,209.796 |
| Wine | 1,768,468.22 | 707,387.285 | 1,802,958.34 | 721,183.336 |
| Dutc and foreign spirits | 26,648,804.72 | 10,659,521.888 | 26,807,988.75 | 10,723,175.50 |
| Salt .h | 1,530,371.215 | 612,148.486 | 1,571,299.94 | 628,519.976 |
| Beer and vinegar | 1,395,692.815 | 558,277.126 | 1,458,763.60 | 583,505.44 |
| Meat | 3,736,233.98 | 1,494,493.592 | 3,890,401.30 | 1,556,160.52 |
| Total | 49,236,464.68 | 19,694,585.946 | 51,074,386.42 | 20,429,754.568 |
| *Gold and silver.* | | | | |
| Taxes | 823,221.685 | 129,288.674 | 337,212.723 | 134,885.09 |
| Assays | 872.205 | 348.882 | 880.40 | 352.16 |
| Total | 324,093.89 | 129,637.556 | 338,098.125 | 185,237.25 |
| *Indirect taxation.* | | | | |
| Stamps | 4,045,352.696 | 1,618,141.076 | 4,242,194.98 | 1,696,877.972 |
| Registration dues | 5,769,617.36 | 2,307,846.95 | 5,884,217.465 | 2,833,886.986 |
| Mortgages | 563,784.06 | 225,513.624 | 592,496.265 | 236,998.506 |
| Succession dues | 15,967,410.475 | 6,386,464.19 | 11,443,963.885 | 4,577,585.554 |
| Total | 26,346,164.59 | 10,538,465.836 | 22,113,872.545 | 8,845,349.018 |
| Domains | 1,900,552.425 | 760,220.97 | 1,706,753.475 | 682,701.39 |
| Post-office | 10,125,028.095 | 4,050,011.23 | 10,750,768.88 | 4,300,307.552 |
| State telegraphs | 2,126,119.32 | 850,447.725 | 2,320,646.00 | 928,258.40 |
| State lottery | 656,540.39 | 262,616.153 | 656,157.335 | 262,462.954 |
| Game and fishing licenses | 139,658.00 | 55,861.20 | 139,085.00 | 55,634.00 |
| Pilotage | 2,219,362.015 | 887,744.806 | 2,122,240.215 | 848,896.086 |
| Total revenue | 138,001,398.685 | 55,200,557.458 | 137,585,583.38 | 55,084,238.352 |

## FISHERIES AND FISH TRADE.

The following figures show the value of the fish sold by auction at the Rotterdam fish market:

| | | | |
|---|---|---|---|
| 1892 | $113,576.54 | 1897 | $124,388.36 |
| 1893 | 113,635.42 | 1898 | 134,585.72 |
| 1894 | 121,776.92 | 1899 | 129,981.42 |
| 1895 | 118,558.34 | 1900 | 136,734.32 |
| 1896 | 131,836.78 | 1901 | 140,607.06 |

The number of salmon caught in the Maas River near Rotterdam, and auctioned at the salmon market of Kralingsche Veer, a suburb of this city, was:

| | | | |
|---|---|---|---|
| 1892 | 66,165 | 1897 | 39,696 |
| 1893 | 75,276 | 1898 | 41,516 |
| 1894 | 57,321 | 1899 | 25,785 |
| 1895 | 48,436 | 1900 | 21,463 |
| 1896 | 49,308 | 1901 | 25,709 |

The following figures show the herring catch of the Netherlands fleet:

| | Barrels. | | Barrels. |
|---|---|---|---|
| 1891 | 375,537 | 1897 | 352,394 |
| 1892 | 591,277 | 1898 | 532,481 |
| 1893 | 585,335 | 1899 | 296,016 |
| 1894 | 585,466 | 1900 | 438,216 |
| 1895 | 494,422 | 1901 | 553,130 |
| 1896 | 530,488 | | |

The exports of herring were:

| Year. | To Germany. | To Belgium. | To the United States. | To other countries. |
|---|---|---|---|---|
| | Tons. | Tons. | Tons. | Tons. |
| 1891 | 177,373 | 21,910 | 10,574 | 8,520 |
| 1892 | 276,353 | 30,708 | 18,127 | 7,883 |
| 1893 | 290,793 | 25,100 | 10,600 | 11,178 |
| 1894 | 292,620 | 21,340 | 18,127 | 18,098 |
| 1895 | 249,133 | 26,333 | 46,107 | 13,947 |
| 1896 | 247,390 | 27,893 | 21,613 | 22,466 |
| 1897 | 208,686 | 32,060 | 26,660 | 4,966 |
| 1898 | 259,380 | 33,540 | 32,940 | 28,473 |
| 1899 | 180,660 | 16,558 | 59,906 | 6,620 |
| 1900 | 276,027 | 23,153 | 63,533 | 20,733 |

## CATTLE TRADE.

Cattle were imported into and exported from the Netherlands in 1901, as follows:

| Kind. | Imported. | Exported. |
|---|---|---|
| Steers, oxen, and cows | 1,591 | 43,617 |
| Calves | 40 | 3,005 |
| Hogs | 30 | 4,976 |
| Sheep | 81,065 | 46,136 |
| Lambs | 924 | 20,383 |

The sales at the Rotterdam weekly cattle market were:

| Year. | Horses. | Cows, steers, calves. | Sheep. | Hogs. | Goats. | Asses. |
|---|---|---|---|---|---|---|
| 1892 | 1,718 | 121,068 | 43,359 | 35,961 | 55 | 16 |
| 1893 | 2,117 | 127,592 | 40,811 | 32,208 | 60 | 12 |
| 1894 | 3,334 | 119,521 | 43,782 | 33,096 | 51 | 33 |
| 1895 | 3,459 | 132,588 | 47,405 | 44,175 | 67 | 11 |
| 1896 | 3,698 | 142,709 | 53,076 | 48,010 | 66 | 13 |
| 1897 | 3,131 | 137,256 | 55,207 | 39,206 | 45 | 19 |
| 1898 | 1,837 | 151,616 | 58,194 | 42,157 | 60 | 14 |
| 1899 | 2,046 | 145,617 | 59,903 | 44,220 | 110 | 38 |
| 1900 | 2,486 | 150,936 | 59,290 | 39,067 | 97 | 13 |
| 1901 | 2,423 | 149,868 | 55,360 | 36,009 | 71 | 8 |

At the Rotterdam slaughterhouse, cattle were slaughtered for export as follows:

| Year. | Cows and steers. | Hogs. | Calves. | Sheep. |
|---|---|---|---|---|
| 1892 | 77 | 15,451 | 8,696 | 77,605 |
| 1893 | 92 | 24,527 | 6,657 | 108,552 |
| 1894 | 168 | 30,250 | 5,998 | 88,603 |
| 1895 | 1,065 | 70,258 | 11,263 | 64,588 |
| 1896 | 273 | 28,733 | 12,158 | 123,650 |
| 1897 | 977 | 18,414 | 19,429 | 203,877 |
| 1898 | 562 | 23,903 | 82,060 | 179,988 |
| 1899 | 3,611 | 45,652 | 36,363 | 178,828 |
| 1900 | 2,321 | 48,261 | 36,338 | 210,489 |
| 1901 | 1,393 | 30,598 | 30,641 | 213,049 |

For Rotterdam consumption, there were killed:

| Year. | Cows, steers, etc. | Calves. | Horses. | Hogs. | Sheep. | Goats. | Asses. |
|---|---|---|---|---|---|---|---|
| 1892 | 16,048 | 8,925 | 1,500 | 21,637 | 2,839 | 350 | 4 |
| 1893 | 17,598 | 8,888 | 1,541 | 20,116 | 3,028 | 347 | 2 |
| 1894 | 16,360 | 8,379 | 1,789 | 24,390 | 2,630 | 412 | 2 |
| 1895 | 16,313 | 7,743 | 1,672 | 30,200 | 2,407 | 559 | 5 |
| 1896 | 15,193 | 7,692 | 2,210 | 34,542 | 2,523 | 457 | 5 |
| 1897 | 19,466 | 8,468 | 2,181 | 31,480 | 2,761 | 643 | 3 |
| 1898 | 23,536 | 10,082 | 4,184 | 30,986 | 2,756 | 893 | 6 |
| 1899 | 25,920 | 10,562 | 4,662 | 37,721 | 2,239 | 964 | 4 |
| 1900 | 27,104 | 11,494 | 5,448 | 38,303 | 2,782 | 1,486 | 5 |
| 1901 | 26,675 | 11,465 | 5,096 | 33,464 | 2,551 | 3,393 | 12 |

The tolls at the cattle market produced in—

| | | | |
|---|---|---|---|
| 1892 | $17,413.60 | 1897 | $19,623.20 |
| 1893 | 17,603.20 | 1898 | 21,192.80 |
| 1894 | 17,044.40 | 1899 | 21,194.40 |
| 1895 | 19,371.20 | 1900 | 21,011.60 |
| 1896 | 20,609.20 | 1901 | 20,504.40 |

### DAIRY INDUSTRY.

The following tables give data relative to this industry:

*Creameries in the Netherlands.*

| Province. | Total number of creameries. | | Quantity of milk made into butter. | | Quantity of butter made. | | Quantity of cheese made in the creameries. | |
|---|---|---|---|---|---|---|---|---|
| | 1899. | 1900. | 1899. | 1900. | 1899. | 1900. | 1899. | 1900. |
| | | | *Imp. gals.* | *Imp. gals.* | *Pounds.* | *Pounds.* | *Pounds.* | *Pounds.* |
| Groningen | 48 | 50 | 6,953,067 | 7,131,512 | 2,197,219 | 2,275,944 | 904,251 | 1,460,571 |
| Freisland | 117 | 127 | 80,804,556 | 88,912,777 | 23,021,324 | 24,621,676 | 32,388,512 | 39,462,848 |
| Drenthe | 92 | 94 | 15,182,467 | 16,838,066 | 5,145,509 | 5,307,064 | 50,310 | 58,099 |
| Overijssel | 77 | 84 | 15,278,667 | 17,107,266 | 5,003,603 | 5,670,276 | 613,030 | 595,820 |
| Gelderland | 86 | 84 | 14,989,933 | 17,987,666 | 5,075,946 | 6,061,044 | 104,104 | 102,245 |
| Utrecht | 10 | 11 | 1,856,844 | 2,116,488 | 546,344 | 668,985 | 419,373 | 381,522 |
| North Holland | 21 | 20 | 2,735,511 | 1,720,488 | 899,906 | 479,677 | 28,950 | 310,290 |
| South Holland | 43 | 47 | 5,179,733 | 6,343,844 | 1,409,364 | 1,339,329 | 1,221,746 | 1,580,414 |
| Zeeland | 17 | 19 | 1,988,333 | 2,038,933 | 629,996 | 687,867 | 14,740 | 6,897 |
| North Braband | 162 | 165 | 14,720,822 | 19,255,711 | 4,965,831 | 5,899,700 | 288,471 | 286,829 |
| Limburg | 156 | 172 | 11,367,888 | 11,602,978 | 3,937,498 | 3,995,473 | | |
| Total | 829 | 873 | 171,057,821 | 191,055,729 | 52,831,540 | 57,007,035 | 36,033,487 | 44,180,035 |

*Cooperative creameries.*

| Province. | Total cooperative creameries. | | Number of cooperators. | | Milk. | | Quantity of butter made in the cooperative creameries. | |
|---|---|---|---|---|---|---|---|---|
| | 1899. | 1900. | 1899. | 1900. | 1899. | 1900. | 1899. | 1900. |
| | | | | | *Imp. gals.* | *Imp. gals.* | *Pounds.* | *Pounds.* |
| Groningen | 31 | 36 | 1,215 | 1,929 | 4,233,358 | 4,811,288 | 1,387,813 | 1,595,799 |
| Friesland | 68 | 76 | 3,681 | 3,662 | 42,538,156 | 44,038,600 | 12,359,079 | 12,841,728 |
| Drenthe | 72 | 72 | 4,606 | 5,042 | 12,245,756 | 13,225,111 | 4,190,899 | 4,527,603 |
| Overijssel | 28 | 32 | 2,546 | 2,185 | 5,267,378 | 6,510,538 | 1,795,402 | 2,227,672 |
| Gelderland | 48 | 51 | 4,683 | 6,065 | 10,737,067 | 1,419,064 | 3,696,717 | 4,808,577 |
| Utrecht | 2 | 8 | 51 | 219 | 172,045 | 966,733 | 61,096 | 338,714 |
| North Holland | 5 | 4 | 124 | 139 | 285,867 | 284,311 | 89,384 | 87,034 |
| South Holland | 8 | 10 | 179 | 173 | 942,654 | 1,219,177 | 291,084 | 398,642 |
| Zeeland | 12 | 11 | 458 | 420 | 1,665,578 | 1,551,467 | 564,010 | 533,320 |
| North Braband | 126 | 130 | 5,805 | 6,661 | 11,402,645 | 14,201,689 | 3,840,494 | 4,742,661 |
| Limburg | 135 | 156 | 5,840 | 7,219 | 8,962,702 | 10,667,711 | 3,075,873 | 3,635,568 |
| Total | 535 | 581 | 29,138 | 33,714 | 98,453,197 | 98,895,684 | 31,351,851 | 35,732,313 |

*Cooperative creameries*—Continued.

| Province. | Quantity of cheese made in the cooperative creameries. | | Number of centrifuges in these creameries. | | | | | |
|---|---|---|---|---|---|---|---|---|
| | | | Steam. | | Hand power. | | Other power. | |
| | 1899. | 1900. | 1899. | 1900. | 1899. | 1900. | 1899. | 1900. |
| | *Pounds.* | *Pounds.* | | | | | | |
| Groningen | 348,550 | 335,078 | 31 | 34 | 17 | 25 | | |
| Friesland | 23,609,779 | 22,564,583 | 115 | 126 | 22 | 25 | 1 | |
| Drenthe | | 53,099 | 45 | 62 | 73 | 77 | | |
| Overijssel | | | 25 | 25 | 24 | 27 | | 1 |
| Gelderland | | | 42 | 53 | 41 | 41 | 1 | 1 |
| Utrecht | | | 1 | 6 | | | | |
| North Holland | | | | | 7 | 7 | | |
| South Holland | 68,833 | 102,788 | 4 | 6 | 7 | 9 | | |
| Zeeland | | | 11 | 10 | 5 | 5 | | |
| North Braband | 251,570 | 227,429 | 17 | 22 | 155 | 160 | | |
| Limburg | | | 2 | 2 | 187 | 161 | | 1 |
| Total | 24,273,732 | 23,282,927 | 298 | 346 | 488 | 530 | 2 | 3 |

*Cheese factories.*

| Province. | Number of cheese factories. | | Milk used. | | Quantity of cheese made. | | Quantity of butter made in the cheese factories. | |
|---|---|---|---|---|---|---|---|---|
| | 1899. | 1900. | 1899. | 1900. | 1899. | 1900. | 1899. | 1900. |
| | | | *Imp. gals.* | *Imp. gals.* | *Pounds.* | *Pounds.* | *Pounds.* | *Pounds.* |
| Groningen | 3 | 7 | 186,222 | 409,689 | 171,085 | 367,101 | | 4,039 |
| North Holland | 64 | 65 | 7,855,778 | 9,226,244 | 6,602,988 | 7,880,453 | 79,262 | 113,951 |
| South Holland | 1 | 1 | (a) | | | | | |
| North Braband | 2 | 3 | 20,000 | 22,222 | 19,800 | 22,000 | 605 | 638 |
| Total | 70 | 76 | 8,061,000 | 9,658,155 | 6,793,873 | 8,269,554 | 79,867 | 118,628 |

a No statistics.

*Cooperative cheese factories.*

| Province where situated. | Number of factories. | | Number of cooperators. | | Milk used. | | Cheese made. | | Butter made in the cheese factories. | |
|---|---|---|---|---|---|---|---|---|---|---|
| | 1899. | 1900. | 1899. | 1900. | 1899. | 1900. | 1899. | 1900. | 1899. | 1900. |
| | | | | | *Imp. gals.* | *Imp. gals.* | *Pounds.* | *Pounds.* | *Pounds.* | *Pounds.* |
| Groningen | 2 | 3 | 88 | 97 | 141,444 | 171,800 | 130,612 | 157,216 | | |
| North Holland | 38 | 48 | 411 | 485 | 4,704,911 | 6,803,600 | 3,979,023 | 5,887,499 | 37,906 | 42,062 |
| Total | 40 | 51 | 499 | 582 | 4,846,355 | 6,975,400 | 4,109,635 | 6,044,715 | 37,906 | 42,062 |

The total quantity of butter and cheese produced in the Netherlands was:

| Origin. | Butter. | | Cheese. | |
|---|---|---|---|---|
| | 1899. | 1900. | 1899. | 1900. |
| | *Pounds.* | *Pounds.* | *Pounds.* | *Pounds.* |
| On farms | 68,932,554 | 65,949,620 | 110,873,664 | 113,469,620 |
| In creameries | 52,831,540 | 54,807,036 | 36,033,487 | 44,240,035 |
| In cheese factories | 79,867 | 118,628 | 6,793,024 | 8,269,554 |
| Total | 121,843,961 | 120,875,284 | 153,700,175 | 165,979,209 |

*Milk centrifuges in use on farms, in creameries, and factories.*

| Province. | Hand power. | | | Animal power. | | | Steam power. | | | Gas, electricity, or petroleum motor power. | | |
|---|---|---|---|---|---|---|---|---|---|---|---|---|
| | 1898. | 1899. | 1900. | 1898. | 1899. | 1900. | 1898. | 1899. | 1900. | 1898. | 1899. | 1900. |
| Groningen | 29 | 30 | 48 | 4 | ..... | ..... | 49 | 51 | 48 | ..... | ..... | ..... |
| Friesland | 118 | 116 | 116 | 4 | 3 | 3 | 181 | 189 | 210 | ..... | 1 | ..... |
| Drenthe | 88 | 94 | 91 | ..... | ..... | ..... | 59 | 63 | 71 | ..... | ..... | ..... |
| Overijssel | 49 | 59 | 78 | 1 | ..... | ..... | 67 | 75 | 78 | 1 | 3 | 3 |
| Gelderland | 83 | 84 | 83 | 3 | 3 | 5 | 67 | 72 | 78 | 8 | 6 | 6 |
| Utrecht | 2 | 6 | 6 | ..... | ..... | ..... | 15 | 16 | 17 | ..... | ..... | ..... |
| North Holland | 30 | 42 | 46 | ..... | 2 | 2 | 17 | 26 | 26 | 1 | 1 | 1 |
| South Holland | 36 | 33 | 36 | 15 | 5 | 6 | 30 | 42 | 47 | 1 | 1 | 1 |
| Zeeland | 134 | 301 | 430 | ..... | ..... | 6 | 18 | 16 | 18 | ..... | ..... | ..... |
| North Braband | 277 | 396 | 463 | 4 | 6 | 14 | 24 | 35 | 39 | 1 | 1 | 1 |
| Limburg | 426 | 537 | 727 | 2 | 11 | 1 | 5 | 5 | 7 | ..... | 1 | 2 |
| Total | 1,272 | 1,698 | 2,119 | 33 | 30 | 37 | 532 | 590 | 639 | 12 | 14 | 14 |

## COAL.

The production of the five principal coal mines of the Netherlands, situated in the province of Limburg, was as follows:

| Year. | Production. | Quantity sold. | Amount realized. | Year. | Production. | Quantity sold. | Amount realized. |
|---|---|---|---|---|---|---|---|
| | *Tons.a* | *Tons.a* | | | *Tons. a* | *Tons. a* | |
| 1890 | 108,807 | 107,727 | $223,330.80 | 1896 | 137,786 | 182,258 | $214,373.60 |
| 1891 | 103,357 | 95,468 | 220,666.00 | 1897 | 150,145 | 145,640 | 244,274.40 |
| 1892 | 96,144 | 91,133 | 173,510.80 | 1898 | 150,398 | 147,286 | 258,075.20 |
| 1893 | 100,776 | 98,352 | 177,771.60 | 1899 | 212,972 | 201,544 | |
| 1894 | 109,278 | 108,074 | 180,319.60 | 1900 | 330,225 | 303,442 | |
| 1895 | 126,615 | 115,716 | 200,272.80 | | | | |

*a Of 2,200 pounds.*

Imports of coal into the Netherlands were, in tons of 1,000 kilograms (about 2,200 pounds):

| Period. | General imports. | For consumption. |
|---|---|---|
| 1900 | 7,714,966 | 5,964,581 |
| 1901 | 7,040,667 | 5,282,269 |
| First half 1902 | 3,908,908 | 2,467,696 |

And at Rotterdam:

| Period. | General imports. | For consumption. |
|---|---|---|
| 1900 | 1,172,813 | 1,172,526 |
| 1901 | 574,065 | 561,734 |
| First half 1902 | 193,021 | 187,733 |

The exports of coal were:

| Period. | From the Netherlands. | From Rotterdam. |
|---|---|---|
| 1900 | 2,728,565 | 691,497 |
| 1901 | 2,037,838 | 380,754 |
| First half 1902 | 1,265,024 | 233,909 |

### PATENT RIGHTS, ETC.

There are are no patent rights in the Netherlands. Information regarding trade-marks, commercial licenses, passports, and quarantine regulations is contained in my report in Commercial Relations, 1896–97, vol. 2, while information as to postal rates is given in the same report and in my report in Commercial Relations, 1899, vol. 2.

### INDUSTRIES AT ROTTERDAM IN 1901.

*Shipbuilding.*—The shipbuilding yards kept busy in 1901 building vessels contracted for while freight rates were still favorable. During the present year shipbuilding, however, has greatly decreased, owing to the large surplus of ship's room, for which there is no demand.

*Machinery.*—Machinery is manufactured for use in the Netherlands and for export to Germany, Belgium, England, France, and the Dutch colonies. The financial results of the several factories have varied. The depressed condition of Rhine navigation influenced the machine shops considerably, and less machinery than usual was needed in this country.

*Driving belts.*—Driving belts are exported to most countries except the United States. The manufacture seems profitable, and the demand increases with the growing application of steam and electricity.

*Fire engines.*—Fire engines are successfully manufactured here for use in the Netherlands.

*Flour mills.*—The flour mills grind principally to supply inland consumers. Owing to the competition from American mills and the import duties levied on flour in several countries, the industry can hardly be considered a paying one.

*Butterine.*—The manufacture of butterine is a very important industry in this city. The factories find a good market for a part of their product in the Netherlands, but they manufacture principally for export to England, Scotland, Denmark, Sweden, South Africa, the Dutch colonies, China, and Japan. The consumption of butterine augments from year to year, but financial results for 1901 were not as good as usual, on account of the high price paid for the raw materials, which are principally imported from the United States.

*Cocoa.*—The cocoa factories supply the Netherlands and export to most European countries, the Dutch colonies, and South America. Some cocoa powder is also exported to the United States. Sales in the Netherlands were satisfactory, but the exports were not. Competition is continually growing; besides, the cocoa beans have been high in price, and costly advertising becomes more and more a necessity for those manufacturers who desire to do a large export business. Cocoa butter commands high prices and is largely in demand abroad. This has led some manufacturers to prepare large quantities of cocoa powder in order to obtain the butter, which resulted in an overproduction of the powder.

*Distilleries.*—The products of the distilleries are exported all over the world and also supply the home demand. The results were not satisfactory in 1901. Great Britain and the colonies purchased less than usual, and in South America, the political situation seems to have had a bad effect on the consumption of gin. Then the competition of whisky is felt more and more, especially abroad. The demand for Dutch brandywine in European countries and the Dutch Indies increased somewhat. For the yeast trade, 1901 was more favorable, owing to better prices; the shipments to foreign countries are, however, decreasing.

*Breweries.*—The breweries produce for home consumption and export to Belgium, France, England, Scotland, Ireland, and the Dutch and British colonies.

*Preserved goods.*—The preserved-goods factories work for home consumption and also export, especially to the Dutch colonies, to England, and to South Africa. The results, although not unsatisfactory, were not as favorable in 1901 as in 1900, on account of the high prices of beef and pork and also of tin and tin plate for canning and packing.

*Cigars.*—Cigars are largely manufactured for consumption in the Netherlands and for export all over the world. The majority of the manufacturers are successful, owing to the very low import duty in this country on raw tobacco, which enables them to compete with their product in foreign markets. In the Netherlands, the competition is very keen.

*Rice mills.*—The rice-cleaning mills work for inland consumption and export to all European countries, except Russia and Spain, and to North America and South Africa. The results in 1901, were not very satisfactory, owing to the damaged condition of rice arriving from British India, which made the percentage of waste larger than usual.

*Cordials.*—Cordials are exported to all the principal ports of the world. The profits for the manufacturers were smaller than in former years, on account of the increased import duties in some of the consuming countries.

*Bed feathers.*—The bed-feather factories work chiefly for consumption in the Netherlands, though small lots are exported to Germany and Switzerland. During the first half of 1901, bed feathers were in good demand, but later, owing to the high prices of the raw material, there were but few buyers.

*Chemical colors.*—The chemical factories sell their products in the Netherlands and export to Belgium, Germany, India, America, and Australia. While the dullness in the building trade influenced sales in this country, the export trade has been very satisfactory. The Dutch products seem to have a good reputation abroad.

*Hats and caps.*—Hats and caps are principally manufactured for use in the Netherlands, but also for export to England. The results are fairly satisfactory to the manufacturers. In military caps and lacquered helmets, the competition with German factories is very severe, the Dutch caps being of somewhat better quality and make, but also somewhat more expensive.

*Carbonic acid.*—Carbonic acid is manufactured for home consumption and for export to Germany, Norway, Sweden, South Africa, and the Dutch East Indies with moderate results.

*White lead.*—The white-lead works, which only supply the Netherlands, had a favorable year. The demand for the Dutch white lead is on the increase.

*Furniture.*—Furniture is principally manufactured for use in the Netherlands; some, however, is exported to the Dutch colonies and South Africa. Unlike other years, none was exported to England in 1901.

*Carpets.*—The carpet and tapestry works chiefly supply the Netherlands market; they export only as much as foreign import duties will permit. The financial results for the year were not very satisfactory.

*Vinegar.*—Notwithstanding the competition of vinegar essences imported from abroad, vinegar is successfully manufactured for home consumption; exportation is made impracticable by heavy import duties levied by most foreign countries.

*Soap.*—Soap is chiefly manufactured for home consumption, but the export trade to the Dutch East Indies is gradually growing. Results for the year were fair.

*Salt works.*—The salt works produce for home consumption and also export to Germany, Belgium, Norway, and England. The results were middling, considering that the Dutch salt makers have to compete with the German syndicate, which charges high prices in Germany and disposes of its overproduction by selling it abroad for almost anything it will bring.

### STEAM ENGINES AND BOILERS AT ROTTERDAM.

On December 31, 1901, 214 industrial concerns at Rotterdam had in use 349 steam boilers, with an aggregate heating surface of 14,292 square meters, and 194 establishments had in use 199 gas motors, while the number of electric motors in use was 269, with an aggregate horsepower of 2,563.

### BRITISH TRADE IN DUTCH AGRICULTURAL PRODUCTS.

*Importation of some of the principal articles of agricultural produce into England, together with the share of the Netherlands therein.*

| 1901. | Total imports. | | Imports from the Netherlands. | |
|---|---|---|---|---|
| | Quantity. | Value. | Quantity. | Value. |
| | *Pounds.* | | *Pounds.* | |
| Fresh beef | 67,128,600 | $5,378,000 | 31,325,800 | $2,968,400 |
| Fresh mutton | 396,904,200 | 31,669,200 | 34,790,800 | 3,415,200 |
| Fresh pork | 85,065,000 | 8,234,800 | 41,476,600 | 3,843,200 |
| Butter | 407,308,000 | 509,440,800 | 32,881,200 | 7,255,200 |
| Butterine | 105,828,800 | 12,312,000 | 99,979,000 | 11,496,800 |
| Cheese | 284,556,800 | 29,890,800 | 34,751,200 | 3,585,600 |

| 1900. | Total imports. | | Imports from the Netherlands. | |
|---|---|---|---|---|
| | Quantity. | Value. | Quantity. | Value. |
| | *Pounds.* | | *Pounds.* | |
| Fresh beef | 57,267,540 | $4,713,720 | 29,305,320 | $2,710,622 |
| Fresh mutton | 373,213,500 | 28,039,516 | 36,445,200 | 3,540,139 |
| Fresh pork | 76,493,450 | 7,417,886 | 42,810,680 | 3,955,368 |
| Butter | 371,636,760 | 83,762,074 | 31,108,550 | 6,789,317 |
| Butterine | 101,245,760 | 11,831,227 | 94,836,940 | 11,016,835 |
| Cheese | 298,298,550 | 32,895,922 | 36,059,870 | 3,842,971 |

### FLAX.

The flax market was rather lively in 1901. Prices were not as high as in 1900, but a large production of flaxseed, a by-product of the flax, made good the difference. The demand was liveliest in the beginning of the year, prices later gradually declining. The supplies on the market were, however, readily bought, and only a small stock remained in the hands of the producers. The arrivals on the Rotterdam market varied from 10,000 to 18,000 stone; on one market day, 20,000 stone was reached. At the end of 1901, prices had reached the lowest point.

### FLAXSEED.

With good prospects for a fine crop, the market in 1901 opened very quietly with 10 florins, or $4 per hectoliter (3.16 bushels) for prime quality. Unfavorable crop reports from Russia and the United States and a rise in linseed-oil prices soon brought about a firmer tone. Quotations went up to 11 florins, or $4.40, and 11.50 florins, or $4.60, and varied but little from these figures during the rest of the season. There was always demand, especially from the oil manufacturers, and the crop was almost entirely disposed of. There was a steady demand from Ireland, and exports of sowing seed thither were somewhat larger than in 1900 and amounted to: To Belfast and Dublin, 22 hogsheads and 1,901 bags; via Grangemouth, 2,262 bags; via Liverpool, 5 hogsheads and 2,049 bags; via Leith, 128 bags; total, 27 hogsheads and 14,340 bags.

### AFRICA TRADE.

The following table shows the quantities in tons (of 1,000 kilograms, or about 2,205 pounds) of the principal articles imported at Rotterdam from the east and west coasts of Africa and sold in this city:

| Articles. | 1901. | 1900. | 1889. | 1898. | 1897. |
|---|---|---|---|---|---|
| Wax | 35 | 57 | 40 | 45 | 51 |
| Hides | | 2 | 5 | 6 | 4 |
| Palm nuts | 2,901 | 3,514 | 2,054 | 3,355 | 3,395 |
| Groundnuts | 95 | 36 | 109 | 125 | 43 |
| Palm oil | 948 | 1,221 | 982 | 1,061 | 1,029 |
| Coffee | 141 | 228 | 271 | 337 | 650 |
| Sesame seed | 1 | 4 | 19 | 38 | 71 |
| India rubber | 334 | 433 | 240 | 259 | 278 |

Considerable quantities of gum copal, piassava, cocoa, ivory, and bark were also imported.

### CEREALS.

*Imports by sea of the five principal cereals at Rotterdam.*

| Year. | Rye. | Wheat. | Barley. | Corn. | Oats. |
|---|---|---|---|---|---|
| | Bushels. | Bushels. | Bushels. | Bushels. | Bushels. |
| 1892 | 6,095,298 | 17,516,098 | 6,663,346 | 6,867,716 | 1,410,060 |
| 1893 | 8,787,017 | 18,495,557 | 11,231,149 | 9,159,596 | 8,364,341 |
| 1894 | 13,395,911 | 22,131,211 | 14,603,621 | 6,705,418 | 11,978,012 |
| 1895 | 15,794,191 | 28,699,936 | 12,475,240 | 4,604,634 | 10,800,293 |
| 1896 | 16,907,784 | 32,124,174 | 11,080,175 | 12,004,680 | 18,133,627 |
| 1897 | 16,889,026 | 34,173,976 | 11,505,664 | 13,940,254 | 14,245,014 |
| 1898 | 14,857,602 | 32,510,910 | 13,735,603 | 20,422,440 | 10,948,115 |
| 1899 | 13,622,202 | 27,726,210 | 11,522,704 | 20,563,616 | 13,911,456 |
| 1900 | 16,788,830 | 30,152,706 | 8,862,163 | 15,939,642 | 18,475,790 |
| 1901 | 17,034,876 | 40,796,486 | 10,835,448 | 11,814,066 | 16,385,408 |

*Imports at Amsterdam and on the river Zaan.*

| Year. | Rye. | Wheat. | Barley. | Corn. | Oats. |
|---|---|---|---|---|---|
| | *Bushels.* | *Bushels.* | *Bushels.* | *Bushels.* | *Bushels.* |
| 1892 | 792,445 | 1,716,610 | 685,312 | 1,379,473 | 11,758 |
| 1893 | 1,891,866 | 1,826,482 | 1,064,068 | 782,136 | 96,361 |
| 1894 | 4,493,704 | 2,572,529 | 2,123,099 | 583,279 | 137,342 |
| 1895 | | | | | 29,138 |
| 1896 | 3,176,612 | 926,720 | 578,082 | 1,190,758 | 375,732 |
| 1897 | 2,236,415 | 835,136 | 287,976 | 1,764,236 | 279,882 |
| 1898 | 1,362,642 | 601,597 | 425,574 | 2,365,237 | 285,335 |
| 1899 | 1,671,539 | 785,885 | | | 429,919 |
| 1900 | | | | | 440,410 |
| 1901 | 1,821,217 | 755,639 | | | 295,048 |

*Supply at Rotterdam (estimated) on January 1.*

| Year. | Rye. | Wheat. | Barley. | Corn. | Oats. |
|---|---|---|---|---|---|
| | *Bushels.* | *Bushels.* | *Bushels.* | *Bushels.* | *Bushels.* |
| 1893 | 369,683 | 208,399 | 570,985 | 86,478 | 34,080 |
| 1894 | 170,400 | 127,800 | 383,400 | 66,030 | |
| 1895 | 417,480 | 119,280 | 187,440 | 93,720 | 25,560 |
| 1896 | 213,000 | 127,800 | 127,800 | 99,514 | |
| 1897 | 340,800 | 93,720 | 144,840 | 63,474 | 56,658 |
| 1898 | 340,800 | 51,120 | 170,400 | 29,820 | 17,040 |
| 1899 | 127,800 | 51,120 | 213,000 | 189,387 | 8,500 |
| 1900 | 170,400 | 127,800 | 170,400 | 213,000 | 42,600 |
| 1901 | 187,440 | 68,160 | 85,200 | 102,240 | 8,520 |
| 1902 | 161,880 | 230,040 | 105,240 | 68,160 | 105,240 |

*Supply at Amsterdam and the river Zaan on January 1.*

| Year. | Rye. | Wheat. | Barley. | Corn. | Oats. |
|---|---|---|---|---|---|
| | *Bushels.* | *Bushels.* | *Bushels.* | *Bushels.* | *Bushels.* |
| 1893 | 352,302 | 424,126 | 70,656 | 8,520 | |
| 1894 | 190,983 | 309,872 | 58,447 | 17,977 | 21,385 |
| 1895 | 814,768 | 590,947 | 99,940 | 2,145 | 8,834 |
| 1896 | 530,114 | 291,640 | 5,964 | 12,524 | |
| 1897 | 568,454 | 596,400 | 14,143 | 15,677 | 88,681 |
| 1898 | 125,755 | 86,734 | 44,780 | 20,583 | 27,434 |
| 1899 | 111,868 | 150,122 | 42,259 | 6,646 | 20,222 |
| 1900 | 182,328 | 168,952 | 58,681 | 12,354 | 37,408 |
| 1901 | 289,680 | 72,420 | 35,611 | 17,466 | 25,134 |
| 1902 | 386,808 | 255,770 | 59,555 | 2,130 | |

*Imports at Rotterdam.*

WHEAT.

| Direct from— | 1901. | 1900. | 1899. | 1898. | 1897. |
|---|---|---|---|---|---|
| | *Bushels.* | *Bushels.* | *Bushels.* | *Bushels.* | *Bushels.* |
| Russian Baltic ports | 2,654,065 | 1,586,935 | 405,637 | 7,903,237 | 6,622,564 |
| Prussian Baltic ports | 690,802 | 1,251,758 | 351,791 | 658,681 | 602,108 |
| Russian Black Sea ports | 8,467,602 | 5,129,466 | 5,022,177 | 8,938,928 | 17,971,236 |
| Turkey | 2,809,129 | 2,902,679 | 846,888 | 2,340,965 | 3,578,144 |
| North America | 21,396,276 | 5,715,472 | 13,275,268 | 10,848,175 | 5,198,308 |
| South America | 3,877,708 | 12,765,090 | 7,544,545 | 984,060 | 84,348 |
| India | 270,680 | | | 327,538 | |
| Various countries and indirect importations | 630,224 | 801,306 | 299,904 | 508,814 | 107,267 |
| Total | 40,796,486 | 30,152,706 | 27,746,210 | 32,510,388 | 34,163,975 |

*Imports at Rotterdam*—Continued.

RYE.

| Direct from— | 1901. | 1900. | 1899. | 1898. | 1897. |
|---|---|---|---|---|---|
| | *Bushels.* | *Bushels.* | *Bushels.* | *Bushels.* | *Bushels.* |
| Archangel | 57,784 | 69,438 | | | |
| St. Petersburg | 842,884 | 2,601,241 | 1,866,849 | 1,924,327 | 1,672,135 |
| Reval, Pernau, etc | 809,996 | 637,211 | 565,984 | 993,091 | 601,342 |
| Riga, etc | 204,450 | 174,916 | 568,540 | 317,029 | 50,127 |
| Libau, Vindau | 514,097 | 889,062 | 147,396 | 179,176 | 83,837 |
| Prussian Baltic ports | 190,081 | 132,401 | 32,802 | 149,867 | 196,890 |
| Russian Black Sea ports | 10,606,292 | 9,910,464 | 7,584,248 | 6,132,611 | 8,508,498 |
| Turkey | 3,651,246 | 2,042,244 | 1,915,466 | 2,530,355 | 4,067,585 |
| America | 146,083 | 194,767 | 782,647 | 2,631,146 | 1,542,631 |
| Various places | 12,013 | 137,087 | 168,270 | | 17,636 |
| Total | 17,034,876 | 16,788,831 | 13,682,212 | 14,857,602 | 16,740,573 |

BARLEY.

| | | | | | |
|---|---|---|---|---|---|
| St. Petersburg | 25,049 | 48,308 | 92,868 | 76,680 | 4,260 |
| Pernau, Reval, etc | 336,881 | 244,524 | 325,208 | 566,836 | 391,920 |
| Riga, etc | 217,004 | 169,292 | 174,916 | 150,122 | 59,981 |
| Libau, Vindau | 65,178 | 6,049 | 116,469 | 48,820 | 53,569 |
| Prussian Baltic ports | 713,976 | 329,990 | 315,155 | 154,723 | 178,409 |
| Russian Black Sea ports | 6,340,158 | 5,240,737 | 7,572,080 | 9,287,429 | 7,046,892 |
| Turkey | 2,441,236 | 1,081,444 | 1,245,454 | 8,073,590 | 2,862,726 |
| Fiume | 292,577 | 323,760 | 634,144 | 148,732 | 138,450 |
| America | 164,521 | 1,299,736 | 712,528 | 197,068 | 737,406 |
| Various places | 238,868 | 148,333 | 98,464 | 84,604 | 52,057 |
| Total | 10,835,448 | 8,862,163 | 11,562,386 | 18,733,604 | 11,505,664 |

CORN.

[By vessel.]

| | | | | | |
|---|---|---|---|---|---|
| New York, etc | 6,021,596 | 10,582,777 | 18,586,917 | 15,087,131 | 10,833,908 |
| New Orleans, etc | 1,321,026 | 3,183,242 | 2,971,350 | 1,992,146 | 1,778,694 |
| Black Sea | 2,942,723 | 1,356,384 | 2,507,692 | 2,505,817 | 1,510,681 |
| South America | 1,509,712 | 702,048 | 1,497,049 | 700,600 | 257,048 |
| Various places | 19,000 | 115,190 | 50,609 | 136,746 | 64,922 |
| Total | 11,814,056 | 15,939,641 | 21,563,617 | 20,422,440 | 18,940,253 |

OATS.

| | | | | | |
|---|---|---|---|---|---|
| Archangel | 368,831 | 291,128 | 42,430 | 82,729 | |
| Russian Baltic ports | 12,315,575 | 13,336,441 | 3,702,707 | 4,652,176 | 3,971,304 |
| Prussian Baltic ports | 319,415 | 690,887 | 1,504,004 | 98,379 | 83,228 |
| Turkey | 656,381 | 216,238 | 1,252,961 | 608,418 | 981,504 |
| Russian Black Sea ports | 1,706,045 | 2,155,560 | 2,017,280 | 409,045 | 1,593,348 |
| North America | 896,304 | 1,608,661 | 5,218,390 | 5,102,372 | 2,664,630 |
| Various places | 122,858 | 176,875 | 163,754 | | |
| Total | 16,385,409 | 18,475,790 | 13,901,456 | 10,948,114 | 14,244,014 |

LINSEED.

| | | | | | |
|---|---|---|---|---|---|
| Northern Russia | 22,408 | 325,879 | 151,315 | 308,424 | 612,588 |
| Southern Russia and the Danube | 947,680 | 1,951,336 | 2,451,630 | 3,418,565 | 5,292,400 |
| Prussian Baltic ports | 45,412 | 164,606 | 184,969 | 71,653 | 78,214 |
| East Indies | | 42,941 | | | |
| North America | 985,168 | 738,002 | 348,950 | 715,424 | 296,174 |
| South America | 2,566,991 | 2,068,997 | 1,798,801 | 257,358 | 3,288 |
| Various places | 178,238 | 123,881 | 13,632 | 4,090 | |
| Total | 4,745,897 | 5,415,142 | 4,944,397 | 4,775,514 | 6,192,714 |

Imports of buckwheat and buckwheat grits at Rotterdam:

| Year. | Buck-wheat. | Buckwheat grits. |
|---|---|---|
| | *Bushels.* | *Bushels.* |
| 1901 | 540,083 | 166,332 |
| 1900 | 450,538 | 238,049 |
| 1899 | 678,618 | 225,091 |
| 1898 | 1,016,095 | 11,161 |
| 1897 | 748,908 | 82,473 |

Quotations at the end of the year for the several cereals were:

Rye:
    South Russian ............................................... $52.00 to $58.00
    Danube ............................................. 52.00 to 60.00
Wheat (per 2,400 kilograms = 5,280 pounds):
    American red winter......................................... 78.00 to 80.00
    South Russian .............................................. 74.00
    Danube .................................................. 66.00 to 72.00
Barley (per 2,000 kilograms = 4,400 pounds):
    Feeding barley.............................................. 48.80 to 52.00
    Distillers' barley .......................................... 56.00 to 58.00
Corn (per 2,000 kilograms = 4,400 pounds):
    American mixed............................................. 57.60
    Odessa .................................................. 50.00
    Cinquantine ............................................... 54.00
Oats (per 100 kilograms = 220 pounds):
    American ................................................. 3.40
Buckwheat (per 2,100 kilograms = 4,620 pounds):
    State.................................................... 68.00

The highest and lowest quotations for the several cereals during the last ten years were:

RYE.

[South Russian, per 2,100 kilograms (4,620 pounds).]

| Year. | Lowest price. | Highest price. | Year. | Lowest price. | Highest price. |
|---|---|---|---|---|---|
| 1892 | $54.00 | $102.00 | 1897 | $38.50 | $60.80 |
| 1893 | 46.00 | 60.00 | 1898 | 45.60 | 80.00 |
| 1894 | 34.00 | 50.00 | 1899 | 54.00 | 60.00 |
| 1895 | 36.00 | 52.00 | 1900 | 52.00 | 62.00 |
| 1896 | 36.00 | 52.00 | 1901 | 48.00 | 60.00 |

BARLEY.

[From Baltic ports, per 1,950 kilograms (4,298 pounds).]

| Year. | Lowest price. | Highest price. | Year. | Lowest price. | Highest price. |
|---|---|---|---|---|---|
| 1892 | $54.00 | $94.00 | 1897 | $46.00 | $52.00 |
| 1893 | 52.00 | 58.00 | 1898 | 48.00 | 60.00 |
| 1894 | 42.00 | 46.00 | 1899 | 54.00 | 60.00 |
| 1895 | 44.00 | 46.00 | 1900 | 52.00 | 60.00 |
| 1896 | 44.60 | 52.00 | 1901 | 54.00 | 60.00 |

FEED BARLEY.

| Year. | Lowest price. | Highest price. | Year. | Lowest price. | Highest price. |
|---|---|---|---|---|---|
| 1892 | $40.00 | $64.00 | 1897 | $32.80 | $46.00 |
| 1893 | 34.00 | 48.00 | 1898 | 38.00 | 60.00 |
| 1894 | 28.00 | 40.00 | 1899 | 40.00 | 52.00 |
| 1895 | 34.00 | 44.00 | 1900 | 47.20 | 76.80 |
| 1896 | 34.00 | 46.00 | 1901 | 44.00 | 52.00 |

## WHEAT.

[Zealand, per 2,400 kilograms (5,291 pounds).]

| Year. | Lowest price. | Highest price. | Year. | Lowest price. | Highest price. |
|---|---|---|---|---|---|
| 1892 | $74.00 | $128.00 | 1897 | $72.00 | $104.00 |
| 1893 | 72.00 | 78.00 | 1898 | 76.80 | 140.00 |
| 1894 | 50.00 | 82.00 | 1899 | 70.00 | 82.00 |
| 1895 | 70.00 | 86.00 | 1900 | 73.20 | 94.00 |
| 1896 | 74.00 | 92.00 | 1901 | 80.00 | 98.00 |

## AMERICAN RED WINTER.

| 1892 | $68.00 | $100.00 | 1897 | ........ | ........ |
|---|---|---|---|---|---|
| 1893 | 70.00 | 80.00 | 1898 | $72.00 | $90.00 |
| 1894 | 54.00 | 66.00 | 1899 | 72.00 | 88.00 |
| 1895 | 62.00 | 80.00 | 1900 | 70.00 | 80.00 |
| 1896 | 62.00 | 86.00 | 1901 | 66.00 | 80.00 |

## BLACK SEA.

| 1892 | $68.00 | $108.00 | 1897 | $68.00 | $96.00 |
|---|---|---|---|---|---|
| 1893 | 60.00 | 70.00 | 1898 | 70.00 | 128.00 |
| 1894 | 40.00 | 66.00 | 1899 | 66.00 | 74.00 |
| 1895 | 44.00 | 70.00 | 1900 | 70.00 | 76.00 |
| 1896 | 54.00 | 86.00 | 1901 | 66.00 | 76.00 |

## CORN.

[American Bunter, per 100 kilograms (220 pounds).]

| 1892 | $2.40 | $3.80 | 1897 | $1.40 | $2.12 |
|---|---|---|---|---|---|
| 1893 | 2.20 | 2.80 | 1898 | 1.60 | 2.50 |
| 1894 | 1.80 | 2.60 | 1899 | 1.90 | 2.20 |
| 1895 | 1.80 | 2.66 | 1900 | 1.84 | 2.45 |
| 1896 | 1.44 | 1.90 | 1901 | 2.04 | 3.12 |

## OATS.

[Prime Russian, per 100 kilograms (220 pounds).]

| 1892 | $3.00 | $3.80 | 1897 | $2.08 | $2.94 |
|---|---|---|---|---|---|
| 1893 | 2.60 | 3.20 | 1898 | 2.56 | 2.90 |
| 1894 | 2.00 | 3.00 | 1899 | 2.36 | 2.60 |
| 1895 | 2.00 | 3.60 | 1900 | 2.30 | 2.88 |
| 1896 | 2.10 | 3.10 | 1901 | 2.46 | 3.24 |

## CEREALS IN 1902.

The cereal market was rather quiet during the first six months of the year, even special inducements failing to cause a revival of business. A good crop was expected in the Netherlands, and from Russia crop reports were not unfavorable. The Netherlands crop, however, did not turn out to be of as fine a quality as was expected; in some provinces wheat and rye did not fully ripen, owing to the unfavorable weather in July and August, although the fields looked promising.

*Wheat.*—Imports were about 20 per cent smaller than last year; about one-third arrived from Odessa. Quotations did not fluctuate much, the nominal value being from 170 florins, or $68, to 175 florins, or $70 per 2,400 kilograms (about 5,280 pounds.) Some business in wheat in stock was done in January, but in February and March there was no question of large transactions; in April prices rose somewhat for wheat in stock or soon to arrive, which improvement continued during May and June. The quality of hard Kansas wheat shipped from Galveston and New Orleans was found satisfactory and not inferior to that of last year; the red winter wheat shipped from the northern ports of the United States was also of good quality, but not as superior as last year's shipments; sometimes parcels arrived slightly heated, not to such an extent, however, that the grain was injured.

*Rye.*—Rye was sold cheap in January by those having stock in this market, notwithstanding that higher prices had to be paid for goods yet to be shipped. February did not bring any change in quotations, but prices went up in March to a point more in accordance with offers from abroad. The stock in the Netherlands gradually decreased, and even parcels already sailing found buyers for consumption on arrival at good prices. Quotations ranged from 130 florins ($52) to 145 florins ($58) per 2,100 kilograms (about 4,620 pounds.) Importations were about one-third smaller than last year; south Russian ports, especially Odessa and Nicolajeff, shipped most; a few lots arrived from the United Sates and also a few lots from north Russian ports.

*Barley.*—Barley brought good prices during the first six months of the year. The stock on hand remained rather small and the demand for direct delivery, especially for the better qualities, was good. Prices rose from 120 florins ($48) to 130 florins ($52) per 1,950 kilograms (4,290 pounds). Importations were about one-third larger than last year and large quantities arrived from Odessa, Nicolajeff, and Novorossisk.

*Oats.*—Quotations did not fluctuate much, the nominal price in January being about 8.40 florins ($3.36) per 100 kilograms (220 pounds) for St. Petersburg quality and practically remaining so until the end of June. There was a regular trade in the article. The stock in the Netherlands was generally small and a fair demand for local consumption kept the price at the aforesaid high rate. Offers for late shipments had little attention. The imports were about 25 per cent smaller than for the same period in 1901. The principal part arrived from Odessa and Nicolajeff, but shipments were also made from St. Petersburg and Libau.

*Corn.*—Owing to the small 1901 crop, American mixed was generally dear. In March, the quotations were so high that importing was considered risky, in view of the prices at which other kinds of corn could be had. A few shipments in April and May did not arrive in sound condition, which caused a drop in prices for local stock, as owners, fearing that the goods would not keep, wanted to get rid of them as soon as practicable. In June, offers for eventual new-crop shipments were made at much lower quotations, but these found little interest. The American mixed is the favorite corn in this market and consumers desire no other kind to replace it, even if it is high in price as in the first months of the year. Of Roumanian corn, the quantities imported in January to meet the demand for consumption in the Netherlands were far too large, and only low prices could be realized. Subsequently the market recovered and large transactions took place. The Roumanian corn is well suited to baking purposes. Considerable business was also done in Odessa corn, while Turkish and La Plata were imported to replace the American mixed. A few lots of Odessa corn arrived slightly heated in April. Importations were about the same as in 1901. The biggest quantities were received from Braila, Sulina, and also from Odessa. Nominal quotations were for American mixed from 111.40 florins ($44.56) to 150 florins ($60). In 1901 quotations were from $43.20 to $44; for Roumanian from 118 florins ($47.20) to 120 florins ($48) per 2,000 kilograms (4,400 pounds).

## PETROLEUM.

The competition between the large petroleum companies, which supply this market with petroleum for consumption, is very keen. In several Dutch towns, petroleum prices varied in accordance with sharpness of local competition. Generally speaking, the quotations are entirely ruled by the American Petroleum Company, German American Petroleum Company, and the Pure Oil Company. Russian petroleum is also trying to enter this market, but this oil has been principally applied for motors; for illuminating purposes, it seems hardly fit for this climate. The specific weight is about 3 per cent heavier than that of American oil.

Petroleum importers endeavor more and more to sell direct to the consumers, not only to save expenses but also to be insured of regular custom, which can not so easily be served by competitors.

In 1901, the quotations at Rotterdam were steady at 11.50 florins ($4.60) per 100 kilograms (220 pounds) for consumption, from the beginning of the year until the end of March, when a gradual decline in prices set in, bringing them down to 9.10 florins ($3.60) in the middle of May. Then a sharp advance followed; prices again rose to 10.75 florins ($4.30), to recede to 10.60 florins ($4.24) in the second half of December.

The consumption in the Netherlands, in barrels of 150 kilograms net (about 350 pounds), was:

| Year. | Barrels. | Year. | Barrels. |
|---|---|---|---|
| 1892 | 819,000 | 1897 | 1,020,000 |
| 1893 | 863,000 | 1898 | 1,065,000 |
| 1894 | 902,000 | 1899 | 1,060,000 |
| 1895 | 970,000 | 1900 | 1,055,000 |
| 1896 | 970,000 | 1901 | 1,080,000 |

The arrivals at Rotterdam and Amsterdam were:

| Year. | Rotterdam. | Amsterdam. | Year. | Rotterdam. | Amsterdam. |
|---|---|---|---|---|---|
| | Barrels. | Barrels. | | Barrels. | Barrels. |
| 1892 | 1,436,000 | 488,000 | 1897 | 1,857,000 | 655,000 |
| 1893 | 1,522,000 | 475,000 | 1898 | 2,020,000 | 680,000 |
| 1894 | 1,525,000 | 520,000 | 1899 | 2,010,000 | 755,000 |
| 1895 | 1,371,000 | 605,000 | 1900 | 1,885,000 | 719,000 |
| 1896 | 1,928,000 | 500,000 | 1901 | 2,205,000 | 818,000 |

## COFFEE.

A review of the Netherlands coffee market was given in the supplement to my last annual report; I add thereto the following statistics:

*Importations of coffee into the Netherlands.*

| Year. | For the Dutch Trading Co. | For private firms. | Total. |
|---|---|---|---|
| | Bales. | Bales. | Bales. |
| 1899 | 164,400 | 1,538,100 | 1,702,500 |
| 1900 | 131,300 | 1,453,300 | 1,584,600 |
| 1901 | 104,500 | 1,616,500 | 1,721,000 |

The coffee imported by the Dutch Trading Company was exclusively from the Dutch East Indies, while that imported by private firms came from the following places:

| | 1901. | 1900. | 1899. | | 1901. | 1900. | 1899. |
|---|---|---|---|---|---|---|---|
| | Bales. | Bales. | Bales. | | Bales. | Bales. | Bales. |
| Java | 259,000 | 408,300 | ,100 | C e n t r a l | | | |
| Padang | 14,000 | 12,600 | ,700 | America | 11,400 | 10,500 | 12,700 |
| Macassar | 21,000 | 14,500 | ,000 | Haiti | 100 | 1,200 | 3,500 |
| Menado | 2,700 | 1,900 | ,900 | Various | 50,200 | 35,000 | 78,400 |
| Africa | 55,700 | 59,900 | 437,400 | | | | |
| Santos | 1,200,200 | 913,700 | 988,100 | Total | 1,616,500 | 1,453,300 | 1,538,100 |
| Venezuela | 2,200 | 700 | 7,300 | | | | |

*Share of Rotterdam in the private arrivals of coffee.*

| | 1901. | 1900. | 1899. | | 1901. | 1900. | 1899. |
|---|---|---|---|---|---|---|---|
| | Bales. | Bales. | Bales. | | Bales. | Bales. | . Bales. |
| Java | 113,576 | 144,963 | 210,288 | C e n t r a l | | | |
| Padang | 1,897 | 2,720 | 410 | America | 5,315 | 8,946 | 9,004 |
| Macassar | | | 708 | Various | 10,500 | 11,800 | 36,300 |
| Africa | 50,516 | 53,787 | 53,763 | | | | |
| Santos | 1,086,242 | 815,040 | 855,774 | Total | 1,269,046 | 1,037,256 | 1,166,242 |
| Venezuela | 2,000 | | | | | | |

*Importations of coffee by private persons from the Dutch East Indies.*

| Year. | The Netherlands. | Rotterdam. |
|---|---|---|
| | Bales. | Bales. |
| 1899 | 457,700 | 211,400 |
| 1900 | 432,300 | 147,700 |
| 1901 | 296,700 | 115,500 |

*Total coffee production of the world.*

| Year. | Bales. | Year. | Bales. |
|---|---|---|---|
| 1891–92 | 11,858,000 | 1897–98 | 16,178,000 |
| 1892–93 | 11,288,000 | 1898–99 | 13,723,000 |
| 1893–94 | 9,219,000 | 1899–1900 | 14,052,000 |
| 1894–95 | 11,636,000 | 1900–1901 | 14,966,000 |
| 1895–96 | 10,355,000 | Estimates for 1901–2 | 19,343,000 |
| 1896–97 | 13,605,000 | Estimates for 1902–3 | 13,005,000 |

*Arrivals of coffee at the principal markets of Europe and the United States.*

| Year. | Bales. | Year. | Bales. |
|---|---|---|---|
| 1892 | 11,878,500 | 1897 | 13,377,000 |
| 1898 | 11,055,700 | 1898 | 14,825,800 |
| 1894 | 11,047,800 | 1899 | 15,139,300 |
| 1895 | 11,240,400 | 1900 | 14,476,600 |
| 1896 | 11,959,700 | 1901 | 16,205,300 |

*Quantities of coffee that changed hands at the several terminal markets.*

| Year. | Havre. | New York. | Hamburg. | London. | Rotter-dam. | Amster-dam. | Antwerp. | Total. |
|---|---|---|---|---|---|---|---|---|
| | Bales. | Bales. | Bales. | Bales. | Bales. | Bales. | Bales. | Bales. |
| 1901 | 11,352,000 | 8,551,400 | 5,695,500 | 3,518,750 | 1,400,000 | 1,431,000 | 61,250 | 32,009,900 |
| 1900 | 10,071,500 | 6,824,450 | 5,804,000 | 4,140,800 | 1,114,000 | 683,550 | 18,350 | 28,606,650 |
| 1899 | 5,787,500 | 4,712,000 | 4,166,000 | 2,179,600 | 386,500 | 486,100 | 28,200 | 17,690,900 |

### TEA.

Quotations for good, ordinary China congou were 0.49, 0.44, 0.51 florin ($0.196, $0.176, $0.204) per half kilogram (1.1 pounds), and those for good ordinary Java leaf 0.28, 0.22, 0.30 florin ($0.112, $0.088, $0.12).

The total imports of China tea in the Netherlands decreased from 68,000 chests (of 40 kilograms or 88 pounds net) in 1900 to 62,000 chests in 1901. Imports of Java tea increased from 159,000 chests to 177,300 chests.

The consumption of China tea in the Netherlands increased from 35,300 to 36,400 chests. Direct imports from Java of Java tea increased from 41,900 to 47,400.

The aggregate imports of Java and China tea increased from 254,100 to 260,800 chests. The aggregate exports decreased from 133,900 to 133,701 chests.

### RICE.

Quotations were in 1901, per 50 kilograms (110 pounds) for uncleaned white Java, 5.75, 5.50 florins ($2.30, $2.20); for uncleaned white Arracan, 4.25, 3.75 florins ($1.70, $1.50).

Arrivals in the Netherlands were, in 1901, 1,822,000 bags; in 1900, 1,553,000 bags, and in 1899, 1,968,000 bags of 90 kilograms (about 190 pounds), of which there arrived from Java 251,200, 211,300, and 353,700 bags, respectively.

### SPICES.

Prices for goods in bond fluctuated as follows in 1901: Nutmegs, Banda, 110 to 115 nuts to the half kilogram, 0.83, 0.56, 0.59 florins (equal to $0.332, $0.224, $0.236) per half kilogram (1.1 pounds); mace, Banda first products, 0.95, 0.88, 0.92 florins ($0.38, $0.352, $0.368) per half kilogram; cloves, Amboyna, 0.305 0.32, 0.31 florins ($0.122, $0.128, $0.124); cloves, Zanzibar, 0.23625, 0.24125, 0.1975, 0.235, 0.225 florins ($0.0945, $0.0965, $0.079, $0.094, $0.09; pepper, Lampong, 0.30½, 0.29875, 0.31875, 0.29875, 0.31875 florins ($0.122, $0.1195, $0.1275, $0.1195, $0.1275).

The importations and stocks in the Netherlands, first and second hand, in bond, amounted to, in tons of 1,000 kilograms (2,205 pounds):

IMPORTS.

| Year | Nutmegs. | Mace. | Cloves. | Pepper. |
|------|----------|-------|---------|---------|
| 1901 | 967 | 289 | 690 | 1,784 |
| 1900 | 982 | 251 | 1,568 | 2,048 |
| 1899 | 719 | 218 | 2,969 | 1,758 |

STOCK ON DECEMBER 31.

| | | | | |
|------|----------|-------|---------|---------|
| 1901 | 987 | 136 | 3,965 | 2,256 |
| 1900 | 1,011 | 172 | 4,834 | 8,698 |
| 1899 | 999 | 194 | 4,606 | 4,972 |

## COCOA.

The course of prices for prime Java kinds was, in 1901, 0.60, 0.44 florins ($0.24, $0.176), and for prime Surinam 0.44, 0.35 florins ($0.176, $0.14) per one-half kilogram (1.1 pound).

First hand sales amounted to 2,448 bags of Java, 109 Surinam, and 150 Trinidad cocoa; together, 2,707 bags against 2,889 bags in 1900 and 2,705 bags in 1899.

## SUGAR.

With few exceptions, sugar quotations retrograded in 1901, as an inevitable result of overproduction. Beet-root sugar opened the year at 11 florins ($4.40) per 100 kilograms (220 pounds), and closed the year with little demand at 8.50 florins ($3.40). At the beginning of the year, there was a rise in prices owing to the reimposition of an import duty in Great Britain, but this rise was soon followed by a continuous decline, broken only by a short-lived improvement in the summer months.

Cane-sugar prices for Java fell from 7 florins ($2.80) for Muscovada to 5.25 florins ($2.10), and for No. 15 from 7.375 florins ($2.95) to 5.50 florins ($2.20).

Imports in the Netherlands for consumption:

| | Tons. |
|---|---|
| Raw sugar | 80,020 |
| Refined sugar | 11,240 |

Exports:

| | |
|---|---|
| Raw sugar | 11,948 |
| Refined sugar | 261,508 |

Stock on December 31, 1901 was:

| | |
|---|---|
| Raw and refined sugar | 142,697 |

## TOBACCO.

*Sumatra.*—Of the 1900 crop (sale year 1901), there were sold 223,544 packages at an average price of 1.12 florins ($0.448) per one-half kilogram (1.1 pound), as against 263,897 packages of the 1899 crop (sale year 1900) at an average price of 0.82 florins ($0.328). The 1900 crop was 40,000 packages smaller in size than the 1899 crop, but the value realized for the 1900 crop amounted to $2,000,000 more.

*Java.*—The 1900 crop (sale year 1901) consisted of 238,885 packages as against 370,897 packages in 1899 (sales year 1900).

The leaf tobacco brought an average price of 0.375 florins ($0.15) per one-half kilogram (1.1 pound), against 0.275 florins ($0.11) for the 1899 crop.

The scrub tobacco brought 0.21 florins ($0.084), against 0.145 florins ($0.0725) for the former crop.

The average selling price of the Java leaf and scrub tobacco (there were 136,852 packages of leaf and 102,033 packages of scrub in the 1900 crop) was 0.305 florins ($0.122), against 0.22 florins ($0.088) in the year before, which indicates that just as with Sumatra tobacco, the shrinkage in production greatly influenced the selling price.

*Dutch Borneo.*—Four thousand two hundred packages arrived, against 7,688 packages the year before. The average price realized was 0.425 florins ($0.17) against $0.198 the year before.

### AMERICAN TOBACCO IN 1902.

*Seedleaf.*—There were no important arrivals; the prices asked and realized in the United States were too high for buyers here.

*Cutting tobaccos.*—Transactions were less important than usual; old crop tobaccos were scarce and dear, and the new crop arrivals came in sparingly. Maryland is to-day the principal tobacco used by the Dutch tobacco manufacturers, yet owing to high prices and the fact that colors do not entirely answer the requirements of the manufacturers, sales were limited. Of sunburn, there was but little in bright colors, which also affected the sale. Very little Virginia, Kentucky, and Burley tobacco arrived in this market; it seems that considerable tobacco which was formerly exported from the United States is now used there. Owing to the small arrivals, prices were brought to too high a level for this market, which prevented large transactions. Of Kentucky lugs, the same may be said.

### MARGARINE, NEUTRAL LARD, COTTON-SEED OIL, ETC.

As all articles in connection with the manufacture of butterine rose in price, 1901 was a profitable year to the dealers in and importers of crude butterine materials. Not so, however, for the manufacturers of butterine, as competition prevented prices from keeping pace with those of raw materials, and attempts of butterine manufacturers to unite, in order to force up prices, failed. For the manufacturers, the year was a poor one. In western and southern Germany, several small butterine factories closed, which will to some extent be felt in this market, as those factories were supplied from Rotterdam with the American commodities.

Imports of oleo and lard were much smaller in 1901 than in 1900, viz, 20,000 tierces of oleo and 28 tierces of neutral lard less.

A dry summer, with high butter prices and high neutral lard quotations, caused a great demand for margarine. Everything cooperated to enhance the prices of the raw butterine materials, and in the middle of September neutral lard was worth as much as 76 florins ($30.40) per 100 kilograms (220 pounds), while fine oleo was quoted as high as 69 florins ($27.60) in October. Then the reaction set in; lard prices went down in the United States and shippers gradually lowered their quotations for oleo to 60 florins ($24) per 100 kilograms (220 pounds); for neutral lard, to 62 to 61 florins ($24.80 to $24.40), and for back-fat neutral lard, to 55 to 54 florins ($22 to $21.60). The decline, however, was but temporary; fine oleo again rose to 63 to 64 florins ($25.20 to $25.60); neutral lard, fresh arrivals, to 68 to 70 florins ($27.20 to $28); back-fat neutral lard, to 63 to 65 florins ($25.20 to $26).

The consumption of oleo stock and of cotton-seed oil was very large, owing to the high prices asked for the other ingredients of butterine. The United States supplied the larger part of the butterine materials, but considerable quantities of oleo were also supplied by Great Britain, France, Austria-Hungary, and Australia.

*Statistics of margarine (oleo).*

|  | 1901. | 1900. | 1899. | 1898. | 1897. | 1896. |
|---|---|---|---|---|---|---|
| First-hand supply American, on Dec. 31, tierces .......................... | 7,600 | 5,410 | 2,477 | 770 | 2,140 | 2,860 |
| Total stock on Dec. 31...........tierces.. | 20,670 | 22,600 | 10,000 | 6,800 | 8,600 | 12,800 |
| Arrivals from the United States (oleo stock included) ................tierces.. | 255,098 | 257,300 | 245,891 | 261,350 | 222,655 | 204,620 |
| Price for prime, per 100 kilograms (220 pounds): |  |  |  |  |  |  |
| Highest ......................dollars.. | 27.60 | 24.00 | 26.40 | 18.80 | 19.20 | 22.00 to 22.40 |
| Lowest .........................do.... | 16.80 | 16.00 | 16.80 | 14.00 | 12.80 | 10.20 |
| Average .......................do.... | 21.40 | 18.80 | 19.40 | 14.80 | 15.20 | 14.00 |

*Neutral lard.*

|  | 1901. | 1900. | 1899. | 1898. | 1897. | 1896. |
|---|---|---|---|---|---|---|
| Total supply on Dec. 31..........tierces.. | 3,910 | 1,600 | 4,000 | 2,600 | 3,000 | 2,300 |
| First hand .................do.... | 720 | 210 | 579 | 300 | 200 | 150 |
| Arrivals from the United States...do.... | 114,000 | 142,000 | 185,000 | 168,260 | 143,200 | 82,900 |
| Price for prime: |  |  |  |  |  |  |
| Highest......................dollars.. | 30.80 | 20.40 to 20.80 | 21.60 to 20.00 | 16.40 | 14.80 to 15.20 | 17.20 to 17.60 |
| Lowest. ........................do.... | 19.20 | 17.60 | 14.80 | 13.60 | 11.20 | 9.60 |
| Average .......................do.... | 22.00 | 18.70 | 16.10 | 15.10 | 12.80 | 18.40 |

*Cotton-seed oil.*—The use of cotton-seed oil increases from year to year, for the manufacture of butterine, for table use, and especially for soap making. Quotations were, in January, 28 florins ($11.20) for prime summer yellow, and 29.50 florins ($11.80) for choice butter oil. Contracts for the new crop were already made in the middle of July at a starting price of 28 florins ($11.20) for choice butter oil delivery, October to December. A little later, prices rose to 30 florins ($12), in August to 32 florins ($12.80), and in September to 32.50 and 33 florins ($13 and $13.20); but in October a decline set in, and in the middle of November large parcels were disposed of at 29 florins ($11.60). The rise in other fats, however, led to a new rise in cotton-seed oil, so that in December 32.50 florins ($13) and at the close of the year 34 florins ($13.60) was paid.

Imports for consumption amounted to 18,851 tons, against 16,915 tons in 1900, while large quantities were imported for exportation. The article becomes more and more important in the Rotterdam market, which is the greatest market for this commodity.

*Arachides oil.*—The trade was lively in 1901. Prices rose in sym-

pathy with those for other fats.    Prime quality rose from 43 florins
($17.20) to 47 florins ($18.80), and inferior grades proportionally.

*Sesame oil.*—This is in good demand, but there are few offers, owing
to the sesame crop failure in most producing countries.    Prices ranged
from 38 to 46 florins ($15.20 to $18.40).

### OLEO AND NEUTRAL LARD IN 1902.

Arrivals of both oleo and neutral lard show a material shortage as
compared with the same period (January 1–June 30) of 1901.

Arrivals were: Of oleo, 79,500 tierces, against 108,000 in 1901 and
114,000 in 1900; of neutral lard, 56,000 tierces, against 71,000 in 1901
and 97,000 in 1900.

Quotations for olio were, per 100 kilograms (220 pounds):

January: 64 florins ($25.60).

February: 64, 62, 58, and 57 florins ($25.60, $24.80, $23.20, and
$22.80).

March: 58, 60, and 61 florins ($23.20, $24, and $24.40).

April: 61, 63, 64.50, 65, 66, 68, 69, and 70 florins ($24.40, $25.20,
$25.80, $26, $26.40, $27.20, $27.60, and $28).

May: 70 florins ($28).

June: 70, 71, 70, and 68 florins ($28, $28.40, $28, and $27.20).

Quotations for neutral lard were:

January: 68, 66.50, 67, 65, 64, 61, and 60 florins ($27.20, $26.60,
$26.80, $26, $25.60, $24.40, and $24).

February: 59 and 57 florins ($23.60 and $22.80).

March: 56, 57, 58, 59.25, 59.50, 60, 61, and 62 florins ($22.40, $22.80,
$23.20, $23.70, $23.80, $24, $24.40, and $24.80).

April: 62, 63, 64, 65, 66.75, 67.50, and 68 florins ($24.80, $25.20,
$25.60, $26, $26.70, $27, and $27.20).

May: 68, 67, and 66 florins ($27.20, $26.80, and $26.40).

June: 65, 65.50, and 66.75 florins ($26, $26.20, and $26.70).

The scarcity of fat cattle and hogs in the United States, owing to
the shortness of last year's corn crop, caused the production of oleo
and lard there to decrease materially, which resulted in the high prices
quoted.

While in the United States, cattle and hogs were short of fat, the
reverse was the case in Europe.    Generally, the cattle were very sleek,
and the butterine manufacturers in the Netherlands were to a great
extent enabled to draw supplies from France, Austria, Great Britain,
and Germany.    The demand for oleo was good, partly owing to the
high quotations ruling for steam lard, and had Europe not been able
to fill the gap in the American supplies, the butterine manufacturers
here would have been very short.    In fact, if the supplies from European sources had not been so plentiful, both lard and oleo would probably have gone up to 90 or 100 florins ($36 or $40).

The cooperation of most of the large packers of oleo and lard in the
United States is also much felt in this market, as it has given great
strength to American prices.

As crops promise to be favorable in the United States this season,
the exports of fat stuffs hence will very likely increase.    It will take
some time, however, before the stock of cattle in the United States
will be up to its old height, and it may be assumed that oleo prices
will not decline much until imports from the United States have
increased to their usual quantities.

## HIDES AND SKINS.

The following information is gleaned from the annual hide and skin circular of the Hide, Skin and Leather Company (Koelit).

The trade in Dutch hides with the United States was limited, owing to the fact that better purchases could be made in other markets. While United States importers were buying prices were steady, but as soon as they stopped quotations dropped. This effected a depression of the trade, especially in South America, and the Netherlands market followed. Quotations went down from 10 to 15 per cent.

Java ox and cow hides were not in demand as much as usual. In 1900, these hides were bought as a substitute for calf and kid leather, but purchasers now have found better and cheaper material in their own neighborhood. The unfavorable conditions in Germany greatly affected the German leather trade; there were some failures, and the German industry purchased little in the Dutch market. The stock on hand in the beginning of 1901 was already large, but in midsummer, first and second hand stock reached the enormous quantity of 200,000 pieces. Owners held up their prices as long as possible, but when the conditions in Germany became well understood, they manifested a willingness to dispose of their stock at 15 to 20 per cent less than former rates. At the reduced prices there was again considerable interest, and the heavy stock was, at the end of the year, reduced to a normal figure.

Prices of leather were rather steady and, though showing an upward tendency, were more in accordance with the prices of the raw material than they had been in late years. Tanners were often able to profit by the cheapness of rawhides.

England was, during the whole of 1901, a buyer of heavy hides for sole and harness leather, and paid good prices, which favorably affected the Dutch ox and bull hides. The lowest quotations for this kind in the spring were 10 per cent higher than last year.

*Java ox and cow hides.*—The demand increased for prime transparent hides, especially for belting leather and laces, partly for chrome tanning. After these kinds had been selected, however, the remainder did not sell so easily. At the end of the year there was good demand for inferior qualities for technical purposes, of which there was only a small stock. Quotations had an upward tendency.

Light qualities for sandals found ready sale for the Orient.

*East Indian buffalo hides.*—Singapores, Saigons, and Rangoons were mostly imported for the local manufacture of leather for technical purposes.

*East Indian ox and cow hides.*—The imports were 14,300 pieces, against 27,598 pieces in 1900.

*Venezuela and West Indian hides.*—Imports were 6,092 pieces, against 10,243 pieces in 1900. Importations depend entirely upon the consumption in the United States, as only those hides are imported here that are not wanted by the Americans, principally second quality.

*Java horsehides.*—Importations were small.

*Java goatskins.*—The demand was strong the whole year, both from Europe and from the United States. Prices were steady, the production not being sufficient to supply the demand, and the importations of Cape and China goatskins having been reduced, owing to the disturbances in these countries. The importations of East Indian goatskins were less, owing to last year's famine.  In midsummer, speculation commenced and prices reached an unknown height.  The reaction, however, came when holders became convinced that prices had been pushed too high.  The large consumers then reduced their manufacture and, consequently, their orders.  At the end of 1901, quotations were the same as at the beginning of the year.

Java bastard goatskins remained almost unaltered in value.  The quality being inferior to that of goatskins and the treatment less careful, the sale is generally difficult and unsatisfactory.

Java deerskins would find a good market at sound prices, if lots sent were of one quality and not mixed with "seconds," "thirds," and "rejections."

*Goatskins from other countries.*—The imports were only 14,600 skins.

*Java lizard and snake skins.*—Although this article is not at present as fashionable as it was some years ago, it still maintains its position on the market.  The demand was mostly for prime selected skins, in large and medium size, and good prices were paid.

*Buffalo hides.*—The trade was small.

*Salted Dutch hides and skins.*—The slaughter of these hides, especially in the cities, improves from year to year, and it may be safely said that a Dutch hide can compete fully, both in slaughter and salting, with that of any other country.

The import of hides in the Netherlands was:

| Year. | Number. | Year. | Number. |
|---|---|---|---|
| 1878 | 326,800 | 1890 | 481,300 |
| 1879 | 354,100 | 1891 | 533,200 |
| 1880 | 356,800 | 1892 | 490,700 |
| 1881 | 380,500 | 1893 | 500,600 |
| 1882 | 444,700 | 1894 | 546,000 |
| 1883 | 497,800 | 1895 | 491,200 |
| 1884 | 491,100 | 1896 | 526,300 |
| 1885 | 506,400 | 1897 | 549,400 |
| 1886 | 385,600 | 1898 | 545,200 |
| 1887 | 490,700 | 1899 | 649,800 |
| 1888 | 460,100 | 1900 | 631,400 |
| 1889 | 472,700 | 1901 | 707,700 |

The import of skins was:

| Year. | Number. | Year. | Number. |
|---|---|---|---|
| 1886 | 147,000 | 1894 | 511,500 |
| 1887 | 168,700 | 1895 | 619,500 |
| 1888 | 110,400 | 1896 | 665,800 |
| 1889 | 142,000 | 1897 | 710,000 |
| 1890 | 138,000 | 1898 | 772,500 |
| 1891 | 166,000 | 1899 | 849,900 |
| 1892 | 280,000 | 1900 | 879,400 |
| 1893 | 549,000 | 1901 | 858,500 |

*Imports into the Netherlands.*

| Description. | 1892. | 1893. | 1894. | 1895. | 1896. |
|---|---|---|---|---|---|
| | *Pieces.* | *Pieces.* | *Pieces.* | *Pieces.* | *Pieces.* |
| Dry Java and Sumatra ox and cow hides | 299,300 | 302,800 | 304,100 | 280,100 | 275,800 |
| Dry Java buffalo hides | 164,300 | 155,100 | 190,500 | 183,200 | 208,400 |
| Dry East Indian ox and cow hides | 5,700 | ...... | 1,280 | 1,150 | 9,300 |
| Dry East Indian buffalo hides | ...... | ...... | 13,000 | 16,700 | 17,600 |
| Dry Buenos Ayres hides | 8,400 | 12,900 | 17,500 | 2,800 | 1,600 |
| Salted Buenos Ayres hides | 3,600 | 21,700 | 11,100 | 3,800 | 10,100 |
| African hides | 7,900 | 3,900 | 2,300 | 1,520 | 1,750 |
| Venezuela and West Indian hides | ...... | 2,400 | 5,600 | 350 | 5,400 |
| Java horsehides | 600 | 1,000 | 700 | 1,600 | 1,400 |
| Java goatskins (about) | } 219,000 | 488,000 | { 392,000 | 501,000 | 496,900 |
| Java bastard goatskins (about) | | | 23,000 | 38,500 | 29,600 |
| Java deerskins (about) | 10,000 | 11,000 | 12,100 | 8,800 | 15,300 |
| Arabian goat and sheep skins (about) | 6,000 | 14,0uu | 21,300 | 16,200 | 8,300 |
| Cape goat and sheep skins | ...... | ...... | 27,500 | 8,300 | 12,700 |
| Goatskins of other countries (about) | ...... | ...... | 55,000 | 98,000 | 55,500 |
| Java lizard and snake skins (about) | 45,000 | 86,000 | 80,600 | 48,700 | 47,500 |
| Buffalo horns (about) | 15,000 | 25,000 | 18,000 | 27,000 | 26,000 |

| Description. | 1897. | 1898. | 1899. | 1900. | 1901. |
|---|---|---|---|---|---|
| | *Pieces.* | *Pieces.* | *Pieces.* | *Pieces.* | *Pieces.* |
| Dry Java and Sumatra ox and cow hides | 310, | 282,793 | 324,112 | 299,214 | 321,559 |
| Dry Java buffalo hides | 185, | 202,749 | 263,751 | 237,914 | 276,412 |
| Dry East Indian ox and cow hides | 8,686 | 6, | 3,889 | 27,598 | 14,300 |
| Dry East Indian buffalo hides | 25,668 | 24,506 | 46,000 | 47,993 | 65,669 |
| Dry Buenos Ayres hides | ...... | 5,668 | 1,168 | ...... | 4,300 |
| Salted Buenos Ayres hides | 11,925 | 13,812 | 2,801 | 2,000 | 1,000 |
| China hides | ...... | ...... | ...... | ...... | 12,300 |
| Australian hides | ...... | ...... | ...... | ...... | 4,500 |
| African hides | 1,797 | 2,177 | 1,224 | 1,598 | 738 |
| Venezuela and West Indian hides | 4,442 | 5,558 | 5,586 | 10,243 | 6,092 |
| Java horsehides | 1,024 | 1,169 | 1,266 | 966 | 820 |
| Java goatskins (about) | 565,900 | 672,000 | 737,700 | 789,000 | 706,000 |
| Java bastard goatskins (about) | 21,000 | 24,000 | 7,500 | 24,500 | 51,500 |
| Java deerskins (about) | 9,200 | 18,100 | 5,600 | 25,800 | 18,700 |
| Arabian goat and sheep skins (about) | 11,300 | 5,300 | 4,200 | 3,400 | 8,100 |
| Cape goat and sheep skins | 14,600 | 10,600 | 16,500 | 2,700 | 2,300 |
| Goatskins of other countries (about) | 46,000 | 30,500 | 23,600 | 19,600 | 14,600 |
| Java lizard and snake skins (about) | 42,000 | 38,000 | 55,200 | 64,400 | 59,700 |
| Buffalo horns (about) | 48,000 | 45,000 | 35,000 | 32,000 | 34,000 |
| Italian salted horsehides | ...... | ...... | ...... | 8,876 | 2,575 |

*Stock in the Netherlands, January 1.*

| Description. | 1893. | 1894. | 1895. | 1896. | 1897. |
|---|---|---|---|---|---|
| | *Pieces.* | *Pieces.* | *Pieces.* | *Pieces.* | *Pieces.* |
| Dry Java, Atjih and Sumatra ox and cow hides | 45,960 | 70,750 | 103,000 | 35,400 | 20,800 |
| Dry Java buffalo hides | 20,520 | 14,100 | 24,700 | 24,000 | 26,200 |
| Dry East Indian ox and cow hides | ...... | ...... | 350 | 450 | 670 |
| Dry Singapore buffalo hides | ...... | ...... | 2,500 | 2,800 | 1,300 |
| Dry Buenos Ayres hides | 4,130 | 6,300 | 10,697 | 1,165 | 565 |
| Salted Buenos Ayres hides | ...... | 4,500 | 400 | 1,300 | 587 |
| African hides | 2,770 | 1,340 | 325 | 320 | ...... |
| Venezuela and Surinam hides | ...... | 500 | 715 | ...... | ...... |
| Java horsehides | 90 | 300 | 360 | 428 | 385 |
| Java goatskins (about) | } 17,000 | 210,000 | { 6,200 | 20,900 | 17,300 |
| Java bastard skins (about) | | | 23,100 | 7,600 | 6,200 |
| Java deerskins | 2,600 | 4,000 | 3,500 | 850 | 7,500 |
| Arabian goat and sheep skins | 1,500 | 5,000 | ...... | ...... | 5,000 |
| Goatskins of other countries | ...... | ...... | 18,000 | 14,300 | 12,900 |
| Java lizard and snake skins | 2,000 | 24,000 | 13,700 | 25,500 | 30,000 |
| Buffalo horns | 5,200 | 4,500 | 2,000 | ...... | ...... |

*Stock in the Netherlands January 1*—Continued.

| Description. | 1898. | 1899. | 1900. | 1901. | 1902. |
|---|---|---|---|---|---|
| | *Pieces.* | *Pieces.* | *Pieces.* | *Pieces.* | *Pieces.* |
| Dry Java, Atjih and Sumatra ox and cow hides ... | 27,700 | 42,488 | 18,268 | 23,458 | 54,925 |
| Dry Java buffalo hides | 21,090 | 31,536 | 17,980 | 10,866 | 20,663 |
| Dry East Indian ox and cow hides | 3,975 | 4,583 | 1,525 | 1,315 | 3,200 |
| Dry Singapore buffalo hides | 2,500 | 7,300 | 6,210 | 5,806 | 7,800 |
| Dry Buenos Ayres hides | | 4,370 | 938 | 300 | 1,617 |
| Salted Buenos Ayres hides | 2,144 | 5,860 | | | |
| China hides | | | | | 3,500 |
| Australian hides | | | | | 500 |
| African hides | | 440 | | 116 | |
| Venezuela and Surinam hides | 322 | 1,950 | 541 | 785 | 47 |
| Java horsehides | 52 | 122 | 850 | 130 | 345 |
| Java goatskins (about) | } 114,200 | 64,200 | { 42,500 | 19,150 | 153,000 |
| Java bastard skins (about) | | | 1,120 | | 21,000 |
| Java deerskins | 6,500 | 1,600 | 1,140 | 160 | 2,900 |
| Arabian goat and sheep skins | 6,000 | 3,000 | 5,100 | 4,200 | 600 |
| Goatskins of other countries | 15,000 | 11,000 | 25,400 | 20,300 | 12,000 |
| Java lizard and snake skins | 40,000 | 50,000 | 35,000 | 36,400 | 27,000 |
| Buffalo horns | | 17,929 | 15,000 | 7,200 | 15,000 |

*Quotations for hides and skins on January 1, 1902, per one-half kilogram (1.1 pounds).*

| Description. | Weight. | Prices quoted per kilo. |
|---|---|---|
| **JAVA OX AND COW HIDES.** | *Kilos.*ᵃ | |
| Batavia | 7 to 9 | $0.20 to $0.208 |
| Samarang: | | |
|   Shaved | 2 to 3 | .273 to .28 |
|   Do | 4 to 5 | .256 to .264 |
|   Do | 5 to 7 | .216 to .224 |
|   Unshaved | 5 to 7 | .18 to .188 |
| Soerabaya | 2 to 4 | .272 to .28 |
|   Do | 5 to 7 | .212 to .22 |
| Tjilatjap | 3 to 6 | .20 to .208 |
| Padang ox and cow hides | 3 to 5 | .18 to .188 |
|   Do | 5 to 7 | .168 to .188 |
| Macassar cow hides | 5 to 9 | .14 to .16 |
| Singapore: | | |
|   Best | 3 to 9 | .14 to .16 |
|   Second | 3 to 9 | .106 to .128 |
| **JAVA BUFFALO HIDES.** | | |
| Batavia: | | |
|   Best, shaved | 14 to 18 | .174 to .18 |
|   Do | 9 to 14 | .18 to .184 |
|   Do | 5 to 9 | .188 to .192 |
|   Second, shaved | 7 to 18 | .148 to .152 |
|   Unshaved | 8 to 13 | .128 to .132 |
| Samarang: | | |
|   Best, shaved | 12 to 17 | .168 to .172 |
|   Do | 9 to 12 | .18 to .184 |
|   Do | 5 to 9 | .188 to .192 |
| Soerabaya: | | |
|   Best, shaved | 8 to 15 | .16 to .18 |
|   Second and unshaved | 8 to 15 | .12 to .14 |
| Tjilatjap | 8 to 12 | .14 to .16 |
| Padang buffalo hides | 8 to 12 | .10 to .12 |
| Macassar | 10 to 15 | .08 to .10 |
| Singapore: | | |
|   Best | 10 to 15 | .108 to .120 |
|   Second | 10 to 15 | .08 to .10 |
| Other Java hides: | | |
|   Horsehides | 3 to 4 | .128 to .148 |
|   Deerskins | 1¼ to 2¼ | .14 to .16 |
|   Goatskins | | ᵇ.43 to .56 |
|   Bastard sheepskins | | ᵇ.20 to .24 |
| Lizard and snake skins | | ᵇ.20 to .40 |
| **BUFFALO HORNS.** | | |
| Buffalo horns | | ᶜ7.20 to 7.60 |
| **SALTED DUTCH HIDES AND SKINS.** | | |
| Cowhides: | | |
|   Vachets | 28 to 30 | .096 to .10 |
|   Town slaughtered | 30 to 32 | .088 to .092 |
|   Do | 28 to 30 | .088 to .092 |

ᵃ1 kilo = 2.046 pounds.    ᵇPer hide or skin.    ᶜPer 50 kilograms (110 pounds.)

*Quotations for hides and skins on January 1, 1902, per one-half kilogram (1.1 pounds)*—Continued.

| Description. | Weight. | Prices quoted per kilo. |
|---|---|---|
| SALTED DUTCH HIDES AND SKINS—continued. | | |
| Cowhides—Continued. | *Kilos.* | |
| Country slaughtered | 24 to 26 | $0.084 to $0.088 |
| Do | 16 to 18 | .088 to .092 |
| Oxhides: | | |
| Town slaughtered | 33 to 35 | .10 to .104 |
| Do | 29 to 30 | .092 to .096 |
| Bullhides: | | |
| Town slaughtered | 35 to 37 | .084 to .088 |
| Do | 32 to 33 | .08 to .084 |
| Vealskins | 9 to 10 | .112 to .116 |
| Without shanks | 9 | .132 to .136 |
| Without heads and shanks | 8 | .148 to .152 |
| Calfskins | 3½ to 4½ | .132 to .136 |
| Horsehides | ........... | a4.00 to 4.400 |

a Per hide or skin.

*Limed pickerbends.*

[Prices are per pound, delivered in England.]

| Description. | Average weight. | Prices quoted (sterling). |
|---|---|---|
| Batavia: | *Pounds.* | *Pence.* |
| Prime, transparent | 20 to 22 | 7½ |
| Do | 15 to 17 | 7¾ |
| Do | 10 to 12 | 8 |
| Do | 6 to 7 | 8¼ |
| Java: | | |
| Prime, unshaved | 20 to 22 | 6¼ |
| Do | 15 to 17 | 6½ |
| Do | 10 to 12 | 6¾ |
| Do | 6 to 7 | 6¾ |
| Batavia: | | |
| Second, transparent | 17 to 18 | 6¾ |
| Do | 12 to 14 | 6¾ |
| Java: | | |
| Second, unshaved | 17 to 18 | 5¾ |
| Do | 12 to 14 | 5¾ |
| Singapore: | | |
| Prime | 11 to 12 | 6¼ |
| Second | 10 to 12 | 5 |
| Rejections | 10 to 12 | 4½ |
| Hide pieces | ........... | 5¼ |
| Hide cuttings | ........... | 3¼ |

## INDIGO.

The imports of Java indigo were:

| Year. | At Rotterdam. | At Amsterdam. | Year. | At Rotterdam. | At Amsterdam. |
|---|---|---|---|---|---|
| | *Chests.* | *Chests.* | | *Chests.* | *Chests.* |
| 1892 | 3,544 | 4,073 | 1897 | 4,062 | 5,180 |
| 1893 | 3,048 | 3,652 | 1898 | 3,844 | 5,659 |
| 1894 | 2,077 | 2,862 | 1899 | 1,787 | 2,292 |
| 1895 | 2,267 | 2,925 | 1900 | 2,184 | 1,688 |
| 1896 | 2,603 | 3,396 | 1901 | 1,654 | 1,681 |

For those engaged in the trade in Java indigo, 1901 was a favorable year. During the first months, transactions were regular at improving prices, about 3 florins ($1.20) being paid per one-half kilogram (1.1 pounds). The summer months were quiet, but the tone again improved, and offerings during the last months were easily placed, as much as 3.25 florins ($1.30) per one-half kilogram being realized.

The Java crop yielded:

| | Pounds. | | | Pounds. |
|---|---|---|---|---|
| 1892 | 1,403,600 | | 1897 | 1,784,000 |
| 1893 | 1,390,400 | | 1898 | 1,988,800 |
| 1894 | 1,089,000 | | 1899 | 1,452,000 |
| 1895 | 1,328,800 | | 1900 | 1,309,000 |
| 1896 | 1,496,000 | | 1901 | 1,135,200 |

### LUMBER.

The following statements, which were kindly furnished me by Messrs. J. C. & Th. H. Leyenaar, lumber importers of this city, show the imports and exports of lumber, hardwood, dyewoods, willows, hoops, staves, etc., at Rotterdam for the first six months of 1901 and 1902.

Lumber for shipbuilding, etc., was imported by sea in full cargoes from the following countries:

[Tons of 1,000 kilograms (2,200 pounds).]

| From— | 1901. | 1902. | From— | 1901. | 1902. |
|---|---|---|---|---|---|
| **UNSAWED:** | | | **SAWED:** | | |
| United States | 1,624 | | United States | 11,311 | 5,700 |
| Russia | 3,018 | | Prussia | 6,277 | |
| Prussia | 986 | | Norway | 274 | 1,949 |
| Sweden | 1,861 | | Russia | 5,548 | 10,188 |
| | | | Sweden | 2,708 | 2,656 |

The value of unsawed lumber imported in other ways was:

| From— | 1901. | 1902. | From— | 1901. | 1902. |
|---|---|---|---|---|---|
| Germany | $137,840.80 | $111,940.80 | Austria | $272,440.00 | $26,162.80 |
| Countries on Danube. | 110,000.00 | 202,584.00 | Italy | 9,600.00 | 140.00 |
| Belgium | 1,220.00 | 558.00 | Dutch East Indies | 58,247.20 | |
| Great Britain | 1,016.00 | 2,992.80 | Greece | 32,080.00 | |
| Russia | 536,174.00 | 159,444.00 | Spain | | 324.00 |
| United States | 2,969,584.00 | 489,304.00 | Japan | | 600.00 |
| Norway | 12,500.00 | 23,584.00 | | | |

Of the above lumber, the following quantities were exported:

| To— | 1901. | 1902. | To— | 1901. | 1902. |
|---|---|---|---|---|---|
| | Pounds. | Pounds. | | Pounds. | Pounds. |
| Belgium | 517,987 | 62,645 | Dutch East Indies | | 20,797 |
| Germany | 43,954,511 | 11,449,447 | Russia | | 66 |
| Great Britain | 292,437 | 273,878 | Denmark | | 116,600 |
| West coast of Africa | 17,600 | | France | | 316,998 |
| Portugal | 6,600 | | | | |

The value of sawed lumber imported in other ways was:

| From— | 1901. | 1902. | From— | 1901. | 1902. |
|---|---|---|---|---|---|
| Belgium | $6,629.60 | $4,987.20 | Russia | $669,888.00 | $477,932.00 |
| Germany | 673,684.40 | 450,030.40 | Sweden | 130,652.00 | 186,544.00 |
| France | 420.00 | 1,140.00 | Countries on the | | |
| Great Britain | 17,959.80 | 10,865.60 | Danube | 272,244.50 | 107,020.60 |
| Norway | 136,958.00 | 306,852.00 | Italy | 10,094.00 | 1,080.00 |
| Spain | 640.00 | 520.00 | Austria | 432.00 | |
| United States | 445,976.40 | 1,042,285.80 | | | |

Of the above lumber, the following quantities were exported:

| To— | 1901. | 1902. | To— | 1901. | 1902. |
|---|---|---|---|---|---|
| | Pounds. | Pounds. | | Pounds. | Pounds. |
| Belgium | 66,755 | 142,435 | Dutch East Indies | 6,215 | |
| Germany | 340,303,398 | 247,749,480 | United States | 141 | |
| Africa (west coast) | 67,540 | 259,415 | Sweden | 1,320 | |
| Denmark | 82,614 | 40,801 | Egypt | 99,000 | |
| France | 6,369 | 1,846 | Algiers | | 35,860 |
| Great Britain | 1,138,108 | 2,124,773 | China | | 22,000 |
| Norway | 4,400 | | | | |

The value of unsawed hard woods for the manufacture of furniture, etc., imported at Rotterdam was:

| From— | 1901. | 1902. | From— | 1901. | 1902. |
|---|---|---|---|---|---|
| Germany | $77,842.00 | $17,314.40 | Dutch East Indies | | $6,818.00 |
| Great Britain | 192,628.00 | 88,139.00 | Russia | $16,000.00 | 2,400.00 |
| France | 6,600.00 | 32,996.00 | Turkey | | 2,800.00 |
| United States | 148,536.00 | 98,800.00 | Belgium | 1,100.00 | 4,104.00 |
| Cuba | 14,720.00 | 54,440.00 | Central America | 8,720.00 | |
| Greece | | 7,320.00 | Mexico | 9,200.00 | |

The quantities of unsawed hard wood exported were:

| From— | 1901. | 1902. | From— | 1901. | 1902. |
|---|---|---|---|---|---|
| | Pounds. | Pounds. | | Pounds. | Pounds. |
| Belgium | 20,460 | 28,556 | France | 39,324 | 660 |
| Germany | 10,540,629 | 5,487,704 | Dutch East Indies | 5,993 | |
| Great Britain | 137,878 | 104,562 | United States | 114,400 | 198 |
| Norway | 64 | | | | |

The value of sawed hard wood imported was:

| From— | 1901. | 1902. | From— | 1901. | 1902. |
|---|---|---|---|---|---|
| Belgium | $2,420.00 | $1,127.20 | United States | $141,240.00 | $68,040.00 |
| Germany | 1,998.00 | 4,634.00 | Italy | 240.00 | |
| France | 80.00 | | Norway | 1,725.60 | |
| Great Britain | 13,133.20 | 25,674.00 | Greece | | 560.00 |
| Countries on the Danube | 20,000.00 | 22,000.00 | Russia | | 13,200.00 |

Of sawed hard woods, the following quantities were exported:

| To— | 1901. | 1902. | To— | 1901. | 1902. |
|---|---|---|---|---|---|
| | Pounds. | Pounds. | | Pounds. | Pounds. |
| Germany | 3,301,678 | 3,005,823 | India | 16,500 | |
| Great Britain | 19,800 | 9 | United States | | 396 |
| Denmark | 13,024 | 8,202 | | | |

*Dyewoods imported at Rotterdam.*

| From— | 1901. | 1902. | From— | 1901. | 1902. |
|---|---|---|---|---|---|
| | Pounds. | Pounds. | | Pounds. | Pounds. |
| Germany | 273,678 | 962,334 | Mexico | 7,299,600 | 4,187,920 |
| Great Britain | 102,540 | 22,189 | Dutch East Indies | 2,435 | 10,892 |
| Haiti | 2,926,000 | | France | | 127,442 |
| Rio de la Plata | 27,278,000 | 3,476,330 | Canada | | 1,256,200 |
| United States | 11,584,650 | 15,354,889 | | | |

*Dyewoods exported form Rotterdam.*

| From— | 1901. | 1902. | From— | 1901. | 1902. |
|---|---|---|---|---|---|
| | *Pounds.* | *Pounds.* | | *Pounds.* | *Pounds.* |
| Belgium | 22,000 | | Great Britain | | 330,220 |
| Germany | 42,138,161 | 34,403,239 | France | | 4,415 |
| Russia | 66,440 | 362,254 | United States | | 17,725 |

*Ground or chopped dyewoods imported at Rotterdam.*

| From— | 1901. | 1902. | From— | 1901. | 1902. |
|---|---|---|---|---|---|
| | *Pounds.* | *Pounds.* | | *Pounds.* | *Pounds.* |
| Belgium | 22,660 | | Germany | 57,116 | 10,010 |
| Great Britain | 15,415 | | France | 242 | |

*Exports of ground or chopped dyewoods.*

| From— | 1901. | 1902. | From— | 1901. | 1902. |
|---|---|---|---|---|---|
| | *Pounds.* | *Pounds.* | | *Pounds.* | *Pounds.* |
| Germany | 63,631 | 52,985 | Norway | | 88,000 |
| Belgium | 22,352 | | United States | | 8,498 |
| Great Britain | | 125 | | | |

*Imports of wood for fuel.*

| From— | 1901. | 1902. | From— | 1901. | 1902. |
|---|---|---|---|---|---|
| | *Pounds.* | *Pounds.* | | *Pounds.* | *Pounds.* |
| Norway | 500,500 | | France | | 125 |
| Germany | 66,000 | 28,647 | Belgium | | 11,715 |

Exports to Great Britain, 74,800 pounds.

*Imports of shoe tacks.*

| From— | 1901. | 1902. | From— | 1901. | 1902. |
|---|---|---|---|---|---|
| | *Pounds.* | | | *Pounds.* | |
| Great Britain | 44 | | Germany | | $40.00 |
| United States | 15,913 | $1,724.00 | | | |

No shoe tacks were exported.

*Sawdust imports.*

| From— | 1901. | 1902. | From— | 1901. | 1902. |
|---|---|---|---|---|---|
| | *Pounds.* | *Pounds.* | | *Pounds.* | *Pounds.* |
| Great Britain | 5,078 | 8,192 | Germany | 36,553 | 47,080 |

*Sawdust exports.*

| To— | 1901. | 1902. | To— | 1901. | 1902. |
|---|---|---|---|---|---|
| | *Pounds.* | *Pounds.* | | *Pounds.* | *Pounds.* |
| Belgium | 37,902 | 16,610 | United States | 77,000 | 220,000 |
| Great Britain | 700,434 | 202,950 | Germany | | 6,798 |
| Java | 11,000 | | | | |

*Imports of willows, twigs, etc.*

| From— | 1901. | 1902. | From— | 1901. | 1902. |
|---|---|---|---|---|---|
| | *Pounds.* | *Pounds.* | | *Pounds.* | *Pounds.* |
| Belgium.............. | 6,204 | 30,560 | France ............. | .............. | 275 |
| Great Britain......... | 1,804 | 297 | | | |

*Exports of willows, twigs, etc.*

| To— | 1901. | 1902. | To— | 1901. | 1902. |
|---|---|---|---|---|---|
| | *Pounds.* | *Pounds.* | | *Pounds.* | *Pounds.* |
| Belgium.............. | 22 | .............. | Denmark............ | 2,963 | 22,970 |
| Great Britain......... | 359,998 | 261,128 | Norway............. | .............. | 5,236 |
| Germany ............. | 7,599 | 2,200 | Sweden............. | .............. | 1,100 |

*Imports of wood wool.*

| From— | 1901. | 1902. | From— | 1901. | 1902. |
|---|---|---|---|---|---|
| | *Pounds.* | *Pounds.* | | *Pounds.* | *Pounds.* |
| Germany .............. | 97,152 | 112,608 | Sweden.............. | 38,500 | 77,000 |

*Exports of wood wool.*

| To— | 1902. | To— | 1902. |
|---|---|---|---|
| | *Pounds.* | | *Pounds.* |
| Great Britain ......................... | 1,100 | Germany ......................... | 88 |

*Hoops imported.*

| From— | 1901. | 1902. | From— | 1901. | 1902. |
|---|---|---|---|---|---|
| | *Pounds.* | *Pounds.* | | *Pounds.* | *Pounds.* |
| France ............... | 15,125 | 16,280 | Great Britain ........ | 260 | .............. |
| United States......... | 1,425 | 1,672 | Norway............. | 22 | .............. |

*Hoops exported.*

| To— | 1901. | 1902. | To— | 1901. | 1902. |
|---|---|---|---|---|---|
| | *Pounds.* | *Pounds.* | | *Pounds.* | *Pounds.* |
| Belgium.............. | 13,365 | 77 | Italy .................... | .............. | 10,076 |
| Great Britain......... | 347,177 | 2,828,993 | Norway ............ | 685,137 | 356,213 |
| Germany ............. | 55,856 | 63,285 | Russia ............. | 22,000 | 5,984 |
| Denmark............. | 136,974 | 33,484 | Sweden ............. | 80,180 | 58,300 |
| France ............. | .............. | 5,874 | United States ........ | 4,840 | .............. |

*Value of staves imported.*

| From— | 1901. | 1902. | From— | 1901. | 1902. |
|---|---|---|---|---|---|
| Norway .............. | $32,738.40 | $13,490.00 | Germany ............ | $63,110.80 | $47,206.80 |
| Austria.............. | 16,600.00 | 800.00 | Great Britain ........ | 10,766.40 | 33,128.80 |
| Russia............... | 2,400.00 | 176.00 | Denmark ........... | 10.80 | 116.00 |
| United States......... | 374,889.60 | 110,851.20 | Sweden ............. | 480.00 | 16,528.00 |
| Belgium.............. | 18,125.60 | 9,672.00 | | | |

*Staves exported.*

| To— | 1901. | 1902. | To— | 1901. | 1902. |
|---|---|---|---|---|---|
| | *Pounds.* | *Pounds.* | | *Pounds.* | *Pounds.* |
| Norway | 75,460 | | Portugal | 143,000 | 358,688 |
| Belgium | 130,306 | 250,562 | Spain | 377,848 | |
| Germany | 13,648,061 | 4,262,822 | Denmark | | 23,122 |
| Africa | 1,596,386 | 1,519,181 | Russia | | 308 |
| Great Britain | 278,146 | 619,557 | Sweden | | 28,600 |
| Italy | | 33,000 | France | | 484,000 |

### AMERICAN MACHINERY, HARDWARE, ETC.

Generally speaking, American manufactured articles are in good demand, and the use of same is always on the increase. The trade in our manufactures would, however, extend more rapidly, if the wishes of the Netherlands importers and dealers with reference to "terms of payment," "sizes and patterns," "extra parts for repairs," "samples," "size of stock," "cost of advertising," etc., could be complied with by the American manufacturers and exporters, and if the latter or their representatives were more frequently on the spot to investigate the needs in that particular branch, to invigorate the efforts of the Dutch agent, and to make concessions to purchasers where such are necessary.

The majority of our manufacturers still adhere to the "cash against documents" system. While this may work very well in the case of commodities of which the Hollanders are in absolute need, it does not work in lines that have to compete with European manufactures. Our shoes, furniture, machinery, hardware, and the like would be more generally used than they are now, were it not for the cash against documents system. The people that exert themselves most to place these manufactures are the merchants or importing agents with modest means—the rich merchant generally handles raw material—and if they are not able to get from thirty to ninety days' credit, they find themselves compelled to look for substitutes in the European markets, as paying cash would, with the small means they generally possess, cripple their business. And why should the American manufacturer not grant the same terms of payment as German, British, French, or Belgian manufacturers? When the character and standing of the Dutch importing agent has once been ascertained (which of course should be done) and found satisfactory, the risk in granting easy terms is comparatively slight, and does not compare with the benefit that may be derived from it.

If more of our machinery and tools, electrical appliances, shoes, and various other articles were permanently exhibited in this country, it would bring about a large increase in sales. I think that manufacturers desirous of supplying this country and the countries along the Rhine should establish stock rooms here. Such stock rooms could first be managed by American representatives, but could in time be turned over to a native agent after he had shown his qualifications and won the confidence of the American manufacturer. The large consumer of American manufactures (such as a ship or machinery constructor) purchases what he can inspect in preference to ordering from a catalogue. Owing to the small stock now kept in the Netherlands, parts of machinery and hardware necessary to replace broken pieces are frequently lacking. Of American shoes, there is always a short ness of sizes and styles. This causes dealers to apply to our British, German, and French competitors.

Some of our manufacturers seem to be of the opinion that the Netherlands is too small a field. They keep such stock as they have in Europe, in Germany, or England. This is a mistake. The Netherlands is a thickly populated country, and is in a position to use a considerable quantity of American manufactures. Besides, from this country, and especially from Rotterdam, a large part of Europe can be worked to advantage, owing to the water connections with Germany, France, and Switzerland. This being the case, the Dutch importer desires direct transactions with the American manufacturer.

There is a lack of American advertisements in Dutch newspapers. At home, our manufacturers advertise a great deal, but here, this is generally left to the importer, who is seldom willing to spend his money in that direction. Manufacturers selling goods in the Netherlands should expend a certain sum annually for advertising here, at least until their goods are well introduced. German manufacturers advertise widely in the Dutch papers.

Germany is our strongest competitor in the Netherlands market. German manufactures are constantly improving in quality and finish, and they are, as a rule, cheaper, besides enjoying lower freight rates. Still the American article is generally of better finish and is renowned for its durability, and will be preferred, provided the price is not too high and the terms of payment are easy.

The following articles, among others, find sale in this country: Pumps, scales, stoves, safes, gas and coal ranges, washing machines, wringers, meat choppers, washboards, tools, refrigerators, mangels, lawn mowers, plows, tin kettles, iron pans, bicycle parts, carpet sweepers, steam and electric machinery, electrical appliances, boilers, rubber tubes, dentist chairs, oak wood mantles, cameras, furniture, lamps, typewriter machines, articles of stationery, pressed glassware, leather, graphophones, shoes, and hats.

### STATISTICS OF THE CITY OF ROTTERDAM.

On December 31, 1901, the city covered a surface of 13,660 acres. On December 31, 1900, it contained 34,867 buildings; in 1901 1,084 buildings were constructed and 429 buildings demolished. The total number of buildings on December 31, 1901, was 35,522, covering an area of about 780 acres. Of the total surface built on, 544 acres was covered by dwellings.

The population of Rotterdam was on December 31—

| | |
|---|---:|
| 1852 | 91,533 |
| 1860 | 107,929 |
| 1870 | 123,097 |
| 1880 | 152,517 |
| 1890 | 209,134 |
| 1900 | 332,185 |
| 1901 | 341,052 |

The present officially estimated population is 345,187.

I desire to acknowledge my indebtedness to the secretary of the Rotterdam Chamber of Commerce and to several prominent merchants for much of the information contained in this report.

S. LISTOE, *Consul-General.*

ROTTERDAM, *October 25, 1902.*

## REPORT FROM CONSULAR AGENCY AT SCHIEDAM.

Schiedam is situated near the mouth of the river Maas and has, according to the last census (December 31, 1901), 27,069 inhabitants, an increase of 353 over the preceding year. At one time, Schiedam established for herself the name of being the leading city in the world for the distillation of gin and alcohol; and yet, in spite of the fact that most of her distilleries have gone out of existence during the last twenty years, the total production of spirits containing 50 per cent alcohol amounted in the year 1901 to 8,194,710 gallons. This quantity was produced by 138 spirit factories (Branderijen), but besides she has 23 distilleries manufacturing gin only, and they import to a very large extent the alcohol used for the production. However, it can not be denied that her gin industry is no longer in the flourishing condition of former days, owing to the low prices now obtained for the product, to the competition in other quarters, and last, but not least, to the great decrease in the demand for yeast, once a very profitable by-product of the distilleries. About half of her once successful distilleries have been abandoned during the last twenty years, and as a matter of course, this has thrown out of employment not only the workers in those establishments, but also a large number of bottle makers, copper workers, coopers, and others engaged in minor industries relying upon the patronage of the large distilleries. Under such conditions, it is no wonder that Schiedam has had a long period of hard times, and it is a rather surprising fact, very much to her credit, that she has been able to go through the ordeal in the manner she has, for, barring a large number of vacant distilleries, she shows to-day no sign of decadence. The partial ruin of her chief industries, which at first naturally enough baffled her, has in recent years aroused her public-spirited citizens, who are now in a fair way to replace the abandoned distilleries with other enterprises. The first start in this direction was made a few years ago, when some Schiedam capitalists established here the now flourishing stearine candle factory, "Apollo," which last year employed over 500 workers, namely, 329 men and boys and 196 women and girls. Other minor factories were added later, and this year one of the largest shipbuilding firms in the Netherlands has located here and is now erecting an extensive p ant. The city government, assisted by the improvement society, "Schiedam vooruit," is doing successful work in encouraging new industries to locate here, and the city's excellent harbor and good railroad and shipping facilities are making their task comparatively easy.

### THE HARBOR.

The Schiedam Harbor is not only considerably nearer the sea than the harbor of Rotterdam, but it also has economical advantages for shipowners; and believing this fact to be of interest to American shippers, I submit tariff of harbor dues in Schiedam for seagoing sailing vessels and steamers, together with that of Rotterdam:

For sailing vessels, per cubic meter for every voyage........................ $0. 02
For steamers and seagoing lighters, per cubic meter.......................... .012
For steamers and seagoing vessels with cargoes of ore only .................. .004

For seagoing vessels arriving at or leaving this port with broken cargo, dues are paid only on such cargo.

For general cargo, per 1,000 kilograms (2,205 pounds)....................... $0. 025
For wood cargo, per 1,000 kilograms (2,205 pounds)......................... 0. 02

Free of harbor dues are craft loading or discharging out or into sea-going vessels in this harbor and leaving twenty-four hours later.

TARIFF OF HARBOR DUES FOR SEAGOING SAILING VESSELS AND STEAMERS AT ROTTERDAM.

Steamers measuring—

| | | | |
|---|---|---|---|
| 650 cubic meters and under | per cubic meter | $0.012 |
| Above 650 cubic meters to 1,000 cubic meters | do | .014 |
| Above 1,000 cubic meters | do | .015 |

Sailing vessels measuring—

| | | | |
|---|---|---|---|
| 600 cubic meters and under | do | .02 |
| Above 600 cubic meters to 700 cubic meters | do | .024 |
| Above 700 cubic meters to 800 cubic meters | do | .028 |
| Above 800 cubic meters to 900 cubic meters | do | .032 |
| Above 900 cubic meters to 1,000 cubic meters | do | .036 |
| Above 1,000 cubic meters to 1,100 cubic meters | do | .04 |
| Above 1,100 cubic meters to 1,200 cubic meters | do | .044 |
| Above 1,200 cubic meters to 1,300 cubic meters | do | .048 |
| Above 1,300 cubic meters to 1,400 cubic meters | do | .052 |
| Above 1,400 cubic meters to 1,500 cubic meters | do | .056 |
| Above 1,500 cubic meters | do | .06 |

Schiedam Harbor has six places with a depth of from 19 to 26 feet at high water where steamers can unload. In the river are four places with a depth of 24 feet at high water. All steam and sailing vessels that can reach Rotterdam can also run in to Schiedam, as they have to pass the last-named city in order to reach the former. Schiedam can be reached from the North Sea in one and a half hours, and no bridges or sluices are found here to occasion delay in reaching the desired place in the harbor. The water in the river is sweet and excellent for the filling of steam boilers.

## IMPORTS FROM THE UNITED STATES.

These consist mainly of corn and barrel staves for use in the distilleries, but as these articles are not imported direct, but via Rotterdam and Antwerp, I have not been able to get accurate figures for the last year. However, it is safe to say that they are considerable, especially in regard to corn.

## THE EXPORTS TO THE UNITED STATES.

As will be seen from the statement of declared exports for the last year, given below, these consist chiefly of pickled herring, old rope, crude glycerin, and gin. The three last-named articles are exported from Schiedam and the herring from Vlaardingen, Maassluis, and Scheveningen. However, the herring export from the two last-named towns is inconsiderable in comparison with that of Vlaardingen, a flourishing city of about 17,000 inhabitants, 4 miles distant from Schiedam. Vlaardingen has devoted herself almost wholly to the fishing industry, which she has developed into gigantic proportions, and stands undoubtedly to-day, in regard to herring fisheries and pickled-herring export, unrivaled by any other city in the world. The exports from this district to the United States during the fiscal year ended June 30, 1902, were:

| Articles. | Value. | Articles. | Value. |
|---|---|---|---|
| Anchovies | $268.89 | Harlem oil | $78.00 |
| Aniline colors | 787.80 | Herring | 736,504.09 |
| Beans | 8,830.76 | Juniper berries | 121.14 |
| Calcined magnesite | 2,214.80 | Mackerel | 2,649.40 |
| Candles | 6,927.75 | Pease, preserved | 540.00 |
| Candle pitch | 5,465. | Poppy seed | 2,797.50 |
| Caraway seed | 1,032. | Preserves | 270.00 |
| Cheese | 4,629. | Rope, old | 56,318.02 |
| Dutch books | 192. | Salted fish | 798.00 |
| Empty bottles in cases | 1,314. | Sardelles | 3,772,45 |
| Fish, preserved | 115. | Sauerkraut | 262.50 |
| Garden seeds | | Show cards and labels | 10.00 |
| Gin | 21, | Yeast press and press sacks | 105.52 |
| Glue | 1,196. | | |
| Glycerin, crude | 34,776. | Total | 894,458.29 |

A. C. NELSON, *Consular Agent.*

SCHIEDAM, *October 24, 1902.*

# PORTUGAL.

## IMPORTS.

In dealing with the statistics of commerce and trade for the year 1901, as compared with those for 1900, and also for the first six months of the present year so far as they are obtainable, I propose to confine myself to the narrative form, and thus avoid tables of figures, which are dry reading and repel rather than invite perusal.

To avoid overloading this report with unnecessary figures, I may here state that 1 conto, or 1,000,000 reis, is equivalent in round numbers to $800.

During the year 1901, the imports from foreign countries for home consumption and reexportation were valued at 73,300 contos ($58,-640,000) and the exports at 44,000 contos ($3,200,000), as compared with 76,000 contos ($60,800,000) and 47,000 contos ($37,600,000), respectively, in the year 1900. This diminution in import value is attributable mainly to the larger home growth of certain cereals, to which I shall allude further on. Judging from the published figures for the first half of 1902, this decrease is still going on, the imports being valued at 33,000 contos ($26,400,000) and the exports at 20,000 contos ($16,000,000).

The largest exporters to Portugal are the following countries: Belgium, Brazil, England, France, Germany, Spain, Sweden and Norway, and the United States. Their joint contributions amounted last year to 57,000 contos ($45,600,000), leaving 16,000 contos ($12,800,000) for the remaining 18 countries separately named or grouped by the statistical department.

The United States stands third on the list, with 7,787 contos ($6,229,600), against England with 20,538 contos ($16,430,400), and Germany with 9,789 contos ($7,831,200). This position America has maintained since 1898. Taking into consideration the lack of ample means of rapid and direct communication because Portugal and the United States (communication is at present limited to 3 steamers flying the Portuguese flag), I think the latter has quite held its own in helping to supply the wants of this country.

Following are a few facts and figures regarding certain items of commerce selected from the 592 classes of merchandise, distributed under six heads, into which the statistical returns are divided. They are treated in alphabetical order for more ready reference.

### AUTOMOBILES.

These are as yet very few in number, their cost being prohibitive except to the rich. The highways of this country, which are not kept in the best state of repair, would also bar the extended adoption of these machines. Thirteen, with a declared value of 16 contos ($12,000) were imported in 1900, and 20, valued at 38 contos ($30,400), in 1901. Up to June 30 of this year, 13 automobiles have come into the country.

### BICYCLES.

In 1900, the number imported was 631, valued at 7½ contos ($6,000), of which 447 came from the States. In 1901, the number was 572, of which 222 were of American make. The number imported during the first six months of 1902 was 301, valued at 6 contos ($4,800).

### BISCUITS.

Of the 27 tons imported in 1900 and the 28 tons in 1901, England was practically the sole exporter. I feel sure that this branch of business is worth looking into by the American trade, and as a novelty in this country, I might suggest "shredded whole wheat," the excellence of which would be appreciated if it were known.

### BOOTS AND SHOES.

In 1900, there were imported 6,112 pairs, valued at 8 contos ($6,400), and in 1901 8,159 pairs, valued at 2 contos ($1,600). A higher priced article, if the customs figures are correct, was imported in the first year. The importation from all countries during the six months ended June 30, 1902, has been 3,707 pairs, valued at nearly 5 contos ($4,000). I commend this branch of commerce to the notice of those interested in the trade.

### BRUSHES AND BROOMS.

Chiefly supplied by Germany and France. Their declared value in 1900 was 17 contos ($13,600), and in 1901 20½ contos ($16,400). The contribution from the United States in the respective years was valued at $25 and $106. The value for the first six months of the present year has been declared at 11 contos ($8,800).

### CEREALS.

In the trade in grain other than wheat and milho (corn), the United States has taken only a small share of the importation, but in the two named varieties it has until lately been a large contributor. For the present, this market is closed to a great extent, owing to the veto put upon importation by the Portuguese Government, except under exceptional circumstances. It was announced in the year 1900 that no more milho (corn) would be imported into Portugal and that this country could supply the demand, but the customs returns give a very different account from what was anticipated.

*Milho or maize.*—In the year 1900, the foreign importation of maize was 71,000 tons, America ,sending 38,000 tons and Roumania 20,000 tons. In 1901, 10,800 tons came from abroad, the American contribution being 3,400 tons and the Roumanian, 1,800 tons. The customs returns up to the end of last June give the foreign importation as 357 tons.

*Wheat.*—The same statement was made, and apparently on good authority, that the importation of wheat would cease. There was, however, imported in 1900 the large quantity of 136,869 tons and in 1901, 92,000 tons. In the first of these years, the United States exported to Portugal 113,610 tons and in the second 84,000 tons, thus securing the bulk of the trade. During the first half of this year, 3,277 tons have been imported.

The Portuguese authorities, it would seem, intend to give effect, as far as they can, to their resolution of 1900. They have had, however, to reckon with the unforeseen, and the proceeds of the late harvest, about which opinions differ considerably both as regards quality and quantity, may lead to a further modification of their resolve. In the interest of the wheat grower, protection is strained to its full extent; the consumer is not so well satisfied, for the home product is inferior to the imported.

### CHEESE.

The importation figures are given as 335 tons, valued at 142 contos ($113,600), in 1900, as against 351 tons, valued at 156 contos ($124,800), in 1901, this increase being well maintained for the first half of the present year.

Holland supplied 293 and 308 tons in the respective years, but of a quality far inferior to good American cheese, which commands a higher price but goes much further and is certainly more wholesome than the Dutch product. Less than a ton was the contribution of the United States in 1900 and 1¼ tons in 1901. The import duty is about 30 cents a kilo (2.2 lbs.). I think there is a good opening for this trade in Portugal.

### CHEMICALS OR CHEMICAL PRODUCTS.

In 1900, out of 13,774 tons of chemical products (25 in all), such as carbonate of soda, sulphate of copper, sulphuric acid, etc., the United States, with two small exceptions, figures only in sulphate of copper, of which it furnished over 254 tons out of 2,759 tons imported; but in 1901 (the total figures under the head of chemical products being somewhat smaller) it exported to Portugal 605 tons, or 25 per cent of the whole quantity of sulphate of copper received.

### COAL.

The importation of coal in 1900 was 883,000 tons, valued at 5,500 contos ($4,400,000), and in 1901, 860,000 tons, valued at 5,100 contos ($4,080,000). Of these amounts, there came from the United States 39,500 tons and 43,000 tons in the respective years. The figures for the first six months of 1902 are 432,000 tons.

A tariff of about 30 cents a ton is levied on coal.

### COLORS AND COLORING MATTER IN POWDER AND CRYSTALS.

Portugal requires at present from 2,250 to 2,300 tons annually. France supplies about two-thirds of the amount imported. America began to send a small quantity—about 4½ tons—last year, and as the total importation during the first six months of this year has increased, the figures in her favor may have also advanced.

### CONSERVES.

*Alimentary, dried, and canned fruits, sweet.*—In 1900 there were imported 341 tons, valued at 121 contos ($96,800), and in 1901, 371 tons, valued at 129 contos ($103,200). The United States contributed in the respective years 2 tons and 5 tons. This item of export, I think, is worthy of greater attention than it has yet received, for I feel sure that America, with its vast supplies, might work up a reasonable export to this country.

### COPPER.

*In finished state for trade appliances, such as tubes, taps, valves, etc.*—This metal is lumped, in the statistical returns, with its compounds or alloys, such as brass, bronze, etc. There was imported, in the year 1900, 240 tons, valued at 288 contos ($230,400), and in 1901, 252 tons, valued at 302 contos ($241,600).

The United States exported to this country in 1900 5 tons, valued at 6½ contos ($5,200), and in 1901, 4 tons, valued at 5¾ contos ($4,600).

*Unfinished copper.*—In the year 1900 Portugal imported under this sub-head 624 tons, valued at 317 contos ($253,600), and in 1901, 861 tons, valued at 391 contos ($312,800). The United States is credited with 31½ tons and 1¼ tons in the respective years. The bulk came from England in both years.

### COTTON.

In the year 1900, there were imported 15,944 tons, valued at 4,476 contos ($3,580,800), of which the United States contributed 6,202 tons and Brazil over 7,000 tons. In the year 1901, there were imported 13,332 tons, valued at 3,855 contos ($3,084,000), of which there came from the United States 6,024 tons and from Brazil 3,944 tons. The importation figures for the first half of 1902 show an increase as compared with those of last year.

### DRUGS.

Of drugs of all kinds and medicinal specifics, the declared value of imports in 1900 was 70 contos ($56,000) and in 1901, 71 contos ($56,800). The popular taste, judging from the figures given, was in favor of the French productions to the extent of 49½ ($36,090) and 54 contos ($43,200) in the respective years. The United States contributed to the value of 4½ ($3,600) and 1½ contos ($1,200), respectively.

I may perhaps be allowed here to mention that patent medicines have to undergo a rigorous analysis at the hands of the Portuguese health department before a license for their sale is granted. On July 6, 1901, I furnished a translation to the director of the Philadelphia Commercial Museum of the thirteen main articles published in the Government Gazette, setting forth all the requirements of the law for the importation and sale of foreign drugs and medicines. The translation is far too long to be embodied in this report, and if epitomized, it might not be intelligible.

### FARINACEOUS FOODS.

For whatever purpose—whether for domestic use or the farmyard—these foods are all lumped by the customs authorities. In 1900, the value of the importation was 398 contos ($316,400), when 10,014 tons were received, and in 1901, 390 contos ($312,000), when 10,670 tons came in. The United States contributed in the respective years, 25½ and 34 tons. Wheat flour does not come under this head, as its importation is prohibited.

### FIREARMS.

*Guns.*—Very few single or double barreled guns, either breechloaders or muzzle-loaders, came from the United States during the two years under review. About 2,500 were reported in 1900—nearly all of German make—America sending only 30 breechloaders; while in 1901, there were imported 2,341, America contributing 88 breechloaders. In this year, Belgium secured the lion's share by supplying 1,560 breechloaders.

*Revolvers.*—Of 838 imported in 1900 and 1,233 in 1901, the United States sent in the respective years 295 and 515. Belgium furnished the largest supply in both years.

### FISH.

Out of the 24,000 tons of dried and salted fish that were imported in 1900, 22,000 tons were cod; and of the 27,000 tons in 1901, 25,000 tons were also cod. The United States contribution in the respective years was 72 and 193 tons. There is no other article of food, whether of home growth or imported, that appeals so much to the taste of the Portuguese as dried fish. All classes like it and the poorer people prefer it to fresh meat. Its wholesale price averages from $5.60 to $6.40 per 60 kilos (132.2 lbs.), and its retail price, 24 to 29 cents a kilo (2.2 lbs.). The import duty is 4 cents a kilo. The demand is more likely to increase than decrease, and this article of commerce is well worth the attention over of our exporters.

### GLASS—BOTTLES, DEMIJOHNS, PLATE GLASS, ETC.

In 1900, there were imported 3,759 tons, valued at 371 contos ($296,800), and in 1901, 3,288 tons, valued at 419 contos ($335,200). The United States contributed 8 and 12 tons in the respective years. Germany was by far the largest exporter, followed at a distance by France. The import trade is likely to fall off considerably, especially in bottles, as a glass manufactory has been started recently, the details of whose operations can not for the present be given.

### GUMS—RESINOUS, ETC.

Of 2,488 tons, valued at 139 contos ($111,200), imported in 1900, 943 tons came from the United States, and of 2,137 tons, valued at 114 contos ($91,200), imported in 1901, 821 tons was of American origin.

## HONEY.

But little honey is imported—351 kilos (774 pounds) in 1900, and 500 (1,102 pounds) in 1901. The national product is of a very inferior quality, of the consistency of thin treacle, but such as it is, the people like it. Their taste in this article should be educated, as it has been in many other articles of consumption which have been imported, and I do not think it would be difficult to induce them to buy honey such as America can produce. The import duty is under 4 cents a kilo (2.2 pounds).

### INSTRUMENTS FOR CALCULATION, LABORATORIES, SURGICAL PURPOSES, TRADE, ETC.

Of 656 tons, valued at 450 contos ($360,000), imported in 1900, 44 tons came from the United States; and of 712 tons, valued at 469 contos ($375,200), imported in 1901, 49 tons represent the American contribution.

The United States might with advantage push this business, for the demand, as shown by the six months' figures of this year, is on the increase. The ability of the United States to turn out articles of the first-class is second to that of no other country.

Germany, France, and England furnished the largest portion—the first named sending 50 per cent of the total imported.

## IRON.

*Finished state, plain and ornamental.*—Rails are excluded and treated under their special heading. In 1900, there were imported under this subdivision 2,559 tons, valued at 538 contos ($460,400), and in 1901, 3,312 tons, valued at 663 contos ($530,400). America exported to Portugal 407 and 185 tons in the respective years. The bulk was supplied by Germany, France, and England.

*Unfinished, cast, galvanized, and wrought.*—Of 54,813 tons, valued at 3,307 contos ($2,645,600), imported in 1900, the United States contributed only 272 tons, and of 58,499 tons in 1901, its share was but 136 tons. The bulk of imports came from England, Belgium, and Germany. Imports for first half of 1902 show a considerable increase.

## JUTE FIBER.

The importation of this article was 1,695 tons, valued at 305 contos ($244,000), in 1900, as against 1,527 tons, valued at 266 contos ($212,800), in 1901.

None was exported from the United States in 1900, but in the next year, an experiment seems to have been made by sending 1½ tons. The 1902 returns to end of June show a marked increase in the importation of this most useful fiber.

## KNICKNACKS.

This title embraces a variety of articles, such as toys, whips, pipes, snuff boxes, hones, pocket compasses, etc. They are all put on the scales and weighed in the customs, however small, and their imported weight in 1900 was 112 tons, the share of the United States being 1 ton. In 1901, it was 130 tons, the United States sending 1½ tons. The declared values of all imports were in the respective years 154 contos

($123,200) and 180 contos ($144,000). Germany and France between them supplied five-sixths of the imports in both years.

The returns for 1902, up to the end of June, show an increased demand for articles under this head which, I would suggest, should claim the attention of the American trade.

LAMPS.

I should have liked to give a few statistical details of this most useful article of import, but I find that it is so hopelessly mixed up with others under the head of "knicknacks" in the statistical tables that it is impossible to segregate the figures. I may, however, venture to remark that American lamps are to be found in fair numbers in this country, and I can safely say that there is none to beat them, either for cheapness or excellence.

LUMBER.

It is difficult to give in a short compass the actual state of the trade. Measures by weight are given in some cases and cubic contents in others; but I may state on the authority of the principal importer in Portugal that European competition has considerably reduced the American import, which until lately held the field for so many years. Perhaps when there is more direct communication than at present exists, the lost ground may be regained.

MACHINERY.

(1) *Agricultural machines.*—These machines, comprising thrashers, reapers, mowers, hay and straw compressors, etc., to the number of 226, with a combined weight of 410 tons and valued at 26 contos ($20,800), were imported in 1900, as against 379, with a total weight of 410 tons and valued at 87 contos ($69,600), in 1901. This branch of industry is making fair progress in Portugal, which is conservative to a degree and clings to the old methods of sowing and reaping its harvests. As a rule, the harvest weather is so fine here that there is no need to hurry, which accords with the national taste, and a string of twenty or thirty men, with diminutive sickles, in a half squatting attitude, creeps leisurely over a field, doing in a week what one good mower or reaper would do in two days if the ground permitted of its use, for the agriculturist pays little or no attention to the removal of surface stones.

(2) *Electrical machines.*—Of this class of machinery, the importation was 98 tons in 1900, but jumped to 282 tons in 1901, the United States sending 166½ tons. The supply from abroad has again fallen during the first six months of the present year, but the decline is probably only temporary.

(3) *Lithographic and* (4) *typewriting machines.*—Seventy-nine machines for these purposes, valued at 18 contos ($14,400), were imported in 1900, and 40, valued at 32 contos ($25,600), in 1901. The United States contributed in the respective years 14 and 20 contos ($11,200 and $16,000) worth.

(5) *Machines for trade purposes.*—It is difficult to compress into a small compass the remarks which I have to offer under this section,

and still more difficult—in fact, quite hopeless—to try to state the number and value of the machines, as the returns include items of gearing, etc., with the machine proper.

The customs tables have divided them into five classes: (1) Those under 50 kilos (110 pounds) in weight; (2) of 50 kilos and up to 100 kilos (110 to 220 pounds); (3) of 100 and up to 500 kilos (220 to 1,102 pounds); (4) of 500 and up to 1,000 kilos (1,102 to 2,204 pounds); (5) above 1,000 kilos, i. e., 1 ton.

The weights and total values of these five classes in 1900 were the following:

(1) Fifty-four and one-half tons, value 34 contos ($29,200); (2) 33 tons, value 19 contos ($15,200); (3) 179½ tons, value 97 contos ($77,600); (4) 607½ tons, value 143 contos ($114,400); (5) 2,818 tons, value 822 contos ($157,600).

The United States contributed in these several classes the following weights:

(1) One and one-half tons; (2) 1 ton; (3) 8¼ tons; (4) 4 tons; (5) 24 tons.

In 1901, they were imported to the following extent as regards weight and value:

(1) Sixty-two tons, valued at 36 contos ($28,800); (2) 29 tons, valued at 18 contos ($14,400); (3) 159 tons, valued at 76 contos ($60,800); (4) 280 tons, valued at 81 contos ($64,800), and (5) 2,532 tons, valued at 803 contos ($642,400).

From the United States there were received the following weights:

(1) Three-fourths of a ton; (2) 1 ton; (3) 6½ tons; (4) 2¾ tons, and (5) 30¼ tons.

There yet remains the item of imported machinery which is classified according to "horsepower" and is not mixed up with gearing and a lot of subordinate fittings. It appears in the customs tables under three divisions: (1) Up to 30 horsepower; (2) from 30 horsepower to 100, and (3) from 100 horsepower upward.

(1) In the year 1900, 148 machines, weighing 248 tons and valued at 95 contos ($76,000) were imported, of which the United States sent 8, weighing 5¼ tons. (2) 14 weighing 70 tons, value 2.3 contos ($18,400); from United States, nil. (3) 15 weighing 451 tons, valued at 134 contos ($107,200); from United States, nil.

(1) In the year 1901, 135 machines, weighing 198 tons, value 71½ contos ($57,200); from United States, nil. (2) 15 machines, weighing 98 tons, value 33 contos ($26,400); from United States, nil. (3) 12 machines, value 200 contos ($160,000) and weighing 661 tons. The United States furnished 3 of an aggregate tonnage of 367 tons, valued at 113 contos ($90,400).

### MEAT (FRESH, SALTED, ETC.).

In the year 1900, there were imported 105 tons, valued at 45½ contos ($36,400), and in the year 1901, 104 tons, valued at 41 contos ($32,800). The United States contributed in the respective years 8 and 23 tons, principally beef, in the latter year furnishing 19 out of the 29 tons imported. This trade is capable of good development. Much more beef is required than Portugal can produce, and the lack of it is noticed occasionally by the press.

## MARGARINE.

The United States supplied 228 out of the 260 tons imported in 1900, and the whole amount (241 tons) received from abroad in 1901. The declared value in the respective years was 59 and 49 contos ($47,200 and $39,200). There is a falling off in the importation of this article during the first six months of 1902.

## MANURES (ARTIFICIAL).

There were imported 28,965 tons, valued at 464 contos ($371,200), in 1900, and 44,853 tons, valued at 737 contos ($589,600), in 1901. None came from the United States in the first year and only 20 tons in 1901. The six months returns of this year show an increased demand. This is a lucrative business and deserves attention.

## MINERAL OILS (ILLUMINATION AND OTHER HOUSEHOLD PURPOSES).

In 1900, according to the customs statistics, there were imported 19,200 tons, and in 1901, 22,553 tons. The import trade is now principally, if not wholly, confined to the American trade.

## MOLASSES.

One thousand five hundred and forty-two tons, valued at 78 contos ($62,400), were imported in 1900, and 1,195 tons, valued at 64 contos ($51,200), in 1901. The United States furnished in the respective years 19 and 161 tons. England and Germany mainly supplied the demand, but the acknowledged superiority of the American product should tempt the trade to make larger purchases from the United States.

## PARAFFIN.

In 1900 there were imported 195½ tons, valued at 47 contos ($37,600), and in 1901, 462 tons, valued at 81 contos ($64,800). The United States supplied, respectively, 26 and 198 tons.

## PHOTOGRAPHY.

Cameras to the number of 1,434, valued at 18 contos ($14,400), were imported in 1900, as against 1,235, valued at 37 contos ($29,680), in 1901. The number imported during the first six months of 1902 shows proportionately a decided increase. The United States furnished 12 in 1900 and 73 in 1901. Germany and France were the principal exporters.

## POTATOES.

France is the principal exporter to Portugal of potatoes, which do well in the soil of this country. The demand is growing for this article of food. Nearly 10,000 tons were imported in 1901, as against 7,000 in 1900. From the United States, there were received only about 2 tons in each year.

## RAILS.

*Iron.*—In 1901, France, Belgium, and Germany shared nearly the whole of the 729 tons imported, the first-named country predominating, and America not appearing at all on the list. But in the previous year (1900), out of 262 tons imported, America and Belgium sent 214 tons between them, in about equal proportions.

*Steel.*—In 1900, Portugal imported 6,070 tons, of which 2,387 came from the United States and the remainder from Germany (figuring at 2,611 tons), England, and Belgium.

In 1901 this country imported 9,208 tons, of which 2,952 came from America, 4,258 from Belgium, 1,658 from Germany, and the balance from France and England. A proportionate increase in this import appears during the first half of 1902.

#### SEWING MACHINES.

In 1900, there were imported 14,415 sewing machines, valued at 218 contos ($174,400), and in 1901, 12,600, valued at 200 contos ($160,000). The United States imports in the respective years were 150 and 965. The majority came from England, to the respective extent of 10,287 and 7,504.

#### SOAP (BAR AND TABLETS).

Forty-seven tons, valued at 31 contos ($24,800), were imported in 1900, as compared with 52 tons, valued at 35½ contos ($28,400), in 1901. The United States contributed about 1½ tons in each year.

#### STAVES.

Staves are shown in the returns in units of a thousand. There were imported in 1900, 3,832 of such units, of which 2,553 were from America, as compared with 3,304 in 1901, of which the American contribution was 1,546. A very short time ago, the trade was principally supplied by the United States, but now the different countries of Europe have become keen competitors.

As I noticed in my last annual report, the making of barrels is still carried on by hand work. Suggestions made for the employment of machinery have been met only with a shrug of the shoulders.

#### STEEL (OTHER THAN RAILS).

*Finished state.*—The returns respecting this metal are under two separate heads, and I adhere to them. One hundred and ninety-three tons of cutlery, springs, umbrella and parasol ribs, etc., were imported in 1900, and 242 tons in 1901, to which America contributed 2 and 1½ tons in the respective years. The export to Portugal in this branch of trade might surely be worked up in the United States. Germany supplied the demand to the largest extent.

*Unfinished state.*—In 1900 there were imported 2,344 tons, and in 1901, 3,074 tons, the United States furnishing a little over 2 tons in the first year and none in the next.

#### SUGAR.

The amount imported in the years 1900 and 1901 was nearly the same, i. e., 29,000 tons, valued at 2,243 contos ($1,794,400) and 2,307 contos ($1,845,600), respectively. The United States sent 3½ tons in the first and 6 tons in the second.

Germany was the principal exporter.

H. Doc. 305, pt 2——37

## TOBACCO.

*Leaf.*—In 1900, Portugal imported 2,682 tons, valued at 569 contos ($455,200), of which 1,865 tons came from the United States; in 1901, 2,564 tons, valued at 476 contos ($380,800), of which 1,772 tons were of American growth. Belgium was the next largest contributor, with 549 and 423 tons in the respective years.

*Cheroots and fine cut.*—These two items are bracketed in the customs returns. Fifty tons were imported in 1900 and 51 in 1901, the respective declared values being 136 and 139 contos ($108,800 and $112,200). Germany, Belgium, and Holland were the chief exporters, while the United States contributed to the value of only 3½ and 7 contos ($2,800 and $5,600) in those years.

## TOOLS.

Tools and utensils for trade purposes, gardening, and field work were imported in 1900 to the extent of 612 tons, and in 1901 to the extent of 654 tons. The United States exported to Portugal about 36 tons in each year. The bulk of the imports came from Germany, England, and France.

## VARNISHES.

Of the 60 tons, valued at 34 contos ($27,200), imported in 1900, 1½ tons came from the United States, and of the 55 tons imported in 1901, only three-fourths of a ton was from America. The bulk came from England. According to the figures for the half year of 1902, the trade seems brisk.

## VEHICLES.

There were 377 vehicles of all kinds, valued at 17 contos ($13,600), imported in 1900, the United States contributing 178; in 1901 the number fell to 204 imported, but the declared value was the same as in 1900.

Of the latter imports, the United States sent 13. In 1901, there were imported for the new electric tramways in this city and suburbs 155 cars (all from the United States), valued at 542 contos.

## WATCHES AND CLOCKS.

*Gold cases.*—Of 4,902 gold watches imported in 1900 and valued at 43½ contos ($34,800), 18 came from the United States; and of 7,125 imported in 1901, and valued at 60 contos ($48,000), 66 came from America. Switzerland in each year almost monopolized the import. Duty, $1.60.

*Silver and other metal.*—Of 43,850 watches with silver cases or of other metal, and valued at 113 contos ($90,400), 277 came from the United States; and of 53,423 watches, valued at 152 contos ($121,600), which came into Portugal, only 92 came from the United States. Switzerland was the chief exporter. Duty, 80 cents.

*Clocks.*—Of all kinds, there were imported 28,000, valued at 44½ contos ($35,600), in 1900, and 30,000, valued at 37 contos ($29,600), in 1901—all charged with an ad valorem duty of 40 per cent. Germany supplied in each year about two-thirds of the whole number, the United States contributing about 6,400 in each of the two years. The imports from January to June, 1902, show a largely increased return.

Wood, other than lumber, wholly or partly prepared for furniture, decorating purposes, and joiner's work generally, was imported in 1900 to the extent of 252 tons, valued at 82 contos ($65,600), of which America contributed 27 tons; and in 1901, 271 tons, valued at 98 contos ($76,400), including a contribution from the United States of 43 tons.

## EXPORTS.

I propose to deal, and but briefly, only with those articles of commerce that were dispatched hence to the United States during the fiscal years ended June, 1901 and 1902.

In the first year, the different items (25 in number) were valued at a total sum of $3,398,706, and in the second year (also 25 in number) at $3,184,735.

Argols, cacao (crude), cork, goatskins, minerals, and rubber (crude) formed the principal articles, absorbing in the respective years $3,020,566 and $2,707,822 of the totals.

During the fiscal year 1901-2, as compared with its predecessor, there was an increase in the declared value of cork and minerals, and a decrease in that of argols, cacao, goatskins, and rubber; in the latter to the extent of nearly 33 per cent.

It will not be out of place to mention two other items, of smaller value than the preceding, furnished by this country to the United States, i. e., soapstock, or green olive pulp, which was exported to the value of $7,252 in 1900-1901 and $27,594 in 1901-2, and wine lees, which in the respective years figured at $41,971 and $63,780.

### GENERAL REMARKS.

#### PACKING.

In my last annual report, I alluded to the packing of goods by United States merchants, and I am able to repeat now what I said then, viz, that this important work is well done.

#### COMMERCIAL TRAVELERS.

I must again touch upon the need of commercial travelers visiting Portugal from the United States, if the latter wishes to maintain its present position in the import trade into this country. No amount of correspondence with buyers will take the place of a personal interview, for a customer naturally likes to see, in sample or diagram, what he is asked to purchase. A commercial traveler can travel in this country without let or hindrance, and he has no tax to pay upon his profession other than a small residential tax, to which every foreigner is liable. If he departs hence by land there is no fee levied, but if by steamer, he must furnish himself with a consular embarking certificate costing $1.

#### PATENTS, ETC.

Patents, copyrights, and trade-marks can be registered after fulfilling the requirements of the department of state charged therewith, and are fully guaranteed.

There are no laws requiring goods to be marked so as to show country of origin.

The dock accommodation at this port has been vastly improved during the past few years, and now, in addition to the discharging of cargo from vessels moored to the quay side, which has 25 feet of water at low tide, passengers by certain lines, such as the Messageries Maritimes, the Hamburg, and South African, can now land by stepping onto the quay and can pass their baggage through a branch establishment of the customs.   This is a boon which only those who have had to disembark by means of a hired boat at the ruined quay of the main customs buildings can fully appreciate.

There are some 25 tugs of various sizes and horsepower belonging to the port authorities, which are said to be ample to meet the wants of present trade and to protect it in case of need.

During the year 1901 and the first six months of 1902, 12 vessels, chiefly sailers, were purchased from foreign countries and arrived in this port.   In Oporto, the purchase consisted of 28 sailing vessels of small tonnage and 2 steamers of 1,700 and 2,000 tons each.   Here, also, there are sufficient tugs to meet ordinary requirements.   No new vessels were built in Lisbon for the mercantile marine within the eighteen months ended last June.   Shipbuilding in Oporto ceased many years ago.

The means of inland transport are good on the main lines of railway, and there are some branch lines in process of construction which will add greatly to the value of the service.

Exchange rates, constantly fluctuating, have been somewhat easier during the last few months, resulting partly from the signing of the convention by which the interest on foreign loans has been diminished, but more especially from the small importation of wheat and maize, for which gold has to be paid.   The rates will rebound at once, should the above cereals have to be imported—a contingency not unlikely.

In conclusion, I may perhaps be allowed to repeat the expression of the wish that I made last year, to see the port of Lisbon the first stopping place of United States vessels en route to the various ports of the Mediterranean.

J. H. THIERIOT, *Consul.*

LISBON, *October 31, 1902.*

# RUSSIA.

## REPORT FROM CONSULATE-GENERAL AT ST. PETERSBURG.

The commercial depression that has prevailed in Russia during the past three years has continued, but there has been an improvement in the general crops which brought relief, and the money market is much easier.   The banks have become more conservative and now make loans at lower rates than at any time during the past few years.

There has been a slight improvement in the cotton industry, but it is by no means satisfactory.

The petroleum industry, which is largely controlled by English capital, is still depressed, and many properties are not paying expenses.

According to the official accounts of receipts and expenditures of the imperial Russian finances, the ordinary receipts for the first six. months were 849,164,000 rubles ($437,319,460), more than 40,000,000 rubles ($20,600,000) above those of the same period of last year. The extraordinary receipts were 195,264,000 rubles ($100,560,960), or nearly thrice as much as last year, making a total of 1,044,428,000 rubles ($537,880,420), against 866,182,000 rubles ($446,083,730) in 1901.

The failure of the Kerch Metallurgical Company, early in the fall, for over 18,000,000 rubles ($9,270,000) increased the depression in the metal trade, and certain French and Russo-French companies, Belgian houses, and three Russian companies are large losers.

The high tariff placed on parts of sewing machines has induced the Singer Sewing Machine Company to erect a large plant at Moscow, which is the leading distributing center for Russia, and it is now manufacturing machines there that were formerly made in the United States.

It was stated early in the year that the Government would expend a large amount of money annually for a number of years in the purchase of rails and other material, to furnish employment to this industry, which threatened to disappear, because of the countermanding of orders by the Government during the war with China. Russian iron works exist practically upon Government orders, as Russia owns practically all the railroads in the Empire. The connection, therefore, between the iron works and the Government is of the closest, and a very slight change of policy of the latter means enormous loss to the former.

### SIBERIAN RAILWAY.

There have been conflicting reports as to the condition of the Trans-Siberian Railroad beyond Irkutsk and as to the probable date of opening for regular traffic. During the latter part of September, Mr. Witte, the Russian minister of finance, in order to satisfy himself of the condition of the road, especially of the Chinese Eastern and Manchurian branch, visited Manchuria. As Mr. Witte traveled by a special, it is presumed that his train made the best time possible between the Baltic and Pacific. At present, the speed of the regular trains averages but 15 miles per hour with stops, and this can not be increased with safety until the rails are at least one-third heavier than those now in use, and properly ballasted. Mr. Witte's train left Moscow September 24, and reached Vladivostok in sixteen days. The distances are as follows: St. Petersburg to Moscow, 400 miles; Moscow to Irkutsk, 3,400 miles; Irkutsk to Baikal—the newly named station on the west bank of Lake Baikal—40 miles; the lake itself, which has to be crossed by boat (or in winter by horses on the ice), 40 miles; from the east bank of Lake Baikal, Misovaya station, to Kaydalovo (where the line branches off to the Russian frontier), 520 miles; thence to the Russian-Chinese frontier station, which is called Manchuria, and across Manchuria to Vladivostok, not less than 1,400 miles. This makes a round total of 5,800 miles covered in sixteen days with stoppages.

As the result of Mr. Witte's visit, the opening of this line, which it was announced would be effected January 1, 1903, has been postponed until January 1, 1907, when coupon tickets will be issued in Russian, French, German, and English, with a translation in Chinese. It is stated that the time between Manchuria and Dalny will be seventy hours, and the fare will be 105.50 rubles ($54.33) for first class, and 66 rubles ($34) for second class. It will require from two and one-half to three days to go by steamer to Shanghai or Nagasaki. The most suitable season for visiting Siberia is summer, China the spring and autumn, and Japan May or September.

While there are yet no through trains from Moscow to Vladivostock, it is possible to travel over the whole line without too much delay or inconvenience. Express trains run regularly from Moscow to Irkutsk; they are comfortable, and well equipped with dining and sleeping cars. This distance can be covered in 185 hours. Beyond Irkutsk, traveling is not so easy and the road is not open for regular passenger through traffic; the Baikal Lake must be crossed on a steamer in the summer and on sledges during the winter. It requires seventy-five hours from Irkutsk to the Manchurian boundary, where there is a stop of twelve hours; from this point to Vladivostock, it requires five days, with a change at Kharbin. There are no sleeping or dining facilities beyond Irkutsk, and the trains are mostly composed of freight cars with only one or two very primitive second-class carriages. The trains from Niuchwang to Manchuria have only second-class cars, and from Manchuria to Irkutsk, first and second class. From Pekin to Irkutsk, sleeping berths can be secured. The passengers must furnish their own bed linen, however, and it is advisable to take a lunch basket along. The whole journey now requires from nineteen to twenty-one days, and costs about $100 first class to Irkutsk and second class from Irkutsk to Vladivostock. The connecting line of track around Lake Baikal is in active construction, and it is expected that it will be completed within a year.

With the increase of traffic on the Siberian railroad, there is a growing demand for mining machinery in Siberia, and this should attract the attention of American manufacturers.

### EXPORTS TO THE UNITED STATES.

The total value of declared exports to the United States from the consular district of St. Petersburg during the fiscal year 1902 amounts to $1,030,887.01. Compared with the fiscal year ended June 30, 1901 ($594,846.51), this represents an increase of $436,040.50.

The principal articles of export from St. Petersburg were flax, bristles, rubber goods and rubber waste, oakum, fish bladders, tarred bolt rope, wool, skins and hides, tow, sheet iron, iridium, and lycopodium. Less important articles are Russian crash, fusel oil, isinglass, dressed leather, machinery, silver articles, and wooden moldings. While there was a considerable increase in bristles, bolt rope, flax, oakum, tow, fish bladders, there was a decrease in wool, rubber waste.

The apparent large increase in flax and tow is due to the fact that these goods were shipped from Archangel and the invoices certified to by the United States consular agent in that town. They are now certified at St. Petersburg.

During the quarter ended September, 1902, the exports amounted to only $237,408.77 against $469,733.81 in 1901, representing a decrease of $232,325.04.

### IMPORTS FROM THE UNITED STATES.

The imports from the United States of machinery and other articles that are covered by the countervailing duty, have practically ceased; these are now supplied by other countries, principally Germany.

As stated in previous annual reports, the Russians prefer goods of American make to those of other countries, because of their superior finish and quality. Lately, frequent demands have been made at this consulate by large importers of general merchandise in St. Petersburg, for novelties of American make. Unfortunately, the retaliatory duty imposed by the Russian Government on certain classes of American goods, especially machinery, hardware, bicycles, etc., is still in force. Most United States goods sold here are not imported direct, but are supplied by the large commission houses in Hamburg and Bremen, where stocks of American goods are kept. These merchants enjoy large capital and can afford to comply with the short credit generally insisted upon by American manufacturers; in turn they send traveling agents all over Russia and allow the long credits that the Russians are accustomed to—nine to twelve months.

### MERCHANT MARINE.

The minister of finance announces the completion of a plan for the promotion of steamship construction in Russia, which has been under consideration by a commission for several months past. The Government will advance to builders of ocean or river steamships two-thirds of the estimated cost of all new iron vessels built of exclusively Russian materials and in Russian dockyards. These loans are to be repaid in five-year installments, without interest. The first payment is due when the new vessel is ready for sea. Until the whole amount of the loan is paid off, the ship will bear on some conspicuous part of the outer hull the legend, "Mortgaged to the State Bank." This latter condition is considered objectionable by many people desirous of availing themselves of the proffered Government assistance. They describe it as a "debtor's brand." The minister of finance expects that a considerable impetus will be given to the lagging home industry by means of these loans, without interest and on easy terms.

Foreign ships have the right of free navigation in Russian waters, but the coasting trade is restricted to the Russian flag. This privilege was granted by the law May 29, 1897 (old style). and extends also to ships navigating beyond seas, i. e., which ply between European ports and Russian ports on the Pacific.

Russian ships in foreign waters are subject to all local laws.

### RELIEF AFFORDED FAMINE SUFFERERS.

The minister of the interior has just issued a statement of which the following is a summary.

It was found difficult to ascertain the extent of relief required in each province. In many cases, the relief asked for far exceeded the actual quantity of foodstuffs, etc., wanted. The total quantity of grains distributed was 58,000,000 poods (29,359,349 tons), of which about one-half was for food and one-half for seed, representing an expenditure of 33,500,000 rubles ($17,252,500). Work was provided by the Government to 50,000 peasants, and over 11,000 persons were transferred from the famine-stricken districts to places where hands were wanted. Medical ·help was also sent by the Government, the Red Cross Society, and the Zemstvo to the stricken provinces.

### THE OWNERSHIP OF LANDS.

Attention has already been called to the change of ownership in land in Russia and the rise of the middle class, who are gradually acquiring the property hitherto held by the nobility. In the manufacturing center, this change has been pretty rapid, and it is now extending to other areas. In the recent list of estates of the nobility put up for sale, for arrears of debt upon money lent by the Government for the improvement of property, the Volga provinces showed much the same tendencies as those of St. Petersburg and Moscow. In the provinces about the Volga, something like 1,500,000 acres of nobles' land are advertised to be sold at auction. In half a dozen provinces of European Russia, mostly devoted to agriculture, an area of 2,300 square miles in the aggregate is passing into the hands of the middle class. The largest area for sale in any single province is in that of Saratov, which was one of the chief centers of the peasant troubles last summer. In this province, 30,000 acres are advertised for sale. The Bank óf the Nobility loses heavily on some of these foreclosures, owing to the depressed condition of the landed estate market; and the losses are all the heavier when the bankrupt properties happen to be situated in frontier governments, foreigners and Jews being ineligible as purchasers.

### BICYCLES AND AUTOMOBILES.

On account of the increase of the Russian duty on wheels of American make to 35 rubles ($18) per wheel (the ordinary schedule being only 18 rubles), the importation has suffered seriously. American wheels are well known here and are in favor with the better classes. Some sell for 135 rubles ($67), but cheaper ones can be bought for about 100 rubles, or $50. Several large German manufacturers of bicycles have taken advantage of the retaliatory duty and·have gained a strong foothold in the principal cities in. Russia. Their wheels are liked principally because they are cheap. Nevertheless, American wheels should sell, if they can be imported at a price that allows a fair profit to the dealer. One of the chief dealers here says that a good wheel must be delivered to him for about 70 rubles ($35), freight and duty paid, so that he can sell it at 100 rubles ($50).

The competition is very keen among local dealers, some of them being even willing to sell a bicycle on monthly installments of 5 rubles ($2.50). Although the summer is very short here, there is a large number of wheels ridden in St. Petersburg and vicinity.

Automobile dealers are of the opinion that Russia offers no market of any importance for that vehicle. There are a few running in this city, chiefly of French and Russian make, but they can not be used in the interior of the Empire, because the roads are mostly narrow and in bad condition.

Parts of bicycles are imported in considerable quantities from foreign countries, and are used in the Russian factories.

### CLOCKS AND WATCHES.

One of the principal dealers in this city says he doubts if a large business in American watches and clocks can be done in this country. The people are used to the Swiss, German, and French clocks, which are imported in large numbers, usually in parts to be put together here. Swiss watches are preferred to the German, because the latter—especially the "Glasshutte" watches—are too expensive. American alarm clocks have been coming to this market in small quantities, and the "Waltham" watch is also known, but the entire business in American clocks is estimated at only $1,500 to $2,000 per annum. The duty on a medium sized alarm clock is 1.70 to 2 rubles (87.3 cents to $1.03), and it should sell at 2.50 rubles ($1.29). Parts of clocks cost 1.12 rubles (58 cents) per pound; watch movements, 1.50 rubles (77 cents) per pound.

### INVOICING AND PACKING OF GOODS SHIPPED TO RUSSIA.

The value of each line of goods must be indicated, as duties imposed on goods imported into Russia are specific and not ad valorem. Attention is called to the need of care in indicating gross and net weights. If, for instance, one package contains various goods, the gross weight of the whole package must be given, together with the net weight of each class of goods contained therein; if these goods are packed in tins, glasses, or jars, it is better to give three kinds of weights, viz, the whole gross weight, the weight of the goods, including the tins, jars, glasses, etc., and the actual net weight. If there are several packages containing the same class of goods, it will be sufficient to state the total gross and net weights. It is, however, safer to give the weights of each package separately. All statements of weights must be signed by the shipper and stamped or sealed with the firm's stamp.

### HIGHWAYS IN RUSSIA.

Prince Hilkoff, minister of ways and communications, is now making a tour of inspection in the Caucasus, with the view of building new and important highways in that province. Russia has few macadamized roads. Their construction began in 1817, and yet there are not more than 14,000 miles in the whole of Russia. In twenty-two governments of European Russia and in the Caucasus, there are none. Macadamized roads are necessary in this country, inasmuch as natural roads, on account of the character of the soil—black earth, clay, and sand—are extremely difficult to keep in good condition; in spring and autumn, they are impassable. The scarcity of Russia's railways, considering the vast area of the Empire, makes the lack of highways lamentable. It hinders the export of grain, especially by small dealers, as they must convey their produce a hundred versts (66 miles) to the nearest railway depot, and must frequently await snowfall before this can be done, for it is only during the winter, when the inequalities of the roads are smoothed by the sleigh runners, that long distances may be comfortably traversed. The repair or macadamizing of natural roads is a pressing necessity. To carry out this project will entail an enormous expenditure, but the Government has resolved upon extending the system as far as its means will allow.   The roads in the Baltic provinces are in excellent condition.

## GOVERNMENT LIQUOR MONOPOLY.

The Government monopoly of the sale of liquor, which was inaugurated a few years since with a view to furnish pure "vodka," and thereby diminish drunkenness and turn the profits into the Government treasury instead of enriching private dealers, has had the effect, it is said, of increasing the general demoralization among the peasant classes, and communal authorities are petitioning the Government to close public houses.

## THE SILK INDUSTRY.

Special inquiry having been made concerning the silk industry in this country, I wish to state that, in European Russia, the culture of silkworms has practically been superseded by more profitable enterprises, and to-day, the south of Russia shows only a few traces of a once flourishing industry.

The conditions are somewhat better in Turkestan, but the local species there is infected with pebrine.   A great effort is being made to support the industry by distributing foreign eggs.   The Government established in 1885 four inspecting stations, to supply the people with sound eggs.   Two foreign houses at Kokand and Samarkand help to introduce the foreign eggs, particularly the species from Corsica and the white species from Bagdad.   Unfortunately, however, experience has shown that these only give satisfactory results the first year, the worm dying during the succeeding season.

The culture of the silkworm in Turkestan requires a continual supply of foreign eggs, and this abnormal condition will cease only when the epidemic has disappeared.   All the cocoons are unwound by means of primitive appliances; therefore, the silk produced is inferior in quality, and very cheap.   This explains why the silk of this region has no commercial importance.

In 1862, before the appearance of the epidemic in the Caucasus, silk culture prospered.   Then the decline set in and continued until 1890, when the industry improved, thanks to the efforts to furnish the people with foreign eggs—which, however, are very expensive.   Imports come from Brusa (Asia Minor), France, and Italy; the quantity varies a great deal, but often reaches 2,500 kilograms (5,511 pounds) of eggs per annum.   In 1900, 1,556 kilograms (3,430 pounds) of eggs were imported, valued at 43,000 rubles ($22,145).   This figure covered 1,261 kilograms (2,780 pounds) of eggs from Turkey; 164 kilograms (361 pounds) from Greece; and 98 kilograms (216 pounds) from France. On the local market, silkworm eggs are sold at about 10 rubles ($5.15) per 100 grams.

In the Caucasus, on account of the lack of modern appliances, the harvest of cocoons is small, being about 1,000 kilograms (2,204 pounds) per 1 kilogram (2.2 pounds) of eggs; but lately, in some parts, a kilogram of eggs has been made to yield 2,000 kilograms (4,409 pounds) of cocoons.

The price of the cocoons varies from 45 to 70 kopecks (23 to 36 cents) per kilogram (2.2 pounds).

The species cultivated in the Caucasus are the green from Japan, the white and yellow from Europe, the white from Bagdad, and those from Var and Khorassan.

The following will permit an estimate of the quality of these different species:

|  |  | Weight. |
|---|---|---|
| 100 cocoons from Japan, green species | grams.. | 6 to 13 |
| 100 cocoons from Europe, white species | do.... | 16 to 27 |
| 100 cocoons from Europe, yellow species | do.... | 12 to 35 |
| 100 cocoons from Khorassan | do.... | 41 |
| 100 cocoons from Bagdad, white species | do.... | 15 to 40 |
| 100 cocoons, local species | do.... | 9 to 19 |

It is very difficult to ascertain the exact quantity of silk produced in the Caucasus, because most of it is used by the people of the country. It is estimated, however, at 2,000 tons of raw silk. One-half of this quantity is worked up by the natives and the other half sold to the Moscow factories at 13 to 16½ rubles ($6.70 to $8.50) per kilogram (2.2 pounds). The best silk-breeding station was erected by the Government in 1887 in Tiflis, and this establishment is considered the most perfectly equipped in Eastern Europe. It publishes reports which contain valuable information regarding experiments, etc., in the culture and raising of the silkworm.

The silkworms are fed in houses, in habitable rooms which are cleared out for this purpose, or else in garrets or sheds in which live stock, hay, straw, etc., are generally kept. The worms crawl about the floor or on a latticework especially prepared for them. They are fed three times a day; very rarely oftener. At first, their food consists of young leaves, and later of boughs with leaves. The food plants are occasionally changed from two to three times during the period of their feeding; often not at all. These and many other irregularities in silkworm culture result from the fact that the growers belong mostly to Asiatic tribes, who hold to their primitive methods and prejudices. The Russian Government long ago directed attention to these imperfect methods, which hinder the development of the silkworm industry, and improvement is expected. The feeding of worms lasts sixty days and sometimes longer, and the harvests are often unsatisfactory. In the governments of southern Russia, the worms are fed from the end of April until July, and in other regions from the end of March until the end of May or the middle of June.

The most destructive diseases to which the silkworms are subject are the pebrine and the pallor; jaundice is a very common malady, but is not usually fatal. The muscardine occurs sporadically, but very seldom. The cocoons are often attacked by the larva called "dermeste lardarius," and in the trans-Caucasia by the ant "crematogaster subdentata."

The raising of silkworms is closely connected with the growing of mulberry trees. In the Russian Empire, two sorts of mulberry trees are grown; the white (*morus alba* L.) and the black (*morus nigra* L.). The white species is found in European Russia up to the border line which passes through St. Petersburg, Moscow, Voronesh, Orenburg, and to the Chinese frontier; also in the Amur regions, in Turkestan, in the trans-Caspian territory, and in the Caucasus, except in the highlands, where the climate is very severe. In St. Petersburg, the mulberry tree winters under straw coverings, but in Moscow, it lives unprotected. In trans-Caucasia and Turkestan, it grows beautifully over all the country, often wild. The black mulberry tree is cultivated only in the Crimea, trans-Caucasia, Turkestan, and the trans-Caspian region.

In trans-Caucasia and Turkestan, there are several species of the white mulberry tree: The ordinary variety, with white, violet, and black fruit; tegeran-tout, bedana, shakh-tout, marvaritak, balkhi, etc., but the varietas tatarica and varietas vulgaris are principally cultivated. The black mulberry tree has no varieties, and is known in Turkestan under the name of shakh-tout, and in trans-Caucasia as khar-tout. The white mulberry tree is cultivated for its fruit, for feeding silkworms, and for many other purposes. The black mulberry tree is grown only for its fruit. The methods of planting these trees are very different. For feeding silkworms, the mulberry tree is set out in the southern governments in bushes, as a hedge; in western trans-Caucasia, it is grown in hedges and also as high trees; in other parts as low trees, very close together, from 60,000 to 70,000 per dessiatine (2.69 acres), the branches being cut off every year.

The extent of mulberry plantations in the Caucasus is estimated at 34,000 dessiatine (91,790 acres).

W. R. HOLLOWAY,
*Consul-General.*

ST. PETERSBURG, *November 12, 1902.*

## RUSSIAN FOREIGN TRADE IN 1902.

The latest statistics published by the department of customs show that the foreign trade of Russia during the first nine months of 1902 attained the sum of 976,096,000 rubles ($502,689,440). The following shows the increase for the same period during the past two years:

| Class. | 1901. | | 1902. | |
|---|---|---|---|---|
| | Rubles. | U. S. currency. | Rubles. | U. S. currency. |
| Exports | 528,204,000 | $272,025,060 | 588,646,000 | $303,152,690 |
| Imports | 399,015,000 | 205,492,725 | 387,451,000 | 199,587,265 |
| Total | 927,219,000 | 477,517,785 | 976,096,000 | 502,689,955 |
| Balance | 129,189,000 | 66,532,335 | 201,194,000 | 103,615,425 |

### EXPORTS.

The classification of exports is as follows:

| Class. | 1901. | | 1902. | |
|---|---|---|---|---|
| | Rubles. | U. S. currency. | Rubles. | U. S. currency. |
| Provisions | 309,279,000 | $159,278,685 | 370,062,000 | $190,581,930 |
| Raw and undressed materials | 188,765,000 | 97,213,975 | 187,919,000 | 96,778,285 |
| Live stock | 13,438,000 | 6,920,570 | 16,331,000 | 8,410,465 |
| Different wares | 16,722,000 | 8,611,830 | 14,322,000 | 7,375,830 |
| Total | 528,204,000 | 272,025,060 | 588,645,000 | 303,152,690 |

The exports increased largely in cereals. The gain in wheat was from 97,138,000 poods (1,579,463 tons) to 123,762,000 poods (2,012,390 tons). A considerable increase is shown also in the export of beet roots, meat, and butter, from 1,536,000 to 23,283,000 poods (24,975 to 378,585 tons): fish, eggs, spirits, flax, bristles, skins, manganese, and pig iron, from 598,000 poods (9,723 tons) to 2,798,000 poods (45,496 tons). A decrease is shown in the export of sugar, timber, hemp, and rubber shoes.

The exports increased to almost all countries, except France (especially in cereals and timber), as shown by the following list:

| Country. | 1901. | | 1902. | |
|---|---|---|---|---|
| | Rubles. | U. S. currency. | Rubles. | U. S. currency. |
| Germany | 135,968,000 | $70,028,520 | 149,215,000 | $76,845,725 |
| England | 110,863,000 | 57,094,445 | 138,909,000 | 71,538,135 |
| Holland | 59,634,000 | 30,711,510 | 71,710,000 | 36,930,650 |
| France | 45,933,000 | 23,655,496 | 38,230,000 | 19,688,450 |
| Austria | 20,142,000 | 10,373,130 | 27,235,000 | 14,026,025 |
| Italy | 27,154,000 | 13,984,310 | 33,049,000 | 17,020,235 |
| Belgium | 14,235,000 | 7,331,025 | 20,663,000 | 10,641,445 |
| Turkey | 14,299,000 | 7,363,985 | 9,932,000 | 5,114,980 |
| Denmark | 16,568,000 | 8,532,520 | 21,160,000 | 10,903,400 |
| Egypt | 8,554,000 | 1,105,310 | 5,325,000 | 2,742,375 |
| Roumania | 5,310,000 | 2,734,650 | 10,989,000 | 5,633,585 |
| Sweden | 5,858,000 | 3,016,870 | 6,888,000 | 3,547,320 |
| Norway | 4,195,000 | 2,160,425 | 4,108,000 | 2,115,620 |
| East Indies | 7,318,000 | 3,768,770 | 3,544,000 | 1,825,160 |
| United States | 2,813,000 | 1,448,695 | 2,904,000 | 1,495,560 |
| China | 2,970,000 | 1,529,550 | 944,000 | 486,160 |
| Other countries | 17,369,000 | 8,945,085 | 19,342,000 | 9,961,130 |

IMPORTS.

The total imports during this period are classified as below:

| Products. | 1901. | | 1902. | |
|---|---|---|---|---|
| | Rubles. | U. S. currency. | Rubles. | U. S. currency. |
| Victuals | 61,525,000 | $31,685,375 | 56,713,000 | $29,207,195 |
| Raw and undressed materials | 213,751,000 | 110,071,765 | 216,795,000 | 111,649,425 |
| Live stock | 1,140,000 | 587,100 | 928,000 | 477,920 |
| Manufactured wares | 122,599,000 | 63,138,485 | 113,015,000 | 58,202,725 |
| Total | 399,015,000 | 205,482,735 | 387,451,000 | 199,537,265 |

A considerable decrease is shown in the imports of rice, herrings, oranges, and wine; of coal and coke, from 184,000,000 poods (2,991,869 tons) to 17,685,000 poods (287,561 tons); pig iron, iron and steel, from 6,172,000 poods (100,357 tons) to 4,236,000 poods (68,878 tons); pewter, zinc, timber, hides, wool, machinery, from 3,383,000 poods (55,009 tons) to 2,866,000 poods (46,602 tons); wire, scythes, sickles, mathematical instruments and watches. On the other hand, the import of the following has increased: Cotton, from 6,444,000 poods (104,780 tons) to 39,200,000 poods (637,236 tons); silk, wax, copper, agricultural implements, manufactured copper, and iron and steel goods.

The imports decreased almost from all countries; they increased only from the United States and Egypt (chiefly in cotton), and from Switzerland, Holland, and East Indies, as seen from the following table:

| Country. | 1901. | | 1902. | |
|---|---|---|---|---|
| | Rubles. | U. S. currency. | Rubles. | U. S. currency. |
| Germany | 155,878,000 | $80,277,170 | 147,338,000 | $75,879,070 |
| England | 81,042,000 | 41,736,630 | 77,717,000 | 40,024,255 |
| France | 19,377,000 | 9,979,155 | 18,035,000 | 9,288,025 |
| Austria | 18,300,000 | 9,424,500 | 5,298,000 | 8,612,860 |
| Belgium | 6,501,000 | 3,348,015 | 16,721,000 | 2,728,470 |
| Italy | 7,770,000 | 4,001,550 | 7,243,000 | 3,730,145 |
| Switzerland | 4,195,000 | 2,160,425 | 4,250,000 | 2,188,750 |
| Turkey | 4,778,000 | 2,460,670 | 4,235,000 | 2,181,025 |
| Holland | 6,495,000 | 3,345,925 | 8,333,000 | 4,291,495 |
| Sweden | 3,872,000 | 1,994,080 | 2,805,000 | 1,444,575 |
| Norway | 4,893,000 | 2,519,895 | 3,662,000 | 1,885,930 |
| Denmark | 4,079,000 | 2,100,685 | 3,074,000 | 1,583,110 |
| Roumania | 1,501,000 | 773,015 | 986,000 | 507,790 |
| United States | 25,828,000 | 13,801,420 | 27,713,000 | 14,272,195 |
| Egypt | 11,246,000 | 5,791,690 | 11,626,000 | 5,987,390 |
| China | 15,811,000 | 8,142,665 | 14,102,000 | 7,262,530 |
| East Indies | 4,524,000 | 2,329,860 | 7,538,000 | 3,882,070 |
| Other countries | 6,746,000 | 3,474,190 | 9,735,000 | 5,012,495 |

It must be remembered that these figures do not state the entire imports from the United States, as most goods shipped from our country are sent through England, Germany, and Denmark and are credited to them.

W. R. Holloway,
*Consul-General.*

St. Petersburg, *December 26, 1902.*

---

## BUDGET OF THE RUSSIAN EMPIRE FOR 1903.

Copies of the report of M. Witte, minister of finance to the Emperor, on the budget of the Russian Empire for 1903 have been received from M. de Routkowsky, financial agent of Russia in the United States, and from Consul-General Holloway.   The following extracts are made:

Of late years the minister of finance, in his reports to Your Imperial Majesty on the budget of the Empire, has had the unpleasant duty of referring to the unfavorable circumstances in which the economic life of the nation was placed.

Unlike the period of 1893—1897-99, which began with excellent harvests and during which money was both cheap and abundant, while at the same time the industry of the country was making rapid strides—the following years were considerably less favorable, the harvests were poor, while the industrial and money markets were in an exceedingly depressed condition.  At the same time, large sums were required for expenditure outside the country, including the expenses entailed by the military operations of 1900.  Moreover, at this very time complications arose in political relations, to which the market is so sensitive, and which greatly increased the general embarrassment.

Thus for several years the country suffered from a combination of bad harvests, stringency in the international money market, and industrial embarrassment.  The minister of finance has more than once reported to Your Majesty on these circumstances and their causes, believing that the above-mentioned unfavorable state of affairs could not continue long, that it might indeed diminish the rapidity of our industrial progress, but could not arrest the general economic development of Russia.

For the first time, after a long interval, the minister of finance has the good fortune of reporting to Your Majesty that the general conditions of our national welfare show evident signs of improvement.

CROPS.

Of these conditions, the most important is the favorable harvest in 1902. According to the data of the central statistical committee, the gross production of all cereals in the 64 provinces of European Russia (including those of the Vistula and Northern Caucasus) amounts to 3,939,000,000 poods (64,048,780 tons).[a] Besides this, Siberia and the Steppe territories yielded 176,000,000 poods (2,861,545 tons); the total harvest for 72 provinces and territories is calculated at 4,115,000,000 poods (66,910,732 tons), or over 1,000,000,000 poods (16,260,163 tons) more than in 1901, which, it is true, was a very unfavorable year. As compared with the last five years, in 46 provinces the crops were above the average, most of the central, New Russia, Little Russia, and southwestern provinces having an especially abundant harvest. However, in judging of the results of this year's harvest, it is necessary to take into account the unfavorable conditions attending the harvesting not only of cereals, but likewise of hay, especially in the north. It must also be borne in mind that this year again, the peasantry in several provinces have had to be assisted with advances for food and seed, and that in several parts of the country the winter crops are threatened. Nevertheless, the harvest as a whole is very satisfactory.

COMMERCE.

In regard to our foreign trade, considerable improvement has taken place during 1902.

*Balance of trade along the European frontier between January 1 and December 10, 1902.*

| Year. | Value of exports. | | Value of imports. | | Excess of exports over imports. | |
|---|---|---|---|---|---|---|
| | Rubles. | U. S. currency. | Rubles. | U. S. currency. | Rubles. | U. S. currency. |
| 1892 .............. | 417,000,000 | $214,755,000 | 329,000,000 | $161,435,000 | 88,000,000 | $45,320,000 |
| 1893 .............. | 539,000,000 | 277,585,000 | 388,000,000 | 199,820,000 | 151,000,000 | 77,765,000 |
| 1894 .............. | 627,000,000 | 322,905,000 | 486,000,000 | 250,290,000 | 141,000,000 | 72,615,000 |
| 1895 .............. | 638,000,000 | 328,570,000 | 468,000,000 | 241,020,000 | 170,000,000 | 87,550,000 |
| 1896 .............. | 632,000,000 | 325,480,000 | 509,000,000 | 262,135,000 | 123,000,000 | 63,345,000 |
| 1897 .............. | 662,000,000 | 340,930,000 | 480,000,000 | 247,200,000 | 182,000,000 | 93,780,000 |
| 1898 .............. | 669,000,000 | 444,535,000 | 531,000,000 | 273,465,000 | 138,000,000 | 71,070,000 |
| 1899 .............. | 570,000,000 | 296,550,000 | 561,000,000 | 288,915,000 | 9,000,000 | 7,635,000 |
| 1900 .............. | 655,000,000 | 337,325,000 | 544,000,000 | 280,160,000 | 111,000,000 | 47,165,000 |
| 1901 .............. | 684,000,000 | 352,260,000 | 495,000,000 | 254,925,000 | 189,000,000 | 97,335,000 |
| 1902 .............. | 783,000,000 | 403,245,000 | 483,000,000 | 248,745,000 | 300,000,000 | 154,500,000 |

These figures show that for the past eleven and one-third months of 1902, the value of our exports was 300,000,000 rubles ($154,500,000) in excess of our imports, i. e., an amount greater than that for any given year of the last decade. This is to be accounted for by the simultaneous effect of the following circumstances: The value of exports in 1902 was considerably greater than that of any preceding year, while at the same time the value of imports fell below that of the preceding four years. Of course, this excess of exports is to a certain extent due to the good harvest of 1902, but it can not be explained by this alone. Since 1899, when the exports hardly exceeded the imports in value, for three consecutive years (of which 1900 and 1901 were not remarkable for abundant harvests) the change in our foreign trade has been twofold—exports have risen and imports have fallen in value. Hence, it may be concluded that some factors more constant than merely a good harvest have effected the alteration in our balance of trade, viz, (1) the increase of exports other than grain and (2) the decrease in imports of machinery and appurtenances for factories and works, and likewise the fact that many articles formerly imported from abroad are now supplied by home production.

In reporting to Your Imperial Majesty on the state of our balance of trade, the minister of finance takes the liberty of referring to a serious doubt on this subject, which has of late years been repeatedly expressed. As is known, during the period of 1887–1891 the excess of our exports over imports reached a very high figure, the average for that time being more than 307,000,000 rubles ($158,105,000) a year. During 1892–1899, partly owing to a fall in the price of grain and then owing to bad harvests, the value of our exports did not increase, and even decreased to a certain extent. At the same time, there was a considerably greater importation of foreign goods, principally machinery, etc., required for our rapidly developing industries.

[a] The equivalents in United States measures and currency in this report have been inserted in the Bureau of Foreign Commerce.

As a result, at that time the excess of our exports over imports fell to less than half of what it had been at the end of the eighties, so that in 1899 it was very inconsiderable. This very naturally led to doubts as to whether the balance of trade might be expected to improve. Without making any conjectures as to the future, it is possible to answer this question in the affirmative with regard to 1902, as the value of our exports during the past eleven and one-third months has almost reached the amount for 1888, the most favorable year in this respect—784,000,000 rubles ($403,-760,000) for twelve months—and the balance of trade is expressed in a sum very close to the average for the above-mentioned five-year period of 1887–1891.

As to the currency system, Minister Witte says:

In general, it is necessary to observe that the stability of our currency has been sufficiently tested by experience, and therefore it is now superfluous to dwell more fully on this question, though it was quite natural to do so during the first few years after the reform in the currency. Of course, the firmest monetary system of any country may be unsettled if any imprudent or injudicious measures be taken in the management of its financial affairs. But the minister of finance entertains no such fears, and is convinced that, so long as the clear and definite regulations for the issue and covering of notes are observed, we are guaranteed against the probability of any serious disturbance in our currency.

The report continues:

### INDUSTRIES.

Having reported to Your Imperial Majesty on some of the improvements in the economic situation of Russia in 1902, the minister of finance considers it his duty to draw attention likewise to the unfavorable points of the same, viz, the embarrassment that is still felt in certain industries. In the report to Your Majesty on the budget for 1902, the principal causes of this embarrassment were shown, and it was pointed out that the fall in the prices of manufactures, as a consequence of increased competition among producers, was in itself advantageous to the bulk of consumers, and that the result attained was the very object of our protective policy, i. e., the provision of the country with cheap manufactures of home production. Nevertheless, the abruptness with which the prices of certain articles fell to a very low level could not but be considered as an unfavorable circumstance. In conclusion, the minister of finance reported to Your Majesty that for a certain time the rapid development of our industries would be arrested, and that some of them would have to reduce their production to a certain extent. But at the same time, he expressed the conviction that the general success attained of late years by our industry as a whole would not be affected by this.

There has been no improvement observable in our industry during the current year. On the contrary, the embarrassment has increased. Nevertheless. the data for this specially heavy year for certain industries testify that the success attained by our home industries in preceding years is insured. In this respect the best indicator is our iron production, as it is a primary business, and the most embarrassed, so that the persons interested are complaining of stagnation in business.

During 1901 and 1902, our iron industry reduced its output. An idea of the extent of this reduction may be gathered from the comparative output of pig iron in former years and lately. These data are presented for Your Majesty's gracious consideration in the following table:

*Output of pig iron.*

| | Poods. | Tons. |
|---|---|---|
| 1877 | 23,000,000 | 373,983 |
| 1887 | 36,000,000 | 585,366 |
| 1892 | 64,000,000 | 1,040,649 |
| 1897 | 113,000,000 | 1,837,398 |
| 1898 | 134,000,000 | 2,178,862 |
| 1899 | 164,000,000 | 2,666,666 |
| 1900 | 176,000,000 | 2,861,626 |
| 1901 | 171,000,000 | 2,780,488 |
| First half of 1901 | 86,000,000 | 1,398,372 |
| First half of 1902 | 84,000,000 | 1,365,853 |

Your Imperial Majesty will deign to call to mind that the increased output of pig iron in 1897 and 1898, as compared with that of preceding years, was considered no insignificant success. The present production of pig iron exceeds that of the years 1897 and 1898 considerably, and nevertheless this important branch of industry must be considered as in a state of embarrassment, because it is far from working to its full extent. This seeming paradox clearly shows the great strides which the iron industry has made on the whole, in spite of two heavy years of stagnation. The same state of affairs is to be observed, though not so conspicuously, in other industries in temporary difficulties; the rapid growth of production has been arrested, there is even some reduction of output, but, on the whole, the success already attained has not been forfeited.

In passing on from the amount of production to prices, it is necessary to remark that in the case of some manufactures, they have fallen.

The best indicators are the prices of pig iron. In places with the greatest production, i. e., the southern works, the prices of this raw material in 1897-1899 stood at 60 to 65 kopecks (30.9 to 33.4 cents) per pood (delivered at the works), and even rose toward the end of this period. At the end of 1900, prices began to decline abruptly, falling as low as 50 to 44 kopecks (25.7 to 22.6 cents) in 1901, and, according to the data for the first half of 1902 now to hand, even still lower. Manufactured metal likewise fell in price, on the whole, but, owing to the great variety of articles made, and of the conditions of production and disposal, the fall in the price of raw material affected them in varying degrees. As an example, we may take the decline in the prices of a very important form of building material, viz, metal H joists, which a short time ago were very dear, being over 1 ruble 40 kopecks (72 cents) per pood at the works, and then fell in 1900 to about 1 ruble 20 kopecks (61.8 cents), and in 1902 to 85 kopecks (43.7 cents) and less. Taking the Ural works, we find a fall in the prices of narrow bar merchant iron, which at the Nizhni-Novgorod fairs of 1899 and 1900 cost about 1 ruble 71 kopecks (88 cents) per pood; in 1901, 1 ruble 50 kopecks (77.2 cents); and in 1902, about 1 ruble 25 kopecks (64.4 cents).

The above figures show what a radical change has in a short time taken place in our metallurgical industry. Several years ago, the production could not meet the demand; the imports of foreign metal increased year by year; prices rose, calling forth complaints of the inaccessibility of such a necessity as iron. At present, the output of our metal works is in excess of the demand, imports of foreign metals have decreased considerably (in 1897-1899, more than 25 per cent of our consumption, expressed in pig iron, was covered by imports, while at the present time these only amount to 10 per cent), and the prices of pig iron and different manufactures are such as cause not unreasonable complaints from owners of works that prices have fallen too low for them to work without loss.

In reporting to Your Imperial Majesty on the straitened condition of some very important branches of our industry, the minister of finance takes the liberty of repeating that he considers such a state of affairs unfavorable not only to private interests but likewise to the national welfare, principally owing to the abruptness of the decline in the prices of certain manufactures. But there is no real cause for alarm in the present embarrassment, if it is to be regarded, not from the point of view of its immediate economic results, but with an eye to the not very distant future. This critical state of affairs can not continue very long, as it brings its own remedy with it. The low prices of manufactured metal, caused by the production of the works outrunning the demand, react (and will continue to do so) simultaneously in two different ways for the restoration of the equilibrium between supply and demand. On the one hand, the production of articles that are especially difficult to dispose of will be somewhat reduced, and certain moribund undertakings must inevitably fall into decline, but the greater number of works will adapt themselves to a sufficiently remunerative production of manufactures, not indeed at the former very high prices, but at rates more accessible to the consumer; there will be a development of the production of articles consumed by the masses—a great want at present; necessity will oblige the producers to organize the disposal of their productions.

On the other hand, the cheapness of manufactures will undoubtedly increase the demand. Articles which the common people could not use on account of the great expense will gradually spread among a great number of consumers, and the masses, having once grown habituated to a wider use of metal articles, will become regular customers. Independently of these fundamental causes which will relieve the industrial embarrassment, there will doubtless be a removal of the indirect cause of the present difficulty, viz, the distrust which at present restricts the trade in certain articles to the satisfaction of immediate requirements, reduces the number of time

H. Doc. 305, pt 2——38

bargains, and retards the establishment of wholesale iron warehouses. Little by little, the demand for the manufactures of the industries now suffering temporary embarrassment will equal the supply; prices will attain a level allowing the producer a sufficient profit, though they will not be so high as in former years.

As a result, the country will come out of its present difficulties with a firmly established metallurgical industry, which will supply the demand of the people for cheap iron—that necessary material both for common use and for the production of agricultural implements and machinery for works and factories.

Extravagant demands are not infrequently made on the resources of our State. At unfavorable times, such demands are necessarily expressed less frequently and less clamorously; but the pressure brought to bear on the Treasury in times of prosperity is all the greater and more decided. Of late years, notwithstanding the exceptionally rapid growth of our budget, the actual receipts of ordinary revenue have always been in excess of the ordinary expenditure. During this time, it has become a matter of course to regard our financial position as favorable, and the necessity for economy in State expenditures has been gradually lost sight of. Applications for the fuller satisfaction of the most varied requirements are presented more and more persistently, while at the same time, and sometimes in the same circles, complaints are made of the burden of taxation, and measures are proposed for the reduction and abolition of certain taxes.

The minister of finance feels it his duty to present to Your Imperial Majesty his considerations in regard to such applications, which have more than once reached Your Majesty.

Efforts to extend the usefulness of the State by increasing grants for that purpose, and likewise attempts to lighten the burden of taxation, especially that falling on the poorer classes, can not but command the fullest sympathy; the attainment of these objects is the care of the financial department. But requirements are innumerable, while the means of satisfaction are limited. In making an application, there is no need to regulate the need to the available resources; but it is necessary to do so when putting new measures into practice—otherwise stern reality, in the shape of a deficit, will not fail to remind us of the disturbance in the balance between the satisfaction of requirements and the means at hand for the purpose. Therefore the minister of finance must turn his attention, not only to the grateful and agreeable business of extending the usefulness of the Government, or of reducing the weight of taxation, but likewise to the difficult and unpopular task of regulating expenditure by revenue, which entails the necessity of discrimination of State requirements; only after means have been found for covering all the most urgent and most important needs is it possible to employ the remaining resources for other requirements.

Now, what requirement is the most pressing? Obviously that on the satisfaction of which depends the very existence of the country, its invulnerability from without. For this purpose, the people give their personal service and pay most of the taxes, receiving in return the priceless consciousness, not to be measured by material benefits, that under the guidance of their Imperial Ruler, every one of Your Majesty's faithful subjects, his family, his property, and his native land are safe from foreign foes. From an economic and humanitarian point of view, it is to be regretted that mankind is not yet imbued with high ideals of universal peace; nevertheless, it must be acknowledged at present, that we are in a grip of an iron law, which decrees that the requirements of culture may be satisfied only from what remains after the expenditure of defense has been covered. When means for the latter purpose are required from the minister of finance, he finds it very difficult, and for the most part even quite impossible, to enter into the question as to how far certain measures are necessary for the defense of the country; but once their necessity is acknowledged, it is his duty to find the means required. Hence proceeds the disagreeable task of taking the initiative in the establishment and increase of taxes, and likewise of opposing the realization of all those measures for which no resources are available, after providing for the above-mentioned urgent requirement of the State.

In laying before Your Majesty the foregoing considerations, called forth by the late enormous increase of applications and demands from all quarters for greater assignments for multifarious requirements, and for the reduction of certain taxes— the minister of finance takes the liberty of expressing his conviction, that by undeviatingly observing, according to Your Majesty's orders, the necessary caution, it will be possible gradually to satisfy the most pressing needs while still preserving the equilibrium of the budget, which has never once been disturbed during Your Imperial Majesty's felicitous reign.

## BATUM.

The principal industries of the Caucasus, as pertaining to trade with other countries, are the production of petroleum, the manufacture of its products, the mining of manganese ore, and the packing of licorice root; there is much wine produced and some cotton, but little of the former and none of the latter is exported; copper mining has also been going on upon a very small scale for some time, but within the last two years, this industry has attracted the attention of foreigners, and a large property about 40 miles from Batum has been bought by a British company, and work commenced upon an extensive scale. I am informed that this company at present employs nearly 1,000 men, but as it has not yet commenced smelting, it is impossible to say what its output is likely to be.

### PETROLEUM TRADE.

In a report from this consulate upon Russian petroleum, dated February 26, 1902,[a] it was stated that great financial depression existed in the trade, which was very clearly due to overproduction, resulting in exceedingly low and unprofitable prices for crude oil and all its products. This depression continues, notwithstanding the price of crude oil is considerably higher now than it was at the beginning of the year; the advance has not been sufficient, however, to make the business generally profitable, and has not been reflected to an adequate extent in the prices of the products manufactured from the crude oil. In the winter, crude at wells sold as low as 4 kopecks per pood (about 17 cents per barrel of 42 gallons), while at present it is 7 to 7½ kopecks per pood (30 to 35 cents per barrel), and at times during the summer, it was even higher; but the advance in refined and lubricating oil prices has not been nearly so great proportionately; the lowest price of the year for refined oil f. o. b. tank cars at Baku was about 6 kopecks per pood (about 0.6 cent per gallon), and all summer it remained under 9 kopecks (4.6 cents) per pood (36.112 pounds), and only within a few weeks advanced to 10 and 11 kopecks (5 to 5.6 cents). Within the last week, sales for delivery during six months have been reported at as high as 12 kopecks per pood. The staple lubricating oil known as "machine" oil was never quoted under 32 kopecks (16.4 cents) per pood, and the latest quotation at hand is 34 kopecks (17.5 cents). This price is undoubtedly profitable, or at least not unprofitable; but as this product constitutes not more than 2½ per cent of the total output, it plays no important rôle in the trade. Refined oil, however, costs more at present than it can be sold for, as upon the basis of 7 kopecks (3.6 cents) per pood for crude at wells and 7¾ kopecks (3.9 cents) per pood for residuum, the cost of a pood of refined at Baku is not less than 13 kopecks (6.6 cents).

That the continuation of the depression in the Russian trade is due to the same cause as its origin—i. e., overproduction—is shown by the fol-

---

[a] Consular Reports, No. 261, June, 1902; Advance Sheets, No. 1312, April 10, 1902.

lowing figures for the crude production of the Baku fields for the first seven months of this year, in comparison with the same time last year:

| Year. | Gross production (barrels of 42 gallons). | Net production (barrels of 42 gallons). |
|---|---|---|
| 1901 | 45,444,755 | 40,022,788 |
| 1902 | 43,137,008 | 38,299,092 |

The figures show a very insignificant falling off in the production in the first seven months of this year, which will probably be more than made up by the production in August and September; for while accurate figures for that period are not yet obtainable, it is known that it was very heavy, estimated at not less than 230,000 barrels per day, as there was a number of large flowing wells reported in those months.

With the exceedingly low prices which have been ruling for Russian petroleum products, and particularly as the price of refined (illuminating oil) has been not much more at Batum than half the American quotation at New York, a very heavy increase in the export of the Russian product might have been reasonably expected; but the following figures for the exports from Batum in the first nine months of 1901 and 1902 show that no material increase in export is so far apparent:

| Class. | 1901. | 1902. |
|---|---|---|
| | *Gallons.* | *Gallons.* |
| Illuminating oils | 224,648,145 | 227,173,990 |
| Illuminating, distillate, and gas oil | 32,381,315 | 31,806,740 |
| Lubricating oils | 30,391,870 | 35,979,060 |
| Residuum | 5,607,240 | 6,501,695 |
| Total | 293,028,570 | 301,461,485 |

This year's export, especially that which goes in cans and cases, was curtailed, however, by the strikes in the early spring in the packing factories here. These strikes commenced in March, and by the middle of that month, all the packing factories were closed and the labor troubles took on such a serious aspect that several hundred of the strikers were arrested and put under a guard of troops. On March 22, a demonstration by the strikers who were free at the prison of those who were under arrest became so boisterous that the crowd was fired upon by the troops, and 13 strikers and onlookers killed, and it is said over 40 wounded; the number of wounded has never been officially stated, but the number of killed is official. Within a few days after this unfortunate occurrence, all but one of the packing factories resumed work, but that one exception was the largest here, the output of which is not far from 25,000 cases per day; and as it remained shut down for nearly four months, the production was undoubtedly reduced 200,000 gallons per day during that time.

### MANGANESE ORE.

This trade has probably been in quite as unfortunate a condition for the past eighteen months as the petroleum trade, and for exactly the same cause, i. e., overproduction. A few years ago, the business appeared to be exceedingly profitable, as unusually heavy return in the mining and shipping of the ore could be shown—on paper at least. The result was the advent of new operators with little or inadequate capital. With the banks advancing operators 70 to 80 per cent of the estimated value of their ore on the railway platforms, it appeared that no great amount of capital was necessary to engage in the business of mining and buying the ore for export; but the increased production necessarily caused a fall in the price to considerably below a profitable figure, and at times to a figure even under cost. One of the results of this state of affairs was the production of much inferior low-grade ore, which, however, was of no assistance, but on the contrary was probably a very unfortunate thing for the trade. It was practically of no assistance, because it could only be worked off upon buyers on the spot, as exporters buy on the basis of the metal in the ore according to assays made at port of receipt. It is said, however, that one cargo of this inferior ore was shipped to the United States and turned out only about 40 per cent metallic manganese, resulting in heavy loss to some one, as it does not pa to ship ore containing less than 50 per cent metal to the United States. Whether or not this one cargo of poor ore was the cause of the great falling off in the export to the United States, I have no means of ascertaining, but that export did fall off materially, as did also export to other countries, and with the increased production, the result was the accumulation of over 500,000 tons in stocks on the platforms at the mines, most of which, it is generally stated, is of very low grade ore. If this ore were known to be high grade, it would be a pretty big bear on the market, representing, as it does, over a year's previous demand; but being reputed low grade makes it even a greater bear, as buyers are afraid of it, and in many cases, it is said, stipulate in their purchase contracts that the delivery must be fresh ore.

A few of the operators may be financially able to hold on to their stocks in the expectation of an advance in prices, but the majority of them are said to be paying all prospective profits in interest upon loans upon their ore, and are consequently compelled to sell at very low prices, which would indicate that an advance is not very near.

From all the information I have been able to obtain, the cost of ore containing 50 per cent metallic manganese on the railway platforms at the railway station at the mines (Chiatoori) is from 6¼ to 7 kopecks (3.3 to 3.6 cents) per pood. From Chiatoori, the ore is shipped by narrow-gauge railway to Sharopan, on the main line of the Trans-Caucasian Railway (about 30 miles) and there transferred into broad-gauge cars and shipped to Poti, the principal port of export on the Black Sea (about 82 miles.) The freight rate is 10 kopecks (5.1 cents) per pood, to which must be added for port dues, shipping expenses, and interest another 3 kopecks (1.5 cents) per pood, making the cost of the ore f. o. b. vessels at Poti not less than 20 kopecks (10 cents) per pood, equivalent to about $6.40 per ton. The latest quotation f. o. b. Poti which I have heard is 21 kopecks (10.8 cents) per pood, and that is what sellers are asking, not what buyers are offering; which, as there seems to be little business doing, must be considerably less.

LICORICE ROOT.

Practically the whole export of this product goes to the United States. The root is gathered on the other side of the Caucasian Mountains, the field producing it extending as far south as the Persian frontier, and north to the Terek River. The root is collected at several stations, where it is pressed into bales and shipped by rail to Batum for export.

Notwithstanding the packing and export of licorice root has been wholly in the hands of three firms, which are not ready to give information regarding the financial results of the business, there is no doubt whatever that up to now, the business has been exceedingly profitable.

The export to the United States has reached over 22,000 tons in a year, and notwithstanding heavy stocks are reported in the United States, the export continues heavy. Recently, however, the business of manufacturing the extract from the root in the United States has gone into the hands of the apparently inevitable "trust." This, up to the present, includes only one of the firms engaged in packing here, and fears seem to be entertained of the eventual "freezing out" of the other two firms, because of a lack of buyers in the United States. Whether or not there is any serious basis for such fears I am unable to state, nor can I say what the result will be if such fears prove well founded; but as I understand that all the licorice root produced in Russia is necessary for the manufacture of chewing tobacco in the United States, it seems reasonable to expect no falling off in the export, whether that business is monopolized or not. There is a possibility, however, of the Russian Government putting an export duty on the root if its export becomes a monopoly, as such a duty has been talked about for years, and at one time was feared by the packers. As the Russian authorities are anything but friendly to monopolies, it is among the possibilities that they may take advantage of an alleged monopolizing of the export of licorice root to impose an export duty upon it.

### TRADE WITH THE UNITED STATES.

Up to the present time, the trade of this section with the United States has been, as far as can be ascertained here, wholly export. There is, however, said to be a heavy import of locomotives, railway material, and agricultural machinery from the United States, for use in the Caucasian and cis-Caucasian districts, but as none of such imports pass through this port, there is absolutely no information concerning them obtainable here.

The principal articles of export to the United States are manganese ore, licorice root, and Russian and Persian wool and rugs. With the exception of manganese (as explained above), there has been a steady increase in the quantities of the above-named articles exported.

There are, or were, several very potent reasons why the imports from the United States have been insignificant, the principal one being the apparent lack of knowledge of the trade on part of American manufacturers, without which knowledge they can not expect to compete with British, Belgian, and German manufacturers, even with better and cheaper goods. The European manufacturers seem to know the trade sufficiently well to have no fears about giving the long credits which seem to be essential to the sale of goods in this country. Such knowledge is acquired only by sending representatives regularly, and by giving this trade as much attention as is given to the home trade. Such a course has very rarely been pursued by American manufacturers; they seem to think that they have only to send their circulars and price lists—generally printed in a language foreign to this country—to the consular representatives in order to get orders for goods. It is possible that their indifference to foreign trade, or at least to this part of it, is due to the fact that they do not consider it of sufficient importance to justify expense—and they should certainly be the best judges of the matter—but it is not a matter of opinion but of fact that they can not hope to materially and permanently extend their trade in this direction by the methods which they have generally made use of; that, without a thorough knowledge of the conditions and the financial standing of the merchants in the trade (which can not be acquired through commercial agencies, but only through actual contact with the people), they are entirely too heavily handicapped in the competition with European manufacturers to hope to make any great headway.

Another very serious obstacle in the way of the introduction of American goods into this section was the almost prohibitive freight rate from United States ports to Black Sea ports. Until this year, goods had to be shipped through some continental or United Kingdom port, at which port they had to be transshipped, which was often so expensive that the freights upon small lots of goods were three times as great as the rates from the same ports direct. The time of small shipments in transit, also, owing to delays in waiting for steamers at the ports of transshipment, was generally nearer four months than three, as against a limit of four weeks from the European ports.

In the spring of this year, however, a German company commenced running monthly steamers from Black Sea ports to New York and return, and reduced the freights to the United States to a rate even lower than the distance would seem to justify in comparison with the rates to European ports. Whether the rates from New York to Black Sea ports have been correspondingly reduced I do not know, but I have no doubt that they have, as outward cargo is quite as important as inward. In addition to this German line, a Russian company advertises that it will soon commence a monthly service from Odessa to New York, via Genoa, and return, and has designated three of its largest and swiftest vessels for the service—vessels which have been running between Odessa and Vladivostock, and which have excellent passenger accommodation and a speed of 17 to 18 knots per hour.

With these two lines in operation, there should be fortnightly sailings from New York to Black Sea ports and freight rates sufficiently low to enable American manufacturers, as far as freights and transit time are concerned, to compete successfully with European manufacturers.

The remaining difficulty which the American manufacturer is compelled to overcome in competing for this trade is the discrimination against American goods by the Russian customs tariff, which was brought about in the effort at retaliation for the differential sugar duties of the United States. This discrimination amounts to 30 per cent more than the duties upon similar goods from other countries, and seems of much more importance than it actually is; for, judging from retail prices in the United States, it seems that the majority of American manufactures, owing to their superiority to those of Europe and their lower cost, can, with everything else equal, in spite of the 30 per cent customs discrimination against them, successfully compete with European goods.

JAMES C. CHAMBERS, *Consul.*

BATUM, *October 9, 1902.*

## MOSCOW.

### RUSSIA'S FOREIGN TRADE IN 1902.

According to statistics published by the custom-house department, Russia's foreign trade for the first half of the current year amounted to 600,840,000 rubles ($300,420,000), against 584,712,000 rubles ($292,356,000) for the corresponding period of 1901, and was classified as follows:

| Class. | 1901. | 1902. |
|---|---|---|
| Export | $159,468,500 | $173,176,500 |
| Import | 132,887,500 | 127,243,500 |

Comparing the two last years, it is found that the amount of exports has increased by 8.6 per cent and the amount of imports has decreased by 4.3 per cent, the total of the trade, therefore, increasing by 4.3 per cent.

The export is classified as follows:

| Class. | 1901. | 1902. |
|---|---|---|
| Victuals | $90,104,000 | $105,461,500 |
| Raw materials | 60,027,000 | 58,138,000 |
| Animals | 3,622,000 | 5,014,500 |
| Manufactures | 5,715,500 | 4,562,500 |
| Total | 159,468,500 | 173,176,500 |

The above figures show an increase in the export of victuals and animals of 17 and 37.1 per cent, respectively, and a decrease in raw materials and manufactures of 3.2 and 20.2 per cent, respectively.

In the first group, the most important item is corn, the export of which is illustrated by the following figures, showing, in comparison with last year, an increase of 15.9 per cent in quantity and of 17.7 per cent in value:

| Year. | Amount. | Value. |
|---|---|---|
| | Tons. | |
| 1901 | 3,264,333 | $72,763,500 |
| 1902 | 3,784,500 | 85,608,500 |

An increase is shown in the export of the following kinds of victuals:

| Articles. | Amount. | Value. | Increase— In amount. | In value |
|---|---|---|---|---|
| | Tons. | | Per cent. | Per cent. |
| Indian corn | 878,983 | $16,167,000 | 505.7 | 572.9 |
| Wheat | 1,222,791 | 32,876,000 | 17.4 | 17.1 |
| Barley | 482,566 | 8,414,500 | 21.9 | 25.4 |

The export of all other victuals, however, shows a decrease, as, for instance, rye 10.6 per cent in quantity and 5.4 per cent in value, and oats 46.3 per cent in quantity and 34.2 per cent in value.

An increase is also shown in the exports of the following articles:

| Articles. | 1901. | | 1902. | |
|---|---|---|---|---|
| | Amount. | Value. | Amount. | Value. |
| Butter...................................................tons.. | 11,616 | $4,472,500 | 16,466 | $5,780,000 |
| Eggs...................................................millions.. | 951 | 8,342,000 | 1,069 | 8,902,500 |
| Flax...................................................tons.. | 90,433 | 13,859,500 | 115,766 | 16,711,000 |
| Manganic minerals.................................do.... | 196,333 | 1,427,500 | 227,650 | 1,586,500 |
| Cast iron...........................................do.... | 3,483 | 152,000 | 15,783 | 1,040,000 |
| Animals, horses...................................head.. | 36,000 | 1,645,500 | 69,000 | 3,291,000 |

The export of meat, spirit, hemp seed, bristles, etc., has also grown; a decline, however, is shown in the export of sugar, tobacco, lumber, flaxseed, hemp, naphtha, cotton fabrics, etc.

A comparison of the exports to the different countries shows that they have increased to all except Germany (which fell off in rye, bran of flour, lumber, and flax), France (in wheat and oats), the United States, and Eastern countries.

| Country. | 1901. | 1902. | Country. | 1901. | 1902. |
|---|---|---|---|---|---|
| Germany............... | $43,097,500 | $42,434,500 | Roumania............ | $1,504,500 | $4,072,500 |
| Great Britain......... | 30,221,500 | 37,517,500 | Sweden............... | 1,317,000 | 1,561,000 |
| Holland............... | 15,486,500 | 20,561,500 | Norway............... | 1,452,500 | 1,149,000 |
| France................ | 14,206,500 | 12,576,500 | East Indies.......... | 3,012,500 | 961,500 |
| Austria-Hungary..... | 6,701,500 | 10,057,500 | United States........ | 821,500 | 562,000 |
| Italy.................. | 8,981,000 | 10,253,000 | China................ | 974,500 | 468,000 |
| Belgium............... | 4,299,000 | 6,975,500 | Other countries...... | 4,962,500 | 5,276,500 |
| Turkey................ | 4,863,500 | 3,225,500 | Finland.............. | 10,140,500 | 7,368,500 |
| Denmark.............. | 4,257,500 | 6,443,500 | | | |
| Egypt................. | 3,175,500 | 1,717,500 | Total............ | 159,468,500 | 173,176,500 |

The total imports are classified shown below:

| Class. | 1901. | 1902. |
|---|---|---|
| Victuals.... | $19,996,000 | $17,795,500 |
| Raw materials......... | 70,630,500 | 71,566,000 |
| Animals................ | 281,000 | 259,500 |
| Manufactures........... | 41,980,000 | 37,622,500 |
| Total ................ | 132,887,500 | 127,243,500 |

The import of raw material shows an increase of 15 per cent over 1901; that of victuals, animals, and manufactures, however, a decrease of 11, 7.7, and 10.5 per cent, respectively.

In the first group is noted a decrease in the import of herrings, fruits, berries, and liquors, and an increase in the import of spices. In the second group, the most important decreases are noted in—

| Articles. | 1901. | 1902. |
|---|---|---|
| | Tons. | Tons. |
| Coal ........ | 1,460,000 | 1,060,000 |
| Coke ........ | 230,000 | 187,800 |
| Iron ........ | 45,100 | 28,400 |

Wax, tallow, dyewood, resin, and gum follow in order.  On the contrary, the import of the following raw materials shows an increase: Raw cotton (from 73,366 to 81,100 tons), raw silk and thread, wool, pile drivers, pulp, copper, and alloy.  The import of machinery and apparatus has fallen off 24.4 per cent—it amounted, in 1901, to $7,775,000; also the import of cast-iron goods, wire, saws, sickles, agricultural machinery, stationery, and cotton materials.

A decrease in the import is shown from all the principal countries, with the exception of Switzerland, Holland, the United States, Egypt, and the East Indies, as per the following data:

| Country. | 1901. | 1902. | Country. | 1901. | 1902. |
|---|---|---|---|---|---|
| Germany | $51,115,000 | $47,412,500 | Denmark | $1,705,500 | $1,106,000 |
| Great Britain | | | | 472,500 | 374,000 |
| France | 6,208,500 | 5,791,000 | United States | 10,369,500 | 11,519,000 |
| Austria-Hungary | 6,218,500 | 5,432,000 | Egypt | 3,662,500 | 5,106,500 |
| Belgium | 2,037,000 | 1,822,500 | China | 4,683,500 | 4,669,500 |
| Italy | 3,090,500 | 2,764,000 | East Indies | 1,701,000 | 3,409,500 |
| Switzerland | 1,432,500 | 1,482,500 | Other countries | 2,171,000 | 3,141,000 |
| Turkey | 1,815,000 | 1,527,000 | Finland | 5,509,500 | 5,255,500 |
| Holland | 2,068,500 | 2,401,500 | | | |
| Sweden | 883,500 | 805,000 | Total | 132,887,500 | 127,243,500 |
| Norway | 1,153,000 | 806,500 | | | |

*Expenditures and income of the Russian Government.*

WHISKY MONOPOLY.

| | Rubles. | Dollars. |
|---|---|---|
| **EXPENDITURE.** | | |
| Cost of construction of 400 distilleries, warehouses, stores, etc., in European Russia | 100,000,000 | 50,000,000 |
| Cost in maintaining the above establishments | 3,000,000 | 1,500,000 |
| Salaries paid to employees, as managers, clerks, etc | 70,000,000 | 35,000,000 |
| Total | 173,000,000 | 86,500,000 |
| **INCOME.** | | |
| Approximate | 390,000,000 | 195,000,000 |

BUDGET OF THE CITY OF MOSCOW FOR 1903.

The budget of the city of Moscow for 1903, which has just been confirmed by the board of aldermen, shows a total of 18,625,818 rubles ($9,312,909), against 17,274,697 rubles ($8,637,348.50) for the current year.  Details follow:

INCOME.

| | |
|---|---|
| Real estate taxes | $2,314,000.00 |
| Trade licenses, merchants' guild dues, etc | 1,232,205.50 |
| Horse and dog taxes | 91,500.00 |
| Sundry taxes | 168,130.00 |
| City property and quitrent accounts | 615,241.50 |
| City enterprises (tramway, waterworks, canalization, and slaughterhouse) | 2,472,964.00 |
| City subventions | 1,991,848.50 |
| Sundry receipts | 99,287.50 |
| City publications | 83,942.50 |
| Receipts from provincial institutions | 157,829.50 |
| Reserve for unforeseen expenses | 15,960.00 |
| | 9,312,909.00 |

## EXPENDITURES.

| | |
|---|---:|
| Contribution toward expenses of Government institutions | $281,347.50 |
| City administration and maintaining of orphan court | 500,791.00 |
| Contribution toward armories | 166,895.00 |
| Police force | 567,820.00 |
| Fire department | 203,296.50 |
| City improvements | 853,382.00 |
| Maintaining of city enterprises | 1,511,714.50 |
| Education | 876,479.00 |
| Charitable institutions | 416,768.50 |
| Board of health | 2,124,575.50 |
| Reimbursement of taxes | 15,726.00 |
| Maintaining of city property | 239,479.00 |
| Payment of city debt | 1,243,584.50 |
| Maintaining of city lombard | 75,861.50 |
| Sundry expenses | 57,214.50 |
| City publications | 46,045.00 |
| Maintaining of prisons | 33,963.00 |
| Charged to reserve capital | 97,966.00 |
| | 9,312,909.00 |

## AMERICAN ENTERPRISES IN RUSSIA.

The New York Brake Company, of New York, has purchased and established large works near Moscow, for the purpose of manufacturing air brakes for Government and private railways in Russia. The expenditure in purchasing and outfitting these works has been estimated at $760,000. There are at present about 300 workmen employed, all the master mechanics of the different departments being Americans. The machinery has been imported from the United States.

The Singer Manufacturing Company has built a large factory in Podolsk, near Moscow, for the purpose of manufacturing sewing machines on an extensive scale. The capacity of the factory at present is 100,000 machines a year, but it can be increased to 200,000. The machinery of the factory has likewise been imported from the United States.

Notwithstanding the high tariff imposed upon the importation of American machinery into this country, both dealers and manufacturers as a rule prefer American articles, which, the consumers find, are better made and more practicable.

There is an excellent opportunity for American shoe factories and steam laundries in this city.

Business conditions in this country are improving. The prospects for the crops over all the country are above the average.

SAMUEL SMITH, *Consul.*

Moscow, *October 27, 1902.*

---

## ODESSA.

### EXPORTS.

As compared with the preceding two years, 1901 shows a larger export of grain from Odessa, the figures being, respectively, 819,000, 1,152,000, and 1,359,000 tons. As compared with 1900, there was an increase in the principal kinds of grain exported; of barley, 180,000 tons; corn, 126,000 tons, and wheat and rye, 90,000 tons. This increase was the result of satisfactory crops in the Odessa district, the first in two years.  Nicolaiev, which draws its grain for export from the same region as Odessa, showed an increase of 468,000 tons over the shipments of 1900, the figures being 972,000 and 504,000 tons, respectively.  Other south Russian ports also exported largely in 1901; the total exports of grain from Russia, in spite of a large falling off at Baltic ports, showing an increase of 900,000 tons.  The statement published by the Odessa customs for 1901 shows that 493,102 tons of wheat was exported, and that the value of same was $10,815,000.  The total exports of wheat from Russia in 1901 are given at 2,490,802 tons, as against 2,110,284 tons in 1900.  Nicolaiev exported 395,802 tons of wheat in 1901, as against 233,208 tons in 1900.  The wheat shipped from Odessa was sent to the following countries: Holland, 170,260 tons; Italy, 97,810 tons; France, 89,460 tons; Great Britain, 72,072 tons; Gibraltar, for orders, 17,640 tons; Germany, 24,210 tons; Belgium, 13,590 tons; Spain, 12,241 tons; Egypt, 5,220 tons; Turkey, 1,629 tons.  The quantity shipped to Holland was really destined for Germany, being transhipped by river.  The quantity of wheat in store at Odessa on January 1, 1902, was 166,320 tons, and on January 1, 1901, 106,470 tons.

### CORN.

Two hundred and forty-two thousand five hundred and fourteen tons of corn was shipped from Odessa in 1901, as against 112,248 tons in 1900.  The total exports of corn from the Empire are given at 531,864 tons for 1901, and 341,730 tons for 1900.  Novoselitsa exported 40,248 tons; Novorossisk, 32,814 tons; Poti, 29,124 tons in 1901.  Nicolaiev exported scarcely any corn.  The value of the corn exported from Odessa is given at $4,635,000.  The Odessa shipments were sent to Great Britain, 121,770 tons; Holland, 48,600 tons; Denmark, 31,330 tons; Belgium, 23,220 tons; Germany, 15,660 tons; France, 8,640 tons; Finland, 1,350 tons.  The amount in store at Odessa on January 1, 1902, was 39,150 tons; on January 1, 1901, 4,230 tons.

### RYE.

Two hundred and forty-two thousand four hundred and fourteen tons of rye was exported from Odessa in 1901, the value of which is given at $4,120,000.  The export in 1890 amounted to 144,396 tons, valued at $3,090,000.  The total exports of rye from the Empire fell off from 1,606,984 tons in 1890 to 1,445,868 tons in 1901, as a result of the unsatisfactory rye crop in other portions of the Empire, where it forms both the principal article of food and the staple grain export.  The rye exports from Nicolaiev last year were 333,140 tons (in 1900 they were 142,380 tons); Rostoff, 228,870 tons (in 1900, 364,374 tons); St. Petersburg, 173,358 tons (in 1900, 296,766 tons); Libau, 91,566 tons (in 1900, 201,618 tons).  The rye exported from Odessa was sent to Holland, 125,370 tons; Scandinavia, 50,760 tons; Germany, 49,050 tons; Denmark, 11,880 tons; Great Britain, 1,260 tons, and to Finland, 1,629 tons.  The Odessa warehouses contained on January 1, 1902, 21,708 tons of rye, and on January 1, 1901, 18,756 tons.

## BARLEY.

Three hundred and forty-four thousand five hundred and thirty-eight tons of barley was shipped from Odessa in 1901, the value of which is given at $6,695,000 (in 1900 the shipments were 156,108 tons, valued at $3,090,000). The total exports of the Empire were increased from 957,276 tons in 1900 to 1,390,500 tons in 1901. Nicolaiev exported 248,904 tons (in 1900, 96,624 tons); Novorossisk, 195,534 tons (in 1900, 100,890 tons); Rostoff on Don, 167,706 tons (in 1900, 192,060 tons). The barley from Odessa was sent to Great Britain, 89,910 tons; Gibraltar, for orders, 13,630 tons; Germany, 97,740 tons; Holland, 89,190 tons; Belgium, 29,700 tons; Scandinavia, 20,430 tons; Denmark, 14,130 tons. The quantity of barley in store at Odessa on January 1, 1902, was 37,458 tons, and on January 1, 1901, 38,466 tons.

## OATS.

Seventeen thousand one hundred and thirty-six tons of oats was exported in 1901, the value of which is given at $412,000 (in 1900 the figures were, respectively, 8,962 tons and $180,250). The total exports of the Empire were 1,430,748 tons (in 1900, 1,418,418 tons). Oats were exported principally by way of St. Petersburg, Libau, Reval, and by rail via Graievo. The exports from Odessa were sent to Great Britain, 9,180 tons; France, 3,510 tons; Holland, 1,710 tons. The stores contained on January 1, 1901, 4,032 tons, and on January 1, 1900, 9,990 tons.

## OILSEEDS.

The export of oilseeds continues to decrease, due partly to the failure of crops, and in a great measure to the increased home demand. The total exports of oilseeds from Odessa in 1901 were only 4,842 tons, as compared with 21,900 tons in 1900. In detail, Odessa exported 1,044 tons of linseed in 1901 and 14,580 tons in 1900; of hempseed, 2,070 tons in 1901 and 1,044 tons in 1900, and of rape seed, 1,768 tons, and in 1900, 6,666 tons. The total exports of linseed from the Empire in 1900 was 304,722 tons; in 1901 it was only 81,936 tons. The linseed exported went to Holland, the hemp seed to France and Great Britain, and the rape seed to Holland and Great Britain. The stock at Odessa on January 1, 1901, was 504 tons of linseed, 234 tons of hemp seed, and 396 tons of rape seed; on January 1, 1902, linseed 936 tons, hemp seed 540 tons, and rape seed 297 tons.

## PULSE.

Fourteen thousand seven hundred and sixty tons of pease, French beans, broad beans, and lentils were exported from Odessa in 1901 (in 1900, 5,008 tons). Scarcely any millet or buckwheat was exported from Odessa last year. Much larger quantities of pulses, especially pease, were exported by Baltic ports and the railroads leading to Germany. Of pease France took 3,780 tons, Italy 1,260 tons, Great Britain 1,080 tons, and Holland 810 tons. Of other pulses, Italy took 2,250 tons, Great Britain 2,160 tons, and France 1,890 tons. The stocks at Odessa on January 1, 1901, were: Pease 216 tons, French beans 756 tons, and beans (little) lentils 18 tons.   On January 1, 1901, there were: Pease 126 tons, French beans 270 tons, beans 135 tons, and lentils 207 tons.

### TOTAL GRAIN EXPORTS.

The total exports of grain products from Russia in 1901 were 7,560,000 tons, and in 1900, 5,760,000 tons.   The points of shipment and the amount from each were:

| Port. | 1901. | 1900. | Port. | 1901. | 1900. |
|---|---|---|---|---|---|
| | *Tons.* | *Tons.* | | *Tons.* | *Tons.* |
| Odessa | 1,350,000 | 423,000 | Mariupol | 126,000 | 189,000 |
| Nicolaiev | 972,000 | 504,000 | Theodosia | 126,000 | 171,000 |
| St. Petersburg a | 774,000 | 918,000 | Graievo | 108,000 | 216,000 |
| Libau | 594,000 | 702,000 | Berdianak | 108,000 | 117,000 |
| Novorossisk | 540,000 | 328,000 | Eupatoria | 90,000 | 90,000 |
| Reval | 207,000 | 270,000 | Kilia | 81,000 | .......... |
| Riga | 198,000 | 252,000 | Ghenichesk | 54,000 | 72,000 |
| Taganrog | 189,000 | 266,000 | Temriuk | 54,000 | .......... |
| Yeisk | 135,000 | 108,000 | Ports on bay of Dzharylgatsk | 13,500 | 7,590 |

a Five hundred and fifty-eight thousand tons of oats were included in the exports from St. Petersburg and 441,000 tons from Libau.

The countries of destination and the amount of grain shipped to each were:

| Country. | 1901. | 1900. | Country. | 1901. | 1900. |
|---|---|---|---|---|---|
| | *Tons.* | *Tons.* | | *Tons.* | *Tons.* |
| Holland | 400,410 | 249,210 | Scandinavia | 55,440 | 14,040 |
| Great Britain | 299,340 | 227,700 | Gibraltar, for orders | 22,900 | 8,820 |
| Germany | 181,440 | 94,800 | Spain | 12,240 | 4,590 |
| Italy | 126,620 | 71,010 | Turkey | 16,800 | 8,230 |
| France | 110,070 | 78,080 | Egypt | 5,220 | 2,610 |
| Belgium | 68,400 | 53,280 | Greece | Very little. | 1,980 |
| Denmark | 60,390 | 2,070 | Finland | 3,600 | .......... |

The total quantity of grain in the warehouses at Odessa on January 1, 1902, was given at 270,000 tons, and on January 1, 1901, 162,000 tons.

In addition to the 1,350,000 tons of raw produce mentioned as having been exported from Odessa in 1901, there should be added the foreign shipments of flour, and also the grain and flour shipped to the far east of Russia, which gives a total export of 1,442,000 tons. The entire transactions in grain and grain produce at Odessa during 1901 amounted to 1,674,000 tons; this includes the grain in store on January 1, 1901, flour, and also the home consumption.   As the grain trade at Odessa is a reflection of the general condition of the trade elsewhere, it may not be devoid of interest to present some statements regarding the crops and surpluses of grain in other grain-growing countries.   The world's crop of wheat in 1901 was, on the whole, satisfactory, and in the United States very large.   It was also good in Italy, the Pyrenean Peninsula, and the Balkan States, with the exception of Servia.   Canada, North Africa, Egypt, India, and Australia also had good crops.   The only grain-exporting countries that had short crops were Argentina and Austria-Hungary.   The grain-importing countries with short crops were France, Belgium, Switzerland, and Denmark.   In Great Britain and Norway, the wheat crops were up to the average; in Russia, the crop of winter wheat was above the average, and the spring wheat about normal. The world's crop of wheat for 1901 and 1900 has been computed as follows:

| Exporting countries. | 1901. | 1900. | Importing countries. | 1901. | 1900. |
|---|---|---|---|---|---|
| | *Tons.* | *Tons.* | | *Tons.* | *Tons.* |
| Russia | 11,700,000 | 12,650,400 | Great Britain | 1,626,228 | 1,585,314 |
| Hungary | 3,824,080 | 4,228,358 | Germany | 3,021,858 | 4,733,316 |
| Roumania | 2,187,432 | 1,712,236 | France | 9,197,262 | 9,349,200 |
| Bulgaria | 1,098,864 | 839,698 | Belgium | 471,636 | 382,680 |
| Servia | 385,884 | 28,822 | Holland | 177,246 | 149,724 |
| Turkey | 2,143,800 | 1,715,040 | Austria | 1,296,648 | 1,224,900 |
| Algiers | 769,194 | 737,802 | Switzerland | 98,622 | 120,060 |
| Tunis | 128,618 | 171,504 | Spain | 3,344,328 | 3,013,056 |
| Egypt | 295,696 | 263,718 | Portugal | 214,880 | 171,504 |
| East Indies | 7,233,336 | 5,351,130 | Italy | 4,287,600 | 3,618,738 |
| United States | 19,485,882 | 15,780,960 | Greece | 162,936 | 120,060 |
| Canada | 2,417,472 | 1,435,096 | Denmark | 23,994 | 81,468 |
| Mexico | 329,652 | 313,182 | Scandinavia | 115,758 | 160,596 |
| Argentina | 2,747,142 | 2,285,546 | | | |
| Uruguay | 197,802 | 214,794 | Total | 23,943,276 | 24,710,616 |
| Chile | 274,362 | 361,566 | | | |
| Australia | 1,573,988 | 1,300,616 | In all | 80,726,810 | 74,446,038 |
| Total | 56,783,084 | 49,785,422 | | | |

The returns show that the exports of wheat, rye, barley, oats, and corn, by countries, were:

WHEAT.

| Country. | July 1, 1900, to July 1, 1901. | | | July 1, 1899, to July 1, 1900. | | |
|---|---|---|---|---|---|---|
| | Total imports. | From Russia. | Percentage. | Total imports. | From Russia. | Percentage. |
| | *Tons.* | *Tons.* | | *Tons.* | *Tons.* | |
| Great Britain | 3,834,754 | 261,196 | 6.8 | 3,961,188 | 102,492 | 2.6 |
| France | 769,178 | 465,624 | 60.9 | 825,488 | 494,856 | 59.9 |
| Italy | 1,228,942 | 895,806 | 79.3 | 642,618 | 496,152 | 77.2 |
| Spain | 192,168 | 85,464 | 44.5 | 388,566 | 159,714 | 41.1 |
| Germany | 1,614,006 | 414,270 | 25.7 | 1,454,094 | 296,044 | 20.4 |
| Belgium | 1,378,382 | 29,484 | 2.1 | 1,309,644 | 25,488 | 1.8 |
| Holland | 1,146,582 | 319,338 | 27.8 | 1,063,270 | 138,978 | 13.2 |
| Switzerland | 413,334 | 241,146 | 58.3 | 402,606 | 223,272 | 55.5 |

RYE.

| | | | | | | |
|---|---|---|---|---|---|---|
| France | 756 | | | 252 | | |
| Germany | 1,065,780 | 984,496 | 92.6 | 639,882 | 615,366 | 89.4 |
| Belgium | 59,508 | 15,192 | 25.5 | 35,622 | 13,122 | 36.8 |
| Holland | 618,768 | 496,042 | 80.5 | 426,276 | 382,599 | 85.1 |

BARLEY.

| | | | | | | |
|---|---|---|---|---|---|---|
| Great Britain | 1,012,156 | 289,620 | 28.6 | 885,402 | 269,460 | 30.4 |
| France | 168,984 | 15,174 | 9 | 101,790 | 13,122 | 16.2 |
| Italy | 5,310 | | | 5,238 | | |
| Germany | 896,866 | 506,124 | 56.3 | 1,044,190 | 431,424 | 40.3 |
| Belgium | 314,226 | 49,914 | 15.9 | 319,130 | 75,510 | 23.7 |
| Holland | 295,484 | 196,020 | 66.3 | 296,388 | 144,014 | 48.6 |
| Switzerland | 8,910 | 1,530 | 17.2 | 10,044 | 1,188 | 11.8 |

OATS.

| | | | | | | |
|---|---|---|---|---|---|---|
| Great Britain | 1,234,580 | 616,068 | 49.9 | 1,016,658 | 448,164 | 44.1 |
| France | 360,396 | 146,988 | 40.8 | 202,784 | 78,784 | 38.9 |
| Italy | 36,540 | | | 52,902 | | |
| Germany | 532,332 | 432,648 | 81.3 | 382,806 | 262,512 | 68.6 |
| Belgium | 69,588 | 21,780 | 31.3 | 72,680 | 32,184 | 44.8 |
| Holland | 399,726 | 333,342 | 83.4 | 361,096 | 313,596 | 61.9 |
| Switzerland | 101,808 | 30,528 | 30 | 103,914 | 18,936 | 18.2 |

CORN.

| Country. | July 1, 1900, to July 1, 1901. | | | July 1, 1899, to July 1, 1900. | | |
|---|---|---|---|---|---|---|
| | Total imports. | From Russia. | Percentage. | Total imports. | From Russia. | Percentage. |
| | Tons. | Tons. | | Tons. | Tons. | |
| Great Britain | 3,090,168 | 87,732 | 2.8 | 3,380,702 | 128,282 | 3.7 |
| France | 378,072 | 52,866 | 14 | 544,770 | 42,252 | 8.3 |
| Italy | 245,880 | | | 137,804 | | |
| Germany | 1,522,620 | 64,188 | 3.9 | 1,769,400 | 94,572 | 5.5 |
| Holland | 677,080 | 11,718 | 1.8 | 809,694 | 29,583 | 3.6 |
| Belgium | 570,690 | 16,938 | 3 | 516,454 | 17,856 | 8.4 |
| Switzerland | 54,986 | 13,752 | 25 | 96,012 | 12,996 | 13.5 |

The rye crops in Austria-Hungary and France were good, and in the other rye-growing countries, either medium or unsatisfactory. In Russia, the crop was medium. Barley gave a normal yield over all Europe, large in the Balkan States, and extremely good in the United States. Oats yielded a medium crop over all Europe, unsatisfactory in Denmark, and poor in the United States. The corn crop was good over all southern Europe (including south Russia), but very unsatisfactory in the United States.

Russia's grain crops for the last three years were:

| Article. | 1901. | 1900. | 1899. |
|---|---|---|---|
| | Tons. | Tons. | Tons. |
| Rye | 21,078,000 | 26,650,000 | 23,256,000 |
| Winter wheat | 5,526,000 | 4,082,000 | 4,230,000 |
| Spring wheat | 7,236,000 | 8,622,000 | 6,912,000 |
| Oats | 9,972,000 | 13,608,000 | 13,104,000 |
| Barley | 5,742,000 | 5,670,000 | 5,400,000 |
| Buckwheat | 864,000 | 990,000 | 1,134,000 |
| Millet | 1,836,000 | 2,034,000 | 2,088,000 |
| Corn | 1,998,000 | 936,000 | 648,000 |
| Total | 54,252,000 | 61,542,000 | 56,772,000 |

The following figures show all grain in store in the principal exporting ports of Russia and on the home market:

| Article. | Jan. 1, 1901. | Jan. 1, 1900. | Article. | Jan. 1, 1901. | Jan. 1, 1900. |
|---|---|---|---|---|---|
| | Tons. | Tons. | | Tons. | Tons. |
| Wheat | 576,900 | 695,142 | Barley | 110,084 | 105,696 |
| Rye | 268,604 | 202,158 | Corn | 11,304 | 5,760 |
| Oats | 207,126 | 201,384 | Flour | 186,094 | 137,962 |

Due to the comparatively good harvest of 1901, the purchase and rent value of farming lands was largely augmented throughout south Russia. In the central provinces, Poltava, for example, the price of land, owing to speculation, was run up to an almost incredible figure. In such provinces as Cherson, Taurida, and Ekaterinoslav, the purchasers were well-to-do peasants or the more affluent German colonists, so that the land passed into hands actually requiring it. During the past two years, numerous complaints have been heard of the lack of labor for farming purposes. This scarcity is causing an increased import of agricultural machinery, about 10,000 tons of which (American) has been purchased for the Odessa region alone. The scarcity of labor is due to the large influx of the rural population into the cities, to emigration to Siberia, and to emigration of well-to-do south Russian farmers to the United States. The migratory movement to America is constantly increasing. It is brought about largely by the ability of these farmers to sell their Russian farms at high prices and purchase land in the United States at low figures. The large, or at least satisfactory, crops of 1901 and 1902 will next year cause a large additional number of farmers to leave Russia for America. These emigrants are in every way a desirable class.

### WHEAT FLOUR.

Thirty-eight thousand four hundred and forty-eight tons of wheat flour was exported from Odessa in 1901, as against 32,472 tons in 1900. Sevastopol exported 2,268 tons in 1901; other places but very little, so that this export about represents the total shipments of wheat flour from the Russian Empire. This flour was nearly all the produce of local mills and was sent to Egypt and Turkey, although 1,620 tons was received by England. The quantity of flour in store at Odessa on January 1, 1901, was 5,634 tons, and on January 1, 1900, 3,816 tons.

### BRAN.

Bran and other grain offal was exported in 1901 to the extent of 16,272 tons, and in 1900, 10,224 tons. The total exports from the Empire in 1901 amounted to 514,224 tons, as against 546,642 tons in 1900. The principal ports of export for bran are Alexandrovo, Mlava, Sosnovitsi, Graievo, and Libau. The bran shipped from Odessa went to Germany (5,004 tons), Holland (3,906 tons), Great Britain (2,610 tons), and Denmark (1,710 tons).

Fires have been so frequent among the flour mills of Russia as to make it an extremely difficult matter to secure adequate insurance from the various companies. This led to the formation among the millers of a mutual insurance company for mills alone. The offices of the company are located at St. Petersburg.

### VEGETABLE OILS.

Vegetable oils have almost ceased to be an article of export from Odessa. Thirty-six tons represents the quantity shipped in 1901, and the greater part of this was aniseed oil for France.

### OIL CAKE.

Twenty-eight thousand four hundred and four tons of oil cake was exported from Odessa in 1901, as against 27,558 tons in 1900, of which Belgium received 8,964 tons; Great Britain, 8,442 tons; Holland, 7,128 tons; Germany, 3,726 tons; France, 1,746 tons, and Denmark, 1,242 tons. Riga, St. Petersburg, Alexandrovo, and Sosnovitsi are the leading places of export. France in 1900 took 6,660 tons of oil cake from Odessa, and the falling off in the shipments to that country in 1901 is due to the fact that the Russian oil cake is not sufficiently pure to satisfy the French market.

H. Doc. 305, pt 2——39

### ALCOHOL.

Four hundred and eleven thousand two hundred and ten vedros of 100 per cent alcohol (equal to 1,110,267 gallons of full-proof alcohol), weighing 28 Russian pounds per vedro, was exported from Odessa in 1901. These shipments were exclusive of the exports to the Russian Pacific ports, which amounted to 469,098 gallons. The alcohol represented 411 cargoes, averaging 2,700 gallons each. Odessa is almost the sole port of export for alcohol; the little exported elsewhere is the crude product, which is not handled here. The alcohol sent from Odessa in 1901 was consigned to Smyria (515,916 gallons), Constantinople (353,160 gallons), and the island of Samos (79,650 gallons); the remainder went to other ports and places in the Levant, the Balkan Peninsula, and to Alexandria. Almost all of the alcohol reaches Odessa by rail. Since its monopoly of this article, the Russian Government has fixed the price of alcohol for 1902 at 19 kopecks per degree, or $4.76 per gallon. The vodka sold for consumption is 40 per cent alcohol.

### SUGAR.

The exports of sugar from Russia have in recent years largely increased, though 1901 shows a smaller export than 1900. According to official returns, the exports of sugar from Odessa amounted in 1901 to 35,910 tons (exclusive of shipments to the Far East possessions of Russia), while in 1900 it was 57,726 tons. This decrease is attributed to the lessened demand for Russian sugar in Italy and Great Britain. The total exports from the Empire have fallen off in a still more remarkable ratio—from 124,470 tons in 1900 to 51,750 tons in 1901. These figures are exclusive of the 40,374 tons exported in 1900 by way of Baku (39,636 tons in 1901), and the 1,044 tons shipped to Finland. The customs returns at Odessa give the total exports from this port at 40,230 tons, including shipments to the Far East. Nearly all of the sugar exported, except that sent to the Far East, is of the quality known as white-sand sugar. Mlawa is the only other European frontier over which sugar was exported, and the quantity shipped was 8,568 tons. Odessa alone exported refined sugar. The sugar exported from Odessa was sent to Turkey (15,048 tons), Italy (6,786 tons—in 1900, 33,391 tons), Egypt (2,646 tons), and Great Britain (270 tons—in 1900, 3,820 tons).

The sugar season of 1900–1901 showed 274 factories in operation, the output of which was 942,519 tons; and to this quantity must be added the hold-over from the previous season, which amounted to 66,006 tons, giving a total of 1,008,525 tons, which under Government regulations was allotted as follows:

| | Tons. | | Tons. |
|---|---|---|---|
| Home consumption | 729,036 | Free reserve | 277,082 |
| Intangible reserve | 26,946 | | |
| | | Total | 1,033,064 |

The estimate for home consumption was increased during the year by 90,073 tons. The season of 1901–2 showed 278 factories in operation, the production of which was 1,071,818 tons. To the latter must be added the quantity available from the reserves from the previous season, in order to understand the distribution according to estimates made by ministry of finance, which amounts to 75,761 tons, making a total of 1,147,579 tons, to be disposed of as follows:

| | Tons. | | Tons. |
|---|---|---|---|
| Home consumption | 756,000 | Free reserve | 301,579 |
| Intangible reserve | 90,000 | | |
| | | Total | 1,147,579 |

The quantity of beetroot used in the season 1901-2 was 9,138,904 tons. The area under cultivation—1,394,643 acres—gave a yield of 117 hundredweight per acre. The consumption of sugar is increasing in Russia, and the latest estimate would equal 11¼ pounds per head.

#### WOOL.

One thousand nine hundred and ninety-eight tons of wool was exported from Odessa in 1901, as against 2,250 tons in 1900. The wool exported was principally washed wool, both merino and the coarser varieties of carpet wool. The total shipments of wool from Russia fell off from 14,778 tons in 1900 to 11,196 tons in 1901. St. Petersburg exported 2,484 tons and Batoum 2,052 tons. Besides small quantities shipped to Austria-Hungary, Holland, and Belgium, Odessa sent Great Britain 1,404 tons of coarse wool intended for transshipment to the United States.

#### CATTLE.

Four thousand four hundred and forty-nine head of cattle were exported from Odessa in 1901, as against 5,979 head in 1900, of which Malta received 3,225 head, Egypt 1,156 head, and Turkey 38 head. The above shipments comprise almost all of the cattle exported from southern Russia by sea. The value of meat animals stood high in 1901 at Odessa, which was due to a considerable extent to the fact that both Warsaw and Moscow bought largely of cattle in the provinces of Kiev and Podolia, and thus diminished the source of the Odessa supply. Good conditioned oxen for export purposes were sold at $83 per head and were difficult to secure at that price. In a report to the Department of State, dated Odessa, August 5, 1899,[*] I mentioned the desire of the Russian Government to induce Great Britain to permit the entrance of Russian cattle, hogs, and animal produce of various kinds into that country. Invitations were freely extended to British expert authority to visit Russia and examine into the conditions prevailing in this country and to suggest improvements in either breed or condition, etc., in the hope that their report would be favorable to the admission of Russian cattle into British ports. Evidently the result has been of a favorable character, because the year 1903 will see large quantities of Russian beef carried in specially constructed steamers from Baltic to English ports. One of the suggestions made by the British commission which visited this country was that high-bred bulls for crossing with the smaller Russian cattle, be introduced, in order that an animal might be produced which would give good weight and fully develop in three years' time. I am informed that this plan has been a success and that each year, commencing with 1903, will see as many as 80,000 head of such cattle slaughtered at the new abattoir

---

[*] See Advance Sheets No. 532 (Sept. 19, 1899).

at Libau and shipped thence to British ports.   It is proposed to carry these cattle by rail from Rostoff on Don to Libau, a distance of 1,221 miles, at the rate of $7.73, and from intermediate points at proportionately lower rates.   The Government has arranged stock yards en route to feed and water and rest the cattle.   The total sales effected at the Odessa cattle market in 1901 amounted in value to $4,868,295, of which the animals exported aggregated $3,469,652 worth and labor cattle $84,861.   The remainder was consumed locally.   Besides the neat cattle just mentioned, 77,000 sheep were exported, of which 46,000 were sent to France and the rest to Greece, Egypt, and Turkey. Odessa is practically the sole Russian port exporting sheep.

### HORSES.

Five hundred and fifty-five horses were exported in 1901 and 230 in 1900, all of which were sent to Turkey for military purposes.   The price paid ranged from $50 to $60 a head.   One hundred and fifty horses were killed at the Odessa abattoir in 1901 and sold as food in local markets.   They were valued at $10 each.

### FOWLS.

Two hundred and fifty thousand fowls were exported from Odessa in 1901 and 359,000 in 1900.   Of these, 166,000 went to France, 22,000 to Turkey.

### HIDES, FURS, AND ANIMAL PRODUCE.

Very little animal produce was exported from Odessa in 1901.   Furs and skins were exported, but not in any large quantity.

Raw hides were exported to the amount of 750 tons; tanned hides, 144 tons, mostly to Great Britain.   The total exports of hides from the Empire decreased from 14,472 tons in 1900 to 12,492 tons in 1901. Riga headed the list with 3,870 tons, St. Petersburg coming next with 2,412 tons, and Libau third with 1,808 tons.

Large quantities of sheep guts were exported to Germany.   Eggs are not exported in large numbers from Odessa by sea, though many are sent abroad by rail.   The number of eggs available for export is evidently limited by the influx into Odessa of eggs from Egypt, which pass through this city in transit to Austria and Germany.

### TALLOW: CANDLES.

One thousand and eighty-five tons of tallow was exported, all of which was sent to Turkey.   In order to supply the wants of her stearine factories, Russia continues to import increasing quantities of tallow—in 1901, 31,000 tons, and in 1900, 21,633 tons.

Tallow candles have ceased to be an article of export, and stearine candles are exported only to the Far East.

### FISH.

Six thousand and thirty tons of fish and fish produce was exported in 1901, all or nearly all of which was sent to the Balkan States.

## MINERAL OILS.

Two hundred and fifty-two tons of lubricating oil was exported from Odessa in 1901 to the Balkan States. One thousand eight hundred and fifty-four tons of kerosene was sent to Persia. These figures seem very small when compared with the 1,178,000 tons shipped abroad from Batoum, and the 329,400 tons from Novorossisk. Still, Odessa has a large trade in the distributing of kerosene over the southwest of Russia and over the adjoining countries. It is estimated that Odessa received, in 1901, 50,760 tons of kerosene, 342 tons of crude oil, 486 tons of oleonaft, and 90 tons of benzine. These figures were obtained from the Odessa brokers, but no doubt they are incorrect, as the Russian Steam Navigation and Trading Company alone brought in their two tank steamers 19,854 tons of kerosene from Batoum to Odessa and 36,630 tons from Novorossisk; also of naphtha residues (ostatki), 16,128 tons was shipped here from Novorossisk. This same company also carried 10,746 tons of kerosene to Nicolaiev, 2,682 tons and 1,800 tons of ostatki to Sevastopol, 5,436 tons of kerosene to Danube ports, 5,040 tons to Vladivostock and Dalni, 1,836 tons to Alexandria, 18,360 tons to Trieste, 1,744 tons of ostatki to Barcelona, 1,944 tons of kerosene to Lisbon, 2,826 tons to Amsterdam, and 8,442 tons to Hamburg. The Baku-Batoum pipe line, which in the section Mikailovo-Batoum, has been in operation since October, 1900, and is to be completed to Baku in 1903. This line is expected to bring back to Batoum much of the petroleum trade that has been diverted to Novorossisk.

## MISCELLANEOUS.

The exports of phosphorites, artificial manures, manganese ore, metal and metal wares, silk and silken goods, woolen goods, felt and carpets, cotton goods, etc., are so small as to be scarcely worth mentioning.

## TOBACCO.

Of the so-called "Turkish" tobacco, there are small exports to Turkey and Austria-Hungary, in the shape of cigarettes; of snuff to Bulgaria, and of leaves to Turkey, Germany, Great Britain, Egypt, Austria-Hungary, and Japan. Odessa has a large trade in tobacco, estimated at about 9,000 tons, nearly all of which is brought to Odessa in coasting vessels from the Crimea and the Caucasus. Only one hundred and twenty-one tons came from abroad in 1901.

## RUSSIAN TIMBER.

Thirty-five thousand one hundred and eighteen tons of timber, chiefly for building purposes, was exported from Odessa in 1901. The total exports from the Empire in 1901 were 141,876 tons of large logs, 99,216 tons of small logs, and 632,484 tons of boards and planks. St. Petersburg, Riga, Libau, Windau, Neshava, and Archangel are the principal exporting points for building timber. Odessa exported 6,480 tons of staves and similar timber in 1901, which was chiefly sent to France. In addition to the Russian, Odessa also exported a large quantity of Austrian timber, which was sent in transit from Galicia.

The quantity thus exported was 140,400 tons, chiefly fir boards. This makes the total export of timber from Odessa in 1901, 175,774 tons. The timber was sent to Egypt (64,080 tons), France (39,960 tons), Holland (26,910 tons), Turkey (20,700 tons), Great Britain (16,740 tons), Belgium (9,360 tons), and Greece (810 tons). The exports to France include those to Algiers, which were 2,790 tons.

Other articles in small quantities were exported during 1901 from Odessa, but their sum total is so small as to make it unnecessary to go into details. The total value of the exports from Odessa during 1901 was $38,625,000, and the quantity 1,350,000 tons. With the transit trade, the amount was 1,494,000 tons, valued at $42,745,000. The increased value over 1900 was $8,755,000, mainly due to grain produce, which represents 72 per cent of the total value, or rather more than the average since 1880. The value of all Russian exports over her western frontiers is computed at $375,950,000, so that Odessa represents, roughly, 10 per cent of the western export trade of Russia.

IMPORTS.

The imports at Odessa during 1901 amounted to 486,000 tons. In addition to this, the transit trade in such articles as tea, tobacco, cotton, olive oil, etc., amounted to 23,400 tons, making a total of 509,400 tons. For 1900, the imports were 590,400 tons. There was a decrease in 1901 of 108,000 tons of coal imported and an increase of 23,400 tons of cotton. There is also more or less increase in a number of small articles of higher value, mainly due to the circumstance that during the previous two years (1900 and 1899) the failure of the crops caused a falling off in the demand for these articles. If the total exports of Odessa are taken at 1,692,000 tons and there is added to that amount the 69,390 tons sent to the Far East, the total will aggregate 1,764,000 tons. These figures show that the weight of the exports and imports compare roughly as 100 to 29, so that fully 70 per cent of the vessels engaged in Odessa's foreign trade arrive here in ballast. The proportion for 1900 was as 100 to 42.5, and for 1899 as 100 to 37, due, to a great extent, to the reduced exports during those years. In good years, the proportion was as low as 100 to 16.5.

The value of all articles on which duty was levied at the Odessa customs has been calculated at $25,389,500. Fifteen thousand three hundred tons of goods in transit (chiefly tea) passed through the Odessa custom-house, the value of which was $9,115,500. Added to the duty-paying goods, this brings the total to $34,505,000. The total value of all imports into Russia over her western frontiers in 1901 is given at $269,499,500, of which the Odessa imports form 9½ per cent, or with the transit trade, 12¾ per cent. In the value of imports Odessa is second only to St. Petersburg.

RICE.

The quantity of rice imported at Odessa in 1901 is not given in the returns thus far obtainable, but it is well known that it was much less than in 1900. The imports of rice over the western frontiers of Russia also show a falling off from 25,200 tons in 1900 to 12,474 tons in 1901. For the same period the imports of rice over the Asiatic frontier increased from 25,524 tons in 1900 to 59,886 tons in 1901. The growth in this trade was due to the very large rice crop in Persia.

STARCH.

About 360 tons of starch was imported at Odessa in 1901.

VEGETABLES.

No particulars are obtainable concerning the quantity of vegetables imported at Odessa last year. The total imports for the Empire, however, have declined from 13,950 tons in 1900 to 13,266 tons in 1901.

FRUIT.

Thirty thousand and seventy-eight tons of fresh fruit was imported at Odessa in 1901, as against 26,550 tons in 1900. The imports consisted principally of oranges and lemons. Grapes are imported in decreasing quantities each year, as the natural consequence of the rapid development of the culture of the vine in Bessarabia, Taurida, Caucasus, Cherson, and Podolia.

One thousand four hundred and twenty-two tons of dried fruits was imported at Odessa in 1901, as against 1,206 tons in 1900. The total imports into Russia of this article have also undergone but very little change. In former years, they were enormous and consisted almost entirely of Greek currants. At that time this fruit, owing to its very low price, less than 50 cents per pood (36.1 pounds), became a popular article of daily consumption, more especially in Lent. Successive failures of the crop, however, caused a great increase in the price, and when the Russian Government added an enormous duty, the trade in currants ceased. The imports for 1901 are given at 108 tons.

One thousand six hundred and thirty-eight tons of olives were imported in 1901, as against 1,556 tons in 1900.

NUTS.

Six thousand eight hundred and forty tons of nuts was imported at Odessa in 1901, as against 5,130 tons in 1900. The total imports of nuts into Russia also increased by 3,240 tons.

The average annual importation of almonds and pistachoes at Odessa has during recent years been about 270 tons. Five hundred and forty tons was also imported over the western frontier and 2,592 tons from Persia.

SPICES.

One thousand five hundred and forty-eight tons of pepper, cloves, caraway, laurel leaf, ginger, vanilla, nutmeg, cinnamon, etc., was imported at Odessa in 1901, as against 1,350 tons in 1900.

COFFEE.

Two thousand six hundred and forty-six tons of coffee was exported at Odessa in 1901, as against 2,232 tons in 1900.

TEA.

Four thousand five hundred and fifty-four tons of tea was imported at Odessa in 1901, and in 1900 4,356 tons. The steady increase in the imports of tea at this port is due to the fact that nearly all of the prominent tea firms are now weighing and sorting their tea here. Formerly, tea was sent in transit to Moscow, where it was weighed and packed and afterwards distributed to the various parts of Russia, Odessa included. The condition is now reversed, and Odessa is the center of the trade. The tea in this market comes both from London and the Orient. A good deal of tea is still sent in transit to Moscow, the quantity of which is estimated at 15,300 tons. Most of the tea imported at Odessa is Ceylon grown. The total imports of tea into Russia over the western frontier in 1901 were 24,084 tons, and over other frontiers 34,416 tons.

### LIQUORS.

Seventy-two tons and 80,000 bottles of spirituous liquor, 558 tons of wine in casks, 74,000 bottles of effervescent wines, and a much less quantity of noneffervescent wines were received at Odessa in 1901.

The importation of mineral waters into the Empire shows a steady increase, which is somewhat surprising, considering the favor with which the mineral waters from the Caucasus have been received. Narzan competes with Giessbubler and Borzhom with Vichy.

### PRESERVED FISH.

One thousand and forty-six tons of preserved fish (chiefly sardines) was imported at Odessa in 1901, as against 846 tons in 1900.

### MINERAL WAX.

Six hundred and forty-eight tons of this article was imported at Odessa in 1901, as against 468 tons in 1900.

### CASTOR SEED AND COPRA.

Thirteen thousand three hundred and two tons was imported in 1901, as against 7,974 tons in 1900. The total imports of castor seed into Russia in 1901 amounted to 21,078 tons, as against 11,754 tons in 1900; of copra, 45,900 tons in 1901, and 41,166 tons in 1900.

### BRICKS AND FIRE BRICKS, TILES AND TUBES.

Fourteen thousand three hundred and ninety-two tons of these articles was imported at Odessa in 1901, as against 7,812 tons in 1900. The total imports for the Empire were, fire bricks, 95,724 tons (160,632 tons in 1900); common bricks, 1,458 tons (13,032 tons in 1900); tubes, 8,028 tons (14,058 tons in 1900). Imports of roof tiles increased from 25,038 tons in 1900 to 32,814 tons in 1901.

### COAL.

One hundred and eight thousand four hundred and sixty-eight tons of coal was imported at Odessa in 1901, as against 287,316 tons in 1900. The total quantity of coal imported into Russia in 1901 was 900,000 tons less than in 1900. Of foreign coal, St. Petersburg received 1,556,532 tons in 1901, as against 1,792,296 tons in 1900; Sosnovitsy, 831,474 tons in 1901 and 864,216 tons in 1900; Riga, 417,582 tons in 1901 and 574,128 tons in 1900, and Libau, 177,858 tons in 1901 and 316,260 tons in 1900. The total imports of coke into Russia in 1901 was 612,000 tons.

### ROSIN.

Four thousand three hundred and two tons of rosin was imported in 1901, as against 2,142 tons in 1900.

## VEGETABLE OIL.

Three thousand six hundred and eighteen tons of this oil was imported in 1901, as against 2,736 tons in 1900.

## TANNING MATERIALS.

Eight thousand five hundred and sixty-eight tons of these materials was imported in 1901, as against 9,976 tons in 1900. The total imports into Russia increased by 19,206 tons.

## NATURAL PAINT AND COLORS.

One thousand eight hundred and thirty-six tons of these was imported in 1901 and 2,124 tons in 1900. White lead or zinc, 1,332 tons in 1901 and 1,314 tons the previous year.

## IRON.

The imports of iron fell off in 1900, but in 1901 there was an increase. Iron and iron industries in Russia have been and still are in a depressed condition. Five hundred and twenty-two tons of cast iron was imported at Odessa in 1901, as against 360 tons in 1900. The total imports of pig iron into Russia in 1901 were 17,442 tons; in 1900, 46,368 tons, and in 1899, 136,134 tons. The iron was imported by way of St. Petersburg and Sosnovitsy in the north and Novorossisk and Mariupol in the south. Of other kinds of iron, Odessa imported 1,440 tons of bars and fashioned iron, 4,158 tons of sheet iron under No. 25, and 7,902 tons of sheet iron over No. 25. The total iron imports of Russia in 1901 were 92,394 tons; in 1900, 97,602 tons, and in 1899, 279,468 tons. The imports entered chiefly at the ports of St. Petersburg and Sosnovitsy. Odessa has ceased to be an important center for imported iron, owing to its proximity to the local iron industries in the provinces of Ekaterinoslay and Cherson.

## STEEL.

Ninety per cent of all the steel for carriage springs and for tools is brought to Odessa from abroad. One thousand nine hundred and eighty tons of steel was imported at Odessa in 1901. Sheet steel was not imported. One thousand seven hundred and twenty-eight tons of ribbon and fashioned steel and 252 tons of steel rails were imported here in 1901. The total imports for the Empire show a falling off of 8,100 tons of steel as compared with 1900. During the last eight years, the production of raw iron in Russia was as follows:

| | Tons. | | Tons. |
|---|---|---|---|
| 1894 | 926,590 | 1898 | 2,219,850 |
| 1895 | 1,452,420 | 1899 | 2,703,890 |
| 1896 | 1,621,100 | 1900 | 2,875,000 |
| 1897 | 1,880,410 | 1901 | 2,784,565 |

The following figures show the imports of raw iron from Germany and Great Britain for the last ten years:

| Year. | Great Britain. | Germany. | Year. | Great Britain. | Germany. |
|---|---|---|---|---|---|
| | Tons. | Tons. | | Tons. | Tons. |
| 1891 | 132,000 | 72,000 | 1896 | 166,000 | 316,000 |
| 1892 | 146,500 | 68,000 | 1897 | 206,000 | 321,000 |
| 1893 | 248,000 | 90,300 | 1898 | 272,000 | 358,000 |
| 1894 | 211,500 | 218,000 | 1899 | 231,000 | 278,000 |
| 1895 | 201,500 | 273,000 | 1900 | 183,500 | 150,300 |

Russia and Germany concluded a' commercial treaty in 1893, and the imports from the latter country rose from 90,300 tons of raw iron in 1893 to 218,000 tons in 1894.

## SCYTHES AND SICKLES.

Of these articles, 414 tons was imported in 1901 and 324 tons in 1900. Nine hundred and fifty-four tons of "hand tools" was imported at Odessa in 1901.

## MACHINES (NOT AGRICULTURAL).

Two thousand four hundred and sixty-six tons of various machines was imported at Odessa in 1901, as against 3,546 tons in 1900.

## AGRICULTURAL MACHINES.

One thousand nine hundred and eight tons of agricultural machines was imported at Odessa in 1901, as against 1,188 tons in 1900.

The total imports of machines and agricultural machines into Russia in 1901 were 108,144 tons and in 1900 155,070 tons. This reduction, however, should not be credited to agricultural machines and implements.

Nineteen hundred and one was a very satisfactory year for the sale of American agricultural machines and implements. The sales of these goods were fully equal to those of the previous year. The increased tariff on certain American machines and other articles has in no way diminished their import. In the matter of bicycles, there has been a slight falling off in the purchases of the American article; but this is in no way due to the increased tariff.

## COTTON.

Thirty-five thousand two hundred and forty-four tons of cotton was imported at Odessa in 1901, as against 11,790 tons in 1900. The total imports of the Empire increased by 1,998 tons. Reval received 40,752 tons, St. Petersburg 29,268 tons, Alexandrovo 27,162 tons, and Libau 432 tons. Of the land frontiers, Sosnovitsy received 6,118 tons and Granitsa 2,430 tons. Russia also imported 17,190 tons of cotton over her Asiatic frontier.

## JUTE.

Four thousand five hundred and thirty-six tons of jute was imported at Odessa in 1901 and 3,006 tons in 1900.

## TOTAL FOREIGN TRADE.

The total foreign trade at Odessa in 1901 amounted to about $64,875,-000, or $14,935,000 in excess of 1900. These figures are exclusive of the transit trade, which was $4,120,000 for exports and $8,755,000 for imports, which would increase the total to $77,250,000. The total exports and imports of Russia over her western frontier amounted in value to $645,295,000, so that Odessa, excluding its transit trade, handled about 10 per cent, and including its transit trade, 12 per cent.

*Foreign shipping at the port of Odessa during the year 1901.*

| Nationality. | Sailing. | | Steam. | | Total. | |
|---|---|---|---|---|---|---|
| | Number of vessels. | Tons. | Number of vessels. | Tons. | Number of vessels. | Tons. |
| British | | | 382 | 689,761 | 382 | 689,761 |
| Russian | | | 159 | 276,483 | 159 | 276,483 |
| Italian | | | 144 | 229,802 | 144 | 229,802 |
| Austro-Hungarian | | | 105 | 111,828 | 105 | 111,828 |
| Greek | 2 | 611 | 45 | 61,878 | 47 | 62,489 |
| German | | | 42 | 55,840 | 42 | 55,840 |
| Norwegian | | | 16 | 27,051 | 16 | 27,051 |
| French | | | 12 | 18,239 | 12 | 18,239 |
| Dutch | | | 11 | 15,241 | 11 | 15,241 |
| Spanish | | | 10 | 12,415 | 10 | 12,415 |
| Danish | | | 9 | 14,833 | 9 | 14,833 |
| Swedish | | | 6 | 12,331 | 6 | 12,331 |
| Turkish | | | 2 | 2,481 | 2 | 2,481 |
| Belgian | | | 1 | 1,327 | 1 | 1,327 |
| Total | 2 | 611 | 941 | 1,529,513 | 946 | 1,530,124 |

The steamers of the Volunteer Fleet carried from Odessa to the Far East 26,450 tons of general cargo and 23,408 tons of Government stores, 357 cabin passengers, 626 third-class and deck passengers, 8,768 recruits and soldiers, 27 soldiers' wives and children, 6,574 emigrants, and 771 convicts. These vessels brought back from the Far East 26,470 tons of general cargo and 1,640 tons of Government stores, 624 cabin passengers, 271 third-class and deck passengers, 17,459 soldiers, 152 soldiers' wives and children, and three convicts. It was formerly the custom to send every year one of these Volunteer Fleet steamers from St. Petersburg to the Far East, and one from the Far East to St. Petersburg, but owing to the completion of the Siberian Railway, this schedule has been abandoned.

There were working at Odessa during the year 1901, 477 factories, with a capital of $34,000,000, and giving employment to 20,629 persons—15,030 men, 512 boys, 4,832 women, and 255 girls.

## TRADE IN 1902.

### AGRICULTURE.

The winter of 1901–2 was in every way favorable to fall sowing. The weather was mild from the beginning and continued so during the entire season. Snow fell at the proper time and in sufficient quantity. The spring opened with abundant rain, and spring-sown grain had all the conditions favorable for a large yield. In a dispatch to the Department of State, dated August 16, 1902, I pointed out that the harvest in Russia would be the largest and most satisfactory that this country had had in the past ten years. Siberia was not included in this statement, and I pointed out that reports from that district were of a very unfavorable character. I can now confirm my predictions, and report a large crop of all cereals except flaxseed.

### AGRICULTURAL IMPLEMENTS.

American agricultural machines and implements were imported in 1902 in larger quantities than in any previous year. I am informed by dealers that the sales were unusually heavy and that the terms were very satisfactory. Labor was scarce during the harvest season, owing to the army maneuvers, which took place on an extensive scale this year. It is the custom to allow the soldiers to work in the fields during harvest time, and this year their absence was severely felt. The result, however, was an increased sale of such articles as mowers, reapers, binders, etc. It is with much satisfaction that I now report that the American plow has at last gained a foothold in this country, and has, I think, come to stay. For years, our plow manufacturers have been trying to introduce the American article into this country, but with little or no success. It is a matter of faith with me that, given a fair chance, any American agricultural machine or implement will make its way in this country and be a success. The first condition necessary is a good article, and that we have. The second condition is a good salesman, one who can not only point out the superiority of the article in question, but can also show the farmer how to operate it, as in the case of a plow, for example. I have met with but one salesman who could plow, and this man came to Russia last year and is still here. His success was immediate. He adopted a suggestion made by me in a report to the Department, dated September 13, 1902,[a] viz, to apply a pair of wheels and an axle to the Amercan plow, thus giving the Russian farmer what he wants. American thrashers have still to make their way in this country. Attempts have been made in the past to introduce these machines into Russia, but the success attending the effort was not very marked. There is no reason why these outfits should not have a large sale in this country. Patience and the expenditure of considerable money in showing what the thrashers can do are absolute necessities. It is not sufficient to send machines here and place them in the hands of an agent, however reliable he may be. Men must be sent with the outfits who understand how to work them to the best advantage. Moreover, these men should be kept permanently in this country.

The Russian-German commercial treaty, which expires at the end of 1903, unless one year's notice to continue it has been given or a new treaty made, is looked forward to with much interest. The treaty of 1832 between Russia and the United States gives us the benefit of the most-favored-nation clause, and consequently the imports from the United States enjoy the reduced rates of the German treaty. Should the Russian-German treaty for any reason be not renewed, it would be a severe blow to all branches of German interests, including shipping. According to the new harbor-dues law, foreign ships of countries that have no treaties of trade and navigation with Russia pay 2 rubles ($1.03) per ton carrying capacity on each voyage. This latter clause would not particularly affect the United States, because no ship carrying the American flag has visited Odessa during the past twenty years.

PREMIUMS FOR RUSSIAN SHIPPING.

The committee appointed to consider the best means of furthering the development of the Russian mercantile marine have presented their report to the marine department of the ministry of finance. The report recommends the granting of premiums to Russian ships (1) in the shape of a navigation premium on the number of miles covered

---

[a] See Advance Sheets No. 1443, September 13, 1902.

and the amount of cargo carried by any Russian ship, irrespective of where the ship is built, and (2) a cargo premium on the number of tons of cargo exported from or brought into Russian ports.    For the furthering of Russian shipbuilding, the committee recommend granting shipowners a premium for ships built in Russian yards, the amount of the premium to be determined by the difference between the cost of constructing the vessel in Russia and abroad.    The committee also add that they consider it advisable that Government vessels should be built entirely at Russian yards, orders being divided equally between the various firms.

### VOLUNTEER FLEET.

Though the law that forbids foreign ships from engaging in the coasting trade of Russia, even when the ports are so far apart as Odessa and Vladivostok, is in full force, still the condition of the merchant marine of Russia is not flourishing.    Three of the newest steamers of the volunteer fleet are laid up in Sevastopol Harbor and others have remained idle at Odessa for the better part of the year. These steamers are heavily subsidized and have been greatly favored in every way by the Government.    The completion of the Siberian Railway has had a marked effect in diminishing the traffic in freights, Government supplies, emigrants, soldiers, and private passengers that the volunteer fleet steamers formerly carried, both from St. Petersburg and Odessa.    The best of these boats are not intended for freight traffic alone, and if engaged in it would not pay expenses.    They are built to move quickly and carry passengers and a limited quantity of freight. It was publicly stated during the year that the directors of the volunteer fleet had decided to run their steamers between Odessa, Italian and other ports, and New York, carrying emigrants and such freight as might be obtainable.    I wrote to the directors for information on this subject, and received a reply to the effect that such a proposition had been under consideration, but it was finally concluded to abandon the idea.

### INDUSTRIAL CONDITIONS.

Industrial undertakings are still suffering from the depression resulting from recent unfortunate speculations.    It is known that during the last two years or more French investors in Russian undertakings have had their investments of $400,000,000 reduced by 50 per cent, while the Belgians have seen their capital of $155,000,000 dwindle to about one-half that sum.    The absence of foreign capital has practically stopped the usual channels of credit, while the absence of large Government orders for rails and public works has tended to keep the industries of the country in a state of stagnation that has become more or less chronic.

### IRON INDUSTRY.

The iron trade seems to have suffered the most, and at a meeting of persons connected with this interest, which was held in Kharkof last fall, under the auspices of the minister of finance, the conclusion reached was that the depressed condition of the trade was due to overproduction, the dearth of Government orders for public works, and the competition of foreign countries.    The only remedy, in their opinion, was to raise still further the import duties.    The minister of finance, however, declined to entertain that proposal, and pointed out that a protective tariff did not exist to protect special industries to an extent which would artificially raise the price of the articles manufactured above the possibility of competition.

According to an official report just issued by the chamber of commerce at Kharkof, the quantities of iron and steel, cast iron, coal, and coke produced during the first six months of 1902 were as follows: Iron and steel, 630,000 tons (in 1901, 586,000 tons); cast iron, 810,000 tons (in 1901, 800,000 tons); coal, 5,500,000 tons (in 1901, 6,400,000 tons); coke, 1,044,000 tons (in 1901, 1,134,000 tons). Four of 18 large collieries have been closed, owing to the decreased demand for coal. Seven of the blast furnaces have also been damped down, leaving 56 in operation. During the six months under review, more than 20,000 work people were discharged. There seems to be at present no prospect of an improvement in the mining or other metal industries of southern Russia. The state of affairs in the other great coal and iron regions of Ekaterinoslav and the Don district is also very depressed.

### PLAGUE AT ODESSA.

The first cases of plague at Odessa in 1902 were in the month of June and the last in October. Forty-nine cases were diagnosed as bubonic plague, and of these 16 died. The advent of this disease, even in its present mild form, had a bad effect on the business world of Odessa. Passenger traffic, both by sea and land, fell off largely, and many local residents left with the intention of not returning.

How the disease entered the city is not known. The local authorities grappled with the trouble in a manner most vigorous. The cases reported were confined solely to the poorer classes, and were found in the parts of the city where the sanitary conditions were least satisfactory. Many of the persons taken ill lived in basements below the level of the streets; and it is the opinion here that these cases were caused by rats. Cultures were developed of that form of typhus fever which is particularly fatal to these rodents and distributed in the cellar and courtyard of every house in Odessa. The entire city was thoroughly cleaned and disinfected. In one locality where the plague seemed to have gained a strong hold, a row of houses was burned down and the owners compensated by the Government. The city authorities declared that they had no money to fight the plague, and St. Petersburg was appealed to for assistance. A grant of 500,000 roubles was placed in the hands of the prefect-general, Count Schouvaloff, by the central Government, and it is a pleasure to state that the money has been well and satisfactorily expended. The mortality at Odessa has never been so low as during the present year, and many people here regard the plague in anything but an alarming light. One authority places the number of rats in Odessa at 20,000,000. Many of these, however, are known to have left the city, as villages and towns many miles from Odessa complain that large numbers of rats have arrived there.

##### ODESSA'S EXPORTS DURING THE FIRST HALF YEAR 1902 (IN TONS OF 2,000 POUNDS.)

Wheat, 301,796; rye, 86,832; corn, 587,953; barley, 83,770; oats, 19,349; potatoes, 673; siftings, 454; beans, 948; pease, 536; French beans, 548; flour, 13,677; bran, 9,542; hemp seed, 675; oil cake, 19,149; sugar, 6,085; raisins, 1,497; wood, 77,160; dry wood, 135; butter, 54; tallow, 420; lentils, 265; rape seed, 265; wool, 10; fish, 8; caviar, 9;

tea, 207; cotton seed, 229; straw, 46; cockle seed, 303; buckwheat, 960; linseed, 106; charcoal, 28; fowls (in number), 187,250; oxen, 990; horses, 320; alcohol (proof), 526,500 gallons.

THOS. E. HEENAN, *Consul.*

ODESSA, *November 30, 1902.*

## RIGA.

The year on record was not prosperous; as in the previous one, strong depression prevailed in almost all business branches. Some enterprises have had to stop work entirely, and numerous factories have been obliged to reduce hours of labor, owing especially to the unprecedented stagnation in the wood trade, which was formerly of importance in Riga's exports. Sea freights dropped during the latter half of the year to a minimum not known for years.

### TRADE WITH THE UNITED STATES.

Almost all American goods arriving here have been transshipped at some European port, to which they are credited by the customs. It is accordingly impossible to ascertain whether new lines of import have been opened or to register the fluctuations in branches already existing. The latter articles embrace, principally, machines, agricultural implements, tools, hardware, lard, rosin, tobacco, etc. Imports of agricultural machines have increased during the year. The public has gradually learned to appreciate the superiority of American patterns. The well-known firm of McCormick has during the year on record opened sale and store rooms in this city.

As regards rosin, the larger part of the quantity imported (a total of 4,200 tons) is of American origin. The French article, formerly preferred on account of its good qualities, has become too expensive.

American coal, I am sorry to say, has not as yet found a market here. It is to be hoped that our exporters will try to get their coal introduced (even if in the commencement they have to work without much profit) before a further development of Russian railways allows native coal to compete in this part of the Empire.

The export to the United States is principally represented by flax, hemp, rubber waste, and skins; other articles of lesser importance are albumen, Hebrew books and ritual goods, horsehair, liquor, etc. The value of the declared exports amounted for the year on record to $392,068, against $394,109 in 1900. In this total, the four principal articles participated in the following proportion:

| | 1900. | 1901. | | 1900. | 1901. |
|---|---|---|---|---|---|
| Flax.......................... | $3,898 | $7,771 | Rubber waste................. | $221,317 | $101,168 |
| Hemp ........................ | 7,512 | 28,347 | Skins .......................... | 98,051 | 207,658 |

The corresponding figures for the first three quarters of 1902 are:

| | | | |
|---|---|---|---|
| Flax......................... | $138,254 | Rubber waste.................. | $61,743 |
| Hemp ...................... | 16,552 | Skins.......................... | 378,555 |

To judge by this, the exports for the current year will reach a considerably higher figure than in the preceding 12 months; they amount already to more than $600,000.

The trade balance for the year on record is far from satisfactory. The value of the goods imported through this port, viz, $25,920,000, shows a decrease of $4,258,000 and $6,708,000 as compared with the figures for 19 0 and 1899, respectively. The export returns, viz, $38,099,700, are more favorable, showing an increase of $500,000 as compared with the foregoing year. Considering the falling off in such branches as cereals, wood, seeds, etc., this result is explicable only through the very considerable development of the butter export.

In this connection, I would call attention to the rapid progress in commercial activity of the neighboring port of Windau, due principally to the circumstance of its being almost free of ice during the winter. For the present, however, its importance is largely confined to the winter trade, but it may later on, thanks to good railway connections with the interior, take a more prominent rank among Baltic ports.

*Cereals.*—In this branch the figures have fallen notably, indicating that the importance of Riga in the grain trade is declining. With the exception of oats, the export of which exceeds that for 1900 by about 16,500 tons, these articles show a total loss of 32,130 tons, viz:

|  | 1901. | Less exports. |
|---|---|---|
|  | *Tons.* | *Tons.* |
| Rye | 73,680 | 20,423 |
| Barley | 17,280 | 1,267 |
| Wheat | 31,750 | 10,450 |

*Seeds (linseed and hemp).*—The decrease during the year on record amounts to 32,000 tons.

*Woods (of different kinds).*—Only 39,850,000 cubic feet was exported, representing a decline of about 7,000,000 feet as compared with the average for the last quinquennial. This is due to less demand on the international market.

*Flax.*—The export—viz, 45,500 tons—is not much less than that of the foregoing year, and Riga maintains its supremacy in this trade among the ports of the Empire.

*Hemp.*—In this line also, Riga takes the first place among Russian ports; 9,180 tons have been shipped, against 6,254 tons in 1900. This is the highest figure reached in this trade since the year 1892, and it represents 22 per cent of the total Russian hemp export. It must not be forgotten, however, that 60 per cent of this export passes over the land frontier.

A considerable increase is also to be noted in oil cakes (16,000 tons more than in 1900), hides and skins, venison, flax tow, peas, etc.

*Eggs.*—This trade, in which Riga takes first rank among Russian ports, is continually increasing. The export has gone up from 31,454 tons in 1900 to 35,100 tons, which is 3,000 tons more than the highest figure hitherto registered, viz, for 1899. Riga's share in the total Russian egg export represents 26¼ per cent. It must be noted that more than a third of the total export passes over the western land frontier and more than 20 per cent over the other land frontiers.

*Butter.*—This branch has attained great development, thanks to the establishment, in 1900, of a fast steamship line between this port and London, the principal market. During the spring of the year on record, a refrigerating establishment was opened in this city, which will further extend this trade. The exports from Riga amounted to:

|  | Tons. |
|---|---|
| 1899 | 277 |
| 1900 | 1,314 |
| 1901 | 12,242 |

The last figure has almost been reached already in the current year. Riga distanced Reval in 1901 by more than 500 tons. This last port has hitherto held the supremacy in this trade. Riga's share of the total Russian butter export has gone up from 7 per cent in 1900 to 40 per cent in 1901, while Reval's export has in the same period fallen from 49 per cent to 38 per cent.

### IMPORTS.

Coals and coke have gone down to 369,700 tons and 14,625 tons from 513,326 tons and 21,700 tons, respectively, in 1900. This very considerable decrease is in no way attributable to enlarged competition on the part of Russian coal, but to the industrial crisis and also to the presence of stocks of fuel in the factories. A rise in this branch is expected.

*Machinery.*—Agricultural machines have (as already mentioned) been imported in greater numbers than during 1900, which, in connection with the increased import of artificial manure, phosphate, etc., indicates that agriculture has prospered more than other industries. The import of machines for industrial purposes has gone down to 5,200 tons from 8,115 in 1900.

A decrease is also to be noted in the import of cast iron and steel, due principally to the competition of the Russian product, the quality of which has been gradually improving.

*Raw cotton.*—The figures were 8,240 tons, against 5,030 tons in 1900. Other branches showing a decline are: Dyewood, rice, herring, chalk, and copra.

A gain is noticed in corkwood, metallic ore, india rubber, soda, etc.

No sensible amelioration in trade and industry had been noticed in 1902, nor will the year be accounted a good one for navigation. Since the opening of navigation, at the end of April, sea freights have been extremely low.

During the past year, this port was visited by 1,839 ships, measuring 1,068,776 registered tons, of which 1,525 were steamers, measuring 999,318 registered tons. Compared with the year 1900, these figures represent a loss of 57 ships and 21,932 registered tons.

H. Doc. 305, pt 2——40

According to nationality, the ships may be classed as follows:

| | | | |
|---|---|---|---|
| Russian | 607 | Belgian | 6 |
| German | 418 | French | 2 |
| Swedish | 164 | British | 279 |
| Norwegian | 98 | Spanish | 6 |
| Danish | 243 | Brazilian | 1 |
| Dutch | 15 | | |

The Stars and Stripes, I am sorry to say, were not seen in this port in 1901.

NIL BORNHOLDT, Consul.

RIGA, *October 24, 1902.*

---

# SPAIN.

### REPORT FROM CONSULATE-GENERAL AT BARCELONA.

A glance at the résumé of the trade statistics of Spain's foreign commerce for 1901 shows a falling off in the value, both of the exports and the imports, as compared with the two preceding years.

The total value of the imports during 1901 amounted to $120,968,135, as against $124,972,276 during 1900 and $136,308,214 during 1899. The exports during 1901 amounted to a declared value of $98,867,226, being $8,788,416 less than in 1900 and $10,874,267 less than in 1899. Spain thus continues to import more than she exports, although with her large natural resources, this ought not to be the case. This unfavorable balance may be seen by the following figures:

| Description. | 1899 | 1900 | 1901 |
|---|---|---|---|
| Imports | $136,308,214 | $124,972,276 | $120,968,135 |
| Exports | 109,741,493 | 107,655,642 | 98,867,226 |
| Difference | 26,566,721 | 17,316,684 | 22,100,909 |

### IMPORTS.

During last year, the imports of raw materials increased from $59,613,191 (their declared value in 1900) to $63,045,772. The imports of coal increased from 1,794,119 tons to 1,955,641, valued at $10,252,109 and $11,175,098, respectively. The value of raw cotton entered during 1901 was $14,051,314, as compared with $11,821,366 during 1900. The value of staves and lumber imported during 1900 was $1,874,493 and $6,001,023, while the corresponding figures for last year were $1,985,843 and $6,045,074. The imports of manufactured goods show a falling off from $44,672,645 in 1900 to $37,320,901 during last year. This decline is attributable to a marked decrease in the importation of iron and steel manufactures, cotton yarns and textiles, linen and hemp yarns and textiles, engines and boilers, machinery, and iron and steel built vessels. Food stuffs show a slight decline of $573,655.

The statistics of the imports of wheat during the past three years were:

WHEAT.

| From— | 1899. | 1900. | 1901. |
|---|---|---|---|
| United States | $943,497 | $164,339 | $451,791 |
| France | 1,814,614 | 63,314 | 55,241 |
| Roumania | | 576,909 | 238,982 |
| Russia | 4,444,356 | 3,606,950 | 2,625,051 |
| Other countries | 6,496,124 | 2,744,292 | 1,415,843 |
| Total | 13,700,591 | 7,155,804 | 4,786,908 |

WHEAT FLOUR.

| | 1899 | 1900 | 1901 |
|---|---|---|---|
| Germany | $3,326 | $455 | $249 |
| Austria | 9 | | |
| Belgium | 18,513 | 4,157 | |
| France | 850,793 | 195,493 | 41,362 |
| Other countries | 171,067 | 90,711 | 98,752 |
| Total | 1,043,708 | 290,816 | 135,363 |

Other cereals, however, show an increase of $240,000. The articles of food of which the importation has also increased during the past year are canned meats, codfish, fresh and salted fish, cocoa beans, and coffee, cheese, preserves, and sparkling wines.

EXPORTS.

Turning to the statistics of the export trade during 1901, we find a falling off in the total figures under each of the three heads raw materials, manufactures, and food stuffs. Raw materials decreased from $44,546,158 in 1899 and $42,430,769 in 1900 to $41,124,662 in 1901, due in a great measure to the declining exports of minerals. Iron ore figures in 1899 for $14,765,377, while in the following year the exports fell to $13,411,320, and to $12,801,111 last year.

Spain continues to be the principal supplier of lead to the United Kingdom. During 1901, 99,147 tons were shipped, as against 87,873 in 1900 and 99,422 in 1899. The shipments to other countries, however, declined, so that the total exports of lead during 1901 were 148,492 tons, against 153,938 tons the year before.

The exports of cotton manufactures were:

| Description. | 1899. | 1900. | 1901. |
|---|---|---|---|
| White cotton tissues | $1,126,153 | $847,936 | $696,450 |
| Dyed or printed tissues | 3,023,975 | 2,514,920 | 2,303,867 |
| Hosiery | 1,552,087 | 1,502,415 | 1,142,704 |
| Total | 5,702,215 | 4,865,271 | 4,143,021 |

Copper, antimony, and manganese have all followed the same course. Wool, on the other hand, was exported in 1900 to the value of $1,147,610, and increased during 1901 to $1,476,984.

In manufactured goods, the total exports for 1901 were valued at $21,301,435, as compared with $24,441,625 during 1900, showing a decrease of $3,140,190. White cotton textiles have contributed to this decline to the extent of $151,486. Silks and velvet show a slight improvement, though silk laces have fallen off by about $7,000. Hand-made linen lace was exported during 1901 to the value of $26,325, as against $5,600 in 1900.

Common soap, which is largely exported from Barcelona to Cuba and South America, figures in the official statistics for 1901 for a total of 7,638 tons, valued at $567,454, as compared with 6,106 tons, valued at $453,631, in 1900.

The exports of wax and stearin candles have been well maintained. In 1899, the declared value was $146,258; in 1900, $256,752, and in 1901, $255,904. The trade in cut corks with foreign countries has somewhat decreased, while the shipments of cork in bulk have advanced, as the following table will show:

| Description. | 1899. | 1900. | 1901. |
|---|---|---|---|
| Cork slabs...................................tons.. | $3,652 | $3,540 | $3,913 |
| Cork cut in squares ...........................M.. | 79,630 | 94,141 | 54,487 |
| Cut corks to France ...........................M.. | 1,366,902 | 1,683,200 | 1,617,902 |
| Cut corks to other countries....................M.. | 711,859 | 1,655,546 | 882,541 |
| Cork in other form..........................tons.. | 1,238 | 3,027 | 4,445 |

Food stuffs show a shrinkage in the exports of $4,450,325 between 1900 and 1901, the figures being $37,803,995 and $33,353,670, respectively. Common red wines, which in 1900 were exported to the value of $10,923,131, in the following year only reached $6,411,634. Sherry wines fell from $760,754 to $126,908. On the other hand, what are known as generous wines improved from $74,577 to $163,939.

The following table gives the quantities in gallons:

| Countries. | 1899. | 1900. | 1901. |
|---|---|---|---|
| Common wines exported to— | *Gallons.* | *Gallons.* | *Gallons.* |
| France ......................................... | 76,078,618 | 56,165,516 | 22,044,110 |
| England........................................ | 4,115,078 | 4,996,046 | 3,427,188 |
| Rest of Europe and Africa..................... | 8,586,066 | 6,620,064 | 8,912,442 |
| Cuba and Porto Rico.......................... | 6,138,682 | 5,957,314 | 6,260,606 |
| Rest of America............................... | 10,151,768 | 9,511,876 | 8,142,266 |
| Asia and Oceania ............................. | 449,570 | 857,296 | 583,022 |
| Total ..................................... | 105,469,782 | 84,108,112 | 49,369,584 |
| Sherry wines exported to— | | | |
| France ......................................... | 256,960 | 357,280 | 30,052 |
| England........................................ | 512,270 | 451,528 | 90,222 |
| Rest of Europe and Africa..................... | 218,190 | 127,754 | 25,718 |
| Cuba and Porto Rico.......................... | 1,320 | 770 | 1,254 |
| Rest of America............................... | 23,628 | 23,628 | 12,672 |
| Asia and Oceania ............................. | 10,230 | 15,334 | 2,948 |
| Total ..................................... | 1,022,538 | 976,294 | 162,866 |
| Exports of generous wines to— | | | |
| France ......................................... | 306,878 | 52,954 | 42,680 |
| England........................................ | 29,304 | 2,046 | 118,602 |
| Rest of Europe and Africa..................... | 204,468 | 19,074 | 80,080 |
| Cuba and Porto Rico .......................... | 19,206 | 4,590 | 10,912 |
| Rest of America............................... | 128,458 | 88,638 | 129,910 |
| Asia and Oceania ............................. | 1,826 | 6,330 | 6,226 |
| Total ..................................... | 690,140 | 176,682 | 388,410 |

Canned fruits and vegetables show a slight improvement (of $323,499) over the returns for 1900, when the amount exported was valued at

$2,472,235. In this branch of trade the cheapness of the products of the soil, coupled with low-priced labor, are factors that go far to aid Spain in her efforts to extend her export trade. The shipments of oranges during 1901 reached a total value of $6,689,230, as compared with $5,576,265 in 1900. Grapes also improved—from $1,316,641 in 1900 to $1,521,549—while raisins dropped from $3,414,003 to $2,958,798.

## SUGAR.

As was foreshadowed in my last annual report, the sugar industry in Spain has been obliged to curtail its output. During the year 1901, Spain produced 28,000 tons of cane sugar and 50,500 of beet sugar, being a decrease of about 5,000 tons of cane sugar and 1,160 tons of beet sugar, as compared with the figures for the preceding year. Considerable stocks have had to be carried over to next season.

## HONEY.

Apiculture is extensively carried on in this country, and though the methods in vogue may be somewhat primitive, it is calculated that there are no less than 1,700,000 hives in Spain, which produce about 19,000 tons of honey and wax annually.

## LUBRICATING OILS.

The declared value of the imports into Spain of lubricating oils, etc., is given as follows: 1899, $260,553; 1900, $266,792; 1901, $370,013. Unfortunately, though imports have increased, the arrivals from the United States have steadily fallen off, owing to the differential tariff, which makes it impossible for our lubricating oils to compete with the Russian product in this market.

The latter are charged a duty of 50 pesetas ($7.50) per 100 kilos (220.4 pounds), while American oils have to pay 60 pesetas ($9) per 100 kilos, or approximately three times the value of the goods themselves, placed free on board at New York. When, as is the case this season, the olive-oil crop is abundant, the sale of foreign oils is rendered very difficult.

## PARAFFIN.

The same remarks as to the high rate of duty charged are applicable to paraffin, which pays 48 pesetas ($7.20) per 100 kilos (220.4 pounds) when imported from the United States and 40 pesetas ($6) when brought from Great Britain. In order to compete with the British sellers, our principal exporters to Spain have been obliged to allow their Spanish buyers a bonus equivalent to the difference in duty, and by this means they have been able to increase their sales here from 457,844 kilos (451 tons) in 1900 to 780,737 kilos (769 tons) in 1901.

The average value of the paraffin imported is not more than the amount of the duty charged. Prior to 1900, the rate was 24 pesetas ($3.60) per 100 kilos on United States paraffin and 20 pesetas ($3) on the British product, but in order to favor the local stearin manufacturers, the tariff was altered and the duty doubled.

Trade relations between the United States and Spain have recovered the position they held before the war; in fact, during the last calendar year the imports from the United States were in excess of those of any other year excepting 1883, aggregating a declared value of several million dollars over those for the years 1899 or 1900.

The exports from Spain also show an improvement over the figures for preceding years. From January 1 to June 30, 1901, Spain imported from the United States $8,988,970 worth of goods, as against $8,189,188 during the same period of the year before, an increase of $799,782; while the exports from Spain are valued at $3,110,718, as compared with $2,875,840 during the first six months of 1900.

During July, 1901, the imports from the United States amounted to $1,156,490, being an increase of $515,801 over those for July, 1900, while the exports from Spain rose from $270,246 in July, 1900, to $634,665 in July of last year.

Of course, the bulk of our exports to Spain is still composed of raw materials, such as cotton, staves, and lumber, but our machine manufacturers are making most encouraging progress in this country and everything points to a steadily increasing sale of American articles.

Spain's exports to the United States are confined principally to fruit and iron ore, and the total declared value is given as $5,409,301 for the last twelve months; the imports from our country during the same period being valued at $15,484,738, against $13,339,680 during the preceding year. Detailed particulars of these totals are not yet available, but the increase in the imports is attributed in a great measure to the larger consumption of cotton—always a healthy sign, as indicating a certain prosperity in the cotton industries of this country.

### MINES IN CATALONIA.

The Government has published some interesting data regarding the mining industry in Spain during 1900. I abstract the following with reference to the principality of Catalonia. In the province of Barcelona, mining is confined to coal, salt, and a small quantity of fluorspar. The salt mines of Cardona, which belong to the Duchess of Denia, gave employment during 1900 to 37 men and 8 boys, and the output amounted to 2,900 tons, valued at 20 pesetas ($3) per ton, which was 300 tons less than the previous year. The coal mines in this neighborhood produced 13,317 tons of screened coal and 23,379 tons of small coal. In the province of Gerona, which lies on the slopes of the Pyrenees, there are 23 mines producing different minerals, the output for the year being 515 tons of arsenic, 195 tons of sulphate of barium, 7,609 tons of steatite, 31,593 tons of coal, 57 tons of lignite, and 246 tons of lead.

The wages paid are the following: Men working under ground, 3.59 pesetas (50 cents); above ground, 2.75 pesetas (39 cents) and 3.10 pesetas (44 cents). Boys under ground, 2 pesetas (28 cents); outside, 1.75 pesetas (25 cents) to 1.93 pesetas (28 cents).

· Nearly all the coal extracted belonged to the mines owned by the railroad company, and was devoted to the manufacture of briquettes, or patent fuel.

Considerable activity has been shown lately in this district, and many of the concessions which have proved unremunerative are now being taken up by new companies in the hope of better success. Chief among these are some auriferous, arsenical, and galena mines, now being worked at a point some 12 miles distant from the town of Ripoll. The claim covers a surface of over 16,000 acres, and, being backed by ample capital, the enterprise is already proving a signal success.

Smelting works have been erected on the seashore in the outskirts of Barcelona, and an extensive plant has also been put up in Barcelona for treating the copper, arsenic, lead, and silver ores obtained from the mines. The chemical and engineering departments of the company are at present under the management of Englishmen. Not only are arsenical pyrites obtained, but the galena ore contains an average of 53 per cent of lead, 60 ounces of silver, and twelve pennyweights of gold to the ton; also, copper ore of about 23 per cent of copper and 20 pennyweights of gold to the ton. Hydraulic cement is produced to the extent of 100,000 tons per annum.

In the province of Lerida, one mine was worked for copper, two for coal, two for lead and zinc, and one for common salt. During the year, 1,050 tons of zinc were extracted, 203 tons of copper, 10,069 tons of lignite, and 3 tons of salt—the latter being restricted to a very limited market.

The province of Tarragona, which forms the remaining district of Catalonia, is given up more to agriculture than to mining. There are, however, four lead mines, which in 1900 produced 1,148 tons of metal, and one sulphate of barium mine, from which 388 tons were obtained.

## HARBOR IMPROVEMENTS.

The work of enlarging and improving the harbor of Barcelona has been actively carried on during the past year. Some of the existing quays are being widened, and large, substantial sheds built upon them, where merchandise can be stored under cover. The plans have been prepared for extending the outer mole for a distance of 4,300 feet in a straight line, almost parallel with the shore, and for constructing others with a view to forming a large outer harbor, that will very materially add to the security of the vessels moored alongside the quays in the present port.

Negotiations are still pending looking to the establishment of a free zone in connection with the harbor, as described in my last annual report, but nothing has as yet been carried into effect.

Hopes are entertained that, after overcoming innumerable obstacles, the large floating dock which has been in course of construction for years will soon be completed and brought into use.

The Barcelona floating coal depot was formally inaugurated on May 2, and is now in complete working order. The hulk, besides being fitted with an ordinary winch with its donkey boiler, has been supplied with one of Grafton's locomotive cranes, which runs on steel rails laid down on the deck, enabling the crane to move by its own machinery from one hold to the other. The coal is raised in steel buckets holding half a ton, and as the crane can without difficulty discharge at the rate of one bucket per minute, when both winch and crane are used at the same time it will be seen that a steamer coming alongside can have her bunkers filled at the rate of 60 tons per hour. Already some 30 or 40 vessels have coaled from the floating depot. The present price for best Welsh coal is 22 shillings ($5.35) per ton f. o. b., if the steamer moors alongside the hulk, or 23 shillings ($5.60) per ton if delivered by lighters.

American vessels visiting Barcelona and requiring to replenish their bunkers should not fail to take advantage of this addition to the harbor improvements.

## FOREIGN TRADE OF SPAIN DURING FIRST FOUR MONTHS OF 1902.

For the first four months of this year, the official returns are more favorable than those of the corresponding months of previous years.

| Description. | 1900. | 1901. | 1902. |
|---|---|---|---|
| IMPORTS. | | | |
| Raw materials | $19,622,586 | $22,080,401 | $21,208,528 |
| Manufactures | 15,169,308 | 13,341,290 | 12,226,326 |
| Food stuffs | 6,483,682 | 7,048,604 | 4,939,012 |
| Total | 41,275,576 | 42,415,295 | 38,368,866 |
| EXPORTS. | | | |
| Raw materials | 13,490,888 | 12,427,968 | 13,918,490 |
| Manufactures | 7,595,694 | 6,747,701 | 5,697,305 |
| Food stuffs | 14,632,475 | 10,061,882 | 12,622,573 |
| Total | 35,719,057 | 29,237,551 | 32,238,368 |

Although the balance is still against the trade of this country, the imports being considerably in excess of the exports, a marked improvement in the relative figures will be noticed.

During the first four months of 1902, Spain was able to reduce her imports of food stuffs by $2,104,592, as compared with the corresponding period of last year. The import of wheat fell from 84,000 tons and 51,000 tons during the past two years to less than 14,000 tons up to the end of April of this year. Of maize, too, Spain has been able to reduce her requirements from abroad from nearly 26,000 tons last year to less than 6,000 this year. This is due to the favorable crops in this country.

The imports of coal, raw cotton, industrial starch, cocoa beans, etc., which are needed for the industries of the country, are all increasing, which is a satisfactory sign.

During the first four months of 1901, eight iron and steel built ships were brought under the Spanish flag, representing a tonnage of over 6,000 and a value of about $400,000.

With regard to exports, minerals have increased considerably, while white cotton goods have fallen off. Such goods as plain linen textiles, cotton hosiery, and woolen goods, especially blankets, show a slight improvement. Bottle corks continue to fall, though a marked increase is reported in the exports during April as compared with the same month in 1900.

Esparto grass, sheepskins, boots and shoes, hams, brined meat, bacon, fish, fresh fruit, and olive oil show an increase in the quantity exported, while the exports of olive oil are double what they were last year.

The unfavorable returns of the exports of wine continue, the total quantity sent out of the country barely reaching the value of $2,000,000.

## TRADE BETWEEN SPAIN AND CUBA.

As was to be expected, trade between Spain and her late chief dependency is a diminishing quantity. From July 1, 1899, to June 30, 1900, the exports to Cuba amounted to $11,387,658 and the imports to $1,006,546. In the following twelve months, the figures were, respectively, $10,268,232 and $579,302, a decrease in the exports of $1,119,426 and in the imports of $427,244.

The details of the above returns are shown below:

*Exports from Spain to Cuba from July 1, 1900, to June 30, 1901.*

| | | | |
|---|---|---|---|
| Books and other printed matter | $144,265 | Paints and colors | $26,352 |
| Paper | 516,998 | Margarine | 64,642 |
| Prepared raw cotton | 14,476 | Lard | 44,596 |
| Biscuits | 7,449 | Cheese | 11,763 |
| Vermicelli | 7,436 | Common soap | 381,910 |
| Candles | 296,426 | Wine (about) | 4,000,000 |
| Crockery | 66,881 | Furniture | 36,006 |
| Clothes | 142,266 | Fans | 20,034 |
| Cotton tissues of all kinds | 1,418,804 | Ropes and twine | 251,649 |
| Silk tissues | 78,091 | Cutlery | 2,009 |
| Woolen tissues | 136,818 | Cigars | 374,668 |
| Boots and shoes | 2,987,070 | Cocoa | 51,788 |
| Leather goods | 89,199 | Coffee | 1,323 |
| Jewelry | 5,941 | Wax | 56 |
| Perfumery | 1,325 | Rum | 2,829 |
| | | Lumber | 27,348 |

## EDUCATION IN SPAIN.

A few remarks on educational facilities may not be out of place in a commercial report. There are in Spain 10 universities, viz, those of Madrid, Barcelona, Valencia, Seville, Saragossa, Granada, Valladolid, Santiago, Oviedo, and Salamanca, besides 49 institutes, one in each province. These are all maintained by the State. There are also in some of the principal cities State schools of commerce and schools for agricultural engineering and public works. Every village has its State school with free education, but the teachers are paid only a small salary, ranging from $12 to $26 per month, while in some parts of Spain even these pittances are months in arrears.

The proportion of illiterates in the country, i. e., those who can not either read or write, is 75 per cent of the entire population.

*Technical education.*—Since the loss of the colonies, the press has made an effort to call public attention to the lack of any proper means of technical education in this country, but so far nothing appears to have been done to remedy this serious hindrance to the advancement of Spain's commerce and industries. It is true that some religious orders have established small technical schools for the laboring classes, but their scope is very limited, so that practically there are no industrial schools in Spain, or any means whereby artisans can obtain the knowledge necessary to enable them to command higher wages.

## COST OF LIVING.

The cost of living, especially in the large towns, is steadily and rapidly increasing; this naturally affects the laboring classes seriously and is, no doubt, the primary origin of the many strikes that are perpetually disturbing the relations between capital and labor.  The depreciation in the value of Spanish currency encourages the exportation of cattle, with a consequent rise in the price of meat; this is the case also in regard to market produce and food stuffs in general.  Considerable quantities of live stock are imported from the north coast of Africa, and some consignments of cattle from the Argentine Republic have also been made, but have resulted in loss to the senders, owing to the heavy expenses at this end.  Meat, as a rule, is of poor quality, and is sold at a high price.  A French firm of butchers has for some years been doing a prosperous trade in Barcelona by providing a better quality of meat than can be purchased elsewhere, and selling it at a slightly higher price.  The meat is kept in refrigerators, which is not done by most dealers.

The question of importing frozen or rather chilled meat in refrigerator ships has been mooted, but no steps have yet been taken to carry it into effect, no refrigerator cars or means of storage being available.  Here, it would seem, is a field for any enterprising concern willing to face some initial difficulties and possible loss, as ultimate success appears all but certain.  It would be necessary to undertake the business on a large scale, and to avoid opposition it would be advisable to enter into relations with the established purveyors.  I should mention that a cold-storage company is already in contemplation in Madrid, and some negotiations have taken place with a view to interesting the Barcelona dealers in the scheme for the purpose of combined action in the matter.

### USE OF ELECTRICITY.

At the end of last year, there were 859 electric works in Spain, of which 648 were for providing electricity to the municipalities of the different towns.  The following is a list of the number in each province:

| | | | |
|---|---|---|---|
| Gerona | 59 | Palencia | 12 |
| Vizcaya | 54 | Leon | 12 |
| Navarra | 47 | Guadalajara | 11 |
| Valencia | 42 | Murcia | 11 |
| Guipuzcoa | 40 | Salamanca | 11 |
| Alicante | 35 | Santander | 11 |
| Madrid | 33 | Caceres | 10 |
| Oviedo | 30 | Soria | 10 |
| Lerida | 27 | Coruña | 10 |
| Zaragoza | 27 | Huesca | 9 |
| Logroño | 25 | Tarragona | 9 |
| Badajoz | 23 | Beleares | 8 |
| Granada | 22 | Castellon | 8 |
| Barcelona | 21 | Pontevedra | 8 |
| Burgos | 20 | Zamora | 8 |
| Cordoba | 19 | Albacete | 8 |
| Cadiz | 18 | Huelva | 7 |
| Sevilla | 18 | Almeria | 6 |
| Valladolid | 17 | Cuenca | 6 |
| Alava | 16 | Avila | 5 |
| Jaen | 15 | Canarias | 5 |
| Malaga | 14 | Lugo | 5 |
| Toledo | 14 | Segovia | 4 |
| Ciudad Real | 13 | Orense | 3 |
| Teruel | 13 | | |

The total number of incandescent lights in public use was 87,112, representing 1,012,945 candlepower, and 1,740 arc lights of 1,136,590 candlepower; while in private houses there were 1,237,836 incandescent lamps of 39,640,641 candlepower, and 2,819 arc lights of 1,292,425 candlepower, a total of 1,329,237 lamps and 43,082,601 candlepower. The streets of Madrid are lighted by 206 arc lights of 155,000 candlepower and 100 incandescent lamps of 500 candlepower, but in private use there are 478,828 incandescent lights of 4,535,626 candlepower and 431 arc lights of 246,652 candlepower. Barcelona follows, with 138 arc lamps of 207,000 candlepower and 30,000 incandescent lamps of 300,000 candlepower, and 886 arc lamps of 265,800 candlepower in private use. Seville has 26,357 incandescent lights of 263,570 candlepower and 313 arc lights of 250,000 candlepower in private use only. The town using most electric light in proportion to the number of its inhabitants is Malaga, which boasts 7 incandescent lamps of 112 candlepower and 39 arc lamps of 40,200 candlepower for the lighting of the town, and 33,208 incandescent lamps of 274,996 candlepower with 275 arc lamps of 191,000 candlepower for use in private houses. The highest prices charged are in the towns of Avila and Leon, where each 10-candlepower lamp costs 5 pesetas (75 cents) per month. In Lugo, the charge is only 50 centimes (7½ cents) kilowatt hour; in Palencia, 65 centimes (9.7 cents); in Soria, 1.14 pesetas (17 cents) per month per 5-candlepower lamp; in Huesca and Logroño, 1.75 (26 cents) per 5-candlepower lamp.

In the other towns and villages, the price ranges from 2.50 pesetas (37½ cents) to 4 pesetas (60 cents) per 10-candlepower lamp; by kilowatt hour the usual price is 1 peseta (15 cents).

Incandescent electric lamps are not manufactured in Spain; a factory was started, but proved a failure and was obliged to liquidate; they are imported from Holland, France, and Austria. The makes chiefly imported are "Phillips," "La Constancia," and "Edison Swan."

The estimated annual consumption is about 100,000. They are usually imported either in small lots of 25 by mail, or in larger quantities, up to 5,000, sold c. i. f. Barcelona. The import duty on incandescent lamps is 20 centimes (3 cents) of a peseta per unit, and they are offered to the trade at 38 centimes (5.7 cents) of a franc gold, or 35 centimes (5.2 cents) per thousand. Unfortunately, the question of cost receives more consideration than that of quality, which is a point that our manufacturers should bear in mind, if they find that their offers are considered too high in this market.

## ELECTRIC TRAMWAYS.

In July last, a new line of tramway was opened from Barcelona to the outlying village of Horta, a distance of nearly 4 miles. The same company's main line, which has been running by steam for many years, is also being changed to electric traction, and will be in working order in a few months. The cars are fitted with two Thomson-Houston motors of 25 horsepower. The trucks were purchased in the United States, but the upper structures of the cars were built in Spain. The Barcelona Tramways Company is at present engaged in fitting the remaining section of its line for electric traction, and by the end of the year horse tramways will be entirely superseded.

A cable railway from the foot of the neighboring hill known as "Tibidabo" to its summit, 1,200 feet above the level of the sea, has been successfully inaugurated. The promoters of the scheme had previously purchased large tracts of ground on both sides of the pro- · posed line, and are now selling them at immense profit for building purposes. Electric cars carry passengers from all parts of the city to the foot of the mountain, from whose summit one of the finest panoramic views in Europe can be obtained.

### AUTOMOBILES.

Up to the present, American automobiles have not found any sale in this country. A few steam and electric cars are imported, but owing to the impossibility of recharging the accumulators (except in the large cities where electric works exist), electric automobiles are of little use here, while the steam motors have never found favor. Nearly all the cars imported are of French make, and are propelled by gasoline motors. Those most in vogue are of 6¼, 8, and 10 horsepower.

So far, "motoring" has been a recreation only of the wealthy, but trials have been made of running motor omnibuses between inland towns having no railroad communications, and it appears certain that ere long, and especially if their cost can be lowered, automobiles will be brought into more general use in Spain.

### SHOES.

Shoes are still being exported to Cuba; this is due to cheap labor and to knowledge of the wants of the people. Prices range from 2 pesetas (30 cents) upward. The upper leather is made from Calcutta kips tanned in Spain. The better qualities of handmade shoes are made from American, German, and French tanned leather, but these are not exported.

### LOOMS.

Looms, which were formerly exclusively imported from Great Britain, are now being made by local machinists. The latter are in a position to turn out 5,000 to 10,000 looms annually, the cost of which is as much as $10 cheaper than those imported from England; in the case of ordinary looms, $20 for drop-box looms, and $50 to $100 for sheeting looms.

### CHEMICALS.

The import returns for chemicals for 1901 show a considerable decrease as compared with the previous year. This is due to the higher prices ruling for these products, caustic soda and other alkaline articles being mainly affected. Feeling the loss of trade, manufacturers decided upon a reduction in prices, to come into force from the beginning of 1902, and the result has proved the wisdom of their decision, business having increased to a marked extent during the first six months of the present year. In imports of this class, the United States has not come to the fore as in other manufactures, and the figures to our credit are insignificant. Acetate of lime for the manufacture of acetic acid is being shipped from New York to makers in this country, and if prices of the acetate continue low, there is every prospect of increased business.

American sulphate of copper is also offered in this market, but does not meet with much favor, although the price is frequently below European figures. Whether this is owing to the lower strength of copper—buyers requiring a guaranty of 98 per cent minimum of pure copper—I have not been able to ascertain. Trade in this product from Great Britain has improved greatly during the past year, and British makers have been able to compete with the home manufacture, in spite of the duty and higher freights. For the present, Spain does not seem likely to be able to dispense with a foreign supply of chemicals, the coarser kinds being shipped from Great Britain, France, and Belgium, and Germany practically holding the monopoly of the finer kinds. A great bar to enterprise in this direction in Spain is the high price of fuel and the cost of transporting raw material. Since my last annual report, I have not found any published account of the electrolytic works therein referred to, but I understand they have made a shipment of their bleaching powder to the United States. It is stated that other chemical works will shortly be built at Figueras, a town in the province of Gerona. With better facilities for shipment, there is no reason why American manufacturers should not come directly into this market.

## COAL.

The total importation of coal into Barcelona during 1901 amounted to 746,566 tons, compared with 662,181 tons in 1900. The increase is due in a great measure to the larger imports from Great Britain, 590,767 tons of British coal having been received here during last year, against 510,505 during 1900. The arrivals of native coal increased by about 10,000 tons, but I regret to report that only 7,236 tons of American coal were imported during 1901, being a falling off of about 9,000 tons from the figures for the preceding year. This is due to the low price of English coal, coupled with the fact that the port dues on vessels from American ports are about 2½ pesetas (37 cents) per ton higher than on those from European ports. Another obstacle to business with the United States is that our sellers exact cash payment through a banker, whereas British firms accept payment by check at thirty days, less 2½ per cent discount, or draw on the buyers at ninety days net. This is a great advantage for coal merchants here, who are obliged to grant long credits to their customers.

The imports from different sources during 1901 were:

| | Tons. |
|---|---|
| Great Britain | 590,767 |
| Spain | 145,616 |
| United States | 7,236 |
| Belgium | 1,097 |
| Holland | 1,850 |
| Total | 746,566 |

JULIUS G. LAY,
*Consul-General.*

BARCELONA, *November 25, 1902.*

## SHIPPING AT THE PORT OF BARCELONA DURING THE YEAR 1901.

### ENTERED.

| Country. | Sailing. | | Steam. | | Total. | |
|---|---|---|---|---|---|---|
| | Number of vessels. | Tons. | Number of vessels. | Tons. | Number of vessels. | Tons. |
| Spain: | | | | | | |
| Coasting | 899 | 47,742 | 1,289 | 979,058 | 2,188 | 1,026,800 |
| Foreign | 57 | 14,106 | 672 | 663,678 | 729 | 677,784 |
| Great Britain | 1 | 145 | 237 | 268,275 | 238 | 268,420 |
| France | 9 | 814 | 75 | 70,051 | 84 | 70,865 |
| Italy | 95 | 29,943 | 190 | 302,927 | 281 | 332,870 |
| Germany | 28 | 27,742 | 62 | 61,208 | 87 | 88,950 |
| Norway and Sweden | 78 | 78,498 | 39 | 81,846 | 117 | 105,339 |
| Denmark | 3 | 259 | 16 | 10,568 | 19 | 10,827 |
| Russia | 2 | 869 | 25 | 18,898 | 27 | 19,762 |
| Greece | 6 | 1,318 | 18 | 22,494 | 24 | 23,812 |
| Austria-Hungary | 4 | 2,507 | 21 | 29,824 | 25 | 82,331 |
| Holland | | | 31 | 18,666 | 31 | 18,666 |
| Belgium | 1 | 1,631 | 1 | 1,500 | 2 | 3,131 |
| United States | | | 2 | 2,912 | 2 | 2,912 |
| Total, 1901 | 1,180 | 200,569 | 2,628 | 2,481,900 | 3,808 | 2,682,469 |
| Total, 1900 | 1,240 | 116,780 | 2,563 | 2,321,154 | 3,804 | 2,437,934 |

### CLEARED.

| Spain: | | | | | | |
|---|---|---|---|---|---|---|
| Coasting | 912 | 50,612 | 1,425 | 1,142,572 | 2,337 | 1,193,184 |
| Foreign | 37 | 9,156 | 645 | 636,452 | 682 | 645,608 |
| Great Britain | 1 | 145 | 234 | 265,951 | 235 | 266,096 |
| France | 9 | 814 | 75 | 70,051 | 84 | 70,865 |
| Italy | 95 | 29,943 | 190 | 302,927 | 285 | 332,870 |
| Germany | 25 | 27,742 | 62 | 61,208 | 87 | 88,950 |
| Norway and Sweden | 75 | 67,582 | 36 | 28,850 | 111 | 96,382 |
| Denmark | 2 | 165 | 15 | 9,952 | 17 | 10,117 |
| Russia | 2 | 869 | 25 | 18,898 | 27 | 19,762 |
| Austria-Hungary | 4 | 2,507 | 21 | 29,824 | 25 | 82,331 |
| Holland | | | 30 | 18,050 | 30 | 18,050 |
| Belgium | 1 | 1,631 | | | 1 | 1,631 |
| Greece | 6 | 1,318 | 18 | 22,494 | 24 | 23,812 |
| United States | | | 2 | 2,912 | 2 | 2,912 |
| Total, 1901 | 1,169 | 192,434 | 2,778 | 2,610,136 | 3,947 | 2,802,570 |
| Total, 1900 | 1,187 | 104,669 | 2,729 | 2,852,617 | 3,916 | 2,957,286 |

*Fluctuations in the rate of exchange on London and Paris during 1900 and 1901.*

| Month. | Francs on Paris. | | Pounds sterling on London. | |
|---|---|---|---|---|
| | 1900. | 1901. | 1900. | 1901. |
| January | 28.45 | 35.65 | 32.35 | 34.09 |
| February | 29.55 | 37.12 | 32.65 | 34.52 |
| March | 30.65 | 35.65 | 32.85 | 34.20 |
| April | 28.90 | 35.20 | 32.40 | 34.05 |
| May | 26.85 | 36.82 | 31.90 | 34.35 |
| June | 26.30 | 38.82 | 31.65 | 34.93 |
| July | 27.15 | 38.37 | 31.90 | 34.86 |
| August | 28.45 | 39.55 | 32.25 | 35.16 |
| September | 29.40 | 41.87 | 32.60 | 35.65 |
| October | 31.85 | 42.05 | 32.95 | 35.70 |
| November | 33.15 | 41.67 | 33.35 | 35.60 |
| December | 33.90 | 36.03 | 33.55 | 34.08 |
| Total | 354.60 | 458.80 | 390.40 | 417.19 |
| Average | 29.55 | 38.23 | 32.58 | 34.76 |

NOTE.—The figures in the case of the francs represent their percentage of premium on the value of the silver peseta, while in the case of the pound sterling they indicate the quoted value of the pound in silver pesetas.

*General commerce of Spain, 1901.*

IMPORTS.

| Description. | 1899. | 1900. | 1901. |
|---|---|---|---|
| | *Pesetas.* | *Pesetas.* | *Pesetas.* |
| Raw materials | 386,552,005 | 417,292,889 | 441,320,408 |
| Manufactured goods | 299,047,809 | 312,708,517 | 261,246,806 |
| Food stuffs | 194,755,078 | 139,238,586 | 136,222,950 |
| Total | 880,354,892 | 869,239,392 | 833,789,666 |
| Gold bullion and coin | 87,996,415 | 161,330 | 814,543 |
| Silver bullion and coin | 35,806,190 | 5,405,070 | 7,672,740 |
| Total | 954,157,497 | 874,805,792 | 846,776,949 |
| (United States currency) | $186,308,214 | $124,972,276 | $120,968,185 |

EXPORTS.

| | | | |
|---|---|---|---|
| Raw materials | 311,823,111 | 297,015,889 | 287,872,634 |
| Manufactured goods | 162,558,010 | 171,091,878 | 149,110,047 |
| Food stuffs | 279,168,717 | 264,627,966 | 233,475,688 |
| Total | 753,549,838 | 732,734,731 | 670,458,369 |
| Gold bullion and coin | 2,855,890 | 745,500 | 334,191 |
| Silver bullion and coin | 11,784,725 | 20,109,268 | 21,278,024 |
| Total | 768,190,453 | 753,589,499 | 692,070,584 |
| (United States currency) | $109,711,493 | $107,655,642 | $98,867,226 |

*Detailed commerce of Spain, 1901.*

IMPORTS.

| Article. | 1899. | 1900. | 1901. |
|---|---|---|---|
| Stones, earths, minerals, glassware, and ceramic products | $10,833,328 | $15,211,447 | $16,098,100 |
| Metals and manufactures in which metal is the chief compound | 3,974,985 | 6,549,998 | 4,993,145 |
| Drugs and chemical products | 10,727,616 | 10,905,731 | 11,428,127 |
| Cotton manufactures and raw cotton | 14,916,974 | 13,458,721 | 15,460,720 |
| Hemp, flax, jute, and other vegetable fibers and their manufactures | 4,106,089 | 3,003,525 | 3,342,354 |
| Wool and hair and their manufactures | 4,249,405 | 3,885,896 | 3,780,862 |
| Silk and its manufactures | 3,928,360 | 3,611,448 | 3,476,225 |
| Paper | 1,399,598 | 1,620,808 | 1,654,656 |
| Wood and its manufactures | 7,674,650 | 8,092,424 | 8,816,644 |
| Animals | 11,782,997 | 11,780,026 | 10,123,950 |
| Machinery | 14,561,519 | 19,314,026 | 13,936,276 |
| Foodstuffs | 28,578,574 | 19,891,219 | 19,817,564 |
| Sundry goods | 1,255,737 | 1,199,840 | 1,173,491 |
| Gold | 5,428,059 | 23,047 | 44,985 |
| Silver | 5,061,444 | 772,153 | 1,096,106 |
| Goods imported at reduced rates | 5,346,677 | 4,491,947 | 6,082,122 |
| Total | 133,790,912 | 124,972,256 | 120,825,277 |

EXPORTS.

| | | | |
|---|---|---|---|
| Stones, earths, minerals, glassware, and ceramic products | $22,541,868 | $22,732,062 | $21,471,216 |
| Metals, and manufactures in which metal is the chief compound | 14,575,569 | 14,488,901 | 14,130,389 |
| Drugs and chemical products | 3,250,660 | 2,879,272 | 2,950,271 |
| Cotton and its manufactures | 5,690,792 | 4,865,271 | 4,143,022 |
| Hemp, flax, jute, and other vegetable fibers and their manufactures | 333,563 | 186,957 | 131,781 |
| Wool and hair and their manufactures | 2,409,222 | 1,397,214 | 1,662,291 |
| Silk and its manufactures | 530,689 | 711,423 | 724,523 |
| Paper | 1,189,080 | 1,209,121 | 1,186,444 |
| Wood and its manufactures | 5,567,257 | 3,665,443 | 6,816,472 |
| Animals | 7,231,986 | 9,356,907 | 8,782,587 |
| Machinery | 104,543 | 113,279 | 113,903 |
| Food stuffs | 37,648,869 | 37,803,995 | 33,353,670 |
| Sundry goods | 438,877 | 266,544 | 313,247 |
| Gold | 406,832 | 106,500 | 47,742 |
| Silver | 1,634,351 | 2,872,753 | 3,089,718 |
| Total | 103,554,108 | 107,655,642 | 98,867,226 |

NOTE.—The figures for 1901 are, according to the Madrid Gazette, only provisional and subject to correction.

Exports (during 1901) from Barcelona.

| | Unit. | France. Quantity. | France. Value. | Great Britain. Quantity. | Great Britain. Value. | Germany. Quantity. | Germany. Value. | Belgium. Quantity. | Belgium. Value. | Italy. Quantity. | Italy. Value. | Other European countries. Quantity. | Other European countries. Value. |
|---|---|---|---|---|---|---|---|---|---|---|---|---|---|
| **MANUFACTURED GOODS.** | | | | | | | | | | | | | |
| Glassware | Pounds | 120,991 | $2,749 | 4,138 | $135 | 297 | $18 | | | 1,061 | $29 | 18,675 | $662 |
| Pottery and porcelain | do | 3,601 | 68 | 41,588 | 620 | | | | | | | 6,782 | 113 |
| Jewelry | do | 220 | 514,296 | 17 | 320 | | | | | | | | |
| Arms | Tons | 1,148 | 1,380 | 6,604 | 12,865 | 7,999 | 15,583 | | | 761 | 1,458 | 2,840 | 4,560 |
| Hardware | Tons | 1,489 | 287,915 | 686 | 41,837 | 19 | 2,214 | 56 | $3,400 | 1,160 | 141,825 | 61 | 5,106 |
| Tartaric acid | Pounds | 7 | 1,928 | 129 | 35,007 | 3 | 739 | 5 | 1,543 | 20 | 5,624 | 19 | 5,259 |
| Candles and matches | | 880 | 94 | 127 | 14 | | | | | | 141 | | |
| Perfumery | | 4,669 | 2,421 | 459 | 239 | | | | | 1,320 | 1,760 | | |
| Drugs | Tons | 2,945 | 285,680 | 90 | 4,866 | | | | | 3,608 | 12,247 | 72 | 6,640 |
| Cotton goods | | 841 | 634,069 | 128 | 113,096 | 41 | 58,298 | 4 | 4,390 | 231 | 358,890 | 6 | 8,117 |
| Linen and jute goods | | 9 | 3,371 | 1 | 726 | | | | | 13 | 4,552 | 2 | 879 |
| Jute sacks | Number | 5,871 | 889 | | | | | | | 1,419 | 921 | 889 | 196 |
| Woolen goods | Pounds | 2,266 | 808 | | | 10 | 3,246 | | | 5 | 1,872 | 13 | 4,245 |
| Cigarette paper | Tons | 6 | 1,945 | 9 | 8,045 | | | | | 7 | 264 | 87 | 23,224 |
| Paper, cardboard, etc | | 28 | 19,780 | 14 | 7,125 | | | | | | 87 | 216 | 20,265 |
| Bottle corks | Number | 3,668,000 | 377,904 | 1,274,000 | 2,370 | 4,587,000 | 9,829 | 844,800 | 789 | 12,463,500 | 26,707 | 9,457,200 | 28,068 |
| Barrel furniture | Tons | 87 | 38,505 | 44 | 8,198 | 58 | 65,567 | | | 17 | 649 | 94 | 119,428 |
| Prepared hides | | 39 | 6 | 1 | 2,064 | | | | | 8 | 9,084 | 11 | 25,888 |
| Boots, shoes, and leather goods | Pounds | 6 | 13,819 | 26 | 2,065 | | 417 | | | 11 | 150 | | |
| Fans | Pounds | 2,516 | 2,451 | | 26 | 402 | 392 | | | 409 | 899 | 2,226 | 2,170 |
| Sandals | Dozen | 7,002 | 8,002 | | | 1,456 | 1,664 | | | 1,448 | 1,655 | 10,174 | 11,627 |
| Playing cards | Pounds | 1,093 | 319 | 200 | 60 | 3,966 | 1,159 | | | 866 | 253 | 2,213 | 647 |
| Umbrellas | Number | 72 | 31 | 31 | 13 | | | | | 120 | 61 | 394 | 169 |
| Hats | | 290 | 207 | 24 | 17 | | | | | 1 | 125 | | |
| Pianofortes | | | 165 | | | | | | | 176 | 301 | | |
| Guitars | Pounds | 96 | | 144 | 247 | 87 | 85 | 13 | 37 | 79 | 106 | 885 | 1,617 |
| Guitar strings | | | | | | 59 | | | | | | | |
| Sundries | Tons | 570 | 116,804 | 11 | 5,096 | 27 | 7,965 | 44 | 8,295 | 87 | 22,673 | 23 | 6,600 |
| **RAW MATERIALS.** | | | | | | | | | | | | | |
| Building material | Tons | 12 | 98 | 136 | 388 | 81 | 11,967 | 275 | 19,687 | 12 | 87 | 5 | 15 |
| Tar, pitch, etc | do | 233 | 8,520 | | | 17 | 849 | 385 | 59,920 | | | 2 | 76 |
| Lead | do | 64 | 4,206 | 26 | 4,822 | 4 | 177 | | | | | 2 | 115 |
| Other metals | do | 351 | 61,017 | 120 | 2,409 | 62 | 4,400 | | | 17 | 4,842 | | |
| Tanning bark | do | 11 | 238 | | | 47 | 7,767 | | | | | 27 | 167 |
| Licorice | do | 30 | 4,221 | | | 15 | 3,125 | | | 7 | 1,207 | 1 | 64 |
| Raw tartar | do | 1,353 | 96,621 | 1,269 | 90,644 | 20 | 3,853 | | | 160 | 18,657 | 172 | 12,292 |
| Glycerin | do | 504 | 82,776 | 4 | 667 | 25 | 2,128 | 16 | 3,619 | 1,040 | 175,212 | 64 | 10,879 |
| Wax and stearin | do | | 64 | 24 | 5,205 | | | 9 | 508 | 15 | 3,277 | 19 | 4,006 |
| Wool and hair | do | 526 | 52,072 | 128 | 16,763 | | | 14 | 4,467 | 190 | 18,189 | 72 | 12,892 |
| Bags and feathers | do | 26 | 1,280 | 45 | 2,308 | | | | | 68 | 8,580 | 6 | 267 |
| Hides | do | 379 | 122,526 | 827 | 116,911 | 88 | 20,865 | | | 210 | 98,279 | 24 | 10,208 |

| | Total | | United States | | Argentine Republic. | | Other American countries. | | Asia and Africa. | | Spanish colonies. | | Total. | |
|---|---|---|---|---|---|---|---|---|---|---|---|---|---|---|

**FOOD STUFFS.**

| | Unit. | | | | | | | | | | | | | |
|---|---|---|---|---|---|---|---|---|---|---|---|---|---|---|
| Fertilisers | do | | | | | | 1,767 | 37,862 | | 3 | 159 | 8,899 | 17½ | 2,821 |
| Sundries | do | | | | | | 7 | 147 | | | 52 | 1,456 | 7 | 446 |
| **Total FOOD STUFFS** | | 1,245 | 28,696 | 1,873 | 40,283 | | 91,685 | | 96,654 | | 1,922 | 328,006 | 576 | 66,448 |
| | | 3,040 | 105,979 | 160 | 5,618 | 2,160 | | 788 | 76 | | | | | |
| | | 7,705 | 565,976 | 4,117 | 285,968 | | | | | | | | | |
| Cattle | Head | | | | | | | | | | | 2 | | |
| Mineral waters | Liters | 422,207 | 48,262 | 18,467 | 1,641 | | | | | 141,500 | 842 | 10,289 | 1,170 | |
| Fish | Kilos | 1,947 | 2,196 | | | 616 | 67 | | | 78,285 | 16,171 | 5,286 | 282 | |
| Garlic | do | 61,451 | 2,112 | 968 | | | | | | 5,146 | 6,474 | 9,823 | 649 | |
| Cereals and flour | do | 9,678 | 675 | 4,745 | | | | 140 | | | 247 | 712 | 43 | |
| Almonds and nuts | do | 600,471 | 111,472 | 19,653 | | 5,765 | 925 | 1 | | | | 12,828 | 1,620 | |
| Fruit | do | 190,448 | 9,982 | 91,545 | 1,972 | 17,470 | 877 | | | 18,816 | 1,581 | 12,550 | 446 | |
| Saffron | do | 23 | 333 | | | | | | 321 | 1,840 | 194 | | | |
| Anise, cumin and pimento | do | 1,756 | 189 | 373 | | 6,215 | 829 | 4 | 457 | 84,845 | 1,457 | 2,069 | 292 | |
| Olive oil | do | 284,351 | 691 | 202 | | 770 | 166 | 3,520 | 4,486 | 16,414 | 5,428 | 8,790 | 513 | |
| Brandy and liqueurs | Liters | 6,571 | 1,138 | 1,596 | | 201,288 | 6,985 | 8,685 | 599 | 50 | 8,527 | 45,287 | 1,286 | |
| Wines | do | 7,883,857 | 228,998 | 518,729 | | 10,706 | 1,126 | 7 | 2,562 | 70 | 6,002 | 229,940 | 8,191 | |
| Sundry comestibles | do | 8,034 | 828 | 5,416 | | | | 3 | 1,304 | 11 | 23,513 | 97,874 | 13,571 | |

**MANUFACTURED GOODS.**

| | Unit. | United States Quantity. | United States Value. | Argentine Republic Quantity. | Argentine Republic Value. | Other American countries Quantity. | Other American countries Value. | Asia and Africa Quantity. | Asia and Africa Value. | Spanish colonies Quantity. | Spanish colonies Value. | Total Quantity. | Total Value. |
|---|---|---|---|---|---|---|---|---|---|---|---|---|---|
| Glassware | Pounds | 39,688 | $1,276 | 70,206 | $3,787 | 299,073 | $17,597 | 2,824 | $117 | 1,443 | $842 | 543,236 | $26,962 |
| Pottery and porcelain | do | | | 36,623 | 1,632 | 1,010,779 | 24,754 | 109,456 | 4,485 | 180,028 | 1,925 | 1,388,767 | 88,467 |
| Jewelry | do | | | | | 87 | | | | | | 237 | 414,606 |
| Arms | Tons | 14,128 | 27,523 | | | 29,061 | 56,653 | 1 | 140 | 20 | 2,584 | 62,061 | 120,047 |
| Hardware | | | | 3 | 342 | 231 | 30,490 | | | | | 3,716 | 465,704 |
| Tartaric acid | Tons | | | | | 78 | 10,129 | | | | | 220 | 60,229 |
| Soap | Tons | 29 | 2,201 | | | 13,838 | 5,804 | 4 | 321 | 19 | 1,457 | 190 | 9,788 |
| Candles and matches | Pounds | | | | | 8,980 | 1,683 | 3,520 | 457 | 84,845 | 5,428 | 104,530 | 7,765 |
| Perfumery | Tons | | | 47 | 6,109 | 196 | 4,665 | 8,685 | 4,486 | 16,414 | 8,527 | 42,765 | 22,098 |
| Drugs | | | | 92 | 96,581 | 2,609 | 24,410 | 7 | 599 | 50 | 6,002 | 2,985 | 395,568 |
| Cotton goods | | | | 6 | 1,987 | 98 | 1,333,573 | 7 | 2,562 | 70 | 23,513 | 4,029 | 2,682,050 |
| Linen and jute goods | Number | | | | | | 43,062 | 3 | 1,304 | 11 | 9,196 | 138 | 65,027 |
| Jute sacks | Pounds | | | | | | | | | 60,946 | 8,700 | 9 | 545 |
| Woolen goods | do | | | 7,851 | 3,569 | 78,706 | 28,643 | | | 3,601 | 8,061 | 66,817 | 88,698 |
| Silk goods | | | | 17,652 | 102,047 | 17,487 | 94,791 | | | | | 89,184 | 194,888 |
| Cigarette paper | Tons | | | 37 | 12,419 | 136 | 44,784 | | | 8 | 2,867 | 85,139 | 74,873 |
| Paper, cardboard, etc. | | | | 1,909 | 688,298 | 1,018 | 465,776 | | | 32 | 10,978 | 224 | 1,215,415 |
| Bottle corks | Number | 7,874,060 | 15,301 | 69,880,000 | 14,998 | 897,240 | | 72,520 | 165 | 8,096 | 99,609 | | |
| Barrel furniture | Tons | 1,496 | 142,602 | 3,052 | 422,296 | 895 | 851 | 1 | 119 | 685,810 | 1,002,795 | | |
| Prepared hides | | | | 40 | 35,271 | 86 | 98,964 | | 28,150 | 27 | 27,858 | 5,807 | 865,744 |
| Boots, shoes, and leather goods | Pounds | | | 50 | 24,113 | 994 | 80,506 | | | | | 848 | 147 |
| Fans | Pounds | | | 23,405 | 22,798 | 182,997 | 129,494 | | | 6,410 | 5,244 | 168,381 | 96,907 |
| Sandals | Dozen | | | 9,982 | 11,905 | 11,067 | 12,636 | | | 5,963 | 6,701 | 46,992 | 163,964 |
| Playing cards | Pounds | | | 30,047 | 8,780 | 172,878 | 49,068 | | | 17,166 | 5,016 | 228,429 | 65,322 |

Exports (during 1901) from Barcelona—Continued.

| Item | Unit | United States Quantity | United States Value | Argentine Republic Quantity | Argentine Republic Value | Other American countries Quantity | Other American countries Value | Asia and Africa Quantity | Asia and Africa Value | Spanish colonies Quantity | Spanish colonies Value | Total Quantity | Total Value |
|---|---|---|---|---|---|---|---|---|---|---|---|---|---|
| **MANUFACTURED GOODS—continued.** | | | | | | | | | | | | | |
| Umbrellas | Number | | | 7,149 | $8,064 | 36,396 | $15,597 | | | 1,017 | $498 | 45,179 | $19,361 |
| Hats | do | | | | | 4,078 | 2,913 | | | | | 4,892 | 8,187 |
| Pianofortes | do | | | | | 68 | 7,875 | | | | | 64 | 8,165 |
| Guitars | do | | | | | 2,107 | 8,612 | | | | | 3,495 | 5,677 |
| Guitar strings | Pounds | | | | | | | | | | | 138 | 190 |
| Sundries | Tons | | | 2 | 984 | 9 | 2,338 | | 87,621 | | 118,761 | 729 | 318,891 |
| **RAW MATERIALS.** | | | | | | | | | | | | | |
| Building material | Tons | | | 4 | 141 | 16 | 49 | | | 18 | 38 | 207 | 600 |
| Tar, pitch, etc | do | | | | | | | | | 14 | 497 | 253 | 9,084 |
| Lead | do | | | | | | | | | 1 | 64 | 780 | 4,884 |
| Other metals | do | | | | | 643 | 32,145 | | | | | 691 | 108,719 |
| Tanning bark | do | | | 4 | 21 | 72 | 12,776 | | | 2 | 36 | 198 | 3,447 |
| Licorice | do | 75 | 82 | | | 12 | 240 | | | | | 76 | 10,977 |
| Raw tartar | do | 45 | 8,242 | 72 | 5,178 | 84 | 5,318 | | | 43 | 8,048 | 4,897 | 821,164 |
| Glycerin | do | 174 | 28,578 | 15 | 2,449 | 946 | 67,560 | | | 12 | 1,991 | 2,880 | 469,381 |
| Wax and stearin | do | | | | | 605 | 99,447 | | | | | 85 | 18,342 |
| Wool and hair | do | | | 8 | 64 | 12 | 2,675 | | | | | 992 | 120,448 |
| Rags and feathers | do | | | | | 40 | 18,640 | | | | | 287 | 12,222 |
| Hides | do | | | | | 4 | 122 | | | 69 | 1,975 | 1,087 | 872,746 |
| Fertilizers | do | | | | | | | | | 285 | 5,046 | 5,460 | 115,667 |
| Sundries | do | | | 84 | 1,474 | 84 | 1,569 | | | 39 | 1,190 | 8,875 | 117,945 |
| Total | | 219b | 31,818 | 189 | 9,927 | 2,418 | 235,681 | | | 418 | 18,880 | | |
| **FOOD STUFFS.** | | | | | | | | | | | | | |
| Mineral waters | Liters | 1,792 | 205 | | | 17,688 | 2,015 | 8,312 | 960 | 7,698 | 878 | | |
| Salt | Kilos | | | | | 5,704 | 187 | | | 75,973 | 5,865 | | |
| Fish | do | | | | | 17,141 | 1,196 | | | 784,986 | 13,798 | | |
| Cereals and flour | do | | | | | 1,012 | 61 | | | | | | |
| Garlic | do | | | | | 106,422 | 14,277 | 5,460 | 615 | 87,297 | 6,460 | | |
| Almonds and nuts | do | | | 84,548 | 14,067 | 5,116 | 2,029 | 3,972 | 178 | 61,504 | 8,092 | | |
| Fruit | do | 1,825 | 61 | 79,749 | 2,943 | 6,142 | | | | 19 | 271 | | |
| Saffron | do | | | | | 198,581 | 26,018 | | | 113 | 10,541 | | |
| Anise, cumin and pimento | do | | | | | 44,609 | 611 | | | 1,096 | 298 | | |
| Olive oil | do | 1,912 | 258 | 59,970 | 7,496 | 146,074 | 41,737 | | | 7,488 | 2,139 | | |
| Brandy and liqueurs | Liters | 1,100 | 114 | 6,706 | 1,846 | | | | | | | | |
| Wines | Liters | 9,558 | 314 | 6,975 | | 5,158,178 | 161,987 | | | 168,224 | 6,006 | | |
| Sundry comestibles | do | 1,640 | 174 | 785,687 | | 246,717 | 27,992 | 189,971 | 16,198 | 705,087 | 88,819 | | |

RECAPITULATION.

[Quantity expressed in tons.]

| | France. | | Great Britain. | | Germany. | | Belgium. | | Italy. | | Other European Countries. | |
|---|---|---|---|---|---|---|---|---|---|---|---|---|
| | Quantity. | Value. | Quantity. | Value. | Quantity. | Value. | Quantity. | Value. | Quantity. | Value. | Quantity. | Value. |
| Raw materials........ | 7,796 | $565,875 | 4,117 | $285,968 | 2,160 | $91,636 | 738 | $96,553 | 1,921 | $313,721 | 578 | $53,446 |
| Food stuffs........... | 1,158 | 164,119 | 123 | 6,497 | 42 | 3,824 |  | 14 | 165 | 16,298 | 144 | 17,299 |
| Manufactured goods....... | 5,493 | 1,691,473 | 1,141 | 237,204 | 161 | 167,101 | 66 | 9,332 | 1,678 | 562,842 | 610 | 241,844 |
| Total........ | 14,447 | 2,421,467 | 5,381 | 528,069 | 2,363 | 262,561 | 804 | 105,899 | 3,764 | 892,861 | 1,332 | 312,589 |

| | United States. | | Argentine Republic. | | Other American countries. | | Asia and Africa. | | Spanish colonies. | | Total. | |
|---|---|---|---|---|---|---|---|---|---|---|---|---|
| | Quantity. | Value. | Quantity. | Value. | Quantity. | Value. | Quantity. | Value. | Quantity. | Value. | Quantity. | Value. |
| Raw materials........ | 219 | $31,818 | 182 | $9,328 | 2,418 | $235,582 | ........ | ........ | 419 | $13,880 | 20,498 | $1,697,747 |
| Food stuffs........... | 5 | 404 | 341 | 40,686 | 581 | 71,606 | 149 | $16,992 | 1,140 | 127,603 | 3,848 | 464,434 |
| Manufactured goods....... | 18 | 1,276 | 3,804 | 1,179,761 | 8,443 | 3,002,061 | 475 | 37,621 | 388 | 118,761 | 22,272 | 7,289,286 |
| Total........ | 242 | 88,686 | 4,277 | 1,229,765 | 11,442 | 3,309,221 | 624 | 54,613 | 1,942 | 260,244 | 46,618 | 9,401,467 |

*Imports at Barcelona in 1901.*

| | Unit. | France. | | Great Britain. | | Germany. | | Belgium. | | Italy. | | Other European countries. | |
|---|---|---|---|---|---|---|---|---|---|---|---|---|---|
| | | Quantity. | Value. | Quantity. | Value. | Quantity. | Value. | Quantity. | Value. | Quantity. | Value. | Quantity. | Value. |
| **MANUFACTURED GOODS.** | | | | | | | | | | | | | |
| Marbles | Tons.... | 8¾ | $465 | 4 | $228 | 24 | $1,837 | 9½ | $965 | 55 | $8,014 | 45½ | $106 |
| Glassware | do | 878 | 22,047 | 102 | 12,905 | 101 | 15,411 | 648 | 61,586 | 71 | 8,021 | 10 | 4,291 |
| Earthenware and porcelain | do | 20 | 2,894 | 808 | 21,780 | 158 | 38,512 | 70 | 1,708 | 15 | 4,670 | 166 | 5,169 |
| Iron and steel goods | do | 171 | 14,919 | 884 | 70,984 | 1,237 | 161,380 | 1,264 | 114,878 | 95 | 11,749 | 3½ | 25,751 |
| Hardware | do | 89 | 29,870 | 64 | 27,146 | 188 | 37,115 | 16 | 88,777 | 57 | 20,205 | | 3,256 |
| Industrial oils | do | 246 | 26,605 | 7 | 777 | 1 | | 1 | 145 | | | | 69 |
| Vegetable and mineral drugs | do | 150 | 26,423 | 167 | 26,357 | 80 | 18,276 | 5½ | 749 | 20 | 3,876 | 889 | 35,738 |
| Color, varnish, and dyes | do | 212 | 84,622 | 154 | 40,045 | 784 | 250,499 | 69 | 11,688 | 12 | 11,776 | 90 | 21,687 |
| Dyeing extracts | do | 1,083 | 155,080 | 471 | 70,735 | 154 | 23,295 | 6 | 1,089 | 267 | 40,082 | 80 | 4,566 |
| Chemical products | do | 10,655 | 405,655 | 12,988 | 498,498 | 4,096 | 311,908 | 1,761 | 88,777 | 300 | 25,492 | 156 | 11,257 |
| Pharmaceutical products | do | 81 | 24,139 | 88 | 28,908 | 12 | 9,373 | | | 2 | 1,681 | 2 | 191 |
| Starch, fecula for commercial purposes | do | 166 | 6,450 | 1,170 | 31,764 | 8,768 | 157,785 | 76 | 41,468 | 828 | 81,775 | 8,717 | 145,220 |
| Perfumery | do | 9½ | 11,188 | 6 | 6,599 | 9 | 15,457 | | | 10 | 11,816 | 4 | 202 |
| Spun and woven cotton goods | do | 18 | 19,065 | 299 | 826,586 | 88 | 12,066 | 468 | 1,057 | 1 | 1,906 | 110 | 4,887 |
| Spun and woven jute goods | do | 148 | 66,584 | 980 | 271,457 | 18 | 83,644 | | 150,979 | 124 | 4,341 | 2 | 47,977 |
| Spun and woven woolen goods | do | 49 | 107,746 | 216 | 284,021 | 1 | 27,086 | | | | 4,688 | 8 | 2,796 |
| Silk goods | do | 64 | 41,099 | 7 | 46,504 | 1 | 6,292 | | | 3 | 18,620 | 8 | 28,698 |
| Paper, cardboard, etc | do | 66 | 19,483 | 78 | 12,625 | 618 | 184,748 | 126 | 84,472 | 29 | 82,568 | 120 | 84,410 |
| Fashioned and wicker ware | do | 70 | 10,957 | 212 | 46,905 | 57 | 14,886 | 48 | 3,067 | 84 | 8,124 | 282 | 48,914 |
| Tanned and leather goods | do | 2 | 8,791 | 81 | 66,469 | 6½ | 12,613 | 1 | 2,494 | 1 | 886 | | 2,001 |
| Pianos, watches etc | Each.. | 109 | 671 | 6 | 66,181 | 15,941 | 12,688 | | | 470 | | 1,414 | 4,380 |
| Machines, tram cars, weighing machines, carriages, etc. | Tons.. | 159 | 86,080 | 2,809 | 527,014 | 1,060 | 250,015 | 480 | 96,176 | 844 | 80,025 | 126 | 28,268 |
| Motor machines and boilers | do | 8 | 1,865 | 477 | 83,814 | 92 | 17,898 | 72 | 12,618 | 14 | 2,512 | | 288 |
| Sewing and cycle machines | do | 1½ | 1,582 | 285 | 201,878 | 43 | 57,222 | | | | 828 | | |
| Shipbuilding material | do | 1½ | 98,771 | 22 | 1,264,000 | | 400 | 6 | 427 | | 20,186 | | |
| Railroad material | do | | | 650 | 84,827 | | | 10 | 8,214 | | | | |
| Sundries | do | 21 | 12,827 | 28 | 16,776 | 26 | 18,700 | | | 10 | 9,406 | 12 | 10,017 |
| **RAW MATERIALS.** | | | | | | | | | | | | | |
| Marble | Tons.. | 14,679 | 107,882 | 1,060 | 8,867 | 13 | 177 | 81 | 1,045 | 8,998 | 47,564 | | |
| Cement | do | 1 | 14 | 568,208 | 8,899,728 | 688 | 6,681 | 972 | 7,015 | 816 | 8,882 | 100 | 782 |
| Coal, charcoal, and coke | do | 69 | 784 | 12 | 204 | 890 | 2,228 | 1,097 | 6,294 | 20,640 | 261,096 | | |
| Pitch, rosin, etc | do | 167 | 6,288 | 826 | 18,268 | 59 | 874 | | 17 | | | 27 | 670 |
| Petroleum and mineral oils | do | 17 | 786 | | | 48 | 2,476 | 286 | 15,816 | 60 | 1,481 | 5,440 | 272,164 |
| Minerals | do | 121 | 5,704 | 2,576 | 92,862 | 58 | 2,295 | | | 2 | | 498 | 22,162 |
| Cast and wrought iron, steel plates, wire, and tin plate | do | | | | | 4,198 | 149,888 | 1,862 | 61,655 | 174 | 5,178 | 468 | 14,696 |
| Copper, tin, and zinc | do | 44 | 16,852 | 180 | 92,561 | 62 | 21,189 | 82 | 7,785 | 19 | 5,891 | 11 | 2,412 |

| | | | | | | | | | | | | | | |
|---|---|---|---|---|---|---|---|---|---|---|---|---|---|---|
| Dye woods | do | 274 | 7,829 | | 682 | 16 | 460 | 11 | 381 | 18 | 808 | | 213 | 18,798 |
| Gums, various woods | do | 1,857 | 86,966 | | | | 62,156 | 306 | | 821 | 2,764 | | | 270 |
| Indigo | do | 2 | 8,966 | | | | | | | | 96 | | 167 | 16,081 |
| Sulphur | do | 59 | 1,849 | | | | | | | | | | | |
| Wax, stearin, and paraffin | do | 88 | 2,488 | 465 | 114,704 | 273 | 76,676 | | 13,700 | | 5,520 | | 4,494 | 802,567 |
| Cotton | do | 79 | 7,101 | 4,227 | 764,579 | 29 | 5,308 | | | 29 | 930,066 | | | |
| Jute, hemp, and other fibers | do | 8 | 11,380 | | | 4 | 2,304 | 4 | 665 | 2,622 | 11,001 | | 2,528 | 1,492 |
| Wool and hair | do | 10 | 6,267 | 1,168 | 804,688 | 887 | 10,124 | 8 | 5,804 | 18 | | | 85,729 | 75,887 |
| Wood pulp | Cubic meters | 88 | 900 | | | 65 | 604 | | | | 74,157 | | | 786,055 |
| Timber | Pieces | 1,000 | 771 | | | | | 87 | | 613,986 | 646 | | | |
| Staves | Tons | 498 | 121 | 629 | 56,667 | 109 | 21,818 | | 848 | 22 | 900 | | 244 | 28,290 |
| Tallow, gum, etc. | do | 362 | 50,566 | 316 | 10,406 | 1 | 30 | 83 | 10,260 | 81 | 99 | | 5 | 168 |
| Manures | do | | 10,966 | | 941 | | 672 | 80 | 878 | | | | | |
| Nacre, ivory, and jet | do | 68 | 184 | 6½ | 11,689 | 9 | 12,452 | | | 149 | 4,702 | | 69 | 188 |
| Gutta-percha | do | 245 | 14,221 | | 7 | 61 | 1,961 | 19½ | 1,986 | 11 | 8,816 | | 4 | 8,877 |
| Pine wood, cork, and hoops | do | 127 | 17,053 | 1,425 | 407,643 | 118 | 82,468 | | 57 | | | | | 1,166 |
| Skins | do | | 26,586 | | | | | | | | | | | |
| **FOOD STUFFS.** | | | | | | | | | | | | | | |
| Live cattle | Head | 1 | 14 | 44 | 76 | 2 | 406 | | | 18 | 987 | | 50 | 2,666 |
| Meat, lard, etc. | Tons | 212 | 190 | 185 | 8,468 | 12½ | 1,197 | | | 4½ | 79 | | 4,004 | 898,880 |
| Stock, and other salt fish | do | | 20,139 | | 17,606 | | | 8 | | | 41 | | 51,586 | 1,656,088 |
| Wheat | do | | | | | | 16 | | | | | | 32,588 | 449,461 |
| Other cereals, and flour | do | 201 | 8,709 | 14 | 6 | 20 | 861 | | 8 | 104 | 53 | | 2,699 | 100,276 |
| Vegetables and garden produce | do | 28 | 89,166 | | 809 | 1 | 52 | | | 24 | 618 | | 160 | 9,108 |
| Fruit | do | | 1,824 | | | | 19 | | | | 142 | | | |
| Sugars, etc. | do | | | 2 | 1,161 | | 249 | | | | | | 2½ | 1,858 |
| Cacao | do | 4½ | 45 | | | | | | | 99 | 521 | | | 262 |
| Coffee | do | | | | | | | | | 2,256 | 2,806 | | | |
| Tea and spices | Gallons | 1,259 | 8,967 | 125 | 64,294 | | 281 | | | | | | 28 | 1,028 |
| Alcohol and spirits | do | 8,185 | 21,842 | 305 | 994 | 142 | 2,825 | | | | 8 | | 824 | 2,675 |
| Wine and beef | Tons | 10 | 457 | 1,987 | 708 | 1,709 | 451 | 105 | 47 | 426½ | 194 | | 1,200 | 7,161 |
| Fodder and grain | Gallons | 72,259 | 82,845 | 1½ | 60 | 10 | 885 | | 40 | 46 | | | 178 | 888 |
| Mineral waters | do | 28 | 6,519 | 8 | 1 | 9 | | 8 | | | | | 1,560 | |
| Sundries | Tons | | | 8 | 2,986 | 3½ | 1,648 | | | | 18,868 | | 286 | 166,091 |

*Imports at Barcelona in 1901—Continued.*

| | Unit. | United States. | | Argentine Republic. | | Other American countries. | | Asia and Africa. | | Spanish colonies. | | Total. | |
|---|---|---|---|---|---|---|---|---|---|---|---|---|---|
| | | Quantity. | Value. | Quantity. | Value. | Quantity. | Value. | Quantity. | Value. | Quantity. | Value. | Quantity. | Value. |
| **MANUFACTURED GOODS.** | | | | | | | | | | | | | |
| Marbles | Tons | 228 | $9,919 | | | | | | | | | 971 | $11,406 |
| Glassware | do | 7 | 652 | | | | | 1 | $923 | | | 1,628 | 134,530 |
| Earthenware and porcelain | do | 149 | 12,741 | 12 | $971 | | | | | | | 1,064 | 76,298 |
| Iron and steel goods | do | 4 | 1,907 | | | | | | | | | 3,919 | 992,873 |
| Hardware | do | 19ᵇ | 6 | | | 43ᵇ | 83 | 37 | 4,455 | 96 | $11,566 | 371½ | 203,825 |
| Industrial oils | do | | | | | | | 36 | 5,764 | | | 858 | 45,681 |
| Vegetable and mineral drugs | do | 53 | 8,868 | | | | 7,175 | | | | | 889† | 121,668 |
| Colors, varnishes, and dyes | do | 11 | 8,146 | | | | | | | | | 1,324 | 378,323 |
| Dyeing extracts | do | 416 | 1,733 | | | 16 | 2,315 | 1 | 158 | | | 1,988 | 298,789 |
| Chemical products | do | 8 | 59,688 | | | 1,402 | 40,140 | | | | | 81,669 | 1,434,185 |
| Pharmaceutical products | do | | 7,167 | ¾ᵇ | 64 | 10 | 6,996 | | | | | 96 | 78,355 |
| Starch, fecula for commercial purposes | do | | | | | | | | | | | 9,718 | 408,422 |
| Perfumery | do | 3ᵇ | 3,565 | | | | | 1ᵇ | 120 | | | 41 | 47,942 |
| Spun and woven cotton goods | do | | 143 | | | | | | 214 | | | 882 | 865,566 |
| Spun and woven jute goods | do | | | | | | | | | | | 1,766† | 674,982 |
| Spun and woven woolen goods | do | | | | | | | | | | | 286 | 423,313 |
| Silk goods | do | | | | | | | 4ᵇ | 82 | | | 24‡ | 302,112 |
| Paper, cardboard, etc | do | 12 | 2,389 | ¾ᵇ | 14 | 1ᵇ | 46 | 4 | 61,134 | | | 1,068 | 371,659 |
| Fashioned and wicker ware | do | 62 | 5,290 | 5ᵇ | 1,428 | 1 | 387 | 8 | 904 | | | 771 | 189,628 |
| Tanned and leather goods | do | 26 | 60,447 | 4 | 8,748 | 1 | 1,805 | 20 | 4,476 | | | 77 | 189,380 |
| Pianos, watches, etc | Each | | | 1 | 114 | 1 | 114 | 4 | 8,892 | | | 17,841 | 21,229 |
| Machines, tram cars, weighing machines, carriages, etc | Tons | 22 | 5,062 | 1½ | 676 | | | | | | | 4,482 | |
| Motor machines and boilers | do | 11 | 2,047 | | | | | | | | | 669 | 120,249 |
| Sewing and cycle machines | do | 28 | 20,202 | | | | | | | | | 303 | 261,450 |
| Shipbuilding material | do | | | | | | | | | | | 24 | 1,378,257 |
| Railroad material | do | | | | | | | | | | | 666 | 37,254 |
| Sundries | do | 8 | 6,240 | | | 6 | 862 | 1 | 724 | | | 111 | 88,072 |
| **RAW MATERIALS.** | | | | | | | | | | | | | |
| Marble | Tons | | 1 | | | | | | | | | 8,798 | 48,781 |
| Cement | do | 2,100 | 12,006 | | | 2 | 12 | | | | | 17,913 | 185,999 |
| Coal, charcoal, and coke | do | 1,597 | 40,061 | | | | | | | | | 617,438 | 8,671,965 |
| Pitch, rosin, etc | do | 691 | 84,487 | | | | | | | | | 1,725 | 42,690 |
| Petroleum and mineral oils | do | | | | | | | | | | | 6,408 | 400,880 |
| Minerals | do | | | | | 880 | 16,286 | | | | | 943 | 41,011 |
| Cast and wrought iron, steel plates, wire, and tin plate | do | 519 | 15,816 | | | 640 | 9,261 | | | | | 10,046 | 843,510 |
| Copper, tin, and zinc | do | 8 | 652 | | | 2 | 680 | ¾ᵇ | 190 | ¾ | 11 | 854 | 148,681 |

| | Unit | | | | | | | | | | | |
|---|---|---|---|---|---|---|---|---|---|---|---|---|
| Dye woods | do | 25 | 1,114 | | 71 | | 199 | 6,712 | 9,648 | 618,801 | | 817 | 17,208 |
| Oleaginous seeds | do | 18,544 | 170,717 | | | 4,622 | 679 | 48,681 | 2 | 8,346 | 11 | 104 | 231,771 |
| Indigo | do | | | | | | 56 | 89,082 | | | 1½ | | 145,709 |
| Sulphur | do | | | | | | | | | | | | 4,108 |
| Wax, stearin, and paraffin | do | 873 | 106,068 | | | | 91 | 248 | 16 | 4,588 | | 430 | 884,588 |
| Cotton | do | 66,719 | 10,128,449 | | ¥ | | 228 | 16,463 | 782 | 130,898 | | 1,626 | 11,950,985 |
| Jute, hemp, and other fibers | do | 92 | 6,599 | | | | 77 | 16,898 | 18,068 | 942,613 | | 66,380 | 1,388,881 |
| Wool and hair | do | | | | | | 10 | 19,873 | | 213 | | 15,981 | 860,135 |
| Wood pulp | do | | | | | 15 | 17,012 | 811 | | | | 1,299 | 86,602 |
| Timber | Cubic meters. | 10,791 | 100,196 | | 10 | 578,167 | | 157,969 | | 100 | | 8,585 | 1,045,940 |
| Staves | Pieces | 1,257 | 152,735 | | 4,880 | 119 | 2,684 | 825,575 | 8½ | | 14 | 118,717 | 227,413 |
| Tallow, guts, etc | Tons | 296 | 98,594 | | 4 | | 72 | 2,079 | | | | 616,258 | 1,169,910 |
| Manures | do | ¥ | | | | 14,721 | 1,801 | 61 | | 205 | 1,718 | 9,424 | 25,541 |
| Nacre, ivory, and jet | do | | 96 | | 315 | 1,015,068 | 948 | 60,065 | 14 | 1,889 | | 821 | 792 |
| Gutta-percha | do | | | | 3,552 | | | 271,053 | 40 | 178,231 | | 81 | 38,611 |
| Fine wood, cork, and hoops | do | 1,185 | 59,504 | | | | | | 606 | | | 8,866 | 164,665 |
| Skins | do | 28 | 6,602 | | | | | | | | 149 | 42,728 | 1,990,856 |
| FOOD STUFFS. | | | | | | | | | | | | | |
| Live cattle | Head | 35 | 5,761 | | 121 | 10,618 | | 8 | 6,037 | 172,466 | | 6,179 | 184,154 |
| Meat, lard, etc | Tons | | 70 | | 4 | 986 | ¥ | | ¥ | 178 | | 187 | 18,078 |
| Stock, and other salt fish | do | 12,117 | 889,491 | | 26,396 | 848,412 | | | | 7 | | 4,418 | 422,890 |
| Wheat | do | 4,976 | 99,529 | | 4,118 | 82,380 | | | 1,685 | 81,680 | | 90,048 | 2,884,441 |
| Other cereals, and flour | do | | | | 10 | 968 | 46 | 12 | 8,091 | 114,828 | | 88,784 | 666,702 |
| Vegetables and garden produce | do | 75½ | 4,084 | | | | 4 | 2,680 | 98 | 5,181 | | 8,240 | 306,156 |
| Fruit | do | 34 | 245 | | | | 752 | 62 | | | 25 | 415 | 28,865 |
| Sugars, etc | do | 64 | 2,857 | | | | 8,945 | 225,683 | | | 10 | 7 | 558 |
| Cacao | do | 812 | 86,974 | | | | 9½ | 1,027,466 | 78 | 22,481 | 1,179 | 1,943 | 551,401 |
| Coffee | do | | | | ¥ | | 651 | 4,387 | 148 | 62,665 | 21 | 3,751 | 1,160,488 |
| Tea and spices | Gallons | 212 | 96 | | | 42 | 4 | 5 | | | 820,168 | 286 | 122,366 |
| Alcohol and spirits | do | | 18 | | | | 1 | 25 | | | 4,577 | 8,498 | 10,163 |
| Wine and beer | Tons. | 4½ | 76 | | 8½ | 186 | | | 869 | 16,820 | | 15,889 | 80,119 |
| Fodder and grain | do | | | | | | | | | | | 672 | 25,208 |
| Mineral waters | Gallons | | | | ¥ | | | | | | | 74,642 | 84,808 |
| Sundries | Tons | 11½ | 7,201 | | | 821 | 1 | 694 | 1½ | 284 | | 887 | 198,587 |

*Imports at Barcelona in 1901*—Continued.

RECAPITULATION.

| Unit | France | | Great Britain | | Germany | | Belgium | | Italy | | Other European countries. | |
|---|---|---|---|---|---|---|---|---|---|---|---|---|
| | Quantity. | Value. | Quantity. | Value. | Quantity. | Value. | Quantity. | Value. | Quantity. | Value. | Quantity. | Value. |
| Raw materials ...... Tons.... | 18,347 | $390,921 | 605,565 | $5,766,019 | 6,396 | $258,117 | 4,294 | $123,170 | 28,526 | $717,725 | 14,355 | $1,280,087 |
| Food stuffs ...... do ... | 2,874 | 120,811 | 381 | 85,383 | 50 | 4,770 | | 43 | 65 | 14,764 | 81,727 | 2,777,244 |
| Manufactured goods ... do ... | 18,612 | 1,177,088 | 22,815 | 4,023,943 | 12,567 | 1,582,479 | 5,104 | 569,210 | 2,187 | 361,884 | 5,214 | 458,549 |
| | 84,838 | 1,688,820 | 628,261 | 9,875,345 | 18,997 | 1,845,876 | 9,389 | 722,428 | 30,778 | 1,094,824 | 101,296 | 4,495,880 |

| Unit | United States. | | Argentine Republic. | | Other American countries. | | Asia and Africa. | | Spanish colonies. | | Total. | |
|---|---|---|---|---|---|---|---|---|---|---|---|---|
| | Quantity. | Value. | Quantity. | Value. | Quantity. | Value. | Quantity. | Value. | Quantity. | Value. | Quantity. | Value. |
| Raw materials ...... Tons.... | 69,146 | $10,782,855 | 8,824 | $1,612,706 | 7,375 | $876,786 | 24,010 | $1,870,508 | 176 | $44,871 | 787,004 | $23,703,166 |
| Food stuffs ...... do ... | 17,544 | 605,286 | 80,587 | 982,092 | 4,157 | 1,260,817 | 5,403 | 254,017 | 1,201 | 324,765 | 146,989 | 6,379,966 |
| Manufactured goods ... do ... | 1,065 | 210,559 | 28 | 11,894 | 1,474 | 59,226 | 115 | 87,769 | 96 | 11,556 | 63,755 | 8,684,106 |
| | 87,755 | 11,698,160 | 89,884 | 2,556,692 | 13,006 | 2,196,779 | 29,528 | 2,212,294 | 1,472 | 381,191 | 994,699 | 38,667,228 |

## TRADE OF SPAIN IN 1902.

Following is a comparative statement of the imports and exports of Spain during the first ten months of the years 1900, 1901, and 1902. These figures have just been published by the Spanish Government:

[Average market value of peseta: In 1900, 14.28 cents; 1901, 15 cents; 1902, 15 cents.]

IMPORTS.

| Articles. | 1900. | | | |
|---|---|---|---|---|
| | Number. | Tonnage. | Pesetas. | United States equivalent. |
| Stones (marble, jasper, alabaster, etc.), minerals, glass, glass goods, pottery | | | 22,336,085 | $3,190,862 |
| Coal | | 1,394,961 | | |
| Coke | | 161,812 | | |
| Metals and metal manufactures | | | 35,676,852 | 5,097,722 |
| Drugs and chemical products | | | 61,675,569 | 8,810,509 |
| Cotton and cotton manufactures | | | 72,095,578 | 10,299,082 |
| Other vegetable fibers and their manufactures | | | 18,435,907 | 2,347,957 |
| Wool and woolen manufactures | | | 24,389,956 | 3,484,279 |
| Silk and silk manufactures | | | 22,508,796 | 3,214,842 |
| Wood pulp, paper, books, maps, etc | | | 9,422,180 | 1,331,740 |
| Timber and manufactures of wood | | | 50,482,957 | 7,211,851 |
| Animals and animal products (skins, hides, grease, manure) | | | 69,683,717 | 9,954,817 |
| Machinery (electrical apparatus and accessories included), carriages (street car and vehicles) | | | 60,886,257 | 8,698,087 |
| Boats of wood having a tonnage up to 50 tons | 19 | 125 | 25,282 | 3,604 |
| Boats and ships of wood with a tonnage of from 51 to 300 tons | 2 | 166 | 41,500 | 5,928 |
| Boats and ships of wood with a tonnage of 301 tons and upward | 1 | 1,436 | 403,800 | 57,714 |
| Boats and ships of iron and steel | 64 | 133,646 | 53,458,410 | 7,636,915 |
| Sailing ships | 2 | 1,278 | 383,400 | 54,771 |
| Food stuffs: | | | | |
| Fowls, salted meat, butter, fish (salted and fresh), shelled rice, etc | | | 28,755,342 | 4,107,906 |
| Wheat— | | | | |
| From United States | | | 999,891 | 142,841 |
| From France | | | 352,872 | 50,410 |
| From Roumania | | | 1,698,420 | 242,631 |
| From Russia | | | 20,221,221 | 2,888,747 |
| From other countries | | | 17,152,786 | 2,450,398 |
| Wheat flour— | | | | |
| From Germany | | | 1,600 | 228 |
| From Belgium | | | 29,098 | 4,157 |
| From France | | | 1,249,039 | 178,484 |
| From other countries | | | 530,163 | 75,788 |
| Barley | | | 1,006,309 | 143,756 |
| Rye | | | 839 | 119 |
| Corn | | | 6,705,456 | 957,922 |
| Other cereals | | | 1,929 | 275 |
| Flour from cereals, wheat excepted | | | 2,199 | 314 |
| Dry vegetables (beans, pease, etc.) | | | 4,561,521 | 651,646 |
| Sugars and sweets | | | 251,878 | 35,845 |
| Cocoa (in the bean) | | | 7,561,412 | 1,080,202 |
| Coffee (in the bean) | | | 10,088,102 | 1,434,014 |
| Tea, spirits, wines, liquors, preserves, biscuits, cakes, cheese, molasses, honey, etc | | | 8,168,739 | 1,152,677 |
| Bones, whalebone, amber, buttons, games, toys, silk, wool, and other laces, elastic woven goods, writing utensils, lamps, etc | | | 6,968,130 | 995,447 |
| Locomotives, wagons, cars, and all other railway material | | | 4,660,324 | 665,760 |
| Machinery for agricultural colonies | | | 109,859 | 15,694 |
| Tobacco and its manufactures | | | 14,937,000 | 2,133,711 |
| Gold: | | | | |
| Bars | | | 37,000 | 5,285 |
| Coin | | | 89,630 | 12,804 |
| Silver: | | | | |
| Bars | | | 1,048,560 | 149,784 |
| Coin | | | 3,997,995 | 571,142 |

IMPORTS—Continued.

| Articles. | 1901. | | | |
|---|---|---|---|---|
| | Number. | Tonnage. | Pesetas. | United States equivalent. |
| Stones (marble, jasper, alabaster, etc.), minerals, glass, glass goods, pottery.................. | | 1,639,270 | 20,318,101 | $3,047,715 |
| Coal.......................................... | | 1,639,270 | ............ | ............ |
| Coke.......................................... | | 161,104 | ............ | ............ |
| Metals and metal manufactures................ | | | 30,380,670 | 4,557,100 |
| Drugs and chemical products ................. | | | 67,207,796 | 9,881,159 |
| Cotton and cotton manufactures............... | | | 79,373,158 | 11,906,973 |
| Other vegetable fibers and their manufactures.. | | | 18,256,519 | 2,738,477 |
| Wool and woolen manufactures................ | | | 24,713,227 | 3,706,984 |
| Silk and silk manufactures.................... | | | 21,634,844 | 3,245,226 |
| Wood pulp, paper, books, maps, etc........... | | | 9,148,945 | 1,372,342 |
| Timber and manufactures of wood ............ | | | 52,623,610 | 7,894,541 |
| Animals and animal products (skins, hides, grease, manure)..................................... | | | 61,992,336 | 9,298,852 |
| Machinery (electrical apparatus and accessories included), carriages (street cars and vehicles).... | 20 | 375 | 56,800,324 | 8,520,049 |
| Boats of wood having a tonnage up to 50 tons...... | 20 | 375 | 74,891 | 11,238 |
| Boats and ships of wood with a tonnage of from 51 to 300 tons..................................... | 3 | 458 | 114,500 | 17,175 |
| Boats and ships of iron and steel .............. | 39 | 60,696 | 24,278,261 | 3,641,739 |
| Sailing ships ................................. | 3 | 398 | 119,420 | 17,913 |
| Food stuffs: | | | | |
| Fowls, salted meat, butter, fish (salted and fresh), shelled rice, etc .................... | | | 30,008,408 | 4,501,261 |
| Wheat— | | | | |
| From United States.................... | | | 1,616,352 | 242,453 |
| From France......................... | | | 226,328 | 33,949 |
| From Roumania....................... | | | 1,486,196 | 222,929 |
| From Russia ......:.................. | | | 15,676,064 | 2,351,409 |
| From other countries.................. | | | 10,118,965 | 1,517,845 |
| Wheat flour— | | | | |
| From Germany ....................... | | | 1,796 | 269 |
| From France ........................ | | | 189,744 | 28,461 |
| From other countries................. | | | 650,208 | 97,530 |
| Barley.................................. | | | 2,142,571 | 321,385 |
| Rye.................................... | | | 777,988 | 116,698 |
| Corn ................................... | | | 10,826,296 | 1,623,944 |
| Other cereals........................... | | | 208,488 | 30,973 |
| Flour from cereals, wheat excepted ...... | | | 2,297 | 344 |
| Dry vegetables (beans, pease, etc.)....... | | | 4,979,443 | 746,916 |
| Sugars and sweets ...................... | | | 62,560 | 9,384 |
| Cocoa (in the bean) .................... | | | 9,416,876 | 1,412,531 |
| Coffee (in the bean) .................... | | | 17,184,278 | 2,577,641 |
| Tea, spirits, wines, liquors, preserves, biscuits, cakes, cheese, molasses, honey, etc.................. | | | 9,283,992 | 1,392,599 |
| Bones, whalebone, amber, buttons, games, toys, silk, wool, and other laces, elastic woven goods, writing utensils, lamps, etc................ | | | 6,992,921 | 1,048,938 |
| Locomotives, wagons, cars, and all other railway material .................................... | | | 15,878,312 | 2,381,747 |
| Machinery for agricultural colonies............. | | | 58,360 | 8,754 |
| Tobacco and its manufactures.................. | | | 20,215,000 | 3,032,250 |
| Gold— | | | | |
| Bars .................................. | | | 103,600 | 15,540 |
| Coin .................................. | | | 183,443 | 27,516 |
| Silver— | | | | |
| Bars....... ........................... | | | 1,351,485 | 202,720 |
| Coin .................................. | | | 4,009,880 | 601,407 |

IMPORTS—Continued.

| Articles. | 1902. | | | |
|---|---|---|---|---|
| | Number. | Tonnage. | Pesetas. | United States equivalent. |
| Stones (marble, jasper, alabaster, etc.), minerals, glass, glass goods, pottery | | | 20,020,019 | $3,008,002 |
| Coal | | 1,784,172 | | |
| Coke | | 146,224 | | |
| Metals and metal manufactures | | | 30,528,288 | 4,579,285 |
| Drugs and chemical products | | | 77,459,736 | 11,518,960 |
| Cotton and cotton manufactures | | | 90,626,907 | 13,594,036 |
| Other vegetable fibers and their manufactures | | | 20,657,302 | 3,098,595 |
| Wool and woolen manufactures | | | 24,246,086 | 3,636,905 |
| Silk and silk manufactures | | | 23,356,789 | 3,508,518 |
| Wood pulp, paper, books, maps, etc | | | 9,900,879 | $1,485,131 |
| Timber and manufactures of wood | | | 41,920,429 | 6,288,064 |
| Animals and animal products (skins, hides, grease, manure) | | | 64,655,184 | 9,698,278 |
| Machinery (electrical apparatus and accessories included), carriages (street car and vehicles) | | | 58,309,223 | 8,746,383 |
| Boats of wood having a tonnage up to 50 tons | 20 | 220 | 43,871 | 6,580 |
| Boats and ships of wood with a tonnage of from 51 to 300 tons | 2 | 168 | 42,085 | 6,305 |
| Boats and ships of wood with a tonnage of 301 tons and upward | 1 | 1,164 | 349,200 | 52,380 |
| Boats and ships of iron and steel | 17 | 11,263 | 4,505,269 | 675,790 |
| Sailing ships | 1 | 1 | 300 | 45 |
| Food stuffs: | | | | |
| Fowls, salted meat, butter, fish (salted and fresh), shelled rice, etc | | | 31,559,859 | 4,133,978 |
| Wheat— | | | | |
| From United States | | | 281,301 | 42,195 |
| From France | | | 25,557 | 3,883 |
| From Russia | | | 10,117,510 | 1,517,626 |
| From other countries | | | 1,325,849 | 198,877 |
| Wheat flour— | | | | |
| From Belgium | | | 1,625 | 243 |
| From France | | | 39,348 | 5,902 |
| From other countries | | | 342,863 | 51,429 |
| Barley | | | 33,645 | 5,047 |
| Rye | | | 100 | 15 |
| Corn | | | 3,951,497 | 592,724 |
| Other cereals | | | 517 | 47 |
| Flour from cereals, wheat excepted | | | 4,378 | 656 |
| Dry vegetables (beans, pease, etc.) | | | 5,687,931 | 853,189 |
| Sugars and sweets | | | 33,223 | 4,983 |
| Cocoa (in the bean) | | | 9,844,782 | 1,476,709 |
| Coffee (in the bean) | | | 14,755,600 | 2,213,340 |
| Tea, spirits, wines, liquors, preserves, biscuits, cakes, cheese, molasses, honey, etc | | | 10,782,903 | 1,637,435 |
| Bones, whalebone, amber, buttons, games, toys, silk, wool, and other laces, elastic woven goods, writing utensils, lamps, etc | | | 7,341,718 | 1,101,257 |
| Locomotives, wagons, cars, and all other railway material | | | 10,344,131 | 1,551,619 |
| Machinery for agricultural colonies | | | 12,059 | 1,808 |
| Tobacco and its manufactures | | | | |
| Gold— | | | 20,514,000 | 3,077,000 |
| Bars | | | 55,500 | 8,325 |
| Coin | | | 1,792,230 | 268,834 |
| Silver— | | | | |
| Bars | | | 1,826,170 | 273,926 |
| Coin | | | 6,973,029 | 1,045,954 |

EXPORTS.

| Articles. | 1900. | | 1901. | | 1902. | |
|---|---|---|---|---|---|---|
| | Pesetas. | U.S. equivalent. | Pesetas. | U.S. equivalent. | Pesetas. | U.S. equivalent. |
| Minerals, pottery, etc ........ | 138,131,604 | $19,733,086 | 132,207,479 | $19,831,121 | 136,606,598 | $20,490,989 |
| Metals and metal manufactures...................... | 78,189,892 | 11,141,411 | 85,950,110 | 12,890,517 | 96,086,041 | 14,512,906 |
| Gold: | | | | | | |
| Bullion ................. | 545,400 | 77,914 | 137,880 | 20,682 | 51,840 | 7,776 |
| Coin ..................... | 358,400 | 50,485 | 180,411 | 27,062 | 147,250 | 22,088 |
| Silver: | | | | | | |
| Bullion ................. | 9,024,990 | 1,289,284 | 8,460,866 | 1,269,130 | 6,665,841 | 999,876 |
| Coin ..................... | 7,286,340 | 1,040,905 | 11,350,163 | 1,702,524 | 5,924,252 | 888,638 |
| Drugs and chemical products, perfumery, common soap, etc............... | 17,524,359 | 2,503,337 | 17,739,440 | 2,660,916 | 16,133,924 | 2,420,088 |
| Cotton manufactures ........ | 29,337,063 | 4,191,009 | 24,018,927 | 3,602,839 | 22,386,472 | 3,357,971 |
| Manufactures of other vegetable fibers................. | 1,136,222 | 162,608 | 776,421 | 116,463 | 1,250,926 | 187,639 |
| Wool and woolen manufactures...................... | 8,080,198 | 1,142,885 | 9,327,017 | 1,399,062 | 13,454,147 | 2,018,122 |
| Silk and silk manufactures.. | 4,122,471 | 588,924 | 4,500,252 | 675,038 | 4,108,089 | 616,213 |
| Paper, books, etc ............. | 6,973,695 | 996,242 | 7,091,064 | 1,063,660 | 6,499,363 | 974,904 |
| Timber, cork, esparto grass, rags, etc................... | 44,622,696 | 6,360,385 | 41,185,361 | 6,277,804 | 33,077,025 | 4,961,554 |
| Animals, animal products (skins, leather), boots and shoes...................... | 54,660,027 | 7,808,575 | 52,359,993 | 7,858,999 | 50,299,226 | 7,544,884 |
| Machinery................... | 673,307 | 96,187 | 637,078 | 95,561 | 620,484 | 93,073 |
| Food stuffs, etc.: | | | | | | |
| Fowls, salted meat, butter, fish (salted and fresh) .................. | 3,795,773 | 542,253 | 3,699,305 | 554,896 | 4,196,658 | 629,798 |
| Rice ..................... | 3,287,018 | 469,574 | 2,374,283 | 356,142 | 2,121,716 | 318,257 |
| Garlic................... | 1,121,840 | 160,232 | 1,253,748 | 188,062 | 1,155,108 | 173,266 |
| Barley, rye, corn, wheat, other cereals, peas, vegetables, almonds, olives ................. | 16,194,119 | 2,313,302 | 20,420,420 | 3,063,063 | 22,566,198 | 3,384,929 |
| Onions................... | 4,300,212 | 614,301 | 5,090,740 | 763,611 | 4,967,454 | 745,118 |
| Wheat flour............. | 746,151 | 106,598 | 199,549 | 29,932 | 136,547 | 20,482 |
| Hazelnuts .............. | 3,042,196 | 433,170 | 2,929,800 | 439,470 | 4,649,380 | 697,407 |
| Chestnuts.............. | 43,449 | 6,207 | 61,280 | 9,192 | 83,867 | 12,580 |
| Walnuts ............... | 85,651 | 7,950 | 44,182 | 6,627 | 7,270 | 1,090 |
| Dried figs ............. | 595,538 | 85,077 | 592,085 | 88,805 | 829,621 | 124,943 |
| Raisins ................ | 19,806,958 | 2,829,565 | 13,172,413 | 1,975,862 | 12,269,046 | 1,840,357 |
| Other dried fruits........ | 180,305 | 25,758 | 226,061 | 33,909 | 183,691 | 27,554 |
| Pomegranates ............ | 347,948 | 49,707 | 552,134 | 82,820 | 629,056 | 94,358 |
| Lemons.................. | 972,854 | 138,979 | 900,760 | 135,114 | 853,827 | 128,074 |
| Oranges................. | 28,178,853 | 4,025,550 | 27,610,117 | 4,141,517 | 39,075,972 | 5,861,396 |
| Grapes.................. | 8,163,666 | 1,136,236 | 9,342,885 | 1,401,433 | 11,041,189 | 1,656,178 |
| Other fresh fruits........ | 2,433,151 | 347,593 | 2,952,195 | 442,829 | 2,688,656 | 403,298 |
| Aniseed................. | 462,999 | 66,128 | 402,429 | 60,364 | 254,562 | 38,184 |
| Saffron................. | 5,870,400 | 838,628 | 6,576,100 | 936,415 | 5,549,300 | 832,395 |
| Peppers and cumin seeds. | 1,156,373 | 165,196 | 1,198,265 | 179,740 | 1,008,082 | 150,462 |
| Olive oil ............. | 30,076,667 | 4,296,667 | 16,602,898 | 2,490,434 | 48,601,286 | 7,290,193 |
| Wines and spirits........ | 70,568,535 | 10,081,219 | 40,336,290 | 6,050,444 | 31,051,800 | 4,657,270 |
| Sausages, chocolate, sweets, preserves, canary seed, etc.......... | 16,065,237 | 2,295,034 | 17,915,573 | 2,687,336 | 20,748,184 | 3,112,227 |
| Fans, hemp shoes, matches, playing cards, etc......... | 2,468,756 | 352,679 | 1,929,890 | 289,489 | 2,726,940 | 409,040 |

*Total value of the imports and exports for the first ten months of the years 1900, 1901, and 1902.*

| | 1900. | | 1901. | | 1902. | |
|---|---|---|---|---|---|---|
| | Pesetas. | U.S. equivalent. | Pesetas. | U.S. equivalent. | Pesetas. | U.S. equivalent. |
| Imports............... | 705,215,708 | $100,745,100 | 688,313,218 | $103,246,982 | 666,041,197 | $99,906,179 |
| Exports............... | 620,712,997 | 88,678,285 | 573,839,506 | 86,075,926 | 611,999,128 | 91,799,869 |

## SHIPPING OF SPAIN.

Following is a comparative statement of the shipping of Spain for the ten months ended October 31, 1900, 1901, and 1902. These figures have just been published by the Spanish Government.

### VESSELS ENTERED.

| | 1900. | | | 1901. | | | 1902. | | |
| | Number of vessels. | Tonnage. | Tons of merchandise carried. | Number of vessels. | Tonnage. | Tons of merchandise carried. | Number of vessels. | Tonnage. | Tons of merchandise carried. |
|---|---|---|---|---|---|---|---|---|---|
| **LOADED.** | | | | | | | | | |
| **Steamers:** | | | | | | | | | |
| Spanish ...... | 4,288 | 3,696,608 | 924,145 | 4,853 | 3,995,252 | 1,014,312 | 4,584 | 3,986,317 | 1,097,268 |
| Foreign ...... | 2,539 | 2,083,943 | 1,714,203 | 2,676 | 2,252,064 | 1,922,171 | 2,601 | 2,267,265 | 1,742,490 |
| **Sailing vessels:** | | | | | | | | | |
| Spanish ...... | 983 | 77,745 | 65,330 | 896 | 68,491 | 57,162 | 940 | 61,594 | 50,518 |
| Foreign ...... | 540 | 133,576 | 137,250 | 610 | 146,427 | 147,165 | 662 | 135,189 | 141,440 |
| **IN BALLAST.** | | | | | | | | | |
| **Steamers:** | | | | | | | | | |
| Spanish ...... | 1,739 | 1,899,912 | ......... | 1,691 | 1,789,043 | ......... | 1,851 | 1,944,506 | ......... |
| Foreign ...... | 3,442 | 3,789,239 | ......... | 3,335 | 3,715,985 | ......... | 3,246 | 3,661,867 | ......... |
| **Sailing vessels:** | | | | | | | | | |
| Spanish ...... | 867 | 18,730 | ......... | 965 | 16,329 | ......... | 1,106 | 21,628 | ......... |
| Foreign ...... | 823 | 69,410 | ......... | 421 | 84,269 | ......... | 393 | 70,921 | ......... |
| Total ....... | 14,661 | 11,769,163 | 2,840,928 | 15,167 | 12,067,860 | 3,140,810 | 15,383 | 12,149,287 | 3,031,716 |

### VESSELS CLEARED.

| | 1900. | | | 1901. | | | 1902. | | |
| | Number of vessels. | Tonnage. | Tons of merchandise carried. | Number of vessels. | Tonnage. | Tons of merchandise carried. | Number of vessels. | Tonnage. | Tons of merchandise carried. |
|---|---|---|---|---|---|---|---|---|---|
| **LOADED.** | | | | | | | | | |
| **Steamers:** | | | | | | | | | |
| Spanish ...... | 4,806 | 4,962,015 | 2,682,115 | 5,344 | 5,256,617 | 2,566,027 | 5,611 | 5,652,006 | 2,985,082 |
| Foreign ...... | 6,011 | 5,516,384 | 6,288,908 | 5,549 | 5,167,612 | 4,811,081 | 5,705 | 5,524,087 | 5,677,152 |
| **Sailing vessels:** | | | | | | | | | |
| Spanish ...... | 1,026 | 64,714 | 44,211 | 896 | 62,518 | 40,296 | 951 | 49,059 | 33,546 |
| Foreign ...... | 515 | 89,630 | 128,228 | 573 | 109,872 | 148,187 | 630 | 96,883 | 119,789 |
| **IN BALLAST.** | | | | | | | | | |
| **Steamers:** | | | | | | | | | |
| Spanish ...... | 721 | 416,864 | ......... | 736 | 449,762 | ......... | 668 | 383,471 | ......... |
| Foreign ...... | 364 | 601,606 | ......... | 372 | 665,366 | ......... | 378 | 613,007 | ......... |
| **Sailing vessels:** | | | | | | | | | |
| Spanish ...... | 364 | 29,901 | ......... | 818 | 18,310 | ......... | 302 | 19,595 | ......... |
| Foreign ...... | 242 | 57,897 | ......... | 287 | 65,543 | ......... | 266 | 65,598 | ......... |
| Total ....... | 14,049 | 11,739,011 | 9,143,463 | 14,075 | 11,795,600 | 7,565,543 | 14,511 | 12,408,206 | 8,815,569 |

The tons referred to are metric tons of 1,000 kilograms (2,205 lbs).

HARRY H. HALLATT,
*Vice-Consul.*

MADRID, *December 16, 1902.*

## REPORT FROM CONSULAR AGENCY AT BILBAO.

The trade in the district of Bilbao decreased continually, and was rather dull toward the end of the year. Notwithstanding these unfavorable circumstances, Bilbao, with its accumulated wealth (see annexed table of companies formed in 1901), principally gained from the products of the iron-ore mines in this province and also from the great number of industrial undertakings established here during the last fifteen years, will hold its position as the center of business and capital for the north of Spain, and it is expected that, when the new harbor works are finished next year and some new railways are added to the good communications already existing, business will develop more than ever.

### STEAMSHIP LINES.

The steamers of "La Compañia Transatlantica," for Cuba and Gulf and Mexican ports, leave here regularly every month. The "Olazarri" (Spanish) and Hamburg lines (German), also make monthly trips to Cuba and South American ports. It is reported that Larriñaga & Co. (Spanish), of Liverpool, have started a new line from New York to the north of Spain, and the first steamer. the *Bernilla*, is expected shortly to arrive.

### COAL.

The coal shippers at Cardiff and Newcastle continue to supply the steel and iron furnaces here, as well as other industrial works, with English fuel. Asturian coals from Gijón and Aviles are also imported in considerable quantities, which importation will undoubtedly increase when more railways are built and more capital is invested in the business.

The blast furnaces, rolling mills, and other ironworks have been working successfully.

Articles that promise well for the future are preserved peppers and raw glycerin. The latter has, up to the present, been shipped only to Elyria and Ivorydale. Glycerin has been sold at various prices between 125 and 144 pesetas, silver; preserved peppers, between 20 and 27.

### PROGRESS OF THE HARBOR WORKS.

During the last season, 24 iron cases, filled with concrete, have been laid down to form the base of the breakwater. There are still 17 cases to be laid, besides a larger one for the foundation of the tower. This tower will be 25 meters in diameter and 8.50 meters in height, and will be built on an inclined wall.

The sum of 1,590,000 pesetas ($238,500) has been paid to contractors during the last year for work executed at the breakwater, which sum, added to the 24,792,000 pesetas ($3,718,800) paid in past years, forms a total of 26,382,000 pesetas ($3,957,300).

The east dock was not finished at the end of last year, but that work will also be completed this season.

## EDUCATION IN THE BASQUE PROVINCES.

Education in the Basque provinces is advancing. Many schools have been opened and the provincial governments, together with the municipal corporations, are making earnest efforts to improve the facilities. I give details below:

Number of schools for—

| | |
|---|---:|
| Children | 12 |
| Adults | 127 |
| Boys— | |
|     Advanced | 2 |
|     Elementary complete | 138 |
|     Elementary incomplete | 1 |
| Girls— | |
|     Elementary complete | 132 |
|     Elementary incomplete | 2 |
| Mixed schools: | |
|     Conducted by masters | 34 |
|     Conducted by mistresses | 26 |
| Number of masters | 193 |
|     Assistants | 26 |
| Number of mistresses | 188 |
|     Assistants | 46 |
| Newspapers published | 1 |
| School savings banks (243 investors, 3,004.70 pesetas) | 4 |
| School colonies: | |
|     For boys | 4 |
|     For girls | 4 |
| Number of boys attending school | 22,264 |
| Number of girls attending school | 16,266 |

| | Pesetas | U. S. currency |
|---|---:|---:|
| Teachers' salaries | 408,130 = | $61,220 |
| Schools requisites | 98,710 = | 14,807 |
| Rewards for pupils | 89,155 = | 13,373 |
| Rents | 39,876 = | 5,981 |
| Total | 635,871 = | 95,381 |

*Classification of masters, mistresses, and assistants, with their annual salaries.*

| Pesetas. | United States currency. | Masters. | Mistresses. | Assistants. |
|---|---|---:|---:|---:|
| 125–250 | $18–37 | 3 | | |
| 250–500 | 37–75 | 12 | 14 | 6 |
| 500–620 | 75–93 | 14 | 10 | |
| 625 | 94 | 44 | 42 | 2 |
| 825 | 124 | 57 | 56 | 4 |
| 1,100 | 165 | 39 | 35 | 7 |
| 1,375 | 206 | 8 | 7 | 18 |
| 1,650 | 248 | 2 | | 29 |
| 2,000 | 300 | 16 | 19 | |

Only one master receives more than 2,000 pesetas ($300).

A school of industrial engineers has been established here, in charge of professors chosen by the minister of public instruction.

## BIRTHS AND DEATHS.

The number of deaths in 1901 reached a total of 2,768, and are accounted for in the following manner: Seven hundred and three from bronchitis, 842 from infectious diseases, 353 from nervous troubles, 144 from diarrhea (from 1 to 4 years of age), 145 from infectious diseases of the organs, 61 from tumors, 82 from debility, 49 from violent death, 10 drowned, 2 suicides, 7 homicides, 8 from advanced age, 61 from other causes, and 127 from causes unknown.  The annual death rate is 33.30 per cent.

The births have been 3,077—1,404 males and 1,314 females legitimate, and 168 males and 191 females illegitimate.  The birth rate is 37.38 per cent.

The population of Bilbao in 1900 was 73,192, and in 1901, 83,213.

*Principal imports to Bilbao during the year 1901.*

| Article. | Total 1901. | Article. | Total 1901. |
|---|---|---|---|
| | *Metric tons.* | | *Metric tons.* |
| Cement, etc.................... | 19,539 | Cotton woven cloth ................. | 174 |
| Carbon coke .................... | 64,987 | Hemp, flax, jute, raw .............. | 120 |
| Carbon mineral.................. | 507,436 | Other metals ...................... | 2,804 |
| Glass, etc....................... | 451 | Silk spun yarn .................... | 3.4 |
| Pottery porcelain ................ | 3,160 | Silk cloth......................... | 2 |
| Slates, blackings, etc ........... | 4,571 | Wood pulp for paper .............. | 9,778 |
| Gold, silver, platinum ........... | ............ | Paper of all sorts................. | 208 |
| Iron castings.................... | 671 | Wood, pitch and pine............. | 76 |
| Iron, forged, rolled ............. | 7,603 | Cut wood and furniture........... | 528 |
| Copper alloys ................... | 394 | Apparatus and machines........... | 81 |
| Colors, dyes, etc ................ | 565 | Railway materials................. | 5,261 |
| Drugs........................... | 2,305 | Animals .......................... | 2 |
| Minerals ........................ | 10 | Meat and fish..................... | 12,856 |
| Staves.......................... | 181 | Grain, flour, dried vegetables ........ | 13,361 |
| Animal fats, grease, artificial manures, etc...................... | 439 | Carriages ......................... | 290 |
| Wool, woven..................... | 103 | Colonial products ................. | 777 |

*Articles imported from the United States in the year 1901 for the Bilbao-Santander Railway Company.*

| Article. | Metric tons. | Article. | Metric tons. |
|---|---|---|---|
| 1901. | | 2 engines, received through the company, for Madrid ................... | 64.5 |
| 65 railway wagons ................. | 240.1 | American organs.................. | 9.1 |
| 2 engines ....................... | 66.1 | | |
| 4 railway carriages, first class........ } | 158.7 | | 642.9 |
| 8 railway carriages, second class ...... } | | | |
| Pieces for the engine.................. | 1.2 | 1902. | |
| 14 wagons....................... | 99.2 | 37 wagons for the railway............ | 184.4 |
| 5 boxes with machines............... | 4 | | |

*Exportations from the port of Bilbao to America in the year 1901.*

| Month. | Hamburguesa Company. | | Transatlantic Company. | | Arrotegui Company. | | Mendraldera-Garteiz. | | Total goods. | Total passengers. |
|---|---|---|---|---|---|---|---|---|---|---|
| | Goods. | Passengers. | Goods. | Passengers. | Goods. | Passengers. | Goods. | Passengers. | | |
| January......... | 380,264 | 37 | 390,116 | 25 | 142,676 | ........ | ........ | ....... | 913,056 | 62 |
| February ....... | 268,929 | 42 | 409,304 | 27 | 113,920 | ........ | ........ | ....... | 792,153 | 69 |
| March .......... | 167,021 | 10 | 333,847 | 9 | 145,063 | ........ | ........ | ....... | 645,951 | 19 |
| April........... | 357,513 | 35 | 314,738 | 16 | 240,051 | ........ | ........ | ....... | 912,602 | 51 |
| May............ | 128,299 | 15 | 359,547 | 22 | 154,551 | ........ | ........ | ....... | 642,390 | 37 |
| June........... | 312,047 | 19 | 248,661 | 5 | 177,217 | ........ | ........ | ....... | 737,925 | 24 |
| July............ | 378,781 | 32 | 282,175 | 10 | 213,235 | ........ | ........ | ....... | 874,141 | 42 |
| August......... | 355,080 | 41 | 252,026 | 14 | 520,546 | ........ | ........ | ....... | 1,127,602 | 55 |
| September ...... | 257,906 | 29 | 119,520 | 28 | 156,220 | 8 | 233,972 | ....... | 767,618 | 65 |
| October......... | 153,311 | 36 | 115,503 | 56 | 131,575 | 10 | 286,078 | ....... | 686,467 | 102 |
| November ...... | 412,941 | 55 | 159,236 | 56 | 235,415 | 7 | 263,615 | ....... | 1,071,207 | 118 |

*Duties collected during the year 1901, Bilbao.*

IMPORTS.

| Month. | Total imports. | | | |
|---|---|---|---|---|
| | Tons. | Kilo-grams. | Pesetas. | U. S. currency. |
| January | 84,867 | 522 | 39,700 | $6,114 |
| February | 76,128 | 417 | 35,792 | 5,512 |
| March | 85,182 | 273 | 39,519 | 6,086 |
| April | 69,401 | 291 | 32,639 | 5,026 |
| May | 86,945 | 592 | 36,713 | 5,654 |
| June | 63,165 | 541 | 31,433 | 4,840 |
| July | 98,001 | 610 | 56,069 | 8,635 |
| August | 62,771 | 722 | 35,441 | 5,458 |
| September | 89,704 | 104 | 47,135 | 7,259 |
| October | 67,090 | 148 | 36,499 | 5,621 |
| November | 97,904 | 044 | 49,328 | 7,597 |
| December | 60,783 | 425 | 25,686 | 3,956 |
| Total | 941,895 | 689 | 465,959 | 71,758 |

EXPORTS.

| Month. | Total exports. | | | |
|---|---|---|---|---|
| | Tons. | Kilo-grams. | Pesetas. | U. S. currency. |
| January | 384,644 | 939 | 191,821 | $29,541 |
| February | 288,542 | 378 | 143,974 | 22,172 |
| March | 285,401 | 121 | 142,530 | 21,949 |
| April | 301,566 | 742 | 150,469 | 23,171 |
| May | 335,171 | 97 | 167,163 | 25,743 |
| June | 350,852 | 712 | 174,980 | 26,947 |
| July | 445,686 | 345 | 222,060 | 34,197 |
| August | 402,761 | 430 | 200,587 | 30,890 |
| September | 382,606 | 802 | 190,871 | 29,394 |
| October | 401,393 | 755 | 200,256 | 30,890 |
| November | 374,400 | 415 | 186,378 | 28,702 |
| December | 342,426 | 231 | 170,687 | 26,286 |
| Total | 4,295,753 | 967 | 2,141,777 | 269,598 |

RECAPITULATION.

| | Tons. | Pesetas. | U. S. currency. |
|---|---|---|---|
| Importation: Coal and general cargo | 941,895 | 465,959.39 | $69,893 |
| Exportation: Mineral and general cargo | 4,295,753 | 2,141,777.72 | 321,266 |
| Total | 5,237,649 | 2,607,737.11 | 391,159 |

*Importation and exportation in the port of Bilbao from 1878 to 1901.*

| Years. | Importation. | Exportation. | Total. |
|---|---|---|---|
| | *Tons.* | *Tons.* | *Tons.* |
| 1878–79 | 144,977 | 1,195,422 | 1,340,399 |
| 1879–80 | 209,893 | 1,791,951 | 2,001,844 |
| 1880–81 | 252,700 | 2,591,660 | 2,844,360 |
| 1881–82 | 247,910 | 2,934,313 | 3,182,223 |
| 1882–83 | 348,546 | 3,758,557 | 4,097,103 |
| 1883–84 | 357,967 | 3,585,468 | 3,943,435 |
| 1884–85 | 383,571 | 3,196,153 | 3,579,724 |
| 1885–86 | 431,340 | 3,434,088 | 3,865,428 |
| 1886–87 | 473,270 | 3,921,164 | 4,394,434 |
| 1887–88 | 548,348 | 4,076,944 | 4,625,288 |
| 1888–89 | 580,155 | 3,879,816 | 4,459,972 |
| 1889–90 | 684,367 | 4,354,038 | 5,038,405 |
| 1890–91 | 822,235 | 3,911,840 | 4,734,075 |
| 1891–92 | 754,568 | 3,764,604 | 4,519,172 |
| 1892–93 | 759,864 | 4,368,967 | 5,128,831 |
| 1893–94 | 774,731 | 4,293,045 | 5,067,776 |
| 1894–95 | 763,158 | 4,219,016 | 4,982,174 |
| 1895–96 | 732,190 | 5,042,772 | 5,775,262 |
| 1896–97 | 838,314 | 4,954,490 | 5,792,804 |
| 1897–98 | 779,878 | 4,894,877 | 5,674,755 |
| 1898–99 | 791,477 | 4,974,149 | 5,765,626 |
| 1899, second half year | 441,318 | 2,894,756 | 3,336,074 |
| 1900 | 973,993 | 4,833,445 | 5,807,438 |
| 1901 | 941,894 | 4,296,751 | 5,237,645 |

From these figures, it will be seen that importation and exportation have been steadily increasing from 1878 to 1901. There was a marked decrease in 1901, especially in reference to exportation, but still the total is an increase of 796,917 tons import and 3,100,329 tons export over the years 1878–79.

*The iron-ingot production in twenty years.*

| Countries. | 1880. | 1900. |
|---|---|---|
| | *Tons.* | *Tons.* |
| Spain | 52,000 | 294,118 |
| United States | 3,896,554 | 14,009,623 |
| Great Britain | 7,800,266 | 9,002,107 |
| Germany and Luxemburg | 2,729,038 | 8,520,390 |
| France | 1,725,298 | 2,699,494 |
| Netherlands | 624,302 | 1,018,507 |
| Austria-Hungary | 750,134 | 1,475,000 |
| Russia | 448,411 | 2,925,600 |
| Sweden | 382,108 | 526,868 |
| Italy | 6,000 | 12,200 |
| Canada | 23,100 | 88,867 |
| Japan | 7,000 | 64,000 |
| Other nations | 40,000 | 150,000 |
| Total | 18,484,206 | 40,786,774 |

*Exportation of mineral during the year 1901 from the harbor of Castro-Urdiales.*

| Loading places. | Number of ships. | Tons. |
|---|---|---|
| Dicido | 82 | 162,487 |
| Saltacaballo | 61 | 154,050 |
| Castro-Alen | 71 | 124,745 |
| Urdiales | 46 | 62,385 |
| Onton | 13 | 20,215 |
| Sonabia | 5 | 6,077 |
| Total | 278 | 529,959 |

*Comparison of the duties collected during the years 1900 and 1901.*

| | 1900. | 1901. | Difference. |
|---|---|---|---|
| IMPORTS. | | | |
| From foreign countries. | *Tons.* | *Tons.* | *Tons.* |
| Coal | 634,450 | 616,594 | − 17,856 |
| General cargo | 163,212 | 170,166 | + 6,954 |
| From Spain: | | | |
| Coal | 106,278 | 84,699 | − 21,579 |
| General cargo | 70,053 | 70,435 | + 382 |
| Total | 973,993 | 941,894 | − 32,099 |
| EXPORTS. | | | |
| Foreign countries: | | | |
| Mineral | 4,584,302 | 4,056,925 | −527,377 |
| General cargo | 40,193 | 52,703 | + 12,510 |
| From Spain: | | | |
| Mineral | 51,549 | 48,811 | − 2,738 |
| General cargo | 157,401 | 137,312 | − 20,089 |
| Total | 4,833,445 | 4,295,751 | −537,694 |
| Comparison | 5,807,438 | 5,237,645 | −569,798 |

*Comparison of the total amount of mineral exported by the different loading places of the river of Bilbao, according to the details received from the respective companies.* .

| Loading places. | 1901. | 1900. | Difference. |
|---|---|---|---|
| | *Tons.* | *Tons.* | *Tons.* |
| Bilbao River and Cantabrian Co., Ltd. (Galdames y Sestao Riv.). | 864,624 | 860,252 | + 3,472 |
| Railway of the— | | | |
| Deportación (Triano) .................................... | 1,016,452 | 1,280,848 | −264,396 |
| Sociedad Franco-Belga, mines at Somorrostro ................ | 748,673 | 721,611 | + 27,072 |
| Luchana Mining Co. ....................................... | 148,886 | 204,233 | − 55,347 |
| Orconera Iron Ore Company, Ltd .......................... | 1,236,452 | 1,408,469 | −172,017 |
| Santander to Bilbao, line of the Cadagno Co ............... | 35,981 | 45,728 | − 9,747 |
| Tram of the mine Primitiva ............................... | 25,146 | 21,526 | + 3,620 |
| Special loading place of: | | | |
| Company de Chavarri y Gandarias ......................... | 342,600 | 59,966 | +282,634 |
| Viuda é Hijos de Pedro Gandarias ......................... | 111,536 | 159,324 | − 47,788 |
| Railway from Bilbao to Portugalet ......................... | 14,685 | .......... | .......... |
| Other loading places at Olareaga ............................ | 237,402 | 229,186 | + 8,356 |
| Total ........ | 4,782,527 | 4,988,093 | .......... |

In these quantities is included the mineral some companies have dispatched for the use of the company of Altos Hornos de Vizcaya by the railway of Galdames, Triano and Orconera. The mineral exported by Castro-Urdiales amounts to 319,700 tons.

*List of societies formed in Bilbao from January 1 to December 31, 1901.*

| Companies. | Capital. | Industry or commerce. |
|---|---|---|
| | *Pesetas.(a)* | |
| Sucesores de L. Schmidt ............................... | 45,000 | Hardware. |
| Vidaurrázaga y Ca. .................................... | 100,000 | Screws. |
| Minera de Peñaflor .................................... | 4,500,000 | Lead mines. |
| Horuraza y Sarasúa .................................... | 50,000 | Cristalery. |
| Goya y Ca. ............................................ | 45,000 | White linen. |
| Sociedad Bilbaina de Artes Gráficas .................... | 500,000 | Typography. |
| Compañía Naviera "Bachi" .............................. | 4,000,000 | Steamship company. |
| Sotar y Azuar ......................................... | 5,000,000 | Mining and Shipping Company. |
| Minas de Teberga ...................................... | 4,000,000 | Coal mines. |
| Bausari, Azula y Ca. ................................... | 80,000 | House building. |
| El Material Industrial ................................. | 100,000 | Machinery. |
| Juan Robert ........................................... | 500,000 | Drugs. |
| Viuda de J. de Olare y Ca .............................. | 25,000 | Sale of coal. |
| Sociedad E. de Droguería General ....................... | 5,000,000 | Drugs. |
| Ceberio y Arauzábal .................................... | 9,250 | Pots (earthenware). |
| Larrinaga y Bilbao ..................................... | 10,000 | Coal. |
| Sindicato Minero de Contratación ....................... | 400,000 | Mines (acquisition). |
| Argentifera de Tras-os-mantes .......................... | 650,000 | Lead mines. |
| Unión Financiera ...................................... | 8,000,000 | Bank. |
| Hidráulica del Fresser. ................................ | 3,000,000 | Waters. |
| Banco Naviero Minero .................................. | 15,000,000 | Bank. |
| E. Coste y Vildosola é Hijo ............................ | 2,283,098 | Flour manufacture. |
| Compañía Minera "La Amistad" ......................... | 300,000 | Iron mines. |
| Trun y Lesaca ......................................... | 5,000,000 | Do. |
| La Estrella ............................................ | 5,000,000 | Steamship company. |
| A. Pascualy Ca. ....................................... | 175,630 | Restaurant. |
| Sociedad Minera de Berástegui ......................... | 2,500,000 | Iron mines. |
| Sociedad Española de Construcciones Metálicas .......... | 13,500,000 | |
| Sierra Almenara ....................................... | 1,500,000 | |
| Eustaquio Hierro y Sobrino ............................ | 40,000 | Boots and manufacture. |
| Pascual Guruceta y Ca. ................................ | 7,750 | Metal foundry. |
| Antón y Vilá. ......................................... | 6,000 | Confectionery. |
| Barón y Ariño ......................................... | 50,000 | Hardware. |
| Arteta y Compañía ..................................... | 5,000 | Electric-light installation. |
| Sanz y García. ........................................ | 40,000 | Typewriter (machines). |
| F. C San Sban á Hernani .............................. | 500,000 | Do. |
| Bilbao-Morata ......................................... | 1,200,000 | Iron mines. |
| E. Estabillo y Hermana ................................ | 2,000 | Hardware. |
| Compañía minera La Firmeza ........................... | 500,000 | Mining. |
| Compañía de Cabarga .................................. | 2,500,000 | Do. |
| Compañía Vasgo Gaditana de Navegación ............... | 2,500,000 | Steamship company. |
| La Constancia ......................................... | 2,500,000 | Copper mines. |
| Electra Ind. Castilla Nueva ............................ | 1,100,000 | Electric light. |

*a* The market value of the peseta is about 15 cents,

*List of societies formed in Bilbao from January 1 to December 31, 1901*—Continued.

| Companies. | Capital. | Industry or commerce. |
|---|---|---|
| | *Pesetas.*(a) | |
| José M Barrenecha y Ca | 1,000,000 | Iron mines. |
| Bilbao y La Justicia | 5,000 | Bakers. |
| Paul Bürger y Ca | 30,000 | Commercial representatives. |
| Banco de Vizcaya | 15,000,000 | Banking. |
| Collado del Lobo | 2,500,000 | Lead mines. |
| Maruri y Yuso | 25,000 | White linen. |
| Vidarte y Ca | 80,000 | Work instruments. |
| La Lealtad Minera | 10,000 | Mines (exploration). |
| La Polar | 100,000,000 | Insurance company. |
| Auxiliar de Ferrocarriles | 4,000,000 | Railway material. |
| Teledinámica del Gállego | 3,000,000 | |
| García, Aguirre y Ca | 5,000 | |
| Bodegas Bilbainas | 6,000,000 | Wines. |
| Eusebio Zabala y Ca | 25,000 | Cement. |
| Minera Euskalduna | 1,000,000 | Mines (acquisition). |
| Centro Minero Bilbaino | 5,000,000 | Do. |
| Sanatorio de Gorbea | 500,000 | Sanitarium. |
| Garteiz Hermanos Yermo y Ca | 425,000 | Machinery. |
| Compañía Minera Ibérica | 4,000,000 | Mines (acquisition). |
| Compañía de vapor "G. Pozzi" | 500,000 | Steamship company. |
| Sociedad Castilla de las Guardas | 7,500,000 | Copper mines. |
| Plomos de Arzuaga y Mestanza | 6,000,000 | Lead mines. |
| Estaños plomos argentíferos | 125,000 | Mining. |
| Lázaro Martinez y Ca | 45,000 | Decoration. |
| Fuerzas motrices del Gándara | 300,000 | Cement. |
| La Hidroeléctrica Ibérica | 20,000,000 | Do. |
| Olavarría v. Luzinaga | 12,000 | Wines. |
| Hulleras de Guardo | 4,000,000 | Coal mines. |
| Tipografía Universal | 40,000 | Lithography. |
| Viuda de F. Hoyos y Krug | 88,661 | Commission. |
| Pedro Llona y Ca | 20,000 | Cloth. |
| Sociedad Minera de Alonsótegui | 1,500,000 | Concession of mines. |
| Los Almadenes | 6,000,000 | Lead mines. |
| Mari-Esperanza de Triano | 225,000 | Iron mines. |
| Angel Uriarte y Ca | 25,000 | Tailor. |
| Santos Fid y Ca | 35,895 | Joinery. |
| David Revuelta y Ca | 6,030 | Bronze articles. |
| Ripalda y Lazcano | 10,000 | Representation. |
| Argentífera de Almagrera | 6,000,000 | Lead mines. |
| Llodio y Ca | 100,000 | Mining. |
| Sociedad Anónima Iris | 500,000 | Decoration. |
| Erice y Mareal | 100,000 | Hardware. |
| Uria, Sunyer y Ca | 161,850 | Portland cement. |
| Banco de Bilbao | 30,000,000 | Bank. |
| Sindicato Minero | 5,500,000 | Mines (acquisition). |
| Sociedad General de Minería | 5,000,000 | Do. |
| Compañía Bilbaina de Electriz | 75,000 | Water. |
| Ahlemeyer (fusion Hisp.) | 30,000,000 | Electricity. |
| Arechavaleta Hermanos | 15,000 | Wines and liquors. |
| Hierros de Celrá | 1,500,000 | Iron mines. |
| A. Zabiaurre Hermanos | 80,000 | |
| Garrote y Ca | 15,000 | Insurance company. |
| Arechavaleta y Richter | 228,888 | Hardware. |
| Estaños de Monterey | 135,000 | Mining. |
| Fábrica de Hierro de Aspe | 1,000,000 | Iron foundry. |
| Meare y Torórntegui | 10,000 | |
| Careaga Gómez y Ca | 100,000 | Mineral oils. |
| Sociedad Minera Vizcaina | 500,000 | Mining. |
| Faustino Pueyo y Ca | 45,737 | Iron mines. |
| Fortuna | 5,000,000 | Clothing. |
| Compañía Ibérica Electricidad Thompson | 10,000,000 | Electrical machinery. |
| Tomás de Zabiria y Ca | 948,625 | Chemistry. |
| Sindicato Vizcaino de Minas | 200,000 | Mines (acquisition). |
| Sociedad Minera de Albarracin | 1,000,000 | Do. |
| Banco del Comercio | 5,000,000 | Bank. |
| Lasa, Ostalosa é Iceta | 34,500 | House building. |
| La Bilbaina | 5,000,000 | Bank. |
| Aristegui Hermanos y Ca | 75,000 | Enameled bricks. |
| Ahlemeyer | 5,000,000 | Electric-light installation. |
| La Atilana | 4,000,000 | Lead mines. |
| Electricista Minera | 500,000 | Water. |
| Minas de Zink de Achando | 850,000 | Zinc mines. |
| Ruiz de Salas y Ca | 18,000 | Material for construction. |
| Tejeiro é Izaurieta | 35,000 | Glassware. |
| Andreu y Galilea | 71,000 | |
| Arana y Ca | 450,000 | Wood. |
| Remigio T. y A. Depics | 50,000 | Glassware. |
| L. Calle y Hermanos | 12,000 | Leather. |
| F. Echevarria é Hijos | 1,000,000 | Industrial company. |
| O. Usabiaga y Ca | 60,000 | Fruits. |
| Laguna y Ca | 10,000 | Colonial produce. |

a The market value of the peseta is about 15 cents.

*List of societies formed in Bilbao from January 1 to December 31, 1901*—Continued.

| Companies. | Capital. | Industry or commerce. |
|---|---|---|
| | *Pesetas.*(a) | |
| Compañía Vascongada de Minería | 12,500,000 | Mines (acquisition). |
| Crédito de la Unión Minera | 20,000,000 | Mining and banking. |
| Constructora Obras Públicas | 10,000,000 | Railway construction. |
| Compañía Minera de M. y Maliaño | 700,000 | Mining. |
| Marisuras de la Asunción | 25,000 | Land draining. |
| Cobres de Menorca | 2,000,000 | Copper mines. |
| La Vizcaína | 3,250,000 | |
| La Vasco Madrileña | 6,000,000 | Lead mines. |
| La Camera Española | 2,000,000 | Mines (acquisition). |
| Aguilar y Ca | 9,000 | Furniture manufacturers. |
| Aguas del Ceruega | 125,000 | Water. |
| Hijos de Rufino Videa | 305,000 | Colonial produce. |
| Cobres de Ruesga | 1,500,000 | Copper mines. |
| Portillo Ibáñez y Ca | 250,000 | Mining and steamship company. |
| Urizar y Aldecoa | 40,000 | Oils. |
| Compañía Minera Bilbao Santander | 5,000,000 | Mining. |
| Empresas Artistas | 50,000 | Artists' instrument. |
| Ochandiano y Ca | 250,000 | Mines. |
| Compañía del Vapor "Katalin" | 90,000 | Steamship company. |
| Compañía Minera de Ampuero | 30,000 | Mining. |
| Ocaña y Ca | 50,000 | Sale of land. |
| Ángel Fernández y Ca | 32,000 | Iron mines. |
| La Papelería Española | 20,000,000 | Paper mills. |
| Total | 482,283,774 | |

a The market value of the peseta is about 15 cents.

*Statement of the Bank of Bilbao, December 31, 1901.*

| Description. | Pesetas. | Description. | Pesetas. |
|---|---|---|---|
| **ACTIVE.** | | **PASSIVE.** | |
| Cash | 11,596,011.84 | Capital | 50,000,000.00 |
| Branch of the Bank of Spain, currency account | 2,078,089.77 | Reserve fund | 3,000,000.00 |
| | | Second reserve fund | 1,200,000.00 |
| Debts of correspondents | 6,638,888.60 | Utilities of unrealized values | 583,674.10 |
| Furniture | 30,681.50 | Creditors in currency account in | |
| Immovable goods | 4,353,009.02 | Bilbao | 26,659,366.15 |
| Effects | 36,034,135.77 | Credits of correspondents | 3,882,541.09 |
| Coupons | 15,993.31 | Debts on effects | 161,239.54 |
| Loans of values | 8,920,130.06 | Effective consignations | 3,760,068.90 |
| Currency accounts of credits, with interest | 26,159,076.91 | Dividends to pay | 929,170.00 |
| | | Credits in realized coupons | 968,334.24 |
| Coupons and amortizations | 682,860.57 | Credits in realized imortizations | 840,965.56 |
| Credits | 3,816.54 | Credits in realized coupons and | |
| General expenditure and salaries | | amortizations | 682,860.57 |
| Savings bank | | From the savings bank | 42,918,645.48 |
| Various credits | 611,758.88 | Sundry credits | 1,589,818.18 |
| Values in hands of correspondents | 8,303,846.26 | Credits of value in hands of correspondents | 3,729,943.95 |
| Shares | 15,000,000.00 | Coupons to collect | |
| Total of debits | 120,428,752.52 | Gains and losses | 25,124.67 |
| Documents in guaranty, necessary, and obligatory | 672,025,675.17 | Total of the credits | 120,428,752.52 |
| | | Deposits | 672,025,675.19 |
| Total | 792,454,427.71 | Total | 792,454,427.71 |

*Exports from the United States to the port of Pasages.*

| Products. | Amount. | Customhouse charges. |
|---|---|---|
| | | *Pesetas.* |
| Petroleum 20 to 30 per cent ... gallons. | 2,245.351 | 372,395.50 |
| Cotton ... metric tons. | 400.753 | 6,833.68 |
| Staves ... do. | 142.706 | 2,130.59 |
| Machines and accessories ... do. | .196 | 47.04 |
| Iron ingot and steel ... do. | 2.720 | 326.40 |
| Total | 2,790.726 | 381,733.21 |

C. YENSEN, *Consular Agent.*

BILBAO, *August 1, 1902.*

### REPORT FROM CONSULAR AGENCY AT GIJON.

The following table shows the relative positions of the countries from which machinery and tools were imported during the year ended December 31, 1901:

| Country. | Value. | Percentage. |
|---|---|---|
| Belgium | $263,100 | 23.44 |
| France | 134,500 | 11.98 |
| Germany | 332,815 | 29.63 |
| United Kingdom | 328,785 | 29.28 |
| United States | 63,750 | 5.67 |
| Total | 1,122,950 | ......... |

The United States has more than doubled her imports of machinery, as compared with the previous year, but still remains at the bottom of the list.

It has been noticed that more American commercial travelers have recently visited this district; but as very few of them are acquainted with any other language than English, their visits have necessarily been largely confined to the limited number of firms that speak that tongue. These visits have undoubtedly resulted in an increase of imports; and if travelers are sent who can speak Spanish or French, a much larger trade with the United States will certainly ensue. Practical men will be able to form the best idea of the requirements of this district.

Greater facilities for doing business should be given to Spanish buyers. The usual custom is to require payment in New York before shipment, while German firms give ninety days, insuring themselves against loss by ascertaining through banking houses whether buyers are trustworthy. Germany stands at the head of the list as regards machinery, the most important of all imports here, and the rapid increase in her trade is largely due to the facilities for doing business.

Commerce with the United States is confined almost exclusively to machinery, wood, grain, and petroleum; certain provisions, such as bacon and lard were, until recently, imported from America, but owing to the high rate of exchange ruling, as well as of freight and of duty, they can not now compete with the Spanish produce.

The importation of grain from the United States is severely handicapped by lack of direct shipment to this district, but that is expected to be altered in two or three years, when the works at the port of Musel are sufficiently advanced to allow steamers of large tonnage to discharge there. These remarks apply also to machinery and wood.

Certain classes of machinery, such as boilers and engines, can not be imported from America, on account of bulk and weight; they involve too much freight and duty to allow them to compete with machinery from European countries. Brass and copper goods are entirely excluded by reason of the heavy duty.

All classes of machinery and tools of a light character, which can be packed in a small compass or are a specialty of American manufacture, are acceptable here. Mining machinery and tools especially find a good market, which should be carefully followed up by American manufacturers, as it offers a wider field for business than any other.

Owing to the backward condition of agriculture in Asturias and to the natural features of the country, the importation of agricultural machinery is almost entirely confined to hillside plows; but cultivators and corn drills should meet with a fair market, if energetically introduced.

I have consulted dealers in machinery regarding the acceptance of samples on the terms of paying 50 per cent before shipment and the balance when the samples are sold, and learn that Messrs. Morgan & Elliot, a responsible firm, is willing to receive samples on these terms.

I am informed by these dealers that shipments of machinery by way of Cadiz and Santander should be avoided, as bad treatment and loss of parts invariably occur; and that Liverpool should be preferred, as it affords better facilities for transshipment.

If weights and measurements in the metric system were given by American manufacturers, it would greatly facilitate business.

ARTHUR LOVELACE,
*Acting Consular Agent.*

GIJON, *May 24, 1902.*

## REPORT FROM CONSULAR AGENCY AT SAN FELIU DE GUIXOLS.

No imports from the United States were entered at this port during the year. The value of the exports to the United States amounted to $566,687.12 gold, consisting mostly of corks and cork shavings.

No changes in the regulations or wharfage dues have been made at this roadstead, but there is a project to construct a harbor; it is expected to commence building within the next six months.

Shipments from this district to the United States go by several routes, to wit, via Bordeaux and Marseilles, France; Genoa, Italy, and Barcelona, Spain.

The movement of shipping between this port and foreign countries has been as follows: Vessels entered, 31; tons register, 25,106. Cleared, 250; tons register, 210,943.

Most of the vessels cleared from this port for foreign countries call from some Spanish port.

The most prominent industries of this district are the manufacture of corks, packing of cork shavings, and fishing. Some of the anchovies caught in these waters are packed here and exported to Italy.

There is no agriculture nor horticulture to speak of in this district, which is mostly hilly land, covered with cork-wood trees.

FRANCIS ESTEVA,
*Consular Agent.*

SAN FELIU DE GUIXOLS, *July 3, 1902.*

*Imports at San Feliu de Guixols for the fiscal year ended June 30, 1902.*

| Articles. | Quantities. | Countries. | Value in United States gold. |
|---|---|---|---|
| Coal............kilos.. | 762,265 | England...................... | $4,252.52 |
| Cork wood............do.... | 129,151 | Italy and Portugal.............. | 8,105.71 |
| Hemp, raw............do.... | 2,698 | Italy.......................... | 376.29 |
| Ivory nuts............do.... | 151,963 | Ecuador and England......... | 4,662.74 |
| Lumber, rough......cubic meters.. | 761 | Russia........................ | 6,898.88 |
| Total .......... | | | 24,296.14 |

*Declared exports from San Feliu de Guixols for the fiscal year ended June 30, 1902.*

| Articles. | Quantities. | Countries. | Value in United States gold. |
|---|---|---|---|
| Anchovies........................kilos.. | 86,910 | Italy.......................................... | $10,909.20 |
| Corks................................M.. | 418,168 | England and Germany................. | 874,828.45 |
| Cork shavings...................kilos.. | 1,646,560 | .....do...................................... | 68,898.72 |
| Cork wood.........................do.... | 28,676 | Germany and France ................. | 2,119.70 |
| Oak bark...........................do.... | 492,891 | Italy...................................... | 9,624.09 |
| Total ................. | | | 966,375.16 |

NOTE.—The exports to the United States are not included in this statement.

## REPORT FROM CONSULAR AGENCY AT TARRAGONA.

*Principal imports at the port of Tarragona for the year ended June 30, 1902.*

| Articles. | Quantities. | Value. | Where produced. |
|---|---|---|---|
| Coal and patent fuel ...............kilos.. | 25,693,000 | $163,754 | England. |
| Cheese and preserved milk.........do.... | 82,257 | 28,208 | Switzerland, Holland. |
| Chemical products...................do.... | 1,089,000 | 72,623 | England, Belgium, France. |
| Cod and stock fish...................do.... | 1,199,590 | 215,737 | Norway, Newfoundland. |
| Deals (pine wood)...................pieces.. | 71,354 | 69,648 | Russia, United States. |
| Glass (plate and wrought).........kilos.. | 4,930 | 1,712 | France, Switzerland. |
| Grains and dried vegetables........do.... | 1,287,700 | 46,319 | Austria, France, Morocco. |
| Guano (artificial)...................do.... | 1,341,864 | 67,235 | France, Algiers. |
| Iron (wrought) .....................do.... | 116,897 | 22,582 | England, Germany. |
| Lime (hydraulic) and cement......do.... | 300,750 | 2,104 | France. |
| Machinery: | | | |
|   Agricultural .....................do.... | 3,319 | 889 | Do. |
|   Various ..........................do.... | 7,542 | 6,203 | Germany, England, Belgium. |
| Meals and feculas ..................do.... | 668,180 | 33,180 | Germany, Holland. |
| Petroleum ..........................do.... | 1,327,913 | 112,312 | United States. |
| Staves: | | | |
|   Chestnut and red oak.......number.. | 996,312 | 69,393 | Italy. |
|   Black oak.........................do.... | 476,689 | 126,463 | United States. |
| Sulphur (brimstone) ...............kilos.. | 1,261,150 | 35,408 | Italy. |
| Wheat ...............................do.... | 14,511,749 | 598,173 | Russia. |
| Wood pulp...........................do.... | 10,100 | 184 | Sweden. |
| Zinc and other metals (pig, sheet, and wrought), kilos. | 18,976 | 3,617 | England, Belgium, Germany. |
| Clay for industrial use..............kilos.. | 55,000 | 670 | United States. |
| Total value...................... | | 1,673,364 | |

*Declared exports from Tarragona during the year ended June 30, 1902.*

| Articles. | Quantities. | Value. | Destination. |
|---|---|---|---|
| Almonds ........................kilos.. | 2,706,375 | $349,750 | England, United States, North Europe, South America. |
| Figs (dried)....................do.... | 340,700 | 11,980 | France, Italy. |
| Filberts.........................do.... | 6,776,200 | 739,800 | England, Germany, Belgium. |
| Grapes (fresh) .................do.... | 200,600 | 7,089 | Germany. |
| Lead ore ........................do.... | 464,725 | 12,823 | Italy, France, Belgium, Holland. |
| Licorice root....................do.... | 57,250 | 2,430 | Italy (probably for transshipment). |
| Oil (olive) .....................do.... | 7,911,500 | 1,403,185 | Italy, France. |
| Pipes (empty casks) ............do.... | 702,210 | 33,192 | France. |
| Tartar (lees and refined)......do.... | 280,600 | 64,526 | England, Germany, France. |
| Wines.......................gallons.. | 8,632,290 | 1,489,830 | France, Germany, England, United States, West Indies, Canada, etc. |
| Total value.................. | | 4,414,605 | |

*Declared exports from Tarragona to the United States during the year ended June 30, 1902.*

| Articles. | Number packages. | Value. | Remarks. |
|---|---|---|---|
| Almonds..........................bags.. | 29,766 | $209,121 | }Exported to the United States. |
| Wines.............................casks.. | 2,684 | 21,318 | |
| Candies and preserved fruit, cases and boxes. | ............ | 2,741 | Exported to Habana. |
| Do.............................. | ............ | 1,871 | Exported to Manila. |
| Total ................................. | ............ | 235,051 | |

*Merchant vessels entered at the port of Tarragona during the year ended June 30, 1902.*

| | Steamers. | Sailing ships. | Registered tonnage. |
|---|---|---|---|
| Spanish ................................. | 794 | ............ | 576,570 |
| Do.......................... | ............ | 260 | 12,545 |
| Foreign ................................. | 347 | ............ | 211,464 |
| Do.......................... | ............ | 75 | 8,358 |
| Total ................................. | 1,141 | 335 | 808,937 |

| Nationalities. | Classification. |
|---|---|
| | *Number.* |
| Spanish ................................. | 1,050 |
| English ................................. | 97 |
| Italian ................................. | 89 |
| Scandinavian ................................. | 94 |
| French ................................. | 56 |
| Dutch ................................. | 46 |
| Russian ................................. | 21 |
| German ................................. | 9 |
| Various (Monaco, Greek, and Turkish) ................................. | 14 |
| Total ................................. | 1,476 |

LOUIS G. AGOSTINI,
*Consular Agent.*

TARRAGONA, *July 1, 1902.*

## REPORT FROM CONSULAR AGENCY AT ALMERIA.

The tables of imports and exports for the calendar year 1901 demonstrate that there has been an improvement in the commerce of Almeria. Progress appears to be slow but substantial, and the increase from year to year indicates a healthy condition of trade.

### TRADE WITH UNITED STATES.

The direct imports from the United States to Almeria were 1,579 cubic meters of timber, with a value of $26,250. Some staves were also imported direct.

The direct exports were chiefly grapes, of which 188,110 barrels and 759 half barrels were shipped from this port, representing a value of about $471,000.

There were also some barrels sent to the United States, by transshipment in England. These, however, do not appear in the figures.

### IRON ORE.

The exports of iron ore from this port were 7,708 tons, representing a value of $15,500.

The indirect imports and exports were small; I have no means of finding out how much they amounted to.

The exportation of iron ore decreased about 18,000 tons as compared with last year. The average price for 50 per cent ore has been about $2.50 per ton.

### SALT.

Owing to the opening of new salt pans at Roquetas, in this district, the exportation of salt has greatly increased. The salt pans, including those at Cape de Gata, produced about 50,000 tons of salt, which was sold at an average price of $1.20 per ton.

### ZINC LEAD.

Nearly all the zinc ore exported from here was sent to Antwerp by the Belgian firm "Société Anonyme Metallurgique Austro-Belge," which ships the ore calcined. There has been a small decrease in the exportation of this metal, the average price being $16 per ton for the calcined ore and $7 for the calamine.

The smelting of lead has been recommenced by the firm "Compañia La Cruz," which intends to push energetically the production of this metal.

### ESPARTO GRASS.

All the esparto grass, with few exceptions, was exported to Great Britain at an average price of $18.75 per ton f. o. b.

### FRUITS.

Grapes, which constitute the principal wealth of this province, have considerably increased in their production. Over 200,000 barrels more than last year was exported, representing an augmentation of $500,000 in the value of exports.

The exportation of grapes to the United States in 1901 was much larger than in former years, owing to the greater production and to the flooding of the British markets, where prices were not favorable. The average price was about $2.50 per barrel.

The exportation of almonds has decreased considerably this year, and about 3,000 boxes less have been shipped. Price, from $5 to $7.50 per box.

The exports of oranges are increasing. About 3,500 cases more than in 1900 were shipped last year. Average price, $2.50 per case.

Over 1,000 cases of figs were exported this year, for the first time in the history of the trade. Price, about $2.25 per case.

### LOCUSTS.

Owing to the great damage done by these insects, the Spanish Government has organized, in this province and others, a campaign for their extinction.

## SUGAR WORKS.

This industry has been suspended on account of a disease in the beet root, caused by the insect *Cassida nebulosa*.

## GENERAL SHIPPING.

No American vessel visited Almeria in the year 1901. In French, Danish, and Norwegian shipping, there has been an increase; in British shipping, a small decrease. As many vessels of other nations called as in the preceding year.

## RAILWAY LINE TO LINARES.

*Statistics of traffic.*

Passenger trains:
Passengers ...................................................number.. 158,713
Luggage (excess) ...............................................tons.. 13
Freight trains:
Ores ...........................................................do.... 227,180
Esparto ........................................................do.... 9,520
Grapes .........................................................do.... 5,513
Sundry..........................................................do.... 214,229

## LOADING STAGES.

Announcement has been made by the firm "The Alguife Mines and Railway Company, Limited," of the proposed construction, by public bids, of mechanical loading stages for loading iron ore. These stages are to be erected outside the port, near the Eastern breakwater.

WILLIAM M. LINDSAY,
*Acting Consular Agent.*

ALMERIA, *June 23, 1902.*

---

*Imports and exports at Almeria in 1901.*

| Articles. | Quantity. | Approximate value. |
|---|---|---|
| **IMPORTS.** | | |
| Coals .................................................tons.. | 28,260 | $226,800 |
| Coke .................................................do... | 2,000 | 19,470 |
| Timber: | | |
| Finland .......................................cubic meters.. | 9,564 | 155,100 |
| America.......................................do... | 1,579 | 26,250 |
| Sweden .......................................do... | 747 | 12,150 |
| Staves ...............................................pieces.. | 390,179 | ............ |
| Railway cars for iron ore...............................number.. | 50 | 30,000 |
| Total, without including staves......................... | ............ | 469,770 |
| **EXPORTS.** | | |
| Iron ore ..............................................tons.. | 230,000 | 575,000 |
| Zinc ore (calcined) ...................................do.... | 1,046 | 16,750 |
| Calamine..............................................do.... | 700 | 5,075 |
| Lead in bars..........................................do.... | 10 | 600 |
| Salt..................................................do.... | 50,000 | 61,600 |
| Esparto ..............................................do.... | 19,400 | 363,750 |
| Grapes ...............................................barrels.. | 1,100,000 | 2,750,000 |
| Do ...............................................half barrels.. | 5,500 | 8,250 |
| Oranges ..............................................cases.. | 13,500 | 33,750 |
| Almonds...............................................boxes.. | 3,600 | 27,000 |
| Figs .................................................cases.. | 1,025 | 2,500 |
| Pomegranates..........................................do.... | 160 | 400 |
| Total................................................. | ............ | 3,844,675 |

*Fruit exported from Almeria in 1901.*

| Ports. | Vessels. | Barrels of grapes. | | Cases of oranges. | Boxes of almonds. | Cases of figs. | Cases of pomegranates. | Cases of prickly pears. | Cases of melons. |
|---|---|---|---|---|---|---|---|---|---|
| | | 50 pounds. | 25 pounds. | | | | | | |
| Liverpool | 70 | 465,512 | 1,484 | 2,576 | 25 | | | | |
| London | 55 | 255,076 | 2,081 | 10,262 | 3,525 | 1,025 | 105 | 9 | 5 |
| New York | 14 | 188,110 | 759 | | 38 | | | | |
| Glasgow | 15 | 83,583 | 416 | 537 | | | | | |
| Hull | 10 | 46,978 | 70 | 152 | | | | | |
| Bristol | 7 | 21,261 | 101 | 16 | | | | | |
| Hamburg | 6 | 15,319 | 239 | | | | | | |
| Newcastle | 3 | 9,852 | 71 | | | | | | |
| St. Petersburg | 1 | 3,608 | 145 | | | | 55 | | |
| Baltic | 1 | 1,773 | 150 | | | | | | |
| Gothenburg | 1 | 1,126 | | | | | | | |
| Christiania | 1 | 1,008 | | | | | | | |
| Total | 184 | 1,093,195 | 5,516 | 13,543 | 3,588 | 1,025 | 160 | 9 | 5 |

*General shipping at the port of Almeria in 1901.*

| Nationality. | Entered. | | Cleared. | |
|---|---|---|---|---|
| | Vessels. | Tons. | Vessels. | Tons. |
| Spanish | 932 | 479,810 | 932 | 479,810 |
| British | 168 | 168,892 | 165 | 164,949 |
| Norwegian | 40 | 21,076 | 40 | 21,076 |
| Italian | 14 | 22,186 | 14 | 22,186 |
| German | 18 | 11,046 | 18 | 11,046 |
| French | 11 | 12,823 | 11 | 12,823 |
| Swedish | 9 | 7,926 | 9 | 7,926 |
| Danish | 9 | 6,077 | 9 | 6,077 |
| Austro-Hungarian | 4 | 4,924 | 4 | 4,924 |
| Russian | 8 | 3,601 | 8 | 3,601 |
| Greek | 1 | 1,302 | 1 | 1,302 |
| Dutch | 1 | 630 | 1 | 630 |
| Belgian | 1 | 584 | 1 | 584 |
| Portuguese | 3 | 358 | 3 | 358 |
| Total | 1,219 | 741,199 | 1,216 | 737,256 |

## CARTAGENA.

Since my last report, business conditions in this district have undergone but little change.

### MINING.

The principal industry is mining, and I regret to say that it has fallen off considerably within the last year. The low prices paid for lead and iron in European markets, added to the excessive taxation imposed upon mining in this country, have caused many mines to cease work.

A slight improvement in the English iron trade, however, has given some impetus to iron ore exports during the last few months, and may lead to better things if it continues.

A government inquiry was instituted some months ago, with the avowed intention of reducing the taxes and collecting them in a way less prejudicial to the miner; but nothing has been done.

### LEAD SMELTING.

The large quantity of lead produced here might, in the absence of explanation, lead to an exaggerated idea of the importance of the local lead mining. It is proper to state that lead ores are arriving constantly by train from the interior, that they come in smaller quantities from the coast, and that occasional cargoes are received from Australia.

## EXCHANGE.

This fluctuates between 36 and 37 per cent premium on gold, with a tendency to rise.

Last winter, a decree was published ordering the payment of certain customs duties in gold,[a] with the intention of providing the treasury with a gold fund, and thus obviating the necessity of making periodical purchases of foreign exchange, for payment of Government obligations abroad. It was believed that the decrease in purchases of sterling and francs would drive down the rate of exchange; but in practice it is not so, for the Government requires as much gold as before, but receives it from a larger number of people, instead of from a few bankers, as formerly.

## ELECTRICITY.

Since my last report, several other towns and villages have adopted the electric light, which is becoming universal throughout this district.

Germany seems to provide most of the machinery and wire, while France, Belgium, and England send smaller quantities. The United States sells nothing.

## CITY IMPROVEMENTS.

The city walls are being demolished. The order was given two months ago, and the work is proceeding rapidly. As the so-called military zones contiguous to the walls have also been abolished, there will probably be much building done within the next few years.

It is intended to turn over to the municipality the existing military barracks, which occupy a considerable part of the city, in exchange for new barracks, to be built on cheaper ground outside the present walls.

## HARBOR.

There is some talk of putting up one or two mechanical loaders for handling iron ore, which at present is shipped by hand.

In this line of engineering, I think that Americans should be able to compete successfully, if they cared to try.

## TRADE WITH THE PHILIPPINES, CUBA, AND PORTO RICO.

The only point worthy of remark in the trade with the Philippines is the large increase of wine shipments from here.

None of the regular lines of steamers to Cuba stop here, and direct business is limited to one steamer, which calls in May or June of each year, and loads 200 or 300 tons of garlic.

I understand that merchandise is sometimes shipped to Malaga, and thence forwarded to Cuban ports.

I know of no shipment to Porto Rico during the past year.

---

[a] See Commercial Relations, 1901, vol. 2, p. 700.

## A COMMON FRAUD.

I receive numerous letters from all parts of the Union with regard to the imprisonment and death of a military officer, who is related by marriage to my correspondents. They have received communications from parties in Spain saying that a valise containing papers of great value is being held by the military court to secure costs. Usually some three or four thousand pesetas are asked for, with which to pay costs, etc.[a]

It is the commonest kind of a swindle—known to every Spaniard— but apparently it catches some victims, or it would not be kept up. It is based on the possession of a directory, wholesale forgery, and a well-founded belief in human credulity or cupidity.

JOS. BOWRON, *Consul.*

CARTAGENA, *July 16, 1902.*

---

*Principal imports of the consular district of Cartagena, from July 1, 1901, to June 30, 1902.*

| Articles. | Countries. | Second half of 1901. | First half of 1902. |
|---|---|---|---|
| **IMPORTS.** | | | |
| Stones and earths (mostly cement)..tons.. | France | 4,535 | 2,149 |
| Fire brick and clay................do.... | England, France | 48 | 69 |
| Pottery and porcelain ware........do.... | Germany | 4 | 12 |
| Coals............................do.... | England | 52,311 | 52,572 |
| Coke.............................do.... | ....do.... | 29,959 | 19,762 |
| Charcoal.........................do.... | Italy | 240 | 242 |
| Glass (hollow or flat)...........do.... | Belgium, France | 18 | 14 |
| Broken glass (cullet)............do.... | Algeria | 19 | 35 |
| Pig iron.........................do.... | England | · 12 | .......... |
| Iron castings....................do.... | France | ... | 7 |
| Merchant iron, sheet and hoop....do.... | Germany, England | 39 | 38 |
| Lead ore ........................do.... | Australia | 1,023 | 4,762 |
| Armor plate......................do.... | France | 141 | .......... |
| Railroad material................do.... | England | 1,635 | 399 |
| Iron tubes or pipes..............do.... | England, Germany | 35 | 6 |
| Bolts, rivets, screws............do.... | Belgium | 1 | 20 |
| Locomotives and tenders..........do.... | England | a3 | b2 |
| Manufactured wire, cable, springs, etc., tons. | Belgium, Germany | 39 | 18 |
| Tools, iron and steel ...........do.... | England, Germany | 15 | 10 |
| Steel rails......................do.... | Belgium, Germany, England | 87 | 35 |
| Steel bars.......................do.... | England | 5 | 17 |
| Machinery and chains.............do.... | England, Germany, Belgium | 692 | 546 |
| Manufactured articles (hardware)..do.... | England, France, Germany | 83 | 63 |
| Iron or steel wire ..............do.... | Germany | 14 | 6 |
| Tin plate........................do.... | England | 21 | 48 |
| Copper and bronze sheets, nails, tubes, and wire, tons. | Germany | 37 | 9 |
| Zinc........................tons.. | ....do.... | 42 | 78 |
| Vegetable oils..................do.... | France | 5 | .......... |
| Prepared colors.................do.... | England, France | 14 | 16 |
| Alkaline, carbonate, and caustic alkalies, tons. | Belgium, England | 17 | 301 |
| Chloride of lime .............tons.. | France | 74 | 90 |
| Nitrate of potash..............do.... | Germany | 156 | 110 |
| Nitrate of soda and sulphate of ammonia, tons. | England, Germany | 514 | 554 |
| Chemical products unenumerated..tons.. | England, Germany, France | 87 | 27 |
| Phosphates and superphosphates of lime, tons. | Algeria, France, England | 793 | 652 |
| Starch........................tons.. | Germany, Holland | 48 | 28 |
| Fecules and dextrines...........do.... | ....do.... | 71 | 75 |
| Hemp cordage ...................do.... | Germany | 24 | 24 |
| Artificial manure ... ...........do.... | France | 1,250 | 3,040 |
| Sawed lumber: | | | |
| Hard wood (small lots)........pieces.. | | 6,237 | 5,787 |
| Do .......................tons.. | England | 50 | 2 |
| Pine........................pieces.. | Canada, Baltic, Austria | 543,601 | 61,546 |
| Do..................cubic meters.. | Russia | 2,115 | .......... |
| Do .......................tons.. | Austria | 104 | .......... |

a See Consular Reports, No. 245; Advance Sheets No. 915.        b Locomotives.

*Principal imports of the consular district of Cartagena, etc.—Continued.*

| Articles. | Countries. | Second half of 1901. | First half of 1902. |
|---|---|---|---|
| **IMPORTS—continued.** | | | • |
| Wooden furniture ...................tons.. | Germany.............................. | 3 | 1 |
| Wrapping and other papers.........do.... | France ............................... | 12 | 9 |
| Animal greases ....................do.... | Germany.............................. | 4 | 3 |
| Engines, with or without boilers...do.... | Belgium............................... | 11 | .......... |
| Salt cod and other similar fish......do.... | Newfoundland, England, Norway, and France. | 2,141 | 2,026 |
| Flour ..............................do.... | France ............................... | 38 | .......... |
| Leguminous seeds for food .........do.... | France................................ | 1,070 | 740 |
| Other seeds .......................do.... | France, Germany .................... | 76 | 10 |
| Cheese ............................do.... | Holland .............................. | 185 | 159 |
| Coffee .............................do.... | ....do................................ | 24 | 51 |
| Potatoes ..........................do.... | France ............................... | 62 | .......... |
| Glycerin ...........................do.... | Belgium, Holland..................... | .......... | 35 |
| Mineral water .....................do.... | France ............................... | 4 | 7 |
| Spices .............................do.... | England, Germany.................... | 51 | 1 |
| Maize .............................do.... | France ............................... | 14 | 20 |
| Intestine skins (casings) ..........do.... | Argentina ............................ | 47 | .......... |
| Other food products ...............do.... | France, England, Germany ........... | 23 | 22 |
| Mules .............................head.. | Algeria............................... | 94 | .......... |
| Oxen ..............................do.... | ....do................................ | .......... | 1,201 |
| Miscellaneous manufactures........tons.. | Germany, Belgium, France, England. | 19 | 16 |
| Unenumerated .....................do.... | Germany, France, England ........... | 19 | 7 |
| Porcelain insulators ...............do.... | Germany.............................. | 17 | .......... |
| Mineral oils........................do.... | ....do................................ | 3 | 45 |
| 2 guns (24 centimeters)............do.... | France ............................... | 46 | .......... |
| Gun carriages and fittings .........do.... | ....do................................ | 19 | .......... |
| **EXPORTS.** | | | |
| Silver..............................cwt.. | France ............................... | 164 | 352 |
| Silver lead ........................tons.. | England, France ..................... | 27,123 | 28,967 |
| Desilverized lead ..................do.... | ....do................................ | 5,520 | 6,348 |
| Old copper and bronze.............do.... | France ............................... | 29 | 9 |
| Sulphur............................do.... | Germany, England.................... | 296 | 986 |
| Copper ores .......................do.... | France ............................... | 210 | 493 |
| Zinc ores..........................do.... | Belgium, England.................... | 17,497 | 21,095 |
| Lead ores .........................do.... | France ............................... | 60 | 40 |
| Iron ores ..........................do.... | England .............................. | 255,305 | 322,859 |
| Iron pyrites .......................do.... | Italy, United States................. | 6,354 | 5,082 |
| Ochers ............................do.... | England .............................. | 426 | 86 |
| Seeds..............................do.... | France ............................... | .......... | 17 |
| Crude esparto .....................do.... | England .............................. | 8,784 | 15,180 |
| Manufactured esparto .............do.... | France ............................... | 47 | 42 |
| Teak ..............................do.... | England .............................. | 22 | .......... |
| Fresh fruits .......................do.... | England, Germany, France........... | 4,040 | 2,965 |
| Almonds ..........................do.... | France ............................... | 178 | 25 |
| Dry figs ...........................do.... | ....do................................ | 106 | 50 |
| Apricot pulp .......................do.... | England, Belgium, Germany.......... | 53 | 117 |
| Capers ............................do.... | France, England ..................... | 48 | 20 |
| Garlic (dried)......................do.... | Cuba, Algeria........................ | .......... | 241 |
| Potatoes ..........................do.... | England .............................. | 254 | 167 |
| Sweet pepper .....................do.... | France, Germany .................... | 234 | 42 |
| Salted fish ........................do.... | Algeria............................... | 78 | 28 |
| Grain .............................do.... | France ............................... | 49 | 75 |
| Other food products...............do.... | Algeria............................... | 2 | 4 |
| Wine...............................do.... | Philippines........................... | 453 | 983 |
| Sacks (empty) .....................do.... | France ............................... | 30 | 10 |
| Donkies ...........................head.. | Algeria............................... | 20 | 37 |
| Mules .............................do.... | ....do................................ | 9 | 31 |
| Unenumerated .....................tons.. | Germany, France..................... | 12 | 13 |

*Declared exports from the consular district of Cartagena from July 1, 1901, to June 30, 1902.*

| Articles. | Second half of 1901. | | First half of 1902. | |
|---|---|---|---|---|
| | United States. | Philippines. | United States. | Philippines. |
| | *Tons.* | | *Tons.* | | *Tons.* | | *Tons.* | |
| Fishing gut.......... | | | | | | $159.76 | | |
| Iron ore............. | | | | | 27,800 | 41,109.83 | | |
| Iron pyrites......... | 4,060 | $9,438.40 | | | | | | |
| Manganiferous ore.. | 4,150 | 6,845.13 | | | 9,950 | 14,816.77 | | |
| Paintings ........... | | 255.49 | | | | | | |
| Wine, in barrels..... | | | 24 | $1,144.36 | | | 38 | $1,607.13 |
| Total.......... | 8,210 | 16,539.02 | 24 | 1,144.36 | 37,750 | 56,086.36 | 38 | 1,607.13 |

*Undeclared exports from the consular district of Cartagena to American colonies and Cuba, from July 1, 1901, to June 30, 1902.*

| Articles. | Second half of 1901. | | First half of 1902. | |
|---|---|---|---|---|
| | Cuba. | Philip-pines. | Cuba. | Philip-pines. |
| | *Tons.* | *Tons.* | *Tons.* | *Tons.* |
| Wine, in barrels | | 436 | | 963 |
| Potatoes | | 10 | | |
| Sweet pepper | | 1 | 1 | |
| Lard | | | | 2 |
| | | *Cwt.* | | *Cwt.* |
| Miscellaneous | | 16 | | 16 |
| Salt | 7,889 | | 8,730 | |
| Garlic | | | 237 | |
| Total | 7,889 | 447½⅜ | 8,968 | 985½⅜ |

### SUPPLEMENTARY.

Exports from this district continue to be light, owing primarily to the depressed conditions of the metal trades, and in the second place to high freight rates.

As to direct American trade, there is none, beyond the occasional arrival of a cargo of pitch pine.

A number of articles of United States manufacture are seen in the retail stores, but they have been imported from European countries, and must necessarily cost much more than if imported direct.

### EXCHANGE.

This has fallen, and gold is to-day worth only 33.50 to 34 per cent premium. During the last few months, the Spanish Government has been in consultation with the leading Madrid bankers, with a view to finding some means of lowering the exchange and bringing it, if possible, to par.

### RAILROADS.

There is room in this district for several standard or narrow-gauge local lines, which could be built cheaply and would do much business. For some of them, concessions have already been obtained.

The real difficulty is to find the capital for building the lines, most foreign capitalists being unnecessarily afraid of possible revolutions, which might imperil their investments.

### SHIPPING.

Since my last report, one more steamer, just built in England, has been acquired by the local shipping company, which was founded a couple of years ago.

### TAXES.

There has been no change. No license is required by commercial travelers, with or without samples; they come and go without let or hindrance.

JOS. BOWRON, *Consul.*

CARTAGENA, *September 29, 1902.*

## MADRID.

Owing to the comparative unimportance of this consular district, no lengthy report can be made. When the heavy handicap American goods have to carry in Spain is taken into consideration, it becomes evident that they are making an excellent showing. Many of the articles imported from the United States come via England and Germany, and no doubt are credited to those countries. The following American goods have been imported into this district during the past year: Refrigerators, typewriters and supplies, shoe polish, cash registers, safes, glassware, hams and many kinds of canned goods, firearms and cartridges, air-rifles, steel-working machinery and hardware of all kinds, locks, windmills, rubber goods, fountain pens, watches, sewing machines, washing machines, phonographs, and novelties of all sorts.

DEAN R. WOOD, *Vice-Consul.*

MADRID, *October 8, 1902.*

---

## MALAGA.

The present year, in so far as the consular district of Malaga is concerned, has been a prosperous one.

The heavy depreciation of the currency, always favorable to exportation, has been unusually beneficial, because of the large and fine crops.

### OLIVE CROP.

The feature of the year is the tremendous yield of olives and olive oil. No olive crop for forty years has equaled or even approached it. The great olive provinces are those of Malaga, Cadiz, Sevilla, Cordoba, Granada, and Jaen, and the total crop of oil this year is variously estimated at from 6,000,000 to 10,000,000 arrobas, or from 75,000 to 125,000 tons.

This has reference, of course, to the crop grown in 1901, from which the oil has been pressed during the present year. In Italy, there was only a half crop, and this has also added largely to the value of the large Spanish yield, of which a considerable percentage has already been marketed at good prices and exported.

Although exporters agree that Italian oil is better and finer than the Spanish product, the fact remains that large quantities of Spanish oil have been exported this year to Italy, and probably marketed there as of Italian production. It is also a matter of fact that Italian oil merchants have been steadily buying Spanish oil at Malaga this year and exporting it direct from here to customers in the United States and elsewhere.

Although there are no reliable statistics, it is believed that upwards of 3,000,000 arrobas (37,500 tons) have already been exported this year from Malaga to the various markets of the world. The only railway line entering the city has been compelled to run special oil trains in order to get the product into Malaga for exportation by sea. This great crop has naturally enriched the Andalusian provinces to a considerable extent; but as is always the case in Spain, the money gets into the hands of a prosperous few and its benefits are not far-reaching.

## OIL TRADE.

A considerable percentage of the great oil crop remains still unsold. This is because the owners are not satisfied with the prices and have thought it best to hold for an increase.

From present indications, there will be another big crop this year. Reports of the Italian crop are also encouraging. Thus it would seem that those who have been holding for higher prices may be disappointed.

Prices this year, f. o. b. Malaga, have ruled from £26 10s. to £29 ($126 to $141) per ton of 1,058 kilograms (2,332 pounds).

## OIL REFINERY WANTED.

It is a remarkable fact that in spite of the great Andalusian olive production, there are no oil refineries of importance in any of the several olive provinces; and the choice table oils consumed here are all imported from France. It is believed that a modern oil refinery at Malaga or Cordoba or Jaen would be a very profitable investment; but as Spaniards are always loath to embark upon any enterprise which does not make money from the outset, they will probably leave this opportunity to foreigners, as is the case with nearly all other modern enterprises in Spain.

## RAISINS AND ALMONDS.

A large crop of raisins and a fair crop of almonds have also served to bring a good deal of money into Andalusia within the past year, and the growers, as well as the middlemen, who buy and export have had no cause for complaint.

## SUGAR CANE DESTROYED.

The unusual frosts of last December and January resulted in the almost complete destruction of the sugar cane in this province; but as this industry is principally in the hands of one large and rich firm which operates five of the principal factories, and as there was already a considerable overproduction of cane sugar, the loss of the cane did not cause much annoyance to the sugar people. The peasants who cultivate the cane were the sufferers.

## MALAGA WINES.

The demand for the famous still wines of Malaga has been fairly good during the year. These wines are no longer exported in any considerable quantities to the United States, but there is a steady demand for them in Europe and South America.

*Malaga wine in tonic form.*—One of the uses to which the famous muscatel wine of Malaga is put is that of a medical tonic. It is the basis of many of the most popular tonics sold to-day in Europe, and in one particular instance, it is known that a famous wine tonic extensively advertised and sold in large quantities over all the world (especially in England and the United States) is nothing more nor less than a fair quality of muscatel wine treated with an extract of cocoa. As a matter of fact, the genuine Malaga muscatel is in itself a wonderful tonic for debilitated persons, and is growing in popularity with chemists and druggists.

## EXPORTS.

No statistics of exportation by countries are kept at Malaga; and it is therefore impossible to offer any exact figures. The two best customers are Great Britain and France. Malaga sends her products, however, over all the world.

*Olive oil.*—Her best customer for olive oil is Russia, where the demand is created by the religion of the country, which requires that olive oil shall be burned in the lamps that are used for illuminating the images of saints in nearly every Russian house. Nearly the whole of the cheaper grade has heretofore been exported to Russia.

*Almonds and raisins.*—Malaga's famous Jordan almonds are exported almost exclusively to Great Britain and the United States. Her Valencia almonds, however, go to almost every other country, as do also her incomparable sun-dried muscatel raisins. Her raisin crop of 1901 was the largest that has been produced since the phyloxera ravaged the country, fifteen years ago. It amounted to more than a million boxes, and sold at good average prices.

*Iron mine.*—Although the province of Malaga is rich in minerals, only one mine of any character is being operated. This is the iron mine at Marbella, which, according to recent reports, is being rapidly exhausted. Ore is exported from this mine to Great Britain and, to a small extent, to the United States.

## LOCAL INDUSTRIES.

*Iron.*—A Belgian company is operating a blast furnace and factory which produces malleable and cast iron, and also makes various castings. This concern gets its ore principally from the mines at Linares, in the interior, about 150 miles north of Malaga. The business of the company this year is reported to have been good.

*Cotton.*—The two great cotton factories at Malaga, which employ between them some 7,500 hands and manufacture cheap cotton prints and white goods for the Spanish, Portuguese, and Morocco markets, are also reported to have had a good year. The raw cotton used by these two concerns amounts to 2,500 to 3,000 metric tons [a] annually and comes exclusively from the United States.

Nearly all the enterprises of the city and province appear to have had a fairly good year, not excepting the Malaga street railway system, which is operated by a Belgian company.

## STRIKES AND DISORDERS.

Although the farmers, manufacturers, and merchants of the district appear to have had a good season, there have been frequent strikes and disorders among the laboring classes, who complain bitterly and aggressively of low wages and increased cost of living. One can not help but wonder what American wage-earners would do under the conditions which exist here. An ordinary field hand is paid 4 reals (about 15 American cents) a day and his board; and in the daily bill of

---

[a] Of 2,204.6 pounds.

fare no meat nor sugar nor any of the better foodstuffs is represented. Carpenters, painters, printers, blacksmiths, and other skilled laborers earn about 3.50 pesetas (40 American cents) a day. Street-car conductors and drivers, who in the summer work fourteen hours a day, earn 2.50 pesetas (35 American cents). Women who work in the almond and raisin warehouses as sorters and packers are glad to earn a peseta (15 American cents) for a day's work of ten hours. They must, of course, feed themselves. The hard-working stevedores who load the ships earn from 3 to 5 pesetas (i. e., from 45 to 75 American cents) a day.

These low wages do not apply solely to manual laborers, but to clerical employees as well. A first-class bookkeeper in Malaga is glad to earn 4,000 pesetas (about $600) a year. Ordinary clerks in the best wholesale houses earn from 100 to 200 pesetas (from $15 to $30) a month.

### HIGH COST OF LIVING.

In view of these apparently trifling wages, one would naturally think that the cost of living is cheap. On the contrary, nearly every wholesome necessity of life costs here (as it does elsewhere in Europe) much more than in the United States.

Fresh meats cost from two to three times as much. Sugar costs from two to two and a half times as much. Coal for cooking costs about twice as much as in the average American city. Almost uneatable butter costs 40 cents a pound. The cheapest ham costs 30 cents a pound. Goat's milk costs 60 centimos (about 8 American cents) a quart. All manufactured articles are much more expensive than in the United States. In short, if a working man lived here as he does in the United States, his daily wage would barely provide a single meal. Fortunately, being accustomed to much less, the Spaniard expects less, and with a bit of bread and a soup made of fish, onions, and oil, he finds he has enough to eat. But this year, the Andalusian workingman has not been content with his lot, and strikes have occurred in nearly every branch of industry. For the first time in the history of this southern country, there has been a serious attempt at organizing the laboring classes into one large federation, but up to this writing it has not been successful, and as a rule the various strikes have failed.

There was until recently a general feeling of unrest lest, among other impending labor troubles, a strike among the dock laborers should occur during the busy vintage season in September and October, when the almond and raisin crops are moving; but this appears to have been averted.

### IMPORTS.

The depreciation of the Spanish currency, which favors exportation, naturally operates, on the other hand, against importation; and although I can not yet present the statistics, it is likely when I do offer them with my supplementary report, that a slight decrease in importation will be shown.

### AMERICAN MANUFACTURED GOODS.

American manufactured goods are more in evidence every day, though it can not be said that there is any significant direct importation. Cheap American hardware, such as spring contrivances to shut doors, coffee grinders, meat choppers, etc., come here from Germany, chiefly through the great importation house of Marks & Co., at Hamburg. American ice-cream freezers are also becoming popular.

*The nickel-in-the-slot machine.*—The American nickel-in-the-slot machine has reached Spain at last and is creating quite a sensation. Malaga claims the distinction of introducing these machines; and the general agency, established here within a year, has not only already extended its business to Seville, Granada, and other Andalusian capitals, but is preparing to enter Madrid and the north.

There are 40 of these machines in use in Malaga alone, and as far as I can learn they are earning a net average of $3.50 each per day. They are nearly all of the gambling variety, and Spaniards are fond of all games of chance.

The most popular of the machines are those with musical box attachments. A 5-centimo piece (1 cent) in the slot not only produces a popular air, but gives the player a chance to strike the lucky combination and realize from 2 to 25 cents.

Several enterprising young business men have formed a partnership for the importation and exploitation of these machines, and with their exclusive rights, are on the way to make the venture profitable.

They are also importing typewriting machines, seed envelopes, belt buckles for ladies, brooches, etc. Incidentally, it may be said that this consulate has been largely instrumental in bringing about the importation of the various American articles referred to, by putting American publications and business pamphlets in the hands of the importers.

*Staves; cotton.*—In spite of the discriminating duty against American staves, there is no material falling off in the importation of this product, which arrives in the ships of all nations except the United States. The same may be said of raw cotton.

### COAL QUESTION.

All American consuls stationed at Mediterranean ports have been watching with keen interest the American coal movement in continental Europe. But in so far as Malaga is concerned, I have nothing encouraging to report. No American coal has yet arrived here, and from what I can ascertain, none is likely to do so. In these reports last year, there was foreshadowed what has since been realized, viz, that England, fearing American competition, would at the very first opportunity, reduce her prices for steam and bunker coal.

Coal now costs here about 3 shillings (73 cents) a ton less than at the same period last year, and last year's prices were lower than those of 1900.

Malaga consumes annually about 50,000 tons of steam and bunker coal, all of which comes from Great Britain. Of this, much the greater part is steam coal from Newcastle. The bunkering coal comes from Cardiff; but ships find it more convenient to coal at Gibraltar, and there is relatively little bunkering at Malaga. Coal dealers are now buying Newcastle steam coal, f. o. b. in Malaga harbor, at from 17 to 20 shillings[a] ($4.13 to $4.86) a ton, according to grade, and Cardiff bunker coal at from 19 to 21 shillings ($4.62 to $5.10). Dealers insist that English ships are now willing to bring the coal from Newcastle or Cardiff to

[a] In addition to the above prices, unloading charges and duties amounting to about 3 shillings (73 cents) a ton should be considered.

Malaga for 5 shillings ($1.21) a ton. It is believed here that English coal will continue to decline in price, and the dealers with whom I have talked do not think there is any present prospect of introducing American coal into Spain. Nevertheless, the largest importer told me that he had written to New York for samples of steam coal.

### EXPORTS TO THE UNITED STATES.

In a supplementary report, I shall forward more general statistics of importation and exportation at this port. Meanwhile, I give a table showing the exports declared at this consulate for the United States during the fiscal year ended June 30, 1902, as compared with 1901:

| Articles. | 1901. | 1902. | Increase. | Decrease. |
|---|---|---|---|---|
| Almonds | $394,996.22 | $416,679.08 | $21,682.86 | |
| Apricots | | 156.70 | 156.70 | |
| Brandy | 962.44 | 1,258.70 | 296.26 | |
| Capers | 444.45 | 359.94 | | $84.51 |
| Figs | 3,297.01 | 522.68 | | 2,774.33 |
| Fish, preserved | | 26.16 | 26.16 | |
| Furniture | 196.32 | 339.62 | 143.30 | |
| Grapes | 9,979.87 | 19,337.22 | 9,357.35 | |
| Iron ore | 44,185.82 | 8,708.16 | | 35,477.66 |
| Iron, oxide of | | 257.25 | 257.25 | |
| Lavender, essence of | | 211.85 | 211.85 | |
| Lemons | 3,823.11 | 2,906.93 | | 916.18 |
| Olives | 264.50 | 4,887.57 | 4,623.07 | |
| Olive oil | 12,147.58 | 249,986.97 | 237,839.39 | |
| Orange peel | 267.31 | 18.63 | | 248.68 |
| Palm-leaf hats | 116,586.93 | 106,611.95 | | 9,974.98 |
| Paint (earth) | | 205.28 | 205.28 | |
| Paintings | 34.06 | | | 34.06 |
| Pepper, red | 1,174.98 | 1,674.72 | 499.74 | |
| Pomegranates | 3,746.54 | 4,702.51 | 955.97 | |
| Rosemary, essence of | | 458.02 | 458.02 | |
| Raisins | 130,146.11 | 126,276.32 | | 3,869.79 |
| Saffron | | 341.46 | 341.46 | |
| Wine | 10,731.96 | 12,263.83 | 1,531.87 | |
| Total | 732,985.21 | 968,191.55 | 278,586.53 | 53,380.19 |

From the above it will be seen that there is considerable increase in the volume of exports, due almost entirely to the enlarged export of olive oil.

### PALM-LEAF HATS.

One interesting feature of Malaga's commerce is the exportation of palm-leaf hats. These are rough, broad-brim straw hats, made by hand by the peasants from the tough palmetto that grows wild on the hills and mountains about Malaga. They are exported in bales to the United States and are there shaped and trimmed, and sold—generally to the negroes in the South. The prices paid here for these hats are pitifully low, considering the amount of handiwork required to produce them; nevertheless, whole families of the peasantry earn their living by making them.

Only two or three firms in the United States receive and complete the hats shipped from here, but as they have something like 600,000 dozens to handle annually, it is clear that they are kept pretty busy.

I am told that similar hats are imported from Mexico into the United States, but they are said to be not so good in quality as those that come from Malaga.

BENJ. H. RIDGELY, *Consul.*

MALAGA, *September 25, 1902.*

## SUPPLEMENTAL.

In transmitting the following statistics to supplement my annual commercial report, I must call attention to the largely decreased imports of raw cotton at this port.

### COTTON.

Malaga has two of the largest cotton mills in southern Europe, and the raw cotton worked in them comes almost exclusively from the United States. The products of these mills—mostly cheap white goods and prints—have always enjoyed a good market in Cuba, Porto Rico, Spain, Portugal, and the Philippines; but the figures given below, showing the largely decreased imports of raw cotton, would seem to indicate that the influence of United States exporters is being felt in the Cuban and Porto Rican markets. In any event, the product of the Malaga mills has this year been considerably below the average, and the smaller demand for Spanish goods in Cuba and Porto Rico is assigned as one of the causes. Another cause is the general bad business, resulting from the almost complete loss of the grape crop in central Spain, where the late and sharp frosts of last spring wrought such havoc.

### OIL EXPORTS.

The figures for the nine months ended September 30, 1902, as compared with the same period of 1901, indicate that 1,224,590 kilograms (i. e., 1,224 metric tons) more were exported in 1901 than in 1902. This is probably an error, as it is generally understood that much more oil has been exported this year than last; but in any event, the figures are misleading, in that they would indicate that last year's crop of oil was larger than this year's crop, whereas, as a matter of fact, it was considerably smaller, and was nearly all sold and exported before the 30th of September, while, on the other hand, nearly half of this year's crop has not yet been marketed, but is being held for better prices.

BENJ. H. RIDGELY, *Consul.*

MALAGA, *October 12, 1902.*

---

*Exports and imports of Malaga from January 1 to September 30, 1902.*

| Articles. | Total. | | 1902. | |
|---|---|---|---|---|
| | 1902. | 1901. | Increase. | Decrease. |
| **EXPORTS.** | | | | |
| Oil .................................metric tons.. | 8,999 | 10,224 | ............ | 1,225 |
| Olives .............................do.... | 52 | 90 | ............ | 38 |
| Aguardiente (brandy) .....................gallons.. | 17,164 | 11,594 | 5,570 | ............ |
| Garlic .............................metric tons.. | 24 | 46 | ............ | 23 |
| Almonds .............................do.... | 1,481 | 940 | 541 | ............ |
| Canary seed .............................do.... | 25 | 59 | ............ | 34 |
| Aniseed .............................do.... | 42 | 38 | 4 | ............ |
| Rice .............................do.... | 731 | 616 | 116 | ............ |
| Nuts, hazel .............................do.... | 12 | 28 | ............ | 16 |
| Orange peel .............................do.... | 4 | 77 | ............ | 72 |
| Chestnuts and other nuts .....................do.... | 21 | 27 | ............ | 6 |
| Onions.............................do.... | 321 | 174 | 148 | ............ |

*Exports and imports of Malaga from January 1 to September 30, 1902*—Continued.

| Articles. | | Total. | | 1902. | |
|---|---|---|---|---|---|
| | | 1902. | 1901. | Increase. | Decrease. |
| Cumin seed ............................metric tons.. | | 15 | 31 | | 16 |
| Preserves.................................do.... | | 27 | 20 | 7 | |
| Chocolate ...............................do.... | | 5 | 21 | | 16 |
| Esparto grass...........................do.... | | 84 | 145 | | 61 |
| Dried fruits.............................do.... | | 129 | 53 | 76 | |
| Green fruits .............................do.... | | 125 | 46 | 78 | |
| Chick-pease .............................do.... | | 1,382 | 2,267 | | 885 |
| Pomegranates...........................do.... | | 19 | 66 | | 47 |
| Figs........................................do.... | | 1,694 | 804 | 890 | |
| Soap.......................................do.... | | 7 | 17 | | 10 |
| Lemons ...................................do.... | | 2,082 | 969 | 1,113 | |
| Minerals..................................do.... | | 9,612 | 6,981 | 2,630 | |
| Oranges...................................do.... | | 609 | 318 | 291 | |
| Palm leaf, manufactured .............do.... | | 26 | 14 | 12 | |
| Raisins....................................do.... | | 1,714 | 2,498 | | 785 |
| Pimento...................................do.... | | 31 | 42 | | 12 |
| Lead .......................................do.... | | 25,433 | 19,597 | 5,835 | |
| Licorice root ............................do.... | | 6 | 11 | | 5 |
| Grapes.....................................do.... | | 768 | 424 | 343 | |
| Wine .................................gallons.. | | 1,424,785 | 1,443,924 | | 19,139 |
| Cotton goods............................metric tons.. | | 27 | 31 | | 4 |
| **IMPORTS.** | | | | | |
| Oils, paints, colors, etc..................metric tons.. | | 191 | 146 | 45 | |
| Alcohol ..............................gallons.. | | 3,533 | 11,190 | | 7,637 |
| Raw cotton ............................metric tons.. | | 930 | 1,534 | | 604 |
| Spun cotton ...........................do.... | | 3 | 3 | | |
| Starch.....................................do.... | | 619 | 732 | | 113 |
| Tar, pitch, asphalt, etc................do.... | | 735 | 926 | | 191 |
| Sugar......................................do.... | | 3 | 24 | | 21 |
| Sulphur and chemical products.......do.... | | 3,187 | 3,830 | | 643 |
| Dried codfish............................do.... | | 3,947 | 4,122 | | 175 |
| Paving stones, brick, cement .........do.... | | 4,564 | 3,789 | 825 | |
| Cocoa......................................do.... | | 8 | 24 | | 16 |
| Coffee.....................................do.... | | 1,426 | 1,817 | | 392 |
| Coal........................................do.... | | 35,538 | 37,928 | | 2,390 |
| Charcoal..................................do.... | | 86 | 49 | 37 | |
| Oats, corn, chick-pease................do.... | | 1,027 | 1,927 | | 900 |
| Beer and sparkling wine................gallons.. | | 71,289 | 61,398 | 9,891 | |
| Leather, hides, etc......................metric tons.. | | 239 | 303 | | 64 |
| Staves.................................pieces.. | | 1,162,217 | 2,437,287 | | 1,275,070 |
| Spices and preserves....................metric tons.. | | 92 | 167 | | 75 |
| Tin, copper, and zinc...................do.... | | 183 | 65 | 118 | |
| Grease.....................................do.... | | 249 | 210 | 39 | |
| Guano......................................do.... | | 11,490 | 15,264 | | 3,775 |
| Manufactured iron of all kinds.........do.... | | 13,468 | 7,824 | 5,644 | |
| Iron wire..................................do.... | | 97 | 110 | | 13 |
| Lard .......................................do.... | | 234 | 131 | 103 | |
| Butter......................................do.... | | 341 | 304 | 37 | |
| Machinery ...............................do.... | | 4,386 | 2,879 | 1,508 | |
| Furniture .................................do.... | | 79 | 63 | 16 | |
| Paper.......................................do.... | | 73 | 59 | 14 | |
| Cheese ....................................do.... | | 337 | 245 | 92 | |
| Lumber ...............................cubic feet.. | | 227,474 | 366,057 | | 138,583 |
| Woven goods of all kinds...............metric tons.. | | 33 | 87 | | 55 |
| Wheat......................................do.... | | 50 | 522 | | 472 |
| Glass and porcelain .....................do.... | | 185 | 170 | 16 | |
| Jute, etc...................................do.... | | 135 | 288 | | 153 |

## TRADE OF MALAGA IN 1902.

In transmitting this report, supplemental to the annual commercial paper sent by my predecessor, I send a table of imports into Malaga exclusively from the United States.

This table has not been included in previous supplemental reports, but certain features of the import trade seem pertinent for notice at this writing.

The pronounced increase in the importation of sulphur and chemical products, lard, and starch, and a like decrease in iron and steel, machinery, wheat, barley and corn, spices and preserves, is perhaps worthy of brief explanation.

## IMPORTS.

American patent medicines are, according to a prominent local druggist, rapidly taking hold in this province, as is shown by the doubled figures last year over those of 1901, when they were first introduced here. Quinine tablets are perhaps the most popular, but the demand for many other medicinal preparations spreads as soon as the merits of the goods become known.

The prospect for laundry starch seems encouraging, the figures showing that the importation of the American article has increased fourfold in a twelvemonth. Prior to 1901, no starch reached Malaga from the United States.

"Octroi" duty—that unpopular municipal tax levied on oil, etc., from the province—has given American lard the much desired opportunity of making its merits felt, inasmuch as imported lard is retailed here at present at less cost than the best cooking oil; consequently, lard for cooking purposes is gradually taking the place of oil.

The decreases are easily explained and should occasion no apprehension. Wheat, corn, and barley were imported from the United States in large quantities in 1901, owing to the almost total failure of the crop in southern Spain, because of inclement weather. Last year, the opposite weather conditions prevailed here, a good crop resulted, and the importations of these articles were practically nil.

The lack of a direct steamship line between Malaga and the United States, of which much complaint has been made in previous reports, is undoubtedly responsible for the falling off in the importation of iron and steel and machinery.

## EXPORT FEATURES.

Two new articles appear in the export list—oxide of iron and earth paint; though a small quantity of the latter was exported for the first time in 1901.

The one feature of the year's work that stands out in bold relief is the unprecedented increase in the olive-oil exportation, as is shown by the output of 22,166 barrels, as against 606 barrels in 1901.

The principal exporters inform me that the olive crop of Italy is again short, and that the Italian demand for the Spanish product will be even greater than last year; and as the crop here is not quite as large, higher prices will prevail.

The heavy exportation of figs was due to the failure of the Smyrna crop. A much higher price was thus obtained for Malaga figs; but as the Smyrna crop is reported to have assumed its normal proportions, local exporters do not look for the same rich harvest during the coming year.

A cold spell in February last played havoc with Jordan almonds, it is said, reducing the crop by one-half, with the inevitable rise in prices.

Failure of the Denia raisin crop is given as the reason for the "good year" experienced by Malaga exporters.

The statistics of the year follow:

1. Declared exports from Malaga to the United States for 1902.
2. Declared exports from Malaga to Porto Rico for 1902.
3. Imports exclusively from the United States at Malaga for 1902.
4. Imports from all countries during the year 1902.
5. Exports from Malaga for the year 1902.

D. R. BIRCH, *Consul.*

MALAGA, *January 20, 1903.*

TABLE No. 3.—*Declared exports from Malaga to the United States for the years 1902 and 1901.*

| Articles. | | 1902. | | 1901. | | Increase 1902. | Decrease 1902. |
|---|---|---|---|---|---|---|---|
| | | Quantity. | Value. | Quantity. | Value. | | |
| Almonds | {bags ... | 160 | } $451,504.53 | { 121 | } $397,999.75 | $53,504.78 | .......... |
| | {boxes. | 65,135 | | 64,479 | | | |
| Apricot stones | boxes. | .......... | .......... | 100 | 156.70 | .......... | $156.70 |
| Brandy | {hogsheads. | .......... | .......... | 1 | } 1,183.72 | 234.14 | .......... |
| | {cases | 315 | 1,417.86 | 244 | | | |
| Capers | barrels. | .......... | .......... | 251 | 804.39 | .......... | 804.39 |
| Figs | frails. | 8,560 | 4,139.25 | 1,603 | 524.87 | 3,614.38 | .......... |
| Fish (preserved) | boxes. | .......... | .......... | .......... | 26.16 | .......... | 26.16 |
| Furniture (antique) | cases. | 7 | 339.62 | .......... | .......... | 339.62 | .......... |
| Grapes | barrels. | 4,474 | 12,173.29 | 9,670 | 19,337.22 | .......... | 7,163.93 |
| Iron ore | tons. | 9,190 | 25,167.04 | 9,200 | 26,163.02 | .......... | 995.98 |
| Iron, oxide of | {barrels. | 17 | } 1,381.21 | .......... | .......... | 1,381.21 | .......... |
| | {bags | 1,663 | | | | | |
| Lavender, essence of | .......... | a 2 | 502.71 | b 5 | 211.85 | 290.86 | .......... |
| Lemons | ½ boxes. | .......... | .......... | 2,702 | 2,906.93 | .......... | 2,906.93 |
| Lead | pigs. | 808 | 2,514.02 | .......... | .......... | 2,514.02 | .......... |
| Olive oil | barrels. | 22,166 | 491,090.10 | 606 | 16,290.54 | 474,799.56 | .......... |
| Olives. | .......... | .......... | 3,205.88 | .......... | 2,035.65 | 1,170.23 | .......... |
| Orange peel | bales. | c 12 | 144.28 | d 78 | 285.94 | .......... | 141.66 |
| Palm-leaf hats | half bales. | 2,384 | 128,351.39 | 2,400 | 105,726.05 | 21,625.34 | .......... |
| Pepper, red | boxes. | 179 | 1,143.97 | 227 | 1,358.60 | .......... | 214.63 |
| Pomegranates | ¼ cases. | 7,274 | 6,346.65 | 5,998 | 4,702.51 | 1,644.14 | .......... |
| Rosemary, essence of | boxes. | .......... | .......... | 12 | 458.02 | .......... | 458.02 |
| Paint earth | bags. | 200 | 152.96 | 50 | 52.32 | 100.64 | .......... |
| Raisins | boxes. | { 6,777 | } 183,529.44 | { 1,795 | } 120,604.37 | 62,925.07 | .......... |
| | | 83,331 | | 68,988 | | | |
| Saffron | do. | 4 | 341.46 | .......... | .......... | 341.46 | .......... |
| Wine. | .......... | .......... | 9,548.61 | .......... | 12,814.37 | .......... | 3,265.76 |
| Total | .......... | .......... | 1,323,084.27 | .......... | 714,642.98 | 624,575.45 | 16,134.16 |

a Drums.    b Boxes.    c Large.    d Small bales.

Increase in 1902, $608,441.29.

*Declared exports from Malaga to Porto Rico for the years 1901 and 1902.*

| Articles. | | 1902. | | 1901. | | Increase, 1902. | Decrease, 1902. |
|---|---|---|---|---|---|---|---|
| | | Quantities. | Value. | Quantities. | Value. | | |
| Aniseed | bags. | 116 | $906.81 | 120 | $696.21 | $210.60 | .......... |
| Canary seed | do. | .......... | .......... | 20 | 73.38 | .......... | $73.38 |
| Chestnuts | cases. | .......... | .......... | 27 | 70.63 | .......... | 70.63 |
| Chick-peas | {bales. | 433 | } 26,178.11 | { 110 | } 22,048.76 | 4,129.35 | .......... |
| | {bags | 2,350 | | 2,351 | | | |
| Cotton goods. | cases. | .......... | .......... | 7 | 774.51 | .......... | 774.51 |
| Cumin seed | bags. | 10 | 22.38 | 40 | 215.95 | .......... | 193.57 |
| Figs | mats. | 142 | 128.50 | 120 | 60.26 | 68.24 | .......... |
| Garlic | {cases. | .......... | .......... | 75 | } 1,084.73 | .......... | 941.30 |
| | {bales. | 14 | 143.43 | 56 | | | |
| Grapes | half barrels. | 2,008 | 2,834.38 | 1,605 | 2,020.13 | 814.25 | .......... |
| Jewelry | boxes. | 1 | 171.71 | .......... | .......... | 171.71 | .......... |
| Lavender | bags. | .......... | .......... | 5 | 20.41 | .......... | 20.41 |
| Lentils | do. | .......... | .......... | 4 | 22.24 | .......... | 22.24 |
| Olive oil | cases. | 459 | 3,705.33 | 820 | 1,977.21 | 1,728.12 | .......... |
| Olives | {boxes | .......... | .......... | 32 | } 1,245.40 | .......... | 853.56 |
| | {small barrels. | 2,000 | 391.84 | 6,100 | | | |
| Pears | cases. | .......... | .......... | 50 | 20.17 | .......... | 20.17 |
| Peaches | boxes. | .......... | .......... | 2 | 26.24 | .......... | 26.24 |
| Pepper, red | do. | 38 | 236.57 | 13 | 79.34 | 157.23 | .......... |
| Pork, pickled | do. | .......... | .......... | 1 | 7.84 | .......... | 7.84 |
| Prunes | do. | 730 | 500.95 | 475 | 324.85 | 176.10 | .......... |
| Raisins | {cases | 126 | } 7,325.64 | { 10 | } 5,270.07 | 2,055.57 | .......... |
| | {boxes. | 7,488 | | 6,585 | | | |
| Sausages | do. | 10 | 50.37 | 27 | 201.20 | .......... | 150.83 |
| Sundries | do. | .......... | .......... | 46 | 258.39 | .......... | 258.39 |
| Sweets. | do. | 34 | 256.08 | .......... | .......... | 256.08 | .......... |
| Wine. | .......... | .......... | 154.31 | .......... | .......... | 154.31 | .......... |
| Total | .......... | .......... | 43,006.41 | .......... | 36,497.92 | 9,921.56 | 3,413.07 |

Total increase, $6,508.49.

*Imports exclusively from the United States at Malaga for the years 1901 and 1902.*

| Articles. | 1901. | 1902. | Increase 1902. | Decrease 1902. |
|---|---|---|---|---|
| Oil, paints, colors, etc ...............................kilos.. | 38,429 | 29,265 | | 9,164 |
| Alcohol ...........................................liters.. | | 2,043 | 2,043 | |
| Raw cotton ........................................kilos.. | 2,097,888 | 2,828,563 | 730,725 | |
| Starch ..............................................do... | 2,128 | 9,315 | 7,187 | |
| Tar, pitch, asphalts, etc ..........................do... | 79,587 | 143,672 | 64,085 | |
| Sulphur and chemical products ...............do... | 201,576 | 475,318 | 273,742 | |
| Paving stones, bricks, and cement ...........do... | 92,566 | 132,412 | 40,846 | |
| Charcoal ...........................................do... | 3,089 | | | 3,089 |
| Barley, corn, etc ..................................do... | 895,405 | 621,833 | | 273,572 |
| Beer and sparkling wine .....................liters.. | 21,836 | 7,421 | | 14,415 |
| Leather, hides, etc ..............................kilos.. | 4,218 | 5,218 | 1,000 | |
| Staves ...........................................pieces.. | 2,587,425 | 2,311,628 | | 275,797 |
| Spices and preserves ..........................kilos.. | 19,825 | 6,364 | | 13,461 |
| Tin, copper, and zinc ............................do... | 4,615 | 12,925 | 8,310 | |
| Grease .............................................do... | 11,897 | 34,415 | 22,518 | |
| Iron and steel ....................................do... | 421,365 | 272,364 | | 149,001 |
| Iron wire ..........................................do... | 21,470 | 12,817 | | 8,653 |
| Lard ...............................................do... | 109,367 | 241,611 | 132,244 | |
| Butter .............................................do... | 5,290 | 14,121 | 8,841 | |
| Machinery .........................................do... | 109,421 | 54,080 | | 55,341 |
| Furniture ..........................................do... | 13,845 | 1,371 | | 12,474 |
| Paper of all kinds ...............................do... | 4,250 | 5,087 | 837 | |
| Cheese .............................................do... | 497 | 262 | | 235 |
| Lumber......................................cubic meters... | 2,084 | 2,090 | 6 | |
| Woven goods of all kinds.......................kilos.. | 1,032 | 1,234 | 202 | |
| Wheat..............................................do... | 475,847 | 263 | | 475,584 |
| Glass and porcelain .............................do... | 5,416 | 9,216 | 3,800 | |
| Jute ...............................................do... | 21,384 | 17,096 | | 4,348 |

*Imports from all countries at Malaga during the year 1902, and totals for 1901.*

| Articles. | England. | France. | Germany. | Belgium. | United States. | Holland. | Norway. | Denmark. | Italy. | Morocco. |
|---|---|---|---|---|---|---|---|---|---|---|
| Oil, paints, colors, etc ...metric tons.. | 102 | 39 | 24.5 | 51.3 | 29 | 9 | 3 | 2 | 1 | 2 |
| Alcohol .......galls.. | 2,070 | 2,758 | 1,342 | 547 | 539 | 456 | 763 | 321 | | |
| Raw cotton, metric tons............... | 4 | 2 | 0.6 | | 2,828.5 | | | | | |
| Cotton yarn, metric tons............... | 1 | 2 | 0.7 | | | | | | | |
| Starch....met. tons.. | 4 | 89.8 | 421 | 410.8 | 9 | 22.8 | | | 17 | |
| Tar, pitch, asphalts, etc .....met. tons.. | 123.9 | 278.5 | 175 | 67.8 | 143.6 | 7.9 | 2.6 | | 38.5 | |
| Sugar........do... | | | 3 | 1 | | | | | 2 | |
| Sulphur and chemical products, met. tons................. | 1,821.5 | 923 | 372.5 | 507 | 475.3 | 107.9 | 42.6 | 18 | 72.3 | 19 |
| Codfish...met. tons.. | 1,103 | 52 | | | | 1,318.4 | 2,110.5 | 120 | | |
| Paving stones, bricks, and cement, met. tons................. | 411 | 5,821 | 672.8 | 102.4 | 132.4 | 190 | | | 102 | 22 |
| Cocoa ....met. tons.. | 9 | | 3 | | | | | | 1 | |
| Coffee ..........do... | 422 | 339 | 568 | 310 | | | | | 15.4 | |
| Coal...........do... | 49,375 | | | | | 7,823 | | | | |
| Charcoal ........do... | 4 | 2 | 5 | 1 | | | | | | 125,000 |
| Barley, corn, chickpeas, etc, metric tons................. | 210.4 | 423 | 62.5 | 32 | 621.8 | | | | | 153.2 |
| Beer and sparkling wines......galls.. | 512 | 13,690 | 55,640 | 1,536 | 1,960 | 6,925 | 692 | 188 | | |
| Leather, hides, etc ......net tons.. | 18.4 | 28.4 | 78 | 2.8 | 5 | 1 | | | 5 | 139.8 |
| Staves .......pieces.. | 39,400 | 92,315 | | | 2,311,628 | | | | 50,000 | |
| Spices and preserves, metric tons........ | 29.3 | 16.4 | 19.3 | 9.9 | 6.1 | 2 | 7 | | 12 | 1.6 |
| Tin, copper, and zinc, metric tons ....... | 24.6 | 58.4 | 15 | 5 | 18 | 82 | 7 | 3 | 1 | |
| Grease..metric tons.. | 123.5 | 51 | 72 | 11 | 34.4 | 2.6 | | | | 9 |
| Guano..........do... | 2,021.3 | 6,721.8 | 3,010.4 | 1,375 | | 628 | | | | 415.7 |
| Iron and steel ..do... | 4,521.3 | 2,410.8 | 2,010 | 6,310 | 272.3 | 1,325 | 51 | 9 | 510.3 | 611.3 |
| Iron wire....do... | 82 | 12 | 9 | 41.6 | 12.8 | 3 | | | 6 | |
| Lard........do... | 18 | 3 | 1.9 | 0.4 | 241.6 | 2 | | | 0.3 | 0.3 |
| Butter.........do... | 10 | 6.8 | 112.3 | 1 | 14 | 210.3 | 2.5 | | 2 | 0.4 |
| Machinery ......do... | 1,628.5 | 982 | 1,171 | 1,320 | 54 | 21.8 | 7 | | 6 | 2.7 |
| Furniture, etc..do... | 5 | 9.3 | 2.8 | 10 | 1.4 | 0.7 | | | 0.3 | 59.3 |
| Paper of all kinds, metric tons........ | 24.3 | 26.5 | 19 | 3 | 5 | 6 | | | 1 | 7.3 |

*Imports from all countries at Malaga during the year 1902, and totals for 1901—Cont'd.*

| Articles. | Eng-land. | France. | Ger-many. | Bel-gium. | United States. | Hol-land. | Nor-way. | Den-mark. | Italy. | Mo-rocco. |
|---|---|---|---|---|---|---|---|---|---|---|
| Cheese ...met. tons.. | 6 | 4.7 | 2 | 0.4 | 0.33 | 410 | | | | |
| Lumber........do... | 636 | 212 | 128 | | 2,278 | | 1,428 | | | |
| Woven goods of all kinds...met. tons.. | 10 | 8.7 | 6 | 5 | 1 | 0.8 | | | 1 | 1 |
| Wheat.........do... | | | | | 0.3 | | | | | 2.3 |
| Glass and porcelain, metric tons | 42 | 61 | 21 | 22 | 9 | 2 | | 3 | 29 | 1 |
| Jute....metric tons.. | 132 | 5 | 2 | 15.8 | 17 | | 1.7 | | | |

*Imports from all countries at Malaga during the year 1902, and totals for 1901—Cont'd.*

| Articles. | Cuba and Porto Rico. | Russia. | Portu-gal. | Aus-tria. | New-found-land. | Total. | | Increase. | Decrease. |
|---|---|---|---|---|---|---|---|---|---|
| | | | | | | 1902. | 1901. | | |
| Oil, paints, colors, etc...metric tons.. | | 2 | 0.7 | 1 | | 268 | 251.3 | 16.6 | ...... |
| Alcohol......galls.. | | | | | | 8,529 | 15,186 | | 6,856 |
| Raw cotton, metric tons | | | | | | 2,835.7 | 2,111.5 | 724 | |
| Cotton yarn, metric tons | | | | 1 | | 6.4 | 5 | 1 | |
| Starch...met. tons. | | | | 5.8 | | 967.3 | 1,004 | | 37 |
| Tar, pitch, asphalts, etc..... met. tons. | | 7 | | 32.8 | | 877.9 | 1,233.9 | | 356 |
| Sugar .........do.. | | | | 1.2 | | 7.8 | 44.3 | | 36.4 |
| Sulphur and chemical products, met. tons | | 2 | | 32 | | 4,393.5 | 5,719.9 | | 1,326.4 |
| Codfish...met. tons.. | | | | | 1,321 | 6,024.9 | 4,877.3 | 1,147.5 | |
| Pavingstones, bricks, and cement, met. tons. | | | | 138.4 | | 7,591.9 | 6,712 | 880 | |
| Cocoa ....met. tons.. | | | | | | 13.5 | 30.4 | | 17 |
| Coffee .........do.. | 211 | | | 38.9 | | 1,924.9 | 2,157.8 | | 233 |
| Coal .........do.. | | | | | | 57,198.4 | 44,725.8 | 12,472.6 | |
| Charcoal ......do.. | | | | 1.2 | | 138.5 | 811.6 | | 673 |
| Barley, corn, chick-peas, etc., metric tons | | | 23 | 416.5 | | 1,491.9 | 2,843.3 | | 1,351.4 |
| Beer and sparkling wines......galls.. | 773 | | | 3,282 | | 89,767 | 101,608 | | 11,941 |
| Leather, hides, etc.....met. tons.. | | | 3.9 | 5 | | 288.6 | 428.6 | | 140 |
| Staves.....pieces.. | | | | | | 2,493,343 | 2,843,709 | | 350,386 |
| Spices and preserves, metric tons | 0.7 | 1 | 1 | 2.9 | | 101 | 242.5 | | 131.6 |
| Tin, copper, and zinc, metric tons | 0.5 | | | 9 | | 213 | 90 | 122.9 | |
| Grease..metric tons.. | | | 1 | 16.3 | | 318.6 | 331.9 | | 18.3 |
| Guano ........do.. | | | | 562 | | 14,784.6 | 19,300.6 | | 4,566 |
| Iron and steel..do.. | | | 471 | 102.3 | | 18,609 | 8,977.3 | 9,631.8 | |
| Iron wire......do.. | | 0.7 | | 1.4 | | 118.9 | 171.5 | | 52.6 |
| Lard .........do.. | | | | 1 | | 269 | 161 | 107.8 | |
| Butter.........do.. | | | | 1 | | 361 | 498.3 | | 137 |
| Machinery.....do.. | 1.8 | | 32 | 39.8 | | 5,211.6 | 3,428.5 | 1,788 | |
| Furniture, etc..do.. | 9 | | | 10 | | 108.7 | 126.7 | | 18 |
| Paper of all kinds, metric tons | | | | 2 | | 96 | 66 | 29 | |
| Cheese....met. tons.. | | | | 3 | | 427 | 295.8 | 131.3 | |
| Lumber.........do.. | | 3,210 | 996 | | | 8,926 | 21,915 | | 12,994 |
| Woven goods of all kinds ......yards.. | | | | 3.2 | | 37.7 | 115 | | 77.6 |
| Wheat....met. tons.. | | | 50 | | | 52.5 | 809.8 | | 757.3 |
| Glass and porcelain, metric tons | | | 2 | 34.6 | | 229 | 237.8 | | 8.9 |
| Jute....metric tons.. | 6.9 | | | 0.7 | | 182 | 353.5 | | 171.3 |

*Exports from Malaga to all countries for the years 1902 and 1901.*

| Articles. | | Total. | | 1902. | |
|---|---|---|---|---|---|
| | | 1902. | 1901. | Increase. | Decrease. |
| Olive oil | metric tons.. | 11,772 | 15,006.5 | .......... | 3,234.6 |
| Olives | do.... | 79 | 184.5 | .......... | 105 |
| Brandy | gallons. | 23,020 | 16,881 | 6,139 | .......... |
| Garlic | metric tons. | 41 | 57 | .......... | 15.6 |
| Almonds | do.... | 2,107 | 1,275 | 832 | .......... |
| Canary seed | do.... | 87 | 72.5 | .......... | 35.6 |
| Aniseed | do.... | 53.7 | 42 | 11.7 | .......... |
| Rice | do.... | 926.6 | 799 | 127.6 | .......... |
| Filberts | do.... | 12.6 | 29.5 | .......... | 16.9 |
| Cocoa shells | do.... | .7 | 8 | .......... | 2 |
| Orange peel | do.... | 6 | 105 | .......... | 99 |
| Walnuts and chestnuts | do.... | 22.8 | 72 | .......... | 49 |
| Onions | do.... | 340.8 | 184 | 156 | .......... |
| Cumin seed | do.... | 18 | 43.5 | .......... | 25 |
| Preserves | do.... | 38 | 26 | 11.8 | .......... |
| Chocolate | do.... | 6.5 | 26 | .......... | 19 |
| Esparto grass | do.... | 109 | 202.5 | .......... | 93.5 |
| Dried fruits | do.... | 317 | 72 | 244.8 | .......... |
| Fresh fruits | do.... | 198 | 51.6 | 146.5 | .......... |
| Chick-peas | do.... | 1,831 | 2,980.5 | .......... | 1,150 |
| Pomegranates | do.... | 140 | 172 | .......... | 31 |
| Figs | do.... | 2,168 | 1,504 | 663.7 | .......... |
| Soap | do.... | 9.4 | 31 | .......... | 21.5 |
| Lemons | do.... | 5,160 | 3,865.4 | 1,294.8 | .......... |
| Minerals | do.... | 14,644.6 | 8,031.4 | 6,613 | .......... |
| Oranges | do.... | 2,653.8 | 1,586.4 | 1,067 | .......... |
| Palm leaf, manufactured | do.... | 39.8 | 40 | .......... | .......... |
| Raisins | do.... | 3,821.9 | 4,487.4 | .......... | 665 |
| Red pepper | do.... | 34.5 | 61.7 | .......... | 27.2 |
| Lead | do.... | 37,303.6 | 29,822 | 7,481 | .......... |
| Licorice root | do.... | 7 | 13.7 | .......... | 6.7 |
| Grapes | do.... | 799.8 | 425 | 374 | .......... |
| Wine | gallons.. | 1,768.9 | 1,914.5 | .......... | 143.5 |
| Cotton goods | metric tons..' | 30.2 | 37 | .......... | 7 |

## VALENCIA.

The only important industrial incidents in this consular district during the past fiscal year have been the large increase in fresh fruit exports and the almost universal labor strikes. The latter resulted in shortening the working day by about an hour and increasing wages 20 per cent.

### FRUIT EXPORTS.

Fruit exports show the following comparative results:

| Description. | Season 1901–2. | Season 1900–1901. |
|---|---|---|
| | *Cases.a* | *Cases.a* |
| Oranges | 4,488,774 | 3,097,535 |
| Onions | 1,332,382 | 1,049,394 |
| Tomatoes | 190,481 | 166,407 |
| Melons | 237,577 | 258,867 |
| Sundry | 135,304 | 184,766 |
| Total | 6,384,518 | 4,756,969 |

a Of 135 pounds net.

The increase for 1901–2 was 1,627,549 cases. The past fruit season, however, has been, on the whole, disastrous for exporters. With the exception of the United Kingdom, all countries importing Valencia oranges admit them only under heavy tariffs; and with the increasing supplies from the United States, Jaffa, Australia, etc., the limit of

British consumption of Valencia oranges at paying rates has apparently been reached, so that under the heavier shipments of the past season the markets collapsed.

## LABOR CONDITIONS.

Although the hours of labor have been shortened and wages increased, the economic condition of the laboring classes has not improved, because of the great increase in cost of the necessaries of life, largely attributable to the depreciation of Spanish currency in international exchanges. Bread, beef, milk, sugar, vegetables, and clothing have advanced fully 30 per cent during the past two years.

## IMPORTS FROM UNITED STATES.

With regard to imports, the obstacles to trade with the United States, referred to in my previous annual reports—lack of a commercial treaty and of direct, rapid, and cheap transport service—still exist. Indeed, so deficient and unreliable is the existing freight service between this port and the United States that an important bicycle consignment, forwarded from Chicago, Ill., on the 26th day of May last, via New York and Liverpool, has not yet arrived here. Still, goods of American manufacture continue in increasing quantities to filter through to Valencia by different indirect routes. Rubber overshoes, ice-cream freezers, typewriters, electric fans, sundry small hardware articles, ingenious knickknacks, and time-saving appliances are visible everywhere. There is also a rapidly increasing demand for electric lamps and fittings. Over 100,000 lamps were imported during the year; but although the superior quality of the American electric lamp and appliances is universally recognized, the higher cost of the American article and the extra duty imposed upon it as coming from a country without treaty rates with Spain, have hitherto prevented successful competition with Dutch, Belgian, and Hungarian manufacturers.

## WINE CROP.

The wines in this consular district have suffered great damage from black rot and heat waves, which literally scorched all the grapes exposed to the sun's rays. In view of the anticipated deficit in the wine crop, merchants are already soliciting samples and quotations from Italy.

R. M. BARTLEMAN, *Consul.*

VALENCIA, *July 30, 1902.*

---

*Exports declared for fiscal year ended June 30, 1901 and 1902.*

UNITED STATES.

| Article. | 1901. | 1902. | Increase (+) or decrease (−), 1902. |
|---|---|---|---|
| Fans | $2,163.61 | $1,023.62 | −$1,139.99 |
| Fan ribs | | 281.81 | + 281.81 |
| Onions | 3,163.02 | 227.28 | − 2,935.74 |
| Oranges | 245.79 | 109.90 | − 135.89 |
| Skins (goat) | 93,546.90 | 155,548.36 | +62,001.46 |
| Saffron | 9,496.49 | 4,371.49 | − 5,125.00 |
| Shoes (bath) | 150.41 | | − 150.41 |
| Wine | 429.98 | 193.22 | − 236.76 |
| Total | 109,196.20 | 161,755.68 | |

*Exports declared for fiscal year ended June 30, 1901 and 1902*—Continued.

PORTO RICO.

| Article. | 1901. | 1902. | Increase (+) or decrease (−), 1902. |
|---|---|---|---|
| Advertisements | $4.00 | .......... | − $4.00 |
| Chufas | 5.34 | .......... | − 5.34 |
| Fans | 851.79 | $281.97 | − 569.82 |
| Furniture | 78.98 | 59.61 | − 19.37 |
| Garlic | 2,009.05 | 1,784.95 | − 224.10 |
| Leather | 198.43 | .......... | −. 198.43 |
| Musical instruments | 96.85 | .......... | − 96.85 |
| Oil (peanut) | 79.41 | 894.50 | + 815.09 |
| Oil (almond) | 850.88 | 1,959.95 | + 1,109.07 |
| Onions | .......... | 124.09 | + 124.09 |
| Paper (wrapping) | 12,792.98 | 6,685.66 | − 6,107.32 |
| Potatoes | 1,083.09 | .......... | − 1,083.09 |
| Preserves | 449.18 | .......... | − 449.18 |
| Pepper (red) | 600.91 | 1,691.55 | + 1,090.64 |
| Rice | 100,254.20 | 54,550.55 | − 45,703.65 |
| Tiles | 197.77 | .......... | − 197.77 |
| Wine | 1,331.08 | 3,286.98 | + 1,955.90 |
| Wood (varnished) | .......... | 147.17 | + 147.17 |
| Total | 120,883.84 | 73,703.28 | .......... |

PHILIPPINE ISLANDS.

| | | | |
|---|---|---|---|
| Wine | .......... | $579.00 | +$579.00 |

CUBA.

| | | | |
|---|---|---|---|
| Fans | a $674.48 | .......... | − $674.48 |
| Oil (cocoa) | a 186.23 | .......... | − 186.23 |
| Seed (canary) | a 373.05 | .......... | − 373.05 |
| Wine | a 203.07 | .......... | − 203.07 |
| Total | 1,436.83 | .......... | .......... |

a Quarters ended Sept. 30 and Dec. 31, 1900.

*Movement of vessels at the port of Valencia during the year 1901.*

ENTERED.

| Nationality. | With cargo. | | | In ballast or transit. | | | Total. | | |
|---|---|---|---|---|---|---|---|---|---|
| | Vessels. | Tons. | Crew. | Vessels. | Tons. | Crew. | Vessels. | Tons. | Crew. |
| British | 121 | 87,278 | 2,188 | 233 | 203,518 | 4,906 | 354 | 290,796 | 7,094 |
| Russian | 16 | 9,565 | 292 | 33 | 22,702 | 666 | 49 | 32,267 | 958 |
| Swedish or Norwegian | 51 | 24,039 | 656 | 107 | 58,779 | 1,547 | 158 | 82,818 | 2,203 |
| Danish | 9 | 5,862 | 155 | 7 | 3,453 | 102 | 16 | 9,315 | 257 |
| German | 37 | 22,972 | 607 | 55 | 38,792 | 995 | 92 | 61,764 | 1,602 |
| Dutch | .......... | .......... | .......... | 35 | 22,142 | 668 | 35 | 22,142 | 668 |
| French | 8 | 1,505 | 77 | 46 | 48,462 | 1,408 | 54 | 49,967 | 1,485 |
| Italian | 65 | 11,426 | 758 | 16 | 12,335 | 341 | 81 | 29,761 | 1,099 |
| Austro-Hungarian | 19 | 25,694 | 519 | 2 | 3,098 | 47 | 21 | 28,727 | 566 |
| Greek | 3 | 4,470 | 71 | .......... | .......... | .......... | 3 | 4,470 | 71 |
| Total | 329 | 198,811 | 5,323 | 534 | 413,276 | 10,680 | 863 | 612,087 | 16,003 |

CLEARED.

| | | | | | | | | | |
|---|---|---|---|---|---|---|---|---|---|
| British | 264 | 225,419 | 5,498 | 90 | 66,116 | 1,599 | 354 | 291,535 | 7,097 |
| Russian | 40 | 26,015 | 795 | 10 | 6,692 | 184 | 50 | 32,707 | 979 |
| Swedish and Norwegian | 124 | 68,657 | 1,823 | 30 | 14,397 | 387 | 154 | 83,054 | 2,210 |
| Danish | 13 | 7,447 | 207 | 3 | 1,868 | 50 | 16 | 9,315 | 257 |
| German | 81 | 54,593 | 1,419 | 10 | 6,302 | 164 | 91 | 60,895 | 1,583 |
| Dutch | 35 | 22,142 | 668 | .......... | .......... | .......... | 35 | 22,142 | 668 |
| French | 8 | 1,505 | 77 | 46 | 48,462 | 1,408 | 54 | 49,967 | 1,485 |
| Italian | 17 | 12,729 | 363 | 64 | 25,270 | 719 | 81 | 37,999 | 1,082 |
| Austro-Hungarian | 18 | 25,503 | 490 | 3 | 3,284 | 76 | 21 | 28,787 | 566 |
| Greek | .......... | .......... | .......... | 3 | 4,470 | 71 | 3 | 4,470 | 71 |
| Total | 600 | 444,010 | 11,340 | 259 | 176,861 | 4,658 | 859 | 620,871 | 15,998 |

*Principal articles of import and export at Valencia for the fiscal year ended June 30, 1902.*

[Custom-house returns.]

IMPORTS.

| Articles and countries. | Quantity. | Articles and countries. | Quantity. |
|---|---|---|---|
| Lime, cement, and earths for building and industrial purposes: | *Tons.* | Sulphate of ammonia, superphosphates and other ingredients of artificial manure: | |
| France | 4,580.2 | | *Tons.* |
| Italy | 76.2 | England | 30,147.5 |
| Belgium | 309.3 | France | 14,058.7 |
| England | 87 | Germany | 3,489.3 |
| Germany | 3.7 | Chile | 1,463.6 |
| Austria | .3 | Belgium | 1,486.1 |
| Coal: | | Algiers | 392.8 |
| England | 123,369.8 | Austria | 249.7 |
| Italy | 80 | Denmark | 16.1 |
| Belgium | 10,883 | Jute (raw): | |
| Petroleum: | | English possessions in India | 2,429.1 |
| United States | 171.4 | Mexico | 4.3 |
| England | 8.1 | England | 78.8 |
| Glass (common blown): | | Belgium | .5 |
| England | 2.6 | Germany | .5 |
| France | 16 | Jute (spun): | |
| Belgium | 20.6 | Belgium | 1,195.9 |
| Germany | 17 | England | 562.7 |
| Austria | .4 | Germany | 59.8 |
| Italy | .3 | Holland | 4.9 |
| Iron and steel, in bars of all kinds: | | Staves: | *Pieces.* |
| England | 24.6 | United States | 3,860,901 |
| France | 8.9 | Italy | 2,180,768 |
| Germany | 27.7 | France | 17,598 |
| Sweden | 191 | Austria | 5,028 |
| Austria | 121.4 | England | 7,468 |
| Belgium | 119 | Wood (common, in planks and logs): | *Cu.meters.* |
| Switzerland | 25.8 | United States | 7,228 |
| Iron (sheet): | | Russia | 9,959 |
| England | 181.5 | Canada | 12,170 |
| Belgium | 193.4 | Austria | 7,612 |
| Germany | 110 | Italy | 1,074 |
| France | 2 | Hides and skins (untanned): | *Tons.* |
| Iron (screws, nails, nuts, and similar articles): | | England, possessions in India | 405.5 |
| France | 36.8 | England | 5.6 |
| Germany | 57.5 | Germany | 118.2 |
| Austria | 15.4 | France | 7.1 |
| Belgium | 24.1 | China | 23.6 |
| England | 3.2 | Denmark | 1.8 |
| Holland | 1.5 | Argentine Republic | 53.6 |
| Iron (manufactures of): | | Algiers | 1.7 |
| United States | .4 | Tallow: | |
| England | 21.4 | France | 10.9 |
| Germany | 89.3 | Belgium | 11.5 |
| France | 66.7 | England | 67 |
| Austria | 10.8 | Germany | 5.3 |
| Switzerland | 39 | Argentine Republic | 345.8 |
| Russia | 1.4 | Austria | 58.6 |
| Belgium | 1.2 | Santo Domingo | 52.7 |
| Italy | 2.5 | Australia | 58.9 |
| Holland | .8 | Intestines: | |
| Copper (wire, sheets, and bronze): | | United States | 8.2 |
| France | 24.4 | France | 37.2 |
| Germany | 27.9 | Argentine Republic | 51.9 |
| Italy | .6 | Germany | 201.1 |
| Tin, in bars, England | 63.2 | Algiers | 1.3 |
| Copra and oleaginous seeds: | | Cod-fish: | |
| United States, possessions in the Philippine Islands | 957 | Norway | 145 |
| England, possessions in Asia | 87.9 | England | 311 |
| Portugal, possessions in Africa | 49.4 | France | 1,306.2 |
| France | 29.3 | Labrador | 919.2 |
| Mozambique | 64.9 | Wheat: | |
| Singapore | 1,236.8 | United States | 3,342 |
| Zanzibar | 172.5 | Russia | 10,794.8 |
| Holland, possessions in India | 140 | Machinery: | |
| Madagascar | 156.5 | United States | 3.7 |
| Soda (caustic) and alkalis: | | France | 134.7 |
| England | 1,464.4 | England | 141.3 |
| France | 565.8 | Germany | 89.1 |
| Germany | 88.8 | Holland | 8.1 |
| Belgium | 292.4 | Belgium | 29.7 |
| Holland | 46.8 | Italy | 11.8 |
| Lime (chloride), France | 325.9 | Austria | 7.4 |
| | | Cocoa: | |
| | | Venezuela | 50.8 |

*Principal articles of import and export at Valencia for the fiscal year ended June 30, 1902*—Continued.

IMPORTS—Continued.

| Articles and countries. | Quantity. | Articles and countries. | Quantity. |
|---|---|---|---|
| Cocoa—Continued. | *Tons.* | Cinnamon—Continued. | *Tons.* |
| Colombia | 15. 3 | China | 27. 2 |
| Guayaquil | 6. 4 | Colombia | 4. 7 |
| Uruguay | 25. 9 | Pepper: | |
| Ecuador | 101. 3 | Singapore | 35. 4 |
| Cinnamon: | | Zanzibar | 17. 6 |
| Ceylon | 41. 2 | | |

EXPORTS.

| Articles and countries. | Quantity. | Articles and countries. | Quantity. |
|---|---|---|---|
| Tiles and mosaics: | | Potatoes: | |
| Philippine Islands | 4. 6 | Philippine Islands | 7. 2 |
| Argentine Republic | 1,187. 2 | England | 372. 2 |
| Uruguay | 57. 5 | France | 76. 1 |
| France | 53. 9 | Cuba | 49 |
| Italy | 88. 2 | Argentine Republic | 4. 4 |
| Canary Islands | 228. 3 | Holland | 26. 5 |
| Morocco | 70. 3 | Italy | 98. 5 |
| Germany | 11. 2 | Raisins: | |
| England | 60. 9 | France | 514. 9 |
| Holland | 30 | England | 1,259. 1 |
| Algiers | 33 | Belgium | 16. 7 |
| Brazil | 15. 3 | Germany | 64. 6 |
| Cuba | 458 | Argentine Republic | 24. 1 |
| Mexico | 41. 1 | Holland | 12. 2 |
| Belgium | 21. 6 | Italy | 33. 5 |
| Argols: | | Canary Islands | 50. 1 |
| Holland | 188. 7 | Norway | 2. 3 |
| France | 577. 1 | Cuba | 1. 6 |
| England | 256. 8 | Oranges: | |
| Belgium | 169. 2 | United States | 14. 3 |
| Peanuts (ground nuts): | | England | 103,319. 6 |
| France | 578. 3 | France | 897. 9 |
| Morocco | 29. 4 | Belgium | 7,966. 2 |
| Algiers | 446. 9 | Germany | 7,569. 7 |
| Canary Islands | 73. 3 | Italy | 213 |
| Holland | 475. 6 | Holland | 5,822. 2 |
| England | 129. 5 | Denmark | 507. 1 |
| Germany | 54. 1 | Norway | 1,486. 8 |
| Italy | 283. 8 | Morocco | 22 |
| Belgium | 15. 2 | Grapes: | |
| Rice: | | England | 65 |
| Porto Rico | 988. 3 | Morocco | .1 |
| Philippine Islands | 15. 1 | France | 985. 5 |
| France | 2,915. 8 | Italy | 1,636. 8 |
| Morocco | 27. 7 | Belgium | 22. 7 |
| Algiers | 261. 9 | Apples, melons, pears, and other fresh | |
| Canary Islands | 140. 1 | fruits: | |
| Uruguay | 30. 6 | Porto Rico | .4 |
| Cuba | 650. 4 | Philippine Islands | 6 |
| Germany | 49. 5 | England | 12,296. 3 |
| Italy | 55. 4 | France | 213. 3 |
| England | 83. 8 | Morocco | .8 |
| Holland | 1,436. 3 | Algiers | 7. 1 |
| Argentine Republic | 1. 7 | Canary Islands | 1. 3 |
| Belgium | .8 | Argentine Republic | 26 |
| Garlic: | | Denmark | 15. 4 |
| Porto Rico | 8 | Germany | 27. 5 |
| Cuba | 103. 1 | Belgium | .7 |
| France | 68. 6 | Saffron: | |
| England | 8. 1 | Philippine Islands | .1 |
| Canary Islands | 1. 6 | France | .5 |
| Italy | 1. 6 | England | 3. 2 |
| Onions: | | Uruguay | 4. 4 |
| Porto Rico | 9. 2 | Argentine Republic | .6 |
| Philippine Islands | 2. 9 | Italy | .2 |
| England | 77,122. 7 | Cuba | .05 |
| Cuba | 76. 3 | Algiers | .4 |
| Denmark | .6 | Canary Islands | .08 |
| Argentine Republic | 12 | Wine. | *Gallons.* |
| Belgium | 24. 1 | United States | 171 |
| Germany | 83. 4 | Porto Rico | 27,742 |
| France | .9 | Philippine Islands | 108,014 |
| Norway | 6 | France | 2,119,724 |
| Pomegranates: | | England | 246,027 |
| England | 1,446. 9 | Germany | 74,578 |
| France | 4. 3 | Italy | 352,206 |

*Principal articles of import and export at Valencia for the fiscal year ended June 30, 1902—Continued.*

EXPORTS—Continued.

| Articles and countries. | Quantity. | Articles and countries. | Quantity. |
|---|---|---|---|
| Wine—Continued. | *Gallons.* | Wine—Continued. | *Gallons.* |
| Canary Islands | 60,479 | Guatemala | 1,643 |
| Morocco | 1,820 | Colombia | 453 |
| Cuba | 767,606 | Fans: | *Tons.* |
| Mexico | 17,335 | United States | .4 |
| Santo Domingo | 2,940 | Porto Rico | .05 |
| Brazil | 149,274 | France | 4 |
| Holland | 157,814 | England | 2.1 |
| Argentine Republic | 748,942 | Argentine Republic | 3.2 |
| Uruguay | 618,113 | Belgium | .4 |
| Singapore | 18,274 | Italy | 8.4 |
| Japan | 107,444 | Canary Islands | .8 |
| Denmark | 28,452 | Uruguay | .3 |
| Belgium | 83,264 | Cuba | .4 |
| Venezuela | 1,862 | Germany | 1 |
| Russia | 10,089 | Mexico | .2 |
| Norway | 9,689 | Brazil | .04 |
| Port Said | 10,929 | Algiers | .05 |

## REPORT FROM CONSULAR AGENCY AT DENIA.

The exports consist chiefly of raisins, and also of some grapes, onions, etc.   They were:

| Articles. | Countries. | Unit. | Quantity. | Value. |
|---|---|---|---|---|
| Raisins | United States | Tons | 1,212 | $92,383.93 |
| | Canada | do | 2,034 | 183,060.00 |
| | England | do | 11,782 | 1,055,880.00 |
| | The Baltic | do | 2,965 | 266,850.00 |
| | Other countries | do | 6,093 | 548,370.00 |
| Grapes | England | {Barrels | 108,436 | } 102,425.00 |
| | | {Cases | 6,228 | |
| Onions | United States | Crates | 162,614 | 47,970.85 |
| | Canada | do | 7,890 | 2,630.00 |
| | England | Cases | 1,186 | 965.00 |
| Almonds | United States | Boxes | 1,206 | 6,080.69 |
| | England | do | 5,290 | 30,420.00 |
| Palm hats | United States | Bales | 145 | 6,283.84 |
| Peppers in oil | do | Cases | 794 | 2,238.21 |
| Oranges | England | do | 18,654 | 27,980.00 |
| Other fruits | Different countries | | | 45,570.00 |
| Total value | | | | 2,419,057.52 |

Imports depend on the regular demand of industry.   Wood for the three sawmills here has been imported as follows:

| From— | | Quantity. | Value. |
|---|---|---|---|
| United States | cubic meters | 448 | $7,690.00 |
| Italy | do | 1,356 | 9,610.00 |
| France | do | 1,442 | 9,818.00 |
| Spain | kilos | 10,983,244 | 91,573.00 |
| Total | | | 118,691.00 |

Pulverized sulphur, guano, etc., come in small quantities from Spanish ports, and other articles, such as flour, sugar, etc., make up an average weekly supply of some 180 tons from Barcelona per coasting steamers.

*Movement of vessels since July 1, 1901.*

| Nationality. | Sailing. | | Steam. | | Total. | |
|---|---|---|---|---|---|---|
| | Vessels. | Tonnage. | Vessels. | Tonnage. | Vessels. | Tonnage. |
| Belgian | | | 1 | 546 | 1 | 546 |
| British | | | 65 | 59,380 | 65 | 59,380 |
| Danish | | | 14 | 10,085 | 14 | 10,085 |
| Dutch | | | 7 | 3,654 | 7 | 3,654 |
| French | | | 2 | 1,830 | 2 | 1,830 |
| German | 8 | | 8 | 4,333 | 8 | 4,333 |
| Italian | 8 | 906 | 1 | 1,829 | 9 | 2,735 |
| Norwegian | | | 25 | 12,918 | 25 | 12,918 |
| Russian | | | 2 | 1,056 | 2 | 1,056 |
| Spanish | 126 | 18,281 | 132 | 57,563 | 258 | 70,844 |
| Swedish | | | 8 | 6,421 | 8 | 6,421 |
| Total | 134 | 14,187 | 265 | 159,615 | 399 | 173,802 |

JOSEPH RAMOS MORAN,
*Consular Agent.*

DENIA, *July 1, 1902.*

# SWEDEN AND NORWAY.

## SWEDEN.

### REPORT FROM CONSULATE-GENERAL AT STOCKHOLM.

The year has shown an average yield in agricultural products throughout southern and central Sweden. In the north, however, and in Lapland crops have been practically a total failure, owing to protracted rains and cold weather during the brief summer season. The people were compelled to request Government aid to enable them to obtain the common necessities of existence. Grants were made from the royal treasury for this purpose, and subscription papers are now in circulation for private donations to the fund.

### SHIPPING.

The total number of ships entering the port of Stockholm from abroad during the last year was 2,049, with an aggregate tonnage of 927,371.

## TRADE.

*Returns of the principal articles of import and export into Sweden during the year 1901.*

### IMPORTS.

| | Quantity. | | Quantity. |
|---|---|---|---|
| Cotton, dyed and undyed.......tons.. | 16,796 | Paper, all kinds.................tons.. | 1,914 |
| Brandy and spirits: | | Salt, unrefined.................sq. ft.. | 2,819,889 |
| In casks, from barley, etc...galls. | 112,860 | Butter: | |
| In casks, from rice, arrack..do.... | 267,036 | Natural....................tons.. | 744 |
| In casks, from grapes, cognac, | | Artificial..................do.... | 243 |
| gallons......................... | 280,808 | Sugar: | |
| In casks, from sugar, rum ..galls.. | 5,280 | Refined, all kinds.........do.... | 235 |
| In other vessels ............do.... | 30,536 | Unrefined, all kinds.......do.... | 315 |
| Fish, salted, dried, etc.: | | Molasses...................do.... | 17,571 |
| Herrings....................tons.. | 40,396 | Grain, unground: | |
| Cod..........................do.... | 2,512 | Wheat.....................do.... | 176,186 |
| Pork ..........................do.... | 10,216 | Barley....................do.... | 255 |
| Manure, all sorts.............do.... | 125,675 | Maize.....................do.... | 15,129 |
| Hides and skins................do.... | 5,911 | Rye.......................do.... | 49,135 |
| Coffee .........................do.... | 28,636 | Grain, ground: | |
| Live stock: | | Wheat meal................do.... | 6,935 |
| Horses ....................head.. | 1,355 | Rye meal..................do.... | 1,224 |
| Cattle ......................do.... | - 2,565 | Coals and coke.............sq. ft.. | 130,014,961 |
| Sheep .......................do.... | 90 | Tallow ....................tons.. | 5,497 |
| Pigs ........................do.... | 925 | Tobacco ...................do.... | 4,578 |
| Meats...........................tons.. | 1,399 | Wool, dyed and undyed .......do.... | 3,816 |
| Machines, tools, and implements, | | Wine: | |
| dollars......................... | 388,640 | In barrels, all kinds .......galls. | 3,325 |
| Iron: | | In other vessels ...........do.... | 125,620 |
| Steel, pig, and ballast iron..tons.. | 40,288 | Textiles, all kinds: | |
| Rails ........................do.... | 55,942 | Silk.......................tons.. | 119 |
| Oleomargarine..................do.... | 1,397 | Cotton....................do.... | 1,478 |
| Oils, mineral ...................do.... | 76,610 | Wool .....................do.... | 1,599 |
| Cheese .........................do.... | 362 | Linen ....................do.... | 473 |

### EXPORTS.

| | Quantity. | | Quantity. |
|---|---|---|---|
| Brandy and spirits...............galls.. | 47,828 | Cheese, all kinds.................tons.. | 1 |
| Fish: | | Paper...........................do.... | 57,947 |
| Fresh herrings ...............tons.. | 9,673 | Wood pulp: | |
| Other kinds ..................do.... | 1,700 | Chemically prepared, dry ..do.... | 144,084 |
| Salted or preserved, dried or | | Chemically prepared, undried, | |
| smoked herrings ..........tons.. | 3,960 | tons ......................... | 10,365 |
| Other kinds....................do.... | 72 | Butter .........................do.... | 18,775 |
| Bacon ..........................do.... | 1,155 | Margarine ......................do.... | 2 |
| Hides and skins..................do.... | 4,991 | Grain, unground: | |
| Live stock: | | Oats ......................do.... | 30,510 |
| Horses ....................head.. | 1,130 | Wheat ....................do.... | 78 |
| Cattle ......................do.... | 3,300 | Barley ....................do.... | 40 |
| Sheep .......................do.... | 1,570 | Rye.......................do.... | 82 |
| Pigs ........................do.... | 85 | Grain, ground: | |
| Meat............................tons.. | 238 | Wheat meal ................do.... | 110 |
| Machines, tools, and implements, | | Rye meal ..................do.... | 7,384 |
| dollars......................... | 3,290,555 | Wood: | |
| Iron: | | Hewn or sawn logs or poles, | |
| Steel, pig, and ballast iron ..tons.. | 84,619 | sq. meters..................... | ........ |
| Ingots.........................do.... | 5,924 | Pit props..............sq. meters.. | 974,000 |
| Blooms.........................do.... | 18,195 | Deals and battens ..........do.... | 2,174,500 |
| Bars...........................do.... | 142,100 | Boards.....................do.... | 1,509,300 |
| Pieces of bars .................do.... | 3,159 | Planed or joined boards ...do.... | 537,700 |
| Iron wire in coils .............do.... | 4,414 | Matches.........................tons.. | 17,595 |
| Sheets.........................do.... | 1,553 | Textiles: | |
| Drawn wire ...................do.... | 982 | Cotton ....................do.... | 130 |
| Nails .........................do.... | 2,992 | Wool......................do.... | 89 |
| Ore: | | | |
| Iron ........................do.... | 1,761,007 | | |
| Zinc..........................do.... | 41,251 | | |

The total imports were valued, according to the latest official figures, at 505,000,000 kroner ($135,740,000). Exports, 358,000,000 kroner ($95,944,000).

The total income from customs, is 59,400,000 kroner ($15,919,200).

The merchant fleet of Sweden comprises:

| Class. | Number. | Tonnage. |
|---|---|---|
| Screw steamers | 872 | 296,421 |
| Sailing vessels | 2,040 | 289,248 |
| Total | 2,912 | 587,669 |

## AGRICULTURE: LUMBER.

The area of land under cultivation is 3,434,000 hectares, or 8,485,-414,000 acres.

The following shows the crops for 1901:

|  | Deciton. |  | Deciton. |
|---|---|---|---|
| Wheat | 1,300,000 | Mixed grains (blends) | 1,946,000 |
| Rye | 6,017,000 | Peas and beans | 623,000 |
| Barley | 3,141,000 | Potatoes | 12,930,000 |
| Oats | 10,434,000 |  |  |

The live stock in Sweden numbers:

|  |  |  |  |
|---|---|---|---|
| Horses | 525,000 | Sheep | 1,284,000 |
| Cows | 1,677,000 | Goats | 81,000 |
| Oxen | 816,000 | Swine | 811,000 |

The forests of Sweden cover about one-half of the land surface of the country. It supplies about one-fifth of the lumber used in the world's markets. The value of the lumber exported annually is 150,000,000 kroner ($39,750,000).

## BUTTER.

Butter is the principal export product of agriculture. The business has grown very rapidly during the past ten years. For 1901, it amounted to 20,000,000 kilograms, or 44,000,000 pounds.

## MINING.

The annual output of iron ore is 2,610,000 tons. From this, there is manufactured 527,000 tons of pig iron and 300,000 tons of steel. The coal produced amounts to 252,000 tons; lead, 1,424 tons; copper, 136 tons; gold, 88 kilograms, or 194.10 pounds; and silver, 1,927 kilograms, or 4,359.49 pounds.

## MANUFACTURES.

The number of factories in Sweden is 10,364, and the number of employees therein is 257,526. The value of annual product is estimated at 950,000,000 kroner ($251,750,000).

## COMMUNICATION.

At present, Sweden has 11,000 kilometers or 6,736 miles of railroads, of which the State owns 4,000 kilometers or 2,449 miles.

The telegraph lines belonging to the State cover 9,000 kilometers or 5,611 miles; telegraph lines along railroads cover 11,000 kilometers or 6,736 miles.

The telephone apparatus in use number 90,000. There are 2,572 post-offices, and the number of pieces of mail matter handled annually is 275,000,000.

EDWARD L. ADAMS,
*Consul-General.*

STOCKHOLM, *October 28, 1902.*

---

### GOTHENBURG.

I submit herewith a few figures as to the commerce during the six months January–June, 1902.

Compared with the corresponding period in 1901, the imports and exports at Gothenburg of some of the more important merchandise have been:

IMPORTS.

| Article. | | 1901. | 1902. |
|---|---|---:|---:|
| Bone dust | tons.. | 1,163 | 1,299 |
| Bicycles, finished | number.. | 1,740 | 1,809 |
| Butter: | | | |
| Natural | pounds.. | 6,819 | 2,552 |
| Artificial | do.... | 133,643 | 7,220 |
| Cheese, all kinds | do.... | 36,943 | 32,619 |
| Coal and coke | bushels.. | 10,386,067 | 9,663,586 |
| Cotton | tons.. | 4,547 | 4,781 |
| Dyestuffs, alizarin, aniline, etc. | pounds.. | 198,863 | 272,489 |
| Eggs | dozen.. | 377,354 | 258,743 |
| Fish, salted, pickled, or smoked: | | | |
| Herring | pounds.. | 17,527,846 | 20,096,188 |
| Codfish | do.... | 166,073 | 111,751 |
| Fertilizers, not specified | tons.. | 8,020 | 13,216 |
| Flour, etc.: | | | |
| Bran | pounds.. | 5,171,183 | 15,650,561 |
| Rice and rice meal | do.... | 305,291 | 540,716 |
| Rye flour | do.... | 62,697 | 21,715 |
| Wheat flour | do.... | 2,199,564 | 4,385,000 |
| Grain: | | | |
| Barley | do.... | 117 | ......... |
| Maize | do.... | 602,032 | 486,308 |
| Oats | do.... | 22,046 | 67,514 |
| Paddy | do.... | 4,890,131 | 8,264,351 |
| Rye | do.... | 65,463 | 2,331,664 |
| Wheat | do.... | 7,727,469 | 8,735,765 |
| Hides and skins | do.... | 1,063,292 | 1,089,526 |
| Hops | do.... | 66,581 | 59,192 |
| Leather: | | | |
| Sole leather | do.... | 288,803 | 183,943 |
| Other kinds | do.... | 181,820 | 258,462 |
| Liquors, in barrels: | | | |
| Brandy, at 40 per cent | gallons.. | 27,065 | 40,055 |
| Arrac, at 50 per cent | do.... | 18,465 | 23,703 |
| Rum, at 50 per cent | do.... | 253 | 345 |
| Whisky, at 50 per cent | do.... | 22,434 | 21,117 |
| Liquors in bottles, etc., all kinds | do.... | 6,987 | 7,711 |
| Machinery and tools, not specified | dollars.. | 493,948 | 509,064 |
| Meat, all kinds | pounds.. | 176,826 | 109,553 |
| Metals, iron and steel: | | | |
| Pig iron | tons.. | 4,934 | 6,479 |
| Pipes or tubes, cast | do.... | 1,671 | 1,266 |
| Pipes, forged, rolled, or drawn | do.... | 486 | 558 |
| Rails | do.... | 5,911 | 13,350 |
| Sheet iron, tinned | do.... | 1,051 | 1,501 |
| Structural iron | do.... | 988 | 1,487 |
| Oils: | | | |
| Mineral, refined | do.... | 1,992 | 3,837 |
| Fat, not specified, in barrels | do.... | 2,085 | 2,010 |
| Oil-seed cakes | do.... | 1,844 | 1,847 |
| Oleomargarine | do.... | 678,127 | 702,847 |
| Paper, all kinds | do.... | 481,780 | 585,141 |
| Pork or bacon | do.... | 1,749,231 | 938,269 |
| Potash, caustic | do.... | 315,105 | 454,981 |
| Potatoes | do.... | 20,872 | 7,580,343 |
| Preserves, all kinds | do.... | 165,453 | 185,504 |

IMPORTS—Continued.

| Article. | 1901. | 1902. |
|---|---|---|
| Rubber: | | |
| Raw .........................................................tons.. | 35,733 | 113,914 |
| Manufacturers of, shoes, etc .............................do.... | 5,946 | 4,931 |
| Saltpeter, Chile ............................................do.... | 1,830,400 | 1,901,408 |
| Salt, common ............................................bushels.. | 306,946 | 349,012 |
| Sewing machines and knitting machines .....................dollars.. | 34,150 | 41,086 |
| Seeds: | | |
| Linseed......................................................tons.. | 3,571 | 4,841 |
| Clover and other grass ..................................pounds.. | 333,029 | 344,002 |
| Shoddy or artificial wool....................................do.... | 566,309 | 585,107 |
| Sugar: | | |
| Refined, all kinds .........................................do.... | 74,165 | 60,714 |
| Raw.........................................................do.... | 154,642 | 26,839 |
| Superphosphate ...........................................tons.. | 1,587 | 2,256 |
| Sirup and molasses........................................pounds.. | 4,694,063 | 3,981,080 |
| Tallow .....................................................do.... | 2,092,723 | 2,627,109 |
| Thread, cotton .............................................do.... | 114,941 | 128,645 |
| Tobacco: | | |
| Raw, leaves and stems ....................................do.... | 515,727 | 887,045 |
| Manufactured, cigars and cigarettes.......................do... | 23,825 | 33,049 |
| Wines: | | |
| In casks or barrels .......................................do.... | 741,731 | 467,994 |
| In bottles, etc ...........................................gallons.. | 17,476 | 12,825 |
| Wool .....................................................pounds.. | 2,285,601 | 2,764,183 |
| Woven fabrics: | | |
| Silk goods, all kinds .....................................do.... | 26,587 | 21,858 |
| Cotton goods ..............................................do.... | 575,848 | 806,268 |
| Linen goods ...............................................do.... | 109,354 | 146,421 |
| Woolen goods .............................................do.... | 387,064 | 392,342 |
| Waterproof carpets........................................do.... | 88,349 | 190,731 |
| Yarn: | | |
| Woolen, all kinds .........................................do.... | 822,121 | 973,972 |
| Cotton......................................................do.... | 799,826 | 978,801 |

EXPORTS.

| | 1901. | 1902. |
|---|---|---|
| Butter..............................................pounds.. | 9,928,734 | 9,890,722 |
| Grain: | | |
| Oats......................................................do...... | 10,055,416 | 11,195,689 |
| Other kinds ..............................................do.... | 1,329,495 | 416,352 |
| Hides and skins............................................do.... | 1,896,049 | 1,912,060 |
| Iron and steel: | | |
| Bars .......................................................tons.. | 24,188 | 25,632 |
| Bar ends ..................................................do.... | 730 | 247 |
| Blooms and rough bars......................................do.... | 5,829 | 3,223 |
| Ingots .....................................................do.... | 1,442 | 775 |
| Nails ......................................................do.... | 1,279 | 1,562 |
| Pig iron ...................................................do.... | 17,418 | 12,964 |
| Plates, rolled or forged....................................do.... | 48 | 55 |
| Wire rods, drawn ..........................................do.... | 30 | 50 |
| Matches ...................................................do.... | 8,056 | 6,544 |
| Paper......................................................do.... | 21,569 | 22,136 |
| Woodenwares: | | |
| Planks and boards ....................................cubic feet.. | 4,405,887 | 4,965,180 |
| Mine timber (pit props)....................................do.... | 6,775,789 | 6,148,082 |
| Beams and rafters.........................................do.... | 2,401 | 1,907 |
| Wood pulp ..................................................tons.. | 43,224 | 37,338 |
| Zinc ore .....................................................do.... | 9,266 | 10,700 |

As to the import from the United States, no reliable statistics can be obtained.

The value of the declared exports from Gothenburg to the United States during the first half of this year shows an increase of $111,873, compared with the declared exports during the same period of 1901. This increase came chiefly from hides and skins, pig iron, wood pulp, wire rods, steel strips, nail rods, matches, liquors, cutlery, and fish.

### FREE PORT.

A few years ago, it was proposed to establish a free port at Gothenburg, but the plan was not realized. The question has now been brought up again, and an association of merchants has sent out experts to study the free ports at Copenhagen and Hamburg, and also mailed circulars to different Swedish manufacturers asking their views.

## CANALS: WATER POWER.

The question of building a modern canal, with large locks, from Lake Venern westward to the sea has been under consideration for some time. Plans and estimates have been made, but, so far as I know, the final decision has not been reached. The old locks and canals are not large enough to accommodate seagoing vessels.

The controversy between the Government and private persons concerning the ownership of waterfalls will soon be settled, and may tend to a more general use of water power.

## PEAT.

The first peat school in Sweden was opened July 1, 1902, at Emmaljunga, near Markaryd, in the county of Kronoberg. This school gives instruction in the proper methods of searching for peat, of estimating value of same as fuel, of draining peat bogs, of manufacturing peat fuel, of storing it, etc. The Government has granted the school an allowance of about $4,800, to be used during a period of five years.

## LIGHT-BUOYS.

Light-buoys using acetylene gas have been used in the harbor here for about a month. They burn quite a long time with each charge and appear to be satisfactory in other ways.

## AGRICULTURE.

It will be noticed in the import list that the import of breadstuffs, with the exception of rye flour, increased during the first half of this year, and I am inclined to believe that the trade will not be less during the coming fall and winter. The crop prospects here do not seem to be very bright. The whole summer has been miserably wet and chilly, which has retarded the growth of everything. An abstract from the official crop report for the month of August may be of interest. In these reports, 5 means very good; 4, good; 3, middling; 2, poor; 1, very poor. The figures were: Winter wheat, 3.5; winter rye, 3.8; barley, 3.4; oats, 3.4; mixed grains, 3.5; legumes, 3.1; potatoes, 3.3; sugar beets, 2.9. The conditions have hardly improved since the above estimate was made.

## EMIGRATION.

I have been informed that 15,011 emigrants left Sweden during the six months January–June, 1902. If this is correct, the total emigration this year will probably be higher than during any other twelve months since 1893. The emigration during the first quarter of 1902 was larger than during any corresponding period in the last seven years. The press has discussed this matter a good deal and several remedies have been proposed: That the Government enact a homestead law and sell public lands on easy terms or lend money to laborers who desire to get a home of their own; that the suffrage or right to vote be extended; that an emigrant tax be adopted.

ROBERT S. S. BERGH, *Consul.*

GOTHENBURG, *September 15, 1902.*

---

## NORWAY.

The figures for import and export in this report are, as on previous occasions, based on returns given in the Norwegian official publication entitled "Norges Handel;" and as this publication generally presents figures covering the trade of the whole kingdom, my report is necessarily compiled in the same manner, showing the trade of the country and not of my consular district only. I have, however, as far as practicable, also given figures for the district separately.

The total trade between Norway and all other countries, Sweden included, has for each of the last five years been as follows:

| Year. | Imports. | Exports. | Excess of imports. |
|---|---|---|---|
| 1897 | $71,275.180 | $45,323,432 | $25,951,748 |
| 1898 | 75,756,750 | 43,054,050 | 32,702,700 |
| 1899 | 83,210,060 | 42,719,200 | 40,490,860 |
| 1900 | 83,255,030 | 46,349,635 | 36,905,895 |
| 1901 | 76,969,600 | 44,246,800 | 32,722,800 |

The large incomes derived from the shipping, and also the incomes from the tourist traffic, serve as an offset to the deficiency in the balance of trade.

Of the imports in 1901, 43.7 per cent of the goods were for purposes of production and 56.3 per cent for purposes of consumption.

The stock of gold in Norges Bank, which was $9,750,000 in December, 1900, is $10,500,000 at the present writing, August 7, 1902.

### IMPORTS.

A classified statement of the values of the entire imports into Norway in the year 1901 is given in the following table, in which also is shown the value of such imports during the previous year and the value of the direct imports from the United States for each of the years 1900 and 1901:

| Article. | Imports by years. | | Direct imports from the United States. | |
|---|---|---|---|---|
| | 1900. | 1901. | 1900. | 1901. |
| Petroleum | $1,062,800 | $1,133,900 | $963,200 | $967,700 |
| Beef, all kinds | 828,468 | 964,000 | 73,960 | 110,700 |
| Pork, all kinds | 1,528,484 | 1,547,320 | 888,200 | 895,100 |
| Leather and skins | 1,863,000 | 2,067,800 | 438,400 | 445,500 |
| Tallow, lard, margarin, etc | 2,006,600 | 2,125,430 | 918,450 | 954,000 |
| Butter | 96,676 | 117,900 | 9,420 | 23,800 |
| Wheat | 256,423 | 242,650 | 11,010 | 83,600 |
| Flour | 1,983,360 | 1,962,400 | 196,000 | 490,400 |
| Corn | 626,070 | 462,800 | 355,550 | 270,600 |
| Corn meal | 4,475 | 6,540 | 1,000 | 2,300 |
| Rye | 5,002,800 | 5,288,650 | .......... | .......... |
| Rye meal | 2,035,755 | 1,100,120 | .......... | .......... |
| Barley | 3,141,300 | 2,265,900 | 7,820 | .......... |
| Barley groats | 95,000 | 66,280 | 8,010 | .......... |
| Barley meal | 120,650 | 83,130 | 1,390 | .......... |

| Article. | Imports by years. | | Direct imports from the United States. | |
|---|---|---|---|---|
| | 1900. | 1901. | 1900. | 1901. |
| Oats | $328,700 | $39,000 | . | |
| Oat groats | 207,150 | 183,800 | $26,540 | $29,300 |
| Oatmeal | 6,673 | 5,100 | 2,510 | 1,300 |
| Malt | 207,900 | 262,600 | | 700 |
| Beans and peas | 200,600 | 171,500 | | |
| Cheese | 131,427 | 120,200 | 410 | 200 |
| Eggs | 57,807 | 46,700 | 10 | |
| Live stock | 634,463 | 798,480 | | |
| Flax, hemp, tow, and jute | 627,200 | 679,100 | | |
| Cotton | 622,560 | 684,000 | 25,100 | 44,200 |
| Rice, sago, etc | 245,450 | 187,700 | | |
| Coffee | 2,506,900 | 2,670,700 | 3,520 | 1,600 |
| Tea and cacao | 235,350 | 227,900 | | |
| Sirup | 366,900 | 446,800 | 30,030 | 46,900 |
| Sugar | 2,311,000 | 2,232,500 | 4,230 | 4,500 |
| Fruits, green and dried | 746,900 | 726,500 | 15,175 | 28,800 |
| Wines | 1,292,200 | 1,196,000 | 3,300 | 900 |
| Spices | 115,000 | 103,600 | | |
| Tobaccoes and cigars | 838,200 | 840,300 | 164,150 | 151,000 |
| Hops | 140,500 | 156,800 | | |
| Vegetables, etc | 482,000 | 287,300 | | |
| Fish, all kinds | 408,430 | 527,100 | | |
| Alcohol and liquors | 649,400 | 697,700 | | |
| Wool and shoddy | 652,000 | 637,430 | | |
| Yarns, threads, cords, and ropes | 2,015,800 | 2,546,900 | 105 | 1,000 |
| Cloth and other manufactures of silk | 562,400 | 582,600 | | |
| Cloth and other manufactures of wool | 2,878,700 | 2,808,000 | | |
| Cloth and other manufactures of cotton | 1,968,250 | 1,886,700 | 1,440 | |
| Cloth and other manufactures of linen, hemp, and jute | 475,140 | 509,700 | 184 | |
| Hats, caps, sundry dry goods, and notions | 812,760 | 866,400 | 410 | |
| Boots, shoes, and other leather goods | 218,770 | 205,400 | 1,667 | 800 |
| Oils, other than petroleum | 1,782,920 | 1,501,500 | 2,770 | 32,500 |
| Varnishes and tar | 279,140 | 283,000 | 3,710 | 1,500 |
| Rubber and rubber goods | 368,940 | 466,900 | 5,900 | 20,600 |
| Seeds and plants | 499,690 | 588,500 | 11,705 | |
| Watches and clocks | 427,220 | 356,400 | 3,484 | 1,900 |
| Musical instruments | 195,560 | 188,300 | 1,072 | 400 |
| Books, pictures, and stationery | 752,860 | 796,700 | 4,475 | 6,800 |
| Woods, oak, ash, etc | 1,956,720 | 1,551,100 | 82,540 | 52,700 |
| Manufactures of wood | 1,202,490 | 916,100 | 6,780 | 22,400 |
| Hair and feathers | 178,170 | 140,800 | 3,100 | 3,200 |
| Soap, perfumery, candles, etc | 40,000 | 135,700 | | |
| Oil cake and similar feed for animals | 335,100 | 282,600 | | |
| Paper and paper articles | 781,060 | 728,200 | 1,275 | 3,200 |
| Cork, bark, and straw | 221,020 | 230,400 | 340 | |
| Coal and coke | 9,422,000 | 8,285,000 | | 17,400 |
| Paints and dyestuffs | 571,750 | 536,200 | | 130 |
| Chemicals | 826,105 | 953,200 | | |
| Cement | 243,050 | 196,900 | | |
| Salt | 614,750 | 485,600 | | |
| Manufactures of clay | 403,500 | 327,300 | | |
| Manufactures of glass | 381,200 | 249,200 | | |
| Pig iron | 472,190 | 292,100 | | |
| Steel | 150,880 | 117,400 | 4,640 | 1,000 |
| Band, bolt, and rod iron | 1,189,360 | 818,000 | 7,000 | 1,900 |
| Sheet and plate iron | 1,146,100 | 1,024,600 | 15,710 | 4,600 |
| Other metals | 695,400 | 759,900 | 1,380 | 4,000 |
| Tools, all kinds | 618,830 | 624,400 | 23,970 | 17,800 |
| Iron pipes, tubes, and beams | 540,050 | 569,000 | 2,895 | 200 |
| Heavy iron castings, rails, etc | 3,798,650 | 3,883,900 | 299,925 | 330,900 |
| Manufactures of other metals | 1,026,500 | 835,000 | 2,430 | 600 |
| Steamships | 2,758,110 | 1,886,000 | | |
| Sail ships | 750,550 | 693,800 | | 23,000 |
| Wagons, carriages, and sleighs | 52,635 | 103,500 | | |
| Locomotives and tenders | 236,270 | 41,000 | | |
| Locomobiles | 17,700 | 19,900 | | |
| Motors | 254,100 | 243,200 | 9,728 | 4,300 |
| Thrashers | 4,150 | 4,000 | | |
| Reapers and mowers | 99,120 | 92,100 | 69,060 | 44,900 |
| Other farm machinery | 113,400 | 137,100 | 22,000 | 13,500 |
| Other machinery | 1,077,840 | 683,200 | 57,650 | 41,700 |
| Parts of machinery | 440,080 | 341,400 | 10,800 | 5,000 |
| Other implements | 180,690 | 35,900 | 81,000 | |
| Sewing and knitting machines | 186,500 | 234,600 | 53 | 700 |
| Electric apparatus and fixtures | 405,300 | 1,117,800 | | |
| Bicycles and bicycle parts | 156,380 | 108,500 | 15,350 | 17,700 |
| Goods not classified | 1,804,099 | 441,870 | 278,687 | 121,470 |
| Total | 83,255,030 | 76,969,600 | 4,575,620 | 4,850,900 |

## UNITED STATES TRADE.

The direct imports from the United States into Norway during the last five years have been:

| | | | |
|---|---|---|---|
| 1897 | $3,240,200 | 1900 | $4,575,620 |
| 1898 | 3,836,700 | 1901 | 4,850,900 |
| 1899 | 5,172,000 | | |

The indirect import of American goods into the country, via England, Germany, and Denmark, through foreign jobbers, may be estimated at over $4,000,000 for the year 1901, and consists principally of the same kind of goods as the direct imports from the United States. The direct importation of American goods is gradually increasing. Among the imports for 1899 was an item of rye to the amount of $808,000, which swells the figures for that year. Since that time, no rye has been bought from America. In the common lines of goods, increases are generally to be observed, and new lines are constantly being tried.

The direct imports from America during the first six months of 1902 have been large. The Copenhagen steamers, running in regular route between New York, Christiania, and Copenhagen, carry, as a rule, heavy cargoes every week. Reliable figures are not as yet obtainable.

If an American salesman would appear occasionally, it would certainly help our trade. American chemicals and drugs, fancy groceries, dry goods, notions, electrical goods, and several other articles should be better introduced. German and British salesmen visit the country regularly, but an American is seldom, if ever, to be seen.

The tax on commercial travelers remains the same as formerly, 100 kroner ($26.80) per thirty days.

The declared exports from Norway to the United States for 1901 and the first six months of 1902 have been:

| Articles. | 1901. | First six months of 1902. |
|---|---|---|
| Wood pulp | $279,119 | $278,475 |
| Salted mackerel | 53,996 | 16,200 |
| Hides | 52,852 | 12,700 |
| Cod-liver oil | 38,725 | 8,821 |
| Oxalic acid | 34,671 | 4,398 |
| Books | 19,530 | 9,473 |
| Other goods | 36,215 | 42,763 |
| Total | 515,106 | 372,825 |

## ORIGIN OF IMPORTS.

Norway conducts the bulk of its trade with two countries, namely, Germany and Great Britain. Its trade with these countries in 1901 was as follows:

| Description. | Germany. | Great Britain. |
|---|---|---|
| Imports | $20,767,800 | $21,197,300 |
| Exports | 5,107,600 | 17,974,600 |

The principal Norwegian imports in 1901 came from the following countries:

From Germany, goods amounting to $20,770,000, consisting principally of woolens and other dry goods, notions, groceries, spices, grains, fruits, tobaccos, oils, electrical goods, tools, machinery, and wines.

From Great Britain, goods amounting to $21,200,000, consisting principally of coal, hardware, machinery, cotton and woolen goods, provisions, paints, oils, and ships.

From Russia, goods amounting to $6,600,000, consisting principally of grain (mostly rye), seeds, woods, hemp, and petroleum.

From Sweden, goods amounting to $6,500,000, consisting of woods, live cattle, iron, tools and machinery, provisions, paper, and a variety of other goods.

From Denmark came grain, beef, and pork, tallow, and margarin, woolens, books, etc., valued at $5,000,000.

From the Netherlands came coffee, cheese, liquors, oils, paints, tallow, and margarin, etc., of a value of $3,500,000.

From Belgium came iron goods, machinery, hardware, grain, coffee, seeds, cotton, etc., of the value of $3,500,000.

From France, Spain, and Italy come, principally, brandies, wines, fruits, vegetables, spices, oils, sulphur, and salt.

Some trade is also conducted with other European countries, and with South America, the West Indies, Asiatic countries, Australia, and Africa.

### EXPORTS.

The Norwegian exports in 1901 are classified in the following statement, the principal markets being also shown:

| Classification. | Value. | Principal markets. |
|---|---|---|
| Lumber | $9,538,700 | Great Britain, Holland, Belgium, and France. |
| Wood pulp | 6,073,100 | Great Britain, France, Belgium, and Spain. |
| Matches | 223,200 | Great Britain, Belgium, and Germany. |
| Turned woods | 59,200 | Great Britain. |
| Fishery products | 13,469,100 | Spain, Germany, Great Britain, Russia, and the Netherlands. |
| Paper, all kinds | 2,646,500 | Great Britain and Germany. |
| Condensed milk | 1,404,300 | Do. |
| Butter | 692,000 | Do. |
| Margarin | 271,700 | Denmark and Great Britain. |
| Hides and furs | 760,000 | Great Britain, the Netherlands, Germany, Sweden, and Denmark. |
| Ores | 595,800 | Great Britain, the Netherlands, Germany, Belgium, and Russia. |
| Copper | 387,200 | Great Britain, Germany, and Sweden. |
| Cut stone and marble | 583,400 | Great Britain and Germany. |
| Canned goods | 566,000 | Great Britain, the Netherlands, and Germany. |
| Ships | 523,400 | Sweden, Great Britain, and Japan. |
| Bran and shorts | 452,400 | Germany. |
| Nails and horseshoe nails | 436,000 | Great Britain and Germany |
| Machines | 261,600 | Sweden and Denmark. |
| Ice | 214,000 | Great Britain and France. |
| Books | 213,000 | Denmark and America. |
| Calcium carbid | 139,000 | Germany and Denmark. |
| Other goods, not classified | 4,737,200 | |
| Total | 44,246,800 | |

Among the exports, not classified, are: Oxalic acid, feldspar, cotton goods, brick, glassware, telephone apparatus, iodine, kelp, leather belting, and live animals.

## TRADE OF NORWEGIAN CITIES.

The total trade of Norway for the year 1901, as before stated, was—

Import............................................................ $76,969,600
Export............................................................ 44,246,800

Of this trade, the three principal cities, Christiania, Bergen, and Trondhjem, had their respective shares as follows:

| City. | Import. | Export. |
|---|---|---|
| Christiania............................................................ | $35,662,000 | $7,837,300 |
| Bergen............................................................ | 13,265,000 | 5,726,000 |
| Trondhjem ............................................................ | 7,001,500 | 1,877,000 |

Other towns of importance are Stavanger, Drammen, Fredrikshald, Skien, Moss, and Christiansand. About one-half of the import trade of the whole country passes through Christiania, whose merchants make good use of its splendid communications by sea and land. Of the American imports into the country, more than four-fifths are handled by Christiana importers.

## TARIFF.

No important tariff changes have been made in the customs rates. It may be mentioned that milliners' feather goods, formerly paying $4 per kilogram (2.2 lbs.), now pay $6.70 per kilogram, and plated wire goods, formerly paying $0.13 per kilogram, now pay $0.67 per kilogram.

The total revenue of the Government for customs on goods imported in 1901 was $9,408,500, of which there was collected at the Christiania custom-house $5,389,700.

## TRADE IN 1902.

Trade statistics for the first half of the present year, 1902, are as yet published in round figures only, and without specification. The figures are:

Import ................................................................ $35,100,000
Export ................................................................ 19,778,000

The same classes of goods given in the statement for 1901 predominate. The import of tobaccos, wire rope and wire fencing, sirups, and many other articles, direct from America, has of late been unusually large.

## FINANCES.

The public debt of Norway was on the 31st day of March, 1901, $61,301,000, and the municipal debts about $21,440,000. The receipts of the public treasury for the year were:

| | | | |
|---|---|---|---|
| Customs ...................... | $9,648,000 | Direct taxes................. | $1,447,000 |
| Liquor revenues............ ...... | 1,428,000 | Inheritance and other fees .. | 241,000 |
| Malt revenues................. | 1,072,000 | | |
| Stamp revenues ............ | 536,000 | Total ................. | 14,372,000 |

The total earnings of the nation for 1901 are estimated at $123,000,000.

The indebtedness of banks is large. Deposits in savings banks are $86,000,000, and the number of depositors 695,524. The municipal taxes in 1901 were $7,500,000. Taxes are very heavy in some communities. The income taxation system is in use.

The amount of money sent from America to relatives in Norway is assuming larger proportions every year. The value sent by postal money orders alone was $637,000 in 1901. It would appear reasonable to believe that at least as much is sent through banks, but of this no report is to be had.

The tourist traffic has been rather light in the past season, on account of the inclemency of the weather.

### AGRICULTURE.

According to the reports of a commission recently appointed to examine into the economic condition of the farmers of the country, the net incomes of the agriculturists amount to about $21,000,000 per annum, deducting all expenditures, even interest on farm loans, while the gross incomes are placed at $62,000,000. The country is best suited for stock raising. Dairies are numerous. Horses, cattle, hogs, sheep, goats, and tame reindeer are the principal domestic animals.

Rye, barley, oats, wheat, and the common vegetables are in most places successfully raised in ordinary seasons.

Considerable fruit, tobacco, and honey are also produced.

The present season has been the worst for the farmers in many years, and the country will have to import unusually large quantities of breadstuffs and provisions. The Government will have to provide seed grain for next season in many tracts.

The number of people depending on agriculture is 838,000, out of a total population of 2,000,000; a large proportion look to the fisheries and the lumber traffic in order to make a living.

### FISHERIES.

In the fisheries are engaged some 100,000 people, most of them being also possessors of small farms. The winter cod fisheries, along the coast from Trondhjem to the Russian border, and in the Lofoten Islands, are of most importance. Then come other coast fisheries, for herring, mackerel, sprat, lobster, halibut, flounders, salmon, etc. The bank fisheries are receiving increased attention every year, and they generally give good returns. The fishermen from the Romsdal district, around Aalesund, are largely interested in the bank fisheries. The catch consists of halibut, ling, and other deep-water fish.

The whale, seal, and walrus fisheries in Arctic waters are also well attended and give fair returns.

The Government expends considerable money on deep-water soundings, in the near portions of the Atlantic and the North Sea, for the purpose of locating new fishing banks. A small fund has also been set aside, out of which loans are furnished to a limited number of fishermen, to enable them to purchase suitable steamboats for use in the bank fisheries.

The total export of fishery products from the country in 1901 was $13,500,000.

The people in northern Norway, who depend largely on the coast fisheries for a living, are petitioning the Storthing (Congress) for the enactment of a law prohibiting the killing of whales in all Norwegian waters. They claim that long experience has taught them that it is the whales in pursuit of herring that drive the latter and other fish from the deep sea nearer to land, where the fishermen are able to make their catch, and that the wholesale killing of whales deprives them of their means of making a living.

Against this, the people interested in the whale fisheries advance the argument that whales are migratory animals, and that the enactment of the proposed law by the Norwegian Government would in a small degree only prevent the destruction of the whales.

### SHIPPING.

The shipping trade continues to be a favored vocation and one of the main supports of the Norwegian people. Their ships are engaged in all parts of the world.

People who are well posted claim, however, that the world's tonnage is becoming too large for the demand. Freights have ruled rather low of late years, and the profits have been uncertain.

As in previous years, there was also in 1901 a decrease in the country's tonnage in sailing ships and an increase in the tonnage in steamships.

The following table shows the growth of the Norwegian merchant marine during the last quarter of a century:

| Year. | Sailing ships. | | Steamships. | |
|---|---|---|---|---|
| | Number. | Tonnage. | Number. | Tonnage. |
| 1875 | 7,596 | 1,349,243 | 218 | 45,965 |
| 1885 | 7,154 | 1,448,912 | 510 | 114,108 |
| 1895 | 6,355 | 1,283,913 | 915 | 821,052 |
| 1898 | 5,881 | 1,120,808 | 1,068 | 437,570 |
| 1899 | 5,698 | 1,052,687 | 1,128 | 482,247 |
| 1900 | 5,642 | 1,002,675 | 1,171 | 505,443 |
| 1901 | 5,518 | 942,400 | 1,218 | 524,600 |

The total tonnage for 1901 was 1,467,000. The valuation placed on the Norwegian merchant fleet at the close of the year 1900 was as follows:

| | |
|---|---|
| 1,171 steamships | $34,218,000 |
| 5,642 sail ships | 17,819,000 |
| Total | 52,037,000 |

The ships engaged in foreign waters in the year 1900 were:

| | Tonnage. |
|---|---|
| 703 steamers | 470,713 |
| 2,628 sail ships | 949,097 |

The gross earnings of these ships were some $38,500,000 for the year.

There were wrecked during 1900 23 steamers, of 12,963 tons burden, and 135 sail ships, of 57,650 tons burden.

The shipping of the country gives employment to about 50,000 seamen.

## MINING.

The common minerals of the country are pyrites, copper, silver, and iron ores. The total valuation of all mineral products was placed at $1,715,000 for the year 1899. Some 2,500 people were engaged. The mining industry is now receiving more attention than ever before in the history of the country. The iron and copper regions in northern Norway are being developed, and promise to prove good investments.

The copper mines in Sulitjelma, Salten, have now been worked a number of years, and have always given very good returns. The iron mines in Gillivari and neighboring places, in Sweden and Norway, have been worked some three years, but none of the stored ore has been shipped, nor will it be till next season, when the railroad connecting the mines with the ocean at the port of Narvik, in Ofoten, will be opened. It is claimed that the annual export of ore from these mines alone will reach 1,000,000 tons. The principal markets will be Germany and England.

The iron mines in the Dunderlandsdal are now being opened by an English syndicate—the "Dunderland Iron Ore Company, Limited"— with $10,000,000 capital, in which considerable American money is also invested. American engineers are now building the railroad, 18 miles long, which is to connect the mines with the sea, at Mo in Ranen. The territory is very mountainous and broken. The ore from the mines is to be treated according to the new Edison system, by electro-magnetism. It is claimed that the region which the company leases from the Norwegian Government holds 75,000,000 to 80,000,000 tons of available ore, and that about 750,000 tons of ore will be shipped annually when the works shall have been completed.

New iron fields have been discovered this summer in the district around the Varanger Bay, in the extreme north. From examinations made, the ore appears plentifully over a large territory, and holds enough iron to be remunerative. The access to the sea is better than in any of the places formerly mentioned.

The old silver mine at Kongsberg and the copper mine at Røraas, which are owned by the Norwegian Government, give fair returns. The Kongsberg mine has given unusually good returns of late, but the price of silver is so low that it requires at least three times as much silver to pay a man's wages now as it did thirty years ago.

Among other metals and minerals found in Norway are zinc, feldspar, rutile, and apatite. Gold appears in Finmarken, in the Tana River district, but so far not in paying quantities. Emeralds appear around Kongsberg. Some pearls are found in the river mussel shells in the Jäderen district. Coal appears on the Andø in Lofoten.

## INDUSTRIES.

The lumber industry is of greater monetary importance to the country than any other. It gives employment to some 35,000 people, including men in the pineries. The exports amounted to about $16,000,000 in the year 1901, not including paper.

In Norway there are still found large tracts covered with pine forest, but the woods easiest of access are becoming exhausted. The wood-pulp and paper mills demand increased quantities of wood every year.

The total number of industrial plants in the country had increased from 3,074 in 1899 to 3,173 at the close of the year 1900. Many of them are very small concerns. The power employed equaled 199,388 horsepower, of which 146,516 was water and 47,796 steam. Water-power is steadily replacing steam in all branches of industry. The number of people employed in industrial plants of all kinds is 79,457, of whom 58,166 are adult men, 12,465 adult women, and the balance young people of both sexes under 18 years; only 600 are under 14 years. The most important industrial plants in the country are woolen and cotton mills; machine shops; wood-pulp, paper, and saw mills; shipyards; glass and porcelain works; chemical laboratories; oil refineries; match factories, and canneries.

## EMIGRATION.

Emigration from Norway has of late assumed such dimensions that it is causing considerable vexation to the authorities.

During the period from 1881 till 1893, the yearly emigration from Norway averaged 21,500 people; from 1894 till 1899 it averaged only 6,600, but since that time there has been a large increase.

The emigration in 1900 was 16,530; in 1901 it was 14,325, and in 1902 it will in all probability fall but little short of 25,000. Nearly all of these people go to the United States. Remembering that the whole population of the country is only a little over 2,000,000 people, these figures are well calculated to create apprehension.

HENRY BORDEWICH,
Consul-General.

CHRISTIANIA, October 10, 1902.

---

## SUPPLEMENTARY.

Official statistics for the year 1901 show that Norway during that period imported directly from the United States goods to the value of nearly $5,000,000, as against about $4,500,000 in 1900. The indirect importations through Germany and England are estimated at $4,000,000, which would make the total import of American goods to the country about $9,000,000 for the year. The direct imports consisted of—

| | | | |
|---|---|---|---|
| Petroleum | $967,700 | Tobaccos | $151,000 |
| Tallow, lard, and margarin | 954,000 | Woods | 52,700 |
| Leather and skins | 445,500 | Railroad rails | 330,900 |
| Pork and beef | 505,800 | Other goods | 598,700 |
| Flour | 490,400 | | |
| Corn | 270,600 | Total | 4,850,900 |
| Wheat | 83,600 | | |

The goods not classified embrace a variety of articles, such as machinery of different kinds, bicycles, tools, paper, rubber goods, sirup, fruits, boots and shoes, etc. The indirect importations consist of the same articles as those in the direct trade, and are bought by Norwegian importers from German and English jobbers.

The total trade of Norway for 1901 was: Exports, $44,246,800; imports, $76,969,600. Of the exports, goods to the value of $515,108 went directly to America; of the imports, 43.7 per cent was for purposes of production, principally for manufacturing purposes, and 56.3 per cent for consumption.

The gross earnings of the Norwegian shipping average $39,000,000 per annum.

The trade between the United States and Norway for the year 1902 has been quite lively and will show increases both as regards export and import. The export of wood pulp and fishery products from Norway to America is increasing, and the first named article shows larger figures than ever before.

Hard times continue in this country. The year 1902 has been a very poor one for the farmers, and the importations of breadstuffs will necessarily be larger than customary. Money is scarce. One of the larger Christiania banks, "Den norske Industriog Vexelbank," which began business in 1897 with a capital of 3,000,000 kroner ($804,000), which was later increased to 6,000,000, was compelled to stop payments a couple of days ago. The bank had invested too much of its money in unprofitable Christiania property during the boom period in 1897 and 1898. This failure is likely to embarrass many of the merchants, and it is quite probable that some of the importers of American goods will be among the number.

Our trade with the country is steadily increasing and American goods are well received. American salesmen with samples in different lines of manufacture should visit the country occasionally, and a little judicious advertising in the local press would also, in my opinion, prove a valuable auxiliary in the advancement of our trade. When credit is asked, the financial standing of the firm should be scrutinized before an account is opened, and in all transactions the terms and other conditions of sale should be thoroughly explained and understood by both parties.

HENRY BORDEWICH,<br>Consul-General.

CHRISTIANIA, *November 25, 1902.*

---

### BERGEN.

#### FISHERIES.

*Herring.*—The quantity of herring caught in the year 1901 was less than in 1900 and much below the average. The prices prevailing were, however, high.

The fat-herring fisheries in 1901 must also be considered a failure, and the total catch was less than in the preceding year, amounting to 185,000 barrels against 285,000 barrels in 1900. Of these, 15,500 barrels were caught in Tromsö, 92,000 in Nordlands, and 54,000 in Tröndelagen.

The seining was comparatively insignificant. The best herring was taken with drift nets on the coast and in the fiords. The fisheries were especially poor during September.

The winter herring fisheries were carried on mostly through drifting in the open sea. More than half was caught outside Christiansand. During the winter, there were caught in all 9,625 mål (14,437.5 barrels), at an average price of 22.61 kroner ($6.06) per barrel, against

13,000 mål (19,500 barrels), at an average price of 13.27 kroner ($3.56) per barrel in 1900–1901.

Outside Stat-Titrau, there were taken in the winter of 1901–2, 95,000 mål (142,500 barrels), valued at 19.36 kroner ($5.19) per barrel. In the winter of 1900–1901, 125,000 mål (187,500 barrels) were taken; price, 13.51 kroner ($3.62) per barrel.

A statistical statement of the herring fisheries on the south coast of Norway (Christiansand) shows the following figures:

| Places. | Boats. | Fisher-men. | Earnings. | | | | | |
|---|---|---|---|---|---|---|---|---|
| | | | Highest rate. | | Lowest rate. | | Aggregate value. | |
| | | | Kroner. | Dollars. | Kroner. | Dollars. | Kroner. | Dollars. |
| Logne | 3 | 12 | 1,200 | 321.60 | 1,800 | 482.40 | 4,700 | 1,259.60 |
| Flekkerö | 21 | 86 | 400 | 107.20 | 4,650 | 1,246.20 | 48,200 | 12,917.60 |
| Lunde | 2 | 8 | 1,800 | 482.40 | 2,000 | 536.00 | 3,800 | 1,018.40 |
| Randosund | 15 | 59 | 600 | 160.80 | 3,300 | 884.40 | 29,150 | 7,812.20 |
| Höwaag | 2 | 8 | 350 | 93.80 | 2,700 | 723.60 | 3,050 | 817.40 |
| Total | 43 | 173 | | | | | 88,900 | 23,825.20 |

| Places. | Average earnings. | | | |
|---|---|---|---|---|
| | Per boat. | | Per man. | |
| | Kroner. | Dollars. | Kroner. | Dollars. |
| Logne | 1,566 | 419.69 | 392 | 105.06 |
| Flekkerö | 2,295 | 605.06 | 560 | 150.08 |
| Lunde | 1,900 | 509.20 | 475 | 127.30 |
| Randosund | 1,943 | 520.72 | 494 | 132.39 |
| Höwaag | 1,525 | 480.70 | 381 | 102.11 |
| Total | 2,067 | 558.96 | 513 | 137.48 |

At present, experimental fisheries are carried on along the coast in all herring districts. In many places, drifting boats are out at sea or in the fjords, in order to force the herrings to go toward land. In others, nets and seines are placed in the bays to lock them in, and the buyers' vessels run between the fishing places in the districts to procure salt and barrels as soon as the catch has been made.

The most important catch some time ago was that of the Leksviken district, amounting to 1,416 mål (2,124 barrels). The total catch at this place should at present be 3,646 mål (5,469 barrels). The catch of bristling and small herring was good on the western coast and in several places in the north.

*Mackerel.*—The summer mackerel fisheries have been improving during the last few years and were excellent in 1900. In 1901 there was less mackerel, but the rates were higher and the pecuniary result was good for the fishermen.

The autumn mackerel fisheries gave a larger output in quantity than any preceding year. Twenty-six thousand five hundred packed barrels were caught in the North Sea, of which 15,000 were split. Twenty-five thousand packed barrels were caught with seines along the coast. During the year 1901, 24,078 barrels of mackerel were exported to the United States, at a value of 1,299,675 kroner ($348,312.91).

*Halibut.*—The bank fisheries were on the whole good. Quantities of halibut were caught by steamboats on the banks out at sea. These fisheries were carried on at Sindmore, particularly from the Aktweggen up to the Shetland coast and outside Storeggen and Nyeggen. The catches were uneven.

*Salmon.*—The salmon fisheries may be considered as average. The river catches were, however, poor.

*Lobster.*—The lobster fisheries were on the whole poor, although very uneven. Some parties had good catches, while others did not even see any lobsters.

*Eel, cod, etc.*—The eel fisheries were better than in 1900. The coalfish (*Gadus vireus*) catches were in many places good. The catches of cod, haddock, etc., were favored by fine weather in Finmarken and gave good results to those who persevered. On the south coast, the catches were variable, although in some places very good. The catch of sprats (*Clupea sprattus*) is followed with great interest, ever since the sprat came into demand as bait for coalfish.

*Seal.*—Eight vessels from the southeast coast took part. The result was poor, the gross profit being only 145,400 kroner ($38,967.20). Storms, high sea, and mist are given as reasons of the poor output. The rates were also lower than in 1900.

*Whale.*—The catch of beaked whale (*Hyperoodon rostratus*) was carried on by 58 ships. The gross value amounted to 668,000 kroner ($179,024). The prices of beaked whale oil were lower than in 1900.

The whalery was carried on in Finmarken by 21 boats. The result was better than in 1900, owing to the larger catch of finback and humpback (*Megaptera boops*). On the Faroes and Iceland, the result was excellent. Twenty-seven Norwegian steam vessels took part in the whaleries around Iceland. In all, 1,192 whales were caught, from which 39,400 barrels of train oil were manufactured. At the Faroes, 5 Norwegian steam vessels were employed, the total catch amounting to 235 whales, giving 6,698 barrels of oil.

The prices of train oil were 19 kroner ($5) per ton less than in 1900, while guano and strong fodder commanded about the same prices as in that year.

### IMPORTS OF NORWAY.

*Corn.*—The aggregate value of the corn imported during 1901 was 45,805,000 kroner ($12,275,740), and of wheat flour, 7,322,400 kroner ($1,962,403.20).

*Metals.*—The next item of importance comprises metals, raw as well as partly manufactured. The total import value in 1901 was 33,805,000 kroner ($9,059,740), of which 11,238,800 kroner ($3,011,998.40) was for raw and half manufactured, and 22,566,200 kroner ($6,047,741.61) for metal wares. Among the first named, 8,403,300 kroner ($2,252,084.40) was paid for pig iron, steel, road iron, and iron plates, the imports of which amounted to 66,947 tons, or somewhat less than in 1900 (69,381 tons).

The import of pig iron amounted to 19,112 tons, against 20,844 tons in 1900. The import of rod and hoop iron in 1901 was 20,672 tons, against 24,745 on an average in 1891–95; 26,036 tons on an average in 1896–1900, and 23,010 in 1900.

The import of iron plates was 25,258 tons, or somewhat more than in 1900 (23,441 tons).

*Manufactures.*—Manufactured goods (including yarns, thread, and rope work) were imported to the value of 34,306,600 kroner ($9,194,168.81).

*Foodstuffs.*—The import of groceries has increased considerably of recent years, and was larger than ever before in 1901, although the value was low compared with the quantity.

The import value of colonial products amounted to 29,979,700 kroner ($8,034,559.61), of which 1,666,500 kroner ($446,622) was for sirup (ordinary) and molasses.

The import value of bacon and meat amounted in 1901 to 9,113,500 kroner ($2,442,418), and that of butter was 481,500 kroner ($129,042). The import of oil, petroleum, etc., amounted to 4,231,000 kroner ($1,133,908).

The coal import was valued at 30,914,000 kroner ($8,284,952); in 1900, at $9,421,272.

### EXPORTS OF NORWAY.

*Wood products.*—The aggregate value of wooden ware and timber exported during 1901 was 59,926,000 kroner ($16,060,168). Of this, 35,592,000 kroner ($9,538,656) was for lumber, 22,661,000 kroner ($6,073,148) for wood pulp and cellulose, 833,000 kroner ($223,244) for matches, and 221,000 kroner ($59,228) for wooden reels, spools, and turned wooden goods.

The export of wood pulp and cellulose during the last five years is shown in the table below:

| Year. | Tons. | Kroner. | Dollars. |
|---|---|---|---|
| 1897 | 302,359 | 18,041,000 | 4,834,988 |
| 1898 | 315,274 | 17,317,000 | 4,640,956 |
| 1899 | 356,162 | 18,297,000 | 4,898,772 |
| 1900 | 384,771 | 23,635,000 | 6,334,180 |
| 1901 | 382,846 | 22,661,000 | 6,073,148 |

These figures do not include Swedish wood pulp and cellulose. The aggregate export of these articles via Norwegian ports in 1901 amounted to about 414,000 tons of cellulose; 82,503 tons of Norwegian, and 12,775 tons of Swedish.

*Fish.*—The following table gives the value of fish and fish products sent to all countries during the calendar year 1901:

| Articles. | Kroner. | Dollars. |
|---|---|---|
| Split cod | 14,866,000 | 3,984,088 |
| Dried fish | 7,229,000 | 1,937,372 |
| Roe | 1,684,000 | 451,312 |
| Train oil | 5,805,000 | 1,555,740 |
| Herring: | | |
| Salted | 10,351,000 | 2,774,068 |
| Fresh | 1,477,000 | 395,836 |
| Salmon, fresh | 1,371,000 | 367,428 |
| Mackerel, fresh | 55,000 | 14,740 |
| Herring, light salted | 1,000 | 268 |
| Other kinds of fresh fish | 1,105,000 | 296,140 |
| Salt fish | 4,155,000 | 1,113,540 |
| Anchovies | 985,000 | 263,980 |
| Lobsters | 619,000 | 165,892 |
| Fish guano | 555,000 | 148,740 |

Other articles exported in 1901 are given below:

| Articles. | Kroner. | Dollars. |
|---|---|---|
| Paper and pasteboard | 9,875,000 | 2,646,500 |
| Condensed milk | 5,240,000 | 1,404,320 |
| Skins | 2,836,000 | 760,048 |
| Butter | 2,582,000 | 691,976 |
| Margarine | 1,014,000 | 271,752 |
| Ores and metals | 2,223,000 | 595,764 |
| Stone, cut | 2,177,000 | 583,436 |
| Hermetic victuals | 2,112,000 | 566,016 |
| Vessels | { 1,953,000<br>1,688,000 | 523,404<br>452,384 |
| Nails and spikes | 1,627,000 | 436,096 |
| Copper, refined, and old metals | 1,445,000 | 337,260 |
| Machines | 980,000 | 262,640 |
| Ice | 797,000 | 213,596 |
| Books | 796,000 | 213,328 |
| Calcium carbide | 518,000 | 138,824 |

Among articles exported in 1901 exceeding in value 100,000 kroner ($26,800) may be mentioned horses, oats, vinegar and acetic acid, rags, rope work, curtains, printed cotton goods, baleens, bone dust, leather straps, petroleum and benzine, lime, coopers' work, oxalic acid, hay, feldspar, iodine, kelp, bricks, bottles and flasks, glassware, pig iron and old iron, as well as telephone and other electric apparatus.

The export of wheat flour (of Norwegian growth) amounted to 2,200 kroner ($589.61).

The export of petroleum and benzine was valued at 144,500 kroner ($38,726).

### NAVIGATION.

The purchase of vessels, steam as well as sail, was less than in 1900, as shown below:

STEAMERS.

| Year. | Number of vessels. | Tonnage. | Value in kroner. | Value in dollars. |
|---|---|---|---|---|
| 1900 | 47 | 34,433 | 10,292,000 | 2,748,256.00 |
| 1901 | 45 | 23,458 | 7,037,000 | 188,591.61 |

SAILING VESSELS.

| | | | | |
|---|---|---|---|---|
| 1900 | 91 | 42,379 | 2,760,000 | 789,680.00 |
| 1901 | 71 | 40,489 | 2,582,000 | 691,976.00 |

The increase of the Norwegian steam fleet during the last four years has been 248,137 tons.

The port of Bergen was, during the year 1901, visited by 14,246 vessels of 2,591,543 tons, apportioned as below:

| Description. | Number. | Tons. |
|---|---|---|
| Sailing vessels | 1,849 | 69,083 |
| Steam vessels | 12,262 | 2,406,441 |
| Total | 14,111 | 2,475,524 |
| Tourist vessels | 32 | 44,537 |
| Pleasure yachts | 46 | 10,839 |
| Men of war | 57 | 60,593 |
| Total | 14,246 | 2,591,543 |

Two new custom-houses have been established in Norway during 1901, at Orje and Narvik.

## STAVANGER.

The principal source of income at the port of Stavanger is from shipping, and the year 1901 must be considered a good one, the sailing vessels, as well as the steamers, having paid their owners fair dividends.

The sailing vessels were principally engaged in the United States and South American waters, and the rates of freight for pitch pine were good.

The steamers traded with herring to the Baltic, or were employed in the fruit trade between United States ports and the West Indies.

The industrial factories of Stavanger have not been very profitable. The wages are too high, which makes it difficult to compete with foreign manufacturers. An exception, however, is found in the Stavanger Stöberi and Dok, which has a large factory for iron castings, is building vessels, and has two dry docks. This concern paid the shareholders 6¼ per cent for 1901.

The canning companies (fish, meat, and game), of which there are 13, made but little profit in 1901, the competition in raw materials being very close, while prices for the products were low.

The herring catch was, unfortunately, poor, so that the exporters had but little to ship.

The crockery company at Egersund sold goods to the value of about 600,000 kroner ($170,000), and paid 7 per cent on the capital invested.

## UNITED STATES GOODS.

There was a marked increase in the import of American goods during the year 1901, especially in machinery, machine tools, and builders' hardware. As I said in my report for 1900, in order to increase commerce with Scandinavia, traveling men with samples and speaking Swedish or Norwegian should be sent here, and commission houses carrying full assortment, of American manufactures should be established in the leading ports.

Our merchants and manufacturers will be required to give (as our English and German competitors do) sixty or ninety days' credit, as dealers here naturally do not care to pay for goods before having examined them.

When I asked a leading importer why he carried so few American goods, he said: "Because your people expect a man to buy a pig in a poke. Other countries allow us to examine their goods and give us three months' time in which to pay for the same."

I hope that our manufacturers will exert themselves a little more to gain trade in Scandinavia.

VICTOR E. NELSON, *Consul.*

BERGEN, *August 27, 1902.*

*Importing houses at Stavanger, Norway.*

| Firm name. | Business. | Firm name. | Business. |
|---|---|---|---|
| Bertelsen & Co ........... | Flour, grain, and beef. | T. Rönneberg............. | Cotton-seed oil. |
| Erik S. Monsen............ | Do. | Motler's Preserving Co ... | Do. |
| T. W. Hölst................ | Do. | John Braadland.......... | Do. |
| Kornelius Olsen ......... | Flour, grain, beef, mar-garin, and lard. | Carl Olsen & Kleppe ..... | Do. |
| | | Claus Andersen's Enke... | Do. |
| Ths. S. Falck .............. | Grain. | Joh. Rasmussen & Racine. | Ironware and steel. |
| Thorstein Bryne .......... | Beef, lard, oils, paints, etc. | Stavanger Stöberi & Dok. | Do. |
| | | Stavanger Reberbane .... | Ropes. |
| Bertel Svendsen ......... | Grain. | E. Berentsen.............. | Do. |
| Stavanger Smörfabrik .... | Margarin. | Störmstenens Darft....... | Lumber and hard wood. |
| Anton Pedersen........... | Beef and flour. | | |
| B. Gundersen ............. | Do. | Madsen & Jespersen...... | Coals. |
| A. Hauge Thiis............ | Cotton-seed oil. | C. Widdelthon .......... | Do. |
| Stavanger Preserving Co.. | Do. | N. B. Sörensen ........... | Do. |
| Chr. Bjelland & Co........ | Do. | | |

*Importing houses at Drontheim, Norway.*

| Firm name. | Business. | Firm name. | Business. |
|---|---|---|---|
| Jacob Halseth............. | Wheat flour. | H. F. Klingenberg........ | Molasses and flour. |
| Jacob Larsen.............. | Do. | Theodor Moe ............ | Do. |
| M. Madsen ............... | Do. | V. C. Frosch ............. | Pork and lard. |
| Lars Storö................ | Do. | Chr. Thaulow ............ | Molasses. |
| T. M. Lykke.............. | Wheat flour and pork. | Arthur Motzfeldt......... | Machinery. |
| L. Wilhelmsen ........... | Do. | A. Eigen ................. | Hardware. |
| V. E. Ryjerd.............. | Molasses and flour. | | |

VICTOR E. NELSON, *Consul.*

BERGEN, *December 20, 1902.*

---

# SWITZERLAND.

## BASEL.

The official returns of imports from the United States during the year 1901 indicate an extremely encouraging state of things with reference to the future of our trade with Switzerland. To people who think that we sell nothing to the little inland Republic, it will come as a surprise to learn that during the year in question, we exported $12,000,000 worth of goods to this country; slightly more than the preceding year, and lacking only two millions of equaling the record year 1898. This is all the more remarkable as it comes at a time of general industrial and commercial depression, not only in Switzerland, but in all Europe. Moreover, the amount of imports has not been swelled abnormally, as in 1898, by the absolute necessity of supplying from abroad the lack of breadstuffs occasioned by the failure of the grain crops in 1898, as well as in the following year. Both 1900 and 1901, on the contrary, were good crop years, and accordingly the importations of our cereals dropped off sufficiently to cover substantially the whole of the loss in sales to Switzerland, as compared with the record year.

It is thus our manufactured goods, especially machines, tools, iron and shoe ware, that, by permanent or increased sales, have kept our exports to this country up to the normal standard.

It is worth while to note the fact that the increase of about three-quarters of a million dollars in the American imports into this country in 1901, as compared with 1900, has taken place under such disadvantages as may have arisen from the application of the general Swiss tariff to American goods since the month of October of the latter year. It was predicted in these reports, at the time when we lost the benefit of the conventional tariff by the termination of our commercial treaty with Switzerland, on the initiative of the United States, that the immediate consequence to our trade would not be very serious. But in no quarter was it supposed that our sales could actually increase, in spite of a change in the tariff which affected rather unfavorably some few articles of considerable importance.

One may fairly conclude, then, that a trade that can increase during a year of decided commercial depression and when impeded by the application of higher import duties and a greatly diminished demand for agricultural products, is on a tolerably solid basis and has no discouraging outlook for the future. This view is fully confirmed by the detailed report of American imports into this country, taken from the official figures published by the Swiss customs authorities, and covering a period of ten years. This interesting table, which is attached to this report, shows a constant gain in our exports and in some details a real conquest of the market for manufactures. During the great trade year 1898, we sold as much as we bought in this country, and though this proportion has not since been maintained, in consequence of the fall in the price of cotton and the diminished market for cereals, the tendency is to recover and surpass it indefinitely, as seems to be shown by the following table, furnished by the Swiss customs department:

*Swiss Trade with United States.*

| Year. | Import, in million dollars. | Per cent of whole import. | Export, in million dollars. | Per cent of total export. |
|---|---|---|---|---|
| 1901 | 12 | 5.84 | 17 | 10.51 |
| 1900 | 11 | 5.14 | 19 | 11.46 |
| 1899 | 12 | 5.33 | 18 | 11.52 |
| 1898 | 14 | 6.85 | 14 | 10.19 |
| 1897 | 10 | 5.03 | 14 | 10.24 |
| 1896 | 8 | 3.95 | 13 | 10.25 |
| 1895 | 8 | 4.24 | 18 | 13.71 |
| 1894 | 7 | 4.25 | 14 | 14.56 |

In connection with the increase of American imports in 1901, it should be further remarked that it took place in a year when the total imports had fallen off no less than $12,000,000, and when no other great exporting country had escaped without a notable decrease of its sales to Switzerland.

But the pleasant prospect for the future, resulting from the trade of last year, would be blighted should the proposed new Swiss tariff [a] be adopted by the Federal Councils and its rigors be enforced without any attenuation in the way of a new treaty with the United States. The increased duties on American products contemplated by the new law are quite another thing than the almost harmless passage from the

[a] See Advance Sheets, Nos. 1293, 1309, and 1507.

conventional to the general tariff, which now presents so ineffectual an obstacle to trade between the two countries.

Apprehension in regard to the effects of the pending tariff changes is freely expressed by the chambers of commerce of the large cities, especially by that of Basel. In respect to the course of business in the more important American articles during the year 1901, the following details may be of interest.

### CEREALS.

Of the immense quantity of wheat imported, the United States furnished about a fourth, coming, as usual, next after Russia. The Argentine Republic and the Danubian countries figure as third and fourth. Wheat of the quality of the Kansas product of last year was never before seen in this market. Curiously enough, even this superb quality was not sufficient to counterbalance the preference for Russian and Danubian wheat, the price of the latter in December being 21.50 francs ($4.05) per quintal (220 pounds) delivered free at the Basel railroad depot, while prime Kansas only brought 20 francs ($3.85) on the same terms. It is this preference which accounts for the relatively unimportant importation of American flour, it being held by the local bakers that the American product is not well adapted to their purposes on account of an alleged lack of gluten. This prejudice may be due to the influence of the Swiss millers, who hold that American wheat, poor in gluten as they allege it to be, nevertheless makes very good flour when subjected to the superior milling process of this country.

In regard to the proposed treatment of grain in the new tariff, the report of the Basel Chamber of Commerce for 1901 makes the following statement:

Under the existing tariff, the duty on grain is only 30 centimes a quintal (about a cent and a half a bushel). This insignificant tax is of no importance in the grain trade, and gives no trouble either to the producer or consumer. If the Swiss Farmers' League (Bauernbund), or its chief, now proposes to abolish it, the true reason for such a course is the hope of creating in the laboring class a feeling in favor of the large increase which the same society proposes in the duties on other articles. The reason which is officially given, however, is that Switzerland is not adapted to the cultivation of grain, the annual product now amounting to only about $5,000,000 in value. This is really a remarkable discovery, for, up to fifty years ago, the country raised all the grain it used, and only a few years ago, Professor Kraemer estimated the value of the yearly product at $14,000,000, which is clearly nearer the truth than the lower figures. If properly conducted, Swiss agriculture could now produce nearly all the cereals the country needs, and it would be nothing less than a national misfortune if this branch of industry were to be suppressed.

### MAIZE.

The failure of the American crop was severely felt in the interior of Europe, and resulted in quite extraordinary prices for an inferior article of corn. In November, 17 francs ($3.28) a quintal was paid at the Basel railway station for a wretched quality of produce, imported for fodder from the Danube and southern Russia.

### MEATS.

The imports of fresh meat, especially from the neighboring French department of Savoy, increased during the year 1901. On the other hand, there was a decline of about 200,000 pounds in salted and smoked meats, all to the prejudice of the American exporter.

On this subject, the report of the Chamber of Commerce contains the following interesting reflections:

The reason why American meats are now introduced in smaller quantities has absolutely nothing to do with their quality. Among the real causes is the extraordinarily high price which has prevailed two years already, and is justified by the unusual demand in America and the incessantly rising price of Indian corn. The demand in South Africa also contributes to raise the price. Finally, the industrial crisis prevailing in our country particularly affects the consumption of this American product, the principal demand for which comes from the factory workmen. Moreover, the Swiss customs duty on the American product is higher than on that coming from competing countries since November 1, 1900, when the tariff of 8 francs ($1.54) per quintal on the gross weight was applied instead of the former rate of 5 francs ($0.96). Already, then, this meat pays not 5 centimes a kilogram (one-half cent a pound), as the opponents of this class of importations are pleased to argue, but 11½ centimes a kilogram (nearly 1 cent a pound), namely, 10 centimes duty on the net weight and 1½ centimes inspection fee. Accordingly, America finds difficulty in the competition with other countries, and this trade is no longer profitable. It is strange and in the highest degree regrettable that our Government has not yet concluded a treaty with the United States, though the latter country has already declared its willingness to enter into arrangements on the basis of reciprocity, and though our exports to America are so important.

Austria and Hungary have made an attempt during the last year to supplant the Americans, encouraged by the relatively low price of their meats, but so far without noticeable success.

The importation of canned beef has also diminished during the year, principally in consequence of the higher price, but at present prices have considerably declined, as the importation into Germany is now forbidden and the market restricted accordingly.

It will be seen from the above that at least one important branch of American trade has already suffered from the mere imposition of the Swiss general tariff. If the proposed new rates were to be actually imposed, no more American meats could be sold in Switzerland.

### FISH.

The importation of frozen salmon from America increases yearly. A far better article, the so-called summer salmon, is now offered in the market.

### HAM.

The prohibition of the use of borax as a means of preservation is causing considerable difficulty. Ham is imported almost exclusively from America and stored up in the spring to be smoked, as circumstances demand, in the course of the year. The principal disadvantage of this method is that the quality suffers from the meat lying too long in pickle. Importers must try to have their supply shipped during the summer, when there is the largest demand for it; otherwise, a large part of the shipments decline materially in value before they are sold. The same is true of imported tongue, so that consumption is diverted to the canned article. A lively business in the latter was expected for the current year.

### LARD.

The chamber of commerce expresses the local feeling in regard to existing and proposed obstacles in the way of the importation of lard in the following vigorous terms:

It seems this article is doomed to be placed in the Index, and no one really knows why. A few weeks before the publication of the proposed new tariff, we read in the unofficial department of the Official Journal of Commerce an extract from a special journal devoted to sanitariums for the cure of consumption. We find it stated there, printed in large type, that the most effective remedy against consumption, the malady that cantonal governments and private benevolence now unite in combating, is hygienic dwellings and the cheapening of meat and fat. Hear! Hear! "Meat and fat!" And thereupon the tariff bill proposes—to speak of fat alone—the following rates of import duty per 100 kilos (220 pounds):

Fresh butter, an increase of 7 francs, making 15 francs ($2.89).
Melted butter, an increase of 10 francs, making 20 francs ($3.86).
Lard, an increase of 5 franks, making 10 francs ($1.93).
Oleomargarine, an increase of 10 francs, making 20 francs ($3.86).

We could hardly believe our eyes; but there it was in black and white. As lard is the real cooking fat of the common workman, we must here protest against such an economically indefensible and injurious system of taxation. As we already pointed out last year, it is not correct to classify lard combined with vegetable oil—the so-called American cooking butter—as "artificial butter" and then impose a duty of $2.89, equivalent to an ad valorem duty of 20 to 30 per cent, because of its American origin. In this way, the importation of cooking butter is rendered impossible and without advantage to anyone, even to the farmer. And now they are going to raise the duty to $3.86 a quintal.

### DRIED FRUIT.

Dried fruit was this year imported in diminished quantities from the United States, there having been a good crop in Switzerland and the price of the American article being high.

### TOBACCO.

Considerably more than half the tobacco used by the important cigar manufacturers of Switzerland during the last year came from the United States. Kentucky tobacco was the leading article in this market, the Virginia brand being neglected on account of the high price.

### LOCAL COMMERCE AND INDUSTRY.

The great industries of Basel—silk ribbon weaving, dyestuffs and chemicals, and waste-silk spinning, as well as the new electrical industry—suffered last year from the general depression prevailing in all parts of Europe. The table of imports and exports attached to this report, showing the provisional estimates of the commerce of the country for the first six months of the current year 1902, indicates that there has been no improvement in the general situation. Both imports and exports have fallen off as compared with the corresponding period of 1901, and when the definite figures are published, it will probably be found that the decline has been nearer five than two million dollars for each of these two commercial branches.

So far as the Basel exporters are concerned, this loss of trade would have been more serious still had it not been for the unusual demand for their goods from the United States. There has been an export of ribbons, in particular, that revives the recollection of the good old times for the Swiss weavers, before Paterson had firmly established a new textile industry in America. While Germany, France, and England, the three principal buyers of silk ribbons, have bought and are still buying cautiously and sparingly—especially England—our country is supplementing its own enormous production by acquiring generous quantities of the old historic Basel fabrics. But it is only the business that is historical. Many of the looms in the factories are imported from the United States—machines of the latest invention and highest perfection. Moreover, the hand looms that continue to produce a considerable quantity of plain ribbons for the manufacturers of this city are now often driven by the electric power derived from the current of the Rhine. There is hardly a more interesting instance of the application of electricity to house industries than the relief thus afforded to the poor peasant of the Canton of Baselland, who has hitherto for generations eked out the slender living derived from his small plot of land by employing his leisure hours and those of his wife and children in the hard labors of the silk loom.

Dyestuffs and chemicals, as well as spun waste silk, have also continued to be largely exported to America during the nine months of 1902 already expired; but from other countries there has been only a feeble demand, and the prices are so depressed as to make the condition of these two branches of manufacture rather discouraging at just this time.

### PUBLIC WORKS AND IMPROVEMENTS.

In the later years of the last century, public improvements and works, together with the annexation of the outlying districts, converted Zurich into one of the great cities of central Europe, taking the lead of Basel in population and the outward signs of prosperity and wealth. The latter city, which hitherto had been the first in Switzerland from both points of view, seems to be imitating Zurich, but in a characteristically sober, deliberate, and circumspect way. It is hoped and expected that this traditional prudence will save the city on the Rhine from the economic headache which in Zurich has followed a great financial debauch. The principal business street has been almost completely rebuilt in a magnificent modern style; most of the narrow, middle-age thoroughfares have been torn away and replaced by wider and much improved ones, while a little river plowing through the place has been arched over and made into a broad avenue; and these improvements, under the direction and often through the intervention of the municipality, are still going on. A new street railway system has been built and is operated by the city, which owns and works all the public franchises. But the glory of the city is its restored city hall and its new schoolhouses, especially the new polytechnic school (Realschule), which is a veritable palace. Indeed, the term "school palace" instead of schoolhouse is often applied to several of the new buildings by citizens who are displeased at the expenditure of so much money for educational purposes.

The justification for bringing this matter into a commercial report lies in the improvements that are still in progress or are about to be taken in hand—works still more important for the transformation of Basel into a modern city than those already completed. First among these are the rebuilding of the stations, passenger and freight, of the three railroads belonging to the Swiss Confederation and to the German Empire (the Elsass-Lothringen road) centering in Basel on the left bank of the Rhine. This involves the changing of the level of the main and side tracks, the removal and rebuilding of all the structures and dependencies, the building of new highways and bridges, the change at great expense of the bridge over the Birsig, formerly belonging to the German railway, into a municipal viaduct, which will facilitate the traffic between two important quarters of the city; in short, the growth of almost a new district, in addition to those which have sprung up within ten years on the outskirts of the old city. On the right bank of the Rhine, the stations and tracks of the three railroads belonging to the Grand Duchy of Baden, two of them of great international importance, are about to undergo a still more radical change and removal; so that the so-called Klein Basel will be given an opportunity to develop and extend even more rapidly than it has hitherto done. The preliminary steps toward carrying out this plan have already been taken.

Of less commercial importance, but of still greater local interest, is the impending removal of the old bridge, which has been the characteristic feature and distinguishing mark of Basel for the last eight hundred years. The new structure, which will take its place between the two bridges built in the latter part of the last century to improve communication between the two halves of the city, will imitate as far as possible the venerable work which it is to replace, but nothing can console the old Baselers for the loss of this familiar monument of their earlier history.

Of great industrial importance, again, is the projected electric plant, where the waters of the Rhine are to supply the city with much-needed force and light. There is already a limited supply of electricity from the works established and owned by the city; but it is quite insufficient for the present needs of the public and the numerous shops and factories. The meanest country villages are now better supplied with power and light by the great establishment at Rheinfelden, where the river has been dammed, than this city of 110,000 inhabitants, and possessing as much wealth per unit of population as any town in the world. It is certain that the city will establish its own works for the production of several thousand horsepower at an early date; but unfortunately, the place and time have not yet been determined, in consequence of conflicting views and interests. The scheme which is most favored at the present time contemplates the building of a canal at Augst, a few miles above the city; but as this plan requires the consent and cooperation of the grand duchy of Baden and of the canton of Baselland, many difficulties have arisen in endeavoring to execute it.

GEO. GIFFORD, Consul.

BASEL, <i>September 30, 1902.</i>

---

Imports into Switzerland from the United States, ten years, 1892–1901.

[Value in thousands of dollars.]

| Articles. | 1892. | 1893. | 1894. | 1895. | 1896. | 1897. | 1898. | 1899. | 1900. | 1901. |
|---|---|---|---|---|---|---|---|---|---|---|
| Waste and fertilizers.... | 0.6 | ...... | 3.8 | ...... | 24.2 | 20.4 | 12.4 | 5.4 | 1.8 | 54.6 |
| Fodder (bran, etc.) . | ...... | ...... | ...... | ...... | 14 | 9.4 | 7.2 | 5.2 | 6.6 | 4.8 |
| Artificial manures .. | .6 | ...... | ...... | ...... | 9.8 | 10.4 | 3.6 | .2 | 3.2 | 49.8 |
| Chemicals, etc.......... | 103.2 | 118.6 | 139.4 | 13.4 | 146.6 | 176.2 | 260.4 | 247.8 | 257 | 228.2 |
| Drugs.............. | 1.6 | 2.8 | 1.8 | 2.6 | 2.4 | 4.2 | 12.6 | 7 | 8.2 | 7.2 |
| Pharmaceutical products .......... | 3.4 | 5.6 | 6 | 5.4 | 10.2 | 10.4 | 7.8 | 6 | 8.8 | 15 |
| Resins.............. | 1.8 | 26 | ...... | ...... | ...... | ...... | ...... | ...... | ...... | ...... |
| Colophony, pitch, etc ............. | ...... | ...... | 26.8 | 21.4 | 21 | 30 | 57 | 63 | 33.6 | 24.2 |
| Tanning liquids .... | .2 | ...... | ...... | .2 | 1.2 | 5 | 2.2 | 6.2 | 5.4 | 15.8 |
| Sulphate of iron, etc.. | ...... | ...... | 2.8 | 5 | 8.4 | 1.4 | 3.6 | 17.8 | 53.4 | 29.4 |
| Coal-tar products ... | 10.8 | 10 | 7 | 7 | 3 | 5.6 | 8.4 | 18.8 | 10.6 | 14.8 |
| Essence of turpentine.............. | 37.8 | 45.6 | 61 | 67.2 | 69.8 | 88.2 | 141.4 | 94.2 | 93.8 | 80.4 |
| Coloring extracts ... | 13.8 | 18 | 18.8 | 14 | 13.8 | 11.2 | 7.6 | 12.4 | 19.2 | 7.2 |

*Imports into Switzerland from the United States, ten years, 1892–1901*—Continued.

| Articles. | 1892. | 1893. | 1894. | 1895. | 1896. | 1897. | 1898. | 1899. | 1900. | 1901. |
|---|---|---|---|---|---|---|---|---|---|---|
| **Chemicals, etc.—Cont'd.** | | | | | | | | | | |
| Aniline colors....... | 13.8 | | | | | | | | | |
| Varnish and lac..... | .8 | 1.6 | 3.4 | 2 | 2 | 10 | 5.2 | 1.6 | 8.2 | 15.4 |
| Wood .............. | 10.8 | 38 | ·75 | 122.8 | 219 | 210 | 325.4 | 424.8 | 287.8 | 293.2 |
| Timber, hard-wood . | | 2 | .8 | 3 | 9.2 | 6.2 | 6.4 | 2.6 | .8 | .2 |
| Shooks ............ | | | .4 | 8.4 | 5 | 13.8 | 15.2 | 9.2 | .8 | 5.4 |
| Other oak, sawn .... | | | | | 2.8 | 6.6 | 22 | 16.2 | 10 | 2.4 |
| Other hard wood, boards ........... | .2 | 1.8 | 3.6 | .6 | 1 | 6.2 | ² 2 | 4.6 | 8.8 | 11 |
| Soft wood, boards ... | 3.2 | 8.2 | 19.6 | 13.4 | 1.4 | 2.6 | .8 | 1.6 | | |
| Cabinetmakers' wood......... | 3 | 1.2 | .2 | 2.2 | 10.2 | 2.8 | 7 | 4.8 | 6 | 8 |
| Cabinetmakers' wood, sawn ...... | | 10.6 | 38.6 | 88.6 | 177.2 | 160.2 | 251.6 | 358.6 | 232.6 | 227.4 |
| Furniture........... | .2 | .6 | .8 | .8 | .8 | 1 | 1 | 1.6 | 2 | 11 |
| Furniture, painted, etc ............... | .4 | .6 | .6 | .8 | 1.6 | 2.4 | 10.4 | 13.8 | 18.8 | 16.2 |
| Seeds............... | .2 | 10.6 | 19.8 | 10.2 | 7.4 | 16.6 | 29 | 21 | 15.6 | 6.4 |
| Grass and clover seeds............. | .2 | 2.4 | 15.8 | 7.6 | 4.4 | 16.6 | 9.8 | 16.2 | 15.6 | 6.2 |
| Other seeds ........ | | 7.6 | 1.8 | 2.4 | 2.8 | | 15.4 | 2 | | |
| Leather and shoe ware . | 347.8 | 485 | 553.4 | 645.8 | 436.8 | 718.8 | 676.4 | 654 | 707.6 | 899.8 |
| Sole leather,........ | 176.6 | 212.8 | 259 | 259.6 | 485.2 | 264.6 | 224.6 | 240.6 | 221 | 222 |
| Leather for straps— calfskin ........... | 17.4 | 4.6 | .4 | .8 | 10.8 | 8.4 | 11.8 | 6.6 | .2 | 1.6 |
| Other leather ....... | 149.4 | 261 | 287.4 | 378.6 | 233.4 | 442.6 | 430.8 | 386.4 | 445 | 513.6 |
| Boots and shoes..... | | | | | | .6 | 3.4 | 7.2 | 16.4 | 20.4 |
| Boots and shoes, rubber ........... | 4.4 | 6.4 | 5.6 | 6.2 | 7.4 | 6 | 2 | 7 | 20.6 | 30.6 |
| Objects relating to literature, science, and art ................ | 29.4 | 58.2 | 53.6 | 48.2 | 59.4 | 55.4 | 45.6 | 89 | 64.8 | 85.4 |
| Oil paintings, engravings, etc...... | 1.2 | .4 | 1 | 1.4 | 1.2 | 1.4 | 1 | 1.2 | 4.4 | 10 |
| Pianos, harmoniums | 4.4 | 3.6 | 9.6 | 7.8 | 2.4 | 11 | 9.2 | 3.2 | 3 | 4.6 |
| Scientific instruments ............. | 5.2 | 6.2 | 7.8 | 7.6 | 8.4 | 8.6 | 5.8 | 9.6 | 9.2 | 22 |
| Electric apparatus .. | .6 | 21 | 1.6 | 3.6 | 4.2 | 5.8 | 4.4 | 25.2 | 12.2 | 24 |
| Orthopedic apparatus ............... | 13.6 | 18.8 | 27.2 | 26 | 39.8 | 23.8 | 22.4 | 38.8 | 28 | 16.4 |
| Watches ........... | 2.6 | 1.8 | 8.6 | 33 | 94.4 | 136.6 | 242.6 | 87.2 | 85.8 | 83.2 |
| Works for watches.. | | 1 | 2.8 | 4.4 | 5 | 6.4 | 7 | 7.6 | 1.6 | 6.4 |
| Nickel cases ....... | .2 | | 5.2 | 26.8 | 88 | 129.2 | 230.2 | 76.2 | 80 | 66.6 |
| Machinery and vehicles. | 27.4 | 52.2 | 86.6 | 99 | 144.6 | 263.4 | 492.8 | 531 | 584 | 442.2 |
| Dynamo-electric machines ......... | .8 | | | | .8 | 1 | 26 | 4.4 | 20.8 | 19.6 |
| Agricultural and household machines............. | 1.6 | 9.2 | 11.6 | 20.6 | 70.8 | 123.2 | 368 | 249.4 | 258.2 | 212 |
| Sewing machines ... | 6.4 | 12.4 | 29.2 | 15 | 17.4 | 5.2 | 13.4 | 32 | 9.8 | 16 |
| Looms and weaving machines ......... | | .2 | .8 | 7.2 | 5.8 | | 19 | | | 4 |
| Tool machines...... | 3 | .6 | 7.6 | 10.2 | 3.6 | 18.8 | 25 | 31.6 | 53.8 | 40.2 |
| Machinery not otherwise mentioned. | 13.8 | 21 | 26.8 | 29.8 | 30.6 | 47 | 119.4 | 82.4 | 142.2 | 71 |
| Agricultural implements............. | .2 | .8 | 1 | 4.2 | 1.4 | 8.8 | 12 | 23.2 | 12.4 | 8.2 |
| Bicycles............ | | .4 | .6 | 1.4 | 1 | 6.6 | 53.6 | 92.6 | 93.4 | 59.4 | 41.8 |
| Iron................ | 23 | 33.2 | 38.8 | 53.2 | 77.4 | 141.6 | 347.4 | 574 | 234.2 | 151 |
| Pig iron............ | | | | | | 27.8 | 15.4 | 29.6 | 6.8 | 9.2 |
| Manufactures of cast iron, rough... | .2 | .2 | .2 | 2.8 | .2 | 1.2 | 1 | 3 | 6 | 4 |
| Manufactures of cast iron, other... | 1.6 | 4 | 6 | 14.4 | 37.2 | 49.4 | 112 | 90 | 116 | 73.2 |
| Pipes, rough ....... | | | | .2 | 7.6 | 24 | 160.2 | 350.2 | 60 | 7.6 |
| Wrought-iron ware— Entirely rough.. | | | | .2 | 1 | 9 | 19 | 59.4 | .8 | 3.8 |
| Other, stew pans | 13.8 | 19.6 | 16.8 | 23.2 | 25.4 | 17 | 24.8 | 25 | 25.4 | 33 |
| Polished, etc.... | 6 | 7 | 9.2 | 10.2 | 4.8 | 4.2 | 7.6 | 10.4 | 11 | 15.4 |
| Copper ............. | 2.2 | 29.2 | 37.4 | 33.4 | 91.8 | 146 | 176 | 103.4 | 187.6 | 178 |
| Copper and brass— Bars.............. | 1.8 | 27.2 | 36.2 | 31.4 | 87.6 | 138.8 | 167.6 | 93.2 | 171 | 115.4 |
| Rolled .......... | | .2 | .4 | .4 | .2 | .8 | 1.2 | 3 | 6.6 | 51 |
| Coppersmiths' wares | .2 | .4 | .6 | 1.4 | 3.8 | 6.2 | 5.8 | 7 | 9 | 5.4 |
| Other metals ....... | 4 | 4.2 | 8.2 | 3.2 | 4.4 | 5.8 | 3.6 | 8.4 | 6.2 | 10 |
| Mineral oils........ | 868.4 | 899.2 | 1,013.2 | 1,112 | 1,151 | 1,145.8 | 1,416.8 | 1,767.8 | 1,755.2 | 1,708.8 |
| Petroleum, etc...... | 824.4 | 840.6 | 948.2 | 1,046.2 | 1,070.2 | 1,076 | 1,349.4 | 1,689.2 | 1,681.8 | 1,622.2 |
| Other mineral oils .. | 41.8 | 54.4 | 58.6 | 60.4 | 76.6 | 65.2 | 61.2 | 70.8 | 66.4 | 71.4 |
| Oils and fats ....... | 55.4 | 98.2 | 69.8 | 67.8 | 69.4 | 75.4 | 102.4 | 232.4 | 303.6 | 321 |
| Table oil in casks... | | 14.4 | 27.2 | 15.4 | | | | | 2 | 2.6 |
| Vegetable oils....... | 46.2 | 58.2 | 36.8 | 46.8 | 64.2 | 62.8 | 90.6 | 216.2 | 261.4 | 272.4 |
| Tallow ............. | 2.8 | 18.6 | .6 | 1.6 | 1.6 | 2.4 | 6.4 | 3.2 | 14.4 | 16.8 |
| Fish oil ............ | 4 | 6 | 5.2 | 4 | 8.6 | 10.2 | 5.4 | 7.6 | 24.6 | 29.2 |

*Imports into Switzerland from the United States, ten years, 1892-1901*—Continued.

| Articles. | 1892. | 1893. | 1894. | 1895. | 1896. | 1897. | 1898. | 1899. | 1900. | 1901. |
|---|---|---|---|---|---|---|---|---|---|---|
| Provisions and groceries | 3,666.2 | 2,773.4 | 1,906.6 | 2,073.6 | 2,321 | 4,198 | 7,883 | 5,220.2 | 3,578.4 | 4,830.4 |
| Lard | 444 | 378.6 | 399.8 | 382.4 | 347.6 | 279.8 | 400.4 | 450.6 | 486.2 | 420.2 |
| Butter, melted, salted | .4 | 8.4 | 8.4 | 11.6 | 16.6 | 10.6 | 24.4 | 43 | 24.8 | 24.6 |
| Fresh fish | | | | 35.8 | .4 | .6 | 13 | 19.4 | 22.4 | 21.2 |
| Dried fish | 1.4 | 2.8 | 6 | 4.4 | 3.8 | 6.2 | 10.6 | 5.4 | 6.6 | .6 |
| Smoked meat and bacon | 216 | 99.6 | 320 | 567.6 | 630 | 518.6 | 741.8 | 525.2 | 395.6 | 347 |
| Sausage | .4 | .2 | .2 | | 2.8 | 9.2 | 9.4 | 12 | 9.8 | 8 |
| Dried fruit | 9.2 | .2 | .6 | 22.4 | 46.4 | 214 | 82.2 | 69 | 55.6 | 13.8 |
| Raisins | | | .4 | 1.8 | 5.6 | 14 | 10.4 | 19.4 | 11.4 | 10.6 |
| Wheat | 2,000.2 | 1,321.8 | 305.2 | 183.2 | 378.4 | 1,931.4 | 4,263.8 | 2,721.8 | 1,389.6 | 2,888.8 |
| Rye | | .8 | | | 1 | 5.2 | 18 | 14.8 | | |
| Oats | 4.2 | 36.4 | 17 | .6 | 15.4 | 198.4 | 866 | 212.4 | 129.8 | 43.4 |
| Barley | 1 | 2.2 | .4 | | | 3.8 | 25.8 | 7.8 | 3.4 | .6 |
| Indian corn | 224.2 | 38.2 | 18.4 | 69 | 97.8 | 133 | 311.8 | 175 | 140.2 | 76 |
| Pease | 1.4 | 32.4 | 3 | | | 4.4 | .8 | 3.2 | .6 | |
| Groats, etc | 63.4 | 22.6 | 1.6 | .8 | 2.8 | 10.6 | 20 | 27.4 | 23.6 | 15.4 |
| Flour | 37.4 | 6.6 | .4 | .2 | | 34.6 | 42.2 | 21.8 | 3 | 3.2 |
| Honey | 5.8 | .6 | 1 | .8 | | 2.8 | 13.2 | 6.2 | 3.4 | 5.8 |
| Tobacco | 615 | 714.4 | 732.2 | 725.4 | 717.6 | 742.2 | 733.4 | 797.2 | 838.6 | 876 |
| Tobacco, smoking, chewing, snuff | 4.2 | 8.8 | 7.2 | 5.4 | 4.2 | 2.4 | 3 | 4. | 2 | 6.8 |
| | 9.6 | 18.2 | 17.4 | 15.8 | 11.4 | 8.8 | 16.4 | 18.6 | 12 | 11.2 |
| Molasses and sirup | 14.6 | 46 | 24.2 | 19.2 | 21.6 | 38.4 | 47.8 | 42.4 | 43.2 | 47.4 |
| Wine in casks | .8 | 11.4 | 20.8 | 12.8 | 10.2 | 4.8 | 11.4 | 4.2 | 8 | 4 |
| Spirits in casks | 1.2 | 9.6 | 10.4 | 3.4 | 2.6 | 5.2 | 5.8 | 3.6 | 3.4 | .8 |
| Cotton | 2,930.4 | 2,968 | 2,887.2 | 3,220.4 | 2,871 | 2,747.4 | 2,573.8 | 2,263 | 3,216.8 | 2,841.8 |
| Cotton | 2,918.2 | 2,964.6 | 2,887 | 3,220.4 | 2,871 | 2,780.6 | 2,567.2 | 2,257 | 3,209.8 | 2,829.6 |
| Cotton waste | 11.2 | 2.6 | | | | 16.8 | 6.4 | 6 | 6.8 | 11.6 |
| India rubber and gutta-percha | 10.4 | 7.2 | 21.2 | 32.2 | 30.8 | 29.8 | 25 | 26.2 | 20.8 | 32.8 |
| Rubber thread | 10.4 | 5 | 19 | 30.4 | 30.2 | 28.4 | 22 | 23.4 | 19 | 28.8 |
| Other textiles | 9.4 | 3.6 | 13 | 5.2 | 4.4 | 2.8 | 8.4 | 3.2 | 6 | 2.4 |
| Animals and animal substances | 29.2 | 41.6 | 70.6 | 60.2 | 90.6 | 236 | 176 | 92.2 | 74.4 | 68.4 |
| Horses | | | | | 33.2 | 188 | 131 | 47 | 18 | 4.4 |
| Oxen | | | 27.4 | 13 | | | | | | |
| Raw hides | 6 | 2.4 | 2 | 7.2 | 5.4 | 8.6 | 5 | 4.4 | 4.4 | 11.6 |
| Raw skins | | .4 | 1.6 | 9.2 | 6.6 | | | .4 | .2 | |
| Animal hair | 4 | | 4.2 | 2.6 | 9 | 6.8 | 9.6 | 6.4 | 13 | 15.8 |
| Bladders, guts, and rennet | 17.2 | 32.2 | 28.8 | 23 | 27.6 | 25.8 | 26.4 | 32 | 34 | 33.2 |
| Other goods | 5.6 | 9.4 | 10.8 | 10.6 | 7 | 13.2 | 16.4 | 16 | 17.6 | 30.6 |
| Common hardware | 1 | 3.4 | 5.2 | 6.2 | 3.2 | 5.2 | 9.4 | 6.2 | 8.4 | 14 |
| **Classified:** | | | | | | | | | | |
| Alimentary substances | 3,037.6 | 2,046.4 | 1,205.8 | 1,355.4 | 1,587.8 | 3,443.6 | 6,930.2 | 4,400.4 | 2,727.8 | 3,989 |
| Raw material | 4,548.8 | 4,778 | 4,821.2 | 5,233 | 5,070.6 | 5,215.2 | 5,321.2 | 5,394.2 | 6,444.6 | 6,084.2 |
| Manufactures | 563.4 | 807 | 989.8 | 1,176.6 | 1,193.2 | 1,678.8 | 2,362.2 | 2,572.8 | 2,241.6 | 2,238.8 |
| Total | 8,149.8 | 7,631.4 | 7,016.8 | 7,765 | 7,851.6 | 10,331.6 | 14,613.6 | 12,367.4 | 11,014 | 11,402 |
| Per cent of total imports | 4.68 | 4.61 | 4.25 | 4.24 | 3.95 | 5.03 | 6.85 | 5.33 | 5.14 | 5.84 |

*Swiss foreign commerce, first six months of the calendar year 1902.*

| Articles. | Imports. | Total. | Exports. | Total. |
|---|---|---|---|---|
| **Colors and chemicals:** | | | | |
| Spirits | $155,225 | | | |
| Artificial colors | 173,995 | | $1,584,776 | |
| Other colors, etc | 502,116 | | 56,473 | |
| | | $831,336 | | $1,641,249 |
| **Glass:** | | | | |
| Window | 108,153 | | | |
| Wares | 143,807 | | 11,263 | |
| | | 251,960 | | 11,263 |
| **Wood:** | | | | |
| Fuel and charcoal | 386,946 | | 79,203 | |
| Timber | 1,118,135 | | 298,764 | |
| Manufactures of | 324,470 | | 127,127 | |
| | | 1,829,551 | | 505,094 |
| Agricultural products | 601,909 | | | 33,722 |

*Swiss foreign commerce, first six months of the calendar year, 1902*—Continued.

| Articles. | Imports. | Total. | Exports. | Total. |
|---|---|---|---|---|
| **Leather:** | | | | |
| Sole leather | $372,321 | | ............ | |
| Harness leather, calf | 98,717 | | ............ | |
| Other leather | 1,279,729 | | $838,780 | |
| Boots and shoes | 414,661 | $2,165,428 | 455,775 | $794,555 |
| **Articles connected with literature, art, and science:** | | | | |
| Books | 851,824 | | ............ | |
| Pianos, harmoniums, etc | 56,635 | | ............ | |
| Electrical apparatus | 109,612 | | ............ | |
| Scientific apparatus | 185,938 | | ............ | |
| Surgical apparatus | 65,228 | 1,269,237 | ............ | 581,909 |
| **Clocks and watches:** | | | | |
| Clocks | ............ | | 18,127 | |
| Music boxes | ............ | | 181,583 | |
| Watches— | | | | |
| Nickel | ............ | | 2,154,250 | |
| Silver | ............ | | 3,469,541 | |
| Gold | ............ | 81,114 | 3,624,792 | 9,443,291 |
| **Machinery:** | | | | |
| Dynamo-electric | 33,635 | | 852,591 | |
| Milling | 21,480 | | 452,398 | |
| Sewing machines | 207,318 | | 44,837 | |
| Spinning machines | 69,534 | | 152,548 | |
| Embroidering machines | 5,832 | | 139,231 | |
| Knitting machines | 6,720 | | 91,699 | |
| Looms | 31,228 | | 442,733 | |
| Machine tools | 88,550 | | 67,462 | |
| Other machinery | 1,202,018 | 1,666,815 | 1,559,602 | 3,803,098 |
| **Metals:** | | | | |
| Lead | 189,461 | | ............ | |
| Pig iron | 554,570 | | ............ | |
| Iron: | | | | |
| Rails, bars, etc | 2,042,643 | | ............ | |
| Cast | 801,233 | | ............ | |
| Malleable | 1,258,828 | | ............ | |
| Copper, zinc, nickel, tin | 1,709,444 | | ............ | |
| Precious metals and coin | 11,855,894 | 17,412,073 | ............ | 6,756,149 |
| **Mineral matters:** | | | | |
| Coal | 4,478,197 | | ............ | |
| Coke | 564,667 | | ............ | |
| Briquets | 1,028,501 | | ............ | |
| Petroleum | 862,356 | | ............ | |
| Other minerals | 256,060 | 7,184,781 | ............ | 230,939 |
| **Provisions and groceries:** | | | | |
| Lard | 181,478 | | ............ | |
| Butter | 532,059 | | ............ | |
| Cacao and cacao shells | 1,134,163 | | ............ | |
| Chocolate | 3,306 | | 1,530,134 | |
| Meat, fresh | 684,297 | | 300,614 | |
| Fruit: | | | | |
| Fresh | 124,295 | | ............ | |
| Evaporated, dried | 60,104 | | ............ | |
| Wheat | 6,927,586 | | ............ | |
| Oats | 1,416,451 | | ............ | |
| Barley | 125,805 | | ............ | |
| Maize | 832,972 | | ............ | |
| Flour, meal, groats | 1,118,726 | | ............ | |
| Coffee | 990,756 | | ............ | |
| Cheese | 247,800 | | 4,182,199 | |
| Malt | 1,427,011 | | ............ | |
| Milk, condensed | ............ | | 3,052,525 | |
| Tobacco and manufactures | 956,329 | | 448,006 | |
| Sugar | 2,067,000 | | ............ | |
| Beer and malt extract | 221,070 | | ............ | |
| Wine in casks | 2,683,000 | | ............ | |
| Other provisions | 3,444,792 | 25,179,000 | 1,598,622 | 10,081,100 |
| **Oils and fats:** | | | | |
| Olive oil in casks | 304,374 | | ............ | |
| Other table oil | 244,375 | | ............ | |
| Other oils and fats | 887,490 | 1,436,239 | ............ | 36,776 |
| Paper | ............ | 411,123 | ............ | 185,751 |
| **Cotton:** | | | | |
| Raw | 3,086,000 | | ............ | |
| Waste | 149,978 | | 151,259 | |
| Yarn | 743,342 | | 1,359,454 | |

*Swiss foreign commerce, first six months of the calendar year 1902*—Continued.

| Articles. | Imports. | Total. | Exports. | Total. |
|---|---|---|---|---|
| **Cotton—Continued.** | | | | |
| Tissues............................................. | $2,061,888 | | $3,327,500 | |
| Embroideries .................................. | 323,327 | | 10,967,500 | |
| | | $6,364,535 | | $15,805,113 |
| Flax and hemp goods ............................ | ............ | 1,041,000 | ............ | 67,111 |
| **Silk:** | | | | |
| Raw and waste........................... | 4,498,112 | | 1,450,093 | |
| Thread and yarn ....................... | 9,136,234 | | 6,700,976 | |
| Piece goods ................................ | 1,162,000 | | 12,061,926 | |
| Ribbons...... | 198,135 | | 3,404,826 | |
| Embroideries and lace .................. | 66,987 | | 775,626 | |
| | | 15,061,468 | | 23,393,447 |
| **Wool:** | | | | |
| Yarn.......................................... | 227,244 | | 863,611 | |
| Tissues....................................... | 2,214,136 | | 303,405 | |
| Embroideries and laces................. | 11,810 | | 19,512 | |
| | | 2,453,190 | | 1,186,528 |
| Rubber ............................................. | ............ | 21,120 | ............ | 139,121 |
| Straw goods ..................................... | ............ | 168,019 | ............ | 1,099,712 |
| **Clothing:** | | | | |
| Cotton .......................................... | 576,201 | | 150,526 | |
| Linen............................................ | 210,950 | | 17,005 | |
| Silk ............................................. | 120,001 | | 28,311 | |
| Wool............................................ | 670,822 | | 37,804 | |
| Knit goods.................................... | 261,813 | | 688,102 | |
| | | 1,839,787 | | 921,748 |
| **Live animals:** | | | | |
| Horses ....................................... | 845,128 | | 205,120 | |
| Neat cattle.................................. | 2,452,011 | | 782,030 | |
| Swine.......................................... | 800,100 | | 6,100 | |
| | | 4,097,239 | | 993,250 |
| Hides and skins ........................... | ............ | 280,815 | ............ | 1,110,785 |
| Earthenware .................................... | ............ | 420,100 | ............ | 71,000 |
| | | | | |
| Total, six months, 1902 ......... | ............ | 93,007,339 | ............ | 77,815,301 |
| Less precious metals................. | ............ | 11,355,894 | ............ | 5,908,125 |
| | | | | |
| | ............ | 81,641,445 | ............ | 71,907,176 |
| Total, six months, 1901 .............. | ............ | 84,100,200 | ............ | 73,968,200 |
| | | | | |
| Decrease in 1902 ............................ | ............ | 2,458,755 | ............ | 2,061,024 |

## BERNE.

Among the industrial nations of the earth, Switzerland occupies a position most remarkable. Without seaports and dependent upon the outside world for its very existence, the Confederation nevertheless holds first rank in commercial activity and commercial progress. Indeed, it may be safely said that one-half of the requirements of Switzerland for sustenance has to be brought into the country from foreign lands; and in order to overcome this heavy handicap, the Swiss are forced to produce for export only goods that command a relatively high price in the world's markets—articles of luxury, the proceeds from the sales of which are depended upon to preserve the financial equilibrium of the little Republic. And in the manufacture of these products, Switzerland owes its sturdy development to the thrift and energy of its people, to whom is due the credit for placing its silk, embroidery, watch, machine, chemical, cheese, and condensed-milk industries upon the high plane which they occupy to-day.

But even with the relatively large sales abroad of these and minor articles, at the close of the financial year, when the books are balanced and the amount of goods sold in other lands is compared with the amount of goods purchased therefrom, a heavy deficit is always to be found. This deficit—$70,000,000 in 1899, $53,000,000 in 1900, and

$41,000,000 in 1901—has to be covered in some manner to insure the commercial prosperity of the country. To a great extent, it is the tourist movement in Switzerland by which this equalization is secured, assisted in a less degree by gains from Swiss undertakings in foreign lands, trading in values, interests, dividends, etc. Every year, from 300,000 to 400,000 travelers come to Switzerland and leave behind them in payment for board, lodging, transportation, souvenirs, tips, and what not, a sum of money that conservatively may be estimated at from $25,000,000 to $35,000,000. The hotel keeper pays the servants, who also receive generous tips, and he pays the butcher and the baker; the little shopkeepers pay their rent, earn a more or less comfortable living, and order carved wooden bears or lions of Lucerne for the next season; the mountain railways flourish; money is dropped here, scattered there, sprinkled everywhere, and thus the Swiss ship of commerce is prevented from listing too far.

## TRADE IN 1901.

Three-quarters of the entire export from Switzerland are manufactured goods, made from raw materials that are imported from the countries to which the finished wares are sent. The special commerce of the Republic may be divided into three great classes—food stuffs, raw materials, and manufactures—the exact figures for which, both in values and percentages, will be found in the following statistical table:

*Imports and exports of Switzerland during the year 1901.*

| Class of goods. | Imports. | | Exports. | |
|---|---|---|---|---|
| | Value. | Per cent. | Value. | Per cent. |
| Food stuffs | $59,178,000 | 29.20 | $20,709,000 | 12.83 |
| Raw materials | 80,221,000 | 39.59 | 17,754,000 | 10.99 |
| Manufactures | 63,251,000 | 31.21 | 122,995,000 | 76.18 |
| Total | 202,650,000 | 100 | 161,458,000 | 100 |

Excess of imports over exports, $41,192,000.

The value of the goods sold to the rest of the world remained practically the same as in the preceding year. The slight falling off in the value of manufactured goods was counterbalanced by an increase in the value of food products sold. The result of the industrial year of 1901, however, was not so favorable as had been expected, although the decrease in imports, particularly raw products, iron and ironware, machines, and textiles (with the exception of silk), brought the deficit down to the $41,000,000 already mentioned. Of the round $12,000,000 decrease in the entire import as compared with the foregoing year, the lower price of silk, cotton, iron, wool, foods, machines, and a few other articles was answerable for $9,800,000, offset only in a slight degree by the rise in the price of leather, shoes, agricultural implements, scientific articles, etc., namely, $580,000, leaving $9,200,000 reduction on account of values alone. In spite of the lower prices paid for wheat, sugar, coffee, and some other food stuffs, Switzerland was compelled to purchase from abroad $1,000,000 worth more than in 1900.

The chief articles of import during the year were:

| | |
|---|---:|
| Food stuffs | $53,000,000 |
| Wheat | 13,900,000 |
| Flour | 1,500,000 |
| Coffee | 2,000,000 |
| Sugars | 4,000,000 |
| Wine | 4,300,000 |
| Meat, poultry, fish | 4,400,000 |
| Eggs | 2,000,000 |
| Silk | 28,000,000 |
| Mineral products | 16,500,000 |
| Cotton | 12,500,000 |
| Iron and manufactures of iron | 10,000,000 |
| Precious metals, uncoined | 10,400,000 |
| Wool | 9,500,000 |
| Animals | 8,600,000 |
| Machines and vehicles | 5,000,000 |
| Wood | 5,000,000 |
| Chemicals | 5,000,000 |
| Tobacco | 2,000,000 |

The chief articles of export during the year were:

| | |
|---|---:|
| Silks | $44,000,000 |
| Cotton embroideries, etc | 29,000,000 |
| Watches and watch materials | 25,000,000 |
| Food products | 20,000,000 |
| Cheese | 8,500,000 |
| Condensed milk | 5,600,000 |
| Chocolate and cocoa | 2,900,000 |
| Children's food | 500,000 |
| Machines | 9,000,000 |
| Chemicals and dyes | 4,000,000 |
| Cigars and cigarettes | 500,000 |

The following table shows the percentage shares of the principal countries in their trade with Switzerland:

| Countries. | Imports. | | Exports. | |
|---|---|---|---|---|
| | 1900. | 1901. | 1900. | 1901. |
| | Per cent. | Per cent. | Per cent. | Per cent. |
| Germany | 31.53 | 30.19 | 24.11 | 23.01 |
| Austria | 6.25 | 6.09 | 5.46 | 5.42 |
| France | 18.66 | 19.57 | 13.15 | 13.06 |
| Italy | 14.58 | 15.03 | 5.28 | 5.51 |
| Belgium | 2.53 | 2.52 | 1.78 | 1.74 |
| Great Britain | 5.61 | 4.48 | 20.99 | 22.55 |
| Russia | 4.82 | 5.52 | 3.23 | 3.02 |
| Spain | 1.15 | 1.04 | 1.75 | 1.85 |
| Egypt | 1.63 | 1.38 | .87 | .89 |
| Japan | .90 | .83 | 1.27 | .72 |
| China | .81 | 1.08 | .77 | 1.02 |
| United States | 5.14 | 5.84 | 11.46 | 10.51 |

## MANUFACTURES.

Owing to the peculiar economic conditions of Switzerland, the energy of her people is necessarily concentrated upon the production of high-priced wares; and minor branches of manufacture, such as iron goods, household and farm utensils, labor-saving devices, articles of daily use, and novelties, are more or less disregarded. The home market is so limited and the field abroad is so occupied by the jostling competition of other countries that the Swiss production in these lines is of small importance. Switzerland, therefore, procures these manufactures from the outside world, and it is Germany, naturally, that occupies first place in supplying them. In fact, more than one-half of the entire Swiss import of this class of goods is furnished by that country—$34,000,000 of the entire import of $65,000,000 in 1901. France comes next with $11,000,000, England with $6,000,000, Austria with $3,500,000, Belgium with $2,200,000, and the United States with $2,100,000, while Italy follows close behind. Ironware and machines, woolen and cotton goods, and leather are the most important of the imports of manufactures.

### TRADE WITH THE UNITED STATES.

Inasmuch as the fluctuations from year to year in the total amount of imports from the United States are caused by the greater or less requirements of Switzerland for food stuffs, it is with satisfaction we note that the imports of manufactured goods from across the Atlantic have increased from $540,000 worth ten years ago to $2,100,000 worth in 1901. It is impossible to ascertain the amount of American goods brought into Switzerland and credited to other countries through which they have passed, but the sum would undoubtedly swell considerably the total value of manufactured articles imported from the United States. The following figures, taken from Swiss sources, show the imports of certain manufactured articles from America for the years 1892 and 1901, respectively:

*Imports of manufactures from the United States.*

| Articles. | 1892. | 1901. |
|---|---|---|
| Total machines | $27,400 | $442,200 |
| Agricultural machines | 1,600 | 212,000 |
| Tool machines | 8,000 | 40,200 |
| Bicycles | | 41,800 |
| Ironware | 23,000 | 151,000 |
| Fine leather shoes | | 20,400 |

The entire import from the United States in 1901 was valued at $11,833,000, of which three-sixths were raw products, two-sixths food stuffs, and one-sixth manufactures. Our share of the Swiss trade was 5.84 per cent of the total, while Switzerland sold us 10.51 per cent of her exports. More favorable freight rates would facilitate greatly our sales to this Republic. A new commercial treaty is also essential to that end.

### SWISS WATCH INDUSTRY.

Watch making, wh'ch had been enjoying increasing prosperity for the past two years, was marked by a reduction of orders toward the close of the year, while the figures for the first half of 1902 are considerably behind those for the corresponding period of 1901—which year, however, witnessed the highest development of the art. The ancient method of producing watches has been cast aside, and machinery now aids in the manufacture of the millions of timepieces that are sold to all quarters of the globe.

The creation of numerous small factories has been made possible by the distribution of electrical energy. There are at present no less than 515 plants in the Cantons Berne, Neuchatel, and Geneva engaged in the production of watches, cases, works, dials, glasses, springs, stones, and other parts of timepieces. The fallacy of the expression "Geneva watch" is shown by the fact that of the 515 factories where the manufacture of watches and parts is carried on, 242 are in Canton Berne,

232 in Canton Neuchatel, and but 41 in Canton Geneva. In these factories there are employed 24,858 persons, of whom 9,000 are females. In addition to that number, 7,594 persons are engaged in the home industry.

The value of the export of watches and parts for the past three years is shown by the following table:

*Exports of watches and parts during the years 1899, 1900, and 1901.*

| Articles. | 1899. | 1900. | 1901. |
|---|---|---|---|
| Gold-cased watches and chronometers............................ | $8,082,239 | $8,626,554 | $9,341,972 |
| Silver-cased watches................................ | 7,311,075 | 7,816,750 | 8,136,880 |
| Nickel and metal watches............................ | 3,921,726 | 4,315,093 | 4,583,943 |
| Finished movements................................ | 559,882 | 660,798 | 858,693 |
| Materials................................ | 1,714,473 | 2,015,230 | 2,190,164 |
| Total................................ | 21,599,385 | 23,434,420 | 25,121,652 |

*Exports of gold, silver, and nickel watches, cases, and finished movements, 1900, 1901, and first half of 1902.*

| Periods. | 1900. | 1901. | 1902. |
|---|---|---|---|
| First quarter................................ | 1,586,723 | 1,936,923 | 1,734,644 |
| Second quarter................................ | 1,826,790 | 2,107,370 | 1,897,427 |
| Third quarter................................ | 1,963,772 | 2,165,624 | ............ |
| Fourth quarter................................ | 2,483,902 | 2,541,854 | ............ |
| Total................................ | 7,861,187 | 8,751,771 | ............ |

There were 2,873,814 nickel and metal cased watches exported in 1901, having an average value of $1.60 each, to these countries: England, 1,056,392; Germany, 363,438; Spain, 241,757; France, 173,702; Italy, 183,540; Austria-Hungary, 164,792; Russia, 50,001; British India, 97,363; China, etc., 72,658; Belgium, 63,559; other countries, 406,612.

The silver-cased watches were valued at an average of $2.30 each, and 3,547,608 were exported to the following countries: England, 1,175,367; Germany, 780,950; Austria-Hungary, 314,742; Italy, 267,018; Russia, 133,828; United States, 140,956; Norway and Sweden, 93,191; China, etc., 76,879; Japan, 57,283; Belgium, 80,012; France, 47,657; British India, 53,426; Netherlands, 75,285; European Turkey, 51,588; other countries, 199,426.

The number of gold-cased watches exported was 919,539, at an average value of $10.81, of which number Germany received 337,514; England, 200,831; Austria-Hungary, 110,175; Russia, 45,986; Italy, 49,350; Belgium, 22,951; France, 7,508; Spain, 18,604; Netherlands, 30,490; United States, 12,102; La Plata, 11,485; Norway and Sweden, 13,735; other countries, 58,808.

The chronometers averaged $32.81 in value, and there were sent to England, 4,369; France, 1,822; United States, 311; other countries, 3,395. The total number exported was 9,897.

The United States took 306,530 of the total of 693,503 finished movements exported; Russia, 134,673; Japan, 94,673; Canada, 66,948; Germany, 69,104; and other countries, 21,575. The average price was $1.25 apiece.

## CUSTOMS TARIFF.

No changes have taken place in the commercial treaties of Switzerland, and no new treaties of importance were entered into between foreign governments and this country. The revision of the Swiss customs tariff was completed by Parliament in the fall of 1902, and before the publication of this report will have been either accepted or rejected by the people, who are at present demanding a referendum. December 31, 1903, marks the period of expiration of the commercial treaties with Germany, Italy, Austria, Spain, and Norway, while the United States, on account of the abrogation of the "most-favored nation" clause of the treaty of 1855, has been paying the present general tariff rates on goods sold to Switzerland since October, 1900. Before the close of 1903, Switzerland will either have entered into new agreements or prolonged the treaties with the countries mentioned, granting reductions in the new tariff, which will be used as a basis.

LEO J. FRANKENTHAL,
*Vice and Deputy Consul.*

BERNE, *November 26, 1902.*

---

## GENEVA.

The industrial and commercial crisis which Germany experienced last year had, as a matter of course, a reflex effect of some importance in Switzerland, which is closely connected with its big northern neighbor. In fact, 30.19 per cent of the total Swiss imports comes from Germany, and 23.01 per cent of the exports is sent to that country. It is generally stated in this district that trade is not what it should be, that business is dull and competition great, but at the same time it would be difficult to indicate a branch of industry or trade which is decidedly bad or decidedly good. "General stagnation" are the words that would best describe conditions in this district.

## TARIF CHANGES.

The denunciation of the commercial treaties with other countries which was to take place on December 31, 1902, to be effective at the end of 1903, will, it is presumed, be postponed until December 31, 1903. In the proposed new general customs tariff, the duty on nearly all articles is increased, as, for instance:

[Per quintal (220 pounds).]

| Articles. | Present duty. | | Proposed duty. | |
|---|---|---|---|---|
| | Francs. | U. S. currency. | Francs. | U. S. currency. |
| Fine boots and shoes | 130 | $25.09 | 150 | $28.95 |
| Bicycles | 100 | 19.30 | *a*20 | 3.86 |
| Dried fruits with stones | *b* | .965 | 5 | .96 |
| Dried fruits without stones | 5 | .965 | 10 | 1.93 |
| Sewing machines | 4 | .772 | 20 | 3.86 |
| Agricultural machines | 4 | .772 | 8 | 1.54 |
| Watch cases: | | | | |
| Finished | 100 | 19.30 | 100 | 19.30 |
| Rough | 100 | 19.30 | 16 | 3.08 |

*a* Apiece.

But it may be added that this proposed tariff does not meet with popular approval as reflected by the press, and it is therefore possible that it may be rejected.

### THE SO-CALLED "FREE ZONE."

Owing to its situation on the frontier of France, being surrounded on three sides by that country, the small Canton of Geneva is more or less dependent on the products coming not only from France at large, but from the immediate vicinity which constitutes (in France), by reciprocal arrangement between the two countries, a free zone. That section of France exported to this district in 1901, 20,150,000 francs ($3,888,950) worth of goods—i. e., an increase of 2,317,000 francs ($447,181) over the preceding year.

### RAILROADS IN SWITZERLAND.

At the end of 1901, the total length of railroads in Switzerland was 4,309 kilometers (2,677 miles), of which 415 kilometers (258 miles) were 1 meter (3 feet) gauge, 172 kilometers (107 miles) were 1 meter (3 feet) gauge, partly cog rails; 91 kilometers (56 miles) were cog rails, 24 kilometers (13 miles) were funicular; and 255 kilometers (141 miles) were tramways. This is 1 kilometer (0.621 mile) per 767 inhabitants.

The first part of the new electric line, which puts the Bernese Oberland in direct communication with the eastern part of Lake Geneva, was inaugurated in December, 1901. It leads from Montreux (400 meters, or 1,312 feet, above sea level) to the Lemanic resort Les Avants (974 meters, or 3,195 feet, elevation).

In the month of August last, the tunnel of Jaman, 2,430 meters (about 1½ miles) long, at an altitude of 1,118 meters (3,668 feet), was successfully pierced, and now that one of the greatest difficulties of the line is overcome, it is expected the work will progress rapidly and that in about two years' time the railroad from Montreux to Zweisimmen will be in full operation. This will shorten the line of travel from this section of Switzerland to Zweisimmen by 78 miles—i. e., three hours.

The second part of the new line which runs from Les Avants to Montbovon, 800 meters (2,635 feet), in the Canton of Fribourg, will connect Montreux with the electric railroad of Bulle-Montbovon. The last part will join at Zweisimmen, 945 meters (3,100 feet), the steam railway Thun-Spiez-Erlenbach.

The total cost of the entire line from Montreux to Zweisimmen will reach 12,300,000 francs ($2,373,900), and its total length, 60 kilometers (37 miles), of which 40 kilometers (25 miles), the most expensive, will be in the Canton of Vaud, in this district. The government of Vaud gives 1,073,400 francs ($207,166) for the new line, and Berne is expected to grant 2,500,000 francs ($482,500). The journey from Montreux to Montbovon will occupy about three hours, and the cost of the trip be 4.50 francs ($0.87). The fare for the whole journey will probably not be more than 7 francs ($1.35). The present cost is 16 francs ($3.08).

The motor of the carriage is strong enough to draw two other carriages, one for travelers and one for goods. The maximum grades will not be heavier than 6 to 7 per cent.

## RAILROAD RATES FOR BAGGAGE.

The Union of Swiss Commercial Travelers has decided to fight the projected increase of tariff for baggage on the railroads of Switzerland, to ask "abonnements" (subscription tickets) by federal district, when all railways shall belong to the Confederation, and to fight the new tariff bill.

### GENEVA COMMERCE.

According to the yearly report of the society administering the bonded warehouses of Geneva, the total amount of goods coming into and taken out of these warehouses reached, in 1901, 747,363 quintals (164,420,000 pounds).

On December 31, 1901, the total of goods stored was 140,268 quintals (20,859,000 pounds), as against 67,051 (14,751,200 pounds) on January 1, and 34,174 (7,518,300 pounds) in May. In that figure are included 124,824 quintals (27,461,000 pounds of corn and 5,482 quintals (1,106,000 pounds) of wine. Only 27,595 quintals (3,311,000 pounds) of wine were bonded in 1901. This last figure is far inferior to that of preceding years. The principal reason of the decrease is overvintage.

On the other side, the amount of corn entered shows a heavy increase. The federal figures also show a large increase over the preceding year—73,217 quintals, i. e., 16,107,740 pounds. The total quantity of corn entered was 336,100 quintals (73,942,000 pounds). This increase is largely due to the important purchases made in August in anticipation of the supposed bad crops, an anticipation which, however, proved ill-founded, since wheat declined 1 franc ($0.19) per quintal (220 pounds) in September.

Nearly all the wheat received in Geneva came through Marseilles from Russia, Roumania and the other Danubian countries. A small portion only comes from the United States and La Plata.

The imports of wheat by Switzerland during the year 1901, according to federal statistics, were: From Russia, 43,333,000 francs ($8,363,300); United States, 14,444,000 francs ($2,787,700); La Plata, 7,855,000 francs ($1,516,000); Danubian countries, 3,025,000 francs ($583,825); Canada and Australia, each, 903,000 francs ($174,300).

It is obvious, therefore, that the greater part of the wheat imported does not enter Switzerland through Geneva.

Oats and maize come from the same countries, and also from Turkey.

The above figures do not by any means show the total quantity of goods consumed in this district, since Geneva is a port of entry not only for Switzerland, but also for all that part of France around this Canton which constitutes the "free zone." The population of the "free zone" is nearly double that of the Canton of Geneva, which contains 130,000 inhabitants.

### RECEIPTS OF CUSTOMS DUTIES IN SWITZERLAND.

The receipts of federal customs for the first six months of 1902 were 1,609,617 francs ($310,736) greater than in 1901, but a decrease of 2,478,433 francs ($478,337) as compared with the same period of 1900. The decrease of receipts during the year 1901 was 1,538,062 francs ($296,846) in a total of 46,471,948 francs, or $8,969,086.

## SWISS BANKS.

Great improvements have taken place in the mutual relations of the Swiss issuing banks. In 1901 there were voted, in addition to other improvements, reciprocal free presentation and payment of commercial bills of exchange; issuance of "general checks" free (these general checks may be presented for payment at any of the Swiss issuing banks); institution of a clearing house; uniformity in rate of official discount; partition of charges for the importation of bullion; regulation, by redemption, of the circulation of bank notes.

All the principal banks, except the Bernese Cantonal Bank, to the number of 36, have accepted these provisions. This leads the way to the creation of the Swiss Central Bank. The act to establish the Federal Bank, which was rejected by the vote of the nation after passage in the Federal Assembly, has not yet been adopted.

## AMERICAN LAUNDRY.

Among the new industries of the Canton of Geneva which will interest our exporters is an American steam laundry in Carouge. This establishment is fitted with American machinery, which gives better results than German imitations used by competitors, the latter requiring a greater amount of water power than the American type. An opening should exist in this line generally, to replace the inferior machines in use.

## AMERICAN SHOE TRADE.

An American shoe store has been established in the most prominent shopping street of Geneva. It is noticeable that American shoes are growing in favor in this district; the field, however, is not properly worked, although there are large possibilities for sales. The chief reasons are that only the better grades of boots and shoes are imported, and that the shape of our boots does not find favor among the people here, who have so long been accustomed to French and German shapes. The large manufacturing firm which first caters to this market by sending a reasonably priced shoe of a shape to please the local markets will find a good business.

The Swiss imports of fine boots and shoes in 1901 were:

| Countries. | Francs. | U. S. currency. |
|---|---|---|
| Germany | 1,887,600 | $364,306 |
| France | 569,800 | 109,971 |
| Austria | 483,000 | 93,220 |
| Italy | 245,300 | 47,342 |

The Swiss exports of boots and shoes in 1901 were:

| Countries. | Francs. | U. S. currency. |
|---|---|---|
| Great Britain | 2,809,300 | $542,195 |
| La Plata | 604,400 | 124,292 |
| France | 558,200 | 106,767 |
| Egypt | 452,100 | 87,255 |
| Chile | 310,950 | 60,013 |
| Germany | 200,000 | 38,600 |

All Swiss boot and shoe factories are in the German part of Switzerland.

The imports of American boots during the past four years were:

| Year. | Francs. | U. S. currency. |
|---|---|---|
| 1898 | 17,000 | $3,281 |
| 1899 | 35,700 | 6,890 |
| 1900 | 82,309 | 15,826 |
| 1901 | 102,000 | 19,686 |

The Swiss general tariff, applied to American goods since November, 1900, imposes a duty of 130 francs ($25.09) per quintal (220 pounds) on American shoes and boots, as against 60 francs ($11.58) in preceding years. This increase seriously handicaps the import trade with America.

The new general tariff, which is now pending before the Federal Chambers, provides a duty of 150 francs ($28.95) per quintal (220 pounds) on boots and shoes, but, as before stated, this tariff has not yet been approved by the nation.

### TELEPHONES.

Switzerland ranks third among nations in the proportionate use of the telephone, as the following figures show: Sweden, 113 subscribers per 10,000 inhabitants; United States, 107, and Switzerland, 93.

### INCREASE IN BUILDING IN GENEVA.

The increase in building operations in all quarters of Geneva is so remarkable that it strikes the attention of even the passing tourist, and is changing the aspect of the city, save in the closely built sections of the old town. Even there, not a few modern buildings are in course of construction. This is explained in part by the activity of French capital, which has recently sought investment in Geneva. The increasing population of the city also naturally creates a demand for a larger number of comfortable dwelling places.

I am unable to obtain statistics relating to the cost of construction, but in 1900, the department of public works issued 310 permits to erect and alter buildings in the Canton (practically the city); in 1901, 419, and in the first six months of 1902, 236.

Apartments of from one to four rooms each increased in number from 22,169 in 1898 to 23,269 in 1900, the greatest increase being in the flats containing three rooms. Apartments of nine rooms increased in the same time from 1,106 to 1,195.

### HOTEL INDUSTRY.

No report on Swiss industries can be complete without a review of the ever-increasing business of hotel keeping. The latest statistics obtainable place the number of hotels in this small country at about 1,900, with 105,000 beds, representing a capital of 550,000,000 francs ($106,150,000), of which 421,000,000 francs ($81,253,000) is invested in buildings and 116,000,000 francs ($22,388,000) in furniture.

One of the interesting points is the increase in the number of hotels at high altitudes, all of which are comfortable and in many cases even luxurious.

Up to 500 meters (1,640 feet) above sea level there are 658 hotels; between 500 and 1,000 meters (3,281 feet), 673; between 1,000 and 2,400 meters (7,874 feet), 565.

The Gornergrat (9,843 feet) and the New Palace (3,610 feet) are the most important among the higher-altitude hotels. The former is near Zermatt and is reached by an electric railway. The latter is an enormous structure at Caux, at the lower end of Lake Geneva.

### TRAINING SCHOOL FOR HOTEL KEEPING.

In order to run these hotels on an increasingly intelligent scale, the Swiss Society of Hotel Keepers (with 800 members) instituted, in 1893, at Ouchy-Lausanne, in this district, a professional school for training persons who contemplated entering upon this calling. In this school, young men are taught both theoretical and practical hotel keeping, including languages, calligraphy, arithmetic, bookkeeping, geography for tourist travel, rules of good behavior, knowledge of food products, etc.

The development of this school has been so rapid that every year, there are three applications for each vacancy.

### TRADE RETURNS.

The following are the statistics of the more important exports and imports of Switzerland:

*Exports from this district to the United States during first three quarters of 1901 and 1902.*

| Exports by quarters. | 1901. | 1902. |
|---|---|---|
| Watches and watch materials: | | |
| First quarter............................................. | $64,318.02 | $69,235.76 |
| Second quarter............................................. | 86,063.30 | 79,550.05 |
| Third quarter............................................. | 116,843.25 | 119,778.90 |
| Chemical products: | | |
| First quarter............................................. | 789.01 | 5,454.53 |
| Second quarter............................................. | 6,611.94 | 7,603.32 |
| Third quarter............................................. | 2,744.05 | 4,222.08 |
| Furs (almost exclusively sealskin garments): | | |
| First quarter............................................. | 1,071.15 | 641.58 |
| Second quarter............................................. | 926.40 | 1,037.38 |
| Third quarter............................................. | 2,448.20 | 3,070.63 |
| Music boxes: | | |
| First quarter............................................. | 13,554.99 | 19,526.30 |
| Second quarter............................................. | 18,035.71 | 21,343.50 |
| Third quarter............................................. | 20,459.30 | 22,151.70 |

*Total imports and exports of Switzerland for the years 1900 and 1901.*

| Year. | Francs. | U. S. currency. |
|---|---|---|
| IMPORTS. | | |
| 1900............................................. | 1,111,109,700 | $214,444,172 |
| 1901............................................. | 1,050,008,557 | 202,650,688 |
| EXPORTS. | | |
| 1900............................................. | 836,079,700 | 161,363,382 |
| 1901............................................. | 836,567,114 | 161,457,453 |

*Imports and exports of Switzerland, by countries, during year 1901.*

| Countries. | Per cent of total imports. | Increase over 1900. | |
|---|---|---|---|
| | | Francs. | U. S. currency. |
| **IMPORTS.** | | | |
| Germany | 30.19 | 33,364,439 | $6,439,337 |
| France | 19.57 | 1,813,028 | 349,914 |
| Italy | 15.08 | 4,163,973 | 808,647 |
| Austria | 6.09 | 5,231,586 | 1,009,696 |
| Great Britain | 4.48 | 15,282,496 | 2,949,522 |
| United States | 5.84 | 4,240,283 | 818,861 |
| Russia | 5.52 | 9,898,450 | 1,909,436 |
| **EXPORTS.** | | | |
| Germany | 23.01 | 9,127,422 | 1,761,598 |
| Great Britain | 22.55 | 13,188,269 | 2,545,336 |
| France | 13.06 | 696,900 | 134,309 |
| United States | 10.51 | 7,813,720 | 1,508,048 |
| Austria | 5.42 | 233,341 | 45,085 |
| Italy | 5.51 | 2,001,413 | 386,273 |
| Russia | 3.02 | 1,658,060 | 320,005 |

*Imports and exports of the United States with Switzerland in 1900 and 1901.*

| Year. | Imports. | | Exports. | |
|---|---|---|---|---|
| | Francs. | U. S. currency. | Francs. | U. S. currency. |
| 1900 | 57,069,517 | $11,014,510 | 95,744,629 | $18,478,800 |
| 1901 | 61,309,800 | 11,382,900 | 87,930,909 | 16,970,700 |

*Details of Swiss trade for the year 1901.*

| Countries. | Primary articles. | | Manufactured articles. | |
|---|---|---|---|---|
| | U. S. currency. | Francs. | U. S. currency. | Francs. |
| **IMPORTS.** | | | | |
| Germany | $20,813,561 | 107,842,286 | $34,221,244 | 177,312,141 |
| Austria | 1,515,667 | 7,853,192 | 3,347,709 | 17,345,644 |
| France | 17,048,358 | 88,333,435 | 11,414,243 | 59,141,158 |
| Italy | 19,662,987 | 101,880,765 | 2,062,337 | 10,685,683 |
| Belgium | 2,602,888 | 13,486,468 | 2,246,778 | 11,641,383 |
| Great Britain | 2,397,789 | 12,423,517 | 6,449,150 | 33,415,286 |
| United States | 5,871,234 | 30,420,903 | 2,160,504 | 11,194,320 |

| Countries. | Alimentary articles. | | Total value. | |
|---|---|---|---|---|
| | U. S. currency. | Francs. | U. S. currency. | Francs. |
| **IMPORTS.** | | | | |
| Germany | $6,144,676 | 31,837,706 | $61,179,481 | 316,992,185 |
| Austria | 7,471,414 | 38,711,992 | 12,334,790 | 63,910,828 |
| France | 11,206,780 | 58,066,223 | 39,669,376 | 205,540,811 |
| Italy | 8,738,688 | 45,278,175 | 30,464,012 | 157,844,623 |
| Belgium | 256,861 | 1,330,889 | 5,106,527 | 26,458,690 |
| Great Britain | 228,744 | 1,185,200 | 9,075,683 | 47,024,003 |
| United States | 3,801,058 | 19,694,577 | 11,832,791 | 61,309,800 |

| Countries. | Primary articles. | | Manufactured articles. | |
|---|---|---|---|---|
| | U. S. currency. | Francs. | U. S. currency. | Francs. |
| **EXPORTS.** | | | | |
| Germany | $10,820,856 | 56,066,613 | $22,757,196 | 117,912,983 |
| Austria | 813,000 | 4,212,485 | 7,196,178 | 37,286,899 |
| France | 3,235,977 | 16,766,722 | 13,352,885 | 69,185,987 |
| Italy | 1,698,362 | 8,799,807 | 5,490,840 | 28,449,949 |
| Belgium | 171,688 | 889,565 | 2,202,016 | 11,409,411 |
| Great Britain | 253,439 | 1,313,155 | 30,920,866 | 160,211,738 |
| United States | 151,194 | 783,391 | 15,735,055 | 81,528,735 |

*Details of Swiss trade for the year 1901*—Continued.

| Countries. | Alimentary articles. | | Total value. | |
|---|---|---|---|---|
| | U. S. currency. | Francs. | U. S. currency. | Francs. |
| **EXPORTS.** | | | | |
| Germany............. | $8,563,972 | 18,466,178 | $37,142,024 | 192,445,724 |
| Austria............. | 735,701 | 3,817,105 | 8,745,879 | 45,315,439 |
| France............. | 4,498,984 | 23,284,629 | 21,082,795 | 109,237,288 |
| Italy............. | 1,723,865 | 8,981,946 | 8,913,087 | 46,151,702 |
| Belgium ............. | 429,056 | 2,228,092 | 2,802,755 | 14,522,056 |
| Great Britain ............. | 5,243,487 | 27,168,071 | 36,417,741 | 188,692,964 |
| United States ............. | 1,084,425 | 5,618,783 | 16,970,674 | 87,980,989 |

*Statistics of number of tourists in Geneva from May 15 to October 15, 1899–1902.*

| Countries. | 1899. | 1900. | 1901. | 1902. |
|---|---|---|---|---|
| Switzerland............. | 17,434 | 18,308 | 22,107 | 31,058 |
| Germany............. | 13,176 | 12,898 | 16,001 | 18,774 |
| England............. | 7,877 | 5,078 | 7,819 | 8,577 |
| Austria-Hungary ............. | 2,071 | 3,187 | 2,697 | 3,070 |
| Africa and Asia............. | 342 | 381 | 521 | 1,091 |
| Australia............. | 89 | 89 | 82 | 62 |
| Belgium ............. | 1,070 | 808 | 1,311 | 1,437 |
| Denmark, Sweden, and Norway............. | 464 | 469 | 458 | 581 |
| Spain and Portugal ............. | 883 | 2,217 | 1,196 | 2,020 |
| United States ............. | 7,348 | 9,143 | 9,354 | 9,879 |
| France............. | 40,752 | 35,743 | 49,543 | 54,357 |
| Netherlands ............. | 1,007 | 944 | 1,196 | 1,623 |
| Italy............. | 4,577 | 6,328 | 8,882 | 6,594 |
| Russia............. | 2,530 | 4,397 | 3,323 | 3,399 |
| Turkey, Greece, etc............. | 710 | 1,329 | 286 | 749 |
| Other countries ............. | 234 | 527 | 201 | 271 |
| Total............. | 100,114 | 102,276 | 126,572 | 143,492 |

The above figures show an increase of 43,878 tourists for the past four years, of whom 2,581 were Americans.

*Total export of watches from Switzerland.*

| Exports. | Pieces. | Value. | | Exports to United States. | |
|---|---|---|---|---|---|
| | | Francs. | U. S. currency. | Francs. | U. S. currency. |
| **1901.** | | | | | |
| Nickel watches............. | 2,873,814 | 23,750,648 | $4,563,875 | 408,008 | $78,745 |
| Silver watches............. | 3,547,608 | 42,159,965 | 8,136,872 | 1,295,832 | 250,095 |
| Gold watches............. | 919,589 | 46,717,286 | 9,016,436 | 851,414 | 164,322 |
| Movements for watches............. | 698,508 | 4,500,602 | 868,616 | 2,091,612 | 403,680 |
| **1900.** | | | | | |
| Nickel watches............. | 2,641,898 | 22,356,007 | 4,315,096 | 358,339 | 69,159 |
| Silver watches............. | 3,805,329 | 40,501,513 | 7,816,792 | 1,007,561 | 193,156 |
| Gold watches............. | 859,829 | 43,086,996 | 8,315,790 | 742,368 | 143,277 |
| Movements for watches............. | 498,892 | 3,423,806 | 660,794 | 1,518,454 | 293,061 |

*Exports of watches, by countries, during 1901.*

| Countries. | Francs. | U. S. currency. |
|---|---|---|
| **NICKEL WATCHES.** | | |
| Germany ............. | 2,940,800 | $567,574 |
| Great Britain ............. | 7,123,858 | 1,374,904 |
| Spain............. | 2,023,526 | 390,540 |
| France............. | 1,796,974 | 346,816 |
| Italy............. | 1,785,418 | 334,236 |
| Austria-Hungary ............. | 1,450,520 | 279,950 |

*Exports of watches, by countries, during 1901*—Continued.

| Countries. | Francs. | U. S. currency. |
|---|---|---|
| **SILVER WATCHES.** | | |
| Germany | 9,275,240 | 1,790,121 |
| Great Britain | 12,169,608 | 2,348,784 |
| Austria-Hungary | 4,019,611 | 775,785 |
| Italy | 2,782,695 | 537,060 |
| Russia | 2,570,362 | 496,060 |
| Sweden and Norway | 1,271,129 | 245,328 |
| China | 1,100,600 | 212,415 |
| **GOLD WATCHES.** | | |
| Germany | 13,974,256 | 2,697,081 |
| Great Britain | 9,292,867 | 1,793,528 |
| Austria-Hungary | 6,101,958 | 1,177,677 |
| Russia | 5,000,755 | 965,145 |
| Italy | 2,373,991 | 458,180 |
| Belgium | 1,257,095 | 242,619 |
| France | 966,486 | 186,532 |
| Spain | 881,480 | 170,116 |
| Netherlands | 856,102 | 165,227 |

*Total imports of watches into Switzerland.*

| Articles. | Francs. | U. S. currency. |
|---|---|---|
| **1901.** | | |
| Nickel watches | 32,876 | $6,345 |
| Silver watches | 4,121 | 795 |
| Gold watches | 192,880 | 37,225 |
| **1900.** | | |
| Nickel watches | 32,704 | 6,312 |
| Silver watches | 5,010 | 967 |
| Gold watches | 109,910 | 21,212 |

*Principal imports from the United States into Switzerland in 1901.*

| Articles. | Francs. | U. S. currency. |
|---|---|---|
| Cabinetmakers' wood, sawn | 1,137,000 | $219,441 |
| Sole leather | 1,110,000 | 214,230 |
| Undressed American hides | 3,068,000 | 592,124 |
| Agricultural machines | 1,060,000 | 204,580 |
| Petroleum and bitumen | 8,111,000 | 1,565,423 |
| Lard | 2,101,000 | 405,493 |
| Meat preserves | 1,735,000 | 334,855 |
| Wheat | 14,444, | 2,787,692 |
| Leaves of tobacco | 4,380, | 845,340 |
| Oils in tank and vegetable wax | 1,362, | 262,866 |
| Cotton in the wool | | 2,730,564 |
| Turpentine oil | | 77,586 |
| Watch cases of common metal | | 64,269 |
| Machine tools | | 38,793 |
| Sewing machines | 80,000 | 15,440 |
| Bicycles | 209,000 | 40,337 |
| Machines of all kinds | 355,000 | 68,515 |
| Copper, pure or alloyed: | | |
| In bars | 577,000 | 111,361 |
| In plates | 255,000 | 49,215 |
| Tar oils | 357,000 | 68,901 |
| Butter oleo and margarin | 123,000 | 23,739 |
| Fish, fresh or frozen | 106,000 | 20,458 |
| Fruits, dried or drained | 69,000 | 13,317 |
| Oats | 217,000 | 41,881 |
| Maize | 380,000 | 73,340 |
| Molasses and sirup | 237,000 | 45,741 |
| Caoutchouc, spun in thread | 144,000 | 27,792 |
| Fish oils, in casks | 146,000 | 28,178 |

*Principal exports to the United States from Switzerland in 1901.*

| Articles. | Francs. | U. S. currency. |
|---|---|---|
| Artificial colors (derived from coal tars) | 3,522,000 | $679,746 |
| Scientific instruments | 111,000 | 21,423 |
| Musical boxes | 436,000 | 84,148 |
| Nickel watches | 408,000 | 78,744 |
| Silver watches | 1,296,000 | 250,128 |
| Gold watches | 851,000 | 164,243 |
| Chronograph and repeater watches | 225,000 | 43,425 |
| Movements for watches | 2,092,000 | 408,756 |
| Embroidering machines | 285,000 | 55,005 |
| Precious stones (unset) | 1,148,000 | 221,564 |
| Chocolate | 144,000 | 27,792 |
| Cheese | 5,094,000 | 983,142 |
| Condensed milk | 176,000 | 33,968 |
| Bleached yarn | 65,000 | 12,555 |
| Tissues, plain, light: | | |
|   Unbleached | 223,000 | 43,089 |
|   Bleached | 360,000 | 69,480 |
| Feather-stitched tissues | 1,850,000 | 357,050 |
| Curtains, crochet embroidery | 3,776,000 | 728,768 |
| Other articles of embroidery | 655,000 | 126,415 |
| Feather-stitched articles | 29,689,000 | 5,729,977 |
| Feather-stitched gowns | 4,882,000 | 942,226 |
| Floss silk: | | |
|   Not thrown | 810,000 | 156,330 |
|   Thrown | 3,056,000 | 589,808 |
| Bolting cloth | 1,208,000 | 233,144 |
|   Pure silk | 8,890,000 | 1,715,770 |
|   Half silk | 3,360,000 | 648,480 |
| Silk ribbons | 2,851,000 | 550,243 |
| Half silk ribbons | 1,945,000 | 374,785 |
| Silk embroidery | 1,323,000 | 255,339 |
| Straw sennit | 697,000 | 134,521 |
| Straw fine wares | 117,000 | 22,581 |
| Cotton hosiery | 688,000 | 132,784 |
| Silk hosiery | 867,000 | 167,331 |
| Wool hosiery | 505,000 | 97,465 |
| Raw hides | 591,000 | 114,063 |
| Raw skins | 48,000 | 9,264 |

HORACE LEE WASHINGTON,
*Consul.*

GENEVA, *October 13, 1902.*

## LUCERNE.

According to statistics published by the Federal customs department at Berne, the total commerce of Switzerland during the twelve months ended December 31, 1901, amounted to $377,314,134—exports, $167,313,423, or an increase of $97,400, and imports, $210,000,711, a decrease of $12,221,200 compared with 1900.

There is a marked decrease of imports—$8,914,400—from the countries bordering upon Switzerland. Germany heads the list, with $6,673,000, followed by Austria, Italy, and France, in the order named. The value of imports from England decreased $3,056,500. A slight decrease is also noted in the export trade with the countries named, except England, which shows an increase of $2,637,600.

### UNITED STATES TRADE.

It is gratifying to note that the imports from the United States for the year 1901 show an increase of $848,057 over the figures for 1900. The exports from Switzerland to the United States show a decrease of $1,562,744. The increase of imports is accounted for principally by the enlarged shipments of food stuffs; the decrease of exports by the reduction in cotton and silk fabrics.

In consideration of the fact that there has been no serious effort on the part of our manufacturers and merchants to capture the Swiss market, it is remarkable to note the strides that articles of American manufacture have made in this country during the past decade. There is scarcely a town or village throughout Switzerland where American articles are not found on sale. Carpenters' tools of American manufacture are universally used here and are admittedly the best in the world.

*Shoes.*—American shoes, which five years ago had no sale whatever in Switzerland, are now sold in all the large shoe stores of the country. They are generally higher in price than the homemade article, but the advance is readily paid by those who care for the style and finish of an American shoe. The demand for American footwear up to the present time has been limited almost entirely to the finer grade articles.

*Shoe machines.*—One of the largest shoe factories in the world, turning out from 5,000 to 8,000 pairs of shoes a day, is situated at Schoenenwerd, in this consular district. It is a large exporter to South American countries. The shoes are made almost entirely on American machinery. Recently the firm has attempted, with fair success, to make an imitation of the American shoe, but the soles are hard and stiff and not as pliable as the genuine article.

*Furniture.*—The success which has been achieved with American office furniture is worthy of notice. Roller-top desks, bookcases, office chairs and tables, typewriters, letter-press tables, and in fact a thousand and one articles for furnishing an office, are coming into general use throughout the country and are regarded highly. Anton Waltisbuehl, who started in a modest way, about six years ago, to import American office furniture and fixtures and purely American novelties, now has large stores at Basel, Zurich, and Lucerne. Many of the articles which he imports have been copied more or less successfully. The mere fact of their having been duplicated locally is evidence of the high consideration in which they are held. "Imitation is the sincerest form of flattery."

*Farm machines.*—American agricultural machinery is finding a market here, but only such machines as are suitable for small farms, as Switzerland could not be called an agricultural country. All the agricultural land is in the hands of small owners. The McCormick Harvesting Machine Company, of Chicago, Ill., is a good illustration of what has for a long time been urged by consular officers—i. e., the advisability of our merchants and manufacturers who desire to do business in foreign countries sending personal representatives abroad. The agent of this firm in Zurich has accomplished results that could not have been reached in any other way than by practical demonstration.

*Bicycles.*—The number of bicycles brought into Switzerland during the year 1901 was 13,088, valued at $539,420, as against 12,923, valued at $547,960, for the preceding year. Of this number, Germany sent 8,858, valued at $354,900; France 2,091, valued at $91,560, and the United States 1,109, valued at $41,720. The reason why we do not get a larger percentage of this trade is the fact that the greater number of bicycles brought here from the United States are of high grade, and are consequently more expensive than either German or French wheels. I think it would be profitable for our manufacturers to investigate the subject.

*General.*—The annual report published by the Federal department of customs, commenting on the commerce between the United States and Switzerland, says:

The commerce with the United States has always been subject to great fluctuations, but we can say that during the last five years, America has gained more ground on our markets than we have on theirs.

Manufactured articles imported from the United States have had more stability than the food stuffs and raw materials. For the last named, the decrease as against 1900 is essentially due to the fall in the price of cotton, as the quantity decreased only 1.6 per cent, whereas the value was 11.8 per cent less. The United States has for the first time furnished us with phosphate for the manufacture of manure ($49,800), and the importation of tobacco and oils for industrial usage, etc., has increased in value, but this increase is offset by the decrease in mineral oils ($54,600) and the decreased importation of horses, fodder, and copper.

More wheat has been imported from America into Switzerland, but the other food stuffs have decreased as against 1900; such, for instance, as lard ($66,000), preserved meats ($55,500), dried fruit ($41,800), oats ($89,900), and maize ($64,200).

Among the manufactured articles, machines and vehicles show a decrease ($141,800); also ornamental castings, especially radiators, which have decreased $48,000; and piping, which represented in 1899 a value of $350,200 and in 1900 $60,000, has fallen to $7,600. As an offset to this loss, ordinary ironworks have increased $12,000. Articles for offices, and also American hardware, appear to enjoy a certain favor, although the quantity received is still very modest in comparison with the total importation. The value of leather and shoes imported from America has increased $191,200, principally on account of the leather being of a lighter quality and more expensive.

The export of raw material to the United States is limited to a very few articles, such as leather and hides, which have increased $50,400, and asphalt, $8,400. An increase is also noted in food stuffs, from $1,020,000 to $1,130,000, thanks to the increased export of cheese of $112,000, whereas the export of manufactured articles has decreased $1,720,000, or about 9.6 per cent. Cotton embroideries and silk tissues (except bolting cloth) have suffered most.

The crops were much less during 1901 than in the preceding year, which necessitated a greater import of food stuffs. Up to the end of the second quarter of the year, 2,000 carloads of wheat in excess of the quantity imported during the same period of 1900 entered Switzerland. During the third and fourth quarters of the year, largely increased quantities of potatoes and vegetables, dried fruits, flour, etc., were also imported. A large part of these food stuffs came from the United States, the freight rates being more favorable than in 1900.

### EXPORTS.

The principal exports from this consular district consist of straw goods, silk, and half-silk ribbons, knit underwear, and drawing instruments. The export of straw goods shows a slight decrease compared with 1900, but the export of silk and half-silk ribbons has increased many fold, especially in the last four months.

The prosperity of the district, and especially Lucerne, is largely dependent upon the number of tourists who visit the country during the season. It is estimated that about 250,000 tourists came to this city during the last season, of whom about 18,000 were Americans. It is roughly calculated that the latter alone expended in the neighborhood of $500,000.

### TRADE IN 1902.

From such statistics as I have been able to obtain, it appears that the commerce of Switzerland for the year 1902 will be greater than that for any other year in the history of the country. The imports for the six months ended June 30, 1902 ($105,796,898), show an increase of about $6,500,000 over the corresponding period of last year, while the exports ($83,570,351) show an increase of about $2,000,000. Large advances are noted in the import of iron, food stuffs, tobacco, raw cotton, silk, and wool. In the export, there is an increase of $1,123,028 in cotton manufactures; $1,211,452 in silks (principally ribbons), and an advance in almost every article traded in, except watches and clocks, which have decreased over $1,000,000.

The imports from the United States for the six months under review amount to $6,090,995, and the exports to our country to $8,967,044. There is a marked increase in the export of manufactured articles, such as ribbons and laces. The import shows but little change from the corresponding period of 1901, except in shoes, which have increased over 100 per cent.

The figures as above given are not absolutely correct, and will be subject to slight changes when the tables for the entire year are made up.

I inclose herewith statistics showing the exports and imports of Switzerland to and from all countries during the years 1899, 1900, and 1901, the percentage of exports and imports of each country, and the increase or decrease of 1901 as against 1900; commerce of Switzerland with the United States during the year ended December 31, 1901; commerce of Switzerland with all countries during the six months ended June 30, 1902; commerce of Switzerland with the United States for the last-mentioned period; also returns for the railways, telegraphs, telephones, and post-offices.

HENRY M. MORGAN, *Consul.*

LUCERNE, *October 10, 1902.*

*Exports and imports of Switzerland during the years ended December 31, 1899, 1900, and 1901, exclusive of precious metals.*

EXPORTS.

| Countries. | 1899. | 1900. | 1901. | Per cent of total. | Increase (+) or decrease(−). |
|---|---|---|---|---|---|
| Germany | $39,716,169 | £40,314,628 | $38,489,145 | 23.01 | −$1,825,483 |
| England | 33,188,695 | 35,100,988 | 37,738,593 | 22.55 | + 2,637,655 |
| France | 19,257,516 | 21,986,637 | 21,847,457 | 13.06 | − 139,180 |
| United States | 18,337,707 | 18,478,800 | 16,970,700 | 10.51 | − 1,562,743 |
| Austria | 9,099,148 | 9,109,756 | 9,063,088 | 5.42 | − 46,668 |
| Italy | 8,396,141 | 8,836,057 | 9,236,340 | 5.51 | + 400,283 |
| Russia | 6,332,199 | 5,392,230 | 5,060,618 | 3.02 | − 331,612 |
| Oriental Asia | 2,108,467 | 3,395,260 | 2,895,510 | 1.74 | − 499,750 |
| Belgium | 2,694,088 | 2,976,418 | 2,904,412 | 1.74 | − 72,006 |
| British India | 2,767,643 | 2,697,857 | 3,030,363 | 1.81 | + 332,506 |
| Spain | 3,002,437 | 2,927,163 | 3,096,785 | 1.85 | + 169,622 |
| Scandinavia | 1,573,192 | 1,252,299 | 1,345,273 | .80 | + 92,974 |
| Danube countries | 1,084,417 | | 1,164,788 | .70 | + 857,715 |
| La Plata | 1,636,724 | 2,045,261 | 1,773,457 | 1.06 | − 271,804 |
| Netherlands | 1,138,354 | 1,140,358 | 1,150,826 | .69 | + 10,468 |
| European Turkey | 809,951 | 745,007 | 870,568 | .52 | + 125,556 |
| Asiatic Turkey | 729,990 | 687,474 | 816,133 | .49 | + 128,659 |
| Brazil | 686,281 | 690,554 | 683,435 | .41 | − 7,119 |
| Central America | 868,532 | 1,238,293 | 1,088,321 | .65 | − 149,972 |
| Australia | 658,337 | 836,198 | 731,469 | .44 | − 104,729 |
| Canada | 809,089 | 840,811 | 909,398 | .54 | + 68,587 |
| Denmark | 648,227 | 613,302 | 667,280 | .40 | + 53,978 |
| Dutch India | 504,947 | 609,217 | 598,722 | .35 | − 15,495 |
| Egypt | 474,229 | 619,778 | 667,880 | .39 | + 48,102 |
| Portugal | 390,380 | 438,155 | 622,858 | .37 | + 184,703 |
| Algiers, Tunis | 387,026 | 390,701 | 469,303 | .28 | + 78,602 |
| Chile, Peru | 294,043 | 649,946 | 583,726 | .35 | + 33,780 |
| Greece | 210,536 | 221,743 | 279,305 | .17 | + 57,562 |
| South American countries | 164,239 | 130,469 | 202,601 | .12 | + 72,132 |
| East Africa | 201,751 | 316,261 | 444,587 | .27 | + 128,326 |
| West Africa | 204,108 | 280,629 | 377,971 | .23 | + 97,342 |
| Uncertain | 833,217 | 876,557 | 922,089 | .55 | + 45,482 |
| Total | 159,202,780 | 167,215,950 | 167,313,423 | 100.00 | + 97,473 |

*Exports and imports of merchandise during the years ended December 31, 1899, 1900, and 1901, arranged by principal countries—Continued.*

IMPORTS.

| Countries. | 1899. | 1900. | 1901. | Per cent of tota. | Increase + or decrease —. |
|---|---|---|---|---|---|
| Germany | | | | 30.19 | —6,672,47 |
| France | | | | 35.57 | — 362,606 |
| Italy | | | | 15.66 | 832,794 |
| United States | | | | 5.44 | 649,057 |
| Austria | | | | 6.39 | — 1,046,216 |
| Russia | | | | 6.52 | — 1,975,691 |
| England | | | | 4.99 | — 3,654,496 |
| Belgium | | | | 2.52 | — 334,630 |
| Oriental Asia | | | | 1.72 | — 334,273 |
| Spain | | | | 1.54 | — 573,446 |
| Egypt | | | | 1.29 | 721,233 |
| Dutch countries | | | | .49 | 673,491 |
| Brazil | | | | .42 | — 299,460 |
| Dutch India | | | | .62 | 46,563 |
| Australia | | | | .62 | 41,402 |
| Central America | | | | .46 | 342,002 |
| La Plata | | | | 1.99 | 50,023 |
| British India | | | | .52 | 149,368 |
| Switzerland | | | | .34 | 4,527 |
| North American countries | | | | .39 + | 63,225 |
| Asiatic Turkey | | | | .14 — | 220 |
| Canada | | | | .17 — | 798,007 |
| Scandinavia | | | | .11 — | 133,549 |
| Greece | | | | .04 — | 85,215 |
| West Africa | | | | .67 — | 70,556 |
| Algiers, Tunis | | | | .06 — | 19,591 |
| European Turkey | | | | .10 — | 8,385 |
| Chile and Peru | | | | .06 — | 14,647 |
| East Africa | | | | .02 — | 11,909 |
| Denmark | | | | .02 + | 16,112 |
| Portugal | | | | .01 + | 1,308 |
| **Total** | 222,464,131 | 222,221,935 | 210,600,711 | 100.00 | — 12,221,214 |

*Commerce with the United States during the year ended December 31, 1901.*

| Articles. | Imports. | Exports. | Increase (+) or decrease (—) of imports over 1899. |
|---|---|---|---|
| Animal products: | | | |
| Raw hides and skins | $11,625 | $127,843 | + $7,104 |
| Bristles | 15,776 | | — 1,068 |
| Bladders, etc | 33,252 | 68 | + 504 |
| Miscellaneous | 2,366 | 1,067 | + 19 |
| Total | 63,019 | 128,978 | + 6,559 |
| Chemicals: | | | |
| Drugs | 7,296 | 263 | — 539 |
| Alkaloids | | 3,463 | |
| Extract of quinine, camphor, etc | | 7,071 | — 65 |
| Pharmaceutical products | 7,200 | 16,120 | — 1,700 |
| Perfumes and cosmetics | 80 | 2,085 | — 920 |
| Colophony, pitch, etc | 24,129 | | — 9,486 |
| Tartaric acid | | 5,022 | |
| Tannin extract | 15,755 | 6,856 | + 10,413 |
| Sulphate of iron, copper, and zinc | 29,134 | | — 24,274 |
| Aniline combinations | | 12,454 | |
| Paraffin, vaseline, etc | 14,706 | | + 4,642 |
| Gallic acid, tannin, etc | 459 | 2,937 | + 459 |
| Essence of turpentine | 80,325 | | — 13,509 |
| Starch | 7,090 | | + 1,732 |
| Gelatin, etc | 705 | 4,410 | + 876 |
| Extracts of coloring matter | 7,276 | 16,988 | — 11,884 |
| Aniline colors | | 704,456 | |
| Varnish | 15,440 | 5 | + 7,320 |
| Miscellaneous | 18,576 | 5,988 | + 8,560 |
| Total | 228,151 | 793,073 | — 28,875 |

*Commerce with the United States during the year ended December 31, 1901—Continued.*

| Articles. | Imports. | Exports. | Increase (+) or decrease (−) of imports over 1899. |
|---|---:|---:|---:|
| **Clocks and watches:** | | | |
| Unfinished parts ............................................. | | $9,428 | − $1,200 |
| Musical boxes ............................................... | $216 | 87,243 | + 12 |
| Finished parts of watches................................... | | 145,197 | |
| Nickel watches .............................................. | 281 | 81,601 | − 158 |
| Silver watches .............................................. | 25 | 259,164 | − 295 |
| Gold watches ............................................... | 840 | 170,281 | + 810 |
| Chronographs, repeaters ..................................... | | 45,045 | |
| Finished movements for watches.............................. | 6,310 | 418,322 | + 4,700 |
| Nickel watch cases.......................................... | 66,685 | 1,058 | − 13,283 |
| Silver watch cases.......................................... | 3 | 1,017 | − 24 |
| Gold watch cases............................................ | 8,708 | 10,203 | + 6,692 |
| Miscellaneous .............................................. | 53 | 784 | − 32 |
| Total ................................................. | 83,121 | 1,229,338 | − 2,778 |
| **Clothing:** | | | |
| Cotton articles ............................................. | 400 | 4,123 | + 400 |
| Silk articles ............................................... | 89 | 9,268 | + 56 |
| Knit goods— | | | |
| Cotton................................................. | | 137,549 | − 210 |
| Linen.................................................. | | 2,286 | |
| Silk................................................... | | 173,422 | |
| Woolen................................................ | | 100,936 | |
| Furs ....................................................... | | 3,476 | |
| Miscellaneous .............................................. | 223 | 1,589 | − 592 |
| Total ................................................. | 712 | 432,649 | − 344 |
| **Cotton:** | | | |
| Raw ....................................................... | 2,829,680 | | − 380,170 |
| Waste ..................................................... | 11,664 | 409 | + 4,786 |
| Threads— | | | |
| Raw.................................................... | | 9,424 | |
| Twisted................................................ | | 7,458 | |
| Bleached............................................... | | 13,091 | |
| Dyed................................................... | | 2,381 | |
| Goods ..................................................... | 500 | 60,063 | + 500 |
| Bleached goods............................................. | | 92,483 | |
| Thread tissues.............................................. | | 12,971 | |
| Colored tissues............................................. | | 33,739 | |
| Printed tissues— | | | |
| Unbleached............................................ | | 2,082 | |
| Bleached............................................... | | 3,968 | |
| Tissues for embroidery— | | | |
| Raw.................................................... | | 5,258 | |
| Bleached............................................... | | 369,933 | |
| Ribbons and braids.......................................... | | 10,670 | |
| Embroidery— | | | |
| Curtains, etc .......................................... | | 886,202 | |
| Etching................................................ | | 5,987,716 | |
| Tulle.................................................. | | 4,317 | |
| Specialties............................................ | | 976,451 | |
| Lace....................................................... | | 2,200 | |
| Miscellaneous .............................................. | | 3,452 | − 120 |
| Total ................................................. | 2,841,844 | 8,434,268 | − 375,004 |
| **Food stuffs:** | | | |
| Lard....................................................... | 420,246 | | − 66,008 |
| Butter, margarine, etc ...................................... | 24,600 | 4 | − 105 |
| Chocolate .................................................. | | 28,835 | |
| Fresh fish.................................................. | 21,248 | | −∙ 7,750 |
| Canned meats, bacon, etc.................................... | 350,013 | 17 | − 55,518 |
| Dried fruits................................................ | 13,787 | 74 | − 41,866 |
| Tropical fruits.............................................. | 10,660 | | − 800 |
| Wheat..................................................... | 2,888,726 | | +1,549,111 |
| Oats....................................................... | 43,322 | | − 89,932 |
| Indian corn................................................ | 76,089 | | − 64,180 |
| Oatmeal, etc............................................... | 15,465 | | − 8,235 |
| Flour...................................................... | 3,234 | | + 134 |
| Cheese .................................................... | 5,856 | 1,018,753 | + 5,856 |
| Condensed milk............................................. | 40 | 35,184 | + 40 |
| Soup stuffs................................................ | 4,284 | 14,798 | + 1,580 |
| Tobacco and snuff........................................... | 882,980 | 1,300 | + 42,322 |
| Cigars und cigarettes........................................ | 11,220 | 7,985 | −∙ 880 |
| Molasses and sirup.......................................... | 47,348 | | + 4,068 |
| Natural wine in bottles...................................... | 12 | 2,488 | + 12 |
| Cognac, rum, etc., in bottles................................ | 280 | 11,625 | + 192 |
| Liqueurs ................................................... | | 6,312 | |

*Commerce with the United States during the year ended December 31, 1901*—Continued.

| Articles. | Imports. | Exports. | Increase (+) or decrease (−) of imports over 1899. |
|---|---|---|---|
| **Food stuffs—Continued.** | | | |
| Wine in casks .................................. | $4,015 | $2,225 | −   $4,039 |
| Cognac, rum, etc., in casks................. | 900 | 869 | −   2,484 |
| Miscellaneous ................................. | 6,222 | 2,572 | −   9,530 |
| Total .................. | 4,830,498 | 1,133,041 | +1,252,018 |
| **Leather and shoes:** | | | |
| Sole leather ................................... | 222,060 | .......... | +   1,140 |
| Harness, strap, and calf leather............ | 1,632 | 13,961 | +   1,428 |
| Other kinds ................................... | 613,700 | 2 | +  168,780 |
| Shoes, finished ............................... | 29,040 | 37 | +  12,720 |
| India-rubber shoes ........................... | 30,690 | .......... | +  10,120 |
| Miscellaneous ................................. | 1,664 | 21 | −   3,044 |
| Total .................. | 898,786 | 14,041 | +  191,144 |
| **Machines and vehicles:** ................... | | | |
| Dynamo-electrical machines.................. | 19,614 | .......... | −   1,207 |
| Steam boilers ................................. | 2,568 | .......... | −     212 |
| Agricultural machinery....................... | 290,311 | 2 | −  50,808 |
| Sewing machines.............................. | 16,080 | 243 | +   6,300 |
| Knitting and embroidery machines ......... | 630 | 64,005 | −   2,450 |
| Weaving machines............................ | 4,060 | 11,905 | +   4,060 |
| Machine implements.......................... | 40,290 | 161 | −   3,448 |
| Machine pieces................................ | 18,188 | .......... | +   5,504 |
| Driving belts ................................. | 3,437 | .......... | +   3,437 |
| Carriages and sleighs......................... | 5,520 | .......... | +   5,520 |
| Bicycles ....................................... | 41,720 | .......... | −  17,640 |
| Miscellaneous ................................. | 74,764 | 13,438 | −  91,416 |
| Total .................. | 442,172 | 89,754 | −  141,765 |
| **Metals:** | | | |
| Aluminum ..................................... | .......... | 4,309 | .......... |
| Iron ore ....................................... | 9,116 | .......... | +   2,221 |
| Iron castings .................................. | 78,104 | 65 | −  48,747 |
| Tubes .......................................... | 7,571 | .......... | −  52,480 |
| Forged iron— | | | |
| Rough..................................... | 3,762 | .......... | +     385 |
| Utensils .................................. | 32,910 | 676 | −   2,530 |
| Tinned, etc. .............................. | 15,420 | 40,575 | +   4,880 |
| Nickeled, etc. ............................ | 6,740 | 336 | +   1,106 |
| Jewelers' tools. ............................... | .......... | 3,266 | .......... |
| Copper and brass— | | | |
| In bars .................................... | 166,864 | .......... | −   4,702 |
| Cast ....................................... | 10,356 | 675 | −   5,207 |
| Jewelry ....................................... | 6,078 | 5,333 | +   3,051 |
| Miscellaneous ................................. | 7,665 | 812 | +  13,370 |
| Total .................. | 339,086 | 56,097 | −  89,123 |
| **Minerals:** | | | |
| Lime, potter's earth, etc .................... | 5,583 | .......... | +   1,482 |
| Precious stones, unmounted ................. | .......... | 229,612 | .......... |
| Asphalt........................................ | 108 | 16,680 | −      12 |
| Petroleum and biproducts.................... | 1,622,282 | .......... | −  59,483 |
| Mineral oils ................................... | 71,385 | .......... | +   4,940 |
| Miscellaneous ................................. | 4,590 | 593 | +   1,745 |
| Total .................. | 1,703,848 | 246,885 | −  51,328 |
| **Science and art:** | | | |
| Books and maps............................... | 4,900 | 17,702 | +     700 |
| Pictures, engravings, etc .................... | 10,045 | 17,151 | +   5,685 |
| Musical instruments.......................... | 6,914 | 756 | +   1,110 |
| Scientific instruments........................ | 22,045 | 22,154 | +  12,989 |
| Electrical apparata........................... | 24,029 | 53 | +  11,868 |
| Surgical instruments......................... | 16,427 | 116 | +  11,482 |
| Miscellaneous ................................. | 1,064 | 2,089 | −     216 |
| Total .................. | 85,424 | 59,971 | +  20,604 |
| **Silks:** | | | |
| Raw silk....................................... | .......... | 2,020 | .......... |
| Thread— | | | |
| Untwisted ................................ | .......... | 162,017 | .......... |
| Twisted ................................... | .......... | 611,249 | .......... |
| Dyed ...................................... | .......... | 4,910 | .......... |
| Bolting cloth.................................. | .......... | 241,586 | .......... |
| Silk in piece................................... | .......... | 1,778,031 | .......... |

*Commerce with the United States during the year ended December 31, 1901*—Continued.

| Articles. | Imports. | Exports. | Increase (+) or decrease (−) of imports over 1899. |
|---|---|---|---|
| **Silks—Continued.** | | | |
| Half silk in piece.... | $39 | $671,973 | + $39 |
| Shawls, scarfs, etc.... | | 2,843 | ............ |
| Ribbons .... | | 570,162 | + 4 |
| Half silk.... | 4 | 388,921 | ............ |
| Embroideries.... | | 264,550 | ............ |
| Silk worked with precious metals.... | | 20,476 | ............ |
| Miscellaneous.... | 1,550 | 2,427 | − 3,101 |
| Total .... | 1,593 | 4,721,115 | − 3,058 |
| **Straw:** | | | |
| Braids.... | | 139,335 | ............ |
| Fine work.... | | 28,482 | − 440 |
| Total .... | | 162,817 | − 440 |
| **Textile goods:** | | | |
| Laces and embroideries.... | | 40,601 | ............ |
| Rubber manufactures.... | 30,956 | | + 11,956 |
| Miscellaneous.... | 1,830 | 7,081 | + 98 |
| Total .... | 32,786 | 47,682 | + 12,054 |
| **Wood:** | | | |
| Oak staves.... | 5,317 | | − 4,727 |
| Boards.... | 13,344 | | + 4,596 |
| Rough.... | 7,982 | | + 1,857 |
| Sawn.... | 227,467 | | − 5,093 |
| Furniture .... | 31,840 | 66 | + 10,870 |
| Wood carvings.... | | 8,513 | ............ |
| Brush handles.... | | 3,713 | ............ |
| Miscellaneous.... | 7,205 | 1,886 | − 2,240 |
| Total .... | 293,105 | 14,178 | + 5,263 |
| **Sundries:** | | | |
| Fodder .... | 4,815 | | − 1,857 |
| Artificial manures.... | 49,717 | | + 49,717 |
| Grass and clover seeds.... | 6,256 | | + 9,560 |
| Oils in barrels.... | 273,278 | | + 11,692 |
| Tallow .... | 16,809 | | + 2,444 |
| Fish oils, bludder, etc.... | 29,169 | 552 | + 4,469 |
| Printing and writing paper.... | 3,720 | 6,364 | + 2,680 |
| Horses.... | 4,350 | | − 13,510 |
| Ironmongery.... | 14,040 | 4,723 | + 5,720 |
| Writing and drawing materials.... | 6,804 | 31 | + 4,284 |
| Antiquities.... | | 4,362 | ............ |
| Sundries.... | 10,337 | 6,263 | − 2,844 |
| Total .... | 417,815 | 22,295 | + 53,135 |

RÉSUMÉ.

| Articles. | Imports. | Exports. | Increase (+) or decrease (−) of imports over 1900. |
|---|---|---|---|
| Animal products.... | $63,019 | $128,978 | + $6,559 |
| Chemicals.... | 228,151 | 793,073 | −− 28,875 |
| Clocks and watches.... | 83,121 | 1,229,338 | − 2,778 |
| Clothing .... | 712 | 432,649 | − 344 |
| Cotton.... | 2,841,844 | 8,431,268 | − 375,004 |
| Foodstuffs.... | 4,830,498 | 1,133,041 | +1,252,013 |
| Leather and shoes.... | 898,786 | 14,011 | + 191,144 |
| Machines and vehicles.... | 442,172 | 89,754 | −− 141,765 |
| Metals.... | 339,086 | 56,097 | − 89,123 |
| Minerals.... | 1,703,848 | 246,885 | − 51,328 |
| Science and art.... | 85,424 | 59,971 | + 20,604 |
| Silks.... | 1,593 | 4,721,115 | − 3,058 |
| Straw .... | | 162,817 | − 440 |
| Textile goods.... | 32,786 | 47,682 | + 12,054 |
| Wood.... | 293,105 | 14,178 | + 5,263 |
| Sundries .... | 417,815 | 22,295 | + 53,135 |
| Total .... | 12,261,960 | 17,586,182 | + 848,067 |

*Imports into Switzerland during the six months ended June 30, 1902, and for the corresponding period of 1901.*

| Articles. | Imports. | | Increase (+) or decrease (−). |
|---|---|---|---|
| | 1902. | 1901. | |
| Agricultural products | $815,456 | $645,262 | + $170,194 |
| Aluminum | 10,585 | 13,902 | − 3,317 |
| Animal products | 971,622 | 982,359 | − 10,787 |
| Beer, wines, etc | 3,037,638 | 2,716,310 | + 321,328 |
| Chemicals | 2,717,262 | 2,337,982 | + 379,280 |
| Copper | 1,274,222 | 1,360,678 | − 86,456 |
| Cotton | 7,443,718 | 6,489,789 | + 953,929 |
| Dyes | 722,783 | 694,029 | + 28,754 |
| Food stuffs, tobacco | 23,812,873 | 22,142,082 | +1,670,791 |
| Glass | 517,878 | 484,629 | + 33,249 |
| Iron | 6,075,055 | 5,215,883 | + 859,172 |
| Lead | 236,477 | 230,276 | + 6,201 |
| Leather and shoes | 2,697,454 | 2,343,075 | + 354,379 |
| Linen | 1,345,736 | 1,194,097 | + 151,639 |
| Live stock | 4,704,588 | 4,100,950 | + 603,638 |
| Machines and vehicles | 2,605,138 | 2,752,457 | − 147,319 |
| Metals | 13,768 | 16,536 | − 2,768 |
| Precious | 4,477,196 | 5,411,598 | − 934,402 |
| Millinery | 2,465,377 | 2,453,115 | + 12,262 |
| Mineral matter | 8,069,746 | 8,026,295 | + 43,451 |
| Nickel | 100,020 | 117,290 | − 17,270 |
| Oils and fat | 1,510,753 | 1,319,289 | + 191,464 |
| Paper | 814,428 | 778,370 | + 36,058 |
| Pharmaceutical objects | 542,415 | 478,867 | + 63,548 |
| Pottery | 511,529 | 487,936 | + 28,598 |
| Rubber | 337,459 | 304,747 | + 32,712 |
| Science and art | 1,745,986 | 1,842,062 | − 96,076 |
| Silk | 15,238,946 | 14,125,224 | +1,113,722 |
| Straw | 248,806 | 215,409 | + 33,397 |
| Tin | 546,220 | 429,676 | + 116,544 |
| Waste and manures | 1,151,442 | 1,194,247 | − 42,805 |
| Watches and clocks | 69,452 | 107,682 | − 38,230 |
| Parts | 228,156 | 248,583 | − 20,377 |
| Wood | 2,523,387 | 2,489,322 | + 34,065 |
| Wool | 5,258,800 | 4,613,433 | + 645,367 |
| Zinc | 161,102 | 153,333 | + 7,769 |
| Miscellaneous | 793,425 | 813,734 | − 20,309 |
| Total | 105,796,898 | 99,330,458 | +6,466,440 |

*Exports from Switzerland during the six months ended June 30, 1902, and for the corresponding period of 1901.*

| Articles. | Exports. | | Increase (+) or decrease (−). |
|---|---|---|---|
| | 1902. | 1901. | |
| Agricultural products | $64,371 | $56,180 | + $8,191 |
| Aluminum | 143,197 | 135,583 | + 7,614 |
| Animal products | 1,239,213 | 1,229,516 | + 9,697 |
| Beer, wines, etc | 66,519 | 77,078 | − 10,559 |
| Chemicals | 713,012 | 658,321 | + 54,691 |
| Copper | 206,235 | 188,812 | + 17,423 |
| Cotton | 16,201,845 | 15,078,817 | +1,123,028 |
| Dyes | 1,635,265 | 1,469,368 | + 165,897 |
| Food stuffs, tobacco | 10,433,045 | 10,137,595 | + 295,450 |
| Glass | 41,118 | 39,483 | + 1,635 |
| Iron | 766,607 | 701,561 | + 65,046 |
| Lead | 26,789 | 26,220 | + 569 |
| Leather and shoes | 931,777 | 1,160,800 | − 229,023 |
| Linen | 190,857 | 164,838 | + 26,019 |
| Live stock | 1,148,776 | 995,462 | + 153,314 |
| Machines and vehicles | 4,452,128 | 4,503,498 | − 51,370 |
| Metals | 206 | 924 | − 718 |
| Precious | 1,618,015 | 1,681,639 | − 63,624 |
| Millinery | 1,191,844 | 1,139,640 | + 52,204 |
| Mineral matter | 532,222 | 497,556 | + 34,666 |
| Nickel | 10,287 | 9,188 | + 1,149 |
| Oils and fat | 51,470 | 53,755 | − 2,285 |
| Paper | 326,554 | 330,081 | − 3,527 |
| Pharmaceutical objects | 712,807 | 640,229 | + 72,578 |
| Pottery | 77,810 | 65,190 | + 12,620 |
| Rubber | 146,670 | 147,915 | − 1,245 |
| Science and art | 908,630 | 913,629 | − 4,999 |
| Silk | 24,881,745 | 23,670,293 | +1,211,452 |

*Exports from Switzerland during the six months ended June 30, 1902, and for the corresponding period of 1901*—Continued.

| Articles. | Exports. | | Increase (+) or decrease (−). |
|---|---|---|---|
| | 1902. | 1901. | |
| Straw | $1,122,185 | $1,067,341 | + 54,844 |
| Tin | 28,180 | 20,205 | + 7,975 |
| Waste and manures | 375,057 | 368,997 | + 6,060 |
| Watches and clocks | 10,090,851 | 11,135,077 | −1,044,226 |
| Parts | 713,257 | 716,382 | − 3,125 |
| Wood | 639,711 | 616,420 | + 23,291 |
| Wool | 1,685,406 | 1,758,387 | − 72,981 |
| Zinc | 19,069 | 17,546 | + 1,523 |
| Miscellaneous | 177,621 | 145,848 | + 31,773 |
| Total | 83,570,351 | 81,619,274 | +1,951,077 |

*Trade of Switzerland with the United States for the six months ended June 30, 1902.*

| Articles. | Imports. | Exports. | Articles. | Imports. | Exports. |
|---|---|---|---|---|---|
| **Animals and animal products:** | | | **Foodstuffs:** | | |
| Horses | $3,300 | | Lard | $123,758 | |
| Rawhides | 781 | $28,690 | Butter | 9,148 | |
| Bladders, etc | 26,031 | 205 | Chocolate | | $9,776 |
| | 30,112 | 28,895 | Preserved meats | 125,410 | 7 |
| | | | Dried fruits | 4,745 | |
| **Agricultural products:** | | | Wheat | 1,824,587 | |
| Grass and clover seed | 5,506 | | Oats | 8,894 | |
| | | | Maize | 1,511 | |
| **Chemicals:** | | | Oatmeal | 6,786 | |
| Benzine, naphtha, etc | | 7,596 | Flour | 2,090 | |
| Glue— | | | Cheese | | 544,065 |
| Prepared | 141 | 3,361 | Condensed milk | | 13,606 |
| Raw | 756 | | Tobacco | 355,410 | |
| Olein | 600 | | Cigars and cigarettes | 2,411 | 3,429 |
| Tartar, raw | | 1,110 | Molasses and sirup | 14,401 | |
| Terebinth | 9,585 | | Natural wines | 852 | 3,814 |
| | 11,082 | 12,067 | Spirits | 456 | 4,260 |
| | | | Liqueurs | | 4,985 |
| **Clothing:** | | | | 2,480,460 | 583,892 |
| Cotton— | | | **Leather:** | | |
| Suits | | 584 | Sole leather | 77,778 | |
| Hosiery | | 97,697 | Harness and strap leather | 125 | 10,439 |
| Underclothing | | 897 | Other fine leather | 368,299 | 3,983 |
| Hats, etc | | 2,076 | Fine shoes | 56,259 | 254 |
| Silk— | | | | 502,461 | 14,676 |
| Clothing | 34 | 3,819 | **Linen:** | | |
| Hosiery | | 83,576 | Laces | | 10,747 |
| Woolen hosiery | | 23,004 | **Machines and vehicles:** | | |
| | 34 | 211,603 | Agricultural machines | 42,540 | |
| | | | Grinding machines | 1,380 | |
| **Coloring matter:** | | | Embroidery machines | | 49,964 |
| Extracts of coloring matter | 6,256 | 10,216 | Weaving machines | 25 | 3,432 |
| Colors from tar | | 377,380 | Machine tools | 11,176 | |
| | 6,256 | 387,596 | Other machines | 29,554 | 8,365 |
| | | | Machine pieces | 8,356 | |
| **Cotton:** | | | Driving belts | 1,611 | |
| Raw | 1,733,718 | | Bicycles, etc | 20,262 | 102 |
| Waste | 638 | | | 114,904 | 61,863 |
| Twisted thread | | 1,474 | | | |
| Bleached threads | | 9,651 | **Metals:** | | |
| Dyed threads | | 932 | Lead | 2,919 | |
| Threads on bobbins | | 1,126 | Iron, worked | 77,196 | 21,772 |
| Tulle | | 1,686 | Watchmakers' tools | | 1,711 |
| Heavy tissues | 384 | 3,601 | Copper and brass | 92,666 | 776 |
| Light tissues | | 15,628 | Precious metals | 695 | 2,251 |
| Bleached tissues | | 55,204 | | 173,476 | 26,510 |
| Colored tissues | | 19,164 | | | |
| Laces | | 175,323 | **Minerals:** | | |
| Ribbons | | 7,257 | Stones for polishing | | 569 |
| Crochet embroideries | | 365,986 | Precious stones, unmounted | | 114,040 |
| Other embroideries | | 3,657,545 | Asphalt | 1 | 8,400 |
| | 1,731,740 | 4,315,577 | | | |

*Trade of Switzerland with the United States for the six months ended June 30, 1902—Cont'd.*

| Articles. | Imports. | Exports. | Articles. | Imports. | Exports. |
|---|---|---|---|---|---|
| **Minerals—Continued.** | | | **Straw—Continued.** | | |
| Petroleum.......... | $719,382 | .......... | Fine goods ......... | .......... | $15,548 |
| Mineral oils and tar . | 37,418 | .......... | | | |
| | | | | .......... | 68,027 |
| | 756,801 | $123,009 | **Waste and manures:** | | |
| **Oils and fats:** | | | Concentrated fodder. | $54,096 | .......... |
| Salad oils, etc ...... | 2,886 | .......... | Rags............... | 40 | .......... |
| Engine oils.......... | 121,212 | .......... | Raw artificial ma- | | |
| Tallow .............. | 12,308 | .......... | nures............. | 11,859 | .......... |
| | 136,356 | .......... | | 65,995 | .......... |
| **Paper:** | | | **Watches and clocks:** | | |
| Dried fibers ......... | 563 | .......... | Musical boxes, etc... | 190 | 44,272 |
| **Rubber:** | | | Nickel watches, pe- | | |
| Rubber threads ..... | 12,960 | .......... | dometers, etc..... | 307 | 37,363 |
| | | | Silver watches ...... | .......... | 73,905 |
| **Science and arts:** | | | Gold watches........ | 82 | 52,465 |
| Books .............. | 3,801 | 6,515 | Chronographs, etc... | .......... | 15,963 |
| Pictures and engrav- | | | Watch movements .. | 1,185 | 158,043 |
| ings .............. | 8,181 | 4,712 | Watch cases— | | |
| Pianos, harmoniums, | | | Nickel.......... | 21,335 | 341 |
| etc ............... | 2,280 | .......... | Gold............ | 1,772 | 1,545 |
| Scientific instru- | | | Finished pieces of | | |
| ments ............ | 5,772 | 9,963 | watches .......... | .......... | 75,679 |
| Electrical appli- | | | | | |
| ances.............. | 2,693 | 2,002 | | 24,771 | 454,576 |
| | 22,727 | 23,212 | **Wood:** | | |
| | | | Sawn oak.......... | 1,490 | .......... |
| **Silks:** | | | Planks, etc ....... | 191 | .......... |
| Raw silk ............ | .......... | 586,738 | Furniture .......... | 1,363 | 3,124 |
| Silk waste .......... | 2,007 | .......... | Carvings .......... | .......... | 1,989 |
| Tissue and cloth .... | 10 | 1,280,336 | Light wood for | | |
| Ribbons, silk and | | | brooms .......... | .......... | 2,041 |
| half silk .......... | .......... | 675,805 | | 3,044 | 7,104 |
| Embroideries, | | | | | |
| scarfs.............. | .......... | 86,045 | **Miscellaneous:** | | |
| Silk worked with | | | Woolen threads ..... | .......... | 246 |
| precious stones .... | .......... | 7,888 | Ironmongery........ | 5,730 | 630 |
| | 2,017 | 2,636,812 | Writing materials ... | 1,000 | 2 |
| **Straw:** | | | | 6,730 | 878 |
| Plaitings ........... | .......... | 52,479 | | | |

## SUMMARY.

| | Imports | Exports | | Imports | Exports |
|---|---|---|---|---|---|
| Animals and animal | | | Oils and fats.......... | $136,356 | .......... |
| products............. | $30,112 | $28,895 | Paper................ | 563 | .......... |
| Agricultural products.. | 5,506 | .......... | Rubber.............. | 12,960 | .......... |
| Chemicals............ | 11,082 | 12,067 | Science and art........ | 22,727 | $23,212 |
| Clothing............. | 34 | 211,603 | Silks................ | 2,017 | 2,636,812 |
| Colors .............. | 6,256 | 387,596 | Straw............... | .......... | 68,027 |
| Cotton.............. | 1,784,740 | 4,315,577 | Waste and manures ... | 65,995 | .......... |
| Foodstuffs ........... | 2,480,460 | 583,892 | Watches and clocks ... | 24,771 | 454,576 |
| Leather ............. | 502,461 | 14,676 | Wood............... | 3,044 | 7,104 |
| Linen ............... | .......... | 10,747 | Sundries ............ | 6,730 | 878 |
| Machines and vehicles.. | 114,904 | 61,863 | | | |
| Metals.............. | 173,476 | 26,510 | Total.............. | 6,090,995 | 8,967,044 |
| Minerals ............ | 756,801 | 123,009 | | | |

*Swiss post-office statistics, 1901.*

| | |
|---|---|
| Number of post-offices in Switzerland.............................. | 1,587 |
| Branch offices: | |
| Post-office business alone ................................. | 1,325 |
| Others.................................................. | 653 |
| Agencies abroad......................................... | 13 |
| Total .................................................. | 3,578 |
| Employees: | |
| Clerical staff ............................................ | 3,571 |
| Other staff (postmen, conductors, etc.) ................... | 6,268 |
| Total .................................................. | 9,839 |

Business in 1901:

Letters—
Inland ........................................................$102, 223, 725
Outward....................................................... 20, 831, 532
Post cards—
Inland ........................................................ 43, 432, 285
Outward....................................................... 17, 388, 638
Printed matter—
Inland ........................................................ 39, 113, 448
Outward....................................................... 9, 302, 598
Samples—
Inland ........................................................ 1, 079, 602
Outward....................................................... 1, 022, 801
Newspapers, inland ............................................ 123, 132, 631
Business papers, outward ...................................... 136, 500
Registered letters—
Inland ........................................................ 3, 450, 479
Outward....................................................... 1, 493, 526
Summons served, inland......................................... 261, 868
Legal notices, inland.......................................... 37, 980
Letters, etc., in transit...................................... 1, 545, 150

Total........................................................ 364, 452, 763

*Receipts and disbursements for 1899, 1900, and 1901.*

| Description. | 1899. | 1900. | 1901. |
|---|---|---|---|
| Receipts................................................... | $6, 795, 462 | $7, 226, 163 | $7, 555, 725 |
| Disbursements ............................................. | 6, 237, 774 | 6, 686, 092 | 6, 943, 019 |
| Balance ................................................. | 557, 688 | 540, 071 | 612, 706 |

*Growth of the Swiss postal system since 1850.*

| Articles. | 1850. | 1860. | 1870. | 1880. | 1890. | 1900. |
|---|---|---|---|---|---|---|
| Letters: | | | | | | |
| Inland........number.. | 11, 420, 971 | 19, 681, 705 | 34, 755, 480 | 46, 590, 793 | 62, 850, 755 | 99, 309, 994 |
| Outward...........do.... | a 5, 319, 263 | 7, 107, 141 | 5, 583, 367 | 9, 444, 708 | 13, 098, 842 | 21, 139, 708 |
| Printed matter and samples: | | | | | | |
| Inland........number.. | a 1, 442, 341 | 1, 999, 454 | 4, 675, 395 | 10, 745, 514 | 21, 024, 367 | 38, 828, 173 |
| Outward...........do.... | | b 2, 301, 991 | 1, 910, 097 | 4, 385, 068 | 5, 822, 364 | 9, 497, 386 |
| Post cards: | | | | | | |
| Inland ...........do.... | | | 678, 476 | 6, 705, 977 | 12, 914, 356 | 39, 606, 414 |
| Outward...........do.... | | | c 22, 419 | 1, 812, 848 | 4, 062, 045 | 15, 657, 275 |
| Parcels...............do.... | 2, 099, 368 | 4, 135, 045 | 4, 756, 515 | 7, 029, 161 | 11, 560, 358 | 19, 258, 661 |
| "Pay on delivery" (remboursement).number.. | | d 244, 405 | 335, 989 | 417, 458 | 899, 938 | 1, 864, 927 |
| "Pay on delivery" (remboursement). amount.. | | $604, 416 | $841, 619 | $1, 301, 695 | $2, 202, 357 | $4, 343, 813 |
| Letters: | | | | | | |
| "Pay on delivery" (remboursement).number.. | | d 882, 348 | 1, 071, 401 | 2, 052, 216 | 3, 161, 641 | 6, 663, 757 |
| "Pay on delivery" (remboursement).amount.. | | $637, 129 | $786, 862 | $1, 780, 920 | $3, 167, 353 | $7, 262, 284 |
| Newspaper subscriptions, number .................... | 8, 481, 060 | 17, 629, 427 | 33, 167, 537 | 50, 128, 836 | 75, 796, 128 | 124, 286, 308 |
| Newspaper subscriptions, amount .................... | $18, 322 | $32, 594 | $53, 146 | $113, 355 | $162, 733 | $248, 565 |
| Stamps sold........number.. | | 1, 216, 586 | 2, 886, 707 | 8, 990, 670 | 14, 544, 749 | 26, 423, 233 |
| Stamped envelopes sold, number................... | | e 351, 743 | 1, 289, 604 | 585, 745 | 10, 618 | f 1, 482 |
| Post cards sold.....number.. | | | $5, 219 | 487, 215 | 886, 944 | 1, 450, 063 |
| Money orders sold....do.... | | | g 142, 801 | 567, 307 | 753, 493 | 1, 026, 576 |
| Postal orders sold .....do.... | | | h 25, 440 | 67, 239 | 109, 094 | ............ |
| Receipts ...................... | $1, 037, 774 | $1, 383, 382 | $1, 900, 768 | $3, 102, 688 | $4, 836, 004 | $7, 226, 163 |
| Expenditures ................ | $886, 132 | $1, 150, 098 | $1, 676, 503 | $2, 700, 315 | $4, 381, 731 | $6, 686, 092 |
| Net profit.............. | $151, 642 | $233, 284 | $224, 265 | $402, 373 | $454, 273 | $540, 071 |

a Commenced in 1855.
b Commenced in 1863.
c Commenced in 1873.
d Commenced in 1866.

e Commenced in 1867.
f Abolished in 1898.
g Commenced in 1876.
h Commenced in 1875.

### Swiss telegraphic statistics.

Number of telegraph offices .................................................... 1,973
Offices open in summer only .................................................... 82
Railway telegraph offices ...................................................... 65
Telegraph receiving offices .................................................... 78

    Total ..................................................................... 2,198

Employees:
    Permanent staff ....................................................... 2,812
    Provisional staff ..................................................... 174

    Total ..................................................................... 2,986

### Telegraph lines.

| Owned by— | Lines. | Wire. |
|---|---|---|
|  | *Miles.* | *Miles.* |
| Government | 3,957 | 13,251 |
| Railways | 749 | 7,789 |
| Private | 678 | 1,280 |
| Total | 5,384 | 22,320 |

### Number of messages in 1901.

| Countries. | Ordinary. | Transit. | Total. |
|---|---|---|---|
| Inland | 3,234,248 | 680,746 | 3,914,994 |
|  | Outward. | Inward. |  |
| Foreign: |  |  |  |
| Germany | 290,358 | 278,874 | 569,232 |
| France | 227,058 | 240,418 | 467,471 |
| Italy | 102,484 | 103,096 | 205,580 |
| Austria | 65,351 | 64,823 | 130,174 |
| England | 56,343 | 71,272 | 127,615 |
| Russia | 21,031 | 23,414 | 44,445 |
| Belgium | 22,084 | 21,720 | 43,804 |
| United States | 15,921 | 19,954 | 35,875 |
| Holland | 11,289 | 10,797 | 22,086 |
| Spain | 7,519 | 7,379 | 14,898 |
| Egypt | 3,152 | 4,169 | 7,321 |
| Algiers and Tunis | 2,486 | 2,984 | 5,470 |
| British India | 2,340 | 2,688 | 5,028 |
| Total | 827,411 | 851,588 | 5,598,993 |

### Accounts for 1900 and 1901.

| Description. | 1900. | 1901. |
|---|---|---|
| Receipts | $606,316 | $605,756 |
| Disbursements | 608,790 | 626,060 |
| Loss | 2,474 | 20,304 |

### Swiss telephone statistics.

Number of telephone nets ....................................................... 324
Telephone stations ............................................................. 44,203
Subscribers .................................................................... 39,988

Employees:
    Permanent staff ....................................................... 662
    Provisional staff ..................................................... 154

                                              816

*Telephone lines.*

| Owned by— | Lines. | Wire. |
|---|---|---|
| | | *Miles.* |
| Government | 8,795 | 98,795 |
| Other | 51 | 241 |
| Total | 8,846 | 99,036 |

*Business in 1901.*

| | |
|---|---|
| Local conversations | 21,935,222 |
| Interurban conversations | 4,735,159 |
| International conversations | 95,903 |
| Conversations with phonogram | 3,711 |
| Forwarding of telegrams per telephone | 233,002 |
| | 27,003,997 |

*Accounts for 1900 and 1901.*

| Description. | 1900. | 1901. |
|---|---|---|
| Receipts | $1,245,971 | $1,311,262 |
| Disbursements | 1,423,041 | 1,499,868 |
| Loss | 177,070 | 188,591 |

*Swiss customs statistics.*

| Description. | 1899. | 1900. | 1901. |
|---|---|---|---|
| **REVENUE.** | | | |
| Import duties | $10,115,737 | $9,498,341 | $9,165,075 |
| Export duties | 26,706 | 26,992 | 27,037 |
| Statistical charges | 29,852 | 31,955 | 32,286 |
| Warehousing, etc., charges | 4,325 | 3,914 | 3,842 |
| Fines and penalties | 2,862 | 2,876 | 2,959 |
| Siezed goods | 9,230 | 10,045 | 11,438 |
| Sale of statistics, formulas, etc | 20,156 | 19,190 | 19,357 |
| Inland spirit duties | 9,483 | 8,689 | 8,396 |
| Total revenue | 10,218,351 | 9,602,002 | 9,294,390 |
| **ARTICLES.** | | | |
| Agricultural products | 8,151 | 8,901 | 9,481 |
| Animals and animal products | 316,672 | 296,445 | 290,909 |
| Chemicals | 342,483 | 368,854 | 862,928 |
| Glassware | 263,178 | 248,075 | 254,684 |
| Leather and shoes | 209,561 | 198,885 | 195,647 |
| Machinery, etc | 361,598 | 292,724 | 232,468 |
| Metals | 959,201 | 914,112 | 766,382 |
| Minerals | 396,805 | 389,699 | 879,982 |
| Oils and fats | 67,276 | 61,173 | 63,173 |
| Paper | 224,926 | 225,810 | 227,499 |
| Provisions | 4,434,836 | 4,120,927 | 4,134,294 |
| Science and arts | 62,999 | 61,725 | 61,026 |
| Stoneware | 194,186 | 174,115 | 159,354 |
| Textile goods | 1,682,031 | 1,618,625 | 1,557,055 |
| Waste and manures | 17,664 | 16,100 | 14,387 |
| Wood | 382,601 | 340,758 | 314,027 |
| Sundries | 172,124 | 166,512 | 165,879 |
| Total | 10,115,737 | 9,498,341 | 9,189,075 |

*Swiss railway statistics.*

Length of railways in Switzerland:

| | Miles. |
|---|---|
| Swiss main lines | 1,451 |
| Swiss branch lines | 524 |
| Foreign lines in Switzerland and under Swiss management | 39 |
| Narrow-gauge lines | 249 |
| Narrow-gauge cog lines | 103 |
| Cable railways | 13.5 |
| Tramways | 153 |

*Rolling stock.*

| Description. | Ordinary and narrow-gauge lines. | Electric lines. | Cable and cog lines. | Tramways. |
|---|---|---|---|---|
| Locomotives | 1,228 | .......... | .......... | .......... |
| Passenger coaches: | | | | |
| Axles | 7,421 | 140 | 438 | 1,422 |
| Places | 130,447 | 1,889 | 7,356 | 21,720 |
| Postal coaches | 242 | .......... | .......... | .......... |
| Luggage vans | 573 | .......... | .......... | .......... |
| Goods wagons | 13,846 | .......... | .......... | .......... |
| Total | 158,757 | 2,029 | 7,794 | 23,142 |

*Traffic in 1901.*

Regular trains:

| | |
|---|---|
| Passenger | 542,184 |
| Mixed | 77,160 |
| Goods | 130,209 |

Special trains:

| | |
|---|---|
| Passenger | 9,055 |
| Mixed | 196 |
| Goods | 35,615 |
| Miles traveled | 17,347,227 |

*Traffic on ordinary lines.*

| | Miles. |
|---|---|
| Main lines | 1,451 |
| Branch lines | 524 |
| Foreign lines under Swiss management | 39 |
| Total | 2,014 |

*Passenger traffic.*

| Years. | Passengers. | Receipts. |
|---|---|---|
| 1900 | 54,889,499 | $10,738,944 |
| 1901 | 55,118,706 | 10,652,870 |

*Goods traffic.*

| Years. | Tons. | Value. |
|---|---|---|
| 1900 | 14,242,391 | $14,602,995 |
| 1901 | 13,520,426 | 14,240,344 |

*Average receipts per mile.*

| Years. | Passengers. | Goods. | Total. |
|---|---|---|---|
| 1900 | $5,532.1 | $7,250.7 | $12,582.8 |
| 1901 | 5,289.5 | 7,070.7 | 12,810.2 |

## ST. GALL.

Imports from the United States into the consular district of St. Gall seem inconsiderable. Among direct imports are wheat, canned meat, dried apples, and office furniture, but efforts to sell American shoes and bicycles have not met with great success.

Exports, mostly embroideries, from this consular district to the United States during the last five calendar years have been:

| | | | |
|---|---|---|---|
| 1897 | $5,734,029 | 1900 | $9,456,387 |
| 1898 | 6,297,025 | 1901 | 8,149,320 |
| 1899 | 8,996,826 | | |

As to exports of embroideries to other countries, there is much complaint, but the American market, always good, is now particularly prosperous.

The following table gives the exports of embroideries, laces, lace curtains, handkerchiefs, etc., from St. Gall to the chief countries of destination:

| Countries. | 1900. | 1901. |
|---|---|---|
| Great Britain | $6,103,230 | $5,389,655 |
| France | 1,222,266 | 1,826,270 |
| Germany | 1,270,000 | 1,282,000 |
| Spain | 710,337 | 605,990 |
| Austria | 342,570 | 374,850 |

## EXCHANGE.

The money market, which was very good during 1898, 1899, and 1900, was dull during 1901, and is still dull. Exchange rates in 1901 fell from 5 to 3¾ per cent, and have remained at this point the first seven months of 1902. For money on deposit for one year and longer, banks pay now 3½ and 3¾ per cent interest, as against 4 and 4½ per cent during the preceding two years. First-class mortgages pay from 4 to 4½ per cent.

### TAXES ON COMMERCIAL TRAVELERS, ETC.

Foreign commercial travelers doing business in Switzerland are required to take out permits which are issued for one year or for six months. The charge for the first is 150 francs ($29) and for the second, 100 francs ($19). These charges, however, are only made for retail travelers. Others have nothing to pay.

Income taxation being in force in the St. Gall consular district, no special taxes are required from merchants on their business, liquor dealers excepted. The latter must have special licenses, for which about $30 per year is charged.

### AMERICAN ENTERPRISES.

The largest embroidery establishments in this district are in the hands of American citizens, but no American labor is engaged therein. The industry is old, and in every respect up to the highest demands.

### NEW RAILROAD.

Final action is pending at Berne on the project of a new railroad to run through the Cantons of St. Gall and Thurgau, from Rapperswil to Romanshorn, a distance of about 50 miles. In all probability the plan will pass with some changes. Correspondence concerning the matter should be addressed to "Schweizerisches Eisenbahn-Departement, Berne."

J. I. McCALLUM, Consul-General.

St. GALL, *August 21, 1902.*

---

# TURKEY.

### DIRECT STEAMSHIP SERVICE.

The service between New York and Constantinople, resuscitated by the German Levant Line last February, is the means of fostering a healthy competition in freights with the British Liverpool lines. In this connection, the discrimination by the British Liverpool lines, noted by Consul-General Dickinson in previous annual reports, against exporters to the United States who failed to ship by the Liverpool companies, still exists. Quite recently, the principal shippers have renewed their agreements with the combination to ship only by its lines, and for this special benefits in the shape of drawbacks and reductions are allowed them. This explains why one of the German Levant Line steamers recently leaving this port for New York secured so little freight. The advantages of importing machinery direct from New York, and thus avoiding the handling necessary for transshipment, are obvious.

### AGRICULTURAL MACHINERY.

It is impossible as yet to give any figures of this year's sales. The harvest, however, promises to be a record one, and there is every reason to believe that the number of American agricultural machines sold will be even larger than last year. I give below a list of the implements exempted from the 8 per cent ad valorem customs duty during a period of ten years from August 17, 1901:

Plows of every kind.
Machines for cutting and binding sheaves.
Machines for mowing grass.
Machines on wheels, drawn by animals, for collecting grass and grain.
Rakes worked by animals.
"Cannon" machines, drawn by animals, for turning, airing, and drying hay.
Presses for making hay into bales.
Machines for spreading manure, drawn by animals.
Harrows of all kinds drawn by animals.
Thrashing machines worked by steam, animal, or water power.
"Locomobile" engines for driving thrashing machines.

Plows driven by steam.

Smooth and toothed rollers of every kind, drawn by animals, for rolling ground and for breaking up clods.

Iron scarifiers for breaking up clods, drawn by animals.

Iron "cultivators" drawn by animals.

Sowing machines drawn by animals.

Sifting machines for cleaning produce, worked by hand, animal, steam, or water power.

Sifting machines for sifting seed grain, worked by hand, animal, steam, or water power.

Machines for granulating maize, worked by hand, animal, steam, or water power.

Beating machines for granulating rice, worked by hand, animal, steam, or water power.

Machines for cutting straw, worked by hand, animal, steam, or water power.

Machines for preparing fodder, worked by hand, animal, steam, or water power.

Machines for cutting beets, worked by hand or animal power.

Machines resembling plows, drawn by animals, for collecting potatoes and beets.

Iron reapers with wooden handles.

"Pulverizer" spraying machines, used in the treatment of diseases attacking vines and other plants.

Centrifugal cream separators, worked by hand, animal power, water power, or steam.

Churns of modern design, made of wood or iron, worked by hand, animal power, water power, or steam.

### FREIGHT RATES.

I must reiterate the complaint, mentioned in Consul-General Dickinson's report of last year, regarding the carelessness of the American exporter in securing a reasonable rate of freight from New York to destination. One can not too forcibly impress upon the American manufacturer the fact that his ability to compete in oriental markets depends more upon the moderation of the freight charges than upon the reduction of his price by a few cents.

### EXPORTS AND IMPORTS.

No further statistics have been published by the Turkish customs since those given in the report for the year ended February 28, 1898.

The total export from this port to the United States, as shown by the invoice book for the year ended June 30, 1902, was $3,579,469.21. Compared with the figures for the previous four years, it was:

Year ended June 30—

| | |
|---|---|
| 1901 | $3,145,608.10 |
| 1900 | 3,725,268.14 |
| 1899 | 1,997,177.73 |
| 1898 | 1,678,065.55 |

The export of Turkish rugs and carpets from Constantinople to the United States reached the record total of $2,224,005.38 for the year ended June 30, 1902. The figures for the previous four years were:

Year ended June 30—

| | |
|---|---|
| 1901 | $1,661,422.93 |
| 1900 | 1,864,031.82 |
| 1899 | 925,699.67 |
| 1898 | 975,969.51 |

### PETROLEUM DEPOSIT.

The English syndicate formed to work the petroleum deposits on the shores of the sea of Marmora has failed to strike oil and has abandoned work. There is no doubt that oil exists, but prospectors have not succeeded in reaching it.

H. Doc. 305, pt 2——48

## TARIFF RATES, ETC.

There has been no change in tariff rates, customs rules, port dues and regulations, lighterage, charges, regulations as to commercial travelers, and passports since the consul-general's report, printed on page 786 in the second volume of Commercial Relations for 1899.

## HARBOR FACILITIES.

The work on the new port and quay at Haidar-Pacha is being pushed with the utmost activity, and two steamers have already been alongside to discharge material. The habor is expected to be opened to the public on the anniversary of the Sultan's accession to the throne, September 1.

## MINING ENTERPRISE.

Mining enterprise in Turkey may be said to be at a low ebb, consequent on the restrictive regulations. The council of state is said to have the question under consideration, and it will no doubt take energetic measures to correct the present state of affairs.

WM. SMITH-LYTE,
*Vice and Deputy Consul-General.*

CONSTANTINOPLE, *July 31, 1902.*

---

## SUPPLEMENTARY.

There has been no radical change in commerce and industries affecting the region in and about Constantinople since my report of 1901; but the facts I have been able to gather indicate a steady increase of American trade. Exact figures are difficult to obtain. There are several chambers of commerce in this city, but none of them are able to give definite figures of the imports from and exports to the United States or any country of Europe. The French Chamber of Commerce is the only one which prints a regular report. It furnishes a full report from its representative at Smyrna, but has only the most meager details of commerce at Constantinople.

## FRENCH TRADE REPORT.

The report from Smyrna indicates a very gratifying growth in American business, especially in agricultural implements, and the following items from the report of the French chamber may be of interest. They contain the estimates of a leading European competitor, and are therefore not likely to be unduly favorable to the United States.

### PLOWS.

The plows (the general-purpose plow, socalled, which is a small article) are imported nearly all from the United States, and sell by the thousand at 15 to 20 francs ($2.90 to $3.86) each. As regards the swivel plows, they also are imported from the United States, and are sold at 25 to 40 francs ($4.83 to $7.72) each. The Oliver plows, which are well known in this country, are also an American product.

### RAKES.

Rakes are also mostly imported from the United States, and are sold at 75 to 100 francs ($14.48 to $19.30) each, according to size and description.

### DISK DRILLS (PLANTERS).

America has also taken the lead in the sale of disk drills, prices being from 350 to 550 francs ($67.55 to $106.15) each.

### REAPERS.

Reapers are exclusively produced by the United States, and are sold at from 375 to 450 francs ($72.38 to $86.85) each.

### THRASHERS AND ENGINES.

The thrashing machines and engines, which are considered as the most important of agricultural machines, were until late years imported from England, but on account of the favorable prices and easy mode of payments allowed by the American manufacturers, they have been able to seize the business out of the hands of the English, and now supply the total demand for these machines.

### GRADERS.

France has the lead in the manufacture of this article, but America has with perseverance been able to produce similar machines.

Some of the leading agricultural machines which were imported in 1901 to Smyrna were the plows, reapers, graders, etc., as enumerated in the following statistics:

American plows, principally Oliver plows, 15,005; Greek plows, 7,804; English plows, 4,732; French plows, 2; American reaping machines, 209; English reaping machines, 2; corn shellers, all from America, 75; graders, from different countries, 12.

The total value of agricultural machines and implements imported to Smyrna in 1901 was 501,766 piasters ($22,078) worth of American goods; 127,085 piasters ($5,592) worth of English goods; 102,240 piasters ($4,499) worth of French goods; 50,726 piasters ($2,232) worth of Greek goods; 31,548 piasters ($1,388) worth of German goods; 1,188 piasters ($52) worth of Austrian goods; total value of goods imported into Smyrna from the above-mentioned countries, 814,555 piasters ($35,840.42).

It thus appears from the reports of the French Chamber of Commerce, whose correspondents are well-known business men of Smyrna, that at that place, the principal port of the Empire for the distribution of agricultural implements and machines, the sales of American goods exceed in value those of all the European countries combined.

The report refers to the sale of American thrashing machines and engines, which monopolize the market, but does not give particulars. Ten of these outfits were furnished to the ministry of agriculture by the American-Oriental agency; one was sold to a firm in Beirut. These machines have been busy thrashing grain throughout the country, and have astonished the peasantry with the rapidity and cleanliness of their work. I hear some complaints, however, that they crack the wheat and break the straw more than was expected, but the experts claim that with a few slight changes this difficulty will be overcome next year.

### INCREASE OF AMERICAN TRADE.

While I am unable to obtain exact figures as to the increase of American trade at this port during the past year, the indications of such increase are unmistakable. This opinion is shared by all the importers of American goods. A number of established concerns, which have for years been engaged in importing English, French, and German manufactures, are becoming large purchasers of American goods.

The combination of American exporters, which was organized in 1899 to exploit the Turkish markets, now finds it profitable to keep a New York representative here and in near-by cities a considerable part of the time.    When this enterprise was started, it was with the greatest difficulty that we were able to interest reliable business men of this city in the project, but now they are seeking the American exporters instead of the latter seeking them.    A New York representative, who arrived here a few days ago, reports that he finds some of the best concerns seeking to make substantial arrangements with the parties he represents, and those with whom the Americans have been doing business are anxious to increase trade relations.    These exporters sold to one concern here during the last year goods to the amount of about $130,000, and also to a single concern in Smyrna goods to the amount of about $50,000.    Their aggregate sales in Beirut, Salonica, and other cities also show a marked increase.    The ball has been fairly set rolling, and will go on now with its own momentum.

One American concern dealing in this market gives the totals of its sales of three articles during the last year as follows: Edible grease (a cheap butter used by the peasants), $200,000; rubber shoes, $30,000; American leather, between $30,000 and $40,000.

The official report of the director of customs of the imports and exports for the Ottoman Empire for the fiscal year March, 1898, to March, 1899, the latest obtainable figures, gives the imports from the United States as amounting in value to $192,886.84, a gain over the previous year, 1897–98, of $34,432.84.    The exports to the United States as reported amounted to $2,222,190.61, an increase over the previous year of $774,972.    These reports are always three years in arrears, and I regard them as of little value except for purposes of comparison.

### DIRECT STEAMSHIP SERVICE.

In all commercial work here during my period of service, direct steam communication between New York and the Levantine ports has seemed of paramount importance.    The heavy freight rate of the long haul by way of Liverpool and Hamburg, and the wharfage and breakage, made competition with European manufacturers on equal terms impossible.

The first direct line established in 1899 encountered the combined opposition of the four Liverpool companies sending ships to these ports, and as a result the sailings of that direct line have been very irregular.    But, as I explained in my last annual report, the low freight rates established as the result of this direct competition have been maintained.    American goods can now reach any of these ports at rates that will enable them to compete with those of European manufacture.

The increase in the volume of trade has also induced other lines to bid sharply for American business; and to this competition is probably due the satisfactory freight rates which now prevail.    The direct line of freight and passenger steamers, started by the Hamburg-American and Deutsche Levante companies last February, continues its monthly sailings.    These companies are, I understand, under contract to continue this direct service for ten years, and they hope there will be such an increase in the volume of business during the present year that they will be able to establish a fortnightly service.    This line has already secured a large percentage of American freights. This is of great importance in maintaining a direct service, as the tonnage from the United States to Turkish ports is far less than that from these ports to the United States. This line makes a close connection with steamers of the Deutsche Levante Line, from Hamburg at Malta, and transshipments are there made for ports where the direct steamers do not call. The result is a speedy and satisfactory service from New York to nearly all the Mediterranean and Black Sea ports, and the merchants using this line speak of it in the highest terms. Goods which can be transshipped at Malta reach any of the Mediterranean ports in less than thirty days. If the goods are heavy or bulky and remain on the direct steamer, which goes by way of Alexandria, about five days' additional time are consumed.

### LOCAL TRANSPORTATION FACILITIES.

There has been some preliminary work during the past summer in connection with the extension of the railroad through Asia Minor from Konia to Bagdad. The only important improvement is the splendid work of preparation which the company has done in building the Haidar Pasha breakwater, elevator, and quays. This work is practically completed. The elevator can accommodate 5,000 tons of grain. Vessels can now lie alongside the quay and receive and discharge cargo in the heaviest weather. The company aims to bring all the freight of Asia Minor the whole length of its railway and discharge it at Haidar Pasha, but it is believed that considerable shipments will continue to be made at Ismidt, at the head of the gulf bearing that name.

Panderma is, next to Ismidt, the most important port of the Marmora, and while it is the natural outlet of a large and fertile region, its commerce is seriously handicapped by lack of harbor facilities. It is now proposed to build there a stone breakwater 220 yards in length, at a cost of $110,000, but there are so many pressing demands upon Turkish finances that I have little faith in the early completion of this work

### POSTAL RATES.

During the past year, the Turkish postal department has reduced the rate of postage to all points outside of this country about 25 per cent. This has been done to take business from the foreign post-offices established in all the seaport cities of the Empire. There is also a new regulation by which a parcel sent through the Turkish post is opened in the presence of the person to whom the parcel is addressed and the customs dues paid without delay, while parcels sent through the other post-offices must be cleared at the custom-house, with considerable extra expense and delay.

### ARTICLES PROHIBITED.

There is a considerable number of articles whose importation is prohibited. These include salt, gunpowder, rifled arms, revolvers, telegraph wire, electrical plants, food products colored with chemicals, patent medicines, unless the formula has been submitted and approved, and cotton-seed oil, unless so adulterated as to prevent its use for food. This last prohibition is in the interest of the manufacturers of olive oil.

The prohibition against American pork products is still in force, though the irade excluding them is about seventeen years old. It is generally believed that nearly all the hams consumed in this country are of American origin, but they are imported by way of other countries.

### CUSTOM-HOUSE DIFFICULTIES.

As already reported, the duty on imported merchandise is 8 per cent ad valorem. In case, however, the importer finds that the valuation of the custom-house expert is too high, he has the right to pay in kind—that is, to leave 8 per cent of the merchandise with the custom-house instead of paying in cash.

Plug tobacco and cigars pay 75 per cent ad valorem duty, while agricultural machinery, which for the past ten years has been exempt from customs charges, has again been relieved from the payment of duty for a further period of ten years.

Storage duties on goods remaining at the custom-house commence on the eighth day after their arrival, and increase in a rapid ratio. All goods exported from the Ottoman Empire pay 1 per cent ad valorem. Merchandise of foreign origin which has paid the 8 per cent duty, if reexported within six months, is entitled to a drawback of 7 per cent of the duty paid. Merchandise of native production is compelled to pay 2 per cent duty when sent from one Turkish port to another; but this regulation is construed to mean that 2 per cent shall be charged each time the same merchandise is sent from one port to another.

Various treaties formally stipulate that foreign merchandise which has once paid the customs duty may circulate freely in the Empire without being obliged to pay any further tax, and until recently no further tax was imposed, but now the custom-house demands that the certificate showing that the duty was paid be deposited with the custom-house, if any part of the consignment is shipped to another port. For example, a merchant imports 100 bales of cotton goods from New York and pays duty here. He sends 11 bales to Samsoun. He pays no interportal duty, as he can show the certificate. But the custom-house keeps the certificate, and when later the merchant sends the remaining 89 bales to some other port he is obliged to pay the 2 per cent interportal duty, as he is unable to produce the certificate. These and other difficulties have injured the distributing business of Constantinople, and merchants of this city are now opening offices in Ismidt and other distributing points.

### NEW COAL MINES.

An English company with a capital of $600,000 has been formed to work the coal fields situated at Kesshan, which is about 24 miles from the harbor of Ibridgi, in the Gulf of Xeros. The coal is reported by gas companies of the United Kingdom as being equal to the celebrated "cannel" coal of England. It is proposed to build a line of rail connecting the coal mines with the sea. At present, the coal is transported by camels.

### RUG INDUSTRY.

Replying to the Department's request for information as to the increase or decrease in exports and imports, I invite attention to the extraordinary advance in the export of rugs from this market during the past year. The total exports from Constantinople to the United States during the quarter ending December 31 passed the million dollar mark—the highest ever reached—and rugs formed a large percentage of these exports. The value of rugs exported during the last quarter was about 50 per cent greater than the value of like exports during the corresponding quarter of 1901, and more than double that of the December quarter of 1900. As there seems to be an unprecedented demand for these goods in the United States, our dealers and purchasers may be interested in a brief statement covering description, quality, and price.

The four great divisions of rugs are Irans, Caucasians, Turkish, and Turkomans, and these are subdivided into different makes, each known by the name of the town where they are manufactured or merely by that of a market place.

*Irans.*—By irans are meant all kinds of Persian rugs and carpets, and they are classed as moderns and antiques.

*Modern irans.*—These are the carpets and rugs now being manufactured in the different rug-producing districts of Persia, and they constitute the bulk of the trade, as they are specially made to suit the tastes and requirements of the United States and European markets. The subdivisions of the modern Irans according to their comparative importance are: Sultanabads, Mushkiabad, Ferahans, Georevans, Heriz, Bakshaish, Kirman, Laver, Korassan, Meshed, Cain, Tourshouz, Tabriz, Sarook, Bidjar, and Sine.

The Sultanabad and Mushkiabad carpets are among the principal articles of export. They consist of three grades, the best of which, Mushkiabads, are worth from 135 to 160 piasters ($5.94 to $7.04) the square meter (10.7 square feet); the second grade, Sultanabads or Extra Persians, are worth from 75 to 90 piasters ($3.30 to $3.96) the square meter, and the third grade, Ferahans, are worth 50 to 65 piasters ($2.20 to $2.86) the square meter. The whole of the Sultanabad district, where these three grades are manufactured, has about 3,000 looms in operation, producing about 200,000 Turkish pounds ($880,000) worth of carpets annually. These carpets are serviceable as floor coverings, but have no ornamental or artistic character, and are not prized by the connoisseur. They are exported in large quantities to the United States and European markets on account of their moderate cost and comparative durability. The total amount imported yearly into the United States, either direct from Persia (transit Constantinople or London) or reexported from Constantinople, can be fairly estimated in value at about 55,000 pounds Turkish ($242,000).

*Heriz.*—The second subdivision is the Heriz carpets. These are mostly known in trade as Gheorevans, and have of late acquired considerable popularity both here and in the United States. These carpets are manufactured in the Heriz district, about 100 miles east of Tabriz. The entire industry, unlike that of the Sultanabad carpets, being in the hands of individuals weaving independently of each other in their huts, it is difficult to estimate the number of looms as well as the yearly output. However, it is safe to reckon the annual supply at about 65,000 to 75,000 pounds Turkish ($286,000 to $330,000), of which nearly two-thirds are shipped to America. These carpets, from the standpoint of design and general coloring, are the nearest approach to old carpets, and being of a moderate cost (110 to 220 piasters) ($4.48 to $8.96) the square meter, the demand for them will doubtless increase.   The name Bakshaish is given to an inferior grade of Heriz weave which is now almost out of the market.

The third subdivision of modern irans is the Kirman and Laver carpets.   These are decidedly the best modern products, as regards workmanship, delicacy of coloring, and elaborateness of design.   As the name implies, they are manufactured in the city of Kirman, and an inferior grade in Laver.   The industry has been considerably developed of late, owing to the increasing demand in the United States and Europe.   In fact, during the past two years the demand has been so great as compared with the supply that from 270 piasters ($11.88) the square meter the price has gone up to 540 piasters ($23.76).   The total output of Kirman carpets and rugs can only be estimated approximately, but 65,000 pounds Turkish ($286,000) a year would be a safe estimate.   Of this, 40,000 to 45,000 pounds ($176,000 to $198,000) are imported into the United States.

Korassan carpets, the fourth subdivision, are manufactured in the eastern province of Persia (Korassan), of which Meshed is the capital. Although Korassan rugs have been woven for many years, the modern Korassan carpet is a recent addition to the market.   These goods are almost exclusively marketed in Constantinople.   Although somewhat limited in supply, the growing demand for them in the United States is increasing the number of looms devoted to this industry.   The yearly export to the United States is estimated at about 15,000 pounds Turkish ($66,000).   The market price for this class ranges from 170 to 240 piasters ($7.48 to $10.56) the square meter.

As the fifth subdivision of irans come the Tabriz carpet and rug, manufactured in the city of Tabriz.   These are very elaborate in design and fine in texture, but have a limited sale on account of their gaudy aniline colors and modern designs.   The city of Tabriz also produces silk rugs and carpets.   They are mostly in the antique design of the Gheordes prayer rug, in delicate shades, and are much prized in the United States by those who can afford to purchase them.   A Tabriz silk rug is worth from 25 to 40 pounds Turkish.   The amount imported into the United States (silk and woolen) varies in value between 15,000 and 17,000 pounds Turkish ($66,000 to $74,800) annually, the market price the square meter being from 300 to 400 piasters ($13.20 to $17.60).

The sixth subdivision comprises the Sarook carpet and rug, which is very much like the Mushkiabad carpet in respect to design and coloring, but is far superior as regards weave and workmanship.   It costs about 400 piasters ($17.60) the square meter (1.196 square yards), and the amount annually imported into the United States may be put down at 8,000 to 10,000 pounds Turkish ($35,200 to $44,000).

The seventh and last subdivision is the Bidjar and Sine carpet, manufactured respectively in the cities of the same name.   Bidjar carpets have a very thick pile and are the most durable of modern makes.   Their designs and colors often resemble those of Ferahans, but they are not valued on account of their thickness and consequent weight.   They are worth from 180 to 220 piasters ($7.92 to $9.68) the square meter (1.196 square yards).

Sines are generally seen in rug sizes.   These have preserved the character of the original Persian design, and some antique specimens of great value may be seen, although the greater demand and consequent carelessness in weaving have brought about a marked decadence in quality. The rug sizes are sold at from 5 to 10 pounds ($22 to $44), and a square meter (1.196 square yards) of Sine carpet is worth from 300 to 400 piasters ($13.20 to $17.60). The total value of these two grades imported annually into the United States may be estimated at 10,000 to 15,000 pounds Turkish ($44,000 to $66,000).

*Antique Irans.*—By this name are meant all rugs and carpets that were manufactured at least fifty years ago. The carpets of this class are not square, like the modern Iran carpets, but long and narrow, the length often being as much as twice or even three times the width. It is among these antique Irans that pieces of great value and high artistic and technical worth are to be found. Pieces such as the famous Ardebil carpet, now among the treasures of the South Kensington Museum, will never even be approached by the modern weaver, either in delicacy of shades or workmanship, all attempts at copying it having proved total failures.

The antique Irans may be subdivided as follows: Kurdistan Sine; Mir, Serebend; Shiraz, Kirmanshah; Koltouk; Soouk Boulak; Herate; Djoshagan; Ispahan. The foregoing are the names worth mentioning, and, as it will be seen, the carpets are named after the town where they originated.

The demand for antique Irans is gradually decreasing, because, besides being expensive, they do not very well satisfy the needs of the customer as a floor covering. Real antiques are becoming scarcer every year, because collectors have during the past twenty years exported whatever was obtainable of real antique, so that all that is left is hardly worthy of the name. Besides the antique carpets, there are also rugs and hall runners manufactured in this class. For these there is a greater demand in the United States than for the carpets, as they are not so expensive and are a very ornamental floor covering.

A class of nomad goods known by the general name of Moussouls is worth noting. These are ancient rugs, generally of coarse texture, having as their origin the villages of Persia, but now collected in the markets of Tabriz and some cities of Mesopotamia, whence they are imported in large quantities into the United States.

*Caucasians.*—Caucasian is a name given to all rugs manufactured in the territory divided by the Caucasus Mountains and bounded by the Black and Caspian seas and the Turkish and Persian frontiers. Caucasian fabrics are generally made in rug sizes, and differ strikingly from the Turkish and Persian rugs in color and the traditional designs which have been faithfully preserved. The different types comprised in the Caucasian group are:

| Types. | Antique. | | Modern. | |
| --- | --- | --- | --- | --- |
| | Piasters. | U. S. currency. | Piasters. | U. S. currency. |
| Shirvans ...........................per piece.. | 260–320 | $11.44–$14.08 | 130–200 | $5.72–$8.80 |
| Guendjes...............................do.... | 200–240 | 8.80– 10.56 | 120–170 | 5.28– 7.48 |
| Kazaks.................................do.... | 280–350 | 12.32– 15.40 | 200–240 | 8.80–10.56 |
| Karabaghs .............................do.... | 80– 90 | 3.52– 3.96 | 60– 75 | 2.64– 3.30 |
| Soumaks ..............................do..... | 1,000–1,300 | 44.00– 57.20 | 400–650 | 17.60–28.60 |

It would be almost impossible to state the quantity of each different type imported yearly to America, but the value of the whole group may be estimated at about 140,000 pounds Turkish ($616,000).

*Turkish.*—This group, as the name implies, comprises all rugs manufactured in Turkish territory. The antique Turkish rug, such as the

Gheordes, Ladik, or Koula, is fast disappearing from the markets, passing into the collectors' hands, and the other antiques, such as Moudjours, Kirshehirs, Bergamas, Meles, Yuruks, etc., are becoming scarcer every day, because nearly all of this class, both in the provinces and Constantinople, have been exported already, so that the value of antique Turkish rugs imported yearly into the United States would barely average 1,000 pounds Turkish.

Among modern Turkish carpets, those manufactured in Smyrna and its vicinity occupy the principal place. Unlike Persian carpets, these are of soft wool, and are delicate in color and elaborate in design. Five years ago, the quantity of Smyrna carpets imported annually into the United States was about 200,000 pounds ($880,000), but since then this figure has rapidly decreased, so that to-day it will hardly exceed in value 50,000 pounds ($220,000).

Next to Smyrna and its environs, Cæsarea produces the greatest number of modern Turkish rugs, the specialty here being the manufacture of silk rugs, mostly in the antique prayer rug Gheordes design, but it is regrettable that the use of aniline dyes and an inferior quality of silk have brought about a marked falling off from the old makes, so that during the last few years the prices have fallen from 1,500 piasters ($66) the piece to about 600 or 700 piasters ($26.40 or $30.80).

*Turkomans.*—This name is applied to all kinds of rugs produced in the vast territory bounded on the east by the Chinese frontier, the west by the Caspian Sea, the north by the Sea of Aral, and the south by the Gulf of Oman.

These rugs are very popular on account of their fineness and durability. The peculiarity about them is their designs, consisting of geometrical figures, which have been faithfully transmitted from generation to generation, and preserved ever since the introduction of the weaving industry. The class to which a Turkoman belongs can be easily ascertained by the feature of the design, each tribe weaving in a design peculiar to itself. The principal types of this group are: Boukharas, Afghans, Beshir, Belouges (Belouchistan), Youmouts, Samarcand. These rugs, as well as the Caucasians, are imported in bond to Constantinople, and are thence reexported. The amount yearly imported into the United States varies between 60,000 and 65,000 pounds Turkish ($264,000 and $286,000).

CHAS. M. DICKINSON,<br>
Consul-General.

CONSTANTINOPLE, *January 8, 1903.*

---

# UNITED KINGDOM.

## REPORT FROM CONSULATE-GENERAL AT LONDON.

The exports from Great Britain in 1901 were, although less than in 1900, higher than in any of the preceding fifteen years, the gross total amounting in value to $1,739,321,340, as against $1,771,868,770 in 1900, a decrease of $32,000,000. Of these exports, those of British and Irish produce totaled $1,400,111,880, against $1,455,959,980 in 1900, or a decrease of over $55,000,000; while the exports of foreign and colonial merchandise showed an increase of $23,000,000, the respective totals being, in 1901, $339,209,460, and in 1900, $315,908,790.

The imports into Great Britain in 1901 showed a small decrease, the figures being, in 1900, $2,615,375,815, and in 1901, $2,609,950,990; but it should not be lost sight of that in 1900 the imports showed a huge increase over 1899, and were indeed greater—much greater—than in any of the preceding fifteen years.

Of the countries importing into Great Britain in 1901, the principal increases were shared by—

Denmark .................................................................... $6,000,000
Germany ................................................................... 5,000,000
Holland .................................................................... 7,500,000
Roumania .................................................................. 13,000,000
United States .............................................................. 11,000,000

The chief decreases were from—

Sweden and Norway ....................................................... $5,000,000
France ..................................................................... 12,000,000
Spain ...................................................................... 9,000,000
Brazil ..................................................................... 5,000,000

On the other hand, the increases in exports from Great Britain were mainly to—

Greece ..................................................................... $3,000,000
Turkey ..................................................................... 9,000,000
China ...................................................................... 6,000,000
British India (nearly) ..................................................... 25,000,000
Natal ...................................................................... 11,500,000
Cape of Good Hope ......................................................... 12,000,000

The most marked decreases were to—

Russia (all ports) ........................................................ $13,000,000
Germany .................................................................... 41,500,000
Belgium .................................................................... 11,000,000
France ..................................................................... 10,000,000
Japan ...................................................................... 8,000,000
Brazil ..................................................................... 8,000,000

Turning to the analysis of articles imported into Great Britain in the year under review, it is noticeable that in bacon and hams there has been a steady increase in the value imported. In 1887, the value declared was $43,668,000, and in 1901, $90,592,000, or more than double. The increase over 1900 alone exceeded $10,000,000. In the imports of beef an even greater increase has occurred, the value of beef imported in 1887 being $7,390,000, and in 1901, $44,534,000, or over 600 per cent. The increase in 1901 over 1900 exceeded $3,700,000. In butter another great increase is seen, 1887 showing imports thereof to the value of $40,000,000, while 1901 totaled $96,000,000, an increase of nearly $10,000,000 over 1900.

The following imports into Great Britain in 1901 show the principal increases, compared with 1900 (in addition to those above mentioned): Barley, oats, raw cotton, hay, wet rawhides, lard, goatskins, sugar (refined). On the other hand, the chief decreases occurred in caoutchouc, cheese, dried currants, raisins, dry rawhides, hops, iron ore, pig and sheet lead, paraffin, petroleum, silk manufactures, tea, wood, and timber (all kinds).

With regard to the exports from Great Britain in 1901 of British and Irish produce, the principal increases were in cotton manufactures (the total value exported being greater than in any year for fifteen years), the increase over 1900 being over $18,000,000 in value; telegraphic wire and apparatus (where again the total value exported was larger than in any of the preceding fifteen years); bulls, fittings, and

machinery of steamships, not registered as British; provisions, locomotives, rails of iron and steel, jute yarn (piece goods).   The exports
of books also showed an increase, which has been steady since 1894.
The principal decreases occurred in chemical products, coal and culm,
coke and cinders, products of coal, textile machinery; iron, pig and
puddled; galvanized iron sheets; steel ingots, bars, and sheets; silk
manufactures, woolen and worsted yarns, and woolen and worsted
manufactures.

In exports of foreign and colonial merchandise, in the gross total
value of which an increase of $23,000,000 is shown, the aggregate being
greater than in any of the preceding fifteen years, although 1889 was
very nearly as great, the principal increases are noticeable in hemp
(the value of which exceeded $10,000,000), raw silk, and silk manufac-
tures; wool, coffee, raw cotton, jute, and jute manufactures; goatskins
and manufactured tobacco and cigars.   Among the chief decreases
are caoutchouc, hides, silver ore (the export of which was less than in
any year for fifteen years); sugar, refined and unrefined, and molasses.

*Aggregate quantity and value of imports into Great Britain in 1901.*

| Articles. | Quantities. | Values. |
|---|---|---|
| Animals: | | |
| Horses .................................................number.. | 40,856 | $5,478,415 |
| Oxen, bulls, cows, and calves.............................do.... | 495,635 | 44,203,320 |
| Sheep and lambs............... ...........do.... | 383,594 | 2,930,695 |
| Arms and ammunition ....................................... | | 2,085,470 |
| Art, works of............................................... | | 1,035,010 |
| Asphalt.............................................tons.. | 73,518 | 948,805 |
| Bacon and hams: | | |
| Bacon .................................hundredweight.. | 5,772,348 | 67,950,880 |
| Hams.................................do..... | 1,860,670 | 22,641,940 |
| Basket ware ................................................ | | 1,323,885 |
| Bead trimmings ............................................. | | 1,255,655 |
| Beef: | | |
| Fresh.................................hundredweight.. | 4,506,746 | 44,584,195 |
| Salted ...................................do..... | 204,396 | 1,336,780 |
| Beer and ale....................................barrels.. | 56,127 | 819,215 |
| Bones (not whalebone)...........................tons.. | 67,269 | 1,369,225 |
| Books, maps, and charts ....................hundredweight.. | 45,977 | 1,255,835 |
| Brimstone..................................do..... | 441,725 | 495,610 |
| Bristles...................................pounds.. | 4,071,863 | 2,633,455 |
| Brush ware ................................................ | | 1,446,155 |
| Butter ....................................hundredweight.. | 3,702,890 | 96,486,980 |
| Buttons and studs (not metal) ......................gross.. | 3,106,573 | 1,286,965 |
| Candles.................................hundredweight.. | 10,394 | 106,735 |
| Canes and sticks, unmounted ............................... | | 843,930 |
| Caoutchouc..............................hundredweight.. | 466,474 | 29,151,120 |
| Caoutchouc, manufactures of— | | |
| Boots and shoes.......................................... | | 1,231,105 |
| Other sorts.............................................. | | 2,219,530 |
| Carriages, wagonettes ..................................... | | 2,898,705 |
| Cement ................................................... | | 1,888,720 |
| Cheese....................................hundredweight.. | 2,586,837 | 31,135,675 |
| Chemical manufactures and products, unenumerated ......... | | 10,100,615 |
| China, porcelain, etc......................hundredweight.. | 408,585 | 4,994,860 |
| Clocks ..................................number.. | 1,783,495 | 2,544,045 |
| Cocoa, raw ..................................pounds.. | 51,798,802 | 7,756,210 |
| Cocoa or chocolate, ground, prepared, or in any way manufactured, | | |
| pounds.. | 8,390,286 | 4,328,235 |
| Coffee...................................hundredweight.. | 958,464 | 16,621,270 |
| Confectionery ...............................do..... | 318,686 | 2,890,630 |
| Cordage, twine, and cable yarn ............................. | | 4,642,520 |
| Cork: | | |
| Unmanufactured..................................tons.. | 27,968 | 1,121,330 |
| Manufactured .................................pounds.. | 13,128,780 | 3,688,930 |
| Corn: | | |
| Wheat ................................hundredweight.. | 69,708,530 | 115,406,860 |
| Barley.....................................do.... | 21,873,480 | 30,815,060 |
| Oats.......................................do.... | 22,470,670 | 31,738,595 |
| Maize......................................do.... | 51,872,700 | 61,986,125 |
| Other kinds .................................do.... | 5,326,741 | 8,838,685 |
| Flour, of wheat .............................do.... | 22,576,490 | 51,707,595 |
| Flour, of other kinds.........................do.... | 2,795,908 | 5,483,580 |
| Total ...... ...........................................do.... | 196,124,409 | 305,876,450 |

*Aggregate quantity and value of imports into Great Britain in 1901*—Continued.

| Articles. | Quantities. | Values. |
|---|---:|---:|
| Cotton: | | |
| Raw ....................................hundredweight.. | 16,336,697 | $209,852,695 |
| Yarn ............................................pounds.. | 4,469,022 | 1,106,055 |
| Cotton waste.........................................do.... | 13,313,073 | 456,705 |
| Cotton manufactures: | | |
| Piece goods .....................................yards.. | 46,625,816 | 4,590,940 |
| Hosiery ...................................... | | 3,538,365 |
| Unenumerated .............................. | | 15,760,740 |
| Diamonds........................................... | | 166,345 |
| Drugs: | | |
| Bark, Peruvian ..................hundredweight.. | 42,546 | 608,350 |
| Opium .........................................pounds.. | 758,095 | 1,948,575 |
| Unenumerated .............................. | | 5,613,775 |
| Dyeing or tanning stuffs: | | |
| Bark...................................hundredweight.. | 441,468 | 862,995 |
| Cutch and gambier............................tons.. | 17,613 | 1,958,865 |
| Extracts ........................................... | | 1,611,975 |
| Dyes from coal tar ........................... | | 3,888,475 |
| Indigo.................................hundredweight.. | 51,359 | 8,944,100 |
| Myrobalans ...................................do.... | 482,036 | 729,650 |
| Sumach .........................................tons.. | 11,258 | 528,775 |
| Valonia ..........................................do.... | 30,533 | 1,620,410 |
| Unenumerated ................hundredweight.. | 187,024 | 1,106,665 |
| Dyewoods ..........................................tons.. | 42,995 | 1,122,660 |
| Eggs.....................................................M.. | 2,048,612 | 27,478,835 |
| Electrical apparatus .............................. | | 4,246,285 |
| Embroidery and needlework ................... | | 6,165,310 |
| Fancy goods........................................ | | 5,175,665 |
| Farinaceous substances........................... | | 7,775,790 |
| Feathers, ornamental ....................pounds.. | 1,177,328 | 6,827,690 |
| Feathers, bed........................hundredweight.. | 34,327 | 458,080 |
| Fish: | | |
| Fresh.............................................do.... | 947,502 | 3,779,275 |
| Cured or salted.............................do.... | 1,354,521 | 14,320,365 |
| Flax and hemp: | | |
| Flax, dressed and undressed................do.... | 1,147,700 | 13,032,875 |
| Tow, or codilla of flax and hemp ........do.... | 452,780 | 2,762,725 |
| Hemp and other like substances..........do.... | 2,789,440 | 20,585,420 |
| Flowers: | | |
| Artificial......................................... | | 2,967,585 |
| Cut and "everlastings" ..................... | | 1,164,565 |
| Fruit: | | |
| Almonds ............................hundredweight.. | 111,322 | 2,070,610 |
| Apples, raw...................................do.... | 1,830,210 | 5,913,910 |
| Bananas, raw..............................bunches.. | 2,228,672 | 4,377,700 |
| Cherries, raw ....................hundredweight.. | 212,688 | 1,067,925 |
| Currants, dried...............................do.... | 962,026 | 5,189,930 |
| Grapes, raw....................................do.... | 679,365 | 3,474,710 |
| Pears, raw......................................do.... | 348,886 | 1,482,055 |
| Plums, raw.....................................do.... | 277,163 | 1,380,275 |
| Raisins...........................................do.... | 522,010 | 4,221,270 |
| Nuts ............................................ | | 3,882,540 |
| Oranges and lemons...............hundredweight.. | 6,358,191 | 12,771,210 |
| Currants, raw ................................do.... | 70,402 | 276,540 |
| Gooseberries, raw ...........................do.... | 21,735 | 57,100 |
| Strawberries, raw ...........................do.... | 88,604 | 256,450 |
| Unenumerated— | | |
| Raw .............................................do.... | 585,247 | 1,510,065 |
| Dried and preserved .......................do.... | 1,886,903 | 61,288,710 |
| Glass: | | |
| Bottles............................................gross.. | 1,689,069 | 3,682,745 |
| Flint, plain, cut, or ornamented ....hundredweight.. | 571,723 | 5,131,235 |
| Of other kinds.................................do.... | 2,000,253 | 8,833,655 |
| Glue, size, and gelatin............................ | | 2,374,690 |
| Guano...................................................tons.. | 22,830 | 524,545 |
| Gum of all sorts .......................hundredweight.. | 460,102 | 6,481,585 |
| Gutta-percha ...................................do.... | 88,488 | 6,913,280 |
| Hair: | | |
| Goats' hair or wool.......................pounds.. | 22,866,281 | 6,712,585 |
| Other ............................................ | | 2,144,500 |
| Manufactures of hair and of goats' wool .............. | | 591,075 |
| Hardware and cutlery........................... | | 5,761,880 |
| Hats or bonnets, trimmed or untrimmed: | | |
| Of straw ......................................dozen.. | 197,717 | 627,880 |
| Of other materials ...........................do.... | 221,189 | 709,395 |
| Hay.......................................................tons.. | 199,976 | 4,000,665 |
| Hides, raw: | | |
| Dry..............................................hundredweight.. | 353,067 | 4,985,660 |
| Wet............................................do.... | 757,175 | 8,918,895 |
| Hops .............................................do.... | 116,042 | 2,306,775 |
| Horns, tips, and pieces of horn. ............tons.. | 4,990 | 822,865 |
| Ice ................................................do.... | 460,946 | 1,849,485 |
| Implements and tools ........................... | | 2,076,610 |
| Isinglass................................hundredweight.. | 7,878 | 513,485 |

*Aggregate quantity and value of imports into Great Britain in 1901*—Continued.

| Articles. | Quantities. | Values. |
|---|---|---|
| Ivory: Teeth, elephants', sea cow, and sea horse....hundredweight.. | 8,825 | $1,678,560 |
| Jute ...............................................................tons.. | 321,331 | 21,630,840 |
| Jute manufactures ......................................................... | ............. | 11,045,280 |
| Laces, and articles thereof................................................ | ............. | 10,696,875 |
| Lard ......................................................hundredweight.. | 1,966,256 | 20,188,445 |
| Leather: | | |
| Undressed.............................................................do.... | 903,131 | 22,790,340 |
| Dressed...............................................................do.... | 412,878 | 17,626,525 |
| Varnished, japanned, or enameled ...................................do.... | 7,824 | 1,191,520 |
| Leather manufactures: | | |
| Boots and shoes...............................................dozen pairs. | 297,504 | 4,694,545 |
| Gloves .............................................................pairs.. | 19,427,592 | 8,321,755 |
| Unenumerated ............................................................. | ............. | 3,172,265 |
| Linen: | | |
| Yarn ............................................................pounds.. | 23,468,952 | 3,821,495 |
| Manufactures............................................................. | ............. | 2,735,180 |
| Locust beans .............................................hundredweight.. | 1,070,318 | 1,197,660 |
| Manures, unenumerated .........................................tons.. | 98,241 | 896,310 |
| Margarin and artificial and imitation butter........hundredweight.. | 962,127 | 12,783,395 |
| Oleomargarine ......................................................do.... | 167,670 | 1,494,060 |
| Matches................................................................... | ............. | 2,116,485 |
| Meat: | | |
| Unenumerated, salted or fresh ..................hundredweight.. | 610,271 | 5,602,235 |
| Preserved, other than salted— | | |
| Beef ................................................................do.... | 464,727 | 6,449,465 |
| Mutton ............................................................do.... | 64,884 | 840,715 |
| Other sorts (not bacon or ham) ......................do.... | 239,737 | 4,121,345 |
| Metals: | | |
| Brass, bronze, and metal bronzed or lacquered, manufactures of ..........................................................hundredweight.. | 48,598 | 1,200,290 |
| Copper, ore of.....................................................tons.. | 100,889 | 6,259,700 |
| Regulus and precipitate............................................do.... | 91,868 | 18,343,315 |
| Unwrought, part wrought, and old .......................do.... | 71,679 | 24,594,985 |
| Manufactures of ......................................................... | ............. | 3,738,975 |
| Iron ore ..........................................................tons.. | 5,548,888 | 22,752,815 |
| Iron and steel, unwrought— | | |
| Iron— | | |
| Pig and puddled .......................................hundredweight.. | 198,500 | 3,961,905 |
| Bar, angle, bolt, and rod.............................do.... | 98,101 | 3,674,560 |
| Steel, unwrought ...............................................do.... | 182,884 | 5,531,825 |
| Iron and steel, wrought or manufactured— | | |
| Girders, beams, and pillars.................hundredweight.. | 122,685 | 4,143,020 |
| Cycles and parts....................................................... | ............. | 881,775 |
| Machinery............................................................... | ............. | 18,062,635 |
| Rails, steel............................................................. | ............. | 2,064,145 |
| Other kinds .......................................hundredweight.. | 321,453 | 18,483,315 |
| Iron, old, broken, etc ...........................................tons.. | 44,017 | 608,865 |
| Lead— | | |
| Ore of .............................................................do.... | 29,472 | 1,221,625 |
| Pig and sheet....................................................do.... | 218,060 | 14,219,980 |
| Manganese, ore of.................................................do.... | 192,654 | 2,293,300 |
| Platinum, wrought or unwrought...................ounces, Troy.. | 158,109 | 1,140,760 |
| Quicksilver .......................................................pounds.. | 2,650,572 | 1,616,390 |
| Silver ore ................................................................ | ............. | 5,309,920 |
| Tin— | | |
| Ore of ..............................................................tons.. | 10,522 | 2,619,425 |
| In blocks, ingots, bars, or slabs..............hundredweight.. | 707,939 | 21,078,190 |
| Zinc— | | |
| Ore of................................................................tons.. | 35,096 | 825,990 |
| Crude, in cakes...................................................do.... | 67,552 | 5,885,355 |
| Manufactures.................................hundredweight.. | 426,858 | 2,451,030 |
| Unenumerated— | | |
| Ores .................................................................tons.. | 75,977 | 1,661,930 |
| Unwrought............................................................do.... | 3,915 | 1,205,500 |
| Wrought or manufactured .....................do.... | 6,236 | 3,542,845 |
| Old ..................................................................do.... | 5,137 | 780,385 |
| Mica, talc, French chalk, steatite, mineral white, silica, and soapstone..............................................hundredweight.. | 140,104 | 707,675 |
| Milk, condensed......................................................do.... | 919,319 | 8,802,580 |
| Mineral water............................................................ | ............. | 1,492,890 |
| Moldings, gilt............................................................ | ............. | 1,391,480 |
| Musical instruments ..................................................... | ............. | 7,024,960 |
| Mutton, fresh .......................................hundredweight.. | 3,606,229 | 32,990,400 |
| Nuts and kernels, used for expressing oil......................tons.. | 50,090 | 3,071,620 |
| Oil: | | |
| Fish .................................................................do.... | 24,384 | 2,269,045 |
| Animal ...................................................hundredweight.. | 91,870 | 602,185 |
| Castor ..............................................................do.... | 107,297 | 777,905 |
| Palm ................................................................do.... | 1,212,111 | 6,853,225 |
| Cocoanut ............................................................do.... | 478,143 | 2,970,770 |
| Olive ...............................................................tons.. | 15,488 | 2,909,465 |
| Seed .................................................................do.... | 48,842 | 5,967,885 |

*Aggregate quantity and value of imports into Great Britain in 1901*—Continued.

| Articles. | Quantities. | Values. |
|---|---|---|
| Oil—Continued. | | |
| Turpentine ......................................hundredweight.. | $643,846 | $4,213,710 |
| Chemical, essential or perfumed..........................pounds.. | 1,941,207 | 1,218,265 |
| Unenumerated ......................................... | .............. | 468,420 |
| Oil-seed cake: | | |
| Linseed cake ..................................................tons.. | 174,072 | 6,360,720 |
| Other kinds ...............................................do.... | 205,527 | 5,707,510 |
| Onions, raw..............................................bushels.. | 7,295,418 | 4,346,985 |
| Painters' colors and pigments ................................. | .............. | 6,489,170 |
| Paper and pasteboard: | | |
| Unprinted .......................................hundredweight.. | 3,654,090 | 14,828,080 |
| Printed or coated ..........................................do.... | 136,350 | 2,109,555 |
| Strawboard, millboard, and wood-pulp boards..............do....| 2,490,867 | 4,773,585 |
| Paper-making materials: | | |
| Linen and cotton rags...........................................tons.. | 15,922 | 733,515 |
| Esparto and other vegetable fiber ......................do.. | 193,937 | 4,012,315 |
| Pulp of wood.............................................do.... | 448,455 | 12,030,420 |
| Other materials .........................................do.... | 16,446 | 490,280 |
| Paraffin and paraffin wax......................hundredweight.. | 839,437 | 5,031,870 |
| Perfumery..............................................pounds.. | 662,019 | 354,725 |
| Petroleum: | | |
| Illuminating................................................gallons.. | 217,209,601 | 19,691,600 |
| Lubricating.................................................do.... | 36,575,145 | 5,661,910 |
| Phosphate of lime and rock................................tons.. | 354,890 | 2,758,825 |
| Pictures and drawings........................................ | .............. | 8,258,565 |
| Plants, shrubs, trees......................................... | .............. | 2,641,895 |
| Plumbago ...................................................tons.. | 18,203 | 1,510,195 |
| Pork......................................................hundredweight.. | 1,038,556 | 10,199,005 |
| Potatoes....................................................do.... | 7,076,726 | 9,257,935 |
| Poultry, game, and rabbits.................................. | .............. | 8,147,915 |
| Pyrites of iron or copper .................................tons.. | 653,584 | 5,606,225 |
| Rice ...............................................hundredweight.. | 6,755,263 | 12,387,325 |
| Rosin......................................................do.... | 1,812,478 | 2,146,510 |
| Saltpeter ..................................................do.... | 240,455 | 1,033,020 |
| Nitrate of soda...........................................do.... | 2,142,160 | 4,550,335 |
| Scientific instruments ....................................... | .............. | 8,554,895 |
| Seeds— | | |
| Clover and grass.......  ....................hundredweight.. | 281,129 | 3,058,090 |
| Cotton .....................................................tons.. | 437,149 | 18,527,985 |
| Flax or linseed............................................quarters.. | 1,684,822 | 21,319,655 |
| Rape ......................................................do.... | 163,329 | 1,492,130 |
| Of all other sorts........................................... | .............. | 5,438,300 |
| Sewing machines............................................ | .............. | 1,752,510 |
| Shells of all kinds.......................................... | .............. | 2,504,575 |
| Silk: | | |
| Knubs or husks and waste......................hundredweight.. | 48,162 | 2,017,745 |
| Raw ......................................................pounds.. | 1,332,480 | 8,841,950 |
| Thrown and spun .........................................do.... | 624,859 | 2,889,930 |
| Silk manufactures: | | |
| Broad stuffs— | | |
| Silk or satin ........................................ | .............. | 31,210,635 |
| Velvet, plain or figured................  ........... | .............. | 2,390,315 |
| Bibbons............................................ | .............. | 10,816,245 |
| Other manufactures ................................. | .............. | 20,734,410 |
| Total of silk manufactures........................... | .............. | 65,151,605 |
| Skins and furs: | | |
| Goat, undressed ...........................................number.. | 19,601,436 | 9,082,980 |
| Seal .......................................................do.... | 840,083 | 1,897,490 |
| Sheep and lamb.............................................do.... | 15,109,399 | 7,363,360 |
| Furs of all sorts, except seal skins........................do.... | 52,913,443 | 7,683,990 |
| Manufactures of ......................................... | .............. | 5,382,860 |
| Soap and soap powder........................................ | .............. | 1,575,130 |
| Spices: | | |
| Pepper ....................................................pounds.. | 15,706,503 | 2,244,185 |
| Of all other sorts .........................................do.... | 13,525,181 | 1,430,365 |
| Spirits: | | |
| Rum.....................................................proof gallons.. | 6,719,452 | 2,549,750 |
| Brandy.....................................................do.... | 3,081,525 | 6,943,170 |
| Other foreign and colonial spirits.........................do.... | 2,617,090 | 2,681,930 |
| Total of spirits ......................  ...........do.... | 12,418,067 | 12,174,850 |
| Sponge .....................................................pounds.. | 1,316,970 | 1,254,315 |
| Stones, marble, etc.: | | |
| Slates ....................................................number.. | 48,300,019 | 1,364,880 |
| Other....................................................tons.. | 1,141,020 | 6,811,860 |
| Straw ......................................................do.... | 40,315 | 499,040 |
| Straw plaiting .............................................pounds.. | 8,310,889 | 2,818,850 |

*Aggregate quantity and value of imports into Great Britain in 1901*—Continued.

| Articles. | Quantities. | Values. |
|---|---|---|
| Sugar: | | |
| Refined and sugar candy— | | |
| Lumps or loaves..........................hundredweight.. | 8,143,155 | $10,556,140 |
| Other sorts .................................do.... | 18,113,691 | 54,188,030 |
| Unrefined: | | |
| Beetroot.......................................do.... | 10,009,438 | 22,665,040 |
| Cane and other sorts .........................do.... | 8,377,705 | 9,225,080 |
| Molasses......................................do.... | 1,709,674 | 1,826,645 |
| Glucose.......................................do.... | 1,497,304 | 3,259,750 |
| Tallow and stearin...............................do.... | 1,785,319 | 11,666,230 |
| Tea..........................................pounds.. | 296,264,142 | 47,201,870 |
| Tobacco: | | |
| Manufactured, cigars and snuff. ..............do.... | 7,411,674 | 10,407,685 |
| Unmanufactured..............................do.... | 84,620,722 | 13,321,755 |
| Tobacco pipes. .................................... | | 1,514,190 |
| Toys ............................................. | | 6,163,625 |
| Vegetables: | | |
| Tomatoes ..................................... | | 3,667,355 |
| Raw, unenumerated ............................ | | 1,949,145 |
| Watches ....................................number. | 2,481,329 | 7,599,290 |
| Wax, including ozokerite and earth wax ..........hundredweight.. | 40,114 | 293,740 |
| Wine: | | |
| In casks ....................................gallons.. | 14,487,625 | 13,896,385 |
| In bottles— | | |
| Still ..........................................do.... | 563,528 | 1,359,100 |
| Sparkling: | | |
| Champagne .............................do.... | 1,235,400 | 8,657,090 |
| Other.....................................do.... | 259,563 | 744,100 |
| Wood and timber: | | |
| Hewn— | | |
| Fir, other than pit wood or fir props...................loads.. | 604,388 | 7,906,350 |
| Pit wood or pit props.............................do.... | 1,879,810 | 10,265,130 |
| Oak.............................................do.... | 178,054 | 4,962,870 |
| Teak ...........................................do.... | 45,768 | 2,773,835 |
| Unenumerated ..................................do.... | 69,925 | 1,372,075 |
| Sawn or split: | | |
| Fir .............................................do.... | 6,095,506 | 78,077,620 |
| Unenumerated ..................................do.... | 185,494 | 8,517,450 |
| Staves .........................................do.... | 140,064 | 3,652,605 |
| Furniture woods and hard woods: | | |
| Mahogany.......................................tons.. | 74,180 | 3,206,505 |
| Unenumerated ..................................do.... | 241,650 | 7,107,785 |
| House frames, fittings, joiners' and cabinet work .............. | | 5,768,795 |
| Woodware turnery, etc .............................. | | 5,647,770 |
| Wool: | | |
| Sheep or lambs...............................pounds.. | 686,956,308 | 107,522,885 |
| Other kinds of flocks.............................do.... | 8,589,140 | 2,010,090 |
| Woolen rags .......................................tons.. | 29,902 | 2,843,540 |
| Woolen and worsted yarn: | | |
| Yarn for weaving .............................pounds.. | 20,841,734 | 10,526,750 |
| For other purposes ..............................do.... | 666,715 | 493,610 |
| Woolen manufactures: | | |
| Cloths.......................................yards.. | 4,466,128 | 3,487,390 |
| Stuffs..........................................do.... | 69,641,927 | 24,381,765 |
| Carpets and rugs................................. | | 2,293,350 |
| Unenumerated.................................... | | 17,725,895 |
| Yeast, dried .....................................hundredweight.. | 180,536 | 1,389,950 |
| All other articles: | | |
| Manufactured ................................... | | 17,151,508 |
| Unmanufactured, unenumerated...................... | | 11,488,675 |
| Total......................................... | | 2,608,638,680 |
| Parcel post (not liable to duty)........... .............. | | 6,312,310 |
| Total imports .................................... | | 2,609,950,990 |

*Exports from Great Britain in 1901 (British and Irish produce).*

| Articles. | Quantities. | Values. |
|---|---|---|
| Aerated waters............................... | | $724,290 |
| Animals: Horses.............................number.. | 27,612 | 30,294,950 |
| Apparel and slops............................ | | 27,856,295 |
| Arms and ammunition: | | |
| Firearms, small ...........................number.. | 111,333 | 1,578,455 |
| Gunpowder...............................pounds.. | 6,865,712 | 857,599 |

*Exports from Great Britain (British and Irish produce)*—Continued.

| Articles. | Quantities. | Values. |
|---|---|---|
| Arms and ammunition—Continued. | | |
| Ammunition, unenumerated ................. | ................. | $7,389,280 |
| Of all other kinds ..................... | ................. | 2,540,586 |
| Bags and sacks, empty ...........................dozen.. | 2,207,400 | 2,504,820 |
| Beer and ale ...............................barrels.. | 522,889 | 8,914,490 |
| Biscuits and bread..........................hundredweight.. | 278,326 | 3,951,930 |
| Bleaching materials.............................do.... | 1,034,400 | 1,717,625 |
| Books, printed ................................do.... | 247,698 | 7,763,860 |
| Bran and pollard ....................... | ................. | 1,275,560 |
| Bricks ....................................thousand.. | 68,727 | 1,053,695 |
| Candles of all sorts .........................pounds.. | 24,586,500 | 2,163,570 |
| Caoutchouc, manufactures of .................. | ................. | 61,312,075 |
| Carriages and wagons: | | |
| Railway, for passengers ................. | ................. | 3,195,715 |
| Railway wagons ........................ | ................. | 9,833,295 |
| Other sorts and parts .................. | ................. | 1,718,345 |
| Cement ...................................hundredweight.. | 6,106,620 | 2,919,870 |
| Chemical products: | | |
| Sulphate of copper..................... | ................. | 4,281,585 |
| Other chemical products ................ | ................. | 12,817,935 |
| Clay, unmanufactured .........................tons.. | 436,522 | 2,422,520 |
| Clocks and parts, and watches................. | ................. | 520,130 |
| Coal, cinders, etc.: | | |
| Coal and culm..............................tons.. | 41,877,081 | 143,724,920 |
| Coke and cinders..............................do.... | 807,671 | 3,503,930 |
| Fuel, manufactured ............................do.... | 1,081,160 | 4,444,890 |
| Products of coal, peat, shale................. | ................. | 5,756,265 |
| Cocoa or chocolate...........................pounds.. | 3,632,273 | 986,670 |
| Cordage and twine .......................hundredweight.. | 233,980 | 2,672,280 |
| Corn, wheat ....................................do.... | 51,591 | 98,545 |
| Wheat flour ..................................do.... | 842,483 | 1,806,330 |
| Other kinds.................................. | ................. | 2,197,850 |
| Cotton yarn and twist: | | |
| Gray ......................................pounds.. | 131,565,200 | 30,554,260 |
| Bleached and dyed ............................do.... | 38,092,800 | 9,330,900 |
| | | |
| Cotton manufactures: | | |
| Piece goods— | | |
| Unbleached.............................yards.. | 2,104,944,200 | 91,546,615 |
| Bleached .............................. | 1,533,349,600 | 78,494,730 |
| Printed ............................... | 909,998,500 | 51,747,275 |
| Dyed or manufactured of dyed yarn.... | 816,269,300 | 60,715,015 |
| Of mixed materials ................... | 38,600 | 4,785 |
| Stockings and socks .................dozen pairs.. | 687,500 | 1,113,185 |
| Thread for sewing ....................pounds.. | 31,058,400 | 17,954,945 |
| Lace and patent net .................... | ................. | 13,834,095 |
| Unenumerated........................... | ................. | 18,682,265 |
| | | |
| Total of cotton manufactures ............ | ................. | 328,542,910 |
| | | |
| Cycles and parts ............................. | ................. | 2,887,060 |
| Dyestuffs: | | |
| Products of coal tar.................... | ................. | 1,051,745 |
| Other sorts, unenumerated .............. | ................. | 648,520 |
| Earthen and china ware: | | |
| Red pottery, brownstone ware and manufactures of clay ...... | ................. | 892,890 |
| Earthenware, china ware, parian, and porcelain.......... | ................. | 9,071,095 |
| Electric-lighting apparatus ................... | ................. | 2,763,885 |
| Fish: | | |
| Herrings...............................barrels.. | 1,878,652 | 11,881,700 |
| Of other sorts ......................... | ................. | 3,472,565 |
| Fishing tackle................................ | ................. | 1,233,490 |
| Flax and hemp, dressed and undressed..........hundredweight.. | 31,628 | 709,000 |
| Furniture, cabinet and upholstery............. | ................. | 8,169,865 |
| Glass: | | |
| Plate, rough and silvered...............hundredweight.. | 66,835 | 576,585 |
| Flint .....................................do.... | 108,501 | 1,252,875 |
| Bottles and manufactures of glass .............do.... | 881,505 | 2,194,085 |
| Of other sorts..............................do.... | 231,074 | 1,262,230 |
| Grease, tallow, and fat ......................do.... | 667,438 | 4,108,890 |
| Haberdashery and millinery.................... | ................. | 7,301,580 |
| Hardware...................................... | ................. | 7,199,130 |
| Cutlery ....................................... | ................. | 8,183,890 |
| Hats: | | |
| Felt......................................dozen.. | 498,014 | 4,062,665 |
| Straw.......................................do.... | 575,834 | 1,997,660 |
| Hides, raw...............................hundredweight.. | 170,097 | 1,551,805 |
| Implements and tools: | | |
| Agricultural ........................... | ................. | 1,968,885 |
| Unenumerated........................... | ................. | 5,491,035 |
| Instruments and apparatus: Surgical, anatomical, and scientific.......... | ................. | 2,513,955 |

*Exports from Great Britain in 1901 (British and Irish produce)*—Continued.

| Articles. | Quantities. | Values. |
|---|---|---|
| Jewelry.................................................... | | $925,155 |
| Jute yarn.........................................pounds.. | 43,014,500 | 2,573,015 |
| Manufactures, piece goods......................yards.. | 215,459,300 | 10,718,650 |
| Leather: | | |
|   Unwrought.............................hundredweight.. | 128,290 | 6,609,130 |
|   Wrought— | | |
|     Boots and shoes.......................dozen pairs.. | 678,543 | 8,265,950 |
|     Of other sorts..................................... | | 2,658,250 |
|   Saddlery and harness............................... | | 2,926,700 |
| Linen yarn..................................pounds.. | 12,971,100 | 4,123,405 |
| Linen manufactures: | | |
|   White or plain...........................yards.. | 137,521,000 | 16,212,485 |
|   Printed, checked, or dyed...............do.... | 8,007,600 | 1,201,875 |
|   Sailcloth and sails.....................do.... | 4,686,700 | 1,271,060 |
|   Thread for sewing......................pounds.. | 1,721,000 | 1,135,595 |
|   Of other sorts..................................... | | 5,281,530 |
|     Total of linen manufactures................... | | 25,102,496 |
| Machinery: | | |
|   Steam engines— | | |
|     Locomotives..................................... | | 9,556,700 |
|     Agricultural..................................... | | 3,104,840 |
|     Other descriptions.............................. | | 8,628,135 |
|   Other sorts— | | |
|     Agricultural..................................... | | 3,614,740 |
|     Textile......................................... | | 23,629,390 |
|     Mining.......................................... | | 2,546,245 |
|     Other........................................... | | 30,171,755 |
| Manures: | | |
|   Sulphate of ammonia.....................tons.. | 149,884 | 8,035,880 |
|   Other descriptions........................do.... | 277,238 | 3,951,675 |
| Medicines................................................ | | 6,699,850 |
| Metals: | | |
|   Iron— | | |
|     Old.......................................tons.. | 85,196 | 1,366,615 |
|     Pig and puddled.........................do.... | 839,182 | 13,152,630 |
|     Bar.....................................do.... | 104,781 | 4,641,795 |
|     Angle, bolt, and rod....................do.... | 13,292 | 565,875 |
|     Railroad— | | |
|       Rails of iron and steel.............do.... | 466,607 | 13,631,320 |
|       Chairs and sleepers.................do.... | 41,919 | 1,209,935 |
|       Unenumerated.......................do.... | 64,198 | 3,281,510 |
|     Wire of iron and steel..................do.... | 47,849 | 4,839,215 |
|     Sheets— | | |
|       Galvanized..........................do.... | 250,285 | 15,964,250 |
|       Not galvanized......................do.... | 35,904 | 2,038,545 |
|     Hoops and hoop iron....................do.... | 89,254 | 1,740,915 |
|     Tinned plates..........................do.... | 271,320 | 18,520,440 |
|     Black plates for tinning................do.... | 51,395 | 2,674,590 |
|     Anchors, grapnels, etc.................do.... | 23,688 | 2,269,470 |
|     Tubes and pipes........................do.... | 55,251 | 5,024,375 |
|     Nails, screws, and rivets...............do.... | 18,640 | 1,959,360 |
|     Bedsteads..............................do.... | 10,584 | 1,289,610 |
|     Cast and manufactures..................do.... | 126,267 | 5,605,975 |
|     Wrought and manufactures..............do.... | 86,941 | 9,032,165 |
|   Steel— | | |
|     Cast in ingots or blooms...............do.... | 5,038 | 196,235 |
|     In bars of all kinds...................do.... | 112,123 | 7,555,965 |
|     Sheets.................................do.... | 96,654 | 4,075,185 |
|     Manufactures of steel or of iron and steel combined, tons.. | 51,851 | 5,724,425 |
|     Total of iron and steel................tons.... | 2,897,719 | 126,410,400 |
| Copper, unwrought— | | |
|   Ingots, cakes, or slabs...............hundredweight.. | 531,209 | 9,761,720 |
| Wrought or partly wrought— | | |
|   Mixed or yellow metal...................do.... | 182,110 | 2,949,175 |
|   Of other sorts.........................do.... | 219,602 | 4,787,870 |
|   Brass of all sorts.......................do.... | 116,239 | 2,965,005 |
| Lead— | | |
|   Pig....................................tons.. | 18,146 | 1,201,880 |
|   Rolled sheet, piping, tubing, etc.........do.... | 19,426 | 1,725,845 |
| Tin, unwrought........................hundredweight.. | 109,919 | 8,897,320 |
| Zinc, wrought and unwrought.............do.... | 172,801 | 724,940 |
| Unenumerated and manufactures................ | | 4,192,220 |
| Milk, condensed.......................hundredweight.. | 207,180 | 1,922,420 |
| Musical instruments..................................... | | 1,126,925 |
| Oil and floor cloth.....................square yards.. | 26,757,900 | 6,490,085 |
| Oil, other than essential or medicinal: | | |
|   Linseed...............................tons.. | 21,024 | 3,307,240 |
|   Cotton seed............................do.... | 17,896 | 1,932,035 |

*Exports from Great Britain in 1901 (British and Irish produce)*—Continued.

| Articles. | Quantities. | Value. |
|---|---|---|
| Oil, other than essential or medicinal—Continued. | | |
| All other seed oils..........................tons.. | 3,946 | $549,065 |
| Other sorts, unenumerated ......................... | | 4,182,985 |
| Oil-seed cake and other animal foods ......................... | | 1,185,810 |
| Painters' colors and materials ......................... | | 10,039,915 |
| Paper and pasteboard: | | |
| Writing or printing paper .................hundredweight.. | 716,857 | 5,476,390 |
| Paper hangings .....................do... | 69,337 | 974,005 |
| Unenumerated .....................do... | 262,059 | 1,892,490 |
| Pickles, vinegar, sauces, and condiments ......................... | | 4,006,500 |
| Confectionery, jams, etc......................... | | 8,747,860 |
| Pictures, drawings, etc......................... | | 2,121,405 |
| Plate and plated ware ......................... | | 2,505,110 |
| Potatoes .....................hundredweight.. | 450,400 | 452,610 |
| Provisions, not otherwise described ......................... | | 9,103,910 |
| Rags and other materials........................tons.. | 65,158 | 1,913,350 |
| Salt.......................do... | 617,203 | 2,545,700 |
| Seeds, of all sorts .....................hundredweight.. | 274,935 | 1,683,765 |
| Sewing machines ......................... | | 7,759,905 |
| Ships and boats, new (not registered as British), with machinery: | | |
| Steamships (gross tonnage, 344,256)— | | |
| Hulls and fittings......................... | | 35,649,205 |
| Machinery......................... | | 9,464,840 |
| Sailing ships......................... | | 633,175 |
| Silk, thrown, twist, and yarn .................pounds.. | 737,000 | 1,471,556 |
| Silk manufactures: | | |
| Broad stuffs— | | |
| Of silk or satin .....................yards.. | 4,255,100 | 2,461,485 |
| Of silk, mixed with other materials.....................do.. | 5,034,800 | 1,884,185 |
| Handkerchiefs, scarfs, and shawls ......................... | | 907,260 |
| Ribbons of all kinds ......................... | | 137,950 |
| Lace ......................... | | 493,860 |
| Other kinds of silk......................... | | 927,145 |
| Other kinds of silk, mixed with other material ......................... | | 335,020 |
| Total of silk manufactures......................... | | 7,146,905 |
| Skins and furs: | | |
| British sheep and lambs, undressed, without the wool ..number.. | 6,090,900 | 1,857,850 |
| British, unenumerated ......................... | | 2,208,330 |
| Foreign, British dressed.....................number.. | 2,423,000 | 2,676,375 |
| Soap .....................hundredweight.. | 947,485 | 4,997,620 |
| Soda compounds .....................do... | 3,726,453 | 5,627,255 |
| Spirits .....................gallons.. | 6,208,975 | 13,161,585 |
| Starch and blue.......................... | | 787,890 |
| Stationery, other than paper......................... | | 6,135,095 |
| Stones and slates: | | |
| Slate for roofing.....................number.. | 20,097,800 | 614,700 |
| Grindstones, millstones, etc.....................tons.. | 46,750 | 800,165 |
| Sugar, refined.....................hundredweight.. | 556,309 | 1,753,805 |
| Molasses, treacle, sirup .....................do... | 228,551 | 677,770 |
| Telegraphic wire and apparatus......................... | | 15,789,925 |
| Tobacco and snuff, manufactured in United Kingdom .... ..pounds.. | 6,620,606 | 8,753,220 |
| Toys and games......................... | | 1,842,090 |
| Umbrellas and parasols......................... | | 2,230,870 |
| Wood and timber, manufactured: Staves and empty casks ......................... | | 2,218,150 |
| Wool: | | |
| Sheep and lambs.....................pounds.. | 20,205,000 | 2,567,840 |
| Flocks and rag wool.....................do... | 10,745,000 | 1,222,185 |
| Noils .....................do... | 9,924,300 | 2,694,045 |
| Waste .....................do... | 1,984,500 | 315,070 |
| Combed or carded and tops .....................do... | 27,111,400 | 6,840,425 |
| Woolen worsted yarn .....................do... | 48,498,400 | 17,438,430 |
| Woolen and worsted manufactures: | | |
| Woolen tissues— | | |
| Heavy broad— | | |
| All wool .....................yards.. | 9,302,800 | 10,130,275 |
| Mixed .....................do... | 13,479,400 | 6,349,610 |
| Light broad— | | |
| All wool.....................do... | 6,137,400 | 4,644,430 |
| Mixed .....................do... | 8,298,100 | 2,648,665 |
| Light narrow— | | |
| All wool.....................do... | 3,026,600 | 897,775 |
| Mixed .....................do... | 3,730,300 | 812,505 |
| Heavy narrow— | | |
| All wool.....................do... | 469,100 | 356,170 |
| Mixed .....................do... | 435,400 | 155,640 |
| Worsted coatings, broad— | | |
| All wool .....................do... | 9,198,800 | 8,971,685 |
| Mixed .....................do... | 5,681,700 | 8,237,505 |
| Worsted coatings, narrow— | | |
| All wool .....................do... | 605,800 | 391,420 |
| Mixed .....................do... | 1,318,700 | 444,460 |

*Exports from Great Britain in 1901 (British and Irish produce)*—Continued.

| Articles. | Quantities. | Values. |
|---|---|---|
| Woolen and worsted manufactures—Continued. | | |
| Worsted coatings, narrow—Continued. | | |
| Flannels ........yards.. | 9,798,500 | $1,756,990 |
| Blankets......pairs.. | 779,300 | 1,485,615 |
| Worsted stuffs, etc.— | | |
| All wool........yards.. | 11,688,200 | 2,724,690 |
| Mixed......do.... | 65,490,900 | 13,460,220 |
| Hosiery ...... | | 4,466,675 |
| Carpets and druggets ......yards.. | 7,540,000 | 4,149,735 |
| Rugs, coverlets, wrappers...... | | 2,219,165 |
| Small wares...... | | 1,210,230 |
| All other...... | | 673,060 |
| Total of woolen and worsted manufactures...... | | 71,186,840 |
| Yarn, alpaca, and mohair......pounds.. | 17,364,900 | 8,754,805 |
| All other articles: | | |
| Manufactured ...... | | 15,218,180 |
| Unmanufactured ...... | | 3,884,965 |
| Total...... | | 1,381,900,035 |
| Parcel post...... | | 18,211,845 |
| Total exports of British and Irish produce ...... | | 1,400,111,880 |

*Exports from Great Britain in 1901 (foreign and colonial merchandise).*

| Articles. | Quantities. | Values. |
|---|---|---|
| Bacon and hams ......hundredweight.. | 262,374 | $3,145,480 |
| Bristles......pounds.. | 1,102,785 | 843,170 |
| Butter......hundredweight.. | 49,956 | 1,273,730 |
| Caoutchouc ......do.... | 293,792 | 18,018,615 |
| Cheese ......do.... | 55,069 | 817,895 |
| Chemical manufactures and products unenumerated...... | | 1,694,400 |
| China or porcelain......hundredweight.. | 72,687 | 1,204,565 |
| Cocoa......pounds.. | 11,201,067 | 1,713,280 |
| Coffee......hundredweight.. | 676,328 | 9,739,155 |
| Cordage, twine, and cable yarn ...... | | 603,630 |
| Cork, manufactured......pounds.. | 2,336,239 | 659,570 |
| Corn: | | |
| Wheat......hundredweight.. | 302,950 | 543,700 |
| Other kinds of corn and grain ......do.... | 442,330 | 625,290 |
| Wheat meal or flour......do.... | 326,026 | 805,475 |
| Cotton: | | |
| Raw......do.... | 1,844,318 | 25,109,810 |
| Waste of......pounds.. | 40,653,308 | 2,290,100 |
| Cotton manufactures: | | |
| Piece goods ......yards.. | 19,956,615 | 1,502,365 |
| Other articles...... | | 1,284,840 |
| Drugs: | | |
| Bark, Peruvian......hundredweight.. | 25,767 | 346,615 |
| Opium......pounds.. | 407,293 | 1,090,385 |
| Unenumerated ...... | | 2,775,630 |
| Dyeing or tanning stuffs: | | |
| Cutch and gambier......tons.. | 4,320 | 491,570 |
| Indigo......hundredweight.. | 31,070 | 2,310,780 |
| Other kinds...... | | 1,024,440 |
| Farinaceous substances...... | | 385,260 |
| Feathers, ornamental ......pounds.. | 503,032 | 3,450,585 |
| Fish, cured or salted......hundredweight.. | 445,912 | 4,237,870 |
| Flax and hemp | | |
| Flax, dressed and undressed ......do.... | 54,080 | 535,295 |
| Tow or codilla of flax and hemp......do.... | 23,840 | 117,185 |
| Hemp and other like substances ......do.... | 1,375,560 | 10,365,650 |
| Fruits: | | |
| Almonds ......do.... | 36,767 | 729,855 |
| Currants......do.... | 68,984 | 456,375 |
| Raisins ......do.... | 42,281 | 278,065 |
| Oranges and lemons ......bushels.. | 279,635 | 657,440 |
| Unenumerated, dried......hundredweight.. | 240,906 | 661,860 |
| Preserved, without sugar, other than dried ......do.... | 98,535 | 587,465 |
| Guano ......tons.. | 1,371 | 45,950 |
| Gum of all sorts ......hundredweight.. | 241,677 | 3,690,105 |
| Gutta-percha ......hundredweight.. | 10,936 | 719,500 |
| Hair: | | |
| Cow, ox, bull, or elk ......do... | 6,058 | 64,160 |
| Other kinds...... | | 504,815 |
| Hardware and cutlery...... | | 1,320,365 |

*Exports from Great Britain in 1901 (foreign and colonial merchandise)*—Continued.

| Articles. | Quantities. | Values. |
|---|---|---|
| Hides, raw, dry, and wet.............................hundredweight.. | 365,834 | $4,862,155 |
| Horns and hoofs...................................................tons.. | 1,703 | 256,805 |
| Ivory, teeth (elephants'), sea cow and sea horse.....hundredweight.. | 5,444 | 1,035,660 |
| Jute ..............................................................tons.. | 121,965 | 8,530,460 |
|    Manufactures of ...................................................... | | 9,158,270 |
| Lace and articles thereof........................................... | | 8,850,740 |
| Lard.........................................................hundredweight.. | 282,282 | 2,757,560 |
| Leather .....................................................pounds.. | 20,783,392 | 7,813,450 |
| Leather gloves..........................................dozen pairs.. | 167,704 | 967,260 |
| Matches .............................................................. | | 576,690 |
| Meat, preserved, salted or fresh, except bacon and hams, hundredweight.. | 125,901 | 1,530,770 |
| Metals: | | |
|    Copper, unwrought, part wrought and old ...................tons.. | 23,191 | 8,171,765 |
|    Iron, bar, angle, bolt, and rod.............................do.... | 12,411 | 583,165 |
|    Iron and steel manufactures— | | |
|       Cycles and parts.......................................... | | 141,100 |
|       Machinery................................................ | | 8,103,490 |
|       Unenumerated .....................................tons.. | 19,121 | 1,545,175 |
|    Lead, pig or sheet ........................................do.... | 12,904 | 822,270 |
|    Platinum, wrought or unwrought .. ...............troy ounces.. | 16,100 | 188,370 |
|    Quicksilver................................................pounds.. | 2,014,753 | 1,194,100 |
|    Silver, ore of............................................... | | 136,780 |
|    Tin in blocks, ingots, bars, or slabs ............hundredweight.. | 418,717 | 12,388,135 |
| Mica and talc ...............................................do.... | 18,118 | 333,635 |
| Milk, condensed ...........................................do.... | 180,344 | 1,772,900 |
| Nuts and kernels (for oil)...................................tons.. | 17,675 | 1,118,525 |
| Oil: | | |
|    Cocoanut................................................hundredweight.. | 162,769 | 109,930 |
|    Olive ................................................................tons.. | 2,984 | 649,575 |
|    Palm ....................................................hundredweight.. | 688,861 | 3,812,135 |
|    Seed ...............................................................tons.. | 3,174 | 372,830 |
| Pictures and drawings............................................... | | 607,855 |
| Plumbago ......................................................tons.... | 3,572 | 350,925 |
| Precious stones, unset............................................... | | 996,675 |
| Rags and other paper-making materials: | | |
|    Linen and cotton rags.......................................tons.. | 6,841 | 259,490 |
|    Other materials .............................................do.... | 8,125 | 296,690 |
| Rice ..........................................................hundredweight.. | 2,515,190 | 5,494,930 |
| Saltpeter ....................................................do.... | 27,614 | 112,035 |
| Cubic niter.....................................................do.... | 96,040 | 210,000 |
| Seeds: | | 2,053,470 |
|    Flax or linseed............................................quarters.. | 170,308 | |
|    Rape .........................................................do.... | 15,423 | 158,915 |
|    Unenumerated, for obtaining oil.............................do.... | 152,242 | 1,623,385 |
| Shells of all kinds ................................................ | | 2,230,555 |
| Silk: | | |
|    Knubs or husks of silk and waste ...............hundredweight.. | 5,370 | 221,295 |
|    Raw ........................................................pounds.. | 244,566 | 765,430 |
|    Thrown and spun..............................................do.... | 48,666 | 208,390 |
| Silk manufactures................................................... | | 5,104,185 |
| Skins and furs: | | |
|    Goat, undressed .............................................number.. | 17,066,619 | 7,826,515 |
|    Seal .........................................................do.... | 51,603 | 507,705 |
|    Sheep, undressed.............................................do.... | 7,761,680 | 3,055,295 |
|    Furs of all sorts (except seal skins) .........................do.... | 38,361,490 | 7,622,860 |
|    Manufactures of ...................................................... | | 1,060,730 |
| Spices, pepper.................................................pounds.. | 11,473,560 | 1,599,125 |
|    Of other sorts.......................................hundredweight.. | 79,722 | 890,250 |
| Spirits: | | |
|    Rum .................................................proof gallons.. | 927,134 | 712,045 |
|    Brandy...........................................................do.... | 60,468 | 216,160 |
|    Geneva and other foreign and colonial spirits..............do.... | 266,246 | 487,005 |
| Straw plaiting for hats and bonnets ...........................pounds.. | 4,013,905 | 1,361,710 |
| Sugar: | | |
|    Refined and candy ..............................hundredweight.. | 70,415 | 246,760 |
|    Unrefined ....................................................do.... | 122,895 | 374,375 |
|    Molasses.......................................................do.... | 50,151 | 79,725 |
| Tallow and stearin..............................................do.... | 949,555 | 6,394,640 |
| Tea...............................................................pounds.. | 43,389,518 | 8,493,470 |
| Tobacco: | | |
|    Unmanufactured ............................................do.... | 5,139,391 | 798,105 |
|    Manufactured, cigars ........................................do.... | 352,965 | 828,730 |
|    Other sorts .................................................do.... | 1,053,141 | 494,735 |
| Wine ...........................................................gallons.. | 1,038,443 | 2,810,395 |
| Wool, sheep, lamb, alpaca, and llama ........................pounds.. | 294,213,768 | 53,554,425 |
| Woolen manufactures: | | |
|    Stuffs ................................................................ | | 2,607,770 |
|    Other kinds.......................................................... | | 1,953,620 |
| All other articles .................................................. | | 27,266,045 |
| Total exports of foreign and colonial produce ................... | | 339,209,460 |
| Total exports of British and foreign goods ...................... | | 1,739,321,240 |

*Value of imports from and exports to foreign countries and British possessions in 1901.*

FOREIGN.

| Countries. | Imports. | Exports. |
|---|---|---|
| Russia: | | |
| Northern ports............................... | $83,825,955 | $61,776,625 |
| Southern ports............................... | 25,691,940 | 9,278,140 |
| Sweden and Norway............................ | 76,760,315 | 46,401,435 |
| Denmark ...................................... | 72,201,160 | 21,202,085 |
| Danish West Indies........................... | 18,960 | 223,006 |
| Germany...................................... | 161,086,070 | 171,105,400 |
| Possessions in West Africa................ | 559,575 | 450,685 |
| Holland...................................... | 164,359,215 | 68,720,105 |
| Java and other possessions in Indian seas | 1,595,725 | 11,813,840 |
| Belgium ...................................... | 123,330,405 | 63,123,455 |
| France....................................... | 256,067,120 | 118,504,100 |
| Algeria ................................... | 3,490,515 | 2,202,070 |
| Possessions in Senegambia ................. | 2,031,925 | 2,825,120 |
| West Indian islands ....................... | 1,510 | 655,605 |
| Portugal..................................... | 16,525,750 | 10,469,960 |
| Azores and Madeira ........................ | 721,555 | 4,718,815 |
| Possessions in West Africa................ | 268,175 | 2,498,095 |
| Possessions in East Africa................ | 240,935 | 3,688,990 |
| Spain ........................................ | 70,200,920 | 27,277,615 |
| Canary Islands ............................ | 5,551,915 | 4,449,920 |
| Possessions in West Africa................ | 86,760 | 122,900 |
| Italy ........................................ | 16,919,290 | 41,467,420 |
| Austria-Hungary.............................. | 5,956,470 | 14,194,520 |
| Greece ....................................... | 7,329,925 | 8,725,875 |
| Bulgaria..................................... | 569,700 | 1,735,655 |
| Roumania .................................... | 19,969,850 | 5,481,310 |
| Turkey....................................... | 29,192,780 | 36,035,270 |
| Egypt........................................ | 59,528,230 | 32,093,785 |
| Tripoli and Tunis............................ | 2,455,910 | 2,017,545 |
| Morocco ..................................... | 2,686,485 | 4,555,400 |
| Persia....................................... | 1,000,620 | 2,916,125 |
| Siam......................................... | 253,800 | 1,286,260 |
| China (not Hongkong and Macao).............. | 10,580,595 | 34,137,730 |
| Japan........................................ | 9,151,450 | 41,047,260 |
| Philippine and Ladrone islands.............. | 13,509,050 | 4,569,390 |
| Islands in Pacific, not elsewhere stated ... | 1,204,895 | 855,885 |
| United States................................ | 705,077,325 | 188,255,750 |
| Cuba and Porto Rico ......................... | 190,350 | 10,120,630 |
| Mexico....................................... | 1,817,580 | 8,365,395 |
| Central American States...................... | 4,556,280 | 4,272,325 |
| Haiti and Santo Domingo ..................... | 274,005 | 1,082,185 |
| Republic of Colombia......................... | 2,522,695 | 4,683,920 |
| Venezuela .................................... | 515,040 | 2,568,400 |
| Ecuador ...................................... | 1,041,105 | 1,461,665 |
| Brazil....................................... | 24,788,970 | 22,200,305 |
| Uruguay ..................................... | 2,872,505 | 6,839,285 |
| Argentine Republic .......................... | 62,074,325 | 34,863,505 |
| Chile........................................ | 21,565,475 | 17,182,500 |
| Peru......................................... | 9,067,525 | 5,619,900 |
| Western coast of Africa...................... | 530,645 | 1,138,680 |
| Other countries ............................. | 1,363,260 | 2,997,880 |
| Total....................................... | 2,082,082,460 | 1,173,729,520 |

BRITISH POSSESSIONS.

| | Imports | Exports |
|---|---|---|
| Channel Islands ............................. | $6,808,270 | $5,787,215 |
| Gibraltar ................................... | 207,605 | 4,274,210 |
| Malta and Gozo............................... | 419,670 | 6,404,510 |
| North American colonies...................... | 101,936,550 | 48,441,995 |
| Bermudas..................................... | 9,790 | 815,305 |
| British West India islands .................. | 9,192,395 | 10,754,235 |
| British Guiana............................... | 2,210,255 | 3,280,215 |
| British Honduras ............................ | 989,370 | 890,195 |
| Australasia.................................. | 121,088,345 | 117,568,310 |
| New Zealand ................................. | 52,972,985 | 30,341,150 |
| British India............................... | 136,958,670 | 178,731,995 |
| Straits Settlements.......................... | 30,551,520 | 16,413,460 |
| Ceylon....................................... | 22,382,760 | 7,972,720 |
| Hongkong .................................... | 3,014,205 | 18,989,890 |
| Mauritius ................................... | 1,591,555 | 5,143,490 |
| Aden ........................................ | 773,160 | 2,362,550 |
| Eastern coast of Africa...................... | 513,080 | 874,110 |
| Natal ....................................... | 2,874,930 | 30,270,310 |
| Cape of Good Hope a.......................... | 22,786,610 | 64,425,425 |

a Value of diamonds exported from the Cape of Good Hope to the United Kingdom, $24,385,210.

*Value of imports from and exports to foreign countries and British possessions in 1901—*
Continued.

BRITISH POSSESSIONS—Continued.

| Countries. | Imports. | Exports. |
|---|---|---|
| Niger Protectorate........................................................ | $5,823,110 | $3,919,210 |
| Lagos...................................................................... | 1,821,285 | 2,591,995 |
| Gold Coast................................................................ | 1,865,840 | 4,997,420 |
| Sierre Leone and Gambia................................................. | 762,665 | 2,073,720 |
| Other possessions........................................................ | 804,005 | 3,767,855 |
| Total of British possessions ........................................... | 527,868,530 | 565,591,820 |
| Total of foreign countries and British possessions................ | 2,109,950,990 | 1,739,321,340 |

### TRADE WITH THE UNITED STATES IN 1901.

The imports from the United States into the United Kingdom in 1901, after showing a decrease of $30,000,000 in 1899—which was wiped off in 1900, and an increase of $63,000,000 shown—again increased in 1901, the aggregate amounting to no less than $705,077,325, a total exceeding any previous year and excelling 1900 by $11,000,000.

The articles which were the chief factors in securing this increase were oxen and bulls, and sheep and lambs (living), butter, caoutchouc, wheat, raw cotton, lard, boots and shoes, bacon, fresh beef, hams, copper regulus and precipitate, and tobacco, manufactured. Although the total value does not affect the aggregate of exports to the United Kingdom from the United States, it is worth noticing that in the case of oranges, the value in 1901 amounted to $94,545, whereas in 1900 it only totaled $19,510; in the case of butter, too, the respective totals are $3,445,820 and $1,238,620, and the value of boots and shoes continues to show steady increase. The same distinction also applies to lard, condensed milk, musical instruments, oilseed cake, poultry and game, toys and games, and staves.

Against the foregoing must be set the following, all of which showed marked decreases, namely: Cheese, clocks, confectionery, barley, oats, maize or indian corn, hops, unwrought and part-wrought copper, iron (pig and puddled); unwrought steel, crude zinc, sawn or split wood, and tallow and grease.

The total exports from the United Kingdom to the United States in 1901 amounted to—

| | |
|---|---|
| British and Irish goods............................................... | $91,969,415 |
| Foreign and colonial ................................................. | 96,286,335 |
| Total........................................................... | 188,255,750 |

In 1900 the respective totals were—

| | |
|---|---|
| British and Irish goods ............................................. | $98,904,155 |

(Thus showing a decrease in 1901 of $7,000,000.)

| | |
|---|---|
| Foreign and colonial goods ......................................... | 87,815,620 |

(Showing an increase in 1901 of nearly $8,500,000.)

| | |
|---|---|
| Total........................................................... | 186,719,775 |

Or a net increase in 1901 of $1,500,000.

In the case of British and Irish goods, exports of horses, jute piece goods, linens, iron (wrought and unwrought), and brass manufactures showed the principal increases, while cement, cotton (entered by the yard), machinery, copper, silk, telegraphic wires and apparatus, and sheep and lambs' wool displayed the greatest falling off in value.

In foreign and colonial merchandise exported to the United States, the chief increases occurred in horses, chinaware, coffee, raw cotton, opium, indigo, ornamental feathers, flax, hemp, jute manufactures, copper (unwrought and part wrought), unset precious stones, seeds (all), shells, goatskins, tea, onions, furniture woods, and woolen cloths and stuffs; and the principal decreases in butter, caoutchouc, preserved fruits, gum kowrie, horsehair, hair (unenumerated), raw hides, bar iron, plaiting of straw, spices, and sheep or lambs' wool.

*Imports into the United Kingdom from the United States in 1901.*

| Articles. | Quantities. | Values. |
|---|---|---|
| Animals, living: | | |
|   Oxen and bulls..............................number.. | 405,288 | $36,586,105 |
|   Cows and calves..............................do.... | 416 | 34,665 |
|   Sheep and lambs..............................do.... | 300,152 | 2,317,595 |
|   Horses— | | |
|     Stallions..............................do.... | 5 | 8,450 |
|     Mares..............................do.... | 9,187 | 1,608,570 |
|     Geldings..............................do.... | 10,168 | 1,679,475 |
|   Unenumerated.............................. | | 3,185 |
| Arms, ammunition, etc.............................. | | 454,125 |
| Blacking and polishes..............................hundredweight.. | 26,443 | 241,450 |
| Bladders, casings, and sausage skins.............. | | 514,395 |
| Books..............................hundredweight.. | 15,428 | 848,155 |
| Butter..............................do.... | 150,121 | 3,445,820 |
| Caoutchouc..............................do.... | 31,493 | 1,276,345 |
|   Manufactures— | | |
|     Boots and shoes..............................dozen pairs.. | 151,806 | 867,405 |
|     Other sorts.............................. | | 606,965 |
| Cards, playing..............................dozen packs.. | 46,070 | 82,005 |
| Carriages, carts, etc..............................number.. | 2,928 | 770,745 |
| Cheese..............................hundredweight.. | 540,102 | 6,370,305 |
| Chemical manufactures and products of all sorts.. | | 1,132,295 |
| China and earthenware..............................hundredweight.. | 31,811 | 88,135 |
| Cider and perry..............................gallons.. | 831,247 | 59,420 |
| Clocks: | | |
|   Complete..............................number.. | 355,390 | 467,650 |
|   Parts thereof.............................. | | 8,720 |
| Cocoa..............................pounds.. | 1,021,404 | 138,265 |
| Coffee, raw..............................hundredweight.. | 101,259 | 1,881,460 |
| Confectionery..............................do.... | 8,329 | 55,475 |
| Cordage, twine, and cable yarn.............................. | | 406,700 |
| Corn: | | |
|   Wheat..............................hundredweight.. | 40,466,300 | 67,377,705 |
|   Barley..............................do.... | 2,630,010 | 4,363,470 |
|   Oats..............................do.... | 4,443,800 | 5,929,640 |
|   Rye..............................do.... | 313,200 | 417,345 |
|   Peas..............................do.... | 440,100 | 767,405 |
|   Maize or Indian corn..............................do.... | 25,564,900 | 29,724,525 |
|   Buckwheat..............................do.... | 2,000 | 3,455 |
|   Wheat meal and flour..............................do.... | 18,999,882 | 43,491,245 |
|   Oatmeal..............................do.... | 740,970 | 2,486,675 |
|   Maize or Indian corn meal..............................do.... | 1,637,226 | 2,285,125 |
|   Meal, unenumerated..............................do.... | 36,220 | 44,160 |
| Cotton: | | |
|   Raw..............................hundredweight.. | 13,221,308 | 161,778,560 |
|   Waste..............................pounds.. | 5,870,786 | 206,105 |
|   Manufactures of, all sorts.............................. | | 1,660,725 |
| Drugs: | | |
|   Opium.....pounds.. | 16,945 | 48,760 |
|   Of all other sorts.............................. | | 1,178,355 |
| Dye stuffs and substances used in tanning and dyeing, extracts...... | | 329,495 |
| Eggs..............................hundred.. | 342,788 | 628,215 |
| Electrical goods.............................. | | 1,940,905 |
| Farinaceous substances: | | |
|   Starch, farina, and dextrine..............................hundredweight.. | 493,609 | 1,017,745 |
|   Of all other sorts.............................. | | 333,820 |
| Feathers: | | |
|   In beds or for beds..............................hundredweight.. | 9,922 | 94,745 |
|   Ornamental..............................pounds.. | 69,307 | 35,085 |
| Fish, of all sorts..............................hundredweight.. | 436,987 | 4,180,885 |
| Fruit: | | |
|   Liable to duty— | | |
|     Plums, dried or preserved..............................hundredweight.. | 10,974 | 88,090 |
|     Prunes..............................do.... | 4,182 | 34,470 |

*Imports into the United Kingdom from the United States in 1901*—Continued.

| Articles. | Quantities. | Values. |
|---|---|---|
| Fruit—Continued. | | |
| Not liable to duty— | | |
| Apples, raw...........................hundredweight.. | 726,366 | $2,439,420 |
| Nuts (other than almonds)...................do.... | 5,256 | 17,080 |
| Oranges ....................................do.... | 19,861 | 94,545 |
| Pears, raw..................................do.... | 38,147 | 229,235 |
| Unenumerated, dried........................do.... | 11,627 | 108,110 |
| Preserved, with or without sugar, not dried ...............do.... | 371,813 | 2,444,820 |
| Glass manufactures............................... | | 166,185 |
| Glue, size, and gelatin .......................hundredweight.. | 21,019 | 202,155 |
| Gum, of all sorts ..............................do.... | 6,345 | 33,420 |
| Hair: | | |
| Horse......................................do.... | 406 | 6,865 |
| Unenumerated .................................. | | 340,735 |
| Hardware (not cutlery).......................hundredweight.. | 157,784 | 2,378,885 |
| Hay ..........................................tons.. | 83,604 | 1,693,200 |
| Hemp: | | |
| Dressed or undressed.......................do.... | 779 | 106,660 |
| Other vegetable, similar substances, unenumerated ........do.... | 118 | 13,540 |
| Hides, raw ..................................hundredweight.. | 4,845 | 48,075 |
| Hops .........................................do.... | 73,660 | 1,447,360 |
| Horns and hoofs ..............................tons.. | 218 | 35,855 |
| Implements and tools............................. | | 1,721,255 |
| Jewelry........................................ | | 82,430 |
| Lamps and lanterns..........................number.. | 97,950 | 103,195 |
| Lard..........................................hundredweight.. | 1,842,054 | 18,878,190 |
| Imitation ..................................do.... | 92,471 | 748,830 |
| Leather ......................................do.... | 624,385 | 16,782,540 |
| Manufactures: | | |
| Boots and shoes.........................dozen pairs.. | 80,697 | 2,028,715 |
| Unenumerated ................................. | | 121,885 |
| Machinery and mill work: | | |
| Steam engines ................................... | | 1,817,670 |
| Not being steam engines— | | |
| Agricultural ................................. | | 1,126,405 |
| Sewing machines............................. | | 737,550 |
| Of all other kinds........................... | | 8,791,330 |
| Manures, phosphate of lime and rock phosphate...................tons.. | 109,700 | 985,420 |
| Margarine cheese............................hundredweight.. | 3,632 | 86,410 |
| Meat (not poultry or game): | | |
| Bacon......................................do.... | 4,244,329 | 46,279,255 |
| Beef— | | |
| Fresh..................................do.... | 3,180,291 | 33,807,935 |
| Salted.................................do.... | 192,000 | 1,284,635 |
| Hams....................................do.... | 1,730,536 | 21,049,080 |
| Pork— | | |
| Fresh..................................do.... | 348,935 | 3,814,965 |
| Salted.................................do.... | 137,680 | 1,039,280 |
| Unenumerated, salted or fresh...............do.... | 174,830 | 1,379,565 |
| Preserved (not by salting) .................do.... | 459,618 | 6,471,520 |
| Metals and ores: | | |
| Brass and bronze, manufactures of...........................do.... | 7,294 | 175,260 |
| Copper— | | |
| Ore of.................................tons.. | 1,027 | 157,940 |
| Regulus and precipitate..................do.... | 20,869 | 3,479,490 |
| Old, fit only to be remanufactured .........do.... | 144 | 29,080 |
| Unwrought and part wrought .............do.... | 18,957 | 6,804,305 |
| Manufactures of .............................. | | 529,320 |
| Iron— | | |
| Pig and puddled .............................tons.. | 35,312 | 664,995 |
| Bar....................................do.... | 3,363 | 124,355 |
| Old broken and old broken steel...........do.... | 989 | 24,220 |
| Steel, unwrought.......................do.... | 50,864 | 1,471,745 |
| Manufactures of iron and steel— | | |
| Girders, beams, and pillars..................do.... | 858 | 28,900 |
| Rails, steel ............................do.... | 25,543 | 938,700 |
| Cycles ....................................... | | 549,950 |
| Of all other kinds .......................hundredweight.. | 900,821 | 3,558,800 |
| Lead, pig and sheet............................tons.. | 43,496 | 2,908,425 |
| Silver, ore of ...................................... | | 823,260 |
| Zinc— | | |
| Ore of.................................tons.. | 1,622 | 61,470 |
| Crude .................................do.... | 4,253 | 310,085 |
| Metal, unenumerated— | | |
| Unwrought............................do.... | 766 | 312,115 |
| Wrought..............................hundredweight.. | 8,254 | 149,580 |
| Old, fit only for remanufacture ............tons.. | 266 | 16,815 |
| Methylic alcohol ..............................gallons.. | 117,102 | 81,920 |
| Milk, condensed ...............................hundredweight.. | 83,016 | 733,530 |
| Moldings ...................................... | | 61,795 |
| Musical instruments............................. | | 1,447,605 |
| Oil: | | |
| Fish, train, and blubber..........................tons.. | 2,911 | 270,975 |
| Animal ....................................hundredweight.. | 32,419 | 259,650 |

*Imports into the United Kingdom from the United States in 1901*—Continued.

| Articles. | Quantities. | Values. |
|---|---|---|
| Oil—Continued. | | |
| Seed...................................................tons.. | 17,238 | $1,852,655 |
| Turpentine....................................hundredweight.. | 618,972 | 4,096,635 |
| Chemical, essential or perfumed....................pounds.. | 75,227 | 81,800 |
| Unenumerated ..................................... | | 221,670 |
| Oil-seed cake.........................................tons.. | 180,964 | 5,746,910 |
| Oleomargarine.................................hundredweight.. | 117,111 | 1,034,585 |
| Painters' colors, unenumerated ..................... | | 982,740 |
| Paper: | | |
| Unprinted....................................hundredweight.. | 505,868 | 1,848,015 |
| Printed...........................................do.... | 26,347 | 300,095 |
| Strawboard and millboard..........................do.... | 80,162 | 179,660 |
| Wood pulp board...................................do.... | 106,936 | 257,580 |
| Paper-making materials: | | |
| Pulp of wood.......................................tons.. | 11,384 | 457,455 |
| Of all other sorts..................................do.... | 1,934 | 58,310 |
| Paraffin .......................................hundredweight.. | 796,867 | 4,723,145 |
| Perfumery (not containing spirit)....................pounds.. | 80,010 | 29,815 |
| Petroleum: | | |
| Illuminating....................................gallons.. | 136,525,182 | 13,197,685 |
| Lubricating.........................................do.... | 26,266,707 | 4,164,135 |
| Pickles and vegetables, in salt or vinegar ..............do.... | 50,454 | 33,650 |
| Pictures and drawings, by hand ...................number.. | 459 | 100,440 |
| Plaiting of straw and other materials for making hats or bonnets .........................................pounds.. | 132,312 | 38,610 |
| Plants, shrubs, trees ................................. | | 73,770 |
| Plumbago .............................................tons.. | 1,448 | 834,875 |
| Poultry and game ................................... | | 1,029,390 |
| Rosin .......................................hundredweight.. | 1,745,970 | 2,082,695 |
| Sauces or condiments.............................pounds.. | 751,835 | 60,970 |
| Scientific instruments (not electrical) ................. | | 1,401,065 |
| Seeds: | | |
| Clover and grass............................hundredweight.. | 70,633 | 820,790 |
| Cotton.............................................tons.. | 17,433 | 528,965 |
| Flax or linseed.....  ...........................quarters.. | 53,808 | 746,425 |
| Of all other kinds................................. | | 23,845 |
| Shells of all kinds.................................. | | 72,350 |
| Silk manufactures, unenumerated ..................... | | 40,940 |
| Skins and furs: | | |
| Seal skins......................................number.. | 42,014 | 808,495 |
| All other kinds....................................do.... | 3,840,737 | 2,284,180 |
| Slates...............................................do.... | 32,474,302 | 981,715 |
| Soap and soap powder.......................hundredweight.. | 228,888 | 1,119,895 |
| Spices of all sorts...............................pounds.. | 868,646 | 71,360 |
| Spirits: | | |
| Rum ....................................proof gallons.. | 245,342 | 87,030 |
| Sweetened or mixed, tested........................do.... | 16,063 | 410,965 |
| All other sorts.................................gallons.. | 21,201 | 71,540 |
| Sponge ........................................pounds.. | 206,335 | 112,420 |
| Stationery, other than paper ......................... | | 896,965 |
| Stones, rough or hewn ............................tons.. | 892 | 41,085 |
| Sugar: | | |
| Molasses .....................................hundredweight.. | 905,314 | 1,546,405 |
| Glucose...........................................do.... | 1,406,444 | 3,029,885 |
| Tallow and stearin....................................do.... | 403,942 | 2,265,370 |
| Tar...............................................do.... | 37,358 | 47,485 |
| Tea............................................pounds.. | 1,042,396 | 158,910 |
| Tobacco: | | |
| Unmanufactured..................................do.... | 76,467,288 | 11,270,055 |
| Manufactured, all kinds...........................do.... | 5,638,050 | 7,660,635 |
| Toys and games..................................... | | 179,320 |
| Varnish, not containing spirit ....................... | | 190,355 |
| Vegetables, raw: | | |
| Tomatoes.....................................hundredweight.. | 872 | 2,965 |
| All other kinds ................................. | | 2,455 |
| Watches: | | |
| Complete .....................................number.. | 108,987 | 284,675 |
| Parts thereof................................... | | 62,910 |
| Wax .........................................hundredweight.. | 4,357 | 65,890 |
| Wine ......................................  ......gallons.. | 144,303 | 117,125 |
| Wood: | | |
| Hewn, of all kinds.............................loads.. | 163,457 | 3,999,945 |
| Sawn or split, of all kinds..........................do.... | 614,415 | 9,935,715 |
| Staves, all dimensions.............................do.... | 36,567 | 1,108,190 |
| Furniture woods and hard woods— | | |
| Mahogany. ...................................tons.. | 5,338 | 276,295 |
| Unenumerated ..................................do.... | 117,567 | 3,748,790 |
| Manufactures of— | | |
| House frames, fittings, etc.........................  ..... | | 2,878,485 |
| Other sorts................................... | | 2,642,215 |
| Wool, sheep or lambs'...........................pounds.. | 557,774 | 62,170 |

*Imports into the United Kingdom from the United States in 1901*—Continued.

| Articles. | Quantities. | Values. |
|---|---|---|
| Woolen manufactures: | | |
| Carpets nad rugs................................................ | ................. | $68,380 |
| Of all other kinds........................................... | ................. | 34,000 |
| All other articles................................................... | ................. | 2,778,705 |
| Total............................................. | ................. | 705,077,825 |

*Exports from the United Kingdom to the United States in 1901 (produce and manufactures of the United Kingdom).*

| Articles. | Quantities. | Values. |
|---|---|---|
| Aerated waters .........................................dozen bottles.. | 844,440 | $279,225 |
| Animals: | | |
| Horses ... .......................................number.. | 574 | 851,915 |
| All other sorts................................................ | ............ | 136,260 |
| Apparel and haberdashery................................. | ............ | 484,350 |
| Arms, ammunition, and military stores................. | ............ | 199,420 |
| Bags and sacks, empty...........................dozen.. | 323,300 | 187,980 |
| Beer and ale.....................................barrels.. | 43,882 | 1,022,115 |
| Books, printed.........................hundredweight.. | 43,933 | 1,724,540 |
| Bricks.................................................M.. | 9,011 | 130,085 |
| Caoutchouc, manufactures of.............................. | ............ | 254,335 |
| Carriages, viz, cycles and parts......................... | ............ | 8,935 |
| Cement...............................................tons.. | 8,102 | 87,645 |
| Chemicals and chemical preparations: | | |
| Bleaching materials....................hundredweight.. | 726,200 | 1,219,585 |
| Soda compounds.............................do.... | 403,902 | 518,560 |
| All other sorts ............................................ | ............ | 2,392,780 |
| Clay, unmanufactured...........................tons.. | 138,909 | 941,030 |
| Clocks, watches, and parts................................ | ............ | 77,765 |
| Coal, coke, and patent fuel ....................tons.. | 181,816 | 560,055 |
| Coal products.................................................. | ............ | 507,890 |
| Cocoa or chocolate, manufactured in the United Kingdom..pounds.. | 271,347 | 66,510 |
| Cordage and twine.......................hundredweight.. | 1,291 | 18,080 |
| Cotton yarn ....................................pounds.. | 2,978,000 | 1,870,090 |
| Cottons: | | |
| Entered by yard ...........................yards.. | 50,936,600 | 7,083,185 |
| Entered at value.......................................... | ............ | 6,170,990 |
| Earthen and china ware..................................... | ............ | 2,561,820 |
| Fish of all sorts.............................................. | ............ | 724,640 |
| Fishing tackle................................................ | ............ | 273,590 |
| Flax and hemp, dressed and undressed............hundredweight.. | 24,825 | 559,675 |
| Furniture, cabinet, and upholstery wares................ | ............ | 248,965 |
| Glass manufactures........................................... | ............ | 658,725 |
| Glues, size, and gelatin..................hundredweight.. | 20,888 | 811,040 |
| Grease, tallow, and animal fat .......................do.... | 48,950 | 190,885 |
| Hardware, unenumerated ..............................do.... | 6,782 | 223,355 |
| Cutlery ....................................................... | ............ | 385,815 |
| Hats of all sorts...................................dozen.. | 5,374 | 54,540 |
| Hides, raw ...............................hundredweight.. | 43,834 | 448,565 |
| Implements and tools ...................................... | ............ | 151,400 |
| Instruments and apparatus—Surgical, anatomical, and scientific ... | ............ | 111,155 |
| Jute yarn.........................................pounds.. | 839,200 | 48,115 |
| Manufactures, piece goods...................yards.. | 121,673,700 | 5,618,670 |
| Leather, wrought and unwrought......................... | ............ | 959,995 |
| Linen yarn .......................................pounds.. | 848,800 | 208,730 |
| Linens: | | |
| Entered by yard ...........................yards.. | 88,839,000 | 10,149,865 |
| Entered at value............................... | ............ | 3,042,120 |
| Machinery and millwork..................................... | ............ | 2,826,385 |
| Manure..............................................tons.. | 11,751 | 589,600 |
| Medicines, drugs, and medicinal preparations ......... | ............ | 235,035 |
| Metals: | | |
| Iron, wrought and unwrought ...................tons.. | 150,943 | 9,742,075 |
| Brass and manufactures of .........hundredweight.. | 9,004 | 121,405 |
| Copper, wrought and unwrought.................do.... | 30,176 | 524,140 |
| Tin, unwrought ...................................do.... | 2,054 | 63,655 |
| Unenumerated, and manufactures thereof............... | ............ | 388,095 |
| Oil: | | |
| Seed..............................................tons.. | 1,521 | 210,710 |
| Other sorts.............................................. | ............ | 412,965 |
| Oil and floor cloth...........................square yards.. | 1,493,300 | 591,940 |
| Painters' colors and materials............................ | ............ | 557,710 |
| Paper of all sorts .....................hundredweight.. | 28,533 | 354,020 |
| Pickles, vinegar, sauces, and condiments. ............. | ............ | 578,590 |

*Exports from the United Kingdom to the United States in 1901 (produce and manufactures of the United Kingdom)—Continued.*

| Articles. | Quantities. | Values. |
|---|---|---|
| Confectionery, jams, and preserved fruits..................pounds.. | 1,153,600 | $115,165 |
| Pictures ...........................................................number.. | 774 | 369,175 |
| Plate and plated ware............................................... | ............ | 80,690 |
| Potatoes ......................................................hundredweight.. | 279,600 | 241,055 |
| Prints, engravings, etc.............................................. | ............ | 119,325 |
| Provisions, unenumerated.......................................... | ............ | 181,940 |
| Rags and other materials for paper making...................tons.. | 29,444 | 1,115,150 |
| Saddlery and harness................................................ | ............ | 298,335 |
| Salt......................................................................tons.. | 74,501 | 500,795 |
| Seeds of all sorts..............................................hundredweight.. | 22,118 | 171,815 |
| Ships and boats, new (not registered as British)......gross tonnage.. | 1,791 | 574,745 |
| Silk: | | |
| Thrown, twist, or yarn...................................pounds.. | 266,700 | 368,870 |
| Manufactures.......................................................... | ............ | 1,018,495 |
| Skins and furs of all sorts.......................................... | ............ | 4,046,020 |
| Soap.......................................................hundredweight.. | 8,536 | 237,580 |
| Spirits, British and Irish .............................proof gallons.. | 603,266 | 1,451,435 |
| Stationery, other than paper ...................................... | ............ | 430,870 |
| Stones and slates ................................................... | ............ | 186,745 |
| Sugar, refined, and candy...........................hundredweight.. | 13,564 | 36,075 |
| Telegraphic wires and apparatus.................................. | ............ | 175,240 |
| Toys and games ..................................................... | ............ | 150,350 |
| Umbrellas, etc ..................................................... | ............ | 60,365 |
| Wool: | | |
| Sheep and lambs' .......................................pounds.. | 15,949,200 | 1,851,640 |
| Noils, waste, combed or carded, and tops..............do.... | 68,100 | 19,835 |
| Woolen and worsted yarn................................do.... | 29,100 | 12,825 |
| Yarn, alpaca, mohair, and other sorts ...................do.... | 17,500 | 8,235 |
| Woolens and worsteds: | | |
| Entered by yard .........................................yards.. | 14,950,500 | 5,212,710 |
| Entered at value ................................................ | ............ | 428,705 |
| All other articles .................................................. | ............ | 2,678,875 |
| Total.......................................................... | ............ | 91,969,415 |

*Exports from the United Kingdom to the United States in 1901 (produce of foreign countries and British colonies).*

| Articles. | Quantities. | Value. |
|---|---|---|
| Animals: Horses......................................number.. | 765 | $552,415 |
| Art, works of.......................................................... | ............ | 54,515 |
| Bladders, casings, and sausage skins.............................. | ............ | 258,890 |
| Bristles ......................................................pounds.. | 348,796 | 416,970 |
| Butter .....................................................hundredweight.. | 250 | 4,770 |
| Caoutchouc ..................................................do.... | 111,690 | 3,959,265 |
| Chemical manufactures and products: | | |
| Saltpeter ....................................................do.... | 1,015 | 3,875 |
| Unenumerated....................................................... | ............ | 732,970 |
| China and earthenware ......................hundredweight.. | 67,263 | 1,119,980 |
| Cocoa...........................................................pounds.. | 2,187,691 | 380,150 |
| Coffee.......................................................hundredweight.. | 44,625 | 654,395 |
| Cordage, twine, and cable yarn................................... | ............ | 62,070 |
| Cork: | | |
| Unmanufactured ............................................tons.. | 2,426 | 236,960 |
| Manufactured .............................................pounds.. | 590,175 | 107,215 |
| Cotton: | | |
| Raw ..................................................hundredweight.. | 527,205 | 9,192,575 |
| Waste .......................................................pounds.. | 741,300 | 46,420 |
| Manufactures.......................................................... | ............ | 367,345 |
| Drugs: | | |
| Bark, Peruvian..........................hundredweight.. | 6,840 | 103,145 |
| Opium ........................................................pounds.. | 207,592 | 503,580 |
| Unenumerated ...................................................... | ............ | 1,052,445 |
| Dyeing or tanning stuffs: | | |
| Cutch or gambier.............................................tons.. | 1,228 | 134,490 |
| Indigo ...........................................hundredweight.. | 15,326 | 1,172,045 |
| Sumach...........................................................tons.. | 997 | 41,350 |
| Unenumerated ..............................hundredweight.. | 8,637 | 56,090 |
| Embroidery and needlework ....................................... | ............ | 57,375 |
| Farinaceous substances: | | |
| Rice, rice meal, and flour .....................hundredweight.. | 100,088 | 225,215 |
| Unenumerated....................................................... | ............ | 118,785 |
| Feathers, ornamental ....................................pounds.. | 147,262 | 1,617,580 |
| Fish, cured or salted .......................hundredweight.. | 60,833 | 375,075 |
| Flax, dressed, undressed, and tow ...........................tons.. | 3,131 | 556,940 |
| Flowers, artificial.................................................... | ............ | 493,465 |

*Exports from the United Kingdom to the United States in 1901 (produce of foreign countries and British colonies)*—Continued.

| Articles. | Quantities. | Value. |
|---|---|---|
| Fruit: | | |
| Currants, dried ...............................hundredweight.. | 8,548 | $50,730 |
| Figs and fig cake................................do.... | 7,107 | 49,500 |
| Grapes, raw ...................................do.... | 65,564 | 340,985 |
| Nuts— | | |
| Almonds .....................................do.... | 12,997 | 291,645 |
| Other nuts used as fruit .....................do.... | 44,856 | 307,835 |
| Oranges and lemons ...........................do.... | 9,582 | 22,025 |
| Raisins ......................................do.... | 2,638 | 19,175 |
| Unenumerated, dried..........................do.... | 68,835 | 162,395 |
| Preserved, with or without sugar or sirup ......do.... | 46,556 | 235,585 |
| Galls........................................do.... | 10,823 | 144,915 |
| Glue, size and gelatine..........................do.... | 11,064 | 133,570 |
| Glue stock, and pieces for making glue...........do.... | 35,357 | 113,645 |
| Gum: | | |
| Kowrie.....................................do.... | 25,841 | 420,440 |
| Lac dye, seed-lac, shellac, and stick-lac .......do.... | 29,225 | 537,160 |
| Of all other sorts............................do.... | 23,626 | 470,575 |
| Gutta-percha...................................do.... | 1,644 | 103,530 |
| Hair: | | |
| Camels .....................................pounds.. | 1,737,424 | 167,330 |
| Cow, ox, bull, or elk ........................hundredweight.. | 5,049 | 43,335 |
| Horse ......................................do.... | 2,011 | 62,075 |
| Unenumerated ..................................... | .............. | 7,760 |
| Hats or bonnets of straw ......................dozens.. | 116,324 | 51,150 |
| Hats of other materials ........................do.... | 54,336 | 38,540 |
| Hemp: | | |
| Dressed, undressed, and tow ...................tons.. | 38,287 | 5,222,465 |
| Other similar vegetable substances ............do.... | 2,081 | 327,100 |
| Hides, raw ...................................hundredweight.. | 175,072 | 2,293,660 |
| Hops .........................................do.... | 3,545 | 58,545 |
| Ivory: teeth, elephants .........................do.... | 1,082 | 254,940 |
| Jute .........................................tons.. | 3,718 | 263,685 |
| Manufactures................................. | .............. | 5,828,145 |
| Lace ........................................... | .............. | 2,836,440 |
| Leather......................................hundredweight.. | 54,516 | 2,304,865 |
| Manufactures................................. | .............. | 243,680 |
| Linen manufactures ............................ | .............. | 90,660 |
| Machinery and mill work ...................... | .............. | 200,530 |
| Matches......................................gross boxes.. | 1,012,320 | 244,190 |
| Metals: | | |
| Copper, unwrought, part wrought, etc.........tons.. | 19,006 | 6,982,595 |
| Iron— | | |
| Ore .......................................do.... | 4,709 | 82,485 |
| Bar........................................do.... | 2,517 | 134,140 |
| Steel, unwrought............................do.... | 1,161 | 52,150 |
| Iron and steel manufactures: | | |
| Cycles and parts ............................ | .............. | 10,850 |
| Unenumerated .............................hundredweight.. | .............. | 235,175 |
| Ores, unenumerated ..........................tons.. | 62,661 | 5,850 |
| Quicksilver...................................pounds.. | 182 | 18,165 |
| Tin, in blocks, ingots, bars, etc .............hundredweight.. | 21,825 | 9,201,755 |
| Unenumerated, unwrought......................tons.. | 310,951 | 192,190 |
| Mica and talc ................................hundredweight.. | 197 | 152,105 |
| Nuts, other sorts, unenumerated, not fruit ........ | .............. | 69,875 |
| Oil: | | |
| Cocoanut ....................................hundredweight.. | 142,399 | 884,000 |
| Olive ........................................tons.. | 978 | 289,405 |
| Palm ........................................hundredweight.. | 49,112 | 271,670 |
| Chemical, essential, or perfumed .............pounds.. | 245,527 | 68,470 |
| Paper-making materials: | | |
| Linen and cotton rags........................tons.. | 6,824 | 256,905 |
| Pulp of wood ................................do.... | 2,275 | 81,500 |
| Of all other sorts ............................do.... | 3,503 | 128,100 |
| Perfumery....................................pounds.. | 3,848 | 18,395 |
| Pictures and drawings .........................number.. | 341 | 284,840 |
| Plaiting of straw ..............................pounds.. | 181,530 | 91,915 |
| Plumbago ....................................tons.. | 1,680 | 162,215 |
| Precious stones: | | |
| Diamonds ...................................carats.. | 2,427 | 126,040 |
| Unset, other descriptions ..................... | .............. | 961,560 |
| Seeds: | | |
| Clover and grass .............................hundredweight.. | 12,023 | 120,345 |
| Flax or linseed...............................quarters.. | 21,126 | 277,770 |
| Garden .....................................pounds.. | 535,089 | 65,905 |
| Unenumerated, for expressing oil................quarters.. | 39,028 | 414,175 |
| Unenumerated, not for oil ....................hundredweight.. | 28,318 | 88,865 |
| All other sorts............................... | .............. | 81,645 |
| Shells of all sorts .............................. | .............. | 920,735 |
| Silk: | | |
| Knubs or husks of silk .......................hundredweight.. | 2,942 | 114,840 |
| Manufactures................................. | .............. | 131,845 |

*Exports from the United Kingdom to the United States in 1901 (produce of foreign countries and British colonies)—Continued.*

| Articles. | | Quantities. | Value. |
|---|---|---|---|
| **Skins:** | | | |
| Goat, undressed | number.. | 15,490,166 | $6,964,525 |
| Sheep | do.... | 4,628,661 | 1,642,950 |
| And furs of all other kinds | do.... | 25,629,589 | 2,305,245 |
| Manufactures of | | | 51,085 |
| Soap and soap powder | hundredweight.. | 9,014 | 53,730 |
| Spices of all sorts | pounds.. | 4,908,383 | 481,690 |
| Spirits, not sweetened, of all sorts | proof gallons.. | 29,815 | 37,800 |
| Sponge | pounds.. | 39,800 | 102,045 |
| Stationery | | | 79,565 |
| Stones, rough and hewn | tons.. | 3,593 | 104,700 |
| **Sugar:** | | | |
| Refined | hundredweight.. | 1,011 | 3,240 |
| Unrefined | do.... | 10,400 | 26,905 |
| Tallow and stearine | do.... | 9,563 | 62,945 |
| Tea | pounds.. | 4,256,095 | 856,975 |
| Tobacco, unmanufactured | do.... | 262,460 | 66,205 |
| Toys | | | 48,870 |
| **Vegetables:** | | | |
| Onions | bushels.. | 420,393 | 243,380 |
| All other sorts | | | 163,600 |
| Watches, and parts thereof | | | 50,265 |
| Wax | hundredweight.. | 3,093 | 44,740 |
| Wine | gallons.. | 51,005 | 259,170 |
| **Wood:** | | | |
| Hewn, teak | loads.. | 451 | 40,145 |
| Furniture, veneers, and hard woods | tons.. | 12,911 | 771,495 |
| Manufactures | | | 149,275 |
| **Wool:** | | | |
| Alpaca, vicuna, and llama | pounds.. | 580,400 | 173,540 |
| Goats' wool and hair | do.... | 96,206 | 32,180 |
| Sheep or lambs | do.... | 47,378,559 | 6,892,785 |
| Other kinds and flocks | do.... | 1,222,237 | 142,490 |
| **Woolen:** | | | |
| Rags (not for manure) | tons.. | 12 | 2,180 |
| Manufactures— | | | |
| Cloths and stuffs | yards.. | 1,702,149 | 823,495 |
| Carpet and rugs | | | 621,820 |
| Unenumerated | | | 248,610 |
| All other articles | | | 1,165,595 |
| | | | |
| Total | | | 96,286,335 |
| Total of British and foreign exports | | | 188,255,750 |

*Declared exports from London to the United States in the years ended June 30, 1901 and 1902.*

| Articles. | 1901. | 1902. | Increase. | Decrease. |
|---|---|---|---|---|
| | | | Per cent. | Per cent. |
| Animals | $167,903.02 | $465,911.26 | 177.54 | |
| Antimony | 77,885.95 | 155,859.44 | 100.10 | |
| Artificial flowers | 6,876.54 | 5,519.08 | | 19.73 |
| Bags and bagging | 62,967.44 | 30,192.48 | | 50.45 |
| Beers, ales, stout, etc | 676,724.04 | 568,593.88 | | 15.97 |
| Blacking | 9,285.01 | 8,069.83 | | 13.07 |
| Books, prints, engravings, etc | 1,699,090.36 | 2,004,193.02 | 17.95 | |
| Bricks and tiles | | 1,824.94 | 100 | |
| Bristles | 504,162.81 | 503,276.56 | | .17 |
| Brushes | 88,489.17 | 91,978.16 | 3.94 | |
| Burlaps | 26,291.86 | 4,528.53 | | 82.76 |
| Buttons | 1,497.05 | 4,357.19 | 19.10 | |
| Card clothing | 160.19 | | | 100 |
| Carpets and rugs | 240,600.38 | 159,108.79 | | 33.86 |
| Cement | 129,279.73 | 145,355.91 | 12.43 | |
| Chalk | 73,488.55 | 77,156.28 | 4.97 | |
| China clay, etc | 4,200.40 | 5,791.48 | 37.88 | |
| Clocks and watches | 93,669.80 | 99,366.14 | 6.07 | |
| Coal and coke | | 2,174.01 | 100 | |
| Cocoa and Chocolate | 369,883.69 | 454,274.47 | 22.81 | |
| Coffee | 514,957.79 | 230,051.16 | | 55.32 |
| Colors, paints, and varnishes | 349,058.18 | 344,204.37 | | 1.38 |
| Confectionery | 80,183.87 | 107,361.60 | 33.89 | |
| Cotton | 12,007.89 | 11,170.49 | | 6.97 |
| Cotton manufactures | 221,805.13 | 288,056.76 | 29.86 | |
| Cutlery | 1,086.23 | 4,653.72 | 355.15 | |
| Cycles | 7,060.47 | 2,087.24 | | 7.43 |
| Drugs, chemicals, dyes, etc | 2,628,157.86 | 2,565,510.71 | | 2.38 |

*Declared exports from London to the United States in the years ended June 30, 1901 and 1902—*Continued.

| Articles. | 1901. | 1902. | Increase. | Decrease. |
|---|---|---|---|---|
| | | | Per cent. | Per cent. |
| Elastic | | | | |
| Emery and polishing powders | $34,286.78 | $45,252.89 | 31.98 | |
| Feathers | 1,145,001.90 | 1,266,972.38 | 10.65 | |
| Fish | 28,966.33 | 33,768.27 | 16.57 | |
| Floor cloth | 282,196.71 | 284,864.21 | .94 | |
| Fruits, nuts, and vegetables | 428,592.00 | 309,288.79 | | 27.83 |
| Fuller's earth | 60,036.79 | 70,194.15 | 16.91 | |
| Furniture | 409,926.90 | 740,550.86 | 80.65 | |
| Glass, china, and earthen ware | 183,285.05 | 187,918.87 | 2.52 | |
| Gloves, hosiery, etc | 489,771.51 | 521,493.64 | 6.27 | |
| Glue and gelatin | 43,768.60 | 69,204.67 | 58.11 | |
| Grease, etc | 220,760.28 | 516,420.11 | 133.92 | |
| Gums | 433,785.03 | 469,037.50 | 5.82 | |
| Hair, cattle, etc | 130,106.69 | 187,446.14 | 44.07 | |
| Hardware | 17,335.88 | 7,263.98 | | 58.09 |
| Hats and felt | 76,660.84 | 108,328.51 | 41.30 | |
| Hemp, flax, tow, etc | 2,785,760.55 | 3,955,318.30 | 41.98 | |
| Indigo | 25,626.52 | 28,201.06 | 10.04 | |
| Ivory | 260,510.31 | 278,233.61 | 6.80 | |
| Jute | 72,517.19 | 47,926.14 | | 33.90 |
| Lace | 26,860.86 | 37,158.66 | 38.33 | |
| Leather, etc | 581,520.61 | 558,052.25 | | 4.03 |
| Linens | 39,919.16 | 109,089.49 | 173.23 | |
| Linseed | 31,849.16 | 168,442.52 | 416.32 | |
| Machinery | 252,956.83 | 207,258.87 | | 18.06 |
| Matches | 7,642.34 | 37,969.71 | 396.84 | |
| Metals: | | | | |
| Iron and steel, and manufactures | 116,402.43 | 182,585.88 | 56.86 | |
| Other | 5,446,603.30 | 6,529,262.52 | 19.87 | |
| Mustard | 246,398.59 | 274,301.41 | 11.32 | |
| Oils | 905,559.94 | 1,219,541.82 | 34.67 | |
| Ores, iron, etc | 17,718.49 | 110,363.31 | 528.52 | |
| Paper and paper hangings | 237,414.53 | 185,919.50 | | 21.69 |
| Paper stock | 158,709.14 | 162,356.96 | 2.29 | |
| Perfumery | 20,097.88 | 20,944.81 | 43.02 | |
| Pitch and tar | 74,099.19 | 89,727.62 | 21.07 | |
| Plumbago | 48,795.90 | 77,828.40 | 59.49 | |
| Precious stones | 4,599,780.10 | 4,938,506.21 | 7.36 | |
| Preserves, pickles, etc | 405,379.47 | 659,293.62 | 62.63 | |
| Provisions, cheese, bacon, etc | 73,422.71 | 196,886.15 | 167.60 | |
| Quicksilver | 50,318.60 | 27,089.49 | | 46.24 |
| Rice | 146,588.83 | 182,747.05 | 24.66 | |
| Rope, string, etc | 135,941.54 | 180,458.53 | 32.73 | |
| Rubber: | | | | |
| Raw | 211,383.73 | 190,688.36 | | 9.78 |
| Clothing and manufactures | 105,120.56 | 148,664.57 | 41.42 | |
| Saddlery | 44,101.03 | 52,716.73 | 19.53 | |
| Salt | 4,901.72 | | | 100 |
| Sausage casings | 12,082.57 | 13,009.95 | 7.67 | |
| Scientific etc., instruments | 121,211.34 | 122,704.07 | 1.23 | |
| Seeds, plants, etc | 470,083.56 | 431,909.86 | | 8.12 |
| Shellac | 133,799.43 | 516,694.12 | 212.60 | |
| Shells | 623,861.03 | 986,745.91 | 58.16 | |
| Silks | 348,157.06 | 374,379.10 | 7.53 | |
| Soaps | 245,123.73 | 226,603.23 | | 7.55 |
| Skins, hides, furs, etc | 7,204,794.76 | 7,434,371.33 | 3.08 | |
| Spices, etc | 345,363.95 | 186,555.22 | | 45.95 |
| Sponges | 94,785.46 | 86,702.40 | | 8.52 |
| Stationery, etc | 332,451.79 | 428,897.60 | 29.01 | |
| Sticks and canes | 34,064.04 | 65,346.54 | 91.83 | |
| Straw plait and braids | 150,442.31 | 140,659.81 | | 6.50 |
| Straw manufactures (other) | 10,951.65 | 6,303.80 | | 42.43 |
| Stuff goods | 138,540.84 | 141,599.37 | 2.20 | |
| Stone, marble, granite, etc | 33,807.48 | 106,208.85 | 214.42 | |
| Sugar | 2,259.00 | 2,277.68 | .79 | |
| Tea | 582,484.37 | 822,688.95 | 58.40 | |
| Thread | 418.65 | 2,688.79 | 543.06 | |
| Tin | 9,198,342.36 | 7,754,732.57 | | 15.25 |
| Tin plates, black plate, etc | | 1,291.14 | 100 | |
| Tobacco and cigarettes | 103,065.17 | 148,411.04 | 43.99 | |
| Wearing apparel, etc | 187,429.34 | 213,345.28 | 13.82 | |
| Wines and spirits | 573,049.16 | 713,141.42 | 22.44 | |
| Woods | 240,978.93 | 429,187.56 | 78.10 | |
| Wool and camel, etc., hair | 2,000,220.97 | 2,152,928.41 | 7.60 | |
| Woolens | 1,445,042.28 | 1,588,325.41 | 9.91 | |
| Works of art | 960,402.30 | 1,261,077.05 | 31.30 | |
| Yarn | 1,927.05 | 3,551.09 | 84.22 | |
| All other articles | 566,088.01 | 534,679.44 | | 5.51 |
| Total | 55,825,874.49 | 60,913,128.01 | | |

Net total increase of $8,219,794.26, or 14.85 per cent.

*Summary.*

| | | | |
|---|---|---|---|
| Total for year ended June 30, 1902. | $60,913,128.01 | Increase in 73 articles | $8,219,794.26 |
| Total for year ended June 30, 1901. | 55,325,874.49 | Decrease in 30 articles | 2,632,540.74 |
| Net total increase | 5,587,253.52 | Net total increase | 5,587,253.52 |

## TRADE WITH CUBA IN 1901.

The imports into the United Kingdom from Cuba in the year under review amounted to $190,350, a decrease of $9,000 from 1900. The exports of British and Irish produce to Cuba in 1901 totaled $6,089,725, compared with $6,196,490, a decrease of a little over $100,000. Cottons showed an increase of $70,000, while linens declined to the extent of $400,000. Machinery and millwork rose from $75,000 in 1900 to over $250,000 in 1901, while iron (wrought and unwrought) declined $190,000. In foreign and colonial merchandise, the total of $3,709,125 shows an increase of over $550,000, the net increase of exports therefore amounting to $448,000. The principal gains in foreign and colonial merchandise were in rice, rice meal, and flour ($375,000), and jute manufactures (over $300,000), and the chief decreases were in cheese ($25,000, or over 50 per cent), hemp ($13,000, or nearly 50 per cent), and meat ($60,000).

*Imports from Cuba into the United Kingdom in 1901.*

| Articles. | Quantities. | Values. |
|---|---|---|
| Wood: | | |
| Mahogany........tons.. | 3,622 | $120,265 |
| Unenumerated........do.... | 1,989 | 63,960 |
| All other articles | | 6,125 |
| Total........ | | 190,350 |

*Exports from the United Kingdom to Cuba in 1901.*

| Articles. | Quantities. | Values. |
|---|---|---|
| PRODUCE OF THE UNITED KINGDOM. | | |
| Apparel and haberdashery | | $87,035 |
| Beer and ale........barrels.. | 5,957 | 128,725 |
| Cement........tons.. | 678 | 6,820 |
| Chemicals and chemical preparations: | | |
| Soda compounds........hundredweight.. | 14,502 | 36,050 |
| All other sorts | | 27,825 |
| Cottons: | | |
| Entered by yard........yards.. | 61,839,800 | 2,712,135 |
| Entered at value | | 451,550 |
| Earthen and china ware | | 82,130 |
| Glass manufactures | | 42,255 |
| Hardware, unenumerated........hundredweight.. | 4,536 | 85,105 |
| Cutlery | | 23,685 |
| Hats, of all sorts........dozens.. | 3,911 | 30,675 |
| Implements and tools | | 78,865 |
| Jute manufactures, piece goods........yards.. | 796,500 | 42,495 |
| Linens: | | |
| Entered by yard........do.... | 6,850,000 | 715,925 |
| Entered at value | | 15,975 |
| Machinery and millwork | | 254,355 |
| Medicines, drugs, etc | | 39,980 |
| Metals: | | |
| Iron, wrought and unwrought........tons.. | 7,664 | 481,855 |
| Brass, and manufactures of........hundredweight.. | 497 | 11,840 |
| Copper, wrought and unwrought........do.... | 2,528 | 61,085 |
| Milk, condensed........do.... | 2,594 | 26,815 |
| Oil, seed........tons.. | 414 | 57,160 |
| Painters' colors and materials | | 90,255 |
| Salt........tons.. | 1,384 | 6,625 |
| Soap........hundredweight.. | 36 | 655 |
| Stationery, other than paper | | 13,120 |

*Exports from the United Kingdom to Cuba in 1901*—Continued.

| Articles. | Quantity. | Values. |
|---|---|---|
| PRODUCE OF THE UNITED KINGDOM—continued. | | |
| Woolens and worsted, entered by the yard ....................yards.. | 796,100 | $822,350 |
| All other articles ....................................................... | | 218,940 |
| Total......................... | | 6,089,725 |
| FOREIGN AND COLONIAL MERCHANDISE. | | |
| Butter ............................................................hundredweight.. | 1,505 | $6,200 |
| Cheese .....................................................................do.... | 1,446 | 21,025 |
| Cotton manufactures ................................................... | | 2,380 |
| Drugs: | | |
| Opium .................................................................pounds.. | 3,814 | 9,810 |
| Unenumerated ......................................................... | | 2,225 |
| Embroidery and needlework .............................................. | | 8,745 |
| Farinaceous substances: | | |
| Rice, rice meal and flour .........................hundredweight.. | 1,011,251 | 2,279,785 |
| Other farinaceous substances.......................................... | | 515 |
| Fish, cured or salted......................................hundredweight.. | 53,355 | 400,700 |
| Hemp, dressed or undressed ....................................tons.. | 88 | 13,610 |
| Jute manufactures...................................................... | | 676,685 |
| Lace ...................................................................... | | 8,080 |
| Meat preserved otherwise than by salting: Beef ....hundredweight.. | 19,143 | 129,840 |
| Metals: Iron and steel manufactures, unenumerated .............do.... | 308 | 1,340 |
| Milk, condensed .......................................................do.... | 5,274 | 53,255 |
| Vegetables ............................................................... | | 16,265 |
| Woolen manufactures of all sorts ...................................... | | 2,755 |
| All other articles ........................................................ | | 46,010 |
| Total........................... | | 3,709,125 |
| Total of British and foreign goods............................ | | 9,798,850 |

## TRADE WITH PORTO RICO IN 1901.

The value of imports from Porto Rico into the United Kingdom was, as in 1897 and 1898, nil, while in 1899 and 1900 the respective totals amounted to only $6,300 and $3,355.

The value of merchandise exported thither from the United Kingdom reached (in goods of British and Irish origin) in 1901, $215,190, against $530,635 in 1900. In goods of foreign and colonial origin, the total in 1901 amounted to $106,590, against $277,880, the aggregate of $321,780 being a decrease of $486,735 compared with 1900 and of $2,632,670 compared with 1899, or 81 per cent decrease since 1899. In British and Irish goods, there was a decrease in every article except implements and tools, which rather more than held their own. Except for jute manufactures, every article of foreign and colonial merchandise also showed a decline.

*Exports from the United Kingdom to Porto Rico in 1901.*

| Articles. | Quantities. | Values. |
|---|---|---|
| PRODUCE OF UNITED KINGDOM. | | |
| Bags and sacks, empty........................................dozen.. | 3,800 | $7,990 |
| Cottons: | | |
| Entered by yard ................................................yards.. | 294,100 | 15,980 |
| Entered at value................................................. | | 28,260 |
| Implements and tools .....,............................................ | | 19,500 |
| Linens, entered by yard ........................................yards.. | 77,700 | 9,505 |
| Machinery and millwork................................................ | | 31,055 |
| Medicines, drugs, and medicinal preparations..................... | | 3,570 |
| Metals: Iron, wrought and unwrought...........................tons.. | 687 | 46,270 |
| Oil seed..............................................................do.... | 43 | 7,805 |
| Painters' colors and materials....................................... | | 9,580 |
| Woolens and worsteds, entered by the yard ....................yards.. | 30,300 | 15,435 |
| All other articles...................................................... | | 24,440 |
| Total.......................................... | | 215,190 |

*Exports from the United Kingdom to Porto Rico in 1901*—Continued.

| Articles. | Quantities. | Values. |
|---|---|---|
| **PRODUCE OF FOREIGN COUNTRIES AND BRITISH COLONIES.** | | |
| Butter ....................................................hundredweight.. | | |
| Candles, of all sorts .................................................do.... | 130 | $1,280 |
| Cheese .....................................................................do.... | 211 | 3,005 |
| Farinaceous substances: Rice, rice meal and flour..............do.... | 8,200 | 15,075 |
| Jute manufactures.............................................................. | | 81,350 |
| Metals: Iron and steel manufactures, unenumerated..hundredweight.. | 217 | 610 |
| All other articles ............................................................... | | 5,290 |
| Total.......................................................... | | 105,590 |
| Total of British and foreign goods............................... | | 321,780 |

## TRADE WITH THE PHILIPPINES IN 1901.

The imports into the United Kingdom from the Philippines in 1901 amounted to $13,509,050, an increase of over $5,000,000, this result being chiefly attributable to larger exports to the United Kingdom of gum, hemp, and manufactured tobacco; on the other hand, decreases occurred in nuts and kernels and unrefined sugar.

The exports from the United Kingdom (of British and Irish produce) to the Philippines in 1901 totaled $4,313,555, a decrease of nearly $1,500,000, principally due to a falling off in cotton yarn, cottons, and machinery, while increases occurred in arms and ammunition, earthen and china ware, and woolens and worsteds.

In exports of foreign and colonial merchandise from the United Kingdom to the Philippines, there was also a decline, amounting to over $30,000, principally due to a decrease in raw cotton, meat, milk (condensed), and cork manufactures. Cement, cotton manufactures, hardware, and woolens showed increases.

*Imports into the United Kingdom from the Philippines in 1901.*

| Articles. | Quantities. | Values. |
|---|---|---|
| Gum of all sorts .......................................hundredweight.. | 8,080 | $42,245 |
| Hemp, dressed, undressed, and tow...........................tons.. | 76,482 | 12,718,380 |
| Nuts and kernels, for expressing oil therefrom .................do.... | 797 | 58,200 |
| Shells of all kinds.......................................................... | | 15,525 |
| Sugar, unrefined.....................................hundredweight.. | 50,465 | 113,960 |
| Tobacco, manufactured, of all sorts ...........................pounds.. | 394,260 | 536,115 |
| All other articles .......................................................... | | 24,625 |
| Total.......................................................... | | 13,509,050 |

*Exports to the Philippines from the United Kingdom in 1901.*

| Articles. | Quantities. | Values. |
|---|---|---|
| **PRODUCE OF THE UNITED KINGDOM.** | | |
| Apparel and haberdashery............................................ | | $21,210 |
| Arms, ammunition, and military stores............................. | | 308,585 |
| Chemicals and chemical preparations—soda compounds, hundredweight.................................................... | 10,342 | 23,305 |
| Coal, coke, and patent fuel...................................tons.. | 369 | 2,875 |
| Cotton yarn...................................................pounds.. | 332,200 | 88,625 |
| Cottons: | | |
| Entered by yard.......................................yards.. | 36,079,700 | 1,947,165 |
| Entered at value............................................ | | 389,695 |
| Earthen and china ware.............................................. | | 46,880 |
| Glass manufactures................................................... | | 13,600 |
| Hardware, unenumerated.........................hundredweight.. | 1,122 | 22,980 |
| Cutlery.................................................................. | | 4,735 |
| Leather, wrought and unwrought.................................. | | 14,515 |

*Exports to the Philippines from the United Kingdom in 1901*—Continued.

| Articles. | Quantities. | Values. |
|---|---|---|
| **PRODUCE OF THE UNITED KINGDOM—continued.** | | |
| Linens, entered by yard...........................................yards.. | 294,100 | $44,835 |
| Machinery and mill work.................................................. | .................. | 198,695 |
| Metals: | | |
|    Iron, wrought and unwrought................................tons.. | 8,359 | 483,605 |
|    Copper, wrought and unwrought.................hundredweight.. | 3,381 | 61,890 |
| Oil, seed....................................................................tons.. | 153 | 28,710 |
| Painters colors and materials............................................ | .................. | 75,945 |
| Pickles, vinegar, sauces, and condiments............................. | .................. | 87,575 |
| Confectionery, jams, and preserved fruits.....................pounds.. | 29,800 | 5,145 |
| Provisions, unenumerated................................................. | .................. | 31,335 |
| Ships and boats, new...............................gross tonnage.. | 806 | 57,040 |
| Silk manufactures........................................................... | .................. | 11,445 |
| Spirits, British and Irish...........................proof gallons.. | 16,736 | 40,810 |
| Woolens and worsteds, entered by yard........................yards.. | 132,500 | 55,580 |
| All other articles........................................................... | .................. | 301,780 |
|     Total............................................................. | .................. | 4,313,555 |
| **FOREIGN AND COLONIAL MERCHANDISE.** | | |
| Butter........................................................hundredweight.. | 101 | 3,370 |
| Cement.........................................................................tons.. | 618 | 5,830 |
| Cheese.......................................................hundredweight.. | 969 | 15,490 |
| Cork manufactures.......................................................pounds.. | 3,485 | 1,060 |
| Cotton, raw.................................................hundredweight.. | 4,061 | 46,515 |
| Cotton manufactures...................................................... | .................. | 16,765 |
| Fish, cured or salted...................................hundredweight.. | 111 | 1,980 |
| Glass of all kinds, except bottles.............................do.... | 111 | 2,805 |
| Hardware (not cutlery).........................................do.... | 196 | 5,025 |
| Lace, and articles thereof................................................ | .................. | 5,290 |
| Machinery and mill work................................................ | .................. | 9,160 |
| Meat (not poultry and game), hams.................hundredweight.. | 325 | 6,545 |
| Metals: | | |
|    Iron, bar, angle, bolt, and rod............................tons. | 158 | 5,340 |
|    Iron and steel manufactures— | | |
|       Rails, steel.......................................do.... | 339 | 22,235 |
|       Unenumerated............................hundredweight.. | 3,386 | 8,115 |
| Milk, condensed..................................................do.... | 703 | 7,665 |
| Paper, unprinted.................................................do.... | 1,086 | 14,875 |
| Silk manufactures......................................................... | .................. | 9,235 |
| Toys......................................................................... | ...... | 5,270 |
| Wine........................................................................gallons.. | 982 | 2,730 |
| Woolen manufactures.................................................... | .................. | 17,610 |
| All other articles.......................................................... | .................. | 42,925 |
|     Total........................................................... | .................. | 255,835 |
|     Total of British and foreign goods................... | .................. | 4,569,390 |

*Total number and tonnage of vessels registered under the merchant shipping acts, belonging to the United Kingdom.*

| Year. | Sailing vessels. | | Steam vessels. | | Total. | |
|---|---|---|---|---|---|---|
| | Number. | Net tonnage. | Number. | Net tonnage. | Number. | Net tonnage. |
| 1901......................... | 10,572 | 2,135,265 | 9,484 | 12,472,584 | 20,056 | 14,607,849 |
| 1900......................... | 10,773 | 2,247,228 | 9,209 | 11,816,924 | 19,982 | 14,064,152 |
|   Increase.............. | .......... | .......... | 275 | 655,660 | 74 | 543,697 |
|   Decrease.............. | 201 | 111,963 | .......... | .......... | .......... | .......... |

*Number and net tonnage of iron, steel, and wooden sailing and steam vessels built in the United Kingdom for foreigners in 1901.*

| | Sailing vessels. | | Steam vessels. | | Total. | |
|---|---|---|---|---|---|---|
| | Number. | Net tonnage. | Number. | Net tonnage. | Number. | Net tonnage. |
| War........................ | .......... | .......... | 10 | 11,000 | 10 | 11,000 |
| Mercantile.............. | 71 | 6,696 | 113 | 189,756 | 184 | 196,452 |
|   Total.................... | 71 | 6,696 | 123 | 200,756 | 194 | 207,452 |

*Total length, paid-up capital, traffic receipts, and working expenses of railways in England and Wales, Scotland and Ireland.*

## ENGLAND AND WALES.

| Years | Length of line open at end of each year | Ordinary | Guaranteed preferential loans and debentures | Total | Number of passengers conveyed, not including season-ticket holders | Weight of goods and minerals conveyed | From passenger traffic | From goods traffic, including live stock | Average receipts per mile of line open | Miscellaneous | Total | Working expenditure | Net receipts | Proportion of working expenses to gross receipts |
|---|---|---|---|---|---|---|---|---|---|---|---|---|---|---|
| | | | | | | Tons. | | | | | | | | Per ct. |
| 1900 | 15,187 | $1,796,888,680 | $98,054,849,225 | $4,960,787,905 | 992,425,769 | 859,594,742 | $138,166,890 | $226,699,810 | $27,645 | $27,094,900 | $446,962,505 | $278,414,050 | $167,548,455 | 63 |
| 1901 | 15,308 | 1,821,186,965 | 3,112,096,865 | 4,983,283,910 | 1,021,178,850 | 851,116,894 | 196,043,705 | 224,474,680 | 27,500 | 31,000,375 | 458,518,850 | 291,748,080 | 161,770,820 | 64 |

## SCOTLAND.

| 1900 | 3,465 | 865,171,295 | 463,272,395 | 880,448,690 | 122,201,102 | 60,268,461 | 23,577,960 | 32,188,465 | 15,995 | 2,278,625 | 58,015,080 | 32,921,075 | 25,098,970 | 57 |
| 1901 | 3,662 | 872,807,420 | 470,506,715 | 843,317,135 | 124,368,718 | 59,999,983 | 23,069,165 | 31,878,980 | 15,990 | 3,185,835 | 60,103,490 | 33,664,640 | 26,438,840 | 56 |

## IRELAND.

| 1900 | 3,183 | 80,444,455 | 118,388,400 | 198,827,865 | 27,649,815 | 5,151,810 | 10,178,585 | 8,494,545 | 5,865 | 363,605 | 19,081,785 | 11,882,478 | 7,649,260 | 60 |
| 1901 | 3,208 | 77,951,160 | 123,320,185 | 201,271,345 | 26,858,382 | 5,186,624 | 10,086,365 | 8,474,185 | 5,770 | 661,195 | 19,171,745 | 12,096,025 | 7,185,720 | 63 |

## UNITED KINGDOM.

| 1900 | 21,855 | 2,345,004,430 | 8,685,005,020 | 5,880,009,450 | 1,142,276,686 | 424,929,618 | 226,919,940 | 267,852,820 | 22,616 | 29,786,880 | 594,009,260 | 328,717,600 | 200,291,690 | 62 |
| 1901 | 22,078 | 2,271,895,585 | 3,705,926,855 | 5,977,822,390 | 1,172,895,900 | 415,968,441 | 233,149,325 | 264,827,845 | 22,555 | 34,816,905 | 582,794,075 | 337,445,690 | 196,345,890 | 63 |

POST-OFFICE.

During the year ended March 31, 1902, the number of postal packets delivered in the United Kingdom was as follows:

| Description. | Number. | Increase. | Average number to each person. |
|---|---|---|---|
| | | Per cent. | |
| Letters | 2,451,500,000 | 5.5 | 58.9 |
| Post cards | 444,900,000 | 6.2 | 10.7 |
| Book packets and circulars | 766,200,000 | 4.6 | 18.4 |
| Newspapers | 169,800,000 | 1.2 | 4.1 |
| Parcels | 86,600,000 | 6.9 | 2.1 |
| Total | 3,919,000,000 | 5.2 | 94.2 |

The number of letters registered in the United Kingdom was 18,800,313, an increase of 6 per cent over the number in the previous year.

The number of undelivered packets dealt with during the year was as follows:

| | Number. |
|---|---|
| Letters | 10,183,866 |
| Post-cards | 1,757,081 |
| Book packets and circulars | 11,523,272 |
| Newspapers | 715,285 |
| Parcels | 242,472 |

The number was larger by 3,500,000 than the figures for five years ago. Out of 10,000,000 letters undelivered, nearly 9,000,000 were reissued to corrected addresses or returned to the senders.

The property found at the returned letter offices in undelivered letters included £18,231 ($88,721) in cash and bank notes, and £650,298 ($3,164,673) in bills, checks, money orders, postal orders, and stamps. The letters posted without address, and containing property, numbered 3,782. They included £179 ($871) cash and bank notes, and £3,434 ($16,712) in checks, etc. The articles found loose in the post numbered 85,640, and included coin to the value of over £1,000 ($4,867), and checks to the value of more than £6,000 ($29,199). A half sovereign, which had evidently been used to seal a parcel, was found to be still adhering to the wax on the arrival of the parcel in London.

The total number of money orders of all kinds dealt with during the year amounted to 13,963,410, as against 13,263,567 in the previous year, an increase of 699,843. The total value of these orders was £42,169,201 ($210,846,005), compared with £39,374,665 ($196,873,325), an increase of £2,794,536 ($13,972,680). The number of postal orders issued during the year was 90,687,404, representing £32,724,681 ($163,623,405).

In the Post-Office Savings Bank, 15,018,645 deposits were made during the year ended December 31, 1901, the total sum deposited being £41,452,051 ($207,260,255), while the number of withdrawals was 5,748,624, amounting in value to £39,890,048 ($199,450,215).

The number of telegrams sent over the wires during the year was 90,432,041, an increase of 95 per cent.

H. CLAY EVANS,
Consul-General.

LONDON, November 6, 1902.

## BRADFORD.

Reviewing the past year, the Bradford trade can be said to have enjoyed a fair degree of prosperity. No special factor can be noted in any one department of the trade, most branches being interested in the commodities which go to make up the full complement of the worsted industry. It has been repeatedly said, and said with some show of reason, that Bradford carries all its eggs in one basket, the wool trade and its varied branches monopolizing the attention of the inhabitants of this city and district. Due credit can be given the business men for their theoretical and practical knowledge of wool and its manufacture. Close observation of the factories and of their products leads one to say that Bradford has, during the past year, turned out wool fabrics which can hold their own in quality, design, and price against all comers, and the amount of goods sold in the home market compares favorably with that of any other season. As the trade of this district has many branches, I will briefly refer to the various departments in which our manufacturers and the textile public generally are interested.

### WOOL.

Wool is paramount in Bradford, and the raw article has enjoyed in merinos the most successful season since the close of 1899. All through the year, fine grades have displayed a rising tendency, a most optimistic feeling pervading the market during the past twelve months. Undoubtedly, the firm belief that consumption had at last overtaken supplies of fine wools has been the leading factor in bringing about the gradual rise in these grades, and the full effect of seven years' drought in Australia is apparent in this district by the absence of stocks of fine wool and tops. There has been no pinch in any department, nor is there likely to be, but perhaps never during the present generation has a time been known when production and consumption were as near together as during the recent months. Three years ago, this district went wild speculating over an anticipated shortage of fine wools; to-day, when a boom would have been far more justified than in 1899, both men and markets have assumed an attitude which has indicated business acumen.

### CROSSBREDS.

Crossbreds, unlike merinos, have been weak and unsteady, and at no time have medium and coarse grades been at such low prices as during the past year. Last December, standard 40s tops or combined wool dropped to as low as 14 cents per pound, while but a few years back the raw wool itself was selling at 4 to 6 cents per pound more. With an increased consumption, and with a continuous rise in merinos, it was thought early in the spring that crossbreds had rounded the corner and that better days were in store. In May, 40s combed tops rose to 18½ cents per pound, and this price at that time showed strong signs of permanency, judging by the increased attention which users were paying to this article. But with the advent of the June-July London wool sales, the market encountered heavy supplies of New England new clip and a serious decline set in, causing the value of this quality of tops to once more settle down to about the lowest price on record, it being possible to buy to-day in Bradford a good 40s prepared top at 14 to 14½ cents per pound. There is no gainsaying the fact that if Bradford enjoys a monopoly, it is in the use and absorption of cross-bred wools, and when this standard article gets down to such a desperate price, it opens a wide field of enterprise not only for Bradford manu-facturers, but also for American users. There is not the least doubt that consumption in this district of crossbred wools is fairly large, but there is a larger production, and this is probably the reason why cross-bred wools have fallen. One leading authority has estimated that whereas in 1895, the proportion of crossbred to merino imported into this country was 31.7 per cent, the proportion has risen in 1901 to 49.3 per cent; or, practically speaking, the imports of Colonial and River Plata wools into Europe are now equally divided between merino and crossbred. There are no sound indications at present for expecting a rise in medium and coarse crossbred wools. The following table shows how prices have moved during the past year for good standard tops:

| Colonial tops. | June 30, 1901. | January 1, 1902. | August 30, 1902. | Colonial tops. | June 30, 1901. | January 1, 1902. | August 30, 1902. |
|---|---|---|---|---|---|---|---|
| | Cents. | Cents. | Cents. | | Cents. | Cents. | Cents. |
| 70s | 41 | 43 | 54 | 50s | 24½ | 22 | 27 |
| 64s | 38 | 42 | 47 | 46s | 18 | 16½ | 18 |
| 60s | 35 | 38½ | 45 | 40s | 15½ | 14 | 14 |
| 56s | 31 | 30 | 35 | 36s | 14½ | 14 | 18 |

## YARNS.

Yarn spinners throughout the past year have been very busy; in fact, the continuous running of machinery has been one of the satisfactory aspects of the market. Complaints have been frequently heard of a scarcity of hands, especially in those departments where the help of young persons is required. Parents of children leaving school are not sending them into the factories, as they did a few years back, the rea-son being that the wages paid are not adequate. It was asserted a few weeks back that the wages of a wool comber, taking the year through, do not average more than $3.25 per week. A fair standard wage for a man working 56½ hours per week is $5, while a few receive $5.76.

### EXPORT YARN TRADE.

There has been some recovery in the export of yarns to the Continent, which has meant a good deal to the spinners of this district. With the slump of 1900, German manufacturers felt keenly their weakened posi-tion, but this year there has been a good trade with the Continent, espe-cially in crossbred and low-quality mohair yarns. Prices for fine merino yarns have advanced anywhere from 6 to 12 cents per pound, according to description and quality, and while at one time even cross-bred yarns were put up in many cases 4 to 6 cents per pound, these can now be bought as low as ever they could. In the early months of this year, some decent weights of medium and fine crossbred yarns were shipped to the United States to meet a temporary demand, but latterly this demand has fallen off. In a word, the spinning industry of Brad-ford has been busy all through the year and frames are being fully run.

### PIECES.

On the whole, Bradford manufacturers have had a normal season. Unfortunately, they have had to encounter many adverse factors, which have during the last two months affected the trade more or less seriously.

Bradford manufacturers prepared for a bright season, hoping with the coronation to be able to do a record trade. "Coronation" cloths were made in all designs and qualities, and early in the season the wholesale houses distributed some heavy weights of material. I need only mention here that at the last moment the coronation festivities had to be postponed, and much disappointment resulted. Retailers in consequence failed to experience that demand for fabrics which they had provided for, and with somewhat "harder times" the general public have not done as much shopping as is customary. A very wet summer has also done much to impede the season's trade, and, with the frequent occurrence of holidays, drapers are left with heavier stocks than usual at the end of the season. All this finds manufacturers to-day in rather a complaining mood, and the outlook is none too bright in the piece departments of the Bradford trade.

### NOVELTIES.

Manufacturers throughout the past season attached considerable importance to the "new things" which they had brought out, and undoubtedly in excellence of design, shade, and finish they surpassed all previous records. One of the leading features in dress goods has been a fabric composed of silk and wool, and in this some big sales have been made, considerable quantities having gone to the United States. The silk blended with the wool has not only given brilliance and color, but the wool has certainly strengthened the fabric so far as wearing qualities are concerned, and had there been an average amount of sunshine, no doubt these goods would have been extensively worn. A leading feature about them is that they drape exceedingly well, the mixture of wool in the fabric preventing them from creasing and cockling, which is such an objectionable feature in pure silk.

The pure luster fabrics which have formed a conspicuous part of the Bradford dress trade during recent years have not been so great a success this season, and mohair and alpaca cloths have experienced a considerable diminution in demand. Fancy effects in all-wool fabrics have had a fair season, and all the leading descriptions of goods in colors have commanded quite a reasonable market.

For the present fall and winter season, zibeline fabrics are the most popular style of goods. These are largely replacing the coverts, which have had such a big run for years past. While the cloth presents an attractive appearance, there is not the wearing property about the zibeline which characterized the covert. Presenting a very rough, hairy appearance, these zibeline fabrics are largely produced out of coarse wool, and, being dyed in almost every imaginable shade, they are no doubt destined to meet with a fair demand both for home and export. Nothing as yet seems to be definitely known concerning the spring season of 1903, but it is expected that colors will once more be run.

## ADVANCE IN FINISHING.

Under the auspices of the Bradford Dyers' Association, rapid strides are being made in the art and science of dyeing and finishing. The Continent, and especially French manufacturers, can no longer boast of having a monopoly of the best shades and of producing more artistic and brighter colors than those produced in this locality. Some firms here are doing work that is equal to anything found elsewhere, while their patent finishes are popularizing Bradford dress goods and coatings in the foreign markets.

## OUTLOOK.

All hands are now preparing for the spring and summer trade of 1903. An endless variety of goods is being shown, but it is as yet too early to say definitely what is likely to be the most popular. The best authorities are of the opinion that fine wools will maintain to-day's prices, but any material improvement is not looked for, while with fine crossbreds moving in sympathy with merinos one is likely to help the other. Medium and coarse crossbreds are struggling despondingly; for, whereas there continues to be a good consumption, supplies are more than adequate to meet all present needs.

## UNITED STATES GOODS.

The past year has shown a greater demand than ever for American goods, and so long as quality is considered an essential element by our exporters, so long may the demand be expected to increase.

*Furniture.*—Attention has previously been called to the lack of finish in furniture. Large quantities of a medium grade find their way here; and while the outside appearance and finish is everything to be desired, there is room for improvement in the internal parts, which are ofttimes roughly made. A great demand exists for both office and household furnishings, and it is suggested that if our manufacturers would only consult the English taste a little more, a much larger amount of business might be done.

*Hardware.*—In some branches of the hardware trade difficulty has arisen in supplying the demand. One firm of importers report that they are unable to obtain the execution of their orders without considerable delay, particularly in regard to steam valves, the explanation being that it is due to increased demand for domestic purposes. This is a condition which undoubtedly should be avoided, if we are to retain the hold already obtained. In joiners' and mechanics' tools there has been a less demand than usual, accounted for partly by a strike in the building trade, which has lasted several months, and by the strenuous endeavors being put forth by English makers to recapture the ground which they have lost. It is stated that at Sheffield and Birmingham new plants have been put up to manufacture on the American principle. American shears still retain their lead. They are to be seen in almost every warehouse and tailoring establishment. Safety razors are also making headway.

*Jewelry.*—Fancy jewelry is finding its way here in increasing quantities. In silverware, the jewelers comment upon the extreme thinness of the metal, which precludes their handling the goods with complete satisfaction. The fancy embossed work is subject to damage with the slightest blow, and they are allowing this trade to go into the hands of miscellaneous fancy dealers, the prices being comparatively low. If a thicker metal could be shown, no doubt the jewelers would be able to do a much larger business.

*Shoes.*—Our boots and shoes are still holding their own. The former complaint as to the poor wearing qualities of the soles, especially in those for men's wear, has been met, and they are now giving complete satisfaction. The English manufacturers have adopted the American style and are importing machinery. Quite recently I had an inquiry from an individual in the trade for the names and addresses of American firms from which he could obtain the necessary machinery for fitting up a plant.

*Meats.*—In regard to the provision trade, there has not been the same demand for our products as heretofore. I can not do better than quote from a correspondent, who is one of the largest importers:

All through the season prices have steadily advanced until, at the present date, they have recorded about the highest, if not the highest, point reached during my knowledge of the trade, extending over the past thirty years, the result being that Canadian produce is being brought more prominently before the consumers of the north of England and is becoming firmly established over that district. The better quality of the meat, compared with the American, its mildness, and more uniform cure are very acceptable to the operative classes, who desire a meat containing a greater portion of lean and a greater freedom from salt. At the present time American hog products have ceased to occupy the premier position, and for the reason herein assigned Canadian meat has attained this position. When the American packers realize that hog products are produced to be consumed and not to gamble with, it will be better for the American provision trade.

### GENERAL REMARKS.

There is one thing in connection with the extension of our foreign trade to which I would again call particular attention, and that is the manner in which would-be exporters attempt to extend their business. It is no uncommon practice for houses to forward catalogues, price lists, or other printed matter (occasionally insufficiently stamped) to firms handling such goods, hoping in this way to induce the recipients to place orders; but in the majority of cases, a casual glance and relegation to the waste-paper basket are all the attention the matter receives. Nor is this to be wondered at at the present day, with the number of travelers constantly on the road, who, coming in personal contact with prospective purchasers, have a great advantage in being able to demonstrate their respective claims. Yorkshiremen are noted as being a hard-headed and rather conservative class of individuals.

The most successful export houses are those having their own representatives in this country periodically calling upon the merchants and able at short notice to supply any demand that may be made. In this way, smaller firms, unable through the limitation of their financial resources to import direct, are enabled to handle quantities of American merchandise.

### EXPORTS.

The accompanying table shows the value of declared exports from this district to the United States for the years ended June 30, 1901 and 1902. The principal increase is in stuffs (dress goods and linings), wool, machinery, cotton cloths, and worsted coatings.

| Articles. | Year ended June 30— | | Increase. | Decrease. |
|---|---|---|---|---|
| | 1901. | 1902. | | |
| Alpaca hair | $152,963.89 | $177,861.63 | $24,897.74 | |
| Animals | 179.74 | 289.64 | 109.90 | |
| Carbon | | 602.23 | 602.23 | |
| Camel's-hair tops and noils | 1,484.33 | | | $1,484.33 |
| Card clothing | 100,207.66 | 101,312.73 | 1,105.07 | |
| Carpets and rugs | 68,258.09 | 70,493.31 | 2,235.22 | |
| Chemicals | 8,328.28 | 4,148.81 | | 4,179.47 |
| Clocks | 366.19 | 56.21 | | 309.98 |
| Cotton | 108.75 | | | 108.75 |
| Cotton cloths | 767,991.11 | 984,543.83 | 216,552.72 | |
| Cotton waste | | 7,376.68 | 7,376.68 | |
| Cow and goat hair | 4,446.95 | 17,047.19 | 12,600.24 | |
| Dyestuffs | 66.92 | 1,623.19 | 1,556.27 | |
| Grease, etc | 18,303.17 | 37,083.36 | 18,780.19 | |
| Haircloths | 706.72 | 1,054.93 | 348.21 | |
| Household furniture | 160.30 | 243.33 | 83.03 | |
| India rubber | 1,458.25 | | | 1,458.25 |
| Iron, steel, etc | 108,088.80 | 135,144.22 | 27,055.42 | |
| Lanterns and slides | 223.15 | | | 223.15 |
| Leather | 40,404.82 | 68,829.05 | 28,424.23 | |
| Linens | 597.77 | 3,340.65 | 2,742.88 | |
| Machinery | 191,586.16 | 445,768.07 | 254,181.91 | |
| Miscellaneous | 267.12 | 655.10 | 387.98 | |
| Mohair (goat hair) | 14,531.12 | 3,868.68 | | 10,662.44 |
| Noils | 4,297.69 | 4,038.37 | | 259.32 |
| Oil paintings | 129.04 | | | 129.04 |
| Paper | 15,065.25 | 16,125.63 | 1,060.38 | |
| Plants | | 1,660.38 | 1,660.38 | |
| Shawls, etc | | 423.14 | 423.14 | |
| Sheepskins | | 54,588.14 | 54,588.14 | |
| Silk goods | 229,067.24 | 268,759.44 | 39,692.20 | |
| Silk waste | 3,276.47 | 1,583.94 | | 1,692.53 |
| Stuff goods | 1,891,956.71 | 2,835,535.00 | 943,578.29 | |
| Tape, braid, etc | 44,321.80 | 24,551.57 | | 19,770.23 |
| Tapestry, damasks, etc | 486.07 | 840.50 | 354.43 | |
| Thread | 3,790.53 | | | 3,790.53 |
| Tops | | 225.56 | 225.56 | |
| Wines and spirits | 455.19 | | | 455.19 |
| Wool | 881,167.30 | 1,343,323.66 | 462,156.36 | |
| Woolen goods | 20,808.16 | 46,121.18 | 25,313.02 | |
| Worsted coatings | 211,801.58 | 345,566.47 | 133,764.89 | |
| Yarns— | | | | |
| Silk | 288,894.10 | 241,437.60 | | 47,456.50 |
| Cotton | 193,195.99 | 198,763.01 | 5,567.02 | |
| Other | 9,394.96 | 68,875.11 | 59,480.15 | |
| Total | 5,278,837.37 | 7,513,761.54 | 2,326,908.88 | 91,979.71 |

Increase, $2,234,924.17.

ERASTUS S. DAY, *Consul.*

BRADFORD, *September 29, 1902.*

---

## FALMOUTH.

### FISHERIES.

The pilchard fishery during the 1901-2 season was, with one exception, the smallest for eleven years. The decrease from the catch of the preceding season was very marked, viz, some 27,500 casks as against some 38,000. The summer catches were fairly heavy, but those of the winter were very slight. Nearly the whole of the total quantity was secured by the drift boats. Italy, as usual, was the destination of the exports, except a few hundreds of casks which went to the United

States, chiefly to the New York market, where there seems to be a slightly increasing demand.

This fishery appears to be of very ancient date. The old process of curing was by dry salting in bulk on the cellar floors. This has for some time been quite superseded by the pickling of the fish in large, tight masonry tanks. The fishermen themselves no longer cure their own fish, but sell them fresh to dealers and curers, who have cellars with tanks at the various curing stations around the south and west coasts of Cornwall. Into these tanks the fish are put as soon as landed, the usual plan being a layer of fish, then a layer of salt, and so on, until the tank is full. After remaining in brine not less than sixteen days the fish are taken out of the tanks, washed, carefully sorted into two qualities, and packed in casks which are put under screw presses. The latter press the fish down in the cask, which is then refilled with fish and again pressed. The casks weigh, on completion, 238 pounds gross each. Some 2 gallons of oil per cask are extracted during the pressing process.

The lobster fishery season has been a successful one throughout Cornwall, but the crab fishery has not been so good.

Some 50 French fishing boats have been engaged during the past summer in fishing for crayfish and other shellfish off the coast of West Cornwal and the Scilly Isles. They have fished outside the 3-mile limit.  l

The important spring mackerel fishery off West Cornwall and the Scilly Isles was prosecuted with unabated energy by an increased number of steam and sailing drifters, but the catch was not as heavy as last year. The winter herring fishery in St. Ives Bay was also below the average.

### IMPORTS.

The imports into this port from foreign countries for the year ended June 30, 1901, were:

| From— | Articles. | Quantities. | Values. |
|---|---|---|---|
| Argentina | Maize ....hundredweight.. | 137,755 | $150,394.31 |
| Roumania | ......do | 95,269 | 121,346.17 |
| Russia | ......do | 71,292 | 91,173.87 |
| Do | Barley....hundredweight.. | 310,578 | 384,361.03 |
| Roumania | ......do | 61,595 | 80,855.64 |
| France | Flour.....hundredweight.. | 7,512 | 15,421.93 |
| Do | Onions .............do.... | 3,600 | 4,112.19 |
| Holland | Sugar ..............do.... | 5,254 | 14,482.70 |
| Chile | Nitrate ............do.... | 30,430 | 68,422.99 |
| Belgium | Explosives ............ | | 28,931.34 |
| Germany | ......do | | 24,536.89 |
| Russia | Timber............loads.. | 9,445 | 109,763.90 |
| Sweden | ......do | 2,055 | 25,490.72 |
| Norway | ......do | 1,510 | 24,269.23 |
| Belgium | Phosphate ..........tons.. | 496 | 2,413.77 |
| France | Guano ............do.... | 100 | 5,109.82 |
| Belgium | ......do | 16 | 817.57 |
| France | Bones .............tons.. | 56 | 1,148.48 |
| Spain | Salt ..............do.... | 180 | 729.97 |
| Portugal | ......do | 50 | 184.92 |
| Spain | Pyrites ............tons.. | 734 | 6,248.56 |
| Do | Sulphur ore.........do.... | 196 | 4,107.32 |
| France | Slates .............do.... | 206 | 3,664.46 |
| Do | Oysters ............... | | 1,362.62 |
| Norway | Ice ...............tons.. | 204 | 744.56 |

The exports for the same period consisted, as usual, of china clay, salted pilchards, and granite.

The declared exports to the United States through this consulate were:

| Articles. | Quarter ending— | | | | Total. |
|---|---|---|---|---|---|
| | Sept. 30, 1901. | Dec. 31, 1901. | Mar. 31, 1902. | June 30, 1902. | |
| China clay | $97,948.16 | $106,929.63 | $120,659.82 | $96,511.68 | $424,049.24 |
| Cornwall stone | | 2,153.44 | | | 2,153.44 |
| Pilchards | 1,188.99 | 3,140.70 | 614.60 | | 4,944.29 |
| Safety fuse | | 364.98 | | | 364.98 |
| Total | 99,137.15 | 114,588.75 | 121,274.42 | 96,511.68 | 431,511.95 |

## SCILLY ISLES.

There has not been any business at this agency since my preceding report.

HOWARD FOX, *Consul.*

FALMOUTH, *October 25, 1902.*

## SUPPLEMENTARY.

### MINING.

The production of Cornish mines and quarries during 1901 was:

| Articles. | Quantities. | Values. |
|---|---|---|
| | *Tons.* | |
| Arsenic | 1,258 | $54,748.12 |
| Arsenical pyrites | 2,334 | 18,560.88 |
| Chert and flint | 933 | 350.38 |
| China clay and china stone | 528,427 | 1,581,492.86 |
| Clay (other kinds) | 47,418 | 11,922.92 |
| Copper ore | 4,251 | 96,016.04 |
| Gravel and sand | 680 | 671.57 |
| Igneous rocks, including granite | 240,248 | 521,625.58 |
| Limestone | 9,250 | 6,014.99 |
| Ocher | 144 | 2,068.39 |
| Sandstone | 2,069 | 8,165.98 |
| Slates and slabs | 31,550 | 152,126.79 |
| Tin ore | 7,278 | 2,228,560.14 |
| Uranium ore | 79 | 14,224.77 |
| Wolfram | 21 | 1,985.68 |
| Zinc ore | 237 | 2,374.86 |

The values were those at the mines or works.

The total number of persons employed above and below ground and outside and inside quarries was 12,443.

The year 1902, which opened with rather a dark outlook, proved, on the whole, satisfactory. Cash tin, which early in the year had declined to about £104 ($506.11) to £105 ($510.98) per ton, began to advance, and before the end of February had reached £117 ($569.37), by the middle of April £126 10 s. ($615.60) and during the following month went still higher.   The strong fluctuations resulted in a declining tendency for a few weeks, after which higher values again ruled until Michaelmas, from which time fluctuations and slightly lower prices have obtained.   Closing prices continue to be rather higher than those of 1901, so that the average values throughout the year have been more than fairly maintained.

### SHIPPING.

The list of arrivals at Falmouth during 1902 for orders and otherwise (exclusive of men-of-war and coasters) was as follows:

| Nationality. | Number of ships. | Registered tonnage. | Nationality. | Number of ships. | Registered tonnage. |
|---|---|---|---|---|---|
| British | 248 | 361,134 | Dutch | 12 | 11,898 |
| Norwegian | 116 | 71,899 | Spanish | 4 | 6,395 |
| German | 100 | 164,337 | Greek | 3 | 4,160 |
| French | 53 | 79,307 | American | 1 | 1,930 |
| Danish | 83 | 14,365 | Austrian | 1 | 1,436 |
| Russian | 23 | 17,249 | Portuguese | 1 | 1,031 |
| Italian | 16 | 16,370 | | | |
| Swedish | 15 | 6,781 | Total | 625 | 758,287 |

Compared with the previous year's figures, the table shows a considerable decrease, the number of vessels being less by 121, with a falling off in the tonnage of 109,692.   An idea of the gradual decline in the volume of floating business at this port is afforded by the fact that twenty years ago, 2,520 vessels (with a tonnage of 1,411,071) put into Falmouth.

The decrease in the past year is most marked in British vessels, there being but 248 as compared with 358 in 1901, while the Italians dropped from 44 to 15.   On the other hand, the French, German, and Norwegian have somewhat increased.   The modern tendency to build large vessels is responsible for the tonnage keeping so high.

The general import trade at the docks, especially in barley and maize, shows an increase, and the same may be said of exports, which consisted of china clay, pickled fish, and granite.   The ship-repairing trade was very quiet.

### AGRICULTURE.

The year just closed has been, on the whole, one of the best that farmers have experienced for some time.   There have been advantages and disadvantages, but on striking a balance there is not much cause for complaint.   It has been a good season for all kinds of stock, which have been healthy and free from disease, and have brought high prices both as stores and fat.   Wheat has been a full average crop, barley and oats above the average.

On the other side, potatoes have been a poor crop, and apples below the average.   The labor bill was very expensive for the corn harvest, and for clearing the land of weeds.

Wheat has dropped in value 10 d. (20 cents) per bushel, barley 4 d. (8 cents), and oats 9 d. (18 cents), prices now being almost as low as they have been for years.

Rather over one-sixth of the county of Cornwall is apportioned to corn growing.   Of this, over one-half, or 67,657 acres, was devoted to oats, 24,101 to wheat, and 31,932 to barley.   Cornish farmers, like all others, know that wheat growing at present prices is unremunerative, and this year it is expected that there will be a further decrease in the area tilled.

## AMERICAN GOODS.

These continue in general demand, but, as previously stated, they are obtained from the large distributing centers in the United Kingdom.

A leading hardware dealer tells me that American wringers and refrigerators hold the field, and that roll-top desks, household woodware, tools of various descriptions, locks (to some extent), clocks, and watches command a ready sale, while the demand for American lamps has somewhat fallen off.

HOWARD FOX, *Consul.*

FALMOUTH, *January 19, 1903.*

## HUDDERSFIELD.

The year ended June, 1902, has been one of exceptional prosperity in the woolen and worsted industries of West Yorkshire—a condition the more gratifying as it was hardly anticipated.

In July, 1901, the situation was discouraging. The year just ended had been one of unusual depression; markets dragging, trade falling off everywhere, and but little promise of improvement in the future. But as the calendar year drew to a close conditions began to change for the better. By November, inquiries and orders began to multiply, and by the beginning of 1902, it was evident that a prosperous season was in sight. From January to July following the mills were running full time and, in some cases, even overtime, and the merchants were busier than for years past.

Moreover, the revival of trade was not confined to special sections, but was general. Domestic, colonial, and foreign markets alike made increased demands. Even the shipments to the United States, though only a fraction of those of former years, have been, with one exception, heavier than in any preceding twelve months since the operation of the 1897 tariff, as will appear from the tables below.

The wool market has been fairly steady during the year. There have been no labor troubles of serious importance. To sum up, the fiscal year, notably the second half, has been exceptionally busy and profitable.

### EXPORTS.

The following tables show the exports to the United States, classified by leading articles, for the year, and also for the six months ended June 30, 1902, as compared with like periods of former years:

| Articles. | Year ending June 30— | | | Six months ending June 30— | | |
|---|---|---|---|---|---|---|
| | 1900. | 1901. | 1902. | 1900. | 1901. | 1902. |
| Woolens | $480,250.57 | $374,200.77 | $481,679.41 | $254,212.56 | $197,107.86 | $261,495.59 |
| Worsteds | 622,909.15 | 379,842.58 | 494,251.42 | 307,737.41 | 191,048.66 | 278,648.44 |
| Other fabrics | 82,297.77 | 39,053.30 | 62,134.15 | 44,587.04 | 19,373.08 | 36,204.51 |
| Wool | 7,493.58 | 13,125.22 | 15,981.06 | 7,493.58 | 3,238.81 | ............. |
| Sewing cottons | 97,519.25 | 45,421.28 | 47,509.88 | 47,408.23 | 1,801.09 | 37,016.89 |
| Card, clothing, and other machinery | 155,064.02 | 100,921.81 | 85,670.55 | 85,258.86 | 37,808.36 | 50,924.27 |
| Chemicals and dyes | 186,948.55 | 161,921.73 | 196,580.40 | 88,286.32 | 99,873.27 | 84,546.78 |
| Miscellaneous | 26,100.57 | 32,819.01 | 46,564.17 | 14,697.48 | 17,360.33 | 25,641.47 |
| Total | 1,658,583.46 | 1,147,305.70 | 1,430,371.04 | 849,681.48 | 567,610.41 | 774,477.95 |

.

## CREDITS.

The topic which has been most widely discussed and which has excited the most lively interest among woolen manufacturers and dealers during the past year is a project to reform existing trade methods, and especially the system of long credits to customers, which have been in vogue for an indefinite period.

The credit system, as is well known, has in all departments of trade in England been pushed to a limit which is not permitted in other manufacturing countries. Although there has been no common rule or understanding in the matter among dealers, the customary periods of credit to wholesale buyers have ranged from six to twelve months, with a discount at maturity of bills, and no inducement worth naming for earlier payments; and with dilatory customers, extensions and other delays aggregating several more months usually intervene before the dealer actually receives his money. The uncertainty disorders business calculations and indirectly increases the cost of production.

The clear-headed leaders of the industry have all along recognized the evil of the situation, but lack of concert and fear of losing trade have hitherto prevented serious efforts at reform. Now, however, there seems to be a concerted and determined effort to grapple with the subject, and a definite scheme to meet the case is proposed.

An association is being formed (of which there are to be branches in the several manufacturing towns of the West Riding) for study and discussion of the question. It is planned to include, if possible, in this association every maker and wholesaler in the woolen trade. Correspondence has been opened with manufacturers of the west of England and of Scottish woolen districts with a view to securing universal cooperation in the plans to be adopted.

A tentative schedule of terms of trade has been prepared, which it is hoped, with possible modifications, will be adopted. It is in substance: (1) Extreme limit of credit to buyers of woolen goods: Four months from date of delivery of the merchandise, with regular trade discount if payment is made at maturity; (2) additional discount at graded rates upon payments before maturity; (3) interest at established rate on all bills after maturity.

The scheme is received with favor throughout the district, and it now seems probable that some general agreement will result.

BENJAMIN F. STONE, *Consul.*

HUDDERSFIELD, *October 31, 1902.*

.

---

## HULL.

The shipping trade of Hull, the great mainstay of its commerce, did not escape the general depression which prevailed in England in 1901. It is no surprise, therefore, to find that this trade appears in an unfavorable light when compared with the figures of the previous year.

Whereas the records for that year show an entry of 3,653 vessels, with an aggregate net tonnage of 2,666,598, those of 1901 show that 181 vessels less were entered, with a proportionate decrease in the carrying capacity of 205,768 tons.

In 1901, 2,718 vessels cleared, the net tonnage of which was 1,964,-526, while the figures of 1900 show that 3,311 vessels cleared, their net tonnage being 2,274,137. This was an increase over the year 1899 of nearly 112,000 tons. The total tonnage entered and cleared for the year 1901 was 4,425,356. These figures do not include the coasting trade, which maintains a fair average.

On the 31st of December, there appeared on the Hull register 235 sailing vessels, with a net tonnage of 15,194, and 629 steam vessels, with a net tonnage of 208,679. On the 31st of December, 1900, the same register showed there were 239 sailing and 643 steam vessels operating in the port, with a total tonnage of 226,654. On the 31st of December, 1899, there were 235 sailing and 632 steam, with a total net tonnage of 213,610. These figures are given with a view of showing that the shipping trade of the port during the last three years exhibits such slight fluctuations that it may be said to have remained stationary. A great many causes contribute to this fact, not the least of these being the dispute between the corporation and the North Eastern Railway, which practically controls all the transportation facilities of the port.

The failure of the new dock scheme is one of the results of this conflict, and Hull finds itself to-day occupying the strange position of being the only important port on the east coast without some practical scheme on hand to enlarge and perfect its dock accommodation. The public have lost all faith in the railway companies, and have now turned to the corporation in the hope that their representatives will bring forward a new scheme for municipalizing the docks, and giving the port all the facilities it needs in that way. If the corporation fails to rise to the necessities of the occasion, the result will be that Hull will soon find itself relegated to the fourth, if not the fifth, position among the ports of Great Britain.

## HULL'S SHIPPING TRADE.

· Hull's shipping trade radiates to nearly every port of importance on the globe, but its paramount interests lie with Russia, Sweden and Norway, Germany, Holland, Belgium, France, Spain, Italy, Austria-Hungary, Turkey, Egypt, Argentine Republic, and the United States. Of the British possessions, India takes the lead, Australia and New Zealand next, with Canada following. The total number of vessels cleared for the United States in 1901, as shown by the Government returns, was 100, with a total net tonnage of 260,992. Of this number, 17 were sail, the remainder being steam. All the steam vessels went to the Atlantic ports, New York and Boston principally, while 11 of the 17 sailing vessels cleared for Pacific ports, chiefly San Francisco. Of the 51 ships that entered during the same period, 21 were from the Atlantic ports, their total net tonnage being 283,763. Thirty grain vessels entered from the Pacific coast, with a total net tonnage of 71,378.

## HULL IMPORTS.

The total value of the cargoes landed in Hull during the year 1901, as shown by the board of trade returns, was close on $160,000,000. This was an increase over the previous year of nearly $2,900,000. It

H. Doc. 305, pt 2——51

shows a still greater increase over the year 1899, when the value of the imports was about $140,000,000. In 1898, the imports were valued at $147,000,000 and in 1897 at $133,000,000. The principal items were: Butter, wheat, barley, oats, indian corn, raw cotton, eggs, fish, fruit, hemp, lard, machinery, margarine, meat, including bacon, fresh and salted beef, hams, etc.; iron and steel, seed oil and cake, paper, petroleum, seeds, including clover and grass, cotton, flax or linseed, rape, etc.; skins, including raw hides and goat skins; sugar, refined and unrefined; molasses and glucose, vegetables, wood, wool, and woolens.

The importations of butter alone were valued at nearly $16,000,000; wheat, $20,000,000; raw cotton, $3,600,000; eggs, $2,300,000; fish, nearly $3,000,000; fruit, $2,150,000; lard, $3,600,000; machinery, $2,375,000; margarine, $2,650,000; meat, including bacon, beef, fresh and salted, and hams, $7,500,000; oil, including fish, olive, seed, and turpentine, $2,700,000; paper, $2,100,000; petroleum, $1,300,000; seeds, including clover and grass, cotton, flax or linseed, rape, etc., $17,500,000; sugar, including refined, unrefined, molasses, and glucose, about $5,000,000; wood of all kinds, about $7,000,000, and wool, $8,250,000.

### HULL EXPORTS.

There is a marked difference between the value of the exports from Hull and that of the imports. The former for 1901 fell short of $76,000,000. It will be seen that with such expansion in the volume of trade, Hull's relation to the home supply entitles it to special distinction as a great distributing port. These exports are for British and Irish produce only and do not take in transshipped merchandise, which appears under the head of foreign and colonial products. The total value of the latter for the year 1901 was $28,000,000. This shows a decline compared with preceding years. A good many items appear on the list of British and Irish products and are put down as Hull exports which have no connection whatever with local trade. All the cotton exports which find their way to Hull from other parts of England were valued at $20,000,000. The same may be said of wool, woolens, and worsted fabrics, the total value of which was between $13,000,000 and $14,000,000. Large consignments of machinery come here from Lincolnshire, Lancashire, and the West Riding of Yorkshire, en route to continental ports. A very large per cent of this class of exports is made up of agricultural and mill-working machinery. Hardware and cutlery, implements and tools, linen yarn, and linen manufactures, including those of brass and copper, fall into the same category.

The following statement shows the value of the declared exports to the United States from Hull for the four quarters of the year ended June 30, 1902:

| Articles | Quarter ending— | | | | Total. |
|---|---|---|---|---|---|
| | Sept. 30. | Dec. 31. | Mar. 31. | June 30. | |
| Alum | | $405 | | $1,550 | $1,955 |
| Ammonia | $5,152 | 10,901 | | 2,171 | 18,224 |
| Beer | | 1,153 | | | 1,153 |
| Bleaching powder | 5,361 | 8,239 | $1,820 | | 15,420 |
| Brass | | | | 150 | 150 |
| Bricks (fire) | 2,621 | | | | 2,621 |
| Calfskins | 5,050 | | | 54,000 | 59,050 |
| Camels hair | 15,582 | 34,711 | 7,843 | 413 | 58,549 |

| Articles. | Quarter ending— | | | | Total. |
|---|---|---|---|---|---|
| | Sept. 30. | Dec. 31. | Mar. 31. | June 30. | |
| Canvas (old) | | | | $352 | $352 |
| Carbolic | | $2,157 | | 1,828 | 3,985 |
| Castor seed | $5,473 | 10,695 | | 8,942 | 25,110 |
| Cement | 272 | 322 | $1,211 | 325 | 2,130 |
| Cliffstone | 4,341 | | | 5,160 | 9,501 |
| Coal | | | | 8,167 | 8,167 |
| Colors | 4,207 | 6,243 | 5,105 | 38,704 | 54,259 |
| Composition | | 279 | 272 | 202 | 753 |
| Cotton seed | | | | 55 | 55 |
| Cotton waste | | | | 6,709 | 6,709 |
| Cowhair | 2,830 | | | | 2,830 |
| Creosote | 219 | | 1,532 | | 1,751 |
| Dogs | 146 | 413 | 176 | 622 | 1,357 |
| Electrical goods | 59 | | | | 59 |
| Fish manure | 2,864 | 5,721 | | | 8,585 |
| Flax | 905 | | | | 905 |
| Gelatin | | 267 | | | 267 |
| Glue | 1,142 | 2,720 | 7,187 | 2,087 | 13,136 |
| Goatskins | 2,171 | | | | 2,171 |
| Grease | 3,173 | 6,495 | 6,276 | 4,688 | 20,632 |
| Herrings | | 5,526 | | | 5,526 |
| Hides and skins | 16,166 | 68,636 | 68,800 | 16,499 | 170,101 |
| Iron ore | | | 2,170 | | 2,170 |
| Iron and steel | | | | 14,594 | 14,594 |
| Leather (walrus) | 1,423 | 583 | 2,858 | 787 | 5,651 |
| Machinery | | | 229 | | 729 |
| Manganese | 47,359 | 9,735 | | | 57,094 |
| Manure | | | | 17,976 | 17,976 |
| Matches | | | 218 | | 218 |
| Oil: | | | | | |
| Creosote | | | | 1,547 | 1,547 |
| Linseed | 2,783 | | | 750 | 3,533 |
| Rape seed | 52,208 | 25,806 | 49,035 | 16,202 | 143,251 |
| Onions | | 710 | | 5,446 | 6,156 |
| Oranges | | | 726 | | 726 |
| Oxide (red) | | | | 895 | 895 |
| Paint | | 350 | 704 | 678 | 1,732 |
| Phosphate | 492 | | | 7,240 | 7,732 |
| Pig iron | 6,154 | 5,875 | | 30,914 | 42,943 |
| Pitch | | 177 | 3,154 | | 3,331 |
| Potatoes | | 27,830 | 120,677 | 21,190 | 169,697 |
| Rope (old) | 17,602 | | 9,383 | 9,606 | 26,591 |
| Silico spiegel | | | | 3,043 | 3,043 |
| Tacks | 115 | | | | 115 |
| Tongues | 1,500 | | | | 1,500 |
| Varnish | | | | 455 | 455 |
| Walnut logs | | 2,770 | | | 2,770 |
| Washing blue | 16,063 | 5,682 | 16,219 | 15,129 | 49,093 |
| Wax (paraffin) | | 780 | | | 780 |
| Whiting | | | | 779 | 779 |
| Wool | 10,841 | 45,526 | 33,580 | 12,264 | 102,161 |
| Total | 234,274 | 302,692 | 339,126 | 192,119 | 1,068,211 |

It might be in order to offer a few words of explanation in reference to four items in the foregoing list, namely, coal, pig iron, potatoes, and steel. The troubles in the coal regions of Pennsylvania are responsible for the first item, while partial failure of the potato crop in the United States last year forced American buyers to draw supplies from foreign markets. Large quantities of this produce came from Continental countries, chiefly Belgium, France, Holland, and Germany, while the remainder was found in the warp land around Doncaster and Goole, a soil that is particularly adapted for the growth of potatoes. The pig iron and steel items are traceable to the great demand for all structural material in the United States and the inability of the mills there to meet this demand. This traffic is one of the shifting features of the commercial panorama in Hull, and might be called the trade sporadic.

### POTATOES AT $5,450 PER TON.

A startling feature of the potato trade was recently brought to light through a report of a transaction at Lincoln market last week. A tuber named the Northern Star was introduced last year by a Mr. Findlay, of Markinch, Scotland, and he parted with a few tons at £1,120 ($5,450) per ton. This is the long ton of 2,240 pounds. To no one would he sell, says a correspondent of the Hull Daily Mail, at a less rate than 10 shillings, or $2.50 per pound, and 2 pounds were purchased by Messrs. Barlow & Blanchard, of Bradney, near Lincoln. From those two pounds they have this year grown 130 pounds, and are so satisfied with the result that they have procured several hundred-weight more from Mr. Findlay at the rate of £500 ($2,430) per ton. A Mr. Kime, of Marcham-le-Fen, in the same county, has purchased a ton at the same figure, and Mr. Blades, of Epworth, after giving £525 ($2,554) for 21 hundredweight, has since procured a further consignment at £30 ($145) per hundredweight, or £600 ($2,919) per ton. Another new potato which has just been placed on the market has also made a tremendous hit. It is named King Edward VII, and is an extremely pretty potato, a peculiarity being a shading of pink around the eyes, while the other end is white. The stock has been held by Mr. Buttler, of Scotter, and Mr. Blades, of Epworth, the former of whom has grown 85 acres of this kind of potato during the present year, while Mr. Blades has grown about 10 acres. Very few circulars were sent out respecting this potato, but there was an extraordinary run upon it, and the price, which commenced at £12 10s. ($60) per ton, has risen to £40, or $194.66, per ton. The whole stock was sold within a fortnight.

### SHIPBUILDING INDUSTRY AT HULL.

The shipbuilding industry in Hull sustained a great loss by the failure of Earles' yard. These extensive premises have been purchased by Mr. Charles H. Wilson, who, with his brother, Mr. Arthur Wilson, controls the vast interests of the Wilson Shipping Company. The yard is now open, but the business so far has been anything but encouraging. The buildings have been partly reconstructed and the entire concern subjected to a general overhauling. Old and obsolete machinery has been thrown out or sold, and its place taken by machines of the latest and most effective type. When the shipbuilding industry of the country resumes a more active state, the new concern will be thoroughly equipped for the transaction of business.

The total number of vessels built at Hull during the year 1901 was 51 sailing vessels, all small craft, with a total tonnage of 4,083, and 21 steam vessels, mostly for the fishing trade, whose total tonnage was 1,204. During the previous year, the total new tonnage turned out, both sail and steam, was 9,258, or nearly twice that of 1901. In 1899, the total tonnage of vessels built was over 14,000. It will be seen by these figures that the shipbuilding industry in Hull is in a very bad state.

### HULL COAL TRADE.

Hull exports each year vast quantities of coal to foreign countries, in addition to the supplies sent out for home consumption. Sweden is its best customer for this product, having taken nearly 400,000 tons in 1901, while the purchases for the previous year amounted to nearly 460,000 tons. Russia comes next, with an aggregate of nearly 340,000 in 1901, and 408,000 tons in 1900. Germany follows with a little over

181,000 tons for 1901, while her purchases for the previous year amounted to close on 250,000 tons. Holland follows on the heels of Germany; then comes France, whose purchases in 1901 dropped to 52,741 tons from 136,383 tons the year before. The purchases for Denmark were not quite so heavy as those of France; they dropped nearly 60 per cent in 1901, from a total of 105,568 in 1900. Belgium, Egypt, Italy, Turkey, and the Channel Islands are also good customers. Africa, which took nearly 72,000 tons in 1900, cried content with 10,719 in 1901. California is credited with having taken 2,442 tons in 1900, but none in 1901. The rest of the United States took about 41,000 tons in 1901, and nearly 48,000 in 1900. The decrease in the exports of Yorkshire coal to foreign countries in the year 1901, as compared with those of the previous year, amounted to nearly 624,000 tons.

The coastwise shipments for 1901 amounted to 313,193 tons, while those of the previous year were 501,709 tons, or a decrease of nearly 189,000 tons.

Various causes are assigned for this marked shrinkage in the coal trade, but those who understand the situation best attribute the result to the adoption of a new policy on the part of the Government, which imposed a tax on coal going out of the country for foreign consumption. The necessities of the revenue, arising out of the war in South Africa, was the real cause, and these influences are still having their effect on the coal trade of the port. Some claim that the coal owners were partly to blame, by standing out for exorbitant prices at the beginning of the year. Their action imparted to Yorkshire coal a fictitious value, with the result that a large portion of the trade was diverted from Hull, and eventually placed with the Tyne ports, Newcastle districts, Scotland, and elsewhere. The loss to Hull was enormous, as will be seen by the statement that in 1900, 4,204,928 tons were brought into the port, as against 3,275,360 tons in 1901, or a decrease of 929,568 tons.

The following table shows the quantity of coal brought to Hull by river and rail each year since 1885, and is taken from the annual report of the Hull coal inspector:

| Year. | Via river. | Via rail. | Total. | Increase over previous year. |
|---|---|---|---|---|
| | Tons. | Tons. | Tons. | Tons. |
| 1885 | 565,600 | 760,952 | 1,326,552 | 24,160 |
| 1886 | 501,720 | 916'008 | 1,417,728 | 91,176 |
| 1887 | 526,888 | 1,264'840 | 1,789,728 | 372,000 |
| 1888 | 514,505 | 1,280,888 | 1,795,332 | 5,604 |
| 1889 | 535,656 | 1,455,312 | 1,990,968 | 195,576 |
| 1890 | 519,392 | 1,677,504 | 2,196,896 | 205,728 |
| 1891 | 503,504 | 1,882,520 | 2,386,024 | 189,328 |
| 1892 | 544,856 | 1,691,312 | 2,236,168 | a 149,856 |
| 1893 | 532,648 | 899,424 | 1,432,072 | a 804,006 |
| 1894 | 537,952 | 1,718,872 | 2,256,824 | 824,752 |
| 1895 | 476,664 | 1,713,352 | 2,190,016 | a 66,808 |
| 1896 | | | | 230,400 |
| 1897 | 577,872 | 2,077,872 | 2,655,744 | 235,328 |
| 1898 | 616,256 | 2,843,232 | 3,459,488 | 803,744 |
| 1899 | 630,568 | 2,912,392 | | |
| 1900 | | | 620 | 661,968 |
| 1901 | 550,648 | 2,724,712 | 3,275,360 | a 929,568 |

a Decreases.

Another cause which may be considered in connection with the trade at Hull is the strike at the Denaby mines in South Yorkshire. These mines employ nearly 5,000 hands, and are reckoned among the largest and best equipped in the country. A very large percentage of their output finds its way to Hull, where it is transshipped and forwarded to all parts of the Continent.

### AMERICAN CATTLE IN HULL.

There has been a complete suspension of the live-cattle trade between Hull and the United States, and the local meat market is gradually showing the effect of this stoppage by the scarcity of supply and the consequent advance in prices.

The splendid cattle landed here by the Wilson Line boats and the superior quality of the meat imparted to this trade a special interest to butchers, who did not hesitate to give it the preference over the native product. I have it from the very best judges that they were the finest cattle ever slaughtered on these shores.

The agent of the cattle owners lays the blame on the butchers, who in turn retaliate by attributing the loss of the trade to the agent's arbitrary and dictatorial business methods. These shipments averaged about 100 prime cattle a week, and always proved a great relief to the local market. A return to the status quo ante is anxiously expected by the entire community, who are beginning to feel the effect of the advance in price and the loss of such a valuable product. The poor, as usual, are largely affected, as an inferior quality of beef and other meat foods have been forced on the market. Hull is a good market for our cattle, and the situation here deserves the serious consideration of the cattlemen in the United States. The trade in prime American cattle could be made to average 250 per week all the year round. The following paragraphs, taken from recent issues of the London Morning Leader, will be of interest in this connection:

### ENGLAND SHORT OF BEEF SUPPLIES.

The present price of meat is a striking commentary on the position that would be likely to arise if we were so foolish as to further restrict our present supplies of one of the chief articles of food by taxing foreign meat to benefit our colonies. It is a simple fact that at present our foreign meat suppliers, instead of being too many, are not numerous enough. The shutting out of Argentine cattle has in consequence been of great advantage to the American exporters, and we are now eagerly looking to Argentina for large shipments of beef to bring down prices. Nothing is gained by shirking the fact that the United States and South America are our best sources of beef supplies. If, as has recently happened, one of these supplies is cut off, we soon become aware of the fact by being placed at the mercy of the remaining available supply. Imagine, then, the folly of supplementing the natural risks of disease and drought by artificially cutting ourselves off from the cheapest and best supplies in the world. That is what is really entailed in the suggestion that we should place a duty upon imported meat, and relax that duty in favor of our colonies. Such an action would be equivalent in its results to the effects of a partial drought in the United States and South America. The simple fact is that every new oversea supply of meat which arises, whether in foreign countries or our colonies, is a source of strength to ourselves, and consequently a source of strength to the Empire in which this country is the predominant partner. The present price of meat, the terrible drought in Australia, the outbreak of foot-and-mouth disease in Argentina, will all prove to be blessings in disguise, if they bring home to this country the simple truths I have endeavored to state.

### CONDITION OF ENGLISH LIVE STOCK.

For some time past, meat has been dearer than for a number of years and the auction sales of sheep and cattle have, as a whole, been of a satisfactory nature. Nor will the weather altogether account for it, though, as will be remembered, the spring of this year was very forbidding and gave no promise of the abundant grass that followed it. The significance of the decrease, in truth, is in this, says a writer in Country Life, that it points to the impoverishment of our farmers during the long period of depression. Owing to circumstances that we need not go into now, the meat supplies from America, Argentina, and New Zealand were considerably affected, with the result that our market went up and farmers could not resist the chance of realizing on their live stock. In other words, "unfinished" animals were hurried off to auction, and even the breeding stock, where it was in anything like condition, was turned into money. No one who understands the position would say this was economical. For the sake of a little capital in hand, many farmers have crippled their resources for years to come. It would have been much better to forego the immediate return and wait for a larger one; but this would have required capital, and capital is precisely what is most lacking among the agricultural classes at the present moment.

### SLAUGHTER OF AMERICAN CATTLE AT HULL.

The Northeastern Railway Company has provided on its own grounds on the river front, in a convenient part of the old town, a large depot and abattoir where American cattle are sold and slaughtered. The buildings are well constructed, all the departments spacious, well-lighted and ventilated, and thoroughly up to date in their sanitary arrangements. The floors are laid in concrete and supplied with the necessary outlets for carrying the waste into the river. There is ample accommodation for cold storage where the meat is held subject to the butcher's order, besides stalls and pens where the live cattle can be housed and fed at a mere nominal cost. Hull has no reason to complain in this respect, as the establishment is one of the best of its kind in England.

### THE HULL PROVISION MARKET.

The reported failure of the corn crop in the United States early in 1901 had a very disquieting effect on the provision market in Great Britain, and led to heavy speculation in this and other districts on the part of buyers who saw, or fancied they saw, in the situation there, unmistakable evidences of an impending advance in prices. The reports that followed proved that their conclusions were drawn rather hastily, and had a very demoralizing effect on the market. The attempt to realize on stocks produced a sudden reaction, and prices fell rapidly. This slump was as short lived as it was sudden, for the market soon recovered itself, under the influence of fresh news from the United States which showed that new forces had been set in motion there to revolutionize the existing state of things, and bring about results that were never foreseen. Prices went up steadily, and have been on the advance ever since, until they have now reached the highest point ever known in this country. The attitude of the American packing houses toward the foreign buyers underwent a complete change, so much so that it was difficult to obtain anything like an adequate supply in proportion to the demand, and wholesale buyers were forced to drive about wherever and whenever they could to find stock for their customers. Every source of supply, both at home and on the Continent, was tapped, but these all fell short. The situation became more acute as time went on, and this is the present position.

### HIGH PRICES FOR AMERICAN PROVISIONS.

The year ended June 30, 1902, will long be remembered by the provision dealers in England, from the lowest to the highest, as one of the worst if not the very worst on record.  The violent fluctuation in prices was another aggravating feature of the situation which added to the general embarrassment.  It will be interesting to note here that American hams, which sold in this market four years ago at $8.75 per hundredweight of 112 pounds, fetched in July last $15.31, while the higher grades or best quality sold for $16.53.  Lard, shoulders, and all portions of bacon are proportionately high and difficult to obtain. The following table shows sundry articles of food imported into Hull each year, from 1896 to 1901 inclusive:

| Articles. | 1896. | 1897. | 1898. | 1899. | 1900. | 1901. |
|---|---|---|---|---|---|---|
| | Cwt. | Cwt. | Cwt. | Cwt. | Cwt. | Cwt. |
| Bacon | 639,294 | 506,688 | 708,569 | 667,573 | 519,352 | 529,261 |
| Beef and pork | 73,500 | 34,120 | 54,424 | 50,718 | 48,410 | 46,154 |
| Hams | 33,487 | 13,565 | 30,059 | 43,374 | 37,027 | 33,092 |
| Meat | 12,037 | 17,544 | 16,818 | 49,992 | 42,058 | 78,296 |
| Butter and margarine | 788,864 | 828,564 | 813,140 | 739,256 | 759,079 | 829,135 |
| Cheese | 37,084 | 39,389 | 29,504 | 31,553 | 31,423 | 33,529 |
| Potatoes | 210,638 | 262,828 | 544,067 | 447,773 | 707,031 | 632,007 |

### FRUIT AND PRODUCE IN HULL.

A further point of interest in Hull is the precarious position of the so-called short trades—that is, the weekly and biweekly services of boats engaged in bringing fruit, yeast, and market produce of all kinds from Antwerp, Rotterdam, Harlingen, Ghent, Amsterdam, Boulogne, and Hamburg.  During the last twenty years, a great part of this trade has been captured by Grimsby and Goole, swifter and more modern boats having been built for that purpose.  To such an extent had the position of Hull become endangered that it became customary to speak of these trades as "doomed."  Lately, however, a change has come over the scene.  The Northeastern Railway Company obtained Parliamentary powers to run boats of its own, as is already done by the Great Central Railway Company from Grimsby.  As yet, this policy is only partially developed, but owing to this and other causes, the continental fruit trade with Hull has rapidly increased.  Year by year reveals an extension of this branch of commerce.  Whole streets in the neighborhood of Humber Dock are now devoted to warehousing and imports. Enormous quantities of fruit and flowers are delivered here during the summer months, and in the winter the shipments of oranges and grapes from Spain are upon a colossal scale.  It is of interest to note that within the past two years, the imports of bananas have multiplied ten or twelve fold.  Auctioned to wholesale dealers from all the great inland towns, they are sold retail in the shops at two for 1½ pence (3 cents), and owing to economies in shipment, will next season be sold at one-half pence (1 cent) each, prime quality.  Curiously enough, few large fortunes are amassed in the fruit trade.  For obvious reasons, it is highly speculative; a buyer who has committed himself in advance to large purchases—say, of Valencia oranges—finds himself the loser by thousands of pounds in a season, owing to a glut in the market, or a severe frost may affect his calculations equally disastrously.  Few trades call for as much skill and judgment on the part of the dealer; consequently, there are few in which the number of business failures are so high.

*Imports of fruits, nuts, and vegetables.*

BY MONTHS, 1901.

[Expressed in packages.]

| Articles. | Countries. | Jan. | Feb. | Mar. | Apr. | May. | June. |
|---|---|---|---|---|---|---|---|
| Apples............. | United States..... | 4,490 | 3,380 | 250 | 500 | 500 | ......... |
| | Portugal.......... | ......... | ......... | ......... | ......... | ......... | 14 |
| Fruit (unclassified).. | Belgium.......... | 1,810 | 2,742 | 6,425 | 1,203 | 76 | 21 |
| | Denmark.......... | ......... | ......... | 2 | ......... | ......... | 3 |
| | France .......... | 4,692 | 2,119 | 10,821 | 1,837 | 6,769 | 54,456 |
| | Germany......... | 8 | 363 | 1,658 | 915 | 1,423 | 16,989 |
| | Holland and Rhine. | 204 | 217 | 342 | 166 | 624 | 55,083 |
| | Norway, Sweden, and Russia. | 7 | 25 | ......... | ......... | ......... | ......... |
| Lemons............. | Italy and Sicily... | 10,294 | 3,373 | 8,068 | 15,585 | 12,156 | 10,565 |
| | Spain............. | | | | | | |
| Oranges ............ | Jaffa and Egypt | | | | | | |
| | Italy and Sicily... | 6,852 | 3,348 | 4,499 | 1,117 | 416 | ......... |
| | Spain............. | 88,067 | 46,794 | 100,797 | 63,257 | 46,610 | 5,743 |
| | St. Michael ...... | ......... | 1,881 | | | | |
| | Portugal.......... | ......... | 640 | | | | |
| Almonds ............. | Italy, Sicily, Spain | 2,026 | 145 | 3,135 | 809 | 77 | 918 |
| Grapes............. | Spain............. | | | | | | |
| Melons ............. | Spain, Malta....... | | | | | | |
| Nuts................ | Belgium, France, Germany, Holland. | 1 | ......... | ......... | 79 | 300 | 30 |
| | Italy and Sicily... | ......... | ......... | 250 | 65 | ......... | ......... |
| | Spain............. | 1,824 | ......... | 500 | ......... | | |
| Pines............. | St. Michaels ...... | ......... | 3,159 | | | | |
| Pomegranates....... | Spain and Malta.... | | | | | | |
| Tomatoes............ | | 80 | 61 | ......... | 67 | 101 | 1,997 |
| Vegetables ......... | France, Belgium.. | 665 | 1,035 | 4,455 | 2,818 | 5,554 | 3,989 |
| | Germany ......... | 20 | 149 | 76 | 78 | 11 | 14 |
| | Holland .......... | 793 | 2,689 | 2,811 | 2,492 | 3,811 | 16,317 |
| Miscellaneous ...... | Other countries... | 66 | 232 | 1 | 10 | ......... | 3 |

| Articles. | Countries. | July. | Aug. | Sept. | Oct. | Nov. | Dec. |
|---|---|---|---|---|---|---|---|
| Apples.............. | United States..... | ......... | ......... | ......... | 100 | 1,382 | 1,925 |
| | Portugal.......... | 4,389 | 1,916 | 27 | ......... | | |
| Fruit (unclassified).. | Belgium.......... | 18,600 | 59,333 | 21,558 | 15,299 | 1,255 | 333 |
| | Denmark.......... | ......... | ......... | ......... | 29 | 1 | 18 |
| | France .......... | 94,615 | 122,316 | 44,751 | 26,169 | 18,082 | 8,540 |
| | Germany......... | 150,523 | 58,612 | 16,015 | 1,506 | 660 | 799 |
| | Holland and Rhine. | 71,928 | 46,768 | 3,096 | 539 | 258 | 636 |
| | Norway, Sweden, and Russia. | 75 | 210 | 880 | 7,322 | 3,872 | 8 |
| Lemons............. | Italy and Sicily .. | 10,127 | 1,480 | 2,214 | 492 | 1,073 | 8,332 |
| | Spain............. | ......... | ......... | 18 | ......... | 61 | ......... |
| Oranges ............ | Jaffa and Egypt .. | ......... | ......... | ......... | 1,169 | ......... | ......... |
| | Italy and Sicily .. | 2,067 | 12 | ......... | ......... | 3,272 | 1,588 |
| | Spain............. | 54 | 9 | ......... | 294 | 46,774 | 100,886 |
| | St. Michael ...... | ......... | ......... | ......... | ......... | ......... | 2,075 |
| | Portugal.......... | ......... | ......... | ......... | ......... | ......... | 1,356 |
| Almonds ............. | Italy, Sicily, Spain | 5 | ......... | 1,748 | 4,554 | 2,263 | 2,191 |
| Grapes............. | Spain............. | 10,271 | 20,626 | 13,879 | 22,161 | 11,705 | ......... |
| Melons ............. | Spain, Malta...... | 5,641 | 6,416 | ,575 | ......... | | |
| Nuts................ | Belgium, France, Germany, Holland. | 12 | 832 | 2,443 | 1,996 | 1,105 | 1,619 |
| | Italy and Sicily... | ......... | 5 | 100 | 210 | 2,820 | 75 |
| | Spain............. | ......... | ......... | ......... | 3,170 | 3,615 | ......... |
| Pines.............. | St. Michaels ...... | ......... | ......... | ......... | ......... | ......... | 80 |
| Pomegranates....... | Spain and Malta.... | ......... | 605 | 7,929 | 104 | ......... | ......... |
| Tomatoes............ | | 7,774 | 1,949 | 6,514 | 735 | ......... | 58 |
| Vegetables ......... | France, Belgium.. | 35,461 | 66,200 | 34,147 | 2,092 | 263 | 126 |
| | Germany ......... | ......... | 5 | ......... | 154 | 198 | 27 |
| | Holland .......... | 21,667 | 26,817 | 6,129 | 1,812 | 2,310 | 2,954 |
| Miscellaneous ...... | Other countries... | 14 | ......... | ......... | 273 | 221 | 383 |

*Imports of fruits, nuts, and vegetables*—Continued.

BY YEARS.

| Articles. | Countries. | 1892. | 1893. | 1894. | 1895. | 1896. |
|---|---|---|---|---|---|---|
| Apples............... | United States..... | 3,969 | 658 | 1,321 | 4,754 | 15,903 |
| | Portugal.......... | 1,492 | 3,057 | 553 | 2,817 | 1,861 |
| Fruit (unclassified).. | Belgium.......... | 266,684 | 316,316 | 473,482 | 173,443 | 124,097 |
| | Denmark.......... | 297 | 850 | 47 | 135 | 273 |
| | France .......... | 142,103 | 338,757 | 476,081 | 199,815 | 256,877 |
| | Germany ......... | 171,636 | 242,283 | 288,544 | 368,007 | 277,020 |
| | Holland and Rhine. | 259,791 | 375,421 | 465,223 | 211,335 | 271,909 |
| | Norway, Sweden, and Russia. | 14,326 | 10,554 | 16,412 | 24,204 | 9,771 |
| Lemons............. | Italy and Sicily... | 41,506 | 57,955 | 89,229 | 63,514 | 84,829 |
| | Spain ............ | 1,767 | 1,389 | 1,435 | 1,219 | 419 |
| Oranges ............ | Jaffa and Egypt .. | 2,895 | 1,251 | 3 | 29 | 45 |
| | Italy and Sicily... | 46,554 | 41,978 | 36,318 | 34,298 | 23,637 |
| | Spain ............ | 331,797 | 264,582 | 401,974 | 443,156 | 408,408 |
| | St. Michael ...... | 27,023 | 19,253 | 21,659 | 39,685 | 25,132 |
| | Portugal ......... | | | | | |
| Almonds ........... | Italy, Sicily, Spain | 5,612 | 8,952 | 7,672 | 5,340 | 14,879 |
| Grapes............. | Spain ............ | 8,018 | 39,516 | 36,091 | 39,192 | 64,728 |
| Melons ............. | Spain, Malta...... | 308 | 1,821 | 3,901 | 1,147 | 5,787 |
| Nuts................ | Belgium, France, Germany, Holland. | 14,112 | 5,391 | 7,674 | 5,098 | 7,927 |
| | Italy and Sicily... | 4,556 | 3,170 | 3,045 | 2,267 | 2,309 |
| | Spain ............ | 5,400 | 12,578 | 7,500 | 15,111 | 13,050 |
| Pines .............. | St. Michaels ...... | 5,875 | 9,121 | 8,160 | 13,294 | 11,205 |
| Pomegranates ...... | Spain and Malta.. | 310 | 2,683 | 2,887 | 3,163 | 6,173 |
| Tomatoes........... | | 4,213 | 6,903 | 9,240 | 20,656 | 13,309 |
| Vegetables ......... | France, Belgium.. | 169,148 | 196,061 | 151,582 | 190,127 | 185,619 |
| | Germany ......... | 1,502 | 1,230 | 727 | 724 | 392 |
| | Holland ......... | 69,327 | 80,365 | 76,570 | 58,221 | 68,605 |
| Miscellaneous ...... | Other countries... | 4,723 | 1,742 | 815 | 1,352 | 7,269 |
| Total ......... | ............ | 2,380,083 | 2,665,493 | 3,336,758 | 2,635,378 | 2,645,452 |

| Articles. | Countries. | 1897. | 1898. | 1899. | 1900. | 1901. |
|---|---|---|---|---|---|---|
| Apples............... | United States..... | 13,068 | 12,538 | 4,962 | 19,022 | 12,527 |
| | Portugal.......... | 4,231 | 2,350 | 10,769 | 1,693 | 6,346 |
| Fruit (unclassified).. | Belgium.......... | 225,262 | 98,600 | 97,928 | 172,785 | 128,655 |
| | Denmark.......... | 809 | 98 | 10 | 701 | 53 |
| | France .......... | 412,346 | 468,929 | 350,833 | 467,930 | 395,167 |
| | Germany ......... | 424,284 | 422,890 | 349,689 | 315,021 | 249,471 |
| | Holland and Rhine. | 244,788 | 211,254 | 104,671 | 175,523 | 179,811 |
| | Norway, Sweden, and Russia. | 367 | 24,237 | 13,497 | 16,286 | 11,899 |
| Lemons............. | Italy and Sicily... | 100,337 | 100,179 | 86,897 | 87,471 | 83,694 |
| | Spain ............ | 738 | 1,006 | 2,040 | 628 | 79 |
| Oranges ............ | Jaffa and Egypt... | ............ | ............ | 2 | ............ | 1,169 |
| | Italy and Sicily .. | 22,077 | 18,013 | 23,246 | 26,658 | 23,171 |
| | Spain ............ | 534,022 | 354,322 | 516,936 | 431,915 | 499,275 |
| | St. Michael ...... | 34,189 | 31,650 | 2,820 | ............ | 3,956 |
| | Portugal.......... | ............ | ............ | 1,105 | ............ | 1,996 |
| Almonds ........... | Italy, Sicily, Spain | 6,710 | 18,990 | 23,423 | 11,129 | 17,871 |
| Grapes............. | Spain ............ | 56,166 | 68,164 | 96,633 | 74,527 | 78,642 |
| Melons ............. | Spain, Malta...... | 5,579 | 10,097 | 6,250 | 10,471 | 12,632 |
| Nuts................ | Belgium, France, Germany, Holland. | 5,962 | 4,548 | 4,250 | 8,830 | 8,417 |
| | Italy and Sicily... | 3,387 | 2,834 | 1,345 | 1,839 | 3,525 |
| | Spain ............ | 13,001 | 3,965 | 12,024 | 2,735 | 8,609 |
| Pines .............. | St. Michaels ...... | 1,582 | 7,629 | 3,561 | ............ | 3,239 |
| Pomegranates ...... | Spain and Malta.. | 5,193 | 6,745 | 8,899 | 5,330 | 8,638 |
| Tomatoes........... | | 20,175 | 17,941 | 22,484 | 16,590 | 19,286 |
| Vegetables ......... | France, Belgium.. | 225,471 | 269,630 | 209,718 | 185,247 | 156,805 |
| | Germany ......... | 2,249 | 711 | 616 | 4,250 | 782 |
| | Holland ......... | 101,152 | 67,582 | 97,389 | 87,013 | 90,602 |
| Miscellaneous ...... | Other countries... | 22,708 | 8,654 | 13,891 | 6,640 | 1,208 |
| Total ......... | ............ | 3,356,608 | 3,386,981 | 3,102,344 | 3,454,979 | 3,260,334 |

### JAMAICA BANANAS IN ENGLAND.

The policy of the British Government to establish closer relations with the colonies has taken practical shape so far as Jamaica is concerned, for this country is now being treated to the largest imports of the products of that island ever known since it became a British possession. Jamaica bananas and oranges are to be found in abundance at all the principal markets, and the attempt is being made to cultivate a taste for these among the masses, who consume vast quantities of fruit when the price places it within their reach. The orange is the great staple with these people, but it is hoped to supplant this eventually by the banana, which is cheaper and more plentiful. To show what a hold this scheme has taken on the people, I have only to point out that there were recently opened in Leeds two large storerooms, specially constructed for the artificial ripening of bananas. They are modeled on the lines observed in the equipment of similar concerns in the United States. Lined with wood, the rooms are kept at temperatures varying from $52°$ to $72°$ F. Over the gas jets which supply the heat are small tanks, the vapor from which keeps the atmosphere humid. The ceiling in both departments is studded with small iron rings, from which are suspended the bunches of fruit. There is accommodation for about 1,000 bunches, which, averaging about 10 dozen in a bunch, means that the establishment provides facilities for ripening over 1,000,000 bananas at a time. Arriving green from the ships, the fruit can be ripened in from seven to twelve days, according to when it is likely to be required for consumption. The effect of this new institution will be, it is claimed, the diminution of the number of unripe and overripe bananas hitherto offered to the public, and by thus improving the general quality of the fruit, it is confidently expected that before another year is over bananas will become as popular as oranges. The information is offered for the special benefit of the masses that a banana with a dark mark on the skin is not necessarily rotten and unfit for consumption. Very often, the black mark is not skin deep, and is due, not to internal, but to external circumstances. In Jamaica, we are told by a writer in the Yorkshire Evening Post—published at Leeds—they do not possess spring carts, and as the fruit is being conveyed down to ships on rickety vehicles, it is sometimes knocked about rather badly, the black marks being the result.

One of the largest shipping concerns in England has taken this trade in hand, and has already perfected arrangements for landing cargoes at ports on the west and southwest coasts of England. This programme is sure to make itself felt on the fruit trade of Hull, which takes its supplies largely from Spain, Italy, Mediterranean ports, France, the Channel Islands, and the Azores. The distribution of this trade from Hull to various ports of England will be checked, and the consequence will be that large quantities of fruit from these countries, particularly oranges, will be thrown on the market and disposed of at a sacrifice. There is considerable alarm in Hull over the prospect, because it means a diversion of a very important element of its trade. The first cargo of Spanish oranges to arrive here this season brought the lowest prices on record. Some of the fruit men I interviewed explained this by saying that they came in an unripe state and were too sour to suit the public taste.  Others say that the Jamaica oranges which found their way into the markets from the distributing ports on the west coast were in better condition, much sweeter, and consequently more marketable.  Bristol is making a great effort to secure this trade, and through the enterprise of its people is going ahead with a great scheme for a new system of docks, while at Hull the conflict between the fruit traders and the Northeastern Railway is little short of a battle royal.  The latter controls the situation, so far as transportation facilities are concerned, and absolutely refuses to yield to the demands of the fruit men, who are constantly clamoring for better dock·arrangements.

### AMERICAN PETROLEUM IN HULL.

The investment of English capital in the Russian oil regions has given quite a fillip to that trade in England, with the result that the Anglo-American Oil Company has had to battle with the forces of a new competition in the market.  Its imports at Hull have not made much progress during the last two years.  That it has been able to hold its own, however, is shown by the returns.  For the year 1901, its imports fell slightly short of 10,000,000 gallons.  For the first six months of the present year, these imports amounted to about 7,000,000 gallons.  It is generally understood that the price will not be affected by this competition, as all the companies concerned have come to an understanding.

### INSPECTION OF UNITED STATES EXPORTS.

The action of Congress in pro i ing a system of inspection for certain articles of export, under the supervision of the Agricultural Department, is having an excellent effect on our trade abroad.  This has special application to our products in England, where the tendency to disparage the quality and merit of foreign produce and manufactures is growing stronger as competition becomes keener each year.  This feeling is partly the outgrowth of a movement directed against what is known, so far as we are concerned, as the "American invasion," in the interests of home and colonial development.  Our cheese exports sustained a severe check some years ago by sheer carelessness on the part of manufacturers, who drifted into the fatal mistake of lowering the standard of quality at the very time the Canadians were making strong efforts to capture the English market.  There was then no system of inspection in force to safeguard these interests, and the result is only too well known.  The feasibility of providing a scrutiny to cover the entire range of our exports is out of the question, yet there are hundreds of articles on our export list that might well be brought within the scope of the present act.  It would have the effect of putting our manufacturers on their guard, by reminding them that as commercial development grows apace, competition becomes a collateral result, and demands new standards and new methods in all the departments of industry.  This is how one of the Leeds papers refers to the operation of the act in question:

## LESSON IN OFFICIAL METHODS.

On a number of boxes of apples in the Leeds market to-day might be seen a yellow label, headed with the official stamp of the U. S. A. Department of Agriculture, and containing the following text, viz:

Contents: Baldwins.

Shipped under the direction of the U. S. Department of Agriculture.

To Messrs. ———. From ———.

Per S. S. *Etruria*, sailing Saturday, November 1, 2 p. m.

Asked whether Britishers attached any importance to these official labels, a prominent fruit merchant replied in the affirmative. "When I receive a box with that label on," said he, "I feel pretty sure about the condition of the contents. It is an absolute guaranty that at the time the fruit was shipped, it was sound and worthy of official recognition. Moreover, it gives us accurate information as to the time the fruit was shipped."

This method of Government assistance to the private trader may be commended to our own authorities. It might be put into operation for a start in Jersey, from which island numbers of boxes of pears are now being received.

## HULL FISHING TRADE AND THE STEAM TRAWLER.

The fishing industry since the development of steam trawling has attained enormous proportions in Hull, between 400 and 500 vessels sailing from the port, which, in order of importance, now ranks next to Grimsby. A noteworthy economic effect of the application of steam power to fishing vessels has been the impoverishment of many of the smaller towns along the coast, where harbor accommodation is defective. From the social point of view, the decay of these fishing villages is a regrettable phenomenon, for the fishing community has always been noted for its sobriety and simple puritanic habits. Another consequence of the improvement of the methods of fishing is its effect upon the supply of fish in the North Sea, upon which the English fish markets have from time immemorial been fed. Scientific authorities are not yet agreed that it is possible to permanently reduce the teeming resources of the sea, but it is certain that the favorite fishing grounds, the Dogger Bank and the Silver Pits, no longer yield remunerative catches, hence the trawlers go farther and farther away, and the Hull and Grimsby markets are now largely supplied from the waters of the coast of Iceland. For the time being, the growth of the industry has been checked owing to the overbuilding of vessels, and also to the belief that many of the existing concerns, floated at a time of great prosperity, are heavily overcapitalized. Whether this check is lasting or merely temporary remains to be seen, but it is a striking fact that the latest returns show, for the first time during a long period, a decline in the number of fishing vessels registered at the port of Hull.

## THE TIMBER TRADE.

As Hull is geographically the nearest port to Scandinavia, it is only to be expected that the timber imports from Norway and Sweden should far exceed those from the United States. None the less, the quantities of American timber shipped here are steadily growing, owing to the increasing taste for fancy woods in house construction. From New York comes yellow pine, canary wood, and black walnut; from New

Orleans, pitch pine, cotton wood, and green wood. California redwood, however, which is steadily growing in favor in the English market, is not brought to Hull, remaining a monopoly of the Liverpool timber trade. Manufacturers of wringing machines in the West Riding buy large quantities of maple wood from Hull importers, owing to the hardness and nonliability to warp when wet. It is to be noted that the ends, or "trimmings" of the rollers when sawn off before shipment, are extensively used in the United States as blocks for the flooring of houses, a striking example of the economy of "by-products" in the building trade. As yet, however, maple wood figures to no considerable extent in the English building industry, although it is predicted that the durability and susceptibility to polish of this material will before long lead to its general use in the erection of houses of the better class, especially as modern English domestic architecture favors the building of large central entrance halls instead of the old-fashioned passage leading from the front door. American pine doors complete, save for the polishing, are largely exported to Hull. Carriage builders display a marked preference for dressed spokes of best American oak, or hickory as it is termed in the United States, and in the London carriage trade, ready-made American wheels are bought in large numbers. Ash oars and hickory handspikes form a small but valuable and constant branch trade between makers of these specialties in the United States and boat builders in England. Curiously enough, the red cherry wood, so highly esteemed on the other side of the Atlantic, finds no market here, owing, it is stated, to the high prices asked.

Generally speaking, it may be said that although the Hull imports of American timber are small in comparison with those landed at Liverpool, the trade is in a healthy condition and is likely to attain larger proportions year by year. Owing to the longer passage, the difference in freight to the two ports represents a handicap of about one-half pence (1 cent) per cubic foot against the Hull merchant, equivalent to a trade profit. Owing, however, to the shorter railway journey, the Hull traders can compete on favorable terms with Liverpool rivals in the Eastern countries, and control especially the extensive Lincoln timber market, which requires a large supply for the manufacture of the agricultural machinery exported from here to Central Europe and Russia.

### AMERICAN LUMBER AT HULL.

The American lumber trade at Hull, so far as the direct imports are concerned, is somewhat irregular. The consumption steadily goes on, but the supplies are mainly from other ports in England. In the year 1900, New York furnished 3,659 tons; Boston, 337 tons; New Orleans, 3,718 tons. In 1901, the imports from New York were 919 tons; from Boston, 556 tons; from New Orleans, 5,721 tons. For the first ten months of 1902, the imports from New York rose to 3,345 tons, making a total for the period named of 7,923 tons.

The imports from Boston during the same period were 429 tons, making a total of 1,322 tons. The imports from New Orleans for the same period were 984 tons, making a total of 10,423 tons. These totals, it will be observed, are for two years, 1900 and 1901, and for the year 1902 up to the end of October.

### AMERICAN WOODWORKING MACHINERY IN ENGLAND.

The transition from timber to woodworking machinery is easy and natural; hence it is that a passing reference to the introduction and use in England of this class of machinery will not be out of place here.

On the line of the Northeastern Railway, halfway between Hull and Leeds, lies the little town of Selby. It is chiefly noted for its abbey, its unpretentious shipyard on the banks of the Ouse, its gas works, its defunct packing house, and its few factories. Thousands of Americans pass through here every summer on their way to the historic town of York, about 15 miles northward. It is safe to say that not one of them, when looking out on the scene and viewing the tall chimneys of these factories, realizes that Ohio machinery is at work in the largest and most prosperous of them, turning out spokes and fellies and wheels, and all sorts of finished woodwork for every conceivable form of wagon for the use of the British Government in various parts of the Empire, and especially in South Africa. Yet such is the case; and such the marvelous success of these machines that the wagon factory here, owned by Messrs. Stagg & Robson, Limited, can turn out their work on shorter notice and in better style than any other firm in England in proportion to its size. The proprietors inform me that their efforts to secure Government contracts are so dependent on the operation of their American plant, that these machines have now become absolutely indispensable as an adjunct of their works.

There are fifteen machines in one department of this factory devoted exclusively to the manufacture of wheels. They are all the product of a well-known concern at Defiance, Ohio, and can turn out ready for tireing about 250 wheels per day. While the output has been increased twenty times over, the enormous decrease in the cost of production enables the proprietors to meet competition at an advantage they never possessed before. The rapid execution of the work at every stage of the process of manufacture and the superior character and excellence of finish attained gives them another great advantage in the matter of dispatch, as affecting the fulfillment of contracts where time limit is an implied or expressed condition. The capacity of the spoke machines is almost unlimited, and their operation so simple and so thorough as to excite the wonder and admiration of everyone who has witnessed it. They turn, tenon, throat, bevel, buff, and complete the spoke in such a short space of time that thousands can be turned out in a single day of eight hours' work. In the same way, fellies are evolved with marvelous rapidity, and every part of the wheel made complete and put together ready for tireing. From every conceivable standpoint, including that of economy, these machines are pronounced to be the finest specimens of American ingenuity ever put down in a wagon factory in England. Their work has been closely inspected by the Government, and it is highly satisfactory to know that it has invariably been approved.

The machines which formerly did this work for Messrs. Stagg & Robson have been relegated to the scrap heap. This fact appeals to us rather comfortably, in view of a recent awakening in the minds of the British public on the aim and scope of the "American invasion."

Considering the advantages enjoyed by Hull, from its position on a splendid estuary 3 miles in width, it is surprising that the possibility of developing the river front for the purpose of unloading vessels has so long been lost sight of. It is a circumstance often deplored by the present generation of citizens that, owing to the lack of foresight displayed in the past, the whole of the frontage to the river within the city boundary, with the exception of a stretch about 200 yards long, has been alienated from public into private hands. It is too late now to undo this mischief, except by a great scheme for the acquisition of the docks from the railway companies, and though public opinion is gradually moving in that direction, the time is not yet ripe for the formulation of a plan. Meanwhile, the absence of river-side accommodation suggests a striking contrast to the condition of affairs at the continental ports. Although the frequent shifting of the channel raises certain difficulties, and the heavy deposits of mud would entail a continual expenditure in dredging, there is a distinct opening for development upon these lines, more especially with regard to the passenger traffic between Hull and the Continent. Every summer, thousands of tourists are brought to Hull, many of them by special trains from London, to be carried by Messrs. Wilson's boats to Norway. Arrived at Hull, they are compelled to find their way through a congeries of shabby streets to a dock situated in a most inconvenient position. The erection of a floating landing stage on the river front, where tourists could embark without delay, would not be a costly affair and would effect one of the most desirable improvements ever carried out here.

Americans who come and go during the tourist season to the northern latitudes are not very favorably impressed with the arrangements provided for handling the passenger traffic at Hull, and do not hesitate to pronounce them the most backward and inconvenient to be found anywhere. This opinion is generally entertained by the business men of Hull, who view with a deep sense of mortification these deplorable conditions, as the result of the irrepressible conflict between the Northeastern Railway and the corporation, aided and abetted by an ancient and venerable institution known as the Humber conservancy board.

### GRIMSBY.

The port of Grimsby, which lies south of the Humber, a short distance from Hull on the Lincolnshire coast, has an extensive trade with foreign countries, principally Russia, Sweden and Norway, Denmark, Germany, Holland, Belgium, and France. It is mainly noted for its fishing industry, in which respect it ranks first port in Great Britain. The combined railways, chief of which is the Great Central, are about to undertake an important work in connection with the enlargement of the present dock accommodation and the construction and equipment of new deep-water docks, which, when completed, will seriously interfere with the trade of Hull.

The total tonnage entered and cleared at Grimsby during the year 1901 was 1,775,637. A very small percentage of this tonnage was concerned with the American trade, for a record of the year shows that 9 vessels, with a total tonnage of 11,489, were entered. Five of these were sailing vessels from the Atlantic and Pacific ports with grain cargoes, while 4 were steam from the Atlantic ports. The clearances during the same year were for 2 sailing vessels and 1 steam, with a total net tonnage of 4,210. Grimsby has very little trade outside of its continental connections. Its coal exports are about equal to those of Goole.

The total value of the imports at Grimsby during the year 1901 was a little less than $46,000,000. The value of the exports for the same period was about $43,500,000. These figures represent both British and Irish produce. The value of the foreign and colonial merchandise, or transshipped cargoes, is put down at a trifle over $500,000. In the brief period of a few years, the exports of native produce have fallen from $50,000,000 to $43,000,000. At Goole, during the same period, there was a shrinkage of nearly $1,000,000, while in Hull there is a palpable reduction in the export values of about $900,000. Butter figures as the leading article of import, with a total value of no less than $9,000,000. This trade finds distribution over the south and west of England, as well as in the midland and northern counties. It is steadily on the increase, having crept up from 235,138 hundredweight of 112 pounds each in 1897 to 317,303 hundredweight in 1901. Margarine shows a proportionate increase, having advanced nearly 16,000 hundredweight during the same period.

The geographical position of Grimsby brings it in close touch with some of the continental ports, through several lines of steamships which operate in connection with a well-equipped railroad service to London and all parts of England. Through this agency, a great bulk of its imports finds easy access to the best markets in the country. No less than 13,481,460 dozens of eggs were landed at the port in 1901. The total valuation of these cargoes is estimated by the board of trade statisticians at $2,208,000.

Glass manufactures are another important item of the import trade which increases with each year. Germany and Belgium are mostly responsible for these products. Musical instruments from various countries on the Continent, principally Germany, are largely imported, as are sugar, wood, woolens, and yarns.

### A MARKET FOR AMERICAN PLATE AND CUT GLASS.

It might be worthy of note to state here, for the benefit of glass manufacturers in the United States, that Belgium and Germany alone exported to England in the year 1901 various glass products valued at $12,000,000. This district obtains a very large share of this trade, a good percentage of which is in the cut and plate glass line. The Charleroi manufacturers are running their English competitors very closely for control of the market for superior cut glass and for the best article of plate glass. I have been told by a large plate-glass merchant in Hull that the Belgians have already succeeded. The rapid development of this business in the United States during the last twenty years and the great improvements that have been made, both as to the quality and style of manufacture, should enable our manufacturers to make a bold bid for an important share of this trade. The English merchants would be glad to see the Americans enter the field.

H. Doc. 305, pt 2——52

Goole, like Grimsby, has a large and flourishing trade with continental ports.   The inward and outward tonnage is about one-half, compared with that of Grimsby.   Its communication with the industrial centers of the West Riding of Yorkshire is maintained by a good system of railways and the splendid waterways of the Aire & Calder Navigation Company.   Its chief exports are coal, textile fabrics, yarns, and machinery.   The total net tonnage for 1901, inward and outward, was nearly 1,000.000 tons.   It has good dock accommodation, and has now under consideration a new scheme for increasing still further its facilities in this respect.   The Lancashire and Yorkshire Railway and the Aire & Calder Navigation Company are jointly interested.

The steamers and sailing craft belonging to this port have to pass Hull on their inward and outward voyages, so that every movement looking toward the enlargement of its docks is closely watched here. The navigation of the Humber between Hull and Goole is beset with many difficulties, owing to the peculiar lie of the channel and the swift tidal currents that are encountered.   The enterprise of the Goole people, however, has succeeded in overcoming these difficulties and in building up a continental trade which should never have been permitted to pass the Hull docks.

The direct trade with the United States is very light, only two sailing ships, with a total tonnage of 1,066, having entered the port during the year 1901.   There were no clearances.

One of the striking features of the Goole trade for 1901 was the enormous import of sugar, chiefly from Germany.   These imports ran up to nearly 100,000 tons, and were forced upon the maket by the financial necessities which arose in Germany during that year.   The subject is well covered by a writer in the Goole Weekly Times, as follows:

Contrary to expectations, the aggregate importations of sugar to Goole are slightly below the amount imported the previous year.   The year 1900 established a record, with an approximate weekly entry of 1,689 tons.   The first month of the year, however, witnessed a diminution in the quantity entering the port, but immediately afterwards, in view of the introduction of the budget and the opinion that the chancellor of the exchequer would find it necessary to impose a duty on sugar with a view to replenishing the impoverished exchequer, the imports went up enormously. Every vessel arriving from France, Germany, and Holland brought a greater or lesser quantity, and as the opinion strengthened that the duty would be imposed, the importations became more, until, in the week immediately preceding April 18, the importations of sugar into Goole reached a total of nearly 3,000 tons.   As soon as the duty was announced, there was a fall, and the depression in the imports was maintained until about the month of September, when the sugar market seemed to have strengthened considerably, and English importers began to buy much more freely.   The financial crisis in Germany has had a result during the last two months of once more causing the entry to be very largely increased.   The German manufacturers have been doing their utmost for the past two or three years to obtain a larger share of patronage in the world's markets in many branches of trade, with the result that at last the banks have had to pull them up and insist on their realizing their stocks.   This has thrown an enormous quantity of sugar onto the market, with the result that English buyers have not been slow to take advantage of the situation, and have bought very largely at the ruinously low rates which the German manufacturers have been compelled to accept.   The effect has been that sugar for the last two months in England has been cheaper than it was before the imposition of the duty.   The English sugar brokers, too, are somewhat nervous lest the increasing financial strain of the war will necessitate the levying of further imposts on commerce, and they anticipate that the sugar duty will be one of the first to be increased, so that what with the advantage offered by the cheapness of German sugar and the desire to anticipate the duty, the result has been that the last three months have probably witnessed a bigger continuous import into this country than any other similar period. This culminated in what was probably the largest weekly entry of sugar into the port being imported during the last week, the total being 3,854 tons. Goole, of course, takes the lead of the Humber ports in this department, and for weeks the ships from Hamburg could almost have carried sugar as ballast if need be, there being such big stocks on the other side waiting to be transshipped to England. Notwithstanding this great rise, however, the total for the year is, up to December 17, as previously stated, under that of 1900, but only to the extent of 100 tons, and as great bulks continue to be poured into the port, by the end of the year it will probably be found that another record has gone by the board.

Prior to the introduction of the duty and for a few months afterwards, saccharine, on which the duty is 1s. 3d (30 cents) per ounce, was largely imported into Goole. The portable nature of saccharine, however, and its great value render it a peculiarly valuable article to smuggle, and with a view to avoid the risk of smuggling, the commissioners of customs restricted the ports of entry of this article, limiting its importation to a certain number of ports, namely, Southampton, Folkestone, Newhaven, Dover, London, and Harwich, and prohibiting its importation in packages of less than 11 pounds. On representations being made, however, that this was seriously curtailing the trade of some of the ports, the commissioners extended the ports of entry so as to include Hull and Leith. Certain inland chambers of commerce, however, pointed out that this was an unfair arrangement, as hitherto they had been able to obtain saccharine through all the east coast ports, and an order was issued in October extending the ports to include Goole, Grimsby, West Hartlepool, and Grangemouth. As a matter of fact, however, we believe that no saccharine has been imported into Goole since the issue of the order restricting it to the Channel ports, London, and Harwich, and the extension of October last has not benefited the port of Goole at all.

Below we give the comparative particulars of the aggregate entries of sugar up to December 17 last, for which we are indebted to Mr. T. Lloyd Williams, sugar broker and agent, of Goole and Hull:

| Year. | - | Bags. | Cases. | Loaves. |
|---|---|---|---|---|
| 1899 | | 570,892 | 236,281 | 98,500 |
| 1900 | | 676,344 | 275,108 | 132,000 |
| 1901 | - | 682,089 | 289,129 | 137,700 |

This gives a total import of 84,387 tons, an average of 1,687 tons per week. By far the greater proportion of this comes from Germany, being shipped by the boats of the Goole Steam Shipping Company and the Cooperative Wholesale Society. France comes next, the Bennett steamers bringing the bulk of the French sugar from Boulogne, while the proportion which comes from Holland is comparatively small.

EXPORTS.

*Coal.*—Goole enjoys excellent transportation facilities with the Yorkshire lines, and for this reason the exports of coal from the port are very heavy. They will average something over 100,000 tons per month, or about 1,250,000 tons per year. They far exceeded this in 1900, when there was an abnormal demand for coal from the Continent.

*Manufactures.*—The manufactured products of the West Riding of Yorkshire, through the excellent connections of the Lancashire and Yorkshire Railway, find a convenient outlet at Goole on their journey to all the countries of Europe. Cotton manufactures figure largely on the list of exports. These come mainly from the Lancashire district, while woolen and worsted yarns (one of the heaviest items on the list) are brought chiefly from the Bradford, Halifax, and Huddersfield districts. Woolen and worsted manufactures are also traceable to these districts.  Machinery and millwork are an important item of its commerce.  Chemicals, too, are largely exported.  The total value of all the exports for the year 1901 was about $30,000,000, including a very small proportion of foreign and colonial merchandise.

### GENERAL IMPORTS.

The value of the imports into Goole for the year 1901 was $26,500,000. These imports are nearly all from the Continent, and consist of butter, chemical manufactures, and products of all sorts, clocks, cocoa, cordage, wheat, yarn and manufactures thereof, dyestuffs, dyewoods, farinaceous substances, flax, fruit, glass, hardware, jute, metals and ores, condensed milk, musical instruments, oil, paper and paper-making materials, plants, rosin, silk, sugar, tobacco, toys and games, vegetables, wine, wood, wool, woolens, and yeast.  The heaviest item on the list is sugar.

### THE CANAL SYSTEM FROM GOOLE TO THE INTERIOR.

Goole owes its prosperity entirely to the fact that it is the port for a remarkable system of canals, affording connection with the populous manufacturing towns of the West Riding.  This port, which in 1820 was a mere hamlet consisting of a few houses, is situated 27 miles up the Humber Estuary west of Hull and about 47 miles from the sea. At the last census (1901), it had a population of 16,500, and its commerce, although necessarily limited by the inability of large vessels to navigate the channels of the Upper Humber, shows every symptom of steady growth.  Its docks have a water area of 23 acres, which is about to be enlarged in order to accommodate the traffic, and are directly connected with the Lancashire and Yorkshire Railway Company and the North Eastern Company, placing the port in communication with the whole of the north of England.  Enormous warehouses have been erected, among which, it is worthy of note, are those of the Wholesale Cooperative Company, an organization consisting of hundreds of thousands of members of the working class, whose capital, representing millions of pounds, has been provided by the accumulated profits of the thousands of retail cooperative establishments in almost every town and village throughout the northern counties of England.  With regard to the wonderful illustration of self-help on the part of the thriftier sections of the artisans, volumes have been written since the early days of the movement under the leadership of the "Rochdale Pioneers;" but as illustrating its scope at the present day, it need only be mentioned that the Leeds cooperative shops alone have an annual turn-over of over $15,000,000.  Cooperative capital is now embarked in almost every branch of productive industry. At Goole, the bulk of the fruit sold in the shops is imported, and cooperative ships run to the Dutch and Belgian ports.  For the rest, regular lines of steamers owned by private companies trade between Goole and London, Antwerp, Rotterdam, Rouen, Boulogne, Ostend, and other ports, and sailing vessels come long distances to the port laden with grain, Spanish ore, logwood from Jamaica (used extensively in the Bradford dyeing trade), and foreign deals, the outward cargo consisting for the most part of the fabrics of the West Riding looms and coal from the pits in the neighborhood of Goole.

Inasmuch as the canals which radiate from Goole inward rank among the most remarkable of the inland waterways of the country, a condensed description will be of value. The principal line extends from Goole to Castleford, for a distance of 24¼ miles, at which point it branches into two arteries, one running to the westward toward Wakefield, a distance of 12 miles, and the other running northward toward Leeds for 11½ miles. At Knottingly, on the main line, a branch runs toward Selby and the river Ouse, a distance of 12 miles. The Aire and Calder Navigation Commissioners, who are the proprietors of this highly remunerative waterway, are also the owners of a canal from Wakefield to Barnsley Basin, near Doncaster, 15 miles in length, together with a small canal, a mile long, connecting the navigable rivers Calder and Hebble with the busy center of the "heavy woolen industry" at Dewsbury. Jointly with the Leeds and Liverpool Canal Company, they own the Bradford Canal, 2¼ miles long, and enjoy certain rights of navigation on the rivers Aire and Calder. The engineering works which converted these rivers into navigable streams are historically of importance, from the circumstance that they were authorized by act of Parliament in 1698, and preceded by more than half a century any similar works in the country, or indeed in Europe; and Priestly, the well-known engineer, was able, as far back as 1831, to comment upon the gratifying fact that a shallow stream had been so completely harnessed to the wheels of commerce (if the figure of speech be permitted) that 150,000 tons of coal were annually carried over it. To-day, the tonnage carried runs into millions yearly. The canal connecting the Aire and Calder with the Ouse at Goole was authorized by statute in 1820, carried out by Rennie, the famous engineer, and opened for traffic in 1826. The immediate result was the creation of the town of Goole as the port of debarkation seaward for the merchandise brought from the interior along the new waterway. Various supplementary enactments authorized the deepening of the canal, the erection of docks, jetties, quays, and warehouses for the handling of the constantly expanding volume of traffic. It may be interesting to mention that the Barnsley Canal was constructed with the object of facilitating the dispatch to the London market of the famous Silkstone coal, which had acquired a high reputation for household purposes. And while the exploitation of the rich mineral deposit of this part of the West Riding was thus stimulated, the owners of the vast areas of marsh land in the district found their property enormously increased in value, owing to the drainage works effected with a view to increasing the depth of water in the canal.

The financial history of the canal is not less remarkable. By an act of George III, the promoters were authorized to raise by loan £43,200 ($210,232) by issuing £100 ($486) shares at £60 ($290) each, and further to borrow £10,000 ($48,660) on mortgage if the original capital did not suffice. In consequence of this measure, the original stockholders were seized with panic, and many sold their £100 shares for £5 ($24), little foreseeing that in thirty years' time, the same shares would be selling on the market at £325 ($1,580).

With respect to the Bradford Canal, a noteworthy feature is that it has hydraulic pumps at each lock, and when one lock is emptied the water is pumped into another lock at a higher level, in order to avoid any loss of water which would otherwise be caused by the passage of vessels. In fact, the ordinary system in operation upon canals where water falls from a higher to a lower level is here completely reversed. At the Bradford terminus, huge warehouses have been erected, and from this great metropolis of the fine-wool industry, a constant traffic is maintained over the canal westward to Liverpool and eastward to Hull.

These great works are still being carried out in a spirited and enterprising manner. At one place, the river Ouse has been diverted from its natural bed into a new channel in order to facilitate navigation, and at the present time, a scheme entailing the expenditure of £250,000 ($1,216,600) is approaching completion with the same object.

One of the characteristic features of traffic on the Aire and Calder navigation is the transport of coal by means of "compartment lighters" constructed of steel, 16 feet long, 20 feet wide, and 8 feet deep, with a carrying capacity of 35 tons. Each is provided with buffers, and they can be connected with each other like railway wagons. An iron cord at each side connects them with the towboat, which by this means dispenses with the necessity for employing a man on each lighter, and the passage is made with ease and rapidity. At Goole are two hydraulic elevators or hoists, where, after the lighters have been detached, they are hoisted singly in a cage and the contents poured into the seagoing vessel lying in the dock below. The lighters can also be covered, and thus employed for the carriage of merchandise susceptible to damage. They are towed in convoys of from 10 to 30, and a total load of 700 tons is regarded as a convoy, which one steam towboat is capable of hauling with ease. For goods requiring prompt conveyance to the port of loading, the company maintains from the heart of Lancashire and Yorkshire a service of rapid-transport barges hauled by steam towing vessels, which are themselves cargo laden.

Altogether, the economic importance of the Aire and Calder Navigation Company, with its bearing upon the various industries of this part of the country, can not well be exaggerated. Its success presents an example of the practical utility of internal water connections which is certain to produce imitators in the future.

### RIVAL INTERESTS AT HULL.

A correct idea of the situation in Hull as regards the relations between the North Eastern Railway and the corporation or town council, and the effect of these relations on the trade and commerce of the port, can be obtained from a retrospective view as it appears to the neutral observer.

The commercial history of Hull during the past twenty-five years is to a great extent bound up with the disputes arising out of the dissatisfaction with the monopoly of railway facilities possessed until recently by the North Eastern Railway Company, and the endeavors of the trading community to establish a rival competing service. For the greater part of a generation, complaints were general that the policy of the company unduly favored rival ports, such as Newcastle and Hartlepool, and withheld from Hull the conditions to which its favorable position entitled it. To representations that commerce was being diverted to the Tyne and the Tees, which ought naturally to come to the Humber, the North Eastern Railway directors turned a deaf ear. The directors, feeling secure of their position, disregarded all appeals, and the breach became inevitable.

The movement took shape in efforts to induce railway systems from the Midlands and Lancashire to extend their lines to Hull. In the light of subsequent history, it is very clear that the success of these attempts would have opened up a better prospect of emancipation for Hull than the actual lines upon which the situation developed. All the roads with which the negotiations were set on foot were powerful combinations, and their advent into Hull would have rendered actual competition for traffic much more keen than could have been the case with a new line. That these companies failed to rise to the opportunity was a misfortune for Hull, and perhaps a greater one for themselves. By this failure, however, the Hull traders were forced to face the problem of building an independent railway and dock for themselves. The leader in the movement was Col. Gerard Smith, a member of an old established banking firm of that name, and subsequently governor of Western Australia. The prospectus of the Hull and Barnsley and West Riding Junction Railway and Dock Company saw the light in 1879, and such was the response of the public to the invitation to subscribe the capital that it was largely oversubscribed, the temporary offices being inundated with applications for shares. In the winter of 1880, the first sod was turned, the occasion being celebrated by a gigantic demonstration. Very soon, however, it became evident that the cost had been greatly underestimated. Owing to the rigorous demands of the board of trade. the cutting of the line and the laying of the permanent way proved the most costly piece of railway construction ever recorded in this country. Additional capital had to be raised by debentures, Parliament consenting to depart so far from precedent as to allow dividends to be paid out of capital during the later stages of the work. Finally, in order to save the whole project from collapse, the Hull corporation obtained Parliamentary powers to invest £500,000 ($2,500,000) of the ratepayers' money, or rather upon the security of the local rates, receiving in return direct representation upon the board of directors. In later years, the Manchester corporation followed this example, when the Manchester Ship Canal had reached the of its end financial resources during the stage of construction.

When the undertaking was opened in 1885, public enthusiasm had been naturally dampened by the checkered history of the concern, but the determination on the part of the large traders to support it had in no way abated. Regarded merely as an engineering feat, it is true it has few points of special interest to offer. From the commercial standpoint, however, it is noteworthy from the fact that it brings Hull into direct contact with the vast undeveloped coal field of the West Riding, and through the Midland Railway, with which it effects a junction at Cudworth near Barnsley, with the great industrial centers of Sheffield and Leeds. Touching, however, no large town upon its system of only 65 miles, the passenger traffic was from the first exceedingly small. Its prospect of success depended entirely upon its ability to carry enormous quantities of coal for shipment abroad. The Alexandra Dock, which constitutes the most important feature of the undertaking, is the finest deep-water dock on the east coast, having sufficient depth of water to admit large vessels at any state of the tide, an advantage hitherto unknown at Hull or any Humber port. It is furnished with the most improved hydraulic appliances for dealing with cargoes of every description, and steam cranes lifting 25, 50, and 100 tons weight. In addition to those completed at the time the dock was opened, several new warehouses have been erected, so that no facility or accommodation is lacking for the dispatch of ships, or the working and storage of cargoes.

At the coal lifts provided at this dock, coal can be shipped with much more ease and rapidity than had hitherto been possible. Indeed, the success with which huge quantities of coal can be handled at Hull has often been cited as a model and example at other ports.

The progress of the line and docks was at first disappointing. In 1891, the hopes of shareholders were raised by the distribution of a 1 per cent dividend, soon, however, to be dashed to the ground by a steady decline in receipts, consequent upon the general depression in the trade of the country which then began to set in. To make matters worse, the year 1893 brought a train of crushing disasters. In the early part of that year, a strike broke out among the dock laborers, which lasted seven weeks and paralyzed the trade of the port, while in the second half, the port suffered another blow from the colossal strike in the coal trade of the country. Since 1895, progress has been marked. The dock has been enlarged in order to meet the growing demands for accommodation, new machinery has been provided, and the annual receipts have grown to nearly $2,250,000, a figure which permits of the payment of the fixed dividend to preference and debenture shareholders, and in addition the distribution of a 2 per cent dividend upon the ordinary stock.

So far, in fact, it would appear as though the enterprise of the citizens had resulted in establishing the permanent independence of the railway and dock. Still, there are dangers ahead, which are at present a source of keen discussion among the commercial community. Owing to a great extent to the excellent facilities offered at the Alexandra Dock, traffic was diverted from the older docks, with the result that in 1893, they passed into the possession of the Northeastern Railway Company. These older docks, constructed at a period when it was impossible to foresee the enormous changes in shipbuilding which the last decade of the nineteenth century witnessed, can not by any tinkering be made capable of dealing with the huge modern steam vessels. Consequently, the inevitable fact faced the proprietors both of the Alexandra and the older docks that entirely new docks would have to be constructed, if the trade of Hull were not to be diverted to other ports where larger and deeper docks have been provided. In 1897, the North Eastern attempted to solve the problem by seeking Parliamentary powers to expend £1,000,000 ($4,866,500) upon deepening the water in their existing docks, by building a wall along the whole of the river front, over two miles in length. This bold scheme was frustrated, owing to the opposition of the owners of small river craft, and an amended scheme introduced into Parliament in the following year was withdrawn because the companies refused to accept certain liabilities. In the examination of the measures, the Hull and Barnsley Company appeared as keen opponents upon various grounds, the real reason no doubt being that they were thereby shut out from sharing the benefit of the development of the shipping trade of the port. A new phase was given to the movement when, in 1899, the two companies appeared before Parliament as joint promoters of a deep-water dock, not far from the eastern boundary of the city. Inasmuch as the financial position of the Hull and Barnsley was not sufficiently secured to enable it to raise capital upon the most favorable terms, it was agreed that the capital should be raised by the North Eastern, and that as security for the regular payment of interest upon the Hull and Barnsley's share, the former should have the right to satisfy themselves, not merely out of the receipts of the dock, but out of the traffic receipts of the railway. This may result in the Hull and Barnsley Company being placed in the hands of their powerful rival. It must be admitted that in face of the previously unconcealed anxiety of the North Eastern to acquire the Hull and Barnsley by some means or other, the position justified the suspicion with which the commercial community regarded the outlook. It is true that effective competition had long ceased to exist, if indeed it could ever be said to exist, inasmuch as the railway and dock rates were identical upon both systems. None the less, substantial advantages are derived from the existence of an independent railway, and both the traders and the citizens as a whole are prepared to make further heavy sacrifices, in order to prevent the Hull and Barnsley from falling into the power of the North Eastern Railway Company.

So far, the proposed joint dock remains "in the air." I was led to believe when writing my report for 1900 that it was an assured fact. Since Parliament sanctioned the project, the whole of the time has been wasted in discussions between the parties concerned, the two companies endeavoring to reduce the scheme to smaller proportions, while the mercantile community, for the most part, stands out for the dock upon the original lines. That the new dock will be built during the next ten years is possible, but in the meantime valuable time is being lost, and trade may easily be diverted to the Continent. This is the real source of danger to Hull. That the port is now face to face with the most serious problem in its history is undeniable, and the future alone can tell whether those who are charged with its solution can work it out to the advantage of the mercantile community who have to stand or fall by the issue.

WM. P. SMYTH, *Consul.*

HULL, *November, 1902.*

---

## JERSEY.

Owing to the operation of the local tonnage act, I am able for the first time to give official statistics with regard to exports from the island, principally to the United Kingdom, for the period between the 1st of April and 22d of November, 1902:

| Articles. | Quantity. | Value. | |
|---|---|---|---|
| | | U. S. currency. | British equivalent. |
| | | | £.    s.   d. |
| Early potatoes .....................................tons.. | 54,473 | $1,581,276.71 | 324,931   0   0 |
| Other vegetables.................................do.... | 199½ | 24,891.17 | 5,114 16   0 |
| Tomatoes ............................................do.... | 507⅛ | 86,661.41 | 17,807 15   0 |
| Other fruits..........................................do.... | 333⅛ | 31,433.33 | 6,459   2   6 |
| Flowers...............................................do.... | 93⅛ | 16,933.23 | 3,479 11   0 |
| Cattle: | | | |
| Bulls and cows...............................head.. | 633 | } 67,881.59 | } 13,948 15   0 |
| Heifers ...........................................do.... | 245 | | |
| Calves ............................................do.... | 120 | | |
| Total .......... ..................................... | 998 | 1,809,077.44 | 371,740 19   6 |

In view of the time of year at which these exports of fruits, vegetables, and flowers took place, it would be correct to say that the figures given show the bulk of exports under these heads, although there is a considerable winter trade in fruits and flowers. Next year, it will be possible to give complete and probably more detailed statistics as regards not only exports, but imports. The latter are not available, except for coal, which is put down at 60,000 tons, of the value of $364,987.50 (£75,000).

The returns of the cattle exported are incomplete. The figures furnished by the Royal Jersey Agricultural Society show that during 1902, 1,150 head of cattle, of the approximate total value of $72,997.50, (£15,000) were exported. Of these cattle, Denmark took 272, the United States of America 181, of the approximate value of $19,466 (£4,000), France 50, and the United Kingdom the balance.

The Jersey breed of cattle has been found by the Agricultural Department of the United States to be free from tuberculosis.

I have every reason to believe, notwithstanding the fact that there is no direct communication between this island and the United States of America, that American goods, in increasing quantities, reach the Jersey market through agencies in the United Kingdom; but a great impetus could be given to the sale of these goods by an enterprising local agency.

E. B. RENOUF, *Consular Agent.*

JERSEY, *December 31, 1902.*

## LIVERPOOL.

### GENERAL REVIEW OF ANGLO-AMERICAN TRADE.

British foreign and colonial trade for the nine months ended September 30, 1902, shows an improvement over the corresponding period of 1901, and the improvement in September was particularly marked. This is true both of imports and exports; and yet, judging by the labor returns, the general trade of the country has not been quite as good this year as last—that is, the home trade has somewhat fallen off. The labor returns show a tendency to a decrease in the number of men employed and also in wages. The probable explanation is that the productive capacity of the country has about caught up with the extra demand created by the boom which started two or three years ago in municipal enterprises, by the increase of shipbuilding, etc. It is worthy of note that within the last year, there has developed a distinct change of sentiment with regard to foreign competition, and more especially with regard to American competition. During the past two years, there has been a persistent effort on the part of publicists and the newspapers to bring about reforms in the methods of business generally, and particularly in methods of manufacture and the relations of workingmen thereto, with a view to more successfully meeting foreign competition—and foreign competition over here means, in most cases, American competition. Beyond a doubt, the warnings that have been sounded and the educational process that has been going on have had their effect to some extent, and American manufacturers must make up their minds that this market will be more difficult to exploit than it has been in the past, and they should also realize that England is more able now to meet competition in neutral markets than she has been in recent years.

## TRADE OF GREAT BRITAIN AND SHARE OF THE UNITED STATES.

The statistics for the year 1901 are very satisfactory from an American standpoint. Probably, few people realize the vastness of the foreign and colonial trade of the United Kingdom—the largest by far of any country in the world. The total for 1901, both in imports and exports, was $4,349,272,330, the imports being $2,609,950,990 and the exports $1,739,321,340. Of this trade, over one-fourth passed through the port of Liverpool, going and coming. The most remarkable feature of British foreign trade is the large proportion of it which is done with the United States, this Anglo-American trade being larger than that between any other two countries in the world. During 1901, the value of the imports from the United States was $705,077,325, being an increase of $11,131,020 over 1900. The value of the imports from the United States into the United Kingdom in 1901 was more than two and one-half times the value of the imports from the next largest seller—which is France; and the United States sent goods here to the value of $177,208,795 in excess of the total value of those sent by all of Great Britain's vast system of colonies, possessions, and protectorates. In view of the popular outcry in this country against goods "made in Germany," it is a very interesting fact that Germany is the only important country (commercially speaking) which receives more goods from Great Britain than Great Britain receives from her. Even little Holland exports more goods to the British Isles than Germany does. The British exports to the United States in 1901 footed up $188,255,750, an increase over 1900 of $1,535,975. It is anticipated that the exports to the United States this year will be larger than those of last year. Of this great trade between the United States and the British Isles, Liverpool receives more goods than any other port, not excepting London, it being the leading entrepôt of the imported products of the American plantation, farm, ranch, and dairy. It is estimated that 80 per cent of the breadstuffs consumed in Great Britain come from abroad, and the United States has the premier place in furnishing these supplies. On account of Liverpool's preeminence as a port, it has become the largest market for grain in the British Empire, and it is claimed that it is now the second largest milling center in the world.

## CANADIAN COMPETITION.

In connection with the importation of farm and dairy products, the British Blue Book for 1901 demonstrates that the United States has more than held its own against the much-talked-of Canadian competition. It should be remembered that Canada is the greatest competitor the United States has in supplying the British market with the products of the forest and farm. The reports from this consulate have several times drawn attention to the extraordinary enterprise and energy of the Canadian government with the view of capturing the British market, or at least (for the present) capturing a much bigger slice of it than Canada has had, with possibilities for the future that have no limit in

Canadian ambition. In view of the efforts put forth, it is surprising to learn that the imports of Canadian products actually fell off last year. In 1901, their value was the smallest in four years. The total was $99,272,925, a decrease of $9,947,180, as compared with 1900. The value of the British exports to Canada in 1901 was $46,252,630, being an increase of $958,685 over 1900. This was probably the greatest value of exports to Canada the United Kingdom has ever reached, and yet the gain does not seem very substantial, considering the preferential tariff this country enjoys in Canada. Let there be no mistake. Canada is very much in earnest in the competitive struggle now going on, and it would be very unwise to dismiss the matter of Canadian competition as a bugaboo. During the past year, greater efforts than ever, both in Canada and in Great Britain, have been made to make this competition stronger. The latest scheme is to sell Canadian products to the British consumer without the intervention of "middlemen." Leaving governmental and political considerations altogether out of the question, and looking exclusively at the comurcial phase of the recent manifestations of "imperialism," Canada has never been so much in evidence in this country as during the current year. The participation of the colonies in the South African war and the demonstrations in connection with the coronation of King Edward developed a wave of what has become known as "imperial sentiment." While it is likely that the lapse of time may chill this popular enthusiasm, yet there undoubtedly has been left a residuum which is being earnestly worked upon by those who belong to the pan-Britannic school. The presence of the colonial premiers has given an impetus to this sentiment, and Canada more than any other colony has been to the front in the "boom," in which all the colonies have more or less participated. For months, the Canadian arch in London proclaimed that Canada was the "granary of the Empire," and leading men of Canada have traveled all over the British Islands prophesying that in course of time, Great Britain would get its food products principally from Canada and the other colonies, instead of from the United States.

### BRITISH COLONIAL TRADE.

The programme of some of the more pronounced imperialists may be extravagant—this programme being the production within the Empire of nearly everything that the Empire consumes. This even includes cotton. Reference has already been made in this series of reports to an attempt to grow cotton on the west coast of Africa. Within the last few weeks, an association of responsible business men, largely of Liverpool and Manchester, has been formed with the avowed object of producing enough cotton in India, British West Africa, and Egypt (which in this connection is considered British) to supply the whole wants of the Empire. The Federation of Master Cotton Spinners' Associations has approved the scheme, and the British Colonial Office and the various colonial governors have undertaken to assist. It is expected that next year, 1,000 bales of West African cotton will be placed on this market, simply to show what can be done. It is significant that during the last five years, there has been a steady growth of British exports to the colonies, rising from $434,821,845 in 1897 to $565,591,820 in 1901, a gain of $130,769,975.

While British exports to foreign countries were $88,018,980 less in 1901 than in 1900, the exports to the colonies show an increase of $55,471,550. There is every reason to believe that during the current year, this growth of colonial trade has extended. Beyond a doubt, there has been a development of sentiment both in the colonies and in the mother country in favor of closer commercial relations. An evidence of this was given only a few days ago by the British Government in issuing an order that all preserved mutton for the use of the army should be the product of British colonies. This is a very serious matter for Argentina, and is in the direct favor of New Zealand and Australia. Canada is certainly not discouraged by her failure so far to get an extra big slice of the British trade, and there are many enterprises under way which will undoubtedly make Canadian competition keener in the future. It is claimed that as a matter of fact, Canadian shipments to Great Britain are much larger than the figures show, for the reason that a large proportion comes by way of the United States in the winter season; and the British Blue Book draws attention to this condition of affairs. But, on the other hand, many shipments from the United States are sent through by way of Quebec and Montreal in the summer season. Although there are many misgivings among Liverpool shipping people as to the success of the enterprise, it is now accepted that in a short time there will be a fast line of steamships between this port and Canada, both in winter and summer. Owners of ships sailing to Canada complain very much of the heavy insurance they have to meet, but the underwriters plead in extenuation the extra danger of the St. Lawrence route. It is said that vast sums of money are being spent by the Canadian Government to render this route less dangerous. But so far, the United States more than maintains its position as the great provider of food products for the British people.

### BRITISH WHEAT IMPORTS.

The ever-increasing value of the food supplies imported into the United Kingdom is really startling, and is a certain indication of the continually growing abandonment of the land of this country for food production. There has been an almost continuous shrinkage in the area of land in the United Kingdom under grain cultivation. In 1900, the acreage was 8,707,602; in 1901 it was 8,476,876—a decrease of 230,726 acres. Permanent pasture land increased by over 1,000,000 acres. Hay is the most profitable crop in England. Within the last few days, the British Government has agreed to render financial assistance to experiments that are being made with a view of "strengthening" British wheat. It is said that in recent years, the wheat grown in this country is not nearly so "strong" or nutritious as that grown in the United States, Canada, and some continental countries. This country is yearly getting more and more dependent upon America for its food supplies. In 1901, the total value of the wheat imported into the British Isles was $115,406,860. Of this the United States supplied wheat to the value of $67,377,655—an increase of $11,211,315 over 1900. Argentina comes next, with $13,351,775—a tremendous drop from 1900, when it was $30,440,615. In spite of all her advertising, Canada sent in 1901 wheat to the value of only $11,080,245, being an increase of but $45,855 over 1900. Australia and New Zealand are coming to the fore, but within the last few years there has been a great drop in the Russian supply. The total value of imported wheat meal and flour in 1901 was $51,707,595, of which the United States sent $43,491,245—an increase of $1,659,965 over 1900 and of $8,045,755 over 1897. Canada comes next to the United States, her contribution in 1901 being $3,143,055, an increase of $289,655 over 1900, but a decrease of $2,628,175 as compared with 1899 and of $873,890 as compared with 1897.

BRITISH MEAT IMPORTS.

The English people are the greatest consumers of bacon in the world. The vast majority of the people eat bacon for breakfast at least six mornings out of every seven throughout the year, so it can easily be understood that the total consumption is enormous. As the British people are ceasing to grow wheat, so they are stopping raising hogs and cattle, and have to depend more and more upon outside sources for supplies. In 1901, the value of the bacon imported was $67,950,880, an increase of $23,611,650 in five years. The United States share was $46,279,255, an increase of $8,819,540 in a year, and of $28,316,080 as compared with 1897. Canada has been making a big bid for this trade. In 1901, she sent over bacon to the value of $4,607,545. Now, while this is a gain of $3,156,130 as compared with 1897, it is an actual decrease, amounting to $769,680, as compared with 1900. The excellence of Canadian bacon can not be disputed. The hogs are fed on pease mostly, and the bacon is well cured, but it is dearer than bacon from the United States, and the American product has within recent years greatly improved in curing and appearance. The English people like mild-cured bacon, and it must be cut in a certain way, and American packers have now become masters in the art of meeting the wishes of their customers over here.

The figures $43,534,195 represent the value of the total importations of fresh beef last year. The value of the contribution of the United States was $33,807,935. Although Argentina can not send live cattle to this country, by reason of the prohibition on account of foot-and-mouth disease, yet she is steadily climbing up in supplying chilled beef to this market. In 1897, the value of the importation from Argentina was only $640,890, while in 1901 the value was $6,091,230. Canada's proportion was insignificant.

The total value of the importation of hams in 1901 was $22,641,940. Of this, the share of the United States was $21,049,080, being an increase of $2,235,510 over 1900. Canada's shipments showed an actual decrease compared with 1900, amounting to $713,795. Curiously, Holland supplies more fresh pork than does any other country, the United States being a good second.

OTHER IMPORTS.

*Barley.*—Russia supplied one-third of the barley imported; next came Asiatic Turkey; Roumania was third, the United States fourth, and Canada was seventh.

*Oats.*—Russia sent more than one-half of the oats imported, and is steadily gaining. Both the United States and Canada are falling behind.

*Eggs.*—In eggs, neither the United States nor Canada kept up with the records of 1900. Russia, Denmark, Germany, Belgium, and France are the principal exporters to this country, in the order named. The number of eggs imported in 1901 was 2,048,612,040, valued at $26,700,427.

*Butter.*—In 1901, butter to the value of $96,486,980 was imported. Denmark supplied almost half. Next in order came France, Russia, and Holland. Russia's trade has grown enormously in the past year. The value of the imports from the United States was $3,445,826, and from Canada $5,040,010, both being substantial increases over 1900, particularly on the part of Canada, but the trade fluctuates very much.

*Lard.*—The United States sent lard to the value of $18,878,190, being nine-tenths of the total value imported, and a gain of $3,708,000 over 1900 and about double that of 1897.

*Cheese.*—Canada is excusably exultant in regard to her importations of cheese to this market, and yet there was a falling off of $507,815 in 1901, as compared with 1900. In 1901, the total value of cheese imported was $31,135,675. The value of the Canadian supply was $18,488,300. The value of the cheese imported from the United States was $6,370,305, a decrease of $2,333,440.

*Apples.*—A few years ago it looked as if Canada would lead the United States in supplying apples, but she is now again second. There were decreased importations from both countries in 1901, the United States, however, leading in the supply. The great feature of the fruit trade in England just now is the growth of the consumption of bananas. It has almost doubled in a year.

*Tobacco.*—The total value of unmanufactured tobacco imported was $13,314,840. Of this, the United States sent $11,263,140.

*Oatmeal.*—The United States furnishes most of the oatmeal imported, the total value in 1901 being $2,730,660; the importations from America being $2,486,675, a gain of $169,630 over 1900. The importations from Canada were $226,025, a loss of $51,795 as compared with 1900.

*Cattle.*—In the absence of competition from Argentina, the United States just now enjoys almost a monopoly in furnishing live cattle for slaughter in this market. In 1901, the total number of oxen and bulls imported was 490,939, valued at $43,801,860. Of this number, the United States sent 405,288, the value being $36,586,105. It had been the anticipation that with the development of the chilled-beef trade, the importations of live cattle would show a falling off, but this has not been the case so far as the United States is concerned. It is fair, however, to expect that when the embargo against cattle from Argentina is removed, the importations from the United States will receive a check. Canada has not shared with the United States the growth in this trade. In 1901, she sent 85,511 head, a decrease of 16,157 as compared with 1900, and a decrease of 38,257 head as compared with 1897. The value of the Canadian cattle sent over here in 1901 was $7,197,730, a decrease of $1,560,355 as compared with 1900, and a decrease of $7,817,100 as compared with 1897; that is, the decrease in value of the Canadian cattle imported into the United Kingdom last year, as compared with five years ago, is greater than the value of all the Canadian cattle imported in 1901.

*Cotton.*—The total importations of cotton in 1901 amounted to $209,852,695, being the largest both in value and weight for the last

five years.  The value of the American cotton imported was $161,778,-
560—nearly four times the value of the cotton brought from Egypt.

*Poultry.*—It was the confident expectation that Canada would make
great gains in the trade in poultry and game exported to this country,
a number of ships being specially provided with refrigerating chambers
for the purpose.  The United States trade only reached $1,029,390,
although with adequate enterprise and proper management, it should
be quadrupled; nevertheless, the United States made a gain of $251,890
over 1900.  Canada sent over poultry and game to the value of only
$52,965—and here again there was a loss ($40,000) as compared with
1900.

*Lumber.*—There was a great falling off in the total importations of
lumber of all kinds, and the United States and Canada shared in the
shrinkage.  Canada continues to lead the United States in supplying
this market (owing to its predominance in fir and spruce).  In 1901,
the importations from Canada were over $20,000,000, a falling off,
however, of about $3,450,000 as compared with 1900.  The importa-
tions from the United States were some $18,315,000 in 1901, a decrease
of about $16,640,000 from 1900.  There was also a noticeable falling
off in the importations of manufactured wood (fittings, frames, joinery,
furniture, etc.) from all the countries of supply.

### IMPORTS OF SHOES.

During the past year, one of the most manifest phases of the
"American invasion" has been the increasing trade in boots and shoes
made in the United States.  There has, indeed, been a great increase
in the sale of continental foot wear, as well as of American, during
the past five years.  In 1901, the total importations were $4,694,545,
an increase of $1,221,055 in a year and of nearly 100 per cent in five
years.  The following figures show how the trade in American boots
and shoes has grown in the United Kingdom: In 1897, the value of
importations was $405,675; in 1898, $369,450; in 1899, $782,330; in
1900, $1,006,325; and in 1901, $2,028,715.  In Liverpool alone, there
are four shops that sell American boots and shoes exclusively, and half
a dozen others that make a specialty of them.  The importations for
1902 will probably show an increase over 1901, but at a meeting of
English manufacturers a few days ago, it was announced that within a
recent period the importations had fallen off.

### IMPORTS OF MACHINERY.

The value of the total importations of machinery and millwork and
parts thereof was $19,815,145, of which the importations from the
United States footed up $12,456,560—a substantial increase over 1900.
It should be remembered that much of this trade is owing to the
movement for the "Americanization" of English factories, with the
specific object of meeting American competition both at home and
abroad.  The total importations of copper in bars, blocks, and ingots
were $23,652,900.  From the United States the importations were
$6,802,970.  There was a decrease in the shipments from the United
States of pig iron, iron bars, angles, and rods.  The importations
from Belgium in these lines have greatly increased.  There was a
marked decrease in importations from the United States of unmanufactured iron and steel.  Rather curiously, Holland has forged to the

front in these lines, increasing her exportations to Great Britain tenfold in a year. Belgium made a gain in iron and steel girders, joists, etc. The United States led in supplying steel rails, sending $938,700 worth in a total of $2,064,145.

The following notes are more particularly from a local standpoint, as regards trade with the United States:

### SHIPPING AND DOCKS.

Of course, the most engrossing subject of local discussion during the past year has been the inclusion of several Liverpool liners in the "shipping combine." In addition to the adverse feeling from a sentimental standpoint, there was at first great alarm over the anticipated injury to the port. Probably the sentimental objection has become modified, but certain it is that Liverpool now feels confident that, no matter who may own or manage the ships—nor, indeed, what flag they may fly—the secured status of this port can be counted upon. The question of the contingent future of Liverpool has been thrashed out time and again. All sorts of schemes are broached; rival ports plan and even carry out enterprises avowedly designed to take trade away from this port. Yet Liverpool keeps on increasing its tonnage and its outward and inward commerce, and its docks still maintain their preeminence. Liverpool is still the home port of the largest ship in the world, and will have the honor of winning back for the British flag the supremacy of the seas for speed. New ships are ever being added, not only to the fleets running to America, but to those going to all parts of the world. The approximate total tonnage inward and outward was 26,616,610 tons for the year ended July 1, 1902, an increase compared with the previous year of 1,319,532 tons. Of steam vessels engaged in the foreign trade paying dock rates, there were 3,912, an increase of 126 over last year, and of the same class paying only harbor dues, 1,198, an increase of 27. Incomplete returns indicate an increase both in ships and tonnage for the current year. The dock board has thought fit to officially contradict published statements that the Liverpool docks can not accommodate the projected new Cunarders, which will be the largest and fastest ships afloat. These new boats will be 750 feet long. It is stated that half a dozen boats 850 feet long and 80 feet beam can be accommodated at one time, and that shortly, a vessel 950 feet long can be accommodated.

### COTTON.

With regard to the importation of cotton into Liverpool, an important alteration has just been made in the system of purchasing American cotton. Dating from October 1, 1902, trading in "spot" and "futures" in Liverpool is to be in the hundredth parts of a penny per pound, instead of sixty-fourth parts as heretofore, and the discount of $1\frac{1}{2}$ per cent formerly allowed will be abolished. This important change in terms will result in a lowering of quotations by approximately $\frac{4}{64}$ to $\frac{7}{64}$, or $\frac{6}{100}$ to $\frac{7}{100}$ pence per pound, being the equivalent of the discount no longer given, the net value thus remaining unaltered. The weight of the American cotton contract for "futures" has also been altered from 47,200 to 48,000 pounds. The object of these changes was to get rid of an obsolete system involving useless calculations, and to simplify the routine of the clerical work.

H. Doc. 305, pt 2——53

## CATTLE.

It will be seen from the appended table that the number of cattle landed at Liverpool, both from the United States and Canada, greatly increased during 1901, the former by 8 per cent and the latter by 28 per cent; whereas the importation of sheep shows a very large increase from the United States, amounting to 136 per cent, and the importation from Canada decreased 24 per cent.  The figures regarding sheep are very striking, but are accounted for by the fact that for two or three years prior to 1899, exceptionally large shipments were made from the United States, so much so that the stocks became depleted, the result being that in 1900 there were very few sheep to export.  In 1901, however, shipments again commenced on a large scale.  There has been for some time past an agitation throughout the country to induce the Government to remove the restriction which was in April, 1900, placed upon cattle and sheep from the Argentine Republic. Owing to the existence of foot-and-mouth disease in that country at that time, the British Government prohibited the importation of live cattle, and only frozen meat has since been entered.  It has been asserted by some authorities that as a result, the importation of frozen meat now exceeds the previous total importations of live stock and frozen meat combined.  But figures are quoted to show that roughly speaking, 78,000 quarters are now annually imported into this country, equal to 19,450 head of cattle, whereas in 1898 and 1899, over 98,000 head of cattle were received.  It is the opinion of many that the board of agriculture will shortly remove the restriction, which action without doubt will tell upon the importation from the United States.  But others in the trade, who claim to speak with authority, say that it is not at all likely that the restriction will be removed for some time, as in their opinion the board of agriculture considers that the importation of dead meat tends more to regulate supplies and keep prices uniform than that of live cattle.  Canadian cattle are subjected to the same restrictions and regulations as those from the United States.

*Cattle, sheep, and horses landed at Liverpool, 1900 and 1901.*

|  | 1900. | | 1901. | |
|---|---|---|---|---|
|  | Number shipped. | Number lost at sea. | Number shipped. | Number lost at sea. |
| AMERICAN. | | | | |
| Cattle | 174,682 | 139 | 190,198 | 175 |
| Sheep | 81,973 | 692 | 193,784 | 1,853 |
| Horses | 11,468 | 244 | 4,904 | 85 |
| CANADIAN. | | | | |
| Cattle | 40,898 | 180 | 52,814 | 161 |
| Sheep | 56,664 | 658 | 43,081 | 612 |

## GREEN FRUIT.

The trade in apples from the United States during the season 1901–2 was very small, owing to the poor crop, but this season, 1902–3, it promises to be a very large one.  Up to the present time, the quantity already arrived from the United States and Canada is over 89,000 barrels, of which at least 77,000 were from the United States, whereas last season, up to the same date, only about 2,000 barrels of American apples had been received on this market. This large increase is accounted for by the good crop in the United States, the superiority of the fruit, both in size and quality, and by the failure of the crops in the United Kingdom and on the Continent of Europe. The prices realized are considered here satisfactory, and should leave a fair return to the fruit growers in the United States. It will be gratifying to the fruit growers to know that there is an increasing demand for American fruits of all varieties, brought about, no doubt, by the experiments instituted by our Government with the early varieties of apples, and also pears and peaches. With regard to the packing and selection of the fruits, I am told by the trade that so far as the United States goes, it is now nearly all that can be desired; in fact, one of the largest importers says that no other country can improve upon the methods of the United States packers, and that that is one point that has helped to make the business a success, even upon the experimental shipments. Fraudulent packing and marking is, however, occasionally resorted to in the United States; but this is done by new packers ignorant of the requirements and methods of foreign markets, who put up poor fruit and cover the barrels with fancy marks, thinking that good prices will result. But these evils quickly work their own cure on this market, as the custom is to turn out into a basket one barrel of each mark, so that buyers can see the packing at the head, tail, sides, and center, and thus the system of putting two or three rows of good apples on the top and at the bottom of the barrels and very inferior fruit in the center is exposed. American pears are coming into decidedly popular favor, but dissatisfaction is expressed at their being packed in barrels, which is considered far too large a package. Owing to the size and the rough handling such packages sometimes receive, the pears very often arrive in an almost worthless condition. If they were packed in cases (as the French pears are packed), it is believed that the fruit would arrive in much better condition, and consequently higher prices would be realized.

### CANNED FRUIT.

The trade in canned fruit with the United States is in a very satisfactory condition. It is noticed and commented upon that while the California fruits are satisfactory as regards size and quality, they should be preserved in a stronger sirup. When such fruit is sent unsweetened, it is not suited to the English palate, and does not tend to the increase of business. With regard to apricot pulp, it is claimed that the Spanish and French pulp contains very much less water than the California pulp, and consequently it requires much less boiling. California pulp contains a large proportion of water; hence it is necessary that it should be evaporated before it can be used successfully to make jam. This materially increases the cost of making jam, which becomes serious when it is remembered that jam has a very large sale in this country. It is suggested that in putting up the pulp, there should be no more water added than is absolutely needed for preservation. At the present time, while the continental pulp is almost solid, the Californian is, to a great extent, liquid. Still, I have heard from the trade here expressions of congratulation to American canners on the general care bestowed in preserving fruit, both canned and dried, and the style of package has very much improved; consequently, the goods are now more readily sold in competition with French and other continental productions.

### IRON AND STEEL.

The iron and steel trade during 1901 was not so satisfactory to British manufacturers as that of the years immediately preceding. The years of 1898 and 1899 were periods of exceptional activity, accompanied by a general advance in prices such as had not been known for a long time. During 1901, the quotations for Scotch pig iron fell from $18.97 to $11.92, but there was not a corresponding reduction in prices of coal or manufactured iron and steel. This may perhaps be accounted for by the fact that wages have not yet fallen to any great extent in these industries (although there is an increasing downward tendency), and it was felt that if trade did not improve during 1902, this matter would have to be dealt with so as to place the cost of production on a fairer basis. Again, owing to the high price of coke during 1901 (which was almost as dear as it was in 1900), pig iron could not be produced at a reasonable profit, and this fact is illustrated by the published returns of some of the large companies. The following figures show the changes that have taken place in the production of pig iron in this country:

| Year. | Production. | Stocks. |
|-------|-------------|---------|
| | *Tons.* | *Tons.* |
| 1898 ........................................................................ | 8,631,115 | 950,000 |
| 1899 ........................................................................ | 9,305,519 | 721,617 |
| 1900 ........................................................................ | 8,908,570 | 455,419 |
| 1901*a* ...................................................................... | 7,800,000 | 550,000 |

*a* Estimated.

The exports for 1901 show a serious reduction of 640,589 tons compared with 1900, but pig iron alone accounts for 588,305 tons of that large total, due to the falling off of German demand. During the last few months of 1901, a new source of supply was opened up, and it is estimated that about 50,000 tons of Canadian pig iron were imported into this country. It is felt that the commanding position which the iron and steel industry of the United States now occupies is bound to influence to a greater extent the future of the English trade. In fact, that influence has already had the effect of bringing home to the manufacturers of this country the necessity of "waking up" to the dangers which are before them, and the need of making their works in every department up to date. Some of the leading houses are moving earnestly in this direction, and it is believed that Great Britain is on the eve of great changes and improvements in the iron and steel trade. The tin-plate trade was exceptionally busy, and the great strike at the tin-plate mills in the United States led to a considerable demand on this country. During the nine months of 1902, ending September, the iron and steel trade maintained a very satisfactory situation, but the fact is not concealed that this was due in a large measure to the exceptional condition of affairs in America. The shipments from this country to the United States for the nine months ended September 30, 1902, were 399,276 tons, compared with

114,026 tons in the corresponding period of 1901, being an increase of 285,150 tons. This was due to the remarkable prosperity of the home trade in the United States. Considerable quantities of unwrought steel have also been shipped to the United States. .Up to the end of last month (September, 1902) 37,924 tons have gone forward, against 9,002 tons in the corresponding period of 1901.

Shipments of galvanized sheets have been exceptionally large during the period named, the quantity being 240,685 tons as compared with 183,502 tons in 1901. The increase has been mainly to South Africa, India, Canada, and Australia. The following table shows the total exports of iron and steel from this country to all parts from January 1 to September 30, 1902:

| Articles. | 1902. | 1901. | 1900. |
|---|---|---|---|
| | *Tons.* | *Tons.* | *Tons.* |
| Pig iron | 739,385 | 653,561 | 1,158,203 |
| Railroads of all kinds | 545,002 | 431,291 | 344,443 |
| Galvanized sheets | 240,685 | 183,502 | 188,940 |
| Cast and wrought iron | 249,144 | 236,206 | 260,715 |
| Steel, unwrought | 222,481 | 160,910 | 253,267 |
| Other descriptions, iron and steel | 318,669 | 284,471 | 335,363 |
| Tin plates and sheets | 229,112 | 196,858 | 204,925 |
| Black plates (for tinning) | 40,902 | 38,899 | 52,146 |
| Total | 2,585,330 | 2,188,698 | 2,798,002 |

JAMES BOYLE, *Consul.*

LIVERPOOL, *October 21, 1902.*

## IMPORTS, EXPORTS, AND NAVIGATION AT THE PORT OF LIVERPOOL DURING THE CALENDAR YEAR 1901.

*Total value of imports of foreign and colonial produce, and total exports, the produce and manufacture of the United Kingdom; also of foreign and colonial produce, at the port of Liverpool, during the years 1897 to 1901.*

| Year. | Total imports of foreign and colonial merchandise. | Exports. | | |
|---|---|---|---|---|
| | | Produce and manufactures of the United Kingdom. | Foreign and colonial merchandise. | Total. |
| 1897 | $495,248,234 | $373,943,874 | $65,729,891 | $439,673,765 |
| 1898 | 538,541,620 | 363,851,165 | 64,427,085 | 428,098,230 |
| 1899 | 535,537,586 | 394,937,995 | 77,856,932 | 472,794,927 |
| 1900 | 606,107,298 | 425,192,569 | 73,311,676 | 498,504,245 |
| 1901 | 639,490,230 | 437,853,943 | 76,373,743 | 514,227,686 |

*Gross amount of customs revenue received at the port of Liverpool during the years 1897 to 1901.*

| | | | |
|---|---|---|---|
| 1897 | $16,428,364 | 1900 | $20,289,493 |
| 1898 | 16,115,079 | 1901 | 24,357,527 |
| 1899 | 17,393,718 | | |

*Quantities of foreign and colonial produce imported at the port of Liverpool during the years of 1900 and 1901.*

| Principal articles. | | 1900. | 1901. |
|---|---|---:|---:|
| **Animals, living:** | | | |
| Oxen, bulls, cows, and calves | number.. | 224,661 | 243,860 |
| Sheep and lambs | do.... | 195,885 | 249,789 |
| Horses | do.... | 12,521 | 5,786 |
| Butter | cwt.. | 90,381 | 186,963 |
| Caoutchouc | do.... | 387,967 | 367,984 |
| Cheese | do.... | 639,277 | 627,381 |
| Caoutchouc, manufactures of | dollars.. | 806,369 | 906,978 |
| **Chemical manufactures and products:** | | | |
| Borax | cwt.. | 289,097 | 277,313 |
| Of all other sorts | dollars.. | 1,172,167 | 1,514,045 |
| Clocks and parts thereof | do.... | 357,069 | 304,075 |
| Cocoa | pounds.. | 13,080,584 | 14,277,966 |
| Coffee, raw | cwt.. | 55,238 | 8,628 |
| Cordage | dollars.. | 289,199 | 301,635 |
| **Cork:** | | | |
| Unmanufactured | tons.. | 7,232 | 10,567 |
| Manufactured | do.. | 2,335,618 | 2,156,132 |
| **Corn:** | | | |
| Wheat | cwt.. | 20,525,870 | 22,297,110 |
| Barley | do.. | 1,236,470 | 1,093,200 |
| Oats | do.. | 729,720 | 841,300 |
| Pease | do.. | 453,372 | 379,570 |
| Beans | do.. | 610,620 | 496,990 |
| Maize, or Indian corn | do.. | 15,825,220 | 14,734,600 |
| Wheatmeal and flour | do.. | 4,250,211 | 4,920,680 |
| Oatmeal and groats | do.. | 285,100 | 303,790 |
| Maize, or Indian corn, meal | do.... | 299,595 | 325,716 |
| **Cotton:** | | | |
| Raw | do.... | 11,850,484 | 12,920,436 |
| Waste | pounds.. | 13,382,738 | 10,143,165 |
| Manufactures of all kinds | dollars.. | 1,244,811 | 1,233,638 |
| **Drugs:** | | | |
| Opium | pounds.. | 296,858 | 158,940 |
| Of all other kinds | dollars.. | 439,688 | 419,218 |
| **Dye stuffs:** | | | |
| Cutch and gambier | tons.. | 6,590 | 5,949 |
| Extracts | dollars.. | 1,185,606 | 1,417,598 |
| Indigo | cwt.. | 3,416 | 4,452 |
| Myrobalans | do.. | 146,230 | 151,805 |
| Valonia | tons.. | 7,040 | 5,276 |
| Of all other kinds | dollars.. | 390,773 | 338,474 |
| Eggs | great hundreds.. | 878,701 | 703,369 |
| Electrical goods | dollars.. | 1,711,259 | 707,504 |
| **Farinaceous substances:** | | | |
| Rice, rice meal and flour | cwt.. | 3,162,137 | 3,744,178 |
| Sago, sago meal, and flour | do.. | 268,869 | 208,072 |
| Of all other kinds | dollars.. | 1,422,419 | 798,949 |
| Fish of all kinds | cwt.. | 621,175 | 586,484 |
| **Fruit, dutiable:** | | | |
| Currants | do.. | 311,564 | 484,646 |
| Figs | do.. | 77,606 | 64,580 |
| Raisins | do.. | 211,296 | 202,402 |
| **Fruit, not liable to duty:** | | | |
| Apples, raw | cwt.. | 976,778 | 758,130 |
| Bananas, raw | bunches.. | 475,965 | 696,650 |
| Grapes, raw | cwt.. | 200,345 | 287,855 |
| Lemons, limes, and citrons | do.. | 365,549 | 435,556 |
| Nuts— | | | |
| Almonds | do.. | 17,375 | 21,411 |
| Other nuts, used as fruit | do.. | 145,590 | 161,008 |
| Oranges | do.. | 1,595,150 | 1,533,370 |
| Raw, of all other kinds | dollars.. | 207,881 | 196,898 |
| Preserved, without sugar, other than dried a | cwt.. | 340,717 | .......... |
| Preserved, with or without sugar, other than dried | do.. | .......... | 388,116 |
| Glass manufactures of all kinds | dollars.. | 618,182 | 687,068 |
| Hardware (other than cutlery) | cwt.. | 39,744 | 41,725 |
| Hay | tons.. | 19,336 | 43,801 |
| Hemp | do.. | 19,046 | 28,090 |
| Hides, raw | cwt.. | 298,670 | 369,206 |
| Hops | do.. | 36,214 | 24,344 |
| Jute, manufactures of | dollars.. | 6,697,614 | 7,188,994 |
| Lard | cwt.. | 853,358 | 958,240 |
| Imitation lard | do.. | 32,133 | 49,987 |
| Leather | do.. | 342,296 | 424,390 |
| Leather manufactures of all kinds | dollars.. | 700,505 | 1,668,676 |
| Machinery and millwork | do.. | | 3,381,296 |
| **Manures:** | | | |
| Nitrate of soda | tons.. | 31,965 | 28,786 |
| Phosphate of lime and rock phosphate | do.. | 48,845 | 47,453 |
| Of all other kinds | do.. | 31,903 | 28,632 |

*a* Included in "Fruit preserved" in 1901.

*Quantities of foreign and colonial produce imported, etc.*—Continued.

| Principal articles. | | 1900. | 1901. |
|---|---|---|---|
| Meat (except poultry and game): | | | |
| Bacon | cwt.. | 2,821,185 | 3,226,551 |
| Beef— | | | |
| Fresh | do... | 2,424,768 | 2,768,378 |
| Salted | do... | 100,551 | 106,942 |
| Hams | do... | 1,294,185 | 1,378,914 |
| Mutton, fresh | do... | 871,815 | 982,750 |
| Pork— | | | |
| Fresh | do... | 213,827 | 298,388 |
| Salted | do... | 108,488 | 116,913 |
| Unenumerated, salted or fresh | do... | 157,125 | 188,925 |
| Preserved, not salted | do... | 164,726 | 194,583 |
| Metals and ores: | | | |
| Copper— | | | |
| Ore of | tons.. | 38,377 | 45,437 |
| Regulus and precipitate | do... | 20,187 | 32,168 |
| Old | do... | 3,495 | 1,282 |
| Unwrought | do... | 29,564 | 31,858 |
| Manufactures of, unenumerated | dollars.. | 2,212,519 | 966,070 |
| Iron— | | | |
| Bar, angle, bolt, and rod | tons.. | 6,333 | 4,545 |
| Pig and puddled | do... | 42,540 | 19,781 |
| Steel, unwrought | do... | 51,807 | 34,799 |
| Manufactures of all kinds | dollars.. | 5,713,792 | 1,974,880 |
| Lead, pig and sheet | tons.. | 24,766 | 25,877 |
| Manganese, ore of | do... | 44,273 | 35,002 |
| Pyrites of iron and copper | do... | 187,237 | 159,880 |
| Silver, ore of | dollars.. | | 1,550,991 |
| Tin, ore of | tons.. | 5,758 | 9,189 |
| Tin, in blocks, ingots, bars, and slabs | cwt.. | 41,972 | 48,838 |
| Zinc, crude, in cakes | tons.. | 15,471 | 9,571 |
| Metal, unenumerated, unwrought | do.... | 914 | 1,840 |
| Metal, unenumerated, old | do.... | 2,049 | 585 |
| Milk, condensed | cwt.. | 75,390 | 86,788 |
| Musical instruments | dollars.. | 824,985 | 884,199 |
| Nuts for expressing oil therefrom | tons.. | 44,884 | 41,982 |
| Oil: | | | |
| Cocoanut | cwt.. | 142,044 | 151,022 |
| Olive | tons.. | 1,664 | 2,999 |
| Palm | cwt.. | 909,788 | 1,121,118 |
| Seed | tons.. | 7,284 | 10,597 |
| Turpentine | cwt.. | 101,959 | 91,191 |
| Oil-seed cake | tons.. | 123,499 | 120,119 |
| Oleomargarine | cwt.. | 83,172 | 47,762 |
| Painters' colors | dollars.. | 1,172,873 | 868,127 |
| Paper, including strawboard, etc | cwt.. | 276,399 | 341,250 |
| Paper-making materials | tons.. | 39,678 | 35,987 |
| Paraffin | cwt.. | 201,083 | 190,649 |
| Petroleum: | | | |
| Illuminating | gallons.. | 24,315,180 | 22,722,059 |
| Lubricating | do... | 9,064,134 | 8,777,101 |
| Piassava and other fibers for brush making | tons.. | 2,746 | 3,473 |
| Poultry and game, alive or dead | dollars.. | 804,466 | 821,753 |
| Rosin | cwt.. | 436,416 | 479,183 |
| Seeds: | | | |
| Cotton | tons.. | 50,061 | 55,866 |
| Flax or linseed | quarters.. | 150,079 | 169,931 |
| Of all other kinds | dollars.. | 890,604 | 1,212,084 |
| Skins: | | | |
| Goat, undressed | number.. | 1,669,318 | 3,507,069 |
| Sheep, undressed | do... | 1,990,289 | 1,791,347 |
| Furs, of all sorts | do... | 3,621,426 | 3,332,321 |
| Soap and soap powder | cwt.. | 102,989 | 166,901 |
| Spirits: | | | |
| Brandy | proof gallons.. | 423,534 | 543,735 |
| Rum | do... | 1,614,686 | 1,760,092 |
| Stones, rough or hewn | tons.. | 17,506 | 15,750 |
| Sugar: | | | |
| Refined | cwt.. | 894,656 | 1,497,390 |
| Unrefined | do... | 5,138,945 | 5,123,829 |
| Molasses | do... | 551,032 | 716,254 |
| Glucose | do... | 320,151 | 259,230 |
| Tallow and stearin | do... | 634,811 | 559,979 |
| Tobacco: | | | |
| Unmanufactured | pounds.. | 56,435,319 | 51,637,025 |
| Manufactured | do... | 3,799,551 | 4,553,968 |
| Vegetables, raw: | | | |
| Onions | bushels.. | 2,080,421 | 1,985,204 |
| Potatoes | cwt.. | 504,315 | 399,312 |
| Tomatoes | do... | 179,427 | 147,734 |
| Of all other kinds | dollars.. | 253,785 | 541,340 |
| Wine | gallons.. | 2,618,452 | 2,645,795 |

*Quantities of foreign and colonial produce imported, etc.—*Continued.

| Principal articles. | 1900. | 1901. |
|---|---|---|
| **Wood:** | | |
| Hewn, of all sorts...............................................loads.. | 155,865 | 148,023 |
| Sawn, of all sorts ...............................................do.... | 634,019 | 505,249 |
| Staves ...............................................do.... | 32,716 | 25,575 |
| Furniture woods of all kinds.......................................tons.. | 112,695 | 107,078 |
| Manufactures of— | | |
| House frames and joiners' work..........................dollars.. | 738,428 | 794,735 |
| Other sorts ...............................................do.... | | 1,258,126 |
| **Wool:** | | |
| Alpaca, vicuna, and llama.......................................pounds.. | 5,795,796 | 5,417,923 |
| Goats' wool, or hair, mohair.......................................do.... | 8,034,282 | 8,923,671 |
| Sheep, or lambs' wool.......................................do.... | 73,971,377 | 101,963,561 |
| Woolen manufactures of all kinds (including manufactures of goats' wool) ...............................................dollars.. | | 521,098 |
| Parcel post (goods free of duty)..........................number of parcels.. | 36,319 | 42,739 |
| All other articles..........................................dollars.. | | 11,879,472 |

*Products and manufactures of the United Kingdom exported at the port of Liverpool during the years 1900 and 1901.*

| Principal articles. | 1900. | 1901. |
|---|---|---|
| Apparel....................................................dollars.. | 3,331,112 | 3,556,557 |
| Beer and ale....................................................barrels.. | 117,640 | 103,961 |
| Carriages, railway ....................................................dollars.. | 3,664,177 | 6,304,712 |
| Chemicals and chemical preparations: | | |
| Alkali....................................................cwt.. | 3,237,492 | |
| Soda compounds a....................................................do.... | | 2,985,908 |
| All other sorts b....................................................dollars.. | | 8,606,413 |
| Cotton yarn .........................................................pounds.. | 51,171,000 | 61,826,800 |
| Cotton manufactures: | | |
| Piece goods......................................................yards.. | 3,536,244,900 | 3,812,282,900 |
| All other kinds....................................................dollars.. | 18,505,159 | 18,850,428 |
| Earthen and china ware ....................................................do.... | 6,176,889 | 5,987,563 |
| Fish ....................................................do.... | 1,770,992 | 1,073,433 |
| Glass ....................................................do.... | 2,673,082 | 2,697,897 |
| Hardware and cutlery....................................................do.... | 3,654,331 | 3,439,373 |
| Implements and tools....................................................do.... | 3,062,057 | 2,968,295 |
| Jute yarn ....................................................pounds.. | 10,708,100 | 16,279,300 |
| Jute piece goods....................................................yards.. | 24,611,700 | 35,327,600 |
| Leather, unwrought and wrought....................................dollars.. | 1,804,240 | 1,832,540 |
| Linen yarn....................................................pounds.. | 4,094,300 | 3,779,400 |
| Linen manufactures: | | |
| Piece goods....................................................yards.. | 89,284,700 | 89,380,500 |
| All other kinds....................................................dollars.. | 3,781,799 | 3,588,361 |
| Machinery and millwork....................................................do.... | 25,655,740 | 25,322,262 |
| Manure ....................................................tons.. | 116,586 | 108,247 |
| Metals: | | |
| Iron, and iron and steel manufactures ......................do... | 801,215 | 746,795 |
| Copper, unwrought and wrought ..........................cwt... | 181,298 | 250,998 |
| Painters' colors and materials ....................................dollars.. | 1,700,475 | 1,591,450 |
| Salt ....................................................tons.. | 396,211 | 459,087 |
| Silk yarn....................................................pounds.. | 847,587 | 484,000 |
| Silk manufactures ....................................................dollars.. | 2,696,143 | 2,349,659 |
| Skins and furs ....................................................do.... | 2,606,014 | 2,635,130 |
| Soap ....................................................cwt.. | 743,654 | 834,090 |
| Wool....................................................pounds.. | 13,729,900 | 10,559,800 |
| Woolen and worsted yarn....................................do.... | 1,660,400 | 1,570,600 |
| Woolen and worsted manufactures: | | |
| Piece goods....................................................yards.. | 71,672,500 | 66,186,800 |
| All other kinds....................................................value.. | 3,102,478 | 2,726,401 |
| Parcels Post....................................number of parcels.. | 114,804 | 125,048 |
| All other articles....................................................dollars.. | 42,133,439 | 41,296,210 |

a Alkali; shown as soda compounds from 1901.
b Bleaching materials and saltpeter were not included prior to 1901.

*Foreign and colonial produce exported at the port of Liverpool during the years 1900 and 1901.*

| Principal articles. | 1900. | 1901. |
|---|---|---|
| Beads of all sorts .................................................pounds.. | 954,263 | 601,006 |
| Bristles.........................................................do... | 130,909 | 110,008 |
| Butter.........................................................cwt.. | 11,299 | 4,632 |
| Caoutchouc .....................................................do... | 182,558 | 188,977 |
| Cheese.........................................................do... | 14,480 | 12,768 |
| Corn: | | |
|   Wheat.........................................................do... | 143,206 | 210,722 |
|   Maize.........................................................do... | 475,512 | 800,452 |
|   Wheat meal or flour...........................................do... | 110,755 | 107,717 |
| Cotton: | | |
|   Raw..........................................................do... | 898,083 | 830,823 |
|   Waste........................................................do... | 6,586,772 | 3,241,806 |
|   Manufactures, piece goods, not muslins ........................yards.. | 14,096,086 | 13,756,190 |
|   Manufactures, unenumerated ...................................dollars.. | 322,383 | 856,199 |
| Drugs...........................................................do... | 340,729 | 264,679 |
| Dye stuffs: Indigo..............................................cwt.. | 1,796 | 3,832 |
| Embroidery and needlework......................................dollars.. | 364,101 | 856,621 |
| Farinaceous substances: Rice, ricemeal, and flour a..............cwt.. | 1,629,498 | 1,710,285 |
| Feathers, ornamental ..........................................pounds.. | 61,240 | 100,563 |
| Fish, cured, unenumerated ......................................cwt.. | 120,193 | 150,752 |
| Flowers, artificial............................................dollars.. | 181,110 | 220,012 |
| Fruit: | | |
|   Preserved, with or without sugar or sirup, other than dried........cwt.. | 52,648 | 20,704 |
|   Raw .........................................................dollars.. | 785,701 | 804,917 |
| Gum............................................................cwt.. | 12,868 | 14,657 |
| Hemp, dressed or undressed......................................tons.. | 3,525 | 11,678 |
| Hides, raw, dry ................................................cwt.. | 40,583 | 15,928 |
| Jute ..........................................................tons.. | 2,993 | 4,221 |
| Jute manufactures.............................................dollars.. | 6,226,763 | 6,523,427 |
| Lace: | | |
|   Of silk ....................................................do... | 305,017 | 335,461 |
|   Of all other materials ......................................do... | 543,270 | 1,160,568 |
| Lard...........................................................cwt.. | 25,020 | 52,480 |
| Leather: | | |
|   Dressed.....................................................do... | 13,146 | 17,159 |
|   Manufactures, gloves ........................................dozen pairs.. | 49,849 | 88,155 |
| Machinery and millwork b .......................................dollars.. | | 894,350 |
| Meat: | | |
|   Bacon.......................................................cwt.. | 65,944 | 68,880 |
|   Hams........................................................do... | 13,426 | 11,786 |
|   Preserved, not salted.......................................do... | 46,343 | 36,781 |
| Metals: | | |
|   Copper, unwrought...........................................tons.. | 4,112 | 7,120 |
|   Iron or steel manufactures, machinery c......................dollars.. | 368,942 | ............. |
|   Iron or steel manufactures, unenumerated ....................cwt.. | 51,264 | 51,690 |
|   Tin in blocks...............................................do... | 9,538 | 12,945 |
| Milk, condensed ................................................do... | 30,684 | 47,763 |
| Nuts for expressing oil therefrom ...............................tons.. | 11,623 | 9,383 |
| Oil, palm......................................................cwt.. | 617,629 | 679,871 |
| Pictures......................................................number.. | 252 | 243 |
| Precious stones: | | |
|   Diamonds d .................................................carats.. | | 2,306 |
|   Unset, other descriptions ...................................dollars.. | 200,338 | 887,197 |
| Seeds, unenumerated: | | |
|   For oil ....................................................quarters.. | 15,275 | 9,383 |
|   Other sorts ................................................cwt.. | 32,382 | 29,895 |
| Silk manufactures.............................................dollars.. | | 821,276 |
| Skins: | | |
|   Goat, undressed ............................................number.. | 1,687,870 | 3,873,601 |
|   Sheep, undressed ...........................................do... | 1,154,451 | 544,056 |
| Furs, unenumerated .............................................do... | 287,751 | 451,950 |
| Sugar, unrefined ...............................................cwt.. | 193,416 | 85,471 |
| Tallow and stearine.............................................do... | 56,408 | 61,881 |
| Tea ...........................................................pounds.. | 291,581 | 1,554,215 |
| Tobacco, unmanufactured .......................................do... | 5,383,940 | 4,185,462 |
| Vegetables, raw ...............................................dollars.. | 227,020 | 257,628 |
| Wine ..........................................................gallons.. | 45,767 | 72,848 |
| Wood: | | |
|   Furniture wood, mahogany ...................................tons.. | 11,070 | 15,000 |
|   Unenumerated ...............................................do... | 4,920 | 8,676 |
|   Manufactures, other sorts e ................................dollars.. | 155,138 | 142,378 |

a Included "Rice" only prior to 1900.
b Not separately recorded prior to 1901, except as to iron and steel machinery, for which see under "Metals."
c Included in "Machinery and millwork" in 1901.
d This account of the exportation of diamonds represents only such diamonds as were declared to the customs on exportation from the 23d March, 1901.
e Not separately recorded prior to 1900.

*Foreign and colonial produce exported at the port of Liverpool, etc.*—Continued.

| Principal articles. | 1900. | 1901. |
|---|---|---|
| Wool: | | |
| Alpaca ......................................................pounds.. | 575,200 | 787,000 |
| Goat, mohair...........................................do... | 205,743 | 118,568 |
| Sheep or lambs.......................................do... | 26,358,229 | 24,441,677 |
| Woolen manufactures: | | |
| Stuffs ......................................................yards.. | 1,614,066 | 2,508,086 |
| Carpet and rugs.....................................dollars.. | 444,077 | 465,656 |
| Unenumerated.........................................do... | 556,824 | 429,099 |
| All other articles ...................................do... | 5,460,824 | 6,410,242 |

*Number and tonnage of British and foreign sailing and steam vessels, including their repeated voyages, that entered and cleared at the port of Liverpool during the year 1901.*

[Vessels in the coastwise trade are not included in this table.]

| | Entered. | | Cleared. | |
|---|---|---|---|---|
| | Vessels. | Tons. | Vessels. | Tons. |
| Russia: | | | | |
| Northern ports............................... | 25 | 17,853 | 25 | 18,508 |
| Southern ports............................... | 29 | 52,610 | 45 | 68,276 |
| Sweden ........................................... | 50 | 38,395 | 83 | 27,150 |
| Norway ........................................... | 126 | 67,125 | 41 | 21,322 |
| Denmark (including Faroe Islands)................. | 39 | 9,062 | 66 | 21,720 |
| Germany........................................... | 154 | 136,606 | 117 | 89,469 |
| Holland........................................... | 59 | 55,491 | 92 | 68,942 |
| Dutch possessions in the Indian Seas— | | | | |
| Java ........................................... | 12 | 17,817 | 22 | 34,886 |
| Dutch West India Islands..................... | 5 | 10,829 | .......... | .......... |
| Belgium........................................... | 114 | 137,275 | 108 | 96,287 |
| France ........................................... | 352 | 173,343 | 225 | 89,111 |
| Algeria ....................................... | 10 | 11,768 | .......... | .......... |
| French possessions in Western Africa........... | 8 | 12,014 | 16 | 18,170 |
| French Indo-China (Cochin China, Cambodia, Annam, and Tonquin)........................... | 4 | 9,628 | .......... | .......... |
| French West India Islands ..................... | 1 | 1,617 | 1 | 312 |
| Portugal ........................................... | 69 | 39,094 | 59 | 31,185 |
| Azores ........................................... | .......... | .......... | 1 | 358 |
| Portuguese possessions in Western Africa ........... | 7 | 18,778 | 20 | 34,111 |
| Portuguese possessions in Eastern Africa........... | .......... | .......... | 1 | 1,446 |
| Spain ........................................... | 345 | 250,838 | 208 | 154,564 |
| Canary Islands................................... | 40 | 23,386 | 35 | 21,849 |
| Italy ........................................... | 30 | 31,577 | 56 | 63,009 |
| Austria-Hungary ................................. | 26 | 35,542 | 87 | 55,590 |
| Greece ........................................... | 21 | 24,957 | 5 | 7,202 |
| Roumania ......................................... | 16 | 22,383 | 31 | 49,381 |
| Turkish dominions: | | | | |
| European Turkey............................... | 39 | 50,695 | 15 | 21,406 |
| Asiatic Turkey (including El Hedjas and Turkish ports on Persian Gulf)......................... | 29 | 35,895 | 18 | 25,518 |
| Egypt ........................................... | 88 | 132,108 | 59 | 90,243 |
| Tunis ........................................... | 9 | 11,897 | .......... | .......... |
| Morocco ........................................... | 2 | 567 | .......... | .......... |
| Congo Free State ................................. | 3 | 5,924 | .......... | .......... |
| Western coast of Africa, not particularly designated..... | 3 | 3,962 | .......... | .......... |
| China (exclusive of Hongkong and Macao)............... | 2 | 4,562 | .......... | .......... |
| Japan............................................. | 9 | 27,881 | 13 | 41,001 |
| Philippine and Ladrone Islands..................... | 18 | 51,753 | 14 | 42,196 |
| Islands in the Pacific, not elsewhere specified........... | 5 | 2,826 | 1 | 1,407 |
| United States of America: | | | | |
| On the Atlantic................................... | 881 | 3,311,397 | 751 | 3,118,751 |
| On the Pacific ................................... | 25 | 57,688 | 14 | 23,483 |
| Cuba............................................. | 3 | 1,269 | 50 | 94,194 |
| Porto Rico ....................................... | .......... | .......... | 8 | 11,127 |
| Haiti and Santo Domingo........................... | 2 | 701 | 4 | 3,795 |
| Mexico ........................................... | 28 | 47,663 | 17 | 29,590 |
| San Salvador ..................................... | .......... | .......... | 1 | 587 |
| Republic of Colombia............................... | 22 | 47,686 | 62 | 133,604 |
| Venezuela ......................................... | 1 | 275 | .......... | .......... |
| Ecuador ........................................... | 1 | 2,531 | 3 | 5,063 |
| Peru ........................................... | 29 | 46,737 | 25 | 45,442 |
| Chile (including the Pacific coast of Patagonia) ......... | 32 | 90,199 | 35 | 91,052 |
| Brazil....1......................................... | 89 | 123,506 | 130 | 176,108 |
| Uruguay ........................................... | 1 | 350 | .......... | .......... |

*Number and tonnage of British and foreign sailing and steam vessels, etc.*—Continued.

| | Entered. | | Cleared. | |
|---|---|---|---|---|
| | Vessels. | Tons. | Vessels. | Tons. |
| Argentine Republic (including the Atlantic coast of Patagonia)........................................ | 146 | 296,260 | 88 | 177,096 |
| Deep-sea fisheries ............................................. | 18 | 1,150 | .......... | .......... |
| Total foreign countries........................... | 3,022 | 5,549,960 | 2,547 | 5,108,462 |
| Total British possessions........................ | 450 | 915,193 | 498 | 1,067,610 |
| Total foreign countries and British possessions........... | 3,472 | 6,465,153 | 3,045 | 6,171,072 |
| Vessels employed by His Majesty's Government in the conveyance of troops, stores, etc., from and to South Africa (not included in above figures).................. | 7 | 23,457 | 25 | 76,281 |

*Number and tonnage of British and foreign sailing and steam vessels that entered and cleared coastwise at the port of Liverpool during the years 1900 and 1901.*

| | Employed in— | | | | Total. | |
|---|---|---|---|---|---|---|
| | General coasting trade. | | Intercourse between Great Britain and Ireland. | | | |
| | Number. | Tons. | Number. | Tons. | Number. | Tons. |
| **1900.** | | | | | | |
| Entered........................... | 11,343 | 1,989,416 | 5,454 | 1,374,695 | 16,797 | 3,314,111 |
| Cleared ........................... | 10,883 | 2,163,900 | 5,623 | 1,328,287 | 16,506 | 3,492,187 |
| **1901.** | | | | | | |
| Entered........................... | 11,220 | 1,849,193 | 5,408 | 1,389,814 | 16,628 | 3,239,007 |
| Cleared ........................... | 11,139 | 2,193,681 | 5,484 | 1,306,851 | 16,623 | 3,500,582 |

*Number and tonnage of sailing and steam vessels of each nation, including their repeated voyages, that entered and cleared with cargoes and in ballast at the port of Liverpool during the year 1901.*

[Vessels in the coastwise trade are not included.]

| | Entered. | | Cleared. | |
|---|---|---|---|---|
| | Vessels. | Tons. | Vessels. | Tons. |
| British................................................ | 2,654 | 5,674,107 | 2,326 | 5,426,581 |
| Russian............................................... | 28 | 17,860 | 25 | 19,264 |
| Swedish.............................................. | 57 | 39,057 | 45 | 28,943 |
| Norwegian........................................... | 270 | 171,350 | 188 | 122,542 |
| Danish................................................ | 50 | 22,455 | 37 | 9,419 |
| German............................................... | 63 | 54,287 | 37 | 38,873 |
| Dutch................................................. | 42 | 44,118 | 25 | 36,453 |
| Belgian............................................... | 53 | 145,875 | 55 | 144,521 |
| French................................................ | 47 | 27,840 | 35 | 17,293 |
| Spanish............................................... | 177 | 218,350 | 245 | 286,490 |
| Italian................................................ | 10 | 11,078 | 8 | 8,279 |
| Austro-Hungarian.................................. | 3 | 6,003 | 1 | 2,381 |
| United States of America ......................... | 6 | 15,904 | 7 | 17,400 |
| All other countries................................. | 12 | 17,869 | 11 | 12,683 |
| Total foreign........................ | 818 | 791,046 | 719 | 744,541 |
| Total British and foreign ........................ | 3,472 | 6,465,153 | 3,045 | 6,171,072 |

## MANCHESTER.

In placing before the Department my report for the nine months ended September 30, 1902, I have to say that, with better returns for the past quarter, the general imports show a gain of £4,410,326 ($19,467,995.26) over the figures for the same nine months of 1901.

This increase is satisfactory, considering that at the end of June the amount to the good was only £323,000 ($1,571,879.50). There is a fair prospect of plentiful and cheap food during the winter.

On the export side there is also an increase for the same period. In June, the exports were £3,204,822 ($15,596,275.99) in arrears compared with last year; now they show an increase of £370,631 ($1,803,675.76).

#### IMPORTS INTO THE UNITED KINGDOM.

The total imports for the first nine months of the present and of the two preceding years were the following:

1902 ............................................... £388,871,037=$1,892,440,901.56
1901 ............................................... 384,460,711= 1,870,978,050.08
1900 ............................................... 379,187,642= 1,845,316,659.79

I give below the principal imports into the United Kingdom from the United States, and from all countries, for the nine months ended September 30, 1902:

*Principal imports.*

| Articles. | From the United States. | | From all countries. | |
|---|---|---|---|---|
| | Quantity. | Value. | Quantity. | Value. |
| Cattle..........number.. | 246,108 | £4,667,759 | $22,715,649.17 | 810,421 | £5,806,895 | $28,258,962.52 |
| Sheep-and lambs.. do.... | 177,533 | 274,730 | 1,396,978.54 | 213,084 | 330,204 | 1,606,987.76 |
| Beef................cwt.. | 1,753,421 | 4,009,966 | 19,514,499.58 | 2,870,206 | 6,109,464 | 29,731,706.55 |
| Bacon.............do.... | 2,505,647 | 6,099,485 | 29,683,148.75 | 3,872,247 | 9,965,366 | 48,496,453.63 |
| Hams.............do.... | 1,030,478 | 2,632,665 | 12,811,864.22 | 1,158,848 | 2,959,318 | 14,401,521.04 |
| Lard..............do.... | 1,185,055 | 2,886,127 | 14,045,387.04 | 1,265,259 | 3,086,706 | 15,021,454.74 |
| Wheat............do.... | 82,861,500 | 11,028,558 | 58,670,477.50 | 59,472,292 | 20,013,314 | 97,394,792.58 |
| Wheat meal and flour, cwt .................... | 10,988,467 | 5,116,342 | 24,898,678.34 | 14,077,998 | 6,473,968 | 31,505,516.60 |
| Tobacco, unmanufactured: | | | | | | |
| Stemmed... pounds.. | 69,236,208 | 1,971,725 | 9,595,399.71 | 71,311,865 | 2,064,346 | 10,046,139.80 |
| Unstemmed... do.... | 12,318,874 | 853,569 | 1,720,643.58 | 17,854,749 | 664,877 | 3,235,623.92 |
| Cigars ..............do.... | 1,184,710 | 940,401 | 4,576,461.46 | 2,108,695 | 1,215,967 | 5,917,508.40 |
| Cigarettes .........do.... | 210,812 | 48,353 | 235,309.87 | 516,817 | 169,180 | 1,698,406.50 |
| Lead,pig and sheet.tons.. | 41,815 | 466,175 | 2,268,640.63 | 176,128 | 1,975,332 | 9,612,958.17 |
| Petroleum: | | | | | | |
| Illuminating..galls.. | 127,478,945 | 2,219,251 | 10,799,984.99 | 197,110,762 | 3,288,693 | 16,004,424.48 |
| Lubricating...do.... | 21,112,870 | 647,241 | 3,149,798.32 | 29,380,783 | 878,267 | 4,274,086.35 |
| Cotton, raw ........cwt.. | 7,269,413 | 17,322,921 | 84,301,995.04 | 9,871,005 | 24,629,705 | 119,860,459.38 |
| Tallow and stearin.do.... | 139,397 | 146,502 | 712,951.98 | 1,553,455 | 2,371,140 | 11,539,152.81 |
| Wood and timber, hewn, loads.................. | 141,184 | 706,370 | 2,437,549.60 | 2,148,040 | 4,159,338 | 20,241,418.37 |
| Leather ............cwt.. | 479,442 | 2,676,784 | 13,026,326.01 | 890,947 | 5,970,895 | 29,057,360.51 |
| Paper (unprinted) on reels .............cwt.. | 173,642 | 102,291 | 497,799.15 | 880,292 | 568,272 | 2,765,495.68 |

#### EXPORTS OF COTTON GOODS.

In the exports of cotton textiles for the nine months ended September 30, 1902, there was a falling off of 733,000 yards in cotton piece goods of all kinds, due to poor markets in Turkey, Bombay, and Madras. Elsewhere, particularly in the United States, China, and Japan, trade has been lively, the total quantity of cotton piece goods sent to these countries from this district having increased slightly. Under all other headings, there are fair expansions.

The exports of cotton piece goods (gray, bleached, printed, and dyed or manufactured of dyed yarn) to the countries named below are the following:

*Cotton piece goods shipped from the United Kingdom to certain countries during the nine months January 1 to September 30, 1900, 1901, and 1902.*

| Countries. | 1900. | 1901. | 1902. | 1900. | 1901. | 1902. |
|---|---|---|---|---|---|---|
| **GRAY.** | *Yards.* | *Yards.* | *Yards.* | | | |
| United States | 7,430,800 | 5,646,900 | 6,493,700 | $721,877.14 | $570,587.39 | $632,085.35 |
| Philippine Islands.. | 8,787,800 | 1,201,400 | 819,300 | 371,683.80 | 55,113.11 | 35,982.99 |
| Egypt | 48,911,500 | 59,463,400 | 58,786,200 | 1,695,907.11 | 2,273,249.21 | 2,158,390.08 |
| Turkey | 68,283,200 | 110,853,100 | 91,796,600 | 2,869,521.92 | 4,825,047.15 | 3,880,269.70 |
| China (including Hongkong) | 201,601,500 | 167,097,000 | 230,831,000 | 8,563,409.72 | 7,669,195.21 | 9,601,988.95 |
| Japan | 52,922,700 | 24,988,800 | 48,002,100 | 2,455,183.31 | 1,287,208.71 | 2,170,527.13 |
| Central America.... | 8,503,500 | 8,090,000 | 7,294,000 | 278,879.64 | 267,448.24 | 217,936.46 |
| Chile | 10,447,300 | 7,039,000 | 9,251,600 | 383,840.32 | 291,187.02 | 335,871.23 |
| Brazil | 849,500 | 814,900 | 1,563,100 | 36,659.34 | 40,314.06 | 71,133.49 |
| Uruguay | 3,060,700 | 4,331,800 | 4,552,700 | 139,761.01 | 187,710.63 | 196,387.60 |
| Argentine Republic. | 16,447,500 | 16,654,900 | 11,991,200 | 653,483.35 | 698,420.61 | 488,830.19 |
| Bombay | 137,833,000 | 222,453,400 | 167,521,600 | 4,764,459.22 | 8,651,201.38 | 6,288,462.10 |
| Bengal and Burma. | 640,623,600 | 649,877,800 | 704,797,400 | 23,502,547.62 | 26,083,009.24 | 27,092,233.75 |
| Madras | 47,053,300 | 61,473,800 | 41,641,000 | 1,943,709.29 | 2,850,450.17 | 1,909,672.99 |
| Straits Settlements.. | 24,281,500 | 36,296,600 | 26,354,700 | 974,910.81 | 1,446,644.98 | 998,401.40 |
| Ceylon | 8,628,500 | 6,623,700 | 3,535,700 | 413,268.04 | 331,763.90 | 171,101.27 |
| British South Africa | 2,275,300 | 2,266,400 | 4,024,000 | 128,120.34 | 126,446.26 | 222,155.72 |
| **BLEACHED.** | | | | | | |
| United States | 12,305,900 | 9,656,500 | 16,738,600 | 1,322,305.91 | 1,117,465.19 | 1,979,371.01 |
| Philippine Islands.. | 15,222,400 | 10,177,800 | 12,024,200 | 660,812.30 | 552,907.39 | 626,727.33 |
| Egypt | 44,852,400 | 53,764,200 | 67,543,800 | 2,075,343.25 | 2,552,123.99 | 3,152,061.24 |
| Turkey | 53,881,100 | 74,073,700 | 70,362,700 | 2,496,115.44 | 3,409,982.21 | 3,189,830.15 |
| China (including Hongkong) | 101,689,500 | 98,952,100 | 146,946,100 | 5,237,872.34 | 5,672,606.52 | 7,600,460.76 |
| Japan | 13,632,200 | 4,359,200 | 11,960,900 | 687,821.37 | 248,600.28 | 597,718.12 |
| Central America.... | 11,028,600 | 9,898,300 | 8,448,500 | 432,179.26 | 420,178.47 | 329,311.18 |
| Chile | 20,858,100 | 20,758,500 | 12,858,500 | 973,952.11 | 1,077,204.64 | 627,021.19 |
| Brazil | 17,166,400 | 11,679,300 | 22,519,000 | 861,535.96 | 636,723.12 | 1,129,300.52 |
| Uruguay | 5,945,900 | 5,373,300 | 8,422,600 | 340,727.99 | 291,561.74 | 470,751.14 |
| Argentine Republic. | 26,553,400 | 17,479,900 | 21,113,900 | 1,674,236.59 | 1,087,562.13 | 1,270,034.83 |
| Bombay | 166,986,100 | 266,263,200 | 159,174,300 | 6,293,299.40 | 11,430,819.65 | 6,106,245.74 |
| Bengal and Burma. | 131,347,000 | 195,626,300 | 135,387,900 | 5,693,843.98 | 8,917,350.26 | 5,922,895.48 |
| Madras | 15,391,300 | 19,436,200 | 12,597,400 | 732,739.17 | 1,051,246.73 | 625,393.91 |
| Straits Settlements.. | 30,606,900 | 31,929,600 | 24,225,600 | 1,486,443.22 | 1,641,762.44 | 1,173,877.66 |
| Ceylon | 6,518,700 | 4,797,500 | 6,514,500 | 370,530.44 | 280,558.59 | 358,364.19 |
| British South Africa. | 5,984,400 | 5,462,300 | 10,658,000 | 488,505.71 | 408,756.80 | 747,002.88 |
| **PRINTED.** | | | | | | |
| United States | 8,532,500 | 4,085,600 | 8,811,900 | 402,440.08 | 488,465.20 | 467,831.24 |
| Philippine Islands.. | 25,405,300 | 7,982,200 | 10,535,500 | 826,343.14 | 390,244.63 | 486,163.35 |
| Egypt | 26,867,700 | 25,542,700 | 29,770,900 | 1,493,227.12 | 1,500,692.33 | 1,740,435.59 |
| Turkey | 64,148,500 | 93,370,000 | 76,024,000 | 3,245,395.85 | 4,769,861.04 | 3,628,112.01 |
| China (including Hongkong) | 30,513,200 | 16,013,800 | 27,359,700 | 1,714,706.40 | 911,860.43 | 1,447,214.36 |
| Japan | 17,255,700 | 3,706,400 | 17,247,200 | 1,032,789.43 | 237,494.98 | 1,019,106.36 |
| Central America.... | 15,587,100 | 7,631,700 | 7,581,400 | 596,929.75 | 355,853.07 | 302,993.15 |
| Chile | 27,283,600 | 12,716,600 | 6,069,500 | 1,284,040.62 | 661,761.26 | 324,104.08 |
| Brazil | 32,339,000 | 21,691,100 | 36,042,300 | 1,738,912.37 | 1,159,949.74 | 1,893,010.10 |
| Uruguay | 8,935,500 | 5,584,600 | 7,654,800 | 438,121.26 | 288,539.65 | 402,858.60 |
| Argentine Republic. | 35,244,100 | 23,414,400 | 20,236,100 | 1,843,537.26 | 1,231,657.61 | 1,079,555.16 |
| Bombay | 62,646,400 | 101,781,600 | 93,698,500 | 2,774,907.49 | 5,098,933.77 | 4,148,457.65 |
| Bengal and Burma.. | 44,889,500 | 46,161,200 | 54,910,600 | 2,218,788.21 | 2,411,156.09 | 2,718,125.17 |
| Madras | 15,764,500 | 17,434,500 | 18,035,300 | 848,313.68 | 963,050.49 | 1,022,865.30 |
| Straits Settlements.. | 22,779,100 | 14,007,100 | 18,023,900 | 1,147,442.83 | 762,916.33 | 902,375.62 |
| Ceylon | 2,593,700 | 3,485,100 | 2,336,100 | 145,683.54 | 190,528.34 | 120,854.66 |
| British South Africa. | 10,174,600 | 12,843,700 | 19,336,600 | 965,323.54 | 846,313.54 | 1,271,893.84 |
| **DYED, OR MANUFAC-TURED OF DYED YARN.** | | | | | | |
| United States | 30,754,700 | 16,516,500 | 21,044,000 | 4,149,854.34 | 2,565,132.15 | 3,576,230.25 |
| Philippine Islands.. | 12,944,500 | 6,636,400 | 6,617,500 | 644,154.27 | 392,346.96 | 427,230.08 |
| Egypt | 10,334,600 | 15,159,200 | 13,236,300 | 627,875.83 | 969,601.46 | 851,428.44 |
| Turkey | 27,693,600 | 44,138,800 | 39,400,500 | 1,651,879.89 | 2,589,795.57 | 2,188,065.99 |
| China (including Hongkong) | 71,370,400 | 67,340,700 | 70,483,300 | 5,671,370.43 | 6,466,707.39 | 5,905,171.69 |

*Cotton piece goods shipped from the United Kingdom to certain countries, etc.—Cont'd.*

| Countries. | 1900. | 1901. | 1902. | 1900. | 1901. | 1902. |
|---|---|---|---|---|---|---|
| DYED, OR MANUFAC- TURED OF DYED YARN—cont'd. | Yards. | Yards. | Yards. | | | |
| Japan............... | 22,026,200 | 7,550,200 | 14,080,600 | $2,248,872.91 | $943,434.28 | $1,460,811.37 |
| Central America.... | 5,251,500 | 6,384,400 | 4,883,400 | 266,961.59 | 351,371.08 | 250,605.28 |
| Chile............... | 19,243,100 | 12,569,700 | 15,810,800 | 1,132,444.28 | 736,316.04 | 870,451.38 |
| Brazil............... | 20,784,900 | 18,010,300 | 28,002,100 | 1,289,335.37 | 1,092,296.65 | 1,593,107.17 |
| Uruguay........... | 7,398,700 | 6,351,200 | 9,858,900 | 460,176.24 | 875,177.96 | 571,760.21 |
| Argentine Republic. | 26,443,800 | 21,696,600 | 24,510,200 | 1,800,955.38 | 1,399,921.72 | 1,452,382.59 |
| Bombay............. | 45,890,900 | 65,319,800 | 60,925,900 | 2,073,182.53 | 2,246,349.68 | 2,726,563.68 |
| Bengal and Burma.. | 65,446,200 | 41,106,100 | 53,289,200 | 3,407,406.50 | 471,948.40 | 2,586,369.55 |
| Madras............. | 12,686,700 | 9,823,400 | 7,836,200 | 688,510.71 | 507,488.35 | 383,567.79 |
| Straits Settlements.. | 13,218,800 | 11,661,300 | 7,455,900 | 901,976.57 | 840,522.41 | 529,596.86 |
| Ceylon ............. | 1,739,400 | 1,546,300 | 1,436,200 | 136,271.73 | 122,553.06 | 103,627.25 |
| British South Africa. | 13,015,900 | 15,943,000 | 23,694,600 | 986,673.14 | 1,248,529.77 | 1,825,852.40 |
| RECAPITULATION. | | | | | | |
| Gray ................ | 1,469,258,700 | 1,562,845,100 | 1,603,700,000 | 59,357,776.00 | 66,682,184.55 | 65,572,651.75 |
| Bleached............ | 979,326,800 | 1,153,429,400 | 1,054,009,700 | 47,827,582.41 | 57,606,463.77 | 52,242,271.69 |
| Printed ............. | 741,519,500 | 672,821,000 | 711,523,400 | 39,523,289.48 | 37,713,321.34 | 38,594,668.82 |
| Dyed, or manufac- tured of dyed yarn. | 632,295,600 | 599,478,900 | 651,020,100 | 44,927,007.28 | 43,972,195.12 | 45,998,386.72 |
| Piece goods of mixed materials, cotton predominating.... | 78,800 | 37,800 | 8,200 | 9,149.02 | 4,443.11 | 1,644.87 |
| Total.......... | 3,822,474,400 | 3,988,612,200 | 4,020,261,400 | 191,644,804.19 | 205,978,607.89 | 202,409,623.85 |

## IRON AND STEEL EXPORTS.

The exports of iron and steel from the United Kingdom during the nine months ended September 30, 1902, were 2,585,330 tons, as compared with 2,188,698 tons last year and 2,798,002 tons in 1900. The value of this year's shipments is £21,314,967 ($103,729,286.90), or about £2,300,000 ($11,192,950) above the figures for 1901, and about £3,500,000 ($17,032,750) less than in 1900. The following statement shows the iron and steel shipments and their value in each month of the first three quarters of the present year:

| Month. | Tons. | Value. | |
|---|---|---|---|
| | | English currency. | United States currency. |
| January.................. | 228,323 | £2,103,174 | $10,235,096.27 |
| February................. | 187,897 | 1,743,653 | 8,485,487.32 |
| March.................... | 264,477 | 2,299,942 | 11,192,667.74 |
| April..................... | 292,883 | 2,449,068 | 11,918,389.42 |
| May...................... | 308,784 | 2,551,291 | 12,415,857.65 |
| June...................... | 288,027 | 2,359,813 | 11,484,029.96 |
| July...................... | 343,561 | 2,686,644 | 13,074,558.02 |
| August................... | 330,358 | 2,466,370 | 12,002,589.60 |
| September................ | 346,080 | 2,655,012 | 12,920,615.89 |

From the following figures it will be seen that the exports of pig iron are still growing, and that this increase is due solely to the abnormal demand from the United States.

| Month. | United States. | | Canada. | |
|---|---|---|---|---|
| | 1901. | 1902. | 1901. | 1902. |
| | Tons. | Tons. | Tons. | Tons. |
| January | 861 | 7,134 | 126 | 505 |
| February | 2,133 | 2,708 | 70 | 425 |
| March | 1,829 | 14,845 | .......... | 350 |
| April | 4,130 | 7,720 | 510 | 3,215 |
| May | 4,651 | 23,177 | 485 | 2,010 |
| June | 6,497 | 26,319 | 1,186 | 5,605 |
| July | 3,293 | 59,442 | 240 | 3,986 |
| August | 4,563 | 69,972 | 1,050 | 4,821 |
| September | 5,408 | 69,827 | 1,365 | 7,740 |
| Total | 33,365 | 281,144 | 5,032 | 28,657 |

The importance of the American demand is exaggerated, for, as a matter of fact, in the last nine months the total pig-iron exports of the United Kingdom have been 400,000 tons less than those for the corresponding period of 1900, although 86,000 tons more than during the first three quarters of 1901. It is said that the home trade generally has not been more active this year than last, and that in some important branches the consumption of pig iron has diminished. This being so, it seems that the high prices quoted for this material are not justified by the American purchases.

MACHINERY EXPORT TRADE.

During the first nine months of the present year, machinery to the value of £473,233 ($2,302,988.39) has been exported to the United States, as compared with £442,379 ($2,152,837.40) worth shipped to that country in the corresponding period of 1901, and £642,817 ($3,128,268.93) in 1900. The total value of the machinery exported to all countries during the above periods are:

```
1902 ............................................... £13,929,373=$67,787,293.70
1901 ...............................................   13,425,301=  65,334,227.31
1900 ...............................................   14,650,540=  71,296,852.91
```

EXPORTS FROM THE MANCHESTER CONSULAR DISTRICT.

I give below a table showing the character and value of declared exports from this consular district to the United States during the nine months ended September 30, 1902; for comparison the corresponding period of 1901 is also exhibited.

| Article. | 1902. | 1901. |
|---|---|---|
| Buttons | $3,340.59 | $2,096.27 |
| Card clothing | 51,873.98 | 56,413.97 |
| Carpets and rugs | 58,082.69 | 75,449.63 |
| Cattle hair and other hair | 49,777.59 | 58,507.79 |
| Chemicals | 120,567.63 | 136,119.71 |
| Colors and dye stuffs | 280,710.46 | 213,512.61 |
| Cotton (American) | 2,378.91 | .......... |
| Cotton and worsted and worsted stuffs | 107,214.44 | 99,364.56 |
| Cotton piece goods | 1,583,810.09 | 957,258.13 |
| Cotton velvets, fustians, etc | 2,012,826.00 | 1,558,648.27 |

| Article. | 1902. | 1901. |
|---|---|---|
| Cotton yarn and thread .............................................. | $1,008,284.77 | $767,897.67 |
| Curtains (lace) .................................................... | 77,223.18 | 66,014.98 |
| Elastic web, cord, etc............................................. | 36,817.64 | 28,579.66 |
| Felt hats and other hats .......................................... | 8,241.49 | 6,912.50 |
| Furniture......................................................... | 5,637.80 | 916.14 |
| Furs, skins, etc .................................................. | 38,911.62 | |
| Glassware, chinaware, and earthenware............................. | 22,959.01 | 11,808.09 |
| Handkerchiefs.................................................... | 35,713.01 | 50,525.05 |
| Hide cuttings.................................................... | 86,554.73 | 85,197.12 |
| Hides............................................................ | 75,789.01 | 54,405.77 |
| Hosiery.......................................................... | 73,066.57 | 82,214.98 |
| India rubber sheets, pouches, etc ................................ | 4,190.11 | 5,328.42 |
| Iron (pig), etc .................................................. | 20,083.63 | 18,652.63 |
| Laces, nets, etc.................................................. | 388,665.39 | 372,616.08 |
| Leather, etc...................................................... | 97,140.44 | 65,898.23 |
| Linens............................................................ | 77,045.62 | 59,495.95 |
| Machinery........................................................ | 908,408.06 | 951,519.02 |
| Mahogany logs, oak logs, etc...................................... | 15,806.32 | 12,821.83 |
| Miscellaneous.................................................... | 26,261.91 | 24,937.42 |
| Needles, pins, etc ............................................... | 15,521.73 | 15,357.92 |
| Paper, paper hangings, etc........................................ | 102,047.81 | 93,348.70 |
| Provisions ...................................................... | 9,926.22 | 2,244.58 |
| Quilts........................................................... | 43,311.21 | 29,801.38 |
| Rags and paper stock............................................. | 311,899.95 | 194,204.91 |
| Shawls........................................................... | 8,117.04 | 6,581.10 |
| Silk and silk and cotton piece goods ............................. | 24,634.89 | 28,634.48 |
| Silk noils and waste ............................................. | 17,064.64 | 16,455.95 |
| Silk yarn ........................................................ | 25,090.30 | 16,811.24 |
| Steel wire, etc .................................................. | 39,070.87 | 19,214.80 |
| Tape and braid .................................................. | 43,137.43 | 55,372.99 |
| Towels........................................................... | 13,865.61 | 13,527.75 |
| Waterproof garments and cloth ................................... | 6,448.56 | 8,564.74 |
| Wool felt, blanketing, lapping, etc............................... | 40,174.41 | 46,020.82 |
| Wool noils and other noils ....................................... | 7,075.13 | |
| Worsted yarn.................................................... | 328.38 | |
| Yarn (other than cotton and silk) ................................ | 8,485.53 | 2,251.04 |
| Returned United States educational exhibits ...................... | | 5,000.00 |
| Total ........................................................ | 7,984,082.22 | 6,356,524.87 |

*Quantities of cotton velvets, cord, and fustians exported hence to the United States during the first nine months of 1901 and 1902.*

| Month. | 1901. | | | 1902. | | |
|---|---|---|---|---|---|---|
| | Dyed. | Undyed. | Total. | Dyed. | Undyed. | Total. |
| | Yards. | Yards. | Yards. | Yards. | Yards. | Yards. |
| January.................... | 353,987 | 452,702½ | 806,689½ | 509,942½ | 596,615½ | 1,106,558 |
| February................... | 314,416½ | 713,484 | 1,027,900½ | 307,672½ | 451,680 | 759,352½ |
| March...................... | 281,870½ | 590,215½ | 872,086 | 240,991½ | 600,696½ | 841,688 |
| April....................... | 298,669½ | 497,383 | 781,052½ | 497,447 | 612,065½ | 1,109,512½ |
| May........................ | 536,286½ | 487,560½ | 1,023,846½ | 943,150½ | 598,911½ | 1,542,062½ |
| June ....................... | 631,556½ | 579,866 | 1,211,422½ | 949,819½ | 652,024½ | 1,601,844½ |
| July........................ | 883,679 | 800,448½ | 1,684,127½ | 1,182,724½ | 540,662½ | 1,723,386½ |
| August..................... | 804,003½ | 712,905½ | 1,516,909½ | 1,106,342 | 680,325½ | 1,786,667½ |
| September ................. | 810,397½ | 659,753½ | 1,470,151½ | 908,392½ | 585,963½ | 1,494,356½ |
| Total.................. | | | 10,399,187 | | | 11,965,428 |

*Exports of cotton yarn to the United States during the first nine months of 1901 and 1902.*

| Month. | 1901. | 1902. | Month. | 1901. | 1902. |
|---|---|---|---|---|---|
| | Pounds. | Pounds. | | Pounds. | Pounds. |
| January.................. | 199,654½ | 288,295 | July...................... | 178,941½ | 274,416½ |
| February................. | 171,451½ | 227,256½ | August................... | 183,475½ | 210,059½ |
| March.................... | 185,180 | 284,520 | September ............... | 174,820½ | 265,155½ |
| April..................... | 156,445½ | 285,515 | | | |
| May...................... | 180,184½ | 335,206 | Total............... | 1,595,126½ | 2,413,779½ |
| June ..................... | 170,864½ | 243,358 | | | |

Increase in 1902, 818,659½ pounds.

## BRITISH COTTON GROWING ASSOCIATION.

Three months ago, chiefly at the instigation of the Oldham Chamber of Commerce, the British Cotton Growing Association was constituted, with a view to obtaining a supply of cotton grown in British colonies, and thus obviate as much as possible the shortages, or rumors of shortages, in the crop of America. To that end, the association proposes to raise a guaranty fund of £50,000 ($243,325) and to dispatch expeditions of experts to various parts of the world for the purpose of reporting upon the best methods of procedure. A considerable part of the guaranty fund of £50,000 ($243,325) has already been promised, and it is said no difficulty is likely to arise through lack of funds. It is significant that the operatives, no less than the manufacturers, are showing themselves anxious to assist in the work.

## THE BRITISH WESTINGHOUSE ELECTRIC AND MANUFACTURING COMPANY, LIMITED.

Following is a brief description of this company's plant at Trafford Park, Manchester: The works occupy some 130 acres of land, on which have been erected six buildings, which include brass and malleable-iron foundries, pattern shops and stores, a steel foundry and forge, a drying and dipping shed, an electrical power generating station, a machine shop, and a box factory.

The machine shop, 1,000 feet long and 450 feet wide, is claimed to be the largest building devoted to this purpose in England. Messrs. Sellers, of Philadelphia, have supplied a 28-foot boring mill for use in this department.

The works at present give employment to some 2,000 hands (a good many of whom are Americans), but this number will be trebled when all the departments are in full operation.

The principal contracts upon which the company is engaged at the present time are as follows:

Dynamo machinery of 1,500 horsepower for the Swansea corporation; 400-horsepower alternator for the New Zealand Electrical Syndicate; electrical power plants of 300 to 800 horsepower for the Birmingham Small Arms Company, Dorman Long & Co., Thomas Smith & Co., of Rodley, and the Oak Bank Oil Company; 650-horsepower rotary converter for the London United Tramways; 500-horsepower alternators for the South Wales Power and Distribution Company, and plant for the Clyde Valley power-generating stations.

## TRADE BETWEEN THE UNITED STATES AND MANCHESTER VIA THE MANCHESTER SHIP CANAL.

As the history and principal physical features of the Manchester Ship Canal are now so well known, the following notes on this waterway refer only to the direct trade between American ports and Manchester passing through it.

Since the opening of the canal in 1894, there has been a steady annual increase in the direct imports and exports via this waterway. New connections with American ports have been formed from time to time, and during the twelve months ended June 30, 1902, the freight landed at the Manchester docks from the United States amounted in weight to 377,750 tons, from which it will be seen that America contributes a goodly proportion toward the 4,000,000 tons of trade annually passing inward and outward through the canal.

It will be seen from the following remarks that every port of importance in the United States seaboard is connected with Manchester, and that ample arrangements have been made to keep the berths well supplied with tonnage.

*New Orleans.*—During the cotton season, steamers are regularly berthed at New Orleans for Manchester, the loading agents being Messrs. Meletta & Stoddart. These steamers are well equipped for the conveyance of cotton and grain, which commodities form the bulk of the cargoes carried. Consignments of lumber, resin, starch, lard, sugar, soap, etc., are also occasionally shipped. During the cotton season of 1901–2, ten steamers loaded at New Orleans for Manchester, bringing here 93,397 bales of cotton, 26,593 tons of grain, and general cargo. The shipments from New Orleans to Manchester usually commence later than from other Gulf ports, but it is expected that the trade during the present season will compare favorably with that of past years.

*Galveston.*—An excellent supply of tonnage for Manchester is provided by Messrs. Fowler & McVittie, of Galveston, the majority of vessels in this service being owned by Messrs. Larrinaga & Co., whose new sheltered-deck steamers with extensive accommodation for cotton cargoes are employed in the trade. The principal items of export from Galveston to Manchester during last season were 171,927 bales of cotton, 5,765 tons of grain, 2,000 tons of pig lead, etc.

The season now opening appears likely to be a record one so far as the direct shipments from Galveston to Manchester are concerned. From the commencement of the season, cotton has been offered very freely, and the evident desire of the shipowners running the service to keep the berth well supplied with tonnage is much appreciated by the shippers. As an indication of the increased shipments this season, it may be mentioned that from September 1 to October 22, 60,644 bales of cotton have been shipped at Galveston for Manchester, as compared with 21,020 bales during the corresponding period of last year.

*Mobile.*—In previous cotton seasons, steamers have been loaded at Mobile for Manchester by various shipping agents, but under a recent agreement, Messrs. Elder Deempster & Co., of Liverpool, are in future to provide all the tonnage necessary at Mobile for loading to ports in the United Kingdom.

*Pensacola.*—The United States Shipping Company is berthing steamers regularly at Pensacola for Manchester. In addition to cotton, lumber, etc., a considerable quantity of phosphate rock finds an outlet at Pensacola for this city, Runcorn, and other points on the Manchester Ship Canal. In the latter connection, it may be mentioned that one of the largest consumers of phosphate rock in England has works on the banks of the Manchester Ship Canal, to which the mineral is delivered direct from the vessel.

*Brunswick, Ga.*—Steamers for Manchester are loaded regularly at this port during the winter season by Messrs. F. D. M. Strachan & Co., the cargoes consisting chiefly of cotton and phosphate rock.

*Savannah.*—The Churchill line maintains a frequent service of steamers between Savannah and Manchester during the cotton season. These steamers secure large quantities of cotton, of which Sea Island

forms a large proportion, also resin, phosphate, etc. Messrs. Minis &
Co., of Savannah, also load steamers occasionally for Manchester.

Sailing vessels with full cargoes of resin from Savannah are frequently ordered to Manchester to discharge. Large stocks of resin
are held at Manchester and distributed to the immediate district and
to towns in Lancashire, Yorkshire, and the Midlands.

*Philadelphia.*—A line of steamers, worked jointly by the Manchester
Limited and the Leyland Shipping Company, was established about
twelve months ago to run regularly between Philadelphia and Manchester. At present, there is one sailing every three weeks, but it is
the intention of the owners shortly to inaugurate a ten days' service.
The steamers running in the trade are first-class boats, with live cattle
accommodation and a dead weight capacity of 6,000 to 8,000 tons.
Since the line commenced operations, large shipments of live cattle,
grain, oil, copper, provisions, flour, lumber, woodenware, starch,
glucose, and other commodities have been made from Philadelphia to
Manchester; and when other boats are added to the service, this will
undoubtedly prove one of the most important lines running into Manchester from American ports. The loading agents at Philadelphia are
Messrs. Charles M. Taylor's Sons, and an important feature in connection with the service is that the Philadelphia and Reading Railroad
Company is closely interested in it; the steamers loading and discharging at the latter's piers.

*New York.*—A regular weekly service between New York and Manchester is maintained all the year round by Messrs. Lamport & Holt.
The steamers employed in this trade make triangular voyages from
Manchester to South America, thence to New York, and from New
York back to Manchester. This line is well known among shippers
and controls a large amount of traffic. The cargoes carried are very
varied, consisting of all descriptions of American produce and manufactures. The steamers occasionally carry live cattle, and the fact that
Messrs. Lamport & Holt have recently added several of their new and
better equipped steamers to the service appears to be much appreciated, both by shippers and consignees. The loading agents in New
York are Messrs. Busk & Jevons.

*Boston.*—The latest steam connection between the United States and
Manchester, and one that is likely to have a far-reaching effect on the
developments of the trade of the Manchester Ship Canal, is the establishment of a line of first-class freight steamers between Boston and
Manchester. It is officially announced that, commencing in January
next, the American Shipping Combine, or, to use the correct title, the
International Mercantile Marine Company, will run steamers regularly
between the two ports, commencing with fortnightly sailings, which
will probably be extended to a weekly service as soon as the line is
firmly established. The steamers employed in the trade will have a
cargo capacity of about 8,000 tons each and will be provided with
refrigerator space for beef and other perishable cargo, and with shelter
decks for live cattle. The steamers will be berthed at the South Boston
terminals of the New York, New Haven and Hartford Railroad, and
the grain elevator and piers controlled by that company are now being
altered to accommodate large ocean-going steamers.

This service will undoubtedly prove a useful outlet for American
commodities, and it is expected that it will be a precursor of steamship lines from other American ports to Manchester, under the auspices

of the International Mercantile Marine Company. The New York, New Haven and Hartford Railroad, with its extensive connecting lines, will deliver to the steamers at the Boston terminals live cattle, chilled beef, provisions, cotton, iron and steel, flour, leather, lumber, machinery, and all other descriptions of American produce, in the shape of food stuffs, raw materials, and manufactured articles, which are so largely consumed in Manchester and the densely populated district of which Manchester forms the center. It may be mentioned that Manchester is not dependent upon local traffic, but is essentially a port of distribution also. In the carting area from the Manchester docks there is a population of 2,000,000, and it is asserted that the district nearer to Manchester than to any other steamship port in the United Kingdom contains a population of no less than 8,000,000 people.

A thorough investigation into the possibilities of trade conducted by a first-class line of steamers between Boston and Manchester tends to show that all the elements are present for the success of the venture.

There should be no lack of export traffic from the United States to Manchester, and plenty of good paying west-bound cargo can undoubtedly be worked through Manchester to all parts of North America via Boston.

WILLIAM F. GRINNELL, *Consul.*

MANCHESTER, *October 30, 1902.*

## NEWCASTLE-UPON-TYNE.

The declared value of the exports from the consular district of Newcastle-upon-Tyne (including the consular agencies of Carlisle, West Hartlepool, and Sunderland) during the last three years ended June 30, were:

| | |
|---|---|
| 1899–1900 | $1,225,298 |
| 1900–1901 | 1,218,568 |
| 1901–2 | 1,641,592 |

consisting of ship's anchors, antimony, antiquities, asphalt (liquid and concrete), aniline oil, binoxide of barium, biscuits, brass (old scrap), basic wire rods, bound books, brattice cloth, bricks (fire bricks), carbonate of barytes, carpets, china clay, coals, coke, composition paint (materials for making), colors, cotton manufactures, cement, chemicals (caustic soda, crystal soda, pearl hardening, and sulphate of ammonia), diamond grit, fireclay, fire tiles, fishing tackle, ferromanganese, ferrosilicon, fertilizers, fire bricks, goatskins (dressed), golf-club heads (aluminum), ground gannister, hats (felt), household and personal effects, iron (pig, Bessemer, Hematite), sulphide of iron, leather (dressed sealskin and dressed Morocco), sealskins, felts, dressed goatskins, linen and union goods, litharge, machinery for ships, minerals (specimens of), ores (fluor spar), paint, paper stock, pictures, red and white lead, rope (old, for papermakers), sanding machine, salt, sheep wash, silico spiegel, spiegeleisen, skins (hare and coney), ship's stores, steel wire rope, grindstones, steel bars, tin cannisters, trees and bushes (young), whisky, wire-rope making machinery, wire rods, woolen goods.

Owing to the extraordinary demand by the United States for pig iron, the shipments of that material from this consular district to America, for the quarter ended June 30, 1902, amount to the value of $1,712,428.

There have also been large shipments, during the last twelve months, of coke and fire bricks to San Francisco, Los Angeles, and Portland, Oreg.

Owing to the great coal strike in the United States, inquiries respecting shipments of coal to America have been made, but so far, no transactions have occurred as regards north country coal. The only shipments of coal to the United States have been from Wales; but this trade, of course, owing to the nature of things, is only temporary.

A larger number of sailing vessels laden with cargo have left the Tyne for American Pacific ports during the past eighteen months than for many years.

### IMPORTS FROM UNITED STATES.

*Miscellaneous goods imported from the United States into the river Tyne, from January 1 to December 31, 1901.*

| | |
|---|---|
| Box and bale goods ..package.. | 1 |
| Soap.....................tons.. | 38 |
| Chemicals, unenumerated, tons....................... | 28 |
| Glucose..................tons.. | 214 |
| Rice .....................do.... | 3 |
| Tobacco, cigars, and snuff.cwt.. | 4 |
| Cotton, jute, linen, and wool goods...................tons.. | 47 |
| Drysalters' stores .......do.... | 30 |
| Glass.....................do.... | 2 |
| Barley ...,..........quarters.. | 36 |
| Maize ....................do.... | 99,295 |
| Oats......................do.... | 9,473 |
| Pease ....................do.... | 5,142 |
| Wheat ...................do.... | 420,221 |
| Cotton and linseed cake, quarters .......................... | 470 |
| Flour and meal...........tons.. | 3,565 |
| Hay and straw...........do.... | 354 |
| Hair .....................do.... | 20 |
| Machinery ..............do.... | 1,067 |
| Forgings and other ironwork, tons....................... | 455 |
| Pig iron .................tons.. | 502 |
| Scrap iron ..............do.... | 817 |
| Steel angles, bars, plates, and sheets ................tons.. | 83 |
| Steel castings ...........do.... | 235 |
| Steel forgings and manufactures, tons .......................... | 35 |
| Steel rails...............tons.. | 552 |
| Steel billets, blooms, and crop ends...................tons.. | 1,298 |
| Litharge and colors......do.... | 111 |
| Pig lead ................do.... | 983 |
| Cows and oxen .......head.... | 819 |
| Manures, phosphates ....tons.. | 4,218 |
| Copper, copper precipitate, and copper ore ............tons.. | 219 |
| Slates ...................do.... | 1,960 |
| Tin and tin lumps.......do.... | 1 |
| Oils (mineral)...........do.... | 15,213 |
| Other oils ..............do.... | 6 |
| Turpentine, varnish, and putty, tons .... | 2 |
| Paper....................tons.. | 719 |
| Pianos and organs.............. | 2 |
| Bacon and pork .........tons.. | 391 |
| Beef ....................do.... | 194 |
| Cheese ..................do.... | 222 |
| Lard ....................do.... | 638 |
| Milk ....................do.... | 1 |
| Preserved meats ........do.... | 506 |
| Sundry goods...........do.... | 303 |
| Resin ...................do.... | 1,286 |
| Tar and pitch..........barrel.. | 1 |
| Deals, battens, and boards, loads ........................ | 4,842 |
| Mahogany ..............tons.. | 94 |
| Staves and headings ....loads.. | 4 |
| Square and other timber.do.... | 19,333 |
| Furniture...........packages.. | 24 |
| Other wood goods .......tons.. | 829 |

*Miscellaneous goods imported from the United States into the Tyne during the six months ended June 30, 1902.*

| | | | | |
|---|---|---|---|---|
| Cotton goods ...........cwt.. | 4 | Slate ................tons.. | 484 |
| Soap.....................tons.. | 1½ | Tin, etc................. cwt.. | 3 |
| Chemicals (unenumerated), | | Mineral oil.............tons.. | 8,289$\frac{7}{10}$ |
| tons ...................... | 37$\frac{3}{10}$ | Tar and pitch (mineral) do.... | 43¼ |
| China clay and china stone, | | Paper..................do.... | 187½ |
| cwt.................... | 13 | Pianos and organs............ | 9 |
| Glucose................tons.. | 105$\frac{3}{10}$ | Bacon and pork.......do.... | 153¼ |
| Drysalters' stores ......tons.. | 10$\frac{1}{10}$ | Beef...................do.... | 55$\frac{2}{10}$ |
| Glass.................do.... | 1½ | Cheese.................do.... | 114$\frac{3}{10}$ |
| Barley .............quarters.. | 7,036 | Lard..................do.... | 267$\frac{1}{10}$ |
| Maize..................do.... | 14,117 | Milk ..................cwt.. | 14 |
| Pease ..................do.... | 976 | Preserved meats ......do.... | 182 |
| Wheat...............do.... | 190,418 | Sundries.............do.... | 173 |
| Flour and meal........tons.. | 1,530$\frac{3}{10}$ | Steel angles, etc........do.... | 5$\frac{1}{10}$ |
| Hay and straw........do.... | 1,315$\frac{3}{10}$ | Steel castings..........do.... | 2$\frac{1}{10}$ |
| Iron castings..........do.... | 3$\frac{9}{10}$ | Steel forgings.........do.... | 3¼ |
| Machinery ..........do.... | 287 | Resin .................do.... | 2,251½ |
| Forgings and other iron work, | | Deals, battens, and boards, | |
| tons ..................... | 65 | loads ..................... | 877 |
| Scrap iron ............tons.. | 179 | Mahogany.............tons.. | 37$\frac{1}{10}$ |
| Lead colors. ..........do.... | 39½ | Staves, etc..........loads.. | 9 |
| Pig lead ...............do.... | 150 | Other timbers......... do.... | 4,277 |
| Cows and oxen.............. | 370 | Furniture........ packages.. | 121 |
| Copper...............cwt.. | 1 | Joinery, etc............tons.. | 265½½ |
| Coal and coke .........tons.. | 1$\frac{1}{10}$ | Wood pulp............ do.... | 15$\frac{1}{10}$ |

### PROSPECTS FOR AMERICAN TRADE.

Owing to the absence of duties on imported manufactured goods, competition is simply a question of freight rates, and after allowing for this difference, goods manufactured in New York or Chicago can compete in price here with goods made in London, Birmingham, or Glasgow. It only remains for firms to have their goods placed through reliable agencies and properly advertised, or to send over here qualified travelers to represent them. All kinds of tinned goods have a big field in England; American boots and shoes are sold extensively; doors and window sashes arrive here regularly, and roofing slates, hair for plasterers' use, farmers' implements, etc., are being more and more imported. Perhaps trade in these lines could be pushed. Print paper also has a market here, and machinery and mechanics' tools, etc., used in the various factories are plainly in evidence. American bicycles are also sold in this country, although having to face keen competition, while cameras and photographers' supplies have a good market and are well spoken of.

### SHIPBUILDING.

The following is a summary of the returns from the Tyne yards for the year 1901:

| | Tons. |
|---|---|
| Sir W. G. Armstrong, Whitworth & Co., Limited ......................... | 39,597 |
| C. S. Swan & Hunter, Limited .................................... | [a]49,087 |
| Wigham, Richardson & Co., Limited ............................. | 36,791 |
| Palmers, Shipbuilding and Iron Company, Limited...................... | [a]61,016 |
| Northumberland Shipbuilding Company..................................... | 31,330 |
| John Redhead & Sons .................................. | [a]26,667 |
| R. & W. Hawthorn, Leslie & Co .......................................... | 24,008 |
| Tyne Iron Shipbuilding Company.......................................... | [a]16,700 |

[a] Gross tonnage, with erections.

| | Tons. |
|---|---|
| Wm. Dobson & Co | 14,712 |
| R. Stephenson & Co. | 13,586 |
| Wood, Skinner & Co | 9,602 |
| Smith's Dock Company, Limited | 2,039 |
| J. P. Reunoldson & Co | 2,609 |
| J. T. Eltringham & Co | 1,114 |
| W. P. Huntley | 205 |
| Hepple & Co | 120 |
| Total | 329,183 |

These figures show an increase of 33,183 tons as compared with 1890. The amount of shipbuilding work on hand (July, 1902) in the yards of the United Kingdom is the lowest since the beginning of the century. The northeast coast ports are worse off; and especially is this noticeable when comparison is made with the conditions of a year ago. On the Tees, for instance, with 24 vessels of 69,353 tons, there is a decrease of 43,000 tons as compared with the total of July, 1901; on the Tyne, with 74 vessels of 192,488 tons, the fall is proportionately almost as great—73,300 tons; at Hartlepool, the drop is about 27,000 tons, the amount of work now being 14 vessels of 64,163 tons, and at Sunderland, where the vessels on the stocks number 42, and measure 155,058 tons, the decrease is 23,500 tons.

The firm of Sir W. G. Armstrong, Whitworth & Co., Limited, has declared (September, 1902), a dividend of 15 per cent on its ordinary shares, after adding $250,000 to the reserve, $400,000 for provision for experimental expenditure, and $150,000 on account of its liability under the workmen's compensation act.

As showing the demand for large ships, it was stated at the annual meeting of Palmer's Shipbuilding and Iron Company (September 29, 1902) that in 1899 the average tonnage of its ships was 2,309 tons, while last year it was 7,627 tons. This firm has done a good deal of work for the British Government lately, building the battle ship *Russell*, which has since passed very successfully through her official trials. It has also finished putting new engines and boilers in H. M. S. *Niger* and the *Gossamer*. The *Medea* and the *Medusa* have been refitted with new boilers; the battle ship *Howe* is now being overhauled. The company has also received from the Admiralty orders for 5 new torpedo-boat destroyers of the improved type, making 21 vessels of that class which have been ordered from the firm for His Majesty's fleet in the last few years.

The largest oil-tank steamer yet built on the Tyne, the *New York*, was dispatched September 29 on her first voyage to New York. This vessel was built to the order of a Dutch firm, and has a carrying capacity of 9,200 tons.

Messrs. Wigham, Richardson & Co., Walker-on-Tyne, has this year built the largest cable ship afloat, the *Colonia*, which on her trial trip developed a speed of 14½ knots per hour, with 5,300-horsepower. This vessel was built to the order of the Telegraph Construction and Maintenance Company, Limited, for the purpose of laying submarine telegraph cables, in conjunction with the *Anglia*, owned by the same firm. The *Colonia* can carry about 4,000 nautical miles of cables, accomodated in four large tanks built in her holds. She is about 500 feet in length, 56 in breadth, and 39 feet in depth, and carries 11,000 tons dead weight. Compared with the *Great Eastern*, the *Colonia* has almost twice the former's cable-carrying capacity.   Moreover, the *Great Eastern* could lay only about 1,800 miles of cable without being reloaded, while the *Colonia* could lay a cable almost twice across the Atlantic.   The vessel left the Tyne in May for Vancouver, via the Suez Canal.

Messrs. C. S. Swan & Hunter, Limited, Wallsend on Tyne, in February last launched a large floating dock for His Majesty's dockyard at Bermuda.   This dock is 515 feet long, and is without gates, hence the length of ship it can take is not restricted.   Its lifting power is 15,500 tons, which can be increased to 17,500 tons, if necessary.

This firm, the following August, launched another floating dock for the port of Durban, Natal.   This dock is of the same type as that described above, though smaller, having a lifting power of only 4,500 tons.   Its extreme length is 365 feet and its width 87 feet.   The distance between the guard timbers on the side walls is 61 feet, so that the dock can accommodate vessels up to 60 feet beam, while, when still retaining a freeboard of 4 feet, it can take a vessel drawing 18 feet over keel blocks 4 feet high.   The dock proper consists of 3 pontoons and two side walls, to which the pontoons are connected by means of movable joints, so that any of the pontoons can when required be removed and lifted by the dock itself, thus making it self-docking in all its parts.

A steel pontoon at North Shields was recently lifted for examination.   The occasion was interesting in so much as when this pontoon was built engineers and others prophesied that frequent renewals of certain parts would be necessary on account of the corrosive action of salt water, which, it was claimed, would prevent pontoons of this class being adopted, ten years being named as about the length of their existence.   The protection afforded by the "bitumastic" enamel coating, however, has proved that instead of lasting only ten years, the pontoons are more likely to last fifty.

Messrs. C. S. Swan & Hunter, Limited, also launched on the same day the Cunard steamship *Carpathia*, which is intended for the Liverpool-Boston service.   She is designed as a saloon and third-class passenger and cargo steamer, with large insulated chambers for chilled meat and ship's stores.   Provision is made for about 200 saloon and about 600 third-class passengers, with ample space for extending either or both classes of accommodation as may hereafter be found desirable. The leading particulars of the vessel are: Length, 558 feet; breadth, 64 feet 3 inches; depth molded to the upper deck, 40 feet 6 inches; depth molded to the shelter deck, 48 feet 6 inches; gross tonnage, about 12,900 tons; speed on trial, about $15\frac{1}{4}$ knots.   The *Carpathia* will be propelled by 2 independent sets of quadruple expansion engines, with cylinders 26, 37, 53, and 76 inches in diameter, and a stroke of 54 inches.   Steam will be supplied by seven large single-ended boilers, fitted with Howden's forced draft.

The same company in 1901 built the steamers *Lake Michigan* and *Lake Manitoba* for the Beaver Line, the latter vessel being of 9,510 tons, and the former of 8,699 tons gross.   Two other vessels of exceptional size that are being constructed are the *Patrician*, of 7,474 gross tons, and the *Santa Fe*, of 5,220 gross tons.   The latter is for the Hamburg and South American Company.

## MARINE ENGINEERING.

The year 1901 was a very successful one for marine engineers on Tyne side. The indicated horsepower put into vessels built by the different firms was as follows:

| | |
|---|---:|
| Palmer's Shipbuilding and Iron Company, Limited | 39,050 |
| C. S. Swan & Hunter, Limited | 23,420 |
| J. T. Eltringham & Co | 1,940 |
| Hepple & Co | 1,050 |
| Sir W. G. Armstrong Whitworth & Co., Limited | 25,750 |
| Wigham, Richardson & Co., Limited | 20,200 |
| Northumberland Shipbuilding Company, Limited | 15,400 |
| John Redhead & Sons | 12,300 |
| R. & W. Hawthorn, Leslie & Co., Limited | 64,050 |
| William Dobson & Co | 7,900 |
| Tyne Iron Shipbuilding Company, Limited | 7,850 |
| J. P. Rennoldson & Co | 3,337 |
| Total | 222,247 |

## THE COAL TRADE.

*Coal and coke shipped from the port of Tyne.*

| Description. | Foreign and coastwise. | | |
|---|---|---|---|
| | 1901. | 1900. | Increase (+) or decrease (−). |
| | *Tons.* | *Tons.* | *Tons.* |
| Coal | 14,558,622 | 14,040,294 | +518,328 |
| Coke | 375,013 | 480,635 | −105,622 |
| Total coal and coke | 14,933,635 | 14,520,929 | +412,706 |

Following are the board of trade returns for the coal shipments from the ports of Amble, Blyth, the Tyne, the Wear, West Hartlepool, and the Tees, during the first five months of 1902:

| | Tons. |
|---|---:|
| January | 28,000 |
| February | 34,000 |
| March | 103,000 |
| April | 25,000 |
| May | 137,000 |
| Total | 327,000 |

Northumbrian steam coals (October 3, 1902) are steady at 11s. 3d. = $2.74 to 11s. 6d. =$2.80 per ton, free on board; best second-class steam, from 9s. =$2.19 to 9s. 9d. =$2.37 per ton, and steam smalls, 5s. =$1.22 per ton. Gas coal is quoted from 9s. =$2.19 to 9s. 9d. =$2.37 per ton, according to quality. In the bunker coal trade, the inquiry is good and supplies are ample. The price of Durham unscreened varies from 8s. 9d. =$2.13 to 9s. 6d. =$2.31 per ton, free on board. In the coke trade, there is a steady demand and good prices are maintained. Best Durham coke for export is about 18s. =$4.38 to 18s. 6d. per ton, free on board, and blast furnace coke, 16s. =$3.89 per ton at the Teeside furnaces.

The river Tyne commissioners are alive to the importance of being able to bunker vessels of large size, and have recently had built two new staiths on the river front, capable of dealing with vessels of any tonnage and at all tides.   They have also just passed a resolution to construct another new river staith southwest of the Albert Edward Dock, at a cost of $258,000.   The staiths both in the dock and on the river have been fitted with anticoal-breakage appliances.   Large vessels can arrive at and depart from these staiths at either high or low water.

A large number of Grimsby steam fishing boats, within the past few weeks, have commenced to take in their bunker coal at Northumberland Dock.   This is a new departure, as hitherto these boats have bunkered at Grimsby, with coal from the Midlands.

Fifty-seven thousand tons of coal are said to have been contracted for shipment to New York and Boston, and one Northumbrian colliery is reported to have arranged to supply 20,000 tons to th · same places.

## STEAMSHIP FREIGHTS.

The freight market has been for some time in a depressed condition, the rates outward being wretchedly low.   The following are the present quotations from Tyne:

Cape, 15s. 6d. = $3.77: Santos, 2,500 coals, 300 coke, 14s. = $3.36 and 16s. = $3.89, respectively; London, 3s. 3d. = 79 cents; Cronstadt, 4s. 3d. = $1.03; Swinemunde, 4s. 3d. = $1.03; Genoa, 4s. 6d. = $1.09 to 4s. 9d. = $1.15.

In homeward chartering, the tone is quiet, with perhaps the exception of Calcutta, where a steady demand exists.   From the Black Sea and Danube, calls are dull.   The American requirements are also very limited.

There are now, however, only about a dozen steamers laid up in the Tyne, as compared with 55 at the commencement of the year

## ELECTRIC TRAMS.

*Newcastle.*—A portion of the street-railway system owned by the municipal corporation was opened for traffic on December 16 last. Since then, nearly the whole system has been put in running order, with a very good service.   Owing to the very high cost of construction, however, there are doubts whether the trams can ultimately be made to pay.   The receipts for the week ended September 27 amounted to $15,030.   It is estimated by some that fares should reach $17,500 weekly to show a profit; but at a meeting on October 1, the chairman of the trams committee stated that the expenses of the system were only about $12,000 a week, while the receipts for the past month averaged $14,750 a week, or a clear profit of $2,500.

*Tyneside tramways*—The new tramway line from Gosforth to New Shields, via Benton, Wallsend, and Willington, constructed by the Tyneside Tramways and Tramroad Company during the last few months, was formally opened on September 29.   The system adopted is the overhead trolley, similar to that of Newcastle and Gateshead line.   Part of the Wallsend-North Shields tram has proved a boon to workmen employed in the shipyards and factories on the river side.   It enters into competition with the North Eastern Railway Company's two lines of railroad from Newcastle to North Shields so strongly that the North Eastern directors are contemplating the early electrification of about 38 miles of their Tyneside tracks.

The system they purpose to adopt is that known as the third-rail system, in which the current is taken from a rail or conductor laid alongside the running rails. Six hundred and fifty volts will be used, which is 150 volts higher than is allowed for tramway purposes. The current will be purchased by the North Eastern Railway Company from the existing station of the Newcastle Electric Power Company, whence it will be sent out at 6,000 volts, and afterwards transformed at the various substations to the working pressure just mentioned. The speed of the trains will be 22 miles per hour.

*South Shields.*—The town council has just resolved (September) to apply for Parliamentary powers authorizing the construction of a system of overhead electric tramways to replace the antiquated horse cars now in vogue. It is estimated that the cost will be $1,066,800.

*Jarrow on Tyne.*—The overhead system of tramways, which is being universally adopted on Tyneside, is expected soon to be in operation in this town. It is also expected that a tramway will shortly be laid from Haworth to South Shields, which will form a line of about 10 miles in length on the south side of the Tyne.

### NEW STEAMSHIP LINES.

A line of steamers between Russia and the Tyne will be established in November next. Messrs. Forwood Brothers & Co., of Newcastle, who have been appointed the agents of the Nord Steamship Company, of Finland, whose head office is in Helsingsfors, will control the service. The project will receive a subsidy from the Russian Government. Three steamers for the new line are now being built on the northeast coast. They are to be fine, powerful vessels, fitted with the very latest improvements in shipbuilding. In them will be built refrigerating plants for Finnish butter and other perishable goods. Most of these imports at present go to Hull, whence they are conveyed by train to Newcastle and other districts. The new steamers will also have accommodation for emigrants; and it is probable that a good many Finns on their way to America will come to Newcastle, thence making the overland journey to Liverpool, where they will take trans-Atlantic steamers. The new line will be a great convenience to exporters, and goods that come from many parts of the country will be shipped from here.

### QUAYS.

Owing to the lack of berthing accommodations, there have for years been many complaints of the detention of vessels coming to Newcastle, and at last the corporation have taken the matter seriously into consideration, and intend very shortly to seek Parliamentary powers to extend the quay a distance of 3,200 feet. The present quay is about 4,600 feet long. Instead of only 30 feet storage room on the quay there will be, under the new plan, a width of 150 to 200 feet for landing goods, a greater depth of water, better lifting appliances, and vessels will be free to arrive or depart on all tides, making Newcastle the finest port on the northeast coast. The rates will be half as cheap as those at London. A tremendous quantity of produce and manufactured goods is shipped from the United States to the north of England, and to these the new improvements will mean much cheaper freight rates. Messrs. Wilson, of Hull, intend to establish a much better and more frequent service of steamers between New York and Newcastle, if the proposed extensions are carried out. The scheme, as originally proposed, was to cost $3,500,000, but after several meetings of the finance committee and of shipowners and merchants, it was finally decided to carry out the improvements only as necessity demanded. To show the immediate demand for additional quay space, no less than 709,000 register tons of shipping came to Newcastle in 1901.

### THE FRUIT TRADE.

A large trade in canned fruits, and also to a certain extent in fresh fruits, exists between the north of England and the United States. A few quotations of the prices realized in the Newcastle market may be of interest to American growers:

Local-grown peaches sell from 4d. (8 cents) to 8d. (16 cents) each, according to size. Pineapples are scarcer, fetching 4s. 6d. ($1.09) each, retail. Filberts are more plentiful, 8d. (16 cents) per pound being asked. Bananas of the finer quality are selling at 1s. 6d. (36 cents) per dozen; the commoner sorts at 1s. (24 cents). English grapes are marked at 1s. (24 cents) to 2s. (49 cents) per pound, according to quality—Guernsey grown can be bought at 8d. (16 cents) a pound. Plums, 4d. (8 cents) to 6d. (12 cents) per pound. Tomatoes can be had in any quantity, the English sorts selling at 8d. (16 cents) a pound, and the commoner kinds at 4d. (8 cents). English melons are selling at 1s. 6d. (36 cents) each, for good ones; foreign ones are retailed at 4d. (8 cents). Canadian apples are retailed at 4d. (8 cents) a pound, and are of fine quality. The English descriptions are rather scarce, the best sorts fetching 3s. (73 cents) a stone, and others about 2s. (49 cents). There is a choice variety of pears on sale. French Williams are retailed at 6d. (12 cents) to 8d. (16 cents) a pound, and the Duchess kind at 8d. (16 cents). English hazels are marked at 3d. (6 cents) and Williams at 4d. (8 cents). Of American fruits, apples, pears, plums, and grapes appear to be in most demand.

### CLOSE OF HISTORIC WORKS.

The historic engineering plant of Messrs. Robert Stephenson & Co. has been dismantled and sold at auction. The firm has moved to Darlington, where it has built works and fitted them with the newest and most improved machinery. In the razing of the workshop of the old plant an interesting link with the past was severed, for in that building was born the first of all locomotives—the "Rocket," of George Stephenson.

At the auction sale, 300 lots were disposed of, ranging from locomotive engines, steam hammers, and chimney stacks to wooden beams and scrap iron. Some of the machines sold had been in constant use for sixty years. The choicest bit of old machinery—the lever-beam engine, designed by George Stephenson to drive the plant of the original factory—did not, however, come under the hammer at all. Working up to a fortnight previous to the sale, this famous old engine had been in use for nearly eighty years. It will shortly be pedestaled in triumph in the new works at Darlington—an honor well won. Messrs. Stephenson & Co. will not sever their connection with Newcastle altogether, as it is their intention still to retain their foundry at Tyneside.

## PAUPERISM.

The following tables are an interesting and encouraging comparison between the amount of pauperism in the county of Northumberland now and thirty years ago:

| Year. | Population. | Paupers. | Per 1,000. |
|---|---|---|---|
| 1871 | 386,645 | 16,648 | 42.6 |
| 1875 | 410,366 | 10,671 | 25.0 |
| 1881 | 434,086 | 11,152 | 25.7 |
| 1886 | 470,058 | 11,036 | 23.6 |
| 1891 | 506,030 | 10,179 | 20.1 |
| 1896 | 564,444 | 11,010 | 19.9 |
| 1901 | 602,859 | 10,446 | 17.3 |

This table gives, for the year 1901, the population, the mean annual number of paupers, and the ratio of pauperism for each of the twelve poor-law unions in Northumberland:

| Union. | Population. | Paupers. | Per 1,000. |
|---|---|---|---|
| Newcastle | 233,150 | 3,858 | 16.5 |
| Tynemouth | 168,881 | 2,658 | 15.8 |
| Castle Ward | 32,406 | 360 | 11.1 |
| Hexham | 34,709 | 929 | 26.8 |
| Haltwhistle | 8,500 | 98 | 11.5 |
| Bellingham | 6,339 | 113 | 17.9 |
| Morpeth | 55,743 | 1,106 | 19.8 |
| Alnwick | 23,661 | 545 | 23.0 |
| Belford | 5,218 | 86 | 16.5 |
| Berwick | 19,491 | 404 | 20.7 |
| Glendale | 8,770 | 188 | 21.4 |
| Rothbury | 5,992 | 90 | 15.1 |

The next table gives details similar to those in the first table, with regard to the Newcastle Union:

| Year. | Population. | Paupers. | Per 1,000. |
|---|---|---|---|
| 1871 | 131,198 | 6,287 | 47.9 |
| 1876 | 140,725 | 2,895 | 20.6 |
| 1881 | 150,252 | 2,735 | 18.2 |
| 1886 | 173,584 | 3,328 | 19.2 |
| 1891 | 196,817 | 3,277 | 16.6 |
| 1896 | 214,983 | 4,037 | 18.8 |
| 1901 | 233,150 | 3,858 | 16.5 |

### PORT OF BLYTH.

Although idle tonnage is accumulating in Blyth Harbor—six steamers of considerable size being laid up in the South Dock—the coal trade is still booming. This is due chiefly to the fact that the coal is being sent to Blyth to be shipped from the Northumberland collieries, instead of to Northumberland Dock, North Shields, as formerly. The coal shipments at Blyth for the week ending September 27, 1902, consisted of 69,284 tons, an increase compared with the corresponding week of last year of 7,642 tons. During the month of August, 283,606 tons were shipped, an increase, compared with the corresponding month of last year, of 21,179 tons. Blyth continues to prosper; and notwithstanding house building has gone on uninterruptedly, there is still a scarcity of homes for the working classes.

### CARLISLE.

In reporting upon the trade of this district twelve months ago, I stated that the previous year had been one of fairly steady progress; that, while wages had not been quite so high as in the previous three years, the working classes generally had never been better off. Very similar remarks would describe the trade of the past twelve months. Probably, however, so far as can be judged from the reports of public companies, the year now ending has been in some respects a more favorable one for capitalists than was its immediate predecessors.

The dividends of the local railway companies have kept well up, and the reports of some of the leading iron companies show that they have passed through a year of very good trade. So far as regards the immediate future, trade prospects are hopeful, always provided that there is no serious labor trouble. Just at the present time, the coal owners of Cumberland are anxious for a reduction of 10 per cent on the wages of the colliers. This proposal is resisted by the latter, but, happily, both parties have agreed to abide by the arbitrament of the neutral chairman of the conciliation board, who is the clerk of the peace for the county. That gentleman is now engaged in hearing evidence. His decision will probably be given before the end of the present month.

The fact that the parties to this dispute have been willing to resort to arbitration may be taken as an evidence that the relations between the coal owners and their workmen are generally amicable.

It was stated in the report which was prepared a year ago that there was a movement on foot looking to the establishment of a technical college for West Cumberland, it being generally felt that those employed in the iron, coal, and kindred trades should receive an education which would enable them better to hold their own with workmen of the United States and of Germany. There is a general desire for the establishment of such a college, and the Cumberland county council has the scheme in hand. There are, however, difficulties in the way of its establishment. In the first place, there is keen contention between Whitehaven and Workington as to which of these towns shall be the site of the college, and there is further difficulty as to what shall be the area of rating for its maintenance.

### THE IRON TRADE.

The reports of the meetings of several of the Workington iron companies afford satisfactory proof of the soundness of the iron trade at the present time. In one case, the chairman announced that about thirteen years ago there was recorded an adverse balance of £18,000 ($87,597); that next year that loss was made good, and that during the following nine years the company had paid dividends amounting to nearly 100 per cent. Since then the company has been reorganized and has now divided 6 per cent on preference shares and 7¼ per cent on ordinary shares. The chairman and another speaker noted the fact that Canada is beginning to take spiegel iron in large quantities from the works, and is likely to continue to do so for some time to come. The inference drawn is that the people of Canada, who have not been in the habit of making steel rails, are now beginning to manufacture them, and for that reason want spiegel from Workington. The report of the proceedings at the meeting of the Moss Bay Iron and Steel Company contains a number of facts indicative of the prosperity of the iron trade of the Workington district. Not so long since the company paid no dividend at all. Later it began to pay a dividend of 2 per cent, then 3 per cent, and now the dividend is equal to 4 per cent.

### HEMATITE ORE.

The hematite ore of Cumberland may be looked upon as the back-bone of the future prosperity of the local iron trade. Roughly speaking, the great bulk of the hematite ore of Cumberland has hitherto been obtained from mines within a radius of 6 or 8 miles of Whitehaven. There is, however, a very valuable deposit at Millom, in the extreme southwestern part of the country. This deposit has been worked with great success for many years and has proved a source of much wealth to the lessees as well as to the owner of the royalty. To guard the mine against possible incursions of the sea, a great sea wall has for some time been in course of erection, at a cost of about half a million sterling ($2,435,250). The fact that so vast an expenditure should have been undertaken for such a purpose is evidence of the extreme value of the iron-ore mines of that neighborhood. Some of the valuable deposits nearer Whitehaven are now getting worked out, and a good deal of prospecting has been going on with the object of tapping hitherto unworked deposits. For some time past, explorations have been proceeding at Beckermet, on the extreme southern verge of what may be termed the Whitehaven iron-ore field, about 10 miles south of that town. It has now transpired that the explorations have been so satisfactory in their results that the mining company which was formed to work the deposits intends sinking shafts and making connections with the railways. This discovery of a new bed of iron ore is regarded as so important that one of the Workington iron companies has taken up half the shares of the company which made the explorations. The capital of the mining company is now being increased, but the iron company will probably continue to hold about half the interest.

### MOTOR CARS.

The alteration of the law, which has allowed the use of motor cars on ordinary highways, must have given great impetus to the manufacture of these vehicles. They are becoming more and more common on the roads of Cumberland and are of almost every imaginable type— good, bad, and indifferent.

There are certain kinds which are quite capable of speeding 30, 40, or even 50 miles an hour; but the magistrates of Cumberland and throughout the country generally are setting their faces determinedly against what they regard as excessive speed, and are inflicting severe fines upon all offenders brought before them. Not only is this so, but some of the more influential residents of the lake district, where many of the roads are narrow and frequently tortuous, have also begun an agitation in favor of a by-law to prevent motor cars using these roads at all. Up till now, that movement has not found much favor, but it may be taken as an indication that there are still several difficulties to be surmounted before the use of motor cars in this district can become very general. There are, however, not a few practical men who fearlessly predict that for ordinary highways the motor car is distinctly the vehicle of the future.

Automobiles are being used, on a small scale, for the conveyance of goods in some parts of Cumberland, and it is understood that their utilization for such purposes is found both economical and convenient. It seems probable that for some years to come a good deal of mechanical skill will be applied to bringing motor cars to a greater standard of perfection, and this will no doubt result in cheapening their cost to within the reach of persons of comparatively small means.

### ELECTRIC TRAMWAYS.

Reference was made in my last annual report to the fact that electric tramways of the overhead trolley system had been introduced into the city of Carlisle. The tram cars have now been running for more than two years, and are of considerable advantage to the public, but, unfortunately, have not yet proved a financial success. This, however, is probably largely due to the fact that while there are six routes, they all converge. There is no through system, and passengers are put to the inconvenience of having to change from one car to another, even where the distances are short. A penny (2 cents) is the minimum fare. It is believed by those who have some practical knowledge of the subject, that the introduction of half-penny (1 cent) fares for short distances would create new traffic, with results that could not fail to be advantageous to shareholders.

Considerably over a year has now elapsed since Parliament gave its sanction to a scheme for constructing an electric tramway between Cleator Moor and Silloth, with direct connections with Whitehaven, Workington, and Maryport. So far, however, no step has been taken toward carrying out the project.

### DOCK AT WORKINGTON.

Other important schemes referred to in previous reports from this district are also in abeyance. The construction of a deep-water dock at Workington, which obtained the sanction of Parliament some time since and is of vital importance, has not yet been begun. The prosecution of the scheme by which it was proposed to supply Carlisle with water by gravitation has also been suspended, and although a large outlay has been incurred, it is at present problematical whether it will ever reach completion.

### BUILDING TRADES.

The building trades are not so brisk as they have been for the last four or five years. Manufacturers are fairly busy.

### DEMAND FOR LABOR.

Generally speaking, farmers are less despondent than they were two or three years since; but all parts of the country complain severely of the dearness of labor and the difficulty of obtaining the services of women for dairy work.

The workmen's compensation act continues to work satisfactorily;

its operation confers a great boon, especially upon those engaged in mining operations. There has been since the close of the war in South Africa a great exodus of miners from the west of Cumberland to that colony. Many who had been in South Africa for some years hastened home on the outbreak of hostilities. These are now returning and taking others with them. It is expected that in the course of a few months many thousands of pounds per annum will be transmitted by these colonists to their relatives in west Cumberland.

TRADE PROSPECTS.

At no other time, perhaps, has there been so decided a leaning toward farm implements of American manufacture as at present—probably incited by the demonstration of their excellence at the Royal Agricultural Show held in Carlisle in 1902. As there is little or no direct trade between this district and the United States, and as the vendors of American goods in most cases lack knowledge of the construction, management, and advantage of the newer machinery, farmers naturally continue their antiquated methods of farming. Were the sale of our farm implements put into more experienced hands, they would undoubtedly become extremely popular. Owing probably to the reasonable price of American goods as compared with British products, people are prejudiced against them, no doubt anticipating inferiority.

Large quantities of patent foods and medicines from the United States are on sale here, although there is no local American store.

There is a daily increasing demand for motor cycles and cars, and in no other branch of trade can the United States compete more successfully.

Unfortunately, only a somewhat inferior make of American bicycle has found its way here, thus condemning the whole.

Whether there is necessity for the import of more fruit may be decided by the fact that good apples and pears are almost unprocurable except during the short English season, and, when this season expires the few tradesmen who retail foreign fruit demand prohibitive prices.

### WEST HARTLEPOOL.

Trade for the year 1901 has been characterized by considerable steadiness, with a further increase in the production of shipping. The tonnage, all steel steamers, launched last year amounted to 150,483, as against 141,145 in 1900; but since the turn of the year, prospects have not been so bright, owing to dullness in the freight market, and there are several empty berths in the largest local shipbuilding yards. The current year will show, therefore, a reduction in the tonnage output, in spite of the fact that prices have been somewhat lower. The freight markets have been very bad, and although some revival is likely to take place during the autumn and early winter, the large quantity of tonnage afloat is bound to prevent any important rise in freights. Ocean carriage will be cheap for some time to come.

The general trade statistics of the port are as follows:

Five thousand three hundred and sixteen vessels (steam and sail) of 1,364,735 tons arrived here during the year ended June 30, 1902, as against 5,651 vessels of 1,438,520 tons for the preceding twelve months.

H. Doc. 305, pt 2——55

The imports and exports consisted of:

| Articles. | | 1902. | 1901. |
|---|---|---|---|
| **IMPORTS.** | | | |
| Timber | loads.. | 388,679 | 523,480 |
| Grain | quarters.. | 55,991 | 12,904 |
| General goods | tons.. | 37,606 | 51,809 |
| Iron ore | do... | 162,700 | 160,452 |
| **EXPORTS.** | | | |
| Coal and coke | tons... | 1,188,468 | 1,215,903 |
| Merchandise goods | do... | 40,924 | 60,656 |

showing a general falling off from last year.

No salt was produced in the port during 1901, but 79,562 tons of cement, 74,220 tons of pig iron, and 88,957 tons of steel and iron plates were manufactured.

In the large woodworking establishments and in the different engine works, American machines are used to some extent, and it would be possible to increase their installation, if good, cheap, and novel designs were offered. American produce, in the shape of flour, bacon, etc., is largely consumed here by the large working-class population, but most of these articles are sent by Atlantic liners to the large distributing centers—Liverpool, Newcastle, Hull, and London—whence they are drawn by rail or small coasting vessels.

The exports to the United States, chiefly pig iron from Middlesbrough, have increased considerably the last six months, as shown by the quarterly returns; and the number of invoices certified (124) at this agency has been larger than for many years. A considerable number of vessels leave this port for the United States, as is shown by the fact that 63 bills of health and visés were issued at this agency between July 1, 1901, and June 30, 1902.

On the whole, business for the period under review may be regarded as not unfavorable; but seeing that the shipbuilding trade, on which the prosperity of this port chiefly depends, is not so brisk, I fear that the coming year will leave much to be desired.

### SUNDERLAND.

The total imports for the year 1901 were: Timber, 76,887 loads, a decrease of 17,752 loads; props, 587,920 dozen, a decrease of 118,400 dozen; iron, 7,589 tons, a decrease of over 3,000 tons; ores, 53,201 tons, an increase of 1,500 tons; grain, 116,537 quarters, a decrease of 47,000 quarters; flour, 217 tons, a decrease of 39 tons; esparto grass, 17,433 tons, a decrease of 227 tons; hay, 111 tons, an increase of 25 tons; straw, 150 tons; petroleum in bulk, 13,008 tons, an increase of 2,500 tons; chalk loam, etc., 44,173 tons, a decrease of 10,300 tons as compared with the preceding year.

The exports for the year ended December 31, 1901, were: Bottles and glass, 4,663 tons, a decrease of 664 tons; lime, 6,496 tons, a decrease of 1,343 tons; iron, 11,772 tons, a decrease of 2,050 tons; patent fuel, none, as against 12,323 tons in 1900; cement, 2,304 tons, a decrease of 1,182 tons.

During the year ended December 31, 1901, the number of vessels cleared from the port of Sunderland was 5,545, registering 2,620,133 tons. The tonnage rates of these vessels amounted to £28,152 13s. 11d. ($137,005). In the year 1900 the number of vessels was 5,777, registering 2,633,937 tons, and the tonnage rates were £28,074 4s. 1d. ($136,623).

The trade of 1901 shows a decrease of 232 vessels and a decrease of tonnage from that of 1900 of 13,804 register tons, or 0.52 per cent.

The decrease of coasting trade is 90,862 register tons, or 6.4 per cent. The increase of European trade is 28,753 register tons, or 2.8 per cent.

The increase of beyond-Europe trade is 48,305 register tons, or 23.8 per cent.

The average payment per ton register is 2.58d. (5.2 cents).

Of the 5,545 vessels which cleared from the port during the year ended December 31, 1901, 2,722 vessels, registering 1,539,616 tons, cleared from the South Dock, the tonnage rates of which were £19,436 14s. 10d. ($94,589).

In the year 1900, the number of vessels was 2,837, registering 1,537,361 tons, and the tonnage rates received were £19,932 8s. 11d. ($97,000).

The quantity of coal, coke, etc., shipped from the port in 1901 was: From the River Wear, 1,943,431 tons; from the North Dock, 4,657 tons; from the South Dock, 2,309,249 tons, a total of 4,257,337 tons.

Compared with 1900, when the total quantity shipped was 4,262,059 tons, this is a decrease of 4,758 tons.

The shipbuilding output of the Wear for the year 1901 again showed an increase of tonnage, the figures exceeding all previous records. The year's output showed that the aggregate tonnage exceeded that of 1900 by 7,547 tons. The total number of vessels launched was 77, as compared with 70 in the previous year, and a gross tonnage of 270,329 tons as compared with 262,782 tons. In addition to these figures, deck erections may be added to the extent of 25,180 tons, which brings the total output up to 295,509 tons.

The average tonnage of the vessels launched on the Wear in 1901 was 3,510 tons, or, including deck erections, 3,837 tons.

The return of vessels launched by the several firms is as follows:

| Firm. | Number of vessels. | Tonnage. | Firm. | Number of vessels. | Tonnage. |
|---|---|---|---|---|---|
| Messrs. J. L. Thompson & Son Limited .................. | 10 | 39,137 | Messrs. Robert Thompson & Sons ...................... | 5 | 16,785 |
| Sir James Laing & Sons, Limited..................... | 8 | 39,050 | Messrs. W. Pickersgill & Sons | 5 | 15,867 |
| Messrs. William Doxford & Sons, Limited .............. | 10 | 35,055 | Messrs. Bartram & Sons...... | 4 | 15,656 |
| Messrs. Short Brothers........ | 7 | 27,297 | Messrs Osbourne, Graham & Co ...................... | 4 | 11,214 |
| The Sunderland Shipbuilding Co., Limited ........... | 5 | 19,463 | Messrs. S. P. Austin & Son, Limited.............. | 5 | 11,189 |
| Messrs John Blumer & Co.... | 6 | 17,766 | Mr. John Crown.............. | 3 | 4,916 |
| Messrs. John Priestman & Co. | 5 | 16,934 | Total................... | 77 | 270,329 |

Messrs. J. L. Thompson & Sons launched four vessels for the North Atlantic Steamship Company, Limited, Messrs. T. Hogan & Sons, managers, New York. Two of these have each a gross tonnage of 4,830 tons and a carrying capacity of 525,000 gross cubic feet; the other two have each a gross tonnage of 3,390 tons and a carrying capacity of 375,000 gross cubic feet. These vessels are for the cattle and general American produce trade with Bristol and other British as well as continental ports.

During the present year, Messrs. J. L. Thompson & Sons have launched the high-class cargo and cattle steamer *Madawaska*, to the order to Messrs. Hogan & Sons, New York. This is the tenth vessel they have built for the North Atlantic Steamship Company, Limited.

Messrs. Short Brothers have also launched during the present year a large steel screw steamer for the America and Japan trade, to the crder of the America and Oriental Steamship Company, Limited, of New York, Messrs. Barber & Co., managers. This vessel, the *Sagami*, has five holds, for the rapid loading and discharging of which nine powerful steam winches have been provided. She has a complete installation of electric light.

The marine engineering trade of the Wear was also good throughout the year. Messrs. Richardsons, Westgarth & Co., Limited, of Hartlepool, Middlesbrough, and Sunderland, now include the Scotia Engine Works, on the Wear. In giving its return this firm embraces the Wear yard.

The following is a summary of the vessels engined by the other firms:

|  | Number of vessels. | Lloyds nominal horse-power. | Indi-cated horse-power. |
|---|---|---|---|
| George Clark & Co., Limited ...................................... | 24 | 8,115 | 48,700 |
| J. Dickinson & Sons, Limited ..................................... | 17 | 5,174 | 31,044 |
| William Doxford & Sons, Limited................................. | 9 | 3,316 | 18,100 |
| Messrs. Maccoll & Pollock ........................................ | 27 | .......... | 10,000 |
| Messrs. John S. Vaux & Co........................................ | 3 | .......... | 1,080 |

To this may be added the approximate indicated horsepower of Messrs Richardson, Westgarth & Co.'s Wear yard, which was a little over 18,000.

The North Eastern Marine Engineering Company, Limited, having works at Wallsend and Sunderland, also includes in one total its returns for both plants. It is therefore impossible to give the returns for the Wear separately. The total figures, however, show an increase of over 4,000 indicated horsepower for the two works.

Generally speaking, the engineering trade indicates an advance over the previous year.

The Sunderland Forge and Engineering Company, Limited, during the year 1901, fitted 17 vessels throughout with the electric light, including several for American steamship companies.

The various works of improvement being carried out by the River Wear commissioners, including the great pier works at Roker and the harbor entrance, are rapidly approaching completion. The success with which these engineering enterprises have been promoted and carried out was recently acknowledged on the occasion of the visit of the North East Coast Institution of Mechanical Engineers, when special praise was bestowed upon Mr. H. H. Wake, C. E., the capable chief engineer to the commissioners.

Some further works of extension are being carried out by Sir John Jackson at the Hudson north dock and the gateway No. 1.

With respect to revenue, the total income of the commissioners for 1901 was £138,143, as compared with £138,823 for 1900. To earn this, in 1901 the commissioners spent £60,467, as compared with £66,299 to earn the income of 1900. The surplus balance of income was therefore £16,978, as compared with £15,536 for 1900.

The commissioners during the year sold their chain, cable, and anchor testing works for £15,000.

The amount spent by the commissioners on the construction of the harbor protecting piers during the year was £43,697, making a total spent upon the piers, up to December 31 last, of £437,400.

Messrs. Doxford & Sons, Limited, during the past year erected at their works a mammoth crane capable of lifting extraordinary weights onto the decks of steamers in the course of construction. This firm has also doubled the space at its works for shipbuilding and marine-engine construction.

Messrs. Sir James Laing & Co. have also extended the number of their berths, and are now laying a new berth that will accommodate vessels upward of 600 feet in length. They have recently launched one ship 500 feet in length.

Messrs. S. P. Austin & Son, Limited, are building a pontoon graving dock, the pontoon for which is being constructed by Messrs. Swan & Hunter, Wallsend. This work is now approaching completion.

The number of vessels built during the first seven months of the current year is fairly up to the average of last year, but there is a scarcity of new orders, and the probability is that the total output for the current year will fall far short of that for 1901.

The Nautilus Steam Shipping Company, Messrs. F. & W. Ritson, managers, Sunderland, has two new turret steamers of large size which are at present on their way to San Francisco to bring grain cargoes to this country. Each carries cargoes of about 7,000 tons. The *Elm Branch*, owned by the same company, is also proceeding to New York, for the purpose of taking a general cargo thence to Australia.

The Neptune Steam Navigation Company, Messrs. W. & T. W. Pinkney, managers, Sunderland, has a regular line running to America, employing eight vessels trading weekly between Rotterdam and Baltimore. The company's Chicago agent is Mr. J. F. Upham, 135 Adams street; its Baltimore agents are Messrs. Dressel, Rauschenberg & Co.; its Rotterdam agents are Messrs. Hudig & Blokhuyzen.

Wheat cargoes are brought to this port from the United States for Messrs. E. C. Robson & Sons and Messrs. Richardson, Bishopwearmouth Mills.

Messrs. Armstrong, Addison & Co., preserved-timber merchants, North Bridge street, Sunderland, import from Mobile pitch pine, telegraph poles, square timber, and deals. The poles are for the telephone companies, and are specially imported on account of their length, which varies from 50 to 80 or 90 feet.

As mentioned in previous reports, the direct trade between the United States and this port is infinitesimal, with the exception of timber, wheat, and petroleum, and even these shipments are small. The reason for this is that steamers are invariably chartered at United States ports to load general goods for Liverpool, Glasgow, London, Hull, or Tyne, whence their cargoes are distributed throughout the various outlying districts. There is no reason why cargoes should not be imported direct to this port, as there is no difficulty regarding sailing rates, and the facilities of the dock company for handling goods are second to none. It only requires enterprise, but somehow the local firms do not show any inclination to import direct. It therefore remains for those who desire to send their goods to this port to take up the venture.

Large consignments of American boots have been purchased from Boston by the Cooperative Wholesale Society. The local dealers report that the footwear is good fitting, meets with a ready sale, is of good quality, and yields a fair profit.

This is a branch of business that is likely to be developed.

                                      HORACE W. METCALF, *Consul.*
NEWCASTLE UPON TYNE, *October 3, 1902.*

---

### NOTTINGHAM.

The fiscal year covered by this report closes the most prosperous season known for years in Nottingham's principal industry—the lace trade—and the approaching season promises equally well. Machines have been busily employed and in some branches have been unable to keep pace with orders. There is also some complaint of tardy delivery. For this condition the American demand is largely responsible; and manufacturers have shown more enterprise in the production of new designs and better-class goods than they have hitherto thought it necessary to exhibit. The increase in lace manufacture in America does not keep pace with growth in other industries, and the steady export of lace machinery from here is not as yet viewed with apprehension. It is, however, but a matter of time when the American demand for machine curtain and levers lace will materially diminish, exactly as the enormous growth in the manufacture of boots and shoes and hosiery in the United States affected those industries here. One hopeful feature, from a local standpoint, is the growing diversification in the character of exports. This is shown by the gradually increasing shipments of manufactures of cotton and woolens, coatings, gloves, muslins, and various forms of haberdashery; in fact, a new industry may be said to have sprung up within the past two years. During idle times, a few enterprising manufacturers tried their machines upon the production of novelties in ladies' and children's wear—caps, aprons, pinafores, blouses, and fancy articles. The product found an immediate market, and from the experiment a profitable and growing trade has been developed. Speculation is still rife as to the practical outcome of the new Matitsch machine (described in Advance Sheets No. 1340; Consular Reports No. 262) for making an imitation of hand-made lace upon a new and economical principle. Negotiations have been opened by several parties, but it is the general impression that the new device will eventually fall into the hands of a leading firm here. That this invention has not so far disturbed conditions to any extent may be inferred from the fact that a local machine builder now has under way an order, given by a local firm, for 50 of the Birkin (single-breadth) machines.

## EXPORTS.

The following table shows the total American exports from this district for the fiscal year, as compared with those of last year:

| Cities. | Year ended— | |
| --- | --- | --- |
| | Sept. 30, 1901. | June 30, 1902. |
| Nottingham | $6,029,609.80 | $6,305,968.29 |
| Derby | 902,515.06 | 1,058,546.44 |
| Leicester | 287,453.42 | 304,964.04 |
| Total | 7,219,578.28 | 7,669,478.77 |

Net increase for district, $449,900.49.

A detailed comparison of Nottingham exports is shown by the following table:

*Comparison of exports for fiscal years ended September 30, 1901, and June 30, 1902.*

| Articles. | Sept. 30, 1901. | June 30, 1902. | Increase. | Decrease. |
| --- | --- | --- | --- | --- |
| Animals | $632.64 | | | $632.64 |
| Braids | 39,529.60 | $23,101.91 | | 16,427.69 |
| Bricks, clinker | 2,271.95 | 2,986.53 | $714.58 | |
| Bed sets | 1,017.04 | 1,231.66 | 214.62 | |
| Beading, cotton | 309.78 | | | 309.78 |
| Cement, Keene's | 5,335.51 | 6,378.02 | 1,042.51 | |
| Clay, crude | 195.16 | | | 195.16 |
| Cloths | 48,879.41 | 18,700.40 | | 30,179.01 |
| Coatings | 17,085.26 | 29,465.13 | 12,429.87 | |
| Coutils | 1,079.11 | | | 1,079.11 |
| Cotton goods | 118,328.12 | 174,718.95 | 56,390.83 | |
| Cricket materials | 265.36 | 272.10 | 6.74 | |
| Designs | 708.19 | 111.92 | | 591.27 |
| Dogs, rough-coated collie | | 145.99 | 145.99 | |
| Elastic webbing | 3,967.81 | 3,629.83 | | 337.98 |
| Embroideries | 500.63 | | | 500.63 |
| Falls | 4,289.43 | 6,488.79 | 2,199.36 | |
| Flooring quarries | 5,283.75 | 7,343.56 | 2,059.81 | |
| French goods | 1,346.89 | 2,407.50 | 1,060.61 | |
| Furniture | 308.40 | 5,024.24 | 4,715.84 | |
| Galloons | 624.14 | 844.87 | 220.73 | |
| Gelatine | | 2,854.27 | 2,854.27 | |
| Gloves | 3,493.35 | 20,171.83 | 16,678.48 | |
| Glue | 10,565.82 | 20,024.11 | 9,458.29 | |
| Gripe water | 510.96 | 510.96 | | |
| Haberdashery | 7,718.93 | 10,090.07 | 2,371.14 | |
| Handkerchiefs | 10,521.62 | 11,403.08 | 881.46 | |
| Hosiery | 218,085.63 | 231,640.82 | 13,555.19 | |
| Household effects | 3,024.39 | 3,649.87 | 625.48 | |
| Hooks | 123.55 | 7.05 | | 116.50 |
| Hardware | | 92.90 | 92.90 | |
| Herbal extracts | | 102.19 | 102.19 | |
| Iron bedsteads | 632.15 | | | 632.15 |
| Jacquard cards | 8,870.03 | 4,383.32 | | 4,486.71 |
| Jewelry | 523.38 | | | 523.38 |
| Lace | 4,525,944.96 | 4,728,971.48 | 203,026.52 | |
| Leather | 20,161.56 | 21,741.95 | 1,580.39 | |
| Loops | 122.99 | | | 122.99 |
| Linen | 160,351.87 | 206,195.56 | 45,843.69 | |
| Lithographs | 362.93 | | | 362.93 |
| Machinery | 277,004.10 | 163,905.42 | | 113,098.68 |
| Metal goods | 449.33 | 97.81 | | 351.32 |
| Mitts | | 2,801.14 | 2,801.14 | |
| Muslins | 28,701.06 | 40,266.00 | 11,564.94 | |
| Needles | 147.93 | | | 147.93 |
| Ribbons | 18,871.47 | 15,183.66 | | 3,287.81 |
| Rubber goods | 41.01 | | | 41.01 |
| Rufflings | 574.37 | | | 574.37 |
| Salted sheepskins | 184,175.05 | 191,362.18 | 7,187.08 | |
| Scarfs, cotton | | 98.85 | 98.85 | |
| Seeds | 2,181.77 | 12,860.27 | 10,678.50 | |
| Shawls, wool | | 187.65 | 187.65 | |
| Silk | 129,079.62 | 134,949.19 | 5,869.57 | |

*Comparison of exports for fiscal years ended September 30, 1901, etc.*—Continued.

| Articles. | Sept. 30, 1901. | June 30, 1902. | Increase. | Decrease. |
|---|---|---|---|---|
| Sod oil .............................. | $14,350.10 | $16,350.79 | $2,000.69 | .......... |
| Stationery ........................... | .......... | 237.43 | 237.43 | .......... |
| Steels ............................... | 344.69 | 255.54 | .......... | $89.15 |
| String................................ | .......... | 230.42 | 230.42 | .......... |
| Silverware............................ | .......... | 218.99 | 218.99 | .......... |
| Swords, old .......................... | .......... | 1,919.31 | 1,919.31 | .......... |
| Tapes................................. | 9,244.17 | 5,302.26 | .......... | 3,941.91 |
| Tapestry covers...................... | 65.81 | .......... | .......... | 65.81 |
| Terra alba ........................... | 1,040.18 | 520.09 | .......... | 520.09 |
| Towels............................... | 494.46 | 2,646.80 | 2,152.34 | .......... |
| Trimmings............................ | 90.61 | .......... | .......... | 90.61 |
| Veilings ............................. | 1,585.87 | 10,812.40 | 9,226.53 | .......... |
| Velvets .............................. | 3,193.02 | 3,786.17 | 593.15 | .......... |
| Velveteens............................ | .......... | 1,032.31 | 1,032.31 | .......... |
| White goods .......................... | 33,685.66 | 56,982.07 | 23,296.41 | .......... |
| Miscellaneous ....................... | 5,497.29 | 6,121.83 | 624.54 | .......... |
| Cases, carriage, packing, seller's commission, etc., not separately included in above......... | 95,924.93 | 92,798.90 | .......... | 3,126.03 |
| Total....................... | 6,029,609.80 | 6,305,968.29 | 458,191.34 | 181,832.85 |

Net increase for the year ended June 30, 1902, $276,358.49.

Especial interest attaches to the exports of lace and hosiery, and machinery used in their production, and a comparative record for three years is given:

| | For fiscal year ended— | | |
|---|---|---|---|
| | Sept. 30, 1900. | Sept. 30, 1901. | June 30, 1902. |
| **LACE.** | | | |
| September 30 ........................... | .......... | .......... | $891,507.63 |
| December 31 ........................... | $1,050,496.69 | $1,223,957.08 | 1,332,064.37 |
| March 31 .............................. | 1,504,546.74 | 1,438,168.70 | 1,420,600.42 |
| June 30 ............................... | 768,354.07 | 972,311.55 | 1,084,799.06 |
| September 30 .......................... | 816,653.68 | 891,507.63 | .......... |
| Total ........................... | 4,140,051.18 | 4,525,944.96 | 4,728,971.48 |
| Increase........................ | .......... | 385,983.78 | 203,026.52 |
| **HOSIERY.** | | | |
| September 30 .......................... | .......... | .......... | 85,627.94 |
| December 31........................... | 19,617.12 | 11,333.18 | 12,492.56 |
| March 31 ............................. | 75,819.14 | 101,272.21 | 95,390.62 |
| June 30 .............................. | 51,434.64 | 19,852.30 | 38,129.70 |
| September 30.......................... | 111,335.91 | 85,627.94 | .......... |
| Total ........................... | 258,206.81 | 218,085.63 | 231,640.82 |
| Decrease........................ | .......... | 40,121.18 | .......... |
| Increase........................ | .......... | .......... | 13,555.19 |
| **MACHINERY.** | | | |
| September 30.......................... | .......... | .......... | 47,872.39 |
| December 31........................... | 22,234.37 | 66,914.19 | 30,584.52 |
| March 31 ............................. | 38,228.47 | 89,546.81 | 39,085.42 |
| June 30 .............................. | 38,371.43 | 72,670.71 | 46,363.09 |
| September 30 ......................... | 39,023.61 | 47,872.39 | .......... |
| Total ........................... | 137,857.88 | 277,004.10 | 163,905.42 |
| Decrease......................... | .......... | .......... | 113,098.68 |
| Increase......................... | .......... | 139,146.22 | .......... |

The following analysis of the three items of lace, hosiery, and machinery for the two preceding fiscal years clearly indicates prevailing market conditions and demands:

| | For fiscal year ended— | | Increase. | Decrease. |
|---|---|---|---|---|
| | Sept. 30, 1901. | June 30, 1902. | | |
| **LACE.** | | | | |
| Cotton lace goods | $3,707,942.11 | $3,906,174.14 | $200,232.03 | .......... |
| Silk lace goods | 120,820.39 | 109,269.29 | .......... | $11,551.10 |
| Cotton nets | 441,419.78 | 458,964.72 | 17,544.94 | .......... |
| Silk nets | 39,362.48 | 36,221.39 | .......... | 3,141.09 |
| Lace curtains | 206,677.23 | 215,181.56 | 8,504.33 | .......... |
| Cotton veilings | 5,981.99 | .......... | .......... | 5,981.99 |
| Silk veilings | 1,860.62 | .......... | .......... | 1,860.62 |
| Silk and cotton lace goods | 1,880.36 | .......... | .......... | 1,880.36 |
| Lace material | .......... | 1,160.38 | 1,160.38 | .......... |
| Total | 4,525,944.96 | 4,728,971.48 | 227,441.68 | 24,415.16 |
| **HOSIERY.** | | | | |
| Cotton hosiery | 65,632.41 | 68,140.90 | 2,508.49 | .......... |
| Woolen hosiery | 25,343.04 | 26,449.53 | 1,106.49 | .......... |
| Silk hosiery | 8,981.09 | 10,380.74 | 1,399.65 | .......... |
| Cashmere hosiery | 1,634.95 | 1,634.95 | .......... | .......... |
| Merino hosiery | 838.46 | 3,144.33 | 2,305.87 | .......... |
| Cotton underwear | 30,273.33 | 37,932.25 | 7,658.92 | .......... |
| Woolen underwear | 78,690.36 | 72,009.50 | .......... | 6,680.86 |
| Silk underwear | 2,376.30 | 2,665.84 | 289.54 | .......... |
| Merino underwear | 4,315.69 | 3,935.71 | .......... | 379.98 |
| Cellular underwear | .......... | 5,072.82 | 5,072.82 | .......... |
| Cashmere underwear | .......... | 274.75 | 274.75 | .......... |
| Total | 218,085.63 | 231,640.82 | 20,616.03 | 7,060.84 |
| **MACHINERY.** | | | | |
| Lace curtain | 87,151.95 | 86,358.45 | .......... | 793.50 |
| Levers | 96,150.49 | 12,096.07 | .......... | 84,054.50 |
| Plain net | 58,326.82 | 46,397.10 | .......... | 11,929.22 |
| Bleaching, dressing, and dyeing | 25,296.64 | 5,883.13 | .......... | 19,413.51 |
| Jacquard | 582.56 | 582.56 | .......... | .......... |
| Punching | 1,601.50 | 636.04 | .......... | 965.46 |
| Warp | 1,435.16 | 1,548.05 | 112.89 | .......... |
| Hosiery | 1,938.31 | 6,777.67 | 4,839.36 | .......... |
| Accessories | 221.36 | .......... | .......... | 221.36 |
| Cornely | 792.87 | .......... | .......... | 792.87 |
| Yarn | 30.58 | .......... | .......... | 30.58 |
| Pleating | 291.99 | .......... | .......... | 291.99 |
| Seaming | 107.91 | .......... | .......... | 107.91 |
| Tucking | 75.42 | .......... | .......... | 75.42 |
| Sugar boiling | .......... | 406.34 | 406.34 | .......... |
| Boiler tubes | .......... | 447.71 | 447.71 | .......... |
| Miscellaneous | 3,001.04 | 2,772.30 | .......... | 228.74 |
| Total | 277,004.10 | 163,905.42 | 5,806.30 | 118,904.98 |

The inequality between exports of levers and curtain machinery for the past year appears to be largely the result of temporary conditions, but there is unquestionably a very decided development in the American lace-curtain industry. Curtain-machine builders here are practically a year behind on American orders. One firm has supplied over 40 machines since January 1, is fully a year ahead on orders, and has recently been obliged to refuse an order for 30 machines. Inevitable future conditions would seem to offer an immense home field for the American machine builder.

## LEICESTER.

Consular Agent Partridge submits the following comment upon trade and industrial conditions at Leicester:

In my report upon American trade in this district for the year ended September 30, 1901, I submitted, for the purpose of comparison, the export returns for that year and for the preceding year, but on this occasion, as the report will only cover the portion of the year from September 30 last, up to the present date, a similar complete comparative table for the year can not, of course, be supplied. Still, taking the corresponding period of last year—September 30, 1900, to August 15, 1901—I find that the differences in exports in the principal lines appear to work out as follows:

|  | Increase. | Decrease. |
|---|---|---|
| Chrome glace kids (leather) | $2,628.06 | |
| Elastic fabrics | | $11,014.08 |
| Gloves: | | |
|    Cotton | | 13,297.31 |
|    Woolen | 25,415.98 | |
| Hosiery, woolen | | 7,779.23 |
| Machinery: | | |
|    Boot and shoe, sewing | | 2,543.78 |
|    Hosiery | | 7,925.27 |
| Photographic apparatus | 1,065.96 | |
| Underwear: | | |
|    Cotton | | 1,233.84 |
|    Silk and wool | | 1,772.22 |
|    Woolen | | 13,237.46 |
| Other lines | | 65.49 |
|     Total | 29,109.95 | 58,868.63 |

It will therefore be seen that for the period referred to the net decrease of exports is about $29,758.68.

For the year ended September 30, 1901, the comparative statement of exports showed an increase of $32,415.68 over the preceding year.

The general dullness of trade in this district, referred to in my report of last year, continues, but in the boot and shoe trade and certain other lines there appears to be some revival.

As regards elastic fabrics, the observations contained in my report of last year are confirmed by the results of the present year's trading.

Another item of decrease is in cotton gloves. It is understood that the manufacture of these goods either has already been, or very shortly will be, commenced in the United States, and naturally the home product will in time supplant the imported article. On the other hand, in the trade in woolen gloves the growth is considerable and represents one of the largest items of increase in the present year's exports.

In the boot and shoe business, the largest industry in this district, I learn that trade is decidedly improving, there being great demand for goods for South Africa, while both in the home and foreign markets a satisfactory increase is claimed. The prohibitory duty entirely shuts out English goods from the United States market. At the same time American producers are largely increasing their trade here, not only in rubber goods, but also in other lines. In nearly all the chief houses in the shoe trade in this town, American goods are being largely stocked, their better style and finish securing popular favor. The only disadvantage pointed out to me in connection with these is their lightness, which renders them unsuitable for the English climate in winter.

As regards hosiery goods, it is claimed here that the local manufacture is very superior to that of the United States. How far this may be true I am not in a position to judge, but in view of the fact that the exports of this commodity have decreased considerably it is fair to assume that there is not much ground for this claim to superiority. The superiority is alleged to exist in the quality of the yarn and the shape of the goods.

### DERBY.

Local conditions at Derby have varied little. Until recently, Consular Agent Eddowes reported dissatisfaction as to the character of American preserved fruit imports and packing methods. He now states that such fruits are of exceptionally good quality, but adds that fresh barreled apples have deteriorated in quality and continue to be poorly packed. He also says that American cured pork does not meet English requirements, the curing process not being sufficiently thorough.

UNITED STATES GOODS ABROAD.

The most significant developments attending the American commercial invasion have not been the absorption of the match industry, the electrification of London, the campaign of the tobacco trust, the mushroom-like growth of the American boot and shoe trade, the encroachments of the meat trust, the all-conquering march of the patent medicine, the spreading grasp of the oil companies, the quiet acquisition of financial premiership, nor yet the transference of the Atlantic carrying trade from British to American ownership. These are the outward and sensational features. The real significance lies in the diversification of the great bulk and body of general exports. Four years ago, not only in the larger provincial cities, but even in London, American goods of almost any description were curiosities. There were sewing machines, typewriters, an occasional roller-top desk, tinned fruits, and a few other Yankee inventions which were amiably tolerated as curiosities; but the idea of serious American competition in any common line was treated with contempt. Within two years that contempt gave way to a wondering apprehension, and in the past year American competition has become a matter of serious national concern, to be discussed ponderously upon every editorial page in the island, in newspapers set by linotype and run off American perfecting machines. By the time England was partially awake, American boots and shoes were selling in Northampton, hosiery in Leicester, cutlery in Sheffield, underwear in Nottingham, while English crops were being cultivated and reaped with American machinery. Agencies for a hundred different lines of manufacture have been established, and the floors and counters of retail stores, not only in the cities but also in the smaller towns and villages, are stocked with American goods. The public does not always know when it buys American goods, and frequently the dealer does not know that he is selling them, for to silence the prejudice of both they generally carry an English label and the address only of the London agency. It is not an infrequent experience to hear an Englishman delightedly descant upon the satisfying progress of British inventions, when all the time he is eulogizing some detested Yankee device that has been an old story in the United States for ten years.

To catalogue the American articles now common on the English market would be simply to enumerate the common utilities—from machinery of all kinds to ladies' patent hair curlers; from fresh meats and provisions to liver pills; from oil stoves to mouse traps; from cotton-seed oil to shaving soap. There have been some distinct failures, in each case attributable to the unusual quickness and enterprise shown by English manufacturers, as well as to the ill-advised and half-hearted efforts of American exporters. One notable illustration was the almost total failure of the American bicycle. Four years ago, this immense market could have been conquered. The English machines were cumbrous, high-priced affairs, and the industry was in no shape to meet competition. Instead of studying the demand and meeting it with good machines and prompt commercial methods, a lot of poor machines wholly unsuited to English requirements were dumped on the market through English wholesalers, and the American bicycle given a reputation from which it will never wholly recover. In the meantime, the English manufacturers greatly improved the character and increased the quantity of their output, so that to-day in every town and village of the country they have excellent and enterprising local agencies and repair shops, and can practically defy competition of whatever kind.

England was also a pioneer in the manufacture of gas engines, and sharp continental competition, especially German, had a tendency to encourage and promote improvements of all kinds. The industry is competent and thoroughly intrenched, and the field an inviting one. The American motor bicycle, however, was the first in that line, and it will be the fault of introductory methods if it does not maintain its prestige and enormously increase its market. In locomobiles, or steam cars, the American machine maintains a lead, for no other apparent rea son than that continental and English manufacturers have paid no atten- tion to this style of car; but the American auto, or petrol car, is scarcely in evidence. This subject alone is a large one, but the gist of the situa- tion is this: English capital is just now paying marked attention to the industry, and in recent speed trials and exhibitions, has had marked success. Continental manufacturers are establishing manufactories or, if not actual manufactories, repair works and agencies, under com- petent supervision and capable of caring for all demands on quick notice. Automobilists, so far, are limited to the wealthy leisure and sporting classes. The national association, which represents practi- cally all the pleasure cars in the island, has now enrolled about 3,000 machines, and the leading factories are from six months to one year behind orders, premiums of from $500 to $1,000 not being uncommon for cars ready to turn out. This class of purchasers are not much influenced by cost price. They want the best, the speediest, the smoothest in operation, the most stylish and comfortable, but they are not going to dicker on details across the Atlantic nor buy machines there, whatever their agreed merits, with no nearer facilities for expert advice, repairs, and alterations. If Americans wish to hold their own in this competition, they must follow continental methods and establish competent repair headquarters here. What has been done, however, is only the commencement. English roads, from one end of the island to the other, are ideal. The cost of maintaining horses and carriages is almost prohibitory to the great middle class. They are waiting for the appearance of a reliable, smooth-running machine to cost in the neighborhood of $500. Whether that machine shall be propelled by steam, petroleum, or the new Edison battery, is immaterial, if its serviceable qualities and cheap maintenance can be demonstrated. This is the present opportunity to compass a market greater than the one now existing for pleasure racers, but it can not be accomplished at long range nor by halting or imperfect methods. Factories here would be unnecessary, but repair shops, and expert representatives with full authority to act in any emergency, are pre- requisite to either substantial or lasting success.

In a general way, English markets are open to any time or labor-saving device for factory, shop, farm or house, the price of which is reason- able, the merits of which are practically demonstrated and the pro- moters of which are able to inaugurate and maintain a campaign of education. There is, for instance, no perceptible limit to the market for American furniture, provided only and always that English styles are conformed to. The American range or cooking stove has been the dream desire of the English middle classes for a century—only they don't know it. No people attempt such economy with coal, and no people ever made a more miserable failure. Three-fourths of their coal goes up the chimney, and no English chimney range is ready for cooking short of from one to two hours stoking. No American housewife would stand this ante-diluvian method for a day, if she could reach an American hardware store; yet to introduce the economical cooking stove will be no easy task.

A self-feeding, easily regulated base-burner for heating purposes, that would use a good quality of English soft coal of even size, hardly to be distinguished from anthracite, would be a household blessing nine months of the year in this damp and chilly climate; but to make the English people believe it, would require a practical demonstration and the uprooting of ancient and sacred prejudices. While public laundries are fairly well equipped with modern machinery, the family washing is still done with the dolly tub, just as it was done two hundred years ago. An American lady in this city was threatened with a strike, because she imported an American washing machine. By great diplomacy and patience, she induced her servants to use it. They tried it to please her, not because they thought washing could be properly done any other way than that of their mothers' and grandmothers'. The result, and its ease of accomplishment, fairly stupefied them. They finally capitulated, and, prejudice once conquered, the wonders of that one common washing machine spread in the most mysterious fashion from servants' quarters to drawing rooms over a large neighboring area.

It is impracticable, within the scope of such a report as this, to cover the industrial field, for each topic involves many particulars peculiar to itself, but in a general way, light can be thrown upon the situation by utilizing characteristic cases. The Hosiery Trade Journal, of Leiscester, is the best English authority in that line. Recently it said:

Some years past, the great cry in our trade was the competition from the continent where a lower rate of wages was paid than the average here, and fears were entertained that it was the idea of the British manufacturer to bring down wages to the continental level. This fear, we are pleased to say, was but a dream, the idea being rather to wait the rise of wages on the continent, and so reduce competition in that way. To-day, a greater competition appears from the other side of the "herring pond," and from one who is far from content with a low wage, but who claims to be about the best paid operative in the industrial world. This being a fact, how can goods made by these operatives be imported into Britain, and to-day be sold side by side with British goods in the large retail shops in all towns throughout Britain is a question of particular interest, and an answer to such question would be of even still greater interest. It has been our opinion for some time that the cause was the greater production at a less cost in spite of the higher wages paid. From inquiries we have made, we find the opinion is is not far from the mark. Our cousins on the other side shun hand labor; everything must be done mechanically, and this by the best and·quickest methods. A machine that needs hand labor, or that is slow, will stand idle, as no operative will work it, and some of our British machinery, we have been told by manufacturers who have come across the pond, would not be tolerated in American factories. A special line of underwear that is being imported into this country at the present time is a fleeced linen garment, and though Britain was the home of the invention of framework knitting, and many machines have been brought out in this country, including the one upon which this class of goods are being made, still the machines now built on the other side are claimed to be simpler and run at more than double the speed of the present day British machine. We are told that a four-feed machine, with three threads at each feeder, can be successfully run at 65 revolutions per minute. Do our machines on plain circular fabric run at this speed? Until our operatives become alive to the fact that old ideas of ten, twenty, and thirty years ago are of no use to-day, and that as other countries progress so must Britain reform her system of trade and commerce, so soon may we expect to keep to the front.  Too much is depended on past laurels, but the present age has no reverence for these, but favors the new and most up-to-date ideas, both as regards machines and commerce.

In another edition, it uttered the following warning to English manufacturers:

The hosiery industry in the United States has grown again by 10 per cent during last year, and there are now 82,955 machines making hosiery, underwear, etc., in that country.  This increase shows that America not only makes goods for the million, but has also started to compete with the German and fancy French patterns. The slow way in getting repeats has helped to bring about this state of affairs. New machines are being put up all the time, and we expect that most of the 10 per cent increase in machines is to be laid to the credit of machines for fancy hose and half hose.

In making deductions from such confessions, American manufacturers should not overlook the fact that for some years now the most progressive of the English factories have been equipping with the latest American improvements, notwithstanding the opposition of trade unionism, which is a topic by itself.  The success of American shoes, now universally sold on their merits, has been unduly emphasized by that considerable proportion of English pessimists who have thrown up both hands and see only a future of industrial disaster.  While they may be excellent prophets in a general way, they have magnified this particular phase of competition.  If the annual consumption of boots and shoes in the United Kingdom be placed at the moderate figure of 10 shillings or $2.50 per head of population, the total reaches the nice aggregate of $100,000,000.  English exports for the same period would aggregate over $5,000,000.  The total of American imports only slightly exceeds $2,000,000.  It must be that the bright, up-to-date stores of the American invaders, with their modish goods, fair prices, and prompt service have dazed the Britishers, or they would not scare at the appearance of a mere skirmish line.  Yet something is the matter with the British industry.  During the winter, matters reached a crisis at both Northampton and Leicester, the centers of manufacture. Some of the operatives at the former place bitterly resented the introduction of new American machinery.  The news of the importation of three machinists to work new apparatus created a riot, and the mayor was roughly handled.  Exciting times followed, with a depression and curtailment of work still existing.  At Leicester matters have been in a similar state.  Failures at both places have been common, the last month witnessing nine at Leicester and six at Northampton.  Only this week, at Bucknall Torkard, one factory employing 70 hands posts a week's notice of permanent closing and offers its machinery for sale. The alleged cause is friction over trades union demands.  A trade paper comments:

The responsible men in the British shoe-manufacturing trade are still clinging to the policy of the ostrich about the present distress in their industry.  They apparently think that by minimizing reports of trouble they can bring better times.  But week by week the list of failures in the trade grows longer.  In view of this the responsible men in the trade, masters and operatives alike, would surely do well to set themselves to find out why a once prosperous trade has lost its place, and how it can regain it.  How far American competition is responsible for this each must judge for himself.  These facts are undisputed.  Our exports of shoes are smaller now than during the corresponding time last year.  American exports to colonies which were once supplied from England have greatly increased. Our home demand for British-made shoes has declined. The sale of American shoes in this country is steadily and largely increasing. The official figures leave no room for dispute on these points. Is it not time, then, for British shoe manufacturers to abandon the ostrich-like policy which they have up to now favored and face the facts?

Commenting upon the serious condition of the industry, the London Mail recently said:

The time has come for frank consideration by masters and men alike in the boot trade of the real state of their industry. About eight months ago, when attention was first called in this paper to the acute and growing distress in the trade, it was deeply resented by employers. The mayor of Northampton wrote to minimize the unfavorable details, and the literary organs of St. Crispin supported him. Since then, despite all disclaimers and denials, the situation has grown steadily worse. The shoe trade expected that though there had been a bad winter there would be a good spring selling season, but it was an unusually bad one. Then it was said that summer and the coronation must mean a revival, but summer brought no revival. The autumn season threatens to be very bad, and there are no present signs of better days. In Leicester and Northampton, the weaker manufacturers are going to the wall, as the list of bankruptcies shows. In Leicester, short time is almost universal, and everywhere masters seize opportunities of closing for a few days on any possible pretext for holidays. Our shoemakers should cease from sneering at their foreign competitors, and ask themselves how it is that they are driving us from the market. Let the leaders of masters and men try intelligently to learn the truth about their rivals and themselves. Do the American workmen turn out more per man than our own, and if so, why? What is it that leads so many English people to purchase American and French shoes in preference to home makes, even at higher prices? Why are our colonial and foreign markets going from us? Sneering at rivals does not help us to beat them. The hour is here for our shoe trade to face the facts.

It should also be borne in mind that the machines and methods to which operatives so strongly object are American; one shoe-machinery organization—the British United Shoe Machinery Company, of Leicester, an offshoot of the American shoe-machine trust—having a grip upon the whole shoemaking industry. The British manufacturer can not, if he is to progress, dispense with its appliances. They are so far ahead of all others that the maker without them is heavily handicapped.

A still more striking contrast between the helplessness or inaptitude of British management and the vigor of American methods is shown by the operation of the meat trust, so called. The American packing houses to-day fix the price of beef in England, and that price now is nearly 30 per cent higher than at the same time last year. Under date of July 9, the London Mail said, in the course of a long article:

Experts in the meat trade smile at the suggestion which has been made that the Americans are about to capture the English meat trade. They say that that would be equivalent to the Dutch taking Holland, and that Smithfield Market has already passed under the absolute control of American houses. The capture has been secret and gradual, but it has been none the less secure. Smithfield Market, the center of the wholesale meat trade, consists of some 300 stalls and refrigerators, under the management of the markets' committee of the city corporation. The turnover of these stalls varies from £4,000 to £50,000 ($19,460 to $243,320) each week, according to the position of the holding. There was a time, less than ten years ago, when no American held a single stall. At that time the Americans sold their meat through English salesmen in Smithfield, paying such salesmen at first 2½ per cent, and afterwards 2 per cent commission. It is estimated that they paid £100,000 ($486,600) yearly in such commission. Then came the American invasion. The Swift Company came first, and the others followed rapidly. In almost every instance the Americans bought up the holdings of the particular commission salesman to whom they had been in the habit of consigning, paying sums ranging downward from one instance in which the purchase price was between £15,000 ($72,997) and £20,000

($97,300), displacing English firms. Here is a list of the principal American firms established in Smithfield:

| Number of stall. | Name. | Previous occupier. |
|---|---|---|
| 73 | Herbert Smith | Frost & Battams. |
| 76, 882. | } Hammond Beef Co., Limited | Harrar & Davis. |
| 138, 139. | | |
| 78 | Edward Morris & Co | Venables. |
| 266 | ....do. | Jennings. |
| 622 | Armour & Co., Limited | Original. |
| 613 | Morris Beef Co., Limited | Do. |
| Central avenue | Archer, Dawson & Sulzberger | A. Hayr and Archer Dawson. |
| 156 | Nelson Morris | E. E. Pool. |
| 162 | Swift Beef Co., Limited | Licensed public house. |
| Central avenue | Cudahy & Co.; agents, Parsons & Elliott. | Fosbery. |
| Do | Hammond & Co.; manager, Jas. Scott | Hickman. |

The country trade, too, as well as that of Smithfield, is passing entirely into American hands. Country buyers who used to get their supplies from Smithfield are now being supplied direct from Liverpool and Southampton depots which the American "ring" has set up. Several English firms which used to cater for this trade have either had to shut their depots or sell them to the Americans, who forced them to these measures by restricting supplies except at prices well above those on which they themselves traded. Possessing the entire supplies of refrigerated beef from the States, the Americans are getting the entire beef trade of the Kingdom into their hands, and are believed to be aiming at the extinction of the English carcass butcher. The American methods of taking care that no unexpected importations of live cattle by English firms shall upset their schemes of quantities and prices for refrigerated beef have been ingenious. To begin with, they have taken practically all the available space on the freight steamers for six months or twelve months at a time, and have run them very much under-laden rather than allow opposition firms any important facilities. Sometimes English firms have chartered steamers and have loaded up with cattle, but in all cases they have found such steamers "nursed" and surrounded by boats of the American "ring," which boats have delivered freight at Deptford in time to make the supply unusually long and cheap just when the British supply came to the market. By signaling either from the Lizard or Gravesend to their incoming freight boats, sending instructions for either promptitude or delay in "making" Deptford, the Americans, regardless almost of the cost, have kept the supply short or long to suit their own moves, their tactics being assisted, of course, by the regulation which provides for the killing of all cattle within ten days of the landing at Deptford. So smart and relentless has been this American competition that now the game has been practically left to them by the disheartened English traders. There is every prospect that beef will be twisted up to record prices before the year has closed. The British side of Smithfield declares that the only thing which can prevent this will be the reopening of the Argentine supply now that the Republic is said to be free from foot-and-mouth disease.

Partially answering the question as to why it is possible for these conditions to exist, a leading authority answered that it was largely because of improved American methods. Continuing, he said:

Of course the Americans are going ahead in our meat markets, not only in London, but in the provinces. The reason is that they supply better stuff and handle it better. Go into the Smithfield market any morning, and you will see the stalls of the great American chilled beef houses the cleanest and brightest there, with their goods displayed to the best advantage. Inquire into prices, and you will find that they get more for their Chicago-killed beef than is given for Scotch cattle. Now, English retail butchers are not fools, and there are good reasons why they prefer to pay heavily for the American article. The Chicago houses have reduced the killing, skinning, cooling, chilling, and transporting of their stock to an exact science. Their stock is hardly touched by hand; it is kept spotless, and it turns up in Smithfield looking better after its ocean journey than does the meat killed the day before by the English butcher 60 miles away. If English cattle raisers want to beat the Americans, they must adopt their cleanliness, their care of their meat, their skill in getting trade, and their straightforward dealings with their trade customers.

Strange as it may seem, the great English public remains dumb to these facts and their significance, and to similar conditions operating daily in almost every field of industry. It eats its American beef with the self-satisfied conviction that no such beef could come from anywhere except Shropshire or Devonshire.

Such facts as have been rehearsed relating to different industries—and examples have been used only for the purposes of illustration—immediately suggest the existence of a peculiar industrial, commercial, and social condition. England may be justly proud of her age, of her old institutions, of her own particular methods; but with them she must carry the burden of antiquity in most things. She can not start anew upon fresh ground and fully utilize the advanced economic systems of newer countries. She must revolutionize the old, and that is a thrice difficult task. Her railroads, for instance, to reap the advantages of recent progress in the handling of freight, must not only discard their vast accumulation of rolling stock of ancient and kindergarten pattern, but alter track distances, enlarge tunnels, and metamorphose terminal and side-track facilities. The cost of this no Englishman has yet been brave enough to estimate, but that a great deal of studying is going on, the pilgrimages to America of various committees and heads of departments bear witness. In the iron and steel industries, not so long ago the boast of English pride, equal incompetency has been admitted, and experts from the leading mills here have crossed to study and profit by American methods. Let it be said here, by way of parenthesis, that they were welcomed in the United States and given every opportunity for the investigation of methods and improvements. To keep history straight, those Americans who have crossed to this side to post themselves upon English methods in various industries should publish their experiences. In this particular industry circumstances have all favored the progressive Englishman as against American competition, for American mills have all been busy with the home market, and even unable to satisfy the home demand. The result has been that such leading concerns as the Consett Iron Company, Vaughn & Co., and Guest, Keen & Co. are being Americanized—transformed, so to speak, into modern plants equipped with American devices—preparatory to meeting the direct American competition of the near future. But all things English can not be so easily reformed, and the British Parliament stands aghast at the task of harmonizing conflicting municipal desires and jealousies into any scheme of general electrical improvement, and against which the vested railroad interests are now also thoroughly aroused. In the practical use of electricity England is twenty years behind the United States, and yet possesses the greatest condensed field for such exploitation in the world. Here, again, arises the interference of age, vested municipal rights, and obstinacy. As cities and towns have grown, they have added independent suburbs, and in the thickly settled portions of the island one town abuts squarely against another. But each has its own government and its own municipal pride. No two want the same style of electric road, the same gauge, or the same cars. When the extent of municipal ownership, or "municipal trading," as as it is called here, is considered, the situation becomes the despair of promoters. Instead of a harmonized, intelligent, and economical scheme of rapid transit between adjacent towns and throughout thickly populated districts, one finds here, where they exist at all, antagonistic systems with separate managements and independent fares, all operated by municipal authorities on money raised by taxing the middle and lower classes. The fad of municipal ownership, involving the extravagant use of public funds and necessitating a very high rate of municipal taxation, is just now receiving much attention. The extent to which it is carried is changing the very basis and scope of local government, and is hardly appreciated in America. It ranges, in various localities, from a monopoly of gas and electric transit, lighting, and power to the furnishing of sterilized milk and baby bottles. There is also a craze for combination in all branches of retail trade, until the "single shopper," as he is called, faces a situation very serious for himself, and the list of failures for last year was headed by 934 retail grocers, with liabilities of over $3,750,000. The cooperative joint stock companies, such as the Home and Colonial, the International Tea Company and Liptons, Limited, increased in capital from $65,000 in 1874 to $340,000,000 in 1890, and the increase, according to Board of Trade estimates, has since been proportionately maintained. In Leeds, for instance, with a population of 367,000, these stores have eighty odd branches and do a grocery business of over $5,000,000 a year, and in other cities in proportion to population. Company shops, operated on similar principles, exist everywhere. One has over 300 branches, another 250, with many running from 60 to 100. These corporations, operated from one central office, invade a town, scatter their stores throughout the retail section and drive the "single shopper" to disaster.

While the industrial situation as a whole is full of suggestions to the American who understands it, it is not necessary to go beyond the admissions of English authorities to find the underlying cause for British backwardness, and hence for the existing industrial chaos. Eminent writers, as well as special investigators appointed by trades bodies, and even trades unions, agree that the solution is to be found in the lack of practical, modern education among the working classes, which carries with it a lack of forceful, individual, and moral character. Eliminating the many and multiplied questions which attach to any study of English social life—the rule of a wealthy and idle aristocracy, the limitations of endeavor enforced by drastic class distinctions, the financial burdens unshouldered by an untaxed landlordism to the backs of the producing people—all critics unite upon the common ground that to meet the world's best competition, which literally means the brains, the character, and the individual force which issue from the American schoolhouse and Germany's educational straitjacket, the common people of England who do the work must be lifted from their present social environment, made to change the public house for the schoolhouse, and be given some hope for the future beyond a supply of black bread and beer for themselves and a similar lifetime diet for their children. Notwithstanding the educational bills pending in Parliament and the spasmodic efforts of well-intentioned people to help in the necessary reform by establishing a few industrial schools and universities, the future of the present generation is as full of hopelessness as the past, and therein lies the somewhat cruel secret of American commercial and industrial supremacy.

S. C. McFARLAND, *Consul.*

NOTTINGHAM, *August 26, 1902.*

## LACE AND HOSIERY TRADE AT NOTTINGHAM IN 1902.

The year 1902 made a new record in the Nottingham lace trade. The previous record year was 1883, following which came a decided slump. Then ensued a reaction which by degrees brought the export trade up to figures overtopping those of 1883. The cause of the extended demand for Nottingham laces during the past year was mainly favoring fashions. The demand was particularly strong for spotted and other varieties of nets. The market was fairly cleared of stocks, and buyers were willing to pay almost any prices in order to accommodate their customers. Quotations were withdrawn and prices were altogether abnormal, the supply being totally inadequate to meet the demand created by the prevalent fashions.

The output of curtains has been extensive, but the demand has remained stationery. Machinery for this product is being spread all all over the world. The building of this machinery for export is becoming an important industry here. The export thereof to the United States is already considerable and is increasing.

The business in silk laces during the year was insignificant, and their manufacture here seems doomed to extinction. Fashions are not favorable, and French makers are disposed to give them more attention than are the local manufacturers.

The manufacture of caps, aprons, blouses, collars, ruffles, and children's wear has greatly enlarged, and a very satisfactory business has been done.

The greatest increase in the export to foreign markets has been to the British colonies. The United States is ranked next. The declared valued of the laces sent to our country from this district last year was about $5,000,000. This is the greatest annual value since 1883, when a decline set in which reached its climax in 1896, after which began a steady gain each year which aggregated about 100 per cent at the end of 1902. Business opens this year with every indication that the gain will continue unabated.

The hosiery trade has been, and the future outlook is, unsatisfactory. This applies generally—not alone to trade with the United States. Time was when hosiery vied with lace in this district in export to our country. Now, that export stands as one to twenty in favor of lace. The change is almost wholly due to the decline of the hosiery business. There was hope that the trade might find relief in prices of wool, but that has been disappointed. A material advance in some grades makes business in certain branches quite impossible—spinners having withdrawn their lists from inability to quote definite prices. Cotton branches are also depressed, especially those engaged with socks and stockings. The term "hosiery" includes underwear, which is in rather better condition than socks and stockings.

FRANK W. MAHIN, *Consul.*

NOTTINGHAM, *January 15, 1903.*

## PLYMOUTH.

An examination of the Board of Trade returns for the first six months of 1902 is not encouraging to the British public. The general depression is shared by the counties of Devon and Cornwall, as a comparison of the following tables, showing the declared exports from this consular district to the United States for the six months ended June 30, 1902, with those previously published, will illustrate:

| Articles. | Quarter ended— | |
|---|---|---|
| | Mar. 31, 1902. | June 30, 1902. |
| Arsenic | $40,593.54 | $17,135.32 |
| Brushes | | 347.14 | 909.76 |
| Clay | 125,299.76 | 112,993.32 |
| Gin | 7,991.46 | 29,110.82 |
| Household effects | | 219.00 |
| Liqueurs | | 762.82 |
| Pottery | | 315.48 |
| Rope | | 5,911.88 |
| Total | 174,231.90 | 167,858.40 |

### IMPORTS.

The import trade, however, continues much the same as during the last six months of 1901. The purchase of American meat has greatly fallen off, owing to the advance in price, but machinery, agricultural implements, and tools have had an improved sale. American carriages have become common sights on the streets of the city, and the sale of American shoes continues to rapidly increase, as does the import of steel rails and of general electrical equipment.

### AGRICULTURE.

It is fully expected that the county of Cornwall will maintain its superiority over Devon, but allowance should be made for the more extensive area of waste land in the larger county, and in cultivated area it can be assumed, for all practical purposes, that Devon is just twice the size of Cornwall. No crop in either county will be below the ten years' averages, as given in the returns issued by the board of agriculture.

In round figures, the area sown in wheat in Devon last year was 7,000 acres less than in 1900, or about 13 per cent, and this year the area will probably show a further reduction. Barley was practically the same, and oats showed only a slight falling off. Wheat last year was the best of the cereals. Potatoes are above the average, but the great supply continues to come from France and the Channel Islands. Last year hay was a failure, but this year it will be far above the ten years' average.

In the two counties there are about 50,000 acres of orchards, but they are so neglected that the crop is of small consequence, and the main supply of fruit comes from the United States.

Jos. G. STEPHENS, Consul.

PLYMOUTH, July 16, 1902.

The official return of the oversea trade of the port of Plymouth for the past year has been issued by the customs authorities, and from the figures it will be seen that the number of vessels and their aggregate tonnage which passed through the port during the last twelve months are considerably in excess of the volume of traffic dealt with in the preceding year, which was ahead of the trade of 1900. The year that has just ended saw 3,372 vessels of 1,000,233 tons arrive and 3,202 vessels of 929,869 tons depart, as compared with 3,160 vessels of 938,911 tons entered, and 3,194 vessels of 872,252 tons cleared in the previous year, and 2,916 vessels of 895,541 tons entered and 2,902 vessels of 832,222 tons cleared in 1900. The foregoing figures do not include the tonnage of British and foreign warships, nor of the many mail and passenger steamers which have called at Plymouth for the purpose of embarking or disembarking passengers, mails, and specie. Plymouth as a port of call is mentioned separately in another part of this report.

## FOREIGN TRADE.

The oversea traffic of Plymouth is principally an import trade, the exports to places beyond the United Kingdom direct from this port being comparatively small. As in past years, the principal business was done with France and the Channel Islands, Germany, the United States, Holland, Norway and Sweden, Belgium, and Russia. In the foreign trade, 581 vessels of 230,693 tons arrived last year, and 584 vessels of 125,225 tons sailed, as against 665 vessels of 231,960 tons arrived and 587 vessels of 108,427 tons cleared in 1901. Last year, although the same number of vessels (33) arrived in ballast as in 1901, the tonnage under this heading was nearly 5,000 tons less; consequently it will be seen that although there is a decline in the actual amount of tonnage that entered the port, the cargo-carrying tonnage was greater by about 4,000 tons. In the "clearances" with cargoes there was little or no fluctuation. The appended table will show at a glance the state of the foreign trade of the port as compared with the previous year:

FOREIGN TRADE.

| Kind of vessel. | Arrivals. | | | | Sailings. | | | |
|---|---|---|---|---|---|---|---|---|
| | 1901. | | 1902. | | 1901. | | 1902. | |
| | Number | Tonnage. | Number. | Tonnage. | Number. | Tonnage. | Number. | Tonnage. |
| Sailing............. | 289 | 49,900 | 241 | 44,590 | 185 | 24,734 | 176 | 21,224 |
| Steamers........... | 343 | 173,145 | 307 | 182,115 | 85 | 8,678 | 94 | 27,379 |
| Sailing (in ballast). | 26 | 5,728 | 22 | 1,991 | 153 | 27,688 | 131 | 20,854 |
| Steamers (in ballast) | 7 | 3,187 | 11 | 1,997 | 164 | 47,327 | 183 | 55,768 |
| Total.......... | 665 | 231,960 | 581 | 230,693 | 587 | 108,427 | 584 | 125,225 |

## THE COASTING TRADE.

The coasting trade of Plymouth was some 103,408 tons in advance of what it was twelve months ago, when an improvement of 99,290 tons was recorded. The number of vessels employed was 5,409, an increase of 307 for the year. The aggregate tonnage of the vessels engaged in the coastwise traffic was 1,574,184 tons, while twelve months ago it was 1,470,776 tons. Last year, 189 vessels of 18,177 tons arrived in ballast, as compared with 147 vessels of 11,581 tons in 1901. In the sailings, too, there has been an increase in the tonnage that left the port in ballast to the extent of over 26.000 tons. In analyzing the return, it will be found that the Irish trade has advanced to the extent of about 11,000 tons. This traffic has shown a steady gain for the past four years. The commerce with ports in Great Britain has also developed. The number of foreign vessels engaged in the British coasting trade was higher than usual, and there was an increase in the foreign tonnage that arrived at Plymouth with cargoes from British ports to the extent of over 6,000 tons. One hundred and forty-five vessels floating a foreign flag were engaged in the British coasting trade, while twelve months ago the number was 112. The nationalities represented were:

| | | | |
|---|---:|---|---:|
| German | 50 | Danish | 10 |
| Norwegian | 30 | Russian | 7 |
| French | 18 | Swedish | 5 |
| Dutch | 13 | Italian | 1 |
| Belgian | 11 | | |

During the five years that I have been stationed at this port, only one American vessel has been employed in the coasting trade, and that for but one voyage. This traffic is not sufficiently remunerative for American ships. The following tables show in brief the state of the coasting trade, as compared with 1901:

GENERAL COASTING TRADE.

| Kind of vessel. | Arrivals. | | | | Sailings. | | | |
|---|---|---|---|---|---|---|---|---|
| | 1901. | | 1902. | | 1901. | | 1902. | |
| | Number. | Tonnage. | Number. | Tonnage. | Number. | Tonnage. | Number. | Tonnage. |
| Sailing | 772 | 61,954 | 899 | 68,091 | 817 | 52,777 | 801 | 51,839 |
| Steamers | 1,361 | 550,303 | 1,449 | 590,636 | 774 | 378,457 | 793 | 391,024 |
| Sailing (in ballast) | 118 | 6,161 | 143 | 6,393 | 165 | 20,904 | 118 | 12,939 |
| Steamers (in ballast) | 14 | 3,287 | 31 | 8,636 | 611 | 219,193 | 661 | 252,798 |
| Total | 2,265 | 621,705 | 2,522 | 673,756 | 2,367 | 671,331 | 2,373 | 708,600 |

THE IRISH TRADE.

| | 1901. | | 1902. | | 1901. | | 1902. | |
|---|---|---|---|---|---|---|---|---|
| Sailing | 49 | 4,375 | 38 | 3,736 | 52 | 4,403 | 42 | 3,457 |
| Steamers | 136 | 69,506 | 150 | 73,518 | 114 | 59,550 | 126 | 63,794 |
| Steamers (in ballast) | 1 | 448 | 4 | 1,070 | 5 | 1,002 | 9 | 3,901 |
| Total | 186 | 74,329 | 192 | 78,324 | 171 | 64,955 | 177 | 71,152 |

FOREIGN VESSELS ENGAGED IN BRITISH COASTING TRADE.

| | 1901. | | 1902. | | 1901. | | 1902. | |
|---|---|---|---|---|---|---|---|---|
| Sailing | 9 | 1,179 | 16 | 1,315 | 7 | 739 | 7 | 667 |
| Steamers | 21 | 8,053 | 50 | 14,167 | 3 | 958 | 2 | 338 |
| Sailing (in ballast) | 12 | 1,423 | 8 | 1,036 | 15 | 3,533 | 17 | 4,524 |
| Steamers (in ballast) | 1 | 262 | 3 | 943 | 44 | 22,309 | 42 | 19,363 |
| Total | 43 | 10,917 | 77 | 17,461 | 69 | 27,539 | 68 | 24,892 |

TOTALS (COASTING TRADE).

| | 1901. | | 1902. | | 1901. | | 1902. | |
|---|---|---|---|---|---|---|---|---|
| Sailing | 830 | 67,508 | 953 | 73,142 | 876 | 57,919 | 850 | 55,963 |
| Steamers | 1,518 | 627,862 | 1,649 | 678,321 | 891 | 438,965 | 921 | 455,156 |
| Sailing (in ballast) | 130 | 7,584 | 151 | 7,429 | 180 | 24,437 | 135 | 17,463 |
| Steamers (in ballast) | 17 | 3,997 | 38 | 10,648 | 660 | 242,504 | 712 | 276,082 |
| Total | 2,495 | 705,951 | 2,791 | 769,540 | 2,607 | 763,825 | 2,618 | 804,644 |

## MILLBAY DOCKS.

The number of vessels which wc. e accommodated at the docks in 1900 was 2,885, of 605,026 net registered tonnage; in 1901, the number of vessels was 2,445, of 597,126 tonnage, and last year 2,263 vessels, of 626,409 tonnage.  The cargo totals, however, show decreases. Details of the year's trade follow:

|  | 1901. | 1902. |
|---|---|---|
| Number of vessels | 2,445 | 2,263 |
| Registered tonnage | 597,126 | 626,409 |

*Cargo.*

|  | 1901. | 1902. |
|---|---|---|
|  | *Tons.* | *Tons.* |
| Coastwise: |  |  |
| Imports | 155,589 | 148,662 |
| Exports | 39,482 | 34,080 |
| Total | 195,021 | 182,742 |
| Foreign: |  |  |
| Imports | 112,614 | 115,541 |
| Exports | 8,072 | 6,099 |
| Total | 120,686 | 121,640 |
| Grand total | 315,707 | 304,382 |

These totals were made up as follows:

|  | 1901. | 1902. |
|---|---|---|
|  | *Tons.* | *Tons.* |
| Coal | 22,556 | 20,920 |
| Clay | 20,967 | 15,392 |
| Grain | 107,813 | 112,715 |
| Manure | 13,476 | 9,108 |
| Ores | 57 | 1,160 |
| Sugar | 8,452 | 7,988 |
| Stone | 5,190 | 1,466 |
| Timber | 11,240 | 12,528 |
| Hay and straw | 364 | 1,008 |
| Sundries | 126,063 | 122,107 |
| Total | 315,707 | 304,382 |

## CATTEWATER.

Last year, 1,496 vessels of 188,475 tons were dealt with in Cattewater, as compared with 1,600 vessels of 175,062 tons in 1901 and 1,527 vessels of 182,848 tons in the previous year.  The amount of cargo that actually passed through Cattewater was 321,710 tons, as against 315,437 tons in the previous year, when a decline of 18,300 tons was recorded in comparison with 1900.  The export traffic was about 2,000 tons heavier than it was twelve months ago, while the imports show an advance of 4,288 tons.  Appended is a comparison of the amount of cargo handled in the export and import traffic of Cattewater during the last two years.

|  | 1901. | 1902. |
|---|---|---|
| Number of vessels | 1,600 | 1,496 |
| Registered tonnage | 175,082 | 188,475 |
| **IMPORTS.** | *Tons.* | *Tons.* |
| Coal and culm | 66,375 | 64,000 |
| Timber, deal, etc | 36,761 | 24,000 |
| Petroleum | 10,807 | 16,743 |
| Pyrites | 11,127 | 10,128 |
| Phosphate | 20,024 | 17,457 |
| Cement | 8,464 | 2,450 |
| Nitrate | | 1,608 |
| Guano | 1,153 | 5,425 |
| Miscellaneous | 14,150 | 26,249 |
| Total | 163,870 | 168,060 |
| **EXPORTS.** | | |
| China clay | 33,698 | 37,354 |
| Fire bricks | 9,861 | 8,793 |
| Manure | 17,003 | 15,456 |
| Pitch | 5,266 | 5,508 |
| Limestone (about) | 70,000 | 70,000 |
| Micellaneous | 15,739 | 16,441 |
| Total | 151,567 | 153,552 |

## SUTTON HARBOR.

Trade has been very brisk in Sutton Harbor during the past twelve months. The number of vessels arriving was 46 over that of the previous year, 1901, and the net tonnage was 23,538 tons greater. The imports of coal have advanced 15,000 tons over 1901, and the general trade has been satisfactory. The imports included coals, timber, corn, feeding cakes, manure, bricks, cement, slate, stone, potatoes, fruit, ice from Norway, and general merchandise. The improvements, which are mentioned elsewhere in this report, have proved of great advantage to the trade, both in the saving of labor and quick dispatch. Excluding the steamers of the Kingsbridge Line, steam trawlers, barges, the vessels of the several fishing fleets, and other small craft, the traffic dealt with in Sutton Harbor last year was represented by 266 steamers and 510 sailing vessels, of an aggregate tonnage of 122,332 tons. Twelve months ago, 236 steamers and 494 sailing vessels, of a total tonnage of 98,794 tons, arrived in the harbor.

## OCEAN MAIL AND PASSENGER TRAFFIC.

The year was a satisfactory one for Plymouth as a port of call. Altogether, some 464 ocean mail and passenger steamers touched at the port, as compared with 444 vessels in 1901 and 421 vessels in 1900. The year 1903, however, owing to recent arrangements of Dutch and German lines, must witness a still greater increase. The homeward bound steamers numbered 361 in 1902 and the outward bound 103. The increase was due to the regular call—going westward and eastward—of the Hamburg-American Line steamers and the eastward call of the North German Lloyd vessels. No less than 60 steamers of the latter line are scheduled to arrive at this port from New York during 1903. There will be 4 steamers a week from New York and probably 3 to New York. To cope with the increased activity at the port, the Great Western Railway Company has arranged to bring to Plymouth an additional passenger tender. During the year, there was landed at Plymouth from New York specie to the value of $7,132,411.43, 4,473 passengers, and 29,000 sacks of mail. The outward bound steamers, intermediate class, of the Hamburg-American Line embarked 685 passengers. These figures would have been much larger but for the mishap to the *Deutschland* in April and again at the close of the year, she being practically out of service for eight months. In addition to the two great German lines, the P. and O. Company, the Orient Pacific Line, the Royal Mail Steam Packet Company, the Union-Castle Line, the British India Company, the Shaw, Savill and Albion Company, the New Zealand Shipping Company, the White Star Australian Line, the Aberdeen Line, the British and African Steamship Company, and the British and Colonial Line have regularly called at Plymouth; the Orient and the Aberdeen company's steamers touched at the port, both homeward and outward bound.

The local lines of passenger steamers have not had a prosperous year, but the freight companies have done a fair trade, viewed from the standpoint of chartering rates. A new line of pleasure steamers, which is having several ships built, will start a service in May.

### FISHING INDUSTRY.

The fishing industry was about the same as usual until the end of the year, when very large catches of herrings were brought to the market by about 250 boats. An additional steam trawler has been added to the Plymouth fleet. During the year, 227 trips have been made to the harbor by steam trawlers, as against 228 trips in the previous year and 171 trips in 1900.

The Devon sea fisheries board reports that fair catches of fish have been brought from the outer grounds, but that the boats working the inner grounds have not met with much success. Trawlers have landed very large catches of dogfish from the outer grounds. The latter appear to be numerous, and are a detriment to other fishing. Plymouth has been most successful as regards whiting. Good prices were obtained for mackerel. Shell fish have been exceedingly scarce. The catches of pilchards have been good, and the market in the United States for these fish is increasing.

### BUNKERING TRADE.

The ordinary bunkering trade of Plymouth amounted to about the same as 1901, but the total output was not as large as had been anticipated. This trade is increased by the large number of war ships that visit the port. Increased facilities are now afforded at Dartmouth for the coaling of steamers.

### TRADE WITH THE CHANNEL ISLANDS.

There was little variation in the trade with the Channel Islands. The Anglo-French Company maintains its regular service, which in April was augmented by a new liner. These steamers have a good freight trade, but owing to their slowness, forfeit the passenger traffic to the very fast boats running out of Southampton and Weymouth.

## TRADE WITH THE UNITED STATES.

The trade of this consular district with the United States, both export and import—especially the latter—continues to increase. The shipments of white powdered arsenic have, owing to increased production in the United States and to Continental competition, rapidly diminished. Notwithstanding a fall of £4 ($19.50) per ton in price, the sales diminished from $136,245.64 to $75,061.19. Large quantities are being produced in Europe; and it is the general opinion that this branch of English export trade is doomed. The local shippers have expressed this conclusion at the consulate, and requested particulars regarding developments in the United States. The sale of woolen goods has completely ceased, and the sale of brushes still declines. Gin and liqueurs have had a larger market. The shipments of china clay show a steady advance—from $502,410.97 in 1901 to $533,677.08 in 1902. The following tables give the declared exports from this district to the United States for the four quarters of the year ended December 31, 1902:

| Article. | Quarter ended— | | | |
|---|---|---|---|---|
|  | Mar. 31. | June 30. | Sept. 30. | Dec. 31. |
| Animals | | | | $121.66 |
| Arsenic | $40,593.54 | $17,135.32 | | |
| Brushes | 347.14 | 909.76 | $1,332.30 | 541.56 |
| Chemicals | | | | 17,832.33 |
| Clay | 125,299.76 | 112,993.32 | 117,142.58 | 178,241.42 |
| Fish | | | | 673.53 |
| Gin | 7,991.46 | 29,110.82 | 29,019.37 | |
| Household effects | | 219.00 | 190.10 | |
| Liqueurs | | 762.82 | | |
| Matches | | | | 110.44 |
| Pictures | | | | 255.41 |
| Pottery | | 315.48 | 266.90 | |
| Rope | | 5,911.88 | | |
| Salted roans | | | | 398.02 |
| Sausage skins | | | 2,001.35 | |
| Show cards | | | 138.78 | |
| Spirits | | | | 3,332.42 |
| Stone | | | | 498.42 |
| Wines | | | | 330.30 |
| Total | 174,231.90 | 167,358.40 | 150,091.38 | 201,830.51 |

As all imports from the States come through agencies in London and Liverpool, no exact figures can be obtained. The amount of American goods and products consumed in this district is great and still increasing. The extension of electric lines and light plants in Plymouth, Devonport, Stonehouse, Exeter, and Torquay will afford a good opportunity for American firms. Their success in the past should be an earnest of the future. The tramway systems are treated under a separate heading. I repeat the statement made in my last annual report, that there has never been a better opportunity for electrical equipment than at the present time.

*Shoes.*—In my last report, I also mentioned the fact that our boots and shoes had captured this part of England, the sales having so encouraged the dealers that several new branches were being established. Another large and imposing store has since then been opened in the best location in the city. The finest three shops in Plymouth are American.

*Meat.*—During the last twelve months, the American beef companies located in Plymouth have sold 10,967 quarters of beef, 7,066 pigs, 1,305 cases of pork loins, and 1,860 cases of sundry provisions. It is needless to say that these figures would have been much greater but for the high price of American beef. The Hammond Company has closed its branch in Plymouth. The Swift and the Morris company, however, continue to extend their connections.

*Wooden ware.*—There appears to be a splendid opening in the counties of Devon and Cornwall for the sale of American wooden ware. A manufacturer from Boston has been here and examined the markets and arranged for early shipments. We are also sending samples to New Zealand.

*Fire extinguishers.*—It appears from conversations that I have had with travelers from the South Island, that there is a chance to sell American fire extinguishers, as nearly all the houses are built of wood, and fires are frequent. Strange as it may seem, many English merchants call at the consulate for information concerning trade conditions in New Zealand, Australia, and Canada; in fact, we get nearly as many inquiries concerning Canada as we do the United States.

*Fruit.*—In our reports for 1901, Consul Boyle, of Liverpool, and myself called attention to the strong competition in tinned fruits in this country. In this trade, I regret to repeat that the United States is not holding its own. Better value is being offered from Spain, Italy, and Singapore, but our trade in general is advancing rapidly. The realization of American resources is growing on the people.

If American merchants make the same earnest efforts that they have in the past, and above all carefully adapt themselves to the buyer's desires and needs, naught but success can crown their work.

### DEVONPORT DOCKYARD.

The importance of the Devonport dockyard in the commercial life of the three towns is shown by the wages and salaries disbursed in the yard during the year that has just closed. The wages for the twelve months amounted to £661,500 ($3,219,189.75), an average of £12,725 ($61,926.21) per week. The number of men on the books of the yard is about 9,700. In addition to the wages, there is necessarily a considerable salary list. During the year, the salaries paid to officers amounted to £61,680 ($300,165.72). Taking salaries and wages together, the amount distributed in the yard is about £14,000 ($68,131) per week.

A table giving the output of the five Government yards since 1890 shows that while the tonnage production of Portsmouth has relatively decreased during the past four years, that of Devonport has greatly increased, and indeed heads the list with a substantial margin. The following tables are from the Glasgow Herald:

| Year. | Portsmouth. | Chatham. | Pembroke. | Devonport. | Sheerness. |
|---|---|---|---|---|---|
| | Tons. | Tons. | Tons. | Tons. | Tons. |
| 1902 | | 20,880 | 9,800 | 20,880 | |
| 1901 | 9,800 | 14,000 | 23,900 | 14,000 | 3,210 |
| 1900 | 2,200 | | | | 3,080 |
| 1899 | 15,000 | 17,200 | 4,700 | 30,000 | |
| 1898 | 15,000 | 27,950 | 11,000 | 15,085 | 1,020 |
| 1897 | 12,950 | 5,800 | 11,000 | | 2,130 |
| 1896 | 26,300 | 14,900 | 14,900 | 11,000 | 4,275 |
| 1895 | 29,800 | 20,500 | 12,350 | 7,700 | |
| 1894 | 5,600 | 14,900 | 1,070 | 3,210 | 1,920 |
| 1893 | 4,360 | 5,480 | 8,720 | 9,630 | 4,350 |
| 1892 | 18,300 | 10,500 | 14,150 | 4,350 | 3,240 |
| 1891 | 21,850 | 24,900 | 14,150 | 3,600 | 3,600 |
| 1890 | 2,575 | 1,340 | 2,575 | 12,500 | 1,470 |

The output work of the Royal yards during the past year is given below. Although Portsmouth and Sheerness have actually contributed nothing to the tonnage total afloat, there are several vessels which are far advanced in construction. The figures are:

|  | Vessels. | Displacement. | |
|---|---|---|---|
|  |  | 1902. | 1901. |
|  |  | Tons. | Tons. |
| Devonport............................................. | 2 | 20, 880 | 14, 000 |
| Chatham ............................................. | 2 | 20, 880 | 14, 000 |
| Pembroke ............................................. | 1 | 9, 800 | 23, 900 |
| Portsmouth ............................................. |  |  | 9, 800 |
| Sheerness............................................. |  |  | 3, 210 |
| Total ............................................. | 5 | 51, 560 | 64, 910 |

| Vessel. | Type. | Displace-ment. |
|---|---|---|
| Devonport: |  | Tons. |
| Queen............................................. | Battle ship.......... | 15, 000 |
| Encounter ............................................. | Cruiser ............. | 5, 800 |
| Total............................................. |  | 20, 800 |
| Chatham: |  |  |
| Prince of Wales............................................. | Battle ship.......... | 15, 000 |
| Challenger............................................. | Cruiser ............. | 5, 880 |
| Total............................................. |  | 20, 880 |
| Pembroke: |  |  |
| Cornwall............................................. | Armored cruiser.... | 9, 800 |

"The gratifying feature in the foregoing figures," says a local paper, "is the unmistakable evidence afforded of the growth of Devonport Dockyard." It continues:

If Plymouth can not yet claim to be the premier naval port, we certainly think the time has come when Devonport may claim to be the principal Government yard of the British Empire. Everything goes to demonstrate this condition. Where Devonport has the great advantage over Portsmouth as a dockyard establishment is in the matter of accommodation, not so much immediate as prospective. The latter yard has virtually been developed to the full limits of its capacity, and therefore it can not go further. Yet, despite this, the congestion of work is a great and growing difficulty with which the authorities are confronted. On the other hand, Devonport has unrivaled opportunities for enlargement, and when the present extension works are completed, the western establishment will certainly be in a position to keep pace with the steadily increasing pressure of naval construction and repairing. Portsmouth has seen the zenith of its prosperity in this aspect of its importance as a service center at any rate, and it must inevitably yield the palm to Devonport. Whether Plymouth will not prove the premier naval port of the near future is also a question which many experts answer in the affirmative. It has great strategic advantages as a base which commands the Channel at its most vulnerable portions, and the Sound is at least as convenient and safe a haven as Portsmouth Harbor, and distinctly more spacious.

The only new marine engineering work completed in the Royal dockyards during the year was the twin-screw triple-expansion engines of the second-class cruiser *Encounter*, of 12,500 indicated horsepower, with 18 Durr boilers, constructed at Devonport dockyard for the cruiser which was built at the western establishment. This compares with 1,400 indicated horsepower—the machinery of a sloop—built at the same works in the previous year.

The original displacement of the new battle ship *King Edward VII*, now being built at Devonport, has been increased to 16,350 tons. Her length will be 425 feet, and her beam 78 feet. Upon normal load draft she will draw 26 feet 9 inches. Her nominal coal endurance is to be 950 tons, which is calculated to give a radius of action of about six days at 14 knots. The twin quadruple expansions of the vessel will develop 18,000 indicated horsepower, and her legend speed is to be 18.5 knots. She will be fitted with Belleville generators of the latest economizer type. The complacement will be 800 of all ranks and ratings. The estimated cost will be £1,400,000 ($6.813,100); the real cost will be substantially more. The battle ship *Queen* has been launched for some time, but is not yet complete.

## MINING.

In Cornwall, 70 mines are at work, giving employment to 6,700 people. The position is very different from that of the palmy days of Cornish mining; but the figures are encouraging in that they show an increase of nearly 400 employees since the previous year. Mining in Devonshire is declining. There are only about 800 hands employed in the 21 mines reported to be at work, showing a decrease of 112 from the previous year. The quarrying industry is still brisk in the two counties which supply so large a proportion of the slate and granite produced in England. The arsenic mines are being closed, but the china clay pits have been rapidly increased in number. The death rate from accident in the mines is 1.30 per thousand per annum, which, considering the dangerous nature of the operations, is very small. Cornwall is covered with deserted mines, and the sight of the desolated country is depressing. This deplorable condition is attributed to (1) extortion of the landlords; (2) abuse of the cost-book system; (3) unwarrantable distribution of profits; (4) inefficient and antiquated mechanical methods; (5) carelessness in working, and (6) waste of mineral raised.

### PLYMOUTH SOUND AND APPROACHES.

The following is taken from a printed statement:

#### UNIFORM BUOYAGE.

Alterations in the buoyage of Plymouth Sound, with its approaches, have been effected in accordance with the uniform system of buoyage, 1883. In carrying this out, the colors adopted for the western channel into the Sound, and hence to Hamoaze, are red and red and red and white as far as the Rubble Bank, and those for the eastern channel, black and black and white as far as the Mallard Shoal; the conical buoys, of whatever single color, are starboard hand buoys; the can buoys, which are either checkered red and white, or checkered black and white, being port hand buoys:

Draystone, can, red and white checkered.
Queen's Grounds, can, red and white checkered.
New Grounds, can, red and white checkered.
Melampus, can, red and white checkered.
Asia, can, red and white checkered.
N. W. Drake's Island, can, red and white checkered.
Cremyll Shoal, can, red and white checkered.
Knap, conical, red, surmounted by staff and globe.
Panther, conical, red.
South Winter, spherical, red and white horizontal stripes, with staff and diamond.
N. W. Winter, spherical, red and white horizontal stripes, with staff and triangle.
Vanguard, conical, red.
Rubble Bank, conical, red.
West Tinker, conical, red.
East Tinker, can, black and white checkered.

Fairway, No. 1, can, black and white checkered.
Fairway, No. 2, can, black and white checkered.
Mewstone Ledge, conical, black.
East Channel, No. 1, conical, black.
East Channel, No. 2, conical, black.
Duke Rock, conical, black.
Mallard Shoal, conical, black.
N. E. Winter, can, black and white checkered.

Bridge buoys have been altered to can buoys, the colors remaining as before—southern, red; northern, white.

Panther buoy has been moved 150 yards W. ¼ N., to a position at the north extreme of the Panther Shoal. It now lies in 7 fathoms at low-water spring tides, with the following marks, bearings, and distance: Roman Catholic church, stone house, shut in with breakwater light-house, N. N. E., ¼ E., Bovisand Bay beacon in line with southeastern extreme of breakwater, E. by S. ¼ S., distant 1½ miles.

### SHAGSTONE BEACON.

A beacon has been erected on the Shagstone, east side of entrance to Plymouth Sound. The beacon, about 21 feet high and 9 feet in diameter at the base, is conical in shape, constructed of open ironwork, and surmounted by a globular top, the whole painted black.

*Rates of pilotage in the Plymouth district.*

[Rates per foot draft.]

| From— | To— | Of 10 feet and under | | Over 10 feet, and under 12 feet | | 12 feet, and under 14 feet | | 14 feet, and under 16 feet | | 16 feet, and under 18 feet | | 18 feet, and over | |
|---|---|---|---|---|---|---|---|---|---|---|---|---|---|
| | | Eng. cur. *s. d.* | U.S. cur. | Eng. cur. *s. d.* | U.S. cur. | Eng. cur. *s. d.* | U.S. cur. | Eng. cur. *s. d.* | U.S. cur. | Eng. cur. *s. d.* | U.S. cur. | Eng. cur. *s. d.* | U.S. cur. |
| Any position between an imaginary line drawn from Rame Head to the Mewstone as the inner line, and the seaward limit of 5 miles as the outer line. | Cawsand Bay or Plymouth Sound, or vice versa. | 3 0 | $0.73 | 3 4 | $0.81 | 3 8 | $0.892 | 4 0 | $0.973 | 4 6 | $1.094 | 4 6 | $1.094 |
| Cawsand Bay or Plymouth Sound | Cattewater, Mill Bay dock, West wharf, Sutton pool, or Hamoaze, or vice versa. | 2 0 | .486 | 2 4 | .567 | 3 0 | .729 | 3 6 | .85 | 4 0 | .973 | 4 6 | 1.094 |
| Sea | Salcombe or the River Yealm, or vice versa. | 4 0 | .973 | 4 0 | .973 | 4 0 | .973 | 4 0 | .973 | 4 0 | .973 | 4 0 | .973 |
| For the pilotage of any vessel between any two of the following places. | Cattewater, Mill Bay dock, West wharf, Sutton pool, and Hamoaze. | 2 0 | .486 | 2 4 | .567 | 3 0 | .73 | 3 6 | .85 | 4 0 | .973 | 4 6 | 1.094 |
| Vessels exempted from pilotage whose masters employ pilots outwards. | Sound or sea to pay (and inwards the rates given for compulsory vessels). | 5 0 | 1.216 | 5 8 | 1.378 | 6 8 | 1.62 | 7 6 | 1.92 | 8 6 | 2.068 | 9 0 | 2.19 |

All ships drawing less than 10 feet of water are to pay the same amount of pilotage as if they were of that draft.

Mail steamers calling to land or embark mails and passengers, and all vessels calling for dispatches only, to pay the rate per foot inward as above, and two shillings and sixpence per foot outward.

The several pilotage rates above specified are subject to a reduction of one-fourth part, in respect of vessels propelled by steam and vessels towed by steam vessels; provided, that if any such vessel shall be propelled by steam or towed by a steam vessel for a part only of the distance for which rate may be payable, the reduction of one-fourth shall be made on such part only of the said rate as shall be proportionate to the distance so propelled or towed.

Steamships putting into Plymouth Sound for bunker coal only are to pay for pilotage in and out the rates above provided for inward only, without the usual deduction for steam.

If a master choose to retain or employ a pilot while at anchor the rate for the lay days is to be 10s. ($2.43) a day, including the day coming in or going out, detention from stress of weather or other unavoidable circumstances not to count.

### PLYMOUTH GAS COMPANY.

A bill is now before Parliament, the object of which is to confer further powers on the Plymouth Gas Company for extending the limit of supply so as to include the parish of Plymstock, and authorizing the raising of £100,000 ($486,600) additional capital. The electric-light plants, which are owned by the corporation of Plymouth, are not satisfactory. It is claimed that municipal ownership of electrical works throughout England has put the country far behind others in this respect. Though the gas manufactured in Plymouth is almost worthless, it will remain for some years paramount to electricity. The following particulars in regard to some of the principal gas undertakings in the west of England are taken from the Gas World Year Book. The price of gas in the different towns depends not only on the illuminating power, but also on the distance of the works from the coal fields, the capital invested, and other circumstances.

| | Annual make. | Candle-power. | Price. | |
|---|---|---|---|---|
| | | | English currency. | United States currency. |
| | *Cubic feet.* | | *s. d.* | |
| Bath | 504,729,000 | 16 | a2 5 | $0.557 |
| Bristol | 2,235,633,000 | 16 | 2 3 | .547 |
| Devonport | 266,220,000 | 15¼ | 2 6 | .608 |
| Exeter | 274,389,000 | 15½ | 3 2 | .77 |
| Falmouth | 89,257,000 | 16 | 3 9 | .912 |
| Gloucester | 833,400,000 | 16¼ | 2 4½ | .587 |
| Plymouth | 970,000,000 | 15 | 1 9 | .425 |

a Less discount.

### CLIMATE.

The climate of Devon and Cornwall is mild and equitable. The summers are cool and balmy, and the winters are almost free from snow and frost. There are no extremes of heat and cold. Outside of the city of Plymouth, the climate is considered extremely healthful. Many Americans spend the summer on the downs and moors of the two counties.

### GENERAL IMPROVEMENTS.

Considerable improvement has been effected during the last twelve months in increasing the facilities for shipping. At the Great Western Railway docks, new gates were opened last year, the undertaking having entailed a large expenditure of money. The gates are manipulated by hydraulic power. A railway swing bridge to cross the new entrance to the floating dock will be completed at an early date. The south wall of the inner basin is being widened about 90 feet, and will give largely increased accommodation. The Trinity pier is being lengthened and doubled in width, the extension being on concrete pillars and arches, and several large new cranes have been placed in position, including a traveling 12-ton crane, available for any part of the docks. The deepening of the entrance in the inner side is proving a long and costly undertaking.

Cattewater Harbor has been receiving considerable attention during the past year. The commissioners have made progress with the dredging of the harbor to a uniform depth of 17 feet at low spring tides, and in connection with Victoria wharves, the new pier of which is rapidly nearing completion. The approach also is being deepened. The recent decision of Plymouth corporation to build a wharf in Cattewater, close to the electrical works, will tend to give that harbor increased importance. When completed, the pier at Victoria wharves will be 500 feet long and 50 feet broad, and on the east side will have minimum depth of 27 feet of water at low tide. The steam cranes and machinery for discharging cargoes at Bayly's wharf have proved particularly helpful, especially the 10-ton steam locomotive cranes.

During the year, Plymouth was visited by several very destructive fires, and property to the value of half a million dollars has been destroyed. In most instances new and imposing buildings are being erected on the sites. Many of the principal streets of the city have been widened and straightened at enormous cost. About 2 acres of tenements have been razed to the ground, and on their site the corporation will erect modern workingmen's homes. The sewerage scheme, now well advanced, will cost about $1,000,000. A large new park has been completed, which gives the Three Towns seven extensive recreation grounds, some of which are among the finest in Europe.

### PLYMOUTH TRAMWAYS.

There are three systems of electric tramways in the aggregate city, producing a revenue averaging about £1,700 ($8,273) per week. Numerous extensions and construction of new lines are being carried out. Either Devonport or Plymouth will build a line to Crownhill. New lines will be laid from the Octagon through Antis street into North road, thence westward to No Place Inn. They are also to be continued from Antis street and North road to the Caprera Hotel, effecting a junction there with the existing tramways. From this place a new road will be built to Pennycomequick. Extensions will be made on Mutley Plain through Alexandra road to the bottom of Lipson Hill, and from the existing terminus at Compton up Manadon Hill to Crownhill.

### CONCLUSION.

The year 1902 has not been marked by any profound change in the life of the southwest of England. This part of the country does not experience the alternations of trade which are acutely felt in other sections of the Kingdom. It does not participate to the full measure in the expansion of industry, nor, on the other hand, does it suffer in the same degree from the recurring cycles of depression. In the three towns, the effects of the South African war have been noticeable. The absence of troops from the garrison was severely felt in Devonport and Stonehouse, and in a lesser degree in Plymouth. Money did not circulate freely and commercial circles were stagnant. A perceptible improvement, however, made itself manifest in the last two months of the year, and the probabilities are that 1903 will be a year of enterprise and prosperity in all branches of industry.

JOS. G. STEPHENS, *Consul.*

PLYMOUTH, *February 10, 1903.*

H. Doc. 305, pt 2——57

## SHEFFIELD.

For the fiscal year ended June 30, 1902, there was an increase in exports from this consular district to the United States, over the previous year, of $113,491.24.

The value of declared exports was—

| | |
|---|---:|
| Sheffield | $2,539,041.26 |
| Barnsley agency | 254,695.10 |
| Total | 2,793,736.36 |

There was a decrease in the value of cutlery exported amounting to $92,677.13, and an increase in the value of raw steel (sheets, bars, plates, etc.) amounting to $109,447.16.

The following shows articles of export and values:

| Articles. | Value. | Articles. | Value. |
|---|---:|---|---:|
| **SHEFFIELD.** | | Saw plates | 5,298.91 |
| | | Shears (sheep and garden) | 56,798.30 |
| Brandy | $576.66 | Sod oil | 866.15 |
| Cutlery | 372,845.59 | Steel, sheets, bars, plates, etc | 1,827,479.58 |
| Die blanks of steel | 6,872.27 | Umbrella ribs | 3,150.78 |
| Edge tools and razors | 35,579.67 | United States machinery returned | 137.69 |
| Electroplated goods | 7,738.68 | Wheels, axles, and tires | 12,420.39 |
| Fiber (vegetable) | 2,674.79 | Miscellaneous | 2,491.88 |
| Files | 899.40 | | |
| Furnaces | 711.72 | Total | 2,539,041.26 |
| Graining combs | 1,249.08 | | |
| Grindstones | 4,896.19 | **BARNSLEY AGENCY.** | |
| Hair | 4,806.28 | | |
| Hardware | 2,221.08 | Chemical compounds | 522.97 |
| Horn, and manufactures of | 87,186.65 | Cotton | 40.80 |
| Leather laces and strips | 1,516.20 | Glue | 85,900.48 |
| Machinery | 5,836.31 | Linens | 12,742.30 |
| Measuring tapes | 32,548.19 | Oil, dead oil in drums | 6,587.10 |
| Palladium | 1,494.86 | Scythe stones | 320.65 |
| Pearl (mother-of-pearl slabs) | 43,771.72 | Sheep dip | 2,710.92 |
| Piston springs and rings | 1,329.15 | Skins (pickled sheepskins) | 144,639.73 |
| Plants and trees | 3,453.11 | Tar, coal tar for sheep dip | 1,289.15 |
| Platinum | 11,228.21 | | |
| Raddle | 2,343.69 | Total | 254,695.10 |

CHURCH HOWE, *Consul.*

SHEFFIELD, *July 10, 1902.*

---

## SOUTHAMPTON.

### THE DOCKS.

There are some 16,000 feet of dock frontage where vessels can load or unload at any state of the tide, some of which has a depth of 30 feet, to accommodate the largest vessels. Alongside the quays abundant storage room is provided for all merchandise, and 25 miles of railway extend alongside the warehouses, enabling all goods to be loaded or unloaded with the greatest convenience and least possible delay.

The Prince of Wales graving dock is 750 feet long, 87½ feet wide at sill, and 112 feet at cope level; the depth to blocks being 32¼ feet. The second graving dock is 520 feet long, and there are three others of less size.

A new graving dock, larger in size than the Prince of Wales, is also nearing completion.

The cold-storage warehouses, commenced in 1899, are now completed, and will be utilized in the coming year.

Dredging and filling is constantly going on, increasing the dock frontage.

## THE CHANNEL.

Time and distance are taken on all vessels for this port at Hurst Castle (the Needles), 21 miles from Southampton. Calshot Castle is about 6 miles from the docks, and "off Netley" is about 2 miles from the docks. From Calshot Castle to Hurst Castle there is a natural channel, needing no deepening. From Calshot Castle to "off Netley," the present depth of channel is from 33 to 54 feet, and from "off Netley" to the docks, 30 feet. These are low-water figures, and as there is a double high tide, vessels are practically certain to find sufficient depth at all times.

The constant and steady increase in the size of steamers, however, and especially in their draft, necessitates deeper channels for the future. Freight vessels and passenger and freight boats combined are now under construction that will draw over 30 feet of water, and probably 35 feet.

The docks are owned by the London and Southwestern Road. It was last week decided to increase the depth of the channel from Calshot Castle to the docks to 35 feet at low water, and to deepen the water at the docks enough to accommodate vessels drawing 35 feet. In view of this expense, the harbor board determined to increase the tonnage dues from 1d. (2 cents) to 1½d. (3 cents) per registered ton.

## TONNAGE OF SOUTHAMPTON.

The net tonnage of Southampton for the year 1901 was as follows:

### INWARD.

| Vessels. | Sail. | Steam. | Total. |
|---|---|---|---|
| | *Tons.* | *Tons.* | *Tons.* |
| Foreign vessels reported calling, vessels not reported, etc......... | 27,710 | 3,372,308 | 3,400,018 |
| Coasting: | | | |
| With cargo .............................................. | 70,158 | 708,054 | 778,207 |
| With ballast and carrying passengers ...................... | 36,951 | 437,022 | 473,973 |
| Total coasting........................................ | 107,104 | 1,140,076 | 1,247,180 |
| Total net tonnage, inward......................... | 134,814 | 4,512,384 | 4,647,198 |
| Steamers cleared other ports, final sailing, Southampton.......... | .......... | .......... | 213,373 |
| Yachts................................................... | .......... | .......... | 11,305 |
| Grand total................................... | .......... | .......... | 4,871,876 |

### OUTWARD.

| Vessels. | Sail. | Steam. | Total. |
|---|---|---|---|
| Foreign vessels clearing, also vessels calling not clearing......... | 25,207 | 3,040,564 | 3,065,771 |
| Coasting: | | | |
| With cargo .............................................. | 65,811 | 453,677 | 519,488 |
| With ballast and carrying passengers ...................... | 39,514 | 816,614 | 856,128 |
| Total coasting........................................ | 105,325 | 1,270,291 | 1,375,616 |
| Total net tonnage, outward....................... | 130,582 | 4,310,855 | 4,441,387 |
| Steamers cleared other ports, final sailing, Southampton.......... | .......... | .......... | 367,429 |
| Yachts................................................... | .......... | .......... | 11,305 |
| Grand total................................... | .......... | .......... | 4,820,121 |

The total net tonnage of this port as compared with 1900 was:

| Description. | 1900. | 1901. | Increase. |
|---|---|---|---|
| Inward | 4,830,519 | 4,871,876 | 41,357 |
| Outward | 4,608,955 | 4,820,121 | 211,166 |
| Total | 9,439,474 | 9,691,997 | 252,523 |

The dock statistics for 1901, as compared with 1900, are the following:

| Description. | 1900. | 1901. | Increase. |
|---|---|---|---|
| Ships entered the docks: | | | |
| Number | 3,208 | 3,349 | 146 |
| Net tonnage | 2,904,594 | 3,122,240 | 217,646 |
| Gross tonnage | 5,525,758 | 5,822,512 | 296,754 |
| Goods, inward ....tons.. | 503,260 | 482,724 | a 20,536 |
| Goods, outward ....tons.. | 396,951 | 398,536 | 1,585 |
| Total | 900,211 | 881,260 | a 18,951 |
| Steam coals: | | | |
| Sea borne ....tons.. | 335,147 | 321,956 | a 13,191 |
| Railway ....do.. | 160,302 | 184,131 | 23,829 |
| Total | 495,449 | 506,087 | 10,638 |
| Passengers in and out | 213,465 | 201,114 | a 12,351 |
| Troops in and out | 132,421 | 151,592 | 19,171 |
| Total | 345,886 | 352,706 | 6,820 |
| Mails and parcel post: | | | |
| Inward | 107,715 | 111,237 | 3,522 |
| Outward | 147,350 | 162,520 | 15,170 |
| Total | 255,065 | 273,757 | 18,692 |

a Decreases.

The American Line, the Hamburg-American Line, and the Nord-Deutscher Lloyd Line are the three companies carrying passengers from this port to New York. Their passenger business in 1901, as compared with 1900, was as follows:

| Line. | 1900. | | | | 1901. | | | |
|---|---|---|---|---|---|---|---|---|
| | First class. | Second class. | Third class. | Total. | First class. | Second class. | Third class. | Total. |
| American | 5,255 | 6,305 | 15,873 | 27,433 | 4,097 | 5,351 | 11,143 | 20,591 |
| Hamburg-American a | 2,189 | 369 | ......... | 2,558 | 2,309 | ......... | ......... | 2,309 |
| Nord-Deutscher Lloyd | 4,329 | 363 | 190 | 4,882 | 3,154 | 220 | ......... | 3,374 |
| Total | 11,773 | 7,037 | 16,063 | 34,873 | 9,560 | 5,571 | 11,143 | 26,274 |

a Carries no third-class passengers.

The number of passengers disembarked returning from New York was:

| Line. | 1900. | | | | 1901. | | | |
|---|---|---|---|---|---|---|---|---|
| | First class. | Second class. | Third class. | Total. | First class. | Second class. | Third class. | Total. |
| American .............. | 7,051 | 5,655 | 8,679 | 21,403 | 4,111 | 3,389 | 5,147 | 12,647 |
| Nord-Deutscher Lloyd...... | 3,444 | 454 | 7 | 3,905 | 2,331 | 252 | ......... | 2,583 |
| Total .............. | 10,495 | 6,109 | 8,704 | 25,308 | 6,442 | 3,641 | 5,147 | 15,230 |

Of the third-class passengers sailing on the American Line, 9,698 embarked during the first nine months of the year. The third-class passengers sailing this year on the American Line, up to September 30, numbered 15,189, and a comparison with the first nine months of 1901, as regards nationality, is shown below:

| Nationality. | 1901. | 1902. | Increase. |
|---|---|---|---|
| Russians (Fins)................. | 2,324 | 4,368 | 2,044 |
| Swedes ..... | 2,371 | 3,210 | 839 |
| Americans. | 1,524 | 2,010 | 486 |
| Unclassified ...... | 712 | 1,522 | 810 |
| English........ | 1,149 | 1,394 | 245 |
| Austrians.... | 387 | 892 | 505 |
| Norwegians , | 545 | 748 | 203 |
| Danes ..... | 525 | 710 | 185 |
| Germans........ | 161 | 335 | 174 |
| Total ........ | 9,698 | 15,189 | 5,491 |

By sex, they were divided as follows:

| Description. | 1901. | 1902. | Increase. |
|---|---|---|---|
| Males.... | 6,072 | 9,861 | 3,789 |
| Females.... | 2,653 | 3,778 | 1,125 |
| Children .... | 793 | 1,260 | 467 |
| Infants...... | 180 | 290 | 110 |
| Total ........ | 9,698 | 15,189 | 5,491 |

Of this number, 43 were deported, as against 29 for the same period in 1901. The deported were:

Russians........................... 13
English........................... 9
Austrians........................... 8
Italians........................... 4
Germans........................... 3
French ........................... 3
Swedes ..................... 2
Roumanians ..................... 1

Males ........................... 31
Females ........................... 11
Infants ........................... 1

Cause of deportation:
Public charge (4 stowaways) .... 29
Diseased (4 insane)............. 12
Contract labor.................. 2

The following are the exports of the principal British products from this port in 1901, together with the amounts going to the United States:

| Articles. | Total exports. | | Exports to United States. | |
|---|---|---|---|---|
| | English currency. | United States currency. | English currency. | United States currency. |
| Apparel | £1,357,143 | $1,738,086 | £10,365 | $50,441 |
| Arms, small | 3,677 | 17,894 | | |
| Arms, ammunition, stores | 38,759 | 188,621 | 26,705 | 129,980 |
| Bags | 38,471 | 187,219 | | |
| Beer | 55,482 | 270,008 | | |
| Biscuits | 78,478 | 381,913 | 4,041 | 19,666 |
| Books | 277,702 | 1,351,437 | 87,733 | 426,953 |
| Brass | 7,969 | 38,635 | | |
| Candles | 8,460 | 41,171 | | |
| Caoutchouc, manufactures | 26,651 | 129,697 | 1,328 | 6,463 |
| Carriages, railroad | 15,711 | 76,458 | | |
| Cycles | 46,574 | 226,652 | | |
| Carriages, vehicles | 10,357 | 50,402 | | |
| Cement | 1,182 | 5,752 | | |
| Chemical products | 112,928 | 549,564 | 7,183 | 34,956 |
| Coal products | 11,002 | 53,541 | | |
| Cocoa | 10,513 | 51,182 | | |
| Confectionery | 61,781 | 300,657 | | |
| Copper, manufactures | 24,676 | 120,086 | | |
| Cordage | 11,333 | 55,152 | | |
| Cotton: | | | | |
| Yarn | 87,822 | 427,386 | 41,429 | 201,614 |
| Manufactures of— | | | | |
| Yards | 2,502,606 | 12,178,942 | 35,864 | 174,582 |
| Value | 608,962 | 2,989,181 | 197,940 | 963,275 |
| Earthenware | 26,547 | 129,191 | 4,202 | 20,449 |
| Electric-lighting apparatus | 20,667 | 100,576 | | |
| Fish: | | | | |
| Herring | 463 | 2,258 | | |
| Other sorts | 41,720 | 203,080 | 2,209 | 10,750 |
| Furniture | 42,296 | 205,843 | 5,541 | 26,969 |
| Grain | 13,565 | 66,014 | | |
| Haberdashery | 299,505 | 1,457,541 | 1,626 | 7,913 |
| Hardware and cutlery | 89,222 | 434,199 | | |
| Hats, all sorts | 163,001 | 798,244 | 2,761 | 13,436 |
| Implements, all sorts | 33,007 | 160,628 | | |
| Instruments | 42,448 | 206,573 | 3,531 | 17,184 |
| Iron and steel | 79,822 | 388,454 | 5,278 | 25,685 |
| Jute: | | | | |
| Yarn | 56,725 | 276,052 | | |
| Manufactured, yards | 86,270 | 419,883 | | |
| Lead, pig and sheet | 9,778 | 47,560 | | |
| Leather | 785,558 | 3,822,918 | 63,174 | 307,436 |
| Linen, manufactures: | | | | |
| Yards | 58,281 | 283,624 | | |
| Value | 29,859 | 145,309 | 3,560 | 17,325 |
| Machinery | 185,146 | 901,013 | 136 | 662 |
| Manure | 7,910 | 38,494 | | |
| Medicines | 117,712 | 572,845 | 8,447 | 41,107 |
| Metals | 35,837 | 172,065 | 7,592 | 36,946 |
| Milk | 55,324 | 269,289 | | |
| Musical instruments | 21,448 | 104,377 | 556 | 2,706 |
| Oilcloth | 19,761 | 96,167 | | |
| Oilseed | 8,919 | 43,404 | | |
| Oil, other sorts | 4,532 | 22,055 | 1,687 | 8,210 |
| Paint | 23,360 | 113,681 | 5,505 | 26,790 |
| Paper | 70,087 | 341,078 | 12,202 | 59,381 |
| Perfumery | 16,698 | 81,261 | 3,216 | 15,651 |
| Pickles | 19,436 | 94,585 | 4,984 | 24,011 |
| Pictures | 12,515 | 60,904 | 10,574 | 51,458 |
| Plate and plated ware | 30,394 | 147,912 | 1,173 | 5,708 |
| Prints | 12,607 | 61,351 | 5,435 | 26,449 |
| Provisions | 145,668 | 708,963 | 3,960 | 19,223 |
| Saddlery | 105,947 | 515,591 | 2,440 | 11,874 |
| Seeds | 8,682 | 42,251 | 4,680 | 22,775 |
| Ships and boats | 30,606 | 148,989 | | |
| Silk: | | | | |
| Yarns | 7,414 | 36,060 | 7,161 | 34,849 |
| Other sort | 96,506 | 469,646 | 36,610 | 178,153 |
| Skins, all sort | 74,841 | 364,214 | 70,107 | 341,176 |
| Soap | 43,936 | 213,815 | 29,222 | 142,209 |
| Spirits | 116,858 | 568,689 | 16,150 | 78,594 |

| Articles. | Total exports. | | Exports to United States. | |
|---|---|---|---|---|
| | English currency. | United States currency. | English currency. | United States currency. |
| Stationery | £143,355 | $697,637 | £17,551 | $85,412 |
| Sugar | 2,550 | 12,410 | | |
| Telegraph wires and apparatus | 15,609 | 75,961 | | |
| Umbrellas | 28,227 | 137,369 | 8,448 | 16,780 |
| Wood manufactures | 7,553 | 37,757 | | |
| Woolen and worsted: | | | | |
| Yards | 535,817 | 2,607,553 | 15,746 | 76,628 |
| Value | 243,820 | 1,186,550 | 8,676 | 42,221 |
| Total | 9,520,516 | 46,381,591 | 781,618 | 3,808,744 |

The following shows the value of the principal articles imported free at Southampton during the year 1901, together with the value of of those coming from the United States:

| Articles. | Principal imports. | | From the United States. | |
|---|---|---|---|---|
| | English currency. | United States currency. | English currency. | United States currency. |
| Animals | £33,070 | $160,935 | | |
| Butter | 1,640,129 | 7,981,688 | £28,891 | $138,596 |
| Caoutchouc | 97,944 | 476,644 | | |
| Manufactures | 35,804 | 174,240 | 35,482 | 172,673 |
| Cheese | 103,380 | 503,099 | 11,410 | 55,527 |
| China and earthen ware | 176,980 | 861,273 | 2,471 | 11,025 |
| Cork, manufactured | 40,291 | 196,076 | | |
| Wheat | 36,242 | 176,372 | 26,690 | 129,887 |
| Barley | 152,480 | 742,044 | 9,567 | 46,558 |
| Oats | 94,823 | 461,456 | 3,400 | 16,546 |
| Corn | 115,726 | 563,181 | 12,990 | 63,216 |
| Flour | 24,883 | 121,093 | 16,985 | 82,414 |
| Cotton: | | | | |
| Manufactures | 50,719 | 246,824 | 29 | 141 |
| Hosiery | 32,546 | 158,385 | | |
| Not otherwise enumerated | 18,347 | 89,386 | 5,738 | 27,924 |
| Drugs | 182,413 | 887,718 | 62,936 | 306,278 |
| Dyestuffs, indigo | 36,136 | 175,856 | | |
| Eggs | 230,549 | 1,121,967 | | |
| Electric goods | 43,781 | 212,817 | 41,843 | 203,609 |
| Embroidery | 35,147 | 181,043 | | |
| Feathers, ornamental | 813,618 | 3,969,448 | | |
| Fish, sardines | 21,481 | 104,587 | | |
| Flowers, fresh | 43,141 | 209,946 | | |
| Fruit: | | | | |
| Apples | 85,999 | 418,514 | 46,450 | 226,049 |
| Cherries | 24,234 | 117,925 | | |
| Grapes | 50,071 | 243,671 | | |
| Nuts | 78,122 | 380,181 | | |
| Oranges | 25,948 | 126,276 | 12,368 | 60,189 |
| Pears | 108,770 | 529,329 | 27,398 | 133,332 |
| Plums | 27,131 | 132,023 | 8,981 | 43,706 |
| Gutta-percha | 132,892 | 646,721 | | |
| Hardware | 65,858 | 320,498 | 62,609 | 304,687 |
| Hides: | | | | |
| Dry | 81,763 | 397,300 | | |
| Wet | 26,076 | 126,899 | | |
| Lard | 37,357 | 181,798 | 35,766 | 174,155 |
| Leather: | | | | |
| Dressed | 62,072 | 302,073 | 56,196 | 273,478 |
| Manufactures of | 168,324 | 819,149 | 75,914 | 369,425 |
| Machinery | 109,896 | 534,809 | 104,558 | 508,832 |
| Meat: | | | | |
| Bacon | 1,047,129 | 5,095,858 | 1,047,129 | 5,095,858 |
| Beef, fresh | 631,097 | 3,071,234 | 527,006 | 2,564,674 |
| Hams | 26,123 | 127,127 | 26,114 | 127,064 |
| Mutton, fresh | 25,258 | 122,918 | 335 | 1,630 |
| Pork, fresh | 42,835 | 208,457 | 19,538 | 95,082 |
| Preserved | 58,055 | 258,192 | | |
| Metals, copper | 153,687 | 747,917 | | |
| Iron manufactures: | | | | |
| Cycles | 24,877 | 121,064 | 24,735 | 120,373 |
| Not otherwise enumerated | 44,191 | 215,055 | 24,293 | 118,222 |

| Articles. | Principal imports. | | From the United States. | |
|---|---|---|---|---|
| | English currency. | United States currency. | English currency. | United States currency. |
| Silver ore | £26,584 | $129,371 | | |
| Milk, cream | 20,000 | 97,380 | | |
| Musical instruments | 25,070 | 122,003 | £20,824 | $101,340 |
| Oil, linseed | 31,081 | 151,256 | 963 | 4,687 |
| Oleomargarine | 24,867 | 121,015 | 7,609 | 37,029 |
| Petroleum | 38,038 | 185,112 | 31,554 | 153,557 |
| Pissava fiber | 29,936 | 145,684 | | |
| Plants | 27,975 | 136,140 | 2,658 | 12,935 |
| Plumbago | 32,080 | 156,117 | 32,080 | 156,117 |
| Poultry | 33,923 | 165,086 | 2,560 | 12,458 |
| Precious stones, unset diamonds | 32,705 | 159,159 | | |
| Scientific instruments | 210,615 | 1,024,968 | 209,930 | 1,021,624 |
| Seeds, clover and grass | 29,182 | 141,771 | | |
| Cotton | 55,591 | 270,534 | | |
| Silk, manufactured: | | | | |
| Broad stuffs | 338,427 | 1,646,965 | | |
| Ribbons | 62,743 | 308,839 | | |
| Skins: | | | | |
| Goat, undressed | 101,822 | 495,517 | | |
| Sheep, undressed | 303,788 | 1,478,384 | | |
| Seal | 54,478 | 265,117 | 36,074 | 175,554 |
| Fur, not otherwise enumerated | 99,102 | 482,280 | 98,532 | 479,506 |
| Spices: | | | | |
| Ginger | 29,343 | 142,796 | | |
| Not otherwise enumerated | 29,021 | 141,231 | | |
| Sugar: | | | | |
| Refined | 23,386 | 113,808 | 236 | 1,148 |
| Unrefined | 23,629 | 114,991 | | |
| Toys and games | 21,279 | 103,564 | 15,541 | 75,630 |
| Vegetables: | | | | |
| Potatoes | 379,175 | 1,845,255 | | |
| Tomatoes | 153,271 | 745,893 | | |
| Not otherwise enumerated | 55,526 | 270,217 | | |
| Watches | 50,617 | 246,328 | 7,462 | 36,314 |
| Wood, sawn, fir | 231,698 | 1,127,558 | 16,489 | 80,244 |
| Wool, goat and sheep | 1,304,022 | 6,346,028 | | |
| Woolen stuffs | 93,653 | 455,762 | | |
| Goods, manufactured, not otherwise enumerated | 44,558 | 216,842 | 34,788 | 169,296 |
| Parcel post from Channel Islands | 78,646 | 382,781 | | |
| Total | 11,288,141 | 54,923,788 | 3,875,070 | 18,858,028 |

The principal dutiable goods entered at this port during 1901, together with the value of those received from the United States, are shown below:

| Articles. | Dutiable goods. | | From the United States. | |
|---|---|---|---|---|
| | English currency. | United States currency. | English currency. | United States currency. |
| Beer | £3,262 | $15,874 | | |
| Cards, playing | 16,284 | 79,246 | £16,238 | $79,022 |
| Cocoa: | | | | |
| Raw | 448,224 | 2,181,282 | | |
| Prepared | 121,529 | 591,421 | | |
| Coffee, raw | 626,880 | 3,050,712 | | |
| Milk, condensed | 14,509 | 70,608 | | |
| Plums, French | 1,041 | 5,066 | | |
| Spirits: | | | | |
| Brandy | 111,318 | 541,729 | | |
| Sweetened | 35,385 | 172,201 | 27,830 | 135,435 |
| Perfumed | 2,939 | 14,303 | 1,834 | 8,925 |
| Sugar: | | | | |
| Refined— | | | | |
| Lump | 44,352 | 215,839 | | |
| Other sorts | 65,627 | 319,373 | | |
| Unrefined | 39,317 | 191,336 | | |
| Glucose | 900 | 4,380 | 900 | 4,380 |
| Tea | 3,488 | 16,974 | 2,500 | 12,166 |
| Tobacco, manufactured | 16,209 | 78,881 | 2,412 | 11,738 |
| Wine | 112,880 | 549,831 | | |
| Total dutiable | 1,664,144 | 8,098,557 | 51,714 | 251,666 |
| Total free | 11,288,141 | 54,933,988 | 3,875,070 | 18,858,028 |
| Grand total | 12,952,285 | 63,032,295 | 3,926,784 | 19,109,694 |

The following shows the imports from the United States and exports to the United States at this port in 1901 and 1900:

IMPORTS.

| Class. | 1900. | | 1901. | |
|---|---|---|---|---|
| | English currency. | United States currency. | English currency. | United States currency. |
| Free | £3,345,510 | $16,280,924 | £3,875,070 | $18,858,028 |
| Dutiable | 47,491 | 231,114 | 51,714 | 251,666 |
| Total | 3,393,001 | 16,512,088 | 3,926,784 | 19,109,694 |
| Increase | | | 533,783 | 2,577,104 |

EXPORTS.

| | | | | |
|---|---|---|---|---|
| British manufactures | £1,123,980 | $5,469,605 | £781,618 | $3,803,743 |
| Foreign | 1,526,003 | 7,426,293 | 1,299,265 | 6,322,878 |
| Total | 2,649,983 | 12,895,898 | 2,080,883 | 10,126,616 |
| Decrease | | | 569,050 | 2,769,282 |

JOHN E. HOPLEY, *Consul.*

SOUTHAMPTON, *November 26, 1902.*

---

## SWANSEA.

The trade of the Swansea Harbor for last year, which I submit in tables, has, for the first time in seven years, shown a decrease instead of an increase as compared with the previous twelve months. The falling off amounted to 6.1 per cent, or 250,000 tons.

The imports have decreased 104,657 tons and exports 147,058 tons. To the decline in exports iron ore contributes 68,700 tons; pig iron, scrap steel, etc., 18,000, and wooden goods 10,792 tons.

The decrease in exports is almost entirely due to coal and patent fuel, which show a shrinkage of 133,720 tons.

### TIN PLATES.

The total shipments of tin plates have increased 6,742 tons. To Russia, 12,000 tons more have been shipped than in the preceding year, and to China and Japan 8,000 tons; but there are the following decreases to be considered: Germany, 9,000 tons; France, 6,000; Holland, 4,000; Belgium, 4,000 tons.

### GENERAL.

The principal event of the year was the passing of an act for the construction of a new dock with large dimensions of lock, large area of water, large width of quays, large extent of sidings, etc.   The following tables how at a glance the trade done at this port:

*Trade by countries.*

| Country. | Imports. | Exports. | Total 1901. | Total 1900. |
|---|---|---|---|---|
| | *Tons.* | *Tons.* | *Tons.* | *Tons.* |
| Russia .................................................. | 20,716 | 94,952 | 115,668 | 112,402 |
| Sweden, Norway, and Denmark ...................... | 27,714 | 111,860 | 139,574 | 140,334 |
| Germany, Holland, and Belgium ...................... | 52,753 | 317,912 | 370,665 | 361,606 |
| Channel Islands ...................................... | 74 | 27,436 | 27,510 | 82,520 |
| France.................................................. | 63,469 | 1,147,239 | 1,210,708 | 1,358,275 |
| Portugal .............................................. | 26,981 | 22,567 | 49,548 | 45,770 |
| Gibraltar, Azores, Madeira, etc ...................... | | 6,065 | 6,065 | 2,452 |
| Spain .................................................. | 82,627 | 142,463 | 225,090 | 223,586 |
| Italy .................................................. | 14,225 | 317,128 | 331,353 | 373,688 |
| Austria, Greece, and Roumania ...................... | 20,883 | 43,742 | 64,625 | 54,734 |
| Algeria, Turkey, Egypt, and Tunis.................... | 8,287 | 186,278 | 194,565 | 194,994 |
| Cape of Good Hope and East and West Africa........ | 28,748 | 42,633 | 71,381 | 73,168 |
| Straits Settlements, China, and Japan............... | 2,247 | 34,684 | 36,931 | 22,422 |
| North America....................................... | 77,740 | 179,159 | 256,899 | 262,556 |
| West Indies........................................... | | 598 | 598 | ......... |
| South America........................................ | 29,320 | 13,015 | 42,335 | 71,856 |
| Australia and New Caledonia ...................... | 7,080 | ......... | 7,080 | 9,582 |
| | 462,814 | 2,687,731 | 3,150,545 | 3,339,795 |
| Coastwise .............................................. | 277,639 | 424,615 | 702,254 | 764,719 |
| Total........................................ | 740,453 | 3,112,346 | 3,852,799 | 4,104,514 |

## SHIPPING.

### COASTWISE AND FOREIGN ENTRANCES.

| Description. | 1891. | | 1900. | | 1901. | |
|---|---|---|---|---|---|---|
| | Vessels. | Registered tonnage. | Vessels. | Registered tonnage. | Vessels. | Registered tonnage. |
| With ballast. ...................... | 2,171 | 907,016 | 2,557 | 1,305,660 | 2,551 | 1,261,564 |
| With cargo.......................... | 2,231 | 442,149 | 2,448 | 736,016 | 2,391 | 684,570 |
| Windbound........................... | 54 | 11,241 | 37 | 6,326 | 27 | 4,114 |
| Total........................ | 4,456 | 1,360,406 | 5,042 | 2,048,002 | 4,969 | 1,950,248 |

### IMPORTS.

| Article. | 1891. | 1900. | 1901. |
|---|---|---|---|
| | *Tons.* | *Tons.* | *Tons.* |
| Gas, coal, tar, and pitch.......................................... | 34,367 | 38,238 | 31,860 |
| Copper, silver, lead, tin, and nickel, with their ores and alloys.......... | 131,641 | 143,033 | 142,628 |
| Zinc, its ore and alloys............................................ | 42,407 | 49,418 | 47,261 |
| Iron ore............................................................ | 87,065 | 154,800 | 86,037 |
| Iron, steel, spiegeleisen, pig iron, castings, and machinery ............. | 71,913 | 126,748 | 108,298 |
| Timber and pitwood ................................................ | 66,400 | 101,948 | 91,109 |
| Bricks, slates, limestones, clay, etc................................ | 22,395 | 32,018 | 28,389 |
| Sulphur ore, pyrites, brimstone, phosphates, salt, etc ................. | 48,647 | 35,749 | 38,903 |
| Flour, grain, potatoes, fruit, hay, etc ............................... | 50,061 | 135,231 | 139,974 |
| Oils, bark, wool, tallow, etc ....................................... | 8,026 | 7,377 | 8,073 |
| Sundries in steamers and general traders not otherwise classified ..... | 36,590 | 20,580 | 17,976 |
| Total ................. ..................................... | 599,532 | 845,110 | 740,453 |

Trade by countries—Continued.

COASTWISE AND FOREIGN CLEARANCES.a

| Description. | 1891. | | 1900. | | 1901. | |
|---|---|---|---|---|---|---|
| | Vessels. | Registered tonnage. | Vessels. | Registered tonnage. | Vessels. | Registered tonnage. |
| With ballast | 588 | 151,655 | 502 | 207,112 | 552 | 310,097 |
| With cargo | 3,821 | 1,208,474 | 4,502 | 1,746,004 | 4,367 | 1,642,065 |
| Total | 4,409 | 1,360,129 | 5,004 | 2,053,116 | 4,919 | 1,952,162 |

a Exclusive of windbound vessels.

EXPORTS.

| Article. | 1891. | 1900. | 1901. |
|---|---|---|---|
| | Tons. | Tons. | Tons. |
| Coal and coke | 1,415,058 | 2,404,798 | 2,294,989 |
| Patent fuel | 353,525 | 503,542 | 479,976 |
| Copper, zinc, copper ores, regulus, silver an l zinc ores | 18,184 | 17,523 | 20,099 |
| Iron, steel, rails, castings, etc. | 19,341 | 32,023 | 17,473 |
| Tin, terne, and black plates | 233,020 | 232,747 | 239,489 |
| Timber | 806 | 835 | 2,774 |
| Bricks and fire cla | 8,968 | 9,992 | 6,030 |
| Alkali, superphosphate, arsenic, powder, etc. | 33,958 | 28,681 | 22,869 |
| Flour, grain, potatoes | 533 | 9,855 | 10,745 |
| Oil, bark, wool, etc | 2,283 | 2,410 | 2,165 |
| Sundries in steamers and general traders not otherwise classified. | 41,713 | 16,708 | 15,787 |
| Total | 2,127,408 | 3,259,404 | 3,112,346 |

| Country. | Imports. | | | | | | | | |
|---|---|---|---|---|---|---|---|---|---|
| | Coal, etc. | Copper, silver, lead. | Iron ore. | Timber, bricks, etc. | Chemicals. | Agricultural produce. | Materials for manufacture. | Miscellaneous. | Total. |
| | Tons. | Tons. | Tons. | Tons. | Tons. | Tons. | Tons. | Tons. | Tons. |
| Russia, northern | | | | 4,067 | | 987 | 361 | 50 | 5,465 |
| Russia, southern | | | | | | 15,251 | | | 15,251 |
| Sweden | | 138 | 1,996 | 4,604 | | | | 100 | 6,838 |
| Norway | | 170 | | 8,533 | 12,047 | | | 50 | 20,800 |
| Denmark | | 22 | 51 | | | | | | 76 |
| Germany | | 2,859 | 7,360 | 51 | 669 | 13,979 | 243 | 850 | 25,511 |
| Holland | | 1,182 | 7,977 | 33 | 806 | 4,888 | 452 | 230 | 15,568 |
| Belgium | | 1,324 | 4,187 | 2,501 | 1,027 | 2,116 | 319 | 250 | 11,674 |
| Channel Islands | | | | | | 74 | | | 74 |
| France | | 6,451 | | 511 | 49,317 | 2,208 | 4,632 | 85 | 320 | 63,469 |
| Portugal | | 1,984 | 11,756 | 6,295 | 6,850 | 96 | | | 26,981 |
| Spain | | 6,231 | 73,243 | 600 | 2,408 | | | 150 | 82,627 |
| Italy | | 14,190 | | 35 | | | | | 14,225 |
| Austrian territories | | | | 120 | | | | | 120 |
| Greece | | 4,454 | | | | | | | 4,454 |
| Roumania | | | | | | 16,309 | | | 16,309 |
| Tunis | | 8,287 | | | | | | | 8,287 |
| Cape of Good Hope | | 28,748 | | | | | | | 28,748 |
| Straits Settlements | | 240 | | | | | | | 240 |
| Bombay | | | | | | 2,007 | | | 2,007 |
| New Caledonia | | 4,450 | | | | | | | 4,450 |
| Australia | | 2,580 | | | | | | | 2,580 |
| Canada | | | | | 10,526 | | 556 | | | 11,082 |
| Newfoundland | | 39,755 | | 30 | | | | | 39,785 |
| United States: | | | | | | | | | |
| On the Atlantic | | 7,609 | 4,279 | 1,791 | | 3,774 | 648 | 130 | 18,231 |
| On the Pacific | | | | | | 8,642 | | | 8,642 |
| Peru | | | | | 1,195 | | | | 1,195 |
| Bolivia | | 759 | | | | | | | 759 |
| Chile | | 11,852 | | | | 11 | | | 11,863 |
| Uruguay | | 1,231 | | | | | | | 1,231 |
| Argentine Republic | | | | | | 14,272 | | | 14,272 |

*Trade by countries*—Continued.

EXPORTS—Continued.

| Country. | Coal and patent fuel. | Copper, silver, lead. | Tin plate. | Fire clay. | Chemicals. | Agricultural produce. | Materials for manufacture. | Miscellaneous. | Total. | Grand total. |
|---|---|---|---|---|---|---|---|---|---|---|
| | Tons. | Tons. | Tons. | Tons. | Tons. | Tons. | Tons. | Tons. | Tons. | Tons. |
| Russia, northern ... | 20,456 | 1,804 | 13,434 | 549 | 29 | ...... | 2 | 30 | 36,304 | 41,769 |
| Russia, southern ... | 11,195 | 261 | 47,102 | 3 | 37 | ...... | ...... | 50 | 58,641 | 78,899 |
| Sweden ............ | 80,258 | 5 | 70 | 30 | ...... | ...... | ...... | ...... | 80,363 | 87,201 |
| Norway ........... | 5,731 | ...... | 30 | ...... | ...... | ...... | ...... | ...... | 5,761 | 26,561 |
| Denmark ......... | 21,727 | 31 | 3,841 | ...... | 26 | 11 | ...... | 100 | 25,736 | 25,812 |
| Germany ......... | 186,831 | 3,021 | 10,330 | 131 | 178 | 402 | 98 | 170 | 200,651 | 226,162 |
| Holland .......... | 81,578 | 5,176 | 14,822 | 108 | 83 | ...... | 3 | 120 | 101,390 | 116,958 |
| Belgium .......... | 5,204 | 334 | 9,185 | 814 | 202 | 17 | 15 | 100 | 15,871 | 27,545 |
| Channel Islands... | 27,434 | ...... | ...... | ...... | 2 | ...... | ...... | ...... | 27,436 | 27,510 |
| France............ | 1,127,435 | 1,453 | 15,208 | 296 | 2,597 | 30 | 43 | 180 | 1,147,239 | 1,210,708 |
| Portugal ......... | 15,671 | 94 | 6,760 | 17 | 15 | ...... | ...... | 10 | 22,567 | 49,548 |
| Madeira .......... | 930 | ...... | ...... | ...... | ...... | ...... | ...... | ...... | 930 | 930 |
| Spain ............ | 142,240 | ...... | 203 | ...... | ...... | ...... | 20 | ...... | 142,463 | 225,090 |
| Gibraltar......... | 1,528 | ...... | ...... | ...... | ...... | ...... | ...... | ...... | 1,528 | 1,528 |
| Azores ........... | 2,680 | ...... | ...... | ...... | ...... | ...... | ...... | ...... | 2,680 | 2,680 |
| Italy ............. | 302,913 | 492 | 8,881 | 1,315 | 3,307 | 58 | 52 | 110 | 317,128 | 331,353 |
| Austrian territories. | 10,950 | 185 | 1,362 | ...... | 252 | 8 | 19 | 30 | 12,806 | 12,926 |
| Greece ........... | 29,879 | ...... | 72 | 10 | 384 | ...... | ...... | 10 | 30,355 | 34,809 |
| European Turkey.. | 5,708 | ...... | ...... | ...... | ...... | ...... | ...... | ...... | 5,708 | 5,708 |
| Roumania ........ | 581 | ...... | ...... | ...... | ...... | ...... | ...... | ...... | 581 | 16,890 |
| Asiatic Turkey..... | 11,113 | ...... | ...... | ...... | ...... | ...... | 10 | ...... | 11,123 | 11,123 |
| Egypt ............ | 21,365 | ...... | ...... | ...... | ...... | ...... | ...... | ...... | 21,365 | 21,365 |
| Tunis ............ | 20,887 | ...... | ...... | ...... | ...... | ...... | ...... | ...... | 20,887 | 29,174 |
| Algeria .......... | 127,192 | ...... | 3 | ...... | .'.... | ...... | ...... | ...... | 127,195 | 127,195 |
| Canary Islands..... | 142 | ...... | ...... | ...... | ...... | ...... | ...... | ...... | 142 | 142 |
| St. Helena........ | 785 | ...... | ...... | ...... | ...... | ...... | ...... | ...... | 785 | 785 |
| Cape of Good Hope. | 38,311 | ...... | 1,833 | 1,972 | 39 | 255 | 663 | 70 | 42,683 | 71,311 |
| Straits Settlements. | 6,261 | 19 | 6,276 | ...... | ...... | ...... | ...... | 10 | 12,566 | 12,806 |
| China............. | 1,131 | 206 | 8,645 | ...... | ...... | ...... | 6 | 20 | 10,008 | 10,008 |
| Japan ............ | 2,466 | 3 | 9,195 | ...... | ...... | ...... | 42 | 10 | 11,716 | 11,716 |
| Bombay........... | ...... | ...... | ...... | ...... | ...... | ...... | ...... | ...... | ...... | 2,007 |
| Java, etc ......... | ...... | ...... | 340 | ...... | 54 | ...... | ...... | ...... | 394 | 394 |
| New Caledonia .... | ...... | ...... | ...... | ...... | ...... | ...... | ...... | ...... | ...... | 4,450 |
| Australia ......... | ...... | ...... | ...... | ...... | ...... | ...... | ...... | ...... | ...... | 2,580 |
| Canada ........... | 7,359 | ...... | ...... | ...... | ...... | ...... | ...... | ...... | 7,359 | 18,441 |
| Newfoundland..... | 5,652 | ...... | 46 | 4 | ...... | 16 | 13 | ...... | 5,731 | 45,516 |
| United States: | | | | | | | | | | |
| On the Atlantic.. | 71,375 | 611 | 36,815 | 814 | 1,840 | ...... | 164 | 180 | 111,799 | 130,040 |
| On the Pacific.. | 54,024 | ...... | ...... | ...... | ...... | ...... | ...... | ...... | 54,024 | 62,666 |
| British West India | | | | | | | | | | |
| Islands.......... | 598 | ...... | ...... | ...... | ...... | ...... | ...... | ...... | 598 | 598 |
| Mexico............ | 246 | ...... | ...... | ...... | ...... | ...... | ...... | ...... | 246 | 246 |
| Peru ............. | ...... | ...... | ...... | ...... | ...... | ...... | ...... | ...... | ...... | 1,195 |
| Bolivia............ | ...... | ...... | ...... | ...... | ...... | ...... | ...... | ...... | ...... | 759 |
| Chile............. | 4,745 | ...... | ...... | ...... | ...... | ...... | ...... | ...... | 4,745 | 16,608 |
| Brazil ........... | 5,870 | ...... | ...... | ...... | ...... | ...... | ...... | ...... | 5,870 | 5,870 |
| Uruguay.......... | ...... | ...... | ...... | ...... | ...... | ...... | ...... | ...... | ...... | 1,231 |
| Argentine Republic | 2,400 | ...... | ...... | ...... | ...... | ...... | ...... | ...... | 2,400 | 16,672 |

RECAPITULATION.

| Article. | Total coastwise. | | Total foreign. | | Grand total. | |
|---|---|---|---|---|---|---|
| | 1900. | 1901. | 1900. | 1901. | 1900. | 1901. |
| **IMPORTS.** | *Tons.* | *Tons.* | *Tons.* | *Tons.* | *Tons.* | *Tons.* |
| Coal, etc ................... | 38,238 | 31,860 | ............ | ............ | 38,238 | 31,860 |
| Copper, silver, lead ........... | 39,213 | 45,368 | 153,238 | 144,516 | 192,451 | 189,884 |
| Iron ore ........................ | 98,566 | 82,992 | 182,982 | 111,343 | 281,548 | 194,335 |
| Timber, bricks, etc ........... | 33,769 | 30,975 | 100,167 | 88,473 | 133,936 | 119,448 |
| Chemicals ..................... | 6,603 | 11,703 | 29,146 | 27,200 | 35,749 | 38,903 |
| Agricultural produce ....... | 57,727 | 52,380 | 77,504 | 87,594 | 135,231 | 139,974 |
| Materials for manufacture ...... | 4,881 | ',015 | 2,496 | 2,058 | 7,377 | 8,073 |
| Miscellaneous ................. | 19,000 | 16,346 | 1,580 | 1,630 | 20,580 | 17,976 |
| Total .................. | 297,997 | 277,639 | 547,113 | 462,814 | 845,110 | 740,453 |
| **EXPORTS.** | | | | | | |
| Coal and patent fuel ............. | 350,068 | 312,564 | 2,558,547 | 2,462,351 | 2,908,685 | 2,774,915 |
| Copper, silver, lead ............. | 8,202 | 6,404 | 9,321 | 13,696 | 17,523 | 20,099 |
| Tin plates ...................... | 63,350 | 63,514 | 201,420 | 198,448 | 264,770 | 256,962 |
| Fire clay ....................... | 3,519 | 2,789 | 7,308 | 6,065 | 10,827 | 8,804 |
| Chemicals ...................... | 15,101 | 13,829 | 13,580 | 9,040 | 28,681 | 22,869 |
| Agricultural produce ........... | 9,582 | 9,948 | 273 | 797 | 9,855 | 10,745 |
| Materials for manufacture ...... | 1,577 | 1,080 | 833 | 1,135 | 2,410 | 2,165 |
| Miscellaneous ................. | 15,308 | 14,587 | 1,400 | 1,200 | 16,708 | 15,787 |
| Total .................. | 466,722 | 424,615 | 2,792,682 | 2,687,731 | 3,259,404 | 3,112,346 |
| Grand total ............... | 764,719 | 702,254 | 3,339,795 | 3,150,545 | 4,104,514 | 3,852,799 |

*Number and tonnage of steamers cleared for the Atlantic ports of North America.*

| Years. | Vessels. | Net registered tonnage. | Years. | Vessels. | Net registered tonnage. |
|---|---|---|---|---|---|
| 1882 ..................... | 20 | 27,396 | 1892 ..................... | 191 | 327,161 |
| 1883 ..................... | 46 | 60,628 | 1893 ..................... | 207 | 356,898 |
| 1884 ..................... | 75 | 105,969 | 1894 ..................... | 236 | 422,904 |
| 1885 ..................... | 88 | 128,372 | 1895 ..................... | 192 | 342,314 |
| 1886 ..................... | 119 | 166,553 | 1896 ..................... | 201 | 335,775 |
| 1887 ..................... | 129 | 182,235 | 1897 ..................... | 190 | 327,502 |
| 1888 ..................... | 99 | 156,382 | 1898 ..................... | 192 | 308,429 |
| 1889 ..................... | 123 | 186,438 | 1899 ..................... | 178 | 292,394 |
| 1890 ..................... | 147 | 246,124 | 1900 ..................... | 158 | 269,830 |
| 1891 ..................... | 144 | 231,720 | 1901 ..................... | 185 | 228,405 |

*Export of tin, terne, and black plates.*

| Years. | Coastwise. | Foreign. | Total net weight. | Years. | Coastwise. | Foreign. | Total net weight. |
|---|---|---|---|---|---|---|---|
| | *Tons.* | *Tons.* | *Tons.* | | *Tons.* | *Tons.* | *Tons.* |
| 1880 ................. | 24,007 | 1,336 | 25,343 | 1891 ................. | 42,971 | 190,049 | 233,020 |
| 1881 ................. | 21,836 | 8,525 | 30,361 | 1892 ................. | 36,398 | 216,228 | 252,626 |
| 1882 ................. | 19,330 | 16,631 | 35,961 | 1893 ................. | 38,321 | 236,709 | 275,030 |
| 1883 ................. | 25,353 | 41,835 | 67,188 | 1894 ................. | 49,198 | 200,412 | 249,610 |
| 1884 ................. | 33,316 | 73,682 | 106,998 | 1895 ................. | 54,653 | 202,943 | 257,596 |
| 1885 ................. | 46,693 | 103,075 | 149,768 | 1896 ................. | 57,979 | 141,963 | 199,942 |
| 1886 ................. | 58,665 | 137,708 | 191,373 | 1897 ................. | 63,007 | 156,007 | 219,014 |
| 1887 ................. | 61,750 | 139,172 | 200,922 | 1898 ................. | 52,792 | 140,058 | 192,850 |
| 1888 ................. | 57,369 | 144,527 | 201,896 | 1899 ................. | 51,956 | 180,518 | 232,474 |
| 1889 ................. | 42,605 | 153,791 | 196,396 | 1900 ................. | 49,420 | 183,327 | 232,747 |
| 1890 ................. | 83,641 | 196,150 | 229,791 | 1901 ................. | 58,821 | 180,668 | 239,489 |

GRIFFITH W. PREES, *Consul.*

SWANSEA, *October 31, 1902.*

## TUNSTALL.

The following statement shows the nature and value of declared exports from this district to the United States for the year 1901 and the totals of each article for the preceding year:

| Articles. | Quarters ended— | | | | Total. | Totals for preceding year. |
|---|---|---|---|---|---|---|
| | Mar. 31. | June 30. | Sept. 30. | Dec. 31. | | |
| Ale ..................... | $256.79 | $118.10 | .......... | .......... | $374.87 | $273.88 |
| China................... | 40,798.30 | 29,086.88 | $62,598.06 | $110,343.02 | 242,771.26 | 187,944.70 |
| Colors.................. | 6,995.90 | 8,003.71 | 5,775.72 | 5,263.87 | 26,039.20 | 18,091.11 |
| Copper plates .......... | .......... | .......... | .......... | 192.49 | 192.49 | .......... |
| Cotton goods (printed) .. | .......... | .......... | 1,588.24 | 272.16 | 1,860.40 | .......... |
| Earthenware ........... | 621,968.87 | 666,964.57 | 578,281.72 | 403,387.69 | 2,270,612.85 | 2,496,219.93 |
| Elastic web.......... | .......... | .......... | .......... | .......... | .......... | .......... |
| Electroplate .......... | .......... | .......... | .......... | .......... | .......... | 19.46 |
| Glass.................. | .......... | 48.67 | .......... | 4,433.39 | 4,482.06 | 199.58 |
| Machinery.............. | 564.03 | 530.69 | 729.06 | 432.80 | 2,256.58 | 1,410.07 |
| Paper ................. | 4,841.84 | 4,074.18 | 2,197.99 | 3,356.54 | 14,470.50 | 8,628.98 |
| Parian ................ | 132.73 | 204.11 | 415.96 | 290.65 | 1,043.45 | 1,150.87 |
| Potters' materials....... | 19,796.98 | 23,827.52 | 14,202.09 | 16,887.95 | 74,714.54 | 90,398.43 |
| Rabbit skins........... | 7,867.08 | 7,686.15 | .......... | 5,990.67 | 21,543.90 | .......... |
| Shrubs ................ | .......... | 252.45 | 176.12 | .......... | 428.57 | .......... |
| Tape .................. | .......... | 2,205.92 | 992.93 | 2,053.01 | 5,251.86 | 7,016.40 |
| Tiles ................. | .......... | 248.19 | .......... | .......... | 248.19 | 183.69 |
| Transfers ............. | 10,141.95 | 13,474.71 | 16,561.24 | 13,641.50 | 53,819.40 | 36,393.42 |
| Trimmings (tailors') .... | .......... | 274.85 | .......... | .......... | 274.85 | 136.26 |
| Velveteen ...:........ | 1,115.65 | .......... | .......... | .......... | 1,115.65 | 1,297.89 |
| Total.............. | 714,500.12 | 756,940.65 | 683,514.13 | 566,545.74 | 2,721,500.64 | 2,849,309.77 |

The following statement shows the nature and value of declared exports from the consular district of Tunstall to the United States during the six months ended June 30, 1902, compared with the figures for the preceding year:

| Articles. | Quarter ended— | | Total. |
|---|---|---|---|
| | Mar. 31, 1902. | June 30, 1902. | |
| Ale........................................ | .......... | $118.09 | $118.09 |
| China...................................... | $59,154.78 | 50,297.45 | 109,452.23 |
| Colors..................................... | 9,787.06 | 10,134.81 | 19,921.87 |
| Cotton goods (printed)..................... | 966.83 | .......... | 966.83 |
| Earthenware............................... | 566,434.81 | 556,601.92 | 1,123,036.73 |
| Machinery................................. | .......... | 319.97 | 319.97 |
| Paper...................................... | 5,703.70 | 5,016.08 | 10,719.78 |
| Potters' materials ......................... | 15,591.61 | 20,867.69 | 36,459.30 |
| Rabbit skins............................... | 4,557.70 | 6,237.19 | 10,794.89 |
| Tape....................................... | .......... | 409.01 | 409.01 |
| Transfers.................................. | 15,571.54 | 20,771.91 | 36,343.45 |
| Trimmings (tailors') ...................... | 168.42 | 136.99 | 305. |
| Total ................................ | 677,936.45 | 670,911.11 | 1,348,847.56 |
| Total for preceding year ................. | 714,500.12 | 756,940.65 | 1,471,440.77 |
| Decrease................................... | 36,563.67 | 86,029.54 | 122,598.21 |

The digest of the invoice book shows that trade on the whole has been worse than last year. The growth of production of ordinary potteryware in the United States has reduced the export trade. Less ordinary and printed earthenware is bought for the United States each quarter. The only ware to hold its own is the finer grade of porcelain, which indeed is exported a little more freely than last year. The shipments of potters' supplies, colors, etc., have increased somewhat during the year.

The bankruptcies during the year 1901 numbered 52, against 26 in 1900. This includes all trades in this district, and only shows that trade in general is not improving. This number of failures does not seem abnormal, in a district where the Government inspector has under his care 1,599 factories and 2,294 workshops, the former using power in some portion of their works, the latter none. Among these there are 362 factories in which the manufacture and decoration of earthenware and china are carried on.

## EXPORTS OF CHINA.

The figures which cause the most alarm are those comparing the exports of china and earthenware from the United Kingdom to the United States with similar exports from other countries. Mr. Bell, the British commercial agent to the United States, is said to have given the following figures to June 30, 1902:

| Exports from— | 1900. | 1901. | 1902. |
|---|---|---|---|
| United Kingdom | $3,175,030 | $3,063,087 | $2,928,341 |
| Austria-Hungary | 516,681 | 622,298 | 696,172 |
| France | 1,463,609 | 1,614,608 | 1,618,657 |
| Germany | 2,876,876 | 3,450,857 | 3,651,264 |
| Rest of Europe | 187,760 | 156,257 | 207,785 |
| Japan | 374,620 | 459,841 | 469,707 |

As will be noted, all nations on the list have increased their exports except the United Kingdom.

## INSURANCE AGAINST LEAD POISONING.

The most noteworthy event in the potteries has been the formation of a society, including practically all the pottery owners, for the purpose of insuring the employees against lead poisoning, with provisions for payment in case of partial or complete incapacity from work. It is the first time, I am told, that such a society has been organized.

## IMPORTS.

Imports from the United States grow; but statistics can not be obtained at this inland post, where merchants buy at secondhand. American oil comes direct in casks from the Liverpool depot. One butcher here has nothing but openly advertised American meat. The plumbers of the district tell me that they are using many American devices. I think the annual meeting of Sanitary Engineers would be a good place in which to introduce more of them. In the older residences here there is a deplorable lack of simple and convenient heating and cooking stoves. There is room for both oil and coal stoves. The former must not smell of kerosene. I imported some oil heaters for my own use, and have inquiries from everyone who sees them as to where such things can be obtained. An inexpensive cooking stove with small fuel (bituminous coal) consumption and a simple water heater is needed. The smallest cottages here have a kind of range built into the fireplace for cooking purposes—a poor substitute, one would think, for our neat cooking stoves.

There is competition among several countries for the introduction of motor carriages into this good, but conservative market. There is room for a good runabout, a surrey, and a wagonette, all of moderate price; particularly the surrey or some two-seated form.

## NOTES.

Manufacturers here are making a strong bid for the trade of Africa, Australia, and the East, and are so successful that the district has had about its usual degree of prosperity.

No American manufactories have been established here since my last annual report.   On the contrary, hardly a day passes but calls are made at the office by relatives of potters who have emigrated to the pottery districts of the United States.

WM. HARRISON BRADLEY, *Consul.*

TUNSTALL, *October 21, 1902.*

## IRELAND.

### BELFAST.

The last six months of 1901 was a very unprofitable period for the linen trade of Belfast.   In the first half of the present year, 1902, however, business greatly increased, notwithstanding the high prices maintained by manufacturers of textile fabrics.

### SHIPBUILDING.

Next in importance to the linen industry comes shipbuilding, which has been in a very prosperous condition.   One of the yards at Belfast ranks well up among the great shipbuilding establishments of the world.

### TOBACCO.

The tobacco trade was considerably disturbed during the year, owing to the appearance of an American company which has entered into very active competition with the English Imperial Tobacco Trust. The result has been a small reduction in prices.

### ROPE AND TWINE.

The manufacturers of rope and twine have made extensive improvements to their plants and greatly increased their output.   This business has been in a highly prosperous condition.

### MISCELLANEOUS.

Whisky is among the products for which Belfast is famous.   Reports show, however, that the business was in a very unsatisfactory condition during the past year.

 Glass and bottle making is progressing satisfactorily.   Tent-making, as well as other canvas working, has increased.   Electrical engineers report a steady increase in the volume of their trade.   Brick and terra cotta works have had a successful year.

On the whole, it may be said that the industries of this consular district have been less prosperous than in the preceding year.   There has been a good deal of pessimistic outcry here in the last few years, and much criticism has been indulged in as to the stereotyped methods of British trade. It is true, generally speaking, that there are indications of a falling off in both exports and imports, but it must be remembered that Germany is suffering from industrial depression, which can not fail to affect British trade adversely. Conditions in the United States, on the other hand, are highly prosperous.

It is remarkable that these two great competitors for British trade—Germany and the United States—should be at opposite poles as regards prosperity, and it is maintained that both conditions militate against the commercial welfare of Great Britain. But there is economic fallacy in this reasoning. The truth really is, Great Britain can no longer hope to enjoy unrivaled the command of the world's markets.

### RETURN OF BELFAST SHIPPING.

Shipping arriving with cargo at Belfast from foreign ports during the year were: British, 361; Norwegian, 26; German, 7; Russian, 3; Danish, 3; Greek, 3; Swedish, 3; Spanish, 1; Dutch, 1; Italian, 1; total, 409.

Cargoes: General, 271; breadstuffs, including maize, wheat, flour, barley, and rye, 50; timber, including deals, boards, sleepers, teakwood, pitch, pine, mahogany, laths, and lathwood, 43; petroleum, 9; flax and hemp, undressed, 7; phosphate, 6; phosphate of lime, 6; sulphur ore, 5; ice, 5; gypsum, 2; tar, 2; cement, 1; waste salt, 1; sugar, 1; total, 409.

### BELFAST CUSTOMS.

The duty paid through the customs in Belfast for the year ended December 31, 1901, amounted in value to $14,649,941, as against $15,376,731 for 1900, or a decrease of $726,790.

### NEW GRAVING DOCK IN BELFAST HARBOR.

The Belfast harbor commissioners have ordered the construction of a new graving dock, the principal dimensions of which are as follows:

|  | Feet. |
|---|---|
| Length of floor | 750 |
| Breadth at bottom | 100 |
| Breadth at top | 128 |
| Breadth at entrance | 96 |
| Depth on sill (10-foot tide) | 34.6 |
| Depth on floor | 36.6 |
| Depth on blocks | 32 |
| Height of blocks | 4.6 |

The dock will be capable of being extended to upward of 1,000 feet in length. The principal material used will be concrete, with a continuous brick invert, and brickwork carried up, at the sides, above low-water mark. The total depth from coping level to foundation will be 60 feet, and the total width over hydraulic-pipe culverts 145 feet, or, exclusive of these, 137 feet 6 inches. The equipment will consist of three 11-ton and two 5-ton hydraulic capstans and a traveling crane with a lift over dock center of 15 tons. The entrance to the dock will be closed by means of a traveling caisson. A number of hydraulic shores are also to be provided. The pumping installation will be actuated by electricity, and electric lights will be provided for the whole plant.

H. Doc. 305, pt 2——58

## SHIPBUILDING.

The year 1901 has shown an unprecedented output of shipping, not only in Belfast, but also throughout the United Kingdom, the tonnage launched during that period exceeding the totals for any previous twelve months. The number of vessels that have been turned out in the United Kingdom is 1,233, with a gross tonnage of about 1,800,000, as compared with 1,660,000 tons in 1900. The following table will show the number of vessels built in Belfast in 1901, together with the name, description, gross tonnage, and indicated horsepower of each:

| Name. | Description. | Gross tonnage. | Indicated horse-power. |
|---|---|---|---|
| Walmer Castle | Twin screw steamer (steel) | 12,546 | 11,800 |
| Athenic | ...do | 12,234 | 4,400 |
| Noordam | ...do | 12,317 | 7,000 |
| Warwickshire | ...do | 7,967 | 5,000 |
| Minnetonka | ...do | 13,398 | 9,800 |
| Corinthic | ...do | 12,231 | 4,400 |
| Ionic | ...do | 12,231 | 4,400 |
| Ionian | ...do | 8,265 | 5,500 |
| Drayton Grange | ...do | 6,592 | 3,700 |
| Oswestry Grange | ...do | 6,591 | 3,700 |
| Niwaru | ...do | 6,782 | 3,700 |
| City of Benares | Steamship | 6,730 | 4,300 |
| Telemachus | ...do | 7,450 | 4,300 |
| Jason | ...do | 7,450 | 4,300 |
| Lord Antrim | ...do | 4,269 | 2,450 |
| Titian | ...do | 4,170 | 3,250 |
| —— | Lighter | 180 | |
| —— | ...do | 180 | |
| Total | | 141,583 | 82,000 |

## FLAX.

The outlook for flax spinners in the early months of the year was far from encouraging, owing to the poor quality of the fiber received from Russia and Belgium. Prices, however, advanced sharply from week to week until they touched $200 per ton, or nearly double the rate for the corresponding period of the preceding year. As the acreage of flax sown in 1901 had increased about 8,000 acres over the planting in the year before, it was hoped that a good many more acres would be sown this year. This hope, however, was not realized, the acreage under flax in Ireland in 1902 showing a decrease of 5,696 acres, or about 10 per cent, as compared with 1901.

## YARNS.

Owing to the disturbed condition of the flax market, the prices of yarns at the beginning of the year were extremely firm. For tow wefts a strong demand existed which, continuing for six months, forced prices higher than at any period last year. The fluctuations during the succeeding half year were only slight.

Tows are extremely scarce, and in case any important demand for coarse goods sets in, prices are very likely again to bound upward.

## BELFAST STOCKS AND SHARES.

Business on the Belfast Stock Exchange has been very quiet during the year and prices in a majority of instances show a decline, the drop in some cases being remarkable. The tone of the market, however, has been better during the two or three months before the close of the year, and a general improvement is anticipated.

## AERATED WATERS.

The home demand for aerated waters seemed to have about held its own, while the export trade was much less than the year preceding. It is claimed that the duty on sugar, which came into force in 1901, told considerably upon the profits of this trade.

## THE BUILDING TRADE.

Various causes have combined to keep the building trade in a rather somnolent condition during the past year.

The duration of the South African war has no doubt adversely affected the industry as a whole, as has also the strike of the carpenters. This difficulty, which was settled amicably shortly before the beginning of the year, both employers and employees conceding several points, caused many people to postpone until a more propitious time the investing of money in any new building venture.

## COAL.

The average decline in the price of coal since the commencement of 1901 has been from 75 to 87 cents per ton, varying, of course, for the different grades, more in some of the mining centers than in others. At the beginning of the year a greater reduction in prices was anticipated; but the downward tendency was retarded from time to time by complications in relation to wages and by restriction of output.

The approximate estimates of British exports of coal for the year ended June 30, 1902, are 40,334,579 tons, as against 42,503,014 for the same period of 1900 and 36,619,132 for 1899. Average prices: 1900, $4; 1901, $3.25. France has been the largest customer of Great Britain, having imported 7,000,000 tons. Germany follows, with 5,500,000 tons, and Italy third, with 5,250,000 tons. Sweden, Spain, Russia, Denmark, Egypt, and Norway come next in order. The shipments of coal to Belfast show a decrease of about 58,000 tons. Reports from the smaller ports in Ulster also show decreases.

## WHOLESALE DRAPERY.

This trade has not during the present year been subjected to the same violent fluctuations in prices of cotton goods which characterized it in 1900. True, there were frequent changes in quotations for the raw material, but as these moved in a narrow compass as compared with last year, the difficulties experienced by buyers were not nearly so great.

Woolen goods were easier to buyers all through the year. The striking feature of this trade in Ireland is the improvement in manufacture and the steadily increasing demand for the different classes of Irish woolens.

There was a time in the history of Ireland when the manufacture of woolen fabrics was well understood, and in certain parts of the country few farmhouses did not contain a loom and a spinning wheel, on which most of the clothing required by the family was made.. Irish woolens were also made for export, and for certain purposes were more sought after than the English or Scotch goods.   This demand is again assuming considerable proportions, and there is a fair prospect for a largely increased sale of Irish tweeds and serges.

The wholesale drapery trade throughout the year has been only an average one, so far as the turnover is concerned.

### BOOTS AND SHOES.

The rapid introduction of American foot wear was an important feature in this trade during the past year.   American boots and shoes, by their all-round superiority, are winning their way to popular favor. People here are becoming aware of and appreciate the excellence of this American production, its ease and comfort, its durability and appearance, and their demand for it has resulted in placing American foot wear in the lead in the markets of this consular district.   I am told that boots and shoes manufactured in the United States are sold in some twenty of the retail establishments in Belfast alone, and that British manufacturers are making strenuous efforts to stem the tide and popularity of the American production.   To that end, they are improving their models, in some instances imitating closely the shape and finish of the imported foot wear.   It is also claimed by them that English leather wears longer and resists the damp much better than that of American tannage.   British dealers have also adopted American methods in the retail trade, of selling all boots and shoes at one price.   Yet, in spite of all this, the demand for the American foot wear seems to be increasing constantly, and it can be said, without exaggeration, that this line of American manufacture has won a permanent place in the markets of Great Britain.

### TIMBER AND SLATES.

Owing to the depression in the general building trade, the turnover in both timber and slate has not been up to the average, and notwithstanding the decrease in imports, stocks are somewhat in excess of what they were at the end of last year.   The total quantity of timber coming to Belfast during the last twelve months amounted to 1,275,506 cubic feet, as against 1,384,727 in the previous year, or a decrease of 109,221 cubic feet.

### GRAIN TRADE.

The fluctuations in values in the grain trade have been unimportant. Indian corn has been in large demand.   The greater portion of this commodity comes from the United States and Argentina, with some few shipments from the Danubian provinces.

### PROVISIONS.

The prices of pigs during the past year stood at a high standard, scarcely ever going below $12.50 per hundredweight and at times touching as high as $13.50 per hundredweight.   As a result, the trade was not by any means a remunerative one for the curers, who, in order to meet the competition of other countries, sold at nearly cost. At the end of the year (June 30, 1902) prices ranged from $12.50 to $12.75 per hundredweight, with little apparent prospect of their reaching a lower level.

Irish bacon sold well throughout the year, in both Lancashire and Yorkshire, where most of it is consumed. Lard also continued in good demand.

Following is a return of the number of pigs in Ireland for the past ten years, as given in the agricultural statistics:

| | | | |
|---|---|---|---|
| 1892 | 1,113,472 | 1897 | 1,327,450 |
| 1893 | 1,152,417 | 1898 | 1,253,912 |
| 1894 | 1,389,324 | 1899 | 1,363,310 |
| 1895 | 1,338,464 | 1900 | 1,268,474 |
| 1896 | 1,404,586 | 1901 | 1,218,999 |

## UNITED STATES TRADE.

Many lines of American manufactured goods have obtained a solid footing in this district and the tendency is to increase both in quantity and variety. Among such goods may be mentioned steel, iron, and woodworking machinery; typewriters, which take the lead in this market; cash registers, which are in general use; office desks and other office furniture; photographic supplies, sewing machines, lawn mowers, which are acknowledged superior to any other make, and a great variety of smaller manufactured articles.

The tobacco in leaf and ribs, used by the manufacturers here for smoking tobacco and cigarettes, is received principally from the United States.

American flour supplies the markets here. Corn flour and indian corn from the United States are also in general use. Fruits from California and canned goods of all kinds from the United States find a ready sale. In fact, in all lines of trade, productions from the United States are to be found.

WILLIAM W. TOUVELLE, *Consul.*

BELFAST, *October 21, 1902.*

---

## CORK.

There has been a considerable decrease in the tonnage of ships entering this port for the year ended September 30, 1902, and a consequent decrease of general business.

### GRAIN.

In the grain trade, the quantities imported have been about as usual. About two-thirds of the wheat received here was from the United States, the remainder being nearly all from Canada, with a small quantity from the river Plata.

Owing to the poor crop and high prices in the United States, the greater portion of maize was brought from the Black Sea and river Plata. Of 58,449 tons shipped to Messrs. R. & H. Hall, of Cork, only 3,681 tons was from the United States.

All the barley used in malting is grown in this country. It is considered superior to any grown elsewhere.

## COAL.

The competition in this trade has been unusually keen during the past year, but prices have, on the average, fallen only 1 shilling (24 cents) per ton. The coal used is brought from England, Wales, and Scotland, as in former years. A Scotch mining company opened a mine at Dromagh, near Kanturk, in Cork, but after spending about $60,000, abandoned it on account of the difficulty of keeping it clear of water and the inferiority of the coal.

## MEATS.

The supply of hogs has been greater this year, as there was a large potato crop in 1901. The yield of potatoes this season also promises to be fine; indeed, all food crops have been good throughout Ireland.

## FLAX, YARNS, ETC.

Flax spinners and weavers report a very poor foreign trade, owing to high prices of flax and yarns, and say they have been selling yarns under cost of production. They also report a good home market, and hope the coming year will be more favorable, as the flax crop is better.

In Ireland the crop is good, but the ground under flax is about 10,000 acres less than in 1901. All over Europe the acreage is greater. A union of flax and cotton has been coming into general use for some years, and the demand for it is increasing.

## WOOLENS.

The woolen industry of the south of Ireland continues to flourish, and the demand has greatly exceeded the output of most of the mills in this district. Some of the mills have put up looms of the latest improved pattern. Besides securing the greater part of the Irish trade, they are now sending their products to England, Scotland, and the Continent. Manufacturers are maintaining the high character for their goods in style and finish and the quality of the wool used. This is one of the most promising industries in Ireland.

## TOBACCO.

In this trade complete disorganization occurred on account of what was known as the tobacco war between the American Tobacco Company and the Imperial Tobacco Company, other manufacturers being unwillingly forced into it. The trade during the year has been well maintained, and were it not for this unhealthy competition, would have been quite satisfactory. Tobacco manufacturing has always been carried on extensively at Cork.

## ELECTRICITY.

The tramways have been doing remarkably well, and have extended their lines since last year. All the rails and machinery are brought from the United States. Owing to the exhibition at Cork this year, they have done a thriving business. Electric lighting is also coming into general use, not only in Cork city, but in many of the small towns and outlying districts.

## EXHIBITION.

The Cork International Exhibition was the great feature of the year, and was a success in every respect. The maufacturers of the United Kingdom were largely represented, and also many of continental nations, Canada and Japan. The exhibits were of a very commendable character, and the grounds and surroundings most picturesque.

The department of agriculture and technical instruction for Ireland took a very active part in the exhibition, and through its assistance the exhibit of the product of mines and quarries was effected, and instruction given in the manufacture of glass and other articles. Several officers of the department remained all the season, and by their courteous attention to visitors aided much in the general success. All visitors to the exhibition expressed themselves as highly pleased.

The lord mayor of Cork and the executive committee now think of purchasing the grounds, with the surplus receipts, and using them as a public park, which is much needed by this city.

DANIEL SWINEY, *Consul.*

QUEENSTOWN, *October 14, 1902.*

————

Under date of December 11, Mr. Swiney adds:

The exhibition closed on the 1st ultimo. The number of visitors was 1,410,000. It has been decided to hold another one in 1903, to be called "The Greater Exhibition."

The final meeting of the executive committee of this year's exhibition was held on the 9th instant, and the liquidator reported that after paying the sum of £3,300 (or $16,059.45) for the shrubberies, grounds, house, and all other liabilities, the committee had in bank a sum of £1,803 13s. (or $8,777.45); and after paying sundry debts, and collecting all moneys due them, they would have a net balance of £1,005 1s. (or $4,891.06).

This balance will be placed at the disposal of the committee of next year's exhibition; also the custody of the grounds and buildings.

————

## SCOTLAND.

### EDINBURGH.

Commercial and industrial conditions in this district in 1902 have not been as good as they were in 1901, which was not a year of prosperity. At the port of Leith, both exports and imports have declined as compared with last year, and, for the most part, mercantile interests have suffered from restricted buying. Production has not been fully maintained in the leading branches of industry, and, as a rule, especially in iron and steel, the margin of profit has been extremely narrow, owing chiefly to German and Belgian competition. The average prices received by the steel companies of Scotland for their products have been about $6.40 per ton less than the prices in 1901, and as the fall in pig iron has been only $3.30 per ton and in coal 75 cents per ton on the relative cost of raw material and finished steel, the balance is $2.35 per ton against them. In the beginning of the year few orders were on hand, and some of the works were practically idle; but the demand from the United States for steel, in the spring, gave a new impetus to the trade, and this demand continuing through the summer, the companies were enabled to carry on their business to some advantage. In the early autumn, however, the depression in steel and finished iron again became severe, being attributed principally to the reduced requirements for shipbuilding, and at this time there are no indications of a change for the better. Leading men in the trade think that the retrograde movement can not long continue, but they have no expectation of a substantial recovery in prices until next year. Prices of manufactured iron—bars, plates, angles, and rails—have declined about $1.15 per ton this year, and as compared with the best prices in the autumn of 1900 the reduction has been fully $10 per ton.

Most of the book printers and publishers have been well employed, and the paper trade is active at a narrow margin of profit.

The brewing and distilling trades have not been prosperous. The consumption of beer has fallen off and prices of raw spirits have weakened, even as compared with the low quotations in 1900 and 1901.

In the tweed industry, trade has been on the whole steady and satisfactory. Scotch goods appear to have regained public favor, which was lost a few years ago to the smoother Yorkshire woolens. Tweed manufacturers are showing a good deal of enterprise in throwing out antiquated machinery and adopting high-speed looms and labor-saving appliances. The margin of profit is rather small, but by economy in production, manufacturers are enabled to compete more keenly. Wool is inclined to rise in value, and the tweed mills have difficulty sometimes in obtaining a corresponding rise in prices of goods. This may act adversely upon the industry, but probably not to a serious extent. Scotch-grown wools are still reasonably low in price, but only the best of these are used in making cheviot suitings, all other qualities being utilized in the manufacture of carpets. Practically all of the wool used in tweed manufacture in South Scotland is imported.

### CREDITS AND GENERAL TRADE TERMS OF BRITISH INDUSTRIES.

Among European countries Germany has long been noted for the free extension of credit in business transactions, both at home and abroad. A close second in this respect is Belgium; next in order, according to the common opinion, is Great Britain. Until a decade ago, British manufacturers had not met with strong competition from their continental neighbors in any part of the world, and they established their trade upon the safe basis of moderate credits. The expanding trade of these progressive nations, especially of Germany, and the vast growth of the industries and commerce of the United States, changed the old easy-going conditions, and for six or seven years the British manufacturer and trader have had to reckon with active competition in almost every market. It is about four years since German manufacturers, in the struggle for markets, began to lengthen credits. Whether they have failed, or how far they have succeeded in their object, need not be here considered. They have at least made more severe the strain upon British industries.

With a view of ascertaining whether or not British manufacturers have been forced to abandon the path of conservatism by the intense competition of other nations, I have made an inquiry into credits and other terms of various industries in the United Kingdom. This investigation has covered the average length of credit, average discounts, and general trade terms to responsible British and foreign customers. It seems needless to say that many difficulties have been encountered in pursuing this inquiry, but I think that a fair measure of success has been attained, and that the results may be useful to American manufacturers and exporters.

The information here presented has been obtained in the respective centers of the industries included in the list, and it is, I believe, as definite and as nearly accurate as any investigation of diverse and competing interests could produce. As to some industries, the statements elicited are vague; but, considered in connection with the facts given in regard to related branches, they are not without value.

It appears to be conclusively shown that among the trades or branches of industries embraced in this inquiry there has been no lengthening of credit in either the home or foreign markets, except in the cutlery, silver and plated ware, and pumps and pumping-engines trades; that there has been, on the contrary, a tendency toward restriction of credit in some industries; that British manufacturers have met the new competition by a reduction of prices or, what means the same thing, an expansion of discounts.

A specially interesting fact is that the cotton-goods trade with China and India at the present time is practically on a cash basis.

The paragraphs have been arranged without reference to the relative importance of the several industries, but in alphabetical order, for convenience.

*Blast-furnace plant.*—As a rule, terms are part of special contract in each case. The ordinary agreement is for payment of one-third on inspection, one-third on shipment, and the balance as soon as the plant is in operation.

*Boilers, steam.*—Net cash on delivery, as a rule. To both home and foreign customers the terms sometimes quoted are one-third with order, one-third on receipt of bill of lading, and the balance in one clear month net.

*Bolt and nut making machinery.*—Generally cash on erection; sometimes one-third with order and the balance on erection, net, or thirty days' grace.

*Brick and tile making machinery.*—Length of credit ranges from three to six months to both British and foreign buyers, but usually one-third of the net price must be paid with order. There has been no lengthening, but rather a restriction of credit.

*Boots and shoes.*—Trade terms vary according to individual circumstances, discounts ranging from 6½ per cent for cash (which practically means within seven days), 5 per cent at the month to a decreased and vanishing discount for a longer period of credit—about five months net. Terms are practically the same to home and foreign buyers, except that the foreign business rests largely upon bills of exchange, not accounts. The length of credit to foreign merchants has not been extended in any general way for several years.

*Chemicals.*—Length of credit is fourteen days net, but 2 per cent discount is allowed for cash and goods guaranteed. This applies to trade in Great Britain and colonies and South America. No trade is done with Russia, as the duty exceeds the cost and freight of chemicals, and if trade were done with that country I am informed that it would mean special terms on account of the great risks involved. There has been no expansion of credit in recent years, and it is not considered that German or other continental or American competition has yet made any material change in British terms.

*Cotton goods.*—In Great Britain, the usual terms to merchants are monthly—that is, goods delivered between the 20th of one month and the 19th of the following month are paid for the first week of the succeeding month; to shippers, however, the terms are seven to fourteen days. To buyers in South Africa the present basis is six months' credit, owing to the general circumstances brought about by the late war. To buyers in China the terms are sixty or ninety days, which means practically cash, as bills of lading are sent through bankers and taken up by payment by the consignees. To Indian buyers the terms are thirty days, and, as the bills of lading go through bankers, this really means cash. The trade in South America has been in a very unsettled state for some time, and failures have hit British houses hard. The bulk of the trade is done on three to six months' credit, but the tendency is to restrict credit in that quarter.

*Cutlery.*—Discounts range from 5 per cent at thirty days in the home trade. Manufacturers offer very extended credit in the foreign trade, six, twelve, or eighteen months being common terms, particularly in Russia, where the longest terms obtain. German competition is most keenly felt in India, where the German manufacturers offer almost any length of credit.

*Cycles and cycle parts.*—The general terms appear to be 5 per cent at thirty days, or three months net, for Great Britain; for the colonies and South America, cash against documents net. No lengthening of credit has been accorded in recent years.

*Dairy machinery.*—From three to six months' credit on bill is allowed to foreign buyers on two-thirds of the net price. The rule is to require one-third with order. In some cases home buyers get more liberal terms.

*Engines, gas.*—Terms in Great Britain are one month, payable during the week following the expiration of the month. Some firms have a deferred system, payment of one-fourth before delivery and the balance spread over eighteen months net. The extensive concerns do all their foreign business through agents, sending out large consignments. Foreign terms are according to circumstances.

*Engines, portable.*—Average terms to responsible buyers do not appear to have changed within the past twenty years to any considerable extent. In most cases these are strictly net prices on delivery. Some large concerns, however, occasionally quote as follows for their foreign trade: One-third with order, one-third on delivery, and one-third at one clear month net.

*Engines, stationary steam.*—Ordinary terms to home and foreign buyers: Cash on delivery. With some manufacturers, cash within a clear month to buyers in Great Britain is the rule.

*Fancy goods.*—Length of credit to British and foreign buyers: Two months at 2½ per cent discount, or one month at 3¾ per cent discount. No expansion of credit within the past five years.

*Forgings, iron and steel.*—General terms in this trade are cash on receipt of bill of lading, which apply to home and foreign markets alike. The exceptions to the rule are few, especially in the foreign trade.

*Furniture.*—The usual credit in the furniture trade is about as follows: Great Britain, six, nine, to twelve months' account, according to status, or 2½ per cent discount for cash in thirty days; colonies, six months' bill or 2½ per cent discount at thirty days and an extra 1¼ per cent prompt; Russia, thirty days' bill or 2½ per cent discount cash against documents. These terms do not appear to have been extended within the past four years.

*Gloves.*—The usual terms of sale are: One month at 3¾ per cent discount, or two months at 2½ per cent discount. Terms are practically the same for all countries. No lengthening of credit within the past five years.

*Hardware.*—As a rule, the terms are 2½ per cent, thirty days' or three months' account net, for Great Britain, and for the colonies and South Africa, cash against documents net; Russia, usually six months' acceptance net. It is said by leading men in the trade that there has been no change in terms or length of credit for some years.

*Hosiery.*—Accounts for goods bought, say, in September at 3¾ per cent discount are due in October, and accounts for goods bought before the 20th of September at 2½ per cent discount are due in November; if purchased after the 20th of September, due in December, 2½ per cent discount. These are the complete terms and general for all countries, having been in vogue for some years.

*Hydraulic machinery and appliances.*—Average terms have not changed for several years. In most cases payment of net prices on delivery is required; but there are foreign transactions on the basis of one-third with order, one-third on delivery, and the balance in thirty days net.

*Laundry machinery.*—Usually to buyers in Great Britain the credit runs from three to six months. There is no common rate of discount, so far as can be ascertained.

To foreign buyers (this trade is not large), the rule is to require one-third with order, one-third in three months, and the balance in four or six months. There has been a restriction of credit in this branch of trade lately, as in some other classes of machinery.

*Locomotives.*—The average terms quoted and the usual terms of the trade are cash on delivery. Latterly, in some cases, a month's credit has been allowed; also, if expressly mentioned in the specifications, one-tenth of the purchase money is retained until an agreed number of miles has been run by the locomotive. Continental competition has had no effect upon terms in this industry.

*Milling machinery.*—The tendency in this trade has been toward a restriction of credit. The length of credit to foreign buyers runs from three to six months. The rule is, where credit is asked, to require one-third with order and one-third in ninety days, and the balance in four or six months. Home buyers have somewhat better terms. Rates of discount vary, and the average rate can not be stated.

*Mining machinery and tools.*—A mining plant is usually contracted for on definite terms of payment, such as one-third on inspection at works, one-third on shipment, and one-third on erection. The average credit on tools, etc., is as follows: Great Britain, three months' account net, at $2\frac{1}{2}$ per cent discount at 30 days; colonies, six months' acceptance or $2\frac{1}{2}$ per cent discount at thirty days and an extra $1\frac{1}{2}$ per cent prompt. South America, sixty days' bills, or $2\frac{1}{2}$ per cent discount at thirty days and an extra $1\frac{1}{2}$ per cent prompt; Russia, thirty days' bill or $2\frac{1}{2}$ per cent discount for cash against documents. Term of credit has not been extended within the past four years.

*Paper.*—Average trade terms at the present time: Great Britain, three months' account net, $2\frac{1}{2}$ per cent discount on monthly account, $3\frac{1}{2}$ per cent discount prompt cash; colonies, six months' bill, $2\frac{1}{2}$ per cent clear thirty days, $3\frac{1}{2}$ per cent prompt cash; South America, three months' bill, $2\frac{1}{2}$ per cent discount clear thirty days, $3\frac{1}{2}$ per cent discount prompt cash; France, the same terms as for South America. There has been no general extension of the period of credit to foreign buyers within five years.

*Papermaking machinery.*—To foreign buyers the average terms are payment of one-third with order, one-third in three months, and one-third in four or six months. British buyers have a longer credit, as a rule, if desired; but there has been no extension of the period of credit in recent years to either the home or foreign customers. Discounts vary according to circumstances and the average rate can not be stated.

*Pottery.*—The general trade terms to home buyers are 5 per cent discount one month from date of invoice, and $2\frac{1}{2}$ per cent discount at three months; but some china manufacturers have different terms, which also differ somewhat from the terms of earthenware concerns. Manufacturers say that there has been no material change in British trade terms due to German or French competition, but that the earthenware industry is suffering from American competition. Terms to foreign buyers are generally cash, but if credit is granted it is usually by three months' bill with 5 per cent discount. The period of credit has not been extended within four years. Most manufacturers doing a foreign trade have no experience of credit transactions, especially in the case of American and colonial buyers.

*Pumps and pumping engines.*—To buyers in Great Britain, the terms are monthly, with no specified discount. The present tendency is toward a lengthening of credit. Export business is not large, and terms can not be ascertained.

*Rolling-mill plant.*—In most cases, definite terms of payment are stated in the contract—usually one-third on inspection, one-third on shipment, and the balance on the erection of the plant.

*Rope and twine making machinery.*—Cash on delivery or thirty days, according to circumstances. Discounts vary from 5 per cent.

*Sanitary appliances.*—Terms in most cases are a matter of arrangement between manufacturer and buyer, trade discounts from catalogue prices being expansive. Taking an average, the following appear to be the terms: Great Britain, three months' account net; monthly account, $2\frac{1}{2}$ per cent discount; colonies, 6 months' bill or $2\frac{1}{2}$ per cent discount at thirty days; Russia, one month's bill or $2\frac{1}{2}$ per cent discount cash; South America, two months' bill or $2\frac{1}{2}$ per cent discount, thirty clear days; no extension of credit period in recent years.

*Silver and plated ware.*—Long credit is given in this trade, varying from six to eighteen months. This applies to both the home and foreign trade. Discounts range from 10 per cent at thirty days. German competition in the cheaper lines has been keen for some years in the British market and abroad, and the length of credit and other terms of British manufacturers have been somewhat affected so far as regards the cheaper goods.

*Springs.*—Average terms in Great Britain, three months' account, $2\frac{1}{2}$ per cent discount at thirty days; for the colonies, six months' acceptance or $2\frac{1}{2}$ per cent discount at thirty days; Russia, thirty days' acceptance or $2\frac{1}{2}$ per cent discount for prompt cash; South America, two months' bill or $2\frac{1}{2}$ per cent discount at thirty days.

*Stoves and ranges.*—General terms of trade are as follows: In Great Britain, the length of credit is usually three months; in continental markets and the colonies, one month from date of delivery, which is practically cash. Discounts vary greatly, ranging from 10 to 33 per cent off price list. German competition has to some extent influenced British prices, and manufacturers in Scotland are making strong efforts to neutralize this competition by arranging suitable terms with customers. But there has been no extension of the credit period in foreign markets; in fact, the tendency is the other way.

*Structural iron and steel.*—Foreign terms are cash on delivery or on receipt of bills of lading. Inland trade is principally by contract, and where cash terms are not quoted the credit is according to special contract terms, which, of course, vary. In this industry a fair amount of shipping is done through London shipping agents, who may quote different terms to foreign customers, especially in South Africa. German or other continental competition has not made itself felt to any noticeable degree in this branch of the iron and steel trade, and the terms are similar to those quoted five years ago.

*Sugar machinery.*—The rule is, payment of net prices on delivery. This applies to both home and foreign customers. Foreign sales are sometimes made on these terms: One-third with order, one-third on delivery, and the balance at one clear month.

*Textile machinery.*—The ordinary terms to colonial and foreign buyers are payment of one-third with order, one-third in ninety days, and the balance in one hundred and twenty or one hundred and eighty days, according to circumstances. To buyers in Great Britain, the terms are somewhat more favorable, but upon the same basis. Of course, in some special cases credit is extended to one or two years, but the tendency of late has been to restrict these special terms and adhere as far as possible to the general. There appear to be no recognized rates of discount, and where this is allowed it is entirely governed by circumstances.

*Tools, hand.*—The trade has not been materially affected by continental competition, the American manufacturers being far more aggressive and successful in several lines of this department of industry. Credit and discounts remain as they were some years ago. Average terms in Great Britain, ninety days' account, 2½ per cent discount at thirty days. Hand tools for the foreign markets are for the most part bought through London merchants. Ordinary terms for the colonies, six months' acceptance or 2½ per cent at thirty days, and an extra 1½ per cent prompt; Russia, one month's bill or 2½ per cent discount for cash; South America, two months' bill or 2½ per cent discount at thirty days and an extra 1½ per cent prompt.

*Tools, machine.*—An average discount of 2½ per cent is allowed and in some cases 5 per cent to merchants in Great Britain who pay at one month; extreme length of credit, six months net. Foreign buyers who ask for credit are, as a rule, required to pay net prices, ordinarily one-third with order if desired, one-third in ninety days, and the balance in one hundred and twenty days. Length of credit to foreign purchasers has not been extended within four years. In the lathe trade, for inquiries made through merchants, the manufacturers allow generally 5 per cent at one month. Goods ordered otherwise than through merchants are, as a rule, payable on receipt of bill of lading. Foreign trade is on the same basis.

*Tubes, iron and steel.*—Average terms to responsible buyers are as follows: Great Britain, three months' account net, 2½ per cent discount on monthly account, 5 per cent discount spot cash; colonies, six months' bill net, 5 per cent discount cash against documents in London; South America, two months' bill net, 5 per cent discount against documents in London; Russia, one month's bill net, 2½ per cent discount cash against documents here. There has apparently been no lengthening of the credit period to foreign buyers within five years.

*Woolen goods.*—Discount about 4 per cent for cash, or 2½ per cent one month. The usual terms for the colonial trade are: Credit, six months' bill net or 2½ per cent at thirty days. Norway, 2½ per cent at thirty days and six months' bill net. Severe losses have been experienced by the British woolen manufacturers in the Russian trade, and they are now practically out of that market, which is largely supplied from Germany. There has been no expansion of credit in the home, colonial, or continental trade within the past four years.

## AMERICAN TRADE IN EAST SCOTLAND.

It is the opinion of importers and merchants that the volume of imports from the United States into this part of Scotland has been equal to that of any previous year. Little corn has been imported from our country for two years, but aside from this one item, the grain and provision trade is quite satisfactory, in view of the reduced purchasing power of the masses, and the shrinkage in almost every branch of business here.

There has been a fair demand for American machinery. Harvesters and other farm machines have sold well, but at prices considerably below the lowest terms heretofore offered by the various companies. Our presses, both for newspaper and book printing, are steadily gaining favor; and this is true also as to our boot and shoe making devices and laundry machines. Our dynamos are used largely, but we have made no great advance in this market as yet in the smaller electrical appliances. Most of the automobiles sold in Scotland are of British manufacture, and of the foreign-made machines, by far the larger number are French, the American manufacturers not having put forth any special efforts in this market. Our sawmilling and rope-making apparatus are in strong favor, also hand and steam pumps. Our machines and instruments for dental surgery have an increasing sale.

The agents of our computing-scale companies have been very successful in East Scotland this year.

The sale of our machine tools and hand tools has been fully up to the average. Our agricultural instruments, such as forks and rakes, hold their place in the trade, but sales have been rather slow; and the same may be said of axes, handles, shovels, spades, picks, etc.

Our boots and shoes of the better grades are getting into the market more largely. Rubber ware does not show a material improvement here, but when the sharp competition is considered the demand is fairly active, giving promise of an increased trade as the merits of our goods become more widely known. Such articles among our household hardware, especially kitchen utensils, as are adapted to this market are winning their way, though somewhat slowly, into general favor. Bolts and nuts are a growing commercial item, although not now a prominent one. Our saddlery hardware is used to some extent and is regarded as excellent and should have a much greater sale than at present. Several patterns of American lawn mowers have been selling more freely this year than ever before. In our furniture, the roll-top desk is the article which seems to be growing most rapidly in commercial importance here. Our roofing slates have secured a permanent place in this market and their sale is extending. Within the past year, there has sprung up a strong demand for our cold-water paint. A local importer of builders' materials informs me that he is receiving heavy orders for this paint, which has gained remarkable popularity, especially for outside work, in a short time. Our radiators are going into many modern houses, particularly public halls and offices, and it is thought that this trade has a prosperous future in Scotland. Our bath tubs and water-closet appliances are also attracting attention and gradually getting the recognition they deserve against very keen competition. The trade in plumbers' supplies and tools has also increased somewhat. Our watches and clocks of the cheaper grades are widely sold. The bicycle trade as a whole has been extremely dull, chiefly on account of the cool and wet weather in the summer, and the sales of American wheels have fallen off with the rest. Our leather has not increased in this district, partly owing to the depression in the boot and shoe manufacture, and further because trunk and portmanteau makers here are now using, to a large extent, American hard fiber as a substitute for leather. Sales of our fencing wire have been good, at rather low prices. Our moldings, both for house interiors and for picture frames, are coming into more general use, but this trade should be far more important than it is at present. Our silverware and plated wares do not as yet compete successfully in Scotland, on a large scale, with the English and German wares; moderate sales of the plainer designs are reported. Our toilet articles, especially soaps and tooth pastes, have been gaining constantly for some years, displacing the French articles. Our medicinal preparations are in high favor with the medical profession in Scotland, owing to the excellent reputation of American manufacturing chemists for care in selecting materials, and also because they are always ready to make any preparation to order. Our cameras and photographic lenses are considered to be fine values at the prices at which they are offered, and there seems no reason why this trade should not grow far beyond its present dimensions. The better grades of our writing inks are sold in moderate quantities, against a decidedly strong competition; the poorer grades can not get into this market. Our typewriters, cash registers, sewing machines, and other standard devices are keeping at the front, although, in common with all similar articles, they have been affected by the depression prevailing during the past two years.

The appended statistics are taken from the abstract of the accounts of the commissioners for the harbor and docks of Leith for the year ended May 15, 1902.

RUFUS FLEMING, *Consul.*

EDINBURGH, *October 27, 1902.*

---

*Imports of grain, flour, and meal, sugar, fruit, esparto, oilcake, wood, guano, flax, hemp and fish, at Leith, from May 15, 1901, to May 15, 1902.*

| Imported from— | Wheat. | Barley. | Oats. | Maize. | Rye. | Other grain. | Total grain. |
|---|---|---|---|---|---|---|---|
| | *Tons.* | *Tons.* | *Tons.* | *Tons.* | *Tons.* | *Tons.* | *Tons.* |
| Scotland | 1,371 | 982 | 8,387 | 800 | | 444 | 11,984 |
| England | 167 | 2,658 | 170 | 1,462 | 1 | 1,476 | 5,934 |
| Ireland | | | 8 | 16 | | 59 | 83 |
| Holland | | | | | | 1,030 | 1,030 |
| Hamburg | 17 | 2,300 | | | | 246 | 2,563 |
| Germany | | 7,466 | 3,781 | 851 | 108 | 3,453 | 15,659 |
| Denmark | | 1,601 | 75 | | 5 | | 1,681 |
| Norway | | | 17 | | | | 17 |
| Russia | 5,344 | 7,712 | 16,845 | | 2,945 | 8,164 | 41,010 |
| France | | 61 | | | | | 61 |
| Roumania | 2,221 | 15,709 | 869 | 43,834 | 4,163 | 724 | 67,520 |
| Austria | | 401 | | | | 1 | 402 |
| Turkey | 882 | 18,643 | | 3,162 | 1,178 | 971 | 24,831 |
| Egypt | | 1,309 | | | | 544 | 1,853 |
| Africa | | 13,649 | | | | 138 | 13,787 |
| New Zealand | 5,050 | | | | | | 5,050 |
| North America: | | | | | | | |
| British | 24,325 | | 712 | 688 | | 678 | 26,348 |
| Foreign | 72,971 | 16,352 | | 3,234 | | 1,330 | 93,887 |
| South America | 2,965 | | | | | | 2,965 |
| Total, 1901–2 | 115,313 | 88,843 | 30,864 | 58,997 | 8,395 | 19,253 | 316,665 |
| Total, 1900–1 | 145,807 | 100,070 | 43,787 | 83,442 | 13,559 | 19,275 | 405,940 |
| Decrease | 30,494 | 11,227 | 12,923 | 29,445 | 5,164 | 22 | 89,275 |

*Imports of grain, flour, etc., at Leith, from May 15, 1901, to May 15, 1902—Continued.*

| Imported from— | Flour and meal. | Sugar. | Fruit. | Espar-to. | Oil-cake. | Wood. | Guano and other ma-nures. | Flax. | Hemp. | Fish, fresh and cured. |
|---|---|---|---|---|---|---|---|---|---|---|
| | Tons. | Tons. | Tons. | Tons. | Tons. | Tons. | Tons. | Tons. | Tons. | Tons. |
| Scotland | 871 | 507 | 5 | | 354 | 1,050 | 648 | 40 | 16 | 30,458 |
| England | 2,122 | 1,446 | 2,504 | | 3,058 | 1,079 | 2,299 | 50 | 2,344 | 2,271 |
| Ireland | 1,426 | | 4 | | 731 | 380 | 320 | 17 | 13 | 15 |
| Holland | 93 | 15,851 | 1,812 | | | | 156 | 479 | | 3 |
| Hamburg | 380 | 48,532 | 820 | | 2,301 | 120 | 10,389 | | 22 | 30 |
| Germany | 104 | 52,132 | 35 | | 152 | 284 | 217 | 55 | 2,796 | 40 |
| Denmark | 28 | 1 | 13 | | | 84 | 340 | 193 | | 2,086 |
| Norway | | | | | | 16,420 | 196 | | | 344 |
| Sweden | | | | | | 7,968 | | | | |
| Russia | 157 | | | | 6,789 | 44,541 | 815 | 6,110 | 893 | |
| Belgium | 424 | 2,279 | 3,578 | | | | 992 | 1,361 | 2 | 3 |
| France | 6,598 | 6,255 | 599 | | 994 | 4 | | 61 | 6 | |
| Spain | | | | 701 | | | | | | |
| Portugal | | | 4 | | | | | | | |
| Austria | 459 | | | | | 1,144 | | | | |
| Turkey | | | 476 | | | | | | | |
| Egypt | | | 1 | | 2,367 | | | | | |
| Africa | | | | 3,754 | | | 4,893 | | | |
| North America: | | | | | | | | | | |
| British | 3,638 | 26 | 38 | | | 6,780 | | | | |
| Foreign | 34,909 | 180 | 83 | | 910 | 8,584 | 5,505 | | | |
| South America | | | | | | | 12,650 | | | |
| Total, 1901-2.. | 51,209 | 127,209 | 9,972 | 4,455 | 17,606 | 88,488 | 38,920 | 8,366 | 6,094 | 35,200 |
| Total, 1900-1.. | 61,247 | 157,576 | 12,127 | 3,695 | 18,898 | 91,895 | 37,859 | 6,918 | 6,339 | 51,937 |
| Increase | | | | 760 | 3,708 | | 1,061 | 1,448 | | |
| Decrease | 10,088 | 30,367 | 2,155 | | | 3,457 | | | 245 | 16,737 |

*General imports and exports at Leith in year ended May 15, 1902.*

| Goods. | Import-ed. | Export-ed. | Goods. | Import-ed. | Export-ed. |
|---|---|---|---|---|---|
| I.—Goods paying at least £25 of rates. | | | I.—Goods paying at least £25 of rates—Continued. | | |
| | Tons. | Tons. | | Tons. | Tons. |
| Ale, beer, and porter: | | | Corn: | | |
| Casks | 5,998 | 77,114 | Barley | 88,216 | 9,850 |
| Cases | 807 | 5,856 | Beans | 4,950 | 657 |
| Ammonia, sulphate of | 14 | 31,616 | Indian corn | 54,008 | 2,820 |
| Asphalt | 2,491 | 874 | Lentils | 1,370 | 355 |
| Bacon, pork, and hams | 3,182 | 1,091 | Malt | 555 | 8,254 |
| Bark | 1,601 | 128 | Oats | 30,655 | 1,160 |
| Barytes, stone | 2,677 | 1,056 | Pease | 10,859 | 833 |
| Basket ware | 542 | 82 | Pease, split | 70 | 1,541 |
| Biscuits | 244 | 3,068 | Rye | 8,298 | 2,231 |
| Bleaching powder | 6,716 | 851 | Tares | 480 | 270 |
| Bone ash, dust and meal | 1,845 | 1,646 | Wheat | 115,081 | 2,946 |
| Bottles | 10,430 | 5,566 | Cork shavings | 1,428 | 1,606 |
| Bricks, common fire clay and bath | 86 | 12,458 | Cotton manufactures | 429 | 1,147 |
| Butter | 18,944 | 227 | Cummings, malt | 204 | 1,220 |
| Cake | 17,715 | 4,118 | Drapery | 726 | 868 |
| Carpets, rugs, etc | 44 | 567 | Drugs | 518 | 594 |
| Casks, empty | 1,965 | 931 | Dreg sediment | 765 | 3,508 |
| | | | Earthenware, etc | 874 | 2,047 |
| Cattle, etc., number: | | | Eggs | 19,787 | 543 |
| Bulls, cows, or oxen | 1,035 | 23 | Electric cables | 518 | 21 |
| Lambs | 7,103 | 1,707 | Envelopes, straw | 1,515 | 70 |
| Sheep | 55,148 | 415 | Esparto | 4,349 | |
| Asses | | 15 | Farina | 2,787 | 2,563 |
| Dogs | 21 | 44 | Fat, grease, etc | 2,657 | 6,540 |
| Horses and ponies | 1,824 | 1,527 | Fire-clay goods | 16 | 2,113 |
| Pigs | 376 | 86 | Fish: | | |
| All other animals | 8 | 5 | Fresh | 4,048 | 208 |
| | | | Cured | 815 | 258 |
| Cattle food | 1,063 | 358 | Dry salt | 3,998 | 1,880 |
| Cement | 43,826 | 2,262 | Shell | 233 | 145 |
| Cheese | 4,588 | 283 | Mussels | 164 | 262 |
| Clay, china, pipe, etc | 11,520 | 150 | Flax | 8,333 | 1,442 |
| Coal and coal dust | 1,574 | 749,856 | Flour: | | |
| Confections | 486 | 889 | Dust, sharps, and bran | 502 | 19,872 |
| Copper | 769 | 888 | Indian corn | 120 | 119 |
| | | | Wheaten | 50,231 | 23,959 |

*General imports and exports at Leith in year ended May 15, 1902*—Continued.

| Goods. | Imported. | Exported. | Goods, | Imported. | Exported. |
|---|---|---|---|---|---|
| I.—*Goods paying at least £25 of rates*—Continued. | Tons. | Tons. | I.—*Goods paying at least £25 of rates*—Continued. | Tons. | Tons. |
| Floor cloth and linoleum ... | 1,773 | 1,387 | Paints and colors............ | 1,831 | 1,626 |
| Fruit: | | | Paper...................... | 18,396 | 29,111 |
|   Apples................... | 3,118 | 93 | Paraffin scale and wax..... | 687 | 6,176 |
|   Cherries and currants ... | 337 | 16 | Petroleum and residuum.... | 1,650 | 13 |
|   Dates.................... | 103 | .......... | Pig heads and feet........ | 2,649 | 871 |
|   Dry almonds............ | 48 | 15 | Phosphate rock........... | 11,231 | 168 |
|   Dry currants........... | 1,015 | 79 | Plants, shrubs, and trees ... | 689 | 30 |
|   Figs.................... | 169 | 20 | Provisions, preserved........ | 1,360 | 880 |
|   Gooseberries............ | 366 | .......... | Pulp of wood............ | 3,269 | 565 |
|   Grapes................. | 5 | 13 | Pyrites .................. | 9,414 | ...... |
|   Lemons ................ | 173 | .......... | Rags..................... | 5,725 | 2,152 |
|   Melons ................ | 34 | 14 | Rice..................... | 4,721 | 862 |
|   Oranges ............... | 451 | 37 | Ropes ................... | 1,261 | 1,996 |
|   Pears.................. | 1,481 | 12 | Resin.................... | 1,115 | 30 |
|   Plums and greengages .. | 1,239 | 19 | Salt: | | |
|   Prunes................. | 69 | 5 |   Refined............... | 2,880 | 740 |
|   Raisins................ | 902 | 113 |   Waste and rock ....... | 8,351 | 848 |
|   Raspberries............ | 4 | .......... | Sand .................... | 5,746 | 161 |
|   Strawberries........... | 9 | .......... | Seeds: | | |
|   Tomatoes............... | 88 | 7 |   Cotton............... | 10,189 | 587 |
|   Other kinds ........... | 18 | 1 |   Flax and linseed...... | 12,671 | 4,445 |
|   Preserved ............. | 470 | 23 |   Grass and clover........ | 6,063 | 9,521 |
| Furniture .................. | 600 | 348 |   Millet .............. | 5,025 | 143 |
| Glass: | | |   Other kinds .......... | 884 | 175 |
|   Window, etc ........... | 4,442 | 582 | Sewing machines.......... | 140 | 1,080 |
|   Hollow ................ | 1,677 | 421 | Sewing machine stands..... | 2 | 1,608 |
| Glue...................... | 1,105 | 527 | Skins, sheep.;.......... | 971 | 29 |
| Gravel..................... | 2,319 | 11 | Slates, roofing........... | 1,129 | 108 |
| Groceries.................. | 24 | 1,243 | Soap, hard and soft ...... | 1,605 | 712 |
| Guano..................... | 8,640 | 2,066 | Soda..................... | 3,026 | 506 |
| Hardware, light............ | 1,359 | 586 |   Ash.................. | 1,965 | 48 |
| Hay ...................... | 3,267 | 489 |   Bicarbonate.......... | 510 | 13 |
| Hemp ..................... | 6,242 | 959 |   Caustic.............. | 2,873 | 386 |
| Herrings: | | | Spelter ................. | 2,761 | 2,578 |
|   In casks, cured......... | 26,307 | 34,721 | Spirits: | | |
|   In cases, etc........... | 217 | 1,585 |   Casks............... | 7,586 | 8,556 |
| Hides..................... | 1,107 | 1,027 |   Cases ............... | 1,568 | 3,774 |
| Hops ..................... | 1,529 | 23 | Starch................... | 2,022 | 800 |
| Husks .................... | 687 | 1,831 | Stones: | | |
| Ice ...................... | 5,244 | 413 |   Grind ............... | 1,077 | 630 |
| India rubber, etc.......... | 569 | 2,296 |   Pavement or flag...... | 6,709 | 2 |
| Instruments, musical, etc... | 788 | 89 | Straw.................... | 5,464 | 458 |
| Iron and steel: | | | Sugar.................... | 128,400 | 55,378 |
|   Angles................ | 300 | 894 | Superphosphate of lime..... | 169 | 3,257 |
|   Bar, bolt, etc.......... | 13,745 | 6,602 | Sirup and treacle ........ | 3,641 | 1,097 |
|   Boilers............... | 68 | 970 | Tar, coal ............... | 965 | 2,860 |
|   Cast, in pipes.......... | 1,658 | 3,505 | Tea..................... | 3,100 | 182 |
|   Girders ............... | 21,742 | 993 | Thread .................. | 32 | 2,231 |
|   Ironwork.............. | 1,999 | 6,167 | Tin...................... | 801 | 288 |
|   Galvanized............ | 111 | 317 | Tobacco.................. | 1,563 | 129 |
|   Machinery, heavy....... | 1,366 | 3,475 | Tow ..................... | 2,418 | 1,607 |
|   Machinery, light....... | 206 | 57 | Toys..................... | 1,387 | 92 |
|   Nails and spikes........ | 1,930 | 676 | Valonia ................. | 1,301 | 14 |
|   Pig iron .............. | 7,797 | 32,191 | Vegetables: | | |
|   Ferrosilicon .......... | .......... | 3,256 |   Carrots.............. | 6,585 | 31 |
|   Rails................. | 610 | 192 |   Onions............... | 6,595 | 106 |
|   Rivets................ | 1,645 | 1,633 |   Potatoes............. | 834 | 6,745 |
|   Wire.................. | 1,355 | 731 |   Other kinds ......... | 1,227 | 19 |
|   Other kinds ........... | 1,589 | 2,417 | Whiting.................. | 3,879 | 605 |
| Jute goods................. | 1,983 | 5,175 | Wood: | | |
| Lard...................... | 2,223 | 215 |   Deals and logs.......... | 75,290 | 3,704 |
| Lead: | | |   Staves............... | 6,621 | 272 |
|   Pipes and sheet ........ | 3,777 | 1,973 |   Fire and lath wood, etc. | 11,410 | 63 |
|   Black, etc ............ | 3,563 | 2,149 |   Boards .............. | 734 | 535 |
|   Pig .................. | 1,618 | 20 |   Other kinds .......... | 158 | 1,254 |
| Locust beans .............. | 7,215 | 692 | Wool h................... | 2,286 | 1,636 |
| Manures, chemical, etc ..... | 994 | 783 | Woolens.................. | 513 | 217 |
| Margarin.................. | 4,759 | 407 | Yarn .................... | 8,571 | 2,876 |
| Matches................... | 540 | 299 | Yarn, hemp and tow ....... | 2,688 | 72 |
| Meal: | | | Zinc and zinc goods........ | 1,798 | 783 |
|   Oat, barley, and rye..... | 1,306 | 3,663 | | | |
|   Groats................ | 542 | 746 | **Miscellaneous packages (numbers)**.......... | 36,917 | 84,158 |
|   Feeding .............. | 8,613 | 3,005 | | | |
|   Nut and oak husks...... | 2,519 | 3,199 |     Total .............. | 1,191,298 | 1,345,086 |
| Milk, preserved........... | 1,691 | 1,226 | II.—*Goods paying less than £25 of rates.* | | |
| Moss, litter .............. | 5,583 | 65 | | | |
| Moldings ................. | 701 | 99 | Miscellaneous — embracing over 300 classes or articles of goods .................. | 43,952 | 29,605 |
| Nitrate of soda ........... | 9,676 | 1,523 | | | |
| Oils: | | |     Grand total........... | 1,235,250 | 1,374,691 |
|   Mineral............... | 9,128 | 17,755 | | | |
|   Vegetable............. | 9,617 | 12,557 | | | |
| Ore, burnt................. | .......... | 4,251 | | | |

*Number and tonnage of vessels arriving at Leith from May 15, 1901, to May 15, 1902.*

| Arrived from— | British. | | | | | | | |
|---|---|---|---|---|---|---|---|---|
| | Sailing vessels. | | | | Steam vessels. | | | |
| | Loaded. | | In ballast. | | Loaded. | | In ballast. | |
| | No. | Tons. | No. | Tons. | No. | Tons. | No. | Tons. |
| Ports in the Firth of Forth | 197 | 5,438 | 127 | 8,123 | 430 | 24,069 | 352 | 42,134 |
| Other ports in Scotland | 137 | 8,442 | 21 | 1,222 | 1,218 | 163,122 | 568 | 43,757 |
| London | 27 | 2,180 | | | 196 | 96,089 | 10 | 8,013 |
| Other ports in England | 79 | 9,233 | 2 | 91 | 799 | 253,133 | 50 | 18,799 |
| Ireland | | | | | 62 | 17,571 | | |
| Holland | 2 | 315 | | | 177 | 82,562 | 7 | 4,462 |
| Hamburg | | | | | 164 | 116,125 | 4 | 1,979 |
| Germany | 1 | 76 | | | 212 | 106,717 | 11 | 9,671 |
| Denmark | | | | | 52 | 41,903 | 6 | 5,022 |
| Norway | | | | | 1 | 548 | 7 | 3,059 |
| Sweden | | | | | 1 | 527 | | |
| Russia | | | | | 75 | 70,722 | | |
| Belgium | | | 2 | 2,715 | 117 | 73,221 | 4 | 2,675 |
| France | 1 | 107 | | | 125 | 51,096 | 2 | 1,676 |
| Spain | | | | | 16 | 11,274 | | |
| Portugal | | | | | 16 | 6,754 | | |
| Roumania | | | | | 17 | 24,511 | | |
| Austria | | | | | 1 | 1,467 | | |
| Turkey | | | | | 10 | 15,470 | | |
| Cyprus | | | | | 4 | 4,096 | | |
| Egypt | | | | | 5 | 4,125 | | |
| Africa | | | | | 11 | 10,418 | | |
| New Zealand | 1 | 1,077 | | | | | | |
| North America: | | | | | | | | |
| British | | | | | 6 | 11,445 | | |
| Foreign | 1 | 1,461 | | | 34 | 71,150 | | |
| South America | 3 | 4,553 | | | 1 | 1,432 | | |
| Total, 1901–2 | 449 | 32,882 | 152 | 12,151 | 3,749 | 1,259,547 | 1,011 | 141,247 |
| Total, 1900–1901 | 557 | 40,582 | 188 | 17,731 | 3,851 | 1,318,232 | 1,094 | 206,491 |
| Decrease | 108 | 7,700 | 36 | 5,580 | 102 | 58,685 | 83 | 65,244 |

| Arrived from— | Foreign. | | | | | | | |
|---|---|---|---|---|---|---|---|---|
| | Sailing vessels. | | | | Steam vessels. | | | |
| | Loaded. | | In ballast. | | Loaded. | | In ballast. | |
| | No. | Tons. | No. | Tons. | No. | Tons. | No. | Tons. |
| Ports in the Firth of Forth | 5 | 2,307 | 15 | 4,814 | 6 | 3,290 | 6 | 1,470 |
| Other ports in Scotland | 3 | 424 | 4 | 982 | 3 | 556 | 1 | 402 |
| London | 30 | 3,112 | 1 | 887 | 1 | 440 | 7 | 3,692 |
| Other ports in England | 47 | 6,111 | 4 | 1,432 | 5 | 1,374 | 8 | 3,162 |
| Holland | 1 | 391 | 1 | 117 | 86 | 50,508 | 9 | 5,956 |
| Hamburg | 4 | 1,465 | | | 5 | 1,029 | 6 | 14,573 |
| Germany | 20 | 2,386 | 1 | 108 | 5 | 1,645 | 2 | 861 |
| Denmark | 20 | 1,673 | 1 | 73 | 103 | 43,519 | 6 | 2,940 |
| Norway | 57 | 9,991 | 1 | 125 | 28 | 10,053 | 6 | 1,982 |
| Sweden | 18 | 4,940 | | | 1 | 564 | 4 | 4,480 |
| Russia | 13 | 3,798 | | | 41 | 24,439 | | |
| Belgium | 1 | 148 | | | 55 | 35,180 | 4 | 2,896 |
| France | 4 | 553 | | | 23 | 10,297 | 4 | 2,551 |
| Portugal | 6 | 1,157 | | | 1 | 630 | | |
| Roumania | | | | | 6 | 9,952 | | |
| Austria | | | | | 1 | 1,148 | | |
| Turkey | | | | | 2 | 2,393 | | |
| Cyprus | | | | | 1 | 1,041 | | |
| Africa | 1 | 76 | | | 7 | 6,088 | | |
| New Zealand | 1 | 983 | | | | | | |
| Australia | 1 | 1,446 | | | | | | |
| North America: | | | | | | | | |
| British | 1 | 915 | | | 7 | 13,975 | | |
| Foreign | 7 | 9,171 | | | 10 | 21,783 | | |
| South America | 6 | 4,564 | | | | | | |
| Total, 1901–2 | 246 | 55,611 | 28 | 8,538 | 397 | 289,854 | 63 | 44,965 |
| Total, 1900–1901 | 257 | 48,610 | 25 | 7,292 | 378 | 218,079 | 70 | 45,618 |
| Increase | | 7,001 | 3 | 1,246 | 19 | 21,775 | | |
| Decrease | 11 | | | | | | 7 | 653 |

*Number and tonnage of vessels arriving at Leith from May 15, 1901, to May 15, 1902*—C't'd.

RECAPITULATION.

| Arrived from— | Total. | | Total for year ended May 15, 1901. | |
|---|---|---|---|---|
| | No. | Tons. | No. | Tons. |
| Ports in the Firth of Forth | 1,138 | 91,645 | 1,336 | 96,559 |
| Other ports in Scotland | 1,945 | 218,907 | 1,929 | 227,876 |
| London | 271 | 114,413 | 298 | 122,592 |
| Other ports in England | 994 | 293,335 | 1,012 | 309,696 |
| Ireland | 62 | 17,571 | 60 | 17,161 |
| Holland | 288 | 144,311 | 324 | 170,242 |
| Hamburg | 183 | 135,171 | 180 | 125,183 |
| Germany | 252 | 121,464 | 248 | 119,202 |
| Denmark | 188 | 96,130 | 192 | 96,604 |
| Norway | 100 | 25,756 | 92 | 22,875 |
| Sweden | 24 | 10,511 | 20 | 6,504 |
| Russia | 129 | 98,959 | 163 | 124,032 |
| Belgium | 183 | 116,835 | 185 | 115,467 |
| France | 159 | 66,280 | 200 | 87,372 |
| Spain | 16 | 11,274 | 17 | 10,506 |
| Portugal | 23 | 8,541 | 13 | 5,017 |
| Roumania | 23 | 34,463 | 4 | 5,029 |
| Austria | 2 | 2,615 | 1 | 1,178 |
| Turkey | 12 | 17,863 | 14 | 19,781 |
| Cyprus | 5 | 5,137 | 2 | 2,057 |
| Egypt | 5 | 4,125 | 8 | 8,508 |
| Africa | 19 | 16,582 | 19 | 16,237 |
| East Indies | | | 1 | 1,877 |
| New Zealand | 2 | 2,060 | | |
| Australia | 1 | 1,446 | | |
| North America: | | | | |
| British | 14 | 26,335 | 14 | 24,740 |
| Foreign | 52 | 103,515 | 76 | 147,448 |
| South America | 10 | 10,549 | 17 | 17,893 |
| Total, 1901-2 | 6,095 | 1,794,795 | 6,420 | 1,902,635 |
| Total, 1900-1901 | 6,420 | 1,902,635 | | |
| Decrease | 325 | 107,840 | | |

*Number and tonnage of vessels sailing from Leith from May 15, 1901, to May 15, 1902.*

| Sailed for— | British. | | | | | | | |
|---|---|---|---|---|---|---|---|---|
| | Sailing vessels. | | | | Steam vessels. | | | |
| | Loaded. | | In ballast. | | Loaded. | | In ballast. | |
| | No. | Tons. | No. | Tons. | No. | Tons. | No. | Tons. |
| Ports in the Firth of Forth | 83 | 5,751 | 318 | 14,646 | 576 | 37,463 | 376 | 88,891 |
| Other ports in Scotland | 136 | 7,486 | 4 | 1,184 | 1,679 | 201,307 | 57 | 7,887 |
| London | 4 | 290 | | | 170 | 97,217 | 3 | 2,221 |
| Other ports in England | 39 | 4,473 | 8 | 997 | 735 | 237,114 | 129 | 69,999 |
| Ireland | | | | | 56 | 16,990 | 1 | 160 |
| Holland | | | | | 181 | 85,127 | | |
| Hamburg | | | | | 152 | 108,577 | 4 | 2,388 |
| Germany | 2 | 159 | | | 193 | 95,037 | | |
| Denmark | | | | | 54 | 43,385 | | |
| Norway | | | | | | | 7 | 3,069 |
| Russia | | | | | 51 | 48,709 | 4 | 3,706 |
| Belgium | | | | | 117 | 68,244 | 1 | 1,304 |
| France | 4 | 527 | | | 119 | 48,190 | | |
| Spain | 1 | 66 | | | 19 | 11,523 | 2 | 2,142 |
| Portugal | | | | | 7 | 2,625 | | |
| Italy | | | | | 7 | 9,106 | | |
| Austria | | | | | 2 | 2,625 | | |
| Greece | | | | | | | 1 | 1,864 |
| Egypt | | | | | 6 | 5,691 | | |
| Africa | 6 | 8,020 | | | 2 | 2,911 | 1 | 22 |
| China | | | | | 1 | 1,467 | | |
| Japan | | | | | 8 | 15,840 | | |
| East Indies | | | | | 1 | 892 | | |
| West Indies | | | | | 1 | 783 | 1 | 1,448 |
| Australia | 1 | 1,724 | | | | | | |
| North America: | | | | | | | | |
| British | | | | | | | 4 | 7,630 |
| Foreign | 1 | 1,479 | | | 16 | 38,172 | 10 | 19,336 |
| South America | 1 | 1,635 | | | 9 | 15,204 | | |
| Total, 1901-2 | 278 | 31,610 | 330 | 16,827 | 4,163 | 1,194,199 | 601 | 212,057 |
| Total, 1900-1901 | 354 | 42,203 | 391 | 20,861 | 4,264 | 1,262,381 | 686 | 266,102 |
| Decrease | 76 | 10,593 | 61 | 4,034 | 101 | 68,132 | 85 | 54,045 |

*Number and tonnage of vessels sailing from Leith from May 15, 1901, to May 15, 1902—*
Continued.

| Sailed for— | Foreign. | | | | | | | |
|---|---|---|---|---|---|---|---|---|
| | Sailing vessels. | | | | Steam vessels. | | | |
| | Loaded. | | In ballast. | | Loaded. | | In ballast. | |
| | No. | Tons. | No. | Tons. | No. | Tons. | No. | Tons. |
| Ports in the Firth of Forth | 4 | 659 | 109 | 15,211 | 13 | 6,075 | 61 | 37,271 |
| Other ports in Scotland | | | 1 | 160 | 4 | 1,950 | 6 | 1,059 |
| Ports in England | 3 | 3,174 | 1 | 1,905 | 4 | 961 | 20 | 16,965 |
| Holland | 1 | 86 | 1 | 117 | 92 | 53,154 | 1 | 2,129 |
| Hamburg | 1 | 87 | | | | | 1 | 2,300 |
| Germany | 30 | 3,251 | | | 8 | 4,075 | | |
| Denmark | 44 | 7,653 | | | 117 | 50,424 | | |
| Norway | 37 | 6,594 | 1 | 750 | 15 | 4,089 | 2 | 824 |
| Sweden | 16 | 6,486 | | | 6 | 5,191 | | |
| Russia | 2 | 418 | 2 | 1,087 | 3 | 2,174 | 5 | 4,188 |
| Belgium | | | | | 59 | 37,065 | | |
| France | 2 | 242 | | | 15 | 6,984 | | |
| Spain | 1 | 647 | | | 6 | 3,179 | 2 | 3,170 |
| Portugal | 1 | 199 | | | 1 | 861 | | |
| Italy | 3 | 1,119 | | | 2 | 2,729 | | |
| Africa | 2 | 1,749 | | | | | 1 | 1,711 |
| China | | | | | 1 | 869 | | |
| West Indies | 1 | 546 | | | | | | |
| Australia | 1 | 1,446 | | | | | | |
| North America: | | | | | | | | |
| British | 2 | 1,290 | 2 | 1,700 | | | 2 | 4,095 |
| Foreign | 3 | 4,405 | 3 | 3,168 | 9 | 19,489 | 1 | 1,953 |
| South America | 2 | 457 | | | 4 | 11,833 | | |
| Total, 1901-2 | 156 | 40,408 | 120 | 24,098 | 359 | 211,052 | 102 | 75,665 |
| Total, 1900-1901 | 169 | 37,715 | 117 | 18,881 | 331 | 183,278 | 116 | 79,769 |
| Increase | | 2,698 | 3 | 5,217 | 28 | 27,774 | | |
| Decrease | 13 | | | | | | 14 | 4,104 |

RECAPITULATION.

| Sailed for— | Total. | | Total for year ending May 15, 1901. | |
|---|---|---|---|---|
| | Number. | Tons. | Number. | Tons. |
| Ports in the Firth of Forth | 1,540 | 205,967 | 1,764 | 226,517 |
| Other ports in Scotland | 1,887 | 221,033 | 1,861 | 217,948 |
| London | 177 | 99,724 | 181 | 105,520 |
| Other ports in England | 940 | 335,588 | 981 | 349,351 |
| Ireland | 57 | 17,150 | 52 | 16,989 |
| Holland | 276 | 140,613 | 269 | 139,725 |
| Hamburg | 158 | 113,352 | 179 | 126,154 |
| Germany | 233 | 102,522 | 227 | 102,207 |
| Denmark | 215 | 101,462 | 224 | 101,802 |
| Norway | 62 | 15,316 | 63 | 19,228 |
| Sweden | 22 | 11,677 | 12 | 4,592 |
| Russia | 67 | 60,282 | 100 | 91,087 |
| Belgium | 177 | 106,613 | 162 | 101,859 |
| France | 140 | 55,943 | 186 | 77,258 |
| Spain | 31 | 20,627 | 28 | 15,638 |
| Portugal | 9 | 3,685 | 9 | 3,363 |
| Roumania | | | 2 | 3,165 |
| Gibraltar | | | 1 | 871 |
| Italy | 12 | 12,954 | 5 | 4,816 |
| Austria | 2 | 2,625 | 5 | 6,635 |
| Greece | 1 | 1,864 | 1 | 1,365 |
| Turkey | | | 1 | 818 |
| Egypt | 6 | 5,691 | 16 | 23,833 |
| Africa | 12 | 14,413 | 5 | 5,128 |
| China | 2 | 2,336 | 1 | 2,679 |
| Japan | 8 | 15,840 | 2 | 2,963 |
| East Indies | 1 | 892 | | |
| West Indies | 3 | 2,777 | 1 | 1,448 |
| Australia | 2 | 3,170 | 2 | 2,514 |
| North America: | | | | |
| British | 10 | 14,715 | 12 | 22,400 |
| Foreign | 43 | 87,952 | 48 | 96,300 |
| South America | 16 | 29,129 | 28 | 36,971 |
| Total, 1901-2 | 6,109 | 1,805,918 | 6,428 | 1,911,140 |
| Total, 1900-1901 | 6,428 | 1,911,140 | | |
| Decrease | 319 | 105,224 | | |

## GLASGOW.

I submit statement showing the exports in the more important lines of merchandise from Glasgow to the United States in the fiscal years 1900, 1901, 1902:

| Articles. | 1900. | 1901. | 1902. |
|---|---|---|---|
| Carpets and rugs | $56,080.07 | $49,671.20 | $60,275.53 |
| Cottons | 1,461,754.60 | 1,056,795.58 | 819,397.02 |
| Chemicals | 325,168.46 | 315,345.35 | 229,802.86 |
| Coal-tar pitch | 63,958.66 | 9,598.38 | 11,993.36 |
| Fishing gut | 33,739.26 | 27,569.23 | 41,882.85 |
| Flax | 172,340.21 | 152,219.29 | 200,445.15 |
| Herrings | 314,682.25 | 305,456.19 | 274,851.19 |
| Hides and skins | 118,035.11 | 57,651.88 | 43,544.48 |
| Iron | 272,681.84 | 38,246.61 | 358,979.71 |
| Linen goods | 23,856.66 | 29,178.54 | 29,970.02 |
| Machinery | 270,365.01 | 163,314.47 | 217,396.90 |
| Muslins | 235,357.02 | 221,789.31 | 231,262.46 |
| Paper and paper stock | 62,517.64 | 53,510.16 | 83,011.15 |
| Silk goods | 75,896.50 | 15,351.45 | 17,822.47 |
| Steel | 168,434.54 | 15,416.08 | 360,268.19 |
| Tobacco pipes | 24,555.93 | 25,462.87 | 29,119.57 |
| Thread | 48,755.10 | 41,194.38 | 22,939.88 |
| Union goods | 64,528.76 | 71,809.82 | 40,279.58 |
| Whisky | 130,871.75 | 172,494.16 | 203,126.39 |
| Wool | 617,066.72 | 785,600.71 | 822,739.92 |
| Woolen goods | 37,885.76 | 35,502.59 | 29,909.84 |

### ELECTRIC TRAMWAYS AT AYR.

The tramway system at Ayr—the capital of Ayrshire, and about 40 miles from Glasgow—is 6¼ miles from end to end. Of this, 4¼ miles is single track and 2 miles double track. There are sixteen double-deck single-truck cars, of good design and finish. The system of traction is by side trolley. The contractor for the road was D. Murray, Glasgow, and for the overhead system, Louden Brothers, Dundee. The cars were supplied by Hurst, Nelson & Co., and the electrical equipment by the British Thomson-Houston Company. Extensions of the tramway system are discussed, but it is said that the corporation has not the resources available, and it is not likely that extensions will be made in the near future. The cars run through the town to Prestwick, 3 miles distant on the one side, and to the Burns cottage and monument, 2¼ miles distant on the other side, making a continuous line of about 6¼ miles.

### ELECTRIC TRAMWAYS AT GREENOCK.

Within this year, the city of Greenock—which has a population of about 70,000, and is situated on the Clyde 21 miles from Glasgow—has substituted electric power for horse traction in its tramway service. The line extends from port Glasgow through Greenock to Gourock, 7½ miles in all. It is partly owned and wholly operated by a private company, the part not owned by the company being leased from the city of Greenock.

As yet, there is very little development of interurban electric-car service in this country. The two lines mentioned are the only ones in operation in this consular district. One or two others are under way. While the needs of the country offer great inducement for the development of electric interurban service, certain physical conditions and illiberal statutory requirements discourage the promotion of such enterprises. The physical conditions are the very narrow highways and the extreme difficulty of obtaining the land on which to lay the rails. Again, no matter how short the line proposed, it is necessary to obtain consent of Parliament to undertake the work. There are no general laws which permit local boards or officers to control this matter. To obtain this consent means a large outlay—from $8,000 or $10,000 up—because the committee appointed by Parliament to hear the case must have all its expenses paid by those inaugurating the proceedings, and it calls witnesses, whose expenses must also be met. In every case the representatives of the steam roads fight the proposition vigorously, thus involving further expense to the promoters. The electric roads already in operation not only seem to pay well, but are undoubtedly of great convenience to the people. It is just as certain, too, that they have affected the patronage of the steam roads, which in this country depend much more on passenger traffic for their income than do those in the United States.

### TRIAL OF AMERICAN PNEUMATIC TOOLS AT GREENOCK.

An important trial of American pneumatic tools adapted for shipbuilding purposes took place recently at the shipbuilding and engineering works of Messrs. Scott & Co., Greenock. The trial lasted over a period of six weeks, and was more exhaustive than those made in Glasgow some time since. The demonstration of the capabilities of these tools was made by the New Taite-Howard Pneumatic Tool Company, of Chicago, which sent some of its best workmen across with the appliances. The tools operated were those used recently on the American liner *Zeeland* at Southampton and later on the Cunard liner *Etruria* at Liverpool. A new stern piece was put on the Cunarder, which required 1½-inch rivets through 9 inches of material—one of the heaviest jobs that have been done by either hand or machinery. At Messrs. Scott & Co.'s yard a 60-foot section of the shell of a ship of 8,000 tons carrying capacity—which would, if completed, be from 430 to 440 feet long—was operated upon by the pneumatic riveting machines. A section of a double bottom, 12 feet square, was also subjected to trial by the pneumatic tools. Invitations were issued to the principal shipbuilders in Great Britain to visit the yard while the task was in progress, and arrangements were made for having a specified number present each day of the six weeks, so that they might have an opportunity of judging of the merits of the work. No detailed results can be given at present, and it may be some time before the notes and observations of those interested can be tabulated and a formal deliverance on the whole subject issued. But, speaking generally, the experiments appear to have given every satisfaction and to have demonstrated the fact that a great saving in time and labor could be effected. However, the use of these machines is not favored by the labor unions, and with native labor they accomplish little, if any, more than is accomplished under the present system, so it will probably be some time before their employment becomes general.

### AUTOMOBILES.

The automobile is becoming fairly popular in this district, and there is every prospect that it will figure more prominently in the future as a means of locomotion. Besides private users, many of the larger warehouses in the city of Glasgow have adopted automobile cars for the delivery of parcels throughout the city. The Scotch prefer to get the benefit of results rather than participate in actual experiments, and the anticipated increase must necessarily be gradual. At the present time, it is estimated that 40 cars are built every month in Glasgow, the major portion of these being turned out by one firm which makes a specialty of this business. The greater number find an English market. Without going into details regarding the particular styles of these cars, I may mention that they are all of the French pattern, and that their motive power is petroleum or gasoline. The prices of these Scotch built cars range from $1,250 to $1,750. No American cars are in use here, so far as I know. In answer to inquiries on the subject from firms in the United States I have endeavored to impress upon them that it is useless to attempt to introduce a car the motive power of which is steam, and again, that in the general build of the car the only pattern which has found favor here is the French. The objections to the American pattern are that "the center of gravity is too high, and in the eyes of the Scotch it does not compare with the French car in general appearance." The main objection to steam is that it "causes too much trouble to keep a sufficient supply."

For the information of those interested in this subject I give the following summary of regulations issued by the secretary for Scotland respecting light locomotives (embracing automobiles) on highways:

The expression "light locomotive" means a vehicle propelled by mechanical power which is under 3 tons in weight, unladen, and is not used for the purpose of drawing more than one vehicle (such vehicle with its locomotive not exceeding in weight, unladen, 4 tons), and is so constructed that no smoke or visible vapor is emitted therefrom except from any temporary or accidental cause. When calculating the weight of a vehicle, unladen, the weight of water, fuel, or accumulators used for the purpose of propulsion shall not be included. No one must drive or allow one to be driven if its exceeds 5 hundredweight, unless it can travel either forward or backward. It shall not exceed 6½ feet in width. The tire of each wheel shall be smooth and flat where it touches the ground. For a machine, unladen, weighing between 15 hundredweight and 1 ton, it must not be less than 2½ inches wide; exceeding 1 ton and not exceeding 2, not less than 3 inches wide; and if exceeding 2 tons, not less than 4 inches. There must be two independent brakes provided to act on two wheels, but in the case of a bicycle it is provided that one wheel will be enough to be acted upon. The name of the owner and place of abode must be painted on locomotives used for haulage, in letters black upon white or white upon black, not less than 1 inch in height. The vehicle shall be built so as not to cause danger to any person on it or on the road, and a competent person must always be in charge. A white light is to be used at night in the front and a red one exhibited at the rear. The vehicle drawn by the locomotive must have a brake, except where the speed is less than 4 miles an hour, and some one must be on the vehicle to work the brake unless it can be worked from the locomotive. The speed must not be greater than is reasonable and proper, and must not exceed 12 miles an hour in any case. If the weight, unladen, is 1½ tons and does not exceed 2 tons, the maximum speed allowed is 8 miles an hour, and if the weight is over 2 tons the speed shall not be greater than 5 miles an hour. If the locomotive is used to draw a vehicle, no matter what its weight is, the speed shall not be greater than 6 miles an hour.

The licenses required for automobiles in Scotland are the following:

| | |
|---|---:|
| Automobiles with four or more wheels, not exceeding 1 ton, unladen | $10.21 |
| Automobiles with four or more wheels, and weight exceeding 1 ton, unladen, but not exceeding 2 tons, unladen: | |
|     If used as an ordinary carriage | 20.43 |
|     If used as a hackney carriage | 13.88 |
| Automobiles with four or more wheels, and weight exceeding 2 tons, unladen: | |
|     If used as an ordinary carriage | 25.54 |
|     If used as a hackney carriage | 18.97 |

Automobiles with less than four wheels, whether used as an ordinary or as a hackney carriage:
- If weight exceeds 1 ton, unladen, but does not exceed 2 tons, unladen.... 13.88
- If weight exceeds 2 tons, unladen ..................................... 18.97

## COMMERCE.

A writer for an English magazine, in a recent article on British export trade as compared with that of the other leading commercial countries between the years 1881 and 1899, makes some interesting revelations. The writer shows that while the British export trade during the period of 1890–1899 amounted to 11,500 million dollars, and was the largest of all the countries—being 2,000 millions greater than that of the United States, which is next largest in the same period—yet the British increase for the period of 1890–1899 over that of 1880–1889 was only 300 million dollars, while that of the United States during the same period increased no less than 2,000 million dollars. Germany during the same time increased 500 millions, Russia 320 millions, Belgium 400 millions, Argentina 375 millions, and Japan 320 millions. Seven countries, in fact, made greater increases in their export trade than did the United Kingdom. From 1890 to 1899 the United Kingdom exported 350 million dollars more of coal than during the period from 1880–1889. It will thus be seen that, omitting the coal increase, the United Kingdom actually had a decrease of about 35 million dollars. During 1895–1899, as compared with 1890–1894, the United Kingdom gained ground in the markets of Belgium, and lost ground in the markets of Germany, United States, France, Holland, Austria-Hungary, Russia, Italy, and Spain. Germany gained ground in the markets of the United States, Belgium, Russia, Italy, and Spain, and lost in the United Kingdom, France, Holland, and Austria-Hungary. The United States gained in the markets of the United Kingdom, Germany, France, Holland, Belgium, Austria-Hungary, Italy, and Spain, and lost in Russia.

Indications are not wanting that manufacturers are becoming more up to date in their methods. The sharp competition to which they have been subjected in the past decade, especially from the United States, has demonstrated the necessity of improvements. In making these improvements they are assisted very materially by their competitors in the United States, in that the latter permit emissaries from this country to inspect their shops and factories. These privileges are not extended in this country. Not only are visiting strangers not admitted to the works, but it is difficult to even ascertain the wages of the workmen. At the present time leading newspapers of this country have special correspondents in the United States, who systematically report business methods and trade conditions in every leading industry, and these reports have created much interest. It is a question if in the last few years United States products have not been overadvertised. To say the least, the "booming" process has awakened much prejudice. In but few lines are sales of United States goods enhanced by the stamp "American." On the other hand, goods manufactured in the United States with that fact not exploited are apt to sell readily on their merits. The people of the United Kingdom, as a rule, are patriotic, and it does not promote their purchases of us to tell them in glaring headlines that their country and its institutions are becoming back numbers in the world of commerce. It is quite as important to retain the trade we already have as it is to acquire new trade, and this can not be done by pursuing methods which, while possibly gratifying to our vanity, are opposed to good business sense and will in due time invite reaction.

SAMUEL M. TAYLOR, *Consul.*

GLASGOW, *October 24, 1902.*

---

### COAL EXPORTS FROM THE UNITED KINGDOM.

The following table shows the exports of coal from Scotland and also Great Britain from 1850 to 1902, inclusive. It will be observed that the increased export from Great Britain in 1902 was 1,281,798 tons, and the total amount exported from Scotland exceeded that of 1901 by 911,550 tons. With the exception of 1900, these are the largest quantities ever exported from Great Britain.

| To— | From Scotland. |
|---|---|
|  | *Tons.* |
| Belgium.................................................................. | 116, 295 |
| Denmark................................................................. | 975, 885 |
| France .................................................................. | 709, 533 |
| Germany................................................................. | 1, 991, 260 |
| Holland.................................................................. | 122, 657 |
| Italy..................................................................... | 418, 692 |
| Norway.................................................................. | 495, 138 |
| Russia................................................................... | 687, 904 |
| Spain.................................................................... | 154, 753 |
| Sweden.................................................................. | 859, 373 |
| Other countries of Europe................................................ | 182, 908 |
| Total ............................................................... | 6, 614, 396 |
| Countries out of Europe................................................. | 490, 646 |
| Total exports......................................................... | 7, 105, 044 |
| Shipments to home ports............................................... | 4, 174, 378 |
| Total shipments in 1902 ............................................... | 11, 279, 422 |
| Total shipments in 1901 ............................................... | 10, 043, 753 |
| Increase in 1902 ...................................................... | 1, 235, 669 |
| The increase is made up thus: | |
| Foreign countries .................................................... | 911, 550 |
| Home ports........................................................... | 824, 119 |
| Total ................................................................ | 1, 235, 669 |

*Exports in previous years.*

| Year. | Scotland. | Great Britain. | Year. | Scotland. | Great Britain. |
|---|---|---|---|---|---|
|  | *Tons.* | *Tons.* |  | *Tons.* | *Tons.* |
| 1850........................ | 329, 722 | 3, 205, 856 | 1890 ...................... | 4, 306, 812 | 28, 738, 241 |
| 1860........................ | 639, 686 | 7, 064, 905 | 1891 ...................... | 4, 501, 493 | 29, 496, 791 |
| 1870........................ | 1, 338, 127 | 11, 177, 976 | 1892 ...................... | 4, 934, 054 | 29, 048, 055 |
| 1880........................ | 1, 928, 448 | 17, 891, 181 | 1893 ...................... | 4, 604, 509 | 27, 619, 933 |
| 1881........................ | 2, 242, 866 | 18, 759, 991 | 1894 ...................... | 3, 359, 938 | 31, 379, 836 |
| 1882........................ | 2, 516, 011 | 19, 926 011 | 1895 ...................... | 4, 700, 860 | 31, 715, 292 |
| 1883........................ | 2, 531, 427 | 21, 669, 926 | 1896 ...................... | 4, 816, 999 | 32, 956, 796 |
| 1884........................ | 2, 646, 353 | 22, 364, 474 | 1897 ...................... | 5, 262, 839 | 35, 317, 278 |
| 1885........................ | 3, 012, 929 | 22, 710, 835 | 1898 ...................... | 6, 355, 402 | 34, 982, 346 |
| 1886........................ | 2, 944, 124 | 22, 107, 144 | 1899 ...................... | 5, 772, 973 | 41, 066, 877 |
| 1887........................ | 3, 125, 246 | 23, 258, 855 | 1900 ...................... | 7, 876, 942 | 44, 088, 405 |
| 1888........................ | 3, 328, 331 | 25, 632, 407 | 1901 ...................... | 6, 193, 494 | 41, 878, 346 |
| 1889........................ | 3, 869, 605 | 27, 504, 911 | 1902 ...................... | 7, 105, 044 | 43, 160, 143 |

The report upon the state of the trade says:

With regard to prospects, these, unfortunately, are not bright, as trade generally is in a depressed state. During the past year low freights have helped exports, but even with this the volume of trade was not sufficient to keep up prices during the early months of the year. There was an easy market until extra orders from France and the unprecedented demand from the United States started and raised prices to their present level. This extra trade was entirely due to short supplies in these countries, owing to strikes of colliers. The demand from France is now normal, but that from the United States still continues, as the shortage caused by the long stoppage of work has not yet been made up. It is anticipated that with the end of the cold weather, this business will stop as suddenly as it began. We shall then have to face a market free from abnormal influences. The figures given on the other side show a slight increase of exports from England and Wales over last year, but as the exports to the United States were greater than this increase, we would, in ordinary course, have had to report a decrease. Indeed, the total increase in the exports from Great Britain represents practically the quantity of coal shipped to replace the shortage in America and France. While it is satisfactory to have secured such a large share of this trade, it is well to remember that when it ceases we must expect to return to the state of matters that prevailed last summer. Unfortunately, the present high prices are severely handicapping exporters in the making of contracts with their regular buyers, with the result that the shipping season will have to be faced with few contracts booked.

S. M. TAYLOR, *Consul.*

GLASGOW, *January 9, 1903.*

---

### DUNFERMLINE.

Linen, coal, floor cloth, and linoleum are the chief industries of this consular district.

The linen trade for the twelve months ended June 30, 1902, has, on the whole, been fairly well maintained. The steady improvement that set in toward the latter half of the year is now having its effect, and great activity prevails in all factories. The close of the South African war has tended to stimulate business generally, and the home trade is showing a decided improvement, which, taken together with the firm American demand, gives promise of a very prosperous year for the linen industry of this district. Manufacturers are at present experiencing difficulty in filling orders in the required time, and there will not be an idle loom in Dunfermline this winter, if sufficient hands can be obtained.

The present prices of linens are likely to remain firm, as yarns continue high and steady, and even though the flax crop should reach the highest estimate, which prospects warrant, it will fall on such a bare market that yarns are bound to remain firm and steady at a good price.

### COAL.

The output of the coal mines of Fife for the year 1901 was 5,666,454 tons, an increase of 184,053 tons over the output for 1900, which surpassed all previous years in the history of the coal industry of the district.

Export prices at present range from 7s. 6d. ($1.83) to 10s. 6d. ($2.55) per ton f. o. b. shipping ports, a decrease of from 1s. to 2s. (25 to 50 cents) per ton compared with last year's prices. The 1s. per ton tax on export coals has operated much more seriously against third-class than against the better grades of coal, the reason being that while there is a difference of from 1s. to 2s. (25 to 50 cents) per ton between first and third-class coals exported from Fife mines, the same tax of 1s. per ton is imposed, and Welsh coals usually bring from 2s. to 3s. (50 to 75 cents) per ton more than Scotch coals, although subject only to the same export tax.

Both masters and miners have protested in vain against this injustice of the tax, as they term it.

### EXHAUSTED PITS.

Three coal pits in the vicinity of Kingseat, Fife, have ceased operations recently, the coal having become exhausted. No. 1 pit, closed about three months ago, had been in operation forty-five years, and Nos. 2 and 3, which were stopped on August 30, had been worked for thirty and twenty-six years, respectively. It is not thought that the closing down of these pits will diminish the annual output of the district.

The wage of Fife miners for eight hours' work at present is 5s. 6d. ($1.34). The wage last year for eight hours' work was 6s. ($1.46), and in 1900 7s. 6d. ($1.83).

Since 1898, the annual output of the Fife mines has steadily increased, and since 1890 prices have steadily fallen. The following is a comparative table of the coal shipments from ports in Dunfermline consular district to September 16, 1902:

| Fife. | Last week. | Previous week. | Corresponding week, 1901. | Total to date. | |
|---|---|---|---|---|---|
| | | | | 1902. | 1901. |
| | Tons. | Tons. | Tons. | Tons. | Tons. |
| Burnt Island | 44,325 | 30,554 | 21,544 | 984,001 | 631,092 |
| Dysart | 651 | 905 | 1,153 | 36,372 | 30,695 |
| Wemyss | 524 | 1,143 | 1,138 | 33,876 | 29,328 |
| Methil | 36,534 | 31,493 | 36,472 | 1,159,381 | 1,091,116 |
| Charleston | 919 | 1,296 | 288 | 25,837 | 26,957 |
| Dundee | | | | | 1,820 |
| Tayport | 198 | 215 | 296 | 11,884 | 18,966 |
| Alloa | 3,181 | 2,921 | 3,653 | 97,308 | 54,228 |
| Total | 86,332 | 68,527 | 64,544 | 2,348,654 | 1,884,202 |

### IMPORTS.

As in former reports, I have to explain that as this is an inland consulate, American imports are distributed from the principal seaport consulates in Great Britain, and therefore no statistics of the imports from the United States consumed in this district are available.

Articles of American manufacture, handled by ironmongers (hardware dealers), referred to in my previous annual report, continue in good demand.

There is also a marked demand for American tinned fruits and meats, pickles, and sundry articles carried by grocers.

### CASH REGISTERS.

I notice also that cash registers are becoming more common, especially among retail grocers.

The national cash register, manufactured at Dayton, Ohio, appears to have a monopoly of the trade, as it is the only kind I have seen or heard of in the district. Agents of this company from the commercial centers solicit orders in the smaller towns here, and no doubt it is owing to their energetic and persistent efforts that the value of a good cash register has been brought to the conservative Scotch mind.

To introduce a new article in Scotland is not an easy matter, but if the article once finds favor and is substantial, its success on the market is assured.

### BOOKCASES.

American sectional bookcases are becoming quite popular in this part of Scotland, and, when more generally known, a good trade can be done, as they are much cheaper than the ordinary bookcase and can be extended from time to time to meet the needs of a growing library, while they occupy small space and add to the appearance of a room.

### BOOTS AND SHOES.

American boots and shoes have evidently grown here very much in the estimation of the public within the past year. The style, finish, and fit of American boots and shoes are their strong features as sellers. Dealers are advertising them in the local press, and those who do not handle them are advertising British boots and shoes made on American models. American rubbers are now sold by dealers generally; they give good satisfaction.

### KIRKCALDY.

The floor-cloth and linoleum industry at Kirkcaldy is in a very flourishing condition owing to the great demand from United States importers.

The declared value of exports of floor cloth and linoleum to America for the quarter ending September 30, 1902, will be considerably in excess of any other quarter since 1878, the year this consular agency was established.

A plant for electric lighting and traction is at present being laid down by the municipal corporation. The overhead system has been adopted for the tramways. The cost of the entire plant will be about £100,000 ($500,000).

Within the past year, a handsome viaduct connecting two parts of the town separated by a ravine has been constructed, at an expenditure of £20,000 ($100,000), and the water commissioners for the town are just completing an additional reservoir, at a cost of about £90,000 ($450,000), previous works having cost about the same amount.

### INVENTIONS.

An improved smoke-consuming and coal-saving apparatus for steam boiler furnaces, an invention of Mr. James Marshall, yarn merchant, Dunfermline, has for the past year been in successful operation in the boiler furnaces of James Marshall & Son, bleachers, Dunfermline.

Mr. Marshall, after a year's test, is thoroughly satisfied that his invention is an improved arrangement for consuming smoke, saving fuel, and increasing boiler efficiency.

Patents have been obtained in Great Britain and in the United States. The American patent is No. 703732. The British patent was accepted May 1, 1902.

*Value of declared exports from the consular district of Dunfermline, including Kirkcaldy agency, to the United States for the year ended June 30, 1902.*

| Article. | Quarter ending— | | | | Total. |
|---|---|---|---|---|---|
| | September 30. | December 31. | March 31. | June 30. | |
| Burlaps | | | $2,505.71 | $7,082.42 | $9,588.13 |
| Chair canvas | | | 360.64 | | 360.64 |
| Cork, prepared | | $39.07 | 228.77 | 362.10 | 629.94 |
| Cottons | $47,437.89 | 39,239.52 | 40,051.21 | 29,945.76 | 156,674.38 |
| Designs, paper | | | 128.07 | | 128.07 |
| Earthenware | 178.43 | 101.54 | | 265.97 | 545.94 |
| Golf cleeks and irons | 97.04 | | | | 97.04 |
| Golf goods | | 460.05 | 314.78 | | 774.83 |
| Jute | 429.16 | | 727.52 | 1,847.78 | 3,004.46 |
| Linens | 464,600.23 | 499,931.27 | 399,368.90 | 261,708.31 | 1,825,608.71 |
| Linoleum, floor cloth, and cork carpet | 52,273.89 | 65,215.85 | 107,517.53 | 64,051.56 | 289,058.88 |
| Oilcloth | | 1,633.09 | | | 1,633.09 |
| Spinning wheels | | | 14.60 | | 14.60 |
| Stone wheels | 574.57 | 458.99 | | | 1,033.56 |
| Onions | 629.30 | 3,290.44 | 6,848.61 | 6,825.51 | 17,593.86 |
| Whisky | 119.63 | 237.84 | 17.11 | | 374.58 |
| Total | 566,340.14 | 610,607.66 | 558,083.45 | 372,089.41 | 2,107,120.66 |

J. N. McCUNN, *Consul.*

DUNFERMLINE, *September 22, 1902.*

---

## WALES.

### CARDIFF.

Since my last annual report, stirring events have occurred in this enterprising town—the "Chicago of Wales."

The first item of interest is:

#### THE OPENING OF THE CORPORATION TRAMWAYS.

In 1898, there was promoted in Parliament the passage of a bill seeking powers to borrow money for various uses, among which were the purchase from Lord Bates of Cathays Park, 60 acres in extent; the erection of a new town hall and law courts; the improvement of streets, and the purchase of lands upon which to construct tramways and the necessary buildings in connection therewith. The amount of money sanctioned to be expended was about $800,000, and the period for repayment was fixed at sixty years for the lands and thirty years for the buildings. All other moneys to be borrowed for tramway purposes, such as plant, equipment, etc., were to be regulated and sanctioned by the board of trade. Mr. W. Harper, the borough engineer, acted as engineer to the scheme during this period. Mr. Arthur Ellis was appointed electrical engineer to the tramways department in June, 1900, and, the following December, was made borough electrical engineer and manager of the electric lighting and tramways undertakings of the corporation. Space will not allow details. An elaborate article on the subject may be found in the Street Railway Journal (New York) for July, 1902. The power station, engine and dynamo room, switch board for both lighting and traction circuits, poles and brackets, main car house, track sprinkler and sweeper, single and double deck cars are up to date and all that can be desired.

The tramway lines were opened on May 1, 1902. The enterprise has proved a profitable investment. The tram cars are well patronized, and the ratepayers expect to realize the benefit of a lighter taxation. The following table of statistics is suggestive and interesting:

*Receipts.*

|  | June. | July. | August. |
|---|---|---|---|
|  | £. s. d. | £. s. d. | £. s. d. |
| Receipts from lines................................... | 7,044 11 7½ | 6,991 7 9 | 7,951 16 6 |
|  | ($34,272) | ($34,023) | ($38,697) |

*Passengers carried.*

| In— | June. | July. | August. |
|---|---|---|---|
| Motor cars........................................................ | 1,460,760 | 1,592,546 | 1,860,164 |
| Horse cars........................................................ | 215,079 | 74,726 | 45,891 |
| Total ......................................................... | 1,675,839 | 1,667,272 | 1,906,055 |

*Distance traveled by cars.*

| By— | June. | July. | August. |
|---|---|---|---|
|  | Miles. | Miles. | Miles. |
| Motor cars........................................................ | 100,893 | 135,468 | 152,550 |
| Horse cars........................................................ | 33,221 | 15,981 | 10,418 |
| Total ......................................................... | 134,114 | 151,449 | 162,968 |

### INDUSTRIAL AGITATIONS.

The most serious question at present disturbing the mining interest of Wales is the sliding scale and minimum rate. This controversy, it is feared, may result in a general strike. The employers desire to continue the sliding scale, while the miners are in favor of abolishing it and substituting the minimum rate. It is argued that the latter principle, which was conceded by the employers in the 1898 agreement, would now prove a failure—that the minimum of 40 per cent demanded by the men is utterly out of the question.

The principle of a sliding scale is a sort of automatic indicator of the price of coal and the consequent wages of the men. The sliding scale has been in operation for over a quarter of a century and has secured regular work to an extent never before known.

### CHANGES IN THE COAL TRADE.

The imposition of a tax of 1s. (24 cents) per ton upon all coal exported from the United Kingdom has aroused the ire of the operators, who, after persistent agitation, have secured from the chancellor of the exchequer a slight modification in regard to small coal. According to the new ruling, the tax ceases to be operative whenever the price of small coal falls to 6s. ($1.46) per ton f. o. b.

During the year 1901 and up to March, 1902, coal prices declined. In December, 1900, best steam coals were quoted 20s. ($4.87), and best small steam coal at 10s. 6d. ($2.55) per ton. In December, 1901, the price of best large steam coal had fallen to 16s. ($3.95); best small steam did not fluctuate. In the first week of March, 1902, the price of best large steam coal was 14s. ($3.50). At the present writing, the very best Cardiff steam coal is quoted at 15s. 6d. ($3.76) per ton, and best small steam coal 7s. 6d. ($1.82).

Freight rates have also been considerably disturbed. Shipowners have had a bad year. Ocean 'freights, both outward and homeward, have been in striking contrast with those of 1900, especially during the last nine months. In January and February, 1902, for instance, 100 steamers were laid up in the Bristol Channel, their owners being unable to run them at a profit; and from March to September, 1902, conditions were hardly better.

### STEEL, TIN-PLATE, AND PIG-IRON INDUSTRIES.

Though not so prosperous as in former years, these industries have improved somewhat. In the early part of 1901, considerable quantities of American and German steel were imported via Cardiff, Newport, and Swansea, and for a time the outlook for the steel trade of the district was very dull. Of late, however, the imports have been insignificant. Now that the Germans have got rid, under pressure, of their heavy stocks, the fear of telling competition from that quarter is slight. The home demand in America is so great, for this year, at least, that imports from the United States will be limited.

The tin-plate and black-plate industries are very prosperous. The big amalgamation in the steel and tin plates during the year, notably those of Guest, Keen, Nettlefords, and Crawshay and Baldwins, is calculated to both develop and give stability to the trades with which the names of these firms have been so long identified.

### TRADE OF CARDIFF.

The imports of iron ore at this port, as per dock returns, for the year ended December 31, 1901, amounted to 697,981 tons, while for the year 1900 they were 772,506 tons.

*Comparative statement of coal and coke shipped from Cardiff during the last two years.*

| Year. | Foreign. | | Coastwise. | |
|---|---|---|---|---|
| | Coal. | Coke. | Coal. | Coke. |
| | Tons. | Tons. | Tons. | Tons. |
| 1900 ...................................................... | 13,461,027 | 75,981 | 2,443,772 | 125 |
| 1901 ...................................................... | 13,537,872 | 55,986 | 2,334,377 | 535 |

*Number and tonnage of British and foreign sailing and steam vessels, including their repeated voyages, that entered and cleared with cargoes and in ballast from and to foreign countries and British possessions, and coastwise, at the ports of Cardiff, Liverpool, and London, during the year 1901.*

| Description. | Entered. | | Cleared. | |
|---|---|---|---|---|
| | Vessels. | Tons. | Vessels. | Tons. |
| **CARDIFF.** | | | | |
| Foreign: | | | | |
| With cargoes............ | 1,461 | 1,263,268 | 6,179 | 7,188,797 |
| In ballast.............. | 2,986 | 3,690,712 | 408 | 601,493 |
| Total............. | 4,397 | 4,953,980 | 6,587 | 7,790,290 |
| Coastwise: | | | | |
| With cargoes............ | 3,727 | 402,984 | 5,622 | 1,346,455 |
| In ballast.............. | 6,571 | 3,933,871 | 2,398 | 369,025 |
| Total............. | 10,298 | 4,336,805 | 8,020 | 1,715,480 |
| **LIVERPOOL.** | | | | |
| Foreign: | | | | |
| With cargoes............ | 3,390 | 6,330,989 | 2,742 | 5,731,193 |
| In ballast.............. | 91 | 163,429 | 319 | 493,576 |
| Total............. | 3,481 | 6,494,418 | 3,061 | 6,224,769 |
| Coastwise: | | | | |
| With cargoes............ | 12,379 | 2,257,982 | 13,241 | 2,338,787 |
| In ballast.............. | 4,249 | 981,075 | 3,395 | 1,195,15? |
| Total............. | 16,628 | 3,239,007 | 16,636 | 3,583,940 |
| **LONDON.** | | | | |
| Foreign: | | | | |
| With cargoes............ | 11,155 | 9,800,306 | 6,610 | 6,191,884 |
| In ballast.............. | 289 | 301,830 | 1,774 | 1,498,362 |
| Total............. | 11,444 | 10,102,136 | 8,384 | 7,690,246 |
| Coastwise: | | | | |
| With cargoes............ | 12,780 | 5,420,291 | 9,826 | 2,251,209 |
| In ballast.............. | 2,231 | 559,155 | 8,739 | 5,670,461 |
| Total............. | 15,011 | 5,979,446 | 18,565 | 7,921,670 |

*Coal, coke, and patent fuel, 1901.*

Coal shipped to foreign ports:                                                        Tons.
 1901.................................................................... 13,537,372
 1900.................................................................... 13,461,027

  Increase .............................................................. 76,345

Coke shipped to foreign ports:
 1901.................................................................... 55,986
 1900.................................................................... 75,981

  Decrease.............................................................. 19,995

Coal shipped coastwise:
 1901.................................................................... 2,324,377
 1900.................................................................... 2,243,772

  Increase.............................................................. 80,605

Patent fuel shipped to foreign ports:
 1901.................................................................... 409,538
 1900.................................................................... 418,546

  Decrease.............................................................. 9,008

Coal, etc., shipped for bunkers in foreign-going vessels:

|  | Tons. |
|---|---|
| 1901 | 2,273,859 |
| 1900 | 1,892,051 |
| Increase | 381,808 |

Estimated quantity of coal, coke, and patent fuel shipped for ships' use on coasters and tugs:

| 1901 | 358,540 |
|---|---|
| 1900 | 359,743 |
| Decrease | 1,203 |

The quantity of coke shipped coastwise was only 535 tons, and of patent fuel, there was none.

The imports of grain and flour into this port for the years ended December 31, 1900 and 1901, were the following:

|  | Tons. |
|---|---|
| 1900 | 299,388 |
| 1901 | 253,095 |

*Timber imports.*

| Year. | Log timber and deals.a | Colliery pit wood. | Total. |
|---|---|---|---|
|  | Tons. | Tons. | Tons. |
| 1900 | 366,844 | 710,968 | 1,077,812 |
| 1901 | 237,739 | 613,204 | 850,943 |

a All timber imports except pitwood.

*Exports of coal at the principal ports for 1900 and 1901 (exclusive of bunkers).*

| Year. | Port of Cardiff. | Tyne ports (including Newcastle, North Shields and South Shields). | Newport. | Blyth. | Glasgow. | Kirkcaldy. |
|---|---|---|---|---|---|---|
|  | Tons. | Tons. | Tons. | Tons. | Tons. | Tons. |
| 1900 | 13,461,627 | 7,476,780 | 2,779,018 | 2,684,500 | 1,131,191 | 1,013,191 |
| 1901 | 13,537,372 | 7,783,382 | 2,618,179 | 2,590,418 | 1,126,821 | 944,950 |

| Year. | Sunderland. | Grangemouth. | Swansea. | Hull. | Methil. | Grimsby. |
|---|---|---|---|---|---|---|
|  | Tons. | Tons. | Tons. | Tons. | Tons. | Tons. |
| 1900 | 1,940,882 | 1,416,783 | 1,859,747 | 1,870,072 | 1,496,318 | 1,071,168 |
| 1901 | 1,894,752 | 1,171,381 | 1,695,874 | 1,424,158 | 1,342,254 | 958,614 |

*Statement showing the imports, exports, and registered tonnage of the Barry Docks for the year 1901.*

Imports:

|  | Tons. | cwts. |
|---|---|---|
| Pit wood (including pit props) | 174,772 | 3 |
| Timber | 33,377 | 1 |
| Tin plates | 911 | 9 |
| Silver sand | 2,813 | 9 |
| Iron and steel | 967 | 18 |
| General merchandise | 21,409 | 12 |
| Total imports | 234,251 | 12 |

Exports:

|  | Tons. | cwts. |
|---|---|---|
| Coal and coke | 7,844,464 | 1 |
| Silver sand | 1,406 | 0 |
| Pitch and fuel | 752 | 5 |
| Iron | 724 | 3 |
| General merchandise | 3,818 | 17 |
| Total exports | 7,851,165 | 6 |
| Total imports and exports | 8,085,416 | 18 |

### REGISTERED TONNAGE.

| Kind of vessel. | Number of vessels. | Tons. |
|---|---|---|
| Steam | 2,932 | 3,715,997 |
| Sail | 182 | 183,840 |
| Total | 3,114 | 3,899,837 |

*Statement showing the imports, exports, and registered tonnage of the Bute docks for the year 1901.*

Imports:

|  | Tons. |
|---|---|
| Iron ore | 697,981 |
| Pig iron | 3,464 |
| Iron and ironwork | 18,577 |
| Timber (round and square) | a 31,390 |
| Deals and deal ends | a 89,660 |
| Mining timber, pit props, and sleepers | a 63,4?? |
| Sundry wood | a 17,554 |
| Pit wood | 435,892 |
| Grain and flour | 253,095 |
| Potatoes | 48,055 |
| Bricks | 1,797 |
| General merchandise | 287,056 |
| Total imports | 1,948,000 |

Exports:

|  | Tons. |
|---|---|
| Coal and coke | 7,216,311 |
| Patent fuel | 430,168 |
| Iron and steel rails | 29,097 |
| Iron (pig, speigel, and other of like nature) | 6,880 |
| Iron (sundry) and ironwork | 46,563 |
| Bricks | 738 |
| General merchandise | 107,403 |
| Total exports | 7,837,160 |
| Total imports and exports | 9,785,160 |

### REGISTERED TONNAGE.

| Kind of vessel. | Number of vessels. | Tons register. |
|---|---|---|
| Steam | 6,285 | 3,653,355 |
| Sailing | 2,550 | 482,483 |
| Total | 8,835 | 4,135,838 |

a Loads.

*Statement of the trade of Penarth Dock and Harbor for the year 1901.*

VESSELS CLEARED.

| Kind of vessel. | Number. | Registered tonnage. |
|---|---|---|
| Steam | 2,347 | 1,596,145 |
| Sailing | 943 | 109,451* |
| Total | 3,290 | 1,705,596 |

| Imports: | Tons. |
|---|---|
| Iron and ironwork | 1,605 |
| Sleepers | 1,280 |
| Flooring boards | 999 |
| Pit wood | 2,540 |
| Pulp (for paper making) | 21,119 |
| Gas coal | 57,598 |
| General merchandise | 38,809 |
| Total imports | 123,950 |

| Exports: | |
|---|---|
| Coal and coke | 3,467,538 |
| Patent fuel | 439 |
| Iron and ironwork | 466 |
| General merchandise | 716 |
| Total exports | 3,469,159 |
| Total imports and exports | 3,593,109 |

### STATUS OF CARDIFF.

As will be observed from the above statistics, Cardiff now leads all other ports in the United Kingdom in shipping clearances to foreign countries and British possessions, and is the premier port in the world for the shipment of coal. It is a wide-awake, enterprising port, and continues to be one of the most profitable customers of the United States.

The Cardiff Railway, begun over a year ago, will soon be opened. New docks are in contemplation and the business prospects are brighter than ever.

DANIEL T. PHILLIPS, *Consul.*

CARDIFF, *September 22, 1902.*

# APPENDIX.

## AUSTRIA-HUNGARY: TRADE IN 1901.

The commercial conditions in Austria-Hungary during the year 1901 were unfavorable. That Austrian manufacturers had to enter into close competition with foreign countries is shown by the fact that the imports rose from $339,500,000 to $340,400,000, while the exports fell from $388,400,000 to $377,800,000. The official statistics as to the foreign commerce of the monarchy are:

| Articles. | Imports. | | Exports. | |
|---|---|---|---|---|
| | 1901. | 1900. | 1901. | 1900. |
| Raw stuffs | $199,500,000 | $199,400,000 | $165,460,000 | $163,820,000 |
| Partially manufactured goods | 47,740,000 | 46,220,000 | 53,320,000 | 60,640,000 |
| Manufactured goods | 93,240,000 | 93,660,000 | 159,040,000 | 163,960,000 |
| Total | 340,480,000 | 339,280,000 | 377,820,000 | 388,420,000 |

A striking reduction in the export of partially and wholly manufactured goods in contrast with the increased exports of raw stuffs, show that the former class had to bear the chief losses of this year. Articles of foreign manufacture were offered more largely than ever before, so that the low prices at which outside countries were ready to unload their goods were made the basis of general business. German competition was most felt. While the entire import into Austria-Hungary from the German Empire sank from $1,438,234,000 to $1,420,146,000, the exports thither from Austria-Hungary rose from $1,130,976,000 to $1,132,737,200. This increase in exports is a consequence of an overstocked domestic market, which compelled manufacturers to make sales at ruinous prices. Among the Austrian imports may be mentioned an increase in chemical products of $600,020; paper, $320,000; and leather, $600,000. In machinery and mechanical apparatus, the import sank from $10,400,000 to $8,800,000; at the same time, the export in this branch decreased by a third from that of the previous year, namely, from $3,080,000 to $2,160,000. In the interior, as well as in foreign countries to which Austria exported machinery, there was a marked shrinkage in industrial investments. The unfavorable business conditions outside of Austria caused the decrease in the value of iron exports ($2,260,000) and that of lumber ($6,500,000). The decline of the import of anthracite coal by $140,000 and the increase of the brown coal export by $2,320,000 is not abnormal, but may be considered a return to the usual state of affairs after the coal strike of 1900. There is a general increase in the import of textiles, while the value of the exports in this line has sunk again during the year in question. The surplus of the import over the export (which in the previous year amounted to $59,020,000) was $60,980,000 in 1901, so that the state of the textile trade has become still worse. The import of wine, an important article in this monarchy, sank in value to the amount of $1,820,000 in consequence of the decrease of the import from Italy. The sugar export was greater in quantity than that of the previous year, being 42,300 tons more, while the value, in consequence of the shrinkage in price, from about 80 cents per 220 pounds for raw sugar, and almost $1 per 220 pounds for refined sugar, showed a decrease of $3,360,000.

### TRADE WITH HUNGARY.

More favorable for Austria than the foreign commerce was the domestic trade with Hungary. While the import into Austria from Hungary decreased from $184,340,000 to $184,080,000, the export from Austria to Hungary rose from $177,040,000 to $185,180,000. Products of agriculture, forestry, and fishing were imported to the value of only $108,640,000 against $111,440,000 in the previous year. Mining and smelting products equal to $4,040,000, were imported against $6,200,000 in 1900, while manufactured articles were imported to the value of $71,400,000, instead of $67,100,000. These changes occurred chiefly through the bad Hungarian crops, which caused a decrease of grain shipments to Austria. The import of Hungarian coal, which was rendered necessary by the strikes of 1900, was also much reduced. The export of Austria to Hungary shows a notable change in manufactures, the value amounting to $164,620,000 against $156,820,000 for 1900. There was a considerable increase in the export of textiles, as well as in iron and iron wares.

### GENERAL EXPORTS.

Austrian commerce with Russia has remained, on the whole, inconsiderable. The export of manufactured articles to Germany, the greatest market for Austrian goods, is likely further to be increased in quantity in the future, although the value of the business may diminish. The Balkan States are not capable of extensive importation. Transoceanic exportation is difficult for Austria on account of the geographical situation of the country which, although covering a territory of 240,942 square miles and having about 46,000,000 inhabitants, has a restricted seaboard. Exports to South Africa, however, have been greater than usual, and, strange to remark, in goods which are not really articles of export from this country, namely, food stuffs, cigars, clothing, and war materials. The importance of India for Austro-Hungarian export has remained unchanged, this trade ranking next to the English in that country. This may be accounted for by the regular steamship communication. The sugar export was especially large. The Austrian product, which goes under the trade name of Austrian crystals, is quoted daily in the India papers; it brings a higher price than any other. All effort to exclude Austrian sugar has been unsuccessful, on account of the preference of the consumers for this variety. The importation of lumber from Austria decreased because of competition from the United States.

## TRADE WITH AMERICA.

The export of Austria-Hungary to the United States has decreased during the year in question. Formerly, manufactured goods were exported thither in large quantities, but now partially manufactured articles and raw stuffs, such as hops, magnesite, ozocerite, ceresin, hides, and skins, are chief in importance. Among the manufactures exported may be mentioned linen damask, colored glassware, porcelain, Gablonz wares, artificial flowers, fans, silk stuffs, musical wind instruments, beer, and sugar. The manufacture of mother-of-pearl buttons, an industry which thrived for many years in Vienna through its large exports to America, but for the last decade has materially decreased, has recently begun again. Only the smallest varieties, on which the duty is less, are being sent. The production of these varieties requires considerable manual preparation. The export of linen fabrics to America, by way of Germany and England, shows a large decrease, because of high prices. The great increase in the silk industry of America has been felt in the Austrian as well as the general European trade. Countries like France and Switzerland, that export silk goods to the United States in large quantities, also compete strongly with domestic goods in this monarchy, so that Austrian mills are compelled to accept orders at a minimum profit, and often at cost prices, in order to keep their looms in motion; and, in spite of all efforts, several mills were forced to slacken work for a few weeks.

American manufacturers are taking increased interest in Austria, and are making good progress. For small articles of merchandise and limited trade, Americans must depend on the local merchant to introduce their goods. Whenever the enterprise is important enough, there must be an intelligent, energetic business man on the spot, speaking the language of the country. Our manufacturers should exhibit at the various trade exhibitions held yearly in Austria. There will probably soon be an opportunity for our business men to have permanent exhibits in Vienna, in a large building to be erected where a former military barracks stood. They could intrust such an exhibit to the agent of some American business house and the cost would be moderate. In spite of opposition to certain American goods, business may be established. Some time ago there were many protests on the part of local manufacturers against the establishment of an American shoe store in Austria; nevertheless the American article has stepped in, and in Vienna alone there are now several stores selling our shoes. An American shoe store can be established with profit, and the prices need not be much higher than for the inferior domestic product.

The same is more or less true of other articles. There are many American products the sale of which will always be limited on account of the high duty and freight rates for small quantities, which make them cost as much again as in America. Inasmuch, however, as these are not standard articles, they are left out of consideration. It is hardly necessary to repeat that American exporters should be very careful to have goods securely and properly packed, to insure against breakage and damage. A business securely established in Austria would be in a position to reap larger benefits, if conditions should change and a more liberal policy be shown toward foreign manufacturers, than a business newly established. For instance, the Government favors any municipal or public enterprise, such as plants for lighting cities and the like, and orders for cars and engines of state railways are distributed among the manufacturers according to their capacity. The Austrian representative of an American firm informs me that he has had to return a machine because it was so poorly made as to be useless, and was refused by a buyer. The agent's business has been doubly injured, because he is out freight and duty and the reputation of his machine has suffered. It is supposed that the order was too hastily filled. Comment is unnecessary.

Credits should be given only against guaranty or on positive knowledge that it is safe to do so.

Austro-Hungarian exporters give considerable attention to trans-Atlantic trade outside of the United States. The attempts of factories and wholesale houses, some two years ago, to gain an interest in the Canadian market resulted favorably in spite of commercial statistics. The exports consisted chiefly of linen, buttons, blankets, brushes, pocketbooks, carpets, and porcelain. The Austrian merchant has also found a market in Mexico. A business in miscellaneous articles is being done with Porto Rico and Cuba. To Brazil Austrian shoes are still exported, although consignments of fans are becoming less important on account of Spanish competition. Chile and Peru are of little importance for Austria commercially, but the Argentine Republic has been a good market, though exports to that country decreased during the last year, especially in textiles, which suffered from the competition of Italy.

### SUGAR.

The sugar industry of Austria-Hungary, which exports more than two-thirds of its entire output, has suffered from the overproduction of sugar in other countries, and was threatened last year with a serious crisis. The price, f. o. b. Aussig, Bohemia, for the first quality of raw sugar sank below $3.60 per 220 pounds, and the average price for the year was $4.51, against $5.39 for 1900. Quotations for the last six month were satisfactory. The season opened at $4.99, and prices were kept up to about $4.80 for the first half of the year. A sharp decline was prevented by the circumstance that England, before the introduction of her sugar duty, imported quantities of sugar. Large shipments were also made to Japan. When these demands were met, the whole market changed. The campaign 1900–1901 closed with large stocks on hand. The beet sowing for 1901–2 was increased by 5 per cent over the previous year, and further increase in production was indicated. In consequence, prices dropped steadily. In July, quotations, f. o. b. Aussig, Bohemia, were still $4.80; in August they had dropped to $4.20, in September to $4, in October and November to $3.90, and in December to $3.60. The export of Austria-Hungary showed an advance in quantity in 1901, being 772,600 tons, against 730,400 tons in the previous year. The surplus consisted entirely of refined sugar, as the raw-sugar export was 60,300 tons less. The export of refined sugar was the greatest of any year during the last decade. Some 300,000 tons went through Hamburg, chiefly to England. The export to the East Indies was, in spite of differential duties, nearly doubled. The export to China was small, being only 3,200 tons, but it showed decided increase when compared with the 1,000 tons exported thither during 1900. On the other hand, Austria's export to Japan sank from 24,100 tons in 1900 to 10,700 tons, a decrease accounted for by the Japanese duties favoring the importation of raw sugar as opposed to refined varieties.

The major portion of the refined product consisted of granulated sugar, of which there was 420,000 tons exported, against 340,000 during the year previous, and 94,399.40 tons ten years ago. Of 628,400 tons, the total export of refined sugar, 81 per cent, or 509,800 tons, came from refineries in Austria, and 19 per cent from Hungarian refineries. The value of the entire sugar export in 1901 was, in spite an increase in the quantity exported, less by $2,800,000 than in 1900. It is of interest to note, in conclusion, that the money value of the total sugar export from Austria-Hungary from 1864 to 1901 amounted to $711,800,000.

### LINEN.

The unfavorable state of the linen industry in 1900, occasioned by the crisis in the flax market, continued into 1901, and was, in fact, rendered even more serious by various causes. During nearly the whole year the flax quotations were abnormally high, and the manufacturer was not able to recoup himself by charging more in proportion for the yarn or woven fabric, because the only prices at which these articles could be sold were below cost. In addition, the export to all countries shrank appreciably. There seems to be little prospect of improvement in this branch until the raw material can be supplied at a lower figure. Although the domestic flax production is highly developed and the Austrian varieties are exported annually in large quanties, the Austrian flax spinners are obliged to purchase abroad about one-half of their raw material. The market for linen fabrics was in a bad condition. The Austrian weavers did not come to an agreement among themselves to limit the output, and the difficulties under which the trade contended were almost unsurmountable. The year under discussion may be considered one of the worst for the linen industry for a long period.

### WOOL.

For the wool trade, 1901 has been termed a year of reconvalescence. The speculation of former years has ended in legitimate business. The manfacturers began to work on a solid basis by reason of brisker demand and normal consumption. A considerable quantity of fine woolen blankets was exported to America.

### SILK.

After the considerable fluctuations in the silk trade during the previous two years, there was manifest a certain firmness for the year under discussion. America has become so important a factor for the raw product that the price variations of the silk markets of Asia, as well as of Europe, are caused by the American buyers. In Austria, several plants have been enlarged and new ones founded. In general, the silk industry in this country has increased, but the situation for the individual manufacturer has been made harder. Wash silks in particular were largely brought and readily sold.

### COTTON.

The condition of the raw cotton market was much quieter than during the previous year.   Generally, the prices showed a backward tendency.   For cotton weavers, the year was unfavorable.   Owing to fluctuations in the raw material and the decrease in prices for same, weavers had to choose between shutting down or running the looms at a loss.   The majority of weavers chose the latter, and it happened that while the prices for raw material kept within certain bounds, the ready fabrics were disposed of under the actual cost price of manufacture.   The lack of an organization among the weavers and a fixed system of payment for goods delivered was felt during the year as never before.   At the beginning of 1902, the demand for raw materials was brisk and the spinning mills were pretty well supplied with orders, so that the hope of improvement seems fairly well founded.

### IRON.

The iron market was affected by the crisis that started in Germany during 1900.   In Austria, the crisis did not come so suddenly as in Germany, and, fortunately for Austrian merchants, was not of the same importance.   Nevertheless, 1901 was decidedly unsatisfactory. There was strong competition with Hungarian works that led to an agreement, during the last months of 1901, among the larger Austrian works, which began negotiations with the Hungarian ones.   According to earlier arrangements, the Austrian works were allowed to send 13,500 tons to Hungary, and Hungarians could export annually to Austria as much as 11,500 tons.   The Hungarian works demanded under the new agreement that they should be privileged to send a greater quantity to Austria, and it was finally settled that they might sell 16,500 tons, while the Austrian side was granted corresponding benefits.

### COPPER.

The use of copper in Austria was not less than during 1900, but the year was unfavorable, as manufacturers were so intimidated by the high prices that they made only the most necessary purchases.   The production of Austrian copper is so small that it can hardly be considered.   American copper, of course, takes the first place on this market, followed by the English, Japanese, and German product.

### CHINA.

The market in stone chinawares remains practically the same as in the previous year.   The prices were, however, somewhat reduced, because the German competitors, not finding an outlet for their large stocks in other countries, sold more in Austria.   Although Austria has coal and all the necessary raw materials to produce stone china, no export in this line has been effected.   The conditions prevailing in the porcelain trade are still more unfavorable than during the previous year.   Of no small influence has been the fact that there were fewer American purchasers in the market.

Manufacturers of tools and tool machinery report a decrease in sales, and there was an apparent lessening of the domestic production. Tools of American manufacture found a good market. The business in agricultural machinery has been unfavorable for Austrian manufacturers, as American agricultural machinery is bought extensively by the larger landowners, a representative of an American firm having recently sold some forty carloads in Galicia.

## AUTOMOBILES.

The automobile business has made decided progress in this country, the number of machines nearly doubling in the past year. The demand for large, heavy wagons has lessened, and smaller machines of light construction are preferred, chiefly on account of cheapness. Some prices paid have been relatively high—$6,000 to $8,000 having been given for fast machines. One American firm has a lucrative agency in Vienna. Machines of foreign manufacture seem to be preferred, and the growth of the automobile business is of more profit to the Frenchman than to the Austrian. The market has increased, but the Austrian industry has not been enlarged in proportion, especially on account of the insufficient protective duties.

## STATISTICS.

*Imports into Austria-Hungary in 1900 and 1901, by countries of origin.*

| Countries. | 1900. | 1901. |
|---|---|---|
| United States of America | $30,564,615.20 | $27,383,069.20 |
| America (not otherwise specified) | 1,682,483.60 | 1,512,666.40 |
| Africa (not otherwise specified) | 642,459.20 | 1,610,944.80 |
| Algeria | 295,951.60 | 481,089.20 |
| Argentine Republic | 888,382.00 | 1,272,875.80 |
| Asia (not otherwise specified) | 779,064.00 | 853,984.40 |
| Belgium | 5,217,308.20 | 6,284,800.20 |
| Brazil | 8,697,780.60 | 7,556,334.60 |
| Bremen (free zone) | 20,440.20 | 3,446.00 |
| British Australia | 750,639.20 | 482,893.00 |
| British India | 16,848,351.00 | 18,998,476.00 |
| British West Indies | 443,537.00 | 465,455.60 |
| British possessions in the Mediterranean | 50,305.40 | 59,142.20 |
| Bulgaria | 847,753.00 | 1,084,568.40 |
| Canada | 31,282.60 | 68,290.20 |
| Capeland | 32,043.40 | 93,457.60 |
| Chile | 2,149,471.80 | 2,516,731.20 |
| China | 1,262,718.20 | 1,173,694.00 |
| Colombia | 22,421.00 | 19,737.20 |
| Cuba | 1,108,690.40 | 1,195,418.80 |
| Denmark | 158,214.80 | 190,290.40 |
| Dutch Indies | 4,094,608.60 | 4,285,290.80 |
| Egypt | 5,534,932.80 | 3,968,897.00 |
| Fiume (free zone) | 10,138.80 | 7,815.20 |
| France | 10,772,788.00 | 23,737,669.40 |
| French Indo-China | 41,888.60 | 6,978.00 |
| German Empire | 126,997,327.20 | 141,228,925.40 |
| German protectorate in Africa | 1,129,814.20 | 237,037.00 |
| Great Britain | 29,788,327.40 | 31,982,862.20 |
| Greece | 3,434,885.00 | 3,308,482.40 |
| Hamburg (free zone) | 57,315.60 | 201,918.40 |
| Italy | 22,859,455.00 | 21,150,042.00 |
| Japan | 793,814.00 | 1,265,341.20 |
| Congo Free State | 99,096.60 | 24,624.00 |
| Mexico | 148,058.00 | 103,987.00 |
| Montenegro | 110,374.00 | 131,373.60 |
| Morocco | 2,875.00 | 3,451.60 |
| Netherlands | 3,268,693.60 | 4,105,555.60 |
| Norway | 800,659.00 | 929,488.80 |
| Oceania | 1,457,646.40 | 913,402.60 |
| Persia | 125,655.00 | 134,371.80 |
| Peru | 22,484.80 | 34,426.20 |

*Imports into Austria-Hungary in 1900 and 1901, by countries of origin—Continued.*

| Countries. | 1900. | 1901. |
|---|---|---|
| Portugal | $186,515.00 | $134,362.00 |
| Roumania | 6,445,419.20 | 7,862,708.20 |
| Russia | 17,829,779.20 | 17,287,974.60 |
| Servia | 8,442,635.60 | 8,457,102.20 |
| Spain | 966,482.40 | 814,614.40 |
| Sweden | 878,140.40 | 1,047,415.00 |
| Switzerland | 11,259,837.40 | 9,873,185.00 |
| Trieste (free zone) | 55,152.00 | 66,968.20 |
| Tunis | 23,150.60 | 31,598.80 |
| Turkey | 8,384,884.00 | 7,550,995.40 |
| Total imports | 339,271,541.40 | 330,528,338.40 |
| Total imports (inclusive of precious metals and specie) | 348,251,259.60 | 365,225,433.20 |

*Imports into Austria-Hungary by classes.*

| Articles. | 1900. | 1901. |
|---|---|---|
| Animals (not neat cattle) | $3,022,084.60 | $3,506,485.60 |
| Animal products | 19,441,201.40 | 19,122,906.20 |
| Art objects | 10,027,628.00 | 10,299,389.00 |
| Base metals and goods thereof | 14,889,556.20 | 14,000,761.60 |
| Brush and sieve makers' goods | 105,700.00 | 119,620.00 |
| Candles and soap | 106,058.40 | 119,925.40 |
| Cattle (neat) | 5,648,276.00 | 5,411,339.60 |
| Chemicals, acids, etc | 5,152,591.60 | 5,512,042.20 |
| Chemical compounds | 4,328,763.20 | 5,826,455.20 |
| Clothing | 3,170,137.80 | 3,156,994.00 |
| Coffee, tea, etc | 11,050,188.60 | 9,738,108.40 |
| Common salt | 159,325.20 | 158,512.40 |
| Cotton yarns and goods thereof | 38,172,374.20 | 33,689,015.00 |
| Drugs and perfumes | 466,562.00 | 462,431.60 |
| Dyeing and tanning materials | 4,334,134.00 | 4,428,061.40 |
| Edibles | 4,615,540.00 | 4,918,667.80 |
| Fats | 3,642,812.60 | 4,014,709.40 |
| Flax, hemp, jute, etc | 10,825,061.00 | 10,764,137.40 |
| Fruit, plants, etc | 14,873,620.80 | 14,191,829.60 |
| Furriers' goods | 1,536,208.00 | 1,769,286.00 |
| Glass and glassware | 837,068.80 | 758,588.80 |
| Grain and leguminous vegetables | 9,996,250.80 | 10,727,494.00 |
| Gum and resin | 2,724,411.60 | 2,636,482.40 |
| Instruments, locks, and fancy goods | 9,805,077.40 | 10,156,768.40 |
| Iron and hardware | 7,500,685.60 | 7,094,414.20 |
| Leather and leather goods | 9,089,524.00 | 9,840,160.00 |
| Machines of wood, iron, and base metals | 10,415,480.00 | 26,360.60 |
| Matches | 48,036.40 | 47,388.40 |
| Minerals | 5,057,380.20 | 5,364,726.00 |
| Mineral oils and brown coal | 1,034,570.40 | 728,464.80 |
| Oilcloth and oil silk | 145,039.80 | 131,864.40 |
| Oils | 4,061,308.60 | 4,021,254.20 |
| Paper and paper goods | 5,110,184.80 | 5,409,415.00 |
| Porcelain | 6,057,575.20 | 5,991,911.80 |
| Pottery | 1,106,367.40 | 1,103,712.80 |
| Precious metals and specie | 979,518.20 | 34,697,094.80 |
| Refuse | 661,724.40 | 4,063,460.00 |
| Rubber, gutta-percha, and goods thereof | 312,218.40 | 3,897,454.00 |
| Silk and silk goods | | 14,350,857.20 |
| Spices | 1,365,163.80 | 1,416,043.40 |
| Straw and chip goods | 2,370,131.80 | 2,079,258.00 |
| Sugar | 10,619.40 | 8,307.20 |
| Tobacco | 11,110,258.20 | 11,241,230.80 |
| Tropical fruits | 4,938,412.60 | 5,405,069.20 |
| Turners' and carvers' goods | 3,211,533.00 | 2,827,512.20 |
| Vehicles | 222,918.40 | 172,473.20 |
| Wines, liquors, etc | 6,663,00 | 4,726,580.60 |
| Wood, coal, and peat | 21,458,60 | 23,479,708.00 |
| Wooden and horn goods | 2,221,40 | 2,272,626.40 |
| Wool and woolen goods | 30,839,80 | 29,847,287.00 |
| Total imports | 339,271,541.40 | 330,528,338.40 |
| Total imports (inclusive of precious metals and specie) | 348,251,059.60 | 365,225,433.20 |

*Exports from Austria-Hungary in 1900 and 1901, by countries of destination.*

| Countries. | 1900. | 1901. |
|---|---|---|
| United States of America | $7,586,922.00 | $6,589,949.60 |
| America, not otherwise specified | 526,486.80 | 578,764.40 |
| Africa, not otherwise specified | 188,615.20 | 127,776.60 |
| Algeria | 195,670.00 | 77,685.60 |
| Argentine Republic | 309,643.80 | 267,626.80 |
| Asia, not otherwise specified | 59,337.60 | 193,761.20 |
| Belgium | 2,977,529.20 | 2,708,188.80 |
| Brazil | 1,072,710.00 | 1,297,780.00 |
| Bremen (free zone) | 767,046.20 | 922,518.80 |
| British Australasia | 128,509.00 | 166,087.60 |
| British India | 2,360,705.00 | 12,071,676.00 |
| British West Indies | 23,722.20 | 18,620.40 |
| British possessions in the Mediterranean | 829,475.80 | 231,621.20 |
| Bulgaria | 1,873,522.60 | 2,382,641.00 |
| Canada | 74,916.60 | 32,245.60 |
| Capeland | 793,942.60 | 956,526.40 |
| Chile | 204,748.60 | 111,766.80 |
| China | 330,297.20 | 414,398.80 |
| Colombia | 8,308.40 | 15,825.40 |
| Cuba | 41,179.80 | 37,245.40 |
| Denmark | 765,041.60 | 785,498.40 |
| Dutch India | 47,572.80 | 66,378.40 |
| Egypt | 5,234,345.60 | 5,268,856.20 |
| Fiume (free zone) | 9,188.80 | 10,515.60 |
| France | 13,696,075.40 | 13,081,015.60 |
| French Indo-China | 20,867.40 | 50,068.20 |
| German Empire | 188,338,188.60 | 182,063,316.60 |
| German Protectorate in Africa | 86,020.60 | 18,683.40 |
| Great Britain | 40,249,980.20 | 37,377,989.60 |
| Greece | 2,677,335.80 | 2,607,940.40 |
| Hamburg (free zone) | 14,162,714.00 | 12,569,309.80 |
| Italy | 29,397,855.40 | 27,294,594.40 |
| Japan | 2,360,705.00 | 1,271,723.40 |
| Kongo Free State | 490.00 | 278.00 |
| Mexico | 149,216.60 | 118,912.20 |
| Montenegro | 74,918.60 | 67,743.80 |
| Morocco | 12,886.60 | 55,780.60 |
| Netherlands | 5,488,435.00 | 5,752,109.00 |
| Norway | 383,339.60 | 325,045.80 |
| Oceania | 84,109.40 | 84,292.60 |
| Persia | 179,713.80 | 163,230.40 |
| Peru | 36,526.60 | 40,299.40 |
| Portugal | 421,382.20 | 490,456.00 |
| Roumania | 8,642,138.60 | 9,561,220.80 |
| Russia | 14,332,242.00 | 14,546,769.40 |
| Servia | 4,834,705.00 | 4,526,887.20 |
| Spain | 1,221,794.60 | 949,007.60 |
| Sweden | 812,246.20 | 1,021,129.20 |
| Switzerland | 13,725,933.60 | 12,895,560.20 |
| Trieste (free zone) | 1,528,776.80 | 1,337,838.20 |
| Tunis | 126,083.40 | 80,837.40 |
| Turkey | 12,723,558.80 | 13,484,561.20 |
| Total exports | 388,400,500.20 | 377,091,508.80 |
| Total exports inclusive of precious metals and specie | 401,709,799.40 | 385,460,524.80 |

*Exports from Austria-Hungary, by classes.*

| Articles. | 1900. | 1901. |
|---|---|---|
| Animals (not neat cattle) | $5,809,866.00 | $4,371,377.80 |
| Animal products | 33,589,922.60 | 32,385,037.80 |
| Art objects | 4,671,129.00 | 4,807,306.00 |
| Base metals and goods thereof | 7,300,416.60 | 6,629,032.20 |
| Brush and sieve makers' goods | 729,896.00 | 548,108.00 |
| Candles and soap | 221,742.60 | 192,267.20 |
| Cattle (neat) | 23,854,477.80 | 24,099,218.60 |
| Chemicals, acids, etc. | 2,564,996.20 | 2,228,815.00 |
| Chemical compounds | 3,773,621.40 | 3,527,682.80 |
| Clothing | 8,524,486.00 | 9,007,473.80 |
| Coffee, tea, etc. | 3,537.20 | 3,880.00 |
| Common salt | 11,490.00 | 21,695.40 |
| Cotton yarns and goods thereof | 5,024,814.60 | 4,897,790.80 |
| Drugs and perfumes | 176,182.00 | 139,388.00 |
| Dyeing and tanning materials | 3,417,346.40 | 3,469,367.60 |
| Edibles | 1,489,328.40 | 3,648,012.20 |
| Fats | 2,942,861.00 | 4,235,631.20 |

*Exports from Austria-Hungary, by classes*—Continued.

| Articles. | 1900. | 1901. |
|---|---|---|
| Flax, hemp, jute, etc | $9,694,258.40 | $9,576,545.00 |
| Fruit, plants, etc | :4,648,804.20 | 17,825,642.20 |
| Furriers' goods | 852,172.00 | 494,240.00 |
| Glass and glassware | 10,546,656.60 | 9,831,097.40 |
| Grain and leguminous vegetables | 27,881,701.00 | 29,742,375.40 |
| Gum and resin | 1,832,348.40 | 1,410,125.20 |
| Instruments, clocks, and fancy goods | 12,206,328.20 | 11,916,856.80 |
| Iron and hardware | 11,136,900.80 | 8,126,573.00 |
| Leather and leather goods | 11,783,397.00 | 11,833,870.60 |
| Machines of wood, iron, and base metals | 2,075,334.60 | 2,160,632.60 |
| Matches | 1,013,353.00 | 887,357.00 |
| Minerals | 6,560,481.00 | 5,678,173.00 |
| Mineral oils and brown coal | 1,428,605.20 | 1,229,522.80 |
| Oilcloth and oil silk | 209,611.60 | 191,154.00 |
| Oils | 144,584.00 | 76,531.00 |
| Paper and paper goods | 1,667,356.40 | 8,521,415.80 |
| Porcelain | 1,491,134.40 | 1,429,843.00 |
| Pottery | 3,835,481.20 | 3,946,023.20 |
| Precious metals and specie | 13,309,299.20 | 8,369,016.00 |
| Refuse | 5,166,695.00 | 4,752,834.00 |
| Rubber, gutta-percha, and goods thereof | 1,667,356.40 | 1,739,864.00 |
| Silk and silk goods | 7,390,734.00 | 6,877,356.80 |
| Spices | 25,947.00 | 36,130.00 |
| Straw and chip goods | 312,041.00 | 298,661.60 |
| Sugar | 37,310,264.60 | 35,338,652.80 |
| Tobacco | 1,109,910.20 | 1,346,117.00 |
| Tropical fruits | 843,873.40 | 828,323.60 |
| Turners' and carvers' goods | 574,015.40 | 510,359.60 |
| Vehicles | 1,293,180.20 | 729,605.80 |
| Wines, liquors, etc | 7,635,160.20 | 7,156,228.40 |
| Wood, coal, and peat | 69,911,332.80 | 65,690,870.20 |
| Wooden and horn goods | 9,761,121.00 | 8,854,734.80 |
| Wool and woolen goods | 13,638,677.20 | 13,850,717.80 |
| Total exports | 388,400,500.20 | 377,091,508.80 |
| Total exports, inclusive of precious metals and specie | 401,709,799.40 | 385,460,524.80 |

CARL BAILEY HURST,
*Consul-General.*

VIENNA, *December 16, 1902.*

## HUNGARY: TRADE IN 1902.

According to preliminary statistics just published, the total value of Hungary's trade in 1902 was 2,468,000,000 crowns ($501,004,000), an increase of 55,000,000 crowns ($11,165,000) over 1901. The export of Hungary to other countries was 42,000,000 crowns ($8,526,000) more, while the import into Hungary increased by only 13,000,000 ($2,630,000).

The export is estimated to have reached the total value of 1,307,000,000 crowns ($265,321,000), the import only 1,161,000,000 ($235,683,000). Hungary, therefore, proudly points to an active balance of 146,000,000 crowns ($29,638,000), which compares well with the 118,000,000 ($23,954,000) balance of 1901. With respect to preceding years, only the balance of 1900, an exceptional year, was larger.

The trade with Austria is characterized by an active balance of 36,000,000 crowns ($7,308,000), the gain being due to Hungary's larger export of grain, flour, animals for slaughter, and animals for industrial purposes.

Textile products and semimanufactures were imported to the amount of 375,710,000 crowns ($76,269,150), forming about one-third of the total import. Austria supplied all of these articles but 12,000,000 ($2,736,000) worth. American exporters should note the fact that this import shows an increase of 21,000,000 crowns ($4,263,000) over that of 1901, though silk goods declined.   Cotton wares advanced most, followed by woolens.

The import of sugar, paper, and chemical products increased, while that of leather, iron, artistic and musical instruments and machines fell off.

The import of cloth and underwear amounted to 64,310,000 crowns ($13,054,950), of which Austria supplied nearly the whole.   Other countries competed in iron and ironware, artistic and musical instruments and machines.   In these groups, United States goods excel those of all other countries, and the market in Hungary ought not to be neglected.   The total import of iron and ironware is valued at 29,698,360 crowns ($6,028,767); of artistic and musical instruments, at 52,711,335 crowns($10,700,401), and of machines, at 44,386,007 crowns($9,010,358).

Imports from the United States in 1902 included the following:

|  | Cubic meters. | Pounds. |
|---|---|---|
| Corn (maize) | 477 = | 105,159 |
| Beans | 9 = | 1,984 |
| Oats | 1 = | 220 |
| Prunes | 5 = | 1,102 |
| Wine (in casks) | 1 = | 220 |
| Shooks and staves | 635 = | 139,992 |
| Refined mineral oil | 1,215 = | 267,858 |
| Crude iron | 400 = | 88,184 |
| Iron and steel bars | 4 = | 881 |

There arrived in Fiume, the port of Hungary, a total of 26 steamships (1 without cargo) and 3 sailing vessels in 1902.

There left Fiume for the United States, in the same year, a total of 31 steamships (1 without cargo) and 1 sailing vessel, empty.

FRANK DYER CHESTER, *Consul.*

BUDAPEST, *February 6, 1903.*

---

## NETHERLANDS: TRADE IN 1902.

The year has not been a profitable one for those interested in ocean shipping.   Freight rates have been low, owing to the abundance of vacant ship room, and with the increased rates demanded for coal and stores, and the raised wages, there could hardly be question of profitable trips.   In fact, the majority of the shipowners and dispatchers considered themselves fortunate if all expenses, including the wear and tear of material, were covered.   The port of Rotterdam has felt the effect of the low freights, and the steady increase in tonnage arriving has not been as large as it usually was previous to 1901.

The total number of ocean-going vessels entered at Rotterdam in 1902, excluding fishing smacks and foreign tugs, was 6,693, with a capacity of 30,193,107 cubic meters (1,065,816,677 cubic feet), against 6,880 ships with a capacity of 29,351,865 cubic meters (1,036,020,834 cubic feet) in 1901.

From 1893 to 1902, the tonnage arrived at Rotterdam has increased as follows:

| | Per cent. | | Per cent. |
|---|---|---|---|
| 1893–94 | 16.1 | 1898–99 | 9.7 |
| 1894–95 | .8 | 1899–1900 | 4.3 |
| 1895–96 | 18.5 | 1900–1901 | 2 |
| 1896–97 | 9.2 | 1901–2 | 3 |
| 1897–98 | 6.3 | | |

Shipbuilding has been greatly influenced by the surplus of ship room. Contracts for new ships can now be made at prices about 15 per cent lower than a year ago, and prices for second-hand ships also retrograded considerably. In some cases, they were sold for 20 per cent less than in the year before. In spite of the dull times, the Netherlands merchant fleet increased in 1902 by 19 steamers with an aggregate capacity of 60,782 tons, while 20 steamers, with a capacity of 45,400 tons (including 15 steamers with a capacity of 31,400 tons on Dutch wharves), are still in course of construction.

### FREIGHT RATES.

The highest and lowest freight rates in 1902 were:

*Home freights.*

| From— | To— | Cargo. | Unit. | British currency. Highest. | British currency. Lowest. | U. S. equivalent. Highest. | U. S. equivalent. Lowest. |
|---|---|---|---|---|---|---|---|
| | | | | s. d. | s. d. | | |
| San Francisco (steamers). | Great Britain or Continent. | Wheat.......... | Ton ...... | 33 0 | 25 6 | $8.0265 | $6.1965 |
| San Francisco (sailing vessels). | .....do ............. | ...do .... | ...do .... | 35 6 | 11 3 | 8.6365 | 2.73 |
| West coast of South America (steamers). | .....do ............. | Saltpeter ......... | ...do .... | 24 6 | 16 3 | 5.9565 | 3.95 |
| West coast of South America (sailing vessels). | .....do ............. | ...do .......... | ...do .... | 25 0 | 12 6 | 6.0765 | 3.04 |
| Saigon ............ | .....do ............. | Rice ........... | ...do .... | 23 9 | 18 0 | 5.7765 | 4.38 |
| Bangkok ......... | .....do ............. | ...do ....... | ...do .... | 26 3 | 23 9 | 6.3365 | 5.7765 |
| Java............... | Great Britain, Continent, or United States. | Sugar, etc ...... | ...do .... | 25 0 | 20 0 | 6.0765 | 4.8665 |
| Burma............ | Great Britain or Continent. | Rice ........... | ...do .... | 24 0 | 15 0 | 5.8365 | 3.65 |
| Bombay .......... | .....do ............. | Manganese ore . | ...do .... | 19 0 | 14 0 | 4.62 | 3.40 |
| Parana River...... | .....do ............. | Grain........... | ...do .... | 18 6 | 11 0 | 4.50 | 2.67 |
| New Orleans or Galveston. | .....do ............. | ...do .......... | ...do .... | 12 0 | 9 0 | 2.92 | 2.19 |
| New York .......... | .....do ............. | ...do .......... | Quarter.. | 3 4½ | 1 6 | .57 | .26 |
| Montreal .......... | Great Britain ..... | Wood.......... | Standard . | 42 6 | 32 6 | 10.333 | 7.9065 |
| Kronstadt.......... | London or east coast of England. | ...do .......... | ...do .... | 28 9 | 17 0 | 6.9865 | 4.13 |
| St. Petersburg ...... | .....do ............. | Grain ......... | Quarter.. | 1 4 | 0 7½ | .32 | .15 |
| Novorossick ....... | Great Britain or Continent. | ...do .......... | Unit, new charter. | 12 0 | 7 3 | 2.92 | 1.76 |
| Odessa.............. | .....do ............. | ...do .......... | ...do .... | 11 6 | 6 6 | 2.79 | 1.58 |
| Danube.............. | .....do ............. | ...do .......... | .....do .... | 15 3 | 7 9 | 3.71 | 1.88 |
| Bilbao ............. | Middelsbro ....... | Ore .......... | Ton ...... | 5 3 | 4 3 | 1.27 | 1.08 |
| Batoum ............ | Calcutta ........... | Petroleum ..... | Case ...... | 0 8 | 0 5¼ | .16 | .105 |

*Freight rates for coal.*

| From— | To— | Unit. | British currency. Highest. | British currency. Lowest. | U. S. equivalent. Highest. | U. S. equivalent. Lowest. |
|---|---|---|---|---|---|---|
| | | | s. d. | s. d. | | |
| Tyne ............. | Kronstadt.................... | Ton .... | 4 6 | 3 6 | $1.09 | $0.85 |
| Do............. | Genoa....................... | ...do ... | 6 3 | 4 3 | 1.52 | 1.03 |
| Cardiff ............ | Constantinople .............. | ...do ... | 7 6 | 4 0 | 1.82 | .97 |
| Do............. | Capetown .................. | ...do ... | 18 0 | 12 9 | 4.38 | 3.10 |
| Do............. | Colombo ................... | ...do ... | 15 0 | 8 6 | 3.65 | 2.06 |
| Do............. | Plate River ................ | ...do ... | 14 6 | 7 1½ | 3.52 | 1.73 |
| Do............. | Singapore .................. | ...do ... | 13 0 | 11 0 | 3.16 | 2.67 |
| Do............. | Hongkong .................. | ...do ... | 20 0 | 13 6 | 4.8665 | 3.28 |

*Imports and exports of principal articles in the Netherlands for 1902.*

| Articles. | Imports. | Exports. | Articles. | Imports. | Exports. |
|---|---|---|---|---|---|
| | *Pounds.* | *Pounds.* | | *Pounds.* | *Pounds.* |
| Ashes.............. | 164,067,200 | 107,023,400 | Mercery ............ | 96,575,600 | 72,870,600 |
| Bark ............. | 21,608,400 | 17,934,400 | Metal articles ..... | 1,552,091,200 | 1,185,305,600 |
| Beer and malt extract............ | 37,897,200 | 52,217,000 | Metal, raw.......... | 3,400,590,600 | 2,859,922,000 |
| Butter............ | 1,630,200 | 50,507,600 | Oils: | | |
| Cereals: | | | Groundnut ..... | 3,284,600 | 6,171,000 |
| Wheat.......... | 3,813,948,600 | 3,239,387,800 | Cotton seed.... | 122,159,400 | 79,655,400 |
| Rye............ | 1,254,008,800 | 770,222,200 | Sesame and other edible.. | 38,328,400 | 42,158,600 |
| Barley.......... | 962,080,800 | 648,155,200 | Palm and other.. | 316,272,000 | 305,855,000 |
| Corn.......... | 988,891,200 | 429,242,000 | Petroleum..... | 991,170,400 | 609,637,600 |
| Oats.......... | 795,707,000 | 790,085,400 | Palm nuts......... | 53,563,400 | 51,737,400 |
| Buckwheat.... | 32,197,000 | 19,272,000 | Paper ............ | 223,698,200 | 393,093,800 |
| Rice.......... | 477,978,600 | 249,420,600 | Potato flour and its | | |
| Other kinds ... | 26,360,400 | .......... | products....... | 82,189,800 | 169,800,400 |
| Cheese........... | .......... | 104,297,600 | Rags............... | .......... | 161,678,000 |
| Coal............... | 8,206,405,800 | 6,850,258,800 | Rattans ........... | 12,284,800 | 11,506,000 |
| Coffee ............ | 284,114,800 | 189,659,800 | Salt............... | 297,096,800 | 95,081,200 |
| Cotton, raw ....... | 155,276,000 | 112,912,800 | Seeds ............ | 873,349,400 | 527,496,200 |
| Drapers' wares ... | 150,847,400 | 141,099,200 | Spices ............ | 17,617,600 | 21,628,200 |
| Drugs, dyestuffs, | | | Spirits ............ | 45,685,200 | 102,183,400 |
| and chemicals.... | 1,140,449,200 | 916,857,200 | Stone ............ | 4,108,715,600 | 974,369,000 |
| Earthenware ...... | 722,486,600 | 288,263,800 | Sugar: | | |
| Engines and machinery .......... | 188,412,400 | 126,517,600 | Raw.......... | 766,484,400 | 407,440,000 |
| Fish ............... | 41,012,400 | 320,826,000 | Other.......... | 104,029,200 | 364,971,200 |
| Fish oil........... | 21,483,000 | 16,599,000 | Sulphur ............ | 21,126,600 | 21,091,400 |
| Flax and hemp .... | 101,681,200 | 164,863,600 | Sirup ............ | 48,584,200 | 57,838,000 |
| Flour............... | 428,117,800 | 59,773,000 | Tallow, suet, etc ... | 114,276,800 | 70,730,000 |
| Fruits ............ | 262,484,200 | 218,983,000 | Tar and pitch ..... | 128,106,000 | 171,963,600 |
| Glass and glassware | 198,294,400 | 168,040,400 | Tea ............... | 22,880,800 | 14,779,600 |
| Groundnuts ....... | 60,049,000 | 26,221,800 | Tobacco and cigars. | 168,960,000 | 129,927,600 |
| Hides, skins, and leather .......... | 100,117,600 | 92,595,800 | Vinegar ........... | .......... | 28,571,400 |
| Lard............... | 58,216,400 | 41,712,000 | Wine ............... | 146,709,200 | 123,972,200 |
| Manure ............ | 603,213,600 | 817,877,200 | Wood: | | |
| Margarine: | | | For shipbuilding and timber | 3,607,793,200 | 1,774,416,600 |
| Butter.......... | 1,012,000 | 109,813,000 | Dyewoods ..... | 60,517,600 | 78,971,200 |
| Raw............. | 76,232,200 | 40,271,000 | Hard woods ... | 93,693,600 | 27,596,800 |
| Meat ............ | 23,663,200 | 161,944,200 | Wool ............... | 96,626,200 | 84,552,600 |
| | | | Yarns ............. | 111,216,600 | 60,240,400 |

*Imports and exports of principal articles at Rotterdam for 1902.*

| Articles. | Imports. | Exports. | Articles. | Imports. | Exports. |
|---|---|---|---|---|---|
| | *Pounds.* | *Pounds.* | | *Pounds.* | *Pounds.* |
| Ashes.............. | 29,321,600 | 13,780,800 | Ground nuts....... | 58,037,600 | 21,170,600 |
| Bark ............. | 2,549,800 | 2,428,800 | Hides, skins, and leather .......... | 39,798,600 | 38,702,400 |
| Beer and malt extract............ | 17,219,400 | 15,393,400 | Lard............... | 50,463,600 | 24,112,000 |
| Butter............ | 1,088,400 | 2,169,200 | Manure ............ | 267,033,800 | 258,305,800 |
| Cereals: | | | Margarine: | | |
| Wheat.......... | 2,513,871,800 | 2,114,388,600 | Butter.......... | 706,400 | 92,098,400 |
| Rye............ | 999,257,600 | 661,619,200 | Raw.......... | 63,036,600 | 17,085,200 |
| Barley.......... | 721,547,200 | 405,244,400 | Meat ............ | 18,570,200 | 58,511,200 |
| Corn.......... | 689,290,800 | 212,647,600 | Mercery ............ | 51,959,600 | 43,456,600 |
| Oats.......... | 713,574,400 | 653,998,400 | Metal articles ..... | 310,547,600 | 325,606,600 |
| Buckwheat.... | 26,419,800 | 14,830,200 | Metal, raw ........ | 912,705,200 | 1,372,694,400 |
| Rice.......... | 182,802,400 | 104,489,000 | Oils: | | |
| Other kinds ... | 17,864,000 | .......... | Ground nut .... | 3,071,200 | 4,754,200 |
| Cheese........... | Not stated. | 43,150,800 | Cotton-seed.... | 114,449,800 | 78,451,400 |
| Coal............... | 816,505,800 | 1,210,737,000 | Sesame and other edible...... | 28,637,400 | 32,186,000 |
| Coffee ............ | 219,846,000 | 104,482,400 | Palm and other. | 198,607,200 | 168,049,200 |
| Cotton, raw........ | 33,660,000 | 12,295,800 | Petroleum..... | 619,007,400 | 427,501,800 |
| Drapers' wares ... | 40,959,600 | 51,169,800 | Palm nuts......... | 47,011,800 | 35,413,400 |
| Drugs, dyestuffs, | | | Paper............... | 91,946,800 | 93,667,200 |
| and chemicals.... | 591,065,200 | 440,367,400 | Potato flour and its products.......... | 58,473,800 | 64,466,600 |
| Earthenware...... | 60,159,000 | 58,680,600 | Rags............... | .......... | 68,809,400 |
| Engines and machinery .......... | 69,170,200 | 48,661,800 | Rattans............ | .......... | 4,586,400 |
| Fish ............... | 20,792,200 | 146,513,400 | Salt............... | 43,509,400 | .......... |
| Fish oil........... | 15,793,800 | 11,035,200 | Seeds ............ | 357,819,000 | 176,341,000 |
| Flax and hemp .... | 44,033,000 | 28,679,200 | Spices ............ | 8,533,200 | 10,069,400 |
| Flour............... | 240,182,800 | 50,248,000 | Spirits ............ | 20,059,600 | 55,844,800 |
| Fruits ............ | 130,935,200 | 115,607,800 | Stone ............ | Not stated. | 245,682,800 |
| Glass and glassware | 43,469,800 | 46,010,800 | | | |

*Imports and exports of principal articles at Rotterdam for 1902*—Continued.

| Articles. | Imports. | Exports. | Articles. | Imports. | Exports. |
|---|---|---|---|---|---|
| | *Pounds.* | *Pounds.* | Vinegar ............. | | 1,271,600 |
| Sugar: | | | Wine ................ | 84,188,000 | 76,654,600 |
| Raw ........... | 289,172,400 | 287,783,600 | Wood: | | |
| Other ......... | 65,678,800 | 53,455,600 | For shipbuild- | | |
| Sulphur ........... | 8,190,600 | 6,019,200 | ing and timber | 1,385,563,200 | 892,372,800 |
| Sirup .............. | 84,240,800 | 80,619,600 | Dyewoods ...... | 40,987,600 | 56,985,800 |
| Tallow, suet, etc.... | 75,748,200 | 80,166,400 | Hard woods .... | 81,270,200 | 16,471,400 |
| Tar and pitch ...... | 8,385,800 | ............... | Wool ............... | 24,686,200 | 14,588,200 |
| Tea ............... | 7,772,600 | ............... | Yarns .............. | 52,714,300 | 29,942,000 |
| Tobacco and cigars. | 77,642,400 | 49,673,800 | | | |

## CEREALS.

The cereal market was a little livelier in 1902 than in the year before. Wheat quotations in the European markets corresponded with those of the New York terminal market, viz, in January, $0.89 to $0.85; February, $0.84; from March to the end of July, $0.82 to $0.78, and from that time to the end of the year, $0.75 to $0.83. Rye quotations, which in the course of 1901 fluctuated between $50 and $54, varied a little more in the past year. Still, the difference between highest and lowest quotations was never greater than $6. Good rye was worth 130 florins, or $52, in January. It was quoted highest in May–June, at 145 florins, or $58, and at the end of the year it was again quoted at 130 florins, or $52, per 2,100 kilograms (about 4,620 pounds). Corn was generally high in price.

The prices of the principal cereals, compared with those of former years, were:

| Cereals. | Unit. | End of— | | | |
|---|---|---|---|---|---|
| | | 1902. | 1901. | 1900. | 1899. |
| Rye ......... | 2,100 kilos, 4,630 pounds ...................... | $54.00 | $54.00 | $54.00 | $56.00 |
| Wheat........ | 2,400 kilos, 5,290 pounds ..................... | 72.00 | 74.00 | 74.00 | 68.60 |
| Barley....... | 1,950 kilos, 4,298 pounds ..................... | 46.00 | 50.00 | 50.00 | 50.00 |
| Corn......... | 2,000 kilos, 4,400 pounds ..................... | 50.00 | 57.60 | 44.00 | 86.00 |
| Oats ......... | 100 kilos, 220 pounds......................... | 2.80 | 3.40 | 2.56 | 2.50 |

*Imports at Rotterdam.*

| Year. | Rye. | Wheat. | Barley. | Corn. | Oats. |
|---|---|---|---|---|---|
| | *Bushels.* | *Bushels.* | *Bushels.* | *Bushels.* | *Bushels.* |
| 1901......................................... | 17,082,076 | 41,816,486 | 10,836,247 | 11,824,056 | 16,429,712 |
| 1902......................................... | 18,287,754 | 40,151,948 | 12,869,204 | 10,945,218 | 18,736,928 |

*Supply at Rotterdam.*

| Date. | Rye. | Wheat. | Barley. | Corn. | Oats. |
|---|---|---|---|---|---|
| January 1— | *Bushels.* | *Bushels.* | *Bushels.* | *Bushels.* | *Bushels.* |
| 1902....................................... | 161,880 | 230,040 | 102,240 | 86,160 | 102,240 |
| 1903....................................... | 170,400 | 110,760 | 170,400 | 68,160 | 68,900 |

## PETROLEUM.

The consumption of petroleum in the Netherlands amounted to about 1,130,000 barrels in 1902, against 1,127,000 in 1901. (The average weight of a barrel is 150 kilograms, or 330 pounds.) At Rotterdam, 1,955,000 barrels were imported in 1902, against 2,205,000 in 1901. At Amsterdam 1,037,000 barrels and 818,000 barrels, respectively, were imported.

## COFFEE.

The Netherlands Trading Company auctioned, in 1902, 112,780 bales and 812 cases. Other first-hand sales amounted to 335,777 bales and 1,784 cases. The totals were:

| Year. | Bales. | Cases. | Year. | Bales. | Cases. |
|---|---|---|---|---|---|
| 1902 | 448,557 | 2,560 | 1898 | 469,327 | 1,887 |
| 1901 | 419,520 | 2,593 | 1897 | 560,902 | 2,408 |
| 1900 | 447,191 | 1,249 | 1896 | 523,693 | 3,406 |
| 1899 | 578,000 | 1,395 | | | |

The sales of Santos and African coffees are not included in the above. As during the two preceding years, only six auctions were held, the imports of Java coffee being too small for nine, the regular number. The choice of varieties aided prices, which were satisfactory.

The aggregate of importations of all the kinds of coffee handled in the Netherlands was again very large in 1902. The Netherlands Trading Company imported 21,900 bales more than in the year before, while private parties imported 153,700 bales more from Java and Padang, but 11,000 bales less from Celebes. The imports of African coffee decreased 7,900 bales, but those of Santos coffee increased 85,900 bales, while the number of bales of Central American coffee imported in 1902 exceeded the number imported in 1901 by 3,300 bales. Still, the consumption of Central American coffee is not increasing, as the cheaper Santos coffee has the preference.

The production of Liberian coffee on the island of Java is growing. There arrived from Java in Netherlands ports 114,300 bales of Liberian coffee in 1902, against 108,000 in 1901, 110,700 in 1900, 96,300 in 1899, and 37,300 in 1898.

The total imports by private parties in the Netherlands of all kinds of coffee amounted to 1,814,300 bales in 1902, 1,593,700 bales in 1901, 1,431,800 bales in 1900, 1,466,000 bales in 1899, 1,240,000 bales in 1898, 1,184,000 bales in 1897, and 978,000 bales in 1896.

Coffee quotations had a downward tendency the whole year, especially those of Santos, owing to the abundant supply. The market closed the year at the lowest point. Java coffee prices fluctuated quite independently of other coffee quotations; there was a fall in June, which was made up for again by a rise in September, but since then prices have receded, especially quotations for Java, West Indian preparation, which retrograded strongly at the end of the year. Prices for African coffee varied but little.

H. Doc. 305, pt 2——61

Quotations were, per one-half kilogram (1.1 pounds):

| For— | Jan. 1. | May. | June. | Sept. | Dec. 30. |
|---|---|---|---|---|---|
| Java: | | | | | |
| Good ordinary | $0.152 | $0.136 | $0.128 | $0. | $0.122 |
| Pale | .16 | .152 | .148 | .1 .. | .146 |
| West Indian preparation, colored | .158 | .128 | .128 | .13 . | .12 |
| Liberian | .106 | .09 | .084 | .088 | .084 |
| Santos | .092 | .07 | .076 | .08 | .07 |
| Africa | .08 | .066 | .062 | .07 | .062 |

The prospects for the coffee trade in 1903 are not bright. The world's supply has greatly augmented, and should it be further increased by a large Brazilian crop, quotations can hardly be expected to rise. The advance in the consumption of coffee by no means keeps pace with the annually growing production, especially of Brazil.

*Imports into the Netherlands.*

| Kind. | Private parties. | | Netherlands Trading Co. | | | |
|---|---|---|---|---|---|---|
| | 1902. | 1901. | 1902. | | 1901. | |
| | *Bales.* | *Bales.* | *Bales.* | *Cases.* | *Bales.* | *Cases.* |
| Java | 411,600 | 258,700 | 124,800 | 14 | 102,200 | ..... |
| Padang | 14,800 | 14,000 | 400 | 491 | 100 | 871 |
| Macassar | 7,100 | 21,000 | 500 | | 1,500 | ..... |
| Menado | 5,600 | 2,800 | | | | |
| Africa | 47,800 | 55,700 | | | | |
| Divers East Indian coffees | | 100 | | | | |
| Santos | 1,285,900 | 1,200,000 | | | | |
| Venezuela | 2,000 | 5,200 | | | | |
| Divers Central American coffees | 39,500 | 36,200 | | | | |
| Total | 1,814,300 | 1,593,700 | 125,700 | 505 | 103,800 | 871 |

*Deliveries.*

| To— | 1902. | | 1901. | |
|---|---|---|---|---|
| | Bales. | Cases. | Bales. | Cases. |
| Netherlands Trading Co | 121,101 | 925 | 132,064 | 474 |
| Private parties | 1,551,500 | 1,748 | 1,474,100 | 2,011 |
| Total | 1,672,601 | 2,673 | 1,606,164 | 2,485 |

*Supply on January 1, 1903.*

| Kind. | Private parties. | Netherlands Trading Co. |
|---|---|---|
| | *Bales.* | *Bales.* |
| Java | 89,300 | 54,000 |
| Padang | 3,800 | ........ |
| Macassar | 8,900 | ........ |
| Menado | 4,100 | 2,100 |
| Africa | 9,600 | ........ |
| Santos | 901,100 | ........ |
| Divers Central American coffees | 1,000 | ........ |
| Total | 1,017,800 | 56,500 |

*Transactions on the terminal market.*

| At— | Kind. | 1902. | 1901. | 1900. |
|---|---|---|---|---|
| | | *Bales.* | *Bales.* | *Bales.* |
| Amsterdam | Santos | 1,892,000 | 1,431,000 | 884,700 |
| Do | Java | 3,000 | 2,000 | |
| Rotterdam | Santos | 1,517,500 | 1,400,000 | 1,112,500 |
| Total | | 3,412,500 | 2,833,000 | 1,997,200 |

The terminal market was livelier than in 1901, although the fluctuations were of less importance.

Owing to lack of interest, the terminal market for Java coffee has been abolished.

## TOBACCO.

Though 1902 has turned out a little better for the tobacco merchants than was expected, results have not been satisfactory, especially for those supplying the cigar manufacturers. The quality of the Sumatra crop was but medium; generally, the tobacco had not sufficiently ripened, and quality and colors often left much to be desired, as of late years bright and gray colors were mostly in demand, while there was no interest in speckled tobacco.

American buyers did not, as they usually do, pay the highest prices; the color varieties bought by Hamburg merchants, which are mostly found in lots of sand leaf, were often better paid for. Still they bought regularly at prices considerably lower than some years ago.

For the tobacco from most of the Sumatra tobacco districts less was realized than in 1902, as shown below:

*Price per one-half kilogram or 1.1 pounds.*

| Varieties. | 1902. | 1901. |
|---|---|---|
| Deli | $0.424 | $0.52 |
| Langkat | .896 | .448 |
| Serdang | .82 | .38 |
| Bedagel | .248 | .272 |
| Batoebahra | .272 | .324 |
| Pagoerawan | .24 | .256 |

Only Padang tobacco brought more in 1902, viz, $0.316, against $0.288 in 1901; for Asahan tobacco the figures are unknown.

The Java tobacco in the market was not of a very satisfactory quality, and results of the sales were far from favorable for the planters. The arrivals being very large, the inscriptions grew in proportion and followed closely upon one another. This had a bad effect upon prices, which receded to abnormally low figures. In the fall, however, they improved a little.

The quantity of British Borneo tobacco on the market was about the same as in 1901, viz, 14,000 bales; the average price—$0.394—realized per one-half kilogram (1.1 pounds) was, however, $0.056 more. This high average must be attributed to the excellent quality and desirable colors produced by one company; 1,348 bales of its tobacco brought $1.156 per one-half kilogram.

The imports of Dutch Borneo tobacco amounted to only 2,772 bales. The average price obtained was a few cents less than in 1901, which is due to the abundant supply of Sumatra tobacco in the market at low prices and to the fact that the quality has not been very good of late years.

The total arrivals and sales of tobacco in the Netherlands in 1902 were:

| Kinds. | Unit. | Arrivals. | Sales. |
|---|---|---|---|
| | | *Bales.* | *Bales.* |
| Java | Bales | 287,371 | 302,786 |
| Sumatra | ....do | 224,270 | 224,270 |
| Borneo | ....do | 17,060 | 17,060 |
| Habana | Mats | 893 | 1,370 |
| Mexico | Bales | 271 | 271 |
| Grecian and Turkish | ....do | 13,987 | 14,860 |
| Paraguay | ....do | 1,335 | 1,335 |
| Seed leaf and cuttings | Cases | 3,307 | 3,271 |
| Virginia, Kentucky, and Mason County | Hogsheads | 2,145 | 2,081 |
| Maryland | ....do | 10,452 | 10,551 |

The amount realized was, per one-half kilogram (1.1 pounds):

| Kind. | Quantity. | Average price. | Total. |
|---|---|---|---|
| | *Bales.* | | |
| Sumatra | 227,511 | $0.376 | $13,000,000 |
| Java | 305,576 | .108 | 5,656,000 |
| British Borneo | 14,288 | .394 | 860,000 |
| Dutch Borneo | 2,772 | .16 | 67,200 |

## SUGAR.

The sugar market opened at very low prices, and, owing to the large surplus stock on the various markets, brought about by the gigantic beet-root crops of the last few years, and the chances for a still further increase of the production, remained depressed.

Toward the last of June, quotations had reached the lowest point. Beet-root sugar 88° was then disposed of at 7.25 florins, or $2.90 per 100 kilograms (220 pounds).

The cold and rainy summer made the prospects for the beet-root crop less favorable than in other years, notwithstanding that the very large stock of sugar on hand somewhat ameliorated prices.

After the commencement of the sugar-manufacturing season, crop reports still remained unfavorable. The early frosts also caused some damage to the crops, at least in the Netherlands and some parts of Germany, for not only was the transportation to the factories delayed, but in many places the beets had not been taken out of the ground. Owing to this, the manufacturing season, which started late, ended earlier than usual; some factories stopped in November, others in December. Prices now rose from 7.25 florins, or $2.90, to 10 florins, or $4, and closed the year at 9.75 florins, or $3.90, per 100 kilograms (220 pounds), against 8.125 florins, or $3.25, in 1901 and 10.875 florins, or $4.35, in 1900.

According to late reports, the stock of beet-root sugar was larger at the end of 1902 than at the end of former years, and a decrease of this stock can only be expected in case it should appear that the quantity of sugar manufactured in December, 1902, and January of this year, is materially less than formerly in the same months. Nothing can, as vet, be stated with certainty as to whether or not the cultivation of beet roots will be limited to some extent this year.

The imports of beet-root sugar into the Netherlands from Belgium and Germany were considerably larger than in 1901, but the exports of refined sugar were less. England was about the only country buying Dutch refined sugar.

A sugar terminal market, on the same basis as the market for coffee, spices, and currents, was established in the Netherlands in 1902. This market is equal in every respect to the other European terminal markets.

In London, the average price for beet-root sugar 88° and Java sugar No. 14 for the last eight years was:

| Years. | Beet-root. | | Java. | |
|---|---|---|---|---|
| | British currency. | American currency. | British currency. | American currency. |
| | *s.* *d.* | | *s.* *d.* | |
| 1902 | 6   8 | $1.62 | 8   0 | $1.94 |
| 1901 | 8   7 | 2.08 | 11   3 | 2.73 |
| 1900 | 10   7 | 2.57 | 13   6 | 3.28 |
| 1899 | 10   0 | 2.43 | 12   1 | 2.94 |
| 1898 | 9   7 | 2.33 | 11   6 | 2.79 |
| 1897 | 8   9 | 2.13 | 10   10 | 2.63 |
| 1896 | 10   6 | 2.55 | 12   7 | 3.06 |
| 1895 | 9   9 | 2.37 | 11   9 | 2.85 |

The controllable supply of sugar was larger than the year before, as the following will indicate:

| Month. | 1902. | 1901. |
|---|---|---|
| | *Tons.* | *Tons.* |
| January | 3,133,000 | 2,613,000 |
| February | 3,760,000 | 2,919,000 |
| March | | |
| April | | 2,956,000 |
| May | 3,445,000 | 2,553,000 |
| June | 3,211,000 | 2,248,000 |
| July | 2,931,000 | 1,962,000 |
| August | 2,636,000 | 1,573,000 |
| September | 2,354,000 | 1,278,000 |
| October | 1,895,000 | 937,000 |
| November | 1,421,000 | 734,000 |
| December | 2,198,000 | 1,825,000 |

The production of the 1902–3 sugar crop is estimated at 5,620,000 tons of beet-root and 3,555,000 tons of cane sugar, making a total of 9,175,000 tons.

### PAINT STUFFS.

*Indigo.*—In the beginning of 1902, the markets for Java as well as for Bengal indigo were affected by the sluggish state of affairs at Calcutta. It was expected then that the demand for Bengal indigo would improve after the Calcutta auctions had started again. These expectations, however, were not realized; business remained very slow, in spite of the fact that the season's production was far below the estimates. Several planters consigned their brands to London, and the effect was for a long time felt on the continental markets.

The Netherlands market for Java indigo was very quiet during the first months of 1902. Prices receded, notwithstanding the very small stock, and purchasers bought no more than they actually needed. When, however, the manufacturing season at Samarang terminated (which occurred already in July, two months earlier than in 1900), and the size of the production and arrivals could be ascertained, purchasers seemed to regain confidence somewhat in the article. The very small estimates for the new Bengal crop contributed thereto, and the result was that during the last five months of the year the lots placed on the Netherlands market could be regularly disposed of at fixed and some-times even at enhanced prices.

For choice varieties, "Old process of manufacture" and "Warm process of manufacture," $1.20 to $1.28 was readily paid. Java indigo, old process of manufacture, is still generally preferred, but the demand for the indigo prepared according to the new "warm process of manufacture," when very fine and of a dark color, seems to increase. The price of this kind has lately receded a little, owing to large offers.

In the last few months, it has again been proven that although the consumption of "indigorine" (artificial indigo) is increasing, the demand for the natural indigo is still large enough to absorb the present production. Limitation thereof seems, therefore, not necessary at present.

The Java crop, which in 1901 produced 7,000 cases, produced in 1902 only 6,800 cases, while the estimate for 1903 is 6,700 cases. As the demand is regular, the supplies in the first and second hand have remained small, and it is expected that the present quotations will be maintained for some time.

The following table shows the imports, sales, and transit, and supplies of the article for the last ten years:

| Years. | Amsterdam. | | | Rotterdam. | | |
| --- | --- | --- | --- | --- | --- | --- |
| | Imports. | Sales and transit. | Supply Dec. 31. | Imports. | Sales and transit. | Supply Dec. 31. |
| | Cases. | Cases. | Cases. | Cases. | Cases. | Cases. |
| 1893 | 3,652 | 3,675 | 547 | 2,979 | 2,804 | 190 |
| 1894 | 2,862 | 2,647 | 762 | 2,077 | 1,879 | 388 |
| 1895 | 2,925 | 3,088 | 599 | 2,267 | 2,242 | 413 |
| 1896 | 3,895 | 2,824 | 1,170 | 2,589 | 1,688 | 1,314 |
| 1897 | 5,180 | 4,774 | 1,576 | 4,062 | 3,211 | 2,165 |
| 1898 | 5,659 | 4,997 | 2,238 | 3,936 | 3,494 | 2,607 |
| 1899 | 2,292 | 3,697 | 833 | 1,787 | 4,112 | 282 |
| 1900 | 1,688 | 2,069 | 452 | 2,181 | 1,499 | 964 |
| 1901 | 1,681 | 2,057 | 76 | 1,674 | 2,808 | 30 |
| 1902 | 1,407 | 1,447 | 36 | 1,625 | 1,520 | 162 |

*Resin.*—Sales were not large in 1902, and most of them covered resin "sailing" or "for future delivery." Lots stored here were readily sold, even in the fall, when prices rose somewhat. Type G, which during the first months of the year fluctuated in price between $1.06 and $1.10, was disposed of in summer at $1 and $1.02 per 50 kilograms (110 pounds) for future delivery. Since September, quotations have been slowly rising again, and at present resin is quoted at $1.14 for spot goods and $1.10 for type F. The American quotations for future delivery are, however, considerably higher.

Of the other types, D was mostly wanted, but very little of it was offered. Choice pale kinds were also more in demand than formerly, and enhanced prices were readily paid. The type WW is now quoted at $2.60 for 50 kilograms (110 pounds).

*Turpentine oil.*—The expectations for a steady market, mentioned in last year's report, were realized. The demand in 1902 was generally good. Prices gradually rose from $7.20 to $9.60 per 50 kilograms (110 pounds). Especially during the last months of the year good deals were closed. Larger offers, brought about by the arrival of two full cargoes, have not affected the market, which closed strongly with the following quotations: Spot goods, $9.60; delivery per sailing vessel or steamer, January–February, $9.90; April–May, $9.15.

*Madder.*—Sales were about equal to those of the last two years, but there was more demand for the inferior and reground than for the choice pale kinds. Quotations for the latter slowly fell, while the first enhanced in price, and there was eventually but little difference in the rates of the several varieties. The new crop appears to be small, which is partly due to the fact that the whole could not be dug on account of the early frosts. Pale varieties are quoted at $7.20 to $7.60 per 50 kilograms (110 pounds). The madder of former crops is nearly all sold, and the offers of reground kinds are getting smaller and smaller. Some lots are yet offered at $4.60 to $5 and at $6.60 to $6.90. "New Racine" has been sold for $6 to $6.20. and is now very scarce.

### RICE.

The Burma crop was the largest ever produced in that country. This, added to the fact that the cereal crops were good in Europe and America, might have had a depressing effect on the market, were it not that there was a constant demand for rice from the famine-stricken districts of British India, and that the crops of Japan, China, and the Indian Archipelago have been short or failed entirely.

During the first half of 1902, the market was generally quiet; quotations rose and fell, according to the demand for rice in British India (which is always felt in Europe by larger or smaller offers from Burma) or according to the reports spread with reference to the cereal crops in the field.

In the second half of August, the market became strong, in consequence of the great demand from Japan; sales of Burma rice then assumed such proportions that scarcely any unshelled rice was offered in the European markets. The unfavorable summer weather in Europe also tended to improve the market; the demand for shelled rice augmented, and very important sales were made for export at slowly rising prices.

The year closed with hardly any offers of Java, Japan, Siam, and Saigon rice. The first hand supply of Java rice is small, while no arrivals of Japan rice are expected in 1903. For Burma rice, the prices remained too high to result in important transactions. At present, $1.60 to $1.65 is asked for Basis Rangoon per 50 kilograms (110 pounds), while this rice in the beginning of 1901 was quoted at $1.55, and in the beginning of 1902 at $1.45.

The part of the coming Burma crop destined for exportation is estimated at 1,960,000 tons, while the estimate for last year was 2,200,000 tons, against 2,935,000 tons for 1900, 1,600,000 for 1899, and 1,900,000 for 1898.

The arrivals in the Netherlands of Burma rice were, 1902, 2,146,000; 1901, 1,814,000; 1900, 1,433,000; 1899, 1,967,000, and 1898, 1,737,000 bales.

The supply at the end of December was (in bales):

| Year. | Java ta-ble rice. | Java rice. | Total. |
|---|---|---|---|
| 1902 | 4,700 | 2,000 | 6,700 |
| 1901 | 11,000 | 33,500 | 44,500 |
| 1900 | 3,125 | 2,675 | 5,800 |
| 1899 | 8,300 | 1,700 | 10,000 |
| 1898 | 21,000 | 17,000 | 38,000 |

The run of prices per 50 kilograms (110 pounds) was:

| Year. | Java table. | | | White Java. | | | Rangoon and Bassein. | | | |
|---|---|---|---|---|---|---|---|---|---|---|
| 1902 | $3.60 | $3.20 | $3.60 | $3.10 | $2.80 | $3.00 | $1.55 | $1.40 | $1.65 | |
| 1901 | 3.10 | 3.80 | 3.70 | 2.60 | 3.50 | 3.30 | 1.60 | 1.50 | 1.65 | $1.55 |
| 1900 | 3.20 | 3.00 | 3.20 | 2.60 | 2.80 | 2.70 | 1.69 | 1.80 | 1.60 | 1.75 |
| 1899 | | 3.60 | 3.20 | 3.00 | 2.50 | 2.70 | 1.80 | 1.50 | 1.80 | |
| 1898 | | 3.80 | 3.60 | 3.10 | 3.50 | 2.90 | 1.30 | 2.00 | 1.80 | |

### SPICES.

*Nutmegs and mace.*—For the two first quarterly auctions there was very little interest, and only part of the goods for sale found purchasers; the lots not disposed of at the auctions were, however, privately sold.

Reports of short crops for this season and crop failures for the next, from Banda and the surrounding islands of the Straits, tended to improve the market. The September auctions were held with fair results; whatever was offered was disposed of at somewhat above the estimated value. Owing to an increasing demand from abroad, the trade augmented, and several lots of nutmegs and mace changed hands at from $0.02 to $0.04 more per half kilogram (1.1 pounds) than had been paid for them in the auctions, something which had not happened for years.

The auctions in December were very lively; purchasers were very willing to pay enhanced prices, and both nutmegs and mace brought from $0.06 to $0.08 more than in the preceding auctions. The nutmegs Nos. 3 and 4 and the so-called "by-kinds," both of nutmegs and mace, generally sold well and also brought more than taxation prices. The coarse Banda nutmegs, of which there are from 80 to 90 to the half kilogram, were quoted the main part of the year at about $0.36, but toward the last they rose to $0.42 per half kilogram. Nutmegs, 110 to 120 to the half kilogram, rose from $0.208 to $0.288, while those of 140 to 150 to the half kilogram rose from $0.152 to $0.192 per half kilogram (1.1 pounds).

*Cloves.*—During almost the whole of the year 1902 there was very little demand for cloves; but lately more interest has been taken in the article, owing to the unfavorable crop reports. In January, cloves were quoted at $0.128; in the following months at $0.116 to $0.12, and of late at $0.128 to $0.132 per half kilogram.

*Pepper.*—White Java: Sixteen hundred bales arrived, 860 were sold, and the first-hand supply was 300 bales. Choice qualities were first quoted at $0.24 to $0.26; subsequently, when there were more offers, at $0.22 to $0.24. Second quality brought from $0.20 to $0.22 per half kilogram (1.1 pounds).

Black Java: Arrivals amounted to 6,300 bales, among which were several lots of excellent quality, which brought from $0.126 to $0.1375 per half kilogram.

Black Lampong: Few spot goods came to the consumption market. The arrivals were either for transit or for the terminal markets. Variations in prices were from $0.016 to $0.02. The year closed with $0.1195.

The total arrivals of pepper in the Netherlands amounted to 40,000 bales, against 36,000 bales in 1901, 30,000 bales in 1900, 33,000 bales in 1899, and 43,000 bales in 1898.

The supply of white and black pepper in London is at present 2,300 tons, against 4,000 tons in 1901, 6,000 tons in 1900, 7,500 tons in 1899, and 9,800 tons in 1898.

The Lampong pepper crop is estimated at about 80,000 bales, against 60,000 bales in 1901 and 1900.

The terminal transactions in pepper amounted to the following:

| Year. | Rotterdam. | Amsterdam. | Year. | Rotterdam. | Amsterdam. |
|---|---|---|---|---|---|
| | *Bales.* | *Bales.* | | *Bales.* | *Bales.* |
| 1902................ | 236,200 | 116,600 | 1899 ................ | 395,000 | 271,000 |
| 1901................ | 207,200 | 107,600 | 1898 ................ | 422,000 | 317,000 |
| 1900................ | 342,000 | 238,000 | | | |

*Imports and first-hand sales and supplies of spices.*

IMPORTS.

| | 1902. | 1901. | 1900. | 1899. | 1898. |
|---|---|---|---|---|---|
| Nutmegs.........................tons.. | 915 | 1,058 | 858 | 828 | 775 |
| Mace.........................do.... | 232 | 295 | 210 | 190 | 226 |
| Amboina cloves.........................bales.. | 2,300 | 275 | .......... | 40 | 2,800 |
| Pepper.........................do.... | 40,000 | 36,000 | 30,000 | 33,000 | 43,000 |

FIRST-HAND SALES.

| | 1902. | 1901. | 1900. | 1899. | 1898. |
|---|---|---|---|---|---|
| Nutmegs.........................packages.. | 13,000 | 19,000 | 10,900 | 13,700 | 13,800 |
| Mace.........................do.... | 4,000 | 5,300 | 4,650 | 4,000 | 4,500 |

FIRST-HAND SUPPLY.

| | 1902. | 1901. | 1900. | 1899. | 1898. |
|---|---|---|---|---|---|
| Nutmegs.........................tons.. | 83 | 160 | 365 | 174 | 282 |
| Mace.........................do.... | 43 | 39 | 25 | 46 | 45 |
| Amboina cloves.........................bales.. | .......... | .......... | 100 | 700 | 740 |
| Pepper.........................do.... | 1,400 | 1,100 | 2,000 | 6,000 | 5,300 |

The supply in bonded warehouses in Rotterdam and Amsterdam was:

| Article. | 1902. | 1901. | 1900. | 1899. | 1898. |
|---|---|---|---|---|---|
| | *Tons.* | *Tons.* | *Tons.* | *Tons.* | *Tons.* |
| Nutmegs ................ | 1,311 | 1,249 | 1,348 | 1,332 | 1,446 |
| Mace ................ | 175 | 181 | 230 | 258 | 533 |
| Cloves ................ | 3,145 | 4,087 | 4,983 | 4,748 | 2,937 |
| Pepper ................ | 2,412 | 2,685 | 3,807 | 5,125 | 5,181 |

## CINCHONA BARK.

Good prices were maintained during the first half of the year. The first auction, which was held in January, opened with an average price of $0.0298 per unit, while the average price in the last auction of 1901 was $0.0306; but in the three succeeding auctions it rose to an average unit price of $0.0346. (The "unit" is the 5 grams of sulphate of quinine contained in the bark.)

Owing to the large arrivals from Java, the unit fell in the June auction to $0.029 and in the July auction to $0.024. The very large August arrivals (1,857,000 pounds) caused the unit to recede to $0.0196. The moderate exports of September caused it to rise again to $0.0272 in October, but with the large offers in the November auction it receded to $0.0242, and closed the year in the December auction at $0.025.

In 1902, 4,409 packages arrived from the Government crop and 73,394 packages from the pri ate crop.

The total sales amounted in 1902 to 74,730 packages (71,269 bales and 3,461 cases), or about 14,305,394 pounds, containing, according to published analysis, 705,021 pounds of sulphate of quinine, while the figures for former years are:

| Year. | Cinchona bark. | Sulphate of quinine. | Year. | Cinchona bark. | Sulphate of quinine. |
|---|---|---|---|---|---|
| | Pounds. | Pounds. | | Pounds. | Pounds. |
| 1901 | 14,517,500 | 718,314 | 1898 | 11,648,696 | 571,545 |
| 1900 | 11,523,010 | 549,296 | 1897 | 10,669,426 | 580,000 |
| 1899 | 12,237,245 | 599,645 | 1896 | 10,729,800 | 579,526 |

The average unit price realized for cinchona bark was, in 1902, $0.0278 per half kilogram, against $0.03312 in 1901, $0.04 in 1900, $0.0284 in 1899, $0.01944 in 1898, $0.0186 in 1897, and $0.0172 in 1896.

The following quantities of the several kinds of cinchona bark were sold at the auctions:

| Description. | Cinchona bark. | Sulphate of quinine. |
|---|---|---|
| GOVERNMENT CROP. | Pounds. | Pounds. |
| Ledgeriana | 662,598 | |
| Officinalis | 23,228 | 45,120 |
| Schuhkraft | 6,631 | |
| Succirubra | 126,878 | 3,362 |
| Total | 819,335 | 48,482 |
| PRIVATE CROP. | | |
| Ledgeriana | 9,351,236 | |
| Hebrides | 1,361,661 | |
| Officinalis | 57,090 | 580,637 |
| Calisaya | 25,311 | |
| Succirubra | 2,454,450 | 63,428 |
| Total | 13,249,748 | 644,065 |

The cinchona bark shipments from Java were:

| December 1 to November 30— | Pounds. |
|---|---|
| 1901–1902 | 14,660,800 |
| 1900–1901 | 13,858,900 |
| 1899–1900 | 11,336,600 |
| 1898–99 | 12,981,980 |

The first-hand supply in the Netherlands on December 31, 1902, was: Government crop, 2,748 packages; private crop, 10,352 packages.

*Sulphate of quinine.*—The prices asked in 1902 by the Amsterdam quinine factory rose from $9.80 and $11.80 to $10.80 and $12.80, then receded to $8.40 and $10.20, and are now again $11.20 and $9.40 per kilogram (2.2 pounds).

### COCOA.

The year 1902 did not bring the favorable results that were expected. Large arrivals, especially from the West Indies, made importers very willing to sell, and important quantities were purchased for consumption. British manufacturers, it is claimed, feared that the British Government would increase the import duties on cocoa, and were anxious to purchase. The British tariff was, however, not raised, and on account thereof the visible supply was much larger than in the same period of former years.

Prices remained steady in the beginning, except for Trinidad cocoa, which receded until they had reached the level of other cocoa prices. Then more interest was felt for this quality. Owing to the late arrival of the summer Ariba crop, the European supplies of Guayaquil cocoa found buyers at fixed prices, whereby most of the other kinds profited, because of the regular demand for consumption. Though the shipments from Guayaquil increased, the prices were maintained with small fluctuations during the rest of the year. Ceylon cocoa was continually in demand and rose steadily in price. Toward the end of the year the demand for this kind, however, became quieter.

In 1903, periodical auctions will be held on January 28, March 11, April 22, June 10, July 29, September 9, October 21, and December 2.

Arrivals from Java were, in 1902, about 11,000 bales; 1901, 22,100; 1900, 19,200; 1899, 16,850; 1898, 16,500, and 1897, 13,800 bales.

The aggregate of the importations of Surinam cocoa into the Netherlands was very small, as the United States imported considerable direct from that colony.

Cocoa quotations remained nearly unchanged the whole of the year, and are at present about $0.152 per half kilogram (1.1 pounds).

There were auctioned at Amsterdam:

| Year. | Java cocoa. | Surinam cocoa. | Other kinds. | Total. |
|---|---|---|---|---|
| | *Bales.a* | *Bales.b* | *Bales.* | *Bales.* |
| 1902 | 13,144 | 617 | .......... | 13,761 |
| 1901 | 19,938 | 635 | 290 | 20,863 |
| 1900 | 18,661 | 744 | 210 | 19,615 |
| 1899 | 16,353 | 1,227 | 205 | 17,785 |

a Bales of 50 kilograms (110 pounds).      b Bales of 80 to 100 kilograms (194 to 220 pounds).

### KAPOK.

At Rotterdam, there were imported. in 1902, 6,693 bales of cleaned kapok, and at Amsterdam 37,870 bales of cleaned, 353 bales of half cleaned, and 635 bales of uncleaned kapok. The sales at Rotterdam amounted to 6,418 bales of cleaned, and at Amsterdam to 43,861 cleaned, 253 half-cleaned, and 635 bales of uncleaned kapok. The supply on December 31 consisted of 425 bales of cleaned kapok at Rotterdam and 9,272 bales of cleaned and 100 bales of half cleaned at Amsterdam.

*Quotations January 15, 1903, per half kilogram.*

East Indian:

Extra cleaned..................................................... $0.128 to $0.132
Prime cleaned ....................................................  .12 to  .128
Cleaned ..........................................................  .10 to  .12
Half cleaned......................................................  .072 to  .08
Uncleaned.........................................................  .04 to  .044

The importations at Rotterdam and Amsterdam amounted to:

| | Bales. | | Bales. |
|---|---|---|---|
| 1893 | 16,806 | 1898 | 32,503 |
| 1894 | 18,450 | 1899 | 37,150 |
| 1895 | 21,530 | 1900 | 41,163 |
| 1896 | 32,381 | 1901 | 47,482 |
| 1897 | 24,746 | 1902 | 45,551 |

## TEA.

*Java.*—There were delivered to importers at Amsterdam, in 1902, 87,268 cases, against 85,249 in 1901, 73,667 in 1900, 69,261 in 1899, and 70,572 cases in 1898.

The sales by 10 auctions at Amsterdam were:

| Year. | Full cases. | Half cases. | Sixteenth cases. | Year. | Full cases. | Half cases. | Sixteenth cases. |
|---|---|---|---|---|---|---|---|
| 1902 | 87,196 | 781 | 1,921 | 1899 | 66,341 | 1,187 | 1,792 |
| 1901 | 91,241 | 836 | 721 | 1898 | 65,485 | 2,056 | 3,308 |
| 1900 | 76,896 | 706 | 1,499 | | | | |

From the tea in the December auction only 95 full cases and 20 sixteenth cases of flowery pekoe remained unsold.

Imports of white pointed varieties were large and the prices remained low during the whole year. Only in the last auctions was some improvement perceived, and the surplus 1901 supply, which had all the year tended to depress prices, could be disposed of.

For ordinary and medium kinds of leaves and dust, good prices were paid in January–March. From April to June the market receded, and became livelier only in November. In December, many kinds could again be quoted at the old figures.

For the better brands, which were not always of a good quality, the demand was slack in March, but since August the tendency has improved. Many plantations shipped better products at the end of the year; some of the lots were marked superior.

*Consumption of the Netherlands for the last five years.*

| | Full cases. |
|---|---|
| 1902 | 46,411 |
| 1901 | 46,424 |
| 1900 | 41,618 |
| 1899 | 35,703 |
| 1898 | 35,642 |

*Exports of Java tea from the Netherlands.*

| | Full cases. |
|---|---|
| 1902 | 40,857 |
| 1901 | 38,825 |
| 1900 | 32,049 |
| 1899 | 33,558 |
| 1898 | 34,930 |

*China.*—At Rotterdam, 875 cases were on the market. First-hand offers for sale at Amsterdam amounted to only 357 half cases and 500 sixteenth cases, against 4,500 half cases in 1902.

There were no British India or Ceylon teas on the Netherlands markets.

### INDIA RUBBER AND GUTTA PERCHA.

*Statistics of india rubber, balata, and gutta-percha during 1902.*

#### RUBBER.

| Description. | Total arrivals. | Stock Jan. 1, 1908. |
|---|---|---|
| | *Pounds.* | *Pounds.* |
| Thimbles red | 850,900 | .......... |
| Kongo balls | 31,680 | .......... |
| Kassai red | 802,340 | .......... |
| Kassai black | 69,300 | .......... |
| Upper Kongo | 725,230 | .......... |
| Sierra Leone | 39,600 | .......... |
| Mozambique | 60,280 | .......... |
| Java and Sumatra | 64,240 | 11,880 |
| Sudan | 25,410 | .......... |
| Sundries | 82,560 | 5,940 |
| Total | 2,201,540 | 17,820 |

#### BALATA.

| | | |
|---|---|---|
| Surinam sheet | 537,900 | .......... |
| Venezuela block | 67,540 | 4,400 |
| Total | 605,440 | 4,400 |

#### GUTTA-PERCHA.

| | Tons. |
|---|---|
| Stock, January 1, 1902 | 263 |
| Arrivals | 267 |
| Total | 530 |
| Sales | 312 |
| Stock, January 1, 1908 | 218 |

### HIDES AND SKINS.

The following information is gleaned from the annual circular of the Hide, Skin and Leather Company "Koelit," formerly Brummer & Co.:

In 1902, the tendency of the market was to gradual improvement in prices. This was not favorable to all concerns interested in the article. There were numerous heavy failures both of tanners and shoe manufacturers. Holders of a good supply profited, of course, but the manufacturers were generally in a disadvantageous position, as the prices of finished leather did not rise with those of hides and skins. The ruling conviction as to a scarcity of raw material in the leading hide and skin markets of the world at the end of the year, and the heavy wants of the tanners, would indicate that the end of the upward course has not yet been reached.

The imports of Java ox and cow hides were 356,149 pieces, against 321,559 in 1901. Owing to the high prices of Calcutta hides, the Java hides were largely used as a substitute.

The strong demand for Java buffalo hides is to be attributed to the extension of chrome tanning in 1902. It is thought that this hide is well adapted for chrome leather. The demand for best transparent quality is still increasing. A good market for sole leather has lately developed. Importations were 232,196, against 276,412 hides in 1901.

East Indian and Straits buffalo hides improved in price with other kinds.

The manufacturers could not raise the price of buffalo bends in proportion to the higher rate they had to pay for the raw material. As is usual in this trade, many had heavy contracts running, while others would have lost customers by raising prices. Endeavors to bring about a combination of the British and continental manufacturers to improve conditions failed entirely, through the discord between the parties concerned.

The imports of East Indian ox and cow hides were 11,700, against 14,300 in 1901.

The quality of Venezuela hides retrograded, and the import trade was neglected. The good hides seem to be exported directly to the United States. The imports were 3,218 pieces, against 6,092 in 1901.

The direct steamship service between Amsterdam and Buenos Ayres did all it could to bring Buenos Ayres hides and skins on the Netherlands markets, but there was little interest in them. The imports were 4,850 hides, against 5,300 in 1901.

Imports of Java horse hides amounted to 376 pieces; those of Java goatskins were 223,000 skins less than in the year before. This is principally due to the large direct shipments from Java to the United States.

There is a regular trade in lizard skins, but prices can not reach the level of some years ago. The imports were 87,000, against 59,700 in 1901; sales amounted to 95,000, against 65,000 in 1901. There is good demand for well-designed and well-measured skins.

*Imports, by years, of hides and skins in the Netherlands.*

| Years. | Hides. | Skins. | Years. | Hides. | Skins. |
|---|---|---|---|---|---|
| | *Pieces.* | *Pieces.* | | *Pieces.* | *Pieces.* |
| 1895 | 491,200 | 619,500 | 1899 | 649,300 | 849,900 |
| 1896 | 526,800 | 665,800 | 1900 | 631,400 | 879,400 |
| 1897 | 549,400 | 710,000 | 1901 | 707,700 | 858,500 |
| 1898 | 545,200 | 772,500 | 1902 | 692,000 | 668,700 |

*Description of imports.*

| Description. | 1899. | 1900. | 1901. | 1902. |
|---|---|---|---|---|
| | *Pieces.* | *Pieces.* | *Pieces.* | *Pieces.* |
| Dry Java and Sumatra ox and cow hides | 324,112 | 299,214 | 321,559 | 356,119 |
| Dry Java Buffalo hides | 263,751 | 237,914 | 276,412 | 232,196 |
| Dry East Indian: | | | | |
| Ox and cow hides | 3,839 | 27,598 | 14,300 | 11,700 |
| Buffalo hides | 46,003 | 47,998 | 65,669 | 73,230 |
| Buenos Aires hides: | | | | |
| Dry | 1,168 | | 4,300 | 2,350 |
| Salted | 2,301 | 2,000 | 1,000 | 2,500 |
| Chinese hides | | | 12,300 | 6,200 |
| Australian hides | | | 4,500 | 2,300 |
| African hides | 1,224 | 1,598 | 788 | 1,755 |
| Venezuela and West Indian hides | 5,586 | 10,243 | 6,092 | 3,218 |
| Java horsehides | 1,266 | 966 | 820 | 376 |
| Java goatskins, about | 737,700 | 739,000 | 706,000 | 483,000 |
| Java bastard skins, goat, about | 7,500 | 24,500 | 51,500 | 46,000 |
| Arabian goat and sheep skins, about | 4,200 | 3,400 | 3,100 | } 4,300 |
| Cape goat and sheep skins, about | 16,500 | 2,700 | 2,300 | |
| Goatskins of other countries, about | 23,600 | 19,600 | 14,600 | 16,800 |
| Java lizard and snake skins, about | 55,200 | 64,400 | 59,700 | 87,000 |
| Java deerskins, about | 5,600 | 25,800 | 18,700 | 31,600 |
| Buffalo horns, about | 35,000 | 32,000 | 34,000 | 26,000 |
| Italian salted horsehides, about | | 3,876 | 2,575 | |

*Stock in the Netherlands.*

| Description. | January 1— | | | |
|---|---|---|---|---|
| | 1900. | 1901. | 1902. | 1903. |
| | *Pieces.* | *Pieces.* | *Pieces.* | *Pieces.* |
| Dry Java, Atjih, and Sumatra ox and cow hides | 13,268 | 23,458 | 54,925 | 23,694 |
| Dry Java buffalo hides | 17,980 | 10,866 | 20,663 | 9,030 |
| Dry East India ox and cow hides | 1,525 | 1,315 | 8,200 | 4,100 |
| Dry Singapore buffalo hides | 6,210 | 5,806 | 7,800 | 1,200 |
| Dry Buenos Aires hides | 938 | 300 | 1,617 | |
| China hides | | | 3,500 | 430 |
| Australian hides | | | 500 | 280 |
| African hides | | 116 | | |
| Venezuela and Surinam hides | 541 | 758 | 47 | |
| Java horsehides | 850 | 130 | 345 | 32 |
| Java goatskins | 42,500 | 19,150 | 153,000 | 24,500 |
| Java bastard goatskins | 1,120 | | 21,000 | 9,000 |
| Java deerskins | 1,140 | 160 | 2,900 | 2,400 |
| Arabian goat and sheep skins | 5,100 | 4,200 | 600 | } 8,200 |
| Goatskins of other countries | 25,400 | 20,300 | 12,000 | |
| Java lizard and snake skins | 35,000 | 36,400 | 27,000 | 9,200 |
| Buffalo horns | 15,000 | 7,200 | 15,000 | 4,000 |

*Salted Dutch hides and skins.*

|  | 1896. | 1897. | 1898. | 1899. | 1900. | 1901. |
|---|---|---|---|---|---|---|
| *Slaughter for home use.* |  |  |  |  |  |  |
| Cows, oxen, and bulls ....... | 221,181 | 268,386 | 282,994 | 300,000 | 270,000 | 287,076 |
| Calves ..................... | 131,540 | 225,021 | 146,755 | 150,000 | 205,000 | 210,624 |
| *Slaughter for export.* |  |  |  |  |  |  |
| Cows, oxen, and bulls ....... | 120,192 | 65,496 | 100/120,000 | 100/120,000 | 30/40,000 | 24,225 |
| Calves ..................... | 21,281 | 190,485 | 200/250,000 | 200/250,000 | 250/260,000 | 25/68/ |

*Quotations for hides and skins on January 1, per one-half kilogram (1.1 pounds).*

| Description. | Weight. | | 1901. | | 1902. | | 1908. | |
|---|---|---|---|---|---|---|---|---|
| *Java ox and cow hides.* | *Kilos.* | | | | | | | |
| Batavia ........................ | 7 to | 9 | $0.232 to $0.24 | | $0.20 to $0.208 | | $0.22 to $0.228 | |
| Samarang: | | | | | | | | |
| Shaved ..................... | 2 | 3 | .304 | .312 | .272 | .28 | .30 | .304 |
| Do ..................... | 4 | 5 | .28 | .288 | .256 | .264 | .28 | .288 |
| Do ..................... | 5 | 7 | .26 | .268 | .216 | .224 | .232 | .24 |
| Unshaved ................... | 5 | 7 | .212 | .22 | .18 | .188 | .20 | .208 |
| Soerabaya ..................... | 2 | 4 | .30 | .308 | .272 | .28 | .30 | .308 |
| Do ..................... | 5 | 7 | .252 | .26 | .212 | .22 | .24 | .248 |
| Tjilatjap ...................... | 3 | 6 | .24 | .248 | .20 | .208 | .232 | .24 |
| Padang: | | | | | | | | |
| Ox and cow hides............... | 3 | 5 | .208 | .216 | .18 | .188 | .224 | .232 |
| Do ..................... | 5 | 7 | .20 | .22 | .168 | .188 | .192 | .212 |
| Macassar, ox and cow hides ..... | 5 | 9 | .18 | .20 | .14 | .16 | .18 | .20 |
| Singapore: | | | | | | | | |
| Best ....................... | 3 | 9 | .16 | .18 | .14 | .16 | .16 | .18 |
| Second ..................... | 3 | 9 | .12 | .14 | .108 | .128 | .128 | .148 |
| *Java buffalo hides.* | | | | | | | | |
| Batavia: | | | | | | | | |
| Best shaved.................... | 14 | 18 | .172 | .176 | .176 | .18 | .20 | .204 |
| Do ..................... | 9 | 14 | .18 | .184 | .18 | .184 | .201 | .208 |
| Do ..................... | 5 | 9 | .188 | .192 | .188 | .192 | .212 | .216 |
| Second shaved ................. | 7 | 18 | .144 | .148 | .148 | .152 | .176 | .18 |
| Unshaved ..................... | 8 | 13 | .128 | .132 | .128 | .132 | .152 | .156 |
| Samarang: | | | | | | | | |
| Best shaved.................... | 12 | 17 | .164 | .168 | .168 | .172 | .192 | .196 |
| Do ..................... | 9 | 12 | .18 | .184 | .18 | .184 | .204 | .208 |
| Do ..................... | 5 | 9 | .188 | .192 | .188 | .192 | .212 | .216 |
| Soerabaya: | | | | | | | | |
| Best shaved ................... | 8 | 15 | .16 | .18 | .16 | .18 | .188 | .208 |
| Second and unshaved ......... | 8 | 15 | .128 | .158 | .12 | .14 | .14 | .16 |
| Tjilatjap ...................... | 8 | 12 | .14 | .16 | .14 | .16 | .168 | .188 |
| Padang buffalo hides ............ | 8 | 12 | .12 | .14 | .10 | .12 | .12 | .14 |
| Macassar ..................... | 10 | 15 | .10 | .12 | .08 | .10 | .108 | .128 |
| Singapore: | | | | | | | | |
| Best ........................ | 10 | 15 | .108 | .128 | .108 | .128 | .132 | .152 |
| Second....................... | 10 | 15 | .08 | .10 | .08 | .10 | .10 | .12 |
| *Java.* | | | | | | | | |
| Horsehides.................... | 3 | 4 | .152 | .172 | .128 | .148 | .14 | .16 |
| Deerskins .................... | 1½ | 2¼ | .16 | .18 | .14 | .16 | .16 | .18 |
| Goatskins .................... | | | a.50 | .60 | a.48 | .56 | a.46 | .52 |
| Bastard sheepskins ............ | | | a.24 | .28 | a.20 | .24 | a.20 | .24 |
| Lizard and snake skins.......... | | | a.20 | .40 | a.20 | .40 | a.18 | .24 |
| *Salted Dutch hides and skins.* | | | | | | | | |
| Cowhides: | | | | | | | | |
| Vachets..................... | 28 to 30 | | .10 | .104 | .096 | .10 | .104 | .108 |
| Town slaughtered ............ | 30 | 32 | .096 | .10 | .088 | .092 | .096 | .10 |
| Do ..................... | 28 | 30 | .096 | .10 | .088 | .092 | .096 | .10 |
| Country slaughtered............. | 24 | 26 | .092 | .096 | .084 | .088 | .088 | .092 |
| Do ..................... | 16 | 18 | .096 | .104 | .088 | .092 | .088 | .092 |
| Oxhides: | | | | | | | | |
| Town slaughtered ............. | 33 | 35 | .092 | .094 | .10 | .104 | .104 | .108 |
| Do ..................... | 29 | 30 | .092 | .096 | .088 | .092 | .096 | .10 |
| Bull hides: | | | | | | | | |
| Town slaughtered ............ | 35 | 37 | .088 | .096 | .084 | .088 | .088 | .092 |
| Do ..................... | 32 | 33 | .084 | .088 | .08 | .084 | .084 | .088 |
| Veal skins ................... | 9 | 10 | .108 | .112 | .112 | .116 | .12 | .124 |
| Without shanks ............. | | 9 | .128 | .13 | .132 | .136 | .132 | .136 |
| Without heads and shanks ...... | | 8 | .148 | .152 | .148 | .152 | .16 | .164 |
| Calfskins..................... | 3½ | 4½ | .128 | .132 | .132 | .136 | .136 | .14 |
| Horsehides.................... | 22 | 30 | a4.00 | 4.40 | a4.00 | 4.40 | a4.00 | 4.40 |

a Per piece.

*Limed pickerbends.*

[Prices are per pound, delivered in England.]

| Description. | Average weight. | 1901. British currency. | 1901. American currency. | 1902. British currency. | 1902. American currency. | 1903. British currency. | 1903. American currency. |
|---|---|---|---|---|---|---|---|
| Batavia: | *Pounds.* | *d.* | | *d.* | | *d.* | |
| Prime transparent .. | 20 to 22 | 7¾ | $0.155 | 7½ | $0.15 | 10 | $0.20 |
| Do............... | 15 17 | 7¾ | .155 | 7½ | .15 | 10 | .20 |
| Do............... | 10 12 | 8 | .16 | 8 | .16 | 10 | .20 |
| Do............... | 6 7 | 8 | .16 | 8¼ | .165 | 10 | .20 |
| Java: | | | | | | | |
| Prime unshaved .... | 20 22 | 6¾ | .135 | 6½ | .13 | 8½ | .17 |
| Do............... | 15 17 | 6½ | .13 | 6¼ | .125 | 8½ | .17 |
| Do............... | 10 12 | 6½ | .13 | 6¼ | .125 | 8½ | .17 |
| Do............... | 6 7 | 6½ | .13 | 6¼ | .125 | 8½ | .17 |
| Batavia: | | | | | | | |
| Second transparent . | 17 18 | 6¾ | .135 | 6¾ | .135 | 9¼ | .185 |
| Do............... | 12 14 | 6¾ | .135 | 6¾ | .135 | 9¼ | .185 |
| Java: | | | | | | | |
| Second unshaved ... | 17 18 | 6 | .12 | 5¾ | .115 | 7¾ | .155 |
| Do............... | 12 14 | 6 | .12 | 5¾ | .115 | 7¾ | .155 |
| Singapore: | | | | | | | |
| Prime ............... | 11 12 | 6½ | .13 | 6½ | .13 | 8¼ | .165 |
| Second ............... | 10 12 | 5 | .10 | 5 | .10 | 7¼ | .145 |
| Rejections........... | 10 12 | 4 | .08 | 4½ | .09 | 5¼ | .105 |
| Hide pieces ............ | .......... | 5 | .10 | 5½ | .11 | 7½ | .15 |
| Hide cuttings ........... | .......... | 3¾ | .075 | 3½ | .07 | 4½ | .09 |

*Buffalo horns.*

[Per 50 kilos (110 pounds).]

| | |
|---|---|
| 1901........................................ | $7.20 to $7.60 |
| 1902........................................ | 7.20 to 7.60 |
| 1903........................................ | 7.40 to 7.60 |

S. LISTOE, *Consul-General.*

ROTTERDAM, *February 12, 1903.*

# INDEX.

O

CPSIA information can be obtained
at www.ICGtesting.com
Printed in the USA
BVHW08*1200170918
527708BV00009B/203/P